Volume 2

CCNA
Certification
Study Guide

WALSALL COLLEGE LRC
WISEMORE CAMPUS
LITTLETON STREET WEST
WALSALL
WS2 8ES

Volume 2
CCNA Certification
Study Guide
Exam 200-301

Todd Lammle

Copyright © 2020 by John Wiley & Sons, Inc., Indianapolis, Indiana

Published simultaneously in Canada

ISBN: 978-1-119-65918-1
ISBN: 978-1-119-66025-5 (ebk.)
ISBN: 978-1-119-66020-0 (ebk.)

Manufactured in the United States of America

No part of this publication may be reproduced, stored in a retrieval system or transmitted in any form or by any means, electronic, mechanical, photocopying, recording, scanning or otherwise, except as permitted under Sections 107 or 108 of the 1976 United States Copyright Act, without either the prior written permission of the Publisher, or authorization through payment of the appropriate per-copy fee to the Copyright Clearance Center, 222 Rosewood Drive, Danvers, MA 01923, (978) 750-8400, fax (978) 646-8600. Requests to the Publisher for permission should be addressed to the Permissions Department, John Wiley & Sons, Inc., 111 River Street, Hoboken, NJ 07030, (201) 748-6011, fax (201) 748-6008, or online at http://www.wiley.com/go/permissions.

Limit of Liability/Disclaimer of Warranty: The publisher and the author make no representations or warranties with respect to the accuracy or completeness of the contents of this work and specifically disclaim all warranties, including without limitation warranties of fitness for a particular purpose. No warranty may be created or extended by sales or promotional materials. The advice and strategies contained herein may not be suitable for every situation. This work is sold with the understanding that the publisher is not engaged in rendering legal, accounting, or other professional services. If professional assistance is required, the services of a competent professional person should be sought. Neither the publisher nor the author shall be liable for damages arising herefrom. The fact that an organization or Web site is referred to in this work as a citation and/or a potential source of further information does not mean that the author or the publisher endorses the information the organization or Web site may provide or recommendations it may make. Further, readers should be aware that Internet Web sites listed in this work may have changed or disappeared between when this work was written and when it is read.

For general information on our other products and services or to obtain technical support, please contact our Customer Care Department within the U.S. at (877) 762-2974, outside the U.S. at (317) 572-3993 or fax (317) 572-4002.

Wiley publishes in a variety of print and electronic formats and by print-on-demand. Some material included with standard print versions of this book may not be included in e-books or in print-on-demand. If this book refers to media such as a CD or DVD that is not included in the version you purchased, you may download this material at http://booksupport.wiley.com. For more information about Wiley products, visit www.wiley.com.

Library of Congress Control Number: 2019953053

TRADEMARKS: Wiley, the Wiley logo, and the Sybex logo are trademarks or registered trademarks of John Wiley & Sons, Inc. and/or its affiliates, in the United States and other countries, and may not be used without written permission. CCNA is a registered trademark of Cisco Technology, Inc. All other trademarks are the property of their respective owners. John Wiley & Sons, Inc. is not associated with any product or vendor mentioned in this book.

SKY10020765_082720

Acknowledgments

There were many people who helped me build the new CCNA books in 2019 and 2020. First, Kenyon Brown helped me put together the direction for the books and managed the internal editing at Wiley, so thank you, Ken, for working diligently for many months keeping these books moving along. Thanks also to Christine O'Connor, my production editor at Wiley for well over a decade now, as well as Judy Flynn my go-to editor who always does an excellent job! Thanks also to Kim Wimpsett for proofreading and to Todd Montgomery for technical proofreading.

The co-author I used in this book was Donald Robb out of Canada. He helped me put together the two wireless chapters and completely wrote the three DevNet chapters (21–23). His knowledge of the subject is second to none and he blew me away! You'll love his work too. You can reach Donald through his popular blog at https://the-packet-thrower.com. He also is a top moderator and contributor at reddit: https://www.reddit.com/r/ccna/.

The top editors I used in the CCNA series included Troy McMillon, who read each chapter in the full series multiple times, making amazing discoveries both technically and editorially. Todd Montgomery was the most excellent tech editor for the complete two book CCNA Series. Also, Monica Lammle read and reread each chapter and really helped me keep the voicing in place throughout the editorial process, which isn't an easy thing to do!

About the Author

Todd Lammle is the authority on Cisco certification and internetworking and is Cisco certified in most Cisco certification categories. He is a world-renowned author, speaker, trainer, and consultant. Todd has three decades of experience working with LANs, WANs, and large enterprise licensed and unlicensed wireless networks, and lately he's been implementing large Cisco Security networks using Firepower/FTD and ISE.

His years of real-world experience are evident in his writing; he is not just an author but an experienced networking engineer with very practical experience from working on the largest networks in the world, at such companies as Xerox, Hughes Aircraft, Texaco, AAA, Cisco, and Toshiba, among many others.

Todd has published almost 100 books, including the very popular *CCNA: Cisco Certified Network Associate Study Guide*, *CCNA Wireless Study Guide*, *CCNA Data Center Study Guide*, *SSFIPS (Firepower)*, and *CCNP Security*, all from Sybex. He runs an international consulting and training company based in Colorado, where he spends his free time in the mountains playing with his golden retrievers.

You can reach Todd through his website at www.lammle.com.

Contents at a Glance

Introduction   *xxv*

Assessment Test   *xl*

Chapter	**1**	Network Fundamentals	1
Chapter	**2**	TCP/IP	29
Chapter	**3**	Easy Subnetting	75
Chapter	**4**	Troubleshooting IP Addressing	105
Chapter	**5**	IP Routing	117
Chapter	**6**	Open Shortest Path First (OSPF)	163
Chapter	**7**	Layer 2 Switching	193
Chapter	**8**	VLANs and Inter-VLAN Routing	219
Chapter	**9**	Enhanced Switched Technologies	251
Chapter	**10**	Access Lists	289
Chapter	**11**	Network Address Translation (NAT)	319
Chapter	**12**	IP Services	337
Chapter	**13**	Security	363
Chapter	**14**	First Hop Redundancy Protocol (HSRP)	411
Chapter	**15**	Virtual Private Networks (VPN's)	433
Chapter	**16**	Quality of Service (QoS)	451
Chapter	**17**	Internet Protocol Version 6 (IPv6)	465
Chapter	**18**	Troubleshooting IP, IPv6, and VLANs	495
Chapter	**19**	Wireless Technologies	549
Chapter	**20**	Configuring Wireless Technologies	595
Chapter	**21**	Virtualization, Automation, and Programmability	661
Chapter	**22**	SDN Controllers	689
Chapter	**23**	Configuration Management	743
Appendix		Answer to Review Questions	787

Index   *809*

Contents

Introduction   *xxv*

Assessment Test   *xl*

Chapter	1	**Network Fundamentals**	**1**
		Network Components	2
		Next-Generation Firewalls and IPS	6
		Network Topology Architectures	10
		The Cisco Three-Layer Hierarchical Model (3-Tier)	10
		Collapsed Core (2-Tier)	13
		Spine-Leaf	14
		WAN	15
		Defining WAN Terms	16
		WAN Connection Bandwidth	17
		Physical Interfaces and Cables	17
		Ethernet Cabling	19
		Straight-Through Cable	20
		Crossover Cable	20
		Fiber Optic	22
		Power over Ethernet (802.3af, 802.3at)	23
		Summary	24
		Exam Essentials	24
		Review Questions	26
Chapter	2	**TCP/IP**	**29**
		Introducing TCP/IP	30
		A Brief History of TCP/IP	30
		TCP/IP and the DoD Model	31
		The Process/Application Layer Protocols	33
		The Host-to-Host or Transport Layer Protocols	42
		The Internet Layer Protocols	51
		IP Addressing	60
		IP Terminology	60
		The Hierarchical IP Addressing Scheme	61
		Private IP Addresses (RFC 1918)	66
		IPv4 Address Types	67
		Layer 2 Broadcasts	68
		Layer 3 Broadcasts	68
		Unicast Address	69
		Multicast Address	70

		Summary	71
		Exam Essentials	71
		Review Questions	73
Chapter	**3**	**Easy Subnetting**	**75**
		Subnetting Basics	76
		How to Create Subnets	77
		Subnet Masks	78
		Classless Inter-Domain Routing (CIDR)	80
		IP Subnet-Zero	81
		Subnetting Class C Addresses	82
		Subnetting Class B Addresses	93
		Summary	102
		Exam Essentials	102
		Review Questions	103
Chapter	**4**	**Troubleshooting IP Addressing**	**105**
		Cisco's Way of Troubleshooting IP	106
		Verify IP Parameters for Operating Systems (OS)	108
		Determining IP Address Problems	109
		Summary	114
		Exam Essentials	114
		Review Questions	115
Chapter	**5**	**IP Routing**	**117**
		Routing Basics	119
		The IP Routing Process	121
		The Cisco Router Internal Process	126
		Testing Your IP Routing Understanding	127
		Configuring IP Routing	132
		Corp Configuration	133
		SF Configuration	135
		LA Configuration	139
		Configuring IP Routing in Our Network	141
		Static Routing	142
		Default Routing	147
		Dynamic Routing	150
		Routing Protocol Basics	150
		Routing Information Protocol (RIP)	152
		Configuring RIP Routing	153
		Holding Down RIP Propagations	156
		Summary	159
		Exam Essentials	159
		Review Questions	161

Contents   xiii

Chapter	6	**Open Shortest Path First (OSPF)**	**163**
		Open Shortest Path First (OSPF) Basics	164
		OSPF Terminology	166
		OSPF Operation	169
		Configuring OSPF	171
		Enabling OSPF	171
		Configuring OSPF Areas	172
		Configuring Our Network with OSPF	175
		OSPF and Loopback Interfaces	179
		Configuring Loopback Interfaces	180
		Verifying OSPF Configuration	182
		The *show ip ospf* Command	183
		The *show ip ospf database* Command	184
		The *show ip ospf interface* Command	185
		The *show ip ospf neighbor* Command	186
		The *show ip protocols* Command	187
		Summary	188
		Exam Essentials	188
		Review Questions	189
Chapter	7	**Layer 2 Switching**	**193**
		Switching Services	194
		Three Switch Functions at Layer 2	195
		Port Security	199
		Configuring Catalyst Switches	204
		Catalyst Switch Configuration	204
		Verifying Cisco Catalyst Switches	212
		Summary	215
		Exam Essentials	215
		Review Questions	216
Chapter	8	**VLANs and Inter-VLAN Routing**	**219**
		VLAN Basics	220
		Broadcast Control	223
		Security	223
		Flexibility and Scalability	224
		Identifying VLANs	224
		Frame Tagging	227
		VLAN Identification Methods	228
		Routing Between VLANs	229
		Configuring VLANs	231
		Assigning Switch Ports to VLANs	234
		Configuring Trunk Ports	236
		Configuring Inter-VLAN Routing	240

		Summary	247
		Exam Essentials	247
		Review Questions	248
Chapter	**9**	**Enhanced Switched Technologies**	**251**
		Spanning Tree Protocol (STP)	252
		Spanning-Tree Terms	253
		Spanning-Tree Operations	257
		Types of Spanning-Tree Protocols	259
		Common Spanning Tree	260
		Per-VLAN Spanning Tree+	261
		Modifying and Verifying the Bridge ID	267
		Spanning-Tree Failure Consequences	273
		PortFast and BPDU Guard	275
		BPDU Guard	276
		EtherChannel	278
		Configuring and Verifying Port Channels	280
		Layer-3 EtherChannel	283
		Summary	284
		Exam Essentials	284
		Review Questions	285
Chapter	**10**	**Access Lists**	**289**
		Perimeter, Firewall, and Internal Routers	290
		Introduction to Access Lists	291
		Mitigating Security Issues with ACLs	294
		Standard Access Lists	295
		Wildcard Masking	296
		Standard Access List Example	298
		Controlling VTY (Telnet/SSH) Access	302
		Extended Access Lists	303
		Extended Access List Example 1	307
		Extended Access List Example 2	308
		Extended Access List Example 3	309
		Named ACLs	310
		Remarks	312
		Monitoring Access Lists	313
		Summary	316
		Exam Essentials	316
		Review Questions	317

Chapter	11	**Network Address Translation (NAT)**	**319**
		When Do We Use NAT?	320
		Types of Network Address Translation	322
		NAT Names	322
		How NAT Works	323
		Static NAT Configuration	325
		Dynamic NAT Configuration	325
		PAT (Overloading) Configuration	326
		Simple Verification of NAT	327
		Testing and Troubleshooting NAT	328
		Summary	333
		Exam Essentials	333
		Review Questions	334
Chapter	12	**IP Services**	**337**
		Exploring Connected Devices Using CDP and LLDP	338
		Getting CDP Timers and Holdtime Information	338
		Gathering Neighbor Information	340
		Documenting a Network Topology Using CDP	344
		Network Time Protocol (NTP)	347
		SNMP	348
		Management Information Base (MIB)	350
		Configuring SNMP	351
		Syslog	352
		Configuring and Verifying Syslog	354
		Secure Shell (SSH)	357
		Summary	358
		Exam Essentials	358
		Review Questions	360
Chapter	13	**Security**	**363**
		Network Security Threats	365
		Three Primary Network Attacks	365
		Network Attacks	366
		Eavesdropping	366
		Denial-of-Service Attacks	368
		Unauthorized Access	370
		WareZ	370
		Masquerade Attack (IP Spoofing)	371
		Session Hijacking or Replaying	371
		Rerouting	371
		Repudiation	371
		Smurfing	372

	Password Attacks	372
	Man-in-the-Middle Attacks	373
	Application-Layer Attacks	373
	Trojan Horse Programs, Viruses, and Worms	373
	HTML Attacks	374
Security Program Elements		374
	User Awareness	374
	Training	375
	Physical Access Control	376
Layer 2 Security Features		378
	Securing Network Access with Cisco AAA	380
Authentication Methods		381
	Windows Authentication	382
	Security Server Authentication	382
	External Authentication Options	383
Managing User Accounts		386
	Disabling Accounts	387
	Setting Up Anonymous Accounts	387
	Limiting Connections	388
	Renaming the Maintenance Account	388
Security Password Policy Elements		389
	Password Management	389
	Managing Passwords	391
	Single Sign-On	395
	Local Authentication	395
	LDAP	395
	Password Alternatives	396
User-Authentication Methods		398
	Public Key Infrastructure (PKI)	398
	Kerberos	399
Setting Passwords		400
	Auxiliary Password	405
Summary		407
Exam Essentials		407
Review Questions		408

Chapter 14   First Hop Redundancy Protocol (HSRP)   411

Client Redundancy Issues	412
Introducing First Hop Redundancy Protocol (FHRP)	414
Hot Standby Router Protocol (HSRP)	416
Virtual MAC Address	418
HSRP Timers	419
Group Roles	421
Configuring and Verifying HSRP	423

		Summary	429
		Exam Essentials	429
		Review Questions	430
Chapter	**15**	**Virtual Private Networks (VPNs)**	**433**
		Virtual Private Networks	434
		Benefits of VPNs	435
		Enterprise- and Provider-Managed VPNs	436
		Introduction to Cisco IOS IPsec	438
		IPsec Transforms	439
		GRE Tunnels	441
		GRE over IPsec	442
		Configuring GRE Tunnels	443
		Verifying GRP Tunnels	445
		Summary	447
		Exam Essentials	447
		Review Questions	448
Chapter	**16**	**Quality of Service (QoS)**	**451**
		Quality of Service	452
		Traffic Characteristics	453
		Trust Boundary	454
		QoS Mechanisms	455
		Classification and Marking	455
		Policing, Shaping, and Re-marking	456
		Tools for Managing Congestion	457
		Tools for Congestion Avoidance	460
		Summary	461
		Exam Essentials	461
		Review Questions	462
Chapter	**17**	**Internet Protocol Version 6 (IPv6)**	**465**
		Why Do We Need IPv6?	467
		The Benefits and Uses of IPv6	467
		IPv6 Addressing and Expressions	469
		Shortened Expression	469
		Address Types	470
		Special Addresses	472
		How IPv6 Works in an Internetwork	473
		Manual Address Assignment	473
		Stateless Autoconfiguration (eui-64)	474
		DHCPv6 (Stateful)	476
		IPv6 Header	477
		ICMPv6	479

		IPv6 Routing Protocols	483
		Static Routing with IPv6	483
		Configuring IPv6 on Our Internetwork	484
		Configuring Routing on Our Internetwork	487
		Summary	490
		Exam Essentials	490
		Review Questions	492
Chapter	**18**	**Troubleshooting IP, IPv6, and VLANs**	**495**
		Endpoints	496
		Desktops/Laptops	496
		Mobile Phones/Tablets	497
		Access Points	497
		IP Phones	497
		Internet of Things	497
		Servers	497
		Server Roles	498
		IP Config	498
		Windows 10	498
		macOS	504
		Ubuntu/Red Hat	506
		Troubleshooting IP Network Connectivity	507
		Using SPAN for Troubleshooting	518
		Configuring and Verifying Extended Access Lists	519
		Troubleshooting IPv6 Network Connectivity	522
		ICMPv6	523
		Troubleshooting VLAN Connectivity	531
		VLAN Troubleshooting	532
		Trunk Troubleshooting	537
		Summary	544
		Exam Essentials	545
		Review Questions	546
Chapter	**19**	**Wireless Technologies**	**549**
		Wireless Networks	551
		Wireless Personal Area Network (WPAN)	552
		Wireless LAN (WLAN)	552
		Wireless Metro Area Network (WMAN)	552
		Wireless Wide Area Network (WWAN)	553
		Basic Wireless Devices	553
		Wireless Access Points	553
		Wireless Network Interface Card (NIC)	555
		Wireless Antennas	556

	Wireless Principles	556
	Independent Basic Service Set (Ad Hoc)	556
	Basic Service Set (BSS)	557
	Infrastructure Basic Service Set	558
	Service Set ID	559
	Extended Service Set	560
	Repeaters	561
	Bridging	562
	Mesh Networks	564
	Nonoverlapping Wi-Fi channels	565
	2.4GHz Band	565
	5GHz Band	566
	Radio Frequency (RF)	569
	Radio Frequency Behaviors	572
	Free Space Path Loss	572
	Absorption	573
	Reflection	574
	Multipath	575
	Refraction	576
	Diffraction	576
	Scattering	577
	RF Operational Requirements	578
	Wireless Security	581
	Authentication and Encryption	581
	WEP	582
	WPA and WPA2: An Overview	583
	WPA3	586
	Summary	588
	Exam Essentials	588
	Review Question	590
Chapter 20	**Configuring Wireless Technologies**	**595**
	WLAN Deployment Models	596
	Stand-Alone Model	597
	Lightweight Model	598
	Cloud Model	600
	Setting Up a Wireless LAN Controller (WLC)	602
	Configuring the Switch	602
	WLC Initial Setup	604
	Joining Access Points (APs)	607
	Manual Method	607
	DNS Method	607
	DHCP Method	608
	Configuring the VLAN	609
	Configuring the Switchport	609

	Wireless LAN Controllers (WLC)	610
	WLC Port Types	611
	WLC Interface Types	614
	Management Interface	615
	Service Port Interface	616
	Redundancy Management	617
	Virtual Interface	618
	Dynamic Interface	619
	Interface Groups	622
	Link Aggregation Group (LAG)	623
	Configuring the AP	625
	AP Modes	629
	AP and WLC Management Access Connections	633
	CDP	634
	Telnet	636
	SSH	637
	HTTP	637
	HTTPS	638
	Console	639
	RADIUS	639
	TACACS+	643
	Connecting the Client	653
	Summary	655
	Exam Essentials	655
	Review Questions	657
Chapter 21	**Virtualization, Automation, and Programmability**	**661**
	Virtual Machine Fundamentals	662
	Virtualization Components	665
	Virtualization Features	666
	Hardware Abstraction	667
	Snapshots	667
	Clones	667
	Migrations	667
	Virtualization Types	668
	Type 1	668
	Type 2	668
	Hardware Virtualized Machine	668
	Paravirtualization	668
	Virtualization Solutions	669
	VMware ESXi	669
	Hyper-V	669
	Xen/KVM	669
	VMware Workstation/Fusion	669
	VirtualBox	670

		Contents	xxi

	Automation Components	670
	Python	670
	JSON	676
	YAML	679
	REST API	679
	Summary	684
	Exam Essentials	684
	Review Questions	685

Chapter 22	**SDN Controllers**	**689**
	Traditional Network Monitoring Systems (NMS)	690
	Configuring SNMP	691
	Network Health	692
	Central Syslog	694
	Central SNMP Traps	695
	Interface Information	695
	Hardware Health	697
	Network Information	697
	Traditional Network Configuration Managers (NCM)	699
	Traditional Networking	702
	Management Plane	702
	Control Plane	703
	Data Plane	703
	Forwarding	704
	Introduction to SDN	706
	Northbound Interfaces	707
	Southbound Interfaces	708
	SDN Solutions	708
	Separating the Control Plane	709
	Controller-Based Architectures	710
	Campus Architecture	711
	Spine/Leaf Architecture	712
	SDN Network Components	712
	Underlay	713
	Overlay	716
	Fabric	718
	DNA Center Overview	718
	Discovery	719
	Network Hierarchy	721
	Templates	723
	Topology	724
	Upgrades	725
	Command Runner	728
	Assurance	729
	Path Trace	731

	EasyQoS	732
	LAN Automation	734
	SD-Access	735
	Restful API	736
Summary		736
Exam Essentials		737
Review Questions		738

Chapter 23   Configuration Management   743

Team Silos		744
DevOps		748
Infrastructure as Code (IaC)		748
Ansible		750
	Installation	751
	Settings	752
	Inventory	753
	Lab Setup	753
	Modules	755
	Ad-Hoc Example	756
	Playbook Example	756
Ansible Tower/AWX		763
Puppet		764
	Installation	764
	Lab Setup	765
	Site Manifest File	766
	DC Manifest File	768
	Installing the Puppet Agent	769
	Verifying the Results	770
	Puppet Enterprise	771
Chef		772
	Installation – Server	774
	Installation – Workstation	775
	Lab Setup	777
	Verifying the Results	781
Summary		781
Exam Essentials		782
Review Questions		783

Appendix   Answer to Review Questions   787

Chapter 1: Network Fundamentals	788
Chapter 2: TCP/IP	788
Chapter 3: Easy Subnetting	789
Chapter 4: Troubleshooting IP Addressing	790

Chapter 5: IP Routing	791
Chapter 6: Open Shortest Path First (OSPF)	792
Chapter 7: Layer 2 Switching	792
Chapter 8: VLANs and Inter-VLAN Routing	794
Chapter 9: Enhanced Switched Technologies	795
Chapter 10: Access Lists	796
Chapter 11: Network Address Translation (NAT)	797
Chapter 12: IP Services	797
Chapter 13: Security	798
Chapter 14: First Hop Redundancy Protocol (HSRP)	799
Chapter 15: Virtual Private Networks (VPNs)	800
Chapter 16: Quality of Service (QoS)	801
Chapter 17: Internet Protocol Version 6 (IPv6)	802
Chapter 18: Troubleshooting IP, IPv6, and VLANs	803
Chapter 19: Wireless Technologies	803
Chapter 20: Configuring Wireless Technologies	805
Chapter 21: Virtualization, Automation, and Programmability	806
Chapter 22: SDN Controllers	806
Chapter 23: Configuration Management	808

Index *809*

Introduction

Welcome to the exciting world of Cisco certification! If you've picked up this book because you want to improve yourself and your life with a better, more satisfying and secure job, you've done the right thing. Whether your plan is to enter the thriving, dynamic IT sector or to enhance your skill set and advance your position within it, being Cisco certified can seriously stack the odds in your favor to help you attain your goals.

Cisco certifications are powerful instruments of success that also just happen to improve your grasp of all things internetworking. As you progress through this book, you'll gain a complete understanding of networking that reaches far beyond Cisco devices. By the end of this book, you'll comprehensively know how disparate network topologies and technologies work together to form the fully operational networks that are vital to today's very way of life in the developed world. The knowledge and expertise you'll gain here are essential for and relevant to every networking job. It's why Cisco certifications are in such high demand—even at companies with few Cisco devices!

For up-to-the-minute updates covering additions or modifications to the Cisco certification exams, as well as additional study tools, review questions, videos, and bonus materials, be sure to visit the Todd Lammle websites and forum at www.lammle.com/ccna

Cisco's Network Certifications

Way back in 1998, obtaining the Cisco Certified Network Associate (CCNA) certification was the first pitch in the Cisco certification climb. It was also the official prerequisite to each of the more advanced levels. But that changed in 2007, when Cisco announced the Cisco Certified Entry Network Technician (CCENT) certification. Then again, in May 2016, Cisco announced new updates to the CCENT and CCNA Routing and Switching (R/S) tests. Today, things have changed dramatically again.

In July of 2019, Cisco switched up the certification process more than they have in the last 20 years! They announced all new certifications that have started in February 2020, which is probably why you're reading this book!

So what's changed? For starters, the CCENT course and exam (ICND1 and ICND2), no longer exist, nor even the terms Routing & Switching (rebranded to Enterprise). On top of that, the CCNA is no longer a prerequisite for any of the higher certifications at all, meaning that you'll be able to jump straight to CCNP without having to take the new CCNA exam.

The new Cisco certification process will look like Figure I.1.

FIGURE I.1 The Cisco certification path

Entry	Associate	Professional	Expert	Architect
Starting point for individuals interested in starting a career as a networking professional.	Master the essentials needed to launch a rewarding career and expand your job possibilities with the latest technologies.	Select a core technology track and a focused concentration exam to customize your professional-level certification.	This certification is accepted worldwide as the most prestigious certification in the technology industry.	The highest level of accreditation achievable and recognizes the architectural expertise of network designers.
CCT	DevNet Associate	DevNet Professional	CCDE	CCAr
	CCNA	CCNP Enterprise	CCIE Enterprise Infrastructure CCIE Enterprise Wireless	
		CCNP Collaboration	CCIE Collaboration	
		CCNP Data Center	CCIE Data Center	
		CCNP Security	CCIE Security	
		CCNP Service Provider	CCIE Service Provider	

First, the CCT, entry-level certification just isn't worth your time. Instead, you'll want to head directly to CCNA, using this book and the abundant resources on www.lammle.com/ccna of course!

The Todd Lammle CCNA program, starting with this book, is a powerful tool to get you started in your CCNA studies, and it's vital to understand that material found in this book and at www.lammle.com/ccna before you go on to conquer any other certifications!

What Does This Book Cover?

This book covers everything you need to know to pass the new CCNA exam. But regardless of which path you choose, as I've said, taking plenty of time to study and practice with routers or a router simulator is the real key to success.

You will learn the following information in this book:

Chapter 1: Network Fundamentals   In Chapter 1, network fundamentals, the Cisco three-layer model, and wide area network are reviewed. Ethernet cabling including fiber optic is discussed. The chapter ends with an overview of PoE. Review questions await you at the end to test your understanding of the material.

Chapter 2: TCP/IP   In this chapter, I'll cover the protocols of TCP/IP. I'll begin by exploring the DoD's version of TCP/IP, then compare that version and its protocols with the OSI reference model that we discussed earlier. Lastly, I dive into the world of IP addressing and the different classes of IP addresses used in networks today. Review questions are at the end of the chapter to test your understanding of the material.

Chapter 3: Introduction to TCP/IP   This chapter will pick up right where we left off in the last chapter and continue to explore the world of IP addressing. I'll open this chapter by showing you how to subnet an IP network. Prepare yourself because being able to subnet quickly and accurately is pretty challenging. Use the review questions to test your ability to understand subnetting; also, use the bonus tools found at www.lammle.com/ccna

Chapter 4: Troubleshooting IP Addressing   In this chapter, we'll cover IP address troubleshooting, while focusing on the steps Cisco recommends following when troubleshooting an IP network. Working through this chapter will hone your knowledge of IP addressing and networking, while refining the essential skills you've attained so far.

Chapter 5: IP Routing   This chapter's focus is on the core topic of the ubiquitous IP routing process. It's integral to networking because it pertains to all routers and configurations that use it—easily the lion's share. IP routing is basically the process of moving packets from one network to another network using routers, and this chapter will cover IP routing in depth.

Chapter 6: Open Shortest Path First (OSPF)   Open Shortest Path First (OSPF) is by far the most popular and important routing protocol in use today—so important, I'm devoting an entire chapter to it! Sticking with the same approach we've taken throughout this book, we'll begin with the basics by completely familiarizing you with key OSPF terminology.

Chapter 7: Managing a Cisco Internetwork   In this chapter, I'm going to cover the finer points of layer 2 switching to make sure you know exactly how it works. You should already know that we rely on switching to break up large collision domains into smaller ones and that a collision domain is a network segment with two or more devices sharing the same bandwidth. Switches have changed the way networks are designed and implemented. If a pure switched design is implemented well, the result will be a clean, cost-effective, and resilient internetwork.

Chapter 8: Virtual LANs and Inter-VLAN Routing (IVR)   This chapter discussed how we break up broadcast domains in a pure switched internetwork. We do this by creating virtual local area networks (VLANs). A VLAN is a logical grouping of network users and resources connected to administratively defined ports on a switch, and I'll show you how to really understand the foundation and the configuration of VLANs and IVR.

Chapter 9: Enhanced Switched Technologies   This chapter will start off with STP protocols and dive into the fundamentals, covering the modes, as well as the various flavors of STP. VLANs, trunks, and troubleshooting. Lastly, PortFast will also be discussed.

Chapter 10: Access List   This chapter covers security and access lists, which are created on routers to filter the network. IP standard, extended, and named access lists are covered in detail. Written and hands-on labs, along with review questions, will help you study for the security and access-list portion of the Cisco exams.

Chapter 11: Network Address Translation (NAT)   In this chapter, we're going to dig into Network Address Translation (NAT), Dynamic NAT, and Port Address Translation (PAT), also known as NAT Overload. Of course, I'll demonstrate all the NAT commands.

Chapter 12: IP Services   This chapter covers how to find neighbor device information using the proprietary Cisco Discovery Protocol (CDP) and the industry-standard Link Layer Discovery protocol (LLDP). I'll also discuss how to make sure our times are synchronized with our devices using Network Time Protocol (NTP). After that, I'll show you the Simple Network Management Protocol (SNMP) and the type of alerts sent to the network management station (NMS). You'll learn about the all-so-important Syslog logging and configuration, and then finally, I'll cover how to configure Secure Shell (SSH).

Chapter 13: Security   New information, commands, troubleshooting, and detailed hands-on labs will help you nail the NAT CCENT objectives.

Chapter 14: First Hop Redundancy Protocol (HSRP)   This chapter will start off by telling you the reasons why we need a layer 3 redundancy protocol, and then move into how to build redundancy and load-balancing features into your network elegantly with routers that you might even have already. You really don't need to buy some overpriced load-balancing device when you know how to configure and use Hot Standby Router Protocol (HSRP).

Chapter 15: Virtual Private Networks (VPNs)   We're going to cover VPNs in depth in this chapter. You'll learn some smart solutions that will help you meet your company's off-site network access needs, and dive deep into how these networks utilize IP security to provide secure communications over a public network via the Internet using VPNs with IPSec. This chapter wraps up by demonstrating how to create a tunnel using GRE (Generic Routing Encapsulation).

Chapter 16: Quality of Service (QoS)   *Quality of service (QoS)* refers to the way resources are controlled so that the quality of services is maintained. In this chapter I'm going to cover how QoS solves problems by using classification and marking tools, policing, shaping and re-marking, providing congestion management and scheduling tools, and finally, link-specific tools.

Chapter 17: Internet Protocol Version 6 (IPv6)   This is a fun chapter chock-full of some great information. IPv6 is not the big, bad scary creature that most people think it is, and it's a really important objective on the latest exam, so study this chapter carefully—don't just skim it.

Chapter 18: Troubleshooting IP, IPv6, and VLANs   This chapter will covered detailed troubleshooting, and since this is such a major focus of the Cisco CCNA objectives, I'd be letting you down if I didn't make sure you've got this important topic down. So to ensure your skills are solid, we're going to begin by diving deep into troubleshooting with IP, IPv6, and virtual LANs (VLANs) now. You absolutely must also have the fundamentals of IP and IPv6 routing and knowledge of VLANs and trunking nailed down tight if you're going to win at this.

Chapter 19: Wireless Technologies   Since I know you've crushed all of the previous chapters, you're ready to dive into this one! If that's not exactly you, just know that the two chapters on switching provide a really nice review on switching and VLANs. So, let's start this chapter by defining a basic wireless network as well as basic wireless principles. We'll talk about different types of wireless networks, discuss the minimum devices required to create a simple wireless network, and look at some basic wireless topologies as well. After that, I'll get into basic security by covering WPA, WPA2, and WPA3.

Chapter 20: Configuring Wireless Technologies   After Chapter 21 you now know how wireless works, so now we're going to guide through configuring a wireless network from beginning to end. We'll start by telling you all about how to get a Cisco Wireless LAN controller up and running before showing you how to join access-points to our new WLC. We'll aslo dig deep into how to configure the WLC to support wireless networks. By the end of this chapter, you'll triumph by having an actual endpoint join your wireless LAN!

Chapter 21: Virtualization, Automation, and Programmability   In this chapter we'll begin to address modern challenges by introducing you to virtualization basics. We'll then walk you through its common components and features to closing the topic by comparing some of the virtualization products on the market as of this writing. After that, we'll explore important automation concepts and components to provide you with sure footing to jump into the SDN and configuration management chapters following this one.

Chapter 22: Software Defined Networks (SDN) Controllers   Automation has gotten popular enough to be included on the CCNA exam—it even has its own Devnet certification track! Even so, most companies still aren't keen on fully managing their network with a bunch of Python scripts on a shared drive. So a better solution is to go with something called a Software Defined Networking (SDN) controller to centrally manage and monitor the network instead of doing everything manually, and that is what this chapter is all about!

Chapter 23: DNA Center Configuration Management   In this chapter we're going to take things to a whole new DNA Center level now, diving deeper into Configuration Management tools like Ansible, Puppet, and Chef. These great features that make it possible to automate almost everything in your infrastructure! We'll explore Ansible, Puppet, and Chef.

Appendix: Answers to Review Questions   This appendix provides the answers to the end-of-chapter review questions.

Interactive Online Learning Environment and Test Bank

The interactive online learning environment that accompanies the *CCNA Certification Study Guide* provides a test bank with study tools to help you prepare for the certification exams and increase your chances of passing them the first time! The test bank includes the following elements:

Sample Tests   All of the questions in this book are provided, including the assessment test, which you'll find at the end of this introduction, and the chapter tests that include the review questions at the end of each chapter. In addition, there are two practice exams. Use these questions to test your knowledge of the study guide material. The online test bank runs on multiple devices.

Electronic Flashcards   The flashcards are included for quick reference and are great tools for learning quick facts. You can even consider these as additional simple practice questions, which is essentially what they are.

Glossary   There is a PDF of a glossary included, which covers the terms used in this book.

The Sybex Interactive Online Test Bank, flashcards, and glossary can be accessed at http://www.wiley.com/go/sybextestprep.

In addition to the materials we provide online as part of the test bank, you can also visit Todd Lammle's website to access other valuable resources.

Todd Lammle Bonus Material and Labs   Be sure to check www.lammle.com/ccna for directions on how to download all the latest bonus material created specifically to help you study for your CCNA exam.

Todd Lammle Videos   I have created a full CCNA series of videos that can be purchased at www.lammle.com/ccna

CCNA Exam Overview

Cisco has designed the new CCNA program to prepare you for today's associate-level job roles in IT technologies. The CCNA now includes security and automation and programmability, and there is even a new CCNA DevNet certification. The new CCNA program has one certification that covers a broad range of fundamentals for IT careers.

The new CCNA certification covers a huge amount of topics, including:

- Network fundamentals
- Network access
- IP connectivity
- IP services
- Security fundamentals
- Wireless
- Automation and programmability

Are there any prerequisites to take before the CCNA exam can be taken?

Not really, but having experience is really helpful. Cisco has no formal prerequisites for CCNA certification, but you should have an understanding of the exam topics before taking the exam.

CCNA candidates often also have:
- One or more years of experience implementing and administering Cisco solutions
- Knowledge of basic IP addressing
- A good understanding of network fundamentals

How to Use This Book

If you want a solid foundation for the serious effort of preparing for the new CCNA exam, then look no further. I've spent hundreds of hours putting together this book with the sole intention of helping you to pass the Cisco exams, as well as really learn how to correctly configure Cisco routers and switches!

This book is loaded with valuable information, and you will get the most out of your study time if you understand why the book is organized the way it is.

So to maximize your benefit from this book, I recommend the following study method:

1. Take the assessment test that's provided at the end of this introduction. (The answers are at the end of the test.) It's okay if you don't know any of the answers; that's why you bought this book! Carefully read over the explanations for any questions you get wrong and note the chapters in which the material relevant to them is covered. This information should help you plan your study strategy.

2. Study each chapter carefully, making sure you fully understand the information and the test objectives listed at the beginning of each one. Pay extra-close attention to any chapter that includes material covered in questions you missed.

3. Answer all of the review questions related to each chapter. (The answers appear in Appendix A.) Note the questions that confuse you and study the topics they cover again until the concepts are crystal clear. And again—do not just skim these questions! Make sure you fully comprehend the reason for each correct answer. Remember that these will not be the exact questions you will find on the exam, but they're written to help you understand the chapter material and ultimately pass the exam!

4. Try your hand at the practice questions that are exclusive to this book. The questions can be found only at http://www.wiley.com/go/sybextestprep. Don't forget to check out www.lammle.com/ccna for the most up-to-date Cisco exam prep questions, videos, hands-on labs, and Todd Lammle boot camps.

5. Test yourself using all the flashcards, which are also found on the download link listed in #4. These are brand-new and updated flashcards to help you prepare for the CCNA exam and a wonderful study tool!

To learn every bit of the material covered in this book, you'll have to apply yourself regularly, and with discipline. Try to set aside the same time period every day to study, and select a comfortable and quiet place to do so. I'm confident that if you work hard, you'll be surprised at how quickly you learn this material!

If you follow these steps and really study—*doing hands-on labs every single day* in addition to using the review questions, the practice exams, the Todd Lammle video sections, and the electronic flashcards, as well as all the written labs—it would actually be hard to fail the Cisco exams. But understand that studying for the Cisco exams is a lot like getting in shape—if you do not go to the gym every day, it's not going to happen!

Where Do You Take the Exam?

You may take the CCNA Composite or any Cisco exam at any of the Pearson VUE authorized testing centers. For information, check www.vue.com or call 877-404-EXAM (3926).

To register for a Cisco exam, follow these steps:

1. Determine the number of the exam you want to take. (The CCNA exam number is 200-301.)
2. Register with the nearest Pearson VUE testing center. At this point, you will be asked to pay in advance for the exam. You can schedule exams up to six weeks in advance or as late as the day you want to take it—but if you fail a Cisco exam, you must wait five days before you will be allowed to retake it. If something comes up and you need to cancel or reschedule your exam appointment, contact Pearson VUE at least 24 hours in advance.
3. When you schedule the exam, you'll get instructions regarding all appointment and cancellation procedures, the ID requirements, and information about the testing-center location.

Tips for Taking Your Cisco Exams

The Cisco exams contain about 50 or more questions and must be completed in about 90 minutes or so. It's hard to write this information down today because it changes so often. You must get a score of about 85 percent to pass this exam, but again, each exam can be different.

Many questions on the exam have answer choices that at first glance look identical—especially the syntax questions! So remember to read through the choices carefully because close just doesn't cut it. If you get commands in the wrong order or forget one measly character, you'll get the question wrong. So, to practice, do the hands-on exercises at the end of this book's chapters over and over again until they feel natural to you.

Also, never forget that the right answer is the Cisco answer. In many cases, more than one appropriate answer is presented, but the *correct* answer is the one that Cisco recommends. On the exam, you will always be told to pick one, two, or three options, never "choose all that apply." The Cisco exam may include the following test formats:

- Multiple-choice single answer
- Multiple-choice multiple answer

- Drag-and-drop
- Router simulations

Cisco proctored exams will not show the steps to follow in completing a router interface configuration, but they do allow partial command responses. For example, show run, sho running, or sh running-config would be acceptable.

Here are some general tips for exam success:

- Arrive early at the exam center so you can relax and review your study materials.
- Read the questions *carefully*. Don't jump to conclusions. Make sure you're clear about *exactly* what each question asks. "Read twice, answer once," is what I always tell my students.
- When answering multiple-choice questions that you're not sure about, use the process of elimination to get rid of the obviously incorrect answers first. Doing this greatly improves your odds if you need to make an educated guess.
- You can no longer move forward and backward through the Cisco exams, so double-check your answer before clicking Next since you can't change your mind.

After you complete an exam, you'll get immediate, online notification of your pass or fail status, a printed examination score report that indicates your pass or fail status, and your exam results by section. (The test administrator will give you the printed score report.)

Test scores are automatically forwarded to Cisco within five working days after you take the test, so you don't need to send your score to them. If you pass the exam, you'll receive confirmation from Cisco, typically within two to four weeks, sometimes a bit longer.

CCNA Certification Exam 200-301 Objectives

1.0 Network Fundamentals	**1, 2, 3, 4, 17, 18**
1.1 Explain the role and function of network components	1
1.1.a Routers	1
1.1.b L2 and L3 switches	1
1.1.c Next-generation firewalls and IPS	1
1.1.d Access points	
1.1.e Controllers (Cisco DNA Center and WLC)	20, 22

1.0 Network Fundamentals	1, 2, 3, 4, 17, 18
1.1.f Endpoints	
1.1.g Servers	
1.2 Describe characteristics of network topology architectures	1
1.2.a 2 tier	1
1.2.b 3 tier	1
1.2.c Spine-leaf	1
1.2.d WAN	
1.2.e Small office/home office (SOHO)	1
1.2.f On-premises and cloud	
1.3 Compare physical interface and cabling types	1
1.3.a Single-mode fiber, multimode fiber, copper	1
1.3.b Connections (Ethernet shared media and point-to-point)	1
1.3.c Concepts of PoE	1
1.4 Identify interface and cable issues (collisions, errors, mismatch duplex, and/or speed)	18
1.5 Compare TCP to UDP	2
1.6 Configure and verify IPv4 addressing and subnetting	2, 3, 4, 18
1.7 Describe the need for private IPv4 addressing	2
1.8 Configure and verify IPv6 addressing and prefix	17, 18
1.9 Compare IPv6 address types	17
1.9.a Global unicast	17
1.9.b Unique local	17
1.9.c Link local	17

1.0 Network Fundamentals	**1, 2, 3, 4, 17, 18**
1.9.d Anycast	17
1.9.e Multicast	17
1.9.f Modified EUI 64	17
1.10 Verify IP parameters for Client OS (Windows, Mac OS, Linux)	4, 18
1.11 Describe wireless principles	19
1.11.a Nonoverlapping Wi-Fi channels	19
1.11.b SSID	19
1.11.c RF	19
1.11.d Encryption	19
1.12 Explain virtualization fundamentals (virtual machines)	21
1.13 Describe switching concepts	7
1.13.a MAC learning and aging	7
1.13.b Frame switching	7
1.13.c Frame flooding	7
1.13.d MAC address table	7

2.0 Network Access	**8, 9, 12, 18**
2.1 Configure and verify VLANs (normal range) spanning multiple switches	8
2.1.a Access ports (data and voice)	8
2.1.b Default VLAN	8
2.1.c Connectivity	8
2.2 Configure and verify interswitch connectivity	8, 18

2.0 Network Access	8, 9, 12, 18
2.2.a Trunk ports	8, 18
2.2.b 802.1Q	8, 18
2.2.c Native VLAN	8, 18
2.3 Configure and verify Layer 2 discovery protocols (Cisco Discovery Protocol and LLDP)	12
2.4 Configure and verify (Layer 2/Layer 3) EtherChannel (LACP)	9
2.5 Describe the need for and basic operations of Rapid PVST+ Spanning Tree Protocol and identify basic operations	9
2.5.a Root port, root bridge (primary/secondary), and other port names	9
2.5.b Port states (forwarding/blocking)	9
2.5.c PortFast benefits	9
2.6 Compare Cisco Wireless Architectures and AP modes	19
2.7 Describe physical infrastructure connections of WLAN components (AP,WLC, access/trunk ports, and LAG)	19
2.8 Describe AP and WLC management access connections (Telnet, SSH, HTTP,HTTPS, console, and TACACS+/RADIUS)	19
2.9 Configure the components of a wireless LAN access for client connectivity using GUI only such as	20
WLAN creation, security settings, QoS profiles, and advanced WLAN settings	

3.0 IP Connectivity	5, 6, 14, 17
3.1 Interpret the components of routing table	5
3.1.a Routing protocol code	5
3.1.b Prefix	5

3.0 IP Connectivity	**5, 6, 14, 17**
3.1.c Network mask	5
3.1.d Next hop	5
3.1.e Administrative distance	5
3.1.f Metric	5
3.1.g Gateway of last resort	5
3.2 Determine how a router makes a forwarding decision by default	5
3.2.a Longest match	5
3.2.b Administrative distance	5
3.2.c Routing protocol metric	5
3.3 Configure and verify IPv4 and IPv6 static routing	5, 17
3.3.a Default route	5
3.3.b Network route	5
3.3.c Host route	5
3.3.d Floating static	5
3.4 Configure and verify single area OSPFv2	6
3.4.a Neighbor adjacencies	6
3.4.b Point-to-point	6
3.4.c Broadcast (DR/BDR selection)	6
3.4.d Router ID	6
3.5 Describe the purpose of first hop redundancy protocol	14

4.0 IP Services	**2, 5, 11, 12, 16**
4.1 Configure and verify inside source NAT using static and pools	11
4.2 Configure and verify NTP operating in a client and server mode	12
4.3 Explain the role of DHCP and DNS within the network	2, 5
4.4 Explain the function of SNMP in network operations	12
4.5 Describe the use of Syslog features including facilities and levels	12
4.6 Configure and verify DHCP client and relay	5
4.7 Explain the forwarding per-hop behavior (PHB) for QoS such as classification, marking, queuing, congestion, policing, shaping	16
4.8 Configure network devices for remote access using SSH	12
4.9 Describe the capabilities and function of TFTP/FTP in the network	2

5.0 Security Fundamentals	**7, 10, 13, 15**
5.1 Define key security concepts (threats, vulnerabilities, exploits, and mitigation techniques)	13
5.2 Describe security program elements (user awareness, training, and physical access control)	13
5.3 Configure device access control using local passwords	13
5.4 Describe security password policies elements, such as management, complexity, and password	13
alternatives (multifactor authentication, certificates, and biometrics)	13
5.5 Describe remote access and site-to-site VPNs	15
5.6 Configure and verify access control lists	10
5.7 Configure Layer 2 security features (DHCP snooping, dynamic ARP inspection, and port security)	7, 13

5.0 Security Fundamentals	7, 10, 13, 15
5.8 Differentiate authentication, authorization, and accounting concepts	13
5.9 Describe wireless security protocols (WPA, WPA2, and WPA3)	19
5.10 Configure WLAN using WPA2 PSK using the GUI	20

6.0 Automation and Programmability	Chapter
6.1 Explain how automation impacts network management	21
6.2 Compare traditional networks with controller-based networking	22
6.3 Describe controller-based and software defined architectures (overlay, underlay, and fabric)	22
6.3.a Separation of control plane and data plane	22
6.3.b North-bound and south-bound APIs	22
6.4 Compare traditional campus device management with Cisco DNA Center enabled device management	22
6.5 Describe characteristics of REST-based APIs (CRUD, HTTP verbs, and data encoding)	21
6.6 Recognize the capabilities of configuration management mechanisms Puppet, Chef, and Ansible	23
6.7 Interpret JSON encoded data	21

Assessment Test

1. What is the sys-id-ext field in a BPDU used for?
   A. It is a 4-bit field inserted into an Ethernet frame to define trunking information between switches.
   B. It is a 12-bit field inserted into an Ethernet frame to define VLANs in an STP instance.
   C. It is a 4-bit field inserted into an non-Ethernet frame to define EtherChannel options.
   D. It is a 12-bit field inserted into an Ethernet frame to define STP root bridges.

2. You have four RSTP PVST+ links between switches and want to aggregate the bandwidth. What solution will you use?
   A. EtherChannel
   B. PortFast
   C. BPDU Channel
   D. VLANs
   E. EtherBundle

3. What configuration parameters must be configured the same between switches for LACP to form a channel? (Choose three.)
   A. Virtual MAC address
   B. Port speeds
   C. Duplex
   D. PortFast enabled
   E. Allowed VLAN information

4. You reload a router with a configuration register setting of 0x2101. What will the router do when it reloads?
   A. The router enters setup mode.
   B. The router enters ROM monitor mode.
   C. The router boots the mini-IOS in ROM.
   D. The router expands the first IOS in flash memory into RAM.

5. Which of the following commands provides the product ID and serial number of a router?
   A. `show license`
   B. `show license feature`
   C. `show version`
   D. `show license udi`

6. Which command allows you to view the technology options and licenses that are supported on your router along with several status variables?
   A. show license
   B. show license feature
   C. show license udi
   D. show version

7. You need to look at past network data in DNA Center. How long can you look back into the DNA snapshot?
   A. 1 Day
   B. 3 Days
   C. 5 Days
   D. 1 Week
   E. 1 Month

8. You want to send a console message to a syslog server, but you only want to send status messages of 3 and lower. Which of the following commands will you use?
   A. logging trap emergencies
   B. logging trap errors
   C. logging trap debugging
   D. logging trap notifications
   E. logging trap critical
   F. logging trap warnings
   G. logging trap alerts

9. You are using the Code Preview feature. Which of the following is this used for? (Choose three.)
   A. Enroll in beta updates for DNA Center
   B. View what a code will do when ran against DNA Center
   C. Generates a sample code snippet to call the Restful API resource in the scripting language to your choice.
   D. Viewing the source code for a DNA Center application

10. You need to connect to a remote IPv6 server in your virtual server farm. You can connect to the IPv4 servers, but not the critical IPv6 server you desperately need. Based on the following output, what could your problem be?

```
C:\>ipconfig
    Connection-specific DNS Suffix  . : localdomain
    IPv6 Address. . . . . . . . . . . : 2001:db8:3c4d:3:ac3b:2ef:1823:8938
    Temporary IPv6 Address. . . . . . : 2001:db8:3c4d:3:2f33:44dd:211:1c3d
```

```
Link-local IPv6 Address . . . . . : fe80::ac3b:2ef:1823:8938%11
IPv4 Address. . . . . . . . . . . : 10.1.1.10
Subnet Mask . . . . . . . . . . . : 255.255.255.0
Default Gateway . . . . . . . . . : 10.1.1.1
```

    A. The global address is in the wrong subnet.

    B. The IPv6 default gateway has not been configured or received from the router.

    C. The link-local address has not been resolved so the host cannot communicate to the router.

    D. There are two IPv6 global addresses configured. One must be removed from the configuration.

11. What command is used to view the IPv6-to-MAC-address resolution table on a Cisco router?

    A. `show ip arp`

    B. `show ipv6 arp`

    C. `show ip neighbors`

    D. `show ipv6 neighbors`

    E. `show arp`

12. An IPv6 ARP entry is listed as with a status of REACH. What can you conclude about the IPv6-to-MAC-address mapping?

    A. The interface has communicated with the neighbor address and the mapping is current.

    B. The interface has not communicated within the neighbor reachable time frame.

    C. The ARP entry has timed out.

    D. IPv6 can reach the neighbor address but the addresses has not yet been resolved.

13. Which configuration management solutions require agents? (Choose two.)

    A. Puppet

    B. Ansible

    C. Chef

    D. Cisco IOS

14. _____ is a Ruby-based configuration management tool that uses custom manifest files to configure devices.

    A. Ansible

    B. Puppet

    C. Chef

    D. Manifold

15. _____ is a Ruby-based configuration tool that uses cookbooks to apply configuration.
    A. Ansible
    B. Puppet
    C. Chef
    D. Manifold

16. You have two OSPF directly configured routers that are not forming an adjacency. What should you check? (Choose three.)
    A. Process ID
    B. Hello and dead timers
    C. Link cost
    D. Area
    E. IP address/subnet mask

17. When do two adjacent routers enter the 2WAY state?
    A. After both routers have received Hello information
    B. After they have exchanged topology databases
    C. When they connect only to a DR or BDR
    D. When they need to exchange RID information

18. You want to use the Command Runner. What is this used for?
    A. Pushing OSPF configuration
    B. Pushing Show commands and viewing the results
    C. Pushing ACL configuration
    D. Pushing Interface configurations
    E. Pushing a banner configuration

19. What type of switching is done in a network fabric?
    A. Layer 2
    B. Layer 3
    C. Layer 4
    D. Layer 7

20. Which statement about GRE is not true?
    A. GRE is stateless and has no flow control.
    B. GRE has security.
    C. GRE has additional overhead for tunneled packets, at least 24 bytes.
    D. GRE uses a protocol-type field in the GRE header so any layer 3 protocol can be used through the tunnel.

21. Which QoS mechanism will drop traffic if a session uses more than the allotted bandwidth?
    A. Congestion management
    B. Shaping
    C. Policing
    D. Marking

22. IPv6 unicast routing is running on the Corp router. Which of the following addresses would show up with the `show ipv6 int brief` command?

    ```
    Corp#sh int f0/0
    FastEthernet0/0 is up, line protocol is up
    Hardware is AmdFE, address is 000d.bd3b.0d80 (bia 000d.bd3b.0d80)
    [output cut]
    ```

    A. FF02::3c3d:0d:bdff:fe3b:0d80
    B. FE80::3c3d:2d:bdff:fe3b:0d80
    C. FE80::3c3d:0d:bdff:fe3b:0d80
    D. FE80::3c3d:2d:ffbd:3bfe:0d80

23. A host sends a type of NDP message providing the MAC address that was requested. Which type of NDP was sent?
    A. NA
    B. RS
    C. RA
    D. NS

24. Each field in an IPv6 address is how many bits long?
    A. 4
    B. 16
    C. 32
    D. 128

25. To enable OSPFv3, which of the following would you use?
    A. `Router(config-if)#ipv6 ospf 10 area 0.0.0.0`
    B. `Router(config-if)#ipv6 router rip 1`
    C. `Router(config)#ipv6 router eigrp 10`
    D. `Router(config-rtr)#no shutdown`
    E. `Router(config-if)#ospf ipv6 10 area 0`

26. What does the command `routerA(config)#line cons 0` allow you to perform next?
    A. Set the Telnet password.
    B. Shut down the router.

C. Set your console password.
D. Disable console connections.

27. Which two statements describe the IP address 10.16.3.65/23? (Choose two.)
    A. The subnet address is 10.16.3.0 255.255.254.0.
    B. The lowest host address in the subnet is 10.16.2.1 255.255.254.0.
    C. The last valid host address in the subnet is 10.16.2.254 255.255.254.0.
    D. The broadcast address of the subnet is 10.16.3.255 255.255.254.0.
    E. The network is not subnetted.

28. On which interface do you configure an IP address for a switch?
    A. `int fa0/0`
    B. `int vty 0 15`
    C. `int vlan 1`
    D. `int s/0/0`

29. Which of the following is the valid host range for the subnet on which the IP address 192.168.168.188 255.255.255.192 resides?
    A. 192.168.168.129–190
    B. 192.168.168.129–191
    C. 192.168.168.128–190
    D. 192.168.168.128–192

30. Which of the following is considered to be the inside host's address after translation?
    A. Inside local
    B. Outside local
    C. Inside global
    D. Outside global

31. Your inside locals are not being translated to the inside global addresses. Which of the following commands will show you if your inside globals are allowed to use the NAT pool?

    ```
    ip nat pool Corp 198.18.41.129 198.18.41.134 netmask 255.255.255.248
    ip nat inside source list 100 int pool Corp overload
    ```

    A. `debug ip nat`
    B. `show access-list`
    C. `show ip nat translation`
    D. `show ip nat statistics`

32. How many collision domains are created when you segment a network with a 12-port switch?
   A. 1
   B. 2
   C. 5
   D. 12

33. Which of the following commands will allow you to set your Telnet password on a Cisco router?
   A. `line telnet 0 4`
   B. `line aux 0 4`
   C. `line vty 0 4`
   D. `line con 0`

34. Which router command allows you to view the entire contents of all access lists?
   A. `show all access-lists`
   B. `show access-lists`
   C. `show ip interface`
   D. `show interface`

35. What does a VLAN do?
   A. Acts as the fastest port to all servers
   B. Provides multiple collision domains on one switch port
   C. Breaks up broadcast domains in a layer 2 switch internetwork
   D. Provides multiple broadcast domains within a single collision domain

36. If you wanted to delete the configuration stored in NVRAM, choose the best answer for the Cisco objectives.
   A. `erase startup`
   B. `delete running`
   C. `erase flash`
   D. `erase running`

37. Which protocol is used to send a destination network unknown message back to originating hosts?
   A. TCP
   B. ARP
   C. ICMP
   D. BootP

38. Which class of IP address provides 15 bits for subnetting?
   A. A
   B. B
   C. C
   D. D

39. What DNS record do you need to create for APs to automatically discover the WLC.
   A. CISCO-WLC-CONTROLLER
   B. WLC-CONTROLLER
   C. CISCO-AP-CONTROLLER
   D. CISCO-DISCOVER-CONTROLLER
   E. CISCO-CAPWAP-CONTROLLER

40. Which one of the following is true regarding VLANs?
   A. Two VLANs are configured by default on all Cisco switches.
   B. VLANs only work if you have a complete Cisco switched internetwork. No off-brand switches are allowed.
   C. You should not have more than 10 switches in the same VTP domain.
   D. You need to have a trunk link configured between switches in order to send information about more than one VLAN down the link.

41. Which two of the following commands will place network 10.2.3.0/24 into area 0? (Choose two.)
   A. `router eigrp 10`
   B. `router ospf 10`
   C. `router rip`
   D. `network 10.0.0.0`
   E. `network 10.2.3.0 255.255.255.0 area 0`
   F. `network 10.2.3.0 0.0.0.255 area0`
   G. `network 10.2.3.0 0.0.0.255 area 0`

42. What command do you use to lookup a module in Ansible?
   A. Ansible-doc
   B. Ansible-execute
   C. Ansible-Playbook
   D. Run-Playbook

43. If routers in a single area are configured with the same priority value, what value does a router use for the OSPF router ID in the absence of a loopback interface?
    A. The lowest IP address of any physical interface
    B. The highest IP address of any physical interface
    C. The lowest IP address of any logical interface
    D. The highest IP address of any logical interface

44. What protocols are used to configure trunking on a switch? (Choose two.)
    A. VLAN Trunking Protocol
    B. VLAN
    C. 802.1q
    D. ISL

45. What's the default QoS queue for a WLAN?
    A. Gold
    B. Platinum
    C. Bronze
    D. Silver
    E. Diamond

46. Where is a hub specified in the OSI model?
    A. Session layer
    B. Physical layer
    C. Data Link layer
    D. Application layer

47. What are the two main types of access control lists (ACLs)? (Choose two.)
    A. Standard
    B. IEEE
    C. Extended
    D. Specialized

48. Which port does TACACS+ use for accounting?
    A. UDP 49
    B. UDP 1645
    C. UDP 1812
    D. UDP 1813
    E. TCP 49

49. What command is used to create a backup configuration?
    A. `copy running backup`
    B. `copy running-config startup-config`

    C. `config mem`

    D. `wr net`

50. 1000Base-T is which IEEE standard?

    A. 802.3f

    B. 802.3z

    C. 802.3ab

    D. 802.3ae

51. Which protocol does DHCP use at the Transport layer?

    A. IP

    B. TCP

    C. UDP

    D. ARP

52. Which of the following best describes a Resource in Restful API?

    A. The specific path to the resource you're trying to access through the API

    B. The security token for the request.

    C. Filtering options for the request

    D. The full URL

53. Which command is used to determine if an access list is enabled on a particular interface?

    A. `show access-lists`

    B. `show interface`

    C. `show ip interface`

    D. `show interface access-lists`

54. Which of the following statements is true with regard to ISL and 802.1q?

    A. 802.1q encapsulates the frame with control information; ISL inserts an ISL field along with tag control information.

    B. 802.1q is Cisco proprietary.

    C. ISL encapsulates the frame with control information; 802.1q inserts an 802.1q field along with tag control information.

    D. ISL is a standard.

55. The protocol data unit (PDU) encapsulation is completed in which order?

    A. Bits, frames, packets, segments, data

    B. Data, bits, segments, frames, packets

    C. Data, segments, packets, frames, bits

    D. Packets, frames, bits, segments, data

56. Based on the configuration shown below, what statement is true?

```
S1(config)#ip routing
S1(config)#int vlan 10
S1(config-if)#ip address 192.168.10.1 255.255.255.0
S1(config-if)#int vlan 20
S1(config-if)#ip address 192.168.20.1 255.255.255.0
```

- **A.** This is a multilayer switch.
- **B.** The two VLANs are in the same subnet.
- **C.** Encapsulation must be configured.
- **D.** VLAN 10 is the management VLAN.

57. You boss read about WPA3 and want you to explain it to him. What replaced the default open authentication with which of the following enhancements?
- **A.** AES
- **B.** OWL
- **C.** OWE
- **D.** TKIP

58. Which AP modes serve wireless traffic? (Choose 2)
- **A.** Local
- **B.** Monitor
- **C.** FlexConnect
- **D.** Sniffer
- **E.** SE-Connect

59. Which of the following choices best defines a token in Restful API?
- **A.** How you filter the response from the Restful API service
- **B.** How you save the output from the Restful API service
- **C.** How you authorize access to the Restful API service
- **D.** How you authenticate to the Restful API service

60. What can the Code Preview feature be used for? (Choose three.)
- **A.** Enroll in beta updates for DNA Center
- **B.** View what a code will do when ran against DNA Center
- **C.** Generates a sample code snippet to call the Restful API resource in the scripting language to your choice
- **D.** Viewing the source code for a DNA Center application

Answers to Assessment Test

1. B. To allow for the PVST+ to operate, there's a field inserted into the BPDU to accommodate the extended system ID so that PVST+ can have a root bridge configured on a per-STP instance. The extended system ID (VLAN ID) is a 12-bit field, and we can even see what this field is carrying via show spanning-tree command output. See Chapter 9 for more information.

2. A. Cisco's EtherChannel can bundle up to eight ports between switches to provide resiliency and more bandwidth between switches. See Chapter 9 for more information.

3. B, C, E. All the ports on both sides of every link must be configured exactly the same between switches or it will not work. Speed, duplex, and allowed VLANs must match. See Chapter 15 for more information.

4. C. 2100 boots the router into ROM monitor mode, 2101 loads the mini-IOS from ROM, and 2102 is the default and loads the IOS from flash. See Chapter 12 for more information.

5. D. The show license udi command displays the unique device identifier (UDI) of the router, which comprises the product ID (PID) and serial number of the router. See Chapter 12 for more information.

6. B. The show license feature command allows you to view the technology package licenses and feature licenses that are supported on your router along with several status variables related to software activation and licensing, both licensed and unlicensed features. See Chapter 12 for more information.

7. D. DNA Center stores the network snapshot for one week.

8. B. There are eight different trap levels. If you choose, for example level 3, level 0 through level 3 messages will be displayed. See Chapter 13 for more information.

9. C. The Code Preview feature in can generate a simple code snippet for several programming languages so you can quickly add it into your script. See Chapter 21 for more information.

10. B. There is no IPv6 default gateway listed in the output, which will be the link-local address of the router interface, sent to the host as a router advertisement. Until this host receives the router address, the host will communicate with IPv6 only on the local subnet. See Chapter 17 for more information.

11. D. The command show ipv6 neighbors provides the ARP cache for on a router. See Chapter 17 for more information.

12. A. If the state is STALE when the interface has not communicated within the neighbor reachable time frame, the next time the neighbor communicates, the state will be REACH. See Chapter 17 for more information.

13. A, C. Puppet and Chef require you to install an agent on the node before the configuration server can manage it. See Chapter 23 for more information.

14. B. Puppet is a Ruby-based configuration management tool that uses custom manifest files to configure devices. See Chapter 23 for more information.

15. C. Chef is a Ruby-based configuration tool that uses cookbooks to apply configuration. See Chapter 23 for more information.

16. B, D, E. In order for two OSPF routers to create an adjacency, the Hello and dead timers must match, and they must both be configured into the same area, as well as being in the same subnet. See Chapter 6 for more information.

17. A. The process starts by sending out Hello packets. Every listening router will then add the originating router to the neighbor database. The responding routers will reply with all of their Hello information so that the originating router can add them to its own neighbor table. At this point, we will have reached the 2WAY state—only certain routers will advance beyond to this. See Chapter 6 for more information.

18. B. The Command Runner is a useful tool for pushing show commands to devices and viewing the results. See Chapter 22 for more information.

19. B. A fabric entirely consists of layer 3 only. See Chapter 22 for more information.

20. B. Generic Routing Encapsulation (GRE) has no built-in security mechanisms. See Chapter 15 for more information.

21. C. When traffic exceeds the allocated rate, the policer can take one of two actions. It can either drop traffic or re-mark it to another class of service. The new class usually has a higher drop probability. See Chapter 16 for more information.

22. B. This can be a hard question if you don't remember to invert the 7th bit of the first octet in the MAC address! Always look for the 7th bit when studying for the Cisco R/S, and when using eui-64, invert it. The eui-64 autoconfiguration then inserts an FF:FE in the middle of the 48-bit MAC address to create a unique IPv6 address. See Chapter 17 for more information.

23. A. The NDP neighbor advertisement (NA) contains the MAC address. A neighbor solicitation (NS) was initially sent asking for the MAC address. See Chapter 17 for more information.

24. B. Each field in an IPv6 address is 16 bits long. An IPv6 address is a total of 128 bits. See Chapter 17 for more information.

25. A. To enable OSPFv3, you enable the protocol at the interface level, as with RIPng. The command string is area-id. It's important to understand that area 0 and area 0.0.0.0 both describe area 0. See Chapter 17 for more information.

26. C. The command `line console 0` places you at a prompt where you can then set your console user-mode password. See Chapter 13 for more information.

Answers to Assessment Test **liii**

27. B, D. The mask 255.255.254.0 (/23) used with a Class A address means that there are 15 subnet bits and 9 host bits. The block size in the third octet is 2 (256–254). So this makes the subnets in the interesting octet 0, 2, 4, 6, etc., all the way to 254. The host 10.16.3.65 is in the 2.0 subnet. The next subnet is 4.0, so the broadcast address for the 2.0 subnet is 3.255. The valid host addresses are 2.1 through 3.254. See Chapter 3 for more information.

28. C. The IP address is configured under a logical interface, called a management domain or VLAN 1, by default. See Chapter 8 for more information.

29. A. 256 – 192 = 64, so 64 is our block size. Just count in increments of 64 to find our subnet: 64 + 64 = 128. 128 + 64 = 192. The subnet is 128, the broadcast address is 191, and the valid host range is the numbers in between, or 129–190. See Chapter 3 for more information.

30. C. An inside global address is considered to be the IP address of the host on the private network after translation. See Chapter 11 for more information.

31. B. Once you create your pool, the command `ip nat inside source` must be used to say which inside locals are allowed to use the pool. In this question, we need to see if access list 100 is configured correctly, if at all, so `show access-list` is the best answer. See Chapter 11 for more information.

32. D. Layer 2 switching creates individual collision domains per port. See Chapter 7 for more information.

33. C. The command line vty 0 4 places you in a prompt that will allow you to set or change your Telnet password. See Chapter 13 for more information.

34. B. To see the contents of all access lists, use the `show access-lists` command. See Chapter 10 for more information.

35. C. VLANs break up broadcast domains at layer 2. See Chapter 8 for more information.

36. A. The command `erase startup-config` deletes the configuration stored in NVRAM. See Chapter 12 for more information.

37. C. ICMP is the protocol at the Network layer that is used to send messages back to an originating router. See Chapter 2 for more information.

38. A. Class A addressing provides 22 bits for host subnetting. Class B provides 16 bits, but only 14 are available for subnetting. Class C provides only 6 bits for subnetting. See Chapter 3 for more information.

39. E. For the DNS method you need to create a A record for CISCO-CAPWAP-CONTROLLER that points to the WLC management IP.

40. D. Switches send information about only one VLAN down a link unless it is configured as a trunk link. See Chapter 8 for more information.

41. B, G. To enable OSPF, you must first start OSPF using a process ID. The number is irrelevant; just choose a number from 1 to 65,535 and you're good to go. After you start the OSPF process, you must configure interfaces on which to activate OSPF using the network command with wildcards and specification of an area. Option F is wrong because there must be a space after the parameter area and before you list the area number. See Chapter 6 for more information.

42. C. Ansible uses the **ansible-doc** command to look up a module and how to use it. See Chapter 23 for more information.

43. B. At the moment of OSPF process startup, the highest IP address on any active interface will be the router ID (RID) of the router. If you have a loopback interface configured (logical interface), then that will override the interface IP address and become the RID of the router automatically. See Chapter 6 for more information.

44. C, D. VLAN Trunking Protocol (VTP) is not right because it has nothing to do with trunking except that it sends VLAN information across a trunk link. 802.1q and ISL encapsulations are used to configure trunking on a port. See Chapter 8 for more information.

45. D. WLANs default to silver queue, which effectively means no QoS is being utilized. See Chapter 20 for more information.

46. B. Hubs regenerate electrical signals, which are specified at the Physical layer. See Chapter 1 for more information.

47. A, C. Standard and extended access control lists (ACLs) are used to configure security on a router. See Chapter 10 for more information.

48. E. TACACS+ uses port TCP 49 for all operations. See Chapter 20 for more information.

49. B. The command to back up the configuration on a router is copy running-config startup-config. See Chapter 12 for more information.

50. C. IEEE 802.3ab is the standard for 1 Gbps on twisted-pair. See Chapter 1 for more information.

51. C. User Datagram Protocol is a connection network service at the Transport layer, and DHCP uses this connectionless service. See Chapter 2 for more information.

52. A. The resource section of the URI points to the specific. See Chapter 21 for more information.

53. C. The show ip interface command will show you if any interfaces have an outbound or inbound access list set. See Chapter 12 for more information.

54. C. Unlike ISL, which encapsulates the frame with control information, 802.1q inserts an 802.1q field along with tag control information. See Chapter 8 for more information.

55. C. The PDU encapsulation method defines how data is encoded as it goes through each layer of the TCP/IP model. Data is segmented at the Transport later, packets created at the Network layer, frames at the Data Link layer, and finally, the Physical layer encodes the 1s and 0s into a digital signal. See Chapter 1 for more information.

56. A. With a multilayer switch, enable IP routing and create one logical interface for each VLAN using the `interface vlan number` command and you're now doing inter-VLAN routing on the backplane of the switch! See Chapter 8 for more information.

57. C. The 802.11 "open" authentication support has been replaced with Opportunistic Wireless Encryption (OWE) enhancement, which is an enhancement, not a mandatory certified setting. See Chapter 19 for more information.

58. A, C. The two AP-Modes listed that can serve wireless traffic are local and flexconnect. See Chapter 20 for more information.

59. D. The token is used to authenticate you to the restful API service. Restful API does not support authorization. See Chapter 21 for more information.

60. C. The Code Preview feature in can generate a simple code snippet for several programming languages so you can quickly add it into your script. See Chapter 22 for more information.

Chapter 1

Network Fundamentals

WE'LL COVER THE FOLLOWING CCNA EXAM TOPICS IN THIS CHAPTER:

1.0 Network Fundamentals

✓ **1.1 Explain the role and function of network components**

- 1.1.a Routers
- 1.1.b L2 and L3 switches
- 1.1.c Next-generation firewalls and IPS

✓ **1.2 Describe characteristics of network topology architectures**

- 1.2.a 2 tier
- 1.2.b 3 tier
- 1.2.c Spine-leaf
- 1.2.d WAN
- 1.2.e Small office/home office (SOHO)

✓ **1.3 Compare physical interface and cabling types**

- 1.3.a Single-mode fiber, multimode fiber, copper
- 1.3.b Connections (Ethernet shared media and point-to-point)
- 1.3.c Concepts of PoE

This chapter is really an internetworking review, focusing on how to connect networks together using Cisco routers and switches. As a heads up, I've written it with the assumption that you have a bit of basic networking knowledge and/or have read the first chapter in the CCNA Part 1: Understanding Cisco Networking Technologies study guide.

That said, there isn't a whole lot of new material here, but even if you're a seasoned network professional, you should still read through *all* chapters to make sure you get how the objectives are currently covered.

Let's start by defining exactly what an internetwork is: You create an internetwork when you connect two or more networks via a router and configure a logical network addressing scheme with protocols like IP or IPv6.

We'll move on to covering network components like routers and switches and defining what exactly creates a Small Office Home Office Network (SOHO). After that, we'll touch on Next Generation Firewalls (NGFWs) and network architect models, and then I'll guide you through an overview of Ethernet and the wiring used in Local Area Networks (LANs) and Wide Area Networks (WANs).

> To find your included bonus material, as well as Todd Lammle videos, practice questions & hands-on labs, please see www.lammle.com/ccna

Network Components

So why is it so important to learn Cisco internetworking anyway?

Networks and networking have grown exponentially over the past 20 years, and understandably so. They've had to evolve at light speed just to keep up with huge increases in basic, mission-critical user needs from simply sharing data and printers to bigger burdens like multimedia remote presentations, conferencing, and the like. Unless everyone who needs to share network resources is located in the same office space, the challenge is to connect relevant networks so all users can share the wealth of whatever services and resources they need, on site or remotely.

Figure 1.1 shows a basic *local area network (LAN)* connected via a *hub*, which is basically an antiquated device, which connects wires together and is typically used in SOHO networks.

Keep in mind that a simple SOHO network like this one would be considered one collision domain and one broadcast domain.

FIGURE 1.1 A very basic SOHO network

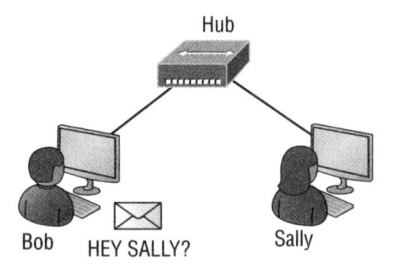

Things really can't get much simpler than this. And yes, though you can still find this configuration in some home networks, even many of those as well as the smallest business networks are more complicated today.

Routers, Switches, and Oh So SOHO!

Figure 1.2 shows a network that's been segmented with a switch, making each network segment that connects to the switch its own separate collision domain. Doing this results in a lot less chaos!

FIGURE 1.2 A switch can break up collision domains.

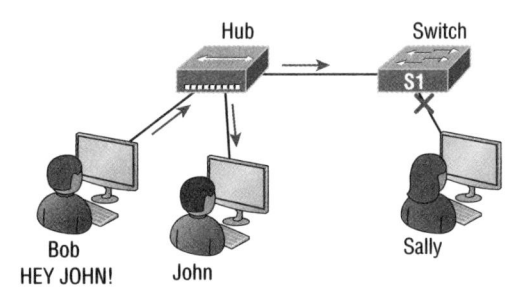

So, this is a great start, but I really want you to note that this network is still just one, single broadcast domain. This means we've really only reduced our PC's chaos—not eliminated it.

For example, if there's some sort of vital announcement that everyone in our network neighborhood needs to hear about, it will definitely still get loud! You can see that the hub used in Figure 1.2 just extended the one collision domain from the switch port. The result is that John received the data from Bob but, happily, Sally did not, which is good because Bob intended to talk with John directly. If he had needed to send a broadcast instead, everyone, including Sally, would have received it, causing unnecessary congestion.

Here's a list of some of the things that commonly cause LAN traffic congestion:

- Too many hosts in a collision or broadcast domain
- Broadcast storms
- Too much multicast traffic
- Low bandwidth
- Adding hubs for connectivity to the network
- A bunch of ARP broadcasts

Take another look at Figure 1.2 and make sure you see that I extended the main hub from Figure 1.1 to a switch in Figure 1.2. I did that because hubs don't segment a network; they just connect network segments. Basically, it's an inexpensive way to connect a couple of PCs, which can work for really simple home use and troubleshooting, but that's about it!

As our community grows, we'll need to add more streets along with traffic control and even some basic security. We'll get this done by adding routers because these convenient devices are used to connect networks and route packets of data from one network to another. Cisco became the de facto standard for routers because of its unparalleled selection of high-quality router products and fantastic service. So never forget that by default, routers are basically employed to efficiently break up a *broadcast domain*—the set of all devices on a network segment, which are allowed to "hear" all broadcasts sent out on that specific segment.

Figure 1.3 depicts a router in our growing network, creating an internetwork and breaking up broadcast domains.

FIGURE 1.3 Routers create an internetwork.

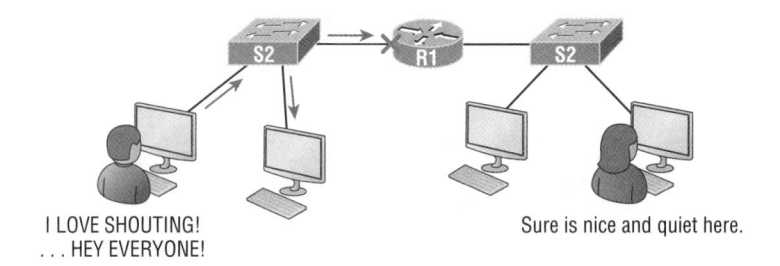

I LOVE SHOUTING!
. . . HEY EVERYONE!

Sure is nice and quiet here.

The network in Figure 1.3 is actually a pretty cool little network. Each host is connected to its own collision domain because of the switch, and the router has created two broadcast domains. So now Sally is happily living in peace in a completely different neighborhood, no longer subjected to Bob's incessant shouting! If Bob wants to talk with Sally, he has to send a packet with a destination address using her IP address—he cannot broadcast for her!

But there's more... Routers provide connections to *wide area network (WAN)* services as well via a serial interface for WAN connections—specifically, a V.35 physical interface on a Cisco router.

Let me make sure you understand why breaking up a broadcast domain is so important. When a host or server sends a network broadcast, every device on the network must read and process that broadcast—unless you have a router. When the router's interface receives this broadcast, it can respond by basically saying, "no thanks," and discard the broadcast without forwarding it on to other networks. Even though routers are known for breaking up broadcast domains by default, it's important to remember that they break up collision domains as well.

There are two advantages to using routers in your network:

- They don't forward broadcasts by default.
- They can filter the network based on layer 3 (Network layer) information such as an IP address.

Conversely, we don't use layer 2 switches to create internetworks because they don't break up broadcast domains by default. Instead, they're employed to add functionality to a network LAN. The main purpose of these switches is to make a LAN work better—to optimize its performance—providing more bandwidth for the LAN's users. Also, these switches don't forward packets to other networks like routers do. Instead, they only "switch" frames from one port to another within the switched network. And don't worry, even though you're probably thinking, "Wait—what are frames and packets?" I promise to completely fill you in later in this chapter. For now, think of a packet as a package containing data.

Okay, so by default, switches break up collision domains, but what are these things? A *Collision domain* is an Ethernet term used to describe a network scenario in which one device sends a packet out on a network segment and every other device on that same segment is forced to pay attention to it no matter what. This isn't efficient because if a different device tries to transmit at the same time, a collision will occur, requiring both devices to retransmit, one at a time—not good! And this happens a lot in a hub environment, where each host segment connects to a hub that represents only one collision domain and a single broadcast domain. By contrast, each and every port on a switch represents its own collision domain, allowing network traffic to flow much more smoothly.

Layer 2 switching is considered hardware-based bridging because it uses specialized hardware called an *application-specific integrated circuit (ASIC)*. ASICs can run up to high gigabit speeds with very low latency rates.

> *Latency* is the time measured from when a frame enters a port to when it exits a port.

Switches read each frame as it passes through the network. The layer 2 device then puts the source hardware address in a filter table and keeps track of which port the frame was received on. This information (logged in the bridge's or switch's filter table) is what helps the machine determine the location of the specific sending device.

Figure 1.4 shows a switch in an internetwork and how John is sending packets to the Internet. Sally doesn't hear his frames because she's in a different collision domain. The destination frame goes directly to the default gateway router, so Sally doesn't even see John's traffic.

FIGURE 1.4 Switches work at layer 2.

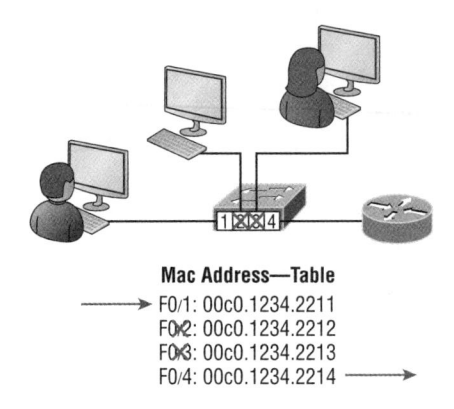

Mac Address—Table
F0/1: 00c0.1234.2211
F0/2: 00c0.1234.2212
F0/3: 00c0.1234.2213
F0/4: 00c0.1234.2214

The real estate business is all about location, location, location, and it's the same way for layer 2 and layer 3 devices. Although both need to be able to negotiate the network, it's crucial to remember that they're concerned with very different parts of it. Primarily, layer 3 machines, like routers, need to locate specific networks, whereas layer 2 machines like switches and bridges need to eventually locate specific devices. So, networks are to routers as individual devices are to switches and bridges. And routing tables that "map" the internetwork are for routers as filter tables that "map" individual devices are for switches and bridges.

After a filter table is built on the layer 2 device, it will forward frames only to the segment where the destination hardware address is located. If the destination device is on the same segment as the source host, the layer 2 device will block the frame from going to any other segments. If the destination is on a different segment, the frame can be transmitted only to that segment. This is called *transparent bridging*.

When a switch interface receives a frame with a destination hardware address that isn't found in the device's filter table, it will forward the frame to all connected segments. If the unknown device that was sent the "mystery frame" replies to this forwarding action, the switch updates its filter table regarding that device's location. But in the event the destination address of the transmitting frame is a broadcast address, the switch will forward all broadcasts to every connected segment by default.

All devices that the broadcast is forwarded to are considered to be in the same broadcast domain. This can be a problem because layer 2 devices propagate layer 2 broadcast storms that can seriously choke performance, and the only way to stop a broadcast storm from propagating through an internetwork is with a layer 3 device—a router!

Next-Generation Firewalls and IPS

Today's networks definitely need security, and as our network grows, we'll need to increase protection for it. Just like we'd add locks to our doors and windows, and then maybe a fence, then even a bigger fence—with a locked gate and even some barbed wire to top it off... We can go on and on here. You get the picture.

There are new devices out that are actually seriously solid firewalls. I'll mention Next Generations Firewalls (NGFW) providing full layer-7 inspection, as though it's just a bump in the wire (meaning little delay), which is mostly true. However, it's totally true that every company, including Cisco, markets their devices like this.

Figure 1.5 pictures devices in a small network and how a basic firewall or NGFW can be placed to provide security in your network.

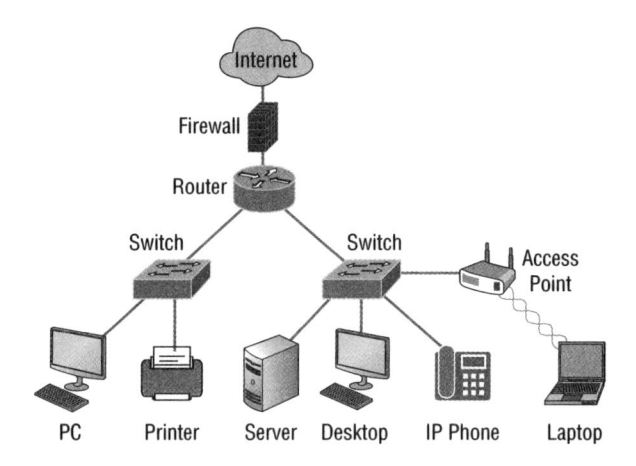

FIGURE 1.5 Physical components of a network

Firewall and NGFW design can be pretty complicated, but we don't need to get into the weeds here. Since this is a Cisco book, we're going to stick with Cisco technologies for our firewall. Cisco has a Next Generation Firewall (NGFW) called Firepower that they acquired from a company called SourceFire in 2013.

> **Note:** Now understand this is going to be a brief introduction to NGFW and Intrusion Prevention Systems (IPS). Why? Because I have a two-book series on CCNP Security Securing Cisco Network Firewalls (SCNF) that covers this topic in depth with well over 1500 pages of information! That's a lot of firewall info. We'll just get our feet wet for now.

So let's start by defining a NGFW and what it has to do with Intrusion Prevention Systems (IPS). NGFWs are considered a third-generation firewall technology that provides full packet reassembly and deep-packet inspect up to and through layer 7.

NGFW's are popular because they permit application visibility and control (AVC) as well as offer intrusion prevention system (IPS) policies, which help us look for attacks on known client vulnerabilities.

And no one said this technology is cheap. For example, the newer firewalls can provide SSL decryption, which sounds simple, but there's a catch. To be able provide that kind of shield at close to wire speed you've got to have hardware encryption acceleration capability, which will cost you plenty!

The NGFWs today have everything but the kitchen sink in their code just to stay competitive, and this causes all sorts of issues for the manufacturers when struggling to keep up with the market.

Here's a taste… All NGFWs must, at a minimum, include the following:

- Be router and switch compatible (L2/L3)
- They must add packet filtering with IPS and Malware inspection capability
- Provide Network Address Translation (NAT)
- Permit stateful inspection
- Permit Virtual Private Networks (VPNs)
- Provide URL and Application filtering
- Implement QoS
- Third-party integration
- Support for REST API

That's not a short list, and the items in it are all absolutely required because NGFWs must pack a powerful security punch in order to lock our modern networks down tight!

Figure 1.6 shows a Cisco Firepower NGFW blocking an attacker trying to exploit a vulnerability on my network, which IPS stopped dead. The red line on top indicates all the attacks and the blue line is for the data. Wow—that's a lot of attacks!

FIGURE 1.6 NGFW can stop attacks in real time.

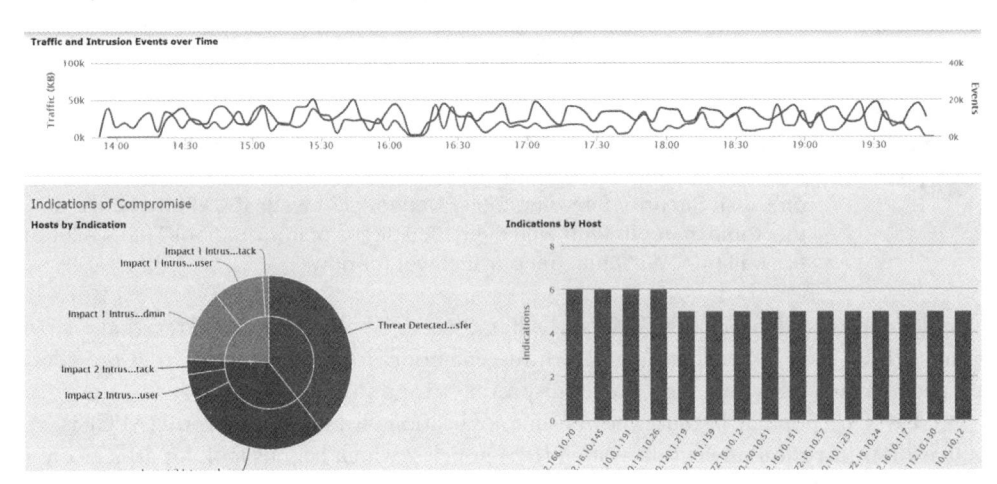

Now, let's dig into those attacks. Well see how the Cisco Firepower NGFW came to the rescue by blocking all those attacks via my IPS policy, as shown in Figure 1.6! Figure 1.7 displays some of the events that were caught by Cisco Firepower.

FIGURE 1.7 Cisco IPS policy to the rescue!

And just so you know, some of those attacks shown in Figure 1.7 were some really serious ones! Figure 1.8 displays all the actual packets that were dropped.

FIGURE 1.8 Cisco Firepower IPS policy dropped the bad guys packets!

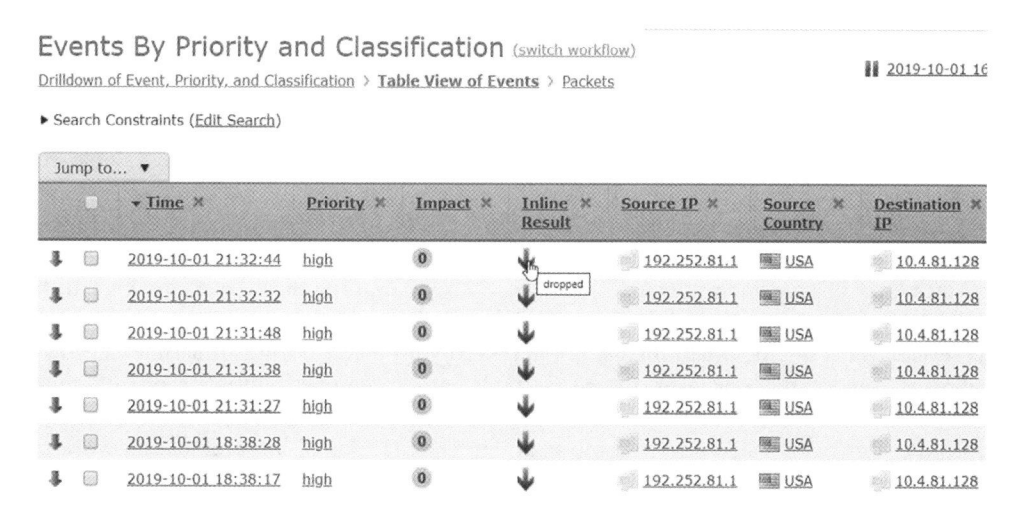

NGFWs perform a deeper inspection compared to your traditional firewall. For instance, the stateful ASA that Cisco is moving away from is being replaced with new Firepower Threat Defense (FTD) devices, which are true NGFW devices.

Network Topology Architectures

Most of us were exposed to hierarchy early in life, and anyone with older siblings learned what it was like to be at the bottom of it. Regardless of where you first discovered the concept of hierarchy, most of us experience it in many aspects of our lives. It's *hierarchy* that helps us understand where things belong, how things fit together, and what functions go where. It brings order to otherwise complex models. If you want a pay raise, for instance, hierarchy dictates that you ask your boss, not your subordinate, because that's the person whose role it is to grant or deny your request. So basically, understanding hierarchy helps us discern where we should go to get what we need.

Hierarchy offers a lot of the same benefits in network design that it does in life. When used properly, it makes networks more predictable and helps us to define which areas should perform certain functions. For example, you can use tools like access lists at certain levels within hierarchical networks and avoid them at others.

Large networks can be extremely complicated, involving multiple protocols, detailed configurations, and diverse technologies. Hierarchy helps us summarize a complex collection of details into an understandable model, bringing order from the chaos. Then, as specific configurations are needed, the model dictates the correct way to apply them.

The Cisco Three-Layer Hierarchical Model (3-Tier)

The Cisco hierarchical model can help you design, implement, and maintain a scalable, reliable, cost-effective hierarchical internetwork.

Cisco defines three layers of hierarchy, as shown in Figure 1.9, each with specific functions, and it's referred to as a 3-tier network architecture.

Each layer has specific responsibilities. Keep in mind that the three layers are logical, so they aren't necessarily physical devices. Consider the OSI model, another logical hierarchy. Its seven layers describe functions but not necessarily protocols, right? Sometimes a protocol maps to more than one layer of the OSI model, and sometimes multiple protocols communicate within a single layer.

In the same way, when we build physical implementations of hierarchical networks, we may have many devices in a single layer, or there may be a single device performing functions at two layers. Just remember that the definition of the layers is logical, not physical!

Let's take a closer look at each of the layers now.

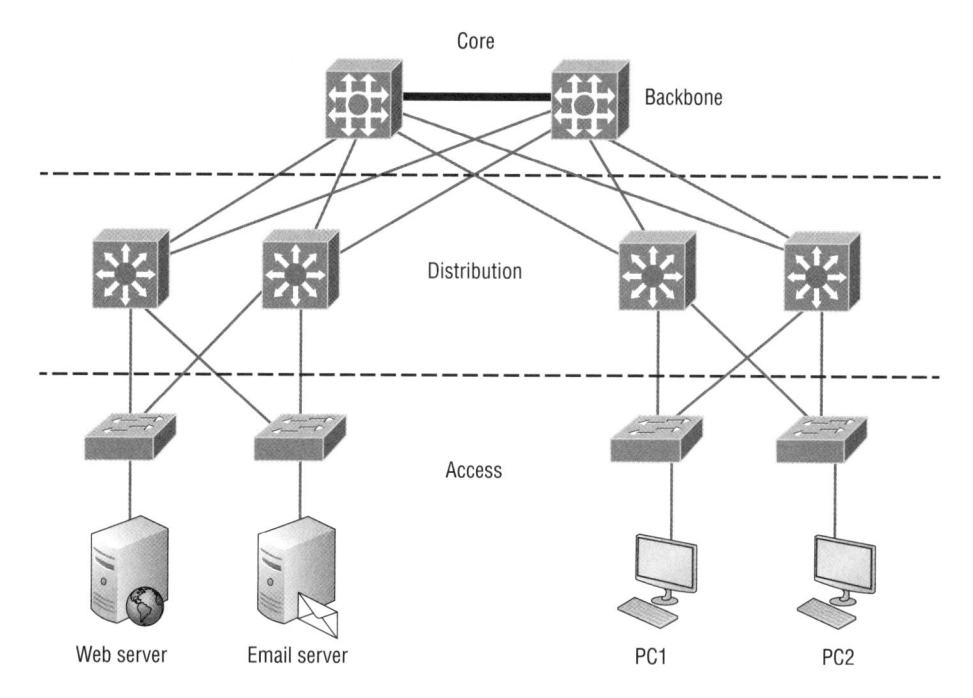

FIGURE 1.9 The Cisco hierarchical model

The Core Layer

The *core layer* is literally the core of the network. At the top of the hierarchy, this layer is responsible for transporting large amounts of traffic both reliably and quickly. The prime purpose of the network's core layer is to switch traffic as fast as possible. The traffic transported across the core is common to a majority of users, but user data is processed at the distribution layer, which forwards the requests to the core if needed.

If there's a failure in the core, *every single user* can be affected! This is why fault tolerance at this layer is so important. The core is likely to see large volumes of traffic, so speed and latency are driving concerns here. Given the function of the core, some vital design specifics come into view. Let's start with things we don't want to happen here:

- Never do anything to slow down traffic. This includes making sure you don't use access lists, perform routing between virtual local area networks, or implement packet filtering.
- Don't support workgroup access here.
- Avoid expanding the core, e.g., adding routers as the internetwork grows. If performance becomes an issue in the core, go with upgrades over expansion.

Here's a list of goals we want to achieve as we design the core:

- Design the core for high reliability. Consider data-link technologies that facilitate both speed and redundancy, like Gigabit Ethernet with redundant links or even 10 Gigabit Ethernet.
- Design with speed in mind. The core should have very little latency.
- Select routing protocols with lower convergence times. Fast and redundant data-link connectivity is no help if your routing tables are shot!

The Distribution Layer

The *distribution layer* is sometimes referred to as the workgroup or aggregation layer and is the communication point between the access layer and the core. The primary functions of the distribution layer are to provide routing, filtering, and WAN access and to determine how packets can access the core, if needed. The distribution layer must determine the fastest way that network service requests are handled—for instance, how a file request is forwarded to a server. After the distribution layer determines the best path, it forwards the request to the core layer if necessary. The core layer then quickly transports the request to the correct service.

The distribution layer is where we implement policies for the network because we have a lot of flexibility in defining network operation here. There are several things that should generally be handled at the distribution layer:

- Routing
- Implementing tools (like access lists), packet filtering, and queuing
- Implementing security and network policies, including address translation and firewalls
- Redistributing between routing protocols, including static routing
- Routing between VLANs and other workgroup support functions
- Defining broadcast and multicast domains

At the distribution layer, it's key to avoid anything limited to functions exclusively belonging to one of the other layers!

The Access Layer

The *access layer* controls user and workgroup access to internetwork resources and is sometimes referred to as the *desktop layer*. The network resources most users need are available locally because the distribution layer handles any traffic for remote services.

Here are some of the tasks the access layer carries out:

- Continued (from distribution layer) use of access control and policies
- Creation of separate collision domains (microsegmentation/switches)
- Workgroup connectivity into the distribution layer
- Device connectivity

- Resiliency and security services
- Advanced technology capabilities (voice/video, etc.)
- QoS Marking

Technologies like Gigabit or Fast Ethernet switching are frequently seen in the access layer as well.

I can't stress this enough—just because there are three separate layers does not imply three separate devices! There could be fewer or there could be more. After all, this is a *layered* approach.

Collapsed Core (2-Tier)

The Collapsed core design is also referred to as 2-tier because it's only 2-layers. But in concept, it's like the 3-tier only less expensive and geared for smaller companies. The design is meant to maximize performance and user availability to the network, while still allowing for design scalability over time.

In a 2-tier, the distribution is merged with the core layer, as shown in Figure 1.10.

FIGURE 1.10 Real-life collapsed core (2-tier) Image

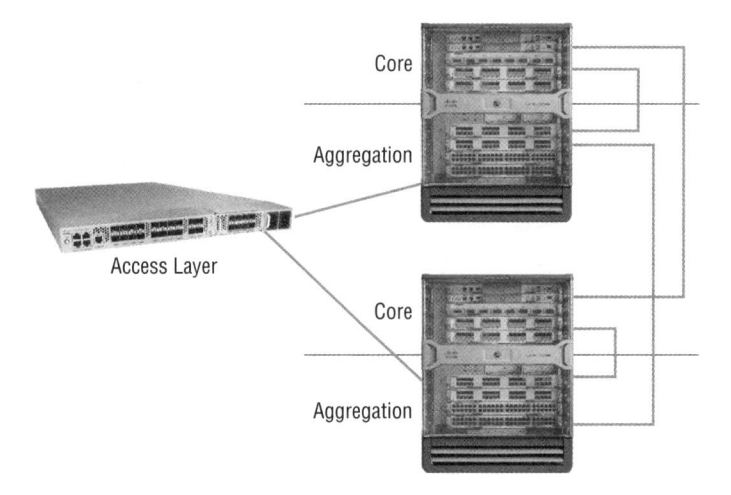

Here you see the Core and Distribution (also called Aggregation) are both running on the same large enterprise switch. The Access layer switches connect into the enterprise switch, only in the defined Aggregation ports.

This design is much more economical and it's still very functional in a campus environment, where your network many not really grow significantly larger over time. It's known as a "collapsed core" and refers to a design in which the distribution layer and core layer functions are implemented by a single device.

The big reason the collapsed core design exists is for reducing network costs, while maintaining most of the benefits of the three-tier hierarchical model.

Spine-Leaf

I've been writing about Cisco's three-tier network design for a really long time, and I just did again. But today's data centers demand a new design, and one was finally created that works really well called a *leaf-and-spine* topology. This design is still pretty old as of this writing, it's just not decades old!

Here's how it works: Your typical data center has racks filled with servers. In the leaf-and-spine design, there are switches found at the top and end of each rack that connect to these servers, with a server connecting into each switch for redundancy.

People refer to this as a top-of-rack (ToR) design because the switches physically reside at the top of a rack. Figure 1.11 pictures a top of rack network design.

FIGURE 1.11   Top of Rack Network Design

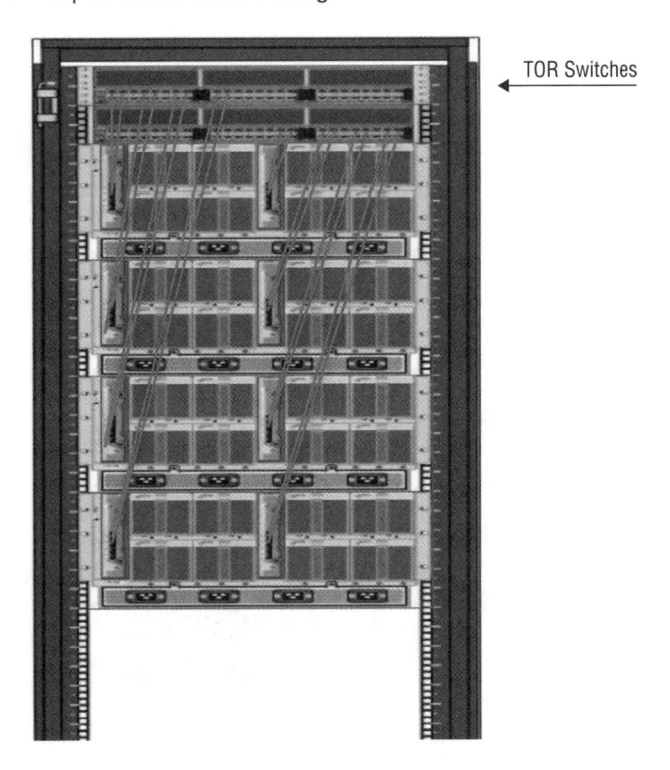

These ToR switches act as the leaves within the leaf-and-spine topology. The ports in the leaf switches connect to a node, e.g., a server in the rack, a firewall, a load-balancing appliance, or a router leaving the data center, as well as to the spine switch. Check out Figure 1.12.

FIGURE 1.12 Spine-leaf design

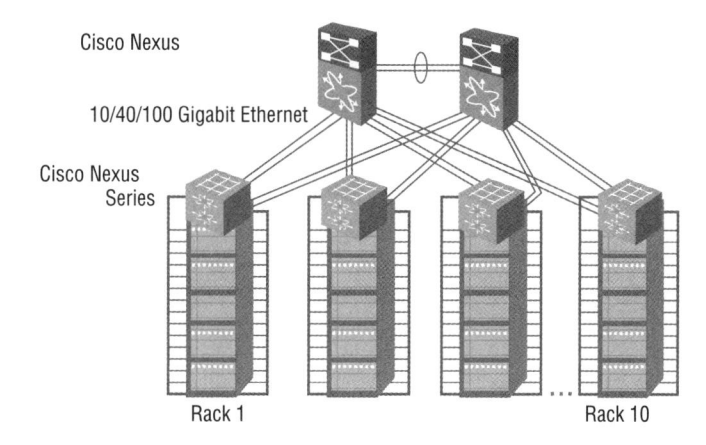

You can see each leaf switch connecting to every spine switch, which is great because it means that we no longer need a gazillion connections between switches. Keep in mind that the spine only connects to leaf devices, not to servers or end devices.

And interestingly enough, when you connect your ToR data center switches in a leaf-and-spine topology, all of your switches are the same distance away from one another (single switch hop).

WAN

Let's begin WAN basics by asking, what's the difference between a wide area network (WAN) and a local area network (LAN)? Clearly there's the distance factor, but modern wireless LANs can cover some serious turf, so there's more to it than that. What about bandwidth? Here again, really big pipes can be had for a price in many places, so that's not it either. So what's the answer we're looking for?

A major distinction between a WAN and a LAN is that while you generally own a LAN infrastructure, you usually lease a WAN infrastructure from a service provider. Modern technologies sometimes blur this characteristic somewhat, but this factor still fits neatly into the context of Cisco's exam objectives.

There are several reasons why WANs are necessary in corporate environments today. LAN technologies provide pretty solid speeds—10/2.5/40/100Gbps is now common—and they're definitely pricey. The thing is, these solutions really only work well in relatively small geographic areas. We still need WANs in a communications environment because some business needs require connections to remote sites for many reasons:

- People in the regional or branch offices of an organization need to be able to communicate and share data.
- Organizations often want to share information with other organizations across large distances.
- Employees who travel on company business frequently need to access information that resides on their corporate networks.

Here are three major characteristics of WANs:

- WANs generally connect devices that are separated by a broader geographic area than a LAN can serve.
- WANs use the services of carriers like telcos, cable companies, satellite systems, and network providers.
- WANs use serial connections of various types to provide access to bandwidth over large geographic areas.

The first key to understanding WAN technologies is to be familiar with the different WAN topologies, terms, and connection types commonly used by service providers to join our LAN networks together.

Defining WAN Terms

Before you run out and order a WAN service type from a provider, you really need to understand the following terms that service providers typically use. Here they are in Figure 1.13:

FIGURE 1.13 WAN terms

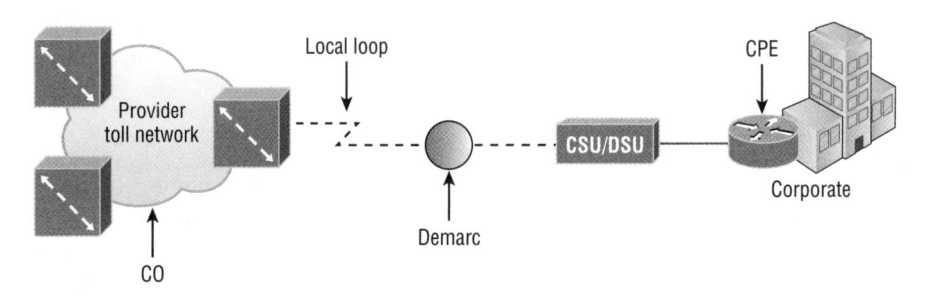

Customer premises equipment (CPE)   *Customer premises equipment (CPE)* is equipment that's typically owned by the subscriber and located on the subscriber's premises.

CSU/DSU   A Channel Service Unit/Data Service Unit (CSU/DSU) is a device that's used to connect a DTE to a digital circuit like a T1/T3 line. A device is considered DTE if it's either a source or destination for digital data—for example, PCs, servers, and routers. In Figure 1.13, the router is considered DTE because it's passing data to the CSU/DSU, which will forward the data to the service provider. Although the CSU/DSU connects to the service provider's infrastructure using a telephone or coaxial cable like a T1 or E1 line, it connects to the router with a serial cable. The most important aspect to remember for the CCNA objectives is the CSU/DSU provides clocking of the line to the router.

Demarcation point   The *demarcation point* (demarc for short) is the precise spot where the service provider's responsibility ends and the CPE begins. It's generally a device in a telecommunications closet owned and installed by the telecommunications company (telco). It's your responsibility to cable (extended demarc) from this box to the CPE, which is usually a connection to a CSU/DSU.

Local loop   The *local loop* connects the demarc to the closest switching office, referred to as the central office.

Central office (CO)   This point connects the customer's network to the provider's switching network. Make a mental note that a *central office (CO)* is sometimes also referred to as a *point of presence (POP)*.

Toll network   The *toll network* is a trunk line inside a WAN provider's network. This network is a collection of switches and facilities owned by the Internet service provider (ISP).

Optical fiber converters   Even though I'm not employing this device in Figure 1.13, optical fiber converters are used where a fiber-optic link terminates to convert optical signals into electrical signals and vice versa. You can also implement the converter as a router or switch module.

Make sure you're comfortable with these terms, what they represent, and where they're located, as shown in Figure 1.13, because they're key to understanding WAN technologies.

WAN Connection Bandwidth

Next, I want you to know these basic but very important bandwidth terms used when referring to WAN connections:

Digital Signal 0 (DS0)   This is the basic digital signaling rate of 64 Kbps, equivalent to one channel. Europe uses the E0 and Japan uses the J0 to reference the same channel speed. Typical to T-carrier transmission, this is the generic term used by several multiplexed digital carrier systems and is also the smallest-capacity digital circuit. 1 DS0 = 1 voice/data line.

T1   Also referred to as a DS1, a T1 comprises 24 DS0 circuits bundled together for a total bandwidth of 1.544 Mbps.

E1   This is the European equivalent of a T1 and comprises 30 DS0 circuits bundled together for a bandwidth of 2.048 Mbps.

T3   Referred to as a DS3, a T3 comprises 28 DS1s bundled together, or 672 DS0s, for a bandwidth of 44.736 Mbps.

OC-3   Optical Carrier (OC) 3 uses fiber and is made up of three DS3s bundled together. It's made up of 2,016 DS0s and avails a total bandwidth of 155.52 Mbps.

OC-12   Optical Carrier 12 is made up of four OC-3s bundled together and contains 8,064 DS0s for a total bandwidth of 622.08 Mbps.

OC-48   Optical Carrier 48 is made up of four OC-12s bundled together and contains 32,256 DS0s for a total bandwidth of 2488.32 Mbps.

Physical Interfaces and Cables

Ethernet was first implemented by a group called DIX, Digital, Intel, and Xerox. They created and implemented the first Ethernet LAN specification, which the IEEE used to create the IEEE 802.3 committee. This was a 10 Mbps network that ran on coax, then eventually twisted-pair and fiber physical media.

The IEEE extended the 802.3 committee to three new committees known as 802.3u (Fast Ethernet), 802.3ab (Gigabit Ethernet on category 5), and then finally 802.3ae (10 Gbps over fiber and coax). There are more standards evolving almost daily, like 100 Gbps Ethernet (802.3ba).

When designing your LAN, it's really important to understand the different types of Ethernet media available to you. Sure, it would be great to run TenGigabit Ethernet to each desktop and 100 Gbps between switches, but I dare you to justify the cost of that network! However, if you mix and match the different types of Ethernet media methods currently available, you can come up with a cost-effective network solution that still works really great.

The *EIA/TIA* (Electronic Industries Alliance and the newer Telecommunications Industry Association) is the standards body that creates the Physical layer specifications for Ethernet. The EIA/TIA specifies that Ethernet use a *registered jack (RJ) connector* on *unshielded twisted-pair (UTP)* cabling (RJ45). But the industry is moving toward simply calling this an 8-pin modular connector.

Every Ethernet cable type that's specified by the EIA/TIA has inherent attenuation, which is defined as the loss of signal strength as it travels the length of a cable and is measured in decibels (dB). The cabling used in corporate and home markets is measured in categories. A higher-quality cable will have a higher-rated category and lower attenuation. For example, category 6 is better than category 5 because category 6 cables have cables have more wire twists per foot and therefore less crosstalk. Crosstalk is the unwanted signal interference from adjacent pairs in the cable.

Here's a list of some of the most common IEEE Ethernet standards, starting with 10 Mbps Ethernet:

10Base-T (IEEE 802.3)   10 Mbps using category 3 unshielded twisted pair (UTP) wiring for runs up to 100 meters. Unlike with the 10Base-2 and 10Base-5 networks, each device must connect into a hub or switch, and you can have only one host per segment or wire. It uses an RJ45 connector (8-pin modular connector) with a physical star topology and a logical bus.

100Base-TX (IEEE 802.3u)   100Base-TX, most commonly known as Fast Ethernet, uses EIA/TIA category 5, 5E, or 6 UTP two-pair wiring. One user per segment and up to 100 meters long, it uses an RJ45 connector with a physical star topology and a logical bus.

100Base-FX (IEEE 802.3u)   Uses fiber cabling 62.5/125-micron multimode fiber. Point-to-point topology and up to 412 meters long. It uses ST and SC connectors, which are media-interface connectors.

1000Base-CX (IEEE 802.3z)   Copper twisted-pair, called twinax, is a balanced coaxial pair that can run only up to 25 meters and uses a special 9-pin connector known as the High Speed Serial Data Connector (HSSDC). This is used in Cisco's Data Center technologies.

1000Base-T (IEEE 802.3ab)   Category 5, four-pair UTP wiring up to 100 meters long and up to 1 Gbps.

1000Base-SX (IEEE 802.3z)   This is the implementation of 1 Gigabit Ethernet, running over multimode fiber-optic cable instead of copper twisted-pair cable, using short wavelength laser. Multimode fiber (MMF) using 62.5- and 50-micron core and uses an 850 nanometer (nm) laser that can go up to 220 meters with 62.5-micron, 550 meters with 50-micron.

1000Base-LX (IEEE 802.3z)   Single-mode fiber that uses a 9-micron core and 1300 nm laser that can go from 3 kilometers up to 10 kilometers.

1000Base-ZX (Cisco standard)   1000BaseZX, or 1000Base-ZX, is a Cisco specified standard for Gigabit Ethernet communication. 1000BaseZX operates on ordinary single-mode fiber-optic links with spans up to 43.5 miles (70 km).

10GBase-T (802.3.an)   10GBase-T is a standard proposed by the IEEE 802.3an committee to provide 10 Gbps connections over conventional UTP cables, (category 5e, 6, or 7 cables). 10GBase-T allows the conventional RJ45 used for Ethernet LANs and can support signal transmission at the full 100-meter distance specified for LAN wiring.

Ethernet Cabling

A discussion about Ethernet cabling is an important one, especially if you are planning on taking the Cisco exams. You need to really understand the following three types of cables:

- Straight-through cable
- Crossover cable
- Rolled cable

We will look at each in the following sections, but first, let's take a look at the most common Ethernet cable used today: the category 5 Enhanced Unshielded Twisted Pair (UTP), shown in Figure 1.14:

FIGURE 1.14   Category 5 Enhanced UTP cable

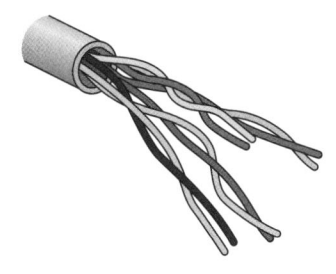

Category 5 Enhanced UTP cable can handle speeds up to a gigabit with a distance of up to 100 meters. Typically we'd use this cable for 100 Mbps and category 6 for a gigabit, but the category 5 Enhanced is rated for gigabit speeds and category 6 is rated for 10 Gbps!

Straight-Through Cable

The *straight-through cable* is used to connect the following devices:

- Host to switch or hub
- Router to switch or hub

Four wires are used in straight-through cable to connect Ethernet devices. It's relatively simple to create this type, and Figure 1.15 shows the four wires used in a straight-through Ethernet cable.

FIGURE 1.15 Straight-through Ethernet cable

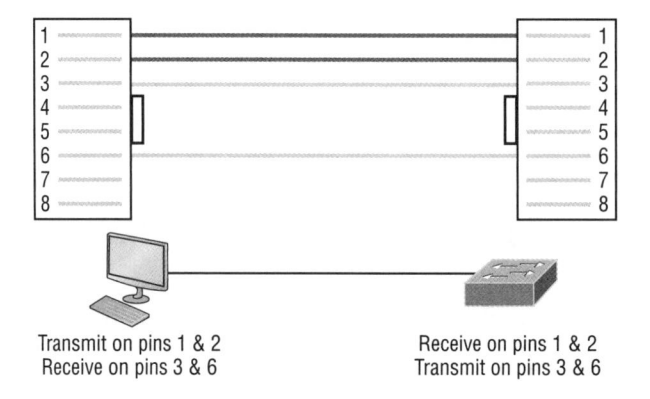

Transmit on pins 1 & 2
Receive on pins 3 & 6

Receive on pins 1 & 2
Transmit on pins 3 & 6

Notice that only pins 1, 2, 3, and 6 are used. Just connect 1 to 1, 2 to 2, 3 to 3, and 6 to 6 and you'll be up and networking stat. Just remember that this would be a 10/100 Mbps Ethernet-only cable and wouldn't work with gigabit, voice, or other LAN or WAN technology.

Crossover Cable

The *crossover cable* can be used to connect these devices:

- Switch to switch
- Hub to hub
- Host to host
- Hub to switch
- Router direct to host
- Router to router

The same four wires used in the straight-through cable are used in this cable; we just connect different pins together. Figure 1.16 shows how the four wires are used in a crossover Ethernet cable.

FIGURE 1.16 Crossover Ethernet cable

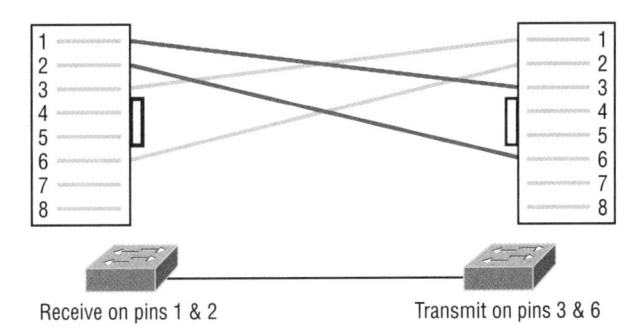

Notice here that instead of connecting 1 to 1, 2 to 2, and so on, here we connect pins 1 to 3 and 2 to 6 on each side of the cable. Figure 1.17 shows some typical uses of straight-through and crossover cables:

FIGURE 1.17 Typical uses for straight-through and cross-over Ethernet cables

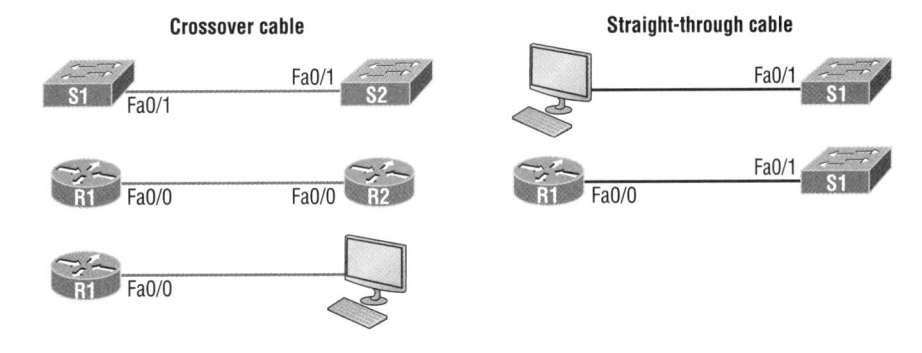

The crossover examples in Figure 1.17 are switch port to switch port, router Ethernet port to router Ethernet port, and router Ethernet port to PC Ethernet port. For the straight-through examples I used PC Ethernet to switch port and router Ethernet port to switch port.

> It's very possible to connect a straight-through cable between two switches, and it will start working because of autodetect mechanisms called auto-mdix. But be advised that the CCNA objectives don't typically consider autodetect mechanisms valid between devices!

UTP Gigabit Wiring (1000Base-T)

In the previous examples of 10Base-T and 100Base-T UTP wiring, only two wire pairs were used. That's definitely not good enough for Gigabit UTP transmission!

The 1000Base-T UTP wiring pictured in Figure 1.18 requires four wire pairs and uses more advanced electronics so that each and every pair in the cable can transmit simultaneously. Even so, gigabit wiring is almost identical to my earlier 10/100 example, except that we'll use the other two pairs in the cable too.

FIGURE 1.18 UTP Gigabit crossover Ethernet cable

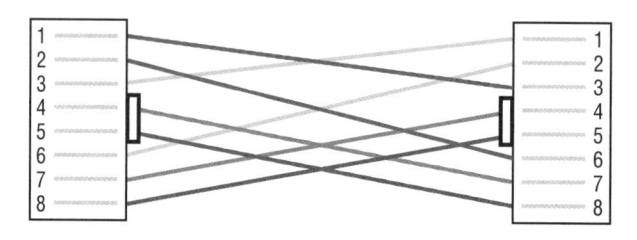

For a straight-through cable it's still 1 to 1, 2 to 2, and so on up to pin 8. And in creating the gigabit crossover cable, you'd still cross 1 to 3 and 2 to 6, but you would add 4 to 7 and 5 to 8—pretty straightforward!

Fiber Optic

Fiber-optic cabling has been around for a long time and provides some solid advantages. The cable allows for very fast transmission of data, is made of glass (even plastic), is very thin, and works as a waveguide to transmit light between two ends of the fiber. Fiber optics has been used to go very long distances, as in intercontinental connections, but it's becoming more and more popular in Ethernet LAN networks due to the fast speeds available. Also, unlike UTP, it's immune to interference like crosstalk.

The main components of this cable are the core and the cladding. The core will hold the light, and the cladding confines the light to the core. Remember, the tighter the cladding, the smaller the core; the smaller the core, the less light sent through it, but it can go faster and farther.

Figure 1.19 pictures a 9-micron core, which is very small and can be measured against a human hair—50 microns!

FIGURE 1.19 Typical fiber cable. Dimensions are in um (10^{-6} meters). Not to scale.

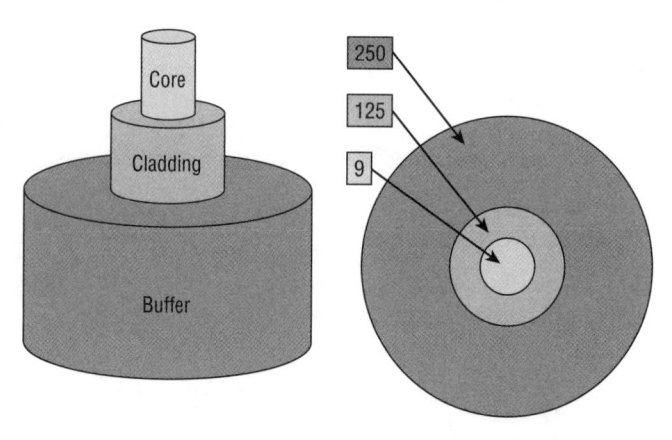

So here, the cladding is 125 microns, which is actually a fiber standard that allows manufacturers to make connectors for all fiber cables. The last piece of this cable is the buffer, which is there to protect the delicate glass.

There are two major types of fiber optics: single-mode and multimode. Figure 1.20 shows the differences between multimode and single-mode fibers.

FIGURE 1.20 Multimode and single-mode fibers

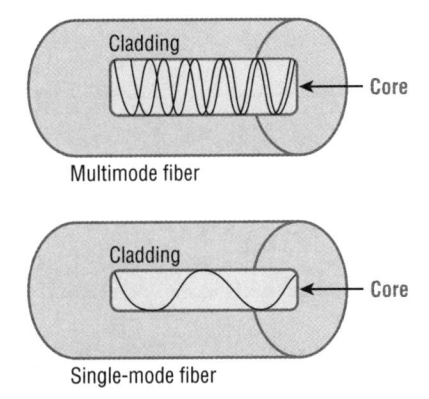

Single-mode is more expensive, has a tighter cladding, and can go much farther distances than multimode. The difference comes in the tightness of the cladding, which as I mentioned, makes a smaller core. It also means that only one mode of light will propagate down the fiber. Multimode is looser and has a larger core so it allows multiple light particles to travel down the glass. These particles have to be put back together at the receiving end. This means the distance is less than that with single-mode fiber, which allows only very few light particles to travel through the fiber.

There are about 70 different connectors for fiber, and Cisco uses a few of them.

Power over Ethernet (802.3af, 802.3at)

Power over Ethernet (PoE and PoE+) technology describes a system for transmitting electrical power, along with data, to remote devices over standard twisted-pair cable in an Ethernet network. This technology is useful for powering IP phones (Voice over IP, or VoIP), wireless LAN access points, network cameras, remote network switches, embedded computers, and other appliances. These are all situations where it would be inconvenient, expensive, and possibly not even feasible to supply power separately. A big reason for this is because the main wiring must be installed by qualified, licensed electricians in order to meet legal and/or insurance mandates.

The IEEE has created a standard for PoE called 802.3af. For PoE+ it's referred to as 802.3at. These standards describe precisely how a powered device is detected and also defines two methods of delivering Power over Ethernet to a given powered device. Keep in mind that PoE+ standard, 802.3at, delivers more power than 802.3af, which is compatible with Gigabit Ethernet with four-wire pairs at 30w.

This process happens one of two ways: either by receiving the power from an Ethernet port on a switch (or other capable device) or via a power injector. And you can't use both approaches to get the job done. And be careful here because doing this wrong can lead to serious trouble! Be sure before connecting.

Figure 1.18 gives you an example of a Cisco Next Generation Firewall (NGFW). It has eight ports that can be routed or switched ports, and ports 7 & 8 are listed as PoE ports at 0.6A. This is an excellent new NGFW that I personally use in my office.

FIGURE 1.21 NGFW ports provide PoE

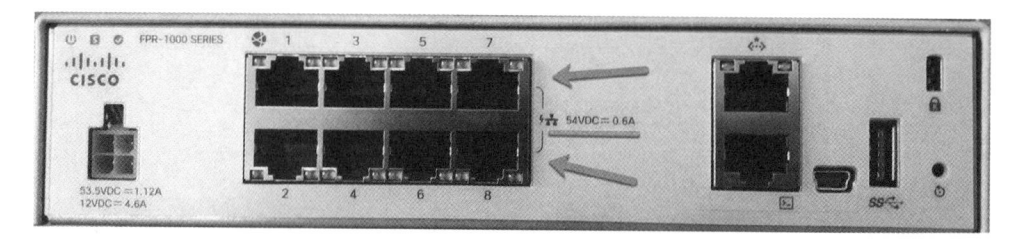

Remember, if you don't have a switch with PoE, you can use a power injector.

> **WARNING**
> Be really careful when using an external power injector! Take your time and make darn sure the power injector provides the voltage level for which your device was manufactured.

Summary

I started this chapter by defining exactly what an internetwork, which was defined as: You create an internetwork when you connect two or more networks via a router and configure a logical network addressing scheme with protocols like IP or IPv6.

I then moved on to covering network components like routers, switches and defining what exactly creates a Small Office Home Office Network (SOHO).

After that, I touched on Next Generation Firewalls (NGFWs), and Cisco's design architecture of 3-tier and 2-tier, and spine-leaf was covered as well.

Finally, a thorough overview of Ethernet and the wiring used in Local Area Networks (LANs) and Wide Area Networks (WANs) was discussed.

Exam Essentials

Differentiate between a Switch and a Router   Switches operate at layer 2 of the OSI model and only read frame hardware addresses in a frame to make a switching decision. Routers read to layer 3 and use routed (logical) address to make forwarding decision on a packet

Understand the term SOHO SOHO means small office, home office, and is small network connecting a user or small handful of users to the internet and office resources such as servers and printers. Usually just one router and a switch or two, plus a firewall.

Define 3-Tier Architecture The Cisco hierarchical model can help you design, implement, and maintain a scalable, reliable, cost-effective hierarchical internetwork. Cisco defines three layers of hierarchy, the core, distribution, and access, each with specific functions, and it's referred to as a 3-tier network architecture.

Define 2-Tier Acthitecture 2-tier architecture is also referred to as the collapsed core design because it's only 2-layers. But in concept, it's like the 3-tier only less expensive and geared for smaller companies. The design is meant to maximize performance and user availability to the network, while still allowing for design scalability over time. In a 2-tier, the distribution layer is merged with the core layer.

Define spine-leaf Also referred to as leaf-and-spine topology, in the leaf-and-spine design, there are switches found at the top of each rack that connect to the servers in the rack, with a server connecting into each switch for redundancy. People refer to this as a top-of-rack (ToR) design because the switches physically reside at the top of a rack.

Review Questions

You can find the answers to these questions in the Appendix.

1. Which one of the following is true about the Cisco core layer in the three-tier design?
   A. Never do anything to slow down traffic. This includes making sure you don't use access lists, perform routing between virtual local area networks, or implement packet filtering.
   B. It's best to support workgroup access here.
   C. Expanding the core, e.g., adding routers as the internetwork grows, is highly recommended as a first step in expansion.
   D. All cables from the Core must connect to the TOR.

2. Which one of the following best describes a SOHO network?
   A. It uses ff:ff:ff:ff:ff:ff as a layer 2 unicast address, which makes it more efficient in a small network
   B. It uses UDP as the Transport layer protocol exclusively, which saves bandwidth in a small network.
   C. A single or small group of users connecting to a switch, with a router providing a connection to the internet
   D. SOHO is the network cabling used from the access layer to the TOR

3. Which two of the following describe the access layer in the three-tier network design? (Choose two.)
   A. Microsegmentation
   B. Broadcast control
   C. PoE
   D. Connections to TOR

4. Which fiber type is a Cisco standard and has a distance of over 40 miles?
   A. 1000Base-SX
   B. 1000Base-LX
   C. 1000Base-ZX
   D. 10GBase-T

5. What is the speed of a T3?
   A. 1.544Mbps
   B. 2.0Mbps
   C. 100Mpbs
   D. 44.736Mbps

6. Which of the following is *not* provided by today's NGFWs?
   A. IPS Inspection
   B. Layer 2 deep packet inspection
   C. Application Visibility and Control (AVC)
   D. Network Address Translation (NAT)

7. Which of the following is the standard for PoE+?
   A. 802.3P
   B. 802.3af
   C. 802.3at
   D. 802.3v6

8. Which of the following defines a two-tier design?
   A. The access layer connects to the distribution layer, and the 2-tiers then connect to the core layer.
   B. In a two-tier design, the distribution layer is merged with the core layer.
   C. It's best to support workgroup access in the two-tier layer
   D. All cables from the core must connect to the two-tier TOR

9. What is the speed of the 802.3.an standard?
   A. 100Mbps
   B. 1Gbps
   C. 10Gbps
   D. 100Gbps

10. In a spine-leaf design, which is true?
   A. The switches are found at the top of each rack that connect to the servers in the rack.
   B. The distribution layer is merged with the core layer.
   C. The access layer connects to the distribution layer, and the two-tiers then connect to the core layer.
   D. All cables from the core must connect to the spine, which connects to the leaf device.

Chapter 2

TCP/IP

THE FOLLOWING CCNA EXAM TOPICS ARE COVERED IN THIS CHAPTER:

1.0 Network Fundamentals

✓ 1.5 Compare TCP to UDP

✓ 1.6 Configure and verify IPv4 addressing and subnetting

✓ 1.7 Describe the need for private IPv4 addressing

4.0 IP Services

✓ 4.3 Explain the role of DHCP and DNS within the network

✓ 4.9 Describe the capabilities and function of TFTP/FTP in the network

The *Transmission Control Protocol/Internet Protocol (TCP/IP)* suite was designed and implemented by the Department of Defense (DoD) to ensure and preserve data integrity as well as maintain communications in the event of catastrophic war. So it follows that if designed and implemented correctly, a TCP/IP network can be a secure, dependable, and resilient one.

In this chapter, I'll cover the protocols of TCP/IP, and throughout this book, you'll learn how to create a solid TCP/IP network with Cisco routers and switches.

We'll begin by exploring the DoD's version of TCP/IP, then compare that version and its protocols with the OSI reference model that we discussed earlier.

Once you understand the protocols and processes used at the various levels of the DoD model, we'll take the next logical step by delving into the world of IP addressing and the different classes of IP addresses used in networks today.

Because having a good grasp of the various IPv4 address types is critical to understanding IP addressing and subnetting, we'll go into these key topics in detail. I'll close this chapter by discussing the various types of IPv4 addresses that you'll need to have down before you move on to through the rest of this book.

> To find your included bonus material, as well as Todd Lammle videos, practice questions & hands-on labs, please see www.lammle.com/ccna.

Introducing TCP/IP

TCP/IP is at the very core of all things networking, so I really want to make sure you have a comprehensive and functional command of it. I'll start by giving you the whole TCP/IP backstory, including its inception, and then move on to describe the important technical goals as defined by its original architects. And of course, I'll include how TCP/IP compares to the theoretical OSI model.

A Brief History of TCP/IP

TCP first came on the scene way back in 1973, and in 1978, it was divided into two distinct protocols: TCP and IP. Later, in 1983, TCP/IP replaced the Network Control Protocol

(NCP) and was authorized as the official means of data transport for anything connecting to ARPAnet, the Internet's ancestor. The DoD's Advanced Research Projects Agency (ARPA) created this ancient network way back in 1957 in a Cold War reaction to the Soviet's launching of *Sputnik*. Also in 1983, ARPA was redubbed DARPA and divided into ARPAnet and MILNET until both were finally dissolved in 1990.

It may be counterintuitive, but most of the development work on TCP/IP happened at UC Berkeley in Northern California, where a group of scientists were simultaneously working on the Berkeley version of UNIX, which soon became known as the Berkeley Software Distribution (BSD) series of UNIX versions. Of course, because TCP/IP worked so well, it was packaged into subsequent releases of BSD Unix and offered to other universities and institutions if they bought the distribution tape. So basically, BSD Unix bundled with TCP/IP began as shareware in the world of academia. As a result, it became the foundation for the tremendous success and unprecedented growth of today's Internet as well as smaller, private and corporate intranets.

As usual, what started as a small group of TCP/IP aficionados evolved, and as it did, the US government created a program to test any new published standards and make sure they passed certain criteria. This was to protect TCP/IP's integrity and to ensure that no developer changed anything too dramatically or added any proprietary features. It's this very quality—this open-systems approach to the TCP/IP family of protocols—that sealed its popularity because it guarantees a solid connection between myriad hardware and software platforms with no strings attached.

TCP/IP and the DoD Model

The DoD model is basically a condensed version of the OSI model that comprises four instead of seven layers:

- Process/Application layer
- Host-to-Host layer or Transport layer
- Internet layer
- Network Access layer or Link layer

Figure 2.1 offers a comparison of the DoD model and the OSI reference model. As you can see, the two are similar in concept, but each has a different number of layers with different names. Cisco may at times use different names for the same layer, such as "Host-to-Host" and Transport" at the layer above the Internet layer, as well as "Network Access" and "Link" used to describe the bottom layer.

FIGURE 2.1 The DoD and OSI models

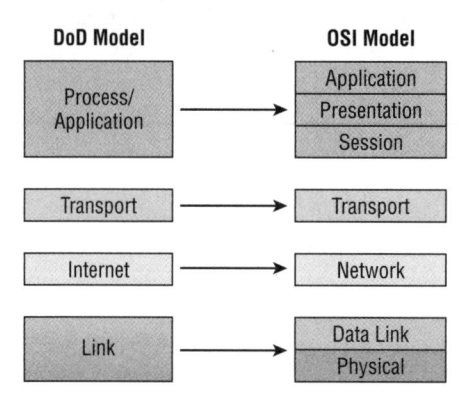

DoD Model	OSI Model
Process/Application	Application / Presentation / Session
Transport	Transport
Internet	Network
Link	Data Link / Physical

A vast array of protocols join forces at the DoD model's *Process/Application layer*. These processes integrate the various activities and duties spanning the focus of the OSI's corresponding top three layers (Application, Presentation, and Session). We'll focus on a few of the most important applications found in the CCNA objectives. In short, the Process/Application layer defines protocols for node-to-node application communication and controls user-interface specifications.

The *Host-to-Host layer or Transport layer* parallels the functions of the OSI's Transport layer, defining protocols for setting up the level of transmission service for applications. It tackles issues like creating reliable end-to-end communication and ensuring the error-free delivery of data. It handles packet sequencing and maintains data integrity.

The *Internet layer* corresponds to the OSI's Network layer, designating the protocols relating to the logical transmission of packets over the entire network. It takes care of the addressing of hosts by giving them an IP (Internet Protocol) address and handles the routing of packets among multiple networks.

At the bottom of the DoD model, the *Network Access layer or Link layer* implements the data exchange between the host and the network. The equivalent of the Data Link and Physical layers of the OSI model, the Network Access layer oversees hardware addressing and defines protocols for the physical transmission of data. Again, the reason TCP/IP became so popular is because there were no set physical layer specifications, meaning it could run on any existing or future physical network!

The DoD and OSI models are alike in design and concept and have similar functions in similar layers. Figure 2.2 shows the TCP/IP protocol suite and how its protocols relate to the DoD model layers.

FIGURE 2.2 The TCP/IP protocol suite

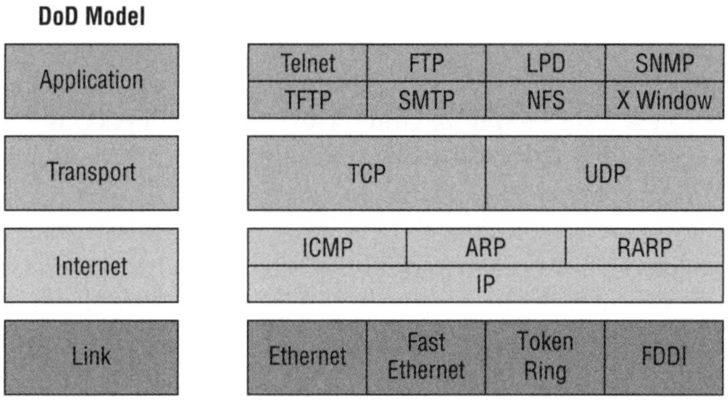

DoD Model				
Application	Telnet	FTP	LPD	SNMP
	TFTP	SMTP	NFS	X Window
Transport	TCP		UDP	
Internet	ICMP	ARP		RARP
	IP			
Link	Ethernet	Fast Ethernet	Token Ring	FDDI

Next, we'll look at the different protocols in more detail, beginning with those found at the Process/Application layer.

The Process/Application Layer Protocols

In this section, I'll describe the different applications and services typically used in IP networks. Although there are many more protocols defined here, we'll focus in on the protocols most relevant to the CCNA objectives. Here's a list of the protocols and applications we'll cover in this section:

- Telnet
- SSH
- FTP
- TFTP
- SNMP
- HTTP
- HTTPS
- NTP
- DNS
- DHCP/BootP
- APIPA

Telnet

Telnet was one of the first Internet standards. It was developed in 1969 and is the chameleon of protocols—its specialty is terminal emulation. It allows a user on a remote client machine, called the Telnet client, to access the resources of another machine, the Telnet server, in order to access a command-line interface. Telnet achieves this by pulling a fast one on the Telnet server and making the client machine appear as though it were a terminal directly attached to the local network. This projection is actually a software image—a virtual terminal that can interact with the chosen remote host. A major drawback is that there are no encryption techniques available within the Telnet protocol, so everything must be sent in clear text—including passwords! Figure 2.3 shows an example of a Telnet client trying to connect to a Telnet server.

FIGURE 2.3 Telnet

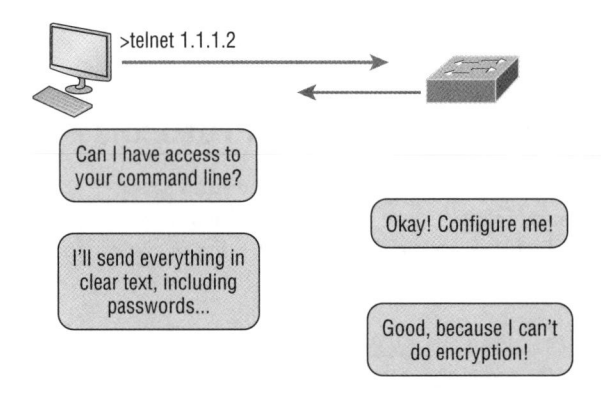

These emulated terminals are of the text-mode type and can execute defined procedures such as displaying menus that give users the opportunity to choose options and access the applications on the duped server. Users begin a Telnet session by running the Telnet client software and then logging into the Telnet server. Telnet uses an 8-bit, byte-oriented data connection over TCP, which makes it very thorough. It's still in use today because it is so simple and easy to use, with very low overhead, but again, as with everything sent in clear text, it's not recommended in production.

Secure Shell (SSH)

Secure Shell (SSH) protocol sets up a secure session that's similar to Telnet over a standard TCP/IP connection. It's used for doing things like logging into systems, running programs on remote systems and moving files from one system to another, and it does all of this while maintaining an encrypted connection. Figure 2.4 shows a SSH client trying to connect to a SSH server. The client must send the data encrypted.

FIGURE 2.4 Secure Shell

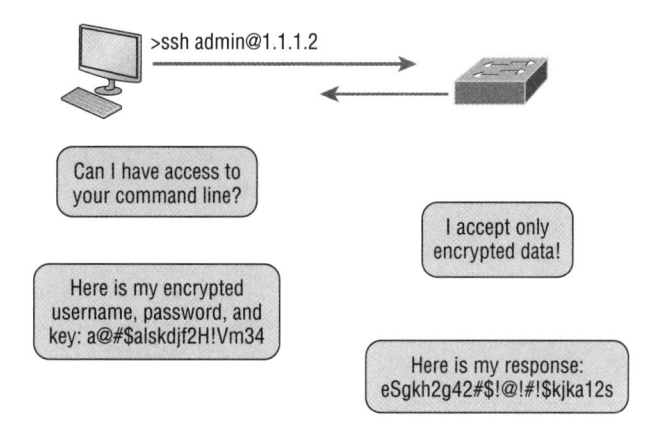

You can think of SSH as the new-generation protocol used in place of the antiquated and very unused *rsh* and *rlogin*—even Telnet.

File Transfer Protocol (FTP)

File Transfer Protocol (FTP) actually lets us transfer files, and it can accomplish this between any two machines using it. But FTP isn't just a protocol; it's also a program. Operating as a protocol, FTP is used by applications. As a program, it's employed by users to perform file tasks by hand. FTP also allows for access to both directories and files and can accomplish certain types of directory operations, such as relocating into different ones (Figure 2.5).

FIGURE 2.5 FTP

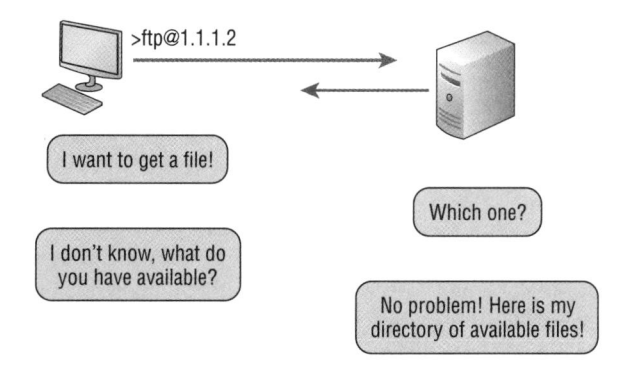

But accessing a host through FTP is only the first step. Users must then be subjected to an authentication login that's usually secured with passwords and usernames implemented by system administrators to restrict access. You can get around this somewhat by adopting the username *anonymous*, but you'll be limited in what you'll be able to access.

Even when employed by users manually as a program, FTP's functions are limited to listing and manipulating directories, typing file contents and copying files between hosts. It can't execute remote files as programs.

Trivial File Transfer Protocol (TFTP)

Trivial File Transfer Protocol (TFTP) is the stripped-down, stock version of FTP. It's the protocol of choice if you know exactly what you want and where to find it because it's so fast and easy to use.

But TFTP doesn't offer the abundance of functions that FTP does because it has no directory-browsing abilities, meaning that it can only send and receive files (Figure 2.6). Still, it's heavily used for managing file systems on Cisco devices.

FIGURE 2.6 TFTP

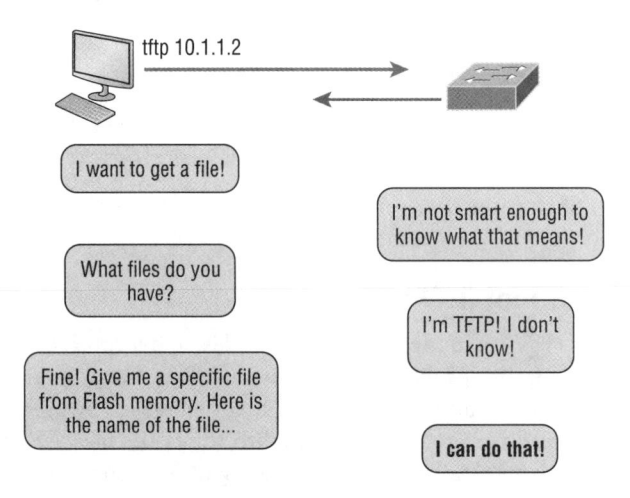

This compact little protocol also skimps in the data department, sending much smaller blocks of data than FTP. Also, there's no authentication as with FTP, so it's even more insecure. Few sites support it because of the inherent security risks.

Real World Scenario

When Should You Use FTP?

Let's say everyone at your San Francisco office needs a 50 GB file emailed to them right away. What do you do? Many email servers would reject that email due to size limits because many ISPs don't allow files larger than 10 MB to be emailed. Even if there are no size limits on the server, it would still take a while to send this huge file... FTP to the rescue!

So if you need to give someone a large file or you need to get a large file from someone, FTP is a nice choice. To use FTP, you would need to set up an FTP server on the Internet so that the files can be shared.

Besides resolving size issues, FTP is faster than email. In addition, because it uses TCP and is connection-oriented, if the session dies, FTP can sometimes start up where it left off. Try that with your email client!

Simple Network Management Protocol (SNMP)

Simple Network Management Protocol (SNMP) collects and manipulates valuable network information, as you can see in Figure 2.7. It gathers data by polling the devices on the network from a network management station (NMS) at fixed or random intervals, requiring them to disclose certain information, or even asking for certain information from the device. In addition, network devices can inform the NMS station about problems as they occur, so the network administrator is alerted.

FIGURE 2.7 SNMP

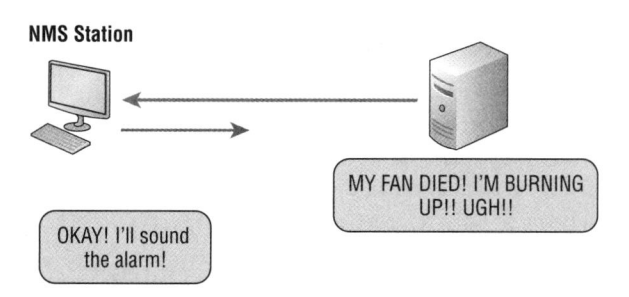

When all is well, SNMP receives something called a *baseline*—a report delimiting the operational traits of a healthy network. This protocol can also stand as a watchdog over the network, quickly notifying managers of any sudden turn of events. These network watchdogs are called *agents*, and when aberrations occur, agents send an alert called a *trap* to the management station.

SNMP Versions 1, 2, and 3

SNMP versions 1 and 2 are pretty much obsolete. This doesn't mean you won't see them in a network now and then, but you'll only come across v1 rarely, if ever. SNMPv2 provided improvements, especially in performance. But one of the best additions was called GETBULK, which allowed a host to retrieve a large amount of data at once. Even so, v2 never really caught on in the networking world and SNMPv3 is now the standard. Unlike v1, which used only UDP, v3 uses both TCP and UDP and added even more security, message integrity, authentication, and encryption.

Hypertext Transfer Protocol (HTTP)

All those snappy websites comprising a mélange of graphics, text, links, ads, and so on rely on the *Hypertext Transfer Protocol (HTTP)* to make it all possible (Figure 2.8). It's used to manage communications between web browsers and web servers and opens the right resource when you click a link, wherever that resource may actually reside.

FIGURE 2.8 HTTP

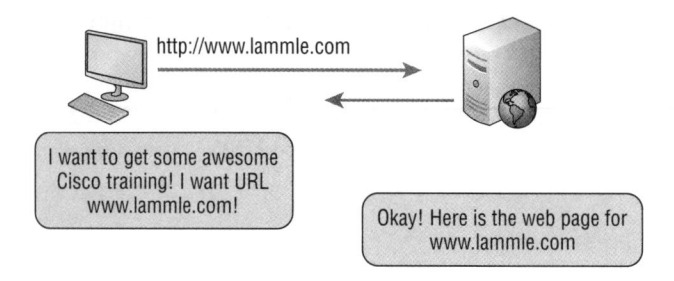

In order for a browser to display a web page, it must first find the exact server that has the right web page, plus the exact details that identify the information requested. This information must be then be sent back to the browser. Nowadays, it's highly doubtful that a web server would have only one page to display!

Your browser can understand what you need when you enter a Uniform Resource Locator (URL), which we usually refer to as a web address, such as, for example, www.lammle.com/ccna and www.lammle.com/blog.

So basically, each URL defines the protocol used to transfer data, the name of the server, and the particular web page on that server.

Hypertext Transfer Protocol Secure (HTTPS)

Hypertext Transfer Protocol Secure (HTTPS) is also known as Secure Hypertext Transfer Protocol. It uses Secure Sockets Layer (SSL). Sometimes you'll see it referred to as SHTTP or S-HTTP, which were slightly different protocols, but since Microsoft supported HTTPS, it became the de facto standard for securing web communication. As indicated, it's a secure version of HTTP that arms you with a whole bunch of security tools for keeping transactions between a web browser and a server secure.

It's what your browser needs to fill out forms, sign in, authenticate, and encrypt an HTTP message when you do things online like make a reservation, access your bank, or buy something.

Network Time Protocol (NTP)

Cheers to Professor David Mills of the University of Delaware for coming up with this handy protocol that's used to synchronize the clocks on our computers to one standard time source (typically, an atomic clock). *Network Time Protocol (NTP)* works by synchronizing devices to ensure that all computers on a given network agree on the time (Figure 2.9).

This may sound pretty simple, but it's very important because so many of the transactions done today are time and date stamped. Think about databases—a server can get messed up pretty badly and crash if it's out of sync with the machines connected to it even by mere seconds. You just can't have a transaction entered by a machine at, say, 1:50 a.m. when the server records that transaction as having occurred at 1:45 a.m. So basically, NTP works to prevent a "back to the future" scenario from bringing down the network—very important indeed!

FIGURE 2.9 NTP

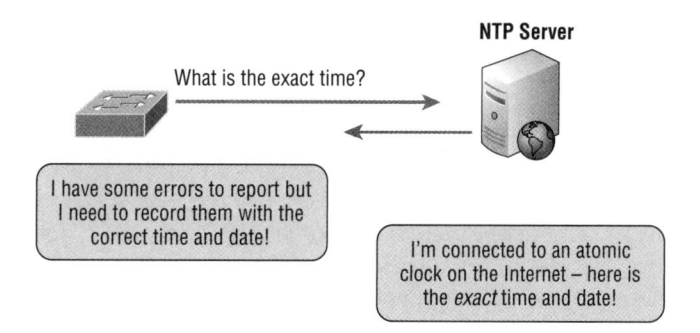

Domain Name Service (DNS)

Domain Name Service (DNS) resolves hostnames—specifically, Internet names, such as www.lammle.com. But you don't have to actually use DNS. You just type in the IP address of any device you want to communicate with and find the IP address of a URL by using the Ping program. For example, >ping www.cisco.com will return the IP address resolved by DNS.

An IP address identifies hosts on a network and the Internet as well, but DNS was designed to make our lives easier. Think about this: What would happen if you wanted to move your web page to a different service provider? The IP address would change and no one would know what the new one is. DNS allows you to use a domain name to specify an IP address. You can change the IP address as often as you want and no one will know the difference.

To resolve a DNS address from a host, you'd typically type in the URL from your favorite browser, which would hand the data to the Application layer interface to be transmitted on the network. The application would look up the DNS address and send a UDP request to your DNS server to resolve the name (Figure 2.10).

FIGURE 2.10 DNS

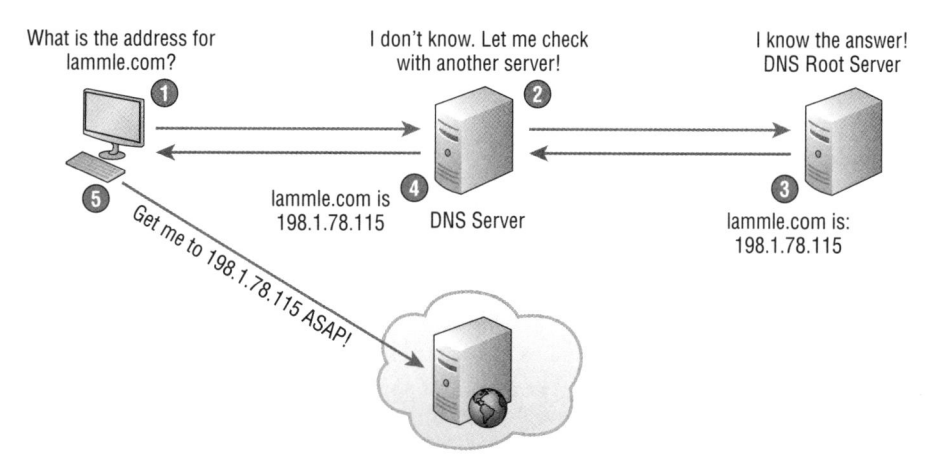

If your first DNS server doesn't know the answer to the query, then the DNS server forwards a TCP request to its root DNS server. Once the query is resolved, the answer is transmitted back to the originating host, which means the host can now request the information from the correct web server.

DNS is used to resolve a *fully qualified domain name (FQDN)*—for example, www.lammle.com or todd.lammle.com. An FQDN is a hierarchy that can logically locate a system based on its domain identifier.

If you want to resolve the name *todd*, you either must type in the FQDN of todd.lammle.com or have a device such as a PC or router add the suffix for you. For example, on a Cisco router, you can use the command *ip domain-name lammle.com* to append each request with the lammle.com domain. If you don't do that, you'll have to type in the FQDN to get DNS to resolve the name.

> An important thing to remember about DNS is that if you can ping a device with an IP address but cannot use its FQDN, then you might have some type of DNS configuration failure.

Dynamic Host Configuration Protocol (DHCP)/Bootstrap Protocol (BootP)

Dynamic Host Configuration Protocol (DHCP) assigns IP addresses to hosts. It allows for easier administration and works well in small to very large network environments. Many types of hardware can be used as a DHCP server, including a Cisco router.

DHCP differs from BootP in that BootP assigns an IP address to a host but the host's hardware address must be entered manually in a BootP table. You can think of DHCP as a dynamic BootP, but remember that BootP is also used to send an operating system that a host can boot from. DHCP can't do that.

Even so, there's still a lot of information a DHCP server can provide to a host when the host is requesting an IP address from the DHCP server. Here's a list of the most common types of information a DHCP server can provide:

- IP address
- Subnet mask
- Domain name
- Default gateway (routers)
- DNS server address
- WINS server address

A client that sends out a DHCP Discover message in order to receive an IP address sends out a broadcast at both layer 2 and layer 3.

- The layer 2 broadcast is all *F*s in hex, which looks like this: ff:ff:ff:ff:ff:ff.
- The layer 3 broadcast is 255.255.255.255, which means all networks and all hosts.

DHCP is connectionless, which means it uses User Datagram Protocol (UDP) at the Transport layer. The Transport layer is also known as the Host-to-Host layer, and we'll talk about this a bit later.

Seeing is believing, so here's an example of output from my analyzer showing the layer 2 and layer 3 broadcasts:

```
Ethernet II, Src: 0.0.0.0 (00:0b:db:99:d3:5e),Dst: Broadcast(ff:ff:ff:ff:ff:ff)
Internet Protocol, Src: 0.0.0.0 (0.0.0.0),Dst: 255.255.255.255(255.255.255.255)
```

The Data Link and Network layers are both sending out "all hands" broadcasts saying, "Help—I don't know my IP address!"

Figure 2.11 shows the process of a client/server relationship using a DHCP connection.

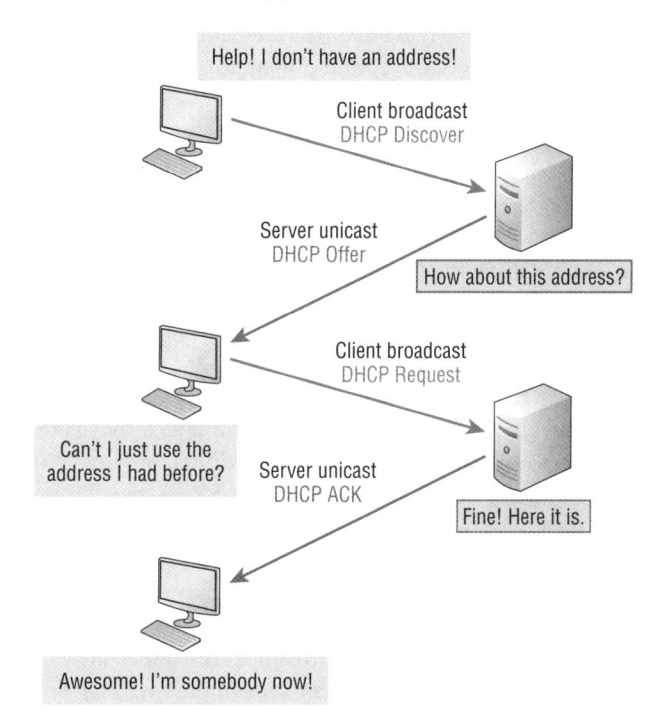

FIGURE 2.11 DHCP client four-step process

This is the four-step process a client takes to receive an IP address from a DHCP server using what we call DORA or Discover, Offer, Request, Acknowledgment:

1. The DHCP client broadcasts a DHCP **Discover** message looking for a DHCP server (Port 67).

2. The DHCP server that received the DHCP Discover message sends a layer 2 unicast DHCP **Offer** message back to the host.

3. The client then broadcasts to the server a DHCP **Request** message asking for the offered IP address and possibly other information.

4. The server finalizes the exchange with a unicast DHCP **Acknowledgment** message.

DHCP Conflicts

A DHCP address conflict occurs when two hosts use the same IP address. This sounds bad, and it is. (We'll never even have to discuss this problem once we get to the chapter on IPv6!)

So during IP address assignment, a DHCP server checks for conflicts using the Ping program to test the availability of the address before it's assigned from the pool. If no host replies, then the DHCP server assumes that the IP address is not already allocated. This helps the server know that it's providing a good address, but what about the host? To provide extra protection against that ugly IP conflict issue, the host can broadcast for its own address.

A host uses something called a gratuitous ARP to help avoid a possible duplicate address. The DHCP client sends an ARP broadcast out on the local LAN or VLAN using its newly assigned address to solve conflicts before they occur.

So, if an IP address conflict is detected, the address is removed from the DHCP pool (scope). And it's really important to remember that the address will not be assigned to a host until the administrator resolves the conflict by hand!

Automatic Private IP Addressing (APIPA)

Okay, so what happens if you have a few hosts connected together with a switch or hub and you don't have a DHCP server? You can add IP information by hand, known as *static IP addressing*, but later Windows operating systems provide a feature called Automatic Private IP Addressing (APIPA). With APIPA, clients can automatically self-configure an IP address and subnet mask—basic IP information that hosts use to communicate—when a DHCP server isn't available. The IP address range for APIPA is 169.254.0.1 through 169.254.255.254. The client also configures itself with a default Class B subnet mask of 255.255.0.0.

But when you're in your corporate network working and you have a DHCP server running, and your host shows that it's using this IP address range, it means that either your DHCP client on the host is not working or the server is down or can't be reached due to some network issue. No one who's seen a host in this address range has been happy about it!

Now, let's take a look at the Transport layer, or what the DoD calls the Host-to-Host layer.

The Host-to-Host or Transport Layer Protocols

The main purpose of the Host-to-Host layer is to shield the upper-layer applications from the complexities of the network. This layer says to the upper layer, "Just give me your data stream, with any instructions, and I'll begin the process of getting your information ready to send."

Next, I'll introduce you to the two protocols at this layer:

- Transmission Control Protocol (TCP)
- User Datagram Protocol (UDP)

In addition, we'll look at some of the key host-to-host protocol concepts, as well as the port numbers.

> Remember, this is still considered layer 4, and Cisco really likes the way layer 4 can use acknowledgments, sequencing, and flow control.

Transmission Control Protocol (TCP)

Transmission Control Protocol (TCP) takes large blocks of information from an application and breaks them into segments. It numbers and sequences each segment so that the destination's TCP stack can put the segments back into the order the application intended. After these segments are sent on the transmitting host, TCP waits for an acknowledgment of the receiving end's TCP virtual circuit session, retransmitting any segments that aren't acknowledged.

Before a transmitting host starts to send segments down the model, the sender's TCP stack contacts the destination's TCP stack to establish a connection. This creates a *virtual circuit*, and this type of communication is known as *connection-oriented*. During this initial handshake, the two TCP layers also agree on the amount of information that's going to be sent before the recipient's TCP sends back an acknowledgment. With everything agreed upon in advance, the path is paved for reliable communication to take place.

TCP is a full-duplex, connection-oriented, reliable, and accurate protocol, but establishing all these terms and conditions, in addition to error checking, is no small task. TCP is very complicated, and so not surprisingly, it's costly in terms of network overhead. And since today's networks are much more reliable than those of yore, this added reliability is often unnecessary. Most programmers use TCP because it removes a lot of programming work, but for real-time video and VoIP, *User Datagram Protocol (UDP)* is often better because using it results in less overhead.

TCP Segment Format

Since the upper layers just send a data stream to the protocols in the Transport layers, I'll use Figure 2.12 to demonstrate how TCP segments a data stream and prepares it for the Internet layer. When the Internet layer receives the data stream, it routes the segments as packets through an internetwork. The segments are handed to the receiving host's Host-to-Host layer protocol, which rebuilds the data stream for the upper-layer applications or protocols.

FIGURE 2.12 TCP segment format

16-bit source port			16-bit destination port
32-bit sequence number			
32-bit acknowledgment number			
4-bit header length	Reserved	Flags	16-bit window size
16-bit TCP checksum			16-bit urgent pointer
Options			
Data			

Figure 2.12 shows the TCP segment format and the different fields within the TCP header. This isn't important to memorize for the Cisco exam objectives, but you need to understand it well because it's really good foundational information.

The TCP header is 20 bytes long, or up to 24 bytes with options. Again, it's good to understand what each field in the TCP segment is in order to build a strong educational foundation:

Source port   This is the port number of the application on the host sending the data, which I'll talk about more thoroughly a little later in this chapter.

Destination port   This is the port number of the application requested on the destination host.

Sequence number   A number used by TCP that puts the data back in the correct order or retransmits missing or damaged data during a process called sequencing.

Acknowledgment number   The value is the TCP octet that is expected next.

Header length   The number of 32-bit words in the TCP header, which indicates where the data begins. The TCP header (even one including options) is an integral number of 32 bits in length.

Reserved   Always set to zero.

Code bits/flags   Controls functions used to set up and terminate a session.

Window   The window size the sender is willing to accept, in octets.

Checksum   The cyclic redundancy check (CRC), used because TCP doesn't trust the lower layers and checks everything. The CRC checks the header and data fields.

Urgent   A valid field only if the Urgent pointer in the code bits is set. If so, this value indicates the offset from the current sequence number, in octets, where the segment of non-urgent data begins.

Options   May be 0, meaning that no options have to be present, or a multiple of 32 bits. However, if any options are used that do not cause the option field to total a multiple of 32 bits, padding of 0s must be used to make sure the data begins on a 32-bit boundary. These boundaries are known as words.

Data   Handed down to the TCP protocol at the Transport layer, which includes the upper-layer headers.

Let's take a look at a TCP segment copied from a network analyzer:

```
TCP - Transport Control Protocol
Source Port: 5973
Destination Port: 23
Sequence Number: 1456389907
Ack Number: 1242056456
Offset: 5
Reserved: %000000
Code: %011000
```

```
Ack is valid
Push Request
Window: 61320
Checksum: 0x61a6
Urgent Pointer: 0
No TCP Options
TCP Data Area:
vL.5.+.5.+.5.+.5 76 4c 19 35 11 2b 19 35 11 2b 19 35 11
2b 19 35 +. 11 2b 19
Frame Check Sequence: 0x0d00000f
```

Did you notice that everything I talked about earlier is in the segment? As you can see from the number of fields in the header, TCP creates a lot of overhead. Again, this is why application developers may opt for efficiency over reliability to save overhead and go with UDP instead. It's also defined at the Transport layer as an alternative to TCP.

User Datagram Protocol (UDP)

User Datagram Protocol (UDP) is basically the scaled-down economy model of TCP, which is why UDP is sometimes referred to as a thin protocol. Like a thin person on a park bench, a thin protocol doesn't take up a lot of room—or in this case, require much bandwidth on a network.

UDP doesn't offer all the bells and whistles of TCP either, but it does do a fabulous job of transporting information that doesn't require reliable delivery, using far less network resources. (UDP is covered thoroughly in Request for Comments (RFC) 768.)

So clearly, there are times that it's wise for developers to opt for UDP rather than TCP, one of them being when reliability is already taken care of at the Process/Application layer. Network File System (NFS) handles its own reliability issues, making the use of TCP both impractical and redundant. But ultimately, it's up to the application developer to opt for using UDP or TCP, not the user who wants to transfer data faster!

UDP does *not* sequence the segments and does not care about the order in which the segments arrive at the destination. It just sends the segments off and forgets about them. It doesn't follow through, check up on them, or even allow for an acknowledgment of safe arrival—complete abandonment! Because of this, it's referred to as an unreliable protocol. This does not mean that UDP is ineffective, only that it doesn't deal with reliability issues at all.

Furthermore, UDP doesn't create a virtual circuit, nor does it contact the destination before delivering information to it. Because of this, it's also considered a *connectionless* protocol. Since UDP assumes that the application will use its own reliability method, it doesn't use any itself. This presents an application developer with a choice when running the Internet Protocol stack: TCP for reliability or UDP for faster transfers.

It's important to know how this process works because if the segments arrive out of order, which is commonplace in IP networks, they'll simply be passed up to the next layer in whatever order they were received. This can result in some seriously garbled data! On the other hand, TCP sequences the segments so they get put back together in exactly the right order—something UDP just can't do.

UDP Segment Format

Figure 2.13 clearly illustrates UDP's markedly lean overhead as compared to TCP's hungry requirements. Look at the figure carefully—can you see that UDP doesn't use windowing or provide for acknowledgments in the UDP header?

FIGURE 2.13   UDP segment

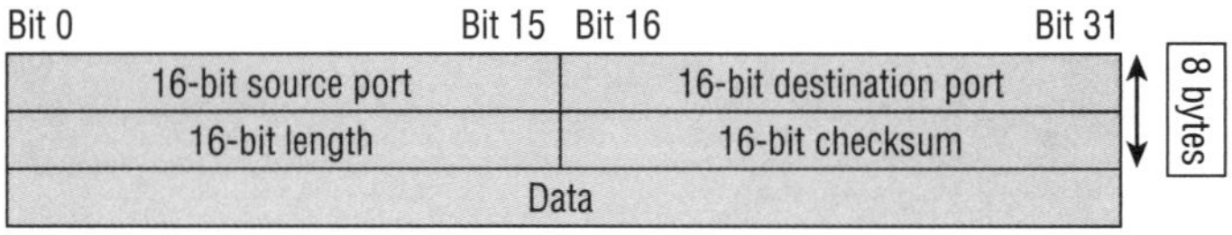

Bit 0	Bit 15	Bit 16	Bit 31	
16-bit source port		16-bit destination port		8 bytes
16-bit length		16-bit checksum		
Data				

It's important for you to understand what each field in the UDP segment is:

Source port   Port number of the application on the host sending the data

Destination port   Port number of the application requested on the destination host

Length   Length of UDP header and UDP data

Checksum   Checksum of both the UDP header and UDP data fields

Data   Upper-layer data

Like TCP, UDP doesn't trust the lower layers and runs its own CRC. Remember that the Frame Check Sequence (FCS) is the field that houses the CRC, which is why you can see the FCS information.

The following shows a UDP segment caught on a network analyzer:

```
UDP - User Datagram Protocol
Source Port: 1085
Destination Port: 5136
Length: 41
Checksum: 0x7a3c
UDP Data Area:
..Z......00 01 5a 96 00 01 00 00 00 00 00 11 0000 00
...C..2._C._C 2e 03 00 43 02 1e 32 0a 00 0a 00 80 43 00 80
Frame Check Sequence: 0x00000000
```

Notice that low overhead! Try to find the sequence number, ack number, and window size in the UDP segment. You can't because they just aren't there!

Key Concepts of Host-to-Host Protocols

Since you've now seen both a connection-oriented (TCP) and connectionless (UDP) protocol in action, it's a good time to summarize the two here. Table 2.1 highlights some of the key concepts about these two protocols for you to memorize.

TABLE 2.1 Key features of TCP and UDP

TCP	UDP
Sequenced	Unsequenced
Reliable	Unreliable
Connection-oriented	Connectionless
Virtual circuit	Low overhead
Acknowledgments	No acknowledgment
Windowing flow control	No windowing or flow control of any type

Just in case all of this isn't quite clear yet, a telephone analogy will really help you understand how TCP works. Most of us know that before you speak to someone on a phone, you must first establish a connection with that other person no matter where they are. This is akin to establishing a virtual circuit with the TCP protocol. If you were giving someone important information during your conversation, you might say something like, "Did you get that?" Saying things like that is a lot like a TCP acknowledgment—it's designed to get you verification. From time to time, especially on mobile phones, people ask, "Are you still there?" And people end their conversations with a "Goodbye" of some kind, putting closure on the phone call, which you can think of as tearing down the virtual circuit that was created for your communication session. TCP performs these types of functions.

Conversely, using UDP is more like sending a postcard. To do that, you don't need to contact the other party first, you simply write your message, address the postcard, and send it off. This is analogous to UDP's connectionless orientation. Since the message on the postcard is probably not vitally important, you don't need an acknowledgment of its receipt. Similarly, UDP does not involve acknowledgments.

Let's take a look at Figure 2.14, which includes TCP, UDP, and the applications associated to each protocol. We'll talk about all of this in the next section.

FIGURE 2.14 Port numbers for TCP and UDP

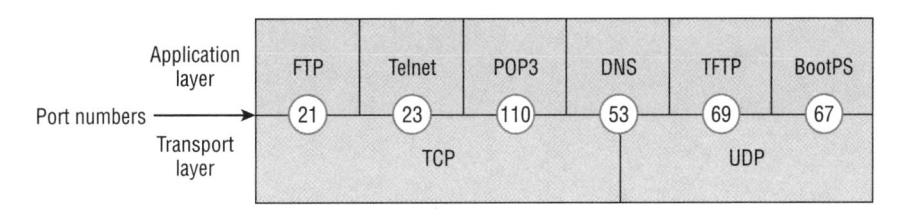

	Application layer	FTP	Telnet	POP3	DNS	TFTP	BootPS
Port numbers		21	23	110	53	69	67
	Transport layer	TCP	TCP	TCP	UDP	UDP	UDP

Port Numbers

TCP and UDP must use *port numbers* to communicate with the upper layers because these are what keep track of different conversations crossing the network simultaneously. Originating-source port numbers are dynamically assigned by the source host and will equal some number starting at 1024. Port number 1023 and below are defined in RFC 3232 (or just see www.iana.org), which discusses what we call well-known port numbers.

Virtual circuits that don't use an application with a well-known port number are assigned port numbers randomly from a specific range instead. These port numbers identify the source and destination application or process in the TCP segment.

> **NOTE** The Requests for Comments (RFCs) form a series of notes about the Internet (originally the ARPAnet) started in 1969. These notes discuss many aspects of computer communication, focusing on networking protocols, procedures, programs, and concepts. They also include meeting notes, opinions, and sometimes even humor. You can find the RFCs by visiting www.iana.org.

Figure 2.14 illustrates how both TCP and UDP use port numbers. I'll cover the different port numbers that can be used next:

- Numbers below 1024 are considered well-known port numbers and are defined in RFC 3232.
- Numbers 1024 and above, often referred to as ephemeral ports, are used by the upper layers to set up sessions with other hosts and by TCP and UDP to use as source and destination addresses in the segment.

TCP Session: Source Port

Let's take a minute to check out analyzer output showing a TCP session I captured with my analyzer software session now:

```
TCP - Transport Control Protocol
Source Port: 5973
Destination Port: 23
Sequence Number: 1456389907
Ack Number: 1242056456
Offset: 5
Reserved: %000000
Code: %011000
Ack is valid
Push Request
Window: 61320
Checksum: 0x61a6
Urgent Pointer: 0
No TCP Options
```

```
TCP Data Area:
vL.5.+.5.+.5.+.5 76 4c 19 35 11 2b 19 35 11 2b 19 35 11
2b 19 35 +. 11 2b 19
Frame Check Sequence: 0x0d00000f
```

Notice that the source host makes up the source port, which in this case is 5973. The destination port is 23, which is used to tell the receiving host the purpose of the intended connection (Telnet).

By looking at this session, you can see that the source host makes up the source port by using numbers from 1024 to 65535. But why does the source make up a port number? The source does that to differentiate between sessions with different hosts because how would a server know where information is coming from if it didn't have a different number from a sending host? TCP and the upper layers don't use hardware and logical addresses to understand the sending host's address like the Data Link and Network layer protocols do. They use port numbers instead.

TCP Session: Destination Port

You'll sometimes look at an analyzer and see that only the source port is above 1024 and the destination port is a well-known port, as shown in the following trace:

```
TCP - Transport Control Protocol
Source Port: 1144
Destination Port: 80 World Wide Web HTTP
Sequence Number: 9356570
Ack Number: 0
Offset: 7
Reserved: %000000
Code: %000010
Synch Sequence
Window: 8192
Checksum: 0x57E7
Urgent Pointer: 0
TCP Options:
Option Type: 2 Maximum Segment Size
Length: 4
MSS: 536
Option Type: 1 No Operation
Option Type: 1 No Operation
Option Type: 4
Length: 2
Opt Value:
No More HTTP Data
Frame Check Sequence: 0x43697363
```

Sure enough—the source port is over 1024, but the destination port is 80, indicating an HTTP service. The server, or receiving host, will change the destination port if it needs to.

In the preceding trace, a "SYN" packet (listed as Synch Sequence in this analysis) is sent to the destination device. This Synch sequence, as shown in the output, is what's used to inform the remote destination device that it wants to create a session.

TCP Session: Syn Packet Acknowledgment

The next trace shows an acknowledgment to the SYN packet:

```
TCP - Transport Control Protocol
Source Port: 80 World Wide Web HTTP
Destination Port: 1144
Sequence Number: 2873580788
Ack Number: 9356571
Offset: 6
Reserved: %000000
Code: %010010
  Ack is valid
  Synch Sequence
Window: 8576
Checksum: 0x5F85
Urgent Pointer: 0
TCP Options:
  Option Type: 2 Maximum Segment Size
  Length: 4
  MSS: 1460
No More HTTP Data
Frame Check Sequence: 0x6E203132
```

Notice the *Ack is valid*, which means that the source port was accepted and the device agreed to create a virtual circuit with the originating host.

So here again, you can see that the response from the server shows that the source is 80 and the destination is the 1144 sent from the originating host—all's well!

Table 2.2 gives you a list of the typical applications used in the TCP/IP suite by showing their well-known port numbers and the Transport layer protocols used by each application or process. It's a really good idea to memorize this table:

TABLE 2.2 Key protocols that use TCP and UDP

TCP	UDP
Telnet 23	SNMP 161
SMTP 25	TFTP 69
HTTP 80	DNS 53
FTP 20, 21	BootP/DHCP 67
DNS 53	
HTTPS 443	NTP 123
SSH 22	
POP3 110	
IMAP4 143	

Notice that DNS uses both TCP and UDP. Whether it opts for one or the other depends on what it's trying to do. Even though it's not the only application that can use both protocols, it's certainly one that you should make sure to remember.

> What makes TCP reliable is sequencing, acknowledgments, and flow control (windowing). Remember... No reliability with UDP!

I want to discuss one more item before we move down to the Internet layer—session multiplexing. Session multiplexing is used by both TCP and UDP and basically allows a single computer, with a single IP address, to have multiple sessions occurring simultaneously. Say you go to www.lammle.com, begin browsing and click a link to another page. Doing this opens another session to your host. Now you go to www.lammle.com/forum from another window and that site opens a window as well. Now you have three sessions open using one IP address because the Session layer is sorting the separate requests based on the Transport layer port number. This is the job of the Session layer: to keep application layer data separate!

The Internet Layer Protocols

In the DoD model, there are two main reasons for the Internet layer's existence: routing and providing a single network interface to the upper layers.

None of the other upper- or lower-layer protocols have any functions relating to routing—that complex and important task belongs entirely to the Internet layer. The Internet layer's second duty is to provide a single network interface to the upper-layer protocols. Without this layer, application programmers would need to write "hooks" into every one of their applications for each different Network Access protocol. This would not only be a pain in the neck, but it would lead to different versions of each application—one for Ethernet, another one for wireless, and so on. To prevent this, IP provides one single network interface for the upper-layer protocols. With that mission accomplished, it's then the job of IP and the various Network Access protocols to get along and work together.

All network roads don't lead to Rome—they lead to IP. And all the other protocols at this layer, as well as all those at the upper layers, use it. Never forget that. All paths through the DoD model go through IP. Here's a list of the important protocols at the Internet layer that I'll cover individually in detail coming up:

- Internet Protocol (IP)
- Internet Control Message Protocol (ICMP)
- Address Resolution Protocol (ARP)

Internet Protocol (IP)

Internet Protocol (IP) essentially is the Internet layer. The other protocols found here merely exist to support it. IP holds the big picture and could be said to "see all," because it's aware of all the interconnected networks. It can do this because all the machines on the network have a software or logical address called an IP address. We'll explore this more thoroughly later in this chapter.

For now, understand that IP looks at each packet's address. Then, using a routing table, it decides where a packet is to be sent next, choosing the best path to send it upon. The protocols of the Network Access layer at the bottom of the DoD model don't possess IP's enlightened scope of the entire network; they deal only with physical links (local networks).

Identifying devices on networks requires answering these two questions: Which network is it on? And what is its ID on that network? The first answer is the *software address*, or *logical address*. You can think of this as the part of the address that specifies the correct street. The second answer is the hardware address, which goes a step further to specify the correct mailbox. All hosts on a network have a logical ID called an IP address. This is the software, or logical, address and contains valuable encoded information, greatly simplifying the complex task of routing. (IP is discussed in RFC 791.)

IP receives segments from the Host-to-Host layer and fragments them into datagrams (packets) if necessary. IP then reassembles datagrams back into segments on the receiving side. Each datagram is assigned the IP address of the sender and that of the recipient. Each router or switch (layer 3 device) that receives a datagram makes routing decisions based on the packet's destination IP address.

Figure 2.15 shows an IP header. This will give you a picture of what the IP protocol has to go through every time user data that's destined for a remote network is sent from the upper layers.

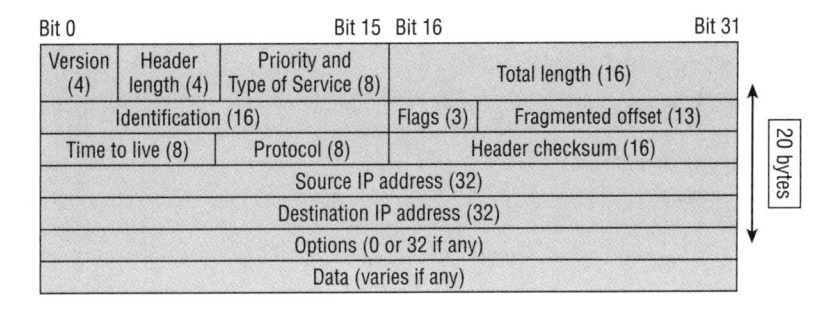

FIGURE 2.15 IP header

Bit 0			Bit 15	Bit 16		Bit 31
Version (4)	Header length (4)	Priority and Type of Service (8)		Total length (16)		
Identification (16)				Flags (3)	Fragmented offset (13)	
Time to live (8)		Protocol (8)		Header checksum (16)		
Source IP address (32)						
Destination IP address (32)						
Options (0 or 32 if any)						
Data (varies if any)						

(20 bytes)

The following fields make up the IP header:

Version   IP version number.

Header length   Header length (HLEN) in 32-bit words.

Priority and Type of Service   Type of Service tells how the datagram should be handled. The first 3 bits are the priority bits, now called the differentiated services bits.

Total length   Length of the packet, including header and data.

Identification   Unique IP-packet value used to differentiate fragmented packets from different datagrams.

Flags   Specifies whether fragmentation should occur.

Fragment offset   Provides fragmentation and reassembly if the packet is too large to put in a frame. It also allows different maximum transmission units (MTUs) on the Internet.

Time To Live   The time to live (TTL) is set into a packet when it's originally generated. If it doesn't get to where it's supposed to go before the TTL expires, boom—it's gone. This stops IP packets from continuously circling the network looking for a home.

Protocol   Port of upper-layer protocol; for example, TCP is port 6 or UDP is port 17. Also supports Network layer protocols (not ports), like ARP and ICMP, and can be referred to as the Type field in some analyzers. We'll talk about this field more in a minute.

Header checksum   Cyclic redundancy check (CRC) on header only.

Source IP address   32-bit IP address of sending station.

Destination IP address   32-bit IP address of the station this packet is destined for.

Options   Used for network testing, debugging, security, and more.

Data   After the IP option field, will be the upper-layer data.

Here's a snapshot of an IP packet caught on a network analyzer. Notice that all the header information discussed previously appears here:

```
IP Header - Internet Protocol Datagram
Version: 4
Header Length: 5
Precedence: 0
Type of Service: %000
Unused: %00
Total Length: 187
Identifier: 22486
Fragmentation Flags: %010 Do Not Fragment
Fragment Offset: 0
Time To Live: 60
IP Type: 0x06 TCP
Header Checksum: 0xd031
Source IP Address: 10.7.1.30
Dest. IP Address: 10.7.1.10
No Internet Datagram Options
```

The Type field is typically a Protocol field, but this analyzer sees it as an IP Type field. This is important... If the header didn't carry the protocol information for the next layer, IP wouldn't know what to do with the data carried in the packet. The preceding example clearly tells IP to hand the segment to TCP.

Figure 2.16 demonstrates how the Network layer sees the protocols at the Transport layer when it needs to hand a packet up to the upper-layer protocols.

FIGURE 2.16 The Protocol field in an IP header

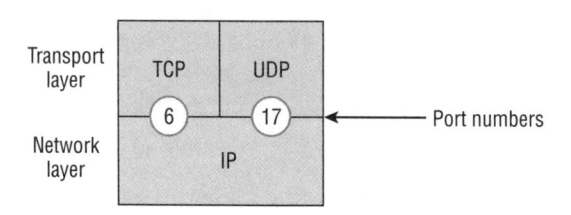

In this example, the Protocol field tells IP to send the data to either TCP 6h or UDP 17h. It will be UDP or TCP only if the data is part of a data stream headed for an upper-layer service or application. It could just as easily be destined for Internet Control Message Protocol (ICMP), Address Resolution Protocol (ARP), or some other type of Network layer protocol.

Table 2.3 is a list of some other popular protocols that can be specified in the Protocol field.

TABLE 2.3 Possible protocols found in the Protocol field of an IP header

Protocol	Protocol Number
ICMP	1
IP in IP (tunneling)	4
TCP	6
UDP	17
EIGRP	88
OSPF	89
IPv6	41
GRE	47
Layer 2 tunnel (L2TP)	115

> You can find a complete list of Protocol field numbers at www.iana.org/assignments/protocol-numbers.

Internet Control Message Protocol (ICMP)

Internet Control Message Protocol (ICMP) works at the Network layer and is used by IP for many different services. ICMP is basically a management protocol and messaging service provider for IP. Its messages are carried as IP datagrams. RFC 1256 is an annex to ICMP, which gives hosts extended capability in discovering routes to gateways.

ICMP packets have the following characteristics:

- They can provide hosts with information about network problems.
- They are encapsulated within IP datagrams.

The following are some common events and messages that ICMP relates to:

Destination unreachable If a router can't send an IP datagram any further, it uses ICMP to send a message back to the sender, advising it of the situation.

For example, take a look at Figure 2.17, which shows that interface e0 of the Lab_B router is down.

FIGURE 2.17 ICMP error message is sent to the sending host from the remote router

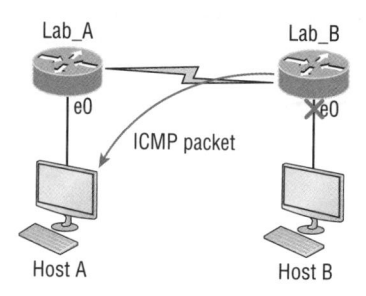

When Host A sends a packet destined for Host B, the Lab_B router will send an ICMP destination unreachable message back to the sending device—Host A in this example.

Buffer full/source quench If a router's memory buffer for receiving incoming datagrams is full, it will use ICMP to send out this message alert until the congestion abates.

Hops/time exceeded Each IP datagram is allotted a certain number of routers, called hops, to pass through. If it reaches its limit of hops before arriving at its destination, the last router to receive that datagram deletes it. The executioner router then uses ICMP to send an obituary message, informing the sending machine of the demise of its datagram.

Ping Packet Internet Groper (Ping) uses ICMP echo request and reply messages to check the physical and logical connectivity of machines on an internetwork.

Traceroute Using ICMP time-outs, Traceroute is used to discover the path a packet takes as it traverses an internetwork.

> **NOTE** Traceroute is usually just called trace. Microsoft Windows uses tracert to allow you to verify address configurations in your internetwork.

The following data is from a network analyzer catching an ICMP echo request:

```
Flags: 0x00
Status: 0x00
Packet Length: 78
Timestamp: 14:04:25.967000 12/20/03
Ethernet Header
Destination: 00:a0:24:6e:0f:a8
Source: 00:80:c7:a8:f0:3d
Ether-Type: 08-00 IP
IP Header - Internet Protocol Datagram
Version: 4
Header Length: 5
Precedence: 0
```

```
Type of Service: %000
Unused: %00
Total Length: 60
Identifier: 56325
Fragmentation Flags: %000
Fragment Offset: 0
Time To Live: 32
IP Type: 0x01 ICMP
Header Checksum: 0x2df0
Source IP Address: 100.100.100.2
Dest. IP Address: 100.100.100.1
No Internet Datagram Options
ICMP - Internet Control Messages Protocol
ICMP Type: 8 Echo Request
Code: 0
Checksum: 0x395c
Identifier: 0x0300
Sequence Number: 4352
ICMP Data Area:
abcdefghijklmnop 61 62 63 64 65 66 67 68 69 6a 6b 6c 6d 6e 6f 70
qrstuvwabcdefghi 71 72 73 74 75 76 77 61 62 63 64 65 66 67 68 69
Frame Check Sequence: 0x00000000
```

Notice anything unusual? Did you catch the fact that even though ICMP works at the Internet (Network) layer, it still uses IP to do the Ping request? The Type field in the IP header is 0x01, which specifies that the data we're carrying is owned by the ICMP protocol. Remember, all segments or data *must* go through IP!

> **Note:** The Ping program uses the alphabet in the data portion of the packet as a payload, typically around 100 bytes by default, unless, of course, you are pinging from a Windows device, which thinks the alphabet stops at the letter *W* (and doesn't include *X*, *Y*, or *Z*) and then starts at *A* again. Go figure!

If you remember reading about the Data Link layer and the different frame types in your CCNA pre-foundation studies, you should be able to look at the preceding trace and tell what type of Ethernet frame this is. The only fields are destination hardware address, source hardware address, and Ether-Type. The only frame that uses an Ether-Type field exclusively is an Ethernet_II frame.

We'll move on soon, but before we get into the ARP protocol, let's take another look at ICMP in action. Figure 2.18 shows an internetwork—it has a router, so it's an internetwork, right?

FIGURE 2.18 ICMP in action

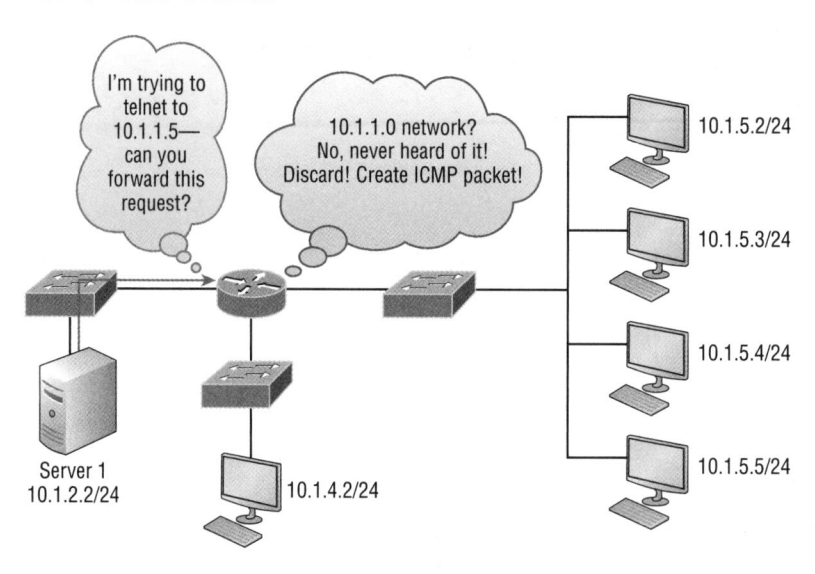

Server 1 (10.1.2.2) telnets to 10.1.1.5 from a DOS prompt. What do you think Server 1 will receive as a response? Server 1 will send the Telnet data to the default gateway, which is the router, and the router will drop the packet because there isn't a network 10.1.1.0 in the routing table. Because of this, Server 1 will receive an ICMP network unreachable back from the router.

Address Resolution Protocol (ARP)

Address Resolution Protocol (ARP) finds the hardware address of a host from a known IP address. Here's how it works: When IP has a datagram to send, it must inform a Network Access protocol, such as Ethernet or wireless, of the destination's hardware address on the local network. Remember that it has already been informed by upper-layer protocols of the destination's IP address. If IP doesn't find the destination host's hardware address in the ARP cache, it uses ARP to find this information.

As IP's detective, ARP interrogates the local network by sending out a broadcast asking the machine with the specified IP address to reply with its hardware address. So basically, ARP translates the software (IP) address into a hardware address—for example, the destination machine's Ethernet adapter address—and from it, deduces its whereabouts on the LAN by broadcasting for this address.

Figure 2.19 shows how an ARP broadcast looks to a local network.

FIGURE 2.19 Local ARP broadcast

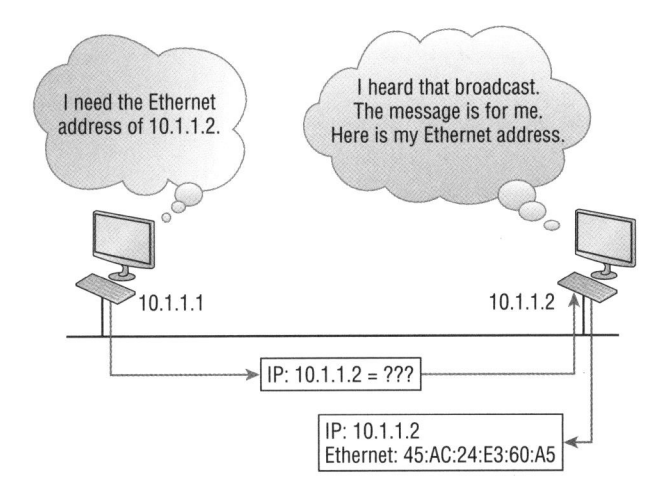

> ARP resolves IP addresses to Ethernet (MAC) addresses.

The following trace shows an ARP broadcast—notice that the destination hardware address is unknown and is all *F*s in hex (all 1s in binary)—and is a hardware address broadcast:

Flags: 0x00
Status: 0x00
Packet Length: 64
Timestamp: 09:17:29.574000 12/06/03
Ethernet Header
Destination: FF:FF:FF:FF:FF:FF Ethernet Broadcast
Source: 00:A0:24:48:60:A5
Protocol Type: 0x0806 IP ARP
ARP - Address Resolution Protocol
Hardware: 1 Ethernet (10Mb)
Protocol: 0x0800 IP
Hardware Address Length: 6
Protocol Address Length: 4
Operation: 1 ARP Request
Sender Hardware Address: 00:A0:24:48:60:A5

```
Sender Internet Address: 172.16.10.3
Target Hardware Address: 00:00:00:00:00:00 (ignored)
Target Internet Address: 172.16.10.10
Extra bytes (Padding):
............... 0A 0A 0A 0A 0A 0A 0A 0A 0A 0A 0A 0A 0A
0A 0A 0A 0A 0A
Frame Check Sequence: 0x00000000
```

IP Addressing

One of the most important topics in any discussion of TCP/IP is IP addressing. An *IP address* is a numeric identifier assigned to each machine on an IP network. It designates the specific location of a device on the network.

An IP address is a software address, not a hardware address—the latter is hard-coded on a network interface card (NIC) and used for finding hosts on a local network. IP addressing was designed to allow hosts on one network to communicate with a host on a different network regardless of the type of LANs the hosts are participating in.

Before we get into the more complicated aspects of IP addressing, you need to understand some of the basics. First, I'm going to explain some of the fundamentals of IP addressing and its terminology. Then you'll learn about the hierarchical IP addressing scheme and private IP addresses.

IP Terminology

Throughout this chapter you're being introduced to several important terms that are vital to understanding the Internet Protocol. Here are a few to get you started:

Bit   A bit is one digit, either a 1 or a 0.

Byte   A byte is 7 or 8 bits, depending on whether parity is used. For the rest of this chapter, always assume a byte is 8 bits.

Octet   An octet, made up of 8 bits, is just an ordinary 8-bit binary number. In this chapter, the terms *byte* and *octet* are completely interchangeable.

Network address   This is the designation used in routing to send packets to a remote network—for example, 10.0.0.0, 172.16.0.0, and 192.168.10.0.

Broadcast address   The address used by applications and hosts to send information to all nodes on a network is called the broadcast address. Examples of layer 3 broadcasts include 255.255.255.255, which is any network, all nodes; 172.16.255.255, which is all subnets and hosts on network 172.16.0.0; and 10.255.255.255, which broadcasts to all subnets and hosts on network 10.0.0.0.

The Hierarchical IP Addressing Scheme

An IP address consists of 32 bits of information. These bits are divided into four sections, referred to as octets or bytes, with each containing 1 byte (8 bits). You can depict an IP address using one of three methods:

- Dotted-decimal, as in 172.16.30.56
- Binary, as in 10101100.00010000.00011110.00111000
- Hexadecimal, as in AC.10.1E.38

All these examples represent the same IP address. Pertaining to IP addressing, hexadecimal isn't used as often as dotted-decimal or binary, but you still might find an IP address stored in hexadecimal in some programs.

The 32-bit IP address is a structured or hierarchical address as opposed to a flat or nonhierarchical address. Although either type of addressing scheme could have been used, *hierarchical addressing* was chosen for a good reason. The advantage of this scheme is that it can handle a large number of addresses, namely, 4.3 billion (a 32-bit address space with two possible values for each position—either 0 or 1—gives you 2^{32}, or 4,294,967,296). The disadvantage of the flat addressing scheme, and the reason it's not used for IP addressing, relates to routing. If every address were unique, all routers on the Internet would need to store the address of each and every machine on the Internet. This would make efficient routing impossible, even if only a fraction of the possible addresses were used!

The solution to this problem is to use a two- or three-level hierarchical addressing scheme that is structured by network and host or by network, subnet, and host.

This two- or three-level scheme can also be compared to a telephone number. The first section, the area code, designates a very large area. The second section, the prefix, narrows the scope to a local calling area. The final segment, the customer number, zooms in on the specific connection. IP addresses use the same type of layered structure. Rather than all 32 bits being treated as a unique identifier as in flat addressing, a part of the address is designated as the network address, and the other part is designated as either the subnet and host or just the node address.

Next, we'll cover IP network addressing and the different classes of address we can use to address our networks.

Network Addressing

The *network address* (which can also be called the network number) uniquely identifies each network. Every machine on the same network shares that network address as part of its IP address. For example, in the IP address 172.16.30.56, 172.16 represents the network address.

The *node address* is assigned to, and uniquely identifies, each machine on a network. This part of the address must be unique because it identifies a particular machine—an individual—as opposed to a network, which is a group. This number can also be referred to as a *host address*. In the sample IP address 172.16.30.56, the 30.56 represents the node address.

The designers of the Internet decided to create classes of networks based on network size. For the small number of networks possessing a very large number of nodes, they created the rank *Class A network*. At the other extreme is the *Class C network*, which is reserved for the numerous networks with a small number of nodes. The class distinction for networks between very large and very small is predictably called the *Class B network*.

Subdividing an IP address into a network and node address is determined by the class designation of one's network. Figure 2.20 summarizes the three classes of networks used to address hosts—a subject I'll explain in much greater detail throughout this chapter.

FIGURE 2.20 Summary of the three classes of networks

	8 bits	8 bits	8 bits	8 bits
Class A:	Network	Host	Host	Host
Class B:	Network	Network	Host	Host
Class C:	Network	Network	Network	Host
Class D:	Multicast			
Class E:	Research			

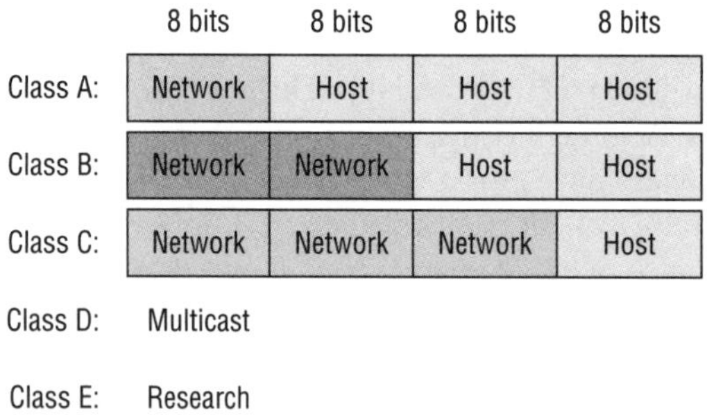

To ensure efficient routing, Internet designers defined a mandate for the leading-bits section of the address for each different network class. For example, since a router knows that a Class A network address always starts with a 0, the router might be able to speed a packet on its way after reading only the first bit of its address. This is where the address schemes define the difference between a Class A, a Class B, and a Class C address. Coming up, I'll discuss the differences between these three classes, followed by a discussion of the Class D and Class E addresses. Classes A, B, and C are the only ranges that are used to address hosts in our networks.

Network Address Range: Class A

The designers of the IP address scheme decided that the first bit of the first byte in a Class A network address must always be off, or 0. This means a Class A address must be between 0 and 127 in the first byte, inclusive.

Consider the following network address:

0xxxxxxx

If we turn the other 7 bits all off and then turn them all on, we find the Class A range of network addresses:

00000000 = 0
01111111 = 127

So, a Class A network is defined in the first octet between 0 and 127, and it can't be less or more. Understand that 0 and 127 are not valid in a Class A network because they're reserved addresses, something I'll go over soon.

Network Address Range: Class B

In a Class B network, the RFCs state that the first bit of the first byte must always be turned on but the second bit must always be turned off (10). If you turn the other 6 bits all off and then all on, you find the range for a Class B network:

10000000 = 128
10111111 = 191

As you can see, a Class B network is defined when the first byte is configured from 128 to 191.

Network Address Range: Class C

For Class C networks, the RFCs define the first 2 bits of the first octet as always turned on, but the third bit can never be on. Following the same process as the previous classes, convert from binary to decimal to find the range. Here's the range for a Class C network:

11000000 = 192
11011111 = 223

So, if you see an IP address that starts at 192 and goes to 223, you'll know it is a Class C IP address.

Network Address Ranges: Classes D and E

The addresses between 224 to 255 are reserved for Class D and E networks. Class D (224–239) is used for multicast addresses and Class E (240–255) for scientific purposes. I'm not going into these types of addresses because they are beyond the scope of knowledge you need to gain from this book.

Network Addresses: Special Purpose

Some IP addresses are reserved for special purposes, so network administrators can't ever assign these addresses to nodes. Table 2.4 lists the members of this exclusive little club and the reasons why they're included in it.

TABLE 2.4 Reserved IP addresses

Address	Function
Network address of all 0s	Interpreted to mean "this network or segment."
Network address of all 1s	Interpreted to mean "all networks."
Network 127.0.0.1	Reserved for loopback tests. Designates the local node and allows that node to send a test packet to itself without generating network traffic.
Node address of all 0s	Interpreted to mean "network address" or any host on a specified network.

TABLE 2.4 Reserved IP addresses *(continued)*

Address	Function
Node address of all 1s	Interpreted to mean "all nodes" on the specified network; for example, 128.2.255.255 means "all nodes" on network 128.2 (Class B address).
Entire IP address set to all 0s	Used by Cisco routers to designate the default route. Could also mean "any network."
Entire IP address set to all 1s (same as 255.255.255.255)	Broadcast to all nodes on the current network; sometimes called an "all 1s broadcast" or local broadcast.

Class A Addresses

In a Class A network address, the first byte is assigned to the network address and the three remaining bytes are used for the node addresses. The Class A format is as follows:

network.node.node.node

For example, in the IP address 49.22.102.70, the 49 is the network address and 22.102.70 is the node address. Every machine on this particular network would have the distinctive network address of 49.

Class A network addresses are 1 byte long, with the first bit of that byte reserved and the 7 remaining bits available for manipulation (addressing). As a result, the maximum number of Class A networks that can be created is 128. Why? Because each of the 7 bit positions can be either a 0 or a 1, thus, 2^7, or 128.

To complicate matters further, the network address of all 0s (0000 0000) is reserved to designate the default route (see Table 2.4 in the previous section). Additionally, the address 127, which is reserved for diagnostics, can't be used either, which means that you can really only use the numbers 1 to 126 to designate Class A network addresses. This means the actual number of usable Class A network addresses is 128 minus 2, or 126.

> **NOTE** The IP address 127.0.0.1 is used to test the IP stack on an individual node and cannot be used as a valid host address. However, the loopback address creates a shortcut method for TCP/IP applications and services that run on the same device to communicate with each other.

Each Class A address has 3 bytes (24-bit positions) for the node address of a machine. This means there are 2^{24}—or 16,777,216—unique combinations and, therefore, precisely that many possible unique node addresses for each Class A network. Because node addresses with the two patterns of all 0s and all 1s are reserved, the actual maximum usable number of nodes for a Class A network is 2^{24} minus 2, which equals 16,777,214. Either way, that's a huge number of hosts on a single network segment!

Class A Valid Host IDs

Here's an example of how to figure out the valid host IDs in a Class A network address:

- All host bits off is the network address: 10.0.0.0.
- All host bits on is the broadcast address: 10.255.255.255.

The valid hosts are the numbers in between the network address and the broadcast address: 10.0.0.1 through 10.255.255.254. Notice that 0s and 255s can be valid host IDs. All you need to remember when trying to find valid host addresses is that the host bits can't all be turned off or on at the same time.

Class B Addresses

In a Class B network address, the first 2 bytes are assigned to the network address and the remaining 2 bytes are used for node addresses. The format is as follows:

network.network.node.node

For example, in the IP address 172.16.30.56, the network address is 172.16, and the node address is 30.56.

With a network address being 2 bytes (8 bits each), you get 2^{16} unique combinations. The Internet designers decided that all Class B network addresses should start with the binary digit 1, then 0. This leaves 14 bit positions to manipulate, therefore 16,384, or 2^{14} unique Class B network addresses.

A Class B address uses 2 bytes for node addresses. This is 2^{16} minus the two reserved patterns of all 0s and all 1s for a total of 65,534 possible node addresses for each Class B network.

Class B Valid Host IDs

Here's an example of how to find the valid hosts in a Class B network:

- All host bits turned off is the network address: 172.16.0.0.
- All host bits turned on is the broadcast address: 172.16.255.255.

The valid hosts would be the numbers in between the network address and the broadcast address: 172.16.0.1 through 172.16.255.254.

Class C Addresses

The first 3 bytes of a Class C network address are dedicated to the network portion of the address, with only 1 measly byte remaining for the node address. Here's the format:

network.network.network.node

Using the example IP address 192.168.100.102, the network address is 192.168.100 and the node address is 102.

In a Class C network address, the first three bit positions are always the binary 110. The calculation is as follows: 3 bytes, or 24 bits, minus 3 reserved positions leaves 21 positions. Hence, there are 2^{21}, or 2,097,152, possible Class C networks.

Each unique Class C network has 1 byte to use for node addresses. This leads to 2^8, or 256, minus the two reserved patterns of all 0s and all 1s, for a total of 254 node addresses for each Class C network.

Class C Valid Host IDs

Here's an example of how to find a valid host ID in a Class C network:

- All host bits turned off is the network ID: 192.168.100.0.
- All host bits turned on is the broadcast address: 192.168.100.255.

The valid hosts would be the numbers in between the network address and the broadcast address: 192.168.100.1 through 192.168.100.254.

Private IP Addresses (RFC 1918)

The people who created the IP addressing scheme also created private IP addresses. These addresses can be used on a private network, but they're not routable through the Internet. This is designed for the purpose of creating a measure of well-needed security, but it also conveniently saves valuable IP address space.

If every host on every network were required to have real routable IP addresses, we would have run out of IP addresses years ago. But by using private IP addresses, ISPs, corporations, and home users only need a relatively tiny group of bona fide IP addresses to connect their networks to the Internet. This is economical because they can use private IP addresses on their inside networks and get along just fine.

To accomplish this task, the ISP and the corporation—the end user, no matter who they are—need to use something called *Network Address Translation (NAT)*, which basically takes a private IP address and converts it for use on the Internet. NAT is covered in Chapter 11, "Network Address Translation (NAT)." Many people can use the same real IP address to transmit out onto the Internet. Doing things this way saves tons of address space—good for us all!

The reserved private addresses are listed in Table 2.5.

TABLE 2.5 Reserved IP address space

Address Class	Reserved Address Space
Class A	10.0.0.0 through 10.255.255.255
Class B	172.16.0.0 through 172.31.255.255
Class C	192.168.0.0 through 192.168.255.255

> **So Which Private IP Address Should I Use?**
>
> That's a really great question: Should you use Class A, Class B, or even Class C private addressing when setting up your network? Let's take Acme Corporation in SF as an example. This company is moving into a new building and needs a whole new network. It has 14 departments, with about 70 users in each. You could probably squeeze one or two Class C addresses to use, or maybe you could use a Class B, or even a Class A just for fun.
>
> The rule of thumb in the consulting world is, when you're setting up a corporate network—regardless of how small it is—you should use a Class A network address because it gives you the most flexibility and growth options. For example, if you used the 10.0.0.0 network address with a /24 mask, then you'd have 65,536 networks, each with 254 hosts. Lots of room for growth with that network!
>
> But if you're setting up a home network, you'd opt for a Class C address because it is the easiest for people to understand and configure. Using the default Class C mask gives you one network with 254 hosts—plenty for a home network.
>
> With the Acme Corporation, a nice 10.1.x.0 with a /24 mask (the x is the subnet for each department) makes this easy to design, install, and troubleshoot.

IPv4 Address Types

Most people use the term *broadcast* as a generic term, and most of the time, we understand what they mean—but not always! For example, you might say, "The host broadcasted through a router to a DHCP server," but, well, it's pretty unlikely that this would ever really happen. What you probably mean—using the correct technical jargon—is, "The DHCP client broadcasted for an IP address and a router then forwarded this as a unicast packet to the DHCP server." Oh, and remember that with IPv4, broadcasts are pretty important, but with IPv6, there aren't any broadcasts sent at all!

So I've referred to IP addresses throughout this chapter, and even showed you some examples, but I really haven't gone into the different terms and uses associated with them yet, and it's about time I did. So here are the address types that I'd like to define for you:

Loopback (localhost) Used to test the IP stack on the local computer. Can be any address from 127.0.0.1 through 127.255.255.254.

Layer 2 broadcasts These are sent to all nodes on a LAN.

Broadcasts (layer 3) These are sent to all nodes on the network.

Unicast This is an address for a single interface, and these are used to send packets to a single destination host.

Multicast These are packets sent from a single source and transmitted to many devices on different networks. Referred to as "one-to-many."

Layer 2 Broadcasts

First, understand that layer 2 broadcasts are also known as hardware broadcasts. They only go out on a LAN and they don't go past the LAN boundary (router).

The typical hardware address is 6 bytes (48 bits) and looks something like 45:AC:24:E3:60:A5. The broadcast would be all 1s in binary, which would be all *F*s in hexadecimal, as in ff:ff:ff:ff:ff:ff as shown in Figure 2.21.

FIGURE 2.21 Local layer 2 broadcasts

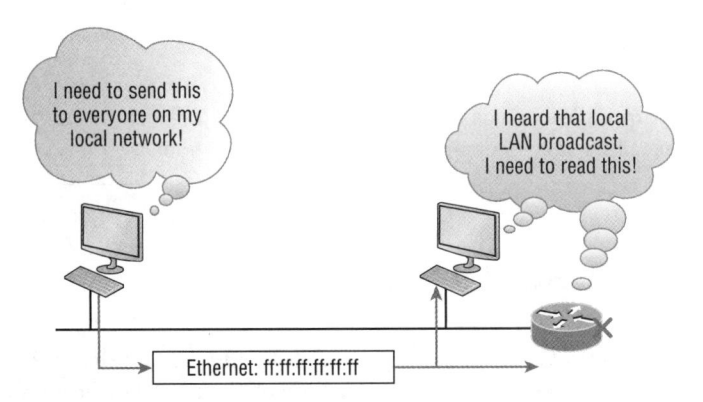

Every network interface card (NIC) will receive and read the frame, including the router, (since this was a layer 2 broadcast), but the router would never, ever forward this!

Layer 3 Broadcasts

Then there are the plain old broadcast addresses at layer 3. Broadcast messages are meant to reach all hosts on a broadcast domain. These are the network broadcasts that have all host bits on.

Here's an example that you're already familiar with: The network address of 172.16.0.0 255.255.0.0 would have a broadcast address of 172.16.255.255—all host bits on. Broadcasts can also be "any network and all hosts," as indicated by 255.255.255.255, and shown in Figure 2.22.

FIGURE 2.22 Layer 3 broadcasts

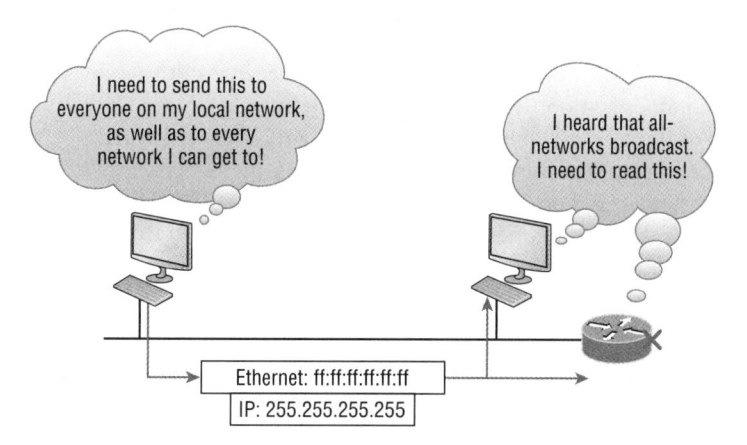

In Figure 2.22, all hosts on the LAN will get this broadcast on their NIC, including the router, but by default, the router would never forward this packet.

Unicast Address

A unicast is defined as a single IP address that's assigned to a network interface card and is the destination IP address in a packet—in other words, it's used for directing packets to a specific host.

In Figure 2.23, both the MAC address and the destination IP address are for a single NIC on the network. All hosts on the broadcast domain would receive this frame and accept it. Only the destination NIC of 10.1.1.2 would accept the packet; the other NICs would discard the packet.

FIGURE 2.23 Unicast address

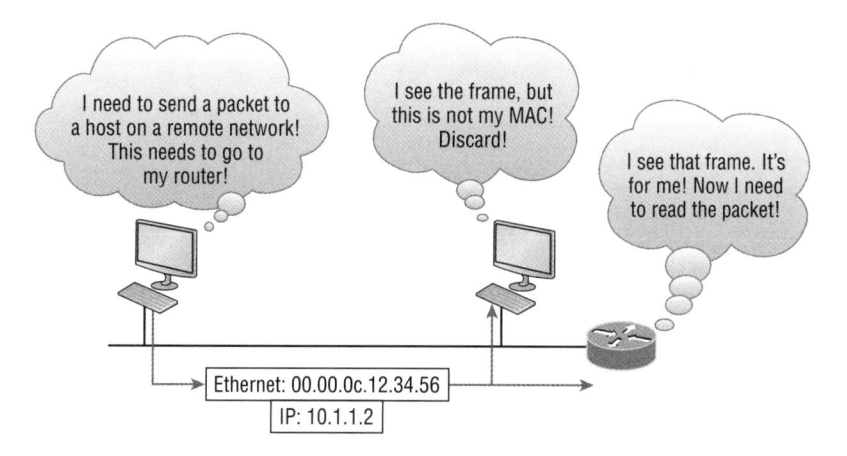

Multicast Address

Multicast is a different beast entirely. At first glance, it appears to be a hybrid of unicast and broadcast communication, but that isn't quite the case. Multicast does allow point-to-multipoint communication, which is similar to broadcasts, but it happens in a different way. The crux of *multicast* is that it enables multiple recipients to receive messages without flooding the messages to all hosts on a broadcast domain. Still, this isn't the default behavior—it's what we *can* do with multicasting if it's configured correctly.

Multicast works by sending messages or data to IP *multicast group* addresses. Unlike with broadcasts, which aren't forwarded, routers then forward copies of the packet out to every interface that has hosts *subscribed* to that group address. This is where multicast differs from broadcast messages—with multicast communication, copies of packets, in theory, are sent only to subscribed hosts. For example, when I say in theory, I mean that the hosts will receive a multicast packet destined for 224.0.0.10. This is an EIGRP packet, and only a router running the EIGRP protocol will read these. All hosts on the broadcast LAN, and Ethernet is a broadcast multi-access LAN technology, will pick up the frame, read the destination address, then immediately discard the frame unless they're in the multicast group. This saves PC processing, not LAN bandwidth. So be warned—multicasting can cause some serious LAN congestion if it's not implemented carefully! Figure 2.24 shows a Cisco router sending an EIGRP multicast packet on the local LAN with only the other Cisco router accepting and reading this packet.

FIGURE 2.24 EIGRP multicast example

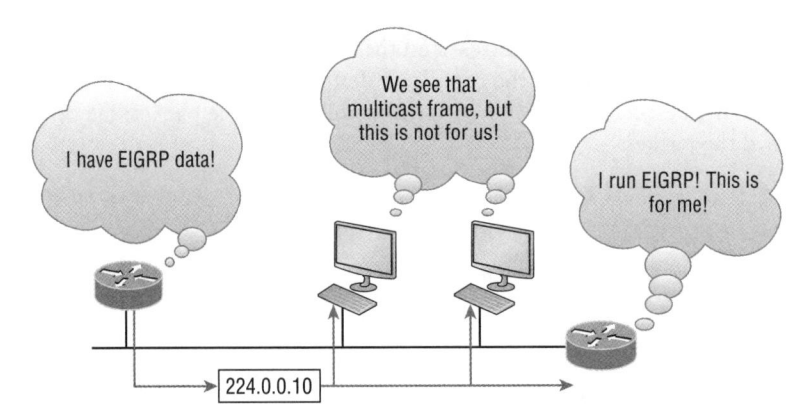

There are several different groups that users or applications can subscribe to. The range of multicast addresses starts with 224.0.0.0 and goes through 239.255.255.255. As you can see, this range of addresses falls within IP Class D address space based on classful IP assignment.

Summary

If you made it this far and understood everything the first time through, fantastic! We really covered a lot of ground in this chapter. If you don't think you completely got it, no worries—it really wouldn't hurt anyone to read this chapter more than once. That's because understanding the information in this chapter is absolutely vital to being able to navigate well through the rest of this book.

There is still a lot of ground to cover and just so you know, there's a lot more! So just make sure you've got this material nailed down to avoid pain later. What we're doing up to this point is building a solid foundation to build upon as you advance.

With that in mind, after you learned about the DoD model, the layers, and associated protocols, you found out about the oh-so-important topic of IP addressing. I discussed in detail the difference between each address class, how to find a network address and broadcast address, plus, what denotes a valid host address range. And not nagging but, I can't stress enough how important it is for you to have this chapter's critical information clearly and completely down before moving on to Chapter 3.

Exam Essentials

Differentiate between the DoD and the OSI network models. The DoD model is a condensed version of the OSI model, composed of four layers instead of seven, but is nonetheless like the OSI model in that it can be used to describe packet creation and devices and protocols can be mapped to its layers.

Identify Host-to-Host layer protocols. Transmission Control Protocol (TCP) is a connection-oriented protocol that provides reliable network service by using acknowledgments and flow control. User Datagram Protocol (UDP) is a connectionless protocol that provides low overhead and is considered unreliable.

Identify Internet layer protocols. Internet Protocol (IP) is a connectionless protocol that provides network address and routing through an internetwork. Address Resolution Protocol (ARP) finds a hardware address from a known IP address. Reverse ARP (RARP) finds an IP address from a known hardware address. Internet Control Message Protocol (ICMP) provides diagnostics and destination unreachable messages.

Describe the functions of DNS and DHCP in the network. Dynamic Host Configuration Protocol (DHCP) provides network configuration information (including IP addresses) to hosts, eliminating the need to perform the configurations manually. Domain Name Service (DNS) resolves hostnames—both Internet names such as `www.lammle.com` and device names such as Workstation 2—to IP addresses, eliminating the need to know the IP address of a device for connection purposes.

Identify what is contained in the TCP header of a connection-oriented transmission. The fields in the TCP header include the source port, destination port, sequence number, acknowledgment number, header length, a field reserved for future use, code bits, window size, checksum, urgent pointer, options field, and finally, the data field.

Identify what is contained in the UDP header of a connectionless transmission. The fields in the UDP header include only the source port, destination port, length, checksum, and data. The smaller number of fields as compared to the TCP header comes at the expense of providing none of the more advanced functions of the TCP frame.

Identify what is contained in the IP header. The fields of an IP header include version, header length, priority or type of service, total length, identification, flags, fragment offset, time to live, protocol, header checksum, source IP address, destination IP address, options, and finally, data.

Compare and contrast UDP and TCP characteristics and features. TCP is connection-oriented, acknowledged, and sequenced and has flow and error control, while UDP is connectionless, unacknowledged, and not sequenced and provides no error or flow control.

Understand the role of port numbers. Port numbers are used to identify the protocol or service that is to be used in the transmission.

Identify the role of ICMP. Internet Control Message Protocol (ICMP) works at the Network layer and is used by IP for many different services. ICMP is a management protocol and messaging service provider for IP.

Define the Class A IP address range. The IP range for a Class A network is 1–126. This provides 8 bits of network addressing and 24 bits of host addressing by default.

Define the Class B IP address range. The IP range for a Class B network is 128–191. Class B addressing provides 16 bits of network addressing and 16 bits of host addressing by default.

Define the Class C IP address range. The IP range for a Class C network is 192 through 223. Class C addressing provides 24 bits of network addressing and 8 bits of host addressing by default.

Identify the private IP ranges. The Class A private address range is 10.0.0.0 through 10.255.255.255. The Class B private address range is 172.16.0.0 through 172.31.255.255. The Class C private address range is 192.168.0.0 through 192.168.255.255.

Understand the difference between a broadcast, unicast, and multicast address. A broadcast is to all devices in a subnet, a unicast is to one device, and a multicast is to some but not all devices.

Review Questions

You can find the answers to these questions in the Appendix.

1. What must happen if a DHCP IP conflict occurs?
   A. Proxy ARP will fix the issue.
   B. The client uses a gratuitous ARP to fix the issue.
   C. The administrator must fix the conflict by hand at the DHCP server.
   D. The DHCP server will reassign new IP addresses to both computers.

2. Which of the following Application layer protocols sets up a secure session that's similar to Telnet?
   A. FTP
   B. SSH
   C. DNS
   D. DHCP

3. Which of the following mechanisms is used by the client to avoid a duplicate IP address during the DHCP process?
   A. Ping
   B. Traceroute
   C. Gratuitous ARP
   D. Pathping

4. Which of the following describe the DHCP Discover message? (Choose two.)
   A. It uses ff:ff:ff:ff:ff:ff as a layer 2 broadcast.
   B. It uses UDP as the Transport layer protocol.
   C. It uses TCP as the Transport layer protocol.
   D. It does not use a layer 2 destination address.

5. Which of the following services use TCP? (Choose three.)
   A. DHCP
   B. SMTP
   C. SNMP
   D. FTP
   E. HTTP
   F. TFTP

6. Which of the following is an example of a multicast address?
   A. 10.6.9.1
   B. 192.168.10.6
   C. 224.0.0.10
   D. 172.16.9.5

7. Which two of the following are private IP addresses?
   A. 12.0.0.1
   B. 168.172.19.39
   C. 172.20.14.36
   D. 172.33.194.30
   E. 192.168.24.43

8. What layer in the TCP/IP stack is equivalent to the Transport layer of the OSI model?
   A. Application
   B. Host-to-Host
   C. Internet
   D. Network Access

9. Which statements are true regarding ICMP packets? (Choose two.)
   A. ICMP guarantees datagram delivery.
   B. ICMP can provide hosts with information about network problems.
   C. ICMP is encapsulated within IP datagrams.
   D. ICMP is encapsulated within UDP datagrams.

10. What is the address range of a Class B network address in binary?
    A. 01xxxxxx
    B. 0xxxxxxx
    C. 10xxxxxx
    D. 110xxxxx

Chapter 3

Easy Subnetting

THE FOLLOWING CCNA EXAM TOPICS ARE COVERED IN THIS CHAPTER:

1.0 Network Fundamentals

✓ 1.6 Configure and verify IPv4 addressing and subnetting

We'll pick up right where we left off in the last chapter and continue to explore the world of IP addressing. I'll open this chapter by showing you how to subnet an IP network—an indispensable skill that's central to mastering networking in general. Forewarned is forearmed, so prepare yourself because being able to subnet quickly and accurately is pretty challenging. You'll definitely need time to practice what you've learned to get good at it. So be patient and don't give up on this key aspect of networking until your skills are seriously sharp!

What I'm about to say might sound weird to you, but you'll be much better off if you just try to forget everything you've already learned about subnetting before reading this chapter—especially if you've been to an official Cisco or Microsoft class! I think these forms of special torture often do more harm than good and sometimes even scare people away from networking completely. Those that survive and persevere usually at least question the sanity of continuing to study in this field. If this is you, relax, and know that you'll find that the way I tackle the issue of subnetting is relatively painless because I'm going to show you a whole new, much easier method to conquer this monster!

After working through this chapter, you'll be able to tame the IP addressing/subnetting beast—just don't give up! I promise that you'll be really glad you didn't. It's one of those things that once you get it down, you'll wonder why you used to think it was so hard.

> **NOTE** To find your included bonus material, as well as Todd Lammle videos, practice questions and hands-on labs, please see www.lammle.com/ccna.

Subnetting Basics

In Chapter 2, "Introduction to TCP/IP," you learned how to define and find the valid host ranges used in a Class A, Class B, and Class C network address by turning the host bits all off and then all on. This is very good, but here's the catch: you were defining only one network, as shown in Figure 3.1.

You probably know that having one large network is not a good thing, so how would you fix the out-of-control problem that Figure 3.1 illustrates? Wouldn't it be nice to be able to break up that one, huge network address and create more manageable networks from it? You bet it would, but to make that happen, you would need to apply the infamous trick of *subnetting* because it's the best way to break up a giant network into a bunch of smaller ones.

FIGURE 3.1 One network

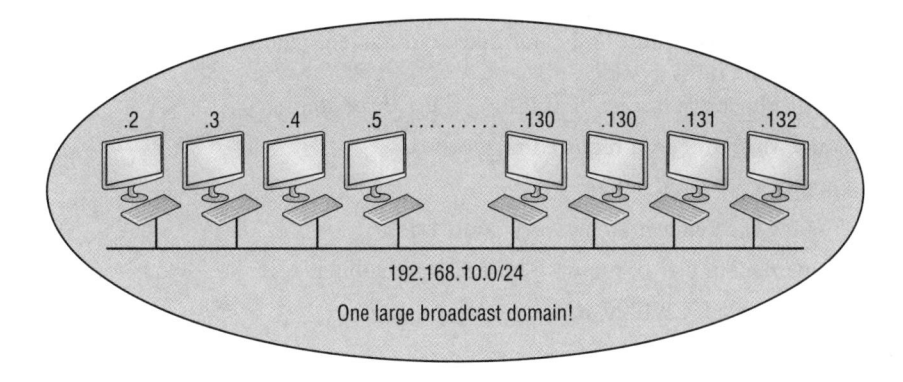

[Figure: One large broadcast domain showing hosts .2, .3, .4, .5 .... .130, .130, .131, .132 on network 192.168.10.0/24]

Check out Figure 3.2 to see how this might look.

FIGURE 3.2 Multiple networks connected together

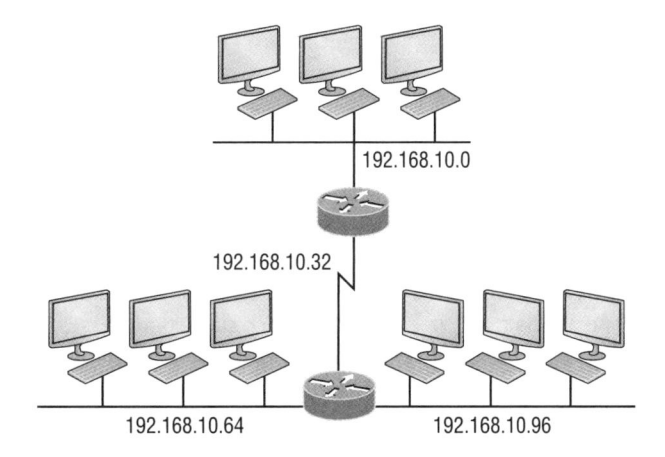

[Figure: Router connecting subnets 192.168.10.0, 192.168.10.32, 192.168.10.64, and 192.168.10.96]

What are those 192.168.10.*x* addresses shown in the figure? Well, that is what this chapter will explain—how to make one network into many networks.

Let's take off from where we left in Chapter 2 and start working in the host section (host bits) of a network address, where we can borrow bits to create subnets.

How to Create Subnets

Creating subnetworks is essentially the act of taking bits from the host portion of the address and reserving them to define the subnet address instead. Clearly this will result in fewer bits being available for defining your hosts, which is something you'll always want to keep in mind.

Later in this chapter, I'll guide you through the entire process of creating subnets starting with Class C addresses. As always in networking, before you actually implement anything, including subnetting, you must first determine your current requirements and make sure to plan for future conditions as well.

To create a subnet, we'll start by fulfilling these three steps:

1. Determine the number of required network IDs:
   - One for each LAN subnet
   - One for each wide area network connection
2. Determine the number of required host IDs per subnet:
   - One for each TCP/IP host
   - One for each router interface
3. Based on the previous requirements, create the following:
   - A unique subnet mask for your entire network
   - A unique subnet ID for each physical segment
   - A range of host IDs for each subnet

Subnet Masks

For the subnet addressing scheme to work, every machine on the network must know which part of the host address will be used as the subnet address. This condition is met by assigning a *subnet mask* to each machine. A subnet mask is a 32-bit value that allows the device that's receiving IP packets to distinguish the network ID portion of the IP address from the host ID portion of the IP address. This 32-bit subnet mask is composed of 1s and 0s, where the 1s represent the positions that refer to the network subnet addresses.

Not all networks need subnets, and if not, it really means that they're using the default subnet mask, which is basically the same as saying that a network doesn't have a subnet address. Table 3.1 shows the default subnet masks for Classes A, B, and C.

TABLE 3.1 Default subnet mask

Class	Format	Default Subnet Mask
A	network.node.node.node	255.0.0.0
B	network.network.node.node	255.255.0.0
C	network.network.network.node	255.255.255.0

Although you can use any mask in any way on an interface, typically it's not usually good to mess with the default masks. In other words, you don't want to make a Class B subnet mask read 255.0.0.0, and some hosts won't even let you type it in. But these days, most devices will. For a Class A network, you wouldn't change the first byte in a subnet mask because it should read 255.0.0.0 at a minimum. Similarly, you wouldn't assign 255.255.255.255 because this is all 1s, which is a broadcast address. A Class B address starts with 255.255.0.0, and a Class C starts with 255.255.255.0, and for the CCNA especially, there is no reason to change the defaults!

> **Understanding the Powers of 2**
>
> Powers of 2 are important to understand and memorize for use with IP subnetting. Reviewing powers of 2, remember that when you see a number noted with an exponent, it means you should multiply the number by itself as many times as the upper number specifies. For example, 2^3 is 2 x 2 x 2, which equals 8. Here's a list of powers of 2 to commit to memory:
>
> $2^1 = 2$
> $2^2 = 4$
> $2^3 = 8$
> $2^4 = 16$
> $2^5 = 32$
> $2^6 = 64$
> $2^7 = 128$
> $2^8 = 256$
> $2^9 = 512$
> $2^{10} = 1,024$
> $2^{11} = 2,048$
> $2^{12} = 4,096$
> $2^{13} = 8,192$
> $2^{14} = 16,384$
>
> Memorizing these powers of 2 is a good idea, but it's not absolutely necessary. Just remember that since you're working with powers of 2, each successive power of 2 is double the previous one.
>
> It works like this—all you have to do to remember the value of 2^9 is to first know that $2^8 = 256$. Why? Because when you double 2 to the eighth power (256), you get 2^9 (or 512). To determine the value of 2^{10}, simply start at $2^8 = 256$, and then double it twice.
>
> You can go the other way as well. If you needed to know what 2^6 is, for example, you just cut 256 in half two times: once to reach 2^7 and then one more time to reach 2^6.

Classless Inter-Domain Routing (CIDR)

Another term you need to familiarize yourself with is *Classless Inter-Domain Routing (CIDR)*. It's basically the method that Internet service providers (ISPs) use to allocate a number of addresses to a company, a home—their customers. They provide addresses in a certain block size, something I'll talk about in greater detail soon.

When you receive a block of addresses from an ISP, what you get will look something like this: 192.168.10.32/28. This is telling you what your subnet mask is. The slash notation (/) means how many bits are turned on (1s). Obviously, the maximum could only be /32 because a byte is 8 bits and there are 4 bytes in an IP address: (4 × 8 = 32). But keep in mind that regardless of the class of address, the largest subnet mask available relevant to the Cisco exam objectives can only be a /30 because you've got to keep at least 2 bits for host bits.

Take, for example, a Class A default subnet mask, which is 255.0.0.0. This tells us that the first byte of the subnet mask is all ones (1s), or 11111111. When referring to a slash notation, you need to count all the 1 bits to figure out your mask. The 255.0.0.0 is considered a /8 because it has 8 bits that are 1s—that is, 8 bits that are turned on.

A Class B default mask would be 255.255.0.0, which is a /16 because 16 bits are ones (1s): 11111111.11111111.00000000.00000000.

Table 3.2 has a listing of every available subnet mask and its equivalent CIDR slash notation.

TABLE 3.2   CIDR values

Subnet Mask	CIDR Value
255.0.0.0	/8
255.128.0.0	/9
255.192.0.0	/10
255.224.0.0	/11
255.240.0.0	/12
255.248.0.0	/13
255.252.0.0	/14
255.254.0.0	/15
255.255.0.0	/16
255.255.128.0	/17

Subnet Mask	CIDR Value
255.255.192.0	/18
255.255.224.0	/19
255.255.240.0	/20
255.255.248.0	/21
255.255.252.0	/22
255.255.254.0	/23
255.255.255.0	/24
255.255.255.128	/25
255.255.255.192	/26
255.255.255.224	/27
255.255.255.240	/28
255.255.255.248	/29
255.255.255.252	/30

The /8 through /15 can only be used with Class A network addresses. /16 through /23 can be used by Class A and B network addresses. /24 through /30 can be used by Class A, B, and C network addresses. This is a big reason why most companies use Class A network addresses. Since they can use all subnet masks, they get the maximum flexibility in network design.

> **NOTE** No, you cannot configure a Cisco router using this slash format. But wouldn't that be nice? Nevertheless, it's *really* important for you to know subnet masks in the slash notation (CIDR).

IP Subnet-Zero

Even though `ip subnet-zero` is not a new command, Cisco courseware and Cisco exam objectives didn't used to cover it. They do now! This command allows you to use the first subnet in your network design. For instance, the Class C mask of 255.255.255.192 provides subnets 64,128 and 192, another facet of subnetting that we'll discuss more thoroughly later in this chapter. But with the ip subnet-zero command, you now get to use subnets 0, 64, 128, and 192. It may not seem like a lot, but this provides two more subnets for every subnet mask we use.

Even though we don't discuss the command-line interface (CLI) here, it's important for you to be at least a little familiar with this command at this point:

```
Router#sh running-config
Building configuration...
Current configuration : 827 bytes
!
hostname Pod1R1
!
ip subnet-zero
!
```

This router output shows that the command ip subnet-zero is enabled on the router. Cisco has turned this command on by default starting with Cisco IOS version 12.*x* and now we're running 15.*x* code.

When taking your Cisco exams, make sure you read very carefully to see if Cisco is asking you *not* to use ip subnet-zero. There are actually instances where this may happen.

Subnetting Class C Addresses

There are many different ways to subnet a network. The right way is the way that works best for you. In a Class C address, only 8 bits are available for defining the hosts. Remember that subnet bits start at the left and move to the right, without skipping bits. This means that the only Class C subnet masks can be the following:

```
Binary    Decimal           CIDR
-----------------------------------------------------------
00000000 = 255.255.255.0   /24
10000000 = 255.255.255.128 /25
11000000 = 255.255.255.192 /26
11100000 = 255.255.255.224 /27
11110000 = 255.255.255.240 /28
11111000 = 255.255.255.248 /29
11111100 = 255.255.255.252 /30
```

We can't use a /31 or /32 because, as I've said, we must have at least 2 host bits for assigning IP addresses to hosts. But this is only mostly true. Certainly we can never use a /32 because that would mean zero host bits available, yet Cisco has various forms of the IOS, as well as the new Cisco Nexus switches operating system, that support the /31 mask. The /31 is above the scope of the CCNA objectives, so we won't be covering it in this book.

Coming up, I'm going to teach you that significantly less painful method of subnetting I promised you at the beginning of this chapter, which makes it ever so much easier to subnet larger numbers in a flash. Excited? Good! Because I'm not kidding when I tell you that you absolutely need to be able to subnet quickly and accurately to succeed in the networking real world and on the exam too.

Subnetting a Class C Address—The Fast Way!

When you've chosen a possible subnet mask for your network and need to determine the number of subnets, valid hosts, and the broadcast addresses of a subnet that mask will provide, all you need to do is answer five simple questions:

- How many subnets does the chosen subnet mask produce?
- How many valid hosts per subnet are available?
- What are the valid subnets?
- What's the broadcast address of each subnet?
- What are the valid hosts in each subnet?

This is where you'll be really glad you followed my advice and took the time to memorize your powers of 2. If you didn't, now would be a good time… Just refer back to the sidebar "Understanding the Powers of 2" earlier if you need to brush up. Here's how you arrive at the answers to those five big questions:

- *How many subnets?* 2^x = number of subnets. x is the number of masked bits, or the 1s. For example, in 11000000, the number of 1s gives us 2^2 subnets. So in this example, there are 4 subnets.

- *How many hosts per subnet?* $2^y - 2$ = number of hosts per subnet. y is the number of unmasked bits, or the 0s. For example, in 11000000, the number of 0s gives us $2^6 - 2$ hosts, or 62 hosts per subnet. You need to subtract 2 for the subnet address and the broadcast address, which are not valid hosts.

- *What are the valid subnets?* 256 – subnet mask = block size, or increment number. An example would be the 255.255.255.192 mask, where the interesting octet is the fourth octet (interesting because that is where our subnet numbers are). Just use this math: 256 – 192 = 64. The block size of a 192 mask is always 64. Start counting at zero in blocks of 64 until you reach the subnet mask value and these are your subnets in the fourth octet: 0, 64, 128, 192. Easy, huh?

- *What's the broadcast address for each subnet?* Now here's the really easy part. Since we counted our subnets in the last section as 0, 64, 128, and 192, the broadcast address is always the number right before the next subnet. For example, the 0 subnet has a broadcast address of 63 because the next subnet is 64. The 64 subnet has a broadcast address of 127 because the next subnet is 128, and so on. Remember, the broadcast address of the last subnet is always 255.

- *What are the valid hosts?* Valid hosts are the numbers between the subnets, omitting the all-0s and all-1s. For example, if 64 is the subnet number and 127 is the broadcast address, then 65–126 is the valid host range. Your valid range is *always* the group of numbers between the subnet address and the broadcast address.

If you're still confused, don't worry because it really isn't as hard as it seems to be at first—just hang in there! To help lift any mental fog, try a few of the practice examples next.

Subnetting Practice Examples: Class C Addresses

Here's your opportunity to practice subnetting Class C addresses using the method I just described. This is so cool. We're going to start with the first Class C subnet mask and work through every subnet that we can, using a Class C address. When we're done, I'll show you how easy this is with Class A and B networks too.

Practice Example #1C: 255.255.255.128 (/25)

Since 128 is 10000000 in binary, there is only 1 bit for subnetting and 7 bits for hosts. We're going to subnet the Class C network address 192.168.10.0.

192.168.10.0 = Network address

255.255.255.128 = Subnet mask

Now, let's answer our big five:

- *How many subnets?* Since 128 is 1 bit on (10000000), the answer would be $2^1 = 2$.
- *How many hosts per subnet?* We have 7 host bits off (10000000), so the equation would be $2^7 - 2 = 126$ hosts. Once you figure out the block size of a mask, the amount of hosts is always the block size minus 2. No need to do extra math if you don't need to!
- *What are the valid subnets?* 256 − 128 = 128. Remember, we'll start at zero and count in our block size, so our subnets are 0, 128. By just counting your subnets when counting in your block size, you really don't need to do steps 1 and 2. We can see we have two subnets, and in the step before this one, just remember that the amount of hosts is always the block size minus 2, and in this example, that gives us 2 subnets, each with 126 hosts.
- *What's the broadcast address for each subnet?* The number right before the value of the next subnet is all host bits turned on and equals the broadcast address. For the zero subnet, the next subnet is 128, so the broadcast of the 0 subnet is 127.
- *What are the valid hosts?* These are the numbers between the subnet and broadcast address. The easiest way to find the hosts is to write out the subnet address and the broadcast address, which makes valid hosts completely obvious. The following table shows the 0 and 128 subnets, the valid host ranges of each, and the broadcast address of both subnets:

Subnet	0	128
First host	1	129
Last host	126	254
Broadcast	127	255

Looking at a Class C /25, it's pretty clear that there are two subnets. But so what—why is this significant? Well actually, it's not because that's not the right question. What you really want to know is what you would do with this information!

The key to understanding subnetting is to understand the very reason you need to do it, and I'm going to demonstrate this by going through the process of building a physical network.

Because we added that router shown in Figure 3.3, in order for the hosts on our internetwork to communicate, they must now have a logical network addressing scheme. We could use IPv6, but IPv4 is still the most popular for now. It's also what we're studying at the moment, so that's what we're going with.

FIGURE 3.3 Implementing a Class C /25 logical network

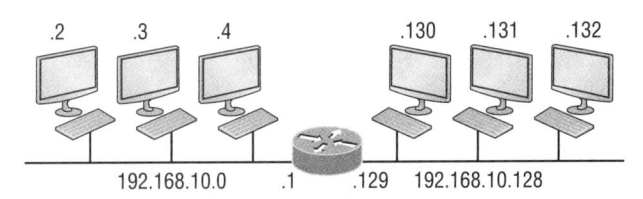

```
Router#show ip route
[output cut]
C 192.168.10.0 is directly connected to Ethernet 0
C 192.168.10.128 is directly connected to Ethernet 1
```

Looking at Figure 3.3, you can see that there are two physical networks, so we're going to implement a logical addressing scheme that allows for two logical networks. As always, it's a really good idea to look ahead and consider likely short- and long-term growth scenarios, but for this example in this book, a /25 gets it done.

Figure 3.3 shows us that both subnets have been assigned to a router interface, which creates our broadcast domains and assigns our subnets. Use the command show ip route to see the routing table on a router. Notice that instead of one large broadcast domain, there are now two smaller broadcast domains, providing for up to 126 hosts in each. The C in the router output translates to "directly connected network," and we can see we have two of those with two broadcast domains and that we created and implemented them. So congratulations—you did it… You have successfully subnetted a network and applied it to a network design. Nice! Let's do it again.

Practice Example #2C: 255.255.255.192 (/26)

This time, we're going to subnet the network address 192.168.10.0 using the subnet mask 255.255.255.192.

192.168.10.0 = Network address

255.255.255.192 = Subnet mask

Now, let's answer the big five:

- *How many subnets?* Since 192 is 2 bits on (**11000000**), the answer would be $2^2 = 4$ subnets.
- *How many hosts per subnet?* We have 6 host bits off (**11000000**), giving us $2^6 - 2 = 62$ hosts. The amount of hosts is always the block size minus 2.

- *What are the valid subnets?* 256 – 192 = 64. Remember to start at zero and count in our block size. This means our subnets are 0, 64, 128, and 192. We can see we have a block size of 64, so we have 4 subnets, each with 62 hosts.
- *What's the broadcast address for each subnet?* The number right before the value of the next subnet is all host bits turned on and equals the broadcast address. For the zero subnet, the next subnet is 64, so the broadcast address for the zero subnet is 63.
- *What are the valid hosts?* These are the numbers between the subnet and broadcast address. As I said, the easiest way to find the hosts is to write out the subnet address and the broadcast address, which clearly delimits our valid hosts. The following table shows the 0, 64, 128, and 192 subnets, the valid host ranges of each, and the broadcast address of each subnet:

The subnets (do this first)	0	64	128	192
Our first host (perform host addressing last)	1	65	129	193
Our last host	62	126	190	254
The broadcast address (do this second)	63	127	191	255

Again, before getting into the next example, you can see that we can now subnet a /26 as long as we can count in increments of 64. And what are you going to do with this fascinating information? Implement it! We'll use Figure 3.4 to practice a /26 network implementation.

FIGURE 3.4 Implementing a class C /26 (with three networks)

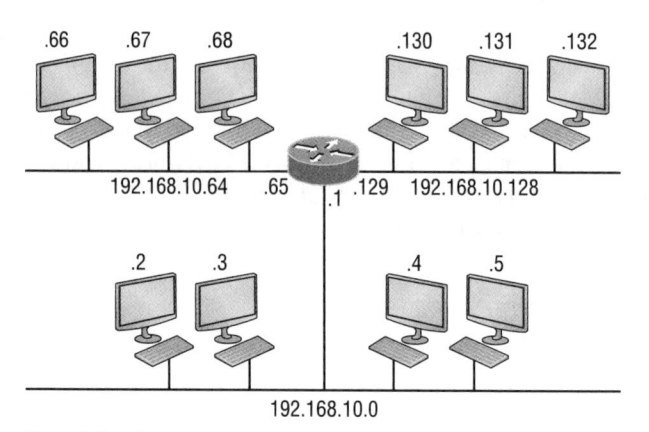

```
Router#show ip route
[output cut]
C 192.168.10.0 is directly connected to Ethernet 0
C 192.168.10.64 is directly connected to Ethernet 1
C 192.168.10.128 is directly connected to Ethernet 2
```

The /26 mask provides four subnetworks, and we need a subnet for each router interface. With this mask, in this example, we actually have room with a spare subnet to add to another router interface in the future. Again, always plan for growth if possible!

Practice Example #3C: 255.255.255.224 (/27)

This time, we'll subnet the network address 192.168.10.0 and subnet mask 255.255.255.224.

192.168.10.0 = Network address

255.255.255.224 = Subnet mask

- *How many subnets?* 224 is 11100000, so our equation would be $2^3 = 8$.
- *How many hosts?* $2^5 - 2 = 30$.
- *What are the valid subnets?* 256 − 224 = 32. We just start at zero and count to the subnet mask value in blocks (increments) of 32: 0, 32, 64, 96, 128, 160, 192, and 224.
- *What's the broadcast address for each subnet?* (Always the number right before the next subnet.)
- *What are the valid hosts?* (The numbers between the subnet number and the broadcast address.)

To answer the last two questions, first just write out the subnets, then write out the broadcast addresses—the number right before the next subnet. Last, fill in the host addresses. The following table gives you all the subnets for the 255.255.255.224 Class C subnet mask:

The subnet address	0	32	64	96	128	160	192	224
The first valid host	1	33	65	97	129	161	193	225
The last valid host	30	62	94	126	158	190	222	254
The broadcast address	31	63	95	127	159	191	223	255

In practice example #3C, we're using a 255.255.255.224 (/27) network, which provides eight subnets as shown previously. We can take these subnets and implement them as shown in Figure 3.5 using any of the subnets available.

Notice that this used six of the eight subnets available for my network design. The lightning bolt symbol in the figure represents a wide area network (WAN), which would be a connection through an ISP or telco. In other words, something you don't own, but it's still a subnet just like any LAN connection on a router. As usual, I used the first valid host in each subnet as the router's interface address. This is just a rule of thumb; you can use any address in the valid host range as long as you remember what address you configured so you can set the default gateways on your hosts to the router address.

FIGURE 3.5 Implementing a Class C /27 logical network

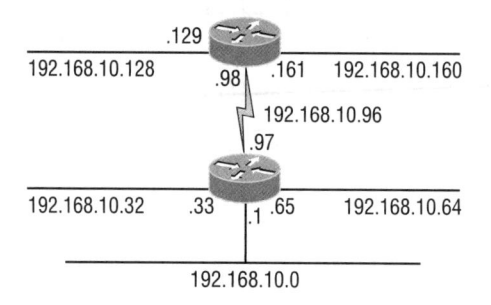

```
                           .129
                     _____
        192.168.10.128  .98 \  .161   192.168.10.160
                              192.168.10.96
                              .97
                     _____
        192.168.10.32   .33 |.1 .65   192.168.10.64
                           192.168.10.0
```

Router#show ip route
[output cut]
C 192.168.10.0 is directly connected to Ethernet 0
C 192.168.10.32 is directly connected to Ethernet 1
C 192.168.10.64 is directly connected to Ethernet 2
C 192.168.10.96 is directly connected to Serial 0

Practice Example #4C: 255.255.255.240 (/28)

Let's practice another one:

192.168.10.0 = Network address

255.255.255.240 = Subnet mask

- *Subnets?* 240 is 11110000 in binary. $2^4 = 16$.
- *Hosts?* 4 host bits, or $2^4 - 2 = 14$.
- *Valid subnets?* 256 − 240 = 16. Start at 0: 0 + 16 = 16. 16 + 16 = 32. 32 + 16 = 48. 48 + 16 = 64. 64 + 16 = 80. 80 + 16 = 96. 96 + 16 = 112. 112 + 16 = 128. 128 + 16 = 144. 144 + 16 = 160. 160 + 16 = 176. 176 + 16 = 192. 192 + 16 = 208. 208 + 16 = 224. 224 + 16 = 240.
- *Broadcast address for each subnet?*
- *Valid hosts?*

To answer the last two questions, check out the following table. It gives you the subnets, valid hosts, and broadcast addresses for each subnet. First, find the address of each subnet using the block size (increment). Second, find the broadcast address of each subnet increment, which is always the number right before the next valid subnet, and then just fill in the host addresses. The following table shows the available subnets, hosts, and broadcast addresses provided from a Class C 255.255.255.240 mask:

Subnet	0	16	32	48	64	80	96	112	128	144	160	176	192	208	224	240
First host	1	17	33	49	65	81	97	113	129	145	161	177	193	209	225	241
Last host	14	30	46	62	78	94	110	126	142	158	174	190	206	222	238	254
Broadcast	15	31	47	63	79	95	111	127	143	159	175	191	207	223	239	255

Subnetting Basics   89

> **TIP:** Cisco has figured out that most people cannot count in 16s and therefore have a hard time finding valid subnets, hosts, and broadcast addresses with the Class C 255.255.255.240 mask. You'd be wise to study this mask.

Practice Example #5C: 255.255.255.248 (/29)

Let's keep practicing:

> 192.168.10.0 = Network address
>
> 255.255.255.248 = Subnet mask

- *Subnets?* 248 in binary = 11111000. 2^5 = 32.
- *Hosts?* $2^3 - 2 = 6$.
- *Valid subnets?* 256 – 248 = 0, 8, 16, 24, 32, 40, 48, 56, 64, 72, 80, 88, 96, 104, 112, 120, 128, 136, 144, 152, 160, 168, 176, 184, 192, 200, 208, 216, 224, 232, 240, and 248.
- *Broadcast address for each subnet?*
- *Valid hosts?*

Take a look at the following table. It shows some of the subnets (first four and last four only), valid hosts, and broadcast addresses for the Class C 255.255.255.248 mask:

Subnet	0	8	16	24	...	224	232	240	248
First host	1	9	17	25	...	225	233	241	249
Last host	6	14	22	30	...	230	238	246	254
Broadcast	7	15	23	31	...	231	239	247	255

> **TIP:** If you try to configure a router interface with the address 192.168.10.6 255.255.255.248 and receive the following error, this means that `ip subnet-zero` is not enabled:
>
> `Bad mask /29 for address 192.168.10.6`
>
> You must be able to subnet to see that the address used in this example is in the zero subnet.

Practice Example #6C: 255.255.255.252 (/30)

Okay—just one more:

> 192.168.10.0 = Network address
>
> 255.255.255.252 = Subnet mask

- *Subnets?* 64.
- *Hosts?* 2.
- *Valid subnets?* 0, 4, 8, 12, etc., all the way to 252.
- *Broadcast address for each subnet?* (Always the number right before the next subnet.)
- *Valid hosts?* (The numbers between the subnet number and the broadcast address.)

The following table shows you the subnet, valid host, and broadcast address of the first four and last four subnets in the 255.255.255.252 Class C subnet:

Subnet	0	4	8	12	...	240	244	248	252
First host	1	5	9	13	...	241	245	249	253
Last host	2	6	10	14	...	242	246	250	254
Broadcast	3	7	11	15	...	243	247	251	255

Real World Scenario

Should We Really Use This Mask That Provides Only Two Hosts?

You are the network administrator for Acme Corporation with dozens of WAN links connecting to your corporate office. Right now your network is a classful network, which means that the same subnet mask is on each host and router interface. You've read about classless routing, where you can have different sized masks, but don't know what to use on your point-to-point WAN links. Is the 255.255.255.252 (/30) a helpful mask in this situation?

Yes, this is a very helpful mask in wide area networks and of course with any type of point-to-point link!

If you were to use the 255.255.255.0 mask in this situation, then each network would have 254 hosts. But you use only 2 addresses with a WAN or point-to-point link, which is a waste of 252 hosts per subnet! If you use the 255.255.255.252 mask, then each subnet has only 2 hosts, and you don't want to waste precious addresses. This is a really important subject, one that we'll address in a lot more detail in the section on VLSM network design in the next chapter.

Subnetting in Your Head: Class C Addresses

Is it really possible to subnet in your head? Yes, and it's not all that hard either—take the following example:

192.168.10.50 = Node address

255.255.255.224 = Subnet mask

First, determine the subnet and broadcast address of the network in which the previous IP address resides. You can do this by answering question 3 of the big 5 questions: 256 – 224 = 32. 0, 32, 64, and so on. The address of 50 falls between the two subnets of 32 and 64 and must be part of the 192.168.10.32 subnet. The next subnet is 64, so the broadcast address of the 32 subnet is 63. Don't forget that the broadcast address of a subnet is always the number right before the next subnet. The valid host range equals the numbers between the subnet and broadcast address, or 33–62. Oh this is just too easy!

Let's try another one. We'll subnet another Class C address:

192.168.10.50 = Node address

255.255.255.240 = Subnet mask

What is the subnet and broadcast address of the network of which the previous IP address is a member? 256 – 240 = 16. Now just count by our increments of 16 until we pass the host address: 0, 16, 32, 48, 64. Bingo—the host address is between the 48 and 64 subnets. The subnet is 192.168.10.48, and the broadcast address is 63 because the next subnet is 64. The valid host range equals the numbers between the subnet number and the broadcast address, or 49–62.

Let's do a couple more to make sure you have this down.

You have a node address of 192.168.10.174 with a mask of 255.255.255.240. What is the valid host range?

The mask is 240, so we'd do a 256 – 240 = 16. This is our block size. Just keep adding 16 until we pass the host address of 174, starting at zero, of course: 0, 16, 32, 48, 64, 80, 96, 112, 128, 144, 160, 176. The host address of 174 is between 160 and 176, so the subnet is 160. The broadcast address is 175; the valid host range is 161–174. That was a tough one!

One more—just for fun. This one is the easiest of all Class C subnetting:

192.168.10.17 = Node address

255.255.255.252 = Subnet mask

What is the subnet and broadcast address of the subnet in which the previous IP address resides? 256 – 252 = 0 (always start at zero unless told otherwise). 0, 4, 8, 12, 16, 20, etc. You've got it! The host address is between the 16 and 20 subnets. The subnet is 192.168.10.16, and the broadcast address is 19. The valid host range is 17–18.

Now that you're all over Class C subnetting, let's move on to Class B subnetting. But before we do, let's go through a quick review.

What Do We Know?

Okay—here's where you can really apply what you've learned so far and begin committing it all to memory. This is a very cool section that I've been using in my classes for years. It will really help you nail down subnetting for good!

When you see a subnet mask or slash notation (CIDR), you should know the following:

/25 What do we know about a /25?

- 128 mask
- 1 bit on and 7 bits off (10000000)
- Block size of 128

- Subnets 0 and 128
- 2 subnets, each with 126 hosts

/26 What do we know about a /26?

- 192 mask
- 2 bits on and 6 bits off (11000000)
- Block size of 64
- Subnets 0, 64, 128, 192
- 4 subnets, each with 62 hosts

/27 What do we know about a /27?

- 224 mask
- 3 bits on and 5 bits off (11100000)
- Block size of 32
- Subnets 0, 32, 64, 96, 128, 160, 192, 224
- 8 subnets, each with 30 hosts

/28 What do we know about a /28?

- 240 mask
- 4 bits on and 4 bits off
- Block size of 16
- Subnets 0, 16, 32, 48, 64, 80, 96, 112, 128, 144, 160, 176, 192, 208, 224, 240
- 16 subnets, each with 14 hosts

/29 What do we know about a /29?

- 248 mask
- 5 bits on and 3 bits off
- Block size of 8
- Subnets 0, 8, 16, 24, 32, 40, 48, etc.
- 32 subnets, each with 6 hosts

/30 What do we know about a /30?

- 252 mask
- 6 bits on and 2 bits off
- Block size of 4
- Subnets 0, 4, 8, 12, 16, 20, 24, etc.
- 64 subnets, each with 2 hosts

Table 3.3 puts all of the previous information into one compact little table. You should practice writing this table out, and if you can do it, write it down before you start your exam!

TABLE 3.3 What do you know?

CIDR Notation	Mask	Bits	Block Size	Subnets	Hosts
/25	128	1 bit on and 7 bits off	128	0 and 128	2 subnets, each with 126 hosts
/26	192	2 bits on and 6 bits off	64	0, 64, 128, 192	4 subnets, each with 62 hosts
/27	224	3 bits on and 5 bits off	32	0, 32, 64, 96, 128, 160, 192, 224	8 subnets, each with 30 hosts
/28	240	4 bits on and 4 bits off	16	0, 16, 32, 48, 64, 80, 96, 112, 128, 144, 160, 176, 192, 208, 224, 240	16 subnets, each with 14 hosts
/29	248	5 bits on and 3 bits off	8	0, 8, 16, 24, 32, 40, 48, etc.	32 subnets, each with 6 hosts
/30	252	6 bits on and 2 bits off	4	0, 4, 8, 12, 16, 20, 24, etc.	64 subnets, each with 2 hosts

Regardless of whether you have a Class A, Class B, or Class C address, the /30 mask will provide you with only two hosts, ever. As suggested by Cisco, this mask is suited almost exclusively for use on point-to-point links.

If you can memorize this "What Do We Know?" section, you'll be much better off in your day-to-day job and in your studies. Try saying it out loud, which helps you memorize things—yes, others nearby may think you've lost it, but they probably already do if you're in the networking field anyway. And if you're not yet in the networking field but are studying all this to break into it, get used to it!

It's also helpful to write these on some type of flashcards and have people test your skill. You'd be amazed at how fast you can get subnetting down if you memorize block sizes as well as this "What Do We Know?" section.

Subnetting Class B Addresses

Before we dive into this, let's look at all the possible Class B subnet masks first. Notice that we have a lot more possible subnet masks than we do with a Class C network address:

```
255.255.0.0     (/16)
255.255.128.0   (/17)   255.255.255.0    (/24)
255.255.192.0   (/18)   255.255.255.128  (/25)
255.255.224.0   (/19)   255.255.255.192  (/26)
255.255.240.0   (/20)   255.255.255.224  (/27)
255.255.248.0   (/21)   255.255.255.240  (/28)
255.255.252.0   (/22)   255.255.255.248  (/29)
255.255.254.0   (/23)   255.255.255.252  (/30)
```

We know the Class B network address has 16 bits available for host addressing. This means we can use up to 14 bits for subnetting because we need to leave at least 2 bits for host addressing. Using a /16 means you are not subnetting with Class B, but it *is* a mask you can use.

> **NOTE** By the way, do you notice anything interesting about that list of subnet values—a pattern, maybe? Ah ha! That's exactly why I had you memorize the binary-to-decimal numbers earlier in Chapter 2, "Ethernet Networking and Data Encapsulation." Since subnet mask bits start on the left and move to the right and bits can't be skipped, the numbers are always the same regardless of the class of address. If you haven't already, memorize this pattern!

The process of subnetting a Class B network is pretty much the same as it is for a Class C, except that you have more host bits and you start in the third octet.

Use the same subnet numbers for the third octet with Class B that you used for the fourth octet with Class C, but add a zero to the network portion and a 255 to the broadcast section in the fourth octet. The following table shows you an example host range of three subnets used in a Class B 240 (/20) subnet mask:

Subnet address	16.0	32.0	48.0
Broadcast address	31.255	47.255	63.255

Just add the valid hosts between the numbers and you're set!

> **NOTE** The preceding example is true only until you get up to /24. After that, it's numerically exactly like Class C.

Subnetting Practice Examples: Class B Addresses

Next, you'll get an opportunity to practice subnetting Class B addresses. Again, I have to mention that this is the same as subnetting with Class C, except we start in the third octet—with the exact same numbers.

Practice Example #1B: 255.255.128.0 (/17)

172.16.0.0 = Network address

255.255.128.0 = Subnet mask

- **Subnets?** 2^1 = 2 (same amount as Class C).
- **Hosts?** 2^{15} − 2 = 32,766 (7 bits in the third octet, and 8 in the fourth).

- *Valid subnets?* 256 − 128 = 128. 0, 128. Remember that subnetting is performed in the third octet, so the subnet numbers are really 0.0 and 128.0, as shown in the next table. These are the exact numbers we used with Class C; we use them in the third octet and add a 0 in the fourth octet for the network address.
- *Broadcast address for each subnet?*
- *Valid hosts?*

This table shows the two subnets available, the valid host range, and the broadcast address of each:

Subnet	0.0	128.0
First host	0.1	128.1
Last host	127.254	255.254
Broadcast	127.255	255.255

Okay, notice that we just added the fourth octet's lowest and highest values and came up with the answers. And again, it's done exactly the same way as for a Class C subnet. We just used the same numbers in the third octet and added 0 and 255 in the fourth octet—pretty simple, huh? I really can't say this enough—it's just not that hard! The numbers never change; we just use them in different octets.

Question: Using the previous subnet mask, do you think 172.16.10.0 is a valid host address? What about 172.16.10.255? Can 0 and 255 in the fourth octet ever be a valid host address? The answer is absolutely, yes, those are valid hosts! Any number between the subnet number and the broadcast address is always a valid host.

Practice Example #2B: 255.255.192.0 (/18)

    172.16.0.0 = Network address

    255.255.192.0 = Subnet mask

- *Subnets?* 2^2 = 4.
- *Hosts?* 2^{14} − 2 = 16,382 (6 bits in the third octet, and 8 in the fourth).
- *Valid subnets?* 256 − 192 = 64. 0, 64, 128, 192. Remember that the subnetting is performed in the third octet, so the subnet numbers are really 0.0, 64.0, 128.0, and 192.0, as shown in the next table.
- *Broadcast address for each subnet?*
- *Valid hosts?*

The following table shows the four subnets available, the valid host range, and the broadcast address of each:

Subnet	0.0	64.0	128.0	192.0
First host	0.1	64.1	128.1	192.1
Last host	63.254	127.254	191.254	255.254
Broadcast	63.255	127.255	191.255	255.255

Again, it's pretty much the same as it is for a Class C subnet—we just added 0 and 255 in the fourth octet for each subnet in the third octet.

Practice Example #3B: 255.255.240.0 (/20)

172.16.0.0 = Network address

255.255.240.0 = Subnet mask

- *Subnets?* 2^4 = 16.
- *Hosts?* $2^{12} - 2$ = 4094.
- *Valid subnets?* 256 – 240 = 0, 16, 32, 48, etc., up to 240. Notice that these are the same numbers as a Class C 240 mask—we just put them in the third octet and add a 0 and 255 in the fourth octet.
- *Broadcast address for each subnet?*
- *Valid hosts?*

The following table shows the first four subnets, valid hosts, and broadcast addresses in a Class B 255.255.240.0 mask:

Subnet	0.0	16.0	32.0	48.0
First host	0.1	16.1	32.1	48.1
Last host	15.254	31.254	47.254	63.254
Broadcast	15.255	31.255	47.255	63.255

Practice Example #4B: 255.255.248.0 (/21)

172.16.0.0 = Network address

255.255.248.0 = Subnet mask

- *Subnets?* 2^5 = 32.
- *Hosts?* $2^{11} - 2$ = 2046.
- *Valid subnets?* 256 – 248 = 0, 8, 16, 24, 32, etc., up to 248.

- *Broadcast address for each subnet?*
- *Valid hosts?*

The following table shows the first five subnets, valid hosts, and broadcast addresses in a Class B 255.255.248.0 mask:

Subnet	0.0	8.0	16.0	24.0	32.0
First host	0.1	8.1	16.1	24.1	32.1
Last host	7.254	15.254	23.254	31.254	39.254
Broadcast	7.255	15.255	23.255	31.255	39.255

Practice Example #5B: 255.255.252.0 (/22)

172.16.0.0 = Network address

255.255.252.0 = Subnet mask

- *Subnets?* 2^6 = 64.
- *Hosts?* $2^{10} - 2$ = 1022.
- *Valid subnets?* 256 − 252 = 0, 4, 8, 12, 16, etc., up to 252.
- *Broadcast address for each subnet?*
- *Valid hosts?*

This table shows the first five subnets, valid hosts, and broadcast addresses in a Class B 255.255.252.0 mask:

Subnet	0.0	4.0	8.0	12.0	16.0
First host	0.1	4.1	8.1	12.1	16.1
Last host	3.254	7.254	11.254	15.254	19.254
Broadcast	3.255	7.255	11.255	15.255	19.255

Practice Example #6B: 255.255.254.0 (/23)

172.16.0.0 = Network address

255.255.254.0 = Subnet mask

- *Subnets?* 2^7 = 128.
- *Hosts?* $2^9 - 2$ = 510.
- *Valid subnets?* 256 − 254 = 0, 2, 4, 6, 8, etc., up to 254.
- *Broadcast address for each subnet?*
- *Valid hosts?*

The next table shows the first five subnets, valid hosts, and broadcast addresses in a Class B 255.255.254.0 mask:

Subnet	0.0	2.0	4.0	6.0	8.0
First host	0.1	2.1	4.1	6.1	8.1
Last host	1.254	3.254	5.254	7.254	9.254
Broadcast	1.255	3.255	5.255	7.255	9.255

Practice Example #7B: 255.255.255.0 (/24)

Contrary to popular belief, 255.255.255.0 used with a Class B network address is not called a Class B network with a Class C subnet mask. It's amazing how many people see this mask used in a Class B network and think it's a Class C subnet mask. This is a Class B subnet mask with 8 bits of subnetting—it's logically different from a Class C mask. Subnetting this address is fairly simple:

172.16.0.0 = Network address

255.255.255.0 = Subnet mask

- *Subnets?* 2^8 = 256.
- *Hosts?* $2^8 - 2$ = 254.
- *Valid subnets?* 256 − 255 = 1. 0, 1, 2, 3, etc., all the way to 255.
- *Broadcast address for each subnet?*
- *Valid hosts?*

The following table shows the first four and last two subnets, the valid hosts, and the broadcast addresses in a Class B 255.255.255.0 mask:

Subnet	0.0	1.0	2.0	3.0	...	254.0	255.0
First host	0.1	1.1	2.1	3.1	...	254.1	255.1
Last host	0.254	1.254	2.254	3.254	...	254.254	255.254
Broadcast	0.255	1.255	2.255	3.255	...	254.255	255.255

Practice Example #8B: 255.255.255.128 (/25)

This is actually one of the hardest subnet masks you can play with. And worse, it actually is a really good subnet to use in production because it creates over 500 subnets with 126 hosts for each subnet—a nice mixture. So, don't skip over it!

172.16.0.0 = Network address

255.255.255.128 = Subnet mask

- *Subnets?* 2^9 = 512.
- *Hosts?* $2^7 - 2$ = 126.

- *Valid subnets?* Now for the tricky part. 256 – 255 = 1. 0, 1, 2, 3, etc., for the third octet. But you can't forget the one subnet bit used in the fourth octet. Remember when I showed you how to figure one subnet bit with a Class C mask? You figure this the same way. You actually get two subnets for each third octet value, hence the 512 subnets. For example, if the third octet is showing subnet 3, the two subnets would actually be 3.0 and 3.128.
- *Broadcast address for each subnet?* The numbers right before the next subnet.
- *Valid hosts?* The numbers between the subnet numbers and the broadcast address.

The following graphic shows how you can create subnets, valid hosts, and broadcast addresses using the Class B 255.255.255.128 subnet mask. The first eight subnets are shown, followed by the last two subnets:

Subnet	0.0	0.128	1.0	1.128	2.0	2.128	3.0	3.128	...	255.0	255.128
First host	0.1	0.129	1.1	1.129	2.1	2.129	3.1	3.129	...	255.1	255.129
Last host	0.126	0.254	1.126	1.254	2.126	2.254	3.126	3.254	...	255.126	255.254
Broadcast	0.127	0.255	1.127	1.255	2.127	2.255	3.127	3.255	...	255.127	255.255

Practice Example #9B: 255.255.255.192 (/26)

Now, this is where Class B subnetting gets easy. Since the third octet has a 255 in the mask section, whatever number is listed in the third octet is a subnet number. And now that we have a subnet number in the fourth octet, we can subnet this octet just as we did with Class C subnetting. Let's try it out:

172.16.0.0 = Network address

255.255.255.192 = Subnet mask

- *Subnets?* 2^{10} = 1024.
- *Hosts?* $2^6 - 2$ = 62.
- *Valid subnets?* 256 – 192 = 64. The subnets are shown in the following table. Do these numbers look familiar?
- *Broadcast address for each subnet?*
- *Valid hosts?*

This table shows the first eight subnet ranges, valid hosts, and broadcast addresses:

Subnet	0.0	0.64	0.128	0.192	1.0	1.64	1.128	1.192
First host	0.1	0.65	0.129	0.193	1.1	1.65	1.129	1.193
Last host	0.62	0.126	0.190	0.254	1.62	1.126	1.190	1.254
Broadcast	0.63	0.127	0.191	0.255	1.63	1.127	1.191	1.255

Notice that for each subnet value in the third octet, you get subnets 0, 64, 128, and 192 in the fourth octet.

Practice Example #10B: 255.255.255.224 (/27)

This one is done the same way as the preceding subnet mask, except that we just have more subnets and fewer hosts per subnet available.

172.16.0.0 = Network address

255.255.255.224 = Subnet mask

- *Subnets?* 2^{11} = 2048.
- *Hosts?* $2^5 - 2$ = 30.
- *Valid subnets?* 256 − 224 = 32. 0, 32, 64, 96, 128, 160, 192, 224.
- *Broadcast address for each subnet?*
- *Valid hosts?*

The following table shows the first eight subnets:

Subnet	0.0	0.32	0.64	0.96	0.128	0.160	0.192	0.224
First host	0.1	0.33	0.65	0.97	0.129	0.161	0.193	0.225
Last host	0.30	0.62	0.94	0.126	0.158	0.190	0.222	0.254
Broadcast	0.31	0.63	0.95	0.127	0.159	0.191	0.223	0.255

This next table shows the last eight subnets:

Subnet	255.0	255.32	255.64	255.96	255.128	255.160	255.192	255.224
First host	255.1	255.33	255.65	255.97	255.129	255.161	255.193	255.225
Last host	255.30	255.62	255.94	255.126	255.158	255.190	255.222	255.254
Broadcast	255.31	255.63	255.95	255.127	255.159	255.191	255.223	255.255

Subnetting in Your Head: Class B Addresses

Are you nuts? Subnet Class B addresses in our heads? It's actually easier than writing it out—I'm not kidding! Let me show you how:

Question: What is the subnet and broadcast address of the subnet in which 172.16.10.33 /27 resides?

Answer: The interesting octet is the fourth one. 256 − 224 = 32. 32 + 32 = 64. You've got it: 33 is between 32 and 64. But remember that the third octet is considered part of the subnet, so the answer would be the 10.32 subnet. The broadcast is 10.63, since 10.64 is the next subnet. That was a pretty easy one.

Question: What subnet and broadcast address is the IP address 172.16.66.10 255.255.192.0 (/18) a member of?

Answer: The interesting octet here is the third octet instead of the fourth one. 256 – 192 = 64. 0, 64, 128. The subnet is 172.16.64.0. The broadcast must be 172.16.127.255 since 128.0 is the next subnet.

Question: What subnet and broadcast address is the IP address 172.16.50.10 255.255.224.0 (/19) a member of?

Answer: 256 – 224 = 0, 32, 64 (remember, we always start counting at 0). The subnet is 172.16.32.0, and the broadcast must be 172.16.63.255 since 64.0 is the next subnet.

Question: What subnet and broadcast address is the IP address 172.16.46.255 255.255.240.0 (/20) a member of?

Answer: 256 – 240 = 16. The third octet is important here: 0, 16, 32, 48. This subnet address must be in the 172.16.32.0 subnet, and the broadcast must be 172.16.47.255 since 48.0 is the next subnet. So, yes, 172.16.46.255 is a valid host.

Question: What subnet and broadcast address is the IP address 172.16.45.14 255.255.255.252 (/30) a member of?

Answer: Where is our interesting octet? 256 – 252 = 0, 4, 8, 12, 16—the fourth. The subnet is 172.16.45.12, with a broadcast of 172.16.45.15 because the next subnet is 172.16.45.16.

Question: What is the subnet and broadcast address of the host 172.16.88.255/20?

Answer: What is a /20 written out in dotted decimal? If you can't answer this, you can't answer this question, can you? A /20 is 255.255.240.0, gives us a block size of 16 in the third octet, and since no subnet bits are on in the fourth octet, the answer is always 0 and 255 in the fourth octet: 0, 16, 32, 48, 64, 80, 96. Because 88 is between 80 and 96, the subnet is 80.0 and the broadcast address is 95.255.

Question: A router receives a packet on an interface with a destination address of 172.16.46.191/26. What will the router do with this packet?

Answer: Discard it. Do you know why? 172.16.46.191/26 is a 255.255.255.192 mask, which gives us a block size of 64. Our subnets are then 0, 64, 128 and 192. 191 is the broadcast address of the 128 subnet, and by default, a router will discard any broadcast packets.

> To get more subnetting practice, head over to www.lammle.com/ccna.

Summary

Were Chapters 2 and 3 crystal clear to you on the first pass? If so, wonderful—congratulations! But you probably really did get lost a couple of times right? No worries—that's usually what happens.

Don't waste time feeling bad if you have to read each chapter more than once, or even 10 times, before you're truly good to go. If you read the chapters more than once, you'll be seriously better off in the long run even if you were pretty comfortable the first time through!

This chapter provided you with critical understanding of IP subnetting—the painless way! And when you've got the material I presented in this chapter completely down, you should be able to subnet IP addresses in your head.

This chapter is extremely essential to your Cisco certification process, so if you just skimmed it, please go back, read it thoroughly, and be sure to practice through all the scenarios too.

Exam Essentials

Identify the advantages of subnetting. Benefits of subnetting a physical network include reduced network traffic, optimized network performance, simplified management, and facilitated spanning of large geographical distances.

Describe the effect of the `ip subnet-zero` command. This command allows you to use the first and last subnet in your network design.

Identify the steps to subnet a classful network. Understand how IP addressing and subnetting work. First, determine your block size by using the 256-subnet mask math. Then count your subnets and determine the broadcast address of each subnet—it is always the number right before the next subnet. Your valid hosts are the numbers between the subnet address and the broadcast address.

Determine possible block sizes. This is an important part of understanding IP addressing and subnetting. The valid block sizes are always 2, 4, 8, 16, 32, 64, 128, etc. You can determine your block size by using the 256-subnet mask math.

Describe the role of a subnet mask in IP addressing. A subnet mask is a 32-bit value that allows the recipient of IP packets to distinguish the network ID portion of the IP address from the host ID portion of the IP address.

Review Questions

You can find the answers to these questions in the Appendix.

1. What is the maximum number of IP addresses that can be assigned to hosts on a local subnet that uses the 255.255.255.224 subnet mask?
   A. 14
   B. 15
   C. 16
   D. 30
   E. 31
   F. 62

2. You have a network that needs 29 subnets while maximizing the number of host addresses available on each subnet. How many bits must you borrow from the host field to provide the correct subnet mask?
   A. 2
   B. 3
   C. 4
   D. 5
   E. 6
   F. 7

3. What is the subnetwork address for a host with the IP address 200.10.5.68/28?
   A. 200.10.5.56
   B. 200.10.5.32
   C. 200.10.5.64
   D. 200.10.5.0

4. The network address of 172.16.0.0/19 provides how many subnets and hosts?
   A. 7 subnets, 30 hosts each
   B. 7 subnets, 2,046 hosts each
   C. 7 subnets, 8,190 hosts each
   D. 8 subnets, 30 hosts each
   E. 8 subnets, 2,046 hosts each
   F. 8 subnets, 8,190 hosts each

5. Which two statements describe the IP address 10.16.3.65/23? (Choose two.)
   A. The subnet address is 10.16.3.0 255.255.254.0.
   B. The lowest host address in the subnet is 10.16.2.1 255.255.254.0.
   C. The last valid host address in the subnet is 10.16.2.254 255.255.254.0.
   D. The broadcast address of the subnet is 10.16.3.255 255.255.254.0.
   E. The network is not subnetted.

6. If a host on a network has the address 172.16.45.14/30, what is the subnetwork this host belongs to?
   A. 172.16.45.0
   B. 172.16.45.4
   C. 172.16.45.8
   D. 172.16.45.12
   E. 172.16.45.16

7. Which mask should you use on point-to-point links in order to reduce the waste of IP addresses?
   A. /27
   B. /28
   C. /29
   D. /30
   E. /31

8. What is the subnetwork number of a host with an IP address of 172.16.66.0/21?
   A. 172.16.36.0
   B. 172.16.48.0
   C. 172.16.64.0
   D. 172.16.0.0

9. You have an interface on a router with the IP address of 192.168.192.10/29. Including the router interface, how many hosts can have IP addresses on the LAN attached to the router interface?
   A. 6
   B. 8
   C. 30
   D. 62
   E. 126

10. You need to configure a server that is on the subnet 192.168.19.24/29. The router has the first available host address. Which of the following should you assign to the server?
    A. 192.168.19.0 255.255.255.0
    B. 192.168.19.33 255.255.255.240
    C. 192.168.19.26 255.255.255.248
    D. 192.168.19.31 255.255.255.248
    E. 192.168.19.34 255.255.255.240

Chapter 4

Troubleshooting IP Addressing

THE FOLLOWING CCNA EXAM TOPICS ARE COVERED IN THIS CHAPTER:

1.0 Network Fundamentals

✓ 1.6 Configure and verify IPv4 addressing and subnetting

✓ 1.10 Verify IP parameters for Client OS (Windows, Mac OS, Linux)

In this chapter, we'll cover IP address troubleshooting, while focusing on the steps Cisco recommends following when troubleshooting an IP network.

The tools I'm going to share with you and the skills you'll gain after learning how to use them will give you a huge advantage when taking the exam. Even more importantly, they'll give you a serious edge in the professional real world! Working through this chapter will hone your knowledge of IP addressing and networking, while refining the essential skills you've attained so far.

So let's get started!

> To find your included bonus material, as well as Todd Lammle videos, practice questions & hands-on labs, please see www.lammle.com/ccna

Cisco's Way of Troubleshooting IP

Because running into trouble now and then in networking is a given, being able to troubleshoot IP addressing is a vital skill. I'm not being negative here—just realistic. The positive here is that if you're the one equipped with the tools to diagnose and clear up inevitable trouble, you get to be the hero when you save the day. And the icing on the cake is you can usually fix an IP network regardless of whether you're on site or not!

We're going to focus on the "Cisco way" of troubleshooting IP addressing, and let's use Figure 4.1 as an example of some basic IP trouble. Poor Sally can't log in to the Windows server. Do you deal with this by calling the Microsoft team to tell them their server is a pile of junk and causing all your problems? Though tempting, a better approach is to first verify your network instead.

FIGURE 4.1 Basic IP troubleshooting

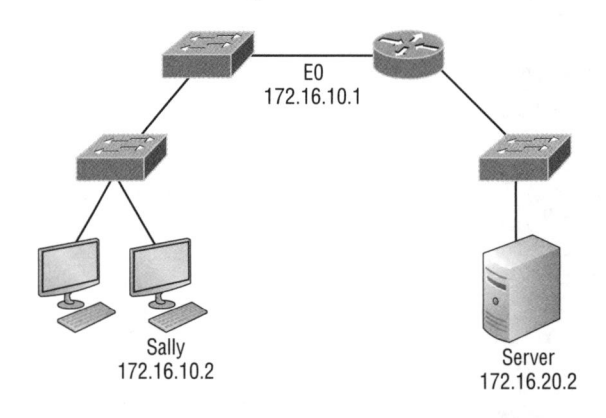

Let's walk through the Cisco Way of troubleshooting using a clear step-by-step approach. These steps are pretty simple—start by imagining you're at a customer host who's complaining they can't communicate to a server, which just happens to be on a remote network. In this scenario, here are the four troubleshooting steps Cisco recommends:

1. Open a Command window and ping 127.0.0.1. This is the diagnostic, or loopback, address, and if you get a successful ping, your IP stack is considered initialized. If it fails, then you have an IP stack failure and need to reinstall TCP/IP on the host:

   ```
   C:\>ping 127.0.0.1
   Pinging 127.0.0.1 with 32 bytes of data:
   Reply from 127.0.0.1: bytes=32 time
   Reply from 127.0.0.1: bytes=32 time
   Reply from 127.0.0.1: bytes=32 time
   Reply from 127.0.0.1: bytes=32 time
   Ping statistics for 127.0.0.1:
   Packets: Sent = 4, Received = 4, Lost = 0 (0% loss),
   Approximate round trip times in milli-seconds:
   Minimum = 0ms, Maximum = 0ms, Average = 0ms
   ```

2. From the Command window, ping the IP address of the local host (we'll assume correct configuration here, but always check the IP configuration too!). If that's successful, your network interface card (NIC) is functioning. If it fails, there is a problem with the NIC. Just so you know, success here doesn't necessarily mean that a cable is plugged into the NIC, only that the IP protocol stack on the host can communicate to the NIC via the LAN driver:

   ```
   C:\>ping 172.16.10.2
   Pinging 172.16.10.2 with 32 bytes of data:
   Reply from 172.16.10.2: bytes=32 time
   Reply from 172.16.10.2: bytes=32 time
   Reply from 172.16.10.2: bytes=32 time
   Reply from 172.16.10.2: bytes=32 time
   Ping statistics for 172.16.10.2:
   Packets: Sent = 4, Received = 4, Lost = 0 (0% loss),
   Approximate round trip times in milli-seconds:
   Minimum = 0ms, Maximum = 0ms, Average = 0ms
   ```

3. From the Command window, ping the default gateway (router). If the ping works, it means that the NIC is plugged into the network and can communicate on the local network. If it fails, you have a local physical network problem that could be anywhere from the NIC to the router:

   ```
   C:\>ping 172.16.10.1
   Pinging 172.16.10.1 with 32 bytes of data:
   Reply from 172.16.10.1: bytes=32 time
   Reply from 172.16.10.1: bytes=32 time
   ```

```
Reply from 172.16.10.1: bytes=32 time
Reply from 172.16.10.1: bytes=32 time
Ping statistics for 172.16.10.1:
Packets: Sent = 4, Received = 4, Lost = 0 (0% loss),
Approximate round trip times in milli-seconds:
Minimum = 0ms, Maximum = 0ms, Average = 0ms
```

4. If steps 1 through 3 were successful, try to ping the remote server. If that works, then you know that you have IP communication between the local host and the remote server. You also know that the remote physical network is working:

```
C:\>ping 172.16.20.2
Pinging 172.16.20.2 with 32 bytes of data:
Reply from 172.16.20.2: bytes=32 time
Reply from 172.16.20.2: bytes=32 time
Reply from 172.16.20.2: bytes=32 time
Reply from 172.16.20.2: bytes=32 time
Ping statistics for 172.16.20.2:
Packets: Sent = 4, Received = 4, Lost = 0 (0% loss),
Approximate round trip times in milli-seconds:
Minimum = 0ms, Maximum = 0ms, Average = 0ms
```

If the user still can't communicate with the server after steps 1 through 4 have been completed successfully, you probably have some type of name resolution problem and need to check your Domain Name System (DNS) settings. But if the ping to the remote server fails, then you know you have some type of remote physical network problem and need to go to the server and work through steps 1 through 3 until you find the snag.

Verify IP Parameters for Operating Systems (OS)

Before we move on to determining IP address problems and how to fix them, I just want to mention some basic commands that you can use to help troubleshoot your network from a Windows PC, Cisco devices, as well as MAC and Linux hosts. Keep in mind that though these commands may do the same thing, they're implemented differently.

ping Uses ICMP echo request and replies to test if a node IP stack is initialized and alive on the network.

traceroute Displays the list of routers on a path to a network destination by using TTL time-outs and ICMP error messages. This command won't work from a command prompt.

tracert Same function as traceroute, but it's a Microsoft Windows command and it won't work on a Cisco router.

arp -a Displays IP-to-MAC-address mappings on a Windows PC.

show ip arp Same function as arp -a, but displays the ARP table on a Cisco router. Like the commands traceroute and tracert, arp -a and show ip arp these aren't interchangeable through Windows and Cisco.

ipconfig /all   Used only from a Windows command prompt; shows you the PC network configuration.

ifconfig   Used by MAC and Linux to get the IP address details of the local machine

ipconfig getifaddr en0   Used to find your IP address if you are connected to a wireless network or use en1 if you are connected to an Ethernet for MAC or Linux.

curl ifconfig.me   This command will display your global Internet IP address in Terminal for MAC or Linux.

curl ipecho.net/plain ; echo   This command will display your global Internet IP address in Terminal for MAC or Linux.

Once you've gone through all these steps and, if necessary, used the appropriate commands, what do you do when you find a problem? How do you go about fixing an IP address configuration error? Time to cover the next step—determining and fixing the issue at hand!

Determining IP Address Problems

It's common for a host, router, or other network device to be configured with the wrong IP address, subnet mask, or default gateway. Because this happens way too often, you've got to know how to find and fix IP address configuration errors.

A good way to start is to draw out the network and IP addressing scheme. If that's already been done, consider yourself lucky because though sensible, it's rarely done. Even if it is, it's usually outdated or inaccurate anyway. So either way, it's a good idea to bite the bullet and start from scratch.

Once you have your network accurately drawn out, including the IP addressing scheme, you need to verify each host's IP address, mask, and default gateway address to establish the problem. Of course, this is assuming that you don't have a physical layer problem, or if you did, that you've already fixed it.

Check out the example illustrated in Figure 4.2.

A user in the sales department calls and tells you that she can't get to ServerA in the marketing department. You ask her if she can get to ServerB in the marketing department, but she doesn't know because she doesn't have rights to log on to that server. What do you do?

First, guide your user through the four troubleshooting steps you learned in the preceding section. Let's say steps 1 through 3 work but step 4 fails. By looking at the figure, can you determine the problem? Look for clues in the network drawing. First, the WAN link between the Lab A router and the Lab B router shows the mask as a /27. You should already know that this mask is 255.255.255.224 and determine that all networks are using this mask. The network address is 192.168.1.0. What are your valid subnets and hosts? 256 – 224 = 32, so this makes our subnets 0, 32, 64, 96, 128, etc. So, by looking at the figure, you can see that subnet 32 is being used by the sales department. The WAN link is using subnet 96, and the marketing department is using subnet 64.

FIGURE 4.2 IP address problem 1

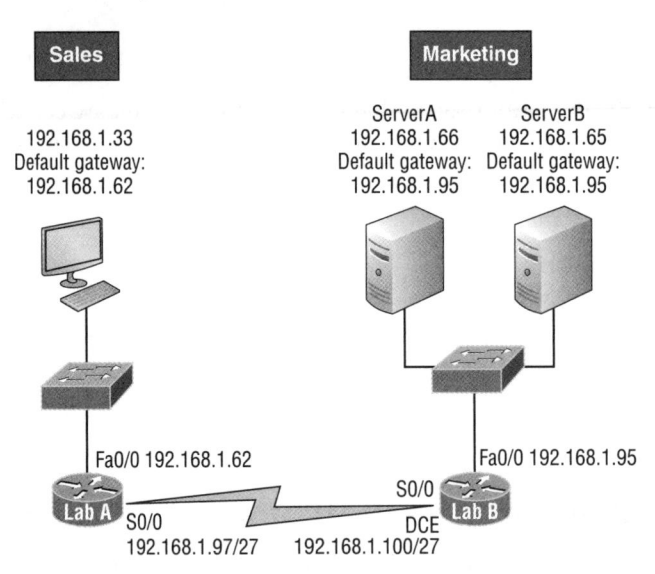

```
                    Sales                              Marketing

                                            ServerA           ServerB
                 192.168.1.33              192.168.1.66      192.168.1.65
                 Default gateway:          Default gateway:  Default gateway:
                 192.168.1.62              192.168.1.95      192.168.1.95


                      Fa0/0 192.168.1.62              Fa0/0 192.168.1.95
                                            S0/0
                    Lab A                          Lab B
                         S0/0              DCE
                         192.168.1.97/27   192.168.1.100/27
```

Next, you've got to establish what the valid host ranges are for each subnet. From what you've learned already, you should now be able to easily determine the subnet address, broadcast addresses, and valid host ranges. The valid hosts for the Sales LAN are 33 through 62, and the broadcast address is 63 because the next subnet is 64, right? For the Marketing LAN, the valid hosts are 65 through 94 (broadcast 95), and for the WAN link, 97 through 126 (broadcast 127). By closely examining the figure, you can determine that the default gateway on the Lab B router is incorrect. That address is the broadcast address for subnet 64, so there's no way it could be a valid host!

> **TIP** If you tried to configure that address on the Lab B router interface, you'd receive a bad mask error. Cisco routers don't let you type in subnet and broadcast addresses as valid hosts!

Did you get all that? Let's try another one to make sure. Figure 4.3 illustrates a network problem.

A user in the Sales LAN can't get to ServerB. You have the user run through the four basic troubleshooting steps and find that the host can communicate to the local network but not to the remote network. Find and define the IP addressing problem.

If you went through the same steps used to solve the last problem, you can see that first, the WAN link again provides the subnet mask to use— /29, or 255.255.255.248. Assuming classful addressing, you need to determine what the valid subnets, broadcast addresses, and valid host ranges are to solve this problem.

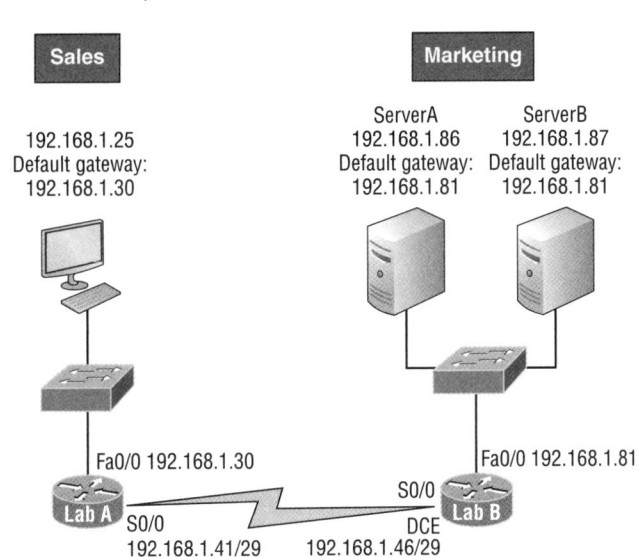

FIGURE 4.3 IP address problem 2

The 248 mask is a block size of 8 (256 − 248 = 8), so the subnets both start and increment in multiples of 8. By looking at the figure, you see that the Sales LAN is in the 24 subnet, the WAN is in the 40 subnet, and the Marketing LAN is in the 80 subnet. Can you see the problem yet? The valid host range for the Sales LAN is 25–30, and the configuration appears correct. The valid host range for the WAN link is 41–46, and this also appears correct. The valid host range for the 80 subnet is 81–86, with a broadcast address of 87 because the next subnet is 88. ServerB has been configured with the broadcast address of the subnet.

Okay, so now that you can figure out misconfigured IP addresses on hosts, what do you do if a host doesn't have an IP address and you need to assign one? You need to scrutinize the other hosts on the LAN and figure out the network, mask, and default gateway. Let's take a look at a couple of examples about how to find and apply valid IP addresses to hosts.

You need to assign a server and router IP addresses on a LAN. The subnet assigned on that segment is 192.168.20.24/29. The router needs to be assigned the first usable address and the server needs the last valid host ID. What is the IP address, mask, and default gateway assigned to the server?

To answer this, you must know that a /29 is a 255.255.255.248 mask, which provides a block size of 8. The subnet is known as 24, the next subnet in a block of 8 is 32, so the broadcast address of the 24 subnet is 31 and the valid host range is 25–30.

Server IP address: 192.168.20.30

Server mask: 255.255.255.248

Default gateway: 192.168.20.25 (router's IP address)

Take a look at Figure 4.4 and solve this problem.

FIGURE 4.4 Find the valid host #1.

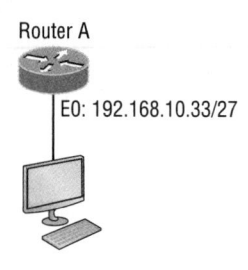

Look at the router's IP address on Ethernet0. What IP address, subnet mask, and valid host range could be assigned to the host?

The IP address of the router's Ethernet0 is 192.168.10.33/27. As you already know, a /27 is a 224 mask with a block size of 32. The router's interface is in the 32 subnet. The next subnet is 64, so that makes the broadcast address of the 32 subnet 63 and the valid host range 33–62.

Host IP address: 192.168.10.34–62 (any address in the range except for 33, which is assigned to the router)

Mask: 255.255.255.224

Default gateway: 192.168.10.33

Figure 4.5 shows two routers with Ethernet configurations already assigned. What are the host addresses and subnet masks of HostA and HostB?

FIGURE 4.5 Find the valid host #2.

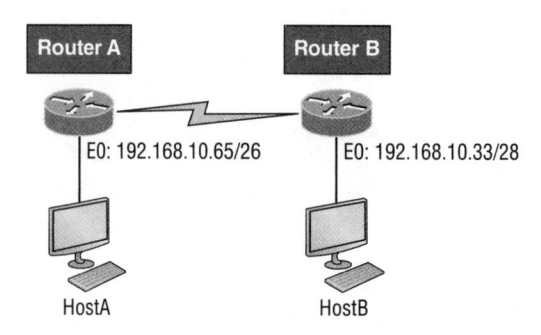

Router A has an IP address of 192.168.10.65/26 and Router B has an IP address of 192.168.10.33/28. What are the host configurations? Router A Ethernet0 is in the 192.168.10.64 subnet and Router B Ethernet0 is in the 192.168.10.32 network.

Host A IP address: 192.168.10.66–126

Host A mask: 255.255.255.192

Host A default gateway: 192.168.10.65

Host B IP address: 192.168.10.34–46

Host B mask: 255.255.255.240

Host B default gateway: 192.168.10.33

Just a couple more examples before you can put this chapter behind you—hang in there!

Figure 4.6 shows two routers. You need to configure the S0/0 interface on RouterA. The IP address assigned to the serial link on RouterA is 172.16.17.0/22 (No, that is not a subnet address, but a valid host IP address on that interface—most people miss this one). Which IP address can be assigned to the router interface on RouterB?

FIGURE 4.6 Find the valid host address #3.

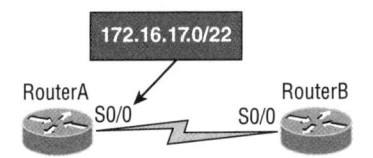

First, know that a /22 CIDR is 255.255.252.0, which makes a block size of 4 in the third octet. Since 17 is listed as the interface IP address, the available range is 16.1 through 19.254, so in this example, the IP address S0/0 on RouterB could be 172.16.18.255 since that's within the range.

Okay, last one! You need to find a classful network address that has one Class C network ID and you need to provide one usable subnet per city while allowing enough usable host addresses for each city specified in Figure 4.7. What is your mask?

FIGURE 4.7 Find the valid subnet mask

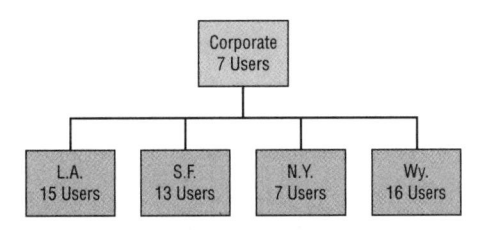

Actually, this is probably the easiest thing you've done all day! I count 5 subnets needed, and the Wyoming office needs 16 users—always look for the network that needs the most hosts! What block size is needed for the Wyoming office? Your answer is 32. You can't use a block size of 16 because you always have to subtract 2. What mask provides you with a block size of 32? 224 is your answer because this provides 8 subnets, each with 30 hosts.

You're done—whew! Time to take a break, but skip the shot and the beer if that's what you had in mind because you need keep going with your studies!

Summary

Again, if you got to this point without getting lost along the way a few times, you're awesome, but if you did get lost, don't stress because most people do! Just be patient and go back over the material that tripped you up until it's all crystal clear. You'll get there!

And make sure you understand and memorize Cisco's troubleshooting methods. You must remember the four steps that Cisco recommends taking when trying to narrow down exactly where a network and/or IP addressing problem is and then know how to proceed systematically to fix it. In addition, you should be able to find valid IP addresses and subnet masks by looking at a network diagram.

Exam Essentials

Describe the benefits of variable length subnet masks (VLSMs). VLSMs enable the creation of subnets of specific sizes and allow the division of a classless network into smaller networks that do not need to be equal in size. This makes use of the address space more efficient because many times IP addresses are wasted with classful subnetting.

Understand the relationship between the subnet mask value and the resulting block size and the allowable IP addresses in each resulting subnet. The relationship between the classful network being subdivided and the subnet mask used determines the number of possible hosts or the block size. It also determines where each subnet begins and ends and which IP addresses cannot be assigned to a host within each subnet.

Describe the process of summarization or route aggregation and its relationship to subnetting. Summarization is the combining of subnets derived from a classful network for the purpose of advertising a single route to neighboring routers instead of multiple routes, reducing the size of routing tables and speeding the route process.

Calculate the summary mask that will advertise a single network representing all subnets. The network address used to advertise the summary address is always the first network address in the block of subnets. The mask is the subnet mask value that yields the same block size.

Remember the four diagnostic steps. The four simple steps that Cisco recommends for troubleshooting are ping the loopback address, ping the NIC, ping the default gateway, and ping the remote device.

Identify and mitigate an IP addressing problem. Once you go through the four troubleshooting steps that Cisco recommends, you must be able to determine the IP addressing problem by drawing out the network and finding the valid and invalid hosts addressed in your network.

Understand the troubleshooting tools that you can use from your host and a Cisco router. The `ping 127.0.0.1` command tests your local IP stack, and `tracert` is a Windows command to track the path a packet takes through an internetwork to a destination. Cisco routers use the command `traceroute`, or just `trace` for short. Don't confuse the Windows and Cisco commands. Although they produce the same output, they don't work from the same prompts. The command `ipconfig /all` will display your PC network configuration from a DOS prompt, and `arp -a` (again from a DOS prompt) will display IP-to-MAC-address mapping on a Windows PC.

Review Questions

You can find the answers to these questions in the Appendix.

1. On a VLSM network, which mask should you use on point-to-point WAN links in order to reduce the waste of IP addresses?
   - **A.** /27
   - **B.** /28
   - **C.** /29
   - **D.** /30
   - **E.** /31

2. If a host is configured with an incorrect default gateway and all the other computers and router are known to be configured correctly, which of the following statements is true?
   - **A.** Host A cannot communicate with the router.
   - **B.** Host A can communicate with other hosts in the same subnet.
   - **C.** With an incorrect gateway, Host A will not be able to communicate with the router or beyond the router but will be able to communicate within the subnet.
   - **D.** Host A can communicate with no other systems.

3. Which of the following troubleshooting steps, if completed successfully, also confirms that the other steps will succeed as well?
   - **A.** Ping a remote computer.
   - **B.** Ping the loopback address.
   - **C.** Ping the NIC.
   - **D.** Ping the default gateway.

4. When a ping to the local host IP address fails, what can you assume?
   - **A.** The IP address of the local host is incorrect.
   - **B.** The IP address of the remote host is incorrect.
   - **C.** The NIC is not functional.
   - **D.** The IP stack has failed to initialize.

5. When a ping to the local host IP address succeeds but a ping to the default gateway IP address fails, what can you rule out? (Choose all that apply.)
   - **A.** The IP address of the local host is incorrect.
   - **B.** The IP address of the gateway is incorrect.
   - **C.** The NIC is not functional.
   - **D.** The IP stack has failed to initialize.

6. What network service is the most likely problem if you can ping a computer by IP address but not by name?
   A. DNS
   B. DHCP
   C. ARP
   D. ICMP

7. When you issue the ping command, what protocol are you using?
   A. DNS
   B. DHCP
   C. ARP
   D. ICMP

8. Which of the following commands displays the networks traversed on a path to a network destination?
   A. ping
   B. traceroute
   C. pingroute
   D. pathroute

9. What command generated the output shown below?

   ```
   Reply from 172.16.10.2: bytes=32 time
   Reply from 172.16.10.2: bytes=32 time
   Reply from 172.16.10.2: bytes=32 time
   Reply from 172.16.10.2: bytes=32 time
   ```

   A. traceroute
   B. show ip route
   C. ping
   D. pathping

10. What switch must be added to the ipconfig command on a PC to verify DNS configuration?
    A. /dns
    B. -dns
    C. /all
    D. showall

Chapter 5

IP Routing

THE FOLLOWING CCNA EXAM TOPICS ARE COVERED IN THIS CHAPTER:

3.0   IP Connectivity

✓ 3.1   Interpret the components of routing table

- 3.1.a Routing protocol code
- 3.1.b Prefix
- 3.1.c Network mask
- 3.1.d Next hop
- 3.1.e Administrative distance
- 3.1.f Metric
- 3.1.g Gateway of last resort

✓ 3.2   Determine how a router makes a forwarding decision by default

- 3.2.a Longest match
- 3.2.b Administrative distance
- 3.2.c Routing protocol metric

✓ 3.3 Configure and verify IPv4 and IPv6 static routing

- 3.3.a Default route
- 3.3.b Network route
- 3.3.c Host route
- 3.3.d Floating static

4.0   IP Services

✓ 4.3   Explain the role of DHCP and DNS within the network

✓ 4.6   Configure and verify DHCP client and relay

This chapter's focus is on the core topic of the ubiquitous IP routing process. It's integral to networking because it pertains to all routers and configurations that use it—easily the lion's share. IP routing is basically the process of moving packets from one network to another network using routers. And by routers, I mean Cisco routers, of course! However, the terms *router* and *layer 3 device* are interchangeable, and throughout this chapter when I use the term *router*, understand that I'm referring to any layer 3 device.

Before jumping into this chapter, I want to make sure you understand the difference between a *routing protocol* and a *routed protocol*. Routers use routing protocols to dynamically find all networks within the greater internetwork and to ensure that all routers have the same routing table. Routing protocols are also employed to determine the best path a packet should take through an internetwork to get to its destination most efficiently. RIP, RIPv2, EIGRP, and OSPF are great examples of the most common routing protocols.

Once all routers know about all networks, a routed protocol can be used to send user data (packets) through the established enterprise. Routed protocols are assigned to an interface and determine the method of packet delivery. Examples of routed protocols are IP and IPv6.

I'm pretty confident you know how crucial it is for you to have this chapter's material down to an almost instinctive level. IP routing is innately what Cisco routers do, and they do it very well, so having a firm grasp of the fundamentals on this topic is vital if you want to excel during the exam and in a real-world networking environment!

I'm going to show you how to configure and verify IP routing with Cisco routers and guide you through these five key subjects:

- Routing basics
- The IP routing process
- Static routing
- Default routing
- Dynamic routing

We'll begin with the basics of how packets actually move through an internetwork.

To find your included bonus material, as well as Todd Lammle videos. practice questions & hands-on labs, please see www.lammle.com/ccna

Routing Basics

Once you create an internetwork by connecting your WANs and LANs to a router, you'll need to configure logical network addresses, like IP addresses, to all hosts on that internetwork to enable them to communicate successfully throughout it.

The term *routing* refers to taking a packet from one device and sending it through the internetwork to another device on a different network. Routers don't really care about hosts—they only care about networks and the best path to each one of them. The logical network address of the destination host is key to getting packets through a routed network. It's the hardware address of the host that's used to deliver the packet from a router and ensure it arrives at the correct destination host.

Here's an important list of the minimum factors a router must know to be able to effectively route packets:

- Destination address
- Neighbor routers from which it can learn about remote networks
- Possible routes to all remote networks
- The best route to each remote network
- How to maintain and verify routing information

The router learns about remote networks from neighboring routers or from an administrator. The router then builds a routing table—a map of the internetwork, describing how to find remote networks. If a network is directly connected, then the router already knows how to get to it.

If a network isn't directly connected to the router, the router must use one of two ways to learn how to get to the remote network. The *static routing* method requires someone to hand-type all network locations into the routing table. Doing this would be a huge labor-intensive task when used on all but the smallest of networks!

But when *dynamic routing* is used, a protocol on one router communicates with the same protocol running on neighboring routers. The routers then update each other about all the networks they know about and place this information into the routing table. If a change occurs in the network, the dynamic routing protocols automatically inform all routers about the event. If static routing is used, the administrator is responsible for updating all changes by hand onto all routers. Most people usually use a combination of dynamic and static routing to administer a large network.

Before we get into the IP routing process, let's take a look at a very simple example that demonstrates how a router uses the routing table to route packets out of an interface. We'll get into a more detailed look at the process soon, but I want to show you something called the "longest match rule" first. Using this rule, IP will scan a routing table to find the longest match as compared to the destination address of a packet. Figure 5.1 offers a picture of this process.

Chapter 5 ▪ IP Routing

FIGURE 5.1 A simple routing example

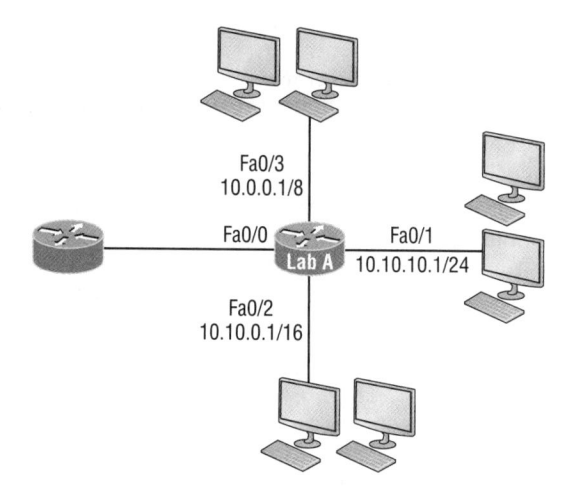

Figure 5.1 illustrates a simple network. Lab_A has four interfaces. Can you see which interface will be used to forward an IP datagram to a host with a destination IP address of 10.10.10.30?

By using the command show ip route on a router, we can see the routing table (map of the internetwork) that Lab_A has used to make its forwarding decisions:

```
Lab_A#sh ip route
Codes: L - local, C - connected, S - static,
[output cut]
10.0.0.0/8 is variably subnetted, 6 subnets, 4 masks
C   10.0.0.0/8 is directly connected, FastEthernet0/3
L   10.0.0.1/32 is directly connected, FastEthernet0/3
C   10.10.0.0/16 is directly connected, FastEthernet0/2
L   10.10.0.1/32 is directly connected, FastEthernet0/2
C   10.10.10.0/24 is directly connected, FastEthernet0/1
L   10.10.10.1/32 is directly connected, FastEthernet0/1
S*  0.0.0.0/0 is directly connected, FastEthernet0/0
```

The C in the routing table output means that the networks listed are directly connected. Until we add a routing protocol like RIPv2, OSPF, etc., to the routers in our internetwork, or enter static routes, only directly connected networks will show up in our routing table. But wait—what about that L in the routing table—that's new, isn't it? Yes! Because in the new Cisco IOS 15 code, Cisco defines a different route, called a local host route. Each local route has a /32 prefix, defining a route just for the one address. So in this example, the router relied upon these routes, which list their own local IP addresses, to more efficiently forward packets to the router itself.

But let's get back to the original question: Looking at the figure and the output of the routing table, what will IP do with a received packet that has a destination IP address of 10.10.10.30? The router will packet-switch the packet to interface FastEthernet 0/1, which will frame the packet and then send it out on the network segment. This is referred to as frame rewrite. Based upon the longest match rule, IP would look for 10.10.10.30, and if that isn't found in the table, then IP would search for 10.10.10.0, then 10.10.0.0, and so on until a route is discovered.

Here's another example: Looking at the output of the next routing table, which interface will a packet with a destination address of 10.10.10.14 be forwarded from?

```
Lab_A#sh ip route
[output cut]
Gateway of last resort is not set
C 10.10.10.16/28 is directly connected, FastEthernet0/0
L 10.10.10.17/32 is directly connected, FastEthernet0/0
C 10.10.10.8/29 is directly connected, FastEthernet0/1
L 10.10.10.9/32 is directly connected, FastEthernet0/1
C 10.10.10.4/30 is directly connected, FastEthernet0/2
L 10.10.10.5/32 is directly connected, FastEthernet0/2
C 10.10.10.0/30 is directly connected, Serial 0/0
L 10.10.10.1/32 is directly connected, Serial0/0
```

To figure this out, look closely at the output until you see that the network is subnetted and each interface has a different mask. I have to tell you—you just can't answer this question if you can't subnet! 10.10.10.14 would be a host in the 10.10.10.8/29 subnet that's connected to the FastEthernet0/1 interface. If you're struggling with this, just go back and reread Chapter 3, "Easy Subnetting," until you've got it.

The IP Routing Process

The IP routing process is actually pretty simple and doesn't change regardless of the size of your network. To give you a picture of this fact, I'll use Figure 5.2 to describe what happens when Host A wants to communicate with Host B on a different network, step-by-step.

FIGURE 5.2 IP routing example using two hosts and one router

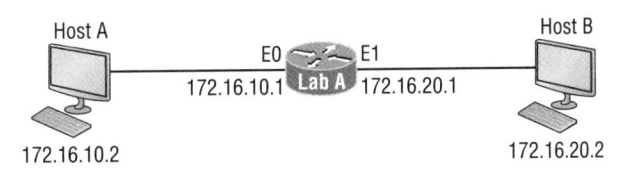

In Figure 5.2 a user on Host_A pinged Host_B's IP address. Routing doesn't get any simpler than this, but it still involves a lot of steps, so let's go through them:

1. Internet Control Message Protocol (ICMP) creates an echo request payload, which is simply the alphabet in the data field.
2. ICMP hands that payload to Internet Protocol (IP), which then creates a packet. At a minimum, this packet contains an IP source address, an IP destination address, and a Protocol field with 01h. Don't forget that Cisco likes to use *0x* in front of hex characters, so this could also look like 0x01. This tells the receiving host which protocol it should hand the payload to when the destination is reached. In this example, it's ICMP.
3. Once the packet is created, IP determines whether the destination IP address is on the local network or a remote one.
4. Since IP has determined that this is a remote request, the packet must be sent to the default gateway so it can be routed to the remote network. The Registry in Windows is parsed to find the configured default gateway.
5. The default gateway of Host_A is configured to 172.16.10.1. For this packet to be sent to the default gateway, the hardware address of the router's interface Ethernet 0, which is configured with the IP address of 172.16.10.1, must be known. Why? So the packet can be handed down to the Data Link layer, framed, and sent to the router's interface that's connected to the 172.16.10.0 network. Because hosts communicate only via hardware addresses on the local LAN, it's important to recognize that for Host_A to communicate to Host_B, it has to send packets to the Media Access Control (MAC) address of the default gateway on the local network.

> **NOTE** MAC addresses are always local on the LAN and never go through and past a router.

6. Next, the Address Resolution Protocol (ARP) cache of the host is checked to see if the IP address of the default gateway has already been resolved to a hardware address.

If it has, the packet is then handed to the Data Link layer for framing. Remember that the hardware destination address is also handed down with that packet. To view the ARP cache on your host:

```
C:\>arp -a
Interface: 172.16.10.2 --- 0x3
Internet Address  Physical Address   Type
172.16.10.1       00-15-05-06-31-b0  dynamic
```

If the hardware address isn't already in the ARP cache of the host, an ARP broadcast will be sent out onto the local network to search for the 172.16.10.1 hardware address. The router then responds to the request, provides the hardware address of Ethernet 0, and the host caches the address.

7. Once the packet and destination hardware address are handed to the Data Link layer, the LAN driver is used to provide media access via the type of LAN—Ethernet, in this case. A frame is then generated, encapsulating the packet with control information. Within that frame are the hardware destination and source addresses plus, in this case, an Ether-Type field, which identifies the specific Network layer protocol that handed the packet to the Data Link layer. Here, it's IP. At the end of the frame is something called a Frame Check Sequence (FCS) field that houses the result of the cyclic redundancy check (CRC). The frame would look something like what I've detailed in Figure 5.3. It contains Host A's hardware (MAC) address and the destination hardware address of the default gateway. It does not include the remote host's MAC address—remember that!

FIGURE 5.3 Frame used from Host A to the Lab_A router when Host B is pinged

Destination MAC (router's E0 MAC address)	Source MAC (Host A MAC address)	Ether-Type field	Packet	FCS CRC

8. Once the frame is completed, it's handed down to the Physical layer to be put on the physical medium one bit at a time. (In this example, twisted-pair wire.)
9. Every device in the collision domain receives these bits and builds the frame. They each run a CRC and check the answer in the FCS field. If the answers don't match, the frame is discarded.
    - If the CRC matches, then the hardware destination address is checked to see if it also matches—in this example, it's the router's interface Ethernet 0.
    - If it's a match, then the Ether-Type field is checked to find the protocol used at the Network layer.
10. The packet is pulled from the frame, and what's left of the frame is discarded. The packet is handed to the protocol listed in the Ether-Type field and given to IP.
11. IP receives the packet and checks the IP destination address. Since the packet's destination address doesn't match any of the addresses configured on the receiving router, the router will look up the destination IP network address in its routing table.
12. The routing table must have an entry for the network 172.16.20.0 or the packet will be discarded immediately and an ICMP message will be sent back to the originating device with a destination network unreachable message.
13. If the router does find an entry for the destination network in its table, the packet is switched to the exit interface—in this example, interface Ethernet 1. The following output displays the Lab_A router's routing table. The C means "directly connected." No routing protocols are needed in this network since all networks (all two of them) are directly connected.

```
Lab_A>sh ip route
C 172.16.10.0 is directly connected, Ethernet0
L 172.16.10.1/32 is directly connected, Ethernet0
C 172.16.20.0 is directly connected, Ethernet1
L 172.16.20.1/32 is directly connected, Ethernet1
```

14. The router packet-switches the packet to the Ethernet 1 buffer.
15. The Ethernet 1 buffer needs to know the hardware address of the destination host and first checks the ARP cache.
    - If the hardware address of Host_B has already been resolved and is in the router's ARP cache, then the packet and the hardware address will be handed down to the Data Link layer to be framed. Let's take a look at the ARP cache on the Lab_A router by using the show ip arp command:

```
Lab_A#sh ip arp
Protocol Address    Age(min) Hardware Addr   Type Interface
Internet 172.16.20.1    -    00d0.58ad.05f4 ARPA Ethernet1
Internet 172.16.20.2    3    0030.9492.a5dd ARPA Ethernet1
Internet 172.16.10.1    -    00d0.58ad.06aa ARPA Ethernet0
Internet 172.16.10.2   12    0030.9492.a4ac ARPA Ethernet0
```

The dash (-) signifies that this is the physical interface on the router. This output shows us that the router knows the 172.16.10.2 (Host_A) and 172.16.20.2 (Host_B) hardware addresses. Cisco routers will keep an entry in the ARP table for 4 hours.

   - Now if the hardware address hasn't already been resolved, the router will send an ARP request out E1 looking for the 172.16.20.2 hardware address. Host_B responds with its hardware address, and the packet and destination hardware addresses are then both sent to the Data Link layer for framing.
16. The Data Link layer creates a frame with the destination and source hardware addresses, Ether-Type field, and FCS field at the end. The frame is then handed to the Physical layer to be sent out on the physical medium one bit at a time.
17. Host_B receives the frame and immediately runs a CRC. If the result matches the information in the FCS field, the hardware destination address will be checked next. If the host finds a match, the Ether-Type field is then checked to determine the protocol that the packet should be handed to at the Network layer—IP in this example.
18. At the Network layer, IP receives the packet and runs a CRC on the IP header. If that passes, IP then checks the destination address. Since a match has finally been made, the Protocol field is checked to find out to whom the payload should be given.
19. The payload is handed to ICMP, which understands that this is an echo request. ICMP responds to this by immediately discarding the packet and generating a new payload as an echo reply.
20. A packet is then created including the source and destination addresses, Protocol field, and payload. The destination device is now Host_A.
21. IP then checks to see whether the destination IP address is a device on the local LAN or on a remote network. Since the destination device is on a remote network, the packet needs to be sent to the default gateway.

22. The default gateway IP address is found in the Registry of the Windows device, and the ARP cache is checked to see if the hardware address has already been resolved from an IP address.
23. Once the hardware address of the default gateway is found, the packet and destination hardware addresses are handed down to the Data Link layer for framing.
24. The Data Link layer frames the packet of information and includes the following in the header:
    - The destination and source hardware addresses
    - The Ether-Type field with 0x0800 (IP) in it
    - The FCS field with the CRC result in tow
25. The frame is now handed down to the Physical layer to be sent out over the network medium one bit at a time.
26. The router's Ethernet 1 interface receives the bits and builds a frame. The CRC is run, and the FCS field is checked to make sure the answers match.
27. Once the CRC is found to be okay, the hardware destination address is checked. Since the router's interface is a match, the packet is pulled from the frame and the Ether-Type field is checked to determine which protocol the packet should be delivered to at the Network layer.
28. The protocol is determined to be IP, so it gets the packet. IP runs a CRC check on the IP header first and then checks the destination IP address.

> **NOTE** IP does not run a complete CRC like the Data Link layer does—it only checks the header for errors.

Since the IP destination address doesn't match any of the router's interfaces, the routing table is checked to see whether it has a route to 172.16.10.0. If it doesn't have a route over to the destination network, the packet will be discarded immediately. I want to point out that this is exactly where the source of confusion begins for a lot of administrators because when a ping fails, most people think the packet never reached the destination host. But as we see here, that's not *always* the case. All it takes for this to happen is for even just one of the remote routers to lack a route back to the originating host's network and—*poof!*—the packet is dropped on the *return trip*, not on its way to the host!

> **TIP** Just a quick note to mention that when (and if) the packet is lost on the way back to the originating host, you will typically see a request timed-out message because it's an unknown error. If the error occurs because of a known issue, such as if a route is not in the routing table on the way to the destination device, you will see a destination unreachable message. This should help you determine if the problem occurred on the way to the destination or on the way back.

29. In this case, the router happens to know how to get to network 172.16.10.0—the exit interface is Ethernet 0—so the packet is switched to interface Ethernet 0.
30. The router then checks the ARP cache to determine whether the hardware address for 172.16.10.2 has already been resolved.
31. Since the hardware address to 172.16.10.2 is already cached from the originating trip to Host_B, the hardware address and packet are then handed to the Data Link layer.
32. The Data Link layer builds a frame with the destination hardware address and source hardware address and then puts IP in the Ether-Type field. A CRC is run on the frame, and the result is placed in the FCS field.
33. The frame is then handed to the Physical layer to be sent out onto the local network one bit at a time.
34. The destination host receives the frame, runs a CRC, checks the destination hardware address, then looks into the Ether-Type field to find out to whom to hand the packet.
35. IP is the designated receiver, and after the packet is handed to IP at the Network layer, it checks the Protocol field for further direction. IP finds instructions to give the payload to ICMP, and ICMP determines the packet to be an ICMP echo reply.
36. ICMP acknowledges that it has received the reply by sending an exclamation point (!) to the user interface. ICMP then attempts to send four more echo requests to the destination host.

You've just experienced Todd's 36 easy steps to understanding IP routing. The key takeaway here is that if you had a much larger network, the process would be the *same*. It's just that the larger the internetwork, the more hops the packet goes through before it finds the destination host.

It's super important to remember that when Host_A sends a packet to Host_B, the destination hardware address used is the default gateway's Ethernet interface. Why? Because frames can't be placed on remote networks—only local networks. So packets destined for remote networks must go through the default gateway.

Let's take a look at Host_A's ARP cache now:

```
C:\ >arp -a
Interface: 172.16.10.2 --- 0x3
Internet Address  Physical Address   Type
172.16.10.1       00-15-05-06-31-b0  dynamic
172.16.20.1       00-15-05-06-31-b0  dynamic
```

Did you notice that the hardware (MAC) address that Host_A uses to get to Host_B is the Lab_A E0 interface? Hardware addresses are *always* local, and they never pass through a router's interface. Understanding this process is very important, so carve this into your memory!

The Cisco Router Internal Process

One more thing before we test how well you understand my 36 steps of IP routing. I think it's important to explain how a router forwards packets internally. For IP to look up a destination address in a routing table on a router, processing in the router must take place, and if there are tens of thousands of routes in that table, the amount of CPU time would be enormous. It results in a potentially overwhelming amount of overhead—think about a router at your ISP that has to calculate millions of packets per second and even subnet to find the correct exit interface! Even with the little network I'm using in this book, lots of processing would need to be done if there were actual hosts connected and sending data.

Cisco uses three types of packet-forwarding techniques.

Process switching   This is actually how many people see routers to this day, because it's true that routers actually did perform this type of bare-bones packet switching back in 1990 when Cisco released their very first router. But the days when traffic demands were unimaginably light are long gone—not in today's networks! This process is now extremely complex and involves looking up every destination in the routing table and finding the exit interface for every packet. This is pretty much how I just explained the process in my 36 steps. But even though what I wrote was absolutely true in concept, the internal process requires much more than packet-switching technology today because of the millions of packets per second that must now be processed. So Cisco came up with some other technologies to help with the "big process problem."

Fast switching   This solution was created to make the slow performance of process switching faster and more efficient. Fast switching uses a cache to store the most recently used destinations so that lookups are not required for every packet. Caching the exit interface of the destination device, plus the layer 2 header, dramatically improved performance, but as our networks evolved with the need for even more speed, Cisco created yet another technology...

Cisco Express Forwarding (CEF)   This is Cisco's newest packet forwarding, performance optimizing creation, and it's the default method used on all the latest Cisco routers. CEF makes many different cache tables that enhance performance and is change triggered, not packet triggered. Translated, this means that when the network topology changes, the cache changes along with it.

> To see which packet switching method your router interface is using, use the command show ip interface.

Testing Your IP Routing Understanding

Since understanding IP routing is so important, it's time for that little test I mentioned earlier... How well do you actually have the IP routing process down so far? Let's find out by having you look at a couple of figures and answering some very basic IP routing questions based upon them.

Figure 5.4 shows a LAN connected to RouterA that's connected via a WAN link to RouterB. RouterB has a LAN connected with an HTTP server attached.

FIGURE 5.4 IP routing example 1

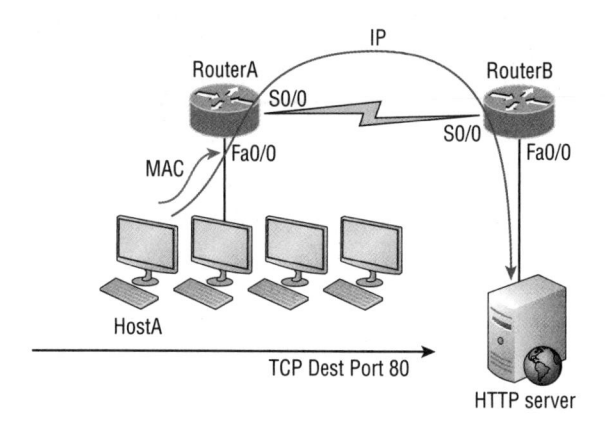

1. The critical information you want to get by looking at this figure is exactly how IP routing will occur in this example. Let's determine the characteristics of a frame as it leaves HostA. Okay so maybe we'll cheat a bit... I'll give you the answer, but I still want you to go back over the figure and see if you can answer example 2 without looking at my three-step answer!
2. The destination address of a frame from HostA would be the MAC address of Router A's Fa0/0 interface.
3. The destination address of a packet would be the IP address of the HTTP server's network interface card (NIC).
4. The destination port number in the segment header would be 80.

That was a pretty straightforward scenario. One thing to remember is that when multiple hosts are communicating to a server via HTTP, they must all use a different source port number. The source and destination IP addresses and port numbers are how the server keeps the data separated at the Transport layer.

Let's complicate things by adding another device into the network. Figure 5.5 shows a network with only one router but two switches.

FIGURE 5.5 IP routing example 2

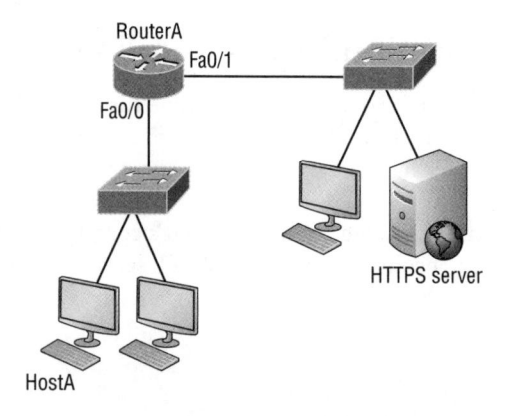

The key thing to zero in on about the IP routing process in this scenario is what happens when HostA sends data to the HTTPS server? Here's your answer:

1. The destination address of a frame from HostA would be the MAC address of RouterA's Fa0/0 interface.
2. The destination address of a packet is the IP address of the HTTPS server's network interface card (NIC).
3. The destination port number in the segment header will have a value of 443.

Did you notice that the switches weren't used as either a default gateway or any other destination? That's because switches have nothing to do with routing. How many of you chose the switch as the default gateway (destination) MAC address for HostA? If you did, don't feel bad—just look into where you went wrong and why. Remember, if your packets are destined for outside the LAN as they were in these last two examples, the destination MAC address will always be the router's interface!

Before moving on into some of the more advanced aspects of IP routing, let's analyze another issue. Take a look at the output of the Corp router's routing table:

```
Corp#sh ip route
[output cut]
R  192.168.215.0 [120/2] via 192.168.20.2, 00:00:23, Serial0/0
R  192.168.115.0 [120/1] via 192.168.20.2, 00:00:23, Serial0/0
R  192.168.30.0 [120/1] via 192.168.20.2, 00:00:23, Serial0/0
C  192.168.20.0 is directly connected, Serial0/0
L  192.168.20.1/32 is directly connected, Serial0/0
C  192.168.214.0 is directly connected, FastEthernet0/0
L  192.168.214.1/32 is directly connected, FastEthernet0/0
```

What do we see here? If I were to tell you that the corporate router received an IP packet with a source IP address of 192.168.214.20 and with destination address 192.168.22.3, what do you think the Corp router will do with this packet?

If you said, "The packet came in on the FastEthernet 0/0 interface, but because the routing table doesn't show a route to network 192.168.22.0 (or a default route), the router will discard the packet and send an ICMP destination unreachable message back out to interface FastEthernet 0/0," you're spot on! The reason that's the right answer is because that's the source LAN where the packet originated from.

Let's check out the next figure and talk about the frames and packets in detail. We're not really going over anything new here; I'm just making sure you totally, completely, thoroughly, understand basic IP routing! It's the crux of this book, and the topic the exam objectives are geared toward. We'll use Figure 5.6 for the next few scenarios.

FIGURE 5.6 Basic IP routing using MAC and IP addresses

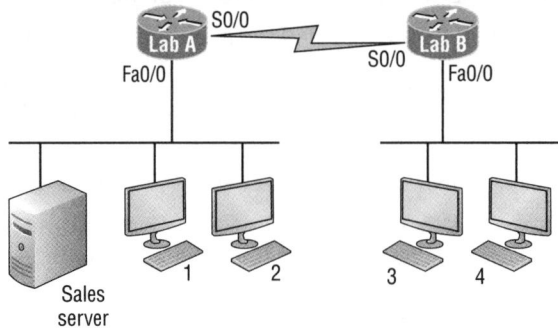

Referring to Figure 5.6, here's a list of all the answers to questions you need:

1. In order to begin communicating with the Sales server, Host 4 sends out an ARP request. How will the devices exhibited in the topology respond to this request?
2. Host 4 has received an ARP reply. Host 4 will now build a packet, then place this packet in the frame. What information will be placed in the header of the packet that leaves Host 4 if Host 4 is going to communicate to the Sales server?
3. The Lab_A router has received the packet and will send it out Fa0/0 onto the LAN toward the server. What will the frame have in the header as the source and destination addresses?
4. Host 4 is displaying two web documents from the Sales server in two browser windows at the same time. How did the data find its way to the correct browser windows?

The following should probably be written in a 3-point font upside down in another part of the book so it would be really hard for you to cheat, but since I'm not mean and you really need to conquer this stuff, here are your answers in the same order that the scenarios were just presented in:

1. In order to begin communicating with the server, Host 4 sends out an ARP request. How will the devices exhibited in the topology respond to this request? Since MAC addresses must stay on the local network, the Lab_B router will respond with the MAC address of the Fa0/0 interface and Host 4 will send all frames to the MAC address of the Lab_B Fa0/0 interface when sending packets to the Sales server.
2. Host 4 has received an ARP reply. Host 4 will now build a packet, then place this packet in the frame. What information will be placed in the header of the packet that leaves Host 4 if Host 4 is going to communicate to the Sales server? Since we're now talking about packets, not frames, the source address will be the IP address of Host 4 and the destination address will be the IP address of the Sales server.
3. Finally, the Lab_A router has received the packet and will send it out Fa0/0 onto the LAN toward the server. What will the frame have in the header as the source and destination addresses? The source MAC address will be the Lab_A router's Fa0/0 interface, and the destination MAC address will be the Sales server's MAC address because all MAC addresses must be local on the LAN.

4. Host 4 is displaying two web documents from the Sales server in two different browser windows at the same time. How did the data find its way to the correct browser windows? TCP port numbers are used to direct the data to the correct application window.

Great! But we're not quite done yet. I've got a few more questions for you before you actually get to configure routing in a real network. Figure 5.7 shows a basic network, and Host 4 needs to get email. Which address will be placed in the destination address field of the frame when it leaves Host 4?

FIGURE 5.7 Testing basic routing knowledge

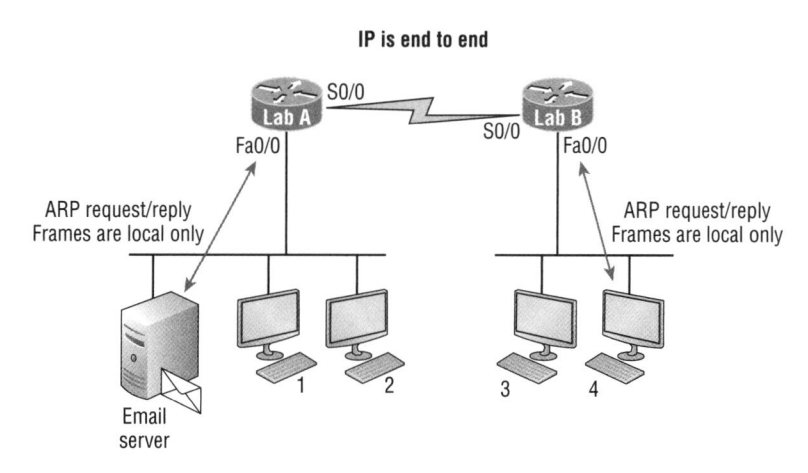

The answer is that Host 4 will use the destination MAC address of the Fa0/0 interface on the Lab_B router—you knew that, right? Look at Figure 5.7 again: What if Host 4 needs to communicate with Host 1—not the server, but with Host 1? Which OSI layer 3 source address will be found in the packet header when it reaches Host 1?

Hopefully you've got this: At layer 3, the source IP address will be Host 4, and the destination address in the packet will be the IP address of Host 1. Of course, the destination MAC address from Host 4 will always be the Fa0/0 address of the Lab_B router, right? And since we have more than one router, we'll need a routing protocol that communicates between both of them so that traffic can be forwarded in the right direction to reach the network that Host 1 is connected to.

Okay—one more scenario... Again, using Figure 5.7, Host 4 is transferring a file to the email server connected to the Lab_A router. What would be the layer 2 destination address leaving Host 4? (Yes, I've asked this question more than once.) But not this one: What will be the source MAC address when the frame is received at the email server?

Hopefully, you answered that the layer 2 destination address leaving Host 4 is the MAC address of the Fa0/0 interface on the Lab_B router and that the source layer 2 address that the email server will receive is the Fa0/0 interface of the Lab_A router.

If you did, you're ready to discover how IP routing is handled in a larger network environment!

Configuring IP Routing

It's time to get serious and configure a real network. Figure 5.8 shows three routers: Corp, SF, and LA. Remember that, by default, these routers only know about networks that are directly connected to them. I'll continue to use this figure and network throughout the rest of this book. As we progress, I'll add more routers and switches as needed.

FIGURE 5.8 Configuring IP routing

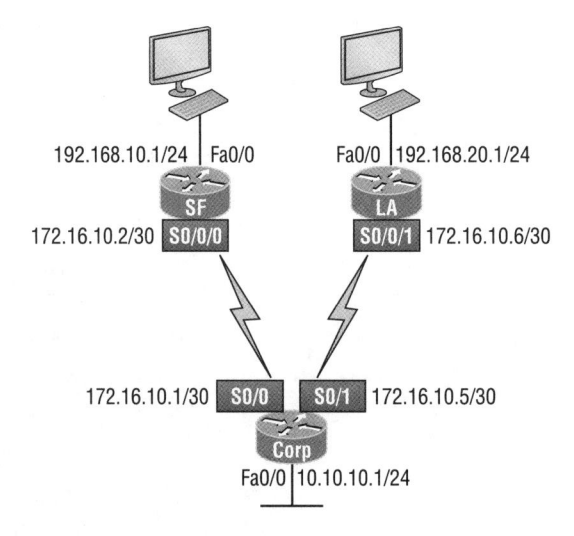

As you might guess, I've got quite a nice collection of routers for us to play with. But you don't need a closet full of devices to perform most, if not all, of the commands we'll use in this book. You can get by nicely with pretty much any router or even with a good router simulator.

Getting back to business… The Corp router has two serial interfaces, which will provide a WAN connection to the SF and LA router and two Fast Ethernet interfaces as well. The two remote routers have two serial interfaces and two Fast Ethernet interfaces.

The first step for this project is to correctly configure each router with an IP address on each interface. The following list shows the IP address scheme I'm going to use to configure the network. After we go over how the network is configured, I'll cover how to configure IP routing. Pay attention to the subnet masks! The LANs all use a /24 mask, but the WANs are using a /30.

Corp

- Serial 0/0: 172.16.10.1/30
- Serial 0/1: 172.16.10.5/30
- Fa0/0: 10.10.10.1/24

SF

- S0/0/0: 172.16.10.2/30
- Fa0/0: 192.168.10.1/24

LA

- S0/0/0: 172.16.10.6/30
- Fa0/0: 192.168.20.1/24

The router configuration is really a pretty straightforward process since you just need to add IP addresses to your interfaces and then perform a no shutdown on those same interfaces. It gets more complex later on, but for right now, let's configure the IP addresses in the network.

Corp Configuration

We need to configure three interfaces to configure the Corp router. And configuring the hostnames of each router will make identification much easier. While we're at it, let's set the interface descriptions, banner, and router passwords too because you need to make a habit of configuring these commands on every router!

To get started, I performed an `erase startup-config` on the router and reloaded, so we'll start in setup mode. I chose no when prompted to enter setup mode, which will get us straight to the username prompt of the console. I'm going to configure all my routers this same way.

Here's how what I just did looks:

```
--- System Configuration Dialog ---
Would you like to enter the initial configuration dialog? [yes/no]: n
Press RETURN to get started!
Router>en
Router#config t
Router(config)#hostname Corp
Corp(config)#enable secret GlobalNet
Corp(config)#no ip domain-lookup
Corp(config)#int f0/0
Corp(config-if)#desc Connection to LAN BackBone
Corp(config-if)#ip address 10.10.10.1 255.255.255.0
Corp(config-if)#no shut
Corp(config-if)#int s0/0
Corp(config-if)#desc WAN connection to SF
Corp(config-if)#ip address 172.16.10.1 255.255.255.252
Corp(config-if)#no shut
Corp(config-if)#int s0/1
```

```
Corp(config-if)#desc WAN connection to LA
Corp(config-if)#ip address 172.16.10.5 255.255.255.252
Corp(config-if)#no shut
Corp(config-if)#line con 0
Corp(config-line)#password console
Corp(config-line)#logging
Corp(config-line)#logging sync
Corp(config-line)#exit
Corp(config)#line vty 0 ?
  <1-181> Last Line number
  <cr>
Corp(config)#line vty 0 181
Corp(config-line)#password telnet
Corp(config-line)#login
Corp(config-line)#exit
Corp(config)#banner motd # This is my Corp Router #
Corp(config)#^Z
Corp#copy run start
Destination filename [startup-config]?
Building configuration...
[OK]
Corp# [OK]
```

Let's talk about the configuration of the Corp router. First, I set the hostname and enabled secret, but what is that `no ip domain-lookup` command? That command stops the router from trying to resolve hostnames, which is an annoying feature unless you've configured a host table or DNS. Next, I configured the three interfaces with descriptions and IP addresses and enabled them with the `no shutdown` command. The console and VTY passwords came next, but what is that `logging sync` command under the console line? The logging synchronous command stops console messages from writing over what you are typing in, meaning it will save your sanity! Last, I set my banner and then saved my configs.

To view the IP routing tables created on a Cisco router, use the command `show ip route`. Here's the command's output:

```
Corp#sh ip route
Codes: L - local, C - connected, S - static, R - RIP, M - mobile, B - BGP
       D - EIGRP, EX - EIGRP external, O - OSPF, IA - OSPF inter area
       N1 - OSPF NSSA external type 1, N2 - OSPF NSSA external type 2
       E1 - OSPF external type 1, E2 - OSPF external type 2
       i - IS-IS, su - IS-IS summary, L1 - IS-IS level-1, L2 - IS-IS level-2
       ia - IS-IS inter area, * - candidate default, U - per-user static route
       o - ODR, P - periodic downloaded static route, H - NHRP, l - LISP
```

```
+ - replicated route, % - next hop override
Gateway of last resort is not set
     10.0.0.0/24 is subnetted, 1 subnets
C       10.10.10.0 is directly connected, FastEthernet0/0
L       10.10.10.1/32 is directly connected, FastEthernet0/0
Corp#
```

So remember—only configured, directly connected networks are going to show up in the routing table. Why is it that only the FastEthernet 0/0 interface shows up in the table? It's not a huge deal—it's just because you won't see the serial interfaces come up until the other side of the links are operational. As soon as we configure our SF and LA routers, those interfaces should pop right up.

One thing, though… Did you notice the C on the left side of the output of the routing table? When you see that there, it means that the network is directly connected. The codes for each type of connection are listed at the top of the show ip route command, along with their descriptions.

> **NOTE** For brevity, the codes at the top of the output will be cut in the rest of this chapter.

SF Configuration

Now we're ready to configure the next router—SF. To make that happen correctly, keep in mind that we have two interfaces to deal with: Serial 0/0/0 and FastEthernet 0/0. Let's make sure not to forget to add the hostname, passwords, interface descriptions, and banners to the router configuration. As I did with the Corp router, I erased the configuration and reloaded since this router had already been configured before.

Here's the configuration I used:

```
R1#erase start
% Incomplete command.
R1#erase startup-config
Erasing the nvram filesystem will remove all configuration files!
Continue? [confirm][enter]
[OK]
Erase of nvram: complete
R1#reload
Proceed with reload? [confirm][enter]
[output cut]
%Error opening tftp://255.255.255.255/network-confg (Timed out)
%Error opening tftp://255.255.255.255/cisconet.cfg (Timed out)
         --- System Configuration Dialog ---
Would you like to enter the initial configuration dialog? [yes/no]: n
```

Before we move on, let's talk about this output for a second. First, notice that beginning with IOS 12.4, ISR routers will no longer take the command erase start. The router has only one command after erase that starts with *s*, as shown here:

```
Router#erase s?
startup-config
```

I know, you'd think that the IOS would continue to accept the command, but nope—sorry! The second thing I want to point out is that the output tells us the router is looking for a TFTP host to see if it can download a configuration. When that fails, it goes straight into setup mode.

Let's get back to configuring our router:

```
Press RETURN to get started!
Router#config t
Router(config)#hostname SF
SF(config)#enable secret GlobalNet
SF(config)#no ip domain-lookup
SF(config)#int s0/0/0
SF(config-if)#desc WAN Connection to Corp
SF(config-if)#ip address 172.16.10.2 255.255.255.252
SF(config-if)#no shut
SF(config-if)#clock rate 1000000
SF(config-if)#int f0/0
SF(config-if)#desc SF LAN
SF(config-if)#ip address 192.168.10.1 255.255.255.0
SF(config-if)#no shut
SF(config-if)#line con 0
SF(config-line)#password console
SF(config-line)#login
SF(config-line)#logging sync
SF(config-line)#exit
SF(config)#line vty 0 ?
  <1-1180>  Last Line number
  <cr>
SF(config)#line vty 0 1180
SF(config-line)#password telnet
SF(config-line)#login
SF(config-line)#banner motd #This is the SF Branch router#
SF(config)#exit
SF#copy run start
Destination filename [startup-config]?
Building configuration...
[OK]
```

Let's take a look at our configuration of the interfaces with the following two commands:

```
SF#sh run | begin int
interface FastEthernet0/0
description SF LAN
ip address 192.168.10.1 255.255.255.0
duplex auto
speed auto
!
interface FastEthernet0/1
no ip address
shutdown
duplex auto
speed auto
!
interface Serial0/0/0
description WAN Connection to Corp
ip address 172.16.10.2 255.255.255.252
clock rate 1000000
!
SF#sh ip int brief
Interface IP-Address OK? Method Status Protocol
FastEthernet0/0 192.168.10.1 YES manual up up
FastEthernet0/1 unassigned YES unset administratively down down
Serial0/0/0 172.16.10.2 YES manual up up
Serial0/0/1 unassigned YES unset administratively down down
SF#
```

Now that both ends of the serial link are configured, the link comes up. Remember, the up/up status for the interfaces are Physical/Data Link layer status indicators that don't reflect the layer 3 status! I ask students in my classes, "If the link shows up/up, can you ping the directly connected network?" And they say, "Yes!" The correct answer is, "I don't know," because we can't see the layer 3 status with this command. We only see layers 1 and 2 and verify that the IP addresses don't have a typo. Remember this!

The show ip route command for the SF router reveals the following:

```
SF#sh ip route
C 192.168.10.0/24 is directly connected, FastEthernet0/0
L 192.168.10.1/32 is directly connected, FastEthernet0/0
172.16.0.0/30 is subnetted, 1 subnets
C 172.16.10.0 is directly connected, Serial0/0/0
L 172.16.10.2/32 is directly connected, Serial0/0/0
```

Notice that router SF knows how to get to networks 172.16.10.0/30 and 192.168.10.0/24; we can now ping to the Corp router from SF:

```
SF#ping 172.16.10.1
Type escape sequence to abort.
Sending 5, 100-byte ICMP Echos to 172.16.10.1, timeout is 2 seconds:
!!!!!
Success rate is 100 percent (5/5), round-trip min/avg/max = 1/3/4 ms
```

Now let's head back to the Corp router and check out the routing table:

```
Corp>sh ip route
172.16.0.0/30 is subnetted, 1 subnets
C 172.16.10.0 is directly connected, Serial0/0
L 172.16.10.1/32 is directly connected, Serial0/0
10.0.0.0/24 is subnetted, 1 subnets
C 10.10.10.0 is directly connected, FastEthernet0/0
L 10.10.10.1/32 is directly connected, FastEthernet0/0
```

On the SF router's serial interface 0/0/0 is a DCE connection, which means a clock rate needs to be set on the interface. Remember that you don't need to use the clock rate command in production.

We can see our clocking with the show controllers command:

```
SF#sh controllers s0/0/0
Interface Serial0/0/0
Hardware is GT96K
DCE V.35, clock rate 1000000

Corp>sh controllers s0/0
Interface Serial0/0
Hardware is PowerQUICC MPC860
DTE V.35 TX and RX clocks detected.
```

Since the SF router has a DCE cable connection, I needed to add clock rate to this interface because DTE receives clock. Keep in mind that the new ISR routers will autodetect this and set the clock rate to 2000000. But you still need to make sure you're able to find an interface that is DCE and set clocking to meet the objectives.

Since the serial links are showing up, we can now see both networks in the Corp routing table. And once we configure LA, we'll see one more network in the routing table of the Corp router. The Corp router can't see the 192.168.10.0 network because we don't have any routing configured yet—routers see only directly connected networks by default.

LA Configuration

To configure LA, we're going to do pretty much the same thing we did with the other two routers. There are two interfaces to deal with, Serial 0/0/1 and FastEthernet 0/0, and again, we'll be sure to add the hostname, passwords, interface descriptions, and a banner to the router configuration:

```
Router(config)#hostname LA
LA(config)#enable secret GlobalNet
LA(config)#no ip domain-lookup
LA(config)#int s0/0/1
LA(config-if)#ip address 172.16.10.6 255.255.255.252
LA(config-if)#no shut
LA(config-if)#clock rate 1000000
LA(config-if)#description WAN To Corporate
LA(config-if)#int f0/0
LA(config-if)#ip address 192.168.20.1 255.255.255.0
LA(config-if)#no shut
LA(config-if)#description LA LAN
LA(config-if)#line con 0
LA(config-line)#password console
LA(config-line)#login
LA(config-line)#logging sync
LA(config-line)#exit
LA(config)#line vty 0 ?
  <1-1180>  Last Line number
  <cr>
LA(config)#line vty 0 1180
LA(config-line)#password telnet
LA(config-line)#login
LA(config-line)#exit
LA(config)#banner motd #This is my LA Router#
LA(config)#exit
LA#copy run start
Destination filename [startup-config]?
Building configuration...
[OK]
```

Nice—everything was pretty straightforward. The following output, which I gained via the show ip route command, displays the directly connected networks of 192.168.20.0 and 172.16.10.0:

```
LA#sh ip route
172.16.0.0/30 is subnetted, 1 subnets
C   172.16.10.4 is directly connected, Serial0/0/1
L   172.16.10.6/32 is directly connected, Serial0/0/1
C   192.168.20.0/24 is directly connected, FastEthernet0/0
L   192.168.20.1/32 is directly connected, FastEthernet0/0
```

So now that we've configured all three routers with IP addresses and administrative functions, we can move on to deal with routing. But I want to do one more thing on the SF and LA routers—since this is a very small network, let's build a DHCP server on the Corp router for each LAN.

Configuring DHCP on Our Corp Router

While it's true that I could approach this task by going to each remote router and creating a pool, why bother with all that when I can easily create two pools on the Corp router and have the remote routers forward requests to the Corp router?

Let's give it a shot:

```
Corp#config t
Corp(config)#ip dhcp excluded-address 192.168.10.1
Corp(config)#ip dhcp excluded-address 192.168.20.1
Corp(config)#ip dhcp pool SF_LAN
Corp(dhcp-config)#network 192.168.10.0 255.255.255.0
Corp(dhcp-config)#default-router 192.168.10.1
Corp(dhcp-config)#dns-server 4.4.4.4
Corp(dhcp-config)#exit
Corp(config)#ip dhcp pool LA_LAN
Corp(dhcp-config)#network 192.168.20.0 255.255.255.0
Corp(dhcp-config)#default-router 192.168.20.1
Corp(dhcp-config)#dns-server 4.4.4.4
Corp(dhcp-config)#exit
Corp(config)#exit
Corp#copy run start
Destination filename [startup-config]?
Building configuration...
```

Creating DHCP pools on a router is actually a simple process, and you would go about the configuration the same way on any router you wish to add a DHCP pool to. To designate a router as a DHCP server, you just create the pool name, add the network/subnet and the default gateway, and then exclude any addresses that you don't want handed out. You definitely want to make sure you've excluded the default gateway address, and you'd usually add a DNS server as well. I always add any exclusions first, and remember that you can conveniently exclude a range of addresses on a single line. But first, we need to figure out why the Corp router still can't get to the remote networks by default.

Now I'm pretty sure I configured DHCP correctly, but I just have this nagging feeling I forgot something important. What could that be? Well, the hosts are remote across a router, so what would I need to do that would allow them to get an address from a DHCP server? If you concluded that I've got to configure the SF and LA F0/0 interfaces to forward the DHCP client requests to the server, you got it!

Here's how we'd go about doing that:

```
LA#config t
LA(config)#int f0/0
LA(config-if)#ip helper-address 172.16.10.5

SF#config t
SF(config)#int f0/0
SF(config-if)#ip helper-address 172.16.10.1
```

I'm pretty sure I did this correctly, but we won't know until I have some type of routing configured and working. So let's get to that next.

Configuring IP Routing in Our Network

So is our network really good to go? After all, I've configured it with IP addressing, administrative functions and even clocking that will automatically occur with the ISR routers. But how will our routers send packets to remote networks when they get their destination information by looking into their tables that only include directions about directly connected networks? And you know routers promptly discard packets they receive with addresses for networks that aren't listed in their routing table, right?

So we're not exactly ready to rock after all. But we will be soon because there are several ways to configure the routing tables to include all the networks in our little internetwork so that packets will be properly forwarded. As usual, one size fits all rarely fits at all, and what's best for one network isn't necessarily what's best for another. That's why understanding the different types of routing will be really helpful when choosing the best solution for your specific environment and business requirements.

These are the three routing methods I'm going to cover with you:

- Static routing
- Default routing
- Dynamic routing

We're going to start with the first way and implement static routing on our network, because if you can implement static routing *and* make it work, you've demonstrated that you definitely have a solid understanding of the internetwork. So let's get started.

Static Routing

Static routing is the process that ensues when you manually add routes in each router's routing table. Predictably, there are pros and cons to static routing, but that's true for all routing approaches.

Here are the pros:

- There is no overhead on the router CPU, which means you could probably make do with a cheaper router than you would need for dynamic routing.
- There is no bandwidth usage between routers, saving you money on WAN links as well, minimizing overhead on the router since you're not using a routing protocol.
- It adds security because you, the administrator, can be very exclusive and choose to allow routing access to certain networks only.

And here are the cons:

- Whoever the administrator is must have a vault-tight knowledge of the internetwork and how each router is connected in order to configure routes correctly. If you don't have a good, accurate map of your internetwork, things will get very messy quickly!
- If you add a network to the internetwork, you have to tediously add a route to it on all routers by hand, which only gets increasingly insane as the network grows.
- Due to the last point, it's just not feasible to use it in most large networks because maintaining it would be a full-time job in itself.

But that list of cons doesn't mean you get to skip learning all about it mainly because of that first disadvantage I listed—the fact that you must have such a solid understanding of a network to configure it properly! So let's dive in and develop some skills. Starting at the beginning, here's the command syntax you use to add a static route to a routing table from global config:

ip route [*destination_network*] [*mask*] [*next-hop_address* or *exitinterface*] [*administrative_distance*] [*permanent*]

This list describes each command in the string:

ip route The command used to create the static route.

destination_network The network you're placing in the routing table.

mask The subnet mask being used on the network.

next-hop_address This is the IP address of the next-hop router that will receive packets and forward them to the remote network, which must signify a router interface that's on a directly connected network. You must be able to successfully ping the router interface before you can add the route. Important note to self is that if you type in the wrong next-hop address or the interface to the correct router is down, the static route will show up in the router's configuration but not in the routing table.

exitinterface   Used in place of the next-hop address if you want, and shows up as a directly connected route.

administrative_distance   By default, static routes have an administrative distance of 1 or 0 if you use an exit interface instead of a next-hop address. You can change the default value by adding an administrative weight at the end of the command. I'll talk a lot more about this later in the chapter when we get to dynamic routing.

permanent   If the interface is shut down or the router can't communicate to the next-hop router, the route will automatically be discarded from the routing table by default. Choosing the permanent option keeps the entry in the routing table no matter what happens.

Before I guide you through configuring static routes, let's take a look at a sample static route to see what we can find out about it:

```
Router(config)#ip route 172.16.3.0 255.255.255.0 192.168.2.4
```

- The `ip route` command tells us simply that it's a static route.
- 172.16.3.0 is the remote network we want to send packets to.
- 255.255.255.0 is the mask of the remote network.
- 192.168.2.4 is the next hop, or router, that packets will be sent to.

But what if the static route looked like this instead?

```
Router(config)#ip route 172.16.3.0 255.255.255.0 192.168.2.4 150
```

That 150 at the end changes the default administrative distance (AD) of 1 to 150. As I said, I'll talk much more about AD when we get into dynamic routing, but for now, just remember that the AD is the trustworthiness of a route, where 0 is best and 255 is worst.

One more example, then we'll start configuring:

```
Router(config)#ip route 172.16.3.0 255.255.255.0 s0/0/0
```

Instead of using a next-hop address, we can use an exit interface that will make the route show up as a directly connected network. Functionally, the next hop and exit interface work exactly the same.

To help you understand how static routes work, I'll demonstrate the configuration on the internetwork shown previously in Figure 5.8. Here it is again in Figure 5.9 to save you the trouble of having to go back and forth to view the same figure.

WALSALL COLLEGE LRC
WISEMORE CAMPUS
LITTLETON STREET WEST
WALSALL
WS2 8ES

FIGURE 5.9 Our internetwork

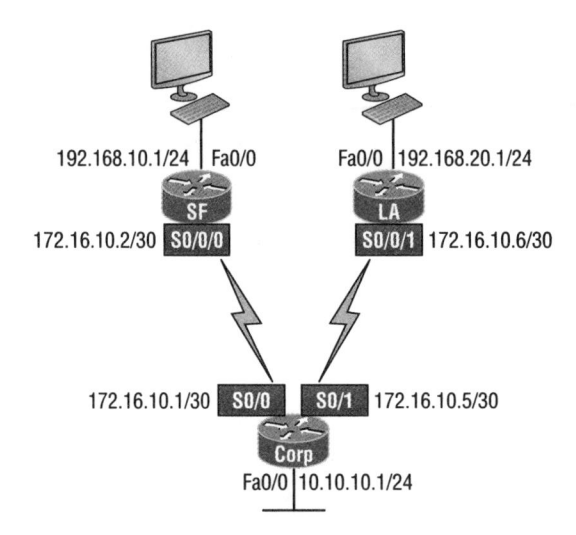

Corp

Each routing table automatically includes directly connected networks. To be able to route to all indirectly connected networks within the internetwork, the routing table must include information that describes where these other networks are located and how to get to them.

The Corp router is connected to three networks. For the Corp router to be able to route to all networks, the following networks have to be configured into its routing table:

- 192.168.10.0
- 192.168.20.0

The next router output shows the static routes on the Corp router and the routing table after the configuration. For the Corp router to find the remote networks, I had to place an entry into the routing table describing the remote network, the remote mask, and where to send the packets. I'm going to add a 150 at the end of each line to raise the administrative distance. You'll see why soon when we get to dynamic routing. Many times this is also referred to as a *floating static route* because the static route has a higher administrative distance than any routing protocol and will only be used if the routes found with the routing protocols (lower AD) go down. Here's the output:

```
Corp#config t
Corp(config)#ip route 192.168.10.0 255.255.255.0 172.16.10.2 150
Corp(config)#ip route 192.168.20.0 255.255.255.0 s0/1 150
Corp(config)#do show run | begin ip route
ip route 192.168.10.0 255.255.255.0 172.16.10.2 150
ip route 192.168.20.0 255.255.255.0 Serial0/1 150
```

I needed to use different paths for networks 192.168.10.0 and 192.168.20.0, so I used a next-hop address for the SF router and an exit interface for the LA router. After the router has been configured, you can just type **show ip route** to see the static routes:

```
Corp(config)#do show ip route
S 192.168.10.0/24 [150/0] via 172.16.10.2
    172.16.0.0/30 is subnetted, 2 subnets
C   172.16.10.4 is directly connected, Serial0/1
L   172.16.10.5/32 is directly connected, Serial0/1
C   172.16.10.0 is directly connected, Serial0/0
L   172.16.10.1/32 is directly connected, Serial0/0
S 192.168.20.0/24 is directly connected, Serial0/1
    10.0.0.0/24 is subnetted, 1 subnets
C   10.10.10.0 is directly connected, FastEthernet0/0
L   10.10.10.1/32 is directly connected, FastEthernet0/0
```

The Corp router is configured to route and know all routes to all networks. But can you see a difference in the routing table for the routes to SF and LA? That's right! The next-hop configuration showed up as via, and the route configured with an exit interface configuration shows up as static but also as directly connected! This demonstrates how they are functionally the same but will display differently in the routing table.

Understand that if the routes don't appear in the routing table, it's because the router can't communicate with the next-hop address you've configured. But you can still use the permanent parameter to keep the route in the routing table even if the next-hop device can't be contacted.

The S in the first routing table entry means that the route is a static entry. The [150/0] stands for the administrative distance and the metric to the remote network, respectively.

Okay—we're good. The Corp router now has all the information it needs to communicate with the other remote networks. Still, keep in mind that if the SF and LA routers aren't configured with all the same information, the packets will be discarded. We can fix this by configuring static routes.

> **NOTE** Don't stress about the 150 at the end of the static route configuration at all, because I promise to get to it really soon in *this* chapter, not a later one! You really don't need to worry about it at this point.

SF

The SF router is directly connected to networks 172.16.10.0/30 and 192.168.10.0/24, which means I've got to configure the following static routes on the SF router:

- 10.10.10.0/24
- 192.168.20.0/24
- 172.16.10.4/30

The configuration for the SF router is revealed in the following output. Remember that we'll never create a static route to any network we're directly connected to as well as the fact that we must use the next hop of 172.16.10.1 since that's our only router connection. Let's check out the commands:

```
SF(config)#ip route 10.10.10.0 255.255.255.0 172.16.10.1 150
SF(config)#ip route 172.16.10.4 255.255.255.252 172.16.10.1 150
SF(config)#ip route 192.168.20.0 255.255.255.0 172.16.10.1 150
SF(config)#do show run | begin ip route
ip route 10.10.10.0 255.255.255.0 172.16.10.1 150
ip route 172.16.10.4 255.255.255.252 172.16.10.1 150
ip route 192.168.20.0 255.255.255.0 172.16.10.1 150
```

By looking at the routing table, you can see that the SF router now understands how to find each network:

```
SF(config)#do show ip route
C 192.168.10.0/24 is directly connected, FastEthernet0/0
L 192.168.10.1/32 is directly connected, FastEthernet0/0
172.16.0.0/30 is subnetted, 3 subnets
S 172.16.10.4 [150/0] via 172.16.10.1
C 172.16.10.0 is directly connected, Serial0/0/0
L 172.16.10.2/32 is directly connected, Serial0/0
S 192.168.20.0/24 [150/0] via 172.16.10.1
10.0.0.0/24 is subnetted, 1 subnets
S 10.10.10.0 [150/0] via 172.16.10.1
```

And we now can rest assured that the SF router has a complete routing table as well. As soon as the LA router has all the networks in its routing table, SF will be able to communicate with all remote networks.

LA

The LA router is directly connected to 192.168.20.0/24 and 172.16.10.4/30, so these are the routes that must be added:

- 10.10.10.0/24
- 172.16.10.0/30
- 192.168.10.0/24

And here's the LA router's configuration:

```
LA#config t
LA(config)#ip route 10.10.10.0 255.255.255.0 172.16.10.5 150
LA(config)#ip route 172.16.10.0 255.255.255.252 172.16.10.5 150
LA(config)#ip route 192.168.10.0 255.255.255.0 172.16.10.5 150
```

```
LA(config)#do show run | begin ip route
ip route 10.10.10.0 255.255.255.0 172.16.10.5 150
ip route 172.16.10.0 255.255.255.252 172.16.10.5 150
ip route 192.168.10.0 255.255.255.0 172.16.10.5 150
```

This output displays the routing table on the LA router:

```
LA(config)#do sho ip route
S    192.168.10.0/24 [150/0] via 172.16.10.5
     172.16.0.0/30 is subnetted, 3 subnets
C       172.16.10.4 is directly connected, Serial0/0/1
L       172.16.10.6/32 is directly connected, Serial0/0/1
S       172.16.10.0 [150/0] via 172.16.10.5
C    192.168.20.0/24 is directly connected, FastEthernet0/0
L    192.168.20.1/32 is directly connected, FastEthernet0/0
     10.0.0.0/24 is subnetted, 1 subnets
S       10.10.10.0 [150/0] via 172.16.10.5
```

LA now shows all five networks in the internetwork, so it too can now communicate with all routers and networks. But before we test our little network, as well as our DHCP server, let's cover one more topic.

Default Routing

The SF and LA routers that I've connected to the Corp router are considered stub routers. A *stub* indicates that the networks in this design have only one way out to reach all other networks, which means that instead of creating multiple static routes, we can just use a single default route. This default route is used by IP to forward any packet with a destination not found in the routing table, which is why it is also called a gateway of last resort. Here's the configuration I could have done on the LA router instead of typing in the static routes due to its stub status:

```
LA#config t
LA(config)#no ip route 10.10.10.0 255.255.255.0 172.16.10.5 150
LA(config)#no ip route 172.16.10.0 255.255.255.252 172.16.10.5 150
LA(config)#no ip route 192.168.10.0 255.255.255.0 172.16.10.5 150
LA(config)#ip route 0.0.0.0 0.0.0.0 172.16.10.5
LA(config)#do sho ip route
[output cut]
Gateway of last resort is 172.16.10.5 to network 0.0.0.0
     172.16.0.0/30 is subnetted, 1 subnets
C       172.16.10.4 is directly connected, Serial0/0/1
L       172.16.10.6/32 is directly connected, Serial0/0/1
```

```
C    192.168.20.0/24 is directly connected, FastEthernet0/0
L    192.168.20.0/32 is directly connected, FastEthernet0/0
S*   0.0.0.0/0 [1/0] via 172.16.10.5
```

Okay—I've removed all the initial static routes I had configured, and adding a default route sure is a lot easier than typing a bunch of static routes! Can you see the default route listed last in the routing table? The S* shows that as a candidate for the default route. And I really want you to notice that the gateway of last resort is now set too. Everything the router receives with a destination not found in the routing table will be forwarded to 172.16.10.5. You need to be really careful where you place default routes because you can easily create a network loop!

So we're there—we've configured all our routing tables. All the routers have the correct routing table, so all routers and hosts should be able to communicate without a hitch—for now. But if you add even one more network or another router to the internetwork, you'll have to update each and every router's routing tables by hand—ugh! Not really a problem at all if you've got a small network like we do, but the task would be a monster when dealing with a large internetwork!

Verifying Your Configuration

We're still not done yet—once all the routers' routing tables are configured, they must be verified. The best way to do this, besides using the show ip route command, is via Ping. I'll start by pinging from the Corp router to the SF router.

Here's the output I got:

```
Corp#ping 192.168.10.1
Type escape sequence to abort.
Sending 5, 100-byte ICMP Echos to 192.168.10.1, timeout is 2 seconds:
!!!!!
Success rate is 100 percent (5/5), round-trip min/avg/max = 4/4/4 ms
Corp#
```

Here you can see that I pinged from the Corp router to the remote interface of the SF router. Now let's ping the remote network on the LA router, and after that, we'll test our DHCP server and see if that is working too:

```
Corp#ping 192.168.20.1
Type escape sequence to abort.
Sending 5, 100-byte ICMP Echos to 192.168.20.1, timeout is 2 seconds:
!!!!!
Success rate is 100 percent (5/5), round-trip min/avg/max = 1/2/4 ms
Corp#
```

And why not test my configuration of the DHCP server on the Corp router while we're at it? I'm going to go to each host on the SF and LA routers and make them DHCP clients.

By the way, I'm using an old router to represent "hosts," which just happens to work great for studying purposes. Here's how I did that:

```
SF_PC(config)#int e0
SF_PC(config-if)#ip address dhcp
SF_PC(config-if)#no shut
Interface Ethernet0 assigned DHCP address 192.168.10.8, mask 255.255.255.0
LA_PC(config)#int e0
LA_PC(config-if)#ip addr dhcp
LA_PC(config-if)#no shut
Interface Ethernet0 assigned DHCP address 192.168.20.4, mask 255.255.255.0
```

Nice! Don't you love it when things just work the first time? Sadly, this just isn't exactly a realistic expectation in the networking world, so we must be able to troubleshoot and verify our networks. Let's verify our DHCP server with a few handy commands:

```
Corp#sh ip dhcp binding
Bindings from all pools not associated with VRF:
IP address Client-ID/ Lease expiration Type
Hardware address/
User name
192.168.10.8 0063.6973.636f.2d30. Sept 16 2013 10:34 AM Automatic
3035.302e.3062.6330.
2e30.3063.632d.4574.
30
192.168.20.4 0063.6973.636f.2d30. Sept 16 2013 10:46 AM Automatic
3030.322e.3137.3632.
2e64.3032.372d.4574.
30
```

We can see from earlier that our little DHCP server is working! Let's try another couple of commands:

```
Corp#sh ip dhcp pool SF_LAN
Pool SF_LAN :
 Utilization mark (high/low) : 100 / 0
 Subnet size (first/next) : 0 / 0
 Total addresses : 254
 Leased addresses : 3
 Pending event : none
 1 subnet is currently in the pool :
 Current index IP address range Leased addresses
 192.168.10.9 192.168.10.1 - 192.168.10.254 3
Corp#sh ip dhcp conflict
IP address Detection method Detection time VRF
```

The last command would tell us if we had two hosts with the same IP address, so it's good news because there are no conflicts reported. Two detection methods are used to confirm this:

- A ping from the DHCP server to make sure no other host responds before handing out an address
- A gratuitous ARP from a host that receives a DHCP address from the server

The DHCP client will send an ARP request with its new IP address looking to see if anyone responds, and if so, it will report the conflict to the server.

Since we can communicate from end to end and to each host without a problem while receiving DHCP addresses from our server, I'd say our static and default route configurations have been a success—cheers!

Dynamic Routing

Dynamic routing is when protocols are used to find networks and update routing tables on routers. This is whole lot easier than using static or default routing, but it will cost you in terms of router CPU processing and bandwidth on network links. A routing protocol defines the set of rules used by a router when it communicates routing information between neighboring routers.

The routing protocol I'm going to talk about in this chapter is Routing Information Protocol (RIP) versions 1 and 2.

Two types of routing protocols are used in internetworks: *interior gateway protocols (IGPs)* and *exterior gateway protocols (EGPs)*. IGPs are used to exchange routing information with routers in the same *autonomous system (AS)*. An AS is either a single network or a collection of networks under a common administrative domain, which basically means that all routers sharing the same routing-table information are in the same AS. EGPs are used to communicate between ASs. An example of an EGP is Border Gateway Protocol (BGP), which we're not going to bother with because it's beyond the scope of this book.

Since routing protocols are so essential to dynamic routing, I'm going to give you the basic information you need to know about them next. Later on in this chapter, we'll focus on configuration.

Routing Protocol Basics

There are some important things you should know about routing protocols before we get deeper into RIP routing. Being familiar with administrative distances and the three different kinds of routing protocols, for example. Let's take a look.

Administrative Distances

The *administrative distance (AD)* is used to rate the trustworthiness of routing information received on a router from a neighbor router. An administrative distance is an integer from 0 to 255, where 0 is the most trusted and 255 means no traffic will be passed via this route.

If a router receives two updates listing the same remote network, the first thing the router checks is the AD. If one of the advertised routes has a lower AD than the other, then the route with the lowest AD will be chosen and placed in the routing table.

If both advertised routes to the same network have the same AD, then routing protocol metrics like *hop count* and/or the bandwidth of the lines will be used to find the best path to the remote network. The advertised route with the lowest metric will be placed in the routing table, but if both advertised routes have the same AD as well as the same metrics, then the routing protocol will load-balance to the remote network, meaning the protocol will send data down each link.

Table 5.1 shows the default administrative distances that a Cisco router uses to decide which route to take to a remote network.

TABLE 5.1 Default administrative distances

Route Source	Default AD
Connected interface	0
Static route	1
External BGP	20
EIGRP	90
OSPF	110
RIP	120
External EIGRP	170
Internal BGP	200
Unknown	255 (This route will never be used.)

If a network is directly connected, the router will always use the interface connected to the network. If you configure a static route, the router will then believe that route over any other ones it learns about. You can change the administrative distance of static routes, but by default, they have an AD of 1. In our previous static route configuration, the AD of each route is set at 150. This AD allows us to configure routing protocols without having to remove the static routes because it's nice to have them there for backup in case the routing protocol experiences some kind of failure.

If you have a static route, an RIP-advertised route, and an EIGRP-advertised route listing the same network, which route will the router go with? That's right—by default, the router will always use the static route unless you change its AD—which we did!

Routing Protocols

There are three classes of routing protocols:

Distance vector   The distance-vector protocols in use today find the best path to a remote network by judging distance. In RIP routing, each instance where a packet goes through a router is called a hop, and the route with the least number of hops to the network will be chosen as the best one. The vector indicates the direction to the remote network. RIP is a distance-vector routing protocol and periodically sends out the entire routing table to directly connected neighbors.

Link state   In link-state protocols, also called shortest-path-first (SPF) protocols, the routers each create three separate tables. One of these tables keeps track of directly attached neighbors, one determines the topology of the entire internetwork, and one is used as the routing table. Link-state routers know more about the internetwork than any distance-vector routing protocol ever could. OSPF is an IP routing protocol that's completely link-state. Link-state routing tables are not exchanged periodically. Instead, triggered updates containing only specific link-state information are sent. Periodic keepalives in the form of hello messages, which are small and efficient, are exchanged between directly connected neighbors to establish and maintain neighbor relationships.

Advanced distance vector   Advanced distance-vector protocols use aspects of both distance-vector and link-state protocols, and EIGRP is a great example. EIGRP may act like a link-state routing protocol because it uses a Hello protocol to discover neighbors and form neighbor relationships and because only partial updates are sent when a change occurs. However, EIGRP is still based on the key distance-vector routing protocol principle that information about the rest of the network is learned from directly connected neighbors.

There's no fixed set of rules to follow that dictate exactly how to broadly configure routing protocols for every situation. It's a task that really must be undertaken on a case-by-case basis, with an eye on specific requirements of each one. If you understand how the different routing protocols work, you can make great decisions that will solidly meet the individual needs of any business!

Routing Information Protocol (RIP)

Routing Information Protocol (RIP) is a true distance-vector routing protocol. RIP sends the complete routing table out of all active interfaces every 30 seconds. It relies on hop count to determine the best way to a remote network, but it has a maximum allowable hop count of 15 by default, so a destination of 16 would be considered unreachable. RIP works okay in very small networks, but it's super inefficient on large networks with slow WAN links or on networks with a large number of routers installed. It's completely useless on networks that have links with variable bandwidths!

RIP version 1 uses only *classful routing*, which means that all devices in the network must use the same subnet mask. This is because RIP version 1 doesn't send updates with subnet mask information in tow. RIP version 2 provides something called *prefix routing* and does send subnet mask information with its route updates. This is called *classless routing*.

So with that, let's configure our current network with RIPv2.

Configuring RIP Routing

To configure RIP routing, just turn on the protocol with the router rip command and tell the RIP routing protocol the networks to advertise. Remember that with static routing, we always configured remote networks and never typed a route to our directly connected networks? Well, dynamic routing is carried out the complete opposite way. You would never type a *remote* network under your routing protocol—only enter your directly connected networks! Let's configure our three-router internetwork, revisited in Figure 5.9, with RIP routing.

Corp

RIP has an administrative distance of 120. Static routes have an AD of 1 by default, and since we currently have static routes configured, the routing tables won't be populated with RIP information by default. We're still good though because I added the 150 to the end of each static route.

You can add the RIP routing protocol by using the router rip command and the network command. The network command tells the routing protocol which classful network to advertise. By doing this, you're activating the RIP routing process on the interfaces whose addressing falls within the specified classful networks configured with the network command under the RIP routing process.

Look at the Corp router configuration to see how easy this is. Oh wait—first, I want to verify my directly connected networks so I know what to configure RIP with:

```
Corp#sh ip int brief
Interface IP-Address OK? Method Status Protocol
FastEthernet0/0 10.10.10.1 YES manual up up
Serial0/0 172.16.10.1 YES manual up up
FastEthernet0/1 unassigned YES unset administratively down down
Serial0/1 172.16.10.5 YES manual up up

Corp#config t
Corp(config)#router rip
Corp(config-router)#network 10.0.0.0
Corp(config-router)#network 172.16.0.0
Corp(config-router)#version 2
Corp(config-router)#no auto-summary
```

That's it—really! Typically just two or three commands and you're done, which sure makes your job a lot easier than dealing with static routes, doesn't it? Be sure to keep in mind the extra router CPU process and bandwidth that you're consuming.

Anyway, so what exactly did I do here? I enabled the RIP routing protocol, added my directly connected networks, made sure I was only running RIPv2, which is a classless routing protocol, and then I disabled auto-summary. We typically don't want our routing protocols summarizing for us because it's better to do that manually and both RIP and EIGRP (before 15.x code) auto-summarize by default. So a general rule of thumb is to disable auto-summary, which allows them to advertise subnets.

Notice I didn't type in subnets, only the classful network address, which is betrayed by the fact that all subnet bits and host bits are off! That's because with dynamic routing, it's not my job—it's up to the routing protocol to find the subnets and populate the routing tables. And since we have no router buddies running RIP, we won't see any RIP routes in the routing table yet.

> Remember that RIP uses the classful address when configuring the network address. To clarify this, refer to the example in our network with an address of 172.16.0.0/24 using subnets 172.16.10.0 and 172.16.20.0. You would only type in the classful network address of 172.16.0.0 and let RIP find the subnets and place them in the routing table. This doesn't mean you are running a classful routing protocol—it's just the way that both RIP and EIGRP are configured.

SF

Let's configure our SF router now, which is connected to two networks. We need to configure both directly connected classful networks, not subnets:

```
SF#sh ip int brief
Interface IP-Address OK? Method Status Protocol
FastEthernet0/0 192.168.10.1 YES manual up up
FastEthernet0/1 unassigned YES unset administratively down down
Serial0/0/0 172.16.10.2 YES manual up up
Serial0/0/1 unassigned YES unset administratively down down
SF#config
SF(config)#router rip
SF(config-router)#network 192.168.10.0
SF(config-router)#network 172.16.0.0
SF(config-router)#version 2
SF(config-router)#no auto-summary
SF(config-router)#do show ip route
C 192.168.10.0/24 is directly connected, FastEthernet0/0
L 192.168.10.1/32 is directly connected, FastEthernet0/0
```

```
172.16.0.0/30 is subnetted, 3 subnets
R    172.16.10.4 [120/1] via 172.16.10.1, 00:00:08, Serial0/0/0
C    172.16.10.0 is directly connected, Serial0/0/0
L    172.16.10.2/32 is directly connected, Serial0/0
S    192.168.20.0/24 [150/0] via 172.16.10.1
     10.0.0.0/24 is subnetted, 1 subnets
R    10.10.10.0 [120/1] via 172.16.10.1, 00:00:08, Serial0/0/0
```

That was pretty straightforward. Let's talk about this routing table... Since we have one RIP buddy out there with whom we are exchanging routing tables, we can see the RIP networks coming from the Corp router. All the other routes still show up as static and local. RIP also found both connections through the Corp router to networks 10.10.10.0 and 172.16.10.4. But we're not done yet!

LA

Let's configure our LA router with RIP, only I'm going to remove the default route first, even though I don't have to. You'll see why soon:

```
LA#config t
LA(config)#no ip route 0.0.0.0 0.0.0.0
LA(config)#router rip
LA(config-router)#network 192.168.20.0
LA(config-router)#network 172.16.0.0
LA(config-router)#no auto
LA(config-router)#vers 2
LA(config-router)#do show ip route
R    192.168.10.0/24 [120/2] via 172.16.10.5, 00:00:10, Serial0/0/1
     172.16.0.0/30 is subnetted, 3 subnets
C    172.16.10.4 is directly connected, Serial0/0/1
L    172.16.10.6/32 is directly connected, Serial0/0/1
R    172.16.10.0 [120/1] via 172.16.10.5, 00:00:10, Serial0/0/1
C    192.168.20.0/24 is directly connected, FastEthernet0/0
L    192.168.20.1/32 is directly connected, FastEthernet0/0
     10.0.0.0/24 is subnetted, 1 subnets
R    10.10.10.0 [120/1] via 172.16.10.5, 00:00:10, Serial0/0/1
```

The routing table is sprouting new R's as we add RIP buddies! We can still see that all routes are in the routing table.

This output shows us basically the same routing table and the same entries that it had when we were using static routes—except for those R's. An R indicates that the networks were added dynamically using the RIP routing protocol. The [120/1] is the administrative distance of the route (120) along with the metric, which for RIP is the number of hops to that remote network (1). From the Corp router, all networks are one hop away.

So, while yes, it's true that RIP has worked in our little internetwork, it's just not a great solution for most enterprises. Its maximum hop count of only 15 is a highly limiting factor. And it performs full routing-table updates every 30 seconds, which would bring a larger internetwork to a crawl in no time!

There's still one more thing I want to show you about RIP routing tables and the parameters used to advertise remote networks. Using a different router on a different network as an example for a second, look into the following output. Can you spot where the following routing table shows [120/15] in the 10.1.3.0 network metric? This means that the administrative distance is 120, the default for RIP, but the hop count is 15. Remember that each time a router sends out an update to a neighbor router, the hop count goes up by one incrementally for each route. Here's that output now:

```
Router#sh ip route
10.0.0.0/24 is subnetted, 12 subnets
C    10.1.11.0 is directly connected, FastEthernet0/1
L    10.1.11.1/32 is directly connected, FastEthernet0/1
C    10.1.10.0 is directly connected, FastEthernet0/0
L    10.1.10.1/32 is directly connected, FastEthernet/0/0
R    10.1.9.0 [120/2] via 10.1.5.1, 00:00:15, Serial0/0/1
R    10.1.8.0 [120/2] via 10.1.5.1, 00:00:15, Serial0/0/1
R    10.1.12.0 [120/1] via 10.1.11.2, 00:00:00, FastEthernet0/1
R    10.1.3.0 [120/15] via 10.1.5.1, 00:00:15, Serial0/0/1
R    10.1.2.0 [120/1] via 10.1.5.1, 00:00:15, Serial0/0/1
R    10.1.1.0 [120/1] via 10.1.5.1, 00:00:15, Serial0/0/1
R    10.1.7.0 [120/2] via 10.1.5.1, 00:00:15, Serial0/0/1
R    10.1.6.0 [120/2] via 10.1.5.1, 00:00:15, Serial0/0/1
C    10.1.5.0 is directly connected, Serial0/0/1
L    10.1.5.1/32 is directly connected, Serial0/0/1
R    10.1.4.0 [120/1] via 10.1.5.1, 00:00:15, Serial0/0/1
```

So this [120/15] is really bad. We're basically doomed because the next router that receives the table from this router will just discard the route to network 10.1.3.0 since the hop count would rise to 16, which is invalid!

> If a router receives a routing update that contains a higher-cost path to a network that's already in its routing table, the update will be ignored.

Holding Down RIP Propagations

You probably don't want your RIP network advertised everywhere on your LAN and WAN. There's enough stress in networking already and not much to be gained by advertising your RIP network to the Internet!

There are a few different ways to stop unwanted RIP updates from propagating across your LANs and WANs, and the easiest one is through the `passive-interface` command. This command prevents RIP update broadcasts from being sent out of a specified interface but still allows that same interface to receive RIP updates.

Here's an example of how to configure a `passive-interface` on the Corp router's Fa0/1 interface, which we will pretend is connected to a LAN that we don't want RIP on (and the interface isn't shown in the figure):

```
Corp#config t
Corp(config)#router rip
Corp(config-router)#passive-interface FastEthernet 0/1
```

This command will prevent RIP updates from being propagated out of FastEthernet interface 0/1, but it can still receive RIP updates.

> ### Real World Scenario
>
> **Should We Really Use RIP in an Internetwork?**
>
> You have been hired as a consultant to install a couple of Cisco routers into a growing network. They have a couple of old Unix routers that they want to keep in the network. These routers do not support any routing protocol except RIP. I guess this means you just have to run RIP on the entire network. If you were balding before, your head now shines like chrome.
>
> No need for hairs abandoning ship though—you can run RIP on a router connecting that old network, but you certainly don't need to run RIP throughout the whole internetwork.
>
> You can do something called *redistribution*, which is basically translating from one type of routing protocol to another. This means that you can support those old routers using RIP but use something much better like Enhanced IGRP on the rest of your network.
>
> This will prevent RIP routes from being sent all over the internetwork gobbling up all that precious bandwidth!

Advertising a Default Route Using RIP

Now I'm going to guide you through how to advertise a way out of your autonomous system to other routers, and you'll see this is completed the same way with OSPF.

Imagine that our Corp router's Fa0/0 interface is connected to some type of Metro-Ethernet as a connection to the Internet. This is a pretty common configuration today that uses a LAN interface to connect to the ISP instead of a serial interface.

If we do add an Internet connection to Corp, all routers in our AS (SF and LA) must know where to send packets destined for networks on the Internet or they'll just drop the packets when they get a remote request. One solution to this little hitch would be to place a default route on every router and funnel the information to Corp, which in turn would have a default route to the ISP. Most people do this type of configuration in small- to medium-size networks because it actually works pretty well!

But since I'm running RIPv2 on all routers, I'll just add a default route on the Corp router to our ISP, as I would normally. I'll then add another command to advertise my network to the other routers in the AS as the default route to show them where to send packets destined for the Internet.

Here's my new Corp configuration:

```
Corp(config)#ip route 0.0.0.0 0.0.0.0 fa0/0
Corp(config)#router rip
Corp(config-router)#default-information originate
```

Now, let's take a look at the last entry found in the Corp routing table:

```
S* 0.0.0.0/0 is directly connected, FastEthernet0/0
```

Let's see if the LA router can see this same entry:

```
LA#sh ip route
Gateway of last resort is 172.16.10.5 to network 0.0.0.0
R   192.168.10.0/24 [120/2] via 172.16.10.5, 00:00:04, Serial0/0/1
    172.16.0.0/30 is subnetted, 2 subnets
C   172.16.10.4 is directly connected, Serial0/0/1
L   172.16.10.5/32 is directly connected, Serial0/0/1
R   172.16.10.0 [120/1] via 172.16.10.5, 00:00:04, Serial0/0/1
C   192.168.20.0/24 is directly connected, FastEthernet0/0
L   192.168.20.1/32 is directly connected, FastEthernet0/0
    10.0.0.0/24 is subnetted, 1 subnets
R   10.10.10.0 [120/1] via 172.16.10.5, 00:00:04, Serial0/0/1
R   192.168.218.0/24 [120/3] via 172.16.10.5, 00:00:04, Serial0/0/1
R   192.168.118.0/24 [120/2] via 172.16.10.5, 00:00:05, Serial0/0/1
R*  0.0.0.0/0 [120/1] via 172.16.10.5, 00:00:05, Serial0/0/1
```

Can you see that last entry? It screams that it's an RIP injected route, but it's also a default route, so our `default-information originate` command is working! Last, notice that the gateway of last resort is now set as well.

Everyone understands that we won't use RIP of any type in a production network today if at all possible. Which is why our next chapter will feature the CCNA star routing protocol, OSPF.

Summary

This chapter covered IP routing in detail. Again, it's extremely important to fully understand the basics we covered in this chapter because everything that's done on a Cisco router will typically have some kind of IP routing configured and running.

You learned how IP routing uses frames to transport packets between routers and to the destination host. From there, we configured static routing on our routers and discussed the administrative distance used by IP to determine the best route to a destination network. You found out that if you have a stub network, you can configure default routing, which sets the gateway of last resort on a router.

We then discussed dynamic routing, specifically RIPv2. You learned how it works on an enterprise, which is not very well!

Exam Essentials

Describe the basic IP routing process. You need to remember that the layer-2 frame changes at each hop but that the packet is never changed or manipulated in any way until it reaches the destination device (the TTL field in the IP header is decremented for each hop, but that's it!).

List the information required by a router to successfully route packets. To be able to route packets, a router must know, at a minimum, the destination address, the location of neighboring routers through which it can reach remote networks, possible routes to all remote networks, the best route to each remote network, and how to maintain and verify routing information.

Describe how MAC addresses are used during the routing process. A MAC (hardware) address will only be used on a local LAN. It will never pass a router's interface. A frame uses MAC (hardware) addresses to send a packet on a LAN. The frame will take the packet to either a host on the LAN or a router's interface (if the packet is destined for a remote network). As packets move from one router to another, the MAC addresses used will change, but normally the original source and destination IP addresses within the packet will not.

View and interpret the routing table of a router. Use the show ip route command to view the routing table. Each route will be listed along with the source of the routing information. A C to the left of the route will indicate directly connected routes, and other letters next to the route can also indicate a particular routing protocol that provided the information, such as, for example, R for RIP.

Differentiate the three types of routing. The three types of routing are static (in which routes are manually configured at the CLI), dynamic (in which the routers share routing information via a routing protocol), and default routing (in which a special route is configured for all traffic without a more specific destination network found in the table).

Compare and contrast static and dynamic routing. Static routing creates no routing update traffic and creates less overhead on the router and network links, but it must be configured manually and does not have the ability to react to link outages. Dynamic routing creates routing update traffic and uses more overhead on the router and network links.

Configure static routes at the CLI. The command syntax to add a route is `ip route` [destination_network] [mask] [next-hop_address or exitinterface] [administrative_distance] [permanent].

Create a default route. To add a default route, use the command syntax `ip route 0.0.0.0 0.0.0.0` *ip-address* or `exit interface type and number`.

Understand administrative distance and its role in the selection of the best route. Administrative distance (AD) is used to rate the trustworthiness of routing information received on a router from a neighbor router. Administrative distance is an integer from 0 to 255, where 0 is the most trusted and 255 means no traffic will be passed via this route. All routing protocols are assigned a default AD, but it can be changed at the CLI.

Differentiate distance-vector, link-state, and hybrid routing protocols. Distance-vector routing protocols make routing decisions based on hop count (think RIP), while link-state routing protocols are able to consider multiple factors such as bandwidth available and building a topology table. Hybrid routing protocols exhibit characteristics of both types.

Configure RIPv2 routing. To configure RIP routing, first you must be in global configuration mode and then you type the command `router rip`. Then you add all directly connected networks, making sure to use the classful address and the `version 2` command and to disable auto-summarization with the `no auto-summary` command.

Review Questions

You can find the answers to these questions in the Appendix.

1. What command was used to generate the following output?
   ```
   Codes: L - local, C - connected, S - static,
   [output cut]
   10.0.0.0/8 is variably subnetted, 6 subnets, 4 masks
   C 10.0.0.0/8 is directly connected, FastEthernet0/3
   L 10.0.0.1/32 is directly connected, FastEthernet0/3
   C 10.10.0.0/16 is directly connected, FastEthernet0/2
   L 10.10.0.1/32 is directly connected, FastEthernet0/2
   C 10.10.10.0/24 is directly connected, FastEthernet0/1
   L 10.10.10.1/32 is directly connected, FastEthernet0/1
   S* 0.0.0.0/0 is directly connected, FastEthernet0/0
   ```
   A. show routing table
   B. show route
   C. Show ip route
   D. Show all route

2. You are viewing the routing table and you see an entry 10.1.1.1/32. What legend code would you expect to see next to this route?
   A. C
   B. L
   C. S
   D. D

3. Which of the following statements are true regarding the command ip route 172.16.4.0 255.255.255.0 192.168.4.2? (Choose two.)
   A. The command is used to establish a static route.
   B. The default administrative distance is used.
   C. The command is used to configure the default route.
   D. The subnet mask for the source address is 255.255.255.0.
   E. The command is used to establish a stub network.

4. Using the output shown, what protocol was used to learn the MAC address for 172.16.10.1?
   ```
   Interface: 172.16.10.2 --- 0x3
   Internet Address Physical Address Type
   172.16.10.1 00-15-05-06-31-b0 dynamic
   ```
   A. ICMP
   B. ARP
   C. TCP
   D. UDP

5. Which of the following is called an advanced distance-vector routing protocol?
   A. OSPF
   B. EIGRP
   C. BGP
   D. RIP

6. When a packet is routed across a network, the _____ in the packet changes at every hop while the _____ does not.
   A. MAC address, IP address
   B. IP address, MAC address
   C. Port number, IP address
   D. IP address, port number

7. When a router looks up the destination in the routing table for every single packet, it is called _____.
   A. dynamic switching
   B. fast switching
   C. process switching
   D. Cisco Express Forwarding

8. What type(s) of route is the following? (Choose all that apply.)
   `S* 0.0.0.0/0 [1/0] via 172.16.10.5`
   A. Default
   B. Subnetted
   C. Static
   D. Local

9. A network administrator views the output from the `show ip route` command. A network that is advertised by both RIP and OSPF appears in the routing table flagged as an OSPF route. Why is the RIP route to this network not used in the routing table?
   A. OSPF has a faster update timer.
   B. OSPF has a lower administrative distance.
   C. RIP has a higher metric value for that route.
   D. The OSPF route has fewer hops.
   E. The RIP path has a routing loop.

10. Which of the following is *not* an advantage of static routing?
    A. Less overhead on the router CPU
    B. No bandwidth usage between routers
    C. Adds security
    D. Recovers automatically from lost routes

Chapter 6

Open Shortest Path First (OSPF)

THE FOLLOWING CCNA EXAM TOPICS ARE COVERED IN THIS CHAPTER:

3.0 IP Connectivity

✓ **3.4 Configure and verify single area OSPFv2**

- 3.4.a Neighbor adjacencies
- 3.4.b Point-to-point
- 3.4.c Broadcast (DR/BDR selection)
- 3.4.d Router ID

Open Shortest Path First (OSPF) is by far the most popular and important routing protocol in use today—so important, I'm devoting an entire chapter to it! Sticking with the same approach we've taken throughout this book, we'll begin with the basics by completely familiarizing you with key OSPF terminology. Once we've covered that thoroughly, I'll guide you through OSPF's internal operation and then move on to tell you all about OSPF's many advantages over RIP.

This chapter isn't just going to be chock full of vitally important information, it's also going to be really exciting because together, we'll explore some critical factors and issues innate to implementing OSPF. I'll walk you through exactly how to implement single-area OSPF in a variety of networking environments and then demonstrate some great techniques you'll need to verify that everything is configured correctly and running smoothly.

> **NOTE** To find your included bonus material, as well as Todd Lammle videos, practice questions & hands-on labs, please see www.lammle.com/ccna

Open Shortest Path First (OSPF) Basics

Open Shortest Path First is an open standard routing protocol that's been implemented by a wide variety of network vendors, including Cisco. And it's that open standard characteristic that's the key to OSPF's flexibility and popularity.

Most people opt for OSPF, which works by using the Dijkstra algorithm to initially construct a shortest path tree and follows that by populating the routing table with the resulting best paths. EIGRP's convergence time may be blindingly fast, but OSPF isn't that far behind, and its quick convergence is another reason it's a favorite. Another two great advantages OSPF offers are that it supports multiple, equal-cost routes to the same destination, and like EIGRP, it also supports both IPv4 and IPv6 routed protocols.

Here's a list that summarizes some of OSPF's best features:

- Allows for the creation of areas and autonomous systems
- Minimizes routing update traffic
- Is highly flexible, versatile, and scalable
- Supports VLSM/CIDR
- Offers an unlimited hop count
- Is open standard and supports multi-vendor deployment

Because OSPF is the first link-state routing protocol that most people run into, it's a good idea to size it up against more traditional distance-vector protocols like RIPv2 and RIPv1. Table 6.1 presents a nice comparison of all three of these common protocols.

TABLE 6.1 OSPF and RIP comparison

Characteristic	OSPF	RIPv2	RIPv1
Type of protocol	Link state	Distance vector	Distance vector
Classless support	Yes	Yes	No
VLSM support	Yes	Yes	No
Auto-summarization	No	Yes	Yes
Manual summarization	Yes	Yes	No
Noncontiguous support	Yes	Yes	No
Route propagation	Multicast on change	Periodic multicast	Periodic broadcast
Path metric	Bandwidth	Hops	Hops
Hop count limit	None	15	15
Convergence	Fast	Slow	Slow
Peer authentication	Yes	Yes	No
Hierarchical network requirement	Yes (using areas)	No (flat only)	No (flat only)
Updates	Event triggered	Periodic	Periodic
Route computation	Dijkstra	Bellman-Ford	Bellman-Ford

OSPF has many features beyond the few I've listed in Table 4.1, and all of them combine to produce a fast, scalable, robust protocol that's also flexible enough to be actively deployed in a vast array of production networks.

One of OSPF's most useful traits is that its design is intended to be hierarchical in use, meaning that it allows us to subdivide the larger internetwork into smaller internetworks called areas. It's a really powerful feature that I recommend using, and I'll show you how to do that later in the chapter.

Here are three of the biggest reasons to implement OSPF in a way that makes full use of its intentional, hierarchical design:

- To decrease routing overhead
- To speed up convergence
- To confine network instability to single areas of the network

Because free lunches are invariably hard to come by, all this wonderful functionality predictably comes at a price and doesn't exactly make configuring OSPF any easier. But no worries—we'll crush it!

Let's start by checking out Figure 6.1, which shows a very typical, yet simple OSPF design. I really want to point out the fact that some routers connect to the backbone area called area 0. OSPF absolutely must have an area 0, and all other areas should connect to it except for those connected via virtual links, which are beyond the scope of this book. A router that connects other areas to the backbone area within an AS is called an *area border router (ABR)*, and even these must have at least one of their interfaces connected to area 0.

FIGURE 6.1 OSPF design example. An OSPF hierarchical design minimizes routing table entries and keeps the impact of any topology changes contained within a specific area.

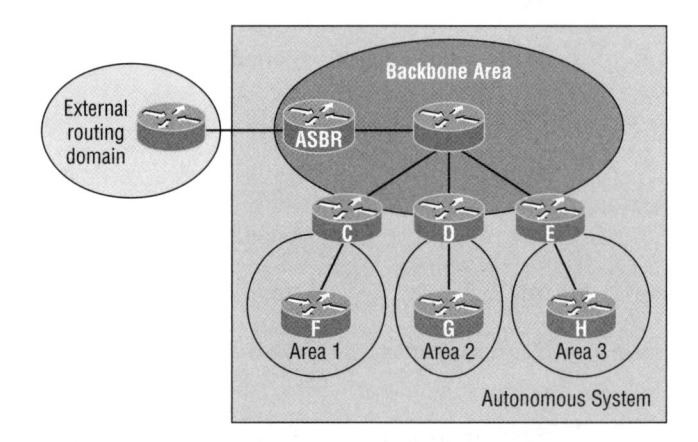

OSPF runs great inside an autonomous system, but it can also connect multiple autonomous systems together. The router that connects these ASs is called an *autonomous system boundary router (ASBR)*. Ideally, you'll want to create other areas of networks to help keep route updates to a minimum, especially in larger networks. Doing this also keeps problems from propagating throughout the network, affectively isolating them to a single area.

So let's take a minute to cover some key OSPF terms that are really essential for you to have down before we move on any further.

OSPF Terminology

Imagine being given a map and compass with no prior concept of east, west, north, or south—not even what rivers, mountains, lakes, or deserts are. I'm guessing that without any ability to orient yourself in a basic way, your cool, new tools wouldn't help you get anywhere but completely lost, right? This is exactly why we're going to begin exploring OSPF by getting you solidly acquainted with a fairly long list of terms before setting out from base camp into the great unknown! Here are those vital terms to commit to memory now:

Link   A *link* is a network or router interface assigned to any given network. When an interface is added to the OSPF process, it's considered to be a link. This link, or interface, will have up or down state information associated with it as well as one or more IP addresses.

Router ID   The *router ID (RID)* is an IP address used to identify the router. Cisco chooses the router ID by using the highest IP address of all configured loopback interfaces. If no loopback interfaces are configured with addresses, OSPF will choose the highest IP address out of all active physical interfaces. To OSPF, this is basically the "name" of each router.

Neighbor   *Neighbors* are two or more routers that have an interface on a common network, such as two routers connected on a point-to-point serial link. OSPF neighbors must have a number of common configuration options to be able to successfully establish a neighbor relationship, and all of these options must be configured exactly the same way:

- Area ID
- Stub area flag
- Authentication password (if using one)
- Hello and Dead intervals

Adjacency   An *adjacency* is a relationship between two OSPF routers that permits the direct exchange of route updates. Unlike EIGRP, which directly shares routes with all of its neighbors, OSPF is really picky about sharing routing information and will directly share routes only with neighbors that have also established adjacencies. And not all neighbors will become adjacent—this depends upon both the type of network and the configuration of the routers. In multi-access networks, routers form adjacencies with designated and backup designated routers. In point-to-point and point-to-multipoint networks, routers form adjacencies with the router on the opposite side of the connection.

Designated router   A *designated router (DR)* is elected whenever OSPF routers are connected to the same broadcast network to minimize the number of adjacencies formed and to publicize received routing information to and from the remaining routers on the broadcast network or link. Elections are won based upon a router's priority level, with the one having the highest priority becoming the winner. If there's a tie, the router ID will be used to break it. All routers on the shared network will establish adjacencies with the DR and the BDR, which ensures that all routers' topology tables are synchronized.

Backup designated router   A *backup designated router (BDR)* is a hot standby for the DR on broadcast, or multi-access, links. The BDR receives all routing updates from OSPF adjacent routers but does not disperse LSA updates.

Hello protocol   The OSPF Hello protocol provides dynamic neighbor discovery and maintains neighbor relationships. Hello packets and Link State Advertisements (LSAs) build and maintain the topological database. Hello packets are addressed to multicast address 224.0.0.5.

Neighborship database The *neighborship database* is a list of all OSPF routers for which Hello packets have been seen. A variety of details, including the router ID and state, are maintained on each router in the neighborship database.

Topological database The *topological database* contains information from all of the Link State Advertisement packets that have been received for an area. The router uses the information from the topology database as input into the Dijkstra algorithm that computes the shortest path to every network.

> LSA packets are used to update and maintain the topological database.

Link State Advertisement A *Link State Advertisement (LSA)* is an OSPF data packet containing link-state and routing information that's shared among OSPF routers. There are different types of LSA packets. An OSPF router will only exchange LSA packets with routers it has established adjacencies for.

OSPF areas An *OSPF area* is a grouping of contiguous networks and routers. All routers in the same area share a common area ID. Because a router can be a member of more than one area at a time, the area ID is associated with specific interfaces on the router. This allows some interfaces to belong to area 1 while the remaining interfaces can belong to area 0. All of the routers within the same area have the same topology table. When configuring OSPF with multiple areas, you've got to remember that there must be an area 0 and that this is typically considered the backbone area. Areas also play a role in establishing a hierarchical network organization—something that really enhances the scalability of OSPF!

Broadcast (multi-access) *Broadcast (multi-access) networks* like Ethernet allow multiple devices to connect to or access the same network, enabling a *broadcast* ability so a single packet can be delivered to all nodes on the network. In OSPF, a DR and BDR must be elected for each broadcast multi-access network.

Nonbroadcast multi-access *Nonbroadcast multi-access (NBMA)* networks like Frame Relay, X.25, and Asynchronous Transfer Mode (ATM) allow for multi-access without broadcast ability like Ethernet. NBMA networks require special OSPF configuration to work.

Point-to-point *Point-to-point* is a type of network topology made up of a direct connection between two routers that provides a single communication path. The point-to-point connection can be physical—for example, a serial cable that directly connects two routers—or logical, where two routers thousands of miles apart are connected by a circuit in a Frame Relay network. Either way, point-to-point configurations eliminate the need for DRs or BDRs.

Point-to-multipoint *Point-to-multipoint* is a network topology made up of a series of connections between a single interface on one router and multiple destination routers.

All interfaces on all routers share the point-to-multipoint connection and belong to the same network. Point-to-multipoint networks can be further classified according to whether they support broadcasts or not. This is important because it defines the kind of OSPF configurations you can deploy.

All of these terms play a critical role when you're trying to understand how OSPF actually works, so again, make sure you're familiar with each of them. Having these terms down will enable you to confidently place them in their proper context as we work through the rest of this chapter.

OSPF Operation

With your newly acquired knowledge of the terms and technologies we just covered, it's now time to get into how OSPF discovers, propagates, and ultimately chooses routes. Once you know how OSPF achieves these tasks, you'll understand how OSPF operates internally really well.

OSPF operation is basically divided into these three categories:

- Neighbor and adjacency initialization
- LSA flooding
- SPF tree calculation

The beginning neighbor/adjacency formation stage is a very big part of OSPF operation. When OSPF is initialized on a router, the router allocates memory for itself, as well as for the maintenance of both neighbor and topology tables. Once the router determines which interfaces have been configured for OSPF, it'll check to see if they're active and begin sending Hello packets as shown in Figure 6.2.

FIGURE 6.2 The Hello protocol

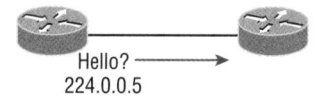

The Hello protocol is used to discover neighbors, establish adjacencies, and maintain relationships with other OSPF routers. Hello packets are periodically sent out of each enabled OSPF interface and in environments that support multicast.

The address used for this is 224.0.0.5, and the frequency with which Hello packets are sent out depends upon the network type and topology. Broadcast and point-to-point networks send Hellos every 10 seconds, but non-broadcast and point-to-multipoint networks send them every 30 seconds.

LSA Flooding

LSA flooding is the method OSPF uses to share routing information. Through Link State Updates (LSU) LSU packets, LSA information containing link-state data is shared with all OSPF routers within an area. The network topology is created from the LSA updates, and flooding is used so that all OSPF routers have the same topology map to make SPF calculations with.

Efficient flooding is achieved through the use of a reserved multicast address: 224.0.0.5 (AllSPFRouters). LSA updates, which indicate that something in the topology has changed, are handled a bit differently. The network type determines the multicast address used for sending updates. Table 6.2 contains the multicast addresses associated with LSA flooding. Point-to-multipoint networks use the adjacent router's unicast IP address.

TABLE 6.2 LSA update multicast addresses

Network Type	Multicast Address	Description
Point-to-point	224.0.0.5	AllSPFRouters
Broadcast	224.0.0.6	AllDRouters
Point-to-multipoint	NA	NA

Once the LSA updates have been flooded throughout the network, each recipient must acknowledge that the flooded update has been received. It's also important for recipients to validate the LSA update.

SPF Tree Calculation

Within an area, each router calculates the best/shortest path to every network in that same area. This calculation is based upon the information collected in the topology database and an algorithm called shortest path first (SPF). Picture each router in an area constructing a tree—much like a family tree—where the router is the root and all other networks are arranged along the branches and leaves. This is the shortest path tree used by the router to insert OSPF routes into the routing table.

Understand that this tree only contains networks that exist in the same area as the router itself does. If a router has interfaces in multiple areas, then separate trees will be constructed for each area. One of the key criteria considered during the route selection process of the SPF algorithm is the metric or cost of each potential path to a network. But this SPF calculation doesn't apply to routes from other areas.

OSPF Metrics

OSPF uses a metric referred to as *cost*. A cost is associated with every outgoing interface included in an SPF tree. The cost of the entire path is the sum of the costs of the outgoing interfaces along the path. Because cost is an arbitrary value as defined in RFC 2338, Cisco had to implement its own method of calculating the cost for each OSPF-enabled interface. Cisco uses a simple equation of $10^8/bandwidth$, where *bandwidth* is the configured bandwidth for the interface. Using this rule, a 100 Mbps Fast Ethernet interface would have a default OSPF cost of 1 and a 1,000 Mbps Ethernet interface would have a cost of 1.

This value can be overridden with the `ip ospf cost` command. The cost is adjusted by changing the value to a number within the range of 1 to 65,535. Because the cost is assigned to each link, the value must be changed on the specific interface you want to change the cost on.

> Cisco bases link cost on bandwidth. Other vendors may use other metrics to calculate a given link's cost. When connecting links between routers from different vendors, you'll probably have to adjust the cost to match another vendor's router because both routers must assign the same cost to the link for OSPF to work well.

Configuring OSPF

Configuring basic OSPF isn't as simple as configuring RIP and EIGRP, and it can get really complex once the many options that are allowed within OSPF are factored in. But you really need to only focus on basic, single-area OSPF configuration for now. Coming up, I'll show you how to configure single-area OSPF.

The two factors that are the basics of OSPF configuration are enabling OSPF and configuring OSPF areas.

Enabling OSPF

The easiest, although least scalable way to configure OSPF, is to just use a single area. Doing this requires a minimum of two commands.

The first command used to activate the OSPF routing process is:

```
Router(config)#router ospf ?
<1-65535>  Process ID
```

A value in the range from 1 to 65,535 identifies the OSPF process ID. It's a unique number on this router that groups a series of OSPF configuration commands under a specific running process. Different OSPF routers don't have to use the same process ID to communicate. It's a purely local value that doesn't mean a lot, but you still need to remember that it can't start at 0 because that's for the backbone. It has to start at a minimum of 1.

You can have more than one OSPF process running simultaneously on the same router if you want, but this isn't the same as running multi-area OSPF. The second process will maintain an entirely separate copy of its topology table and manage its communications independently of the first one. It comes into play when you want OSPF to connect multiple ASs together. Also, because the Cisco exam objectives only cover single-area OSPF with each router running a single OSPF process, that's what we'll focus on in this book.

> The OSPF process ID is needed to identify a unique instance of an OSPF database and is locally significant.

Configuring OSPF Areas

After identifying the OSPF process, you've got to identify the interfaces that you want to activate OSPF communications on as well as the area in which each resides. This will also configure the networks you're going to advertise to others.

Here's an example of a basic OSPF configuration showing our second minimum command needed—the network command:

```
Router#config t
Router(config)#router ospf 1
Router(config-router)#network 10.0.0.0 0.255.255.255 area ?
  <0-4294967295>  OSPF area ID as a decimal value
  A.B.C.D         OSPF area ID in IP address format
Router(config-router)#network 10.0.0.0 0.255.255.255 area 0
```

> The areas can be any number from 0 to 4.2 billion. Don't get these numbers confused with the process ID, which ranges from 1 to 65,535.

Remember, the OSPF process ID number is irrelevant. It can be the same on every router on the network, or it can be different—doesn't matter. It's locally significant and just enables the OSPF routing on the router.

The arguments of the network command are the network number (10.0.0.0) and the wildcard mask (0.255.255.255). The combination of these two numbers identifies the interfaces that OSPF will operate on and will also be included in its OSPF LSA advertisements. Based on the example configuration, OSPF will use this command to find any interface on the router configured in the 10.0.0.0 network and will place any interface it finds into area 0.

Even though you can create about 4.2 billion areas, a router wouldn't actually let you create that many. But you can name them using numbers up to 4.2 billion. You can also label an area using an IP address format.

Let me give you a quick explanation of wildcards: A 0 octet in the wildcard mask indicates that the corresponding octet in the network must match exactly. On the other hand, a 255 indicates that you don't care what the corresponding octet is in the network number. A network and wildcard mask combination of 1.1.1.1 0.0.0.0 would match an interface configured exactly with 1.1.1.1 only, and nothing else. This is really useful if you want to activate OSPF on a specific interface in a very clear and simple way. If you want to match a range of networks, the network and wildcard mask combination of 1.1.0.0 0.0.255.255 would match any interface in the range of 1.1.0.0 to 1.1.255.255. Because of this, it's simpler and safer to stick to using wildcard masks of 0.0.0.0 and identify each OSPF interface individually. Once configured, they'll function exactly the same.

The final factor is the area number, which indicates the area that the interfaces identified in the network and wildcard mask belong. Remember that OSPF routers will become neighbors only if their interfaces share a network that's configured to belong to the same area number. The format of the area number is either a decimal value from the range 0 to 4,294,967,295 or a value represented in standard dotted-decimal notation. For example, area 0.0.0.0 is a legitimate area and is identical to area 0.

Wildcard Example

Before configuring our network, let's take a quick look at a more complex OSPF network configuration to find out what our OSPF network statements would be if we were using subnets and wildcards.

In this scenario, you have a router with these four subnets connected to four different interfaces:

- 192.168.10.64/28
- 192.168.10.80/28
- 192.168.10.96/28
- 192.168.10.8/30

All interfaces need to be in area 0, so it seems to me the easiest configuration would look like this:

Test#**config t**
Test(config)#**router ospf 1**
Test(config-router)#**network 192.168.10.0 0.0.0.255 area 0**

Okay—I'll admit that preceding example is actually pretty simple, but easy isn't always best—especially when dealing with OSPF! So even though this is an easy-button way to configure OSPF, it doesn't make good use of its capabilities and what fun is that? Worse yet, the objectives aren't likely to present you with something this simple! So let's create a separate network statement for each interface using the subnet numbers and wildcards. Doing that would look something like this:

Test#**config t**
Test(config)#**router ospf 1**
Test(config-router)#**network 192.168.10.64 0.0.0.15 area 0**
Test(config-router)#**network 192.168.10.80 0.0.0.15 area 0**
Test(config-router)#**network 192.168.10.96 0.0.0.15 area 0**
Test(config-router)#**network 192.168.10.8 0.0.0.3 area 0**

Wow, now that's different! Truthfully, OSPF would work exactly the same way as it would with the easy configuration I showed you first—but unlike the easy configuration, this one covers the objectives!

And although this looks a bit complicated, it really isn't. All you need is to fully understand block sizes. Just remember that when configuring wildcards, they're always one less than the block size. A /28 is a block size of 16, so we would add our network statement using the subnet number and then add a wildcard of 15 in the interesting octet. For the /30, which is a block size of 4, we would go with a wildcard of 3. Once you practice this a few times, it gets really easy. And do practice because we'll deal with them again when we get to access lists later on!

Let's use Figure 6.3 as an example and configure that network with OSPF using wildcards. The figure shows a three-router network with the IP addresses of each interface.

FIGURE 6.3 Sample OSPF wildcard configuration

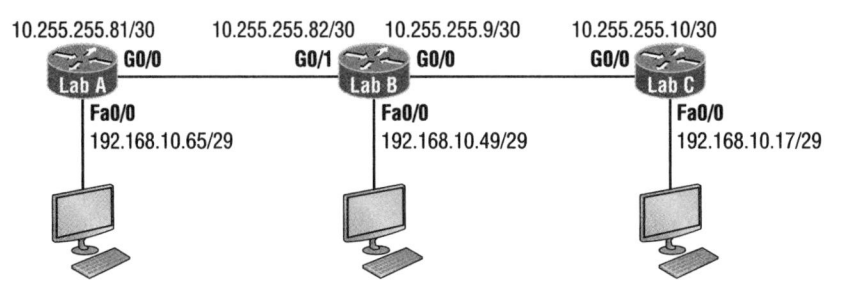

The very first thing you need to be able to do is to look at each interface and determine the subnet that the addresses are in. Wait, I know what you're thinking: "Why don't I just use the exact IP addresses of the interface with the 0.0.0.0 wildcard?" You can, but we're paying attention to Cisco exam objectives here, not just what's easiest!

The IP addresses for each interface are shown in the figure. The Lab_A router has two directly connected subnets: 192.168.10.64/29 and 10.255.255.80/30. Here's the OSPF configuration using wildcards:

```
Lab_A#config t
Lab_A(config)#router ospf 1
Lab_A(config-router)#network 192.168.10.64 0.0.0.7 area 0
Lab_A(config-router)#network 10.255.255.80 0.0.0.3 area 0
```

The Lab_A router is using a /29, or 255.255.255.248, mask on the Fa0/0 interface. This is a block size of 8, which is a wildcard of 7. The G0/0 interface is a mask of 255.255.255.252—block size of 4, with a wildcard of 3. Did you notice that I typed in the network number, not the interface number? You can't configure OSPF this way if you can't look at the IP address and slash notation and figure out the subnet, mask, and wildcard! So don't take your exam until you're good at this.

Here are other two configurations to help you practice:

```
Lab_B#config t
Lab_B(config)#router ospf 1
Lab_B(config-router)#network 192.168.10.48 0.0.0.7 area 0
Lab_B(config-router)#network 10.255.255.80 0.0.0.3 area 0
Lab_B(config-router)#network 10.255.255.8 0.0.0.3 area 0

Lab_C#config t
Lab_C(config)#router ospf 1
```

```
Lab_C(config-router)#network 192.168.10.16 0.0.0.7 area 0
Lab_C(config-router)#network 10.255.255.8 0.0.0.3 area 0
```

As I mentioned with the Lab_A configuration, you've got to be able to determine the subnet, mask, and wildcard just by looking at the IP address and mask of an interface. If you can't do that, you won't be able to configure OSPF using wildcards. So again, keep at this until you're really comfortable with it!

Configuring Our Network with OSPF

Let's have some fun and configure our internetwork with OSPF using just area 0. OSPF has an administrative distance of 110, but let's remove RIP while we're at it because you shouldn't get in the habit of having RIP running on your network.

There's a bunch of different ways to configure OSPF, and as I said, the simplest and easiest is to use the wildcard mask 0.0.0.0. But I want to show you that we can configure each router differently with OSPF and still come up with the exact same result. This is one reason why OSPF is more fun and challenging than other routing protocols—it gives us all a lot more ways to screw things up, which automatically provides a troubleshooting opportunity!

We'll use our network as shown in Figure 6.4 to configure OSPF and by the way, notice I added a new router!

FIGURE 6.4 Our new network layout

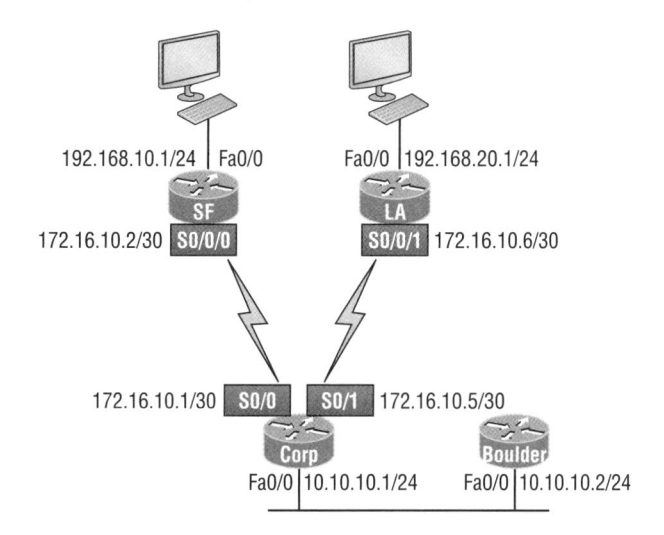

Corp

Here's the Corp router's configuration:

```
Corp#sh ip int brief
Interface        IP-Address    OK? Method Status              Protocol
FastEthernet0/0  10.10.10.1    YES manual up                  up
```

```
Serial0/0          172.16.10.1      YES manual up                        up
FastEthernet0/1    unassigned       YES unset  administratively down down
Serial0/1          172.16.10.5      YES manual up                        up
Corp#config t
Corp(config)#no router rip
Corp(config)#router ospf 132
Corp(config-router)#network 10.10.10.1 0.0.0.0 area 0
Corp(config-router)#network 172.16.10.1 0.0.0.0 area 0
Corp(config-router)#network 172.16.10.5 0.0.0.0 area 0
```

So it looks like we have a few things to talk about here... First, I removed RIP and then added OSPF. Why did I use OSPF 132? It really doesn't matter—the number is irrelevant. I guess it just felt good to use 132. But notice that I started with the show ip int brief command, just like when I was configuring RIP. I did this because it's always important to verify exactly what you are directly connected to. Doing this really helps prevent typos!

The network commands are pretty straightforward. I typed in the IP address of each interface and used the wildcard mask of 0.0.0.0, which means that the IP address must precisely match each octet. This is actually one of those times where easier is better, so just do this:

```
Corp(config)#router ospf 132
Corp(config-router)#network 172.16.10.0 0.0.0.255 area 0
```

Nice—there's only one line instead of two for the 172.16.10.0 network! I really want you to understand that OSPF will work the same here no matter which way you configure the network statement. Now, let's move on to SF. To simplify things, we're going to use our same sample configuration.

SF

The SF router has two directly connected networks. I'll use the IP addresses on each interface to configure this router.

```
SF#sh ip int brief
Interface        IP-Address       OK? Method Status                Protocol
FastEthernet0/0  192.168.10.1     YES manual up                        up
FastEthernet0/1  unassigned       YES unset  administratively down down
Serial0/0/0      172.16.10.2      YES manual up                        up
Serial0/0/1      unassigned       YES unset  administratively down down
SF#config t
SF(config)#no router rip
SF(config)#router ospf 300
SF(config-router)#network 192.168.10.1 0.0.0.0 area 0
SF(config-router)#network 172.16.10.2 0.0.0.0 area 0
*Apr 30 00:25:43.810: %OSPF-5-ADJCHG: Process 300, Nbr 172.16.10.5 on
Serial0/0/0 from LOADING to FULL, Loading Done
```

All I did was to first disable RIP, turn on OSPF routing process 300, and then I added my two directly connected networks. Now let's move on to LA…

LA

The LA router is directly connected to two networks:

```
LA#sh ip int brief
Interface       IP-Address      OK? Method Status                Protocol
FastEthernet0/0 192.168.20.1    YES manual up                    up
FastEthernet0/1 unassigned      YES unset  administratively down down
Serial0/0/0     unassigned      YES unset  administratively down down
Serial0/0/1     172.16.10.6     YES manual up                    up
LA#config t
LA(config)#router ospf 100
LA(config-router)#network 192.168.20.0 0.0.0.255 area 0
LA(config-router)#network 172.16.0.0 0.0.255.255 area 0
*Apr 30 00:56:37.090: %OSPF-5-ADJCHG: Process 100, Nbr 172.16.10.5 on
Serial0/0/1 from LOADING to FULL, Loading Done
```

Remember that when you're configuring dynamic routing, using the show ip int brief command first will make it all so much easier!

And don't forget, I can use any process ID I want, as long as it's a value from 1 to 65,535, because it doesn't matter if all routers use the same process ID. Also, notice that I used different wildcards in this example. Doing this works really well too.

Okay, I want you to think about something for a second before we move onto more advanced OSPF topics: What if the Fa0/1 interface of the LA router was connected to a link that we didn't want, or need to have on in order to have OSPF working, as shown in Figure 6.5?

FIGURE 6.5 Adding a non-OSPF network to LA router

```
LA(config)#router ospf 100
LA(config-router)#passive-interface fastEthernet 0/1
```

Even though this is pretty simple, you've really got to be careful before you configure this command on your router! I added it as an example on interface Fa0/1, which happens to be an interface we're not using in this network because I want OSPF to work on my other router's interfaces.

Now it's time to configure the Corp router to advertise a default route to the SF and LA routers because doing so will make our lives a lot easier. Instead of having to configure all our routers with a default route, we'll only configure one router and then advertise that this router is the one that holds the default route—efficient!

Looking at Figure 6.4, keep in mind that for now, the corporate router is connected to the Internet off of Fa0/0. We'll create a default route toward this imaginary Internet and then tell the other routers that this is the route they'll use to get to the Internet. Here's the configuration:

```
Corp#config t
Corp(config)#ip route 0.0.0.0 0.0.0.0 Fa0/0
Corp(config)#router ospf 1
Corp(config-router)#default-information originate
```

Now, let's check and see if our other routers have received this default route from the Corp router:

```
SF#show ip route
[output cut]
E1 - OSPF external type 1, E2 - OSPF external type 2
[output cut]
O*E2 0.0.0.0/0 [110/1] via 172.16.10.1, 00:01:54, Serial0/0/0
SF#
```

Sure enough—the last line in the SF router shows that it received the advertisement from the Corp router regarding the fact that the corporate router is the one holding the default route out of the AS.

But wait... I need to configure our new router into my lab to create the example network we'll use from here on. Here's the configuration of the new router that I connected to the same network that the Corp router is connected to via the Fa0/0 interface:

```
Router#config t
Router(config)#hostname Boulder
Boulder(config)#int f0/0
Boulder(config-if)#ip address 10.10.10.2 255.255.255.0
Boulder(config-if)#no shut
*Apr  6 18:01:38.007: %LINEPROTO-5-UPDOWN: Line protocol on Interface
FastEthernet0/0, changed state to up
Boulder(config-if)#router ospf 2
Boulder(config-router)#network 10.0.0.0 0.255.255.255 area 0
*Apr  6 18:03:27.267: %OSPF-5-ADJCHG: Process 2, Nbr 223.255.255.254 on
FastEthernet0/0 from LOADING to FULL, Loading Done
```

This is all good, but I need to make sure that you don't follow my example to a tee here because I just quickly brought a router up without setting my passwords first. I can get away with this only because I am in a nonproduction network, so don't do this in the real world where security is vital!

Anyway, now that I have my new router nicely connected with a basic configuration, we're going to move on to cover loopback interfaces, how to set the router ID (RID) used with OSPF, and, finally, how to verify OSPF.

OSPF and Loopback Interfaces

You've got make sure to configure loopback interfaces when using OSPF. In fact, Cisco suggests using them whenever you configure OSPF on a router for stability.

Loopback interfaces are logical interfaces, which means they're virtual, software-only interfaces, not actual, physical router interfaces. A big reason we use loopback interfaces with OSPF configurations is because they ensure an interface is always active and available for OSPF processes.

Loopback interfaces also come in very handy for diagnostic purposes as well as for OSPF configuration. Understand that if you don't configure a loopback interface on a router, the highest active IP address on a router will become that router's RID during bootup!

Figure 6.6 illustrates how routers know each other by their router ID.

FIGURE 6.6 OSPF router ID (RID)

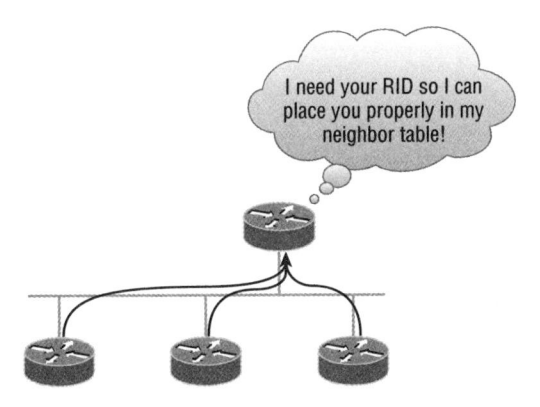

The RID is not only used to advertise routes; it's also used to elect the designated router (DR) and the backup designated router (BDR). These designated routers create adjacencies when a new router comes up and exchanges LSAs to build topological databases.

> **NOTE** By default, OSPF uses the highest IP address on any active interface at the moment OSPF starts up to determine the RID of the router. But you can override this via a logical interface. Remember—the highest IP address of any logical interface will always become a router's RID!

Let's configure logical loopback interfaces and learn how to verify them, as well as verify RIDs.

Configuring Loopback Interfaces

Configuring loopback interfaces rocks mostly because it's the easiest part of OSPF configuration, and we all need a break about now—right?

First, let's see what the RID is on the Corp router with the show ip ospf command:

```
Corp#sh ip ospf
 Routing Process "ospf 1" with ID 172.16.10.5
[output cut]
```

You can see that the RID is 172.16.10.5—the Serial0/1 interface of the router. So let's configure a loopback interface using a completely different IP addressing scheme:

```
Corp(config)#int loopback 0
*Mar 22 01:23:14.206: %LINEPROTO-5-UPDOWN: Line protocol on Interface
    Loopback0, changed state to up
Corp(config-if)#ip address 172.31.1.1 255.255.255.255
```

The IP scheme really doesn't matter here, but each one being in a separate subnet does! By using the /32 mask, we can use any IP address we want as long as the addresses are never the same on any two routers.

Let's configure the other routers now:

```
SF#config t
SF(config)#int loopback 0
*Mar 22 01:25:11.206: %LINEPROTO-5-UPDOWN: Line protocol on Interface
    Loopback0, changed state to up
SF(config-if)#ip address 172.31.1.2 255.255.255.255
```

Here's the configuration of the loopback interface on LA:

```
LA#config t
LA(config)#int loopback 0
*Mar 22 02:21:59.686: %LINEPROTO-5-UPDOWN: Line protocol on Interface
    Loopback0, changed state to up
LA(config-if)#ip address 172.31.1.3 255.255.255.255
```

I'm pretty sure you're wondering what the IP address mask of 255.255.255.255 (/32) means and why we don't just use 255.255.255.0 instead. While it's true that either mask works, the /32 mask is called a host mask and works fine for loopback interfaces. It also allows us to save subnets. Notice how I was able to use 172.31.1.1, .2, .3, and .4? If I didn't use the /32, I'd have to use a separate subnet for each and every router—not good!

One important question to answer before we move on is did we actually change the RIDs of our router by setting the loopback interfaces? Let's find out by taking a look at the Corp's RID:

```
Corp#sh ip ospf
 Routing Process "ospf 1" with ID 172.16.10.5
```

Okay—what happened here? You would think that because we set logical interfaces, the IP addresses under them would automatically become the RID of the router, right? Well, sort of, but only if you do one of two things: either reboot the router or delete OSPF and re-create the database on your router. Neither is a good option, so try to remember to create your logical interfaces before you start OSPF routing. That way, the loopback interface would always become your RID straight away!

With all this in mind, I'm going with rebooting the Corp router because it's the easier of the two options I have right now.

Now let's look and see what our RID is:

```
Corp#sh ip ospf
 Routing Process "ospf 1" with ID 172.31.1.1
```

That did the trick! The Corp router now has a new RID, so I guess I'll just go ahead and reboot all my routers to get their RIDs reset to our logical addresses. But should I really do that?

Maybe not, because there is *one* other way... What do you think about adding a new RID for the router right under the router ospf *process-id* command instead? Sounds good, so let's give that a shot. Here's an example of doing that on the Corp router:

```
Corp#config t
Corp(config)#router ospf 1
Corp(config-router)#router-id 223.255.255.254
Reload or use "clear ip ospf process" command, for this to take effect
Corp(config-router)#do clear ip ospf process
Reset ALL OSPF processes? [no]: yes
*Jan 16 14:20:36.906: %OSPF-5-ADJCHG: Process 1, Nbr 192.168.20.1
on Serial0/1 from FULL to DOWN, Neighbor Down: Interface down
or detached
*Jan 16 14:20:36.906: %OSPF-5-ADJCHG: Process 1, Nbr 192.168.10.1
on Serial0/0 from FULL to DOWN, Neighbor Down: Interface down
or detached
*Jan 16 14:20:36.982: %OSPF-5-ADJCHG: Process 1, Nbr 192.168.20.1
on Serial0/1 from LOADING to FULL, Loading Done
*Jan 16 14:20:36.982: %OSPF-5-ADJCHG: Process 1, Nbr 192.168.10.1
on Serial0/0 from LOADING to FULL, Loading Done
Corp(config-router)#do sh ip ospf
 Routing Process "ospf 1" with ID 223.255.255.254
```

It worked... We changed the RID without reloading the router! But wait—remember, we set a logical loopback interface earlier. Does that mean the loopback interface will win over the `router-id` command? Well, we can see our answer... A loopback interface will *not* override the `router-id` command, and we don't have to reboot the router to make it take effect as the RID!

So this process follows this hierarchy:

1. Highest active interface by default.
2. Highest logical interface overrides a physical interface.
3. The `router-id` overrides the interface and loopback interface.

The only thing left now is to decide whether you want to advertise the loopback interfaces under OSPF. There are pros and cons to using an address that won't be advertised versus using an address that will be. Using an unadvertised address saves on real IP address space, but the address won't appear in the OSPF table, which means you can't ping it.

So basically, what you're faced with here is a choice that equals a trade-off between the ease of debugging the network and conservation of address space—what to do? A really great strategy is to use a private IP address scheme as I did. Do this and all will be well!

Now that we've configured all the routers with OSPF, what's next? Miller time? Nope—not yet. It's verification time again. We still have to make sure that OSPF is really working, and that's exactly what we're going to do next.

Verifying OSPF Configuration

There are several ways to verify proper OSPF configuration and operation, so next, I'm going to demonstrate the various OSPF show commands you need to know in order to achieve the goal. We're going to start by taking a quick look at the routing table of the Corp router.

First, let's issue a `show ip route` command on the Corp router:

```
O    192.168.10.0/24 [110/65] via 172.16.10.2, 1d17h, Serial0/0
     172.131.0.0/32 is subnetted, 1 subnets
     172.131.0.0/32 is subnetted, 1 subnets
C       172.131.1.1 is directly connected, Loopback0
     172.16.0.0/30 is subnetted, 4 subnets
C       172.16.10.4 is directly connected, Serial0/1
L       172.16.10.5/32 is directly connected, Serial0/1
C       172.16.10.0 is directly connected, Serial0/0
L       172.16.10.1/32 is directly connected, Serial0/0
O    192.168.20.0/24 [110/65] via 172.16.10.6, 1d17h, Serial0/1
     10.0.0.0/24 is subnetted, 2 subnets
C       10.10.10.0 is directly connected, FastEthernet0/0
L       10.10.10.1/32 is directly connected, FastEthernet0/0
```

The Corp router shows only two dynamic routes for the internetwork, with the O representing OSPF internal routes. The Cs are clearly our directly connected networks, and our two remote networks are showing up too—nice! Notice the 110/65—that's our administrative distance/metric.

Now that's a nice looking OSPF routing table! It's important to make it easier to troubleshoot and fix an OSPF network, which is why I always use the show ip int brief command when configuring my routing protocols. It's very easy to make little mistakes with OSPF, so keep your eyes on the details!

It's time to show you all the OSPF verification commands that you need in your toolbox for now.

The *show ip ospf* Command

The show ip ospf command is what you'll need to display OSPF information for one or all OSPF processes running on the router. Information contained therein includes the router ID, area information, SPF statistics and LSA timer information. Let's check out the output from the Corp router:

```
Corp#sh ip ospf
 Routing Process "ospf 1" with ID 223.255.255.254
 Start time: 00:08:41.724, Time elapsed: 2d16h
 Supports only single TOS(TOS0) routes
 Supports opaque LSA
 Supports Link-local Signaling (LLS)
 Supports area transit capability
 Router is not originating router-LSAs with maximum metric
 Initial SPF schedule delay 5000 msecs
 Minimum hold time between two consecutive SPFs 10000 msecs
 Maximum wait time between two consecutive SPFs 10000 msecs
 Incremental-SPF disabled
 Minimum LSA interval 5 secs
 Minimum LSA arrival 1000 msecs
 LSA group pacing timer 240 secs
 Interface flood pacing timer 33 msecs
 Retransmission pacing timer 66 msecs
 Number of external LSA 0. Checksum Sum 0x000000
 Number of opaque AS LSA 0. Checksum Sum 0x000000
 Number of DCbitless external and opaque AS LSA 0
 Number of DoNotAge external and opaque AS LSA 0
 Number of areas in this router is 1. 1 normal 0 stub 0 nssa
 Number of areas transit capable is 0
 External flood list length 0
 IETF NSF helper support enabled
```

```
    Cisco NSF helper support enabled
       Area BACKBONE(0)
           Number of interfaces in this area is 3
           Area has no authentication
           SPF algorithm last executed 00:11:08.760 ago
           SPF algorithm executed 5 times
           Area ranges are
           Number of LSA 6. Checksum Sum 0x03B054
           Number of opaque link LSA 0. Checksum Sum 0x000000
           Number of DCbitless LSA 0
           Number of indication LSA 0
           Number of DoNotAge LSA 0
           Flood list length 0
```

Notice the router ID (RID) of 223.255.255.254, which is the highest IP address configured on the router. Hopefully, you also noticed that I set the RID of the corporate router to the highest available IP address available with IPv4.

The *show ip ospf database* Command

Using the show ip ospf database command will give you information about the number of routers in the internetwork (AS) plus the neighboring router's ID—the topology database I mentioned earlier. Unlike the show ip eigrp topology command, this command reveals the OSPF routers, but not each and every link in the AS like EIGRP does.

The output is broken down by area. Here's a sample output, again from Corp:

```
Corp#sh ip ospf database

            OSPF Router with ID (223.255.255.254) (Process ID 1)
Router Link States (Area 0)

Link ID          ADV Router       Age       Seq#        Checksum Link count
10.10.10.2       10.10.10.2       966       0x80000001  0x007162 1
172.31.1.4       172.31.1.4       885       0x80000002  0x00D27E 1
192.168.10.1     192.168.10.1     886       0x8000007A  0x00BC95 3
192.168.20.1     192.168.20.1     1133      0x8000007A  0x00E348 3
223.255.255.254  223.255.255.254  925       0x8000004D  0x000B90 5

            Net Link States (Area 0)

Link ID          ADV Router       Age       Seq#        Checksum
10.10.10.1       223.255.255.254  884       0x80000002  0x008CFE
```

You can see all the routers and the RID of each router—the highest IP address on each of them. For example, the Link ID and ADV Router of my new Boulder router shows up twice: once with the directly connected IP address (10.10.10.2) and as the RID that I set under the OSPF process (172.31.1.4).

The router output shows the link ID—remember that an interface is also a link—and the RID of the router on that link under the ADV router, or advertising router.

The *show ip ospf interface* Command

The show ip ospf interface command reveals all interface-related OSPF information. Data is displayed about OSPF information for all OSPF-enabled interfaces or for specified interfaces. I'll highlight some of the more important factors for you. Here's the output:

```
Corp#sh ip ospf int f0/0
FastEthernet0/0 is up, line protocol is up
  Internet Address 10.10.10.1/24, Area 0
  Process ID 1, Router ID 223.255.255.254, Network Type BROADCAST, Cost: 1
  Transmit Delay is 1 sec, State DR, Priority 1
  Designated Router (ID) 223.255.255.254, Interface address 10.10.10.1
  Backup Designated router (ID) 172.31.1.4, Interface address 10.10.10.2
  Timer intervals configured, Hello 10, Dead 40, Wait 40, Retransmit 5
    oob-resync timeout 40
    Hello due in 00:00:08
  Supports Link-local Signaling (LLS)
  Cisco NSF helper support enabled
  IETF NSF helper support enabled
  Index 3/3, flood queue length 0
  Next 0x0(0)/0x0(0)
  Last flood scan length is 1, maximum is 1
  Last flood scan time is 0 msec, maximum is 0 msec
  Neighbor Count is 1, Adjacent neighbor count is 1
    Adjacent with neighbor 172.31.1.  Suppress hello for 0 neighbor(s)
```

Okay—so this command has given us the following information:

- Interface IP address
- Area assignment
- Process ID
- Router ID
- Network type
- Cost
- Priority

- DR/BDR election information (if applicable)
- Hello and Dead timer intervals
- Adjacent neighbor information

The reason I used the `show ip ospf interface f0/0` command is because I knew that there would be a designated router elected on the FastEthernet broadcast multi-access network between our Corp and Boulder routers. The information that I highlighted is all very important, so make sure you've noted it! A good question to ask you here is what are the Hello and Dead timers set to by default?

Type in the `show ip ospf interface` command and receive this response:

```
Corp#sh ip ospf int f0/0
%OSPF: OSPF not enabled on FastEthernet0/0
```

This error occurs when OSPF is enabled on the router, but not the interface. When this happens, you need to check your network statements because it means that the interface you're trying to verify is not in your OSPF process!

The *show ip ospf neighbor* Command

The `show ip ospf neighbor` command is really useful because it summarizes the pertinent OSPF information regarding neighbors and the adjacency state. If a DR or BDR exists, that information will also be displayed. Here's a sample:

```
Corp#sh ip ospf neighbor

Neighbor ID     Pri   State        Dead Time    Address        Interface
172.31.1.4      1     FULL/BDR     00:00:34     10.10.10.2     FastEthernet0/0
192.168.20.1    0     FULL/  -     00:00:31     172.16.10.6    Serial0/1
192.168.10.1    0     FULL/  -     00:00:32     172.16.10.2    Serial0/0
```

Real World Scenario

An Admin Connects Two Disparate Routers Together with OSPF and the Link Between Them Never Comes Up

A while back, an admin called me in a panic because he couldn't get OSPF working between two routers, one of which was an older router that they needed to use while they were waiting for their new router to be shipped to them.

OSPF can be used in a multi-vendor network so he was confused as to why this wasn't working. He turned on RIP and it worked so he was super confused with why OSPF was not creating adjacencies. I had him use the `show ip ospf interface` command to look

> at the link between the two routers and sure enough, the hello and dead timers didn't match. I had him configure the mismatched parameters so they would match, but it still wouldn't create an adjacency. Looking more closely at the show ip ospf interface command, I noticed the cost did not match! Cisco calculated the bandwidth differently than the other vendor. Once I had him configure both as the same value, the link came up! Always remember, just because OSPF can be used in a multi-vendor network, does not mean it will work out of the box!

This is a critical command to understand because it's extremely useful in production networks. Let's take a look at the Boulder router output:

```
Boulder>sh ip ospf neighbor

Neighbor ID       Pri    State      Dead Time    Address       Interface
223.255.255.254   1      FULL/DR    00:00:31     10.10.10.1    FastEthernet0/0
```

Here we can see that since there's an Ethernet link (broadcast multi-access) on the link between the Boulder and the Corp router, there's going to be an election to determine who will be the designated router (DR) and who will be the backup designated router (BDR). We can see that the Corp became the designated router, and it won because it had the highest IP address on the network—the highest RID.

Now the reason that the Corp connections to SF and LA don't have a DR or BDR listed in the output is that by default, elections don't happen on point-to-point links and they show FULL/ - . But we can still determine that the Corp router is fully adjacent to all three routers from its output.

The *show ip protocols* Command

The show ip protocols command is also highly useful, whether you're running OSPF, EIGRP, RIP, BGP, IS-IS, or any other routing protocol that can be configured on your router. It provides an excellent overview of the actual operation of all currently running protocols!

Check out the output from the Corp router:

```
Corp#sh ip protocols
Routing Protocol is "ospf 1"
  Outgoing update filter list for all interfaces is not set
  Incoming update filter list for all interfaces is not set
  Router ID 223.255.255.254
  Number of areas in this router is 1. 1 normal 0 stub 0 nssa
  Maximum path: 4
  Routing for Networks:
    10.10.10.1 0.0.0.0 area 0
    172.16.10.1 0.0.0.0 area 0
    172.16.10.5 0.0.0.0 area 0
```

```
Reference bandwidth unit is 100 mbps
Routing Information Sources:
    Gateway           Distance      Last Update
    192.168.10.1         110        00:21:53
    192.168.20.1         110        00:21:53
Distance: (default is 110) Distance: (default is 110)
```

From looking at this output, you can determine the OSPF process ID, OSPF router ID, type of OSPF area, networks and areas configured for OSPF, and the OSPF router IDs of neighbors—that's a lot. It's super-efficient!

Summary

This chapter gave you a great deal of information about OSPF. It's really difficult to include everything about OSPF because so much of it falls outside the scope of this chapter and book, but I've given you a few tips here and there, so you're good to go—as long as you make sure you've got what I presented to you dialed in!

I talked about a lot of OSPF topics, including terminology, operations, and configuration as well as verification and monitoring.

Each of these topics encompasses quite a bit of information—the terminology section just scratched the surface of OSPF. But you've got the goods you really need for your studies. Finally, I gave you a tight survey of commands highly useful for observing the operation of OSPF so you can verify that things are moving along as they should.

Exam Essentials

Compare OSPF and RIPv1.   OSPF is a link-state protocol that supports VLSM and classless routing; RIPv1 is a distance-vector protocol that does not support VLSM and supports only classful routing.

Know how OSPF routers become neighbors and/or adjacent.   OSPF routers become neighbors when each router sees the other's Hello packets.

Be able to configure single-area OSPF.   A minimal single-area configuration involves only two commands: router ospf *process-id* and network *x.x.x.x y.y.y.y* area *Z*.

Be able to verify the operation of OSPF.   There are many show commands that provide useful details on OSPF, and it is useful to be completely familiar with the output of each: show ip ospf, show ip ospf database, show ip ospf interface, show ip ospf neighbor, and show ip protocols.

Review Questions

The answers to these questions can be found in the Appendix.

1. Which of the following describe the process identifier that is used to run OSPF on a router? (Choose two.)
   A. It is locally significant.
   B. It is globally significant.
   C. It is needed to identify a unique instance of an OSPF database.
   D. It is an optional parameter required only if multiple OSPF processes are running on the router.
   E. All routes in the same OSPF area must have the same process ID if they are to exchange routing information.

2. All of the following must match for two OSPF routers to become neighbors except which?
   A. Area ID
   B. Router ID
   C. Stub area flag
   D. Authentication password if using one

3. You get a call from a network administrator who tells you that he typed the following into his router:

   Router(config)#**router ospf 1**
   Router(config-router)#**network 10.0.0.0 255.0.0.0 area 0**

   He tells you he still can't see any routes in the routing table. What configuration error did the administrator make?
   A. The wildcard mask is incorrect.
   B. The OSPF area is wrong.
   C. The OSPF process ID is incorrect.
   D. The AS configuration is wrong.

4. Which of the following statements is true with regard to the output shown?

   ```
   Corp#sh ip ospf neighbor
   Neighbor ID     Pri   State        Dead Time   Address       Interface
   172.31.1.4       1    FULL/BDR     00:00:34    10.10.10.2    FastEthernet0/0
   192.168.20.1     0    FULL/    -   00:00:31    172.16.10.6   Serial0/1
   192.168.10.1     0    FULL/    -   00:00:32    172.16.10.2   Serial0/0
   ```
   A. There is no DR on the link to 192.168.20.1.
   B. The Corp router is the BDR on the link to 172.31.1.4.
   C. The Corp router is the DR on the link to 192.168.20.1.
   D. The link to 192.168.10.1 is 32 hops away.

5. What is the administrative distance of OSPF?
   A. 90
   B. 100
   C. 120
   D. 110

6. In OSPF, Hellos are sent to what IP address?
   A. 224.0.0.5
   B. 224.0.0.9
   C. 224.0.0.10
   D. 224.0.0.1

7. Updates addressed to 224.0.0.6 are destined for which type of OSPF router?
   A. DR
   B. ASBR
   C. ABR
   D. All OSPF routers

8. For some reason, you cannot establish an adjacency relationship on a common Ethernet link between two routers. Looking at this output, what is the cause of the problem?

   ```
   RouterA#
   Ethernet0/0 is up, line protocol is up
     Internet Address 172.16.1.2/16, Area 0
     Process ID 2, Router ID 172.126.1.2, Network Type BROADCAST, Cost: 10
     Transmit Delay is 1 sec, State DR, Priority 1
     Designated Router (ID) 172.16.1.2, interface address 172.16.1.1
     No backup designated router on this network
     Timer intervals configured, Hello 5, Dead 20, Wait 20, Retransmit 5


   RouterB#
   Ethernet0/0 is up, line protocol is up
     Internet Address 172.16.1.1/16, Area 0
     Process ID 2, Router ID 172.126.1.1, Network Type BROADCAST, Cost: 10
     Transmit Delay is 1 sec, State DR, Priority 1
     Designated Router (ID) 172.16.1.1, interface address 172.16.1.2
     No backup designated router on this network
     Timer intervals configured, Hello 10, Dead 40, Wait 40, Retransmit 5
   ```

   A. The OSPF area is not configured properly.
   B. The priority on RouterA should be set higher.

C. The cost on RouterA should be set higher.
D. The Hello and Dead timers are not configured properly.
E. A backup designated router needs to be added to the network.
F. The OSPF process ID numbers must match.

9. Given the following output, which statement or statements can be determined to be true? (Choose all that apply.)

```
RouterA2# show ip ospf neighbor
Neighbor ID Pri State Dead Time Address Interface
192.168.23.2 1 FULL/BDR 00:00:29 10.24.4.2 FastEthernet1/0
192.168.45.2 2 FULL/BDR 00:00:24 10.1.0.5 FastEthernet0/0
192.168.85.1 1 FULL/- 00:00:33 10.6.4.10 Serial0/1
192.168.90.3 1 FULL/DR 00:00:32 10.5.5.2 FastEthernet0/1
192.168.67.3 1 FULL/DR 00:00:20 10.4.9.20 FastEthernet0/2
192.168.90.1 1 FULL/BDR 00:00:23 10.5.5.4 FastEthernet0/1
<<output omitted>>
```

A. The DR for the network connected to Fa0/0 has an interface priority higher than 2.
B. This router (A2) is the BDR for subnet 10.1.0.0.
C. The DR for the network connected to Fa0/1 has a router ID of 10.5.5.2.
D. The DR for the serial subnet is 192.168.85.1

10. A(n) _____ is an OSPF data packet containing link-state and routing information that is shared among OSPF routers.
A. LSA
B. TSA
C. Hello
D. SPF

Chapter 7

Layer 2 Switching

THE FOLLOWING CCNA EXAM TOPICS ARE COVERED IN THIS CHAPTER:

1.0 Network Fundamentals

✓ **1.13 Describe switching concepts**

- 1.13.a MAC learning and aging
- 1.13.b Frame switching
- 1.13.c Frame flooding
- 1.13.d MAC address table

5.0 Security Fundamentals

✓ **5.7 Configure Layer 2 security features (DHCP snooping, dynamic ARP inspection, and port security)**

When Cisco brings up switching in the Cisco exam objectives, they mean layer 2 switching unless they say otherwise. Layer 2 switching is the process of using the hardware address of devices on a LAN to segment a network. So, in this chapter, we're going to cover the finer points of layer 2 switching to make sure you know exactly how it works.

You should already know that we rely on switching to break up large collision domains into smaller ones and that a collision domain is a network segment with two or more devices sharing the same bandwidth. A hub network is a good example of this type of technology, but since each port on a switch is actually its own collision domain, we can create a much more efficient network simply by replacing hubs with switches.

Switches have changed the way networks are designed and implemented. If a pure switched design is implemented well, the result will be a clean, cost-effective, and resilient internetwork. Coming up, I'll compare how networks were designed before and after switching technologies were introduced.

I'll be using three switches to begin configuring our switched network and we'll continue configuring them in Chapter 8, "VLANs and Inter-VLAN Routing."

To find your included bonus material, as well as Todd Lammle videos, practice questions & hands-on labs, please see www.lammle.com/ccna

Switching Services

Bridges use software to create and manage a Content Addressable Memory (CAM) filter table. Instead, the fast switches we use today rely upon application-specific integrated circuits (ASICs) to build and maintain their MAC filter tables. This is a big difference, but it's still okay to think of a layer 2 switch as a multiport bridge because their basic reason for being is the same: to break up collision domains.

Layer 2 switches and bridges are faster than routers because they don't waste time looking at the Network layer header information. Instead, they look at the frame's hardware addresses before deciding to either forward, flood, or drop the frame.

Unlike hubs, switches create private, dedicated collision domains and provide independent bandwidth exclusive on each port.

Here's a list of four important advantages we gain when using layer 2 switching:

- Hardware-based bridging (ASICs)
- Wire speed
- Low latency
- Low cost

A big reason layer 2 switching is so efficient is that no modification to the data packet takes place. The device only reads the frame encapsulating the packet, which makes the switching process considerably faster and less vulnerable to errors than routing processes are.

Plus, if you use layer 2 switching for both workgroup connectivity and network segmentation (breaking up collision domains), you can create more network segments than you can with traditional routed networks. Another nice benefit gained via layer 2 switching is it increases bandwidth for each user because, again, each connection, or interface into the switch, is its own, self-contained collision domain.

Three Switch Functions at Layer 2

There are three distinct functions of layer 2 switching you need to remember: *address learning*, *forward/filter decisions*, and *loop avoidance*.

Address learning   Layer 2 switches remember the source hardware address of each frame received on an interface and enter this information into a MAC database called a forward/filter table. The old name for this table was called Content Addressable Memory (CAM), and the table is still sometimes referred either way.

Forward/filter decisions   When a frame is received on an interface, the switch looks at the destination hardware address, then chooses the appropriate exit interface for it in the MAC database. This way, the frame is only forwarded out of the correct destination port.

Loop avoidance   If multiple connections between switches are created for redundancy, network loops can occur. Spanning Tree Protocol (STP) is used to prevent network loops while still permitting redundancy.

Next, I'm going to talk about address learning and forward/filtering decisions. Loop avoidance is beyond the scope of the objectives being covered in this chapter.

Address Learning

When a switch is first powered on, the MAC forward/filter table (CAM) is empty, as shown in Figure 7.1.

FIGURE 7.1 Empty forward/filter table on a switch

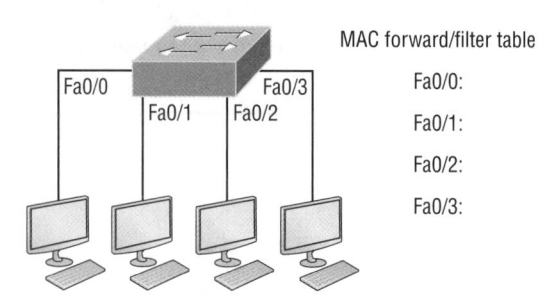

MAC forward/filter table

Fa0/0:
Fa0/1:
Fa0/2:
Fa0/3:

When a device transmits and an interface receives a frame, the switch places the frame's source address in the MAC forward/filter table, allowing it to refer to the precise interface the sending device is located on. The switch then has no choice but to flood the network with this frame out of every port except the source port because it has no idea where the destination device is actually located.

If a device answers this flooded frame and sends a frame back, then the switch will take the source address from that frame and place that MAC address in its database as well, associating this address with the interface that received the frame. Because the switch now has both of the relevant MAC addresses in its filtering table, the two devices can now make a point-to-point connection. The switch doesn't need to flood the frame as it did the first time because now the frames will only be forwarded between these two devices. This is exactly why layer 2 switches are so superior to hubs. In a hub network, all frames are forwarded out all ports every time—no matter what.

Figure 7.2 shows the processes involved in building a MAC database.

FIGURE 7.2 How switches learn hosts' locations

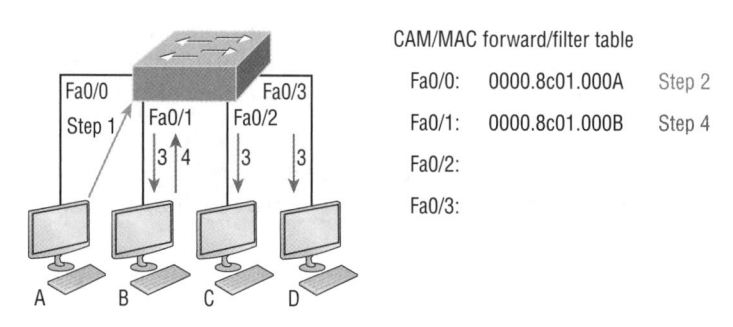

CAM/MAC forward/filter table

Fa0/0:   0000.8c01.000A   Step 2
Fa0/1:   0000.8c01.000B   Step 4
Fa0/2:
Fa0/3:

This figure shows four hosts attached to a switch. When the switch is powered on, it has nothing in its MAC address forward/filter table, just as in Figure 7.1. But when the hosts start communicating, the switch places the source hardware address of each frame into the table along with the port that the frame's source address corresponds to.

Let me give you an example of how a forward/filter table is populated using Figure 7.2:

1. Host A sends a frame to Host B. Host A's MAC address is 0000.8c01.000A; Host B's MAC address is 0000.8c01.000B.
2. The switch receives the frame on the Fa0/0 interface and places the source address in the MAC address table.
3. Since the destination address isn't in the MAC database, the frame is forwarded out all interfaces except the source port.
4. Host B receives the frame and responds to Host A. The switch receives this frame on interface Fa0/1 and places the source hardware address in the MAC database.
5. Host A and Host B can now make a point-to-point connection, and only these specific devices will receive the frames. Hosts C and D won't see the frames, nor will their MAC addresses be found in the database because they haven't sent a frame to the switch yet.

If Host A and Host B don't communicate to the switch again within a certain time period, the switch will flush their entries from the database to keep it current.

Forward/Filter Decisions

When a frame arrives at a switch interface, the destination hardware address is compared to the forward/filter MAC database. If the destination hardware address is known and listed in the database, the frame is only sent out of the appropriate exit interface. The switch won't transmit the frame out any interface except for the destination interface, which preserves bandwidth on the other network segments. This process is called *frame filtering*.

But if the destination hardware address isn't listed in the MAC database, then the frame will be flooded out all active interfaces except the interface it was received on. If a device answers the flooded frame, the MAC database is then updated with the device's location—its correct interface.

If a host or server sends a broadcast on the LAN, by default, the switch will flood the frame out all active ports except the source port. Remember, the switch creates smaller collision domains, but it's always still one large broadcast domain by default.

In Figure 7.3, Host A sends a data frame to Host D. What do you think the switch will do when it receives the frame from Host A?

FIGURE 7.3   Forward/filter table

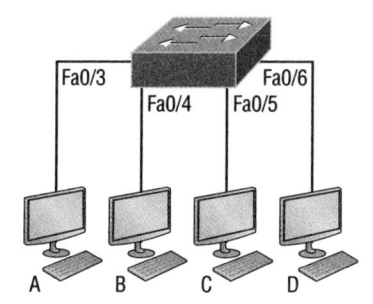

Switch# show mac address-table

VLAN	Mac Address	Ports
1	0005.dccb.d74b	Fa0/4
1	000a.f467.9e80	Fa0/5
1	000a.f467.9e8b	Fa0/6

Let's examine Figure 7.4 to find the answer.

FIGURE 7.4 Forward/filter table answer

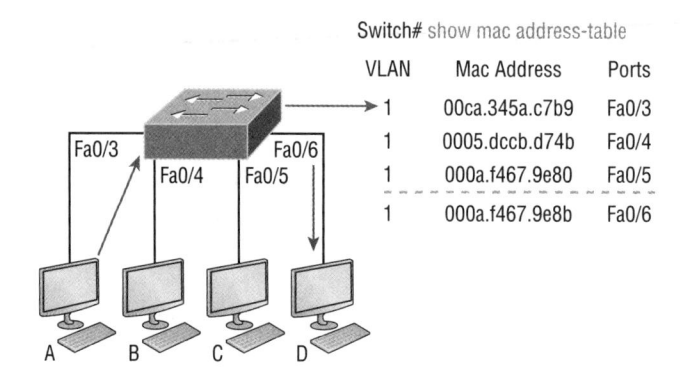

```
Switch# show mac address-table
VLAN    Mac Address      Ports
  1     00ca.345a.c7b9   Fa0/3
  1     0005.dccb.d74b   Fa0/4
  1     000a.f467.9e80   Fa0/5
  1     000a.f467.9e8b   Fa0/6
```

Since Host A's MAC address is not in the forward/filter table, the switch will add the source address and port to the MAC address table, then forward the frame to Host D. It's important to remember that the source MAC is always checked first to make sure it's in the CAM table. After that, if Host D's MAC address wasn't found in the forward/filter table, the switch would've flooded the frame out all ports except for port Fa0/3 because that's the specific port the frame was received on.

Now let's take a look at the output that results from using a show mac address-table command:

```
Switch#sh mac address-table
Vlan Mac Address Type Ports]]> ---- ----------- -------- -----
1 0005.dccb.d74b DYNAMIC Fa0/1
1 000a.f467.9e80 DYNAMIC Fa0/3
1 000a.f467.9e8b DYNAMIC Fa0/4
1 000a.f467.9e8c DYNAMIC Fa0/3
1 0010.7b7f.c2b0 DYNAMIC Fa0/3
1 0030.80dc.460b DYNAMIC Fa0/3
1 0030.9492.a5dd DYNAMIC Fa0/1
1 00d0.58ad.05f4 DYNAMIC Fa0/1
```

Now, let's say the preceding switch received a frame with the following MAC addresses:
Source MAC: 0005.dccb.d74b
Destination MAC: 000a.f467.9e8c
How will the switch handle this frame? The right answer is that the destination MAC address will be found in the MAC address table, and the frame will only be forwarded out Fa0/3. Never forget that if the destination MAC address isn't found in the forward/filter table, the frame will be forwarded out all of the switch's ports except for the one on which it was originally received in an attempt to locate the destination device. Now that you can

see the MAC address table and how switches add host addresses to the forward filter table, how do think we can secure it from unauthorized users?

Port Security

It's usually a bad idea to have your switches available for anyone to just plug into and play around with. We worry about wireless security, so why wouldn't we demand switch security just as much, if not more?

But just how do we actually prevent someone from simply plugging a host into one of our switch ports—or worse, adding a hub, switch, or access point into the Ethernet jack in their office? By default, MAC addresses will dynamically appear in your MAC forward/filter database, and you can stop them in their tracks by using port security!

Figure 7.5 shows two hosts connected to the single switch port Fa0/3 via either a hub or access point (AP).

FIGURE 7.5 "Port security" on a switch port restricts port access by MAC address.

Port Fa0/3 is configured to observe and allow only certain MAC addresses to associate with the specific port. So in this example, Host A is denied access, but Host B is allowed to associate with the port.

By using port security, you can limit the number of MAC addresses that can be assigned dynamically to a port, set static MAC addresses, and—here's my favorite part—set penalties for users who abuse your policy! Personally, I like to have the port shut down when the security policy is violated. Making abusers bring me a memo from their boss explaining why they violated the security policy is just so satisfying, so I'll also require something like that before I'll enable their port again. Things like this really help people remember to behave!

This is all good, but you still need to balance your particular security needs with the time that implementing and managing them will require. If you have tons of time on your hands, then go ahead and seriously lock your network down like a vault, but if you're busy like the rest of us, rest assured that there are ways to secure things nicely without an overwhelming amount of administrative overhead. First, and painlessly, always remember to shut down unused ports or assign them to an unused VLAN. All ports are enabled by default, so you need to make sure there's no access to unused switch ports!

Here are your options for configuring port security:

```
Switch#config t
Switch(config)#int f0/1
Switch(config-if)#switchport mode access
Switch(config-if)#switchport port-security
Switch(config-if)#switchport port-security ?
aging Port-security aging commands
mac-address Secure mac address
maximum Max secure addresses
violation Security violation mode
<cr>
```

Most Cisco switches ship with their ports in desirable mode, which means those ports will desire to trunk when they sense another switch has been connected. So first, we need to change the port and make it an access port instead. If we don't do that, we won't be able to configure port security on it at all. Once that's out of the way, we can move on using our `port-security` commands, never forgetting to enable port security on the interface with the basic command `switchport port-security`. Notice that I did this after I made the port an access port!

The preceding output clearly illustrates that the `switchport port-security` command can be used with four options. While it's true you can use the `switchport port-security mac-address` *mac-address* command to assign individual MAC addresses to each switch port, if you go with that option, you'd better have boatloads of time on your hands!

You can configure the device to take one of the following actions when a security violation occurs by using the `switchport port-security` command:

- Protect: The protect violation mode drops packets with unknown source addresses until you remove enough secure MAC addresses to drop below the maximum value.

- Restrict: The restrict violation mode also drops packets with unknown source addresses until you remove enough secure MAC addresses to drop below the maximum value. It also generates a log message, causes the security violation counter to increment, and sends an SNMP trap.

- Shutdown: Shutdown is the default violation mode. The shutdown violation mode puts the interface into an error-disabled state immediately. The entire port is shut down. Also, in this mode, the system generates a log message, sends an SNMP trap, and increments the violation counter. To make the interface usable, you must do a shut/no shut on the interface.

If you want to set up a switch port to allow only one host per port and make sure the port will shut down if this rule is violated, use the following commands like this:

```
Switch(config-if)#switchport port-security maximum 1
Switch(config-if)#switchport port-security violation shutdown
```

These commands are probably the most popular because they prevent random users from connecting to a specific switch or access point in their office. The port security default that's immediately set on a port when it's enabled is `maximum 1` and `violation shutdown`. This sounds good, but the drawback is that it only allows a single MAC address to be used on the port. So if anyone, including you, tries to add another host on that segment, the switch port will immediately enter error-disabled state, and the port will turn amber. When that happens, you have to manually go into the switch and re-enable the port by cycling it with a `shutdown` and then a `no shutdown` command.

Probably one of my favorite commands is the sticky command, and not just because it's got a cool name. It also makes very cool things happen. You can find this command under the mac-address command:

```
Switch(config-if)#switchport port-security mac-address sticky
Switch(config-if)#switchport port-security maximum 2
Switch(config-if)#switchport port-security violation shutdown
```

Basically, with the sticky command you can provide static MAC address security without having to type in absolutely everyone's MAC address on the network. I like things that save me time like that!

In the preceding example, the first two MAC addresses coming into the port "stick" to it as static addresses and will be placed in the running-config, but when a third address tried to connect, the port would shut down immediately.

Here's one more example... Figure 7.6 displays a host in a company lobby that needs to be secured against the Ethernet cable used by anyone other than one, authorized individual.

FIGURE 7.6 Protecting a PC in a lobby

What can you do to ensure that only the MAC address of the lobby PC is allowed by switch port Fa0/1?

The solution is pretty straightforward because in this case, the defaults for port security will work well. All I have left to do is add a static MAC entry:

```
Switch(config-if)#switchport port-security
Switch(config-if)#switchport port-security violation restrict
Switch(config-if)#switchport port-security mac-address aa.bb.cc.dd.ee.ff
```

To protect the lobby PC, we would set the maximum allowed MAC addresses to 1 and the violation to `restrict` so the port doesn't get shut down every time someone tries to use the Ethernet cable (which would be constantly). By using `violation restrict`, the unauthorized frames would just be dropped. But did you notice that I enabled `port-security` and then set a static MAC address? Remember that as soon as you enable `port-security` on a port, it defaults to `violation shutdown` and a maximum of 1. So all I needed to do was change the violation mode and add the static MAC address!

> ### Real World Scenario
>
> **Lobby PC Always Being Disconnected Becomes a Security Risk**
>
> At a large Fortune 50 company in San Jose, California, there was a PC in the lobby that held the company directory. With no security guard present in the lobby, the Ethernet cable connecting the PC was free game to all vendors, contractors, and visitors waiting in the lobby.
>
> Port security to the rescue! When port security was enabled on the port with the `switchport port-security` command, the switch port connecting to the PC was automatically secured with the defaults of allowing only one MAC address to associate to the port and violation shutdown. However, the port was always going into err-shutdown mode whenever anyone tried to use the Ethernet port. When the violation mode was changed to restrict and a static MAC address was set for the port with the `switchport port-security mac-address` command, only the Lobby PC was able to connect and communicate on the network! Problem solved!

Loop Avoidance

Redundant links between switches are important to have in place because they help prevent network failures in the event that one link stops working.

But while it's true that redundant links can be extremely helpful, they can also cause more problems than they solve! This is because frames can be flooded down all redundant links simultaneously, creating network loops as well as other evils. Here's a list of some of the ugliest problems that can occur:

- If no loop avoidance schemes are put in place, the switches will flood broadcasts endlessly throughout the internetwork. This is sometimes referred to as a *broadcast storm*, but most of the time, they're referred to in more unprintable ways! Figure 7.7 illustrates how a broadcast can be propagated throughout the network. Observe how a frame is continually being flooded through the internetwork's physical network media.

- A device can receive multiple copies of the same frame because that frame can arrive from different segments at the same time. Figure 7.8 demonstrates how a whole bunch of frames can arrive from multiple segments simultaneously.

- The server in the figure sends a unicast frame to Router C. Because it's a unicast frame, Switch A forwards the frame and Switch B provides the same service—it forwards the unicast. This is bad because it means that Router C receives that unicast frame twice, causing additional overhead on the network.

FIGURE 7.7 Broadcast storm

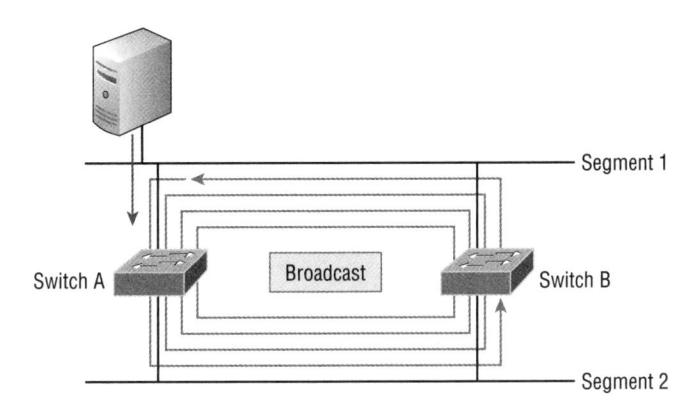

FIGURE 7.8 Multiple frame copies

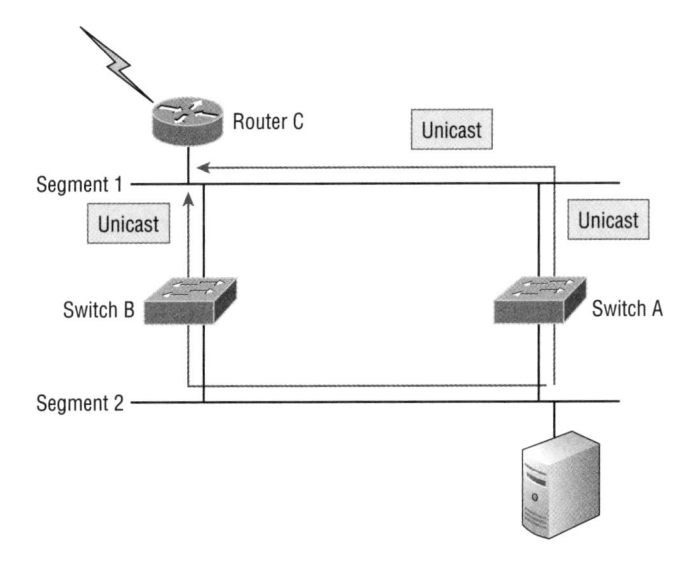

- You may have thought of this one: The MAC address filter table could be totally confused about the source device's location because the switch can receive the frame from more than one link. Worse, the bewildered switch could get so caught up in constantly updating the MAC filter table with source hardware address locations that it will fail to forward a frame! This is called thrashing the MAC table.
- One of the most vile events is when multiple loops propagate throughout a network. Loops can occur within other loops, and if a broadcast storm were to occur simultaneously, the network wouldn't be able to perform frame switching—period!

All of these problems spell disaster or close, and they're all really bad situations that must be avoided or fixed somehow. That's where the Spanning Tree Protocol comes into play. It was actually developed to solve every one of the problems I just told you about!

Now that I explained the issues that can occur when you have redundant links, or when you have links that are improperly implemented, I'm sure you understand how vital it is to prevent them.

I'll be honest here—the best solutions are beyond the scope of this chapter. We'll get into that territory when we explore the more advanced Cisco exam objectives coming up in Chapter 9. For now, let's focus on configuring some switching!

Configuring Catalyst Switches

You get a lot of variety when it comes to Cisco Catalyst switches. Some run 10 Mbps, while others can speed all the way up to 10 Gbps or higher switched ports with a combination of twisted-pair and fiber. These newer switches, like the 3850, also have more intelligence, so they can give you data fast—mixed media services, too!

Coming up, I'm going to show you how to start up and configure a Cisco Catalyst switch using the command-line interface (CLI). After you get the basic commands down in this chapter, you'll learn to configure virtual LANs (VLANs), plus Inter-Switch Link (ISL) and 802.1q trunking in the next one.

Here's a list of the basic tasks we'll be covering next:

- Administrative functions
- Configuring the IP address and subnet mask
- Setting the IP default gateway
- Setting port security
- Testing and verifying the network

> You can learn all about the Cisco family of Catalyst switches at https://www.cisco.com/c/en/us/products/switches/index.html

Catalyst Switch Configuration

Before we actually get into configuring one of the Catalyst switches, I want you to be familiar with the boot process of these switches. Figure 7.9 shows a typical Cisco Catalyst switch.

FIGURE 7.9 A Cisco Catalyst switch

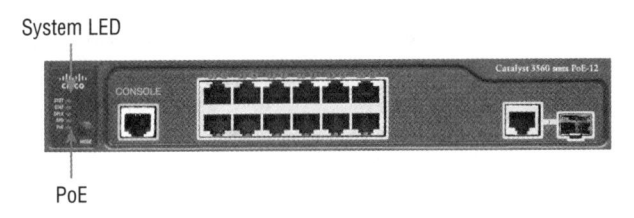

The first thing I want to point out is that the console port for Catalyst switches is typically found on the back of the switch. On a smaller switch like the 3560 shown in the figure, the console is right in the front to make it easier to use. The eight-port 2960 looks exactly the same.

If the POST completes successfully, the system LED turns green, but if the POST fails, it will turn amber. That amber glow is an ominous thing—typically fatal. So keep a spare switch around, especially in case a production switch dies on you! The bottom button is used to indicate which lights are providing Power over Ethernet (PoE). You can see this by pressing the Mode button. The PoE is a very cool feature because it allows me to power my access point and phone by just connecting them into the switch with an Ethernet cable—sweet.

Figure 7.10 shows the switched network we'll be working on.

FIGURE 7.10 Our switched network

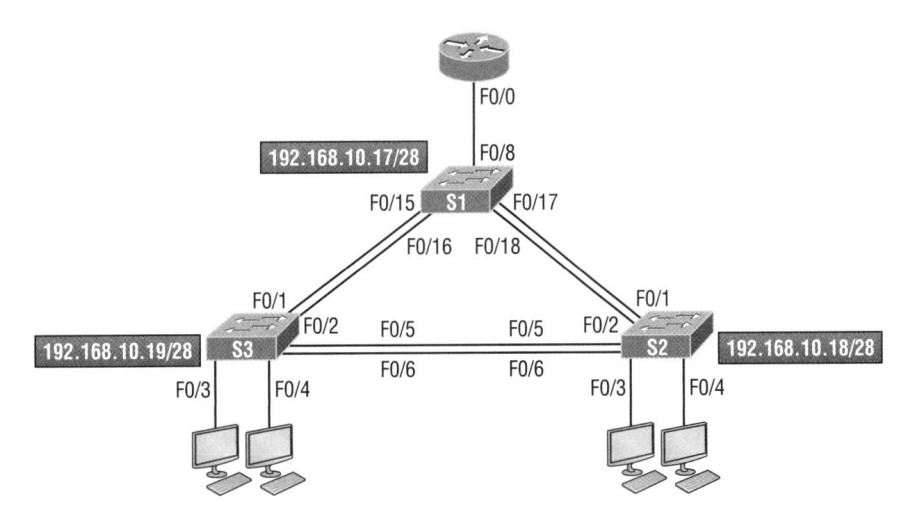

You can use any layer 2 switches for this chapter to follow the configuration, but when we get to Chapter 8, you'll need at least one router plus a layer 3 switch, like my 3560.

Now if we connect our switches to each other, as shown in Figure 7.10, first we'll need a crossover cable between the switches. My 3560 switches autodetect the connection type, so I was able to use straight-through cables—not all switches autodetect the cable type. Different switches have different needs and abilities, so keep this in mind when connecting various switches together. Make a mental note that in the Cisco exam objectives, switches never autodetect!

Okay—so when you first connect the switch ports to each other, the link lights are amber and then turn green, indicating normal operation. What you're actually watching is spanning-tree converging, and this process takes around 50 seconds with no extensions enabled. If you connect into a switch port and the switch port LED is alternating green and amber, it means the port is experiencing errors. When this happens, check the host NIC or the cabling, possibly even the duplex settings on the port to make sure they match the host setting.

Do We Need to Put an IP Address on a Switch?

Absolutely not! Switches have all ports enabled and ready to rock. Take the switch out of the box, plug it in, and the switch starts learning MAC addresses in the CAM. So why would I need an IP address since switches are providing layer 2 services? Because you still need it for in-band management purposes! Telnet, SSH, SNMP, etc., all need an IP address in order to communicate with the switch through the network in-band. Remember, since all ports are enabled by default, you need to shut down unused ports or assign them to an unused VLAN for security reasons.

So where do we put this management IP address the switch needs for management purposes? On the predictably named management VLAN interface—a routed interface on every Cisco switch called interface VLAN 1. This management interface can be changed, and Cisco recommends that you do change this to a different management interface for better security.

Let's configure our switches now.

S1

We're going to begin by connecting into each switch and setting the administrative functions. We'll also assign an IP address to each switch, but as I said, doing that isn't really necessary to make our network function. The only reason we're going to do that is so we can manage/administer it remotely, via Telnet for example. Let's use a simple IP scheme like 192.168.10.16/28. This mask should be familiar to you! Check out the following output:

```
Switch>en
Switch#config t
Switch(config)#hostname S1
S1(config)#enable secret todd
S1(config)#int f0/15
S1(config-if)#description 1st connection to S3
S1(config-if)#int f0/16
S1(config-if)#description 2nd connection to S3
S1(config-if)#int f0/17
```

```
S1(config-if)#description 1st connection to S2
S1(config-if)#int f0/18
S1(config-if)#description 2nd connection to S2
S1(config-if)#int f0/8
S1(config-if)#desc Connection to IVR
S1(config-if)#line con 0
S1(config-line)#password console
S1(config-line)#login
S1(config-line)#line vty 0 15
S1(config-line)#password telnet
S1(config-line)#login
S1(config-line)#int vlan 1
S1(config-if)#ip address 192.168.10.17 255.255.255.240
S1(config-if)#no shut
S1(config-if)#exit
S1(config)#banner motd #this is my S1 switch#
S1(config)#exit
S1#copy run start
Destination filename [startup-config]? [enter]
Building configuration...
[OK]
S1#
```

The first thing to notice here is that there's no IP address configured on the switch's physical interfaces. Since all ports on a switch are enabled by default, there's not really a whole lot to configure. The IP address is configured under a logical interface, called a management domain or VLAN. You can use the default VLAN 1 to manage a switched network just as we're doing here, but you can opt to use a different VLAN for management.

The rest of the configuration is basically the same as the process you go through for router configuration. So remember... no IP addresses on physical switch interfaces, no routing protocols, and so on. We're performing layer 2 switching at this point, not routing! Also, make a note to self that there is no AUX port on Cisco switches.

S2

Here is the S2 configuration:

```
Switch#config t
Switch(config)#hostname S2
S2(config)#enable secret todd
S2(config)#int f0/1
S2(config-if)#desc 1st connection to S1
S2(config-if)#int f0/2
```

```
S2(config-if)#desc 2nd connection to s1
S2(config-if)#int f0/5
S2(config-if)#desc 1st connection to S3
S2(config-if)#int f0/6
S2(config-if)#desc 2nd connection to s3
S2(config-if)#line con 0
S2(config-line)#password console
S2(config-line)#login
S2(config-line)#line vty 0 15
S2(config-line)#password telnet
S2(config-line)#login
S2(config-line)#int vlan 1
S2(config-if)#ip address 192.168.10.18 255.255.255.240
S2(config)#exit
S2#copy run start
Destination filename [startup-config]?[enter]
Building configuration...
[OK]
S2#
```

We should now be able to ping from S2 to S1. Let's try it:

```
S2#ping 192.168.10.17
Type escape sequence to abort.
Sending 5, 100-byte ICMP Echos to 192.168.10.17, timeout is 2 seconds:
.!!!!
Success rate is 80 percent (4/5), round-trip min/avg/max = 1/1/1 ms
S2#
```

Okay—now why did I get only four pings to work instead of five? The first period [.] is a time-out, but the exclamation point [!] is a success.

It's a good question, and here's your answer: the first ping didn't work because of the time that ARP takes to resolve the IP address to its corresponding hardware MAC address.

S3

Check out the S3 switch configuration:

```
Switch>en
Switch#config t
SW-3(config)#hostname S3
S3(config)#enable secret todd
S3(config)#int f0/1
S3(config-if)#desc 1st connection to S1
```

```
S3(config-if)#int f0/2
S3(config-if)#desc 2nd connection to S1
S3(config-if)#int f0/5
S3(config-if)#desc 1st connection to S2
S3(config-if)#int f0/6
S3(config-if)#desc 2nd connection to S2
S3(config-if)#line con 0
S3(config-line)#password console
S3(config-line)#login
S3(config-line)#line vty 0 15
S3(config-line)#password telnet
S3(config-line)#login
S3(config-line)#int vlan 1
S3(config-if)#ip address 192.168.10.19 255.255.255.240
S3(config-if)#no shut
S3(config-if)#banner motd #This is the S3 switch#
S3(config)#exit
S3#copy run start
Destination filename [startup-config]?[enter]
Building configuration...
[OK]
S3#
```

Let's ping to S1 and S2 from the S3 switch and see what happens:

```
S3#ping 192.168.10.17
Type escape sequence to abort.
Sending 5, 100-byte ICMP Echos to 192.168.10.17, timeout is 2 seconds:
.!!!!
Success rate is 80 percent (4/5), round-trip min/avg/max = 1/3/9 ms
S3#ping 192.168.10.18
Type escape sequence to abort.
Sending 5, 100-byte ICMP Echos to 192.168.10.18, timeout is 2 seconds:
.!!!!
Success rate is 80 percent (4/5), round-trip min/avg/max = 1/3/9 ms
S3#sh ip arp
Protocol Address Age (min) Hardware Addr Type Interface
Internet 192.168.10.17 0 001c.575e.c8c0 ARPA Vlan1
Internet 192.168.10.18 0 b414.89d9.18c0 ARPA Vlan1
Internet 192.168.10.19 - ecc8.8202.82c0 ARPA Vlan1
S3#
```

In the output of the show ip arp command, the dash (-) in the minutes column means that it is the physical interface of the device.

Now, before we move on to verifying the switch configurations, there's one more command you need to know about, even though we don't really need it in our current network because we don't have a router involved yet. It's the ip default-gateway command. If you want to manage your switches from outside your LAN, you must set a default gateway on the switches just as you would with a host, and you do this from global config. Here's an example where we introduce our router with an IP address using the last IP address in our subnet range:

S3#**config t**
S3(config)#**ip default-gateway 192.168.10.30**

Now that we have all three switches basically configured, let's have some fun with them!

Port Security

A secured switch port can associate anywhere from 1 to 8,192 MAC addresses, but the 3560s I am using can support only 6,144, but that's more than enough. You can choose to allow the switch to learn these values dynamically, or you can set static addresses for each port using the switchport port-security mac-address *mac-address* command.

So let's set port security on our S3 switch now. Ports Fa0/3 and Fa0/4 will have only one device connected in our lab. By using port security, we're assured that no other device can connect once our hosts in ports Fa0/3 and in Fa0/4 are connected. Here's how to easily do that with just a couple commands:

S3#**config t**
S3(config)#**int range f0/3-4**
S3(config-if-range)#**switchport mode access**
S3(config-if-range)#**switchport port-security**
S3(config-if-range)#**do show port-security int f0/3**
Port Security : Enabled
Port Status : Secure-down
Violation Mode : Shutdown
Aging Time : 0 mins
Aging Type : Absolute
SecureStatic Address Aging : Disabled
Maximum MAC Addresses : 1
Total MAC Addresses : 0
Configured MAC Addresses : 0
Sticky MAC Addresses : 0
Last Source Address:Vlan : 0000.0000.0000:0
Security Violation Count : 0

The first command sets the mode of the ports to "access" ports. These ports must be access or trunk ports to enable port security. By using the command `switchport port-security` on the interface, I've enabled port security with a maximum MAC address of 1 and violation of shutdown. These are the defaults, and you can see them in the highlighted output of the `show port-security int f0/3` command in the preceding code.

Port security is enabled, as displayed on the first line, but the second line shows Secure-down because I haven't connected my hosts into the ports yet. Once I do, the status will show Secure-up and would become Secure-shutdown if a violation occurs.

I've just got to point out this important fact one more time: It's very important to remember that you can set parameters for port security but it won't work until you enable port security at the interface level. Notice the output for port F0/6:

```
S3#config t
S3(config)#int range f0/6
S3(config-if-range)#switchport mode access
S3(config-if-range)#switchport port-security violation restrict
S3(config-if-range)#do show port-security int f0/6
Port Security : Disabled
Port Status : Secure-up
Violation Mode : restrict
[output cut]
```

Port Fa0/6 has been configured with a violation of restrict, but the first line shows that port security has not been enabled on the port yet. Remember, you must use this command at interface level to enable port security on a port:

```
S3(config-if-range)#switchport port-security
```

There are two other modes you can use instead of just shutting down the port. The restrict and protect modes mean that another host can connect up to the maximum MAC addresses allowed, but after the maximum has been met, all frames will just be dropped and the port won't be shut down. Both the restrict and shutdown violation modes alert you via SNMP that a violation has occurred on a port. You can then call the abuser and tell them they're busted—you can see them, you know what they did last summer and they're in trouble!

If you've configured ports with the violation shutdown command, then the ports will look like this when a violation occurs:

```
S3#sh port-security int f0/3
Port Security : Enabled
Port Status : Secure-shutdown
Violation Mode : Shutdown
Aging Time : 0 mins
Aging Type : Absolute
SecureStatic Address Aging : Disabled
```

```
Maximum MAC Addresses : 1
Total MAC Addresses : 2
Configured MAC Addresses : 0
Sticky MAC Addresses : 0
Last Source Address:Vlan : 0013:0ca69:00bb3:00ba8:1
Security Violation Count : 1
```

Here you can see that the port is in Secure-shutdown mode and the light for the port would be amber. To enable the port again, you'd need to do this:

```
S3(config-if)#shutdown
S3(config-if)#no shutdown
```

Let's verify our switch configurations before we move onto VLANs in the next chapter. Beware that even though some switches will show err-disabled instead of Secure-shutdown as my switch shows, there is no difference between the two.

Verifying Cisco Catalyst Switches

The first thing I like to do with any router or switch is to run through the configurations with a show running-config command. Why? Because doing this gives me a really great overview of each device. It's time consuming, and showing you all the configs would take up way too many pages in this book. Besides, we can run other commands that will still stock us up with really good information.

For example, to verify the IP address set on a switch, we can use the show interface command. Here's the output:

```
S3#sh int vlan 1
Vlan1 is up, line protocol is up
Hardware is EtherSVI, address is ecc8.8202.82c0 (bia ecc8.8202.82c0)
Internet address is 192.168.10.19/28
MTU 1500 bytes, BW 1000000 Kbit/sec, DLY 10 usec,
reliability 255/255, txload 1/255, rxload 1/255
Encapsulation ARPA, loopback not set
[output cut]
```

The previous output shows the interface is in up/up status. Remember to always check this interface, either with this command or the show ip interface brief command. Lots of people tend to forget that this interface is shutdown by default.

> **NOTE** Never forget that IP addresses aren't needed on a switch for it to operate. The only reason we would set an IP address, mask, and default gateway is for management purposes.

show mac address-table

I'm sure you remember being shown this command earlier in the chapter. Using it displays the forward filter table, also called a content addressable memory (CAM) table. Here's the output from the S1 switch:

```
S3#sh mac address-table
Mac Address Table]]> -----------------------------------------
Vlan Mac Address Type Ports]]> ---- ----------- -------- -----
All 0100.0ccc.cccc STATIC CPU
[output cut]
1 000e.83b2.e34b DYNAMIC Fa0/1
1 0011.1191.556f DYNAMIC Fa0/1
1 0011.3206.25cb DYNAMIC Fa0/1
1 001a.2f55.c9e8 DYNAMIC Fa0/1
1 001a.4d55.2f7e DYNAMIC Fa0/1
1 001c.575e.c891 DYNAMIC Fa0/1
1 b414.89d9.1886 DYNAMIC Fa0/5
1 b414.89d9.1887 DYNAMIC Fa0/6
```

The switches use base MAC addresses, which are assigned to the CPU. The first one listed is the base mac address of the switch. From the preceding output, you can see that we have six MAC addresses dynamically assigned to Fa0/1, meaning that port Fa0/1 is connected to another switch. Ports Fa0/5 and Fa0/6 have only one MAC address assigned, and all ports are assigned to VLAN 1.

Let's take a look at the S2 switch CAM and see what we can find out.

```
S2#sh mac address-table
Mac Address Table]]> -----------------------------------------
Vlan Mac Address Type Ports]]> ---- ----------- -------- -----
All 0100.0ccc.cccc STATIC CPU
[output cut
1 000e.83b2.e34b DYNAMIC Fa0/5
1 0011.1191.556f DYNAMIC Fa0/5
1 0011.3206.25cb DYNAMIC Fa0/5
1 001a.4d55.2f7e DYNAMIC Fa0/5
1 581f.aaff.86b8 DYNAMIC Fa0/5
1 ecc8.8202.8286 DYNAMIC Fa0/5
1 ecc8.8202.82c0 DYNAMIC Fa0/5
Total Mac Addresses for this criterion: 27
S2#
```

This output tells us that we have seven MAC addresses assigned to Fa0/5, which is our connection to S3. But where's port 6? Since port 6 is a redundant link to S3, STP placed Fa0/6 into blocking mode.

Assigning Static MAC Addresses

You can set a static MAC address in the MAC address table, but like setting static MAC port security without the `sticky` command, it's a ton of work. Just in case you want to do it, here's how:

```
S3(config)#mac address-table ?
aging-time    Set MAC address table entry maximum age
learning      Enable MAC table learning feature
move          Move keyword
notification  Enable/Disable MAC Notification on the switch
static        static keyword
S3(config)#mac address-table static aaaa.bbbb.cccc vlan 1 int fa0/7
S3(config)#do show mac address-table
Mac Address Table]]> ------------------------------------------

Vlan Mac Address Type Ports]]> ---- ----------- -------- -----
All  0100.0ccc.cccc    STATIC   CPU
[output cut]
1    000e.83b2.e34b    DYNAMIC  Fa0/1
1    0011.1191.556f    DYNAMIC  Fa0/1
1    0011.3206.25cb    DYNAMIC  Fa0/1
1    001a.4d55.2f7e    DYNAMIC  Fa0/1
1    001b.d40a.0538    DYNAMIC  Fa0/1
1    001c.575e.c891    DYNAMIC  Fa0/1
1    aaaa.bbbb.0ccc    STATIC   Fa0/7
[output cut]
Total Mac Addresses for this criterion: 59
```

On the left side of the output you can see that a static MAC address has now been assigned permanently to interface Fa0/7 and that it's also been assigned to VLAN 1 only.

This chapter offered lots of great information. You've learned a lot and just maybe even had a little fun along the way! You've configured and verified all switches and set port security, which means you're ready to learn all about virtual LANs.

I'm going to save all our switch configurations so we'll be able to start right from here in Chapter 8.

Summary

In this chapter, I talked about the differences between switches and bridges and how they both work at layer 2. They create MAC address forward/filter tables in order to make decisions on whether to forward or flood a frame.

Although everything in this chapter is important, I wrote two port-security sections—one to provide a foundation and one with a configuration example. You must know both these sections in detail.

I also covered some problems that can occur if you have multiple links between bridges (switches).

Finally, we went through a detailed configuration of Cisco's Catalyst switches, including verifying the configuration itself.

Exam Essentials

Remember the three switch functions.   Address learning, forward/filter decisions, and loop avoidance are the functions of a switch.

Remember the command show mac address-table.   The command show mac address-table will show you the forward/filter table used on the LAN switch.

Understand the reason for port security.   Port security restricts access to a switch based on MAC addresses.

Know the command to enable port security.   To enable port security on a port, you must first make sure the port is an access port with switchport mode access and then use the switchport port-security command at the interface level. You can set the port security parameters before or after enabling port security.

Know the commands to verify port security.   To verify port security, use the show port-security, show port-security interface *interface*, and show running-config commands.

Review Questions

You can find the answers to these questions in the Appendix.

1. Which of the following statements is *not* true with regard to layer 2 switching?
   A. Layer 2 switches and bridges are faster than routers because they don't take up time looking at the Network layer header information.
   B. Layer 2 switches and bridges look at the frame's hardware addresses before deciding to forward, flood, or drop the frame.
   C. Switches create private, dedicated collision domains and provide independent bandwidth on each port.
   D. Switches use application-specific integrated circuits (ASICs) to build and maintain their MAC filter tables.

2. What statement(s) is/are true about the output shown here? (Choose all that apply.)

   ```
   S3#sh port-security int f0/3
   Port Security : Enabled
   Port Status : Secure-shutdown
   Violation Mode : Shutdown
   Aging Time : 0 mins
   Aging Type : Absolute
   SecureStatic Address Aging : Disabled
   Maximum MAC Addresses : 1
   Total MAC Addresses : 2
   Configured MAC Addresses : 0
   Sticky MAC Addresses : 0
   Last Source Address:Vlan : 0013:0ca69:00bb3:00ba8:1
   Security Violation Count : 1
   ```

   A. The port light for F0/3 will be amber in color.
   B. The F0/3 port is forwarding frames.
   C. This problem will resolve itself in a few minutes.
   D. This port requires the `shutdown` command to function.

3. Which of the following commands in this configuration is a prerequisite for the other commands to function?

   ```
   S3#config t
   S(config)#int fa0/3
   S3(config-if#switchport port-security
   S3(config-if#switchport port-security maximum 3
   S3(config-if#switchport port-security violation restrict
   S3(config-if#Switchport mode-security aging time 10
   ```

A. `switchport mode-security aging time 10`
B. `switchport port-security`
C. `switchport port-security maximum 3`
D. `switchport port-security violation restrict`

4. Which if the following is *not* an issue addressed by STP?
   A. Broadcast storms
   B. Gateway redundancy
   C. A device receiving multiple copies of the same frame
   D. Constant updating of the MAC filter table

5. Which two of the following switch port violation modes will alert you via SNMP that a violation has occurred on a port?
   A. `Restrict`
   B. `Protect`
   C. `Shutdown`
   D. `Err-disable`

6. On which default interface have you configured an IP address for a switch?
   A. `int fa0/0`
   B. `int vty 0 15`
   C. `int vlan 1`
   D. `int s/0/0`

7. Which Cisco IOS command is used to verify the port security configuration of a switch port?
   A. `show interfaces port-security`
   B. `show port-security interface`
   C. `show ip interface`
   D. `show interfaces switchport`

8. Which of the following methods will ensure that only one specific host can connect to port Fa0/3 on a switch? (Choose two. Each correct answer is a separate solution.)
   A. Configure port security on F0/3 to accept traffic other than that of the MAC address of the host.
   B. Configure the MAC address of the host as a static entry associated with port F0/3.
   C. Configure an inbound access control list on port F0/3 limiting traffic to the IP address of the host.
   D. Configure port security on F0/3 to accept traffic only from the MAC address of the host.

9. What will be the effect of executing the following command on port F0/1?

    `switch(config-if)# switchport port-security mac-address 00C0.35F0.8301`

    A. The command configures an inbound access control list on port F0/1, limiting traffic to the IP address of the host.
    B. The command expressly prohibits the MAC address of 00c0.35F0.8301 as an allowed host on the switch port.
    C. The command encrypts all traffic on the port from the MAC address of 00c0.35F0.8301.
    D. The command statically defines the MAC address of 00c0.35F0.8301 as an allowed host on the switch port.

10. The conference room has a switch port available for use by the presenter during classes, and each presenter uses the same PC attached to the port. You would like to prevent other PCs from using that port. You have completely removed the former configuration in order to start anew. Which of the following steps is *not* required to prevent any other PCs from using that port?

    A. Enable port security.
    B. Assign the MAC address of the PC to the port.
    C. Make the port an access port.
    D. Make the port a trunk port.

Chapter 8

VLANs and Inter-VLAN Routing

2.0 Network Access

✓ **2.1 Configure and verify VLANs (normal range) spanning multiple switches**

- 2.1.a Access ports (data and voice)
- 2.1.b Default VLAN
- 2.1.c Connectivity

✓ **2.2 Configure and verify interswitch connectivity**

- 2.2.a Trunk ports
- 2.2.b 802.1Q
- 2.2.c Native VLAN

By default, switches break up collision domains, and routers break up broadcast domains.

In contrast to the networks of yesterday that were based on collapsed backbones, thanks to switches, today's network design is characterized by a flatter architecture. So now what? How do we break up broadcast domains in a pure switched internetwork? By creating virtual local area networks (VLANs). A VLAN is a logical grouping of network users and resources connected to administratively defined ports on a switch. When you create VLANs, you're given the ability to create smaller broadcast domains within a layer 2 switched internetwork by assigning different ports on the switch to service different subnetworks. A VLAN is treated like its own subnet or broadcast domain, meaning that frames broadcast onto the network are only switched between the ports logically grouped within the same VLAN.

So, does this mean we no longer need routers? Maybe yes; maybe no. It really depends on what your specific networking needs and goals are. By default, hosts in a specific VLAN can't communicate with hosts that are members of another VLAN, so if you want inter-VLAN communication, the answer is that you still need a router or Inter-VLAN Routing (IVR).

Coming up I'm going to walk you through exactly what a VLAN is and how VLAN memberships are used in a switched networking environment. You'll learn what a trunk link is, plus how to configure and verify them.

Towards the end of this chapter, I'll demonstrate how inter-VLAN communication works by introducing a router into our switched network.

Of course, you'll be working with the same, switched network layout we used in the last chapter. We'll create VLANs, implement trunking and configure Inter-VLAN routing on a layer 3 switch by building switched virtual interfaces (SVIs).

> To find your included bonus material, as well as Todd Lammle videos, practice questions & hands-on labs, please see www.lammle.com/ccna

VLAN Basics

Figure 8.1 illustrates the flat network architecture that used to be standard for layer 2 switched networks. With this type of configuration, every broadcast packet transmitted is seen by every device on the network regardless of whether the device needs to receive that data or not.

VLAN Basics

FIGURE 8.1 Flat network structure

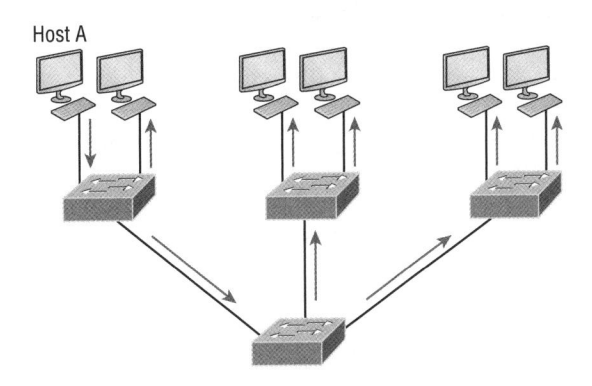

By default, routers allow broadcasts to occur only within the originating network, whereas switches forward broadcasts to all segments. The reason it's called a *flat network* is because it's one *broadcast domain*, not because the actual design is physically flat. In Figure 8.1 we see Host A sending out a broadcast and all ports on all switches forwarding it—all except the port that originally received it.

Now check out Figure 8.2. It pictures a switched network and shows Host A sending a frame with Host D as its destination. Clearly, the important factor here is that the frame is only forwarded out the port where Host D is located.

FIGURE 8.2 The benefit of a switched network

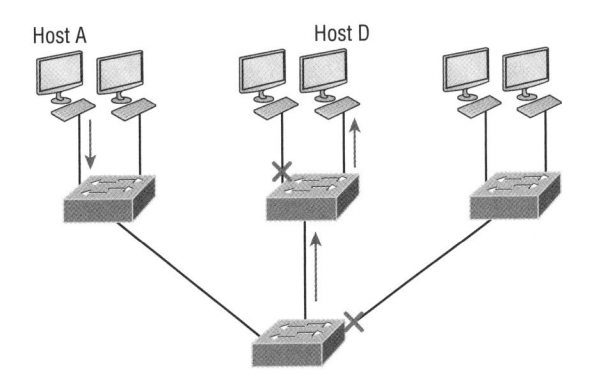

This is a huge improvement over the old hub networks that only offer one huge collision domain by default!

The biggest benefit gained by having a layer 2 switched network is that it creates individual collision domain segments for each device plugged into each port on the switch. It frees us from the old Ethernet density constraints and allows us to build larger networks. But it's not all sunshine here—the more users and devices that populate and use a network, the more broadcasts and packets each switch has to deal with.

And there's another big downside—security! Rather, the lack thereof because within the typical layer 2 switched internetwork, all users can see all devices by default. And you can't stop devices from broadcasting, plus you can't stop users from trying to respond to broadcasts. This means your security options are dismally limited to placing passwords on your servers and other devices.

But wait—there's hope! We can solve a slew of layer 2 switching snags by creating VLANs, as you'll soon see.

VLANs work like this: Figure 8.3 shows all hosts in this very small company connected to one switch. This means all hosts will receive all frames because that's the default behavior of all switches.

FIGURE 8.3 One switch, one LAN: Before VLANs, there were no separations between hosts.

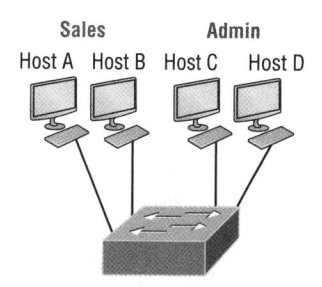

If we want to separate the host's data, we could either buy another switch or create virtual LANs, as shown in Figure 8.4.

FIGURE 8.4 One switch, two virtual LANs (*logical* separation between hosts): Still physically one switch, but this switch can act as many separate devices.

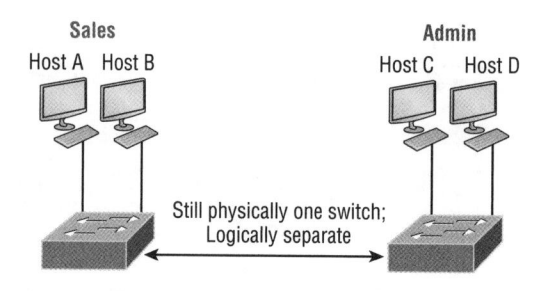

In Figure 8.4, I configured the switch to be two separate LANs, two subnets, two broadcast domains, two VLANs—they all mean the same thing—without buying another switch. We can do this 1,000 times on most Cisco switches, which saves thousands of dollars and more!

Notice that even though the separation is virtual and the hosts are all still connected to the same switch, the LANs can't send data to each other by default. This is because they are still separate networks. We'll get into inter-VLAN communication later in this chapter.

Here's a short list of ways VLANs simplify network management:

- Network adds, moves, and changes are achieved with ease by just configuring a port into the appropriate VLAN.
- A group of users that need an unusually high level of security can be put into its own VLAN so that users outside of that VLAN can't communicate with that group's users.
- As a logical grouping of users by function, VLANs can be considered independent from their physical or geographic locations.
- VLANs greatly enhance network security if implemented correctly.
- VLANs increase the number of broadcast domains while decreasing their size.

Next, we'll explore the world of switching to discover how and why switches provide us with much better network services than hubs can in our networks today.

Broadcast Control

Broadcasts occur in every protocol, but how often they occur depends upon three things:

- The type of protocol
- The application(s) running on the internetwork
- How these services are used

Some older applications have been rewritten to reduce their bandwidth consumption, but the legion of multimedia applications around today consume even generous amounts of bandwidth in no time. Most of these apps use both broadcasts and multicasts extensively. As if that weren't enough of a challenge, factors like faulty equipment, inadequate segmentation, and poorly designed firewalls can seriously compound the problems already caused by these broadcast-intensive applications. All of this added a major new dimension to network design and presents a bunch of new challenges for an administrator. Positively making sure your network is properly segmented so you can quickly isolate a single segment's problems to prevent them from propagating throughout your entire internetwork is now imperative. The most effective way to do that is through strategic switching and routing.

Since switches have become more affordable, most everyone has replaced their flat hub networks with pure switched network and VLAN environments. All devices within a VLAN are members of the same broadcast domain and receive all broadcasts relevant to it. By default, these broadcasts are filtered from all ports on a switch that aren't members of the same VLAN. This is wonderful because you get all the benefits you would with a switched design without getting hit with all the problems you'd have if all your users were in the same broadcast domain!

Security

But there's always a catch, right? Time to get back to those security issues. A flat internetwork's security used to be tackled by connecting hubs and switches together with routers. So it was basically the router's job to maintain security. This arrangement was pretty ineffective for several reasons. First, anyone connecting to the physical network could access the network resources located on that particular physical LAN. Second, all anyone had to do to observe any and all traffic traversing that network was to simply plug a network analyzer into the hub. And like that last, scary fact, users could easily join a workgroup by just plugging their workstations into the existing hub!

But that's exactly what makes VLANs so cool. If you build them and create multiple broadcast groups, you can still have total control over each port and user. So the days when anyone could just plug their workstations into any switch port and gain access to network resources are history because now you get to control each port and any resources it can access.

And that's not even all—VLANs can be created in harmony with a specific user's need for the network resources. Plus, switches can be configured to inform a network management station about unauthorized access to those vital network resources. And if you need inter-VLAN communication, you can implement restrictions on a router to make sure this all happens securely. You can also place restrictions on hardware addresses, protocols, and applications. *Now* we're talking security!

Flexibility and Scalability

As we know, layer 2 switches only read frames for filtering because they don't look at the Network layer protocol. And by default, switches forward broadcasts to all ports. But if you create and implement VLANs, you're essentially creating smaller broadcast domains at layer 2.

As a result, broadcasts sent out from a node in one VLAN won't be forwarded to ports configured to belong to a different VLAN. But if we assign switch ports or users to VLAN groups on a switch or on a group of connected switches, we gain the flexibility to exclusively add only the users we want to let into that broadcast domain regardless of their physical location. This setup can also work to block broadcast storms caused by a faulty network interface card (NIC) as well as prevent an intermediate device from propagating broadcast storms throughout the entire internetwork. Those evils can still happen on the VLAN where the problem originated, but the disease will be fully contained in that one ailing VLAN.

Another advantage is that when a VLAN gets too big, you can simply create more VLANs to keep the broadcasts from consuming too much bandwidth. The fewer users in a VLAN, the fewer users affected by broadcasts. This is all good, but you seriously need to keep network services in mind and understand how the users connect to these services when creating a VLAN. A good strategy is to try to keep all services, except for the email and Internet access that everyone needs, local to all users whenever possible.

Identifying VLANs

Switch ports are layer 2–only interfaces that are associated with a physical port that can belong to only one VLAN if it's an access port or all VLANs if it's a trunk port.

Switches are definitely busy devices. As myriad frames are switched throughout the network, they have to be able to keep track of all frames, plus understand what to do with them depending on their associated hardware addresses. And remember—frames are handled differently according to the type of link they're traversing.

There are two different types of ports in a switched environment. Let's take a look at the first type in Figure 8.5.

FIGURE 8.5 Access ports

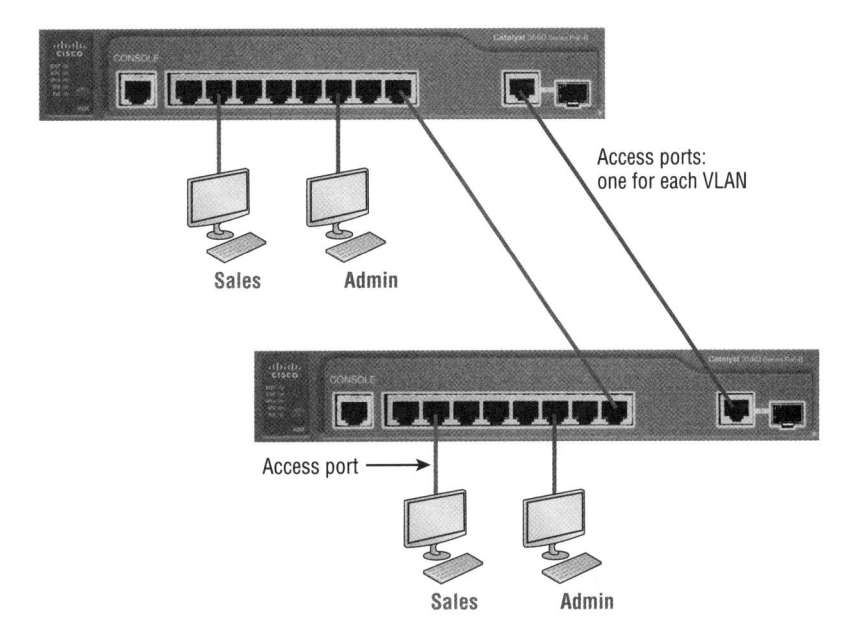

Notice there are access ports for each host and an access port between switches—one for each VLAN.

Access ports An *access port* belongs to and carries the traffic of only one VLAN. Traffic is both received and sent in native formats with no VLAN information (tagging) at all. Anything arriving on an access port is simply assumed to belong to the VLAN assigned to the port. Because an access port doesn't look at the source address, tagged traffic—a frame with added VLAN information—can be correctly forwarded and received only on trunk ports.

With an access link, this can be referred to as the *configured VLAN* of the port. Any device attached to an *access link* is unaware of a VLAN membership—the device just assumes it's part of some broadcast domain. But it doesn't have the big picture, so it doesn't understand the physical network topology at all.

Another good bit of information to know is that switches remove any VLAN information from the frame before it's forwarded out to an access-link device. Remember that access-link devices can't communicate with devices outside their VLAN unless the packet is routed. Also, you can only create a switch port to be either an access port or a trunk port—not both. So you've got to choose one or the other and know that if you make it an access port, that port can be assigned to one VLAN only.

In Figure 8.5, only the hosts in the Sales VLAN can talk to other hosts in the same VLAN. This is the same with the Admin VLAN, and they can both communicate to hosts on the other switch because of an access link for each VLAN configured between switches.

Voice access ports   Not to confuse you, but all that I just said about the fact that an access port can be assigned to only one VLAN is really only sort of true. Nowadays, most switches will allow you to add a second VLAN to an access port on a switch port for your voice traffic, called the voice VLAN. The voice VLAN used to be called the auxiliary VLAN, which allowed it to be overlaid on top of the data VLAN, enabling both types of traffic to travel through the same port. Even though this is technically considered to be a different type of link, it's still just an access port that can be configured for both data and voice VLANs. This allows you to connect both a phone and a PC device to one switch port but still have each device in a separate VLAN.

Trunk ports   Believe it or not, the term *trunk port* was inspired by the telephone system trunks, which carry multiple telephone conversations at a time. So it follows that trunk ports can similarly carry multiple VLANs at a time as well.

A *trunk link* is a 100, 1,000, 10,000 Mbps, or more, point-to-point link between two switches, between a switch and router, or even between a switch and server, and it carries the traffic of multiple VLANs—from 1 to 4,094 VLANs at a time. But the amount is really only up to 1,001 unless you're going with extended VLANs.

Instead of an access link for each VLAN between switches, we'll create a trunk link as seen in Figure 8.6.

FIGURE 8.6   VLANs can span multiple switches by using trunk links, which carry traffic for multiple VLANs.

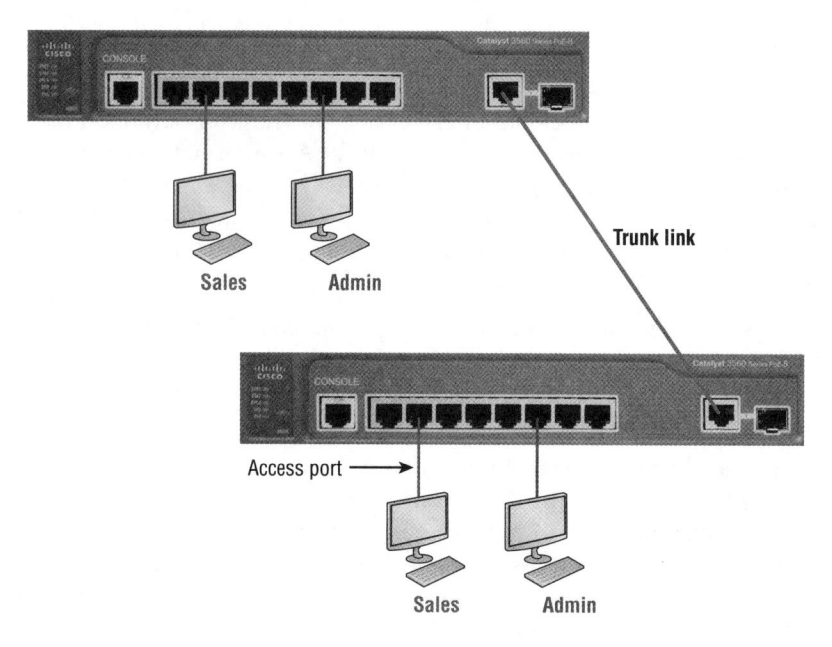

Trunking can offer a real advantage because with it, you get to make a single port part of a whole bunch of different VLANs at the same time. This is a great feature because you can actually set ports up to have a server in two separate broadcast domains simultaneously so your users won't have to cross a layer 3 device (router) to log in and access it. Another benefit to trunking comes into play when you're connecting switches. Trunk links can carry the frames of various VLANs across them, but by default, if the links between your switches aren't trunked, only information from the configured access VLAN will be switched across that link.

Also good to know is that all VLANs send information on a trunked link unless you clear each VLAN by hand. I'll show you how to clear individual VLANs from a trunk in a bit.

It's finally time to tell you about frame tagging and the VLAN identification methods used in it across our trunk links.

Frame Tagging

As you now know, you can set up your VLANs to span more than one connected switch. You can see that going on in Figure 8.6, which depicts hosts from two VLANs spread across two switches. This flexible, power-packed capability is probably the main advantage to implementing VLANs, and we can do this with up to a thousand VLANs and thousands upon thousands of hosts!

All this can get kind of complicated—even for a switch—so there needs to be a way for each one to keep track of all the users and frames as they travel the switch fabric and VLANs. When I say "switch fabric," I'm just referring to a group of switches that share the same VLAN information. And this just happens to be where *frame tagging* enters the scene. This frame identification method uniquely assigns a user-defined VLAN ID to each frame.

Here's how it works: Once within the switch fabric, each switch that the frame reaches must first identify the VLAN ID from the frame tag. It then finds out what to do with the frame by looking at the information in what's known as the filter table. If the frame reaches a switch that has another trunked link, the frame will be forwarded out of the trunk-link port.

Once the frame reaches an exit that's determined by the forward/filter table to be an access link matching the frame's VLAN ID, the switch will remove the VLAN identifier. This is so the destination device can receive the frames without being required to understand their VLAN identification information.

Another great thing about trunk ports is that they'll support tagged and untagged traffic simultaneously—if you're using 802.1q trunking, which we will talk about next. The trunk port is assigned a default port VLAN ID (PVID) for a VLAN upon which all untagged traffic will travel. This VLAN is also called the native VLAN and is always VLAN 1 by default, but it can be changed to any VLAN number.

Similarly, any untagged or tagged traffic with a NULL (unassigned) VLAN ID is assumed to belong to the VLAN with the port default PVID. Again, this would be VLAN 1 by default. A packet with a VLAN ID equal to the outgoing port native VLAN is sent untagged and can communicate to only hosts or devices in that same VLAN. All other

VLAN traffic has to be sent with a VLAN tag to communicate within a particular VLAN that corresponds with that tag.

VLAN Identification Methods

VLAN identification is what switches use to keep track of all those frames as they're traversing a switch fabric. It's how switches identify which frames belong to which VLANs, and there's more than one trunking method.

Inter-Switch Link (ISL)

Inter-Switch Link (ISL) is a way of explicitly tagging VLAN information onto an Ethernet frame. This tagging information allows VLANs to be multiplexed over a trunk link through an external encapsulation method. This allows the switch to identify the VLAN membership of a frame received over the trunked link.

By running ISL, you can interconnect multiple switches and still maintain VLAN information as traffic travels between switches on trunk links. ISL functions at layer 2 by encapsulating a data frame with a new header and by performing a new cyclic redundancy check (CRC).

Of note is that ISL is proprietary to Cisco switches, but it's pretty versatile too. ISL can be used on a switch port, router interfaces, and server interface cards to trunk a server. Although some Cisco switches still support ISL frame tagging, Cisco has moved toward using only 802.1q.

IEEE 802.1q

Created by the IEEE as a standard method of frame tagging, IEEE 802.1q actually inserts a field into the frame to identify the VLAN. If you're trunking between a Cisco switched link and a different brand of switch, you've got to use 802.1q for the trunk to work.

Unlike ISL, which encapsulates the frame with control information, 802.1q inserts an 802.1q field along with tag control information, as shown in Figure 8.7.

FIGURE 8.7 IEEE 802.1q encapsulation with and without the 802.1q tag

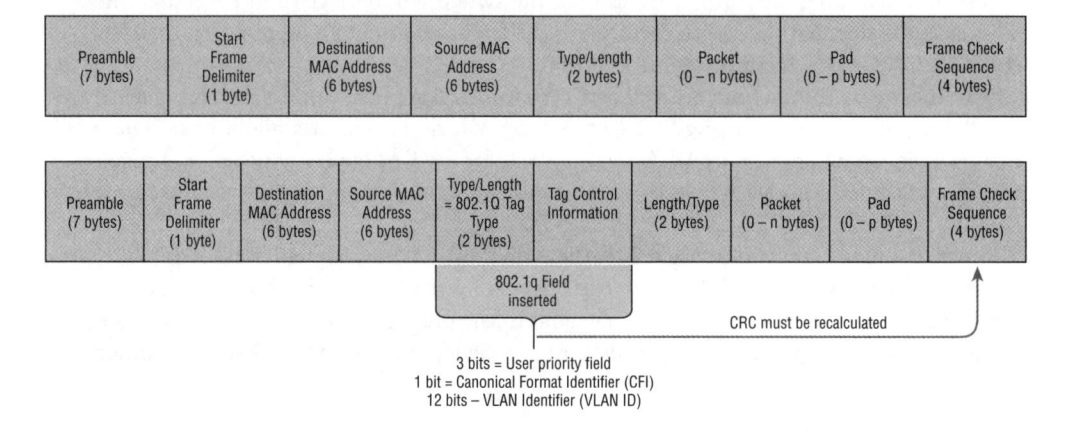

| Preamble (7 bytes) | Start Frame Delimiter (1 byte) | Destination MAC Address (6 bytes) | Source MAC Address (6 bytes) | Type/Length (2 bytes) | Packet (0 – n bytes) | Pad (0 – p bytes) | Frame Check Sequence (4 bytes) |

| Preamble (7 bytes) | Start Frame Delimiter (1 byte) | Destination MAC Address (6 bytes) | Source MAC Address (6 bytes) | Type/Length = 802.1Q Tag Type (2 bytes) | Tag Control Information | Length/Type (2 bytes) | Packet (0 – n bytes) | Pad (0 – p bytes) | Frame Check Sequence (4 bytes) |

802.1q Field inserted

CRC must be recalculated

3 bits = User priority field
1 bit = Canonical Format Identifier (CFI)
12 bits – VLAN Identifier (VLAN ID)

For the Cisco exam objectives, it's only the 12-bit VLAN ID that matters. This field identifies the VLAN and can be 2 to the 12th, minus 2 for the 0, and 4,095 reserved VLANs, which means an 802.1q tagged frame can carry information for 4,094 VLANs.

It works like this: You first designate each port that's going to be a trunk with 802.1q encapsulation. The other ports must be assigned a specific VLAN ID in order for them to communicate. VLAN 1 is the default native VLAN, and when using 802.1q, all traffic for a native VLAN is untagged. The ports that populate the same trunk create a group with this native VLAN, and each port gets tagged with an identification number reflecting that. Again, the default is VLAN 1. The native VLAN allows the trunks to accept information that was received without any VLAN identification or frame tag.

Most 2960 model switches only support the IEEE 802.1q trunking protocol. The 3560 will support both the ISL and IEEE methods, which you'll see later in this chapter.

> The basic purpose of ISL and 802.1q frame-tagging methods is to provide inter-switch VLAN communication. Remember that any ISL or 802.1q frame tagging is removed if a frame is forwarded out an access link—tagging is used internally and across trunk links only!

Routing Between VLANs

Hosts in a VLAN live in their own broadcast domain and can communicate freely. VLANs create network partitioning and traffic separation at layer 2 of the OSI. As I said when I told you why we still need routers, if you want hosts or any other IP-addressable device to communicate between VLANs, you must have a layer 3 device to provide routing.

For this, you can use a router that has an interface for each VLAN or a router that supports ISL or 802.1q routing. The least expensive router that supports ISL or 802.1q routing is the 2600 series router. You'd have to buy that from a used-equipment reseller because they are end-of-life, or EOL. I'd recommend at least a 2800 as a bare minimum, but even that only supports 802.1q; Cisco is really moving away from ISL, so you probably should only be using 802.1q anyway. Some 2800s may support both ISL and 802.1q; I've just never seen it supported.

Anyway, as shown in Figure 8.8, if you had two or three VLANs, you could get by with a router equipped with two or three FastEthernet connections. And 10Base-T is okay for home study purposes, and I mean only for your studies, but for anything else I'd highly recommend Gigabit or higher interfaces for real power under the hood!

What we see in Figure 8.8 is that each router interface is plugged into an access link. This means that each of the routers' interface IP addresses would then become the default gateway address for each host in each respective VLAN.

FIGURE 8.8 Router connecting three VLANs together for inter-VLAN communication, one router interface for each VLAN

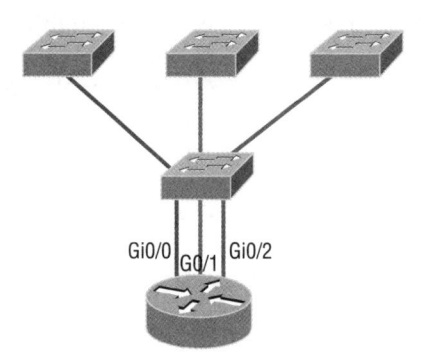

If you have more VLANs available than router interfaces, you can configure trunking on one FastEthernet interface or buy a layer 3 switch, like the old and now cheap 3560 or a higher-end switch like a 3850. You could even opt for a 6800 if you're feeling spendy.

Instead of using a router interface for each VLAN, you can use one FastEthernet interface and run ISL or 802.1q trunking. Figure 8.9 shows how a FastEthernet interface on a router will look when configured with ISL or 802.1q trunking. This allows all VLANs to communicate through one interface. Cisco calls this a router on a stick (ROAS), and this is what's used on the CCNA objectives for Inter-VLAN routing.

FIGURE 8.9 Router on a stick: single router interface connecting all three VLANs together for inter-VLAN communication

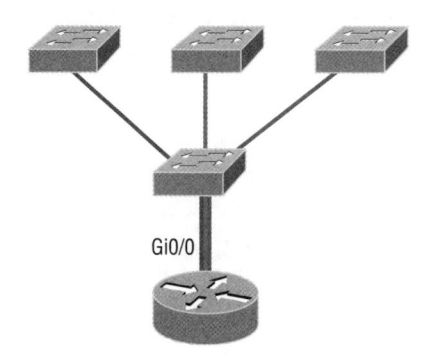

I really want to point out that this creates a potential bottleneck, as well as a single point of failure, so your host/VLAN count is limited. To how many? Well, that depends on your traffic level. To really make things right, you'd be better off using a higher-end switch and routing on the backplane. But if you just happen to have a router sitting around, configuring this method is free, right?

Figure 8.10 shows how we would create a router on a stick using a router's physical interface by creating logical interfaces—one for each VLAN.

FIGURE 8.10 A router creates logical interfaces.

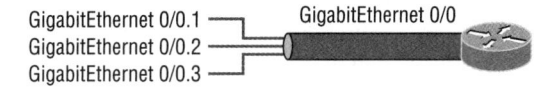

Here we see one physical interface divided into multiple subinterfaces, with one subnet assigned per VLAN, and each subinterface being the default gateway address for each VLAN/subnet. An encapsulation identifier must be assigned to each subinterface to define the VLAN ID of that subinterface. In the next section where I'll configure VLANs and inter-VLAN routing, I'll configure our switched network with a router on a stick to demonstrate this for you.

But wait, there's still one more way to go about routing! Instead of using an external router interface for each VLAN or an external router on a stick, we can configure logical interfaces on the backplane of the layer 3 switch; this is called inter-VLAN routing (IVR), and it's configured with a switched virtual interface (SVI).

Figure 8.11 shows how hosts see these virtual interfaces.

FIGURE 8.11 With IVR, routing runs on the backplane of the switch, and it appears to the hosts that a router is present.

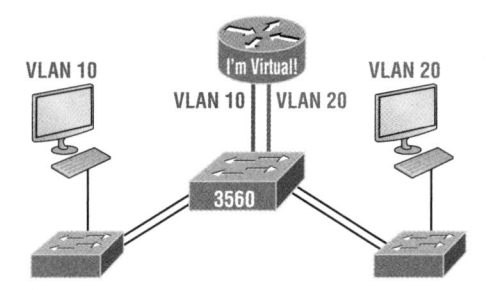

In Figure 8.11, it appears there's a router present, but there is no physical router present as there was when we used router on a stick. The IVR process takes little effort, but it's easy to implement, which makes it very cool! Plus, it's a lot more efficient for inter-VLAN routing than an external router is.

To implement IVR on a multilayer switch, we just need to create logical interfaces in the switch configuration for each VLAN. We'll configure this method in a minute, but first let's take our existing switched network from Chapter 7, "Layer 2 Switching," add some VLANs, and then we'll configure VLAN memberships and trunk links between our switches.

Configuring VLANs

Configuring VLANs is actually pretty easy. It's just that figuring out which users you want in each VLAN is not easy, and doing that can eat up a lot of your time. Once you've decided on the number of VLANs you want to create and established which users you want belonging to each one, it's time to bring your first VLAN into the world.

To configure VLANs on a Cisco Catalyst switch, use the global `config vlan` command. In the following example, I'm going to demonstrate how to configure VLANs on the S1 switch by creating three VLANs for three different departments—again, remember that VLAN 1 is the native and management VLAN by default:

```
S1(config)#vlan ?
  WORD        ISL VLAN IDs 1-4094
  access-map  Create vlan access-map or enter vlan access-map command mode
  dot1q       dot1q parameters
  filter      Apply a VLAN Map
  group       Create a vlan group
  internal    internal VLAN
S1(config)#vlan 2
S1(config-vlan)#name Sales
S1(config-vlan)#vlan 3
S1(config-vlan)#name Marketing
S1(config-vlan)#vlan 4
S1(config-vlan)#name Accounting
S1(config-vlan)#vlan 5
S1(config-vlan)#name Voice
S1(config-vlan)#^Z
S1#
```

In this output, you can see that you can create VLANs from 1 to 4094. But this is only mostly true. As I said, VLANs can really only be created up to 1001, and you can't use, change, rename, or delete VLANs 1 or 1002 through 1005 because they're reserved. The VLAN numbers above 1005 are called extended VLANs and won't be saved in the database unless your switch is set to what is called VLAN Trunking Protocol (VTP) transparent mode.

You won't see these VLAN numbers used too often in production. Here's an example of me attempting to set my S1 switch to VLAN 4000 when my switch is set to VTP server mode (the default VTP mode):

```
S1#config t
S1(config)#vlan 4000
S1(config-vlan)#^Z
% Failed to create VLANs 4000
Extended VLAN(s) not allowed in current VTP mode.
%Failed to commit extended VLAN(s) changes.
```

After you create the VLANs that you want, you can use the `show vlan` command to check them out. But notice that, by default, all ports on the switch are in VLAN 1. To change the VLAN associated with a port, you need to go to each interface and specifically tell it which VLAN to be a part of.

Configuring VLANs 233

> **NOTE** Remember that a created VLAN is unused until it is assigned to a switch port or ports and that all ports are always assigned in VLAN 1 unless set otherwise.

Once the VLANs are created, verify your configuration with the show vlan command (sh vlan for short):

```
S1#sh vlan
VLAN Name Status Ports
---- ------------------------ --------- -------------------------------
1 default active Fa0/1, Fa0/2, Fa0/3, Fa0/4
Fa0/5, Fa0/6, Fa0/7, Fa0/8
Fa0/9, Fa0/10, Fa0/11, Fa0/12
Fa0/13, Fa0/14, Fa0/19, Fa0/20
Fa0/21, Fa0/22, Fa0/23, Gi0/1
Gi0/2
2 Sales active
3 Marketing active
4 Accounting active
5 Voice active
[output cut]
```

This may seem repetitive, but it's important, and I want you to remember it: You can't change, delete, or rename VLAN 1 because it's the default VLAN, and you just can't change that—period. It's also the native VLAN of all switches by default, and Cisco recommends that you use it as your management VLAN. If you're worried about security issues, then just change the management VLAN. Basically, any ports that aren't specifically assigned to a different VLAN will be sent down to the native VLAN—VLAN 1.

In the preceding S1 output, you can see that ports Fa0/1 through Fa0/14, Fa0/19 through 23, and Gi0/1 and Gi0/2 uplinks are all in VLAN 1. But where are ports 15 through 18? First, understand that the command show vlan only displays access ports, so now that you know what you're looking at with the show vlan command, where do you think ports Fa15–18 are?

That's right! They are trunked ports. Cisco switches run a proprietary protocol called *Dynamic Trunk Protocol (DTP)*, and if there is a compatible switch connected, they will start trunking automatically, which is precisely where my four ports are. You have to use the show interfaces trunk command to see your trunked ports like this:

```
S1# show interfaces trunk
Port Mode Encapsulation Status Native vlan
Fa0/15 desirable n-isl trunking 1
Fa0/16 desirable n-isl trunking 1
Fa0/17 desirable n-isl trunking 1
Fa0/18 desirable n-isl trunking 1
```

```
Port Vlans allowed on trunk
Fa0/15 1-4094
Fa0/16 1-4094
Fa0/17 1-4094
Fa0/18 1-4094
[output cut]
```

This output reveals that the VLANs from 1 to 4094 are allowed across the trunk by default. Another helpful command, which is also part of the Cisco exam objectives, is the `show interfaces` *interface* `switchport` command:

```
S1#sh interfaces fastEthernet 0/15 switchport
Name: Fa0/15
Switchport: Enabled
Administrative Mode: dynamic desirable
Operational Mode: trunk
Administrative Trunking Encapsulation: negotiate
Operational Trunking Encapsulation: isl
Negotiation of Trunking: On
Access Mode VLAN: 1 (default)
Trunking Native Mode VLAN: 1 (default)
Administrative Native VLAN tagging: enabled
Voice VLAN: none
[output cut]
```

The highlighted output shows us the administrative mode of `dynamic desirable`, that the port is a trunk port, and that DTP was used to negotiate the frame-tagging method of ISL. It also predictably shows that the native VLAN is the default of 1.

Now that we can see the VLANs created, we can assign switch ports to specific ones. Each port can be part of only one VLAN, with the exception of voice access ports. Using trunking, you can make a port available to traffic from all VLANs. I'll cover that next.

Assigning Switch Ports to VLANs

You configure a port to belong to a VLAN by assigning a membership mode that specifies the kind of traffic the port carries plus the number of VLANs it can belong to. You can also configure each port on a switch to be in a specific VLAN (access port) by using the `interface switchport` command. You can even configure multiple ports at the same time with the `interface range` command.

In the next example, I'll configure interface Fa0/3 to VLAN 3. This is the connection from the S3 switch to the host device:

```
S3#config t
S3(config)#int fa0/3
S3(config-if)#switchport ?
```

```
access          Set access mode characteristics of the interface
autostate       Include or exclude this port from vlan link up calculation
backup          Set backup for the interface
block           Disable forwarding of unknown uni/multi cast addresses
host            Set port host
mode            Set trunking mode of the interface
nonegotiate     Device will not engage in negotiation protocol on this
                interface
port-security   Security related command
priority        Set appliance 802.1p priority
private-vlan    Set the private VLAN configuration
protected       Configure an interface to be a protected port
trunk           Set trunking characteristics of the interface
voice           Voice appliance attributes voice
```

Well now, what do we have here? There's some new stuff showing up in our output now. We can see various commands—some that I've already covered, but no worries because I'm going to cover the access, mode, nonegotiate, and trunk commands coming up.

However, let's start with setting an access port on S1, which is probably the most widely used type of port you'll find on production switches that have VLANs configured:

```
S3(config-if)#switchport mode ?
access        Set trunking mode to ACCESS unconditionally
dot1q-tunnel  set trunking mode to TUNNEL unconditionally
dynamic       Set trunking mode to dynamically negotiate access or trunk mode
private-vlan  Set private-vlan mode
trunk         Set trunking mode to TRUNK unconditionally
S3(config-if)#switchport mode access
S3(config-if)#switchport access vlan 3
S3(config-if)#switchport voice vlan 5
```

By starting with the `switchport mode access` command, you're telling the switch that this is a nontrunking layer 2 port. You can then assign a VLAN to the port with the `switchport access` command, as well as configure the same port to be a member of a different type of VLAN, called the voice VLAN.

This allows you to connect a laptop into a phone, and the phone into a single switch port. Remember, you can choose many ports to configure simultaneously with the `interface range` command.

Let's take a look at our VLANs now:

```
S3#show vlan
VLAN Name           Status    Ports
---- -------------- --------- -------------------------------
1    default        active    Fa0/4, Fa0/5, Fa0/6, Fa0/7
Fa0/8, Fa0/9, Fa0/10, Fa0/11,
```

```
Fa0/12, Fa0/13, Fa0/14, Fa0/19,
Fa0/20, Fa0/21, Fa0/22, Fa0/23,
Gi0/1 ,Gi0/2
2 Sales active
3 Marketing active Fa0/3]]> 5 Voice active Fa0/3
```

Notice that port Fa0/3 is now a member of VLAN 3 and VLAN 5—two different types of VLANs. But, can you tell me where ports 1 and 2 are? And why aren't they showing up in the output of show vlan? That's right, because they are trunk ports!

We can also see this with the show interfaces interface switchport command:

```
S3#sh int fa0/3 switchport
Name: Fa0/3
Switchport: Enabled
Administrative Mode: static access
Operational Mode: static access
Administrative Trunking Encapsulation: negotiate
Negotiation of Trunking: Off
```

Access Mode VLAN: 3 (Marketing) Trunking Native Mode VLAN: 1 (default) Administrative Native VLAN tagging: enabled Voice VLAN: 5 (Voice)

The highlighted output shows that Fa0/3 is an access port and a member of VLAN 3 (Marketing), as well as a member of the Voice VLAN 5.

That's it. Well, sort of. If you plugged devices into each VLAN port, they can only talk to other devices in the same VLAN. But as soon as you learn a bit more about trunking, we're going to enable inter-VLAN communication!

Configuring Trunk Ports

The 2960 switch only runs the IEEE 802.1q encapsulation method. To configure trunking on a FastEthernet port, use the interface command switchport mode trunk. It's a tad different on the 3560 switch.

The following switch output shows the trunk configuration on interfaces Fa0/15–18 as set to trunk:

```
S1(config)#int range f0/15-18
S1(config-if-range)#switchport trunk encapsulation dot1q
S1(config-if-range)#switchport mode trunk
```

I want to point out here that if you have a switch that only runs the 802.1q encapsulation method, you wouldn't use the encapsulation command as I did in the preceding output. Let's check out our trunk ports now:

```
S1(config-if-range)#do sh int f0/15 swi
Name: Fa0/15
Switchport: Enabled
```

```
Administrative Mode: trunk
Operational Mode: trunk
Administrative Trunking Encapsulation: dot1q
Operational Trunking Encapsulation: dot1q
Negotiation of Trunking: On
Access Mode VLAN: 1 (default)
Trunking Native Mode VLAN: 1 (default)
Administrative Native VLAN tagging: enabled
Voice VLAN: none
```

Notice that port Fa0/15 is a trunk and running 802.1q. Let's take another look:

```
S1(config-if-range)#do sh int trunk
Port Mode Encapsulation Status Native vlan
Fa0/15 on 802.1q trunking 1
Fa0/16 on 802.1q trunking 1
Fa0/17 on 802.1q trunking 1
Fa0/18 on 802.1q trunking 1
Port Vlans allowed on trunk
Fa0/15 1-4094
Fa0/16 1-4094
Fa0/17 1-4094
Fa0/18 1-4094
```

Take note of the fact that ports 15–18 are now in the trunk mode of on and the encapsulation is now 802.1q instead of the negotiated ISL. Here's a description of the different options available when configuring a switch interface:

switchport mode access   I touched on this in the previous section… It puts the interface (access port) into permanent nontrunking mode and negotiates to convert the link into a nontrunk link. The interface becomes a nontrunk interface regardless of whether the neighboring interface is a trunk interface. The port would be a dedicated layer 2 access port.

switchport mode dynamic auto   This mode makes the interface able to convert the link to a trunk link. The interface becomes a trunk interface if the neighboring interface is set to trunk or desirable mode. The default is dynamic auto on a lot of Cisco switches, but that default trunk method is changing to dynamic desirable on most new models.

switchport mode dynamic desirable   This one makes the interface actively attempt to convert the link to a trunk link. The interface becomes a trunk interface if the neighboring interface is set to trunk, desirable, or auto mode. I used to see this mode as the default on some switches, but not anymore. It's now the default switch port mode for all Ethernet interfaces on all new Cisco switches.

switchport mode trunk   Puts the interface into permanent trunking mode and negotiates to convert the neighboring link into a trunk link. The interface becomes a trunk interface even if the neighboring interface isn't a trunk interface.

switchport nonegotiate   Prevents the interface from generating DTP frames. You can use this command only when the interface switchport mode is access or trunk. You must manually configure the neighboring interface as a trunk interface to establish a trunk link.

> Dynamic Trunking Protocol (DTP) is used for negotiating trunking on a link between two devices as well as negotiating the encapsulation type of either 802.1q or ISL. I use the `nonegotiate` command when I want dedicated trunk ports; no questions asked.

To disable trunking on an interface, use the `switchport mode access` command, which sets the port back to a dedicated layer 2 access switch port.

Defining the Allowed VLANs on a Trunk

As I've mentioned, trunk ports send and receive information from all VLANs by default, and if a frame is untagged, it's sent to the management VLAN. Know that this applies to the extended range VLANs too.

We can remove VLANs from the allowed list to prevent traffic from certain VLANs from traversing a trunked link. I'll show you how you'd do that, but first let me again demonstrate that all VLANs are allowed across the trunk link by default:

```
S1#sh int trunk
[output cut]
Port      Vlans allowed on trunk
Fa0/15    1-4094
Fa0/16    1-4094
Fa0/17    1-4094
Fa0/18    1-4094
S1(config)#int f0/15
S1(config-if)#switchport trunk allowed vlan 4,6,12,15
S1(config-if)#do show int trunk
[output cut]
Port      Vlans allowed on trunk
Fa0/15    4,6,12,15
Fa0/16    1-4094
Fa0/17    1-4094
Fa0/18    1-4094
```

The preceding command affected the trunk link configured on S1 port F0/15, causing it to permit all traffic sent and received for VLANs 4, 6, 12, and 15. You can try to remove VLAN 1 on a trunk link, but it will still send and receive management like CDP, DTP, and VTP, so what's the point?

To remove a range of VLANs, just use the hyphen:

```
S1(config-if)#switchport trunk allowed vlan remove 4-8
```

If by chance someone has removed some VLANs from a trunk link and you want to set the trunk back to default, just use this command:

`S1(config-if)#`**`switchport trunk allowed vlan all`**

Next, I want to show you how to configure a native VLAN for a trunk before we start routing between VLANs.

Changing or Modifying the Trunk Native VLAN

You can change the trunk port native VLAN from VLAN 1, which many people do for security reasons. To change the native VLAN, use the following command:

```
S1(config)#int f0/15
S1(config-if)#switchport trunk native vlan ?
<1-4094> VLAN ID of the native VLAN when this port is in trunking mode
S1(config-if)#switchport trunk native vlan 4
1w6d: %CDP-4-NATIVE_VLAN_MISMATCH: Native VLAN mismatch discovered on
FastEthernet0/15 (4), with S3 FastEthernet0/1 (1).
```

So we've changed our native VLAN on our trunk link to 4, and by using the show running-config command, I can see the configuration under the trunk link:

```
S1#sh run int f0/15
Building configuration...
Current configuration : 202 bytes
!
interface FastEthernet0/15
 description 1st connection to S3
 switchport trunk encapsulation dot1q
 switchport trunk native vlan 4
 switchport trunk allowed vlan 4,6,12,15
 switchport mode trunk
end
S1#!
```

Oops—wait a minute! You didn't think it would just start working, did you? Of course not! Here's the rub: If all switches don't have the same native VLAN configured on the given trunk links, then we'll start to receive this error, which happened immediately after I entered the command:

```
1w6d: %CDP-4-NATIVE_VLAN_MISMATCH: Native VLAN mismatch discovered
on FastEthernet0/15 (4), with S3 FastEthernet0/1 (1).
```

Actually, this is a good, noncryptic error, so I can either go to the other end of our trunk link(s) and change the native VLAN or set the native VLAN back to the default to fix it. Here's how to do that:

```
S1(config-if)#no switchport trunk native vlan
1w6d: %SPANTREE-2-UNBLOCK_CONSIST_PORT: Unblocking FastEthernet0/15
on VLAN0004. Port consistency restored.
```

Okay—now our trunk link is using the default VLAN 1 as the native VLAN. Just remember that all switches on a given trunk must use the same native VLAN or you'll have some ugly management problems. These issues won't affect user data, just management traffic between switches. Now, let's mix it up by connecting a router into our switched network and configure inter-VLAN communication.

Configuring Inter-VLAN Routing

By default, only hosts that are members of the same VLAN can communicate. To change this and allow inter-VLAN communication, you need a router or a layer 3 switch. I'm going to start with the router approach.

To support ISL or 802.1q routing on a FastEthernet interface, the router's interface is divided into logical interfaces—one for each VLAN—as was shown in Figure 8.10. These are called *subinterfaces*. From a FastEthernet or Gigabit interface, you can set the interface to trunk with the encapsulation command:

```
ISR#config t
ISR(config)#int f0/0.1
ISR(config-subif)#encapsulation ?
dot1Q  IEEE 802.1Q Virtual LAN
ISR(config-subif)#encapsulation dot1Q ?
<1-4094>  IEEE 802.1Q VLAN ID
```

Notice that my 2811 router (named ISR) only supports 802.1q. We'd need an older-model router to run the ISL encapsulation, but why bother?

The subinterface number is only locally significant, so it doesn't matter which subinterface numbers are configured on the router. Most of the time, I'll configure a subinterface with the same number as the VLAN I want to route. It's easy to remember that way since the subinterface number is used only for administrative purposes.

It's really important that you understand that each VLAN is actually a separate subnet. True, I know—they don't *have* to be, but it really is smart to configure your VLANs as separate subnets.

Before we move on, I want to define *upstream routing*. This is a term used to define the router on a stick. This router will provide inter-VLAN routing, but it can also be used to forward traffic upstream from the switched network to other parts of the corporate network or Internet.

So let's make sure you're fully prepared to configure inter-VLAN routing and that you can determine the IP addresses of hosts connected in a switched VLAN environment. As always, it's also a good idea to be able to fix any problems that may arise. To set you up for success, let me give you few examples.

First, start by looking at Figure 8.12 and read the router and switch configuration within it. By this point in the book, you should be able to determine the IP address, masks, and default gateways of each of the hosts in the VLANs.

FIGURE 8.12 Configuring inter-VLAN example 1

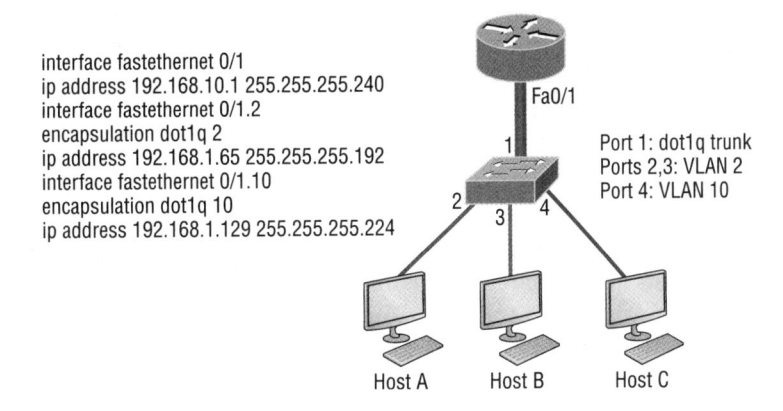

```
interface fastethernet 0/1
ip address 192.168.10.1 255.255.255.240
interface fastethernet 0/1.2
encapsulation dot1q 2
ip address 192.168.1.65 255.255.255.192
interface fastethernet 0/1.10
encapsulation dot1q 10
ip address 192.168.1.129 255.255.255.224
```

Fa0/1

Port 1: dot1q trunk
Ports 2,3: VLAN 2
Port 4: VLAN 10

Host A   Host B   Host C

The next step is to figure out which subnets are being used. By looking at the router configuration in the figure, you can see that we're using 192.168.10.0/28 for VLAN1, 192.168.1.64/26 with VLAN 2, and 192.168.1.128/27 for VLAN 10.

By looking at the switch configuration, you can see that ports 2 and 3 are in VLAN 2 and port 4 is in VLAN 10. This means that Host A and Host B are in VLAN 2 and Host C is in VLAN 10.

But wait—what's that IP address doing there under the physical interface? Can we even do that? Sure, we can! If we place an IP address under the physical interface, the result is that frames sent from the IP address would be untagged. So what VLAN would those frames be a member of? By default, they would belong to VLAN 1, our management VLAN. This means the address 192.168.10.1 /28 is my native VLAN IP address for this switch.

Here's what the hosts' IP addresses should be:

Host A: 192.168.1.66, 255.255.255.192, default gateway 192.168.1.65

Host B: 192.168.1.67, 255.255.255.192, default gateway 192.168.1.65

Host C: 192.168.1.130, 255.255.255.224, default gateway 192.168.1.129

The hosts could be any address in the range—I just chose the first available IP address after the default gateway address. That wasn't so hard, was it?

Now, again using Figure 8.12, let's go through the commands necessary to configure switch port 1 so it will establish a link with the router and provide inter-VLAN communication using the IEEE version for encapsulation. Keep in mind that the commands can vary slightly depending on what type of switch you're dealing with.

For a 2960 switch, use the following:

2960#**config t**
2960(config)#**interface fa0/1**
2960(config-if)#**switchport mode trunk**

That's it! As you already know, the 2960 switch can only run the 802.1q encapsulation, so there's no need to specify it. You can't anyway. For a 3560, it's basically the same, but because it can run ISL and 802.1q, you have to specify the trunking encapsulation protocol you're going to use.

> Remember that when you create a trunked link, all VLANs are allowed to pass data by default.

Let's take a look at Figure 8.13 and see what we can determine. This figure shows three VLANs, with two hosts in each of them. The router in Figure 8.13 is connected to the Fa0/1 switch port, and VLAN 4 is configured on port F0/6.

When looking at this diagram, keep in mind that these three factors are what Cisco expects you to know:

- The router is connected to the switch using subinterfaces and is named ISR.
- The switch port connecting to the router is a trunk port.
- The switch is a 2960, and the switch ports connecting to the clients and the hub are access ports, not trunk ports.

FIGURE 8.13 Inter-VLAN example 2

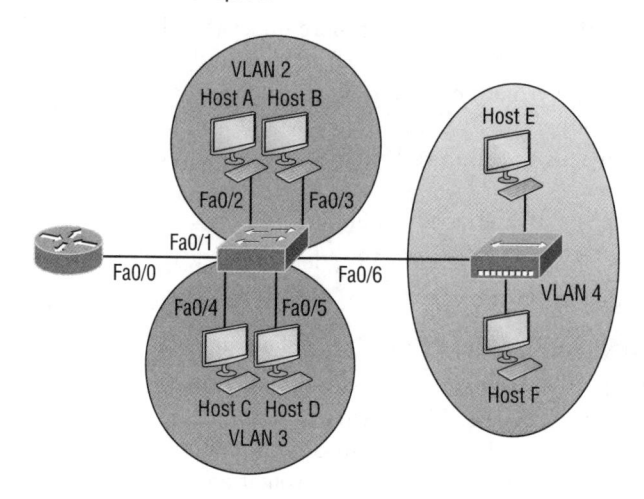

The configuration of the switch would look something like this:

```
2960#config t
2960(config)#int f0/1
2960(config-if)#switchport mode trunk
2960(config-if)#int f0/2
2960(config-if)#switchport access vlan 2
2960(config-if)#int f0/3
```

```
2960(config-if)#switchport access vlan 2
2960(config-if)#int f0/4
2960(config-if)#switchport access vlan 3
2960(config-if)#int f0/5
2960(config-if)#switchport access vlan 3
2960(config-if)#int f0/6
2960(config-if)#switchport access vlan 4
```

Before we configure the router, we need to design our logical network:

VLAN 1: 192.168.10.0/28

VLAN 2: 192.168.10.16/28

VLAN 3: 192.168.10.32/28

VLAN 4: 192.168.10.48/28

The configuration of the router would then look like this:

```
ISR#config t
ISR(config)#int fa0/0
ISR(config-if)#ip address 192.168.10.1 255.255.255.240
ISR(config-if)#no shutdown
ISR(config-if)#int f0/0.2
ISR(config-subif)#encapsulation dot1q 2
ISR(config-subif)#ip address 192.168.10.17 255.255.255.240
ISR(config-subif)#int f0/0.3
ISR(config-subif)#encapsulation dot1q 3
ISR(config-subif)#ip address 192.168.10.33 255.255.255.240
ISR(config-subif)#int f0/0.4
ISR(config-subif)#encapsulation dot1q 4
ISR(config-subif)#ip address 192.168.10.49 255.255.255.240
```

Notice I didn't tag VLAN 1. Even though I could have created a subinterface and tagged VLAN 1, it's not necessary with 802.1q because untagged frames are members of the native VLAN.

The hosts in each VLAN would be assigned an address from their subnet range, and the default gateway would be the IP address assigned to the router's subinterface in that VLAN.

Now, let's take a look at another figure and see if you can determine the switch and router configurations without looking at the answer—no cheating! Figure 8.14 shows a router connected to a 2960 switch with two VLANs. One host in each VLAN is assigned an IP address. What would your router and switch configurations be based on these IP addresses?

FIGURE 8.14 Inter-VLAN example 3

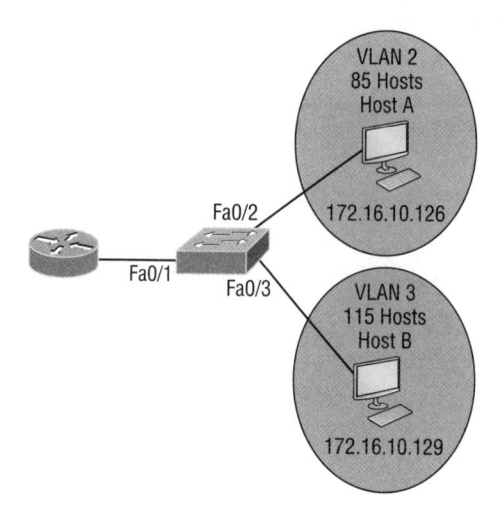

Since the hosts don't list a subnet mask, you have to look for the number of hosts used in each VLAN to figure out the block size. VLAN 2 has 85 hosts, and VLAN 3 has 115 hosts. Each of these will fit in a block size of 128, which is a /25 mask, or 255.255.255.128.

You should know by now that the subnets are 0 and 128; the 0 subnet (VLAN 2) has a host range of 1–126, and the 128 subnet (VLAN 3) has a range of 129–254. You can almost be fooled since Host A has an IP address of 126, which makes it *almost* seem that Host A and B are in the same subnet. But they're not, and you're way too smart by now to be fooled by this one, right?

Here's the switch configuration:

```
2960#config t
2960(config)#int f0/1
2960(config-if)#switchport mode trunk
2960(config-if)#int f0/2
2960(config-if)#switchport access vlan 2
2960(config-if)#int f0/3
2960(config-if)#switchport access vlan 3
```

Here's the router configuration:

```
ISR#config t
ISR(config)#int f0/0
ISR(config-if)#ip address 192.168.10.1 255.255.255.0
ISR(config-if)#no shutdown
ISR(config-if)#int f0/0.2
ISR(config-subif)#encapsulation dot1q 2
```

```
ISR(config-subif)#ip address 172.16.10.1 255.255.255.128
ISR(config-subif)#int f0/0.3
ISR(config-subif)#encapsulation dot1q 3
ISR(config-subif)#ip address 172.16.10.254 255.255.255.128
```

I used the first address in the host range for VLAN 2 and the last address in the range for VLAN 3, but any address in the range would work. You would just have to configure the host's default gateway to whatever you make the router's address. Also, I used a different subnet for my physical interface, which is my management VLAN router's address.

Before we go on to the next example, let's make sure you know how to set the IP address on the switch. Since VLAN 1 is typically the administrative VLAN, we'll use an IP address from out of that pool of addresses. Here's how to set the IP address of the switch (not nagging, but you really should know this already!):

```
2960#config t
2960(config)#int vlan 1
2960(config-if)#ip address 192.168.10.2 255.255.255.0
2960(config-if)#no shutdown
2960(config-if)#exit
2960(config)#ip default-gateway 192.168.10.1
```

Yes, you have to execute a no shutdown on the VLAN interface and set the ip default-gateway address to the router.

One more example, and then we'll move on to IVR using a multilayer switch—another important subject that you definitely don't want to miss.

In Figure 8.15 there are two VLANs, plus the management VLAN 1. By looking at the router configuration, what's the IP address, subnet mask, and default gateway of Host A? Use the last IP address in the range for Host A's address.

If you look really carefully at the router configuration (the hostname in this configuration is just Router), there's a simple and quick answer. All subnets are using a /28, which is a 255.255.255.240 mask. This is a block size of 16. The router's address for VLAN 2 is in subnet 128. The next subnet is 144, so the broadcast address of VLAN 2 is 143 and the valid host range is 129–142. So the host address would be this:

IP address: 192.168.10.142

Mask: 255.255.255.240

Default gateway: 192.168.10.129

This section was probably the hardest part of this book so far, and I honestly created the simplest configuration you can possibly get away with using to help you through it!

I'll use Figure 8.16 to demonstrate configuring inter-VLAN routing (IVR) with a multi-layer switch, using interface fa0/0, which is often referred to as a switched virtual interface (SVI). I'm going to use the same network that I used to discuss a multilayer switch back in Figure 8.11, and I'll use this IP address scheme: 192.168.x.0/24, where x represents the VLAN subnet. In my example this will be the same as the VLAN number.

FIGURE 8.15 Inter-VLAN example 4

```
Router#config t
Router(config)#int fa0/0
Router(config-if)#ip address 192.168.10.1 255.255.255.240
Router(config-if)#no shutdown
Router(config-if)#int f0/0.2
Router(config-subif)#encapsulation dot1q 2
Router(config-subif)#ip address 192.168.10.129 255.255.255.240
Router(config-subif)#int fa0/0.3
Router(config-subif)#encapsulation dot1q 3
Router(config-subif)#ip address 192.168.10.46 255.255.255.240
```

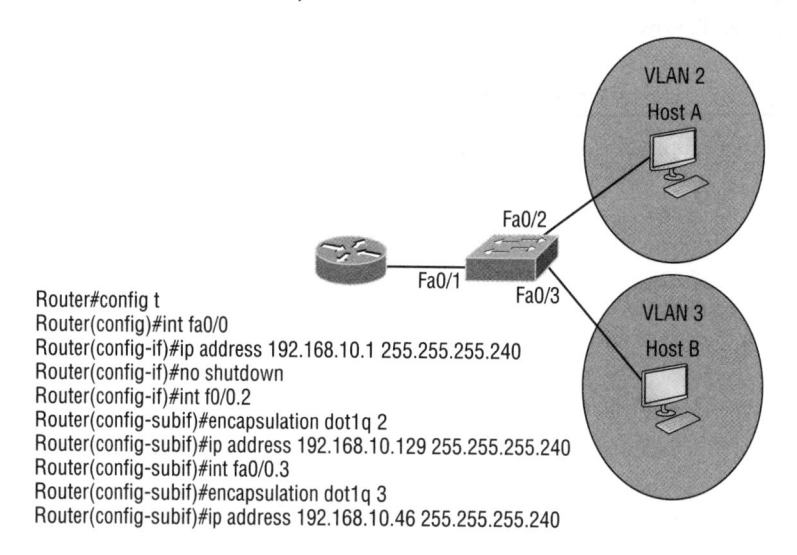

FIGURE 8.16 Inter-VLAN routing with a multilayer switch

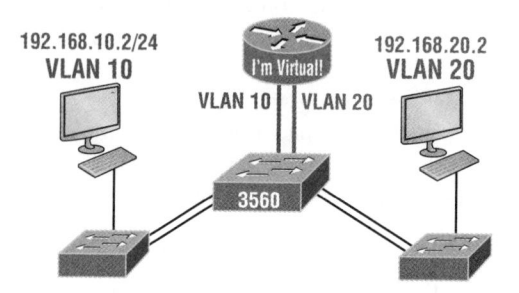

The hosts are already configured with the IP address, subnet mask, and default gateway address using the first address in the range. Now I just need to configure the routing on the switch, which is pretty simple actually:

```
S1(config)#ip routing
S1(config)#int vlan 10
S1(config-if)#ip address 192.168.10.1 255.255.255.0
S1(config-if)#int vlan 20
S1(config-if)#ip address 192.168.20.1 255.255.255.0
```

And that's it! Enable IP routing and create one logical interface for each VLAN using the interface vlan number command and voilà! You've now accomplished making inter-VLAN routing work on the backplane of the switch.

Summary

This chapter introduced you to the world of virtual LANs and described how Cisco switches can use them. We talked about how VLANs break up broadcast domains in a switched internetwork. This is a very important thing because layer 2 switches only break up collision domains, and by default, all switches make up one large broadcast domain. I also described access links to you, and we went over how trunked VLANs work across a FastEthernet or faster link.

Trunking is a crucial technology to understand really well when you're dealing with a network populated by multiple switches that are running several VLANs.

You were also presented with some key troubleshooting and configuration examples for access and trunk ports, configuring trunking options, and a huge section on IVR.

Exam Essentials

Understand the term *frame tagging*. Frame tagging refers to VLAN identification; this is what switches use to keep track of all those frames as they're traversing a switch fabric. It's how switches identify which frames belong to which VLANs.

Understand the 802.1q VLAN identification method. This is a nonproprietary IEEE method of frame tagging. If you're trunking between a Cisco switched link and a different brand of switch, you have to use 802.1q for the trunk to work.

Remember how to set a trunk port on a 2960 switch. To set a port to trunking on a 2960, use the `switchport mode trunk` command.

Remember to check a switch port's VLAN assignment when plugging in a new host. If you plug a new host into a switch, then you must verify the VLAN membership of that port. If the membership is different than what is needed for that host, the host will not be able to reach the needed network services, such as a workgroup server or printer.

Remember how to create a Cisco router on a stick to provide inter-VLAN communication. You can use a Cisco FastEthernet or Gigabit Ethernet interface to provide inter-VLAN routing. The switch port connected to the router must be a trunk port; then you must create virtual interfaces (subinterfaces) on the router port for each VLAN connecting to it. The hosts in each VLAN will use this subinterface address as their default gateway address.

Remember how to provide inter-VLAN routing with a layer 3 switch. You can use a layer 3 (multilayer) switch to provide IVR just as with a router on a stick, but using a layer 3 switch is more efficient and faster. First you start the routing process with the command `ip routing`, then create a virtual interface for each VLAN using the command `interface vlan vlan`, and then apply the IP address for that VLAN under that logical interface.

Review Questions

You can find the answers to these questions in the Appendix.

1. Which of the following statements is true with regard to VLANs?
   A. VLANs greatly reduce network security.
   B. VLANs increase the number of collision domains while decreasing their size.
   C. VLANs decrease the number of broadcast domains while decreasing their size.
   D. Network adds, moves, and changes are achieved with ease by just configuring a port into the appropriate VLAN.

2. You can only add one data VLAN to a switch port when configured as an Access port. What is the second type of VLAN that can be added to an Access port?
   A. Secondary
   B. Voice
   C. Primary
   D. Trunk

3. In the following configuration, what command is missing in the creation of the VLAN interface?

   2960#**config t**
   2960(config)#**int vlan 1**
   2960(config-if)#**ip address 192.168.10.2 255.255.255.0**
   2960(config-if)#**exit**
   2960(config)#**ip default-gateway 192.168.10.1**

   A. `no shutdown` under int vlan 1
   B. `encapsulation dot1q 1` under int vlan 1
   C. `switchport access vlan 1`
   D. `passive-interface`

4. Which of the following statements is true with regard to ISL and 802.1q?
   A. 802.1q encapsulates the frame with control information; ISL inserts an ISL field along with tag control information.
   B. 802.1q is Cisco proprietary.
   C. ISL encapsulates the frame with control information; 802.1q inserts an 802.1q field along with tag control information.
   D. ISL is a standard.

5. Based on the configuration shown here, what statement is true?

    ```
    S1(config)#ip routing
    S1(config)#int vlan 10
    S1(config-if)#ip address 192.168.10.1 255.255.255.0
    S1(config-if)#int vlan 20
    S1(config-if)#ip address 192.168.20.1 255.255.255.0
    ```

    A. This is a multilayer switch.
    B. The two VLANs are in the same subnet.
    C. Encapsulation must be configured.
    D. VLAN 10 is the management VLAN.

6. What is true of the output shown here?

    ```
    S1#sh vlan
    VLAN Name Status Ports
    ---- -------------------- --------- --------------------------------
    1 default active Fa0/1, Fa0/2, Fa0/3, Fa0/4
    Fa0/5, Fa0/6, Fa0/7, Fa0/8
    Fa0/9, Fa0/10, Fa0/11, Fa0/12
    Fa0/13, Fa0/14, Fa0/19, Fa0/20,
    Fa0/22, Fa0/23, Gi0/1, Gi0/2
    2 Sales active
    3 Marketing active Fa0/21
    4 Accounting active
    [output cut]
    ```

    A. Interface F0/15 is a trunk port.
    B. Interface F0/17 is an access port.
    C. Interface F0/21 is a trunk port.
    D. VLAN 1 was populated manually.

7. 802.1q untagged frames are members of which VLAN.

    A. Auxiliary
    B. Voice
    C. Native
    D. Private

8. In the switch output of question 6 how many broadcast domains are shown?

    A. 1
    B. 2
    C. 4
    D. 1001

9. What is the purpose of frame tagging in virtual LAN (VLAN) configurations?
   A. Inter-VLAN routing
   B. Encryption of network packets
   C. Frame identification over trunk links
   D. Frame identification over access links

10. Which statement is true regarding 802.1q frame tagging?
    A. 802.1q adds a 26-byte trailer and 4-byte header.
    B. 802.1q uses a native VLAN.
    C. The original Ethernet frame is not modified.
    D. 802.1q only works with Cisco switches.

Chapter 9

Enhanced Switched Technologies

THE FOLLOWING CCNA EXAM TOPICS ARE COVERED IN THIS CHAPTER:

- ✓ 2.4 Configure and verify (Layer 2/Layer 3) EtherChannel (LACP)

- ✓ 2.5 Describe the need for and basic operations of Rapid PVST+ Spanning Tree Protocol and identify basic operations
  - 2.5.a Root port, root bridge (primary/secondary), and other port names
  - 2.5.b Port states (forwarding/blocking)
  - 2.5.c PortFast benefits

Long ago, a company called Digital Equipment Corporation (DEC) created the original version of *Spanning Tree Protocol (STP)*. The IEEE later created its own version of STP called 802.1d. Cisco has moved toward another industry standard in its newer switches called 802.1w. We'll explore both the old and new versions of STP in this chapter, but first, I'll define some important STP basics.

Routing protocols like RIP, EIGRP, and OSPF have processes for preventing loops from occurring at the Network layer, but if you have redundant physical links between your switches, these protocols won't do a thing to stop loops from occurring at the Data Link layer.

That's exactly why STP was developed—to put an end to loop issues in a layer 2 switched network. It's also why we'll be thoroughly exploring the key features of this vital protocol and how it works within a switched network in this chapter.

After covering STP in detail, we'll move on to explore PortFast and EtherChannel.

> To find your included bonus material, as well as Todd Lammle videos, practice questions & hands-on labs, please see www.lammle.com/ccna

Spanning Tree Protocol (STP)

Spanning Tree Protocol (STP) achieves its primary objective of preventing network loops on layer 2 network bridges or switches by monitoring the network to track all links and shut down the redundant ones. STP uses the spanning-tree algorithm (STA) to create a topology database and then search out and disable redundant links. With STP running, frames will be forwarded on only premium, STP-chosen links.

The Spanning Tree Protocol is a great protocol to use in networks like the one shown in Figure 9.1.

This is a switched network with a redundant topology that includes switching loops. Without some type of layer 2 mechanism in place to prevent a network loop, this network is vulnerable to issues like broadcast storms, multiple frame copies, and MAC table thrashing!

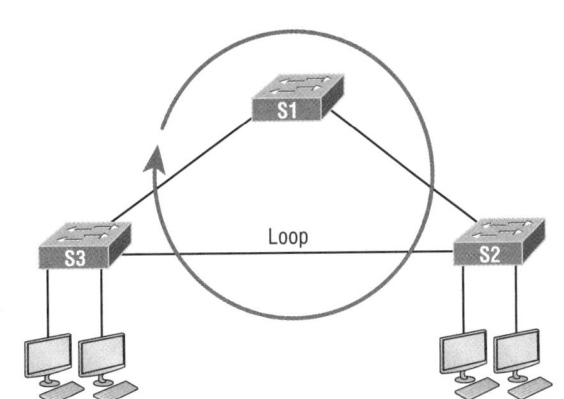

FIGURE 9.1 A switched network with switching loops

Figure 9.2 shows how this network would work with STP working on the switches.

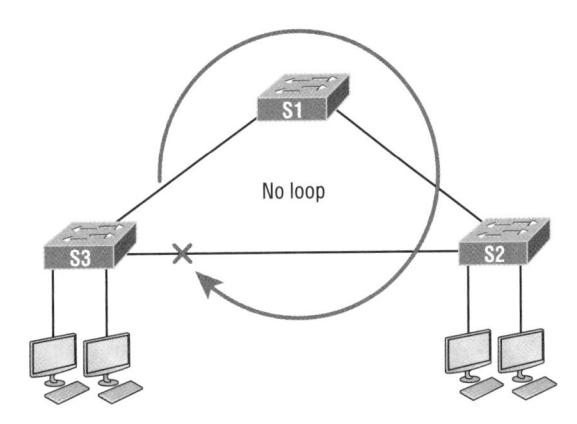

FIGURE 9.2 A switched network with STP

There are few types of spanning-tree protocols, but I'll start with the IEEE version 802.1d, which happens to be the default on all Cisco IOS switches.

Spanning-Tree Terms

Before I get into describing the details of how STP works within a network, it would be good for you to have these basic ideas and terms down first:

Root bridge The *root bridge* is the bridge with the lowest and, therefore, the best bridge ID. The switches within the STP network elect a root bridge, which becomes the focal point in the network. All other decisions in the network, like which ports on the non-root bridges should be blocked or put in forwarding mode, are made from the perspective of the root bridge. Once it has been elected, all other bridges must create a single path to it. The port with the best path to the root bridge is called the root port.

Non-root bridges These are all bridges that aren't the root bridge. Non-root bridges exchange BPDUs with all the other bridges and update the STP topology database on all switches. This prevents loops and helps prevent link failures.

BPDU All switches exchange information to use for the subsequent configuration of the network. Each switch compares the parameters in the *Bridge Protocol Data Unit (BPDU)* that it sends to a neighbor with the parameters in the BPDU that it receives from other neighbors. Inside the BPDU is the bridge ID.

Bridge ID The bridge ID is how STP keeps track of all the switches in the network. It's determined by a combination of the bridge priority, 32,768 by default on all Cisco switches, and the base MAC address. The bridge with the lowest bridge ID becomes the root bridge in the network. Once the root bridge is established, every other switch must make a single path to it. Most networks benefit by forcing a specific bridge or switch to be the Root Bridge by setting its bridge priority lower than the default value.

Port cost Port cost determines the best path when multiple links are used between two switches. The cost of a link is determined by the bandwidth of a link, and this path cost is the deciding factor used by every bridge to find the most efficient path to the root bridge.

Path cost A switch may encounter one or more switches on its path to the root bridge, and there may be more than one possible path to it. All unique paths are analyzed individually and a path cost is calculated for each by adding the individual port costs encountered on the way to the root bridge.

Bridge Port Roles

STP uses roles to determine how a port on a switch will act within the spanning-tree algorithm.

Root port The root port is the link with the lowest path cost to the root bridge. If more than one link connects to the root bridge, then a port cost is found by checking the bandwidth of each link. The higher the link speed, the lower the related cost of the link, and then the lowest cost port becomes the root port. When multiple links connect to the same device, the port connected to the lowest port number on the upstream switch will be the one that's used. The root bridge can never have a root port designation, while every other switch in a network must have only one root port.

Designated port A *designated port* is one that's been determined to have the best (lowest) cost to get to on a given network segment compared to other ports on that segment. A designated port will be marked as a forwarding port, and you can have only one forwarding port per network segment.

Non-designated port A *non-designated port* is one with a higher cost than the designated port. These are basically the ones left over after the root ports and designated ports have been determined. Non-designated ports are put in blocking or discarding mode—they are not forwarding ports!

Forwarding port A forwarding port forwards frames and will be either a root port or a designated port.

Blocked port   A blocked port won't forward frames in order to prevent loops. A blocked port will still always listen to BPDU frames from neighbor switches, but it will drop any and all other frames received and will never transmit a frame.

Alternate port   This corresponds to the blocking state of 802.1d and is a term used with the newer 802.1w (Cisco Rapid Spanning Tree Protocol). An alternative port is located on a switch connected to a LAN segment with two or more switches connected, and one of the other switches holds the designated port.

Backup port   This corresponds to the blocking state of 802.1d and is a term now used with 802.1w. A backup port is connected to a LAN segment wherein another port on that switch is acting as the designated port.

Spanning-Tree Port States

Okay, so you plug your host into a switch port and the light turns amber and your host doesn't get a DHCP address from the server. You wait and wait and finally the light goes green after almost a full minute—that's an eternity in today's networks! This is the spanning-tree algorithm (SPA) transitioning through the different port states verifying that you didn't just create a loop with the device you just plugged in. STP would rather time out your new host than allow a loop into the network because that would effectively bring your network to its knees.

So now, I'm going to talk about the transition states. Later in this chapter I'll demonstrate how to speed this process up.

The ports on a bridge or switch running IEEE 802.1d STP can transition through five different states:

Disabled (technically, not a transition state)   A port in the administratively disabled state doesn't participate in frame forwarding or STP. A port in the disabled state is virtually nonoperational.

Blocking   As I mentioned, a blocked port won't forward frames—it just listens to BPDUs. The purpose of the blocking state is to prevent the use of looped paths. All ports are in blocking state by default when the switch is powered up.

Listening   This port listens to BPDUs to make sure no loops occur on the network before passing data frames. A port in listening state prepares to forward data frames without populating the MAC address table.

Learning   The switch port listens to BPDUs and learns all the paths in the switched network. A port in learning state populates the MAC address table but still doesn't forward data frames. Forward delay refers to the time it takes to transition a port from listening to learning mode, or from learning to forwarding mode, which is set to 15 seconds by default and can be seen in the show spanning-tree output.

Forwarding   This port sends and receives all data frames on the bridged port. If the port is still a designated or root port at the end of the learning state, it will enter the forwarding state.

> **NOTE**   Switches populate the MAC address table in learning and forwarding modes only.

Switch ports are most often in either the blocking or forwarding state. A forwarding port is typically the one that's been determined to have the lowest (best) cost to the root bridge. But when and if the network experiences a topology change due to a failed link or because someone has added in a new switch, you'll see the ports on a switch transitioning through listening and learning states.

As I said earlier, blocking ports is a good strategy for preventing network loops. Once a switch determines the best path to the root bridge for its root port and any designated ports, all other redundant ports will be in blocking mode. Blocked ports can still receive BPDUs—they just don't send out any frames.

If a switch determines that a blocked port should become the designated or root port because of a topology change, it will go into listening mode and check all BPDUs it receives to make sure it won't create a loop once the port moves into forwarding mode.

Convergence

Convergence occurs when all ports on bridges and switches have transitioned to either forwarding or blocking modes. No data will be forwarded until convergence is complete. Yes—you read that right: When STP is converging, all host data stops transmitting through the switches! So if you want to remain on speaking terms with your network's users, or remain employed for any length of time, you must make sure that your switched network is physically designed solidly, allowing STP to converge quickly!

Convergence is vital because it ensures that all devices have a coherent database. Making sure this happens efficiently definitely requires your time and attention. The original STP (802.1d) takes 50 seconds to go from blocking to forwarding mode by default and I don't recommend changing the default STP timers. You can adjust those timers for a large network, but the better solution is simply to opt out of using 802.1d completely. We'll get to the various STP versions in a minute.

Link Costs

Now that you know about the different port roles and states, you need to really understand all about path cost before we put this all together. Port cost is based on the speed of the link, and Table 9.1 breaks down the need-to-know path costs for you. Port cost is the cost of a single link, whereas path cost is the sum of the various port costs to the root bridge.

TABLE 9.1 IEEE STP link costs

Speed	Cost
10 Mb/s	100
100 Mb/s	19
1000 Mb/s	4
10,000 Mb/s	2

These costs will be used in STP calculations to choose a single root port on each bridge. You absolutely need to memorize this table, and I'll guide you through lots of examples to help you do that!

Let's take everything you've learned so far and put it all together now.

Spanning-Tree Operations

I'll begin by summarizing what you've learned so far using the simple three-switch network connected together, as shown in Figure 9.3.

FIGURE 9.3 STP operations

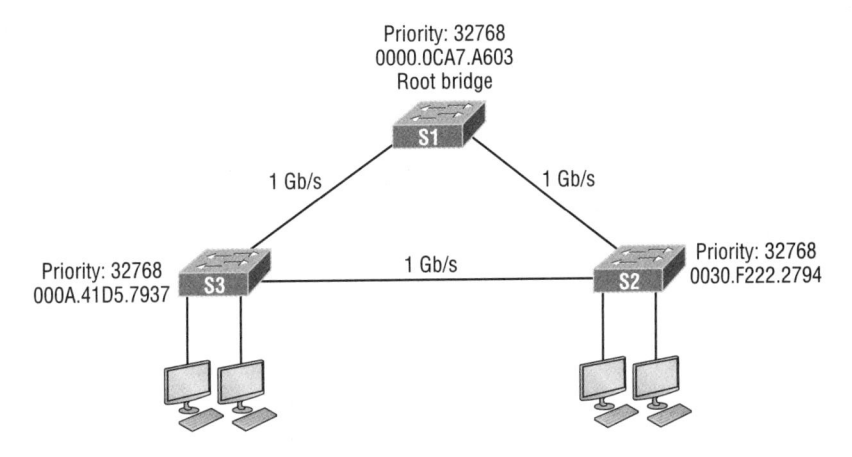

Basically, STP's job is to find all the links in the network and shut down any redundant ones, thereby preventing network loops from occurring. It achieves this by first electing a root bridge that will have all ports forwarding and will also act as a point of reference for all other devices within the STP domain.

In Figure 9.3, S1 has been elected the root bridge based on bridge ID. Since the priorities are all equal to 32,768, we'll compare MAC addresses and find the MAC address of S1 is lower than that of S2 and S3. Of course, this means that S1 has a better bridge ID.

Once all switches agree on the root bridge, they must then determine their one and only root port—the single path to the root bridge. It's really important to remember that a bridge can go through many other bridges to get to the root, so it's not always the shortest path that'll be chosen. That role will be given to the port that offers the highest, fastest bandwidth.

Figure 9.4 shows the root ports for both non-root bridges (the **RP** signifies a root port, and the **F** signifies a designated forwarding port).

FIGURE 9.4 STP operations

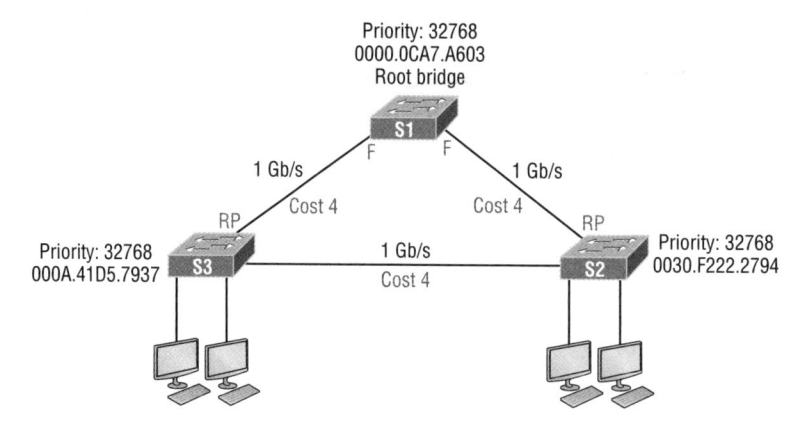

Looking at the cost of each link, it's clear why S2 and S3 are using their directly connected links—because a gigabit link has a cost of 4. For example, if S3 chose the path through S2 as its root port, we'd have to add up each port cost along the way to the root, which would be 4 + 4 for a total cost of 8.

Every port on the root bridge is a designated, or forwarding, port for a segment. After the dust settles on all other non-root bridges, any port connection between switches that isn't either a root port or a designated port will predictably become a non-designated port. These will again be put into the blocking state to prevent switching loops.

Okay—at this point, we have our root bridge with all ports in forwarding state, and we've found our root ports for each non-root bridge. Now the only thing left to do is to choose the one forwarding port on the segment between S2 and S3. Both bridges can't be forwarding on a segment because that's exactly how we would end up with loops. So, based on the bridge ID, the port with the best and lowest would become the only bridge forwarding on that segment. The one with the one having the highest, worst bridge ID would be put into blocking mode.

Figure 9.5 shows the network after STP has converged.

FIGURE 9.5 STP converged

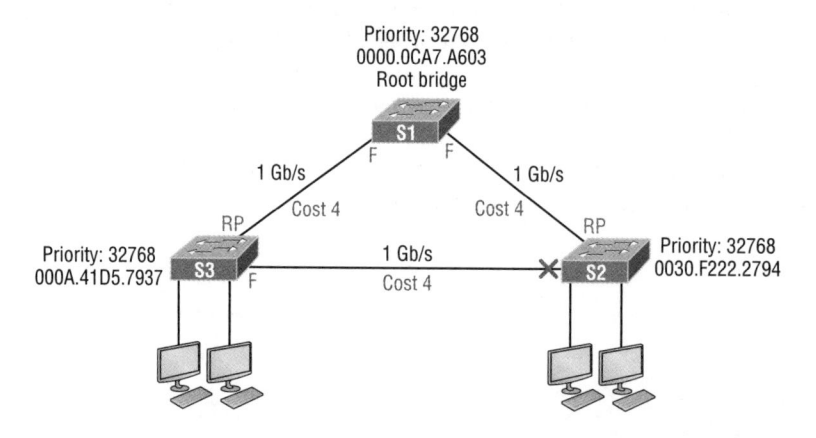

Since S3 had a lower bridge ID (better), S2's port went into blocking mode. Let's discuss the root bridge election process more completely now.

Selecting the Root Bridge

The bridge ID is used to elect the root bridge in the STP domain and to determine the root port for each of the remaining devices when there's more than one potential root port available because they have equal-cost paths. This key bridge ID is 8 bytes long and includes both the priority and the MAC address of the device, as illustrated in Figure 9.6. Remember—the default priority on all devices running the IEEE STP version is 32,768.

FIGURE 9.6 STP operations

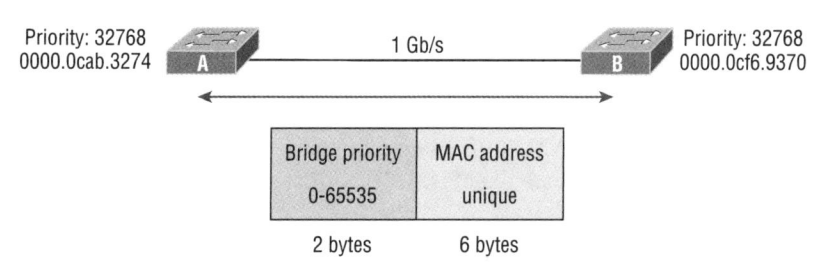

So, to determine the root bridge, you combine the priority of each bridge with its MAC address. If two switches or bridges happen to have the same priority value, the MAC address becomes the tiebreaker for figuring out which one has the lowest and, therefore, best ID. This means that because the two switches in Figure 9.6 are both using the default priority of 32,768, the MAC address will be the determining factor instead. And because Switch A's MAC address is 0000.0cab.3274 and Switch B's MAC address is 0000.0cf6.9370, Switch A wins and will become the root bridge. A really easy way to figure out the lowest MAC address is to just start reading from the left toward the right until you find a lesser value. For Switch A, I only needed to get to 0000.0ca before stopping. Switch A wins since switch B is 0000.0cf. Never forget that the lower value is always the better one when it comes to electing a root bridge.

I want to point out that prior to the election of the root bridge, BPDUs are sent every 2 seconds out all active ports on a bridge/switch by default, and they're received and processed by all bridges. The root bridge is elected based on this information. You can change the bridge's ID by lowering its priority so that it will become a root bridge automatically. Being able to do that is important in a large switched network because it ensures that the best paths will actually be the ones chosen. Efficiency is always awesome in networking!

Types of Spanning-Tree Protocols

There are several varieties of spanning-tree protocols in use today:

IEEE 802.1d   The original standard for bridging and STP, which is really slow but requires very little bridge resources. It's also referred to as Common Spanning Tree (CST).

PVST+ (Cisco default version)   The Cisco proprietary enhancement for STP that provides a separate 802.1d spanning-tree instance for each VLAN. Know that this is just as slow as the CST protocol, but with it, we get to have multiple root bridges. This creates more efficiency of the links in the network, but it does use more bridge resources than CST does.

IEEE 802.1w   Also called Rapid Spanning Tree Protocol (RSTP), this iteration enhanced the BPDU exchange and paved the way for much faster network convergence. But it still only allows for one root bridge per network like CST. The bridge resources used with RSTP are higher than CST's but less than PVST+.

802.1s (MSTP)   This is the IEEE standard that started out as Cisco propriety MISTP. It maps multiple VLANs into the same spanning-tree instance to save processing on the switch. It's basically a spanning-tree protocol that rides on top of another spanning-tree protocol.

Rapid PVST+   This is Cisco's version of RSTP that also uses PVST+ and provides a separate instance of 802.1w per VLAN. It offers up really fast convergence times and optimal traffic flow but predictably requires the most CPU and memory of all.

Common Spanning Tree

If you're running Common Spanning Tree (CST) in your switched network with redundant links, there will be an election to choose what STP considers to be the best root bridge for your network. That switch will also become the root for all VLANs in your network, and all bridges in your network will create a single path to it. You can manually override this selection and pick whichever bridge you want if it makes sense for your particular network.

Figure 9.7 shows how a typical root bridge would look on your switched network when running CST.

FIGURE 9.7   Common STP example

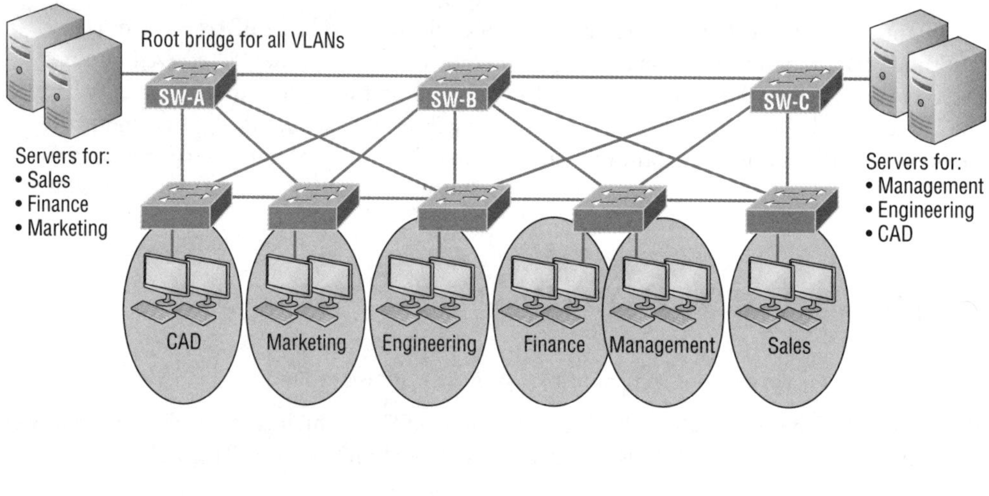

Notice that switch A is the root bridge for all VLANs even though it's really not the best path for some VLANs because all switches must make a single path to it. This is where Per-VLAN Spanning Tree+ (PVST+) comes into play. Because it allows for a separate instance of STP for each VLAN, it frees up the option to individually select the most optimal path!

Per-VLAN Spanning Tree+

PVST+ is a Cisco proprietary extension to 801.2d STP that provides a separate 802.1 spanning-tree instance for each VLAN configured on your switches. All of Cisco proprietary extensions were created to improve convergence times, which is 50 seconds by default. Cisco IOS switches run 802.1d PVST+ by default, which means you'll have optimal path selection, but the convergence time will still be slow.

Creating a per-VLAN STP instance for each VLAN is worth the increased CPU and memory requirements because it allows for per-VLAN root bridges. This feature allows the STP tree to be optimized for the traffic of each VLAN by allowing you to configure the root bridge in the center of each of them. Figure 9.8 shows how PVST+ would look in an optimized switched network with multiple redundant links.

FIGURE 9.8 PVST+ provides efficient root bridge selection.

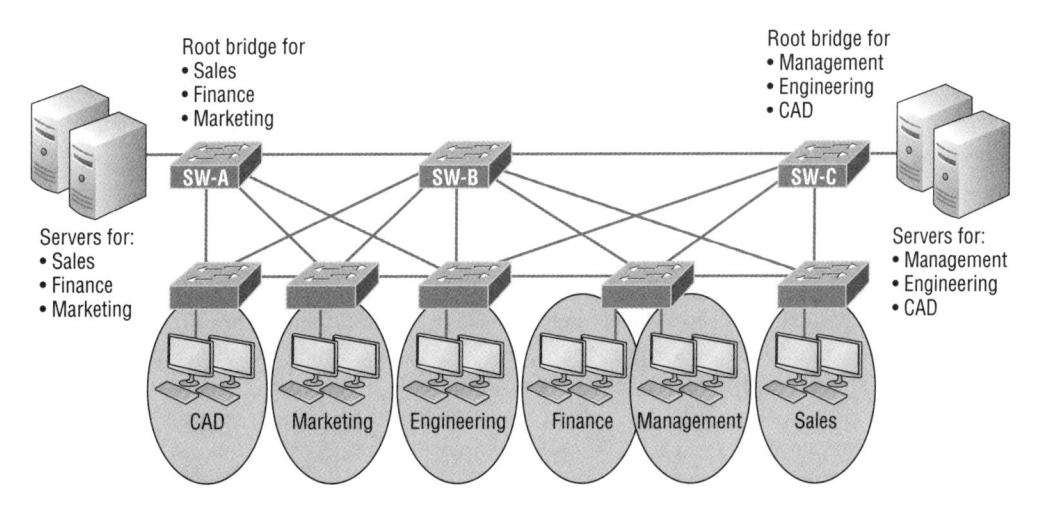

This root bridge placement clearly enables faster convergence as well as optimal path determination. This version's convergence is really similar to 802.1 CST's, which has one instance of STP no matter how many VLANs you have configured on your network. The difference is that with PVST+, convergence happens on a per-VLAN basis, with each VLAN running its own instance of STP. Figure 9.8 shows us that we now have a nice, efficient root bridge selection for each VLAN.

To allow PVST+ to operate, there's a field inserted into the BPDU to accommodate the extended system ID so that PVST+ can have a root bridge configured on a per-STP instance, shown in Figure 9.9.

FIGURE 9.9 PVST+ unique bridge ID

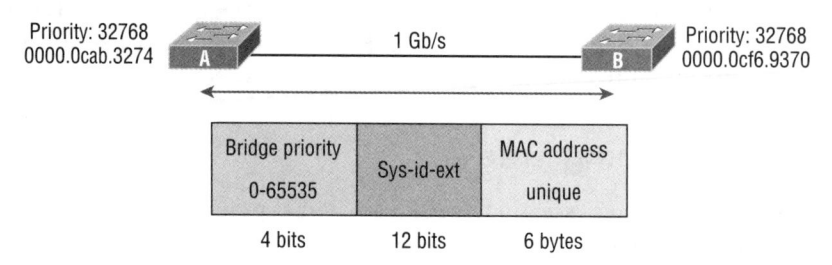

The bridge ID actually becomes smaller—only 4 bits—which means that we would configure the bridge priority in blocks of 4,096 rather than in increments of 1 as we did with CST. The extended system ID (VLAN ID) is a 12-bit field, and we can even see what this field is carrying via `show spanning-tree` command output, which I'll show you soon.

But still, isn't there a way we can do better than a 50-second convergence time? That's a really long time in today's world!

Rapid Spanning Tree Protocol 802.1w

Wouldn't it be wonderful to have a solid STP configuration running on your switched network, regardless of switch type, and still have all the features we just discussed built in and enabled on every one of your switches too? Rapid Spanning Tree Protocol (RSTP) provides exactly this amazing capacity!

Cisco created proprietary extensions to "fix" all the potholes and liabilities the IEEE 802.1d standard threw at us, with the main drawback to them being they require extra configuration because they're Cisco proprietary. But RSTP, the new 802.1w standard, brings us most of the patches needed in one concise solution. Again, efficiency is golden!

RSTP, or IEEE 802.1w, is essentially an evolution of STP that allows for much faster convergence. But even though it does address all the convergence issues, it still only permits a single STP instance, so it doesn't help to take the edge off suboptimal traffic flow issues. And as I mentioned, to support that faster convergence, the CPU usage and memory demands are slightly higher than CST's. The good news is that Cisco IOS can run the Rapid PVST+ protocol—a Cisco enhancement of RSTP that provides a separate 802.1w spanning-tree instance for each VLAN configured within the network. But all that power needs fuel, and although this version addresses both convergence and traffic flow issues, it also demands the most CPU and memory of all solutions. And it's also good news that Cisco's newest switches don't have a problem with this protocol running on them.

> Keep in mind that Cisco documentation may say STP 802.1d and RSTP 802.1w, but it is referring to the PVST+ enhancement of each version.

Understand that RSTP wasn't meant to be something completely new and different. The protocol is more of an evolution rather than an innovation of the 802.1d standard, which offers faster convergence whenever a topology change occurs. Backward compatibility was a must when 802.1w was created.

So, RSTP helps with convergence issues that were the bane of traditional STP. Rapid PVST+ is based on the 802.1w standard in the same way that PVST+ is based on 802.1d. The operation of Rapid PVST+ is simply a separate instance of 802.1w for each VLAN. Here's a list to clarify how this all breaks down:

- RSTP speeds the recalculation of the spanning tree when the layer 2 network topology changes.
- It's an IEEE standard that redefines STP port roles, states, and BPDUs.
- RSTP is extremely proactive and very quick, so it doesn't need the 802.1d delay timers.
- RSTP (802.1w) supersedes 802.1d while remaining backward compatible.
- Much of the 802.1d terminology and most parameters remain unchanged.
- 802.1w is capable of reverting to 802.1d to interoperate with traditional switches on a per-port basis.

And to clear up confusion, there are also five terminology adjustments between 802.1d's five port states to 802.1w's, compared here, respectively:

802.1d State		802.1w State
Disabled	=	Discarding
Blocking	=	Discarding
Listening	=	Discarding
Learning	=	Learning
Forwarding	=	Forwarding

Make note of the fact that RSTP basically just goes from discarding to learning to forwarding, whereas 802.1d requires five states to transition.

The task of determining the root bridge, root ports, and designated ports hasn't changed from 802.1d to RSTP, and understanding the cost of each link is still key to making these decisions well.

Let's take a look at an example of how to determine ports using the revised IEEE cost specifications in Figure 9.10.

FIGURE 9.10 RSTP example 1

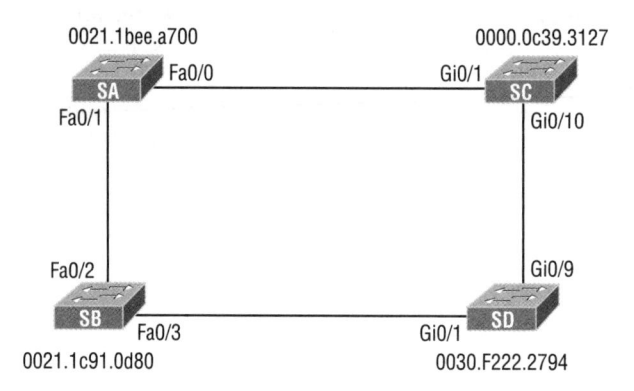

Can you figure out which is the root bridge? How about which port is the root and which ones are designated? Well, because SC has the lowest MAC address, it becomes the root bridge, and since all ports on a root bridge are forwarding designated ports, that's easy, right? Ports Gi0/1 and Gi0/10 become designated forwarding ports on SC.

But which one would be the root port for SA? To figure that out, we must first find the port cost for the direct link between SA and SC. Even though the root bridge (SC) has a Gigabit Ethernet port, it's running at 100 Mbps because SA's port is a 100-Mbps port, giving it a cost of 19. If the paths between SA and SC were both Gigabit Ethernet, their costs would only be 4, but because they're running 100 Mbps links instead, the cost jumps to a whopping 19!

Can you find SD's root port? A quick glance at the link between SC and SD tells us that it's a Gigabit Ethernet link with a cost of 4, so the root port for SD would be its Gi0/9 port.

The cost of the link between SB and SD is also 19 because it's also a Fast Ethernet link, bringing the full cost from SB to SD to the root (SC) to a total cost of 19 + 4 = 23. If SB were to go through SA to get to SC, then the cost would be 19 + 19, or 38, so the root port of SB becomes the Fa0/3 port.

The root port for SA would be the Fa0/0 port since it's a direct link with a cost of 19. Going through SB to SD would be 19 + 19 + 4 = 42, so we'll use that as a backup link for SA to get to the root just in case we need to.

Now, all we need is a forwarding port on the link between SA and SB. Because SA has the lowest bridge ID, Fa0/1 on SA wins that role. Also, the Gi0/1 port on SD would become a designated forwarding port. This is because the SB Fa0/3 port is a designed root port and you must have a forwarding port on a network segment! This leaves us with the Fa0/2 port on SB. Since it isn't a root port or designated forwarding port, it will be placed into blocking mode, preventing loops in our network.

Let's take a look at this example network when it has converged in Figure 9.11.

Types of Spanning-Tree Protocols

FIGURE 9.11 RSTP example 1 answer

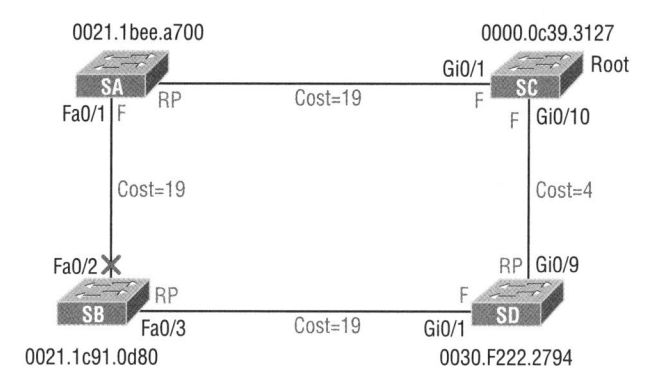

```
0021.1bee.a700                          0000.0c39.3127
        SA          Gi0/1      SC         Root
        RP    Cost=19       F
Fa0/1 F                        F  Gi0/10

      Cost=19                     Cost=4

Fa0/2 X                         RP  Gi0/9
        RP                     F
   SB                             SD
      Fa0/3  Cost=19   Gi0/1
0021.1c91.0d80              0030.F222.2794
```

If this isn't clear and still seems confusing, just remember to always tackle this process following these three steps:

1. Find your root bridge by looking at bridge IDs.
2. Determine your root ports by finding the lowest path cost to the root bridge.
3. Find your designated ports by looking at bridge IDs.

As usual, the best way to nail this down is to practice, so let's explore another scenario, shown in Figure 9.12.

FIGURE 9.12 RSTP example 2

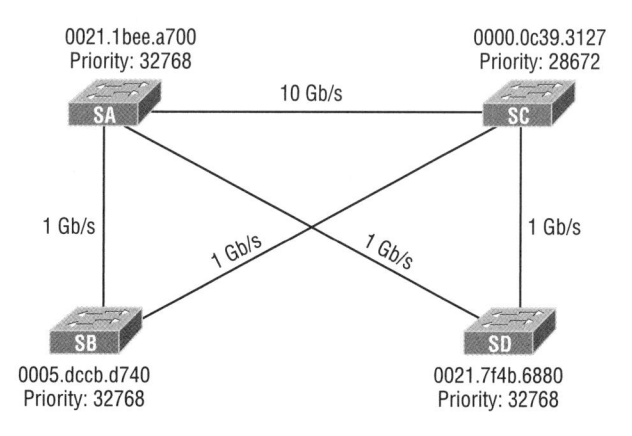

```
0021.1bee.a700                    0000.0c39.3127
Priority: 32768                   Priority: 28672
        SA         10 Gb/s           SC

   1 Gb/s                            1 Gb/s
              1 Gb/s      1 Gb/s

        SB                            SD
0005.dccb.d740                   0021.7f4b.6880
Priority: 32768                  Priority: 32768
```

So which bridge is our root bridge? Checking priorities first tells us that SC is the root bridge, which means all ports on SC are designated forwarding ports. Now we need to find our root ports.

We can quickly see that SA has a 10-gigabit port to SC, so that would be a port cost of 2, and it would be our root port. SD has a direct Gigabit Ethernet port to SC, so that would be the root port for SD with a port cost of 4. SB's best path would also be the direct Gigabit Ethernet port to SC with a port cost of 4.

Now that we've determined our root bridge and found the three root ports we need, we've got to find our designated ports next. Whatever is left over simply goes into the discarding role. Let's take a look at Figure 9.13 and see what we have.

FIGURE 9.13 RSTP example 2, answer 1

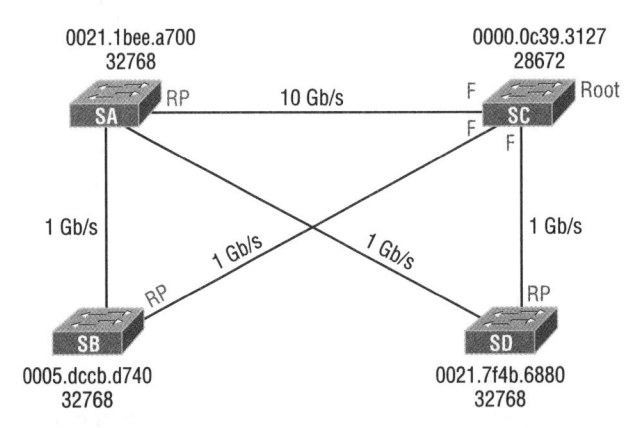

All right, it looks like there are two links to choose between to find one designated port per segment. Let's start with the link between SA and SD. Which one has the best bridge ID? They're both running the same default priority, so by looking at the MAC address, we can see that SD has the better bridge ID (lower), so the SA port toward SD will go into a discarding role. Or will it? The SD port will go into discarding mode, because the link from SA to the root has the lowest accumulated path costs to the root bridge, and that is used before the bridge ID in this circumstance. It makes sense to let the bridge with the fastest path to the root bridge be a designated forwarding port. Let's talk about this a little more in depth.

As you know, once your root bridge and root ports have been chosen, you're left with finding your designated ports. Anything left over goes into a discarding role. But how are the designated ports chosen? Is it just bridge ID? Here are the rules:

1. To choose the switch that will forward on the segment, we select the switch with the lowest accumulated path cost to the root bridge. We must have the fastest path to the root bridge.

2. If there is a tie on the accumulated path cost from both switches to the root bridge, then we'll use bridge ID, which was what we used in our previous example. We didn't use it with this latest RSTP example—not with a 10-Gigabit Ethernet link to the root bridge available!

3. Port priorities can be set manually if we want a specific port chosen. The default priority is 32768, but we can lower that if needed.

4. If there are two links between switches and if the bridge ID and priority are tied, the port with the lowest number will be chosen—for example, Fa0/1 would be chosen over Fa0/2.

Let's take a look at our answer now, but before we do, can you find the forwarding port between SA and SB?

Take a look at Figure 9.14 for the answer.

FIGURE 9.14 RSTP example 2, answer 2

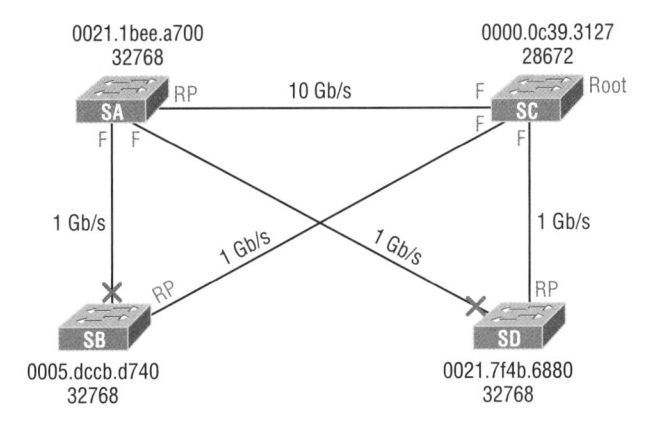

Again, to get the right answer to this question we're going to let the switch on the network segment with the lowest accumulated path cost to the root bridge forward on that segment. This is definitely SA, meaning the SB port goes into discarding role—not so hard at all!

802.1s (MSTP)

Multiple Spanning Tree Protocol (MSTP), also known as IEEE 802.ls, gives us the same fast convergence as RSTP but reduces the number of required STP instances by allowing us to map multiple VLANs with the same traffic flow requirements into the same spanning-tree instance. It essentially allows us to create VLAN sets and basically is a spanning-tree protocol that runs on top of another spanning-tree protocol.

So clearly, you would opt to use MSTP over RSTP when you've got a configuration involving lots VLANs, resulting in CPU and memory requirements that would be too high otherwise. But there's no free lunch—though MSTP reduces the demands of Rapid PVST+, you've got to configure it correctly because MSTP does nothing by itself!

Modifying and Verifying the Bridge ID

To verify spanning tree on a Cisco switch, just use the command show spanning-tree. From its output, we can determine our root bridge, priorities, root ports, and designated and blocking/discarding ports.

Let's use the same simple three-switch network we used earlier as the base to play around as we configure STP. Figure 9.15 shows the network we'll work with in this section.

FIGURE 9.15 Our simple three-switch network

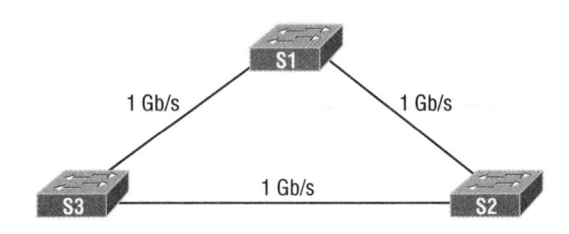

Let's start by taking a look at the output from S1:

```
S1#sh spanning-tree vlan 1
VLAN0001
  Spanning tree enabled protocol ieee
  Root ID     Priority    32769
              Address     0001.42A7.A603
              This bridge is the root
              Hello Time  2 sec  Max Age 20 sec  Forward Delay 15 sec
  Bridge ID   Priority    32769  (priority 32768 sys-id-ext 1)
              Address     0001.42A7.A603 him
              Hello Time  2 sec  Max Age 20 sec  Forward Delay 15 sec
              Aging Time  20

Interface         Role Sts Cost      Prio.Nbr Type
----------------  ---- --- --------- -------- --------------------------------
Gi1/1             Desg FWD 4         128.25   P2p
Gi1/2             Desg FWD 4         128.26   P2p
```

First, we can see that we're running the IEEE 802.1d STP version by default, and don't forget that this is really 802.1d PVST+! Looking at the output, we can see that S1 is the root bridge for VLAN 1. When you use this command, the top information is about the root bridge, and the Bridge ID output refers to the specific bridge you're looking at. In this example, they are one and the same. Notice the sys-id-ext 1 (for VLAN 1). This is the 12-bit PVST+ field that is placed into the BPDU so it can carry multiple-VLAN information. You add the priority and sys-id-ext to come up with the true priority for the VLAN. We can also see from the output that both Gigabit Ethernet interfaces are designated forwarding ports. You will not see a blocked/discarding port on a root bridge. Now let's take a look at S3's output:

```
S3#sh spanning-tree
VLAN0001
  Spanning tree enabled protocol ieee
  Root ID     Priority    32769
              Address     0001.42A7.A603
```

Modifying and Verifying the Bridge ID   269

```
              Cost         4
              Port         26(GigabitEthernet1/2)
              Hello Time  2 sec  Max Age 20 sec  Forward Delay 15 sec

  Bridge ID  Priority    32769  (priority 32768 sys-id-ext 1)
             Address     000A.41D5.7937
             Hello Time  2 sec  Max Age 20 sec  Forward Delay 15 sec
             Aging Time  20

Interface        Role Sts Cost      Prio.Nbr Type
---------------- ---- --- --------- -------- --------------------------------
Gi1/1            Desg FWD 4         128.25   P2p
Gi1/2            Root FWD 4         128.26   P2p
```

Looking at the Root ID, it's easy to see that S3 isn't the root bridge, but the output tells us it's a cost of 4 to get to the root bridge and that it's located out port 26 of the switch (Gi1/2). This tells us that the root bridge is one Gigabit Ethernet link away, which we already know is S1, but we can confirm this with the show cdp neighbors command:

```
Switch#sh cdp nei
Capability Codes: R - Router, T - Trans Bridge, B - Source Route Bridge
                  S - Switch, H - Host, I - IGMP, r - Repeater, P - Phone
Device ID    Local Intrfce   Holdtme    Capability  Platform   Port ID
S3           Gig 1/1         135                S   2960       Gig 1/1
S1           Gig 1/2         135                S   2960       Gig 1/1
```

That's how simple it is to find your root bridge if you don't have the nice figure as we do. Use the show spanning-tree command, find your root port, and then use the show cdp neighbors command. Let's see what S2's output has to tell us now:

```
S2#sh spanning-tree
VLAN0001
  Spanning tree enabled protocol ieee
  Root ID    Priority    32769
             Address     0001.42A7.A603
             Cost        4
             Port        26(GigabitEthernet1/2)
             Hello Time  2 sec  Max Age 20 sec  Forward Delay 15 sec

  Bridge ID  Priority    32769  (priority 32768 sys-id-ext 1)
             Address     0030.F222.2794
             Hello Time  2 sec  Max Age 20 sec  Forward Delay 15 sec
```

```
      Aging Time   20

Interface          Role Sts Cost       Prio.Nbr  Type
---------------    ---- --- ---------  --------  --------------------------------
Gi1/1              Altn BLK 4          128.25    P2p
Gi1/2              Root FWD 4          128.26    P2p
```

We're certainly not looking at a root bridge since we're seeing a blocked port, which is S2's connection to S3!

Let's have some fun by making S2 the root bridge for VLAN 2 and for VLAN 3. Here's how easy that is:

```
S2#sh spanning-tree vlan 2
VLAN0002
  Spanning tree enabled protocol ieee
  Root ID    Priority    32770
             Address     0001.42A7.A603
             Cost        4
             Port        26(GigabitEthernet1/2)
             Hello Time  2 sec   Max Age 20 sec   Forward Delay 15 sec

  Bridge ID  Priority    32770   (priority 32768 sys-id-ext 2)
             Address     0030.F222.2794
             Hello Time  2 sec   Max Age 20 sec   Forward Delay 15 sec
             Aging Time  20

Interface          Role Sts Cost       Prio.Nbr  Type
---------------    ---- --- ---------  --------  --------------------------------
Gi1/1              Altn BLK 4          128.25    P2p
Gi1/2              Root FWD 4          128.26    P2p
```

We can see that the root bridge cost is 4, meaning that the root bridge is one-gigabit link away. One more key factor I want to talk about before making S2 the root bridge for VLANs 2 and 3 is the sys-id-ext, which shows up as 2 in this output because this output is for VLAN 2. This sys-id-ext is added to the bridge priority, which in this case in 32768 + 2, which makes the priority 32770. Okay, now that you understand what that output is telling us, let's make S2 the root bridge:

```
S2(config)#spanning-tree vlan 2 ?
  priority  Set the bridge priority for the spanning tree
  root      Configure switch as root
  <cr>
S2(config)#spanning-tree vlan 2 priority ?
```

Modifying and Verifying the Bridge ID

```
    <0-61440>  bridge priority in increments of 4096
S2(config)#spanning-tree vlan 2 priority 16384
```

You can set the priority to any value from 0 through 61440 in increments of 4096. Setting it to zero (0) means that the switch will always be a root as long as it has a lower MAC address than another switch that also has its bridge ID set to 0. If you want to set a switch to be the root bridge for every VLAN in your network, then you have to change the priority for each VLAN, with 0 being the lowest priority you can use. But trust me—it's never a good idea to set all switches to a priority of 0!

Furthermore, you don't actually need to change priorities because there is yet another way to configure the root bridge. Take a look:

```
S2(config)#spanning-tree vlan 3 root ?
  primary    Configure this switch as primary root for this spanning tree
  secondary  Configure switch as secondary root
S2(config)#spanning-tree vlan 3 root primary
```

Notice that you can set a bridge to either primary or secondary—very cool! If both the primary and secondary switches go down, then the next highest priority will take over as root.

Let's check to see if S2 is actually the root bridge for VLANs 2 and 3 now:

```
S2#sh spanning-tree vlan 2
VLAN0002
  Spanning tree enabled protocol ieee
  Root ID    Priority   16386
             Address    0030.F222.2794
             This bridge is the root
             Hello Time  2 sec  Max Age 20 sec  Forward Delay 15 sec

  Bridge ID  Priority   16386  (priority 16384 sys-id-ext 2)
             Address    0030.F222.2794
             Hello Time  2 sec  Max Age 20 sec  Forward Delay 15 sec
             Aging Time 20

Interface        Role Sts Cost      Prio.Nbr Type
---------------- ---- --- --------- -------- --------------------------------
Gi1/1            Desg FWD 4         128.25   P2p
Gi1/2            Desg FWD 4         128.26   P2p
```

Nice—S2 is the root bridge for VLAN 2, with a priority of 16386 (16384 + 2). Let's take a look to see the root bridge for VLAN 3. I'll use a different command for that this time. Here's the output:

```
S2#sh spanning-tree summary
Switch is in pvst mode
```

Root bridge for: VLAN0002 VLAN0003
```
Extended system ID              is enabled
Portfast Default                is disabled
PortFast BPDU Guard Default     is disabled
Portfast BPDU Filter Default    is disabled
Loopguard Default               is disabled
EtherChannel misconfig guard    is disabled
UplinkFast                      is disabled
BackboneFast                    is disabled
Configured Pathcost method used is short

Name                    Blocking Listening Learning Forwarding STP Active
----------------------  -------- --------- -------- ---------- ----------
VLAN0001                       1         0        0          1          2
VLAN0002                       0         0        0          2          2
VLAN0003                       0         0        0          2          2

----------------------  -------- --------- -------- ---------- ----------
3 vlans                        1         0        0          5          6
```

This output tells us that S2 is the root for the two VLANs, but we can see we have a blocked port for VLAN 1 on S2, so it's not the root bridge for VLAN 1. This is because there's another bridge with a better bridge ID for VLAN 1 than S2's.

One last burning question: How do you enable RSTP on a Cisco switch? Well, doing that is actually the easiest part of this chapter! Take a look:

```
S2(config)#spanning-tree mode rapid-pvst
```

Is that really all there is to it? Yes, because it's a global command, not per VLAN. Let's verify we're running RSTP now:

```
S2#sh spanning-tree
VLAN0001
  Spanning tree enabled protocol rstp
  Root ID    Priority    32769
             Address     0001.42A7.A603
             Cost        4
             Port        26(GigabitEthernet1/2)
             Hello Time  2 sec  Max Age 20 sec  Forward Delay 15 sec
[output cut]
S2#sh spanning-tree summary
Switch is in rapid-pvst mode
Root bridge for: VLAN0002 VLAN0003
```

Looks like we're set! We're running RSTP, S1 is our root bridge for VLAN 1, and S2 is the root bridge for VLANs 2 and 3. I know this doesn't seem hard, and it really isn't, but you still need to practice what we've covered so far in this chapter to make sure your skills are solid!

Spanning-Tree Failure Consequences

Clearly, there will be consequences when a routing protocol fails on a single router. Mainly, you'll just lose connectivity to the networks directly connected to that router, but it usually doesn't affect the rest of your network. This definitely makes it easier to troubleshoot and fix the issue.

There are two failure types with STP. One of them causes the same type of issue I mentioned with a routing protocol, when certain ports have been placed in a blocking state when they should be forwarding on a network segment instead. This situation makes the network segment unusable, but the rest of the network will still be working. But what happens when blocked ports are placed into forwarding state when they should be blocking? Let's work through this second failure issue now, using the same layout we used in the last section.

Let's start with Figure 9.16 and then find out what happens when STP fails. It isn't pretty!

Looking at Figure 9.16, what do you think will happen if switch SD transitions its blocked port to the forwarding state?

FIGURE 9.16 STP stopping loops

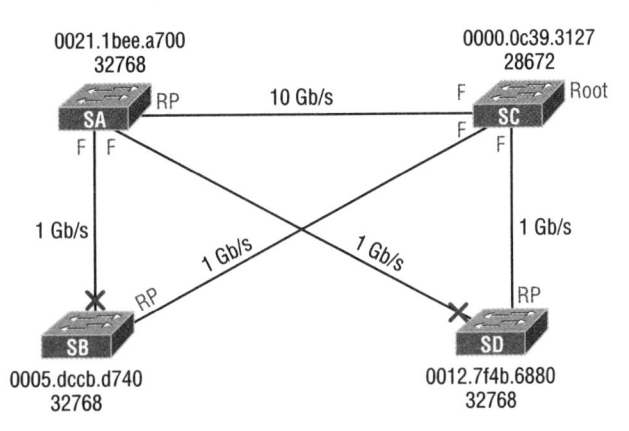

Clearly, the consequences to the entire network will be pretty devastating! Frames that already had a destination address recorded in the MAC address table of the switches are forwarded to the port they're associated with. But any broadcast, multicast, and unicasts not in the CAM are now in an endless loop!

Figure 9.17 shows us the carnage—when you see all the lights on each port blinking super-fast amber/green, this means serious errors are occurring—lots of them!

FIGURE 9.17 STP failure

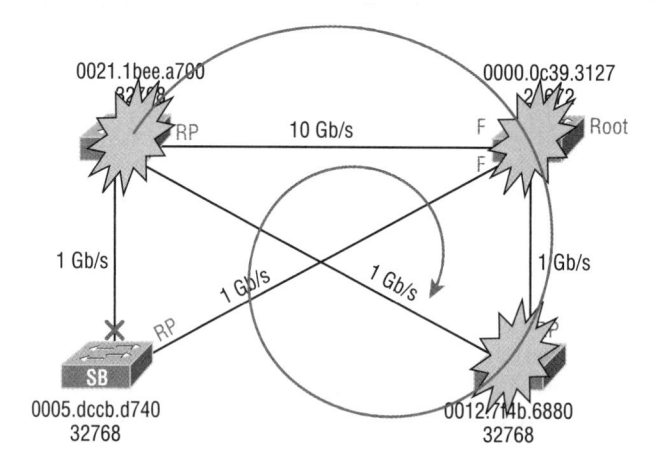

As frames begin building up on the network, the bandwidth starts getting saturated. The CPU percentage goes way up on the switches until they'll just give up and stop working completely. And all this happens within a few seconds!

Here's a list of the problems that will occur in a failed STP network that you must be aware of and you must be able to find in your production network. Of course, you must also understand them to meet the exam objectives:

- The load on all links begins increasing and more and more frames enter the loop. Remember, this loop affects all the other links in the network because these frames are always flooded out all ports. This scenario is a little less dire if the loop occurs within a single VLAN. In that case, the snag will be isolated to ports only in that VLAN membership, plus all trunk links that carry information for that VLAN.

- If you have more than one loop, traffic will increase on the switches because all the circling frames actually get duplicated. Switches basically receive a frame, make a copy of it, and send it out all ports. And they do this over and over and over again with the same frame, as well as for any new ones!

- The MAC address table is now completely unstable. It no longer knows where any source MAC address hosts are actually located because the same source address comes in via multiple ports on the switch.

- With the overwhelmingly high load on the links and the CPUs, now possibly at 100% or close to that, the devices become unresponsive, making it impossible to troubleshoot—it's a terrible thing!

At this point your only option is to systematically remove every redundant link between switches until you can find the source of the problem. And don't freak because, eventually, your ravaged network will calm down and come back to life after STP converges. Your fried switches will regain consciousness, but the network will need some serious therapy, so you're not out of the woods yet!

Now is when you start troubleshooting to find out what caused the disaster in the first place. A good strategy is to place the redundant links back into your network one at a time and wait to see when a problem begins to occur. You could have a failing switch port, or even a dead switch. Once you've replaced all your redundant links, you need to carefully monitor the network and have a back-out plan to quickly isolate the problem if it reoccurs. You don't want to go through this again!

You're probably wondering how to prevent these STP problems from ever darkening your doorstep in the first place. Well, just hang on, because after the next section, I'll tell you all about EtherChannel, which can stop ports from being placed in the blocked/discarding state on redundant links to save the day! But before we add more links to our switches and then bundle them, let's talk about PortFast.

PortFast and BPDU Guard

If you have a server or other devices connected into your switch that you're totally sure won't create a switching loop if STP is disabled, you can use a Cisco proprietary extension to the 802.1d standard called PortFast on these ports. With this tool, the port won't spend the usual 50 seconds to come up into forwarding mode while STP is converging, which is what makes it so cool.

Since ports will transition from blocking to forwarding state immediately, PortFast can prevent our hosts from being potentially unable to receive a DHCP address due to STP's slow convergence. If the host's DHCP request times out or if every time you plug a host in you're just tired of looking at the switch port being amber for almost a minute before it transitions to forwarding state and turns green, PortFast can really help you out.

Figure 9.18 illustrates a network with three switches, each with a trunk to each of the others and a host and server off the S1 switch.

FIGURE 9.18 PortFast

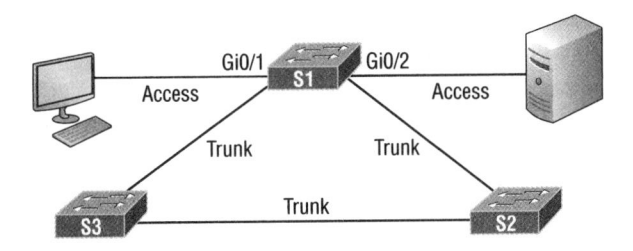

We can use PortFast on the ports on S1 to help them transition to the STP forwarding state immediately upon connecting to the switch.

Here are the commands, first from global config mode—they're pretty simple:

```
S1(config)#spanning-tree portfast ?
  bpdufilter  Enable portfast bdpu filter on this switch
  bpduguard   Enable portfast bpdu guard on this switch
  default     Enable portfast by default on all access ports
```

If you were to type spanning-tree portfast default, you would enable all nontrunking ports with PortFast. From interface mode, you can be more specific, which is the better way to go:

```
S1(config-if)#spanning-tree portfast ?
  disable  Disable portfast for this interface
  trunk    Enable portfast on the interface even in trunk mode
  <cr>
```

From interface mode you can actually configure PortFast on a trunk port, but you would do that only if the port connects to a server or router, not to another switch, so we won't use that here. So let's take a look at the message I get when I turn on PortFast on an interface Gi0/1:

```
S1#config t
S1#config)#int range gi0/1 - 2
S1(config-if)#spanning-tree portfast
%Warning: portfast should only be enabled on ports connected to a single
 host. Connecting hubs, concentrators, switches, bridges, etc... to this
 interface  when portfast is enabled, can cause temporary bridging loops.
 Use with CAUTION

%Portfast has been configured on GigabitEthernet0/1 but will only
 have effect when the interface is in a non-trunking mode.
```

PortFast is enabled on port Gi0/1 and Gi0/2, but notice that you get a pretty long message that's essentially telling you to be careful. This is because when using PortFast, you definitely don't want to create a network loop by plugging another switch or hub into a port that's also configured with PortFast! Why? Because if you let this happen, even though the network may still sort of work, data will pass super slowly, and worse, it could take you a really long time to find the source of the problem, making you very unpopular. So proceed with caution!

At this juncture, you would be happy to know that there are some safeguard commands to have handy when using PortFast just in case someone causes a loop in a port that's configured with PortFast enabled. Let's talk a really key safeguard command now.

BPDU Guard

If you turn on PortFast for a switch port, it's a really good idea to turn on BPDU Guard as well. In fact, it's such a great idea, I personally feel that it should be enabled by default whenever a port is configured with PortFast!

This is because if a switch port that has PortFast enabled receives a BPDU on that port, it will place the port into error disabled (shutdown) state, effectively preventing anyone from accidentally connecting another switch or hub port into a switch port configured with PortFast. Basically, you're preventing (guarding) your network from being severely crippled or even brought down. So let's configure our S1 interface, which is already configured with PortFast, with BPDU Guard now:

Here's how to set it globally:

```
S1(config)# spanning-tree portfast bpduguard default
```

And specifically on an interface:

```
S1(config-if)#spanning-tree bpduguard enable
```

It's important to know that you would only configure this command on your access layer switches—switches where users are directly connected.

> ## Real World Scenario
>
> ### Hedging My Bets Created Bad Switch Ports During the Super Bowl
>
> A junior admin called me frantically telling me all switch ports have just gone bad on the core switch, which was located at the data center where I was lead consultant for a data center upgrade. Now these things happen, but keep in mind that I just happened to be at a Super Bowl party having a great time watching my favorite team play in the "Big One" when I received this call! So I took a deep breath to refocus. I needed to find out some key information to determine just how bad the situation really was, and my client was in as big of a hurry as I was to get to a solution!
>
> First I asked the junior admin exactly what he did. Of course, he said, "Nothing, I swear!" I figured that's what he'd say, so I pressed him for more info and finally asked for stats on the switch. The admin told me that all the ports on the 10/100/1000 line card went amber at the same time—finally some information I could use! I confirmed that, as suspected, these ports trunked to uplink distribution switches. Okay, wow—this was not good!
>
> At this point, though, I found it hard to believe that all 24 ports would suddenly go bad, but it's possible, so I asked if he had a spare card to try. He told me that he had already put in the new card but the same thing was still happening. Well, okay—it's not the card, or the ports, but maybe something happened with the other switches. I knew there were a lot of switches involved, so someone must have screwed something up to make this catastrophe happen! Or, maybe the fiber distribution closet went down somehow? If so, how? Was there a fire in the closet or something? Some serious internal shenanigans would be the only answer if that were the cause!
>
> So remaining calm, (because, to quote Dr. House, "Patients lie"), I again had to ask the admin exactly what he did, and sure enough, he finally admitted that he tried to plug his personal laptop into the core switch so he could watch the Super Bowl, and quickly added, "…but that's it, I didn't do anything else!" I'll skip over the fact that this guy was

about to have the ugliest Monday ever, but something still didn't make sense, and here's why.

Knowing that the ports on that card would all connect to distribution switches, I configured the ports with PortFast so they wouldn't have to transition through the STP process. And because I wanted to make sure no one plugged a switch into any of those ports, I enabled BPDU Guard on the entire line card.

A host just would not bring down those ports, so I asked him if he had plugged in the laptop directly or used something in between. He admitted that he had indeed used another switch because, turns out, there were lots of people from the office who wanted to plug into the core switch and watch the game too. Was he kidding me? The security policy wouldn't allow connecting from their offices, so wouldn't you think they'd consider the core even more off-limits? Some people!

But wait... This still doesn't explain all ports turning amber, because only the one he plugged into should be doing that. It took me a second, but I figured out what he did and finally got him to confess. When he plugged the switch in, the port turned amber so he thought it went bad. So what do think he did? Well, if at first you don't succeed, try, try again, and that's just what he did—he actually kept trying ports—all 24 of them to be exact! Now that's what I call determined!

Sad to say, I got back to the party in time just to watch my team lose in the last few minutes! A dark day, indeed.

EtherChannel

Know that almost all Ethernet networks today will typically have multiple links between switches because this kind of design provides redundancy and resiliency. On a physical design that includes multiple links between switches, STP will do its job and put a port or ports into blocking mode. In addition to that, routing protocols like OSPF and EIGRP could see all these redundant links as individual ones, depending on the configuration, which can mean an increase in routing overhead.

We can gain the benefits from multiple links between switches by using port channeling. EtherChannel is a port channel technology that was originally developed by Cisco as a switch-to-switch technique for grouping several Fast Ethernet or Gigabit Ethernet ports into one logical channel.

Also important is that once your port channel (EtherChannel) is up and working, layer 2 STP and layer 3 routing protocols will treat those bundled links as a single one, which would stop STP from performing blocking. An additional benefit is that because the routing protocols now only see this as a single link, a single adjacency across the link can be formed—elegant!

Figure 9.19 shows how a network would look if we had four connections between switches, before and after configuring port channels.

FIGURE 9.19 Before and after port channels

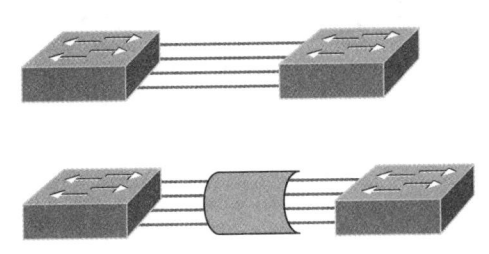

So as usual, there's the Cisco version and the IEEE version of port channel negotiation protocols to choose from—take your pick. Cisco's version is called Port Aggregation Protocol (PAgP), and the IEEE 802.3ad standard is called Link Aggregation Control Protocol (LACP). Both versions work equally well, but the way you configure each is slightly different. Keep in mind that both PAgP and LACP are negotiation protocols and that EtherChannel can actually be statically configured without PAgP or LACP. Still, it's better to use one of these protocols to help with compatibility issues as well as to manage link additions and failures between two switches.

Cisco EtherChannel allows us to bundle up to 8 ports active between switches. The links must have the same speed, duplex setting, and VLAN configuration—in other words you can't mix interface types and configurations into the same bundle.

There are a few differences in configuring PAgP and LACP, but first, let's go over some terms so you don't get confused:

Port channeling Refers to combining two-to-eight Fast Ethernet or two-Gigabit Ethernet ports together between two switches into one aggregated logical link to achieve more bandwidth and resiliency.

EtherChannel Cisco's proprietary term for port channeling.

PAgP This is a Cisco proprietary port channel negotiation protocol that aids in the automatic creation for EtherChannel links. All links in the bundle must match the same parameters (speed, duplex, VLAN info), and when PAgP identifies matched links, it groups the links into an EtherChannel. This is then added to STP as a single bridge port. At this point, PAgP's job is to send packets every 30 seconds to manage the link for consistency, any link additions, and failures.

LACP (802.3ad) This has the exact same purpose as PAgP, but is nonproprietary so it can work between multi-vendor networks.

`Channel-group` This is a command on Ethernet interfaces used to add the specified interface to a single EtherChannel. The number following this command is the port channel ID.

`Interface port-channel` Here's the command that creates the bundled interface. Ports can be added to this interface with the `channel-group` command. Keep in mind that the interface number must match the group number.

Okay, now let's see if you can make some sense out of all these terms by actually configuring something!

Configuring and Verifying Port Channels

Let's use Figure 9.20 for our simple example of how to configure port channels.

FIGURE 9.20 EtherChannel example

You can enable your `channel-group` for each channel by setting the channel mode for each interface to either `active` or `passive` if using LACP. When a port is configured in passive mode, it will respond to the LACP packets it receives, but it won't initiate an LACP negotiation. When a port is configured for active mode, the port initiates negotiations with other ports by sending LACP packets.

Next, I'll show you a simple example of configuring port channels and then verifying them. First I'll go to global configuration mode and create a port channel interface, and then I'll add this port channel to the physical interfaces.

Remember, all parameters and configurations of the ports must be the same, so I'll start by trunking the interfaces before I configure EtherChannel, like this:

```
S1(config)#int range g0/1 - 2
S1(config-if-range)#switchport trunk encapsulation dot1q
S1(config-if-range)#switchport mode trunk
```

All ports in your bundles must be configured the same, so I'll configure both sides with the same trunking configuration. Now I can assign these ports to a bundle:

```
S1(config-if-range)#channel-group 1 mode ?
  active     Enable LACP unconditionally
  auto       Enable PAgP only if a PAgP device is detected
  desirable  Enable PAgP unconditionally
  on         Enable Etherchannel only
  passive    Enable LACP only if a LACP device is detected
S1(config-if-range)#channel-group 1 mode active
S1(config-if-range)#exit
```

To configure the IEEE nonproprietary LACP, I'll use the `active` or `passive` command; if I wanted to use Cisco's PAgP, I'd use the `auto` or `desirable` command. You can't mix and match these on either end of the bundle, and really, it doesn't matter which one you use in a pure Cisco environment, as long as you configure them the same on both ends. Setting the mode to on would be statically configuring your EtherChannel bundle. At this point in the configuration, I'd have to set the mode to `active` on the S2 interfaces if I wanted the bundle to

EtherChannel

come up with LACP because, again, all parameters must be the same on both ends of the link. Let's create our port channel interface now with the `interface port-channel` command:

```
S1(config)#int port-channel 1
S1(config-if)#switchport trunk encapsulation dot1q
S1(config-if)#switchport mode trunk
S1(config-if)#switchport trunk allowed vlan 1,2,3
```

Notice that I set the same trunking method under the port channel interface as I did the physical interfaces—the VLAN information too.

Time to configure the interfaces, channel groups, and port channel interface on the S2 switch:

```
S2(config)#int range g0/13 - 14
S2(config-if-range)#switchport trunk encapsulation dot1q
S2(config-if-range)#switchport mode trunk
S2(config-if-range)#channel-group 1 mode active
S2(config-if-range)#exit
S2(config)#int port-channel 1
S2(config-if)#switchport trunk encapsulation dot1q
S2(config-if)#switchport mode trunk
S2(config-if)#switchport trunk allowed vlan 1,2,3
```

On each switch, I configured the ports I wanted to bundle with the same configuration, then created the port channel. After that, I added the ports into the port channel with the channel-group command, and the port channel is created.

Remember, for LACP we'll use either active/active on each side of the bundle or active/passive, but you can't use passive/passive. Same goes for PAgP—you can use it with desirable/desirable or auto/desirable, but not auto/auto.

Let's verify our EtherChannel with a few commands. We'll start with the `show etherchannel port-channel` command to see information about a specific port channel interface:

```
S2#sh etherchannel port-channel
              Channel-group listing:
              ----------------------

Group: 1
----------
              Port-channels in the group:
              ---------------------------

Port-channel: Po1    (Primary Aggregator)
------------

Age of the Port-channel   = 00d:00h:46m:49s
```

```
Logical slot/port   = 2/1         Number of ports = 2
GC                  = 0x00000000     HotStandBy port = null
Port state          = Port-channel
Protocol            =    LACP
Port Security       = Disabled

Ports in the Port-channel:

Index   Load   Port     EC state         No of bits
------+------+------+------------------+-----------
  0     00    Gig0/2   Active             0
  0     00    Gig0/1   Active             0
Time since last port bundled:    00d:00h:46m:47s    Gig0/1
S2#
```

Notice that we have one group and that we're running the IEEE LACP version of port channeling. We're in Active mode, and that Port-channel: Po1 interface has two physical interfaces. The heading Load is not the load over the interfaces, it's a hexadecimal value that decides which interface will be chosen to specify the flow of traffic.

The show etherchannel summary command displays one line of information per port channel:

```
S2#sh etherchannel summary
Flags:  D - down         P - in port-channel
        I - stand-alone  s - suspended
        H - Hot-standby (LACP only)
        R - Layer3       S - Layer2
        U - in use       f - failed to allocate aggregator
        u - unsuitable for bundling
        w - waiting to be aggregated
        d - default port

Number of channel-groups in use: 1
Number of aggregators:           1

Group  Port-channel  Protocol    Ports
------+-------------+-----------+-----------------------------------------
1      Po1(SU)         LACP      Gig0/1(P) Gig0/2(P)
```

This command shows that we have one group, that we're running LACP, and Gig0/1 and Gig0/2 or (P), which means these ports are in port-channel mode. This command isn't really all that helpful unless you have multiple channel groups, but it does tell us our group is working well!

Layer-3 EtherChannel

One last item to discuss before we finish this chapter is layer 3 EtherChannel. You'd use layer 3 EtherChannel when connecting a switch to multiple ports on a router, for example.

You wouldn't put IP addresses under the physical interface, you'd actually add the IP address of the bundle under the logical port-channel interface.

Here's an example on how to create the logical port channel 1 and assign 20.2.2.2 as its IP address:

```
Router#config t
Router(config)#int port-channel 1
Router(config-if)#ip address 20.2.2.2 255.255.255.0
```

Now we need to add the physical port into port channel 1:

```
Router(config-if)#int range g0/0-1
Router(config-if-range)#channel-group 1
GigabitEthernet0/0 added as member-1 to port-channel1
GigabitEthernet0/1 added as member-2 to port-channel1
```

Now let's take a look at the running-config and notice there are no IP addresses under the physical interface of the router:

```
!
interface Port-channel1
 ip address 20.2.2.2 255.255.255.0
 load-interval 30
!
 interface GigabitEthernet0/0
 no ip address
 load-interval 30
 duplex auto
 speed auto
 channel-group 1
!
 interface GigabitEthernet0/1
 no ip address
 load-interval 30
 duplex auto
 speed auto
 channel-group 1
!
```

Any configuration added in the port-channel configuration are inherited in each interface in the group. We now have bundled router interfaces to our switch. Nice!

Summary

This chapter was all about switching technologies, with a particular focus on the Spanning Tree Protocol (STP) and its evolution to newer versions like RSTP and then Cisco's PVST+.

You learned about the problems that can occur if you have multiple links between bridges (switches) and the solutions attained with STP.

I also talked about and demonstrated issues that can occur if you have multiple links between bridges (switches), plus how to solve these problems by using the Spanning Tree Protocol (STP).

I walked you through a detailed configuration of Cisco's Catalyst switches, including verifying the configuration, setting the Cisco STP extensions, and changing the root bridge by setting a bridge priority.

Finally, we discussed, configured, and verified the EtherChannel technology that helps us bundle multiple links between switches.

Exam Essentials

Understand the main purpose of the Spanning Tree Protocol in a switched LAN. The main purpose of STP is to prevent switching loops in a network with redundant switched paths.

Remember the states of STP. The purpose of the blocking state is to prevent the use of looped paths. A port in listening state prepares to forward data frames without populating the MAC address table. A port in learning state populates the MAC address table but doesn't forward data frames. A port in forwarding state sends and receives all data frames on the bridged port. Also, a port in the disabled state is virtually nonoperational.

Remember the command `show spanning-tree`. You must be familiar with the command `show spanning-tree` and how to determine the root bridge of each VLAN. You can also use the `show spanning-tree summary` command to help you get a quick glimpse of your STP network and root bridges.

Understand what PortFast and BPDU Guard provides. PortFast allows a port to transition to the forwarding state immediately upon a connection. Because you don't want other switches connecting to this port, BPDU Guard will shut down a PortFast port if it receives a BPDU.

Understand what EtherChannel is and how to configure it. EtherChannel allows you to bundle links to get more bandwidth instead of allowing STP to shut down redundant ports. You can configure Cisco's PAgP or the IEEE version, LACP, by creating a port channel interface and assigning the port channel group number to the interfaces you're bundling.

Review Questions

The answers to these questions can be found in the Appendix.

1. You receive the following output from a switch:

    ```
    S2#sh spanning-tree
    VLAN0001
    Spanning tree enabled protocol rstp
    Root ID    Priority    32769
               Address     0001.42A7.A603
               Cost        4
               Port        26(GigabitEthernet1/2)
               Hello Time  2 sec  Max Age 20 sec  Forward Delay 15 sec
    [output cut]
    ```

    Which are true regarding this switch? (Choose two.)
    - **A.** The switch is a root bridge.
    - **B.** The switch is a non-root bridge.
    - **C.** The root bridge is four switches away.
    - **D.** The switch is running 802.1w.
    - **E.** The switch is running STP PVST+.

2. You have configured your switches with the `spanning-tree vlan x root primary` and `spanning-tree vlan x root secondary` commands. Which of the following tertiary switch will take over if both switches fail?
    - **A.** A switch with priority 4096
    - **B.** A switch with priority 8192
    - **C.** A switch with priority 12288
    - **D.** A switch with priority 20480

3. Which of the following would you use to find the VLANs for which your switch is the root bridge? (Choose two.)
    - **A.** `show spanning-tree`
    - **B.** `show root all`
    - **C.** `show spanning-tree port root VLAN`
    - **D.** `show spanning-tree summary`

4. You want to run the new 802.1w on your switches. Which of the following would enable this protocol?

  A. `Switch(config)#spanning-tree mode rapid-pvst`
  B. `Switch#spanning-tree mode rapid-pvst`
  C. `Switch(config)#spanning-tree mode 802.1w`
  D. `Switch#spanning-tree mode 802.1w`

5. Which of the following is a layer 2 protocol used to maintain a loop-free network?

  A. VTP
  B. STP
  C. RIP
  D. CDP

6. Which statement describes a spanning-tree network that has converged?

  A. All switch and bridge ports are in the forwarding state.
  B. All switch and bridge ports are assigned as either root or designated ports.
  C. All switch and bridge ports are in either the forwarding or blocking state.
  D. All switch and bridge ports are either blocking or looping.

7. Which of the following modes enable LACP EtherChannel? (Choose two.)

  A. On
  B. Prevent
  C. Passive
  D. Auto
  E. Active
  F. Desirable

8. Which of the following are true regarding RSTP? (Choose three.)

  A. RSTP speeds the recalculation of the spanning tree when the layer 2 network topology changes.
  B. RSTP is an IEEE standard that redefines STP port roles, states, and BPDUs.
  C. RSTP is extremely proactive and very quick, and therefore it absolutely needs the 802.1 delay timers.
  D. RSTP (802.1w) supersedes 802.1d while remaining proprietary.
  E. All of the 802.1d terminology and most parameters have been changed.
  F. 802.1w is capable of reverting to 802.1d to interoperate with traditional switches on a per-port basis.

9. What does BPDU Guard perform?
    A. Makes sure the port is receiving BPDUs from the correct upstream switch.
    B. Makes sure the port is not receiving BPDUs from the upstream switch, only the root.
    C. If a BPDU is received on a BPDU Guard port, PortFast is used to shut down the port.
    D. Shuts down a port if a BPDU is seen on that port.
10. How many bits is the sys-id-ext field in a BPDU?
    A. 4
    B. 8
    C. 12
    D. 16

Chapter 10

Access Lists

THE FOLLOWING CCNA EXAM TOPICS ARE COVERED IN THIS CHAPTER:

5.0 Security Fundamentals

✓ 5.6 Configure and verify access control lists

If you're a sys admin, I'm guessing that shielding sensitive, critical data and your network's resources is a major priority of yours, right? Well, you're going to like this chapter. Cisco has some very effective tools to use as the security solutions you'll need to protect your network from danger!

The first power tool I'm going to hand you is the access control list (ACL). Being able to execute an ACL proficiently is an integral part of Cisco's security solution, so I'm going to begin by showing you how to create and implement simple ACLs. From there, I'll move to demonstrating more advanced ACLs and describe how to implement them strategically to provide serious armor for an internetwork in today's challenging, high-risk environment.

The proper use and configuration of access lists is a vital part of router configuration partly because they're so versatile. Contributing mightily to the efficiency and operation of your network, ACLs give us a huge amount of control over traffic flow throughout the enterprise. With them, we can simply gather basic statistics on packet flow or use them to deploy smart security policies. These dynamic tools make us able to protect sensitive devices from the constantly present dangers of unauthorized access. We're going to cover ACLs for TCP/IP and explore effective ways to test and monitor how well applied access lists are functioning.

So let's begin with a quick overview of the usual hardware devices involved and then I'll introduce you to ACLs.

To find your included bonus material, as well as Todd Lammle videos, practice questions & hands-on labs, please see www.lammle.com/ccna

Perimeter, Firewall, and Internal Routers

You see this a lot—typically, in medium to large enterprise networks—the various strategies for security are based on some mix of internal and perimeter routers, plus firewall devices. Internal routers provide additional security by screening traffic to various parts of the protected corporate network. They achieve this by using access lists.

You can see where each of these types of devices would be found in Figure 10.1.

FIGURE 10.1 A typical secured network

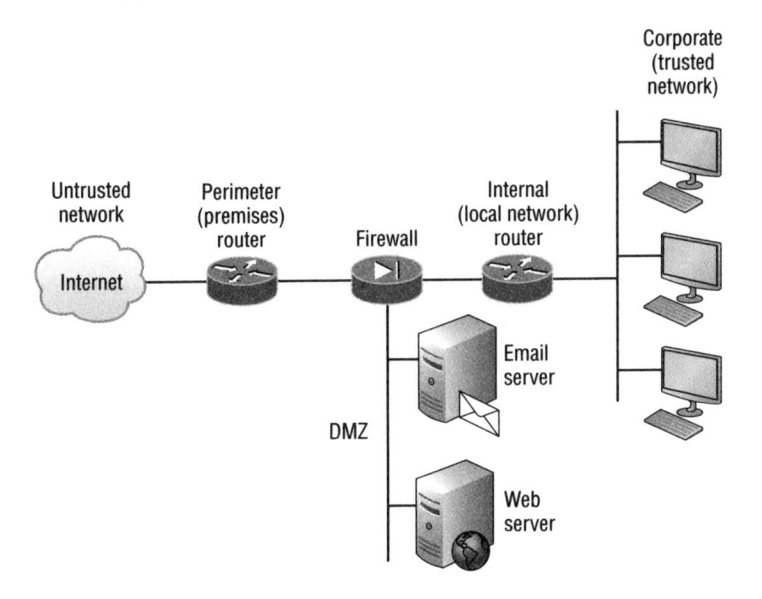

I'll use the terms *trusted network* and *untrusted network* throughout this chapter, so it's important that you can see where they're found in a typical secured network. The demilitarized zone (DMZ) can be global (real) Internet addresses or private addresses, depending on how you configure your firewall. This is typically where you'll find the HTTP, DNS, email, and other Internet-type corporate servers.

As you now know, instead of using routers, we can create VLANs with switches on the inside, trusted network. Multilayer switches containing their own security features can sometimes replace internal (LAN) routers to provide higher performance in VLAN architectures.

Let's look at some ways of protecting the internetwork using access lists.

Introduction to Access Lists

An *access list* is essentially a list of conditions that categorize packets, and they really come in handy when you need to exercise control over network traffic. An ACL would be your tool of choice for decision making in these situations.

One of the most common and easiest-to-understand uses of access lists is to filter unwanted packets when implementing security policies. For example, you can set them up to make very specific decisions about regulating traffic patterns so that they'll allow only certain hosts to access web resources on the Internet while restricting others. With the right combination of access lists, network managers have the power to enforce nearly any security policy they can invent.

Creating access lists is a lot like programming a series of if-then statements—if a given condition is met, then a given action is taken. If the specific condition isn't met, nothing happens and the next statement is evaluated. Access-list statements are basically packet filters that packets are compared against, categorized by, and acted upon accordingly. Once the lists are built, they can be applied to either inbound or outbound traffic on any interface. Applying an access list causes the router to analyze every packet crossing that interface in the specified direction and take the appropriate action.

There are three important rules that a packet follows when it's being compared with an access list:

- The packet is always compared with each line of the access list in sequential order—it will always start with the first line of the access list, move on to line 2, then line 3, and so on.
- The packet is compared with lines of the access list only until a match is made. Once it matches the condition on a line of the access list, the packet is acted upon and no further comparisons take place.
- There is an implicit "deny" at the end of each access list—this means that if a packet doesn't match the condition on any of the lines in the access list, the packet will be discarded.

Each of these rules has some powerful ramifications when filtering IP packets with access lists, so keep in mind that creating really effective ACLs definitely takes some practice!

There are two, main types of access lists:

Standard access lists   These ACLs use only the source IP address in an IP packet as the condition test. All decisions are made based on the source IP address. This means that standard access lists basically permit or deny an entire suite of protocols. They don't distinguish between any of the many types of IP traffic such as Web, Telnet, UDP, and so on.

Extended access lists   Extended access lists can evaluate many of the other fields in the layer 3 and layer 4 headers of an IP packet. They can evaluate source and destination IP addresses, the Protocol field in the Network layer header, and the port number at the Transport layer header. This gives extended access lists the ability to make much more granular decisions when controlling traffic.

Named access lists   Hey, wait a minute—I said there were only two types of access lists but listed three! Well, technically there really are only two since *named access lists* are either standard or extended and not actually a distinct type. I'm just distinguishing them because they're created and referred to differently than standard and extended access lists are, but they're still functionally the same.

> **NOTE**   We'll cover these types of access lists in more detail later in the chapter.

Creating an access list is just the beginning because it's not going to do anything until you apply it. Yes, they're there on the router, but they're inactive until you tell that router what to do with them. To use an access list as a packet filter, you need to apply it to an interface on the router where you want the traffic filtered. And you've got to specify which direction of traffic you want the access list applied to. There's a good reason for this—you may want different controls in place for traffic leaving your enterprise destined for the Internet than you'd want for traffic coming into your enterprise from the Internet. So, by specifying the direction of traffic, you can and must use different access lists for inbound and outbound traffic on a single interface:

Inbound access lists   When an access list is applied to inbound packets on an interface, those packets are processed through the access list before being routed to the outbound interface. Any packets that are denied won't be routed because they're discarded before the routing process is invoked.

Outbound access lists   When an access list is applied to outbound packets on an interface, packets are routed to the outbound interface and then processed through the access list before being queued.

There are some general access-list guidelines that you should keep in mind when creating and implementing access lists on a router:

- You can assign only one access list per interface per protocol per direction. This means that when applying IP access lists, you can have only one inbound access list and one outbound access list per interface.

> **NOTE**   When you consider the implications of the implicit deny at the end of any access list, it makes sense that you can't have multiple access lists applied on the same interface in the same direction for the same protocol. That's because any packets that don't match some condition in the first access list would be denied, and there wouldn't be any packets left over to compare against a second access list!

- Organize your access lists so that the more specific tests are at the top.
- Anytime a new entry is added to the access list, it will be placed at the bottom of the list, which is why I highly recommend using a text editor for access lists.
- You can't remove one line from an access list. If you try to do this, you will remove the entire list. This is why it's best to copy the access list to a text editor before trying to edit the list. The only exception is when you're using named access lists.

> **NOTE**   You can edit, add, or delete a single line from a named access list. I'll show you how soon.

- Unless your access list ends with a `permit any` command, all packets will be discarded if they do not meet any of the list's tests. This means every list should have at least one `permit` statement or it will deny all traffic.
- Create access list permit and deny statements first and then apply them to an interface. Any access list applied to an interface without access list test statements already created will not filter traffic.
- Access lists are designed to filter traffic going through the router. They will not filter traffic that has originated from the router.
- Place IP standard access lists as close to the destination as possible. This is the reason we don't really want to use standard access lists in our networks. You can't put a standard access list close to the source host or network because you can only filter based on source address and all destinations would be affected as a result.
- Place IP extended access lists as close to the source as possible. Since extended access lists can filter on very specific addresses and protocols, you don't want traffic to traverse the entire network just to be denied. By placing this list as close to the source address as possible, you can filter traffic before it uses up precious bandwidth.

Before demonstrating how to configure basic and extended ACLs, let's talk about how they can be used to mitigate the security threats I mentioned earlier.

Mitigating Security Issues with ACLs

The most common attack is a denial of service (DoS) attack. Although ACLs can help with a DoS, you really need an intrusion detection system (IDS) and intrusion prevention system (IPS) to help prevent these common attacks. Cisco sells the new Firepower and Firepower Threat Defense (FTD) products that is the best next generation firewall (NGFW) in the industry.

Here's a list of the many security threats you can mitigate with ACLs:

- IP address spoofing, inbound
- IP address spoofing, outbound
- Denial of service (DoS) TCP SYN attacks, blocking external attacks
- DoS TCP SYN attacks, using TCP Intercept
- DoS smurf attacks
- Denying/filtering ICMP messages, inbound
- Denying/filtering ICMP messages, outbound
- Denying/filtering Traceroute

Note: This is not an "introduction to security" book, so you may have to research some of the preceding terms if you don't understand them.

It's generally a bad idea to allow any external IP packets that contain the source address of any internal hosts or networks into a private network—just don't permit it!

Here's a list of rules to live by when configuring ACLs from the Internet to your production network to mitigate security problems:

- Deny any source addresses from your internal networks.
- Deny any local host addresses (127.0.0.0/8).
- Deny any reserved private addresses (RFC 1918).
- Deny any addresses in the IP multicast address range (224.0.0.0/4).

None of these source addresses should ever be allowed to enter your internetwork. Now finally, let's get our hands dirty and configure some access lists!

Standard Access Lists

Standard IP access lists filter network traffic by examining the source IP address in a packet. You create a *standard IP access list* by using the access-list numbers 1–99 or numbers in the expanded range of 1300–1999 because the type of ACL is generally differentiated numerically. Based on the number used when the access list is created, the router knows which type of syntax to expect as the list is entered. By using numbers 1–99 or 1300–1999, you're telling the router that you want to create a standard IP access list, so the router will expect syntax specifying only the source IP address in the test lines.

The following output displays a good example of the many access-list number ranges that you can use to filter traffic on your network. The IOS version delimits the protocols you can specify access for:

```
Corp(config)#access-list ?
<1-99>       IP standard access list
<100-199>    IP extended access list
<1000-1099>  IPX SAP access list
<1100-1199>  Extended 48-bit MAC address access list
<1200-1299>  IPX summary address access list
<1300-1999>  IP standard access list (expanded range)
<200-299>    Protocol type-code access list
<2000-2699>  IP extended access list (expanded range)
<2700-2799>  MPLS access list
<300-399>    DECnet access list
<700-799>    48-bit MAC address access list
<800-899>    IPX standard access list
<900-999>    IPX extended access list
dynamic-extended Extend the dynamic ACL absolute timer
rate-limit   Simple rate-limit specific access list
```

Wow—there sure are whole lot of old protocols listed in that output! IPX and DECnet would no longer be used in any of today's networks. Let's take a look at the syntax used when creating a standard IP access list:

```
Corp(config)#access-list 10 ?
deny Specify packets to reject
permit Specify packets to forward
remark Access list entry comment
```

As I said, by using the access-list numbers 1–99 or 1300–1999, you're telling the router that you want to create a standard IP access list, which means you can only filter on source IP address.

Once you've chosen the access-list number, you need to decide whether you're creating a permit or deny statement. I'm going to create a deny statement now:

```
Corp(config)#access-list 10 deny ?
Hostname or A.B.C.D Address to match
any Any source host
host A single host address
```

The next step is more detailed because there are three options available in it:

1. The first option is any parameter, used to permit or deny any source host or network.
2. The second choice is to use an IP address to specify either a single host or a range of them.
3. The last option is to use the host command to specify a specific host only.

The any command is pretty obvious—any source address matches the statement, so every packet compared against this line will match. The host command is relatively simple too, as you can see here:

```
Corp(config)#access-list 10 deny host ?
Hostname or A.B.C.D Host address
Corp(config)#access-list 10 deny host 172.16.30.2
```

This tells the list to deny any packets from host 172.16.30.2. The default parameter is host. In other words, if you type **access-list 10 deny 172.16.30.2**, the router assumes you mean host 172.16.30.2 and that's exactly how it will show in your running-config.

But there's another way to specify either a particular host or a range of hosts known as wildcard masking. In fact, to specify any range of hosts, you must use wildcard masking in the access list.

So exactly what is wildcard masking? Coming up, I'm going to show you using a standard access list example. I'll also guide you through how to control access to a virtual terminal.

Wildcard Masking

Wildcards are used with access lists to specify an individual host, a network, or a specific range of a network or networks. The block sizes you learned about earlier used to specify a range of addresses are key to understanding wildcards.

Standard Access Lists

So let's do a quick review of block sizes before we go any further. I'm sure you remember that the different block sizes available are 64, 32, 16, 8, and 4. When you need to specify a range of addresses, you choose the next-largest block size for your needs. So if you need to specify 34 networks, you need a block size of 64. If you want to specify 18 hosts, you need a block size of 32. If you specify only 2 networks, then go with a block size of 4.

Wildcards are used with the host or network address to tell the router a range of available addresses to filter. To specify a host, the address would look like this:

`172.16.30.5 0.0.0.0`

The four zeros represent each octet of the address. Whenever a zero is present, it indicates that the octet in the address must match the corresponding reference octet exactly. To specify that an octet can be any value, use the value 255. Here's an example of how a /24 subnet is specified with a wildcard mask:

`172.16.30.0 0.0.0.255`

This tells the router to match up the first three octets exactly, but the fourth octet can be any value.

Okay—that was the easy part. But what if you want to specify only a small range of subnets? This is where block sizes come in. You have to specify the range of values in a block size, so you can't choose to specify 20 networks. You can only specify the exact amount that the block size value allows. This means that the range would have to be either 16 or 32, but not 20.

Let's say that you want to block access to the part of the network that ranges from 172.16.8.0 through 172.16.15.0. To do that, you would go with a block size of 8, your network number would be 172.16.8.0, and the wildcard would be 0.0.7.255. The 7.255 equals the value the router will use to determine the block size. So together, the network number and the wildcard tell the router to begin at 172.16.8.0 and go up a block size of eight addresses to network 172.16.15.0.

This really is easier than it looks! I could certainly go through the binary math for you, but no one needs that kind of pain because all you have to do is remember that the wildcard is always one number less than the block size. So, in our example, the wildcard would be 7 since our block size is 8. If you used a block size of 16, the wildcard would be 15. Easy, right?

Just to make sure you've got this, we'll go through some examples to be sure. The following one tells the router to match the first three octets exactly but that the fourth octet can be anything:

`Corp(config)#access-list 10 deny 172.16.10.0 0.0.0.255`

The next example tells the router to match the first two octets and that the last two octets can be any value:

`Corp(config)#access-list 10 deny 172.16.0.0 0.0.255.255`

Now, try to figure out this next line:

`Corp(config)#access-list 10 deny 172.16.16.0 0.0.3.255`

This configuration tells the router to start at network 172.16.16.0 and use a block size of 4. The range would then be 172.16.16.0 through 172.16.19.255, and by the way, the Cisco objectives seem to really like this one!

Let's keep practicing. What about this next one?

```
Corp(config)#access-list 10 deny 172.16.16.0 0.0.7.255
```

This example reveals an access list starting at 172.16.16.0 going up a block size of 8 to 172.16.23.255.

Let's keep at it... What do you think the range of this one is?

```
Corp(config)#access-list 10 deny 172.16.32.0 0.0.15.255
```

This one begins at network 172.16.32.0 and goes up a block size of 16 to 172.16.47.255. You're almost done... After a couple more, we'll configure some real ACLs.

```
Corp(config)#access-list 10 deny 172.16.64.0 0.0.63.255
```

This example starts at network 172.16.64.0 and goes up a block size of 64 to 172.16.127.255.

What about this last example?

```
Corp(config)#access-list 10 deny 192.168.160.0 0.0.31.255
```

This one shows us that it begins at network 192.168.160.0 and goes up a block size of 32 to 192.168.191.255.

Here are two more things to keep in mind when working with block sizes and wildcards:

- Each block size must start at 0 or a multiple of the block size. For example, you can't say that you want a block size of 8 and then start at 12. You must use 0–7, 8–15, 16–23, etc. For a block size of 32, the ranges are 0–31, 32–63, 64–95, etc.
- The command any is the same thing as writing out the wildcard 0.0.0.0 255.255.255.255.

> **NOTE** Wildcard masking is a crucial skill to master when creating IP access lists. It's the same whether you're creating standard or extended IP access lists.

Standard Access List Example

In this section, you'll learn how to use a standard access list to stop specific users from gaining access to the Finance department LAN.

In Figure 10.2, a router has three LAN connections and one WAN connection to the Internet. You don't want users on the Sales LAN to have access to the Finance LAN, but they should be able to access the Internet and the marketing department files. The Marketing LAN needs to access the Finance LAN for application services.

Standard Access Lists

FIGURE 10.2 IP access list example with three LANs and a WAN connection

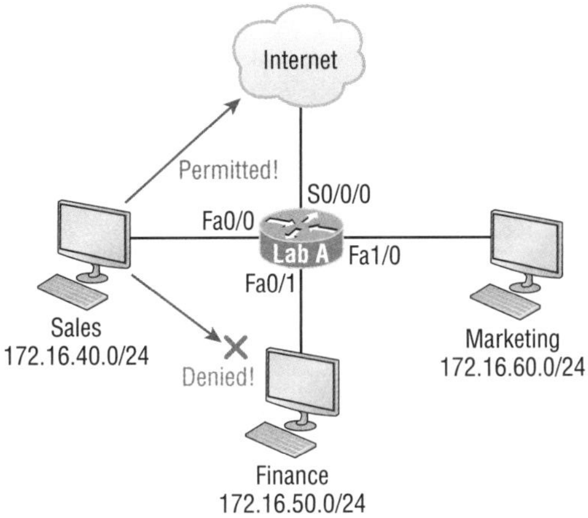

We can see that the following standard IP access list is configured on the router:

```
Lab_A#config t
Lab_A(config)#access-list 10 deny 172.16.40.0 0.0.0.255
Lab_A(config)#access-list 10 permit any
```

It's very important to remember that the any command is the same thing as saying the following using wildcard masking:

```
Lab_A(config)#access-list 10 permit 0.0.0.0 255.255.255.255
```

Since the wildcard mask says that none of the octets are to be evaluated, every address matches the test condition, so this is functionally doing the same as using the any keyword.

At this point, the access list is configured to deny source addresses from the Sales LAN to the Finance LAN and to allow everyone else. But remember, no action will be taken until the access list is applied on an interface in a specific direction!

Where should this access list be placed? If you place it as an incoming access list on Fa0/0, you might as well shut down the FastEthernet interface because all of the Sales LAN devices will be denied access to all networks attached to the router. The best place to apply this access list is on the Fa0/1 interface as an outbound list:

```
Lab_A(config)#int fa0/1
Lab_A(config-if)#ip access-group 10 out
```

Doing this completely stops traffic from 172.16.40.0 from getting out FastEthernet0/1. It has no effect on the hosts from the Sales LAN accessing the Marketing LAN and the Internet because traffic to those destinations doesn't go through interface Fa0/1. Any packet trying to exit out Fa0/1 will have to go through the access list first. If there were an inbound list placed on F0/0, then any packet trying to enter interface F0/0 would have to go through the access list before being routed to an exit interface.

Let's take a look at another standard access list example. Figure 10.3 shows an internetwork of two routers with four LANs.

FIGURE 10.3 IP standard access list example 2

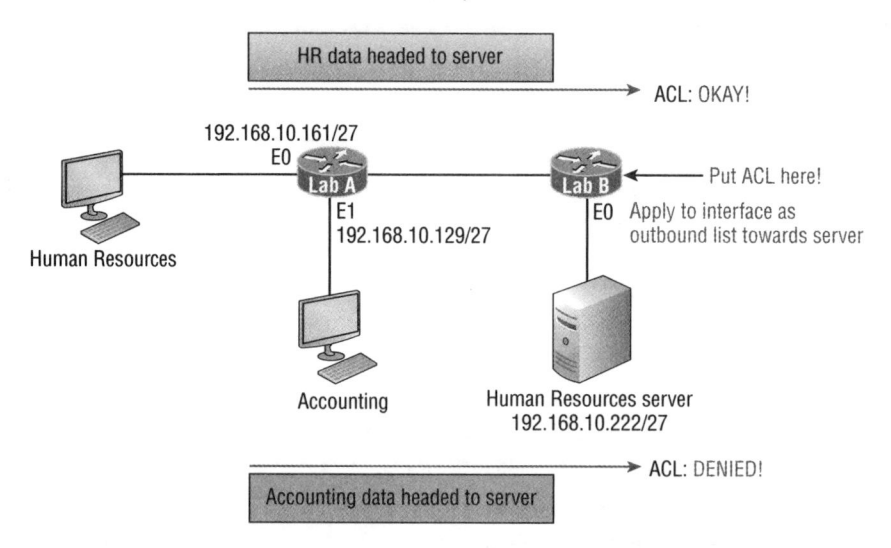

We're going to stop the Accounting users from accessing the Human Resources server attached to the Lab_B router but allow all other users access to that LAN using a standard ACL. What kind of standard access list would we need to create and where would we place it to achieve our goals?

The real answer is that we should use an extended access list and place it closest to the source! But this question specifies using a standard access list, and as a rule, standard ACLs are placed closest to the destination.

In this example, Ethernet 0 is the outbound interface on the Lab_B router, and here's the access list that should be placed on it:

```
Lab_B#config t
Lab_B(config)#access-list 10 deny 192.168.10.128 0.0.0.31
Lab_B(config)#access-list 10 permit any
Lab_B(config)#interface Ethernet 0
Lab_B(config-if)#ip access-group 10 out
```

Keep in mind that to be able to answer this question correctly, you really need to understand subnetting, wildcard masks, and how to configure and implement ACLs. The accounting subnet is the 192.168.10.128/27, which is a 255.255.255.224, with a block size of 32 in the fourth octet.

With all this in mind and before we move on to restricting Telnet access on a router, let's take a look at one more standard access list example. This one is going to require some thought. In Figure 10.4, you have a router with four LAN connections and one WAN connection to the Internet.

FIGURE 10.4 IP standard access list example 3

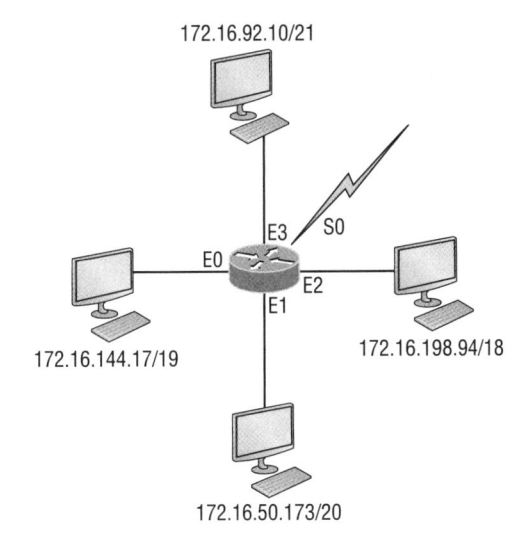

You need to write an access list that will stop access from each of the four LANs shown in the diagram to the Internet. Each of the LANs reveals a single host's IP address, which you need to use to determine the subnet and wildcards of each LAN to configure the access list.

Here's an example of what your answer should look like, beginning with the network on E0 and working through to E3:

```
Router(config)#access-list 1 deny 172.16.128.0 0.0.31.255
Router(config)#access-list 1 deny 172.16.48.0 0.0.15.255
Router(config)#access-list 1 deny 172.16.192.0 0.0.63.255
Router(config)#access-list 1 deny 172.16.88.0 0.0.7.255
Router(config)#access-list 1 permit any
Router(config)#interface serial 0
Router(config-if)#ip access-group 1 out
```

Sure, you could have done this with one line:

```
Router(config)#access-list 1 deny 172.16.0.0 0.0.255.255
```

But what fun is that?

And remember the reasons for creating this list. If you actually applied this ACL on the router, you'd effectively shut down access to the Internet, so why even have an Internet connection? I included this exercise so you can practice how to use block sizes with access lists, which is vital for succeeding when you take the Cisco exam!

Controlling VTY (Telnet/SSH) Access

Trying to stop users from telnetting or trying to SSH to a router is really challenging because any active interface on a router is fair game for VTY/SSH access. Creating an extended IP ACL that limits access to every IP address on the router may sound like a solution, but if you did that, you'd have to apply it inbound on every interface, which really wouldn't scale well if you happen to have dozens, even hundreds, of interfaces, now would it? And think of all the latency dragging down your network as a result of each and every router checking every packet just in case the packet was trying to access your VTY lines—horrible!

Don't give up—there's always a solution! And in this case, a much better one, which employs a standard IP access list to control access to the VTY lines themselves.

Why does this work so well? Because when you apply an access list to the VTY lines, you don't need to specify the protocol since access to the VTY already implies terminal access via the Telnet or SSH protocols. You also don't need to specify a destination address because it really doesn't matter which interface address the user used as a target for the Telnet session. All you really need control of is where the user is coming from, which is betrayed by their source IP address.

You need to do these two things to make this happen:

1. Create a standard IP access list that permits only the host or hosts you want to be able to telnet into the routers.
2. Apply the access list to the VTY line with the `access-class in` command.

Here, I'm allowing only host 172.16.10.3 to telnet into a router:

```
Lab_A(config)#access-list 50 permit host 172.16.10.3
Lab_A(config)#line vty 0 4
Lab_A(config-line)#access-class 50 in
```

Because of the implied deny any at the end of the list, the ACL stops any host from telnetting into the router except the host 172.16.10.3 regardless of the individual IP address on the router being used as a target. It's a good idea to include an admin subnet address as the source instead of a single host, but the reason I demonstrated this was to show you how to create security on your VTY lines without adding latency to your router.

> **Real World Scenario**
>
> **Should You Secure Your VTY Lines on a Router?**
>
> You're monitoring your network and notice that someone has telnetted into your core router by using the `show users` command. You use the disconnect command and they're disconnected from the router, but you notice that they're right back in there a few minutes later. You consider putting an ACL on the router interfaces, but you don't want to add latency on each interface since your router is already pushing a lot of packets. At this point,

you think about putting an access list on the VTY lines themselves, but not having done this before, you're not sure if this is a safe alternative to putting an ACL on each interface. Would placing an ACL on the VTY lines be a good idea for this network?

Yes—absolutely! And the `access-class` command covered in this chapter is the way to do it. Why? Because it doesn't use an access list that just sits on an interface looking at every packet, resulting in unnecessary overhead and latency.

When you put the `access-class in` command on the VTY lines, only packets trying to telnet into the router will be checked and compared, providing easy-to-configure yet solid security for your router!

> Just a reminder—Cisco recommends using Secure Shell (SSH) instead of Telnet on the VTY lines of a router, as we covered in Chapter 6, "Cisco's Internetworking Operating System (IOS)," so review that chapter if you need a refresher on SSH and how to configure it on your routers and switches.

Extended Access Lists

Let's go back to the standard IP access list example where you had to block all access from the Sales LAN to the finance department and add a new requirement. You must now allow Sales to gain access to a certain server on the Finance LAN but not to other network services for security reasons. What's the solution? Applying a standard IP access list won't allow users to get to one network service but not another because a standard ACL won't allow you to make decisions based on both source and destination addresses. It makes decisions based only on source address, so we need another way to achieve our new goal—but what is it?

Using an *extended access list* will save the day because extended ACLs allow us to specify source and destination addresses as well as the protocol and port number, which identify the upper-layer protocol or application. An extended ACL is just what we need to affectively allow users access to a physical LAN while denying them access to specific hosts—even specific services on those hosts!

We're going to take a look at the commands we have in our arsenal, but first, you need to know that you must use the extended access-list range from 100 to 199. The 2000–2699 range is also available for extended IP access lists.

After choosing a number in the extended range, you need to decide what type of list entry to make. For this example, I'm going with a deny list entry:

```
Corp(config)#access-list 110 ?
deny    Specify packets to reject
dynamic Specify a DYNAMIC list of PERMITs or DENYs
permit  Specify packets to forward
remark  Access list entry comment
```

And once you've settled on the type of ACL, you need to then select a protocol field entry:

```
Corp(config)#access-list 110 deny ?
<0-255>  An IP protocol number
ahp      Authentication Header Protocol
eigrp    Cisco's EIGRP routing protocol
esp      Encapsulation Security Payload
gre      Cisco's GRE tunneling
icmp     Internet Control Message Protocol
igmp     Internet Gateway Message Protocol
ip       Any Internet Protocol
ipinip   IP in IP tunneling
nos      KA9Q NOS compatible IP over IP tunneling
ospf     OSPF routing protocol
pcp      Payload Compression Protocol
pim      Protocol Independent Multicast
tcp      Transmission Control Protocol
udp      User Datagram Protocol
```

> **NOTE** If you want to filter by Application layer protocol, you have to choose the appropriate layer 4 transport protocol after the `permit` or `deny` statement. For example, to filter Telnet or FTP, choose TCP since both Telnet and FTP use TCP at the Transport layer. Selecting IP wouldn't allow you to specify a particular application protocol later and only filter based on source and destination addresses.

So now, let's filter an Application layer protocol that uses TCP by selecting TCP as the protocol and indicating the specific destination TCP port at the end of the line. Next, we'll be prompted for the source IP address of the host or network and we'll choose the any command to allow any source address:

```
Corp(config)#access-list 110 deny tcp ?
A.B.C.D  Source address
any      Any source host
host     A single source host
```

After we've selected the source address, we can then choose the specific destination address:

```
Corp(config)#access-list 110 deny tcp any ?
A.B.C.D  Destination address
any      Any destination host
eq       Match only packets on a given port number
gt       Match only packets with a greater port number
```

```
host  A single destination host
lt    Match only packets with a lower port number
neq   Match only packets not on a given port number
range Match only packets in the range of port numbers
```

In this output, you can see that any source IP address that has a destination IP address of 172.16.30.2 has been denied:

```
Corp(config)#access-list 110 deny tcp any host 172.16.30.2 ?
ack         Match on the ACK bit
dscp        Match packets with given dscp value
eq          Match only packets on a given port number
established Match established connections
fin         Match on the FIN bit
fragments   Check non-initial fragments
gt          Match only packets with a greater port number
log         Log matches against this entry
log-input   Log matches against this entry, including input interface
lt          Match only packets with a lower port number
neq         Match only packets not on a given port number
precedence  Match packets with given precedence value
psh         Match on the PSH bit
range       Match only packets in the range of port numbers
rst         Match on the RST bit
syn         Match on the SYN bit
time-range  Specify a time-range
tos         Match packets with given TOS value
urg         Match on the URG bit
<cr>
```

And once we have the destination host addresses in place, we just need to specify the type of service to deny using the equal to command, entered as eq. The following help screen reveals the options available now. You can choose a port number or use the application name:

```
Corp(config)#access-list 110 deny tcp any host 172.16.30.2 eq ?
<0-65535> Port number
bgp       Border Gateway Protocol (179)
chargen   Character generator (19)
cmd       Remote commands (rcmd, 514)
daytime   Daytime (13)
discard   Discard (9)
domain    Domain Name Service (53)
drip      Dynamic Routing Information Protocol (3949)
```

```
echo Echo (7)
exec Exec (rsh, 512)
finger Finger (79)
ftp File Transfer Protocol (21)
ftp-data FTP data connections (20)
gopher Gopher (70)
hostname NIC hostname server (101)
ident Ident Protocol (113)
irc Internet Relay Chat (194)
klogin Kerberos login (543)
kshell Kerberos shell (544)
login Login (rlogin, 513)
lpd Printer service (515)
nntp Network News Transport Protocol (119)
pim-auto-rp PIM Auto-RP (496)
pop2 Post Office Protocol v2 (109)
pop3 Post Office Protocol v3 (110)
smtp Simple Mail Transport Protocol (25)
sunrpc Sun Remote Procedure Call (111)
syslog Syslog (514)
tacacs TAC Access Control System (49)
talk Talk (517)
telnet Telnet (23)
time Time (37)
uucp Unix-to-Unix Copy Program (540)
whois Nicname (43)
www World Wide Web (HTTP, 80)
```

Now let's block Telnet (port 23) to host 172.16.30.2 only. If the users want to use FTP, fine—that's allowed. The `log` command is used to log messages every time the access list entry is hit. This can be an extremely cool way to monitor inappropriate access attempts, but be careful because in a large network, this command can overload your console's screen with messages!

Here's our result:

```
Corp(config)#access-list 110 deny tcp any host 172.16.30.2 eq 23 log
```

This line says to deny any source host trying to telnet to destination host 172.16.30.2. Keep in mind that the next line is an implicit deny by default. If you apply this access list to an interface, you might as well just shut the interface down because by default, there's an implicit deny all at the end of every access list. So we've got to follow up the access list with the following command:

```
Corp(config)#access-list 110 permit ip any any
```

The IP in this line is important because it will permit the IP stack. If TCP was used instead of IP in this line, then UDP, etc., would all be denied. Remember, the `0.0.0.0 255.255.255.255` is the same command as any, so the command could also look like this:

```
Corp(config)#access-list 110 permit ip 0.0.0.0 255.255.255.255
0.0.0.0 255.255.255.255
```

But if you did this, when you looked at the running-config, the commands would be replaced with the any any. I like efficiency, so I'll just use the any command because it requires less typing.

As always, once our access list is created, we must apply it to an interface with the same command used for the IP standard list:

```
Corp(config-if)#ip access-group 110 in
```

Or this:

```
Corp(config-if)#ip access-group 110 out
```

Next, we'll check out some examples of how to use an extended access list.

Extended Access List Example 1

For our first scenario, we'll use Figure 10.5. What do we need to do to deny access to a host at 172.16.50.5 on the finance department LAN for both Telnet and FTP services? All other services on this and all other hosts are fine for the sales and marketing departments to access.

FIGURE 10.5 Extended ACL example 1

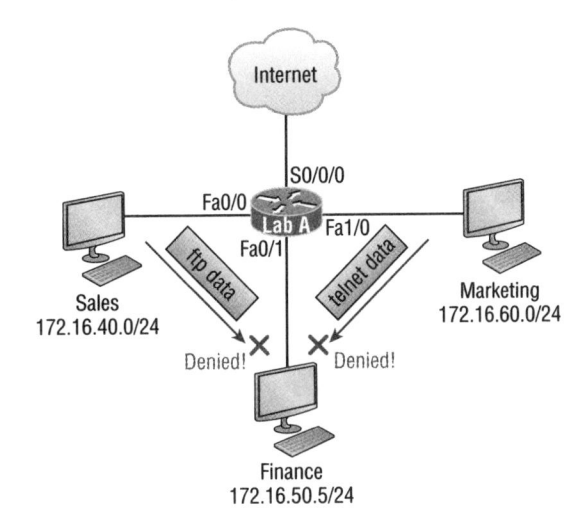

Here's the ACL we must create:

```
Lab_A#config t
Lab_A(config)#access-list 110 deny tcp any host 172.16.50.5 eq 21
Lab_A(config)#access-list 110 deny tcp any host 172.16.50.5 eq 23
Lab_A(config)#access-list 110 permit ip any any
```

The access-list 110 tells the router we're creating an extended IP ACL. The tcp is the protocol field in the Network layer header. If the list doesn't say tcp here, you cannot filter by TCP port numbers 21 and 23 as shown in the example. Remember that these values indicate FTP and Telnet, which both use TCP for connection-oriented services. The any command is the source, which means any source IP address, and the host is the destination IP address. This ACL says that all IP traffic will be permitted from any host except FTP and Telnet to host 172.16.50.5 from any source.

> **Note:** Remember that instead of the host 172.16.50.5 command when we created the extended access list, we could have entered 172.16.50.5 0.0.0.0. There would be no difference in the result other than the router would change the command to host 172.16.50.5 in the running-config.

After the list is created, it must be applied to the FastEthernet 0/1 interface outbound because we want to block all traffic from getting to host 172.16.50.5 and performing FTP and Telnet. If this list was created to block access only from the Sales LAN to host 172.16.50.5, then we'd have put this list closer to the source—on FastEthernet 0/0. In that situation, we'd apply the list to inbound traffic. This highlights the fact that you really need to analyze each situation carefully before creating and applying ACLs!

Now let's go ahead and apply the list to interface Fa0/1 to block all outside FTP and Telnet access to the host 172.16.50.5:

```
Lab_A(config)#int fa0/1
Lab_A(config-if)#ip access-group 110 out
```

Extended Access List Example 2

We're going to use Figure 9.4 again, which has four LANs and a serial connection. We need to prevent Telnet access to the networks attached to the E1 and E2 interfaces.

The configuration on the router would look something like this, although the answer can vary:

```
Router(config)#access-list 110 deny tcp any 172.16.48.0 0.0.15.255 eq 23
Router(config)#access-list 110 deny tcp any 172.16.192.0 0.0.63.255 eq 23
Router(config)#access-list 110 permit ip any any
Router(config)#interface Ethernet 1
```

```
Router(config-if)#ip access-group 110 out
Router(config-if)#interface Ethernet 2
Router(config-if)#ip access-group 110 out
```

Here are the key factors to understand from this list:

- First, you need to verify that the number range is correct for the type of access list you are creating. In this example, it's extended, so the range must be 100–199.
- Second, you must verify that the protocol field matches the upper-layer process or application, which in this case, is TCP port 23 (Telnet).

> The protocol parameter must be TCP since Telnet uses TCP. If it were TFTP instead, then the protocol parameter would have to be UDP because TFTP uses UDP at the Transport layer.

- Third, verify that the destination port number matches the application you're filtering for. In this case, port 23 matches Telnet, which is correct, but know that you can also type **telnet** at the end of the line instead of 23.
- Finally, the test statement `permit ip any any` is important to have there at the end of the list because it means to enable all packets other than Telnet packets destined for the LANs connected to Ethernet 1 and Ethernet 2.

Extended Access List Example 3

I want to guide you through one more extended ACL example before we move on to named ACLs. Figure 10.6 displays the network we're going to use for this last scenario.

FIGURE 10.6 Extended ACL example 3

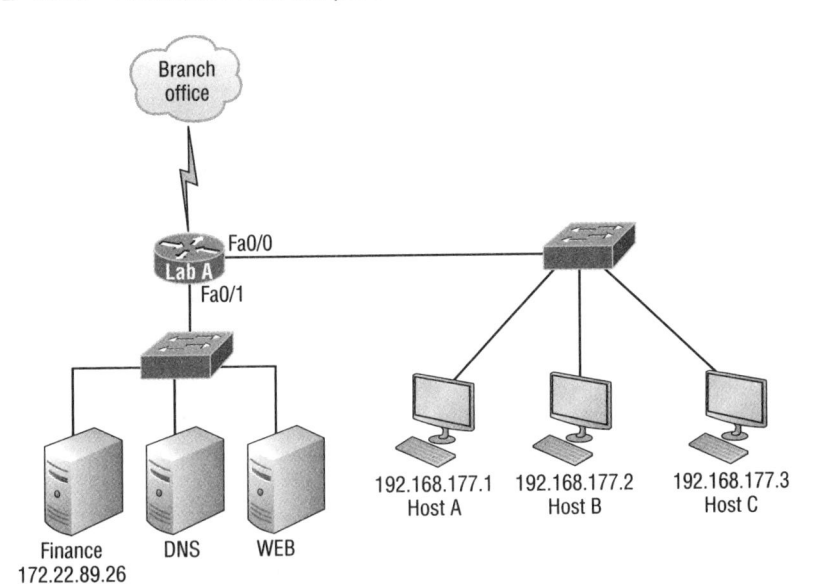

In this example, we're going to allow HTTP access to the Finance server from source Host B only. All other traffic will be permitted. We need to be able to configure this in only three test statements, and then we'll need to add the interface configuration.

So take what you've learned and knock this one out:

Lab_A#**config t**
Lab_A(config)#**access-list 110 permit tcp host 192.168.177.2 host 172.22.89.26 eq 80**
Lab_A(config)#**access-list 110 deny tcp any host 172.22.89.26 eq 80**
Lab_A(config)#**access-list 110 permit ip any any**

This is really pretty simple! First we need to permit Host B HTTP access to the Finance server. But since all other traffic must be allowed, we must detail who cannot HTTP to the Finance server, so the second test statement is there to deny anyone else from using HTTP on the Finance server. Finally, now that Host B can HTTP to the Finance server and everyone else can't, we'll permit all other traffic with our third test statement.

Not so bad—this just takes a little thought! But wait—we're not done yet because we still need to apply this to an interface. Since extended access lists are typically applied closest to the source, we should simply place this inbound on F0/0, right?

Well, this is one time we're not going to follow the rules. Our challenge required us to allow only HTTP traffic to the Finance server from Host B. If we apply the ACL inbound on Fa0/0, then the branch office would be able to access the Finance server and perform HTTP. So in this example, we need to place the ACL closest to the destination:

Lab_A(config)#**interface fastethernet 0/1**
Lab_A(config-if)#**ip access-group 110 out**

Perfect! Now let's get into how to create ACLs using names.

Named ACLs

As I said earlier, *named* access lists are just another way to create standard and extended access lists. In medium to large enterprises, managing ACLs can become a real hassle over time! A handy way to make things easier is to copy the access list to a text editor, edit the list, and then paste the new list back into the router. This works pretty well if it weren't for the "pack rat" mentality. It's really common to think things like, "What if I find a problem with the new list and need to back out of the change?" This and other factors cause people to hoard unapplied ACLs, and over time, they can seriously build up on a router, leading to more questions, like, "What were these ACLs for? Are they important? Do I need them?" All good questions, and named access lists are the answer to this problem!

And of course, this kind of thing can also apply to access lists that are up and running. Let's say you come into an existing network and are looking at access lists on a router. Suppose you find an access list 177, which happens to be an extended access list that's a whopping 93 lines long. This generates the same bunch of questions and on really bad days, existential despair! Instead, wouldn't it be a whole lot easier to identify an access list with a name like "FinanceLAN" rather than one obscurely dubbed "177"?

To our collective relief, named access lists allow us to use names for creating and applying either standard or extended access lists. There's really nothing new or different about these ACLs aside from being readily identifiable in a way that makes sense to humans. Still, there are some subtle changes to the syntax. So let's re-create the standard access list we created earlier for our test network in Figure 10.2 using a named access list:

```
Lab_A#config t
Lab_A(config)#ip access-list ?
extended    Extended Access List
log-update  Control access list log updates
logging     Control access list logging
resequence  Resequence Access List
standard    Standard Access List
```

Notice that I started by typing **ip access-list**, not **access-list**. Doing this allows me to enter a named access list. Next, I'll need to specify it as a standard access list:

```
Lab_A(config)#ip access-list standard ?
<1-99>      Standard IP access-list number
<1300-1999> Standard IP access-list number (expanded range)
WORD        Access-list name
Lab_A(config)#ip access-list standard BlockSales
Lab_A(config-std-nacl)#
```

I've specified a standard access list, then added the name, BlockSales. I definitely could've used a number for a standard access list, but instead, I chose to use a nice, clear, descriptive name. And notice that after entering the name, I hit Enter and the router prompt changed. This confirms that I'm now in named access list configuration mode and that I'm entering the named access list:

```
Lab_A(config-std-nacl)#?
Standard Access List configuration commands:
default  Set a command to its defaults
deny     Specify packets to reject
exit     Exit from access-list configuration mode
no       Negate a command or set its defaults
permit   Specify packets to forward
Lab_A(config-std-nacl)#deny 172.16.40.0 0.0.0.255
Lab_A(config-std-nacl)#permit any
Lab_A(config-std-nacl)#exit
Lab_A(config)#^Z
Lab_A#
```

So I've entered the access list and then exited configuration mode. Next, I'll take a look at the running configuration to verify that the access list is indeed in the router:

```
Lab_A#sh running-config | begin ip access
ip access-list standard BlockSales
deny 172.16.40.0 0.0.0.255
permit any
!
```

And there it is: the BlockSales access list has truly been created and is in the running-config of the router. Next, I'll need to apply the access list to the correct interface:

```
Lab_A#config t
Lab_A(config)#int fa0/1
Lab_A(config-if)#ip access-group BlockSales out
```

Clear skies! At this point, we've re-created the work done earlier using a named access list. But let's take our IP extended example, shown in Figure 10.6, and redo that list using a named ACL instead as well.

Same business requirements: Allow HTTP access to the Finance server from source Host B only. All other traffic is permitted.

```
Lab_A#config t
Lab_A(config)#ip access-list extended 110
Lab_A(config-ext-nacl)#permit tcp host 192.168.177.2 host 172.22.89.26 eq 80
Lab_A(config-ext-nacl)#deny tcp any host 172.22.89.26 eq 80
Lab_A(config-ext-nacl)#permit ip any any
Lab_A(config-ext-nacl)#int fa0/1
Lab_A(config-if)#ip access-group 110 out
```

Okay—true—I named the extended list with a number, but sometimes it's okay to do that! I'm guessing that named ACLs don't seem all that exciting or different to you, do they? Maybe not in this configuration, except that I don't need to start every line with `access-list 110`, which is nice. But where named ACLs really shine is that they allow us to insert, delete, or edit a single line. That isn't just nice, it's wonderful! Numbered ACLs just can't compare with that, and I'll demonstrate this in a minute.

Remarks

The remark keyword is really important because it gives you the ability to include comments (remarks) regarding the entries you've made in both your IP standard and extended ACLs. Remarks are very cool because they efficiently increase your ability to examine and understand your ACLs to superhero level! Without them, you'd be caught in a quagmire of potentially meaningless numbers without anything to help you recall what all those numbers mean.

Even though you have the option of placing your remarks either before or after a permit or deny statement, I totally recommend that you position them consistently so you don't get confused about which remark is relevant to a specific permit or deny statement.

To get this going for both standard and extended ACLs, just use the access-list *access-list number* remark *remark* global configuration command like this:

```
R2#config t
R2(config)#access-list 110 remark Permit Bob from Sales Only To Finance
R2(config)#access-list 110 permit ip host 172.16.40.1 172.16.50.0 0.0.0.255
R2(config)#access-list 110 deny ip 172.16.40.0 0.0.0.255 172.16.50.0 0.0.0.255
R2(config)#ip access-list extended No_Telnet
R2(config-ext-nacl)#remark Deny all of Sales from Telnetting to Marketing
R2(config-ext-nacl)#deny tcp 172.16.40.0 0.0.0.255 172.16.60.0 0.0.0.255 eq 23
R2(config-ext-nacl)#permit ip any any
R2(config-ext-nacl)#do show run
[output cut]
!
ip access-list extended No_Telnet
remark Stop all of Sales from Telnetting to Marketing
deny tcp 172.16.40.0 0.0.0.255 172.16.60.0 0.0.0.255 eq telnet
permit ip any any
!
access-list 110 remark Permit Bob from Sales Only To Finance
access-list 110 permit ip host 172.16.40.1 172.16.50.0 0.0.0.255
access-list 110 deny ip 172.16.40.0 0.0.0.255 172.16.50.0 0.0.0.255
access-list 110 permit ip any any
!
```

Okay—I was able to add a remark to both an extended list and a named access list. By the way, you can't see these remarks in the output of the show access-list command, which we'll cover next, because they only show up in the running-config.

Speaking of ACLs, I still need to show you how to monitor and verify them. This is an important topic—stay with me!

Monitoring Access Lists

It's always good to be able to verify a router's configuration. Table 10.1 lists the commands that we can use to achieve that.

TABLE 10.1 Commands used to verify access-list configuration

Command	Effect
show access-list	Displays all access lists and their parameters configured on the router. Also shows statistics about how many times the line either permitted or denied a packet. This command does not show you which interface the list is applied on.
show access-list 110	Reveals only the parameters for access list 110. Again, this command will not reveal the specific interface the list is set on.
show ip access-list	Shows only the IP access lists configured on the router.
show ip interface	Displays which interfaces have access lists set on them.
show running-config	Shows the access lists and the specific interfaces that have ACLs applied on them.

We've already used the show running-config command to verify that a named access list was in the router, so now let's look at the output from some of the other commands.

The show access-list command will list all ACLs on the router, whether they're applied to an interface or not:

```
Lab_A#show access-list
Standard IP access list 10
10 deny 172.16.40.0, wildcard bits 0.0.0.255
20 permit any
Standard IP access list BlockSales
10 deny 172.16.40.0, wildcard bits 0.0.0.255
20 permit any
Extended IP access list 110
10 deny tcp any host 172.16.30.5 eq ftp
20 deny tcp any host 172.16.30.5 eq telnet
30 permit ip any any
40 permit tcp host 192.168.177.2 host 172.22.89.26 eq www
50 deny tcp any host 172.22.89.26 eq www
Lab_A#
```

First, notice that access list 10 as well as both of our named access lists appear on this list—remember, my extended named ACL was named 110! Second, notice that even though I entered actual numbers for TCP ports in access list 110, the show command gives us the protocol names rather than TCP ports for serious clarity.

Monitoring Access Lists

But wait! The best part is those numbers on the left side: 10, 20, 30, etc. Those are called sequence numbers, and they allow us to edit our named ACL. Here's an example where I added a line into the named extended ACL 110:

```
Lab_A (config)#ip access-list extended 110
Lab_A (config-ext-nacl)#21 deny udp any host 172.16.30.5 eq 69
Lab_A#show access-list
[output cut]
Extended IP access list 110
10 deny tcp any host 172.16.30.5 eq ftp
20 deny tcp any host 172.16.30.5 eq telnet
21 deny udp any host 172.16.30.5 eq tftp
30 permit ip any any
40 permit tcp host 192.168.177.2 host 172.22.89.26 eq www
50 deny tcp any host 172.22.89.26 eq www
```

You can see that I added line 21. I could have deleted a line or edited an existing line as well—very nice!

Here's the output of the show ip interface command:

```
Lab_A#show ip interface fa0/1
FastEthernet0/1 is up, line protocol is up
Internet address is 172.16.30.1/24
Broadcast address is 255.255.255.255
Address determined by non-volatile memory
MTU is 1500 bytes
Helper address is not set
Directed broadcast forwarding is disabled
Outgoing access list is 110
Inbound access list is not set
Proxy ARP is enabled
Security level is default
Split horizon is enabled
[output cut]
```

Be sure to notice the bold line indicating that the outgoing list on this interface is 110, yet the inbound access list isn't set. What happened to BlockSales? I had configured that outbound on Fa0/1! That's true, I did, but I configured my extended named ACL 110 and applied it to Fa0/1 as well. You can't have two lists on the same interface, in the same direction, so what happened here is that my last configuration overwrote the BlockSales configuration.

And as I've already mentioned, you can use the show running-config command to see any and all access lists.

Summary

You've now learned how to configure standard access lists to properly filter IP traffic. You discovered what a standard access list is and how to apply it to a Cisco router to add security to your network. You also learned how to configure extended access lists to further filter IP traffic. We also covered the key differences between standard and extended access lists as well as how to apply them to Cisco routers.

Further on, you found out how to configure named access lists and apply them to interfaces on the router and learned that named access lists offer the huge advantage of being easily identifiable. Because of that, they're a whole lot easier to manage than mysterious access lists that are simply referred to by obscure numbers.

The chapter wrapped up by showing you how to monitor and verify selected access-list configurations on a router.

Exam Essentials

Remember the standard and extended IP access-list number ranges.   The number ranges you can use to configure a standard IP access list are 1–99 and 1300–1999. The number ranges for an extended IP access list are 100–199 and 2000–2699.

Understand the term *implicit deny*.   At the end of every access list is an implicit deny. This means is that if a packet does not match any of the lines in the access list, it will be discarded. Also, if you have nothing but deny statements in your list, the list will not permit any packets.

Understand the standard IP access-list configuration command.   To configure a standard IP access list, use the access-list numbers 1–99 or 1300–1999 in global configuration mode. Choose permit or deny, then choose the source IP address you want to filter on using one of the three techniques covered in this chapter.

Understand the extended IP access-list configuration command.   To configure an extended IP access list, use the access-list numbers 100–199 or 2000–2699 in global configuration mode. Choose permit or deny, the Network layer protocol field, the source IP address you want to filter on, the destination address you want to filter on, and finally, the Transport layer port number if TCP or UDP has been specified as the protocol.

Remember the command to verify an access list on a router interface.   To see whether an access list is set on an interface and in which direction it is filtering, use the show ip interface command. This command will not show you the contents of the access list, merely which access lists are applied on the interface.

Remember the command to verify the access-list configuration.   To see the configured access lists on your router, use the show access-list command. This command will not show you which interfaces have an access list set or not.

Review Questions

You can find the answers to these questions in the Appendix.

1. Which of the following statements is false when a packet is being compared to an access list?
   A. It's always compared with each line of the access list in sequential order.
   B. Once the packet matches the condition on a line of the access list, the packet is acted upon and no further comparisons take place.
   C. There is an implicit deny at the end of each access list.
   D. Until all lines have been analyzed, the comparison is not over.

2. You need to create an access list that will prevent hosts in the network range of 192.168.160.0 to 192.168.191.0. Which of the following lists will you use?
   A. access-list 10 deny 192.168.160.0 255.255.224.0
   B. access-list 10 deny 192.168.160.0 0.0.191.255
   C. access-list 10 deny 192.168.160.0 0.0.31.255
   D. access-list 10 deny 192.168.0.0 0.0.31.255

3. You have created a named access list called BlockSales. Which of the following is a valid command for applying this to packets trying to enter interface Fa0/0 of your router?
   A. (config)#ip access-group 110 in
   B. (config-if)#ip access-group 110 in
   C. (config-if)#ip access-group Blocksales in
   D. (config-if)#BlockSales ip access-list in

4. Which access list statement will permit all HTTP sessions to network 192.168.144.0/24 containing web servers?
   A. access-list 110 permit tcp 192.168.144.0 0.0.0.255 any eq 80
   B. access-list 110 permit tcp any 192.168.144.0 0.0.0.255 eq 80
   C. access-list 110 permit tcp 192.168.144.0 0.0.0.255 192.168.144.0 0.0.0.255 any eq 80
   D. access-list 110 permit udp any 192.168.144.0 eq 80

5. Which of the following access lists will allow only HTTP traffic into network 196.15.7.0?
   A. access-list 100 permit tcp any 196.15.7.0 0.0.0.255 eq www
   B. access-list 10 deny tcp any 196.15.7.0 eq www
   C. access-list 100 permit 196.15.7.0 0.0.0.255 eq www
   D. access-list 110 permit ip any 196.15.7.0 0.0.0.255
   E. access-list 110 permit www 196.15.7.0 0.0.0.255

6. What router command allows you to determine whether an IP access list is enabled on a particular interface?
   A. show ip port
   B. show access-lists
   C. show ip interface
   D. show access-lists interface

7. If you wanted to deny all Telnet connections to only network 192.168.10.0, which command could you use?
   A. access-list 100 deny tcp 192.168.10.0 255.255.255.0 eq telnet
   B. access-list 100 deny tcp 192.168.10.0 0.255.255.255 eq telnet
   C. access-list 100 deny tcp any 192.168.10.0 0.0.0.255 eq 23
   D. access-list 100 deny 192.168.10.0 0.0.0.255 any eq 23

8. If you wanted to deny FTP access from network 200.200.10.0 to network 200.199.11.0 but allow everything else, which of the following command strings is valid?
   A. access-list 110 deny 200.200.10.0 to network 200.199.11.0 eq ftp
   B. access-list 111 permit ip any 0.0.0.0 255.255.255.255
   C. access-list 1 deny ftp 200.200.10.0 200.199.11.0 any any
   D. access-list 100 deny tcp 200.200.10.0 0.0.0.255 200.199.11.0 0.0.0.255 eq ftp
   E. access-list 198 deny tcp 200.200.10.0 0.0.0.255 200.199.11.0 0.0.0.255 eq ftp
      access-list 198 permit ip any 0.0.0.0 255.255.255.255

9. You want to create an extended access list that denies the subnet of the following host: 172.16.50.172/20. Which of the following would you start your list with?
   A. access-list 110 deny ip 172.16.48.0 255.255.240.0 any
   B. access-list 110 udp deny 172.16.0.0 0.0.255.255 ip any
   C. access-list 110 deny tcp 172.16.64.0 0.0.31.255 any eq 80
   D. access-list 110 deny ip 172.16.48.0 0.0.15.255 any

10. Which of the following is the wildcard (inverse) version of a /27 mask?
    A. 0.0.0.7
    B. 0.0.0.31
    C. 0.0.0.27
    D. 0.0.31.255

Chapter 11

Network Address Translation (NAT)

THE FOLLOWING CCNA EXAM TOPICS ARE COVERED IN THIS CHAPTER:

4.0   IP Services

✓ 4.1   Configure and verify inside source NAT using static and pools

In this chapter, we're going to dig into Network Address Translation (NAT), Dynamic NAT, and Port Address Translation (PAT), also known as NAT Overload. Of course, I'll demonstrate all the NAT commands. I also provided some fantastic hands-on labs for you to configure at the end of this chapter, so be sure not to miss those!

It's important to understand the Cisco objective for this chapter, and it's very straightforward: you have hosts on your inside Corporate network using RFC 1918 addresses, and you need to allow those hosts access to the Internet by configuring NAT translations.

Because we'll be using ACLs in our NAT configurations, it's clearly important to be really comfortable with the skills you just learned in the last chapter!

> **NOTE** To find your included bonus material, as well as Todd Lammle videos and practice questions, please see www.lammle.com/ccna

When Do We Use NAT?

Network Address Translation (NAT) is similar to Classless Inter-Domain Routing (CIDR) in that the original intention for NAT was to slow the depletion of available IP address space by allowing multiple, private IP addresses to be represented by a much smaller number of public IP addresses.

Since then, we've discovered that NAT is also really useful for network migrations and mergers, server load sharing, and creating virtual servers. Before we dive deep into this chapter, I'm going to describe the basics of NAT functionality and common NAT terminology.

Because NAT decreases the overwhelming amount of public IP addresses required in a networking environment, it comes in really handy when two companies that have duplicate internal addressing schemes merge. NAT is also a great tool to use when an organization changes its Internet service provider (ISP) but the sys admin wants to avoid changing the internal address scheme.

Here's a list of situations when NAT is super helpful:

- When you need to connect to the Internet and your hosts don't have globally unique IP addresses
- When you've changed to a new ISP that requires you to renumber your network
- When you need to merge two intranets with duplicate addresses

You typically use NAT on a border router. In Figure 11.1, NAT is placed on the Corporate router connected to the Internet.

FIGURE 11.1 Where to configure NAT

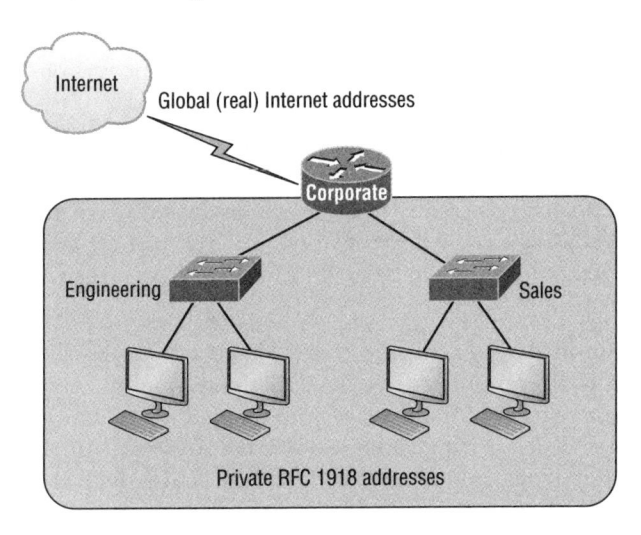

So maybe you're thinking, "NAT's totally cool and I just gotta have it!" But don't get too excited yet because there's some downside to using NAT that you should consider first. Don't get me wrong—it can be a lifesaver sometimes, but NAT has a bit of a dark side you need to know about too. For the pros and cons linked to using NAT, check out Table 11.1.

TABLE 11.1 Advantages and disadvantages of implementing NAT

Advantages	Disadvantages
Conserves legally registered addresses.	Translation results in switching path delays.
Remedies address overlap events.	Causes loss of end-to-end IP traceability.
Increases flexibility when connecting to the Internet.	Certain applications will not function with NAT enabled.
Eliminates address renumbering as a network evolves.	Complicates tunneling protocols such as IPsec because NAT modifies the values in the header.

> **NOTE** The most obvious advantage associated with NAT is that it allows you to conserve your legally registered address scheme. But a version of it known as PAT is also why we've only just recently run out of IPv4 addresses. Without NAT/PAT, we'd have run out of IPv4 addresses more than a decade ago!

Types of Network Address Translation

Let's cover go the three types of NATs now:

Static NAT (one-to-one)   This type of NAT is designed to allow one-to-one mapping between local and global addresses. Keep in mind that the static version requires you to have one real Internet IP address for every host on your network.

Dynamic NAT (many-to-many)   This version gives you the ability to map an unregistered IP address to a registered IP address from a pool of registered IP addresses. You don't have to statically configure your router to map each inside address to an individual outside address as you would using static NAT, but you do have to have enough real, bona fide IP addresses for everyone who's going to be sending packets to and receiving them from the Internet at the same time.

Overloading (one-to-many)   This is the most popular type of NAT configuration. Overloading is really a form of dynamic NAT that maps multiple unregistered IP addresses to a single registered IP address (many-to-one) by using different source ports. Why is this so special? It's also known as *Port Address Translation (PAT)*, which is also commonly referred to as NAT Overload. Using PAT allows you to permit thousands of users to connect to the Internet using only one real global IP address! Seriously, NAT Overload is the real reason we haven't run out of valid IP addresses on the Internet.

NAT Names

The names used to describe the addresses used with NAT are easy to remember. Addresses used after NAT translations are called *global addresses*. These are usually the public addresses used on the Internet, which you don't need if you aren't going on the Internet.

Local addresses are the ones used before NAT translation. This means that the inside local address is actually the private address of the sending host that's attempting to get to the Internet. The outside local address would typically be the router interface connected to your ISP and is also usually a public address used as the packet begins its journey.

After translation, the inside local address is then called the *inside global address*, and the outside global address then becomes the address of the destination host.

Table 11.2 lists all this terminology and offers a clear picture of the various names used with NAT. Keep in mind that these terms and their definitions vary a bit based on implementation. The table shows how they're used according to the Cisco exam objectives.

TABLE 11.2 NAT terms

Names	Meaning
Inside local	Source host inside address before translation—typically an RFC 1918 address.
Outside local	Address of an outside host as it appears to the inside network. This is usually the address of the router interface connected to ISP—the actual Internet address.
Inside global	Source host address used after translation to get onto the Internet. This is also the actual Internet address.
Outside global	Address of outside destination host and, again, the real Internet address.

How NAT Works

So let's see how this whole NAT thing works. I'm going to start by using Figure 11.2 to describe basic NAT translation.

FIGURE 11.2 Basic NAT translation

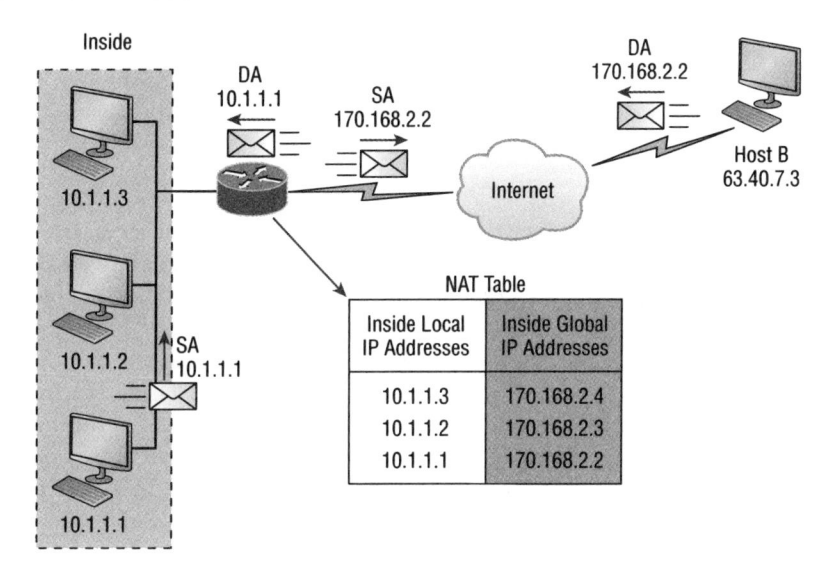

In this figure, we can see host 10.1.1.1 sending an Internet-bound packet to the border router configured with NAT. The router identifies the source IP address as an inside local IP address destined for an outside network, translates the source IP address in the packet, and documents the translation in the NAT table.

The packet is sent to the outside interface with the new, translated source address. The external host returns the packet to the destination host and the NAT router translates the inside global IP address back to the inside local IP address using the NAT table. This is as simple as it gets!

Next, I'm going to show you a more complex configuration using overloading, also referred to as PAT. I'll use Figure 11.3 to demonstrate how PAT works by having an inside host HTTP to a server on the Internet.

FIGURE 11.3 NAT overloading example (PAT)

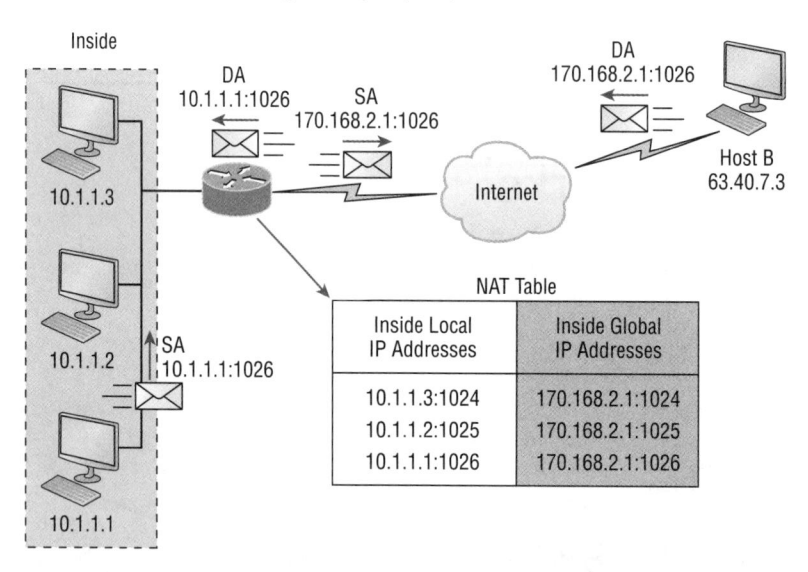

Inside Local IP Addresses	Inside Global IP Addresses
10.1.1.3:1024	170.168.2.1:1024
10.1.1.2:1025	170.168.2.1:1025
10.1.1.1:1026	170.168.2.1:1026

With PAT, all inside hosts get translated to one single IP address, hence the term *overloading*. Again, the reason we've only recently run out of available global IP addresses on the Internet is because of overloading (PAT).

Take a look at the NAT table in Figure 11.3 again. In addition to the inside local IP address and inside global IP address, we now have port numbers. These port numbers help the router identify which host should receive the return traffic. The router uses the source port number from each host to differentiate the traffic from each of the hosts. In this example, the packet has a destination port number of 80 when it leaves the router, and the HTTP server sends back the data with a destination port number of 1026. This allows the NAT translation router to differentiate between hosts in the NAT table and then translate the destination IP address back to the inside local address.

Port numbers are used at the Transport layer to identify the local host. If we had to use real global IP addresses to identify the source hosts, that's called *static NAT* and we would run out of addresses. PAT allows us to use the Transport layer to identify the hosts, which in turn allows us to theoretically use up to about 65,000 hosts with only one real IP address!

Static NAT Configuration

Let's take a look at a simple example of a basic static NAT configuration:

```
ip nat inside source static 10.1.1.1 170.46.2.2
!
interface Ethernet0
ip address 10.1.1.10 255.255.255.0
ip nat inside
!
interface Serial0
ip address 170.46.2.1 255.255.255.0
ip nat outside
!
```

In this output, we can see that the ip nat inside source command identifies which IP addresses will be translated. The ip nat inside source command configures a static translation between the inside local IP address 10.1.1.1 and the outside global IP address 170.46.2.2.

Scrolling farther down in the configuration, we find an ip nat command under each interface. The ip nat inside command identifies that interface as the inside interface, and the ip nat outside command identifies that interface as the outside interface. When you look back at the ip nat inside source command, you can see that the command is referencing the inside interface as the source or starting point of the translation. You could also use the command like this: ip nat outside source. This option indicates the interface that you designated as the outside interface should become the source or starting point for the translation.

Dynamic NAT Configuration

Basically, dynamic NAT really means we have a pool of addresses that we'll use to provide real IP addresses to a group of users on the inside. Because we don't use port numbers, we must have real IP addresses for every user who's trying to get outside the local network simultaneously.

Here's the sample output of a dynamic NAT configuration:

```
ip nat pool todd 170.168.2.3 170.168.2.254
netmask 255.255.255.0
ip nat inside source list 1 pool todd
!
```

```
interface Ethernet0
ip address 10.1.1.10 255.255.255.0
ip nat inside
!
interface Serial0
ip address 170.168.2.1 255.255.255.0
ip nat outside
!
access-list 1 permit 10.1.1.0 0.0.0.255
!
```

The `ip nat inside source list 1 pool todd` command tells the router to translate IP addresses that match `access-list 1` to an address found in the IP NAT pool named todd. Here the ACL isn't there to filter traffic for security reasons by permitting or denying traffic. In this case, it's there to select or designate what we often call interesting traffic. When interesting traffic has been matched with the access list, it's pulled into the NAT process to be translated. This is actually a common use for access lists, which aren't always there just blocking traffic at an interface!

The command `ip nat pool todd 170.168.2.3 170.168.2.254 netmask 255.255.255.0` creates a pool of addresses that will be distributed to the specific hosts requiring global addresses. When troubleshooting NAT for the Cisco objectives, always check this pool to confirm that there are enough addresses in it to provide translation for all the inside hosts. Lastly, check to make sure the pool names match exactly on both lines, remembering that they're case sensitive. If they don't match, the pool won't work!

> **NOTE** One of the most common issues on the exam is misconfiguration of inside and outside on the interfaces.

PAT (Overloading) Configuration

This last example shows how to configure inside global address overloading. This is the form of NAT that we typically use today. It's actually pretty rare to use static or dynamic NAT now unless it's for something like statically mapping a server.

Here's a sample output of a PAT configuration:

```
ip nat pool globalnet 170.168.2.1 170.168.2.1 netmask 255.255.255.0
ip nat inside source list 1 pool globalnet overload
!
interface Ethernet0/0
ip address 10.1.1.10 255.255.255.0
ip nat inside
!
```

```
interface Serial0/0
ip address 170.168.2.1 255.255.255.0
ip nat outside
!
access-list 1 permit 10.1.1.0 0.0.0.255
```

One nice thing about PAT is that there are only a few differences between this configuration and the previous dynamic NAT configuration:

- Our pool of addresses has shrunk to only one IP address.
- We included the overload keyword at the end of our ip nat inside source command.

A key factor here is that the one IP address that's in the pool for us to use is the IP address of the outside interface. This is perfect if you are configuring NAT Overload for yourself at home or for a small office that has only one IP address from your ISP. You could, however, use an additional address such as 170.168.2.2. if you had that address available to you as well. Doing that would work great for a large implementation where you've got a bunch of simultaneously active internal users. Not hard to imagine that situation needing more than one overloaded IP address on the outside!

Simple Verification of NAT

As always, once you've chosen and configured the type of NAT you're going to run, typically PAT, you'll need to verify your configuration.

To see basic IP address translation information, use the following command:

Router#**show ip nat translations**

When looking at the IP NAT translations, you'll probably see lots of translations from the same host to the corresponding host at the destination. This is normal when there are many connections to the same server.

You can also verify your NAT configuration via the debug ip nat command. The output will show the sending address, the translation, and the destination address on each debug line:

Router#**debug ip nat**

But wait—how do you clear your NAT entries from the translation table? Just use the clear ip nat translation command, and if you want to clear all entries from the NAT table, just use an asterisk (*) at the end of the command.

Testing and Troubleshooting NAT

Cisco's NAT gives you some serious power—and it does so without a whole lot of effort, because the configurations are really pretty simple. Still, we all know nothing's perfect, so when something goes wrong, you can figure out some of the more common culprits by running through this list of potential causes:

- Check the dynamic pools. Are they composed of the right scope of addresses?
- Check to see if any dynamic pools overlap.
- Check to see if the addresses used for static mapping and those in the dynamic pools overlap.
- Ensure that your access lists specify the correct addresses for translation.
- Make sure there aren't any addresses left out that need to be there, and ensure that none are included that shouldn't be.
- Check to make sure you've got both the inside and outside interfaces delimited properly.

One of the most common problems with a new NAT configuration often isn't specific to NAT at all—it usually involves a routing blooper. So, because you're changing a source or destination address in a packet, make sure your router still knows what to do with the new address after the translation!

The first command you should use is the show ip nat translations command:

```
Router#show ip nat trans
Pro Inside global Inside local Outside local Outside global
--- 192.2.2.1 10.1.1.1 --- ---
--- 192.2.2.2 10.1.1.2 --- ---
```

After checking out this output, can you tell me if the configuration on the router is static or dynamic NAT? The answer is yes, either static or dynamic NAT is configured because there's a one-to-one translation from the inside local to the inside global. Basically, by looking at the output, you can't tell if it's static or dynamic per se, but you absolutely can tell that you're not using PAT because there are no port numbers.

Let's take a look at another output:

```
Router#sh ip nat trans
Pro Inside global Inside local Outside local Outside global
tcp 170.168.2.1:11003 10.1.1.1:11003 172.40.2.2:23 172.40.2.2:23
tcp 170.168.2.1:1067 10.1.1.1:1067 172.40.2.3:23 172.40.2.3:23
```

Here you can easily see that the previous output is using NAT Overload (PAT). The protocol in this output is TCP, and the inside global address is the same for both entries.

Supposedly the sky's the limit regarding the number of mappings the NAT table can hold. But this is reality, so things like memory and CPU, or even the boundaries set in place by the scope of available addresses or ports, can cause limitations on the actual number of entries. Consider that each NAT mapping devours about 160 bytes of memory. And even though it doesn't happen a lot, sometimes the amount of entries must be limited for the sake of performance or because of policy restrictions. In situations like these, just go to the ip nat translation max-entries command for help.

Another handy command for troubleshooting is show ip nat statistics. Deploying this gives you a summary of the NAT configuration, and it will count the number of active translation types too. Also counted are hits to an existing mapping as well any misses, with the latter causing an attempt to create a mapping. This command will also reveal expired translations. If you want to check into dynamic pools, their types, the total available addresses, how many addresses have been allocated and how many have failed, plus the number of translations that have occurred, just use the pool keyword after statistics.

Here's the result using the basic NAT debugging command:

```
Router#debug ip nat
NAT: s=10.1.1.1->192.168.2.1, d=172.16.2.2 [0]
NAT: s=172.16.2.2, d=192.168.2.1->10.1.1.1 [0]
NAT: s=10.1.1.1->192.168.2.1, d=172.16.2.2 [1]
NAT: s=10.1.1.1->192.168.2.1, d=172.16.2.2 [2]
NAT: s=10.1.1.1->192.168.2.1, d=172.16.2.2 [3]
NAT*: s=172.16.2.2, d=192.168.2.1->10.1.1.1 [1]
```

Notice the last line in the output and how the NAT at the beginning of the line has an asterisk (*). This means the packet was translated and fast-switched to the destination. You remember the term fast-switched, right? Just in case it's a vague memory, here's a brief refresh: Fast-switching has gone by several aliases such as cache-based switching and this nicely descriptive name, "route once switch many." The fast-switching process is used on Cisco routers to create a cache of layer 3 routing information to be accessed at layer 2 so packets can be forwarded quickly through a router without the routing table having to be parsed for every packet. As packets are packet switched (looked up in the routing table), this information is stored in the cache for later use if needed for faster routing processing.

Okay—let's get back to verifying NAT. Did you know you can manually clear dynamic NAT entries from the NAT table? You can, and doing this comes in seriously handy if you need to get rid of a specific rotten entry without sitting around waiting for the timeout to expire! A manual clear is also really useful when you want to clear the whole NAT table to reconfigure a pool of addresses.

You also need to know that the Cisco IOS software just won't allow you to change or delete an address pool if any of that pool's addresses are mapped in the NAT table. The clear ip nat translations command clears entries. You can indicate a single entry via the global and local address and through TCP and UDP translations, including ports, or you can just type in an asterisk (*) to wipe out the entire table. But know that if you do that, only dynamic entries will be cleared because this command won't remove static entries.

Oh, and there's more—any outside device's packet destination address that happens to be responding to any inside device is known as the inside global (IG) address. This means that the initial mapping has to be held in the NAT table so that all packets arriving from a specific connection get translated consistently. Holding entries in the NAT table also cuts down on repeated translation operations happening each time the same inside machine sends packets to the same outside destinations on a regular basis.

Let me clarify: When an entry is placed into the NAT table the first time, a timer begins ticking and its duration is known as the translation timeout. Each time a packet for a given entry translates through the router, the timer gets reset. If the timer expires, the entry will be removed from the NAT table and the dynamically assigned address will then be returned to the pool. Cisco's default translation timeout is 86,400 seconds (24 hours), but you can change that with the `ip nat translation timeout` command.

Before we move on to the configuration section and actually use the commands I just talked about, let's go through a couple of NAT examples and see if you can figure out the best configuration to go with. To start, look at Figure 11.4 and ask yourself two things: Where would you implement NAT in this design? What type of NAT would you configure?

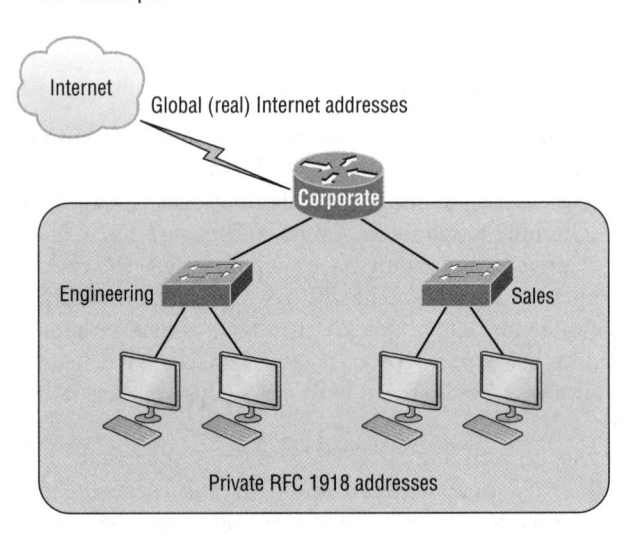

FIGURE 11.4 NAT example

In Figure 11.4, the NAT configuration would be placed on the corporate router, just as I demonstrated with Figure 11.1, and the configuration would be dynamic NAT with overload (PAT).

In this example, what type of NAT is being used?

```
ip nat pool todd-nat 170.168.10.10 170.168.10.20 netmask 255.255.255.0
ip nat inside source list 1 pool todd-nat
```

The preceding command uses dynamic NAT without PAT. The pool in the command gives the answer away as dynamic. Plus there's more than one address in the pool and there's no `overload` command at the end of our `ip nat inside source` command. This means we are not using PAT!

In the next NAT example, refer to Figure 11.5 and see if you can come up with the configuration needed.

FIGURE 11.5 Another NAT example

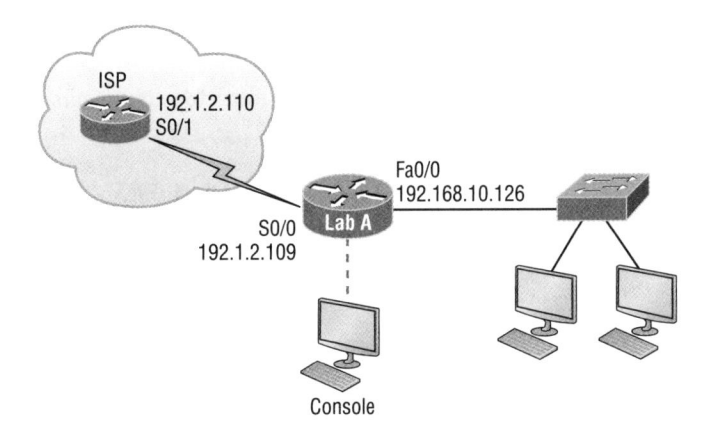

Figure 11.5 shows a border router that needs to be configured with NAT to allow the use of six public IP addresses to the inside locals, 192.1.2.109 through 192.1.2.114. But on the inside network, you have 62 hosts that use the private addresses of 192.168.10.65 through 192.168.10.126. What would your NAT configuration be on the border router?

Actually, two different answers would both work here, but the following would be my first choice based on the exam objectives:

```
ip nat pool Todd 192.1.2.109 192.1.2.109 netmask 255.255.255.248
access-list 1 permit 192.168.10.64 0.0.0.63
ip nat inside source list 1 pool Todd overload
```

The command `ip nat pool Todd 192.1.2.109 192.1.2.109 netmask 255.255.255.248` sets the pool name as Todd and creates a dynamic pool of only one address using NAT address 192.1.2.109. Instead of the netmask command, you can use the `prefix-length 29` statement. In case you're wondering, you can't do this on router interfaces too!

The second answer would get you the exact same result of having only 192.1.2.109 as your inside global, but you can type this in and it will also work: `ip nat pool Todd 192.1.2.109 192.1.2.114 netmask 255.255.255.248`. This option is really a waste because the second through sixth addresses would only be used if there were a conflict with a TCP port number. You would use something like what I've shown in this example if you actually had about ten thousand hosts with one Internet connection for some reason! You would need it to help with the TCP-Reset issue when two hosts are trying to use the same source port number and get a negative acknowledgment (NAK). But in our example, we've only got up to 62 hosts connecting to the Internet at the same time, so having more than one inside global gets us nothing.

This isn't difficult to grasp because it's easy to see in this access-list line that it's just the *network number* and *wildcard* used with that command. I always say, "Every question is a subnet question," and this one is no exception. The inside locals in this example were 192.168.10.65–126, which is a block of 64, or a 255.255.255.192 mask. See that? I wasn't kidding—you really need to be able to subnet quickly!

The command `ip nat inside source list 1 pool Todd overload` sets the dynamic pool to use PAT by using the `overload` command.

And be sure to add the `ip nat inside` and `ip nat outside` statements on the appropriate interfaces.

One more example:

The network in Figure 11.6 is already configured with IP addresses as shown in the figure and there is only one configured host. Now, you need to add 25 more hosts to the LAN and all 26 hosts must be able to get to the Internet at the same time.

FIGURE 11.6 Last NAT example

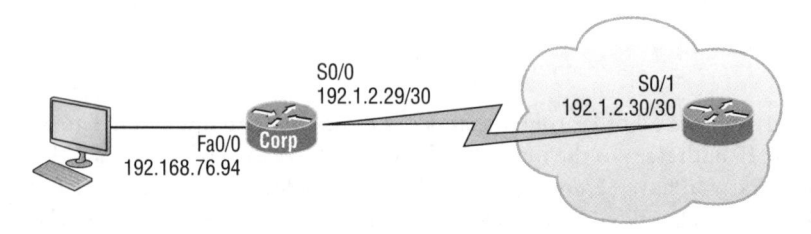

By looking at the configured network, use only the following inside addresses to configure NAT on the Corp router to allow all hosts to reach the Internet:

- Inside globals: 198.18.41.129 through 198.18.41.134
- Inside locals: 192.168.76.65 through 192.168.76.94

This one's a bit more challenging because all we have to help us figure out the configuration is the inside globals and the inside locals. We can still configure this correctly with these crumbs of information, plus the IP addresses of the router interfaces shown in the figure.

To do that, we first determine what our block sizes are so we can get our subnet mask for our NAT pool. This will also equip us to configure the wildcard for the access list.

You should easily be able to see that the block size of the inside globals is 8 and the block size of the inside locals is 32. Know that it's critical not to stumble on this foundational information!

Let's configure NAT now that we have our block sizes:

```
ip nat pool Corp 198.18.41.129 198.18.41.134 netmask 255.255.255.248
ip nat inside source list 1 pool Corp overload
access-list 1 permit 192.168.76.64 0.0.0.31
```

Since we had a block of only 8 for our pool, I had to use the `overload` command to make sure all 26 hosts can get to the Internet at the same time.

There's one other simple way to configure NAT, and I use this command at my home office to connect to my ISP. One command line and it's done! Here it is:

```
ip nat inside source list 1 int s0/0/0 overload
```

I can't say enough how much I love efficiency and being able to achieve something cool using one measly line always makes me happy! My lone, powerfully elegant line basically says, "Use my outside local as my inside global and overload it." Nice! Of course, I still had to create ACL 1 and add the inside and outside interface commands to the configuration, but this is a really nice, fast way to configure NAT if you don't have a pool of addresses to use.

Summary

In this chapter, you learned a lot about Network Address Translation (NAT) and how it's configured as static and dynamic as well as with Port Address Translation (PAT), also called NAT Overload.

I also described how each variety of NAT is used in a network, plus how each type is configured.

We finished up by going through some verification and troubleshooting commands. So don't forget to practice all the wonderfully helpful labs until you've got them down tight!

Exam Essentials

Understand the term *NAT*. This may come as news to you, because I didn't—okay, failed to—mention it earlier, but NAT has a few nicknames. In the industry, it's referred to as network masquerading, IP-masquerading, and (for those who are besieged with OCD and compelled to spell everything out) Network Address Translation. Whatever you want to dub it, basically, they all refer to the process of rewriting the source/destination addresses of IP packets when they go through a router or firewall. Just focus on the process that's occurring and your understanding of it—the important part, and you're golden.

Remember the three methods of NAT. The three methods are static, dynamic, and overloading; the latter is also called PAT.

Understand static NAT. This type of NAT is designed to allow one-to-one mapping between local and global addresses.

Understand dynamic NAT. This version gives you the ability to map a range of unregistered IP addresses to a registered IP address from out of a pool of registered IP addresses.

Understand overloading. Overloading is really a form of dynamic NAT that maps multiple unregistered IP addresses to a single registered IP address (many-to-one) by using different ports. It's also known as *PAT*.

Review Questions

You can find the answers to these questions in the Appendix.

1. Which of the following are disadvantages of using NAT? (Choose three.)
   A. Translation introduces switching path delays.
   B. NAT conserves legally registered addresses.
   C. NAT causes loss of end-to-end IP traceability.
   D. NAT increases flexibility when connecting to the Internet.
   E. Certain applications will not function with NAT enabled.
   F. NAT reduces address overlap occurrence.

2. Which of the following are advantages of using NAT? (Choose three.)
   A. Translation introduces switching path delays.
   B. NAT conserves legally registered addresses.
   C. NAT causes loss of end-to-end IP traceability.
   D. NAT increases flexibility when connecting to the Internet.
   E. Certain applications will not function with NAT enabled.
   F. NAT remedies address overlap occurrence.

3. Which command will allow you to see real-time translations on your router?
   A. show ip nat translations
   B. show ip nat statistics
   C. debug ip nat
   D. clear ip nat translations *

4. Which command will show you all the translations active on your router?
   A. show ip nat translations
   B. show ip nat statistics
   C. debug ip nat
   D. clear ip nat translations *

5. Which command will clear all the translations active on your router?
   A. show ip nat translations
   B. show ip nat statistics
   C. debug ip nat
   D. clear ip nat translations *

6. Which command will show you the summary of the NAT configuration?

 A. `show ip nat translations`

 B. `show ip nat statistics`

 C. `debug ip nat`

 D. `clear ip nat translations *`

 E. `clear ip nat sh config summ *`

7. Which command will create a dynamic pool named Todd that will provide you with 30 global addresses?

 A. `ip nat pool Todd 171.16.10.65 171.16.10.94 net 255.255.255.240`

 B. `ip nat pool Todd 171.16.10.65 171.16.10.94 net 255.255.255.224`

 C. `ip nat pool todd 171.16.10.65 171.16.10.94 net 255.255.255.224`

 D. `ip nat pool Todd 171.16.10.1 171.16.10.254 net 255.255.255.0`

8. Which of the following are methods of NAT? (Choose three.)

 A. Static

 B. IP NAT pool

 C. Dynamic

 D. NAT double-translation

 E. Overload

9. When creating a pool of global addresses, which of the following can be used instead of the netmask command?

 A. / (slash notation)

 B. `prefix-length`

 C. `no mask`

 D. `block-size`

10. Which of the following would be a good starting point for troubleshooting if your router is not translating?

 A. Reboot.

 B. Call Cisco.

 C. Check your interfaces for the correct configuration.

 D. Run the `debug all` command.

Chapter 12

IP Services

THE FOLLOWING CCNA EXAM TOPICS ARE COVERED IN THIS CHAPTER:

2.0 Network Access

✓ 2.3 Configure and verify Layer 2 discovery protocols (Cisco Discovery Protocol and LLDP)

4.0 IP Services

✓ 4.2 Configure and verify NTP operating in a client and server mode

✓ 4.4 Explain the function of SNMP in network operations

✓ 4.5 Describe the use of syslog features including facilities and levels

✓ 4.8 Configure network devices for remote access using SSH

We're going to start off the chapter talking about how to find neighbor device information using the proprietary Cisco Discovery Protocol (CDP) and the industry standard Link Layer Discovery protocol (LLDP). Next, I'll show you how to make sure our times are synchronized with our devices using Network Time Protocol (NTP). After that, we'll look at Simple Network Management Protocol (SNMP) and the type of alerts sent to the network management station (NMS). You'll learn about the all-so-important Syslog logging and configuration, and then finally, I'll cover how to configure Secure Shell (SSH).

> **NOTE** To find your included bonus material, as well as Todd Lammle videos, practice questions & hands-on labs, please see www.lammle.com/ccna

Exploring Connected Devices Using CDP and LLDP

Cisco Discovery Protocol (CDP) is a proprietary protocol designed by Cisco to help us collect information about locally attached devices. Using CDP, we can gather hardware and protocol information about neighbor devices—vital information for documenting and troubleshooting the network! Another dynamic discovery protocol is Link Layer Discovery Protocol (LLDP), but it's not proprietary like CDP.

We'll start by covering the CDP timer and other CDP commands used to verify our network.

Getting CDP Timers and Holdtime Information

The show cdp command (sh cdp for short) is great for getting information about two CDP global parameters typically configured on Cisco devices:

- *CDP timer* delimits how often CDP packets are transmitted out all active interfaces.
- *CDP holdtime* delimits the amount of time that the device will hold packets received from neighbor devices.

Both Cisco routers and switches use the same parameters. Figure 12.1 shows how CDP works within a switched network.

FIGURE 12.1 Cisco Discovery Protocol

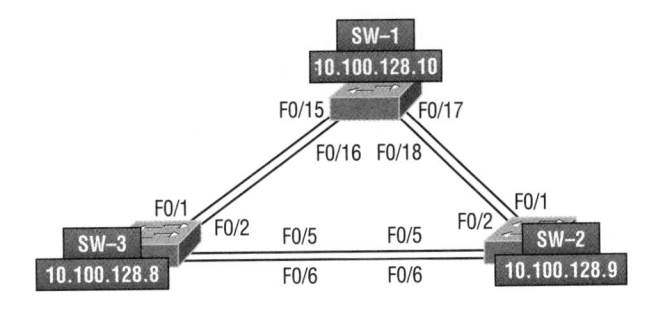

The output on my 3560 SW-3 looks like this:

```
SW-3#sh cdp
Global CDP information:
        Sending CDP packets every 60 seconds
        Sending a holdtime value of 180 seconds
        Sending CDPv2 advertisements is enabled
```

This output tells us that the default transmits every 60 seconds and will hold packets from a neighbor in the CDP table for 180 seconds. I can use the global commands cdp holdtime and cdp timer to configure the CDP holdtime and timer on a router like this:

```
SW-3(config)#cdp ?
  advertise-v2  CDP sends version-2 advertisements
  holdtime      Specify the holdtime (in sec) to be sent in packets
  run           Enable CDP
  timer         Specify the rate at which CDP packets are sent (in sec)
  tlv           Enable exchange of specific tlv information

SW-3(config)#cdp holdtime ?
  <10-255>  Length of time (in sec) that receiver must keep this packet

SW-3(config)#cdp timer ?
  <5-254>  Rate at which CDP packets are sent (in sec)
```

You can turn off CDP completely with the no cdp run command from global configuration mode of a router and enable it with the cdp run command:

```
SW-3(config)#no cdp run
SW-3(config)#cdp run
```

To turn CDP off or on for an interface, use the no cdp enable and cdp enable commands.

Gathering Neighbor Information

The show cdp neighbor command (sh cdp nei for short) delivers information about directly connected devices. It's important to remember that CDP packets aren't passed through a Cisco switch and that you only see what's directly attached. This means that if your router is connected to a switch, you won't see any of the Cisco devices connected to that switch!

This output shows the show cdp neighbor command I used on SW-3:

```
SW-3#sh cdp neighbors
Capability Codes: R - Router, T - Trans Bridge, B - Source Route Bridge
                  S - Switch, H - Host, I - IGMP, r - Repeater, P - Phone,
                  D - Remote, C - CVTA, M - Two-port Mac Relay Device ID Local Intrfce Holdtme
Capability Platform Port ID
SW-1 Fas 0/1 150 S I WS-C3560- Fas 0/15
SW-1 Fas 0/2 150 S I WS-C3560- Fas 0/16
SW-2 Fas 0/5 162 S I WS-C3560- Fas 0/5
SW-2 Fas 0/6 162 S I WS-C3560- Fas 0/6
```

Okay—we can see that I'm directly connected with a console cable to the SW-3 switch and also that SW-3 is directly connected to two other switches. But do we really need the figure to draw out our network? We don't! CDP allows me to see who my directly connected neighbors are and gather information about them. From the SW-3 switch, you can see that there are two connections to SW-1 and two connections to SW-2. SW-3 connects to SW-1 with ports Fas 0/1 and Fas 0/2, and there are connections to SW-2 with local interfaces Fas 0/5 and Fas 0/6. Both the SW-1 and SW-2 switches are 3650 switches. SW-1 is using ports Fas 0/15 and Fas 0/16 to connect to SW-3. SW-2 is using ports Fas 0/5 and Fas 0/6.

To sum this up, the device ID shows the configured hostname of the connected device, that the local interface is our interface, and the port ID is the remote device's directly connected interface. Remember that all you get to view are directly connected devices!

Table 12.1 summarizes the information displayed by the show cdp neighbor command for each device.

TABLE 12.1 Output of the show cdp neighbors command

Field	Description
Device ID	The hostname of the device directly connected.
Local Interface	The port or interface that you're receiving CDP packets on.
Holdtime	The amount of time the router will hold the information before discarding it if no more CDP packets are received.

Field	Description
Capability	The capability of the neighbor—the router, switch, or repeater. The capability codes are listed at the top of the command output.
Platform	The type of Cisco device directly connected. In the previous output, the SW-3 shows it's directly connected to two 3560 switches.
Port ID	The neighbor device's port or interface that CDP packets are multicast from.

> **Note:** You must be able to look at the output of a show cdp neighbors command and understand the information it's given you about the neighbor device's capability. It tells us whether it's a router or switch, the model number (platform), of the port connecting to that device (local interface), and the port of the neighbor connecting to you (port ID).

Another command that will deliver the goods on neighbor information is the show cdp neighbors detail command (show cdp nei de for short). This command can be run on both routers and switches, and it displays detailed information about each device connected to the device you're running the command on. Check out the router output:

```
SW-3#sh cdp neighbors detail
-------------------------
Device ID: SW-1
Device ID: SW-1
Entry address(es):
  IP address: 10.100.128.10
Platform: cisco WS-C3560-24TS,  Capabilities: Switch IGMP
Interface: FastEthernet0/1,  Port ID (outgoing port): FastEthernet0/15
Holdtime : 135 sec

Version :
Cisco IOS Software, C3560 Software (C3560-IPSERVICESK9-M), Version 12.2(55)SE5,
RELEASE SOFTWARE (fc1)
Technical Support: http://www.cisco.com/techsupport
Copyright (c) 1986-2013 by Cisco Systems, Inc.
Compiled Mon 28-Jan-13 10:10 by prod_rel_team

advertisement version: 2
```

```
Protocol Hello:  OUI=0x00000C, Protocol ID=0x0112; payload len=25,
value=00000000FFFFFFFF010221FF000000000000001C555EC880Fc00f000
VTP Management Domain: 'NULL'
Native VLAN: 1
Duplex: full
Power Available TLV:

    Power request id: 0, Power management id: 1, Power available: 0, Power
management level: -1
Management address(es):
  IP address: 10.100.128.10
------------------------

[ouput cut]


------------------------
Device ID: SW-2
Entry address(es):
  IP address: 10.100.128.9
Platform: cisco WS-C3560-8PC,  Capabilities: Switch IGMP
Interface: FastEthernet0/5,  Port ID (outgoing port): FastEthernet0/5
Holdtime : 129 sec

Version :
Cisco IOS Software, C3560 Software (C3560-IPBASE-M), Version 12.2(35)SE5,
RELEASE SOFTWARE (fc1)
Copyright (c) 1986-2005 by Cisco Systems, Inc.
Compiled Thu 19-Jul-05 18:15 by nachen

advertisement version: 2
Protocol Hello:  OUI=0x00000C, Protocol ID=0x0112; payload len=25,
value=00000000FFFFFFFF010221FF000000000000B41489D91880Fc00f000
VTP Management Domain: 'NULL'
Native VLAN: 1
Duplex: full
Power Available TLV:

    Power request id: 0, Power management id: 1, Power available: 0, Power
management level: -1
Management address(es):
  IP address: 10.100.128.9
[output cut]
```

So what do we see here? First, we've been given the hostname and IP address of all directly connected devices. In addition to the same information displayed by the `show cdp neighbors` command, the `show cdp neighbors detail` command tells us the IOS version and IP address of the neighbor device—nice!

The `show cdp entry *` command displays the same information as the `show cdp neighbors detail` command. There really isn't any difference between these commands.

> ### Real World Scenario
>
> **CDP Can Save Lives!**
>
> Karen has just been hired as a senior network consultant at a large hospital in Dallas, Texas, so she's expected to be able to take care of any and all problems that crop up. As if that weren't enough pressure, she also has to worry about the awful possibility that people won't receive correct health care solutions—even the correct medications—if the network goes down... a potential life-or-death situation!
>
> But Karen is confident and begins optimistically. Of course, it's not long before the network reveals that it has a few problems. Unfazed, she asks one of the junior administrators for a network map so she can troubleshoot the network. This person tells her that the old senior administrator, whom she replaced, had them with him and now no one can find them! The sky begins to darken a bit.
>
> Doctors are now calling every couple of minutes because they can't get the necessary information they need to take care of their patients. What should she do?
>
> It's CDP to the rescue! And it's a gift that this hospital happens to be running Cisco routers and switches exclusively, because CDP is enabled by default on all Cisco devices. Karen is also in luck because the disgruntled former administrator didn't turn off CDP on any devices before he left!
>
> So all Karen has to do now is to use the show CDP neighbor detail command to find all the information she needs about each device to help draw out the hospital's network. With the command's critical information, she brings the network back up to speed and the personnel relying so heavily upon it can get back to the important business of saving lives!
>
> The only snag to nailing this in your own network is if you don't know the passwords of all those devices. Your only hope then is to somehow find out the access passwords or to perform password recovery on them.
>
> So, use CDP—you never know when you may end up saving someone's life.
>
> By the way, this is a true story!

Documenting a Network Topology Using CDP

With that real-life scenario in mind, I'm going to show you how to document a sample network by using CDP. You'll learn to determine the appropriate router types, interface types, and IP addresses of various interfaces using only CDP commands and the show running-config command. Our rules for this exercise are:

- We can only console into the Lab_A router to document the network.
- You'll have to assign any remote routers the next IP address in each range.

We'll use a different figure for this example—Figure 12.2—to help us complete the required documentation.

FIGURE 12.2 Documenting a network topology using CDP

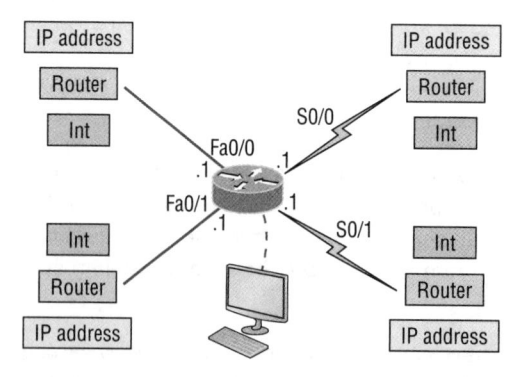

In this output, you can see we have a router with four interfaces: two Fast Ethernet and two serial. So first, let's find out the IP addresses of each interface using the show running-config command like this:

```
Lab_A#sh running-config
Building configuration...
Current configuration : 960 bytes
!
version 12.2
service timestamps debug uptime
service timestamps log uptime
no service password-encryption
!
hostname Lab_A
!
ip subnet-zero
!
!
```

```
interface FastEthernet0/0
ip address 192.168.21.1 255.255.255.0
duplex auto
!
interface FastEthernet0/1
ip address 192.168.18.1 255.255.255.0
duplex auto
!
interface Serial0/0
ip address 192.168.23.1 255.255.255.0
!
interface Serial0/1
ip address 192.168.28.1 255.255.255.0
!
ip classless
!
line con 0
line aux 0
line vty 0 4
!
end
```

With this step completed, we can document the IP addresses of the Lab_A router's four interfaces. Next, we've got to determine the type of device on the other end of each of these interfaces. For that, we'll use the show cdp neighbors command:

```
Lab_A#sh cdp neighbors
Capability Codes: R - Router, T - Trans Bridge, B - Source Route Bridge
                  S - Switch, H - Host, I - IGMP, r - Repeater
Device ID  Local Intrfce  Holdtme  Capability  Platform  Port ID
Lab_B      Fas 0/0        158      R           2501      E0
Lab_C      Fas 0/1        135      R           2621      Fa0/0
Lab_D      Ser 0/0        158      R           2514      S1
Lab_E      Ser 0/1        135      R           2620      S0/1
```

Wow—looks like we're connected to some old routers! It's not our job to judge—our mission is to draw out the network and we've got some nice information to meet that challenge with now. Using both the show running-config and show cdp neighbors commands, we have the IP addresses of the Lab_A router, the types of routers connected to each of the Lab_A router's links, plus all the interfaces of the remote routers.

Equipped with all the information gathered via show running-config and show cdp neighbors, we can accurately create the topology in Figure 12.3.

FIGURE 12.3 Network topology documented

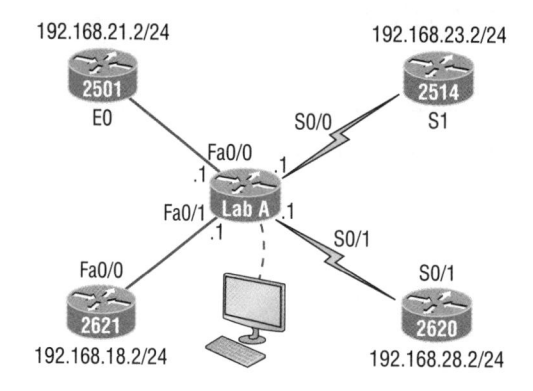

```
         192.168.21.2/24              192.168.23.2/24
              [2501]                      [2514]
                E0        S0/0             S1
                      Fa0/0
                        .1    .1
                 Fa0/1 [Lab A] .1
                        .1     S0/1
              Fa0/0                         S0/1
              [2621]                       [2620]
         192.168.18.2/24              192.168.28.2/24
```

If we needed to, we could've also used the `show cdp neighbors detail` command to view the neighbor's IP addresses. But since we know the IP addresses of each link on the Lab_A router, we already know what the next available IP address is going to be.

Link Layer Discovery Protocol (LLDP)

Before moving on from CDP, I want to tell you about a nonproprietary discovery protocol that provides pretty much the same information as CDP but works in multi-vendor networks.

The IEEE created a new standardized discovery protocol called 802.1AB for Station and Media Access Control Connectivity Discovery. We'll just call it *Link Layer Discovery Protocol (LLDP)*.

LLDP defines basic discovery capabilities, but it was also enhanced to specifically address voice applications. This version is called LLDP-MED (Media Endpoint Discovery). An important factor to remember is that LLDP and LLDP-MED are not compatible!

LLDP has the following configuration guidelines and limitations:

- LLDP must be enabled on the device before you can enable or disable it on any interface.
- LLDP is supported only on physical interfaces.
- LLDP can discover up to one device per port.
- LLDP can discover Linux servers.

You can turn off LLDP completely with the `no lldp run` command from global configuration mode and enable it with the `lldp run` command. Doing this enables it on all interfaces:

SW-3(config)#**no lldp run**
SW-3(config)#**lldp run**

To turn LLDP off or on for an interface, use the `lldp transmit` and `lldp receive` commands:

```
SW-3(config-if)#no lldp transmit
SW-3(config-if)#no lldp receive

SW-3(config-if)#lldp transmit
SW-3(config-if)#lldp receive
```

Next, we'll make sure that all our devices are in sync with the same time by covering Network Time Protocol.

Network Time Protocol (NTP)

Network Time Protocol provides pretty much what it describes: time to all your network devices. More specifically, NTP synchronizes clocks of computer systems over packet-switched, variable-latency data networks.

Typically you'll have an NTP server that connects through the Internet to an atomic clock. This time can then be synchronized throughout the network to keep all routers, switches, servers, etc., receiving the same time information and in sync.

Correct network time within the network is important because:

- It allows the tracking of events in the network in the correct order.
- Clock synchronization is critical for the correct interpretation of events within the syslog data.
- Clock synchronization is critical for digital certificates.

Having all your devices synchronized with the correct time is critical to your routers and switches for analyzing logs to find security issues or other maintenance tasks. These devices issue log messages when different events take place, like when an interface goes down and back up or not. You already know that all messages generated by the IOS go only to the console port by default; however, those console messages can be directed to a syslog server.

A syslog server saves copies of console messages and can time-stamp them so you can view them later. And this is actually really easy to do. Here would be your configuration on the SF router:

```
SF(config)#service timestamps log datetime msec
```

So even though I had the messages time-stamped with the command `service timestamps log datetime msec`, this doesn't mean that we'll know the exact time using default clock sources.

To make sure all devices are synchronized with the same time information, I'm going to configure our devices to get accurate time information from a centralized server, as shown here, in Figure 12.4:

```
SF(config)#ntp server 172.16.10.1 version 4
```

FIGURE 12.4 Synchronizing time information

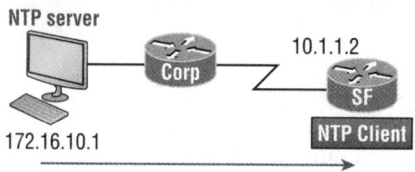

Just use that single command on all your devices, and each of them will receive the same, exact time and date information accurately. You can also make your router or switch an NTP server with the `ntp master` command.

Okay—to verify that our NTP client is receiving clocking information, use the following commands:

```
SF#sh ntp ?
  associations  NTP associations
  status        NTP status  status    VTP domain status

SF#sh ntp status
Clock is unsynchronized, stratum 16, no reference clock
nominal freq is 119.2092 Hz, actual freq is 119.2092 Hz, precision is 2**18
reference time is 00000000.00000000 (00:00:00.000 UTC Mon Jan 1 1900)
clock offset is 0.0000 msec, root delay is 0.00 msec
S1#sh ntp associations

address         ref clock    st   when  poll reach  delay   offset    disp
~172.16.10.1    0.0.0.0      16   -     64   0      0.0     0.00      16000.
* master (synced), # master (unsynced), + selected, - candidate, ~ configured
```

In this example, we can see that the NTP client in SF isn't synchronized with the server via the show `ntp status` command. The stratum value is a number from 1 to 15, and a lower stratum value indicates a higher NTP priority—16 means there's no clocking being received.

There's a bunch of additional ways to configure an NTP client like NTP authentication, making a router or switch foolproof to things like an intruder being able to change the time of an attack.

SNMP

Although *Simple Network Management Protocol (SNMP)* certainly isn't the oldest protocol ever, it's still pretty old, considering it was created way back in 1988 (RFC 1065)!

SNMP is an Application layer protocol that provides a message format for agents on a variety of devices to communicate with network management stations (NMSs). A couple of examples are Cisco Prime and SolarWinds. Agents send messages to the NMS station, which then either reads or writes information into a database stored on the NMS called a Management Information Base (MIB).

NMS periodically queries or polls the SNMP agent on a device to gather and analyze statistics via GET messages. End devices running SNMP agents would send an SNMP trap to the NMS if a problem occurs. This process is demonstrated in Figure 12.5.

FIGURE 12.5 SNMP GET and TRAP messages

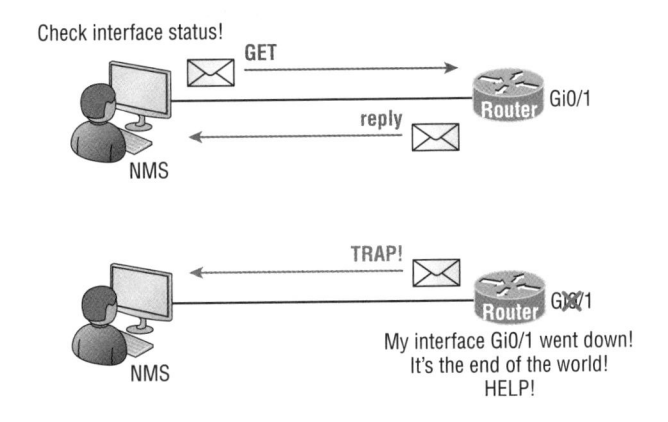

We can also use SNMP to provide agents with SET messages. In addition to polling for statistics, SNMP can analyze information and compile it into a report or even a graph. When thresholds are exceeded, a process is triggered alerting about the event. Graphing tools are used to monitor the CPU statistics of Cisco devices, such as core routers. The CPU should be monitored continuously, and the NMS can graph the statistics. Notifications are sent when any threshold you've set is exceeded.

SNMP has three versions, with version 1 being rarely, if ever implemented today. Here's a list of these three versions:

SNMPv1   Supports plaintext authentication with community strings and uses only UDP.

SNMPv2c   Supports plaintext authentication with community strings with no encryption but provides GET BULK, which is a way to gather abundant information at once and minimize the number of GET requests. It offers a more detailed error message via a reporting method called INFORM, but it's not really more secure than v1. It uses UDP even though it can be configured to use TCP.

SNMPv3   Supports strong authentication with MD5 or SHA, providing confidentiality (encryption) and data integrity of messages via DES or DES-256 encryption between agents and managers. GET BULK is a supported feature of SNMPv3, and this version also uses TCP.

Management Information Base (MIB)

With so many kinds of devices and so much data that can be accessed, there needed to be a standard way to organize this deluge of data. It's MIB to the rescue! A *management information base (MIB)* is a collection of information that's organized hierarchically that can be accessed by protocols like SNMP. RFCs define some common public variables, but most organizations define their own private branches along with basic SNMP standards. Organizational IDs (OIDs) are laid out as a tree with different levels assigned by different organizations. Top-level MIB OIDs belong to various standards organizations.

Vendors assign private branches in their own products. Let's take a look at Cisco's OIDs, which are described in words or numbers to locate a particular variable in the tree, as shown in Figure 12.6.

FIGURE 12.6 Cisco's MIB OIDs

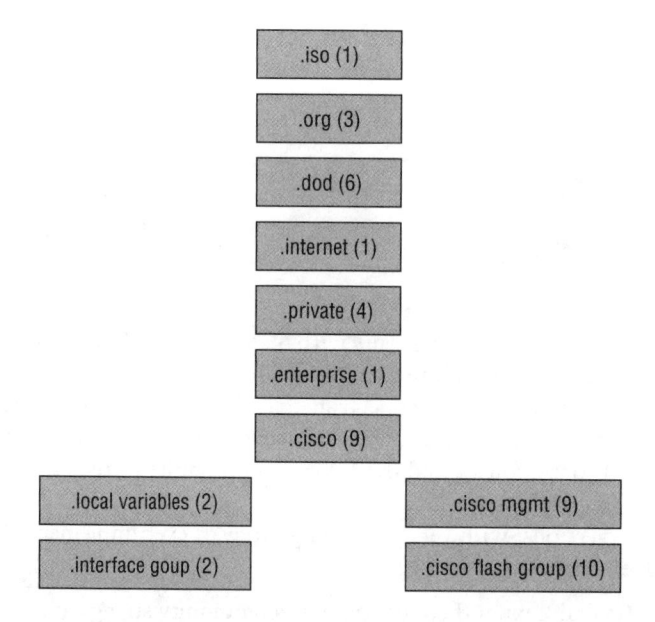

```
                    .iso (1)
                    .org (3)
                    .dod (6)
                    .internet (1)
                    .private (4)
                    .enterprise (1)
                    .cisco (9)
   .local variables (2)        .cisco mgmt (9)
   .interface goup (2)         .cisco flash group (10)
```

Luckily, you don't need to memorize the OIDs in Figure 12.6 for the Cisco exams!

To obtain information from the MIB on the SNMP agent, you can use several different operations:

- GET: This operation is used to get information from the MIB to an SNMP manager.
- SET: This operation is used to get information to the MIB from an SNMP agent.
- WALK: This operation is used to list information from successive MIB objects within a specified MIB.
- TRAP: This operation is used by the SNMP agent to send a triggered piece of information to the SNMP manager.
- INFORM: This operation is the same as a trap, but it adds an acknowledgment, which traps don't provide.

Configuring SNMP

Configuring SNMP is a pretty straightforward process following four steps, and you only need a few commands. Here are the steps you need to run through to configure a Cisco device for SNMP access:

1. Enable SNMP read-write access to the router.
2. Configure SNMP contact information.
3. Configure SNMP location.
4. Configure an ACL to restrict SNMP access to the NMS hosts.

The only required configuration is the community string because the other three are optional. Here's an example of a typical SNMP router configuration:

```
Router(config)#snmp-server community ?
  WORD   SNMP community string

Router(config)#snmp-server community Todd ?
  <1-99>       Std IP accesslist allowing access with this community string
  <1300-1999>  Expanded IP accesslist allowing access with this community
               string
  WORD         Access-list name
  ipv6         Specify IPv6 Named Access-List
  ro           Read-only access with this community string
  rw           Read-write access with this community string
  view         Restrict this community to a named MIB view
  <cr>

Router(config)#snmp-server community Todd rw
Router(config)#snmp-server location Boulder
Router(config)#snmp-server contact Todd Lammle
Router(config)#ip access-list standard Protect_NMS_Station
Router(config-std-nacl)#permit host 192.168.10.254
```

Entering the snmp-server command enables SNMPv1 on the Cisco device.

You can enter the ACL directly in the SNMP configuration to provide security, using either a number or a name. Here's an example:

```
Router(config)#snmp-server community Todd Protect_NMS_Station rw
```

Notice that even though there's a boatload of configuration options under SNMP, you only really need to work with a few of them to configure a basic SNMP trap setup on a router. First, I chose the community name of Todd with RW access (read-write), which means the NMS will be able to retrieve and modify MIB objects from the router. Location and contact information comes in really handy for troubleshooting the configuration. Make sure you understand that the ACL protects the NMS from access, not the actual devices with the agents!

Here's a short list defining the SNMP read and write options:

Read-only   Gives authorized management stations read-access to all objects in the MIB except the community strings and doesn't allow write-access

Read-write   Gives authorized management stations read-and write-access to all objects in the MIB but doesn't allow access to the community strings

There are still more ways to gather information from Cisco devices, and next, we'll get into logging with Syslog. Personally I like this approach a lot better than SNMP since there are a lot more Syslog messages available within IOS compared to just SNMP Trap messages.

Syslog

Reading system messages from a switch's or router's internal buffer is a popular and efficient method of seeing what's going on with your network at a particular time. But the best way is to log messages to a *syslog* server, which stores messages from you. It can even timestamp and sequence them for you, plus it's easy to set up and configure!

Syslog allows you to display, sort, and even search messages, all of which makes it a really great troubleshooting tool. The search feature is especially powerful because you can use keywords and even severity levels. And the server can even email admins based on the severity level of the message.

Network devices can be configured to generate a syslog message and forward it to various destinations. These four examples are popular ways to gather messages from Cisco devices:

- Logging buffer (on by default)
- Console line (on by default)
- Terminal lines (using the terminal monitor command)
- Syslog server

So, you already know that all system messages and debug output generated by the IOS go out only the console port by default and are also logged in buffers in RAM. And you also know that Cisco routers aren't exactly shy about sending messages! To send message to the VTY lines, use the `terminal monitor` command. We'll also add a small configuration needed for syslog, which I'll show you soon in the configuration section.

By default, we'd see something like this on our console line:

```
*Oct 21 15:33:50.565:%LINK-5-CHANGED:Interface FastEthernet0/0, changed state to administratively down
*Oct 21 15:33:51.565:%LINEPROTO-5-UPDOWN:Line protocol on Interface FastEthernet0/0, changed state to down
```

And the Cisco router would send a general version of the message to the syslog server that would be formatted into something like this:

```
Seq no:timestamp: %facility-severity-MNEMONIC:description
```

The system message format can be broken down in this way:

seq no   This stamp logs messages with a sequence number, but not by default. If you want this output, you've got to configure it.

Timestamp   Data and time of the message or event, which again will show up only if configured.

Facility   The facility to which the message refers.

Severity   A single-digit code from 0 to 5 that indicates the severity of the message.

MNEMONIC   Text string that uniquely describes the message.

Description   Text string containing detailed information about the event being reported.

The severity levels, from the most severe level to the least, are explained in Table 12.2. "Informational" is the default, and will result in all messages being sent to the buffers and console.

TABLE 12.2   Severity levels

Severity Level	Explanation
Emergency (severity 0)	System is unusable.
Alert (severity 1)	Immediate action is needed.
Critical (severity 2)	Critical condition.
Error (severity 3)	Error condition.
Warning (severity 4)	Warning condition.
Notification (severity 5)	Normal but significant condition.
Informational (severity 6)	Normal information message.
Debugging (severity 5)	Debugging message.

If you're studying for your Cisco exam, you'll need to memorize Table 12.2. Here's a handy mnemonic for doing that: Every Awesome Cisco Engineer Will Need Icecream Daily.

Know that only emergency-level messages will be displayed if you've configured severity level 0. But if you go with level 4 instead, you'll see level 0 through 4 displayed, giving you emergency, alert, critical, error, and warning messages too. Level 5 is the highest-level security option and displays everything, but just be warned that opting for it can have a pretty serious impact on a device's performance! So always use debugging commands carefully choosing only the messages you really need to meet your specific business requirements.

Configuring and Verifying Syslog

So Cisco devices send all log messages of the severity level you've chosen to the console. They'll also go to the buffer, and both happen by default. Because of this, it's good to know that you can disable and enable these features with the following commands:

```
Router(config)#logging ?
Hostname or A.B.C.D  IP address of the logging host
buffered       Set buffered logging parameters
buginf         Enable buginf logging for debugging
cns-events     Set CNS Event logging level
console        Set console logging parameters
count          Count every log message and timestamp last occurrence
esm            Set ESM filter restrictions
exception      Limit size of exception flush output
facility       Facility parameter for syslog messages
filter         Specify logging filter
history        Configure syslog history table
host           Set syslog server IP address and parameters
monitor        Set terminal line (monitor) logging parameters
on             Enable logging to all enabled destinations
origin-id      Add origin ID to syslog messages
queue-limit    Set logger message queue size
rate-limit     Set messages per second limit
reload         Set reload logging level
server-arp     Enable sending ARP requests for syslog servers when
               first configured
source-interface  Specify interface for source address in logging
               transactions
trap           Set syslog server logging level
userinfo       Enable logging of user info on privileged mode enabling

Router(config)#logging console
Router(config)#logging buffered
```

Wow—as you can see, you've got plenty of options available via the logging command! The preceding configuration enabled the console and buffer to receive all log messages of all severities, and don't forget that this is the default setting for all Cisco IOS devices. If you want to disable the defaults, use the following commands:

```
Router(config)#no logging console
Router(config)#no logging buffered
```

I like leaving the console and buffer commands on in order to receive the logging info, but that's up to you. You can see the buffers with the show logging command here:

```
Router#sh logging
Syslog logging: enabled (11 messages dropped, 1 messages rate-limited,
 0 flushes, 0 overruns, xml disabled, filtering disabled)
    Console logging: level debugging, 29 messages logged, xml disabled,
                    filtering disabled
    Monitor logging: level debugging, 0 messages logged, xml disabled,
                    filtering disabled
    Buffer logging: level debugging, 1 messages logged, xml disabled,
                    filtering disabled
    Logging Exception size (4096 bytes)
    Count and timestamp logging messages: disabled
No active filter modules.

    Trap logging: level informational, 33 message lines logged

Log Buffer (4096 bytes):
*Jun 21 23:09:35.822: %SYS-5-CONFIG_I: Configured from console by console
Router#
```

The default trap (message from device to NMS) level is debugging, but you can change this too. And now that you've seen the system message format on a Cisco device, I'm going to show you how you can also control the format of your messages via sequence numbers and time stamps because they aren't enabled by default. We'll begin with a basic example of how to configure a device to send messages to a syslog server, pictured in Figure 12.7.

FIGURE 12.7 Messages sent to a syslog server

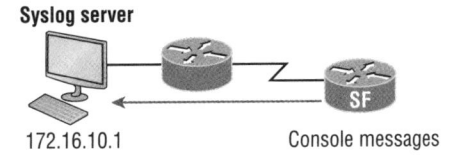

A syslog server saves copies of console messages and can time-stamp them for viewing at a later time. This is actually pretty easy to configure, and here's how doing that would look on the SF router:

```
SF(config)#logging 172.16.10.1
SF(config)#logging informational
```

This is awesome—now all the console messages will be stored in one location to be viewed at our convenience! I typically use the `logging host ip_address` command, but `logging IP_address` without the host keyword gets the same result.

We can limit the amount of messages sent to the syslog server, based on severity, with the following command:

```
SF(config)#logging trap ?
  <0-5> Logging severity level
  alerts         Immediate action needed       (severity=1)
  critical       Critical conditions           (severity=2)
  debugging      Debugging messages            (severity=5)
  emergencies    System is unusable            (severity=0)
  errors         Error conditions              (severity=3)
  informational  Informational messages        (severity=6)
  notifications  Normal but significant conditions (severity=5)
  warnings       Warning conditions            (severity=4)
  <cr>
SF(config)#logging trap informational
```

Notice that we can use either the number or the actual severity level name—and that they're in alphabetical order, not severity order. This "feature" makes it a pain to memorize the order! (Thanks, Cisco!) Since I went with severity level 6 (Informational), I'll receive messages for levels 0 through 6. These are referred to as local levels as well, such as, for example, local6—no difference.

Now let's configure the router to use sequence numbers:

```
SF(config)#no service timestamps
SF(config)#service sequence-numbers
SF(config)#^Z
000038: %SYS-5-CONFIG_I: Configured from console by console
```

When you exit configuration mode, the router will send a message like the one shown in the preceding code lines. Without the time stamps enabled, we'll no longer see a time and date, but we will see a sequence number.

So we now have the following:

- Sequence number: 000038
- Facility: %SYS
- Severity level: 5
- MNEMONIC: CONFIG_I
- Description: Configured from console by console

Out of all of these, you need to pay the closest attention to the severity level for the Cisco exams as well as for a means to control the number of messages sent to the syslog server!

Secure Shell (SSH)

I'm strongly recommending that you use Secure Shell (SSH) instead of Telnet to connect to your devices because it creates a more secure session. Telnet uses an unencrypted data stream, where SSH uses encryption keys to send data so your username and password aren't sent in the clear, vulnerable to poaching!

Here are the steps for setting up SSH on your Cisco devices:

1. Set your hostname:

    Router(config)#**hostname Todd**

2. Set the domain name—both the hostname and domain name are required for the encryption keys to be generated:

    Todd(config)#**ip domain-name Lammle.com**

3. Set the username to allow SSH client access:

    Todd(config)#**username Todd password Lammle**

4. Generate the encryption keys for securing the session:

    ```
    Todd(config)#crypto key generate rsa
    The name for the keys will be: Todd.Lammle.com
    Choose the size of the key modulus in the range of 360 to
    4096 for your General Purpose Keys. Choosing a key modulus
    Greater than 512 may take a few minutes.
    How many bits in the modulus [512]: 1024
    % Generating 1024 bit RSA keys, keys will be non-exportable...
    [OK] (elapsed time was 6 seconds)
    Todd(config)#
    1d14h: %SSH-5-ENABLED: SSH 1.99 has been enabled*June 24
    19:25:30.035: %SSH-5-ENABLED: SSH 1.99 has been enabled
    ```

5. Enable SSH version 2 on the device—not mandatory, but strongly suggested:

    Todd(config)#**ip ssh version 2**

6. Connect to the VTY lines of the switch or router:

    Todd(config)#**line vty 0 15**

7. Tell the lines to use the local database for password:

    Todd(config-line)#**login local**

8. Configure your access protocols:

    Todd(config-line)#**transport input ?**
    all All protocols

```
none    No protocols
ssh     TCP/IP SSH protocol
telnet  TCP/IP Telnet protocol
```

Beware of this next line, and make sure you never use it in production because it's a horrendous security risk:

```
Todd(config-line)#transport input all
```

I recommend using the next line instead to secure your VTY lines with SSH:

```
Todd(config-line)#transport input ssh ?
  telnet  TCP/IP Telnet protocol
  <cr>
```

I actually do use Telnet once in a while when a situation arises that specifically calls for it. It just doesn't happen very often. But if you want to go with SSH & Telnet on a device, here's how you do that:

```
Todd(config-line)#transport input ssh telnet
```

Know that if you don't use the keyword telnet at the end of the command string, then only SSH will work on the device. You can go with either, just so long as you understand that SSH is way more secure than Telnet.

Summary

I began this chapter by providing detailed information on how to find neighbor device information using the proprietary Cisco Discovery Protocol (CDP) and industry-standard Link Layer Discovery protocol (LLDP). We then synchronized the time for our devices using Network Time Protocol (NTP).

After that, I walked you through Simple Network Management Protocol (SNMP), an Application layer protocol that provides a message format for agents on a variety of devices to communicate to network management stations (NMSs). You also learned about the type of alerts sent to the network management station (NMS). We then moved on to the very important Syslog, which was covered in depth, and finally, I demonstrated how to configure SSH.

Exam Essentials

Describe the value of CDP and LLDP. Cisco Discovery Protocol can be used to help you document and troubleshoot your network. LLDP is a nonproprietary protocol that can provide the same information as CDP.

Understand the information provided by the output of the show cdp neighbors **command.** The show cdp neighbors command provides the following information: device ID, local interface, holdtime, capability, platform, and port ID (remote interface).

List Understand how to configure NTP. It's pretty simple to configure NTP, and you don't have to remember all of the options! Most important are configuring syslog to mark the time and date and enabling NTP:

SF(config)#**service timestamps log datetime msec**
SF(config)#**ntp server 172.16.10.1 version 4**

Understand the various levels of syslog. Though it's simple to configure syslog, there are a bunch of options you have to remember for the exam. Use this mneumonic: "Every Awesome Cisco Engineer Will Need Icecream Daily" in order to remember this table:

Severity Level	Explanation
Emergency (severity 0)	System is unusable.
Alert (severity 1)	Immediate action is needed.
Critical (severity 2)	Critical condition.
Error (severity 3)	Error condition.
Warning (severity 4)	Warning condition.
Notification (severity 5)	Normal but significant condition.
Informational (severity 6)	Normal information message.
Debugging (severity 5)	Debugging message.

Remember the differences between SNMPv2 and SNMPv3. SNMPv2 uses UDP but can use TCP. SNMPv2 still sends data to the NMS station in clear text, exactly like SNMPv1. SNMPv2 implemented GETBULK and INFORM messages. SNMPv3 uses TCP and authenticates users, plus it can use ACLs in the SNMP strings to protect the NMS station from unauthorized use.

Describe the advantages of using Secure Shell and list its requirements. Secure Shell (SSH) uses encrypted keys to send data so that usernames and passwords are not sent in the clear. It requires that a hostname and domain name be configured for encryption keys to be generated.

Review Questions

You can find the answers to these questions in the Appendix.

1. How can you efficiently restrict the read-only function of a requesting SNMP management station based on the IP address?
    A. Place an ACL on the logical control plane.
    B. Place an ACL on the line when configuring the RO community string.
    C. Place an ACL on the VTY line.
    D. Place an ACL on all router interfaces.

2. A switch is configured with the `snmp-server community Cisco RO` command running SNMPv2c. An NMS is trying to communicate to this router via SNMP. What can be performed by the NMS? (Choose two.)
    A. The NMS can only graph obtained results.
    B. The NMS can graph obtained results and change the hostname of the router.
    C. The NMS can only change the hostname of the router.
    D. The NMS can use GETBULK and return many results.

3. Which is true regarding SNMP? (Choose two.)
    A. SNMPv2c offers more security than SNMPv1.
    B. SNMPv3 uses TCP and introduced the GETBULK operation.
    C. SNMPv2c introduced the INFORM operation.
    D. SNMPv3 provides the best security of the three versions.

4. Which command can you use to determine the IP address of a directly connected neighbor?
    A. `show cdp`
    B. `show cdp neighbors`
    C. `show cdp neighbors detail`
    D. `show neighbor detail`

5. According to the output, which interface does SW-2 use to connect to SW-3?

    ```
    SW-3#sh cdp neighbors
    Capability Codes: R - Router, T - Trans Bridge, B - Source Route BridgeS -
    Switch, H - Host, I - IGMP, r - Repeater, P - Phone, D - Remote, C - CVTA, M
    - Two-port Mac Relay Device ID
    Local Intrfce     Holdtme    Capability  Platform    Port ID
    SW-1    Fas 0/1     170         S I      WS-C3560-  Fas 0/15
    SW-1    Fas 0/2     170         S I      WS-C3560-  Fas 0/16
    SW-2    Fas 0/5     162         S I      WS-C3560-  Fas 0/2
    ```

- **A.** Fas 0/1
- **B.** Fas 0/16
- **C.** Fas 0/2
- **D.** Fas 0/5

6. Which of the following commands enables syslog on a Cisco device with debugging as the level?
   - **A.** `syslog 172.16.10.1`
   - **B.** `logging 172.16.10.1`
   - **C.** `remote console 172.16.10.1 syslog debugging`
   - **D.** `transmit console messages level 7 172.16.10.1`

7. What is the default syslog facility level?
   - **A.** local4
   - **B.** local5
   - **C.** local6
   - **D.** local7

8. Which three statements about syslog utilization are true? (Choose three.)
   - **A.** Utilizing syslog improves network performance.
   - **B.** The syslog server automatically notifies the network administrator of network problems.
   - **C.** A syslog server provides the storage space necessary to store log files without using router disk space.
   - **D.** There are more syslog messages available within Cisco IOS than there are comparable SNMP trap messages.
   - **E.** Enabling syslog on a router automatically enables NTP for accurate time stamping.
   - **F.** A syslog server helps in aggregation of logs and alerts.

9. You need to configure all your routers and switches so they synchronize their clocks from one time source. Which command will you type for each device?
   - **A.** `clock synchronization` *ip_address*
   - **B.** `ntp master ip_address`
   - **C.** `sync ntp ip_address`
   - **D.** `ntp server` *ip_address* `version` *number*

10. A network administrator enters the following command on a router: `logging trap 3`. Choose the three message types that will be sent to the syslog server:
    - **A.** Informational
    - **B.** Emergency
    - **C.** Warning
    - **D.** Critical
    - **E.** Debug
    - **F.** Error

11. Which two of the following commands are required when configuring SSH on your router? (Choose two.)

   A. `enable secret password`
   B. `exec-timeout 0 0`
   C. `ip domain-name` *name*
   D. `username name password` *password*
   E. `ip ssh version 2`

Chapter 13

Security

THE FOLLOWING CCNA EXAM TOPICS ARE COVERED IN THIS CHAPTER:

5.0 Security Fundamentals

- ✓ 5.1 Define key security concepts (threats, vulnerabilities, exploits, and mitigation techniques)

- ✓ 5.2 Describe security program elements (user awareness, training, and physical access control)

- ✓ 5.3 Configure device access control using local passwords

- ✓ 5.4 Describe security password policies elements, such as management, complexity, and password alternatives (multifactor authentication, certificates, and biometrics)

- ✓ 5.7 Configure Layer 2 security features (DHCP snooping, dynamic ARP inspection, and port security)

- ✓ 5.8 Differentiate authentication, authorization, and accounting concepts

Network security has grown from a consideration into a critically important essential. In an age of increasing use and dependence on the Internet, nearly everyone—from individuals and small businesses, to huge corporations, institutions, and worldwide organizations—is now a potential victim of hackers and E-crime. And although our defense techniques continue to improve with time, so does the sophistication and weaponry used by the bad guys.

Today's tightest security will be laughably transparent three years from now, making it absolutely necessary for administrators to stay up with the industry's quickly evolving security trends.

Among additional important technologies, this chapter will cover Authentication, Authorization, and Accounting, or AAA. AAA is a technology that gives us substantial control over users and what they're permitted to do inside of our networks. That's just the beginning—there are more tools in the box! RADIUS and TACACS+ security servers like Integrated Services Engine ISE help us implement a centralized security plan by recording network events to the security server, or to a Syslog server via logging.

Solid security hasn't just become imperative, it's also becoming increasingly complex. Cisco continues to develop and extend its features to meet these demands by providing us with a whole suite of hardware and software solutions.

ISE (Identity Security Engine), Cisco Prime, Tetration, ACI, and other powerful tools like Next Generation Firewall (NGFW), also called Cisco Firepower & Firepower Threat Defense (FTD), will be covered in my new CCNP Security books. For now, just know that the new FTD, and even older ASA devices, can be used to send authentication to the server.

In this chapter, we'll also be covering user accounts, password security and user authentication methods, and we'll finish up by demonstrating how to set passwords on your Cisco devices.

I know all of this sounds pretty complicated, and truthfully, it is. That's why I'm devoting a whole chapter to these crucial topics!

So, let's look into the specific types of threats your network is probably vulnerable to now.

> To find your included bonus material, as well as Todd Lammle videos, practice questions & hands-on labs, please see www.lammle.com/ccna

Network Security Threats

There are four primary threats to network security you must be familiar with as well as being able to define the type of attacker:

Unstructured Threats These are threats typically originated by curious people that have downloaded information from the Internet and want to feel the sense of power this provides them. Sure, some of these types called Script Kiddies can be pretty nasty, but most of them are just doing it for the rush, thrills, and bragging rights. They're not talented, experienced hackers.

Structured Threats This kind of hacker is much more sophisticated, technically competent and calculating. They're dedicated to their work, and they usually understand network design and how to exploit routing and network vulnerabilities. They can create hacking scripts that allow them to penetrate deep into the network's systems and tend to be repeat offenders. Both structured and unstructured threats typically come from the Internet.

External Threats These typically come from people on the Internet or from someone who has found a hole in your network from the outside. These serious threats have become ubiquitous now that all companies have an Internet presence. External threats generally make their way into your network via the Internet.

Internal Threats These come from users on your network, typically employees. These are probably the scariest of all threats because they're really hard to catch and stop. Worse, since these hackers are authorized to be on the network, they can do some serious damage in less time because they're already in and know their way around. Add that to the profile of an angry, disgruntled employee or contractor out for revenge and you've got a real problem! We all know doing this is illegal but some of us also know it's pretty easy to cause a lot of damage really fast, and the odds aren't bad that they'll get away with it!

Three Primary Network Attacks

Now you know your enemy, but what, exactly, are they up to? The better you understand that, the more equipped you'll be to handle anything an attacker may throw at you. Most network attacks fall into these three categories:

Reconnaissance Attacks *Reconnaissance attacks* are basically an unauthorized familiarization session. An attacker on reconnaissance is out for discovery—mapping the network, its resources, systems, and vulnerabilities. This is often preliminary. The information gathered will often be used to attack the network later.

Access Attacks *Access attacks* are waged against networks or systems to retrieve data, gain access, and/or escalate their access privilege. This can be as easy as finding network shares with no passwords. Some access attacks are just for the intellectual challenge, but beware. Darker motivations include actual theft, corporate espionage, or using you as camouflage, making their dirty work appear to originate from your network!

Denial of Service (DoS) Attacks *Denial of service (DoS) attacks* are always vile, and they deny legitimate users from accessing the network resources. Their sole purpose is to disable or corrupt network services. The result of a DoS attack will usually either crash a system or slow it down to the point that it's rendered useless. DoS attacks are usually aimed at web servers and are surprisingly easy to carry out.

Network Attacks

There's a whole bunch of ways to gather information about a network, compromise corporate information or destroy corporate web servers and services. Most of them are pretty common. TCP/IP teams up with operating systems to provide lots of weak, exploitable spots into our networks, and some are so bad, they're almost like an outright invitation!

Here's a list of the most common threats:

- Eavesdropping
- Denial-of-service attacks
- Unauthorized Access
- WareZ
- Masquerade attack (IP spoofing)
- Session replaying or hijacking
- Rerouting
- Repudiation
- Smurfing
- Password attacks
- Man-in-the-middle attacks
- Application-layer attacks
- HTML attacks

It's your job to protect your company's network from these attacks. You've got to effectively prevent the theft, destruction, and corruption of sensitive, corporate information, as well as block the introduction of corrupt information that can cause irreparable damage.

Eavesdropping

Eavesdropping, otherwise known as network snooping and packet sniffing, is the act of a hacker "listening in" to your system. There's a really cool product called a packet sniffer that enables us to read packets of information sent across a network because a network's packets aren't encrypted by default. You can just imagine how helpful sniffers can be when trying to optimize or troubleshoot a network! But it's not a stretch to imagine hackers using them for evil and breaking into a network to gather up sensitive corporate info, right?

And gather they can! Some applications send all information across the network in clear text, an especially convenient feature for someone striving to nick usernames and passwords gain access to corporate resources. A bad guy only needs to jack the right account and they've got the run of your network. Worse, if they manage to gain admin or root access, they can even create a new user ID to use at any time as a back door into your network and its resources. The network belongs to the hacker—kiss it goodbye!

> **Simple Eavesdropping**
>
> Here's an example of eavesdropping when I was checking my email that demonstrates how easy it is to find usernames and passwords!
>
> The network analyzer I'm using shows the first packet has the username in cleartext in the output below:
>
> **TCP - Transport Control Protocol**
>
> ```
> Source Port:          3207
> Destination Port:     110  pop3
> Sequence Number:      1904801173
> Ack Number:           1883396251
> Offset:               5 (20 bytes)
> Reserved:             %000000
> Flags:                %011000
>                       0. .... (No Urgent pointer)
>                       .1 .... Ack
>                       .. 1... Push
>                       .. .0.. (No Reset)
>                       .. ..0. (No SYN)
>                       .. ...0 (No FIN)
> Window:               64166
> Checksum:             0x078F
> Urgent Pointer:       0
> No TCP Options
> POP - Post Office Protocol
>   Line 1:             USER tlammle1<CR><LF>
> FCS - Frame Check Sequence
>   FCS (Calculated):   0x0CFCA80E
> ```

> This next packet has the password. Everything needed to break into the system is seen in this packet! In this case, it's an email address and username/password):
>
> **TCP - Transport Control Protocol**
>
> | | |
> |---|---|
> | Source Port: | 3207 |
> | Destination Port: | 110 *pop3* |
> | Sequence Number: | 1904801188 |
> | Ack Number: | 1883396256 |
> | Offset: | 5 *(20 bytes)* |
> | Reserved: | %000000 |
> | Flags: | %011000 |
> | | 0. .... (No Urgent pointer) |
> | | .1 .... Ack |
> | | .. 1... Push |
> | | .. .0.. (No Reset) |
> | | .. ..0. (No SYN) |
> | | .. ...0 (No FIN) |
> | Window: | 64161 |
> | Checksum: | 0x078F |
> | Urgent Pointer: | 0 |
> | No TCP Options | |
> | POP - Post Office Protocol | |
> | Line 1: | PASS secretpass<CR><LF> |
>
> Both the username, "tlammle1," and the password, "secretpass," are right there in clear text for everyone's viewing pleasure!

So worse yet, eavesdropping is also used for stealing information and identities. Imagine the intruder, hacking into some financial institution, snaking credit card numbers, account, and other personal information from the institution's network computers or data crossing its network. Voila! The hacker now has everything needed for some serious identity theft.

Of course, there's something we can do about this and again; the solution stems from having a nice, tight network security policy in place. To counteract eavesdropping, create a policy forbidding the use of protocols with known susceptibilities to eavesdropping and make sure all sensitive, important network traffic is encrypted.

Denial-of-Service Attacks

The most debilitating of all, denial-of-service (DoS) attacks can force a corporation to its knees by crippling its ability to conduct business!

And unfortunately, these attacks are alarmingly simple in design and execution. The basic idea is to keep open all available connections supported by the key server. This locks out valid attempts to gain access because legitimate users like customers and employees are shut out due to all services being overwhelmed and all bandwidth consumed.

DoS attacks are often implemented using common Internet protocols like TCP and ICMP—TCP/IP weaknesses for which Cisco offers some safeguards, but nothing we could call bulletproof.

TCP attacks are carried out when a hacker opens up more sessions than the targeted server can handle rendering it inaccessible to anyone else.

ICMP attacks, sometimes called "The Ping of Death," are executed by an attacker in one of two ways: The first way is by sending so many pings to a server; it's thoroughly overwhelmed dealing with pings instead of serving its corporation. The second method is achieved by modifying the IP portion of a header, making the server believe there's more data in the packet than there really is. If enough of these packets are sent, they'll overwhelm and crash the server.

Here's a list describing some of the other kinds of DoS attacks you should know about:

Chargen   Massive amounts of UDP packets are sent to a device resulting in tremendous congestion on the network.

SYN flood   Randomly opens up lots of TCP ports, tying up the network equipment with bogus requests, denying sessions to real users.

Packet fragmentation and reassembly   This attack exploits the buffer overrun bug in hosts or internetwork equipment, creating fragments that can't be reassembled, crashing the system. Having packet reassembly on an interface is very efficient for your network; however, you should disable this on your outside interface/zone.

Accidental   DoS of service attacks can happen by legitimate users using misconfigured network devices.

E-mail bombs   Many free programs exist that allow users to send bulk e-mail to individuals, groups, lists, or domains, taking up all the e-mail service.

Land.c   Uses the TCP SYN packet that specifies the target host's address as both the source and destination. Land.c also uses the same port on the target host as source and destination, causing the target to crash.

The Cisco IOS gives us some nice firewall features to help stop DoS attacks, but you just can't prevent them completely right now without cutting off legitimate users. Here's a list of Cisco's safeguards:

Context-Based Access Control (CBAC)   CBAC provides advanced traffic filtering services and can be used as an integral part of your network's firewall.

Java blocking   Helps stop hostile Java applet attacks.

DoS detection and monitoring   You've really have to understand exactly how much protective power your network actually needs from this feature because going with too much will keep out attackers as well as legitimate users! Carefully assess your specific network needs, and weigh the pros and cons to use DoS monitoring system wisely.

Audit trails   Audit trails are great for keeping track of who's attacking you, which is awesome because you can then send those logs to the FBI.

Real-time alerts log   Keeping a log of the attacks in real-time is helpful in exactly the same way audit trails are: For helping the authorities go after the bad guys.

> The Cisco TCP intercept feature implements software to protect TCP servers from a type of DoS attack called TCP SYN-flooding.

Unauthorized Access

Intruders love gaining access to the root or administrator because they can exploit that access to powerful privileges. The /etc/password file on the UNIX host allows them to view important passwords. Adding additional accounts to use as backdoors permits them access any time they want.

Sometimes intruders gain access into a network so they can place unauthorized files or resources on another system for ready access by other intruders. Other goals could be to steal software and distribute it if possible—more on that in a bit.

Again the Cisco IOS offers us help with something called Lock and Key. Another tool is Terminal Access Controller Access Control System (TACACS+) server—a remote authentication server. There's also an authentication protocol called Challenge Handshake Authentication Protocol (CHAP). All of these technologies provide additional security against unauthorized access attempts.

In addition to a TACACS+ server and CHAP, you can implement a mechanism that authenticates a user beyond an IP network address. It supports things like password token cards and creates other challenges to gaining access. This mechanism also requires remote reauthorization during period of inactivity—another safeguard!

WareZ

WareZ applies to unauthorized distribution of software. The intruder's goal is theft and piracy—they want to either sell someone else's software or distribute the unlicensed versions of it for free on the Internet. It's a favorite of present or former employees, but could be executed by anyone on the Internet with a cracked version of the software. As you can imagine, WareZ is a huge problem!

There are many ways to provide free software on the Internet and a legion of servers in the Far East that offer blatantly pirated downloads of free software because they know there is nothing anyone can do about it. The only thing that can protect products from a WareZ is to include some type of activation key and licensing preventing illegal use.

Masquerade Attack (IP Spoofing)

Masquerading *or* IP spoofing is pretty easy to prevent once you understand how it works. An IP spoofing attack happens when someone outside your network pretends to be a trusted computer by using an IP address that's within the range of your network's IP addresses. The attacker's plan is to steal an IP address from a trusted source for use in gaining access to network resources. A trusted computer is one that you either have administrative control over or one you've decided to trust on your network.

You can head off this attack by placing an access control list (ACL) on the corporate router's interface to the Internet denying access to your internal addresses from that interface. This approach easily stops IP spoofing but only if the attacker is coming in from outside the network.

In order to spoof a network ID, a hacker would need to change the routing tables in your router in order to receive any packets. Once they do that, the odds are good that they'll gain access to user accounts and passwords. And if your hacker happens to understand messaging protocols, he or she just might add a little twist and send e-mail messages from some poor employee's company e-mail account to other users in the company. That way, it looks like that user sent the messages, and many hackers get a real kick out of embarrassing corporate users. IP spoofing helps them achieve that goal.

Session Hijacking or Replaying

When two hosts communicate, they typically use the TCP protocol at the Transport layer to set up a reliable session. This session can be "hijacked," by making the hosts believe that they are sending packets to a valid host, when in fact, they're delivering their packets to a hijacker.

You don't see this so much anymore because a network sniffer can gather much more information, but it still happens now and then, so you should still be aware of it. You can protect yourself from *session hijacking* or *replaying* by using a strongly authenticated, encrypted management protocol.

Rerouting

A *rerouting* attack is launched by a hacker who understands IP routing. The hacker breaks into the corporate router and then changes the routing table to alter the course of IP packets so they'll go to the attacker's unauthorized destination instead. Some types of cookies and Java or Active X scripts can also be used to manipulate routing tables on hosts.

To stop a rerouting attack, you can use access control with an ASA and/or Cisco Firepower device.

Repudiation

Repudiation is a denial of a transaction so that no communications can be traced by erasing or altering logs to hide the trail providing deniability. Doing this can prevent a third party from being able to prove that a communication between two other parties ever took place.

Non-repudiation is the opposite—a third party can prove that a communication between two other parties took place. So because you generally want the ability to trace your communications, as well as prove they actually did take place, non-repudiation is the preferred transaction.

Attackers who want to create repudiation attack can use Java or Active X scripts to do so. They can also use scanning tools that confirm TCP ports for specific services, network or system architecture, and OS. Once information is obtained, the attacker will try and find vulnerabilities associated with those entities.

To stop repudiation, set your browser security setting to "high." You can also block any corporate access to public e-mail sites. In addition, add access control and authentication on your network. Non-repudiation can be used with digital signatures, which are discussed in Chapter 7.

Smurfing

The latest trend in the attacker game is the *smurf attack*. This attack sends a large amount of ICMP (Internet Control Message Protocol) echo (ping) traffic to IP broadcast addresses from a supposedly valid host that is traceable. The framed host then gets blamed for the attack. The targets IP address is used as the source address in the ping and all system reply to the target eating up its resources.

Smurf attacks send a layer two (Data-Link layer) broadcast. Most hosts on the attacked IP network will reply to each ICMP echo request with an echo reply, multiplying the traffic by the number of hosts responding. This eats up tons of bandwidth and results in a denial of service to valid users because the network traffic is so high.

The smurf attack's cousin is called *fraggle*, which uses UDP echo packets in the same fashion as the ICMP echo packets. Fraggle is a simple rewrite of smurf to use a layer 4 (Transport layer) broadcast.

To stop a smurf attack, all networks should perform filtering either at the edge of the network where customers connect (the access layer), or at the edge of the network with connections to the upstream providers. Your goal is to prevent source-address-spoofed packets from entering from downstream networks or leaving for upstream ones.

Password Attacks

These days, it's a rare user that isn't aware of password issues, but you can still depend on them to pick the name of their dog, significant other, or child because those things are nice and easy to remember. But you've been wise and set policies to stop these easy-to-guess passwords, no worries—right?

Well, almost. You've definitely saved yourself a good bit of grief. It's just that even if your users pick really great passwords, programs that record a username and password can still be used to gather them up. If a hacker creates a program that repeatedly attempts to identify a user account and/or password, it's called a *brute-force attack*. And if it's successful, the hacker will gain access to all resources the stolen username and password usually provides to the now ripped-off corporate user. As you can imagine, it's especially dark day when the bad guy manages to jack the username and password of an administrator account.

Man-in-the-Middle Attacks

A *man-in-the-middle* attack is just that—a person that is between you and the network you are connected to gathering everything you are sent and received. For a man-in-the middle attack to be possible, the attacker must have access to network packets traveling across the networks. This means your middleman could be an internal user, someone who spoofed—even someone who works for an Internet service provider (ISP). Man-in-the-middle attacks are usually implemented by using network packet sniffers, routing protocols, or even Transport layer protocols.

Your middleman attacker's goal is any or all of the following:

- Theft of information
- Hijacking of an ongoing session to gain access to your internal network resources
- Traffic analysis to derive information about your network and its users
- Denial of service
- Corruption of transmitted data
- Introduction of new information into network sessions

Application-Layer Attacks

An *Application-layer attack* involves an application with well-known weaknesses that can be easily exploited. Sendmail, PostScript, and FTP are a few really good examples. The idea here is to gain access to a computer with the permissions of the account running the application, which is usually a privileged, system-level account.

Trojan Horse Programs, Viruses, and Worms

I hate to admit this but, the *Trojan horse attack* is actually a very cool attack—that is, if you look at the way it's implemented, and, more importantly, if it's not happening to you. See, the Trojan horse creates a substitute for a common program, duping users into thinking they are in a valid program when they're not. They're in the horse. This gives the attacker the power to monitor login attempts and to capture user account and password information. This attack can even mix it up a notch and allow the horse's rider to modify application behavior and receive all your corporate e-mail messages instead of you. Pretty stylin' huh! I told you it was cool.

Both worms and viruses spread and infect multiple systems. The differentiator between the two is that viruses require some form of human intervention to spread, and worms do that on their own. Since viruses, Trojan horses, and worms are conceptually alike, they're all considered to be the same form of attack. They're all software programs created for and aimed at destroying your data. And some variants of these weapons can also deny legitimate users' access to resources and consume bandwidth, memory, disk space, and CPU cycles.

So be smart—use a virus program and update it regularly!

HTML Attacks

Another new attack on the Internet scene exploits several new technologies: the Hypertext Markup Language (HTML) specification, web browser functionality, and HTTP.

HTML attacks can include Java applets and ActiveX controls, and their modus operandi is to pass destructive programs across the network and load them through a user's browser.

Microsoft promotes an Authenticode technology for ActiveX. Only, it doesn't do much except to provide a false sense of security to users. This is because attackers can use a properly signed and totally bug-free ActiveX control to create a Trojan horse!

This particular approach is unique because it's teamwork—the attacker and you. Part one of this attack—the bad guy's part—is to modify a program and set it up so that you, the user, actually initiate the attack when you either start the program or choose a function within it. And these attacks aren't hardware dependent. They're very flexible because of the portability of the programs.

Security Program Elements

A security program backed by a security policy is one of the best ways to maintain a secure posture at all times. Solid programs cover many elements, but three are key:

- User awareness
- Training
- Physical security

User Awareness

Attacks are often successful because users aren't wise to the type of social engineering attacks confronting them. Moving beyond figuring out they're being played, users must also be skilled enough to avoid being set up and trapped as the inevitable dangers are encountered. Social engineering attacks and attackers use believable language, manipulation, and user gullibility to get the goods they're after like user credentials or other sensitive, confidential information. Common threats that you want your people to be able to identify and understand include phishing/pharming, shoulder surfing, identity theft, and dumpster diving.

Phishing/Pharming

When phishing, attackers try to learn personal information, including credit card information and financial data. A very popular phishing technique is to put up a mock web site that very closely resembles a legitimate one. Users visit the site, and enter their data, including credentials, essentially handing the bad guys facets of their valuable identity! Spear phishing is when an attack is carried out against a specific target by learning about the chosen mark's habits and likes. Because of the detailed background information required, these attacks take longer to carry out.

Pharming is similar to phishing only pharming actually pollutes the contents of a computer's DNS cache so that requests to a legitimate site are actually routed to an alternate one.

Malware

Malicious software, or malware, is any software designed to perform malicious acts.

Here are the four classes of malware you should understand:

- Virus: Any malware that attaches itself to another application to replicate or distribute itself.
- Worm: Any malware that replicates itself but doesn't need another application or human interaction to propagate.
- Trojan horse: Any malware that disguises itself as a needed application while carrying out malicious actions.
- Spyware: Any malware that collects private user data, including browsing history or keyboard input.

The best defense against malicious software is to implement anti-virus and anti-malware software. Today, most vendors package these two types of protection together. Keeping anti-virus and anti-malware software up to date is vital, especially ensuring that the latest virus and malware definitions have been installed.

Training

The best countermeasure against social engineering threats is to provide user security awareness training. This training should be required and must occur on a regular basis because social engineering techniques evolve constantly.

Caution users against using any links embedded in e-mail messages, even if the message appears to have come from a legitimate entity. Users should also scrutinize a site's address bar any time they access a site where their personal information is required to verify the site is genuine and SSL is being used. The latter is indicated either by a padlock icon or an HTTPS designation at the beginning of the URL address.

Physical Access Control

With no physical security, logical or technical methods are pretty useless. For example, if someone can physically access your routers and switches, they can erase your configuration and take ownership of the devices! Likewise, physical access to a workstation can permit a hacker to boot to an operating system on a flash drive and access data.

Physical security is a grab bag of elements added to an environment to aid in securing it. Let's look at a few examples now.

Mantrap

Think of a mantrap like a series of two doors with a small room between them. The person who wants in is authenticated at the first door and then allowed into the room. Next, additional verification like a guard visually identifying them is required to permit them through the second door. Most of the time, mantraps are used only in very high-security situations and typically require the first door to be closed before opening the second one.

Figure 13.1 shows a mantrap design.

FIGURE 13.1 Aerial view of a mantrap

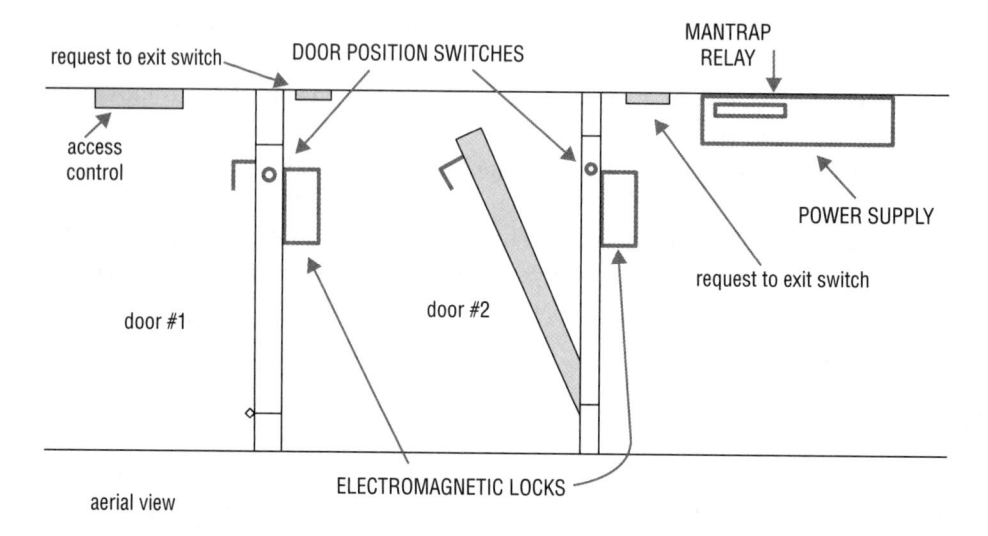

Badge reader

Radio Frequency Identification (RFID) is a wireless, no-contact technology used with badges or cards and their accompanying reader. The reader is connected to the workstation and validates against the security system. This is an upgrade for authentication process security because the user must be in physical possession of the badge to access resources. An obvious drawback here is if the card is lost or stolen, anybody with the card can access those resources! Badge readers are used to provide access to devices and to open doors as well.

Smart Card

A smart card is basically a fancy badge or card that gives you access to myriad resources, including buildings, parking lots, and computers. It's embedded with your identity and access privilege information, and each area or device you access has a card scanner to insert your card into or swipe.

Smart cards are tough to counterfeit but easy to steal, and once a thief has it, they can access anything the card allows. To counteract this, most organizations avoid placing identifying marks on their smart cards, which definitely does make it harder for thieves to use them. Taking things further, modern smart cards often require a password or PIN to activate it plus encryption to protect the card's contents.

Security Guard

Sometimes, nothing takes the place of a human being. Security guards rely on the training, intuition, and common sense that automated systems lack to head off intruders. They can even be armed.

Door Lock

One of the easiest ways to prevent people with bad intentions from physically entering your environment is to lock your doors. Door locks are the most universal form of physical barrier and are a key point of access control for protecting network systems and devices. One door is good, but more doors are better, and the most effective physical barrier implementations are called multiple-barrier systems.

Ideally, you should have a minimum of three physical barriers to be effective. The first one is the external entrance to the building called the perimeter, which is protected by alarms, external walls, fencing, surveillance, and so on. Keep an accurate access list of who can enter and be verified by a guard or someone else in authority. The second barrier is the actual entrance into the building. Use things like ID badges verified by security guards to permit access here. The third barrier is the entrance to the computer room itself. Here's where things like fobs and smart cards are used for gaining access. (If sufficiently paranoid and loaded with cash, you could go even go with a biometric system!) Of course, each of these entrances should be individually secured, monitored, and protected with alarm systems.

> **TIP** Think of the three barriers this way: Outer = fence, Middle = guards, locks and mantraps, Inner = key fobs/smart cards.

Yes, the truly determined can still break in, but these three barriers will probably slow an intruder down enough for law enforcement to respond before they can get away!

Layer 2 Security Features

The Cisco hierarchical model is a great reference in designing, implementing and maintaining a scalable, reliable and cost-effective internetwork.

The bottom layer of this model, the Access Layer, controls user and workgroup access to internetwork resources. Sometimes it's referred to as the desktop layer. The network resources most users need are available locally because the Distribution Layer above handles traffic for remote services.

Here's a list of some of some Access Layer functions:

- Continued use of access control lists and policies from Distribution Layer
- Creation of separate collision domains with microsegmentation
- Workgroup connectivity into the Distribution Layer
- Device connectivity
- Resiliency and security services
- Advanced technological capabilities (voice/video, PoE, port-security, QoS, etc.)
- Gigabit switching

The Access Layer is where user devices connect to the network, and it's also the connection point between the network and client device. So clearly, safeguarding this layer is vital to protecting users, applications, and the network itself from attacks.

Some ways to protect the access layer are pictured in Figure 13.2.

FIGURE 13.2 Mitigating Threats at the Access Layer

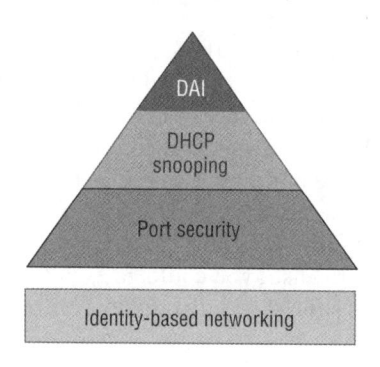

Port Security   Yes—you're already familiar with port security. It's the most common way to defend the access layer by restricting a port to a specific set of MAC addresses.

DHCP Snooping   DHCP snooping is a Layer 2 security feature that validates DHCP messages by acting like a firewall between trusted hosts and untrusted DHCP servers.

In order to stop rogue DHCP servers within the network, switch interfaces are configured as trusted or untrusted. Trusted interfaces allow all types of DHCP messages but untrusted interfaces only permit requests. Trusted interfaces connect to a legitimate DHCP server or an uplink towards the legitimate DHCP server as shown in Figure 13.3.

FIGURE 13.3 DHCP Snooping

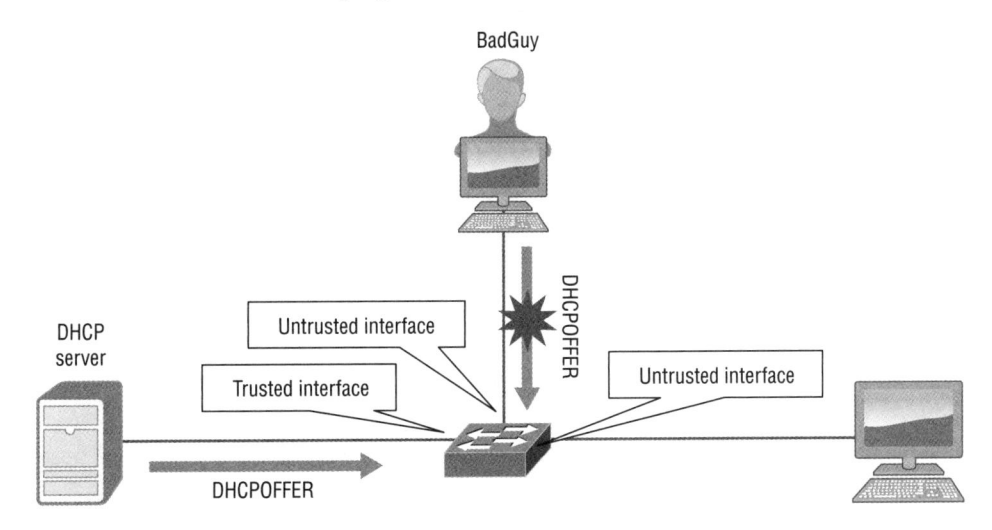

With DHCP snooping enabled, a switch also builds a DHCP snooping binding database. Each entry includes the MAC and IP address of the host, as well as the DHCP lease time, binding type, VLAN, and interface. Dynamic ARP Inspection also uses the DHCP snooping binding database.

Dynamic ARP Inspection (DAI)   DAI, used with DHCP snooping, tracks IP-to-MAC bindings from DHCP transactions to protect against ARP poisoning. You need DHCP snooping in order to build the MAC-to-IP bindings for DAI validation.

Identity Based Networking   Identity-based networking is a concept that ties together several authentication, access control, and user policy components to provide users with only the network services you want them to access.

In the past, for a user to connect to the Finance services, they had to be plugged into the Finance LAN or VLAN. But with user mobility as one of the core requirements of modern networks, this is no longer practical, nor does it provide sufficient security.

Identity-based networking allows us to verify users when they connect to a switch port by authenticating them, placing them in the right VLAN and applying security and QoS policies based upon their identity. Users who fail to pass the authentication process might simply be placed in a guest VLAN, but their access can be rejected too! Figure 13.4 illustrates this process.

Note: ISE and DNA center are Identity-Based Networking products from Cisco.

FIGURE 13.4 Identity-Based Networking

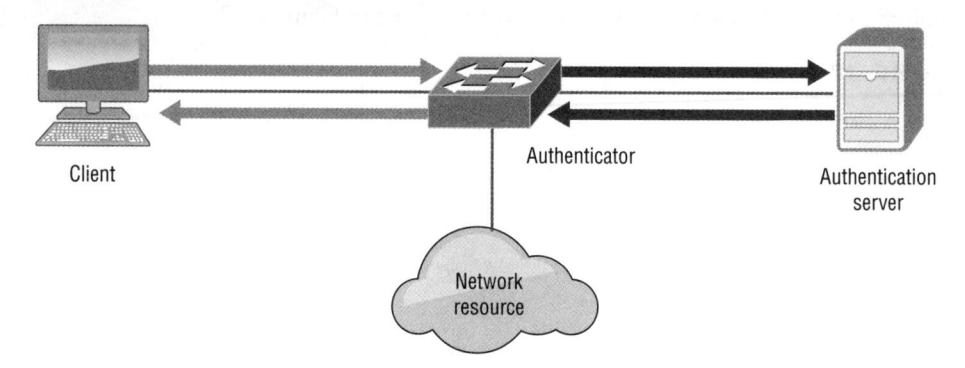

The IEEE 802.1x standard permits the implementation of identity-based networking on wired and wireless hosts by using client-server access control. There are three roles:

- Client: also referred to as a supplicant, is software that runs on a client, which is 802.1x compliant
- Authenticator: Typically, a switch, VPN server, or wireless AP, controls physical access to the network, and is a proxy between the client and the authentication server
- Authentication server (RADIUS): Server that authenticates each client before making any services available

Securing Network Access with Cisco AAA

A really nice feature of authentication, authorization, and accounting (AAA) architecture is that it enables systematic access security both locally and remotely. AAA technologies work within the remote client system and the security server to secure access. Here's a definition of each of the "A"s in AAA:

- **Authentication** requires users to prove that they are who they say they are in one of these three ways:
  - Name and password
  - Challenge and response
  - Token cards
- **Authorization** only takes place after authentication is validated. Authorization provides the needed resources specifically allowed to a certain user and permits the operations that specific user is allowed to perform.
- **Accounting** and auditing records what the user actually did on the network as well as which resources they accessed. It also keeps track of how much time they spent using network resources.

Authentication Methods

With a terminal server configuration, a router authenticates a user coming in on it by ensuring that the person attempting to connect is valid and truly permitted access. The most common way the router determines that is via either a password or a combination of a username and a password. First, the user submits the needed information to the router, then the router checks to see if that information is correct. If so, the user is then authenticated and allowed access to the console.

But that's only one way for routers to authenticate users from outside its boundaries. There are several different authentication methods you can apply that involve the operating system, security server, PAP, and CHAP authentication. CHAP is rarely in use today. I'm going to tell you about all of these techniques shortly, but first, I want to go into more detail about the way authentication is achieved most often—via usernames and passwords.

Username/password methods range from weak to strong in their authentication power—it depends on how vigilant you want to be. A database of usernames and passwords is employed at the simpler and least secure end of the range while more advanced methods utilize one-time passwords, multi-factor, certificates, and biometrics.

The list below begins from the least secure authentication progressing through to the most:

- **No username or password**: Obviously, this is the least secure method. It provides ease of connectivity, but absolutely no security to network equipment or network resources. An attacker simply has to find the server or network address to gain access.

- **Username/password (static):** Set up by a network administrator and remains in place and unchanged until the network administrator changes it. It's better than nothing, but hackers can easily decipher usernames and passwords using snooping devices.

- **Aging username/password:** These expire after a set time (usually between 30 and 90 days) and must be reset—most often, by the user. The administrator configures the time period. This is tighter than the static usernames and password method, but it's still susceptible to playback attacks, eavesdropping, theft, and password cracking.

- **One-time passwords (OTP):** This is a very secure username/password method. Most OTP systems are based on a "secret pass-phrase," which is used to generate a list of passwords. They're only good for one login so they're useless to anyone who manages to eavesdrop and capture them. A list of accessible passwords is typically generated by S/KEY server software and is then distributed to users.

- **Token cards/soft tokens:** This is the most secure authentication method. An administrator passes out a token card and a personal identification number (PIN) to each user. Token cards are typically the size of a credit card and are provided by a vendor to the administrator when they buy a token card server. This type of security usually consists of a remote client computer, security device such as the Cisco ASA/FTD, and a security server running token security software.

Figure 13.5 pictures a typical RSA token card, although an authenticator app on a smart phone is common today as well.

FIGURE 13.5   RSA token card

- Token cards and servers generally work like this:
    - A OTP is generated by the user with the token card using a security algorithm.
    - The user enters this password into the authentication screen generated on the client.
    - The passwords is sent to the token server via the network and a device.
    - On the token server, an algorithm is used—the same one running on the client—to verify the password and authenticate the user.

The network security policy you've created provides you with the guidelines you need to determine the kind of authentication method you choose to implement on your network.

Windows Authentication

Everyone knows that Microsoft so graciously includes many captivating bugs and flaws with its OS, but at least it does manage to provide an initial authentication screen and users need to authenticate to log into Windows!

If those users happen to be local, they log in to the device via the Windows logon dialog box. If they're remote, they log in to the Windows remote dialog box using PPP (Point to Point Protocol) and TCP/IP over the communication line to the security server.

Generally, that security server is responsible for authenticating users, but it doesn't have to be. A user's identity (username and password) can also be validated using an AAA security server.

The AAA server can then access the MS AD server's user database.

Security Server Authentication

Cisco AAA access control gives you options—it provides either a local security database or a remote one. Your Cisco devices such as the ASA, or the new Cisco FTD, runs the local database for a small group of users, and if you simply have one or two devices, you can opt for local authentication through it. All the remote security data is on a separate server that runs the AAA security protocol, which provides services for both network equipment and a big group of users.

While it's true that local authentication and line security offer an adequate level of security, you're way better off going there if you have fairly small network. That's because they require a whole bunch of administration. Picture a really huge network with, say, 300 routers. Every time a password needs to be changed, the entire roost of routers—that's all 300—must be modified individually to reflect that change. That's right—*individually* by the administrator—YOU!

This is exactly why it's so much smarter to use security servers if your network is even somewhat large. Security servers provide centralized management of usernames and passwords and this is how they work: When a router wants to authenticate a user, it collects the username and password information from them and submits that information to the ISE security server. The security server then compares the information it's been given to the user database to see if the user should be allowed access to the router. All usernames and passwords are stored centrally on the single or redundant pair of security servers.

This AAA four-step process is pictured in Figure 13.6.

FIGURE 13.6 External Authentication options

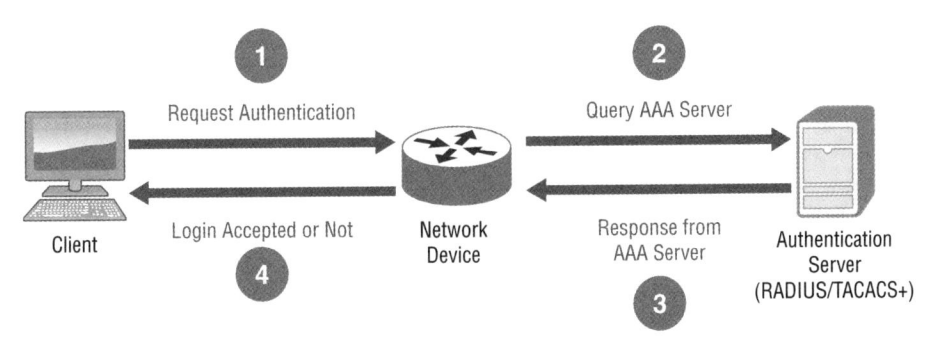

With administration consolidated on a single device like this, managing millions of users is a day at the beach!

There are three types of security server protocols supported by Cisco routers: RADIUS, TACACS+, and Kerberos. Let's take a look at each of these now.

External Authentication Options

Of course we only want authorized IT folks to have administrative access to our network devices such as routers and switches, and in a small to medium-sized network, using just local authentication is sufficient.

But if you have hundreds of devices, managing administrative connectivity would be nearly impossible since you'd have to configure each device by hand. So if you changed just one password, it could take hours to update your network!

Since maintaining the local database for each network device individually in a very large network is unwise, you can use an external AAA server to manage all user and administrative access needs for an entire network.

The two most popular options for external AAA are:

RADIUS

Remote Authentication Dial-In User Service (RADIUS) was developed by the Internet Engineering Task Force—the IETF. It's basically a security system that works to guard the network against unauthorized access. RADIUS, which uses only UDP, is an open standard implemented by most major vendors. It's one of the most popular types of security servers around because it combines authentication and authorization services into a single process. So after users are authenticated, they are then authorized for network services.

RADIUS implements a client/server architecture, where the typical client is a router, switch or AP, and the typical server, a Windows or Unix device that's running RADIUS software.

The authentication process has three distinct stages:

- First, the user is prompted for a username and password.
- Second, the username and encrypted password are sent over the network to the RADIUS server.
- And finally, the RADIUS server replies with one of the following:

Response	Meaning
Accept	The user has been successfully authenticated.
Reject	The username and password are not valid.
Challenge	The RADIUS server requests additional information.
Change Password	The user should select a new password.

It's important to remember that RADIUS encrypts only the password in the access-request packet, from the client to the server. The remainder of the packet is unencrypted.

Configuring RADIUS

To configure a RADIUS server for console and VTY access, first you need to enable AAA services so you can configure all the AAA commands. Configure the **aaa new-model** command in global configuration mode:

```
Router(config)# aaa new-model
```

The **aaa new-model** command immediately applies local authentication to all lines and interfaces—except line con 0. So, to avoid being locked out of the router or switch, you should define a local username and password before starting the AAA configuration.

Now, configure a local user:

`Router(config)#`**`username Todd password Lammle`**

Creating this user is super important because you can use this same locally created user to gain access if the external authentication server fails! If you don't do this and you can't get to the server, you're going to end up doing a password recovery.

Next, configure a RADIUS server of any name and the RADIUS key that is configured on the server:

`Router(config)#`**`radius server SecureLogin`**
`Router(config-radius-server)#`**`address ipv4 10.10.10.254`**
`Router(config-radius-server)#`**`key MyRadiusPassword`**

Now, add your newly created RADIUS server to a AAA group of any name:

`Router(config)#`**`aaa group server radius MyRadiusGroup`**
`Router(config-sg-radius)#`**`server name SecureLogin`**

Lastly, configure this newly created group to be used for AAA login authentication. If the RADIUS server fails, the fallback to local authentication should be set:

`Router(config)#` **`aaa authentication login default group MyRadiusGroup local`**

TACACS+

Terminal Access Controller Access Control System (TACACS+) is also a Cisco proprietary security server that uses TCP. It's really similar in many ways to RADIUS and does all RADIUS does only more, including multiprotocol support.

TACACS+ was developed by Cisco Systems and was later released as an open standard, so it was originally designed specifically to interact with Cisco's AAA services. If you're using TACACS+, you have the entire menu of AAA features available to you, and it handles each security aspect separately, unlike RADIUS:

- Authentication includes messaging support in addition to login and password functions.
- Authorization enables explicit control over user capabilities.
- Accounting supplies detailed information about user activities.

> **NOTE** Understand that authentication and authorization are treated as separate processes.

Configuring TACACS+

This is pretty much identical to the RADIUS configuration.

To configure a TACACS+ server for console and VTY access, first you need to enable AAA services and configure all the AAA commands. Configure the **aaa new-model** command in the global configuration mode if it isn't already enabled:

Router(config)# **aaa new-model**

Now, configure a local user if you haven't already:

Router(config)#**username Todd password Lammle**

Next, configure a TACACS+ server of any name and the key that is configured on the server:

Router(config)#**tacacs-server SecureLoginTACACS+**
Router(config-radius-server)#**address ipv4 10.10.10.254**
Router(config-radius-server)#**key MyTACACS+Password**

Add your newly created TACACS+ server to a AAA group of any name:

Router(config)#**aaa group server tacacs+ MyTACACS+Group**
Router(config-sg-radius)#**server name SecureLoginTACACS+**

Lastly, configure this newly created group to be used for AAA login authentication. If the TACACS+ server fails, the fallback to local authentication should be set:

Router(config)# **aaa authentication login default group MyTACACS+Group local**

Managing User Accounts

There's a whole bunch of authentication schemes used today, and although it's important to know about them and how they work, all that knowledge doesn't equal power if your network's users aren't schooled on how to manage their account names and passwords correctly.

Clearly, if the wrong people get their hands-on usernames and passwords, they've got a way to get into your network. Worse, if a hacker gains the administrator account name and password for your network, it doesn't matter what authentication protocol or server you're using. That hacker is going to get in with the escalated rights that type of account allows and can do some serious damage!

So, let's look at some solid ways to manage user accounts and passwords and follow that up by talking about the key authentication methods in use today.

Usernames and passwords are vital to network security because their whole purpose is to control initial access to a device. Even if the system administrator assigns individuals their usernames and passwords, users can and often do change them, so you need to make sure your network's users know the difference between a good password and a bad one, and how to keep their passwords safe from theft.

Your first step in managing access to network resources is through user accounts and the rights you assign to the network resources. System administrators usually maintain user accounts on a daily basis, doing things like renaming accounts, groups and setting the number of simultaneous connections. You can also designate where users can log in, how often, and when, plus adjust how often their passwords expire and their accounts expire too.

Disabling Accounts

This is important… When a user leaves the organization, you have these three options:

- Leave the account in place.
- Delete the account.
- Disable the account.

The first option isn't so good because if you just leave the account in place, anyone (including the user to whom it belonged) can still log in as that user if they know the password. But deleting the account presents its own set of problems because if you delete an account and then create a new one, the numeric ID associated with that user (UID in Unix, SID in Windows Server) will be lost. It's through this magic number that passwords and rights to network resources are associated with the user account. This can be good, but if you create a new user account with the same name as the one you deleted, the identification number of the new account will be different from the old one, so all of its settings will be removed for the new account.

This leaves you with disabling an account until you've made a decision about what should happen to it. It's really your best bet because you'll probably just want to rename the account when someone new is hired. When you disable an account, it still exists, but no one can use it to log in. Another good time to disable an account is when someone will be gone for an extended period when taking a leave, going on sabbatical, or even an extended vacation.

Another scenario that's fairly common is if a company employs contract and temporary employees. These people will need temporary accounts used for only a short time and then disabled. So knowing how to manage them is important! If you know it in advance, just set the employee's account to expire on their expected last day of work.

Setting Up Anonymous Accounts

Anonymous accounts allow only extremely limited access for a large number of users who all log in with the same username—for instance, *anonymous* or *guest*. These logins are frequently used to access public Wi-Fi service and FTP files—access is gained when you log in with the username *anonymous* and enter your email address as the password.

It's a very bad idea to use anonymous accounts for regular network access because you just can't track them. All Windows Server products from Windows NT onward come with the anonymous account Guest disabled, and it's usually good to leave it that way. When you want to enable that account, like at a public WiFi kiosk, make sure you carefully manage what it's able to access by implementing strict group policies.

Some web servers create an Internet user account to allow anonymous access to the website through which a user is allowed to access the web server over the network. The password is always blank, and you never see a request to log in to the server because it's done automatically. Without this kind of account, no one would be able to access your web pages!

Limiting Connections

It's smart to limit how many times a user can connect to the network. Because they can only be in one place at a time, users should normally be logged in to the network for one instance only. So if your system is telling you that someone is logged in from more than one place, it's probably because someone else is using their account. By limiting simultaneous connections to one, only a single user at a single workstation can gain access to the network using a specific user account.

There are times that some users need to log in multiple times to use certain applications or perform certain tasks, and you can allow that specific user to have multiple concurrent connections.

Some people limit a particular user to logging in from specific location from their own workstations. Sounds good but I wouldn't usually do this because users move around without taking their computers with them and sometimes log in at someone else's machine to get their jobs done or collaborate. So unless you require extra tight security, this rule will just complicate your job because it requires a lot of administration. Windows Server products can limit which station(s) a user is allowed to log in from, but they don't do so by default. A Windows feature that's enabled by default is preventing average users from logging in at the server console. Some serious damage can be done even by accident!

Renaming the Maintenance Account

Network operating systems automatically give the network maintenance (administration) account a default name. On Windows servers, it's Administrator, and for Unix it's root. Clearly, if you don't change this account name, bad guys already have half the information they need to break into your network. The only thing missing is the password!

So yes, definitely rename that account to something cool and creative that you'll remember but that would be really hard for someone to guess—and don't write it on a Post-it and stick it to the server. Here's a "do not use" list of names:

- Admin
- Administrator
- Analyst
- Audit
- Comptroller
- Controller
- Manager
- Root

- Super
- Superuser
- Supervisor
- Wizard
- Any variation on the above

Security Password Policy Elements

Managing passwords is one the most important parts of access management. In this section well discuss common considerations and offer some alternatives to simple passwords.

Password Management

One of the strongest ways to keep a system safe is to employ strong passwords and educate your users in the best security practices. In this section, you'll explore various techniques that can enhance the security of your user passwords.

Setting Strong Passwords

Passwords should be as long as possible. Most security experts believe a password of 10 characters is the minimum that should be used if security is a real concern. If you use only the lowercase letters of the alphabet, you have 26 characters with which to work. If you add the numeric values 0 through 9, you'll get another 10 characters. If you go one step further and add the uppercase letters, you'll then have an additional 26 characters, giving you a total of 62 characters with which to construct a password.

> **TIP** Most vendors recommend that you use nonalphabetical characters such as #, $, and % in your password, and some go so far as to require it.

If you used a 4-character password, this would be 62 × 62 × 62 × 62 (62^4), or approximately 14 million password possibilities. If you used five characters in your password, this would give you 62 to the fifth power (62^5), or approximately 920 million password possibilities. If you used a 10-character password, this would give you 62 to the tenth power (62^{10}), or 8.4×10^{17} (a very big number) possibilities.

As you can see, these numbers increase exponentially with each character added to the password. The 4-digit password could probably be broken in a fraction of a day, whereas the 10-digit password would take considerably longer and consume much more processing power.

If your password used only the 26 lowercase letters from the alphabet, the 4-digit password would have 26 to the fourth power, or 456,000 password combinations. A

5-character password would have 26 to the fifth power, or more than 11 million, and a 10-character password would have 26 to the tenth power, or 1.4×10^{14}. This is still a big number, but it would take considerably less time to break it. As noted earlier, NIST now considers password length more important than complexity.

> **NOTE** To see tables on how quickly passwords can be surmised, visit www.lockdown.co.uk/?pg=combi&s=articles

Password Expiration

The longer that a password is used, the more likely it is that it will be compromised in some way. It is for this reason that requiring users to change their passwords at certain intervals increases the security of their passwords. You should require users to set a new password every 30 days (more frequently for higher-security networks), and you must also prevent them from reusing old passwords. Most password management systems have the ability to track previously used password and to disallow users from recycling old passwords.

Password Complexity

You can set up many different parameters and standards to force the people in your organization to conform with security practices. In establishing these parameters, it's important that you consider the capabilities of the people who will be working with these policies. If you're working in an environment where people aren't computer savvy, you may spend a lot of time helping them remember and recover passwords. Many organizations have had to reevaluate their security guidelines after they've invested great time and expense to implement high-security systems.

Setting authentication security, especially in supporting users, can become a high-maintenance activity for network administrators. On one hand, you want people to be able to authenticate themselves easily; on the other hand, you want to establish security that protects your company's resources. In a Windows server domain, password policies can be configured at the domain level using Group Policy objects. Variables you can configure include password complexity, length, and time between allowed changes.

A good password includes both uppercase and lowercase letters as well as numbers and symbols. In the past an accepted practice was to make passwords complex (using at least three of the four-character types: uppercase, lowercase, numbers, and non-numeric figures), but recently the NIST has recommended that longer and simpler passwords are more secure than shorter and more complex ones.

Screensaver Required Password

A screensaver should automatically start after a short period of idle time, and that screensaver should require a password before the user can begin the session again. This method of locking the workstation adds one more level of security.

BIOS/UEFI Passwords

Passwords should be configured and required to access either the BIOS or UEFI settings on all devices. If this is not the case, it would be possible for someone to reboot a device, enter the settings, change the boot order, boot to an operating system residing on a USB or optical drive, and use that OS as a platform to access data located on the other drives. While this is a worst-case scenario, there is also less significant mayhem a malicious person could cause in the BIOS and UEFI.

Requiring Passwords

Make absolutely certain you require passwords (such a simple thing to overlook in a small network) for all accounts and change the default passwords on system accounts.

Managing Passwords

Like any other aspect of network security, passwords must be managed, and doing that involves ensuring that all passwords for user accounts follow security guidelines so black hats can't easily crack them. You've also got to implement certain features of your network operating system to prevent unauthorized access.

A strong password is some combination of alphanumeric and special characters that's easy for you to remember but really hard for someone else to guess. Like server account names, they should never be written down on anything that is then put into your desk or stuck onto your machines. In a perfect world, everyone is smart and avoids doing those things, but users tend to make things easy by choosing passwords that are also easy to guess. Let's look at some characteristics of strong passwords.

Minimum Length

Strong passwords should be at least 8 characters (the more, the merrier), but they shouldn't be any longer than 15 characters to make them easier to remember. You absolutely must specify a minimum length for passwords because a short password is easily cracked—after all, there are only so many combinations of three-character types, right? The upper limit depends on the capabilities of your operating system and the ability of your users to remember complex passwords. Here's what I call "The Weak List" for passwords—never use them!

- The word *password* (not kidding—people actually still do this!)
- Proper names
- Your pet's name
- Your spouse's name
- Your children's names
- Any word in the dictionary
- A license plate number

- Birth dates
- Anniversary dates
- Your username
- The word *server*
- Any text or label on the PC or monitor
- Your company's name
- Your occupation
- Your favorite color
- Any of the above with a leading number
- Any of the above with a trailing number
- Any of the above spelled backward

There are more, but you get the idea!

Real World Scenario

Security Audits

A great way to begin a basic security audit and get a feel for any potential threats to your network is to simply take a walk through the company's halls and offices. I've done this a lot, and it always pays off because invariably I happen upon some new and different way that people are trying to "beat the system" regarding security. This doesn't necessarily indicate that a given user is trying to cause damage on purpose. It's just that following the rules can be inconvenient—especially when it comes to adhering to strict password policies. Your average user just doesn't get how important their role is in maintaining the security of the network (maybe even their job security as well) by sticking to the network's security policy, so you have to make sure they do.

Think about it. If you can easily discover user passwords just by taking a little tour of the premises, so can someone else, and once they have a username and a password, it's pretty easy to hack into resources. I wasn't kidding about people slapping sticky notes with their usernames and/or passwords right on their monitors—this happens a lot more than you would think. Some users, thinking they're actually being really careful, glue them to the back of their keyboards instead, but you don't have to be Sherlock Holmes to think about looking there either, right? People wouldn't think of leaving their cars unlocked with the windows down and the keys in the ignition, but that's exactly what they're doing by leaving sensitive info anywhere on or near their workstations.

Even though it might not make you Mr. or Ms. Popularity when you search workspaces or even inside desks for notes with interesting or odd words written on them, do it anyway. People will try to hide these goodies anywhere. Sometimes, not so much... I had a user

> who actually wrote his password on the border of his monitor with a Sharpie, and when his password expired, he just crossed it off and wrote the new one underneath it. Sheer genius! But my personal favorite was when I glanced at this one guy's keyboard and noticed that some of the letter keys had numbers written on them. All you had to do was follow the numbers that (surprise!) led straight to his password. Oh sure—he'd followed policy to the, ahem, letter by choosing random letters and numbers, but a lot of good that did—he had to draw himself a little map in plain sight on his keyboard to remember the password.
>
> So, like it or not, you have to walk your beat to find out if users are managing their accounts properly. If you find someone doing things the right way, praise them for it openly. If not, it's time for more training—or maybe worse, termination.

Using Characters to Make a Strong Password

The good news is that solid passwords don't have to be in ancient Mayan to be hard to crack. They just need to include a combination of numbers, letters, and special characters—that's it. Special characters aren't letters or numbers but symbols like $ % ^ # @). Here's an example of a strong password: tqbf4#jotld. Looks like gibberish, but remember that famous sentence, "The quick brown fox jumped over the lazy dog"? Well, this particular password uses the first letter of each word in that sentence with a 4# thrown in the middle of it. Sweet, solid and easy to remember! You can do this with favorite quotes, song lyrics, and so on, with a couple of numbers and symbols stuck in the middle. Just make sure you don't actually sing the song every time you log in!

If you want to test the strength of passwords to make sure they're nice and tight, you can use auditing tools like crack programs that try to guess passwords. Clearly, if that program has a really tough time or even fails to crack the password, you have a good one. By the way, don't just use a regular word preceded by or ending with a special character because good crack programs strip off the leading and trailing characters during decryption attempts.

Password-Management Features

All network operating systems include built-in features for managing passwords to help ensure that your system remains secure and that passwords cannot be easily hacked with crack programs. These features usually include automatic account lockouts and password expiration.

Automatic Account Lockouts

Hackers, and even people who forget their passwords, usually try to log in by guessing passwords. This is why most network operating systems will lock you out after a few unsuccessful attempts. Some will even disable the account. Once that happens, the user won't be able to log in to that account even if they enter the correct password. This feature prevents a potential hacker from running an automated script to crack account passwords by continuously attempting to log in using different character combinations.

When an account is on lockdown, guards—I mean, network staff—will have to unlock the account if the network operating system doesn't unlock it after a preset period. In any high-security network, it's a good idea to require an administrator to manually unlock every locked account instead of setting the network operating system to do it automatically. This way, you will be sure to know about any possible security breaches.

> **WARNING** Be careful not to lock yourself out! With many network operating systems, only administrators can reset passwords, so if you happen to be the administrator and you lock yourself out, only another administrator can unlock your account. Embarrassing, yes, but what if you're the only administrator? That's real trouble because even though many network operating system vendors have solutions to this humiliating issue, the cost of those solutions isn't cheap!

> **TIP** It's good to know that Windows-based servers allow you to configure accounts to be locked out after a number of bad login attempts, yet the default Administrator account is exempt from this happening. This might sound convenient for you, but it's actually a security risk. You should definitely rename this account, and it's also a good idea not to use it for day-to-day administration. Create a new administrator account (with a different name, of course), and use it for management instead.

Password Expiration and Password Histories

Unlike a good wine, even really good passwords don't age well over time; they just become more likely to be cracked. This is why it's good to set passwords so that they expire after a specific amount of time. Most organizations set up passwords to expire every 30 to 45 days, after which the network's users all must reset their passwords either immediately or during a preset grace period. The grace period is usually limited to a specific number of login attempts, or it may allow a couple of days.

> **TIP** By default, each network operating system delimits a specific password-expiration period and any hacker with skills knows about it. So make sure you reset that time period to something other than the default!

Older network OSs allowed users to reset their passwords back to their original form after using an intermediary password for a while. Today's network OSs prevent this via password histories—a record of the past several passwords used by a specific user, which prevents them from using recent passwords stored in the history. If they try, the password will fail, and the operating system will then request a password change. What this means to you is that if your security policy dictates that passwords be reset every two weeks, you should make sure your password history can hold at least 20 passwords. This prevents a user from reusing a password until the password is at least 10 months old (two changes per month)!

By the way, your more experienced users know about this history feature, and because coming up with a really tight password takes a little thought, when savvy users create ones they really like, they may have a hard time letting go. Maybe they just want to avoid the hassle of creating a tight new password and remembering it, so they'll try to find ways to get out of doing that by getting around the password-history feature. I knew one guy who actually admitted that he just changed his password as many times as it took to defeat the history log and then changed it one last time to his beloved, original password, which only took him only about five minutes!

You can force users to change their passwords to ones that are unique because the latest operating systems require unique passwords and can, depending on the network operating system, store more than 20 passwords. This feature makes it a whole lot harder to revert to any previous passwords. But it's still possible for users to beat the system by beating the minimum password age setting, so don't rely completely on it.

Single Sign-On

In Today's, modern enterprises, users sometimes get overwhelmed by the number of points in the network where they're required to identify themselves. Most have to log onto the domain to have network access at all, and there are company websites requiring an authentication process to access databases, SharePoint sites, secured drives, personal folders, and so on!

When users have to remember multiple passwords, as the number increases, they begin to resort to unsafe security practices like writing passwords on sticky notes, hiding passwords in their drawers, and even sharing them with coworkers. All of these practices undermine the security of the network.

Single sign-on (SSO) solves this problem because when the user logs into the domain, the domain controller issues them an access token. This access token contains a list of all the resources including folders, drives, websites, databases, etc., to which they're permitted access. As a result, anytime the user accesses a resource, the token is verified behind the scenes, shielding users from having to provide multiple passwords!

Local Authentication

Users authenticate to either to a domain or to the local machine. When local authentication is performed the users local account and password are verified with the local user database. This local user database is called Security Accounts Manager (SAM) and it's located in c:\windows\system32\config\.

In Linux, the database is a text file, */etc/passwd* (called the password file), which lists all valid usernames and their associated information.

LDAP

Microsoft Active Directory as a common user database designed to centralize data management regarding network subjects and objects. A typical directory contains a hierarchy including users, groups, systems, servers, client workstations, and so on. Because the directory service contains data about users and other network entities, it can be used by many applications that require access to that information. A common directory service standard is Lightweight Directory Access Protocol (LDAP), which is based on the earlier standard X.500.

X.500 uses Directory Access Protocol (DAP). In X.500, the distinguished name (DN) provides the full path in the X.500 database where the entry is found. The relative distinguished name (RDN) in X.500 is an entry's name without the full path.

LDAP is simpler than X.500. LDAP supports DN and RDN, but it includes more attributes, such as the common name (CN), domain component (DC), and organizational unit (OU) attributes. Using a client/server architecture, LDAP uses TCP port 389 to communicate. If advanced security is needed, LDAP over SSL communicates via TCP port 636.

Password Alternatives

Passwords are considered the lowest form of authentication but can be effective when combined with other methods. Let's look at some of these.

Certificates

Instead of clunky usernames and passwords, we'll use certificates as a key to unlock the door.

A digital *certificate* provides an entity, usually a user, with the credentials to prove its identity and associates that identity with a public key. At minimum, a digital certification must provide the serial number, the issuer, the subject (owner), and the public key.

A certificate is a text document that ties a user account to a public and private key pair created by a certificate server or certificate authority (CA).

An X.509 certificate contains the following fields:

- Version
- Serial Number
- Algorithm ID
- Issuer
- Validity
- Subject
- Subject Public Key Info
- Public Key Algorithm
- Subject Public Key
- Issuer Unique Identifier (optional)
- Subject Unique Identifier (optional)
- Extensions (optional)

VeriSign first introduced the following digital certificate classes:
- Class 1: For individuals intended for e-mail. These certificates get saved by Web browsers.
- Class 2: For organizations that must provide proof of identity.
- Class 3: For servers and software signing in which independent verification and identity and authority checking is done by the issuing CA.

Multifactor Authentication

Multifactor authentication is designed to add an additional level of security to the authentication process by verifying more than one characteristic of a user before allowing access to a resource. Users can be identified in one of three ways:
- By something they know (password)
- By something they are (retinas, fingerprint, facial recognition)
- By something they possess (smart card)
- By somewhere they are (location)
- By something they do (behavior)

Two-factor authentication is when two of the above factors are being tested, while multifactor is when more than two of the above factors are being tested. An example of two-factor authentication would be requiring both a smart card and a PIN to log onto the network. The possession of either by itself would not be sufficient to authenticate. This protects against the loss and theft of the card as well as the loss of the password. An example of multifactor would be when three items are required, such as a smart card, PIN, and a fingerprint scan.

This process can get as involved as the security requires. In an extremely high-security situation, you might require a smart card, a password, a retina scan, and a fingerprint scan. The trade-off to all the increased security is an inconvenient authentication process for the user and the high cost of biometric authentication devices.

Biometrics

For high security scenarios that warrant the additional cost and administrative effort involved, biometrics is a viable option. Biometric devices use physical characteristics to identify the user. Such devices are becoming more common in the business environment. Biometric systems include hand scanners, retinal scanners, and soon, possibly, DNA scanners. To gain access to resources, you must pass a physical screening process. In the case of a hand scanner, this may include identifying fingerprints, scars, and markings on your hand. Retinal scanners compare your eye's retinal pattern, which are as unique as fingerprints to a stored retinal pattern to verify your identity. DNA scanners will examine a unique portion of your DNA structure to verify that you are who you say you are.

With the passing of time, the definition of *biometric* is expanding from simply identifying physical attributes about a person to being able to describe patterns in their behavior. Recent advances have been made in the ability to authenticate someone based on the key pattern they use when entering their password (how long they pause between each key, the amount of time each key is held down, and so forth). A company adopting biometric technologies needs to consider the controversy they may face (some authentication methods are considered more intrusive than others). It also needs to consider the error rate and that errors can include both false positives and false negatives.

User-Authentication Methods

There are a number of authentication systems in use today, but I'm going to focus on the ones you're likely to be confronted with in the objectives.

Public Key Infrastructure (PKI)

Public Key Infrastructure (PKI) is a system that links users to public keys and verifies a user's identity by using a *certificate authority (CA)*. Think of a CA as an online notary public—an organization that's responsible for validating user IDs and issuing unique identifiers to confirmed individuals to certify that their identity can really be trusted. Figure 13.7 shows how the CA process works in relation to two users.

FIGURE 13.7 The certificate authority process

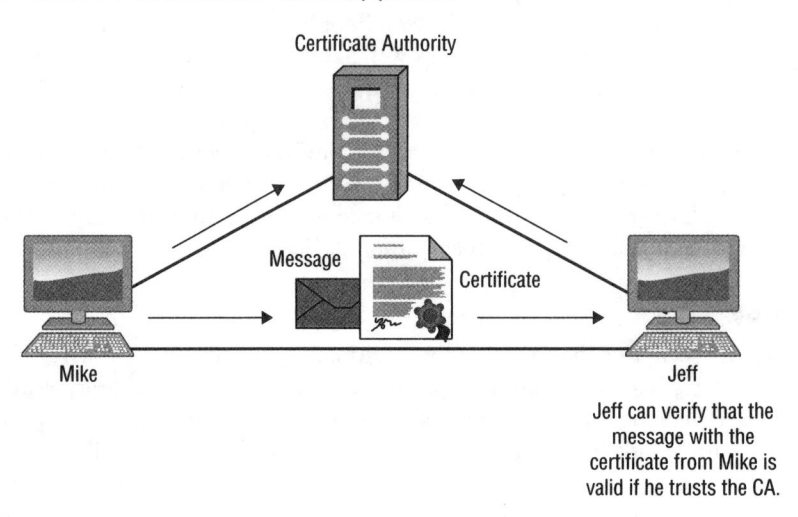

PKI allows people to communicate with each other with the confidence that they're talking to whom they think they are talking to. It's used to establish confidentiality and to ensure message integrity without knowing anything about the other party prior to the conversation. It's also used to verify the digital signature of a private key's owner.

Public-key encryption operates through asymmetric cryptography, meaning that a different key is used to encrypt and decrypt the message, respectively. Symmetric cryptography uses the same key to encrypt and decrypt, so it's a lot less secure. Here's how it works: If I sent you a message using PKI, I'd use your public key to encrypt the message. When you received the message, you would use your private key, which is theoretically the only thing that can be used to decrypt the message back into something readable by humans. If a digital signature was required, you would use a hash algorithm to generate a message digest of the message, then encrypt the hash with your private key, and anyone with access to your public key would be able to verify that only you could have encrypted the hash and then the hash can be used to verify the integrity of the message itself. So clearly, you should be the only one who has access to your private key. Figure 13.8 illustrates what I just described.

FIGURE 13.8 PKI Encryption Process in action

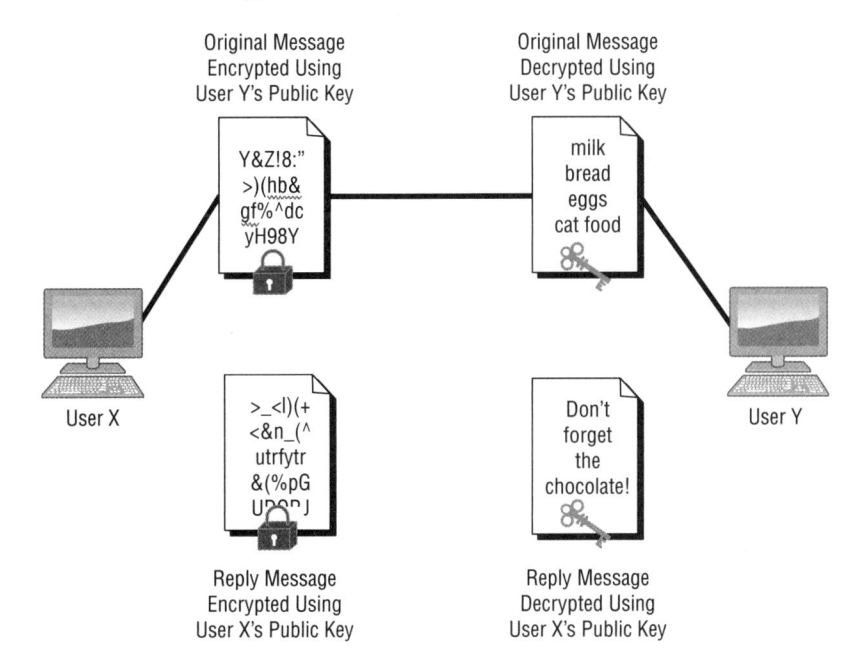

This type of authentication is often hidden in the background of websites that perform transactions. You've probably experienced shopping online and having an error message pop up notifying you that a certain site's certificate or key has expired and asking if you want to proceed with the transaction. If you do, it's time to rethink things—you're probably way too trusting. Just say no!

Kerberos

Kerberos, created at MIT, isn't just a protocol, it's an entire security system that establishes a user's identity when they first log on to a system running it. It employs strong encryption for all transactions and communication, and it's readily available. The source code for Kerberos can be freely downloaded from lots of places on the Internet.

Figure 13.9 shows the 5 steps that Kerberos users to authenticate a user.

FIGURE 13.9 The Kerberos authentication process

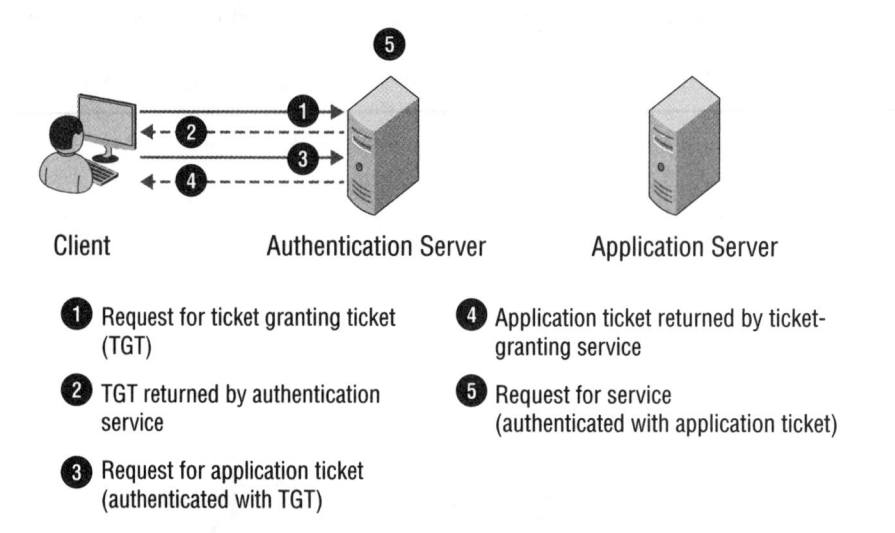

1. Request for ticket granting ticket (TGT)
2. TGT returned by authentication service
3. Request for application ticket (authenticated with TGT)
4. Application ticket returned by ticket-granting service
5. Request for service (authenticated with application ticket)

Kerberos works by issuing tickets to users who log in, kind of like going to an amusement park—as long as you have your ticket to ride, you're good to go. Even though the tickets expire quickly, they're automatically refreshed as long as you remain logged in. Because of this refresh feature, all systems participating in a Kerberos domain must have synchronized clocks. This synchronicity is a bit complicated to set up, although in Microsoft servers and Domains the process is automatic, requiring only access to a recognized time server (which Microsoft also operates). The real negative hits come if you have only one Kerberos authentication server—if it goes down, no one can log in to the network!

So when running Kerberos, having redundant servers is vital. You should also know that because all users' secret keys are stored in one centralized database, if that's compromised, you have a security tsunami on your hands. Luckily these keys are stored in an encrypted state.

Setting Passwords

There are five passwords you'll need to secure your Cisco routers: console, auxiliary, telnet (VTY), enable password, and enable secret. The enable secret and enable password are the ones used to set the password for securing privileged mode. Once the `enable` commands are set, users will be prompted for a password when entering privileged mode.

The other three are used to configure a password when user mode is accessed through the console port, through the auxiliary port, or via Telnet.

The most common form of router authentication is line authentication, also called *character-mode access*. It uses different passwords to authenticate users depending on the line the user is connecting through.

Let's start by configuring a Cisco device with the *enable* password.

Enable Passwords

You set the enable passwords from global configuration mode like this:

```
Todd(config)#enable ?
last-resort  Define enable action if no TACACS servers
             respond
password     Assign the privileged level password
secret       Assign the privileged level secret
use-tacacs   Use TACACS to check enable passwords
```

The following list describes the enable password parameters:

last-resort This allows you to still enter the device if you set up authentication through a TACACS server and it's not available. It won't be used if the TACACS server is working.

password This sets the enable password on older, pre-10.3 systems and isn't ever used if an enable secret is set.

secret The newer, encrypted password that overrides the enable password if it has been set.

use-tacacs This tells the router or switch to authenticate through a TACACS server. It comes in really handy when you have lots of routers because changing the password on a multitude of them can be insanely tedious. It's much easier to simply go through the TACACS server and change the password only once!

Here's an example that shows how to set the enable passwords:

```
Todd(config)#enable secret todd
Todd(config)#enable password todd
The enable password you have chosen is the same as your
enable secret. This is not recommended. Re-enter the
enable password.
```

If you try to set the enable secret and enable passwords the same, the device will give you a polite warning to change the second password. Make a note to yourself that if there aren't any old legacy routers involved, you don't even bother to use the enable password!

User-mode passwords are assigned via the line command like this:

```
Todd(config)#line ?
<0-16>   First Line number
console  Primary terminal line
vty      Virtual terminal
```

And these two lines are especially important for the exam objectives:

console   Sets a console user-mode password.

vty   Sets a Telnet password on the device. If this password isn't set, then by default, Telnet can't be used.

Aux   Sets a password on the Aux line, used for modem connection.

To configure user-mode passwords, choose the line you want and configure it using the `login` command to make the switch prompt for authentication. Let's focus in on the configuration of individual lines now.

Console Password

We set the console password with the `line console 0` command, but look at what happened when I tried to type **line console ?** from the (config-line)# prompt—I received an error! Here's the example:

```
Todd(config-line)#line console ?
% Unrecognized command
Todd(config-line)#exit
Todd(config)#line console ?
  <0-0>  First Line number
Todd(config)#line console 0
Todd(config-line)#password console
Todd(config-line)#login
```

You can still type **line console 0** and that will be accepted, but the help screens just don't work from that prompt. Type **exit** to go back one level, and you'll find that your help screens now work. This is a "feature." Really.

Because there's only one console port, I can only choose line console 0. You can set all your line passwords to the same password, but doing this isn't exactly a brilliant security move!

And it's also important to remember to apply the `login` command or the console port won't prompt for authentication. The way Cisco has this process set up means you can't set the `login` command before a password is set on a line because if you set it but don't then set a password, that line won't be usable. You'll actually get prompted for a password that doesn't exist, so Cisco's method isn't just a hassle; it makes sense and is a feature after all!

> **NOTE**   Definitely remember that although Cisco has this "password feature" on its routers starting with IOS 12.2 and above, it's not included in older IOSs.

Okay, there are a few other important commands you need to know regarding the console port.

For one, the `exec-timeout 0 0` command sets the time-out for the console EXEC session to zero, ensuring that it never times out. The default time-out is 10 minutes.

> **Tip:** If you're feeling mischievous, try this on people at work: Set the `exec-timeout` command to 0 1. This will make the console time out in 1 second, and to fix it, you have to continually press the down arrow key while changing the time-out time with your free hand!

Logging synchronous is such a cool command that it should be a default, but it's not. It's great because it's the antidote for those annoying console messages that disrupt the input you're trying to type. The messages will still pop up, but at least you get returned to your device prompt without your input being interrupted! This makes your input messages oh-so-much easier to read!

Here's an example of how to configure both commands:

```
Todd(config-line)#line con 0
Todd(config-line)#exec-timeout ?
  <0-35791>  Timeout in minutes
Todd(config-line)#exec-timeout 0 ?
  <0-2147483>  Timeout in seconds
  <cr>
Todd(config-line)#exec-timeout 0 0
Todd(config-line)#logging synchronous
```

> **Note:** You can set the console to go from never timing out (0 0) to timing out in 35,791 minutes and 2,147,483 seconds. Remember that the default is 10 minutes.

Telnet Password

Its hard to believe, but as I've mentioned before a lot of my customers still use telnet, even though I try hard to get them to move to SSH. Jump back to Chapter 12 real quick if you need to review the SSH configuration.

> **Note:** Most people would not use Telnet in production, or so you'd think. I see a lot of customers who still use telnet, when they should be using SSH. Why do they still use telnet? Because it's easy... Same reason I use it on my own private labs.

To set the user-mode password for Telnet access into the router or switch, use the `line vty` command. IOS switches typically have 16 lines, but routers running the Enterprise edition have considerably more. The best way to find out how many lines you have is to use that handy question mark like this:

```
Todd(config-line)#line vty 0 ?
% Unrecognized command
Todd(config-line)#exit
Todd(config)#line vty 0 ?
  <1-15>  Last Line number
  <cr>
Todd(config)#line vty 0 15
Todd(config-line)#password telnet
Todd(config-line)#login
```

This output clearly shows that you cannot get help from your (config-line)# prompt. You must go back to global config mode in order to use the question mark (?).

As a reminder, to enable SSH, use the following command under your lines:

```
Todd(config)#line vty 0 15
Todd(config-line)#transport input ssh
```

This effectively disabled telnet and enables only SSH on your device.

So what will happen if you try to telnet into a device that doesn't have a VTY password set? You'll receive an error saying the connection has been refused because the password isn't set. So, if you telnet into a switch and receive a message like this one that I got from Switch B:

```
Todd#telnet SwitchB
Trying SwitchB (10.0.0.1)...Open
Password required, but none set
[Connection to SwitchB closed by foreign host]
Todd#
```

This means the switch doesn't have the VTY password set. But you can still get around this and tell the switch to allow Telnet connections without a password by using the no login command:

```
SwitchB(config-line)#line vty 0 15
SwitchB(config-line)#no login
```

> **WARNING** I definitely do not recommend using the no login command to allow Telnet connections without a password, unless you're in a testing or classroom environment. In a production network, always set your VTY password!

After your IOS devices are configured with an IP address, you can use the Telnet program to configure and check your routers instead of having to use a console cable. You can use the Telnet program by typing telnet from any command prompt (DOS or Cisco).

Auxiliary Password

To configure the auxiliary password on a router, go into global configuration mode and type **line aux ?**. And by the way, you won't find these ports on a switch. This output shows that you only get a choice of 0–0, which is because there's only one port:

```
Todd#config t
Todd(config)#line aux ?
  <0-0>  First Line number
Todd(config)#line aux 0
Todd(config-line)#login
% Login disabled on line 1, until 'password' is set
Todd(config-line)#password aux
Todd(config-line)#login
```

Encrypting Your Passwords

Because only the enable secret password is encrypted by default, you'll need to manually configure the user-mode and enable passwords for encryption.

Notice that you can see all the passwords except the enable secret when performing a show running-config on a switch:

```
Todd#sh running-config
Building configuration...
Current configuration : 1020 bytes
!
! Last configuration change at 00:03:11 UTC Mon Mar 1 1993
!
version 15.0
no service pad
service timestamps debug datetime msec
service timestamps log datetime msec
no service password-encryption
!
hostname Todd
!
enable secret 4 ykw.3/tgsOuy9.6qmgG/EeYOYgBvfX4v.S8UNA9Rddg
enable password todd
!
[output cut]
!
line con 0
 password console
 login
line vty 0 4
```

```
password telnet
login
line vty 5 15
password telnet
login
!
end
```

To manually encrypt your passwords, use the service password-encryption command. Here's how:

```
Todd#config t
Todd(config)#service password-encryption
Todd(config)#exit
Todd#show run
Building configuration...
!
!
enable secret 4 ykw.3/tgsOuy9.6qmgG/EeYOYgBvfX4v.S8UNA9Rddg
enable password 7 1506040800
!
[output cut]
!
!
line con 0
password 7 050809013243420C
login
line vty 0 4
password 7 06120A2D424B1D
login
line vty 5 15
password 7 06120A2D424B1D
login
!
end
Todd#config t
Todd(config)#no service password-encryption
Todd(config)#^Z
Todd#
```

Nicely done—the passwords will now be encrypted. All you need to do is encrypt the passwords, perform a show run, then turn off the command if you want. This output clearly shows us that the enable password and the line passwords are all encrypted.

Before we finish this chapter, I want to stress some points about password encryption. As I said, if you set your passwords and then turn on the service password-encryption command, you have to perform a show running-config before you turn off the encryption service or your passwords won't be encrypted.

However, you don't have to turn off the encryption service at all—you'd only do that if your switch is running low on processes. And if you turn on the service before you set your passwords, then you don't even have to view them to have them encrypted.

Summary

This chapter started by covering the understanding security program elements. I then covered Authentication, Authorization, and Accounting, or AAA services, is a technology that gives us substantial control over users and what they're permitted to do inside of our networks.

In this chapter I also covered user accounts, password security and user authentication methods, and I finished this chapter by showing how to set passwords on your Cisco devices.

Exam Essentials

Know which attacks can occur because of TCP/IP's weakness. There are many attacks that can occur because of TCP/IP's inherent weaknesses. The most important to remember being spoofing, man-in-the-middle and session replaying.

Understand security program elements. The three security program elements are: User Awareness, Training & Physical Security.

Remember the security password policy elements. Password management is important and that goes without saying, but you my set strong password, have expirations, complexity, screen saver passwords, and BIOS passwords.

Practice setting Cisco passwords. On your Cisco devices, practice setting your console, telnet, AUX, and Enable secret passwords as shown in the chapter.

Understand how to mitigate threats at the access layer. You can mitigate threats at the access layer by using port security, DHCP snooping, Dynamic ARP inspection, and identity-based networking.

Understand TACACS+ and RADIUS. TACACS+ is Cisco proprietary, uses TCP, and can separate services. RADIUS is an open standard, uses UDP, and cannot separate services.

Understand PKI. *Public Key Infrastructure (PKI)* is a system that links users to public keys and verifies a user's identity by using a *certificate authority (CA)*.

Understand Kerberos. *Kerberos*, created at MIT, isn't just a protocol; it's an entire security system that establishes a user's identity when they first log on to a system that's running it.

Review Questions

The answers to these questions can be found in the Appendix.

1. Which of the following commands will enable AAA on a router?
   A. aaa enable
   B. enable aaa
   C. new-model aaa
   D. aaa new-model

2. Which of the following will mitigate access layer threats? (Choose two.)
   A. Port security
   B. Access lists
   C. Dynamic ARP inspection
   D. AAA

3. Which of the following is not true about DHCP snooping? (Choose two.)
   A. Validates DHCP messages received from untrusted sources and filters out invalid messages.
   B. Builds and maintains the DHCP snooping binding database, which contains information about trusted hosts with leased IP addresses.
   C. Rate-limits DHCP traffic from trusted and untrusted sources.
   D. DHCP snooping is a layer 2 security feature that acts like a firewall between hosts.

4. Which of the following are true about TACACS+? (Choose two.)
   A. TACACS+ is a Cisco proprietary security mechanism.
   B. TACACS+ uses UDP.
   C. TACACS+ combines authentication and authorization services as a single process—after users are authenticated, they are also authorized.
   D. TACACS+ offers multiprotocol support.

5. Which of the following is not true about RADIUS?
   A. RADIUS is an open standard protocol.
   B. RADIUS separates AAA services.
   C. RADIUS uses UDP.
   D. RADIUS encrypts only the password in the access-request packet, from the client to the server. The remainder of the packet is unencrypted.

6. You want to configure RADIUS so your network devices have external authentication, but you also need to make sure you can fallback to local authentication. Which command will you use?
   A. `aaa authentication login local group MyRadiusGroup`
   B. `aaa authentication login group MyRadiusGroup fallback local`
   C. `aaa authentication login default group MyRadiusGroup external local`
   D. `aaa authentication login default group MyRadiusGroup local`

7. Which is true about DAI?
   A. It must use TCP, BootP, and DHCP snooping in order to work.
   B. DHCP snooping is required in order to build the MAC-to-IP bindings for DAI validation.
   C. DAI is required in order to build the MAC-to-IP which protects against man in the middle attacks.
   D. DAI tracks ICMP-to-MAC bindings from DHCP.

8. The IEEE 802.1x standard allows you to implement identity-based networking on wired and wireless hosts by using client-server access control. There are three roles. Which of the following are these three roles?
   A. Client
   B. Forwarder
   C. Security Access Control
   D. Authenticator
   E. Authentication Server

9. Which of the following is *not* a password alternative?
   A. Multi-Factor Authentication (MFA)
   B. Malware lookups
   C. Biometrics
   D. Certificates

10. Security Awareness is *not* defined by which of the following?
    A. Smart card
    B. User awareness
    C. Training
    D. Physical security

11. Which of the following are examples of a TCP/IP weakness? (Choose three.)
    A. Trojan horse
    B. HTML attack
    C. Session replaying
    D. Application-layer attack
    E. SNMP
    F. SMTP

12. Which Cisco IOS feature would you use to protect TCP server from TCP SYN-flooding attacks?
    A. Rerouting
    B. TCP intercept
    C. Access control lists
    D. Encryption

13. Which of the following can be used to counter an unauthorized access attempt? (Choose three.)
    A. Encrypted data
    B. Cisco Lock and Key
    C. Access Lists
    D. PAP
    E. CHAP
    F. IKE
    G. TACACS

14. Which one of the following threats is an example of snooping and network sniffing?
    A. Repudiation
    B. Masquerade threats
    C. Eavesdropping
    D. DoS

15. In a masquerade attack, what does an attacker steal when pretending to come from a trusted host?
    A. Account identification
    B. User group
    C. IP address
    D. CHAP password

Chapter 14

First Hop Redundancy Protocol (HSRP)

THE FOLLOWING CCNA EXAM TOPIC IS COVERED IN THIS CHAPTER:

3.0 IP Connectivity

✓ 3.5 Describe the purpose of first hop redundancy protocol

You're about to learn how to build redundancy and load-balancing features into your network elegantly with routers that you might even have already. You really don't need to buy some overpriced load-balancing device when you know how to configure and use Hot Standby Router Protocol (HSRP).

I'm going to get started with telling you the reasons why we need a layer 3 redundancy protocol.

> To find your included bonus material, as well as Todd Lammle videos, practice questions & hands-on labs, please see www.lammle.com/ccna

Client Redundancy Issues

How could it be possible to configure a client to send data off its local link when its default gateway router has gone down? It usually isn't because most host operating systems just don't allow you to change data routing. Sure, if a host's default gateway router goes down, the rest of the network will still converge, but it won't share that information with the hosts!

Take a look at Figure 14.1 to see what I am talking about.

There are actually two routers available to forward data for the local subnet, but the hosts only know about one of them. They learn about this router when you provide them with the default gateway either statically or through DHCP.

But is there another way to use the second active router? The answer is a bit complicated, so bear with me. There is a feature that's enabled by default on Cisco routers called Proxy Address Resolution Protocol (Proxy ARP). Proxy ARP enables hosts, which have no knowledge of routing options, to obtain the MAC address of a gateway router that can forward packets for them.

FIGURE 14.1 Default gateway

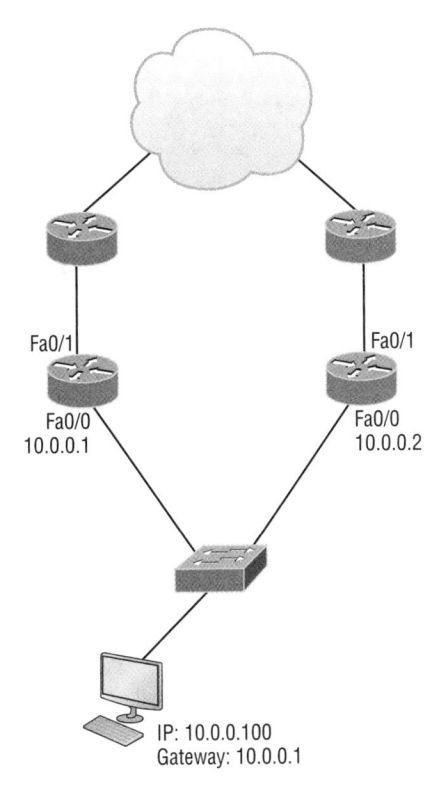

You can see how this happens in Figure 14.2. If a Proxy ARP–enabled router receives an ARP request for an IP address that it knows isn't on the same subnet as the requesting host, it will respond with an ARP reply packet to the host.

The router will give its own local MAC address—the MAC address of its interface on the host's subnet—as the destination MAC address for the IP address that the host is seeking to be resolved. After receiving the destination MAC address, the host will send all the packets to the router, not knowing that what it thinks is the destination host is really a router. The router will then forward the packets toward the intended host.

So with Proxy ARP, the host device sends traffic as if the destination device were located on its own network segment. If the router that responded to the ARP request fails, the source host continues to send packets for that destination to the same MAC address. But because they're being sent to a failed router, the packets will be sent to the other router that is also responding to ARP requests for remote hosts.

FIGURE 14.2 Proxy ARP

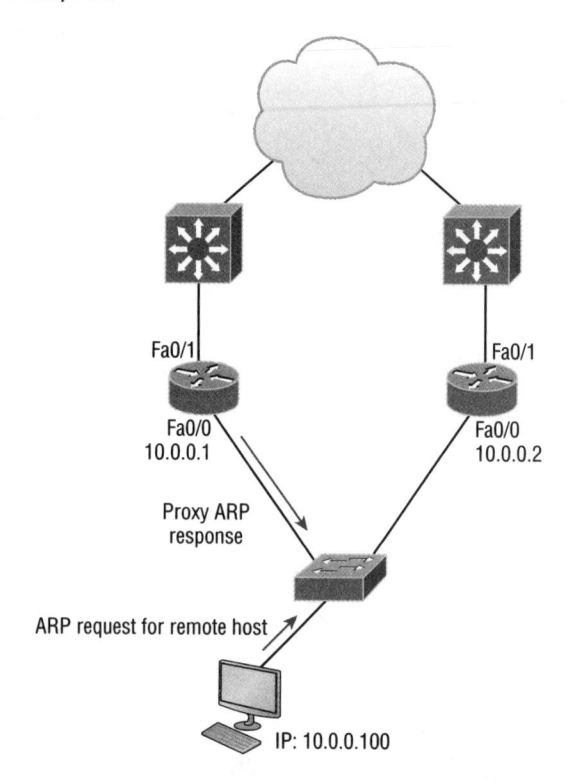

After the time-out period on the host, the proxy ARP MAC address ages out of the ARP cache. The host can then make a new ARP request for the destination and get the address of another proxy ARP router. Keep in mind that the host cannot send packets off of its subnet during the failover time. This isn't exactly ideal, so there's got to be a better way, right? There is! Our solution is found through the use of redundancy protocols.

Introducing First Hop Redundancy Protocol (FHRP)

First hop redundancy protocols (FHRPs) work by giving you a way to configure more than one physical router to appear as if they were only a single logical one. This makes client configuration and communication easier because you can simply configure a single default gateway and the host machine can use its standard protocols to communicate. *First hop* is a reference to the default router being the first router, or first router hop, that a packet will pass through.

So how does a redundancy protocol get this done? Basically by presenting a virtual router to all of the clients. The virtual router has its own IP and MAC addresses. The virtual IP address is the address that's configured on each of the host machines as the default gateway. The virtual MAC address is the address that will be returned when an ARP request is sent by a host. The hosts don't know or care which physical router is actually forwarding the traffic, as you can see in Figure 14.3.

FIGURE 14.3 FHRPs use a virtual router with a virtual IP address and virtual MAC address.

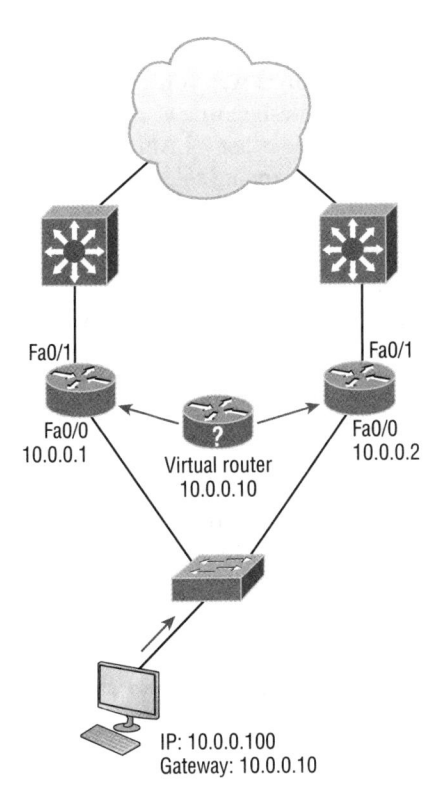

It's the responsibility of the redundancy protocol to decide which physical router will actively forward traffic and which one will be placed on standby in case the active router fails. Even if the active router fails, the transition to the standby router will be transparent to the hosts because the virtual router that's identified by the virtual IP and MAC addresses is now used by the standby router. The hosts never change default gateway information, so traffic keeps flowing.

> **NOTE** Fault-tolerant solutions ensure continued operation in the event of a device failure, and load-balancing solutions distribute the workload over multiple devices.

There are three important redundancy protocols, but only one is covered on the CCNA objectives now:

Hot Standby Router Protocol (HSRP)   HSRP has got to be Cisco's favorite protocol ever! Don't buy just one router; buy up to eight routers to provide the same service, and keep seven as backup in case of failure! HSRP is a Cisco proprietary protocol that provides a redundant gateway for hosts on a local subnet. The drawback here is that this isn't a load-balanced solution. HSRP allows you to configure two or more routers into a standby group that shares an IP and MAC address and provides a default gateway. When the IP and MAC addresses are independent from the routers' physical addresses—on a virtual interface and not tied to a specific interface—they can swap control of an address if the current active forwarding router fails. There is actually a way you can sort of achieve load balancing with HSRP. By using multiple VLANs and designating a specific router active for one VLAN, then an alternate router as active for the other VLAN via trunking. This is really just rigging things and still isn't a true load-balancing solution. It's not nearly as solid as what you can achieve using Gateway Load Balancing Protocol!

Virtual Router Redundancy Protocol (VRRP)   Also provides a redundant gateway for hosts on a local subnet, but again, not a load-balanced one. It's an open standard protocol that functions almost identically to HSRP. We'll sift through the fine differences that exist between these protocols later in the chapter.

Gateway Load Balancing Protocol (GLBP)   For the life of me I can't figure out how GLBP isn't a CCNA objective anymore! GLBP doesn't stop at providing us with a redundant gateway, it's a true load-balancing solution for routers. GLBP allows a maximum of four routers in each forwarding group. By default, the active router directs the traffic from hosts to each successive router in the group using a round-robin algorithm. The hosts are directed to send their traffic toward a specific router by being given the MAC address of the next router in line for deployment.

Hot Standby Router Protocol (HSRP)

So again, HSRP is a Cisco proprietary protocol that can be run on most, but not all Cisco's router and multilayer switch models. It defines a standby group, and each standby group that you define includes the following routers:

- Active router
- Standby router
- Virtual router
- Any other routers that maybe attached to the subnet

The problem with HSRP is that with it, only one router is active and two or more routers just sit there in standby mode and won't be used unless a failure occurs—not very cost effective or efficient! Figure 14.4 shows how only one router is used at a time in an HSRP group.

FIGURE 14.4 HSRP active and standby routers

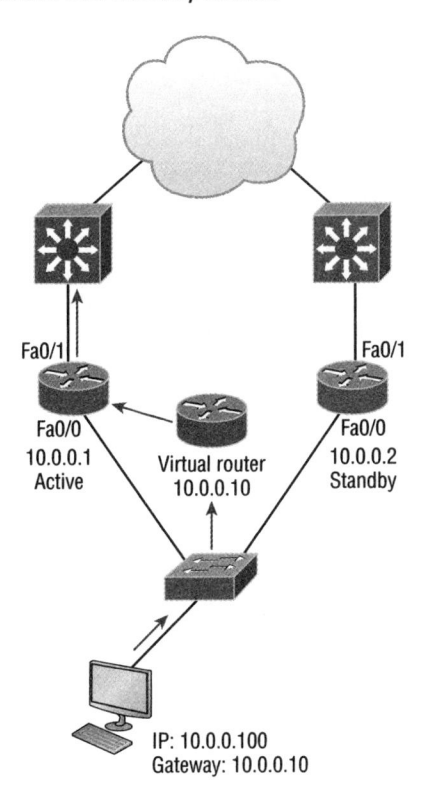

The standby group will always have at least two routers participating in it. The primary players in the group are the one active router and one standby router that communicate to each other using multicast Hello messages. The Hello messages provide all of the required communication for the routers. They contain the information required to accomplish the election, which determines the active and standby router positions. They also hold the key to the failover process. If the standby router stops receiving Hello packets from the active router, it then takes over the active router role, as shown in Figure 14.5.

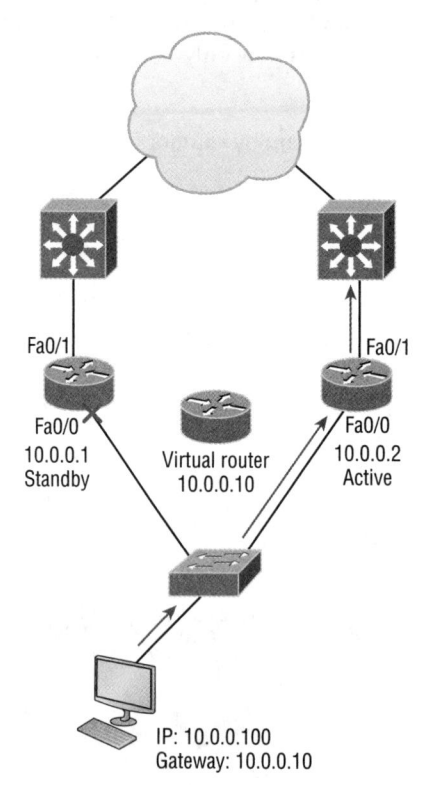

FIGURE 14.5 Example of HSRP active and standby routers swapping interfaces

As soon as the active router stops responding to Hellos, the standby router automatically becomes the active router and starts responding to host requests.

Virtual MAC Address

A virtual router in an HSRP group has a virtual IP address and a virtual MAC address. So where does that virtual MAC come from? The virtual IP address isn't that hard to figure out; it just has to be a unique IP address on the same subnet as the hosts defined in the configuration. But MAC addresses are a little different, right? Or are they? The answer is yes—sort of. With HSRP, you create a totally new, made-up MAC address in addition to the IP address.

The HSRP MAC address has only one variable piece in it. The first 24 bits still identify the vendor who manufactured the device (the organizationally unique identifier, or OUI). The next 16 bits in the address tell us that the MAC address is a well-known HSRP MAC address. Finally, the last 8 bits of the address are the hexadecimal representation of the HSRP group number.

Let me clarify all this with a picture of what an HSRP MAC address would look like:

0000.0c07.ac0a

- The first 24 bits (0000.0c) are the vendor ID of the address; in the case of HSRP being a Cisco protocol, the ID is assigned to Cisco.
- The next 16 bits (07.ac) are the well-known HSRP ID. This part of the address was assigned by Cisco in the protocol, so it's always easy to recognize that this address is for use with HSRP.
- The last 8 bits (0a) are the only variable bits and represent the HSRP group number that you assign. In this case, the group number is 10 and converted to hexadecimal when placed in the MAC address, where it becomes the 0a that you see.

You can see this displayed with every MAC address added to the ARP cache of every router in the HSRP group. There will be the translation from the IP address to the MAC address, as well as the interface it's located on.

HSRP Timers

Before we get deeper into the roles that each of the routers can have in an HSRP group, I want to define the HSRP timers. The timers are very important to HSRP function because they ensure communication between the routers, and if something goes wrong, they allow the standby router to take over. The HSRP timers include *hello*, *hold*, *active*, and *standby*.

Hello timer The hello timer is the defined interval during which each of the routers send out Hello messages. Their default interval is 3 seconds, and they identify the state that each router is in. This is important because the particular state determines the specific role of each router and, as a result, the actions each will take within the group. Figure 14.6 shows the Hello messages being sent and the router using the hello timer to keep the network flowing in case of a failure.

This timer can be changed, but people used to avoid doing so because it was thought that lowering the hello value would place an unnecessary load on the routers. That isn't true with most of the routers today; in fact, you can configure the timers in milliseconds, meaning the failover time can be in milliseconds! Keep in mind that increasing the value will make the standby router wait longer before taking over for the active router when it fails or can't communicate.

Hold timer The hold timer specifies the interval the standby router uses to determine whether the active router is offline or out of communication. By default, the hold timer is 10 seconds, roughly three times the default for the hello timer. If one timer is changed for some reason, I recommend using this multiplier to adjust the other timers too. By setting the hold timer at three times the hello timer, you ensure that the standby router doesn't take over the active role every time there's a short break in communication.

FIGURE 14.6 HSRP Hellos

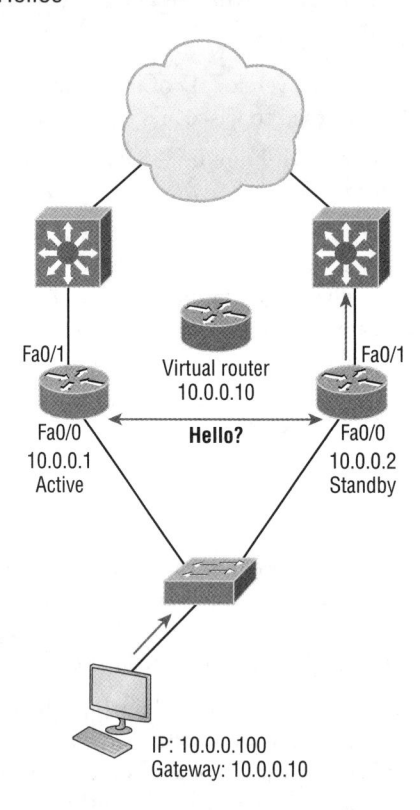

Active timer   The active timer monitors the state of the active router. The timer resets each time a router in the standby group receives a Hello packet from the active router. This timer expires based on the hold time value that's set in the corresponding field of the HSRP hello message.

Standby timer   The standby timer is used to monitor the state of the standby router. The timer resets anytime a router in the standby group receives a Hello packet from the standby router and expires based on the hold time value that's set in the respective Hello packet.

Real World Scenario

Large Enterprise Network Outages with FHRPs

Years ago when HSRP was all the rage, and before VRRP and GLBP, enterprises used hundreds of HSRP groups. With the hello timer set to 3 seconds and a hold time of 10 seconds, these timers worked just fine and we had great redundancy with our core routers.

Hot Standby Router Protocol (HSRP)

> But now, and certainly in the future, 10 seconds is a lifetime! Some of my customers have started complaining about the failover time and loss of connectivity to their virtual server farm.
>
> So lately I've been changing the timers to well below the defaults. Cisco changed the timers so you could use sub-second times for failover. Because these are multicast packets, the overhead seen on a current high-speed network is almost nothing.
>
> The hello timer is typically set to 200 msec and the hold time is 700 msec. The command is as follows:
>
> (config-if)#**Standby 1 timers msec 200 msec 700**
>
> This almost ensures that not even a single packet is lost when there's an outage!

Group Roles

Each of the routers in the standby group has a specific function and role to fulfill. The three main roles are as virtual router, active router, and standby router. Additional routers can also be included in the group.

Virtual router As its name implies, the virtual router is not a physical entity. It really just defines the role that's held by one of the physical routers. The physical router that communicates as the virtual router is the current active router. The virtual router is nothing more than a separate IP address and MAC address that packets are sent to.

Active router The active router is the physical router that receives data sent to the virtual router address and routes it onward to its various destinations. As I mentioned, this router accepts all the data sent to the MAC address of the virtual router in addition to the data that's been sent to its own physical MAC address. The active router processes the data that's being forwarded and will also answer any ARP requests destined for the virtual router's IP address.

Standby router The standby router is the backup to the active router. Its job is to monitor the status of the HSRP group and quickly take over packet-forwarding responsibilities if the active router fails or loses communication. Both the active and standby routers transmit Hello messages to inform all other routers in the group of their role and status.

Other routers An HSRP group can include additional routers (up to 255 per group), which are members of the group but that don't take the primary roles of either active or standby states. These routers monitor the Hello messages sent by the active and standby routers to ensure that an active and standby router exists for the HSRP group that they belong to. They will forward data that's specifically addressed to their own IP addresses, but they will never forward data addressed to the virtual router unless elected to the active or standby state. These routers send "speak" messages based on the hello timer interval that informs other routers of their position in an election.

Interface Tracking

By now, you probably understand why having a virtual router on a LAN is a great idea. It's a very good thing that the active router can change dynamically, giving us much needed redundancy on our inside network. But what about the links to the upstream network or the Internet connection off of those HSRP-enabled routers? And how will the inside hosts know if an outside interface goes down or if they are sending packets to an active router that can't route to a remote network? Key questions and HSRP do provide a solution for them called interface tracking.

Figure 14.7 shows how HSRP-enabled routers can keep track of the interface status of the outside interfaces and how they can switch the inside active router as needed to keep the inside hosts from losing connectivity upstream.

FIGURE 14.7 Interface tracking setup

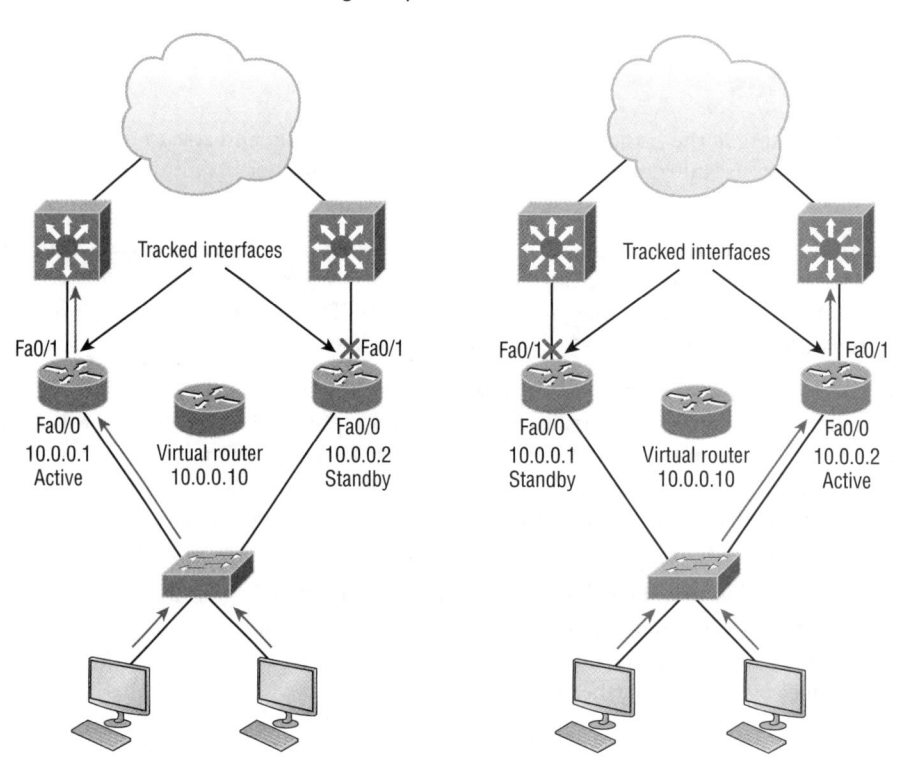

If the outside link of the active router goes down, the standby router will take over and become the active router. There is a default priority of 100 on routers configured with an HSRP interface, and if you raise this priority, which we'll do in a bit, it means your router has a higher priority to become the active router. The reason I'm bringing this up now is because when a tracked interface goes down, it decrements the priority of this router.

Configuring and Verifying HSRP

Configuring and verifying the different FHRPs can be pretty simple, especially regarding the Cisco objectives, but as with most technologies, you can quickly get into advanced configurations and territory with the different FHRPs.

The Cisco objectives don't cover much about the configuration of FHRPs, but verification and troubleshooting is important, so I'll use a simple configuration on two routers here. Figure 14.8 shows the network I'll use to demonstrate HSRP.

FIGURE 14.8 HSRP configuration and verification

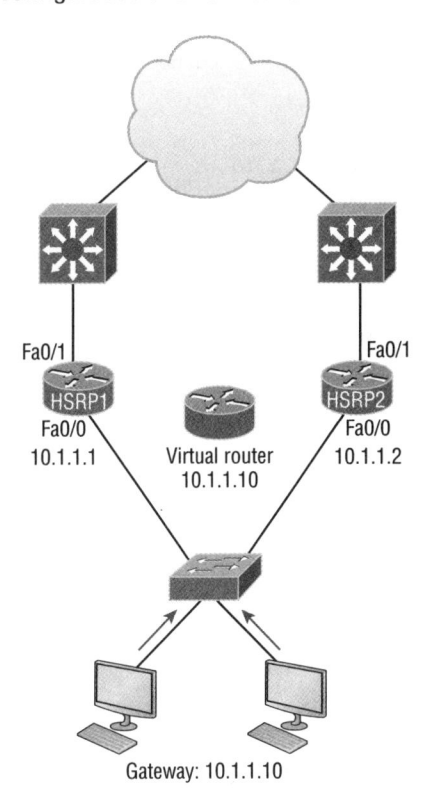

This is a simple configuration that you really need only one command for: standby *group ip virtual_ip*. After using this single mandatory command, I'll name the group and set the interface on router HSRP1 so it wins the election and becomes the active router by default.

```
HSRP1#config t
HSRP1(config)#int fa0/0
HSRP1(config-if)#standby ?
  <0-255>          group number
  authentication   Authentication
```

```
  delay           HSRP initialisation delay
  ip              Enable HSRP and set the virtual IP address
  mac-address     Virtual MAC address
  name            Redundancy name string
  preempt         Overthrow lower priority Active routers
  priority        Priority level
  redirect        Configure sending of ICMP Redirect messages with an HSRP
                  virtual IP address as the gateway IP address
  timers          Hello and hold timers
  track           Priority tracking
  use-bia         HSRP uses interface's burned in address
  version         HSRP version
```

```
HSRP1(config-if)#standby 1 ip 10.1.1.10
HSRP1(config-if)#standby 1 name HSRP_Test
HSRP1(config-if)#standby 1 priority ?
  <0-255>  Priority value

HSRP1(config-if)#standby 1 priority 110
000047: %HSRP-5-STATECHANGE: FastEthernet0/0 Grp 1 state Speak -> Standby
000048: %HSRP-5-STATECHANGE: FastEthernet0/0 Grp 1 state Standby -> Active110
```

There are quite a few commands available to use in an advanced setting with the standby command, but we'll stick with the simple commands that follow the Cisco objectives. First, I numbered the group (1), which must be the same on all routers sharing HSRP duties; then I added the virtual IP address shared by all routers in the HSRP group. Optionally, I named the group and then set the priority of HSRP1 to 110, and I left HSRP2 to a default of 100. The router with the highest priority will win the election to become the active router. Let's configure the HSRP2 router now:

```
HSRP2#config t
HSRP2(config)#int fa0/0
HSRP2(config-if)#standby 1 ip 10.1.1.10
HSRP2(config-if)#standby 1 name HSRP_Test
*Jun 23 21:40:10.699:%HSRP-5-STATECHANGE:FastEthernet0/0 Grp 1 state
Speak -> Standby
```

I really only needed the first command—naming it was for administrative purposes only. Notice that the link came up and HSRP2 became the standby router because it had the lower priority of 100 (the default). Make a note that this priority comes into play only if both routers were to come up at the same time. This means that HSRP2 would be the active router, regardless of priority, if it comes up first.

Preemption

According to the dictionary, *preempt* means "to replace with something considered to be of greater value or priority."

Using preemption, one router can take over another router only during an election, and preemption is the only way to force an election when a device hasn't gone down.

By using the command standby 1 preempt, you can have a particular device always be the active (forwarding) device. Since I want router 1 to always be the forwarding router if possible, our configuration of router 1 would now look like this:

```
HSRP1(config-if)#standby 1 ip 10.1.1.10
HSRP1(config-if)#standby 1 name HSRP_Test
HSRP1(config-if)#standby 1 priority 110
HSRP1(config-if)#standby 1 prempt
```

HSRP Verification

Let's take a look at the configurations with the show standby and show standby brief commands:

```
HSRP1(config-if)#do show standby
FastEthernet0/0 - Group 1
  State is Active
    2 state changes, last state change 00:03:40
  Virtual IP address is 10.1.1.10
  Active virtual MAC address is 0000.0c07.ac01
    Local virtual MAC address is 0000.0c07.ac01 (v1 default)
  Hello time 3 sec, hold time 10 sec
    Next hello sent in 1.076 secs
  Preemption disabled
  Active router is local
  Standby router is 10.1.1.2, priority 100 (expires in 7.448 sec)
  Priority 110 (configured 110)
  IP redundancy name is "HSRP_Test" (cfgd)

HSRP1(config-if)#do show standby brief
                     P indicates configured to preempt.
                     |
Interface   Grp Prio P State    Active          Standby         Virtual IP
Fa0/0       1   110    Active   local           10.1.1.2        10.1.1.10
```

Notice the group number in each output—it's a key troubleshooting spot! Each router must be configured in the same group or they won't work. Also, you can see the virtual MAC and configured virtual IP address, as well as the hello time of 3 seconds. The standby and virtual IP addresses are also displayed.

HSRP2's output tells us that it's in standby mode:

```
HSRP2(config-if)#do show standby brief
                     P indicates configured to preempt.
                     |
Interface   Grp Prio P State    Active      Standby      Virtual IP
Fa0/0       1   100    Standby  10.1.1.1    local        10.1.1.10
HRSP2(config-if)#
```

Also notice that so far that you've seen HSRP states of Active and Standby, but watch what happens when I disable Fa0/0:

```
HSRP1#config t
HSRP1(config)#interface Fa0/0
HSRP1(config-if)#shutdown
*Nov 20 10:06:52.369: %HSRP-5-STATECHANGE: Ethernet0/0 Grp 1 state Active -> Init
```

The HSRP State went into Init state, meaning it's trying to initialize with a peer. The possible interface states for HSRP are shown in Table 14.1.

TABLE 14.1 HSRP States

State	Definition
Initial (INIT)	This is the state at the start. This state indicates that HSRP does not run. This state is entered through a configuration change or when an interface first becomes available.
Learn	The router has not determined the virtual IP address and has not yet seen an authenticated hello message from the active router. In this state, the router still waits to hear from the active router.
Listen	The router knows the virtual IP address, but the router is neither the active router nor the standby router. It listens for hello messages from those routers.
Speak	The router sends periodic hello messages and actively participates in the election of the active and/or standby router. A router can't enter the speak state unless the router has the virtual IP address.
Standby	The router is a candidate to become the next active router and sends periodic hello messages. With the exclusion of transient conditions, there is, at most, one router in the group in standby state.
Active	The router currently forwards packets that are sent to the group virtual MAC address. The router sends periodic hello messages. With the exclusion of transient conditions, there must be, at most, one router in active state in the group.

There's one other command that I want to cover. If you really want to understand HSRP, learn to use this debug command and have your active and standby routers move. You'll really get to see what's going on!

```
HSRP2#debug standby
*Sep 15 00:07:32.344:HSRP:Fa0/0 Interface UP
*Sep 15 00:07:32.344:HSRP:Fa0/0 Initialize swsb, Intf state Up
*Sep 15 00:07:32.344:HSRP:Fa0/0 Starting minimum intf delay (1 secs)
*Sep 15 00:07:32.344:HSRP:Fa0/0 Grp 1 Set virtual MAC 0000.0c07.ac01
type: v1 default
*Sep 15 00:07:32.344:HSRP:Fa0/0 MAC hash entry 0000.0c07.ac01, Added
Fa0/0 Grp 1 to list
*Sep 15 00:07:32.348:HSRP:Fa0/0 Added 10.1.1.10 to hash table
*Sep 15 00:07:32.348:HSRP:Fa0/0 Grp 1 Has mac changed? cur 0000.0c07.ac01
new 0000.0c07.ac01
*Sep 15 00:07:32.348:HSRP:Fa0/0 Grp 1 Disabled -> Init
*Sep 15 00:07:32.348:HSRP:Fa0/0 Grp 1 Redundancy "hsrp-Fa0/0-1" state Disabled -> Init
*Sep 15 00:07:32.348:HSRP:Fa0/0 IP Redundancy "hsrp-Fa0/0-1" added
*Sep 15 00:07:32.348:HSRP:Fa0/0 IP Redundancy "hsrp-Fa0/0-1" update,
Disabled -> Init
*Sep 15 00:07:33.352:HSRP:Fa0/0 Intf min delay expired
*Sep 15 00:07:39.936:HSRP:Fa0/0 Grp 1 MAC addr update Delete from SMF  0000.0c07.ac01
*Sep 15 00:07:39.936:HSRP:Fa0/0 Grp 1 MAC addr update Delete from SMF  0000.0c07.ac01
*Sep 15 00:07:39.940:HSRP:Fa0/0 ARP reload
```

HSRP Load Balancing

As you know, HSRP doesn't really perform true load balancing, but it can be configured to use more than one router at a time for use with different VLANs. This is different from the true load balancing that's possible with GLBP, but HSRP still performs a load-balancing act of sorts. Figure 14.9 shows how load balancing would look with HSRP.

How can you get two HSRP routers active at the same time? Well for the same subnet with this simple configuration you can't, but by trunking the links to each router, they'll run and be configured with a "router on a stick" (ROAS) configuration. This means that each router can be the default gateway for different VLANs, but you still only have one active router per VLAN.

In a more advanced setting you usually wouldn't go with HSRP for load balancing. Instead, opt for GLBP. But you can do load-sharing with HSRP, which is the topic of an objective, so you'll remember that, right? It comes in handy because it prevents situations where a single point of failure causes traffic interruptions. This HSRP feature improves network resilience by allowing for load-balancing and redundancy capabilities between subnets and VLANs.

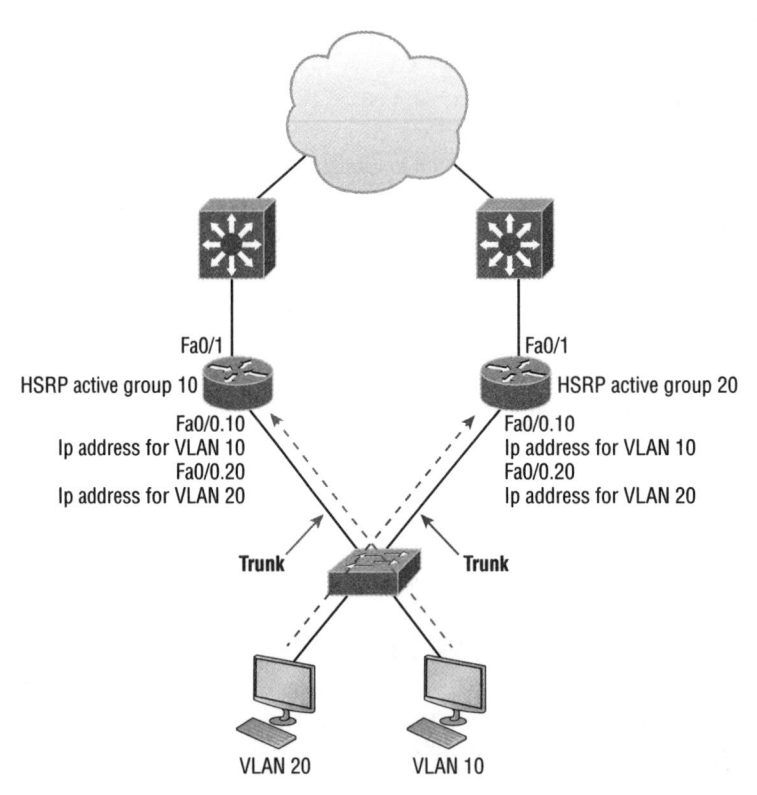

FIGURE 14.9 HSRP load balancing per VLAN

HSRP Troubleshooting

Besides the HSRP verification, troubleshooting HSRP is the Cisco objective hotspot, so let's explore that now.

Most of your HSRP misconfiguration issues can be solved by checking the output of the show standby command. In the output, you can see the active IP and the MAC address, the timers, the active router, and more, as shown in the verification section above.

There are several possible misconfigurations of HSRP, but the following ones are the focus for your CCNA:

Different HSRP virtual IP addresses configured on the peers   Console messages will notify you about this of course, but if you configure it this way and the active router fails, the standby router takes over with a virtual IP address. This is different to the one used previously, and different to the one configured as the default-gateway address for end devices, so your hosts stop working, defeating the purpose of a FHRP.

Different HSRP groups are configured on the peers   This misconfiguration leads to both peers becoming active, and you'll start receiving duplicate IP address warnings. This seems easy to troubleshoot, but the next issue results in the same warnings.

Different HSRP versions are configured on the peers or ports blocked   HSRP comes in 2 versions, 1 and 2. If there's a version mismatch, both routers will become active and you'll get duplicate IP address warnings again.

In version 1, HSRP messages are sent to the multicast IP address 224.0.0.2 and UDP port 1985. HSRP version 2 uses and the multicast IP address 224.0.0.102 and UDP port 1985. These IP addresses and ports need to be permitted in the inbound access lists. If the packets are blocked, the peers won't see each other, meaning there will be no HSRP redundancy.

Summary

We began this chapter with a talk about how to mitigate security threats at the access layer and also discussed external authentication for our network devices for ease of management.

I showed you how to integrate redundancy and load-balancing features into your network with existing routers you probably already have. We explored the Cisco proprietary HSRP as well as GLBP and you learned how to configure and use Hot Standby Router Protocol (HSRP).

Exam Essentials

Understand FHRP's, especially HSRP.   The FHRPs are HSRP, VRRP and GLBP, with HSRP and GLBP being Cisco proprietary.

Remember the HSRP Virtual address   The HSRP MAC address has only one variable piece in it. The first 24 bits still identify the vendor who manufactured the device (the organizationally unique identifier, or OUI). The next 16 bits in the address tell us that the MAC address is a well-known HSRP MAC address. Finally, the last 8 bits of the address are the hexadecimal representation of the HSRP group number.

An example of what an HSRP MAC address would look like:

```
0000.0c07.ac0a
```

Review Questions

The answers to these questions can be found in the Appendix.

1. What is the default priority setting on an HSRP router?
   A. 25
   B. 50
   C. 100
   D. 125

2. What is a true regarding any type of FHRP? (Choose two.)
   A. The FHRP supplies hosts with routing information.
   B. The FHRP is a routing protocol.
   C. The FHRP provides default gateway redundancy.
   D. The FHRP is only standards-based.

3. Which of the following are an HSRP state? (Choose two.)
   A. INIT
   B. ACTIVE
   C. ESTABLISHED
   D. IDLE

4. Which command configures an interface to enable HSRP with the virtual router IP address 10.1.1.10?
   A. `standby 1 ip 10.1.1.10`
   B. `ip hsrp 1 standby 10.1.1.10`
   C. `hsrp 1 ip 10.1.1.10`
   D. `standby 1 hsrp ip 10.1.1.10`

5. Which command displays the status of all HSRP groups on a Cisco router or layer 3 switch?
   A. `show ip hsrp`
   B. `show hsrp`
   C. `show standby hsrp`
   D. `show standby`
   E. `show hsrp groups`

6. Two routers are part of an HSRP standby group and there's no priority configured on the routers for the HSRP group. Which of the following statements is correct?
   A. Both router will be in the active state.
   B. Both routers will be in the standby state.
   C. Both routers will be in the listen state.
   D. One router will be active the other standby.

7. Which of the following statements is true about the HSRP version 1 hello packet?
   A. HSRP hello packets are sent to multicast address 224.0.0.5.
   B. HSRP RP hello packets are sent to multicast address 224.0.0.2 with TCP port 1985.
   C. HSRP hello packets are sent to multicast address 224.0.0.2 with UDP port 1985.
   D. HSRP hello packets are sent to multicast address 224.0.0.10 with UDP port 1986.

8. Routers HSRP1 and HSRP2 are in HSRP group 1. HSRP1 is the active router with a priority of 120 and HSRP2 has the default priority. When HSRP1 reboots, HSRP2 will become the active router. Once HSRP1 comes back up, which of the following statements will be true? (Choose two.)
   A. HSRP1 will become the active router.
   B. HSRP2 will stay the active router.
   C. HSRP1 will become the active router if it is also configured to preempt.
   D. Both routers will go into Speak state.

9. What's the multicast and port number used for HSRP version 2?
   A. 224.0.0.2, UDP port 1985
   B. 224.0.0.2. TCP port 1985
   C. 224.0.0.102, UDP port 1985
   D. 224.0.0.102, TCP port 1985

Chapter 15

Virtual Private Networks (VPNs)

THE FOLLOWING CCNA EXAM TOPIC IS COVERED IN THIS CHAPTER:

5.0 Security Fundamentals

✓ 5.5 Describe remote access and site-to-site VPNs

We're going to cover VPNs in depth in this chapter. You'll learn some smart solutions that will help you meet your company's off-site network access needs. We'll dive deep into how these networks utilize IP security to provide secure communications over a public network via the Internet using VPN's with IPSec

I'll wrap up the chapter by demonstrating how to create a tunnel using GRE (Generic Routing Encapsulation).

> To find your included bonus material, as well as Todd Lammle videos, practice questions & hands-on labs, please see www.lammle.com/ccna

Virtual Private Networks

Of course, you've heard the term *VPN* before and you probably have a pretty good idea of what one is, but just in case: A *virtual private network (VPN)* allows the creation of private networks across the Internet, providing privacy and the tunneling of IP and non-TCP/IP protocols. VPNs are used daily to give remote users and disparate networks connectivity over a public medium like the Internet instead of using more expensive, permanent means.

VPNs are actually pretty easy to understand. A VPN fits somewhere between a LAN and WAN, with the WAN often simulating a LAN link. Basically, your computer on one LAN connects to a different, remote LAN and uses its resources remotely. The challenge when using VPNs is a big one—security! This may sound a lot like connecting a LAN (or VLAN) to a WAN, but a VPN is so much more.

Here's the key difference: A typical WAN connects two or more remote LANs together using a router and someone else's network, like your Internet service provider's (ISP's). Your local host and router see these networks as remote not local networks or local resources.

A VPN actually makes your local host part of the remote network by using the WAN link that connects you to the remote LAN. The VPN will make your host appear as though it's actually local on the remote network. This means we gain access to the remote LAN's resources, and that access is also very secure.

And this may also sound a lot like a VLAN definition because the concept is the same: "Take my host and make it appear local to the remote network's resources." Just remember this key distinction: For networks that are physically local, using VLANs is a good solution, but for physically remote networks that span a WAN you need to use VPNs instead.

Here's a simple VPN example using my home office in Colorado. Here, I have my personal host, but I want it to appear as if it's on a LAN in my corporate office in Texas, so I can get to my remote servers. I'm going to go with VPN to achieve my goal.

Figure 15.1 pictures my host using a VPN connection from Colorado to Texas. This allows me to access the remote network services and servers as if my host were right there on the same VLAN.

FIGURE 15.1 Example of using a VPN

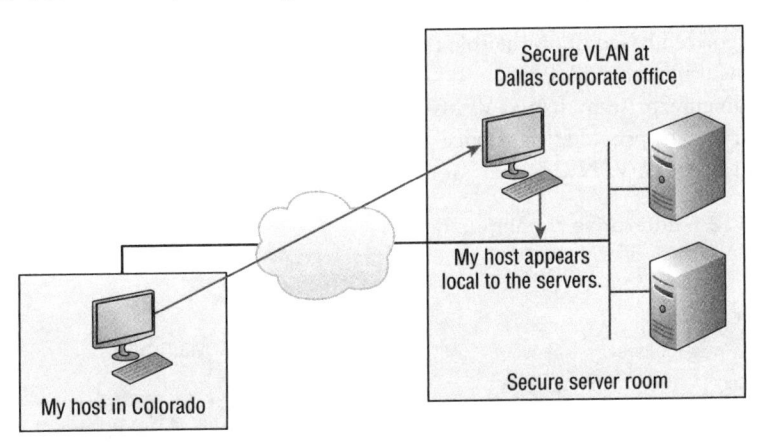

Why is this so important? If you answered, "Because my servers in Texas are secure, and only the hosts on the same VLAN are allowed to connect to them and use the resources of these servers," you nailed it! A VPN allows me to connect to these resources by locally attaching to the VLAN through a VPN across the WAN. My other option is to open up my network and servers to everyone on the Internet so clearly, it's vital for me to have a VPN!

Benefits of VPNs

There are many benefits to using VPNs on your corporate and even home network. The ones covered in the CCNA R/S objectives are:

Security VPNs provide security using advanced encryption and authentication protocols, which help protect your network from unauthorized access. IPsec and SSL fall into this category. Secure Sockets Layer (SSL) is an encryption technology used with web browsers and has native SSL encryption known as Web VPN. You can also use the Cisco AnyConnect SSL VPN client installed on your PC to provide an SSL VPN solution, as well as the Clientless Cisco SSL VPN.

Cost Savings By connecting the corporate remote offices to their closest Internet provider and creating a VPN tunnel with encryption and authentication, I gain a huge savings over opting for traditional leased point-to-point lines. This also permits higher bandwidth links and security, all for far less money than traditional connections.

Scalability VPNs scale very well to quickly bring up new offices or have mobile users connect securely.

Compatibility with broadband technology For remote and traveling users and remote offices, any Internet access can provide a connection to the corporate VPN. This allows users to take advantage of the high-speed Internet access DSL or cable modems offer.

Enterprise- and Provider-Managed VPNs

VPNs are categorized based upon the role they play in a business, such as enterprise-managed VPNs and provider-managed VPNs.

You'll use an enterprise-managed VPNs if your company manages its own VPNs. This is a very popular way to provide this service and it's pictured in Figure 15.2. The ASA in the Main Site is used as the VPN Concentrator.

FIGURE 15.2 Enterprise-managed VPNs

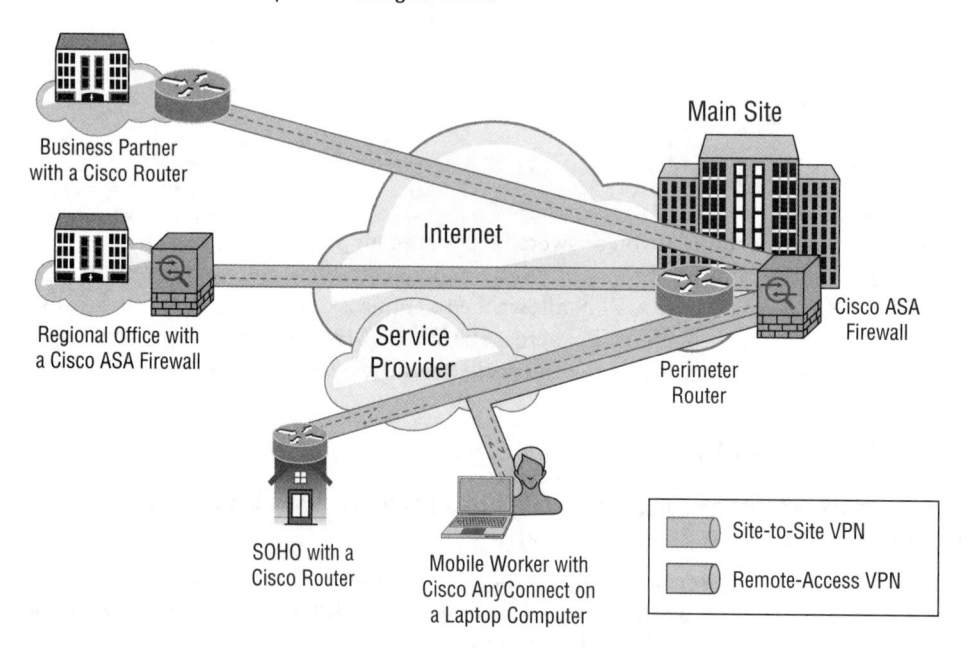

There are three different categories of enterprise-managed VPNs:

Remote access VPNs allow remote users like telecommuters to securely access the corporate network wherever and whenever they need to.

Site-to-site VPNs, or intranet VPNs, allow a company to connect its remote sites to the corporate backbone securely over a public medium like the Internet instead of requiring more expensive WAN connections like Frame Relay.

Extranet VPNs allow an organization's suppliers, partners, and customers to be connected to the corporate network in a limited way for business-to-business (B2B) communications.

Provider-managed VPNs are illustrated in Figure 15.3.

FIGURE 15.3 Provider-managed VPNs

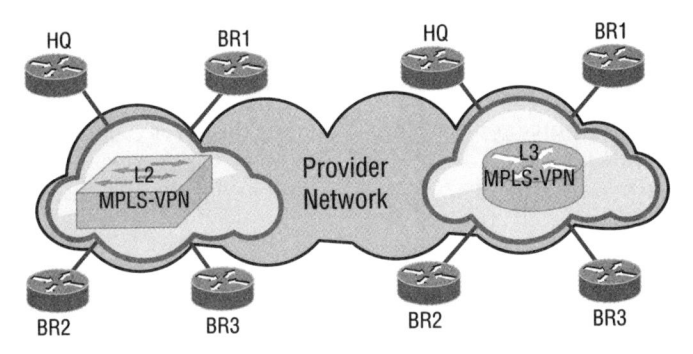

Layer 2 MPLS VPN (VPLS and VPWS):
- Customer routers exchange routes directly.
- Some applications need Layer 2 connectivity to work.

Layer 3 MPLS VPN:
- Customer routers exchange routes with SP routers.
- It provides Layer 3 service across the backbone.

There are two different categories of provider-managed VPNs:

Layer 2 MPLS VPN, Layer 2 VPNs are a type of virtual private network (VPN) that uses MPLS labels to transport data. The communication occurs between routers known as *Provider Edge* routers (PEs) because they sit on the edge of the provider's network, next to the customer's network.

ISPs that have an existing layer 2 network may choose to use these VPNs instead of the other common layer 3 MPLS VPNs.

The two typical technologies of Layer 2 MPLS VPN are:

Virtual private wire service (VPWS) VPWS is the simplest form for enabling Ethernet services over MPLS. It's also known as ETHoMPLS (Ethernet over MPLS), or VLL (Virtual Leased Line). VPWS is characterized by a fixed relationship between an attachment-virtual circuit and an emulated virtual circuit. For example, VPWS-based services are point-to-point Frame-Relay/ATM/Ethernet services over IP/MPLS.

Virtual private LAN switching service (VPLS) This is an end-to-end service and is virtual because multiple instances of this service share the same Ethernet broadcast domain virtually. Still, each connection is independent and isolated from the others in the network. A learned, dynamic relationship exists between an attachment-virtual circuit and emulated virtual circuits that's determined by customer MAC address.

In this type of network, the customer manages its own routing protocols. One advantage that Layer 2 VPN has over its layer 3 counterpart is that some applications won't work if nodes aren't in the same Layer 2 network.

Layer 3 MPLS VPN Layer 3 MPLS VPN provides a Layer 3 service across the backbone and a different IP subnet connects each site. Since you will typically deploy a routing protocol over this VPN, you need to communicate with the service provider in order to participate in the exchange of routes. Neighbor adjacency is established between your router (called CE) and provider router (called PE). The service provider network has many core routers (called P routers) and the job of the P routers is to provide connectivity between the PE routers.

If you want to totally outsource your Layer 3 VPN, then this service is for you. Your service provider will maintain and manage routing for all your sites. From your perspective as a customer who's outsourced your VPN's, it will seem like your ISP's network is one, big virtual switch.

Because they're inexpensive and secure, I'm guessing that you really want to know how to create VPNs now, right? Great! So there's more than one way to bring a VPN into being. The first approach uses IPsec to build authentication and encryption services between endpoints on an IP network. The second way is via tunneling protocols, which allow you to establish a tunnel between endpoints on a network. Understand that the tunnel itself is a way for data or protocols to be encapsulated inside another protocol—pretty clean!

We'll get to IPsec in a minute, but first, you need to know about four of the most common tunneling protocols in use today:

Layer 2 Forwarding (L2F)

A Cisco-proprietary tunneling protocol that was Cisco's first and created for virtual private dial-up networks (VPDNs). A VPDN allows a device to use a dial-up connection to create a secure connection to a corporate network. L2F was later replaced by L2TP, which is backward compatible with L2F.

Point-to-Point Tunneling Protocol (PPTP)

PPTP was created by Microsoft with others to allow for the secure transfer of data from remote networks to the corporate network.

Layer 2 Tunneling Protocol (L2TP)

L2TP was created by Cisco and Microsoft to replace L2F and PPTP. It merges the capabilities of both L2F and PPTP into one tunneling protocol.

Generic Routing Encapsulation (GRE)

GRE is the predominate encapsulation protocol in use today. Another Cisco-proprietary tunneling protocol, GRE forms virtual point-to-point links, allowing for a variety of protocols to be encapsulated in IP tunnels. I'll cover GRE in more detail, including how to configure it, at the end of this chapter.

So now that you're clear on both exactly what a VPN is and the various types of VPNs available, it's time to dive into IPsec.

Introduction to Cisco IOS IPsec

Simply put, IPsec is an industry-wide standard framework of protocols and algorithms that allows for secure data transmission over an IP-based network. It functions at the layer 3 Network layer of the OSI model.

Did you notice I said IP-based network? That's really important because by itself, IPsec can't be used to encrypt non-IP traffic. This means that if you run into a situation where you have to encrypt non-IP traffic, you'll need to create a Generic Routing Encapsulation (GRE) tunnel for it and then use IPsec to encrypt that tunnel!

IPsec Transforms

An *IPsec transform* specifies a single security protocol with its corresponding security algorithm; without these transforms, IPsec wouldn't be able to give us its glory. It's important to be familiar with these technologies, so let me take a second to define the security protocols. I'll also briefly introduce the supporting encryption and hashing algorithms that IPsec relies upon.

Security Protocols

The two primary security protocols used by IPsec are *Authentication Header (AH)* and *Encapsulating Security Payload (ESP)*.

Authentication Header (AH)

The AH protocol provides authentication for the data and the IP header of a packet using a one-way hash for packet authentication. It works like this: The sender generates a one-way hash, then the receiver generates the same one-way hash. If the packet has changed in any way, it won't be authenticated and will be dropped because the hash value no longer matched. So basically, IPsec relies upon AH to guarantee authenticity.

Let's take a look at this using Figure 15.4.

FIGURE 15.4 Security Protocols

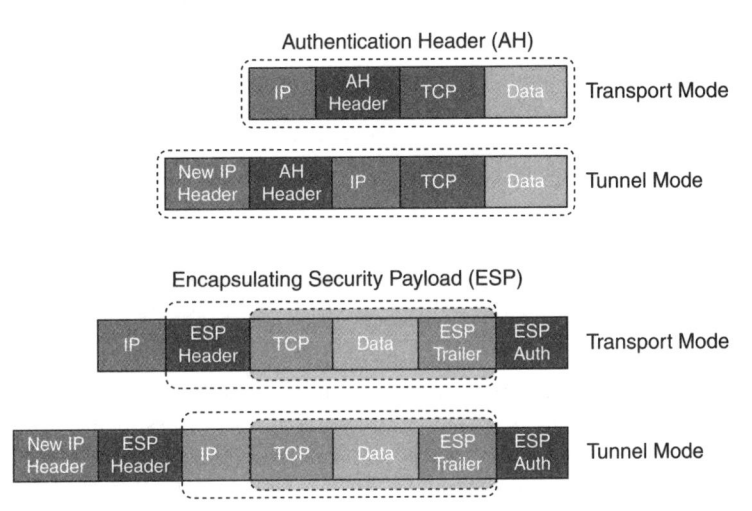

AH checks the entire packet when in tunnel mode, but it doesn't offer any encryption services. However, using AH in transport mode checks only the payload.

This is unlike ESP, which only provides an integrity check on the data of a packet when in transport mode. However, using AH in tunnel mode ESP encrypts the whole packet.

Encapsulating Security Payload (ESP)

So ESP won't tell you when or how the NASDAQ's gonna bounce up and down like a superball, but ESP does a lot for you! It provides confidentiality, data origin authentication, connectionless integrity, anti-replay service, and limited traffic-flow confidentiality by defeating traffic flow analysis—which is almost as good as AH without the possible encryption! Here's a description of ESPs five big features:

Confidentiality (encryption) Confidentiality allows the sending device to encrypt the packets before transmitting in order to prevent eavesdropping and is provided through the use of symmetric encryption algorithms like DES 3DES, however, AES is the most common in use today. It can be selected separately from all other services, but the type of confidentiality must be the same on both endpoints of your VPN.

Data integrity Data integrity allows the receiver to verify that the data received hasn't been altered in any way along the way. IPsec uses checksums as a simple way to check of the data.

Authentication Authentication ensures that the connection is made with the correct partner. The receiver can authenticate the source of the packet by guaranteeing and certifying the source of the information.

Anti-replay service Anti-replay election is based upon the receiver, meaning the service is effective only if the receiver checks the sequence number. In case you were wondering, a replay attack is when a hacker nicks a copy of an authenticated packet and later transmits it to the intended destination. When the duplicate, authenticated IP packet gets to the destination, it can disrupt services and generally wreak havoc. The *Sequence Number* field is designed to foil this type of attack.

Traffic flow For traffic flow confidentiality to work, you've got to have at least tunnel mode selected. It's most effective if it's implemented at a security gateway where tons of traffic amasses because that's precisely the kind of environment that can mask the true source-destination patterns to bad guys trying to breach your security.

Encryption

VPNs create a private network over a public network infrastructure, but to maintain confidentiality and security, we really need to use IPsec with our VPNs. IPsec uses various types of protocols to perform encryption. The types of encryption algorithms used today are:

Symmetric encryption This type of encryption requires a shared secret to encrypt and decrypt. Each computer encrypts the data before sending info across the network, with this same key being used to both encrypt and decrypt the data. Examples of symmetric key encryption are Data Encryption Standard (DES), Triple DES (3DES), and Advanced Encryption Standard (AES).

Asymmetric encryption Devices that use asymmetric encryption use different keys for encryption than they do for decryption. These keys are called private and public keys.

Private keys encrypt a hash from the message to create a digital signature, which is then verified via decryption using the public key. Public keys encrypt a symmetric key for secure distribution to the receiving host, which then decrypts that symmetric key using its exclusively held private key. It's not possible to encrypt and decrypt using the same key. Asymmetric decryption is a variant of public key encryption that also uses a combination of both a public and private keys. An example of an asymmetric encryption is Rivest, Shamir, and Adleman (RSA).

Looking at Figure 15.5, you can see the complex encryption process.

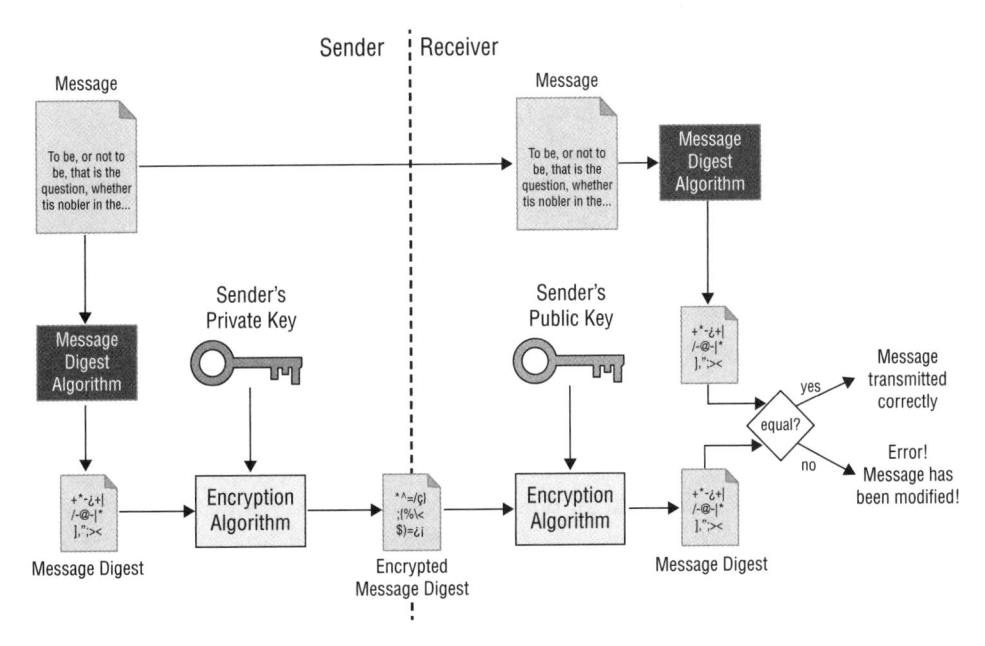

FIGURE 15.5 Encryption Process

As you can see from the amount of information I've thrown at you so far, establishing a VPN connection between two sites takes some study, time, and practice. And I'm just scratching the surface here! I know it can be difficult at times, and it definitely takes patience. Cisco does have some GUI interfaces to help with this process, which also come in handy for configuring VPNs with IPsec. Though highly useful and very interesting, they're just beyond the scope of this book, so I'm not going into this topic further here.

GRE Tunnels

Generic Routing Encapsulation (GRE) is a tunneling protocol that can encapsulate many protocols inside IP tunnels. Some examples would be routing protocols such as EIGRP and OSPF and the routed protocol IPv6. Figure 15.6 shows the different pieces of a GRE header.

FIGURE 15.6 Generic Routing Encapsulation (GRE) tunnel structure

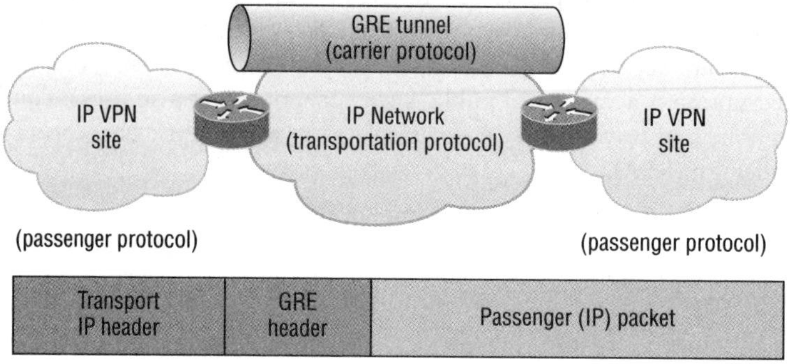

A GRE tunnel interface supports a header for each of the following:

- A passenger protocol or encapsulated protocols like IP or IPv6, which is the protocol being encapsulated by GRE
- GRE encapsulation protocol
- A Transport delivery protocol, typically IP

GRE tunnels have the following characteristics:

- GRE uses a protocol-type field in the GRE header so any layer 3 protocol can be used through the tunnel.
- GRE is stateless and has no flow control.
- GRE offers no security.
- GRE creates additional overhead for tunneled packets—at least 24 bytes.

GRE over IPsec

So as I mentioned, by itself, GRE offers no security—no form of payload confidentiality or encryption whatsoever. If the packets are sniffed over the public network, their contents are in plain text. Although IPsec provides a secure method for tunneling data across an IP network, it definitely has its limitations.

IPsec doesn't support IP broadcast or IP multicast, preventing the use of protocols that need them like routing protocols. IPsec also does not support the use of multiprotocol traffic. But GRE can be used to "carry" other passenger protocols like IP broadcast or IP multicast, plus non-IP protocols as well. Using GRE tunnels with IPsec allows you to run a routing protocol, IP multicast, as well as multiprotocol traffic across your network.

With a generic hub-and-spoke topology like Corp to Branch, you can typically implement static tunnels (usually GRE over IPsec) between the corporate office and branch offices. When you want to add a new spoke to the network, you just need to configure it on the hub router and then a small configuration on the corp router. Also, the traffic between spokes has to traverse the hub, where it must exit one tunnel and enter another. Static tunnels are an appropriate solution for small networks, but not so much as the network grows larger with an increasing number of spokes!

Cisco DMVPN (Cisco Proprietary)

The Cisco Dynamic Multipoint Virtual Private Network (DMVPN) feature enables you to easily scale large and small IPsec VPNs. The Cisco DMVPN is Cisco's answer for allowing a corporate office to connect to branch offices with low cost, easy configuration and flexibility. DMVPN is comprised of one central router like a corporate router, which is referred to as the hub, and the branches as spokes. So the corporate to branch connection is referred to as the hub and spoke interconnection. The spoke-to-spoke design is also supported for branch-to-branch interconnections. If you're thinking this design sounds really similar to your old Frame Relay network, you're right! The DMPVN features enable you to configure a single GRE tunnel interface and a single IPsec profile on the hub router to manage all spoke routers. This keeps the size of the configuration on the hub router basically the same even if you add more spoke routers to the network. DMVPN also allows a spoke router to dynamically create VPN tunnels between them as network data travels from one spoke to another.

Cisco IPsec VTI (Cisco Proprietary)

The IPSec Virtual Tunnel Interface (VTI) mode of an IPsec configuration can seriously simplify a VPN configuration when protection is needed for remote access. And it's a simpler option than GRE or L2TP for the encapsulation and crypto maps used with IPSec. Like GRE, it sends routing protocol and multicast traffic, just without GRE and all the overhead it brings. Simple configuration and routing adjacency directly over the VTI are great benefits! Understand that all traffic is encrypted and that it supports only one protocol—either IPv4 or IPv6 just like standard IPsec.

So let's get ready to configure a GRE tunnel now. It's actually pretty simple.

Configuring GRE Tunnels

Before you attempt to configure a GRE tunnel, you need to create an implementation plan. Here's a checklist of what you need do to configure and implement a GRE tunnel:

- Use IP addressing.
- Create the logical tunnel interfaces.
- Specify that you're using GRE tunnel mode under the tunnel interface. This is optional since it's the default tunnel mode.
- Specify the tunnel source and destination IP addresses.
- Configure an IP address for the tunnel interface.

We're now ready to bring up a simple GRE tunnel. Figure 15.7 pictures the network with two routers.

FIGURE 15.7 Example of GRE configuration

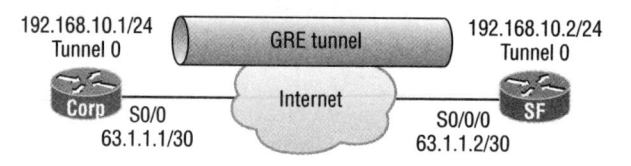

First, we need to make the logical tunnel with the interface tunnel number command. We can use any number up to 2.14 billion.

```
Corp(config)#int s0/0/0
Corp(config-if)#ip address 63.1.1.1 255.255.255.252
Corp(config)#int tunnel ?
  <0-2147483647>  Tunnel interface number
Corp(config)#int tunnel 0
*Jan 5 16:58:22.719:%LINEPROTO-5-UPDOWN: Line protocol on Interface Tunnel0,
changed state to down
```

Once we've configured our interface and created the logical tunnel, we need to configure the mode and then transport protocol:

```
Corp(config-if)#tunnel mode ?
  aurp      AURP TunnelTalk AppleTalk encapsulation
  cayman    Cayman TunnelTalk AppleTalk encapsulation
  dvmrp     DVMRP multicast tunnel
  eon       EON compatible CLNS tunnel
  gre       generic route encapsulation protocol
  ipip      IP over IP encapsulation
  ipsec     IPSec tunnel encapsulation
  iptalk    Apple IPTalk encapsulation
  ipv6      Generic packet tunneling in IPv6
  ipv6ip    IPv6 over IP encapsulation
  nos       IP over IP encapsulation (KA9Q/NOS compatible)
  rbscp     RBSCP in IP tunnel
Corp(config-if)#tunnel mode gre ?
  ip          over IP
  ipv6        over IPv6
  multipoint  over IP (multipoint)

Corp(config-if)#tunnel mode gre ip
```

Now that we've created the tunnel interface, the type, and the transport protocol, we've got to configure our IP addresses for use inside of the tunnel. Of course, we must use our actual physical interface IP for the tunnel to send traffic across the Internet, but we also need to configure the tunnel source and tunnel destination addresses:

```
Corp(config-if)#ip address 192.168.10.1 255.255.255.0
Corp(config-if)#tunnel source 63.1.1.1
Corp(config-if)#tunnel destination 63.1.1.2

Corp#sho run interface tunnel 0
Building configuration...

Current configuration : 117 bytes
!
interface Tunnel0
 ip address 192.168.10.1 255.255.255.0
 tunnel source 63.1.1.1
 tunnel destination 63.1.1.2
end
```

Time to configure the other end of the serial link and watch the tunnel pop up!

```
SF(config)#int s0/0/0
SF(config-if)#ip address 63.1.1.2 255.255.255.252
SF(config-if)#int t0
SF(config-if)#ip address 192.168.10.2 255.255.255.0
SF(config-if)#tunnel source 63.1.1.2
SF(config-if)#tun destination 63.1.1.1
*May 19 22:46:37.099: %LINEPROTO-5-UPDOWN: Line protocol on Interface Tunnel0,
changed state to up
```

Oops—did I forget to set my tunnel mode and transport to GRE and IP on the SF router? No, I didn't need to because it's the default tunnel mode on Cisco IOS. Nice! So, first I set the physical interface IP address—which used a global address even though I didn't have to—then I created the tunnel interface and set the IP address of the tunnel interface. It's important that you remember to configure the tunnel interface with the actual source and destination IP addresses to use or the tunnel won't come up. In my example, the 63.1.1.2 was the source and 63.1.1.1 was the destination.

Verifying GRP Tunnels

As usual I'll start with my favorite troubleshooting command, show ip interface brief.

```
Corp#sh ip int brief
Interface        IP-Address    OK? Method Status                Protocol
FastEthernet0/0  10.10.10.5    YES manual up                    up
```

Chapter 15 • Virtual Private Networks (VPNs)

```
Serial0/0          63.1.1.1         YES manual up                         up
FastEthernet0/1    unassigned       YES unset  administratively down      down
Serial0/1          unassigned       YES unset  administratively down      down
Tunnel0            192.168.10.1     YES manual up                         up
```

In this output, you can see that the tunnel interface is now showing up as an interface on my router. You can see the IP address of the tunnel interface, and the Physical and Data Link status show as up/up. So far so good! Let's take a look at the interface with the show interfaces tunnel 0 command:

```
Corp#sh int tun 0
Tunnel0 is up, line protocol is up
  Hardware is Tunnel
  Internet address is 192.168.10.1/24
  MTU 1514 bytes, BW 9 Kbit, DLY 500000 usec,
     reliability 255/255, txload 1/255, rxload 1/255
  Encapsulation TUNNEL, loopback not set
  Keepalive not set
  Tunnel source 63.1.1.1, destination 63.1.1.2
  Tunnel protocol/transport GRE/IP
    Key disabled, sequencing disabled
    Checksumming of packets disabled
  Tunnel TTL 255
  Fast tunneling enabled
  Tunnel transmit bandwidth 8000 (kbps)
  Tunnel receive bandwidth 8000 (kbps)
```

The show interfaces command shows the configuration settings and the interface status as well as the IP address, tunnel source, and destination address. The output also shows the tunnel protocol, which is GRE/IP. Last, let's take a look at the routing table with the show ip route command:

```
Corp#sh ip route
[output cut]
     192.168.10.0/24 is subnetted, 2 subnets
C       192.168.10.0/24 is directly connected, Tunnel0
L       192.168.10.1/32 is directly connected, Tunnel0
     63.0.0.0/30 is subnetted, 2 subnets
C       63.1.1.0 is directly connected, Serial0/0
L       63.1.1.1/32 is directly connected, Serial0/0
```

The tunnel0 interface shows up as a directly connected interface. And even though it's a logical interface, the router treats it as a physical interface, just like serial 0/0 in the routing table:

Corp#**ping 192.168.10.2**

```
Type escape sequence to abort.
Sending 5, 100-byte ICMP Echos to 192.168.10.2, timeout is 2 seconds:
!!!!!
Success rate is 100 percent (5/5)
```

Did you notice that I just pinged 192.168.10.2 across the Internet? One last thing before we close and move on... troubleshooting an output that shows a tunnel routing error. If you configure your GRE tunnel and receive this GRE flapping message:

```
          Line protocol on Interface Tunnel0, changed state to up
07:11:55: %TUN-5-RECURDOWN:
          Tunnel0 temporarily disabled due to recursive routing
07:11:59: %LINEPROTO-5-UPDOWN:
          Line protocol on Interface Tunnel0, changed state to down
07:12:59: %LINEPROTO-5-UPDOWN:
```

It means that you've misconfigured your tunnel, which will cause your router to try and route to the tunnel destination address using the tunnel interface itself!

Summary

In this chapter, you got the concept of virtual private networks completely down, and you learned of solutions to meet your company's off-site network access needs. You discovered how these networks utilize IP security to provide secure communications over a public network such as the Internet using VPN's with IPSec. We then moved on to exploring IPsec and encryption.

As the chapter closed, you were introduced to GRE and found out how to create a tunnel using GRE on virtual private networks and then verify it.

Exam Essentials

Understand the term virtual private network. You must understand why and how to use a VPN between two sites and the purpose that IPsec serves with VPNs.

Understand how to configure and verify a GRE tunnel. To configure GRE, first configure the logical tunnel with the `interface tunnel` *number* command. Configure the mode and transport, if needed, with the `tunnel mode` *mode protocol* command, then configure the IP addresses on the tunnel interfaces, the tunnel source and tunnel destination addresses, and your physical interfaces with global addresses. Verify with the `show interface tunnel` command as well as the ping protocol.

Review Questions

The answers to these questions can be found in the Appendix.

1. Which two of the following are GRE characteristics? (Choose two.)
    - **A.** GRE encapsulation uses a protocol-type field in the GRE header to support the encapsulation of any OSI layer 3 protocol.
    - **B.** GRE itself is stateful. It includes flow-control mechanisms, by default.
    - **C.** GRE includes strong security mechanisms to protect its payload.
    - **D.** The GRE header, together with the tunneling IP header, creates at least 24 bytes of additional overhead for tunneled packets

2. A GRE tunnel is flapping with the following error message:

    ```
    07:11:49: %LINEPROTO-5-UPDOWN:
        Line protocol on Interface Tunnel0, changed state to up
    07:11:55: %TUN-5-RECURDOWN:
        Tunnel0 temporarily disabled due to recursive routing
    07:11:59: %LINEPROTO-5-UPDOWN:
        Line protocol on Interface Tunnel0, changed state to down
    07:12:59: %LINEPROTO-5-UPDOWN:
    ```

    What could be the reason for this?
    - **A.** IP routing hasn't been enabled on tunnel interface.
    - **B.** There is an MTU issue on the tunnel interface.
    - **C.** The router is trying to route to the tunnel destination address using the tunnel interface itself.
    - **D.** Access-list is blocking traffic on the tunnel interface.

3. Which of the following commands will not tell you if the GRE tunnel 0 is in "up/up" state?
    - **A.** `show ip interface | brief`
    - **B.** `show interface tunnel 0`
    - **C.** `show ip interface tunnel 0`
    - **D.** `show run interface tunnel 0`

4. You've configured a serial interface with GRE IP commands on a corporate router with a point-to-point link to a remote office. Which command will show you the IP addresses and tunnel source and destination addresses of the interfaces?
   A. `show int serial 0/0`
   B. `show ip int brief`
   C. `show interface tunnel 0`
   D. `show tunnel ip status`
   E. `debug ip interface tunnel`

5. You want to allow remote users to send protected packets to the corporate site, but you don't want to install software on the remote client machines. What's the best solution you could implement?
   A. GRE tunnel
   B. Web VPN
   C. VPN Anywhere
   D. IPsec

6. Which of the following are benefits to using a VPN in your internetwork? (Choose three.)
   A. Security
   B. Private high-bandwidth links
   C. Cost savings
   D. Incompatibility with broadband technologies
   E. Scalability

7. Which two technologies are examples of layer 2 MPLS VPN technologies? (Choose two.)
   A. VPLS
   B. DMVPM
   C. GETVPN
   D. VPWS

8. Which of the following is an industry-wide standard suite of protocols and algorithms that allows for secure data transmission over an IP-based network that functions at the layer 3 Network layer of the OSI model?
   A. HDLC
   B. Cable
   C. VPN
   D. IPsec
   E. xDSL

9. Which of the following describes the creation of private networks across the Internet, enabling privacy and tunneling of non-TCP/IP protocols?

   A. HDLC
   B. Cable
   C. VPN
   D. IPsec
   E. xDSL

10. Which two VPNs are examples of service provider-managed VPNs? (Choose two.)

   A. Remote-access VPNs
   B. Layer 2 MPLS VPN
   C. Layer 3 MPLS VPN
   D. DMVPN

Chapter 16

Quality of Service (QoS)

THE FOLLOWING CCNA EXAM TOPIC IS COVERED IN THIS CHAPTER:

4.0 IP Services

✓ **4.7 Explain the forwarding per-hop behavior (PHB) for QoS such as classification, marking, queuing, congestion, policing, shaping**

Quality of service (QoS) refers to the way resources are controlled so that the quality of services is maintained.
In this chapter I'm going to cover how QoS solves problems by using classification and marking tools, policing, shaping and re-marking, providing congestion management and scheduling tools, and finally, link specific tools.

> **NOTE** To find your included bonus material, as well as Todd Lammle videos, practice questions & hands-on labs, please see www.lammle.com/ccna

Quality of Service

Quality of service (QoS) provides the ability to assign a different priority to one or more types of traffic over others for different applications, data flows, or users so a certain level of performance can be guaranteed. QoS is used to manage contention for network resources for a better end-user experience

QoS methods focus on one of five problems that can affect data as it traverses network cable:

1. Delay Data can run into congested lines or take a less-than-ideal route to the destination, and delays like these can make some applications, such as VoIP, fail. This is the best reason to implement QoS when real-time applications are in use in the network—to prioritize delay-sensitive traffic.

2. Dropped Packets Some routers will drop packets if they receive a packet while their buffers are full. If the receiving application is waiting for the packets but doesn't get them, it will usually request that the packets be retransmitted, another common cause of a service(s) delay. With QoS, when there is contention on a link, less important traffic is delayed or dropped in favor of delay-sensitive and/or otherwise prioritized traffic.

3. Error Packets can be corrupted in transit and arrive at the destination in an unacceptable format, again requiring retransmission and resulting in delays.

4. Jitter Not every packet takes the same route to the destination, so some will be more delayed than others if they travel through a slower or busier network connection. The variation in packet delay is called *jitter*, which can have a particularly negative impact on programs that communicate in real time.

5. Out-of-Order Delivery Out-of-order delivery is also a result of packets taking different paths through the network to their destination. The application at the receiving end needs to put them back together in the right order for the message to be completed. So if there are significant delays, or the packets are reassembled out of order, users will experience the decline of an application's quality.

QoS can ensure that applications with a required bit rate receive the necessary bandwidth to work properly. Clearly, this isn't a factor on networks with excess bandwidth, but the more limited your bandwidth is, the more important QoS becomes!

Traffic Characteristics

Today's networks will typically have a mix of data, voice, and video traffic traversing them. Each traffic type has different properties.

Figure 16.1 shows the different traffic characteristics for data, voice and video.

FIGURE 16.1 Traffic characteristics

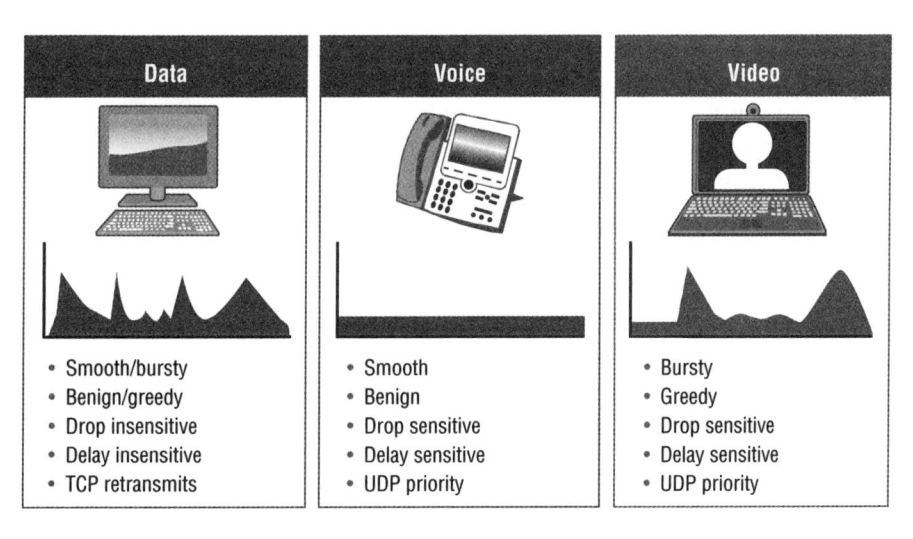

Data	Voice	Video
• Smooth/bursty • Benign/greedy • Drop insensitive • Delay insensitive • TCP retransmits	• Smooth • Benign • Drop sensitive • Delay sensitive • UDP priority	• Bursty • Greedy • Drop sensitive • Delay sensitive • UDP priority

Data traffic is not real-time traffic. Data packet traffic is bursty, and unpredictable making packet arrival vary by quite a bit.

The following are data characteristics we can see in Figure 16.1:

- Smooth/bursty
- Benign/greedy
- Drop insensate
- Delay insensitive
- TCP retransmits

Data traffic doesn't really require special handling in modern networks, especially if TCP is used. Voice traffic is real-time traffic that requires and consumes a consistent amount of bandwidth with known packet arrival times.

These are the characteristics of voice traffic on a network:

- Smooth
- Benign
- Drop sensate
- Delay sensate
- UDP priority

And these are the voice requirements for one-way traffic:

- Latency of less than or equal to 150 milliseconds
- Jitter of less than or equal to 30 milliseconds
- Loss of less than or equal to 1%
- Bandwidth of only 128 kbps

There's quite a variety of video traffic types around today on the Internet. Netflix, Hulu and other apps, gaming and remote collaboration require streaming video, real-time interactive video and video conferencing.

Video requirements for one-way traffic are:

- Latency of less than or equal to 200-400 milliseconds
- Jitter of less than or equal to 30-50 milliseconds
- Loss of less than or equal to 0.1-1%
- Bandwidth 384 Kbps to 20 Mbps or greater

Trust Boundary

The trust boundary refers to a point in the network where packet markings aren't necessarily trusted and is where we can create, remove, or rewrite markings. The borders of a trust domain are the network locations where packet markings are accepted and acted upon. Figure 16.2 illustrates some typical trust boundaries.

FIGURE 16.2 Trust boundary

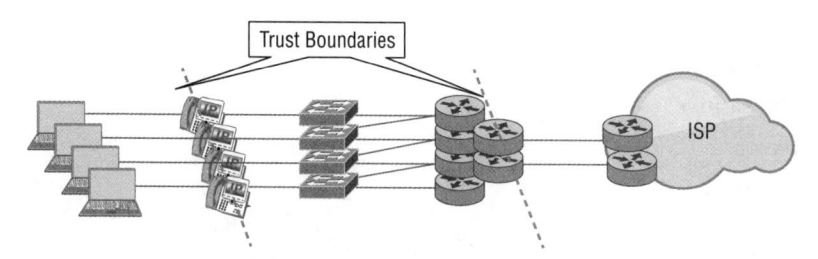

The figure shows that IP phones and router interfaces are typically trusted, but not beyond a certain point. Those points are trust boundaries.

To meet the exam objectives, understand these three things:

Untrusted domain   This is the part of the network you're not actively managing populated by PCs, printers, etc.

Trusted domain   This is part of the network with only administrator-managed devices like switches, routers, etc.

Trust boundary   Where packets are classified and marked. In an enterprise campus network, the trust boundary is almost always at the edge switch.

So traffic at the trust boundary is classified and marked before being forwarded to the trusted domain. Markings on traffic coming from an untrusted domain are usually ignored to prevent end-user-controlled markings from taking unfair advantage of the network QoS configuration.

QoS Mechanisms

Next, we're going to explore the following mechanisms:

- Classification and marking tools
- Policing, shaping, and re-marking tools
- Congestion management or scheduling tools
- Link-specific tools

Let's take a detailed look at each one now.

Classification and Marking

A classifier inspects a field within a packet to identify the type of traffic that the packet is carrying so that QoS can determine which traffic class it belongs to and how the packet should be treated. Traffic is then directed to a policy-enforcement mechanism called policing. It's important this isn't a constant cycle for traffic because it takes up time and resources!

Policy enforcement mechanisms include marking, queuing, policing, and shaping, and there are various layer 2 and layer 3 fields in a frame and packet for marking traffic. Understanding these marking techniques is important for the objectives, so here you go:

Class of Service (CoS)   An Ethernet frame marking at layer 2 containing 3 bits. This is called the Priority Code Point (PCP) within an Ethernet frame header when VLAN tagged frames as defined by IEEE 802.1Q are used.

Type of Service (ToS)   ToS comprises 8 bits, 3 of which are designated as the IP precedence field in an IPv4 packet header. The IPv6 header field is called Traffic Class.

Differentiated Services Code Point (DSCP or DiffServ)   One of the methods that can be used for classifying and managing network traffic and providing QoS on modern

IP networks is DSCP. It uses a 6-bit differentiated services code point in the 8-bit, Differentiated Services field (DS field) within the IP header for packet classification. This permits us to create traffic classes needed for assigning priorities. While IP precedence is the old way to mark ToS, DSCP is the new way. DSCP is backwards-compatible with IP precedence.

Layer 3 packet marking with IP precedence and DSCP is the most widely deployed marking option because Layer 3 packet markings have end-to-end significance.

Class Selector   Class selector uses the same 3 bits of the field as IP precedence and is used to indicate a 3-bit subset of DSCP values.

Traffic Identifier (TID)   TID is for wireless frames and describes a 3-bit field within the QoS control field in 802.11. Very similar to CoS—just remember CoS is wired Ethernet and TID is wireless.

Classification Marking Tools

As we talked about, the classification of traffic determines which type of traffic the packets or frames belong to. Once that's been determined we can apply policies to it by marking, shaping, and policing. Always try to mark traffic as close to the trust boundary as possible.

We typically use three ways to classify traffic:

Markings   This looks at header information on existing layer 2 or 3 settings. Classification is based on existing markings.

Addressing   This classification technique looks at header information using source and destinations of interfaces, layer 2 and 3 address, and layer 4 port numbers. We can group traffic with the device using IP and by type using port numbers.

Application signatures   This technique is the way to look at the information in the payload called deep packet inspection.

I'm going to dive a bit deeper into deep packet inspection by introducing you to Network Based Application recognition (NBAR).

NBAR is a classifier that provides deep-packet inspection on layer 4 to 7 on a packet. Compared to using addresses (IP or ports), or ACLs, using NBAR is the most CPU intensive technique.

Since it's not always possible to identify applications by looking at just layer 3 and 4, NBAR looks deep into the packet payload and compares the payload content against its signature database called a Packet description Language Model (PDLM).

There are two different modes of operation used with NBAR:

- **Passive mode:** Using passive mode will give you real-time statistics on applications by protocol or interface, as well as packet bit rate, packet, and byte counts.
- **Active mode:** Classifies applications for traffic marking so QoS policies can be applied.

Policing, Shaping, and Re-marking

So now that we've identified and marked traffic, it's time to put some action on your packet. We do this with bandwidth assignments, policing, shaping, queuing or dropping.

For example, if some traffic exceeds bandwidth, it might be delayed, dropped, or even remarked in order to avoid congestion.

Policers and shapers are two tools that identify and respond to traffic problems. Both are rate-limiters and Figure 16.3 shows how they differ.

FIGURE 16.3 Policing and shaping rate limiters

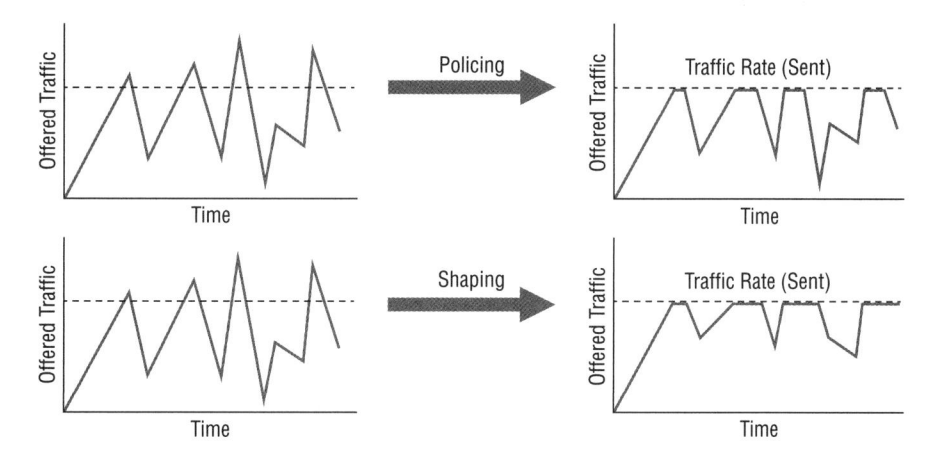

Policers and shapers identify traffic violations in a similar way, but they differ in their responses:

Policers Since the policers make instant decisions, you want to deploy on the ingress if possible—you want to drop traffic as soon as you receive it if it's going to be dropped anyway, right? Still, you can place policers on an egress to control the amount of traffic per class. When traffic is exceeded, policers don't delay it by introducing jitter or delay; they just check the traffic and drop or remark it. Just know that due to the higher drop probability, you can end up with a whole bunch of TCP resends.

Shapers Shapers are usually deployed between an enterprise network and the ISPs on the egress side to make sure you stay within the contract rate. If the rate is exceeded, it gets policed by the provider and dropped. This allows the traffic to meet the Service Level Agreement (SLA). Shaping introduces jitter and delay and results in fewer TCP resends than policers.

> Basically, remember that policers drop traffic and shapers delay it. Shapers introduce delay and jitter, but policers do not. Policers cause significant TCP resends, but shapers do not.

Tools for Managing Congestion

Next up is a couple of important sections on congestion issues. If traffic exceeds network resources, the traffic gets queued into the temporary storage of backed-up packets. Queuing is done in order to avoid dropping packets and isn't a bad thing because without it, packets that can't be processed immediately would be dropped. Also, traffic classes like VoIP are actually better off being immediately dropped unless you can somehow guarantee enough delay-free bandwidth for it!

When congestion occurs, there are two types of congestion management are activated, as shown in Figure 16.4.

FIGURE 16.4 Congestion management

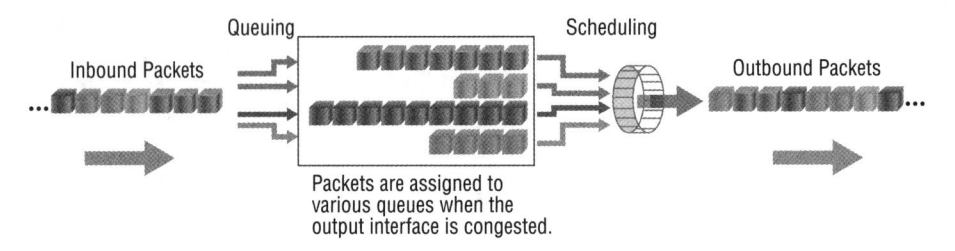

Let's take a closer look at congestion management:

Queuing (or buffering)   Buffering is the logic of ordering packets in output buffers and is only activated when congestion occurs. When queues fill up, packets can be reordered so that the higher-priority ones are sent out of the exit interface sooner than lower priority traffic.

Scheduling   This is the process of deciding which packet should be sent out next and occurs whether or not there is congestion on the link. Make sure you're familiar with these three scheduling mechanisms:

Strict priority scheduling   Scheduling low priority queues only happens once the high priority queues are empty. This is great if you're sending the high-priority traffic, but it's possible for low-priority queues to never be processed. We call this traffic or queue starvation.

Round-robin scheduling   This sounds like a fair technique because queues are serviced in a set sequence. You won't find starving queues here, but real-time traffic suffers badly!

Weighted fair scheduling   By weighing the queues, the scheduling process will service some queues more often than others—an upgrade over round-robin. You won't find any starvation carnage here either, but unlike round-robin, you can give priority to real-time traffic. The inevitable disclaimer coming at us here is that we get no guarantees for actual bandwidth availability.

Okay, let's run back over and finish queueing. Queuing is typically a layer 3 process, but some queueing can occur at layer 2 or even layer 1. Interestingly, if a layer 2 queue fills up, the data can be pushed into layer 3 queues, and when layer 1—called the transmit ring or TX-ring queue, fills up—the data is pushed to layer 2 and 3 queues. This is when QoS becomes active on the device.

There are many different queuing mechanisms, with only two of them typically used today. Even so, it won't hurt to take a quick look at legacy queuing methods:

First In First Out (FIFO)   A single queue, with packets being processed in the exact order they arrived in.

Priority Queuing (PQ)   Similar to round-robin scheduling, lower-priority queues are only served when the higher-priority queues are empty. There are only four queues, and low priority traffic may never be sent.

Custom Queueing (CQ)   With up to 16 queues and round-robin scheduling, CQ prevents low-level queue starvation and gives us traffic guarantees. But it doesn't provide strict priority for real-time traffic so VoIP traffic could still end up being dropped.

Weighted Fair Queuing (WFQ)   WFQ is the Cisco default queuing mechanism. WFQ is actually a pretty popular way of queuing for a long time because it divided up the bandwidth by the number of flows. This provided bandwidth for all applications and worked great for real-time traffic, but there weren't any guarantees for a particular flow.

So now that you know about the queuing methods not to use, let's focus on the two newer queuing mechanisms recommended for today's rich-media networks—Class Based Weighted Fair Queuing (CBWFQ) and Low Latency Queuing (LLQ). Check out Figure 16.5.

FIGURE 16.5   Modern queuing mechanisms

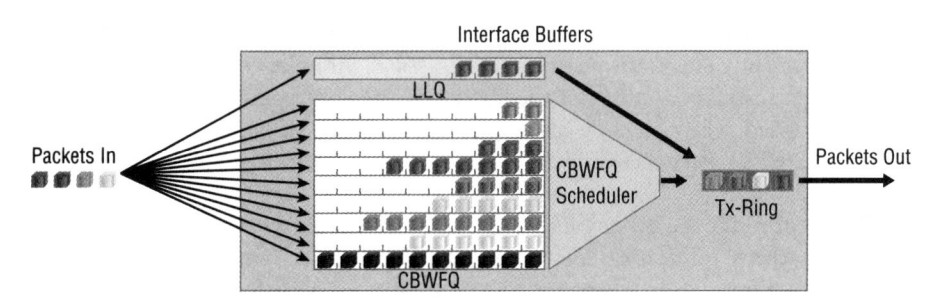

And here's a brief description of CBWFQ and LLQ:

Class Based Weighted Fair Queuing (CBWFQ):   Provides fairness and bandwidth guarantees for all traffic, but doesn't provide a latency guarantee. It's typically only used for data traffic management

Low Latency Queuing (LLQ):   LLQ is really the same thing as CBWFQ but with stricter priorities for real time traffic. LLQ is great for both data and real time traffic because it provides both latency and bandwidth guarantees.

In Figure 16.6, you can see the LLQ queuing mechanism working great for real time traffic.

FIGURE 16.6 LLQ queuing mechanisms

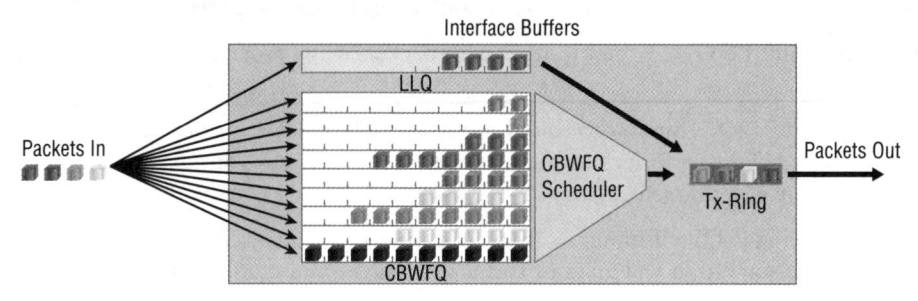

If you remove the low-latency queue (at the top), you're left with CBWFQ, which is only used for data-traffic networks!

Tools for Congestion Avoidance

TCP changed our networking world when it introduced sliding windows as a flow-control mechanism in the middle 1990s. Flow control is a way for the receiving device to control the amount of traffic from a transmitting device.

If a problem occurred during a data transmission, the previous flow control methods employed by TCP and other layer 4 protocols like SPX before sliding windows would just cut the transmission rate in half and leave it at the same rate, or lower, for the duration of the connection. Clearly, this was less than popular with users!

Sure, TCP certainly cuts transmission rates drastically if a flow control issue occurs, but it increases the transmission rate after the missing segments are resolved or when packets are finally processed. This behavior, although awesome at the time, can result in something called tail drop, which isn't acceptable in today's networks because bandwidth isn't used effectively.

What's tail drop? It's the dropping of packets as they arrive when the queues on the receiving interface are full. This is a terrible waste of bandwidth since TCP will just keep resending the data until it's happy again when it finally receives an ACK. Enter another new term—TCP global synchronization—wherein each sender reduces their transmission rate simultaneously when packet loss occurs.

Congestion avoidance starts dropping packets before a queue fills using traffic weights instead of just randomness. Cisco uses something called weighted random early detection, (WRED), a queuing method that ensures high-precedence traffic has lower loss rates than other traffic during times of congestion. This prevents more important traffic, like VoIP, from being dropped by prioritizing it over less important traffic like a connection to Facebook.

> Queuing algorithms manage the front of the queue, and congestion mechanisms manage the back of the queue.

Figure 16.7 shows how congestion avoidance works.

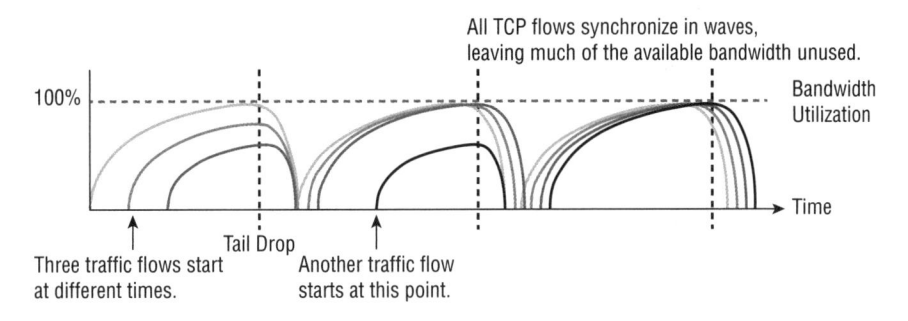

FIGURE 16.7 Congestion avoidance

We can see three traffic flows beginning at different times, resulting in congestion. In a situation like this, you know that TCP may cause tail drop because it drops the traffic as soon as it's received if the buffers are full! At that point, TCP would begin another traffic flow, synchronizing the TCP flows in waves, which sadly leaves much of the bandwidth unused!

Summary

Quality of service (QoS) refers to the way the resources are controlled so that the quality of services is maintained.

In this chapter we discussed how QoS solves problems by using classification and marking tools, policing, shaping and re-marking, providing congestion management and scheduling tools. We wrapped it up covering link specific tools.

Exam Essentials

Have a deep understanding of QoS.   You must understand QoS, specifically marking, device trust, and prioritization for voice, video, and data. Also in the need to know category: shaping, policing, and congestion management. Understand all of these in detail.

Remember the two queuing mechanisms used in today's networks.   The two queuing mechanisms you should now use in today's network are CBWFQ (class based weighted fair queuing) and LLQ (low latency queuing).

Remember the two tools that identify and respond to traffic problems.   Policers and shapers are two tools that identify and respond to traffic problems and are both rate-limiters.

Review Questions

You can find the answers in the Appendix.

1. Which of the following is a congestion-avoidance mechanism?
   A. LMI
   B. WRED
   C. QPM
   D. QoS

2. Which three features are properties and one-way requirements for voice traffic? (Choose three.)
   A. Bursty voice traffic
   B. Smooth voice traffic
   C. Latency should be below 400ms
   D. Latency should be below 150ms
   E. Bandwidth is roughly between 30 and 128Kbps
   F. Bandwidth is roughly between 0.5 and 20 Mbps

3. Which statement about QoS trust boundaries or domains is true?
   A. The trust boundary is always a router.
   B. PCs, printers and tablets are usually part of a trusted domain.
   C. An IP phone is a common trust boundary.
   D. Routing will not work unless the service provider and the enterprise network are one single trust domain.

4. Which advanced classification tool can be used to classify data applications?
   A. NBAR
   B. MPLS
   C. APIC-EM
   D. ToS

5. The DSCP field constitutes how many fields in the IP header?
   A. 3 bits
   B. 4 bits
   C. 6 bits
   D. 8 bits

6. Which option is a layer 2 QoS marking?
   A. EXP
   B. QoS group
   C. DSCP
   D. CoS
7. Which QoS mechanism will drop traffic if a session uses more than the allotted bandwidth?
   A. Congestion management
   B. Shaping
   C. Policing
   D. Marking

Chapter 17

Internet Protocol Version 6 (IPv6)

THE FOLLOWING CCNA EXAM TOPICS ARE COVERED IN THIS CHAPTER:

1.0 Network Fundamentals

✓ **1.8 Configure and verify IPv6 addressing and prefix**

✓ **1.9 Compare IPv6 address types**

- 1.9.a Global unicast
- 1.9.b Unique local
- 1.9.c Link local
- 1.9.d Anycast
- 1.9.e Multicast
- 1.9.f Modified EUI 64

3.0 IP Connectivity

✓ **3.3 Configure and verify IPv4 and IPv6 static routing**

We've covered a lot of ground in this book, and though the journey has been tough at times, it's been well worth it! But our networking expedition isn't quite over yet because we still have the vastly important frontier of IPv6 to explore. There's still some expansive territory to cover with this subject, so gear up and get ready to discover all you need to know about IPv6. Understanding IPv6 is vital now, so you'll be much better equipped and prepared to meet today's real-world networking challenges as well as to ace the exam. This chapter is packed and brimming with all the IPv6 information you'll need to complete your Cisco exam trek successfully, so get psyched—we're in the home stretch!

I probably don't need to say this, but I will anyway because I really want to go the distance and do everything I can to ensure that you arrive and achieve You absolutely must have a solid hold on IPv4 by now, but if you're still not confident with it, or feel you could use a refresher, just page back to the chapters on TCP/IP and subnetting. And if you're not crystal clear on the address problems inherent to IPv4, you really need to review Chapter 11, "Network Address Translation (NAT)," before we decamp for this chapter's IPv6 summit push!

People refer to IPv6 as "the next-generation Internet protocol," and it was originally created as the solution to IPv4's inevitable and impending address-exhaustion crisis. Though you've probably heard a thing or two about IPv6 already, it has been improved even further in the quest to bring us the flexibility, efficiency, capability, and optimized functionality that can effectively meet our world's seemingly insatiable thirst for ever-evolving technologies and increasing access. The capacity of its predecessor, IPv4, pales wan and ghostly in comparison, which is why IPv4 is destined to fade into history completely, making way for IPv6 and the future.

The IPv6 header and address structure has been completely overhauled, and many of the features that were basically just afterthoughts and addenda in IPv4 are now included as full-blown standards in IPv6. It's power-packed, well equipped with robust and elegant features, poised and prepared to manage the mind-blowing demands of the Internet to come!

After an introduction like that, I understand if you're a little apprehensive, but I promise—really—to make this chapter and its VIP topic pretty painless for you. In fact, you might even find yourself actually enjoying it—I definitely did! Because IPv6 is so complex, while still being so elegant, innovative, and powerful, it fascinates me like some weird combination of a sleek, new Aston Martin and a riveting futuristic novel. Hopefully you'll experience this chapter as an awesome ride and enjoy reading it as much as I did writing it!

> **NOTE** To find your included bonus material, as well as Todd Lammle videos, practice questions & hands-on labs, please see www.lammle.com/ccna

Why Do We Need IPv6?

Well, the short answer is because we need to communicate, and our current system isn't really cutting it anymore. It's kind of like the Pony Express trying to compete with airmail! Consider how much time and effort we've been investing for years while we scratch our heads to resourcefully come up with slick new ways to conserve bandwidth and IP addresses. Sure, variable length subnet masks (VLSMs) are wonderful and cool, but they're really just another invention to help us cope while we desperately struggle to overcome the worsening address drought.

I'm not exaggerating, at all, about how dire things are getting, because it's simply reality. The number of people and devices that connect to networks increases dramatically each and every day, which is not a bad thing. We're just finding new and exciting ways to communicate to more people, more often, which is good thing. And it's not likely to go away or even decrease in the littlest bit, because communicating and making connections are, in fact, basic human needs—they're in our very nature. But with our numbers increasing along with the rising tide of people joining the communications party increasing as well, the forecast for our current system isn't exactly clear skies and smooth sailing. IPv4, upon which our ability to do all this connecting and communicating is presently dependent, is quickly running out of addresses for us to use.

IPv4 has only about 4.3 billion addresses available—in theory—and we know that we don't even get to use most of those! Sure, the use of Classless Inter-Domain Routing (CIDR) and Network Address Translation (NAT) has helped to extend the inevitable dearth of addresses, but we will still run out of them, and it's going to happen within a few years. China is barely online, and we know there's a huge population of people and corporations there that surely want to be. There are myriad reports that give us all kinds of numbers, but all you really need to think about to realize that I'm not just being an alarmist is this: there are about 7 billion people in the world today, and it's estimated that only just under half of the population is currently connected to the Internet—wow!

That statistic is basically screaming at us the ugly truth that based on IPv4's capacity, every person can't even have a computer, let alone all the other IP devices we use with them! I have more than one computer, and it's pretty likely that you do too, and I'm not even including phones, laptops, game consoles, fax machines, routers, switches, and a mother lode of other devices we use every day into the mix! So I think I've made it pretty clear that we've got to do something before we run out of addresses and lose the ability to connect with each other as we know it. And that "something" just happens to be implementing IPv6.

The Benefits and Uses of IPv6

So what's so fabulous about IPv6? Is it really the answer to our coming dilemma? Is it really worth it to upgrade from IPv4? All good questions—you may even think of a few more. Of course, there's going to be that group of people with the time-tested "resistance to change syndrome," but don't listen to them. If we had done that years ago, we'd still be waiting weeks, even months for our mail to arrive via horseback. Instead, just know that the answer is a resounding *yes*, it is really the answer, and it is worth the upgrade! Not only does IPv6 give us lots of addresses (3.4×10^{38} = definitely enough), there are tons of other features built into this version that make it well worth the cost, time, and effort required to migrate to it.

Today's networks, as well as the Internet, have a ton of unforeseen requirements that simply weren't even considerations when IPv4 was created. We've tried to compensate with a collection of add-ons that can actually make implementing them more difficult than they would be if they were required by a standard. By default, IPv6 has improved upon and included many of those features as standard and mandatory. One of these sweet new standards is IPsec—a feature that provides end-to-end security.

But it's the efficiency features that are really going to rock the house! For starters, the headers in an IPv6 packet have half the fields, and they are aligned to 64 bits, which gives us some seriously souped-up processing speed. Compared to IPv4, lookups happen at light speed! Most of the information that used to be bound into the IPv4 header was taken out, and now you can choose to put it, or parts of it, back into the header in the form of optional extension headers that follow the basic header fields.

And of course there's that whole new universe of addresses—the 3.4×10^{38} I just mentioned—but where did we get them? Did some genie just suddenly arrive and make them magically appear? That huge proliferation of addresses had to come from somewhere! Well it just so happens that IPv6 gives us a substantially larger address space, meaning the address itself is a whole lot bigger—four times bigger as a matter of fact! An IPv6 address is actually 128 bits in length, and no worries—I'm going to break down the address piece by piece and show you exactly what it looks like coming up in the section "IPv6 Addressing and Expressions." For now, let me just say that all that additional room permits more levels of hierarchy inside the address space and a more flexible addressing architecture. It also makes routing much more efficient and scalable because the addresses can be aggregated a lot more effectively. And IPv6 also allows multiple addresses for hosts and networks. This is especially important for enterprises veritably drooling for enhanced access and availability. Plus, the new version of IP now includes an expanded use of multicast communication—one device sending to many hosts or to a select group—that joins in to seriously boost efficiency on networks because communications will be more specific.

IPv4 uses broadcasts quite prolifically, causing a bunch of problems, the worst of which is of course the dreaded broadcast storm. This is that uncontrolled deluge of forwarded broadcast traffic that can bring an entire network to its knees and devour every last bit of bandwidth! Another nasty thing about broadcast traffic is that it interrupts each and every device on the network. When a broadcast is sent out, every machine has to stop what it's doing and respond to the traffic whether the broadcast is relevant to it or not.

But smile assuredly, everyone. There's no such thing as a broadcast in IPv6 because it uses multicast traffic instead. And there are two other types of communications as well: unicast, which is the same as it is in IPv4, and a new type called *anycast*. Anycast communication allows the same address to be placed on more than one device so that when traffic is sent to the device service addressed in this way, it's routed to the nearest host that shares the same address. And this is just the beginning—we'll get into the various types of communication later in the section called "Address Types."

IPv6 Addressing and Expressions

Just as understanding how IP addresses are structured and used is critical with IPv4 addressing, it's also vital when it comes to IPv6. You've already read about the fact that at 128 bits, an IPv6 address is much larger than an IPv4 address. Because of this, as well as the new ways the addresses can be used, you've probably guessed that IPv6 will be more complicated to manage. But no worries! As I said, I'll break down the basics and show you what the address looks like and how you can write it as well as many of its common uses. It's going to be a little weird at first, but before you know it, you'll have it nailed!

So let's take a look at Figure 17.1, which has a sample IPv6 address broken down into sections.

FIGURE 17.1 IPv6 address example

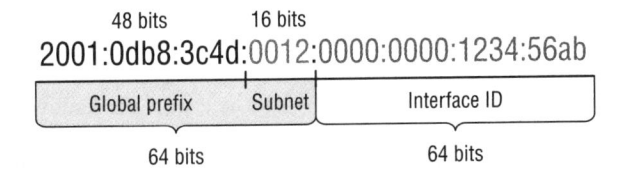

```
      48 bits       16 bits
2001:0db8:3c4d:0012:0000:0000:1234:56ab
    Global prefix  Subnet      Interface ID
         64 bits                 64 bits
```

As you can clearly see, the address is definitely much larger. But what else is different? Well, first, notice that it has eight groups of numbers instead of four and also that those groups are separated by colons instead of periods. And hey, wait a second there are letters in that address! Yep, the address is expressed in hexadecimal just like a MAC address is, so you could say this address has eight 16-bit hexadecimal colon-delimited blocks. That's already quite a mouthful, and you probably haven't even tried to say the address out loud yet!

> **NOTE** There are four hexadecimal characters (16 bits) in each IPv6 field (with eight fields total), separated by colons.

Shortened Expression

The good news is there are a few tricks to help rescue us when writing these monster addresses. For one thing, you can actually leave out parts of the address to abbreviate it, but to get away with doing that you have to follow a couple of rules. First, you can drop any leading zeros in each of the individual blocks. After you do that, the sample address from earlier would then look like this:

`2001:db8:3c4d:12:0:0:1234:56ab`

That's a definite improvement—at least we don't have to write all of those extra zeros! But what about whole blocks that don't have anything in them except zeros? Well, we can kind of lose those too—at least some of them. Again referring to our sample address, we can remove the two consecutive blocks of zeros by replacing them with a doubled colon, like this:

`2001:db8:3c4d:12::1234:56ab`

Cool—we replaced the blocks of all zeros with a doubled colon. The rule you have to follow to get away with this is that you can replace only one contiguous block of such zeros in an address. So if my address has four blocks of zeros and each of them were separated, I just don't get to replace them all because I can replace only one contiguous block with a doubled colon. Check out this example:

`2001:0000:0000:0012:0000:0000:1234:56ab`

And just know that you *can't* do this:

`2001::12::1234:56ab`

Instead, the best you can do is this:

`2001::12:0:0:1234:56ab`

The reason the preceding example is our best shot is that if we remove two sets of zeros, the device looking at the address will have no way of knowing where the zeros go back in. Basically, the router would look at the incorrect address and say, "Well, do I place two blocks into the first set of doubled colons and two into the second set, or do I place three blocks into the first set and one block into the second set?" And on and on it would go because the information the router needs just isn't there.

Address Types

We're all familiar with IPv4's unicast, broadcast, and multicast addresses that basically define who or at least how many other devices we're talking to. But as I mentioned, IPv6 modifies that trio and introduces the anycast. Broadcasts, as we know them, have been eliminated in IPv6 because of their cumbersome inefficiency and basic tendency to drive us insane!

So let's find out what each of these types of IPv6 addressing and communication methods do for us:

Unicast Packets addressed to a unicast address are delivered to a single interface. For load balancing, multiple interfaces across several devices can use the same address, but we'll call that an anycast address. There are a few different types of unicast addresses, but we don't need to get further into that here.

Global unicast addresses (2000::/3)   These are your typical publicly routable addresses and they're the same as in IPv4. Global addresses start at 2000::/3. Figure 17.2 shows how a unicast address breaks down. The ISP can provide you with a minimum /48 network ID, which in turn provides you 16-bits to create a unique 64-bit router interface address. The last 64-bits are the unique host ID.

FIGURE 17.2   IPv6 global unicast addresses

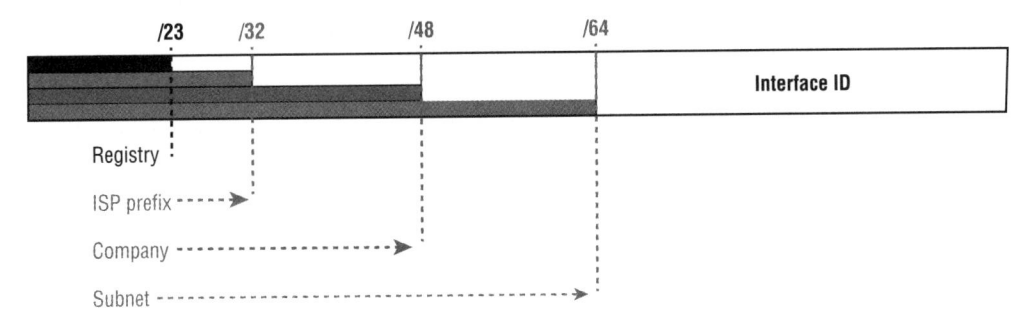

Link-local addresses (FE80::/10)   These are like the Automatic Private IP Address (APIPA) addresses that Microsoft uses to automatically provide addresses in IPv4 in that they're not meant to be routed. In IPv6 they start with FE80::/10, as shown in Figure 17.3. Think of these addresses as handy tools that give you the ability to throw a temporary LAN together for meetings or create a small LAN that's not going to be routed but still needs to share and access files and services locally.

FIGURE 17.3   IPv6 link local FE80::/10: The first 10 bits define the address type.

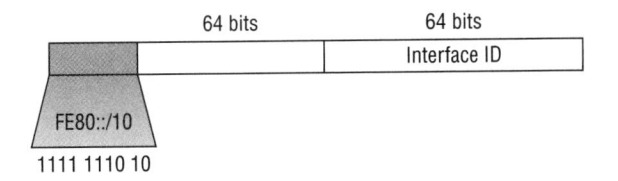

Unique local addresses (FC00::/7)   These addresses are also intended for nonrouting purposes over the Internet, but they are nearly globally unique, so it's unlikely you'll ever have one of them overlap. Unique local addresses were designed to replace site-local addresses, so they basically do almost exactly what IPv4 private addresses do: allow communication throughout a site while being routable to multiple local networks. Site-local addresses were deprecated as of September 2004.

Multicast (FF00::/8) Again, as in IPv4, packets addressed to a multicast address are delivered to all interfaces tuned into the multicast address. Sometimes people call them "one-to-many" addresses. It's really easy to spot a multicast address in IPv6 because they always start with *FF*. We'll get deeper into multicast operation coming up, in "How IPv6 Works in an Internetwork."

Anycast Like multicast addresses, an anycast address identifies multiple interfaces on multiple devices. But there's a big difference: the anycast packet is delivered to only one device—actually, to the closest one it finds defined in terms of routing distance. And again, this address is special because you can apply a single address to more than one host. These are referred to as "one-to-nearest" addresses. Anycast addresses are typically only configured on routers, never hosts, and a source address could never be an anycast address. Of note is that the IETF did reserve the top 128 addresses for each /64 for use with anycast addresses.

You're probably wondering if there are any special, reserved addresses in IPv6 because you know they're there in IPv4. Well there are—plenty of them! Let's go over those now.

Special Addresses

I'm going to list some of the addresses and address ranges (in Table 17.1) that you should definitely make sure to remember because you'll eventually use them. They're all special or reserved for a specific use, but unlike IPv4, IPv6 gives us a galaxy of addresses, so reserving a few here and there doesn't hurt at all!

TABLE 17.1 Special IPv6 addresses

Address	Meaning
0:0:0:0:0:0:0:0	Equals ::. This is the equivalent of IPv4's 0.0.0.0 and is typically the source address of a host before the host receives an IP address when you're using DHCP-driven stateful configuration.
0:0:0:0:0:0:0:1	Equals ::1. The equivalent of 127.0.0.1 in IPv4.
0:0:0:0:0:0:192.168.100.1	This is how an IPv4 address would be written in a mixed IPv6/IPv4 network environment.
2000::/3	The global unicast address range.
FC00::/7	The unique local unicast range.
FE80::/10	The link-local unicast range.
FF00::/8	The multicast range.

Address	Meaning
3FFF:FFFF::/32	Reserved for examples and documentation.
2001:0DB8::/32	Also reserved for examples and documentation.
2002::/16	Used with 6-to-4 tunneling, which is an IPv4-to-IPv6 transition system. The structure allows IPv6 packets to be transmitted over an IPv4 network without the need to configure explicit tunnels.

> When you run IPv4 and IPv6 on a router, you have what is called "dual-stack."

Let me show you how IPv6 actually works in an internetwork. We all know how IPv4 works, so let's see what's new!

How IPv6 Works in an Internetwork

It's time to explore the finer points of IPv6. A great place to start is by showing you how to address a host and what gives it the ability to find other hosts and resources on a network.

I'll also demonstrate a device's ability to automatically address itself—something called stateless autoconfiguration—plus another type of autoconfiguration known as stateful. Keep in mind that stateful autoconfiguration uses a DHCP server in a very similar way to how it's used in an IPv4 configuration. I'll also show you how Internet Control Message Protocol (ICMP) and multicasting works for us in an IPv6 network environment.

Manual Address Assignment

In order to enable IPv6 on a router, you have to use the `ipv6 unicast-routing` global configuration command:

`Corp(config)#ipv6 unicast-routing`

By default, IPv6 traffic forwarding is disabled, so using this command enables it. Also, as you've probably guessed, IPv6 isn't enabled by default on any interfaces either, so we have to go to each interface individually and enable it.

There are a few different ways to do this, but a really easy way is to just add an address to the interface. You use the interface configuration command `ipv6 address <ipv6prefix>/<prefix-length> [eui-64]` to get this done.

Here's an example:

`Corp(config-if)#ipv6 address 2001:db8:3c4d:1:0260:d6FF.FE73:1987/64`

You can specify the entire 128-bit global IPv6 address as I just demonstrated with the preceding command, or you can use the EUI-64 option. Remember, the EUI-64 (extended unique identifier) format allows the device to use its MAC address and pad it to make the interface ID. Check it out:

`Corp(config-if)#`**`ipv6 address 2001:db8:3c4d:1::/64 eui-64`**

As an alternative to typing in an IPv6 address on a router, you can enable the interface instead to permit the application of an automatic link-local address.

To configure a router so that it uses only link-local addresses, use the `ipv6 enable` interface configuration command:

`Corp(config-if)#`**`ipv6 enable`**

> Remember, if you have only a link-local address, you will be able to communicate only on that local subnet.

Stateless Autoconfiguration (eui-64)

Autoconfiguration is an especially useful solution because it allows devices on a network to address themselves with a link-local unicast address as well as with a global unicast address. This process happens through first learning the prefix information from the router and then appending the device's own interface address as the interface ID. But where does it get that interface ID? Well, you know every device on an Ethernet network has a physical MAC address, which is exactly what's used for the interface ID. But since the interface ID in an IPv6 address is 64 bits in length and a MAC address is only 48 bits, where do the extra 16 bits come from? The MAC address is padded in the middle with the extra bits—it's padded with FFFE.

For example, let's say I have a device with a MAC address that looks like this: 0060:d673:1987. After it's been padded, it would look like this: 0260:d6FF:FE73:1987. Figure 17.4 illustrates what an EUI-64 address looks like.

FIGURE 17.4 EUI-64 interface ID assignment

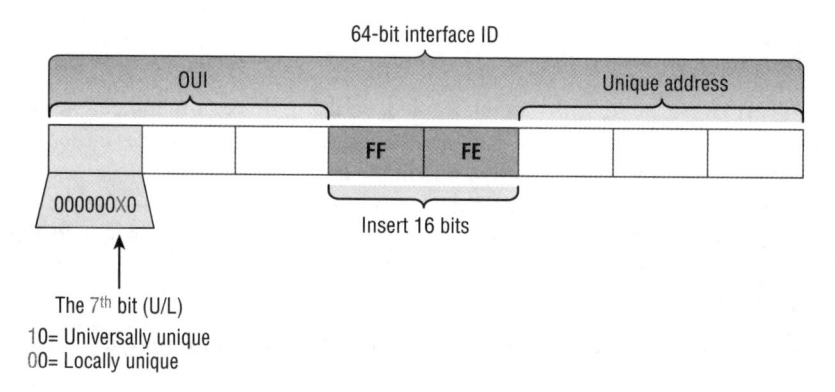

So where did that 2 in the beginning of the address come from? Another good question. You see that part of the process of padding, called modified EUI-64 format, changes a bit to specify if the address is locally unique or globally unique. And the bit that gets changed is the 7th bit in the address.

The reason for modifying the U/L bit is that, when using manually assigned addresses on an interface, it means you can simply assign the address 2001:db8:1:9::1/64 instead of the much longer 2001:db8:1:9:0200::1/64. Also, if you are going to manually assign a link-local address, you can assign the short address fe80::1 instead of the long fe80::0200:0:0:1 or fe80:0:0:0:0200::1. So, even though at first glance it seems the IETF made this harder for you to simply understand IPv6 addressing by flipping the 7th bit, in reality this made addressing much simpler. Also, since most people don't typically override the burned-in address, the U/L bit is a 0, which means that you'll see this inverted to a 1 most of the time. But because you're studying the Cisco exam objectives, you'll need to look at inverting it both ways.

Here are a few examples:

- MAC address 0090:2716:fd0f
- IPv6 EUI-64 address: 2001:0db8:0:1:0290:27ff:fe16:fd0f

That one was easy! Too easy for the Cisco exam, so let's do another:

- MAC address aa12:bcbc:1234
- IPv6 EUI-64 address: 2001:0db8:0:1:a812:bcff:febc:1234

10101010 represents the first 8 bits of the MAC address (aa), which when inverting the 7th bit becomes 10101000. The answer becomes A8. I can't tell you how important this is for you to understand, so bear with me and work through a couple more!

- MAC address 0c0c:dede:1234
- IPv6 EUI-64 address: 2001:0db8:0:1:0e0c:deff:fede:1234

0c is 00001100 in the first 8 bits of the MAC address, which then becomes 00001110 when flipping the 7th bit. The answer is then 0e. Let's practice one more:

- MAC address 0b34:ba12:1234
- IPv6 EUI-64 address: 2001:0db8:0:1:0934:baff:fe12:1234

0b in binary is 00001011, the first 8 bits of the MAC address, which then becomes 00001001. The answer is 09.

To perform autoconfiguration, a host goes through a basic two-step process:

1. First, the host needs the prefix information, similar to the network portion of an IPv4 address, to configure its interface, so it sends a router solicitation (RS) request for it. This RS is then sent out as a multicast to all routers (FF02::2). The actual information being sent is a type of ICMP message, and like everything in networking, this ICMP message has a number that identifies it. The RS message is ICMP type 133.

2. The router answers back with the required prefix information via a router advertisement (RA). An RA message also happens to be a multicast packet that's sent to the all-nodes multicast address (FF02::1) and is ICMP type 134. RA messages are sent on a periodic basis, but the host sends the RS for an immediate response so it doesn't have to wait until the next scheduled RA to get what it needs.

These two steps are shown in Figure 17.5.

FIGURE 17.5 Two steps to IPv6 autoconfiguration

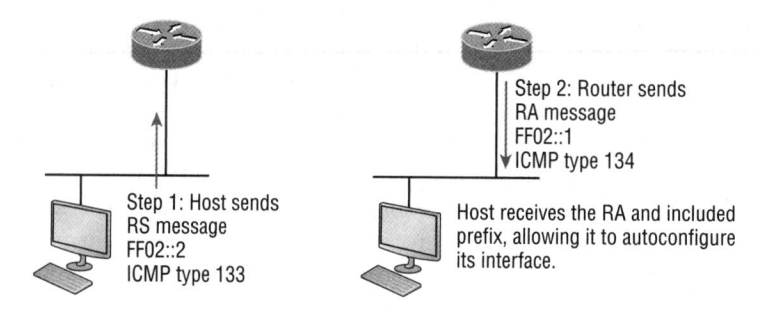

Step 1: Host sends RS message FF02::2 ICMP type 133

Step 2: Router sends RA message FF02::1 ICMP type 134

Host receives the RA and included prefix, allowing it to autoconfigure its interface.

By the way, this type of autoconfiguration is also known as stateless autoconfiguration because it doesn't contact or connect to and receive any further information from the other device. We'll get to stateful configuration when we talk about DHCPv6 next.

But before we do that, first take a look at Figure 17.6. In this figure, the Branch router needs to be configured, but I just don't feel like typing in an IPv6 address on the interface connecting to the Corp router. I also don't feel like typing in any routing commands, but I need more than a link-local address on that interface, so I'm going to have to do something! So basically, I want to have the Branch router work with IPv6 on the internetwork with the least amount of effort from me. Let's see if I can get away with that.

FIGURE 17.6 IPv6 autoconfiguration example

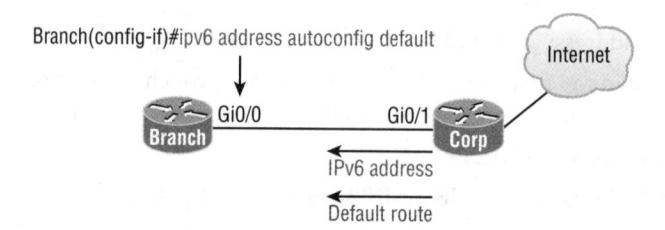

Branch(config-if)#ipv6 address autoconfig default

Branch Gi0/0 — Gi0/1 Corp — Internet

IPv6 address
Default route

Ah ha—there is an easy way! I love IPv6 because it allows me to be relatively lazy when dealing with some parts of my network, yet it still works really well. By using the command `ipv6 address autoconfig`, the interface will listen for RAs and then, via the EUI-64 format, it will assign itself a global address—sweet!

This is all really great, but you're hopefully wondering what that `default` is doing there at the end of the command. If so, good catch! It happens to be a wonderful, optional part of the command that smoothly delivers a default route received from the Corp router, which will be automatically injected it into my routing table and set as the default route—so easy!

DHCPv6 (Stateful)

DHCPv6 works pretty much the same way DHCP does in v4, with the obvious difference that it supports IPv6's new addressing scheme. And it might come as a surprise, but there are a couple of other options that DHCP still provides for us that autoconfiguration doesn't. And no, I'm not kidding—in autoconfiguration, there's absolutely no mention of DNS servers, domain names, or many of the other options that DHCP has always generously provided for us via IPv4. This is a big reason that the odds favor DHCP's continued use into the future in IPv6 at least partially—maybe even most of the time!

Upon booting up in IPv4, a client sends out a DHCP Discover message looking for a server to give it the information it needs. But remember, in IPv6, the RS and RA process happens first, so if there's a DHCPv6 server on the network, the RA that comes back to the client will tell it if DHCP is available for use. If a router isn't found, the client will respond by sending out a DHCP Solicit message, which is actually a multicast message addressed with a destination of ff02::1:2 that calls out, "All DHCP agents, both servers and relays."

It's good to know that there's some support for DHCPv6 in the Cisco IOS even though it's limited. This rather miserly support is reserved for stateless DHCP servers and tells us it doesn't offer any address management of the pool or the options available for configuring that address pool other than the DNS, domain name, default gateway, and SIP servers.

This means that you're definitely going to need another server around to supply and dispense all the additional, required information—maybe to even manage the address assignment, if needed!

> Remember for the objectives that both stateless and stateful autoconfiguration can dynamically assign IPv6 addresses.

IPv6 Header

An IPv4 header is 20 bytes long, so since an IPv6 address is four times the size of IPv4 at 128 bits, its header must then be 80 bytes long, right? That makes sense and is totally intuitive, but it's also completely wrong! When IPv6 designers devised the header, they created fewer, streamlined fields that would also result in a faster routed protocol at the same time.

Let's take a look at the streamlined IPv6 header using Figure 17.7.

FIGURE 17.7 IPv6 header

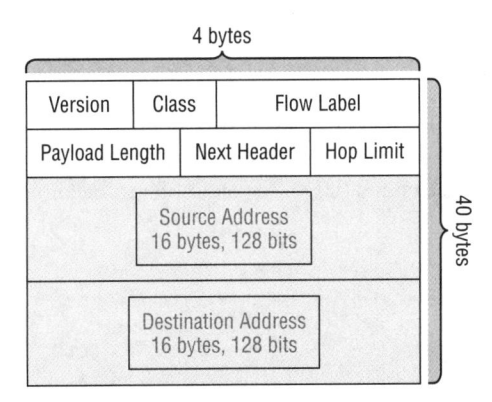

The basic IPv6 header contains eight fields, making it only twice as large as an IP header at 40 bytes. Let's zoom in on these fields:

Version   This 4-bit field contains the number 6, instead of the number 4 as in IPv4.

Traffic Class   This 8-bit field is like the Type of Service (ToS) field in IPv4.

Flow Label   This new field, which is 24 bits long, is used to mark packets and traffic flows. A flow is a sequence of packets from a single source to a single destination host, an anycast or multicast address. The field enables efficient IPv6 flow classification.

Payload Length   IPv4 had a total length field delimiting the length of the packet. IPv6's payload length describes the length of the payload only.

Next Header   Since there are optional extension headers with IPv6, this field defines the next header to be read. This is in contrast to IPv4, which demands static headers with each packet.

Hop Limit   This field specifies the maximum number of hops that an IPv6 packet can traverse.

> For objectives remember that the Hop Limit field is equivalent to the TTL field in IPv4's header, and the Extension header (after the destination address and not shown in the figure) is used instead of the IPv4 Fragmentation field.

Source Address   This field of 16 bytes, or 128 bits, identifies the source of the packet.

Destination Address   This field of 16 bytes, or 128 bits, identifies the destination of the packet.

There are also some optional extension headers following these eight fields, which carry other Network layer information. These header lengths are not a fixed number—they're of variable size.

So what's different in the IPv6 header from the IPv4 header? Let's look at that:

- The Internet Header Length field was removed because it is no longer required. Unlike the variable-length IPv4 header, the IPv6 header is fixed at 40 bytes.

- Fragmentation is processed differently in IPv6 and does not need the Flags field in the basic IPv4 header. In IPv6, routers no longer process fragmentation; the host is responsible for fragmentation.

- The Header Checksum field at the IP layer was removed because most Data Link layer technologies already perform checksum and error control, which forces formerly optional upper-layer checksums (UDP, for example) to become mandatory.

> **Tip:** For the objectives, remember that unlike IPv4 headers, IPv6 headers have a fixed length, use an extension header instead of the IPv4 Fragmentation field, and eliminate the IPv4 checksum field.

It's time to move on to talk about another IPv4 familiar face and find out how a certain very important, built-in protocol has evolved in IPv6.

ICMPv6

IPv4 used the ICMP workhorse for lots of tasks, including error messages like destination unreachable and troubleshooting functions like Ping and Traceroute. ICMPv6 still does those things for us, but unlike its predecessor, the v6 flavor isn't implemented as a separate layer 3 protocol. Instead, it's an integrated part of IPv6 and is carried after the basic IPv6 header information as an extension header. And ICMPv6 gives us another really cool feature—by default, it prevents IPv6 from doing any fragmentation through an ICMPv6 process called path MTU discovery. Figure 17.8 shows how ICMPv6 has evolved to become part of the IPv6 packet itself.

FIGURE 17.8 ICMPv6

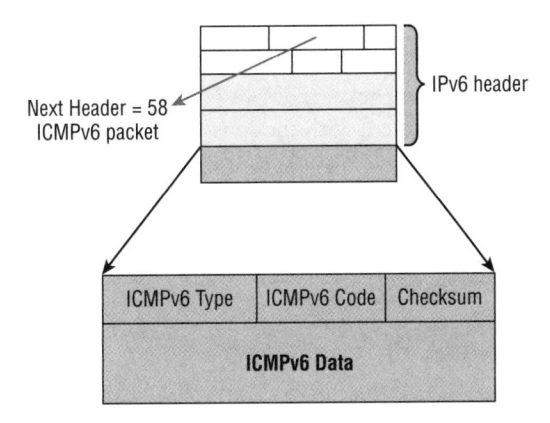

The ICMPv6 packet is identified by the value 58 in the Next Header field, located inside the ICMPv6 packet. The Type field identifies the particular kind of ICMP message that's being carried, and the Code field further details the specifics of the message. The Data field contains the ICMPv6 payload.

Table 17.2 shows the ICMP Type codes.

TABLE 17.2 ICMPv6 types

ICMPv6 Type	Description
1	Destination Unreachable
128	Echo Request
129	Echo Reply
133	Router Solicitation
134	Router Advertisement
135	Neighbor Solicitation
136	Neighbor Advertisement

And this is how it works: The source node of a connection sends a packet that's equal to the MTU size of its local link's MTU. As this packet traverses the path toward its destination, any link that has an MTU smaller than the size of the current packet will force the intermediate router to send a "packet too big" message back to the source machine. This message tells the source node the maximum size the restrictive link will allow and asks the source to send a new, scaled-down packet that can pass through. This process will continue until the destination is finally reached, with the source node now sporting the new path's MTU. So now, when the rest of the data packets are transmitted, they'll be protected from fragmentation.

ICMPv6 is used for router solicitation and advertisement, for neighbor solicitation and advertisement (i.e., finding the MAC data addresses for IPv6 neighbors), and for redirecting the host to the best router (default gateway).

Neighbor Discovery (NDP)

ICMPv6 also takes over the task of finding the address of other devices on the local link. The Address Resolution Protocol is used to perform this function for IPv4, but that's been renamed neighbor discovery (ND) in ICMPv6. This process is now achieved via a multicast address called the solicited-node address because all hosts join this multicast group upon connecting to the network.

Neighbor discovery enables these functions:

- Determining the MAC address of neighbors
- Router solicitation (RS) FF02::2 type code 133
- Router advertisements (RA) FF02::1 type code 134
- Neighbor solicitation (NS) Type code 135

- Neighbor advertisement (NA) Type code 136
- Duplicate address detection (DAD)

The part of the IPv6 address designated by the 24 bits farthest to the right is added to the end of the multicast address FF02:0:0:0:0:1:FF/104 prefix and is referred to as the *solicited-node address*. When this address is queried, the corresponding host will send back its layer 2 address.

Devices can find and keep track of other neighbor devices on the network in pretty much the same way. When I talked about RA and RS messages earlier and told you that they use multicast traffic to request and send address information, that too is actually a function of ICMPv6—specifically, neighbor discovery.

In IPv4, the protocol IGMP was used to allow a host device to tell its local router that it was joining a multicast group and would like to receive the traffic for that group. This IGMP function has been replaced by ICMPv6, and the process has been renamed multicast listener discovery.

With IPv4, our hosts could have only one default gateway configured, and if that router went down we had to either fix the router, change the default gateway, or run some type of virtual default gateway with other protocols created as a solution for this inadequacy in IPv4. Figure 17.9 shows how IPv6 devices find their default gateways using neighbor discovery.

FIGURE 17.9 Router solicitation (RS) and router advertisement (RA)

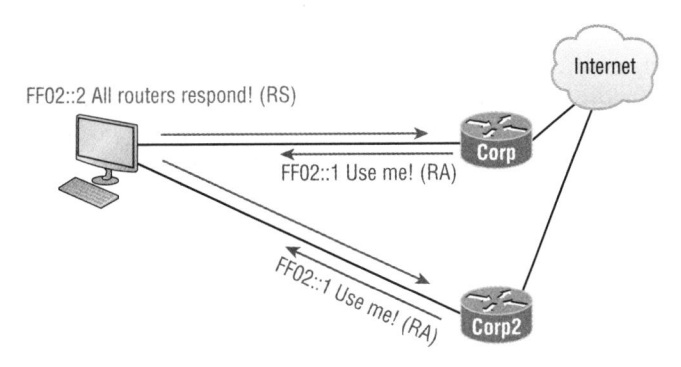

IPv6 hosts send a router solicitation (RS) onto their data link asking for all routers to respond, and they use the multicast address FF02::2 to achieve this. Routers on the same link respond with a unicast to the requesting host, or with a router advertisement (RA) using FF02::1.

But that's not all! Hosts also can send solicitations and advertisements between themselves using a neighbor solicitation (NS) and neighbor advertisement (NA), as shown in Figure 17.10. Remember that RA and RS gather or provide information about routers, and NS and NA gather information about hosts. Remember that a "neighbor" is a host on the same data link or VLAN.

FIGURE 17.10 Neighbor solicitation (NS) and neighbor advertisement (NA)

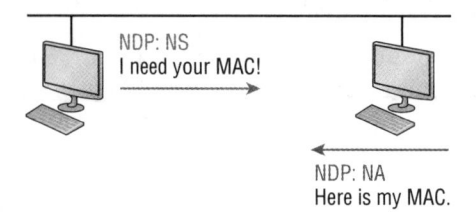

Solicited-Node and Multicast Mapping over Ethernet

If an IPv6 address is known, then the associated IPv6 solicited-node multicast address is known, and if an IPv6 multicast address is known, then the associated Ethernet MAC address is known.

For example, the IPv6 address 2001:DB8:2002:F:2C0:10FF:FE18:FC0F will have a known solicited-node address of FF02::1:FF18:FC0F.

Now we'll form the multicast Ethernet addresses by adding the last 32 bits of the IPv6 multicast address to 33:33.

For example, if the IPv6 solicited-node multicast address is FF02::1:FF18:FC0F, the associated Ethernet MAC address is 33:33:FF:18:FC:0F and is a virtual address.

Duplicate Address Detection (DAD)

So what do you think are the odds that two hosts will assign themselves the same random IPv6 address? Personally, I think you could probably win the lotto every day for a year and still not come close to the odds against two hosts on the same data link duplicating an IPv6 address! Still, to make sure this doesn't ever happen, duplicate address detection (DAD) was created, which isn't an actual protocol, but a function of the NS/NA messages.

Figure 17.11 shows how a host sends an NDP NS when it receives or creates an IPv6 address.

FIGURE 17.11 Duplicate address detection (DAD)

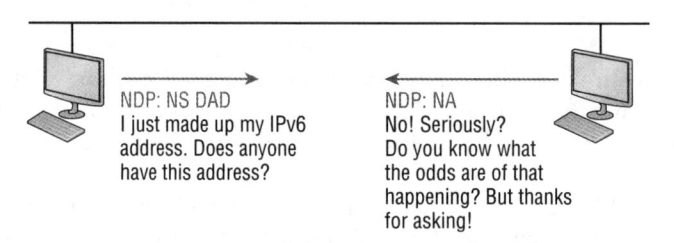

When hosts make up or receive an IPv6 address, they send three DADs out via NDP NS asking if anyone has this same address. The odds are unlikely that this will ever happen, but they ask anyway.

> Remember for the objectives that ICMPv6 uses type 134 for router advertisement messages, and the advertised prefix must be 64 bits in length.

IPv6 Routing Protocols

All of the routing protocols we've already discussed have been tweaked and upgraded for use in IPv6 networks, so it figures that many of the functions and configurations that you've already learned will be used in almost the same way as they are now. Knowing that broadcasts have been eliminated in IPv6, it's safe to conclude that any protocols relying entirely on broadcast traffic will go the way of the dodo. But unlike with the dodo, it'll be really nice to say goodbye to these bandwidth-hogging, performance-annihilating little gremlins!

The routing protocols we'll still use in IPv6 have been renovated and given new names. Even though this chapter's focus is on the Cisco exam objectives, which cover only static and default routing, I want to discuss a few of the more important ones too.

First on the list is the IPv6 RIPng (next generation). Those of you who've been in IT for a while know that RIP has worked pretty well for us on smaller networks. This happens to be the very reason it didn't get whacked and will still be around in IPv6. And we still have EIGRPv6 because EIGRP already had protocol-dependent modules and all we had to do was add a new one to it to fit in nicely with the IPv6 protocol. Rounding out our group of protocol survivors is OSPFv3—that's not a typo, it really is v3! OSPF for IPv4 was actually v2, so when it got its upgrade to IPv6, it became OSPFv3. Lastly, for the new objectives, we'll list MP-BGP4 as a multiprotocol BGP-4 protocol for IPv6. Please understand for the objectives at this point in the book, we only need to understand static and default routing.

Static Routing with IPv6

Okay, now don't let the heading of this section scare you into looking on Monster.com for some job that has nothing to do with networking! I know that static routing has always run a chill up our collective spines because it's cumbersome, difficult, and really easy to screw up. And I won't lie to you—it's certainly not any easier with IPv6's longer addresses, but you can do it!

We know that to make static routing work, whether in IP or IPv6, you need these three tools:

- An accurate, up-to-date network map of your entire internetwork
- Next-hop address and exit interface for each neighbor connection
- All the remote subnet IDs

Of course, we don't need to have any of these for dynamic routing, which is why we mostly use dynamic routing. It's just so awesome to have the routing protocol do all that work for us by finding all the remote subnets and automatically placing them into the routing table!

Figure 17.12 shows a really good example of how to use static routing with IPv6. It really doesn't have to be that hard, but just as with IPv4, you absolutely need an accurate network map to make static routing work!

FIGURE 17.12 IPv6 static and default routing

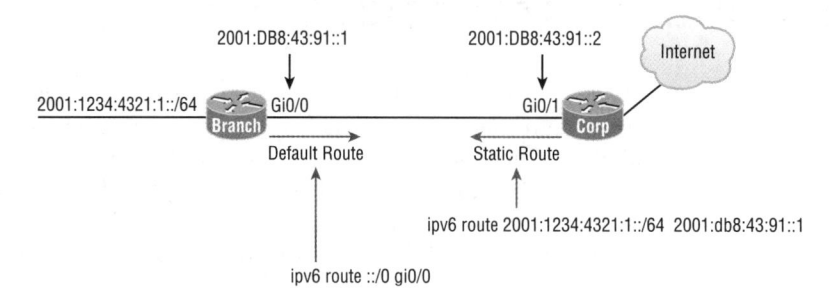

So here's what I did: First, I created a static route on the Corp router to the remote network 2001:1234:4321:1::/64 using the next hop address. I could've just as easily used the Corp router's exit interface. Next, I just set up a default route for the Branch router with ::/0 and the Branch exit interface of Gi0/0—not so bad!

Configuring IPv6 on Our Internetwork

We're going to continue working on the same internetwork we've been configuring throughout this book, as shown in Figure 17.13. Let's add IPv6 to the Corp, SF, and LA routers by using a simple subnet scheme of 11, 12, 13, 14, and 15. After that, we'll add the OSPFv3 routing protocol. Notice in Figure 17.13 how the subnet numbers are the same on each end of the WAN links. Keep in mind that we'll finish this chapter by running through some verification commands.

FIGURE 17.13 Our internetwork

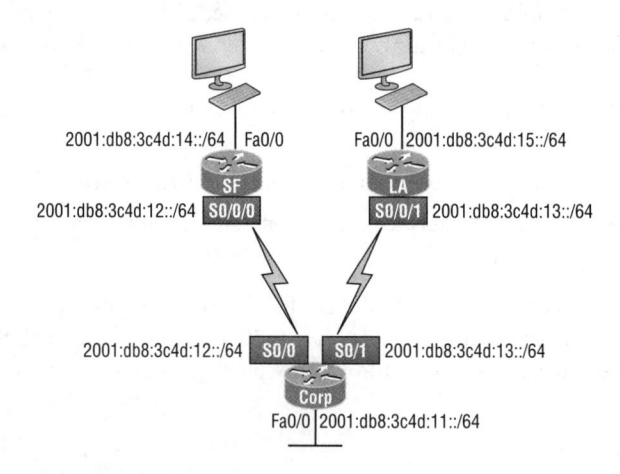

As usual, I'll start with the Corp router:

```
Corp#config t
Corp(config)#ipv6 unicast-routing
Corp(config)#int f0/0
Corp(config-if)#ipv6 address 2001:db8:3c4d:11::/64 eui-64
Corp(config-if)#int s0/0
Corp(config-if)#ipv6 address 2001:db8:3c4d:12::/64 eui-64
Corp(config-if)#int s0/1
Corp(config-if)#ipv6 address 2001:db8:3c4d:13::/64 eui-64
Corp(config-if)#^Z
Corp#copy run start
Destination filename [startup-config]?[enter]
Building configuration...
[OK]
```

Pretty simple! In the previous configuration, I only changed the subnet address for each interface slightly. Let's take a look at the routing table now:

```
Corp(config-if)#do sho ipv6 route
C 2001:DB8:3C4D:11::/64 [0/0]
   via ::, FastEthernet0/0
L 2001:DB8:3C4D:11:20D:BDFF:FE3B:D80/128 [0/0]
   via ::, FastEthernet0/0
C 2001:DB8:3C4D:12::/64 [0/0]
   via ::, Serial0/0
L 2001:DB8:3C4D:12:20D:BDFF:FE3B:D80/128 [0/0]
   via ::, Serial0/0
C 2001:DB8:3C4D:13::/64 [0/0]
   via ::, Serial0/1
L 2001:DB8:3C4D:13:20D:BDFF:FE3B:D80/128 [0/0]
   via ::, Serial0/1
L FE80::/10 [0/0]
   via ::, Null0
L FF00::/8 [0/0]
   via ::, Null0
Corp(config-if)#
```

Alright, but what's up with those two addresses for each interface? One shows C for connected, one shows L. The connected address indicates the IPv6 address I configured on each interface and the L is the link-local that's been automatically assigned. Notice in the link-local address that the FF:FE is inserted into the address to create the EUI-64 address.

Let's configure the SF router now:

```
SF#config t
SF(config)#ipv6 unicast-routing
SF(config)#int s0/0/0
SF(config-if)#ipv6 address 2001:db8:3c4d:12::/64
% 2001:DB8:3C4D:12::/64 should not be configured on Serial0/0/0, a subnet router anycast
SF(config-if)#ipv6 address 2001:db8:3c4d:12::/64 eui-64
SF(config-if)#int fa0/0
SF(config-if)#ipv6 address 2001:db8:3c4d:14::/64 eui-64
SF(config-if)#^Z
SF#show ipv6 route
C 2001:DB8:3C4D:12::/64 [0/0]
via ::, Serial0/0/0
L 2001:DB8:3C4D:12::/128 [0/0]
via ::, Serial0/0/0
L 2001:DB8:3C4D:12:21A:2FFF:FEE7:4398/128 [0/0]
via ::, Serial0/0/0
C 2001:DB8:3C4D:14::/64 [0/0]
via ::, FastEthernet0/0
L 2001:DB8:3C4D:14:21A:2FFF:FEE7:4398/128 [0/0]
via ::, FastEthernet0/0
L FE80::/10 [0/0]
via ::, Null0
L FF00::/8 [0/0]
via ::, Null0
```

Did you notice that I used the exact IPv6 subnet addresses on each side of the serial link? Good... but wait—what's with that anycast error I received when trying to configure the interfaces on the SF router? I didn't mean to create that error; it happened because I forgot to add the `eui-64` at the end of the address. Still, what's behind that error? An anycast address is a host address of all 0s, meaning the last 64 bits are all off, but by typing in /64 without the `eui-64`, I was telling the interface that the unique identifier would be nothing but zeros, and that's not allowed!

Let's configure the LA router now:

```
SF#config t
SF(config)#ipv6 unicast-routing
SF(config)#int s0/0/1
SF(config-if)#ipv6 address 2001:db8:3c4d:13::/64 eui-64
SF(config-if)#int f0/0
SF(config-if)#ipv6 address 2001:db8:3c4d:15::/64 eui-64
```

```
SF(config-if)#do show ipv6 route
C 2001:DB8:3C4D:13::/64 [0/0]
via ::, Serial0/0/1
L 2001:DB8:3C4D:13:21A:6CFF:FEA1:1F48/128 [0/0]
via ::, Serial0/0/1
C 2001:DB8:3C4D:15::/64 [0/0]
via ::, FastEthernet0/0
L 2001:DB8:3C4D:15:21A:6CFF:FEA1:1F48/128 [0/0]
via ::, FastEthernet0/0
L FE80::/10 [0/0]
via ::, Null0
L FF00::/8 [0/0]
via ::, Null0
```

This looks good, but I want you to notice that I used the exact same IPv6 subnet addresses on each side of the links from the Corp router to the SF router as well as from the Corp to the LA router.

Configuring Routing on Our Internetwork

I'll start at the Corp router and add simple static routes. Check it out:

```
Corp(config)#ipv6 route 2001:db8:3c4d:14::/64
2001:DB8:3C4D:12:21A:2FFF:FEE7:4398 150
Corp(config)#ipv6 route 2001:DB8:3C4D:15::/64 s0/1 150
Corp(config)#do sho ipv6 route static
[output cut]
S 2001:DB8:3C4D:14::/64 [150/0]
via 2001:DB8:3C4D:12:21A:2FFF:FEE7:4398
```

Okay—I agree that first static route line was pretty long because I used the next-hop address, but notice that I used the exit interface on the second entry. But it still wasn't really all that hard to create the longer static route entry. I just went to the SF router, used the command show ipv6 int brief, and then copied and pasted the interface address used for the next hop. You'll get used to IPv6 addresses (you'll get used to doing a lot of copy/paste moves!).

Now since I put an AD of 150 on the static routes, once I configure a routing protocol such as OSPF, they'll be replaced with an OSPF injected route since it has a lower AD (remember this is called a floating static route). Let's go to the SF and LA routers and put a single entry in each router to get to remote subnet 11.

```
SF(config)#ipv6 route 2001:db8:3c4d:11::/64 s0/0/0 150
```

That's it! I'm going to head over to LA and put a default route on that router now:

```
LA(config)#ipv6 route ::/0 s0/0/1
```

Let's take a peek at the Corp router's routing table and see if our static routes are in there.

```
Corp#sh ipv6 route static
[output cut]
S 2001:DB8:3C4D:14::/64 [150/0]
via 2001:DB8:3C4D:12:21A:2FFF:FEE7:4398
S 2001:DB8:3C4D:15::/64 [150/0]
via ::, Serial0/1
```

Voilà! I can see both of my static routes in the routing table, so IPv6 can now route to those networks. But we're not done because we still need to test our network! First I'm going to go to the SF router and get the IPv6 address of the Fa0/0 interface:

```
SF#sh ipv6 int brief
FastEthernet0/0 [up/up]
FE80::21A:2FFF:FEE7:4398
2001:DB8:3C4D:14:21A:2FFF:FEE7:4398
FastEthernet0/1 [administratively down/down]
Serial0/0/0 [up/up]
FE80::21A:2FFF:FEE7:4398
2001:DB8:3C4D:12:21A:2FFF:FEE7:4398
```

Next, I'm going to go back to the Corporate router and ping that remote interface by copying and pasting in the address. No sense doing all that typing when copy/paste works great!

```
Corp#ping ipv6 2001:DB8:3C4D:14:21A:2FFF:FEE7:4398
Type escape sequence to abort.
Sending 5, 100-byte ICMP Echos to 2001:DB8:3C4D:14:21A:2FFF:FEE7:4398, timeout is 2 seconds:
!!!!!
Success rate is 100 percent (5/5), round-trip min/avg/max = 0/0/0 ms
Corp#
```

We can see that static route worked, so next, I'll go get the IPv6 address of the LA router and ping that remote interface as well:

```
LA#sh ipv6 int brief
FastEthernet0/0 [up/up]
FE80::21A:6CFF:FEA1:1F48
```

```
2001:DB8:3C4D:15:21A:6CFF:FEA1:1F48
Serial0/0/1 [up/up]
FE80::21A:6CFF:FEA1:1F48
2001:DB8:3C4D:13:21A:6CFF:FEA1:1F48
```

It's time to head over to Corp and ping LA:

```
Corp#ping ipv6 2001:DB8:3C4D:15:21A:6CFF:FEA1:1F48
Type escape sequence to abort.
Sending 5, 100-byte ICMP Echos to 2001:DB8:3C4D:15:21A:6CFF:FEA1:1F48, timeout
is 2 seconds:
!!!!!
Success rate is 100 percent (5/5), round-trip min/avg/max = 4/4/4 ms
Corp#
```

Now let's use one of my favorite commands:

```
Corp#sh ipv6 int brief
FastEthernet0/0 [up/up]
FE80::20D:BDFF:FE3B:D80
2001:DB8:3C4D:11:20D:BDFF:FE3B:D80
Serial0/0 [up/up]
FE80::20D:BDFF:FE3B:D80
2001:DB8:3C4D:12:20D:BDFF:FE3B:D80
FastEthernet0/1 [administratively down/down]
unassigned
Serial0/1 [up/up]
FE80::20D:BDFF:FE3B:D80
2001:DB8:3C4D:13:20D:BDFF:FE3B:D80
Loopback0 [up/up]
unassigned
Corp#
```

What a nice output! All our interfaces are up/up, and we can see the link-local and assigned global address.

Static routing really isn't so bad with IPv6! I'm not saying I'd like to do this in a ginormous network—no way—I wouldn't want to opt for doing that with IPv4 either! But you can see that it can be done. Also, notice how easy it was to ping an IPv6 address. Copy/paste really is your friend!

Before we finish the chapter, let's add another router to our network and connect it to the Corp Fa0/0 LAN. For our new router I really don't feel like doing any work, so I'll just type this:

```
Boulder#config t
Boulder(config)#int f0/0
Boulder(config-if)#ipv6 address autoconfig default
```

Nice and easy! This configures stateless autoconfiguration on the interface, and the `default` keyword will advertise itself as the default route for the local link!

I hope you found this chapter as rewarding as I did. The best thing you can do to learn IPv6 is to get some routers and just go at it. Don't give up because it's seriously worth your time!

Summary

This last chapter introduced you to some very key IPv6 structural elements as well as how to make IPv6 work within a Cisco internetwork. You now know that even when covering and configuring IPv6 basics, there's still a great deal to understand—and we just scratched the surface! But you're still well equipped with all you need to meet the Cisco exam objectives.

You learned the vital reasons why we need IPv6 and the benefits associated with it. I covered IPv6 addressing and the importance of using the shortened expressions. As I covered addressing with IPv6, I also showed you the different address types, plus the special addresses reserved in IPv6.

IPv6 will mostly be deployed automatically, meaning hosts will employ autoconfiguration. I demonstrated how IPv6 utilizes autoconfiguration and how it comes into play when configuring a Cisco router. You also learned that in IPv6, we can and still should use a DHCP server to the router to provide options to hosts just as we've been doing for years with IPv4—not necessarily IPv6 addresses, but other mission-critical options like providing a DNS server address.

From there, I discussed the evolution of the more integral and familiar protocol like ICMP. They've been upgraded to work in the IPv6 environment, but these networking workhorses are still vital and relevant to operations, and I detailed how ICMP works with IPv6

I wrapped up this pivotal chapter by demonstrating key methods to use when verifying that all is running correctly in your IPv6 network.

Exam Essentials

Understand why we need IPv6.   Without IPv6, the world would be depleted of IP addresses.

Understand link-local.   Link-local is like an IPv4 APIPA IP address, and it can't be routed at all, not even in your organization.

Understand unique local.   This, like link-local, is like a private IP address in IPv4 and cannot be routed to the Internet. However, the difference between link-local and unique local is that unique local can be routed within your organization or company.

Remember IPv6 addressing. IPv6 addressing is not like IPv4 addressing. IPv6 addressing has much more address space, is 128 bits long, and represented in hexadecimal, unlike IPv4, which is only 32 bits long and represented in decimal.

Understand and be able to read a EUI-64 address with the 7th bit inverted. Hosts can use autoconfiguration to obtain an IPv6 address, and one of the ways it can do that is through what is called EUI-64. This takes the unique MAC address of a host and inserts FF:FE in the middle of the address to change a 48-bit MAC address to a 64-bit interface ID. In addition to inserting the 16 bits into the interface ID, the 7th bit of the 1st byte is inverted, typically from a 0 to a 1.

Review Questions

The answers to these questions can be found in the Appendix.

1. How is an EUI-64 format interface ID created from a 48-bit MAC address?
   A. By appending 0xFF to the MAC address
   B. By prefixing the MAC address with 0xFFEE
   C. By prefixing the MAC address with 0xFF and appending 0xFF to it
   D. By inserting 0xFFFE between the upper 3 bytes and the lower 3 bytes of the MAC address

2. Which option is a valid IPv6 address?
   A. 2001:0000:130F::099a::12a
   B. 2002:7654:A1AD:61:81AF:CCC1
   C. FEC0:ABCD:WXYZ:0067::2A4
   D. 2004:1:25A4:886F::1

3. Which three statements about IPv6 prefixes are true? (Choose three.)
   A. FF00::/8 is used for IPv6 multicast.
   B. FE80::/10 is used for link-local unicast.
   C. FC00::/7 is used in private networks.
   D. 2001::1/127 is used for loopback addresses.
   E. FE80::/8 is used for link-local unicast.
   F. FEC0::/10 is used for IPv6 broadcast.

4. What are three approaches that are used when migrating from an IPv4 addressing scheme to an IPv6 scheme? (Choose three.)
   A. Enable dual-stack routing.
   B. Configure IPv6 directly.
   C. Configure IPv4 tunnels between IPv6 islands.
   D. Use proxying and translation to translate IPv6 packets into IPv4 packets.
   E. Use DHCPv6 to map IPv4 addresses to IPv6 addresses.

5. Which two statements about IPv6 router advertisement messages are true? (Choose two.)
   A. They use ICMPv6 type 134.
   B. The advertised prefix length must be 64 bits.
   C. The advertised prefix length must be 48 bits.
   D. They are sourced from the configured IPv6 interface address.
   E. Their destination is always the link-local address of the neighboring node.

6. Which of the following is true when describing an IPv6 anycast address? (Choose three.)
   A. One-to-many communication model
   B. One-to-nearest communication model
   C. Any-to-many communication model
   D. A unique IPv6 address for each device in the group
   E. The same address for multiple devices in the group
   F. Delivery of packets to the group interface that is closest to the sending device

7. You want to ping the loopback address of your IPv6 local host. What will you type?
   A. ping 127.0.0.1
   B. ping 0.0.0.0
   C. ping ::1
   D. trace 0.0.::1

8. What are three features of the IPv6 protocol? (Choose three.)
   A. Optional IPsec
   B. Autoconfiguration
   C. No broadcasts
   D. Complicated header
   E. Plug-and-play
   F. Checksums

9. Which two statements describe characteristics of IPv6 unicast addressing? (Choose two.)
   A. Global addresses start with 2000::/3.
   B. Link-local addresses start with FE00:/12.
   C. Link-local addresses start with FF00::/10.
   D. There is only one loopback address and it is ::1.
   E. If a global address is assigned to an interface, then that is the only allowable address for the interface.

10. A host sends a router solicitation (RS) on the data link. What destination address is sent with this request?
    A. FF02::A
    B. FF02::9
    C. FF02::2
    D. FF02::1
    E. FF02::5

Chapter 18

Troubleshooting IP, IPv6, and VLANs

THE FOLLOWING CCNA EXAM TOPICS ARE COVERED IN THIS CHAPTER:

1.0 **Network Fundamentals**

✓ 1.4 Identify interface and cable issues (collisions, errors, mismatch duplex, and/or speed)

✓ 1.6 Configure and verify IPv4 addressing and subnetting

✓ 1.8 Configure and verify IPv6 addressing and prefix

✓ 1.10 Verify IP parameters for Client OS (Windows, Mac OS, Linux)

2.0 **Network Access**

✓ 2.2 Configure and verify interswitch connectivity

- 2.2.a Trunk ports
- 2.2.b 802.1Q
- 2.2.c Native VLAN

Especially at first, it's going to seem like we're covering the same ground already covered in other chapters. It's just that troubleshooting is such a major focus of the Cisco CCNA objectives I'd be letting you down if I didn't make sure you've seriously got it down. So to make sure your skills are solid, we're going start with a deep dive into troubleshooting with IP, IPv6, and virtual LANs (VLANs). Having the fundamentals of IP and IPv6 routing, plus a working knowledge of VLANs and trunking nailed down tight is also key if you're going to win at this!

Although it's hard to predict exactly what the CCNA exam will throw at you, I'll use carefully planned scenarios to guide you through Cisco's troubleshooting steps. With the skills you'll gain pushing through the scenarios, you'll be able to successfully solve the problems you're likely to face on the exam and in the real world. This chapter is specifically designed to solidify your troubleshooting foundation, so let's get started!

Let's get started by looking at the components we're going to connect to our network and find out how to quickly get them online for testing in the lab or workplace.

> To find your included bonus material, as well as Todd Lammle videos, practice questions & hands-on labs, please see www.lammle.com/ccna

Endpoints

An endpoint is basically just something that connects to the network through a wired or wireless connection. Most vendors license based upon how many active endpoints on the network are using the service the product provides. I'll quickly cover some common endpoints now.

Desktops/Laptops

Desktops and Laptops are by far the most prevalent kind of endpoint in our networks because pretty much every employee has at least one of these assigned to them.

Most companies are either on Microsoft Windows 10 or in process of upgrading to it from Windows 7. Some also have a few Apple Mac computers in the mix, but you usually won't find Linux on the end user side of things.

And of course, all computers can use wired or wireless connections interchangeably.

Mobile Phones/Tablets

It's also pretty common for staff to be issued a mobile phone and/or a tablet that will often connect to a SSID provided by the office. Most companies also allow employees to use their own devices on the network, but access is usually restricted via security policies.

Typical mobile devices would be Apple iPhone/iPad or some Android variant, which all tend to use wireless connections exclusively.

Access Points

Even though these devices are actually there to provide wireless access to your endpoints, they connect to the network too, so they're also considered endpoints.

Access Points typically use wired connections for power supply and to get on the network, but they can also use wireless connections in more advanced configurations.

IP Phones

Most companies either have a Voice over IP (VoIP) solution or they're talking about it. Because of this, phones hog lots of switch ports, so to save on cabling requirements, office computers are often connected to the IP Phone's built-in switch. That way, it's only the phone that gets connected to the access switch.

IP Phones typically use wired ethernet connections for power rather than plugging into the wall.

Internet of Things

With the genesis of the IoT, everything from light bulbs to fridges and alarm systems are all the network now and they're all endpoints too!

Servers

Just like your server at a restaurant, the server on the network delivers what you've ordered. Servers are basically higher end computers used to provide infrastructure or application services to users and they tend to come in these three forms:

Tower   Tower end servers are pretty much just standard computer towers that can provide a few more resources than a regular computer.

Rack Server   The most common type of server is a rack-mounted simple server that's usually one rack unit (RU) in size but can be bigger. People sometimes call rack servers pizza boxes because they're often large squares.

Blade Server   This is the most complex type of server, which is actually a blade that connects into a large chassis. These systems are designed to be very redundant and resilient.

Server Roles

There are way too many different server roles out there for me to talk about all of them in this chapter, but here's list the most common kinds of servers found in a network:

Active Directory   Microsoft AD is Windows Server's flagship role for User and Computer management and it's used one way or another by almost every company in existence!

DNS   Using the Internet in any kind of efficient way depends on DNS because without it, we would all be surfing by memorizing IP addresses.

DHCP   Covered earlier, DHCP is how your endpoints dynamically learn their IP address to get on the network.

Hypervisor   I'll talk about this role more when we get into virtualization, but for now, just know it's what allows us to run virtual machines.

RADIUS   This role is largely used by wireless to authenticate connections into the network.

TACACS+   This role is used for device administration and can control what a user has access to when they log into a device.

Email   The type of server that manages sending and receiving email messages.

File   File servers store a large number of files for users to access.

Databases   These servers store data in mysterious tables ran by crazy wizards known as DBAs. Avoid DBAs at all cost!

Web   This type of server runs the webpages we browse on the Internet.

IP Config

It's a fact that at some point in your Cisco studies, you'll need to know how to verify and change the IP address on the operating system you're using. Doing this is really helpful for labs that use PCs for testing since you can adjust the IP to suit your lab environment.

Clearly, being good at this is vital in the real world because most servers use static IP addresses—not every subnet will have DHCP running and you'll probably need to troubleshoot an end user's connection from time to time.

Windows 10

On Windows operating systems you can set the IP address from Network Connections. The easiest way to get there is to type **ncpa.cpl** in the search bar or from the Run command.

You can also get there through the Control panel by selecting **Network and Sharing Center** then **Change adapter settings**. Once you're in, just right-click the network adapter you want to set the IP on and then left-click on **properties** as shown in Figure 18.1.

FIGURE 18.1 Network Connections page

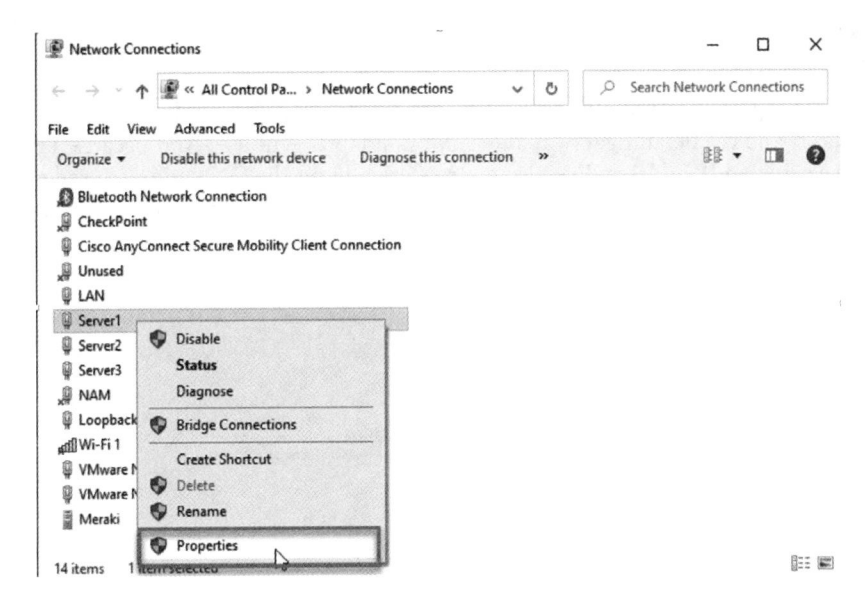

The properties page has a bunch of protocol information that we can adjust for the network adapter. For now, I'm going to choose Internet Protocol Version 4 (TCP/IP) and I'm going to click on properties as pictured in Figure 18.2.

FIGURE 18.2 IPv4 Properties Page

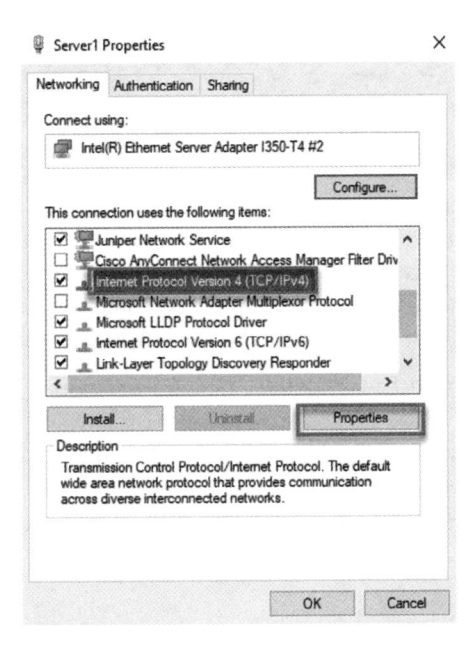

NOTE If you want to change the IPv6 address you'd go into the Version 6 properties instead.

On the next page, I can finally set my IP address information including the IP address, subnet mask, and the default gateway the network adapter will use. And because I'm statically setting an IP address, I've also got to statically set the DNS address used to resolve domain names too since the network adapter won't be learning it via DHCP (See Figure 18.3.).

FIGURE 18.3 Setting the IP and DNS addresses

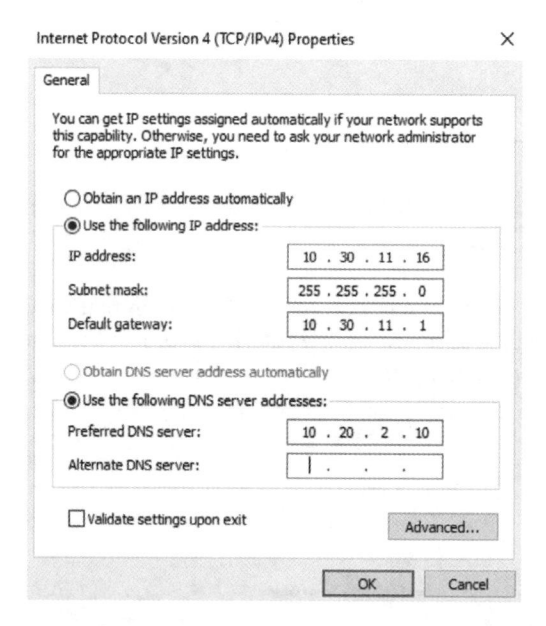

Now that the network adapter's IP and DNS is set, I could just hit OK to apply the changes. But I'm not going to do that just yet because I want to introduce you to a couple of important items under the Advanced button first. This is where you can add additional IP addresses under the interface. This is like adding a secondary IP address on a Cisco router interface where you can add as many additional IPs as you want. Check out Figure 18.4.

This comes in really handy for web servers where each web site may want to bind to a different IP address on the system.

Like a Cisco router, Windows also has a routing table. So if you have multiple active interfaces on your computer, you can choose to adjust the interface metric, making it either more or less desirable when the computer needs to pick an interface to route traffic out of.

FIGURE 18.4 Advanced tab

The last thing I want to point out here in these properties is the DNS tab. This is where you can choose to add more DNS servers if you have more than two, as shown in Figure 18.5.

FIGURE 18.5 DNS tab

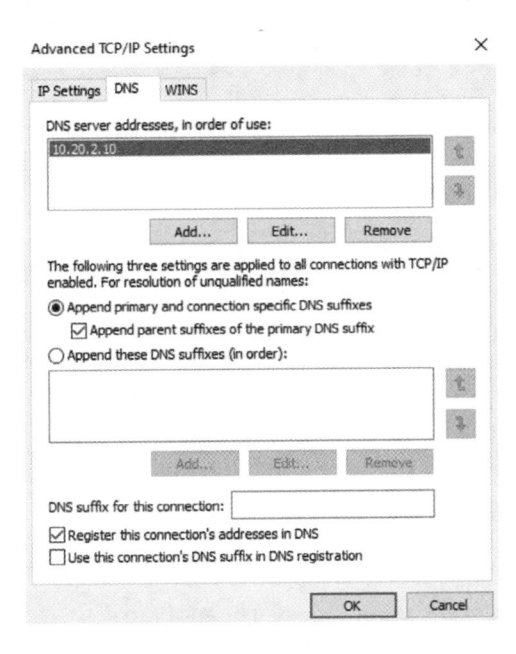

502 Chapter 18 ▪ Troubleshooting IP, IPv6, and VLANs

Oh—and I can also choose to append domain names to my DNS queries! If I add **testlab.com** I just need to type **web01** to reach **web01.testlab.com** because it will append the name for me—cool.

So with all that out of the way, I'll hit OK on all the dialogs until I'm back to Network Connections screen.

And if I want to verify the IP change from Network Connections, I'll just double-click the network adapter and then click Details. From there, I can see the IP information pictured in Figure 18.6.

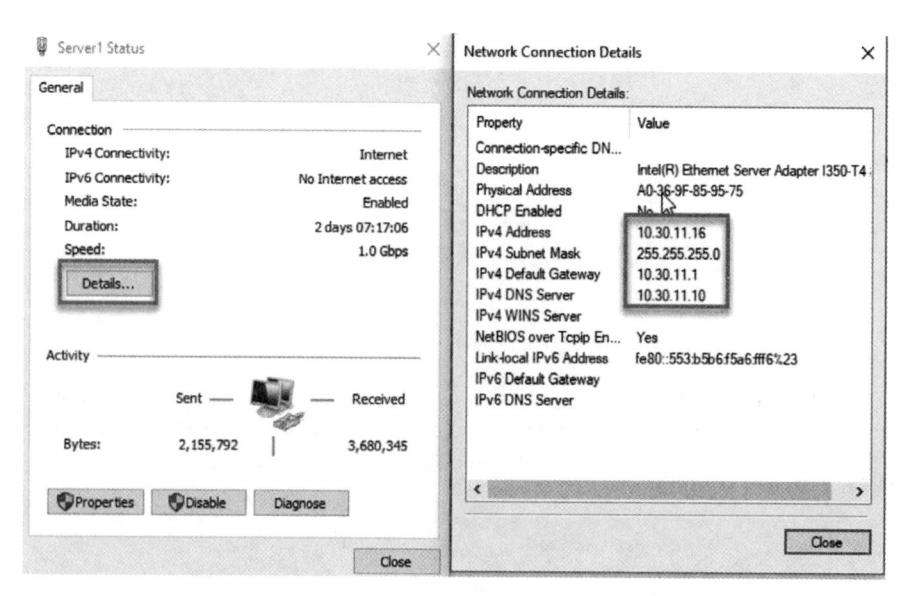

FIGURE 18.6 Verifying IP information

Good to know is that you can also use the **ipconfig** command to get the IP address information from Windows's command prompt. This will give you the IP address, subnet mask and default gateway for each interface as shown in Figure 18.7.

FIGURE 18.7 IPconfig

```
PS C:\> ipconfig

Windows IP Configuration

Ethernet adapter LAN:

   Connection-specific DNS Suffix  . :
   Link-local IPv6 Address . . . . . : fe80::c8f:7f3f:e84:4953%11
   IPv4 Address. . . . . . . . . . . : 10.30.10.16
   Subnet Mask . . . . . . . . . . . : 255.255.255.0
   Default Gateway . . . . . . . . . : 10.30.10.1

Ethernet adapter Server1:

   Connection-specific DNS Suffix  . :
   Link-local IPv6 Address . . . . . : fe80::553:b5b6:f5a6:fff6%23
   IPv4 Address. . . . . . . . . . . : 10.30.11.16
   Subnet Mask . . . . . . . . . . . : 255.255.255.0
   Default Gateway . . . . . . . . . : 10.30.11.1
```

And if you want to check out information like DNS servers as well, just go with the **ipconfig /all** command to see all information about the network adapters on the system (See Figure 18.8.).

FIGURE 18.8 IPConfig /all

```
PS C:\> ipconfig /all

Windows IP Configuration

   Host Name . . . . . . . . . . . . : home01
   Primary Dns Suffix  . . . . . . . : testlab.com
   Node Type . . . . . . . . . . . . : Hybrid
   IP Routing Enabled. . . . . . . . : No
   WINS Proxy Enabled. . . . . . . . : No
   DNS Suffix Search List. . . . . . : testlab.com

Ethernet adapter LAN:

   Connection-specific DNS Suffix  . :
   Description . . . . . . . . . . . : Intel(R) Ethernet Server Adapter I350-T4
   Physical Address. . . . . . . . . : A0-36-9F-85-95-74
   DHCP Enabled. . . . . . . . . . . : No
   Autoconfiguration Enabled . . . . : Yes
   Link-local IPv6 Address . . . . . : fe80::c8f:7f3f:e84:4953%11(Preferred)
   IPv4 Address. . . . . . . . . . . : 10.30.10.16(Preferred)
   Subnet Mask . . . . . . . . . . . : 255.255.255.0
   Default Gateway . . . . . . . . . : 10.30.10.1
   DHCPv6 IAID . . . . . . . . . . . : 111163039
   DHCPv6 Client DUID. . . . . . . . : 00-01-00-01-25-0B-09-00-40-8D-5C-FF-2C-34
   DNS Servers . . . . . . . . . . . : 10.30.11.10
                                       10.20.2.10
   NetBIOS over Tcpip. . . . . . . . : Enabled

Ethernet adapter Server1:

   Connection-specific DNS Suffix  . :
   Description . . . . . . . . . . . : Intel(R) Ethernet Server Adapter I350-T4 #2
   Physical Address. . . . . . . . . : A0-36-9F-85-95-75
   DHCP Enabled. . . . . . . . . . . : No
   Autoconfiguration Enabled . . . . : Yes
   Link-local IPv6 Address . . . . . : fe80::553:b5b6:f5a6:fff6%23(Preferred)
   IPv4 Address. . . . . . . . . . . : 10.30.11.16(Preferred)
   Subnet Mask . . . . . . . . . . . : 255.255.255.0
   Default Gateway . . . . . . . . . : 10.30.11.1
   DHCPv6 IAID . . . . . . . . . . . : 211826335
   DHCPv6 Client DUID. . . . . . . . : 00-01-00-01-25-0B-09-00-40-8D-5C-FF-2C-34
```

Okay—so you know that the ipconfig method works fine, but it's an older command. The new way to do things in Microsoft products is to use powershell instead of CMD. The main advantage to this is that you can filter the output you get back instead of getting all the network adapters every time you type ipconfig.

In powershell, I can use the Get-NetIPAddress cmdlet to get the IP address and netmask and I can also opt to just see my Server1 interface and only IPv4 addresses (See Figure 18.9.).

FIGURE 18.9 Powershell

```
PS C:\> Get-NetIPAddress -InterfaceAlias Server1 -AddressFamily ipv4

IPAddress         : 10.30.11.16
InterfaceIndex    : 23
InterfaceAlias    : Server1
AddressFamily     : IPv4
Type              : Unicast
PrefixLength      : 24
PrefixOrigin      : Manual
SuffixOrigin      : Manual
AddressState      : Preferred
ValidLifetime     : Infinite ([TimeSpan]::MaxValue)
PreferredLifetime : Infinite ([TimeSpan]::MaxValue)
SkipAsSource      : False
PolicyStore       : ActiveStore
```

Just understand that this won't return any default gateway or DNS information because powershell likes to keep its commands very focused. So, I would need to use the Get-DnsClientServerAddress command to get DNS information, and Get-NetRoute to see routing information.

macOS

To verify IP information on a Mac, open Network Preferences by either clicking the Wireless signal on the top right of the desktop or by opening System Preferences and selecting it from there (See Figure 18.10.).

FIGURE 18.10   MAC OS

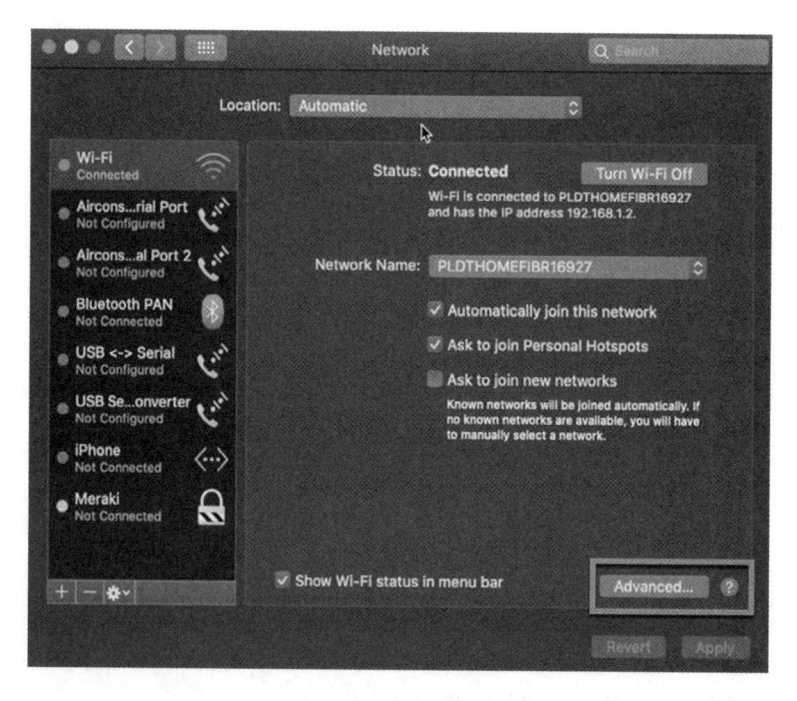

From there, you can see the IP address by choosing the network you're connected to. You won't see any other information unless you click on Advanced and once you, you'll get the screen shown in Figure 18.11.

Under the TCP/IP tab, I can set the IP address, subnet mask, and gateway.

FIGURE 18.11   MAC TCP/IP Screen

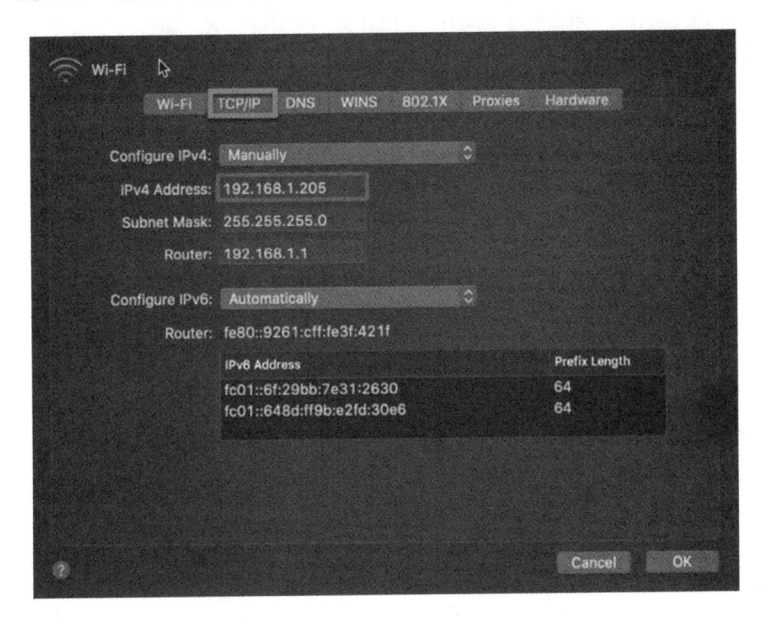

Under the DNS tab shown in Figure 18.12, I can add DNS servers, which appends domain names to DNS queries just like in Windows.

FIGURE 18.12   MAC DNS tab

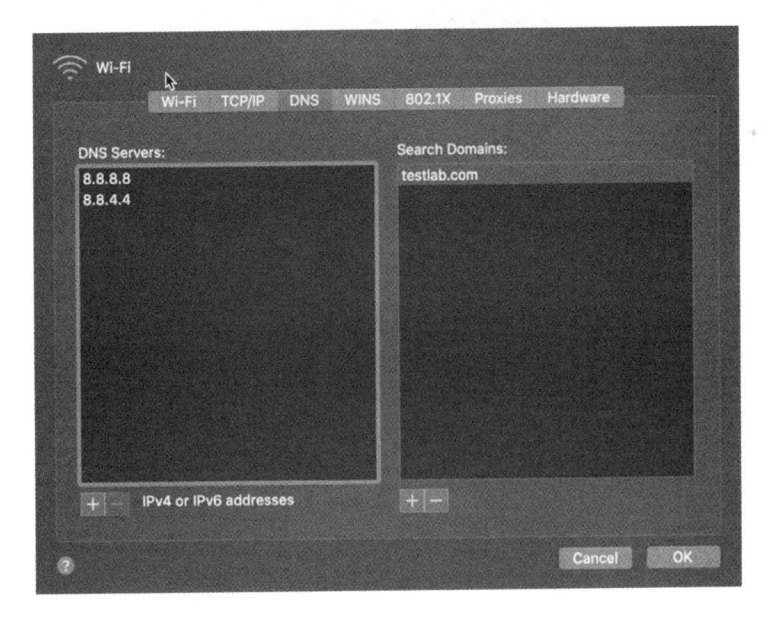

Now if I want to verify the IP information from CLI, I'll use the **ifconfig** command, which can also be used to set an IP address. Just know that the static IP won't survive a reboot. Check out Figure 18.13.

FIGURE 18.13   MAC ifconfig

```
Donalds-MacBook-Pro:~ drobb$ ifconfig en0
en0: flags=8863<UP,BROADCAST,SMART,RUNNING,SIMPLEX,MULTICAST> mtu 1500
        options=400<CHANNEL_IO>
        ether a4:83:e7:c4:e8:b8
        inet6 fe80::b8:9238:1f3c:a398%en0 prefixlen 64 secured scopeid 0x6
        inet 10.30.10.114 netmask 0xffffff00 broadcast 10.30.10.255
        nd6 options=201<PERFORMNUD,DAD>
        media: autoselect
        status: active
Donalds-MacBook-Pro:~ drobb$
```

Ubuntu/Red Hat

Both Ubuntu and Redhat based Linux desktops actually go through the same steps to change an IP address via the GUI. They only differ in how you change the IP address in the Linux shell.

To verify or change the IP address in Ubuntu or Fedora/Centos, open Settings and then Network. You can also click the network on the top right of the screen and then select the connection's settings as shown in Figure 18.14.

FIGURE 18.14   Ubuntu IP Settings

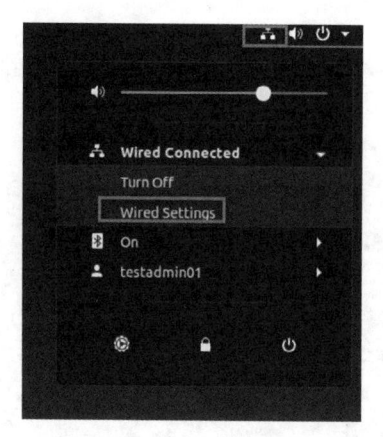

From there, click the gear icon to see the network information on the Linux box show in Figure 18.15. This is where you can adjust the IP address, subnet mask, default gateway, and the DNS servers.

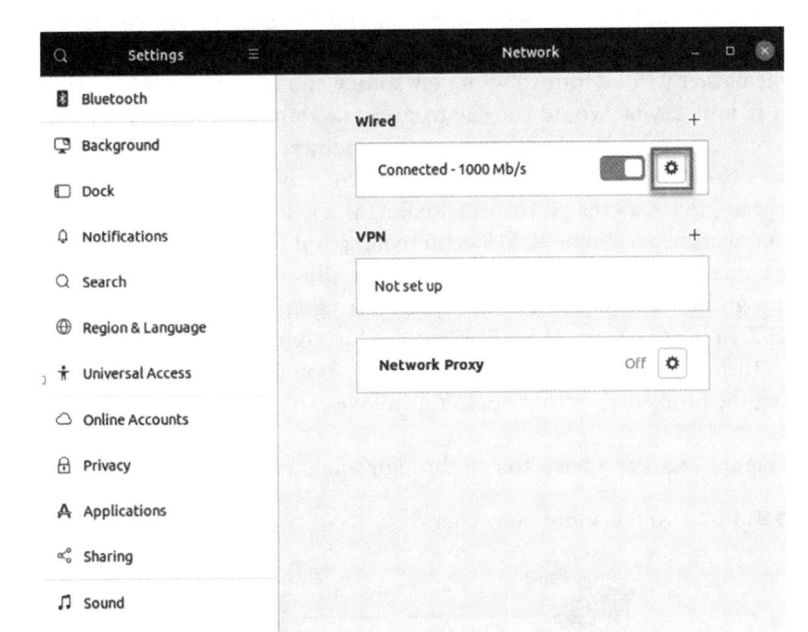

FIGURE 18.15 the Linux gear icon

When you're done, just hit the Apply button to make the changes active.

Finally, to verify the IP address, use the **ifconfig** command, just like we did on the Mac OS example.

Troubleshooting IP Network Connectivity

Let's begin troubleshooting now with a short, sweet review of IP routing. When a host wants to transmit a packet, IP looks at the destination address to determine if it's a local or remote request. If it's local, IP just broadcasts a frame over the local network to find the host using an ARP request. If it's a remote request, the host will send out an ARP request to the default gateway to discover the MAC address of the router.

Once the hosts have the default gateway address, they'll send each other a packet to then be transmitted to the Data Link layer for framing. The newly framed packets are then sent out on the local collision domain. The router will receive the frame and remove the packet, and IP will parse the routing table looking for the exit interface on the router. If the destination is found in the routing table, it will packet-switch the packet to the exit interface. At this point, the packet will be framed with new source and destination MAC addresses.

With that in mind, what would you say to someone claiming they weren't able to get to a server on a remote network? Other than reboot Windows, what's the first thing you would have this user do, or do yourself, to test network connectivity? If you came up with using the Ping program, that's a great start because Ping is a helpful tool to find out if a host is alive on the network via a simple ICMP echo request and reply. But being able to ping the host as well as the server still doesn't guarantee that all is well in the network. There's more to the Ping program than just using it as a quick testing protocol.

To be prepared for the exam objectives, get used to connecting to various routers and pinging from them. Of course, pinging from a router is not as good as pinging from the host reporting the problem, but that doesn't mean we can't isolate problems from the routers themselves.

Let's use Figure 18.16 as a basis to run through some troubleshooting scenarios.

FIGURE 18.16 Troubleshooting scenario

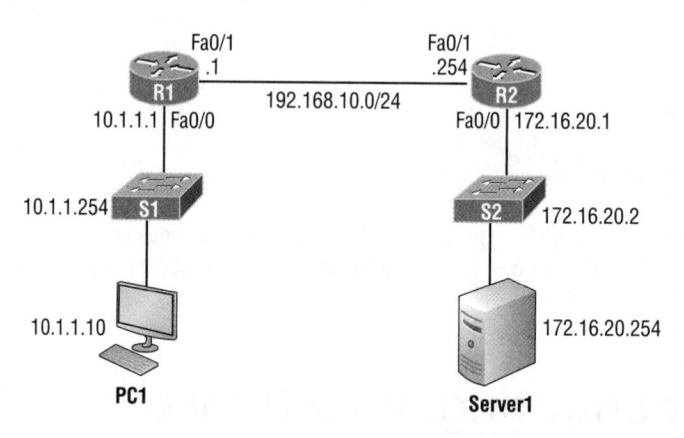

In this first scenario, a manager contacts you saying that he can't log in to Server1 from PC1. Your job is to find out why and fix it. The Cisco objectives are clear on the troubleshooting steps to take when a problem has been reported, and here they are:

1. Check the cables to see if there's a faulty cable or interface in the mix and verify the interface's statistics.
2. Make sure that devices are determining the correct path from the source to the destination. Correct the routing information if needed.
3. Verify that the default gateway is correct.
4. Verify that name resolution settings are correct.
5. Verify there aren't any access control lists (ACLs) blocking traffic.

To effectively troubleshoot this problem, we'll narrow down the possibilities by process of elimination. We'll start with PC1 and verify that it's configured correctly and also that IP is working correctly.

There are four steps for checking the PC1 configuration:

1. Test that the local IP stack is working by pinging the loopback address.
2. Test that the local IP stack is talking to the Data Link layer (LAN driver) by pinging the local IP address.
3. Test that the host is working on the LAN by pinging the default gateway.
4. Test that the host can get to remote networks by pinging remote Server1.

Let's check out the PC1 configuration by using the `ipconfig` command, or `ifconfig` on a Mac or Linux device:

```
C:\Users\Todd Lammle>ipconfig

Windows IP Configuration

Ethernet adapter Local Area Connection:

   Connection-specific DNS Suffix  . : localdomain
   Link-local IPv6 Address . . . . . : fe80::64e3:76a2:541f:ebcb%11
   IPv4 Address. . . . . . . . . . . : 10.1.1.10
   Subnet Mask . . . . . . . . . . . : 255.255.255.0
   Default Gateway . . . . . . . . . : 10.1.1.1
```

We can also check the route table on the host with the `route print` command to see if it knows the default gateway:

```
C:\Users\Todd Lammle>route print
[output cut]
IPv4 Route Table
===========================================================================
Active Routes:
Network Destination        Netmask          Gateway       Interface  Metric
          0.0.0.0          0.0.0.0         10.1.1.10       10.1.1.1     10
[output cut]
```

Between the output of the `ipconfig` command and the `route print` command, we can rest assured that the hosts are aware of the correct default gateway.

> **Note:** To meet Cisco's objectives, it's extremely important to be able to check and verify the default gateway on a host and that this address also matches the router's interface!

Let's verify that the local IP stack is initialized by pinging the loopback address:

```
C:\Users\Todd Lammle>ping 127.0.0.1

Pinging 127.0.0.1 with 32 bytes of data:
Reply from 127.0.0.1: bytes=32 time<1ms TTL=128
Reply from 127.0.0.1: bytes=32 time<1ms TTL=128
Reply from 127.0.0.1: bytes=32 time<1ms TTL=128
Reply from 127.0.0.1: bytes=32 time<1ms TTL=128

Ping statistics for 127.0.0.1:
    Packets: Sent = 4, Received = 4, Lost = 0 (0% loss),
Approximate round trip times in milli-seconds:
    Minimum = 0ms, Maximum = 0ms, Average = 0ms
```

This first output confirms the IP address and configured default gateway of the host. Then I verified the fact that the local IP stack is working. Our next move is to verify that the IP stack is talking to the LAN driver by pinging the local IP address:

```
C:\Users\Todd Lammle>ping 10.1.1.10

Pinging 10.1.1.10 with 32 bytes of data:
Reply from 10.1.1.10: bytes=32 time<1ms TTL=128
Reply from 10.1.1.10: bytes=32 time<1ms TTL=128
Reply from 10.1.1.10: bytes=32 time<1ms TTL=128
Reply from 10.1.1.10: bytes=32 time<1ms TTL=128

Ping statistics for 10.1.1.10:
    Packets: Sent = 4, Received = 4, Lost = 0 (0% loss),
Approximate round trip times in milli-seconds:
    Minimum = 0ms, Maximum = 0ms, Average = 0ms
```

And now that we know the local stack is solid and the IP stack is communicating to the LAN driver, it's time to check our local LAN connectivity by pinging the default gateway:

```
C:\Users\Todd Lammle>ping 10.1.1.1

Pinging 10.1.1.1 with 32 bytes of data:
Reply from 10.1.1.1: bytes=32 time<1ms TTL=128
Reply from 10.1.1.1: bytes=32 time<1ms TTL=128
Reply from 10.1.1.1: bytes=32 time<1ms TTL=128
Reply from 10.1.1.1: bytes=32 time<1ms TTL=128

Ping statistics for 10.1.1.1:
    Packets: Sent = 4, Received = 4, Lost = 0 (0% loss),
Approximate round trip times in milli-seconds:
    Minimum = 0ms, Maximum = 0ms, Average = 0ms
```

Looking good! I'd say our host is in good shape. Let's try to ping the remote server next to see if our host is actually getting off the local LAN to communicate remotely:

```
C:\Users\Todd Lammle>ping 172.16.20.254

Pinging 172.16.20.254 with 32 bytes of data:
Request timed out.
Request timed out.
Request timed out.
Request timed out.

Ping statistics for 172.16.20.254:
    Packets: Sent = 4, Received = 0, Lost = 4 (100% loss),
```

Well, looks like we've confirmed local connectivity but not remote connectivity, so we're going to have to dig deeper to isolate the problem. But first, and just as important, it's key to make note of what we can rule out at this point:

1. The PC is configured with the correct IP address and the local IP stack is working.
2. The default gateway is configured correctly and the PC's default gateway configuration matches the router interface IP address.
3. The local switch is working because we can ping through the switch to the router.
4. We don't have a local LAN issue, meaning our Physical layer is good because we can ping the router. If we couldn't ping the router, we would need to verify our physical cables and interfaces.

Let's see if we can narrow the problem down further using the traceroute command:

```
C:\Users\Todd Lammle>tracert 172.16.20.254

Tracing route to 172.16.20.254 over a maximum of 30 hops

  1    1 ms     1 ms    <1 ms   10.1.1.1
  2    *        *        *      Request timed out.
  3    *        *        *      Request timed out.
```

Well, we didn't get beyond our default gateway, so let's go over to R2 and see if we can talk locally to the server:

```
R2#ping 172.16.20.254

Pinging 172.16.20.254 with 32 bytes of data:
Reply from 172.16.20.254: bytes=32 time<1ms TTL=128
Reply from 172.16.20.254: bytes=32 time<1ms TTL=128
Reply from 172.16.20.254: bytes=32 time<1ms TTL=128
Reply from 172.16.20.254: bytes=32 time<1ms TTL=128

Ping statistics for 172.16.20.254:
    Packets: Sent = 4, Received = 0, Lost = 4 (100% loss),
```

Okay—we just eliminated a local LAN problem by connecting to Server1 from the R2 router, so we're good there. Let's summarize what we know so far:

1. PC1 is configured correctly.
2. The switch located on the 10.1.1.0 LAN is working.
3. PC1's default gateway is configured correctly.
4. R2 can communicate to the Server1 so we don't have a remote LAN issue.

But something is still clearly wrong, so what do we check next? Now would be a great time to verify the Server1 IP configuration and make sure the default gateway is configured correctly. Let's take a look:

```
C:\Users\Server1>ipconfig

Windows IP Configuration

Ethernet adapter Local Area Connection:

   Connection-specific DNS Suffix  . : localdomain
   Link-local IPv6 Address . . . . . : fe80::7723:76a2:e73c:2acb%11
   IPv4 Address. . . . . . . . . . . : 172.16.20.254
   Subnet Mask . . . . . . . . . . . : 255.255.255.0
   Default Gateway . . . . . . . . . : 172.16.20.1
```

The Server1 configuration looks good and the R2 router can ping the server, so it seems that the server's local LAN is solid, the local switch is working, and there are no cable or interface issues. But let's zoom in on interface Fa0/0 on R2 and talk about what to expect if there were errors on this interface:

```
R2#sh int fa0/0
FastEthernet0/0 is up, line protocol is up
[output cut]
  Full-duplex, 100Mb/s, 100BaseTX/FX
  ARP type: ARPA, ARP Timeout 04:00:00
  Last input 00:00:05, output 00:00:01, output hang never
  Last clearing of "show interface" counters never
  Input queue: 0/75/0/0 (size/max/drops/flushes); Total output drops: 0
  Queueing strategy: fifo
  Output queue: 0/40 (size/max)
  5 minute input rate 0 bits/sec, 0 packets/sec
  5 minute output rate 0 bits/sec, 0 packets/sec
     1325 packets input, 157823 bytes
     Received 1157 broadcasts (0 IP multicasts)
     0 runts, 0 giants, 0 throttles
     0 input errors, 0 CRC, 0 frame, 0 overrun, 0 ignored
```

```
  0 watchdog
  0 input packets with dribble condition detected
  2294 packets output, 244630 bytes, 0 underruns
  0 output errors, 0 collisions, 3 interface resets
  347 unknown protocol drops
  0 babbles, 0 late collision, 0 deferred
  4 lost carrier, 0 no carrier
  0 output buffer failures, 0 output buffers swapped out
```

You've got to be able to analyze interface statistics to find problems there if they exist, so let's pick out the important factors relevant to achieving that goal next.

Speed and duplex settings   Good to know that the most common cause of interface errors is a mismatched duplex mode between two ends of an Ethernet link. This is why it's so important to make sure that the switch and its hosts (PCs, router interfaces, etc.) have the same speed setting. If not, they just won't connect. Worse, if they do have mismatched duplex settings, you'll receive a legion of errors, which will cause nasty performance issues, intermittent connectivity—even loss of communication!

Using autonegotiation for speed and duplex is a common practice that's enabled by default. But if this fails for some reason, you'll have to set the configuration manually like this:

```
Switch(config)#int gi0/1
Switch(config-if)#speed ?
  10    Force 10 Mbps operation
  100   Force 100 Mbps operation
  1000  Force 1000 Mbps operation
  auto  Enable AUTO speed configuration
Switch(config-if)#speed 1000
Switch(config-if)#duplex  ?
  auto  Enable AUTO duplex configuration
  full  Force full duplex operation
  half  Force half-duplex operation
Switch(config-if)#duplex  full
```

If you have a duplex mismatch, a telling sign is that the late collision counter will increment.

Input queue drops   If the input queue drops counter increments, it signifies that more traffic is being delivered to the router than it can process. If this is consistently high, try to determine exactly when these counters are increasing and how the events relate to CPU usage. You'll see the ignored and throttle counters increment as well.

Output queue drops   This counter indicates that packets were dropped due to interface congestion, leading to packet drops and queuing delays. When this occurs, applications like VoIP will experience performance issues. If you observe this constantly incrementing, consider QoS.

Input errors Input errors often indicate high errors like CRCs, which can point to cabling problems, hardware issues, or duplex mismatches.

Output errors This is the total number of frames that the port tried to transmit when an issue such as a collision occurred.

We're going to move on in our troubleshooting process of elimination by analyzing the routers' actual configurations. Here's R1's routing table:

```
R1>sh ip route
[output cut]
Gateway of last resort is 192.168.10.254 to network 0.0.0.0

S*      0.0.0.0/0 [1/0] via 192.168.10.254
        10.0.0.0/8 is variably subnetted, 2 subnets, 2 masks
C          10.1.1.0/24 is directly connected, FastEthernet0/0
L          10.1.1.1/32 is directly connected, FastEthernet0/0
        192.168.10.0/24 is variably subnetted, 2 subnets, 2 masks
C          192.168.10.0/24 is directly connected, FastEthernet0/1
L          192.168.10.1/32 is directly connected, FastEthernet0/1
```

This actually looks pretty good! Both of our directly connected networks are in the table and we can confirm that we have a default route going to the R2 router. So now let's verify the connectivity to R2 from R1:

```
R1>sh ip int brief
Interface            IP-Address       OK? Method Status                Protocol
FastEthernet0/0      10.1.1.1         YES manual up                    up
FastEthernet0/1      192.168.10.1     YES manual up                    up
Serial0/0/0          unassigned       YES unset  administratively down down
Serial0/1/0          unassigned       YES unset  administratively down down
R1>ping 192.168.10.254
Type escape sequence to abort.
Sending 5, 100-byte ICMP Echos to 192.168.10.254, timeout is 2 seconds:
!!!!!
Success rate is 100 percent (5/5), round-trip min/avg/max = 1/2/4 ms
```

This looks great too! Our interfaces are correctly configured with the right IP address and the Physical and Data Link layers are up. By the way, I also tested layer 3 connectivity by pinging the R2 Fa0/1 interface.

Since everything looks good so far, our next step is to check into the status of R2's interfaces:

```
R2>sh ip int brief
Interface            IP-Address       OK? Method Status                Protocol
FastEthernet0/0      172.16.20.1      YES manual up                    up
```

```
FastEthernet0/1         192.168.10.254  YES manual up                    up
R2>ping 192.168.10.1
Type escape sequence to abort.
Sending 5, 100-byte ICMP Echos to 192.168.10.1, timeout is 2 seconds:
!!!!!
Success rate is 100 percent (5/5), round-trip min/avg/max = 1/2/4 ms
```

Well, everything still checks out at this point. The IP addresses are correct and the Physical and Data Link layers are up. I also tested layer 3 connectivity with a ping to R1, so we're all good so far. We'll examine the routing table next:

```
R2>sh ip route
[output cut]
Gateway of last resort is not set

    10.0.0.0/24 is subnetted, 1 subnets
S      10.1.1.0 is directly connected, FastEthernet0/0
    172.16.0.0/16 is variably subnetted, 2 subnets, 2 masks
C      172.16.20.0/24 is directly connected, FastEthernet0/0
L      172.16.20.1/32 is directly connected, FastEthernet0/0
    192.168.10.0/24 is variably subnetted, 2 subnets, 2 masks
C      192.168.10.0/24 is directly connected, FastEthernet0/1
L      192.168.10.254/32 is directly connected, FastEthernet0/1
```

Okay—we can see that all our local interfaces are in the table, as well as a static route to the 10.1.1.0 network. But do you see the problem? Look closely at the static route. The route was entered with an exit interface of Fa0/0, and the path to the 10.1.1.0 network is out Fa0/1! Aha! We've found our problem! Let's fix R2:

```
R2#config t
R2(config)#no ip route 10.1.1.0 255.255.255.0 fa0/0
R2(config)#ip route 10.1.1.0 255.255.255.0 192.168.10.1
```

That should do it. Let's verify from PC1:

```
C:\Users\Todd Lammle>ping 172.16.20.254

Pinging 172.16.20.254 with 32 bytes of data:
Reply from 172.16.20.254: bytes=32 time<1ms TTL=128
Reply from 172.16.20.254: bytes=32 time<1ms TTL=128
Reply from 172.16.20.254: bytes=32 time<1ms TTL=128
Reply from 172.16.20.254: bytes=32 time<1ms TTL=128

Ping statistics for 172.16.20.254
    Packets: Sent = 4, Received = 4, Lost = 0 (0% loss),
Approximate round trip times in milli-seconds:
    Minimum = 0ms, Maximum = 0ms, Average = 0ms
```

Our snag appears to be solved, but just to make sure, we really need to verify with a higher-level protocol like Telnet:

```
C:\Users\Todd Lammle>telnet 172.16.20.254
Connecting To 172.16.20.254...Could not open connection to the host, on
port 23: Connect failed
```

Okay, that's not good! We can ping to the Server1, but we can't telnet to it. In the past, I've verified that telnetting to this server worked, but it's still possible that we have a failure on the server side. To find out, let's verify our network first, starting at R1:

```
R1>ping 172.16.20.254
Type escape sequence to abort.
Sending 5, 100-byte ICMP Echos to 172.16.20.254, timeout is 2 seconds:
!!!!!
Success rate is 100 percent (5/5), round-trip min/avg/max = 1/1/4 ms
R1>telnet 172.16.20.254
Trying 172.16.20.254 ...
% Destination unreachable; gateway or host down
```

This is some pretty ominous output! Let's try from R2 and see what happens:

```
R2#telnet 172.16.20.254
Trying 172.16.20.254 ... Open

User Access Verification

Password:
```

Oh my—I can ping the server from a remote network, but I can't telnet to it, yet the local router R2 can! These factors eliminate the server being a problem since I can telnet to the server when I'm on the local LAN.

And we know we don't have a routing problem because we fixed that already. So what's next? Let's check to see if there's an ACL on R2:

```
R2>sh access-lists
Extended IP access list 110
    10 permit icmp any any (25 matches)
```

Seriously? What a loopy access list to have on a router! This ridiculous list permits ICMP, but that's it. It denies everything except ICMP due to the implicit deny ip any any at the end of every ACL. But before we uncork the champagne, we need to see if this foolish list has been applied to our interfaces on R2 to confirm that this is really our problem:

```
R2>sh ip int fa0/0
FastEthernet0/0 is up, line protocol is up
  Internet address is 172.16.20.1/24
```

         Broadcast address is 255.255.255.255
         Address determined by setup command
         MTU is 1500 bytes
         Helper address is not set
         Directed broadcast forwarding is disabled
         <u>**Outgoing access list is 110**</u>
         <u>**Inbound access list is not set**</u>

There it is—that's our problem all right! In case you're wondering why R2 could telnet to Server1, it's because an ACL filters only packets trying to go through the router—not packets generated at the router. Let's get to work and fix this:

R2#**config t**
R2(config)#**no access-list 110**

I just verified that I can telnet from PC1 to Server1, but let's try telnetting from R1 again:

R1#**telnet 172.16.20.254**
Trying 172.16.20.254 ... Open

User Access Verification

Password:

Nice—looks like we're set, but what about using the name?

R1#**telnet Server1**
Translating "Server1"...domain server (255.255.255.255)

% Bad IP address or host name

Well, we're not all set just yet. Let's fix R1 so that it can provide name resolution:

R1(config)#**ip host Server1 172.16.20.254**
R1(config)#**^Z**
R1#**telnet Server1**
Trying Server1 (172.16.20.254)... Open

User Access Verification

Password:

Great—things are looking good from the router, but if the customer can't telnet to the remote host using the name, we've got to check the DNS server to confirm connectivity and for the correct entry to the server. Another option would be to configure the local host table manually on PC1.

The last thing to do is to check the server to see if it's responding to HTTP requests via the `telnet` command, believe it or not! Here's an example:

R1#**telnet 172.16.20.254 80**
Trying 172.16.20.254, 80 ... Open

Yes—finally! Server1 is responding to requests on port 80, so we're in the clear.

Using SPAN for Troubleshooting

A traffic sniffer can be a valuable tool for monitoring and troubleshooting your network. However, since the inception of switches into our networks more than 20 years ago, troubleshooting has become tougher because we can't just plug an analyzer into a switch port and be able to read all the network traffic. Before we had switches, we used hubs, and when a hub received a digital signal on one port, the hub sent that digital signal out on all ports except the port it was received on. This allows a traffic sniffer that's connected to a hub port to receive all traffic in the network.

Modern local networks are essentially switched networks. After a switch boots, it starts to build up a layer 2 forwarding table based on the source MAC addresses of the different packets that the switch receives. After the switch builds this forwarding table, it forwards traffic destined for a known MAC address directly to the exit port associated with that MAC address. By default, this prevents a traffic sniffer connected to another port from receiving the unicast traffic.

The SPAN feature was introduced on switches to help solve this problem, as shown in Figure 18.17.

FIGURE 18.17 Using SPAN for troubleshooting

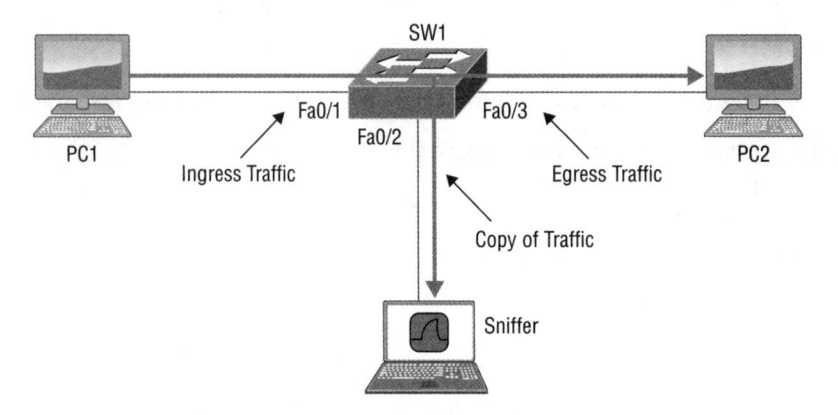

SPAN helps us analyze network traffic passing through the port by sending a copy of the traffic to another port on the switch that's been connected to a network analyzer or other monitoring device. SPAN copies the traffic that the device receives and/or sends on source ports to a destination port for analysis.

For example, if you would like to analyze the traffic flowing from PC1 to PC2, shown in Figure 18.17, you need to specify a source port where you want to capture the data. You can either configure the interface Fa0/1 to capture the ingress traffic or configure the interface Fa0/3 to capture the egress traffic—your choice. Next, specify the destination port interface where the sniffer is connected and will capture the data, in this example, Fa0/2. The traffic flowing from PC1 to PC2 will then be copied to that interface and you'll be able to analyze it with a traffic sniffer.

Step 1: Associate a SPAN session number with the source port of what you want to monitor.

```
S1(config)#monitor session 1 source interface f0/1
```

Step 2: Associate a SPAN session number of the sniffer with the destination interface.

```
S1(config)#monitor session 1 dest interface f0/2
```

Step 3: Verify that the SPAN session has been configured correctly.

```
S1(config)#do sh monitor
Session 1
---------
Type                   : Local Session
Source Ports           :
    Both               : Fa0/1
Destination Ports      : Fa0/2
    Encapsulation      : Native
         Ingress       : Disabled
```

Now connect up your network analyzer into port F0/2 and enjoy!

Configuring and Verifying Extended Access Lists

Even though I went through some very basic troubleshooting with ACLs earlier in this chapter, let's dig a little deeper to make sure you really understand extended named ACLs before hitting IPv6.

As you know, standard access lists focus only on IP or IPv6 source addresses. Extended ACLs, however, filter based on the source and destination layer 3 addresses at a minimum. In addition, they can filter using the protocol field in the IP header (Next Header field in IPv6), as well as the source and destination port numbers at layer 4, all shown in Figure 18.18.

FIGURE 18.18 Extended ACLs

An Example from a TCP/IP Packet

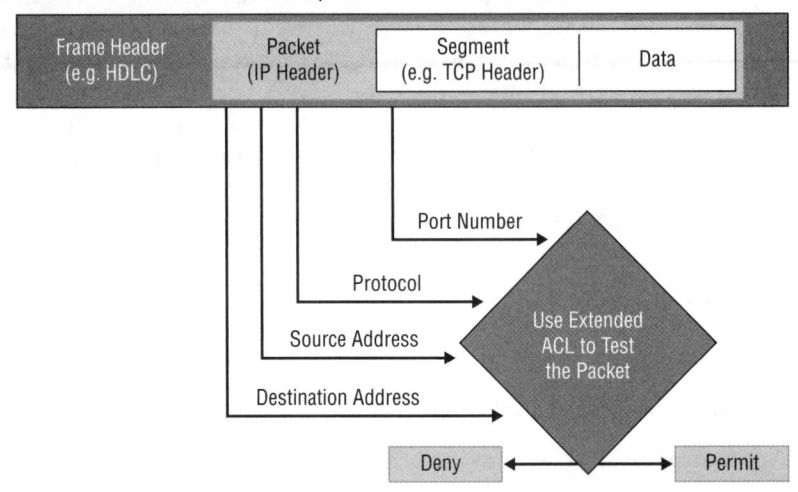

Using the network layout in Figure 18.16, let's create an extended named ACL that blocks Telnet to the 172.16.20.254 server from 10.1.1.10. It's an extended list, so we'll place it closest to the source address as possible.

Step 1: Test that you can telnet to the remote host.

```
R1#telnet 172.16.20.254
Trying 172.16.20.254 ... Open
Server1>
```

Okay, great!

Step 2: Create an ACL on R1 that prevents telnetting to the remote host of 172.16.20.254. Using a named ACL, start with the protocol (IP or IPv6), choose either a standard or extended list, and then name it. The name is absolutely case sensitive when applying to an interface.

```
R1(config)#ip access-list extended Block_Telnet
R1(config-ext-nacl)#
```

Step 3: Once you've created the named list, add your test parameters:

```
R1(config-ext-nacl)#deny tcp host 10.1.1.1 host 172.16.20.254 eq 23
R1(config-ext-nacl)#permit ip any any
```

Step 4: Verify your access list:

```
R1(config-ext-nacl)#do sh access-list
```

```
Extended IP access list Block_Telnet
    10 deny tcp host 10.1.1.1 host 172.16.20.254 eq telnet
    20 permit ip any any
```

Notice the numbers 10 and 20 on the left side of each test statement. These are called sequence numbers and we can use them to edit a single line, delete it, or even add a new line in between two sequence numbers. Named ACLs can be edited; numbered ACLs can't!

Step 5: Configure your ACL on your router interface.

Since we're adding this to the R1 router in Figure 18.16, we'll add it inbound to interface FastEthernet 0/0, stopping traffic closest to the source:

```
R1(config)#int fa0/0
R1(config-if)#ip access-group Block_Telnet in
```

Step 6: Test your access list:

```
R1#telnet 172.16.20.254
Trying 172.16.20.254 ... Open
Server1>
```

Hmm... that didn't work because I'm still able to telnet to the remote host. Let's take a look at our list, verify our interface and fix the problem.

```
R1#sh access-list
Extended IP access list Block_Telnet
    10 deny tcp host 10.1.1.1 host 172.16.20.254 eq telnet
    20 permit ip any any
```

By verifying the IP addresses in the deny statement in line sequence 10, you can see that my source address is 10.1.1.1 It should have been 10.1.1.10.

Step 7: Fix and/or edit your access list. Delete the bad line and reconfigure the ACL to the correct IP:

```
R1(config)#ip access-list extended Block_Telnet
R1(config-ext-nacl)#no 10
R1(config-ext-nacl)#10 deny tcp host 10.1.1.10 host 172.16.20.254 eq 23
```

Verify that your list is working:

```
R1#telnet 172.16.20.254
Trying 172.16.20.254 ...
% Destination unreachable; gateway or host down
```

Step 8: Display the ACL again and check the updated hit counters with each line. Also verify that the interface is set with the ACL:

```
R1#sh access-list
Extended IP access list Block_Telnet
    10 deny tcp host 10.1.1.10 host 172.16.20.254 eq telnet (58 matches)
    20 permit ip any any (86 matches)

R1#sh ip int f0/0
FastEthernet0/0 is up, line protocol is up
  Internet address is 10.10.10.1/24
  Broadcast address is 255.255.255.255
  Address determined by non-volatile memory
  MTU is 1500 bytes
  Helper address is not set
  Directed broadcast forwarding is disabled
  Multicast reserved groups joined: 224.0.0.10
  Outgoing access list is not set
  Inbound  access list is Block_Telnet
  Proxy ARP is enabled
[output cut]
```

The interface was up and working, so verifying at this point was a little overkill. Know that you must be able to look at an interface and troubleshoot issues, such as ACLs set on an interface and be sure to remember the show ip interface command!

Next, let's mix things up a little by adding IPv6 to our network and work through the same troubleshooting steps.

Troubleshooting IPv6 Network Connectivity

I'm going to be straight with you: There isn't a lot that's going to be much different regarding IPv6 and the process you just went through in the IPv4 troubleshooting steps. Except the addressing, of course! So other than that key factor, we'll take the same approach. Using Figure 18.19 specifically because I really want to highlight the differences associated with IPv6. So the problem scenario I'm going to use will also stay the same: PC1 cannot communicate to Server1.

I want to point out that this is not an "Introduction to IPv6" chapter, so I'm assuming you've got some IPv6 fundamentals down.

FIGURE 18.19 IPv6 troubleshooting scenario

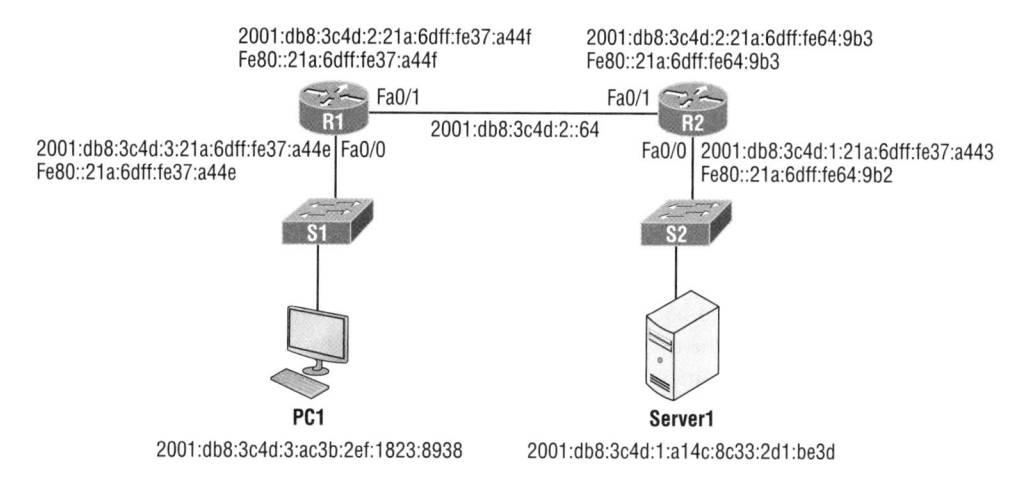

```
2001:db8:3c4d:2:21a:6dff:fe37:a44f     2001:db8:3c4d:2:21a:6dff:fe64:9b3
Fe80::21a:6dff:fe37:a44f               Fe80::21a:6dff:fe64:9b3
                        Fa0/1               Fa0/1
                     R1                               R2
                          2001:db8:3c4d:2::64
2001:db8:3c4d:3:21a:6dff:fe37:a44e Fa0/0     Fa0/0  2001:db8:3c4d:1:21a:6dff:fe37:a443
Fe80::21a:6dff:fe37:a44e                            Fe80::21a:6dff:fe64:9b2
                     S1                               S2

                    PC1                             Server1
       2001:db8:3c4d:3:ac3b:2ef:1823:8938   2001:db8:3c4d:1:a14c:8c33:2d1:be3d
```

Notice that I documented both the link-local and global addresses assigned to each router interface in Figure 18.19. We need both in order to troubleshoot, so right away, you can see that things get a bit more complicated because of the longer addresses and the fact that there are multiple addresses per interface involved!

But *before* we start troubleshooting the IPv6 network in Figure 18.19, I want to refresh your memory on the ICMPv6 protocol, which is an important protocol in our troubleshooting arsenal.

ICMPv6

IPv4 used the ICMP workhorse for lots of tasks, including error messages like destination unreachable and troubleshooting functions like Ping and Traceroute. ICMPv6 still does those things for us, but unlike its predecessor, the v6 version isn't implemented as a separate layer 3 protocol. Instead, it's an integrated part of IPv6 and is carried after the basic IPv6 header information as an extension header.

ICMPv6 is used for router solicitation and advertisement, for neighbor solicitation and advertisement (i.e., finding the MAC addresses for IPv6 neighbors), and for redirecting the host to the best router (default gateway).

Neighbor Discovery (NDP)

ICMPv6 also takes over the task of finding the address of other devices on the local link. The Address Resolution Protocol is used to perform this function for IPv4, but that's been renamed Neighbor Discovery (ND or NDP) in ICMPv6. This process is now achieved via a multicast address called the solicited node address because all hosts join this multicast group upon connecting to the network.

Neighbor discovery enables these functions:

- Determining the MAC address of neighbors
- Router solicitation (RS) FF02::2
- Router advertisements (RA) FF02::1
- Neighbor solicitation (NS)
- Neighbor advertisement (NA)
- Duplicate address detection (DAD)

The part of the IPv6 address designated by the 24 bits farthest to the right is added to the end of the multicast address FF02:0:0:0:0:1:FF/104. When this address is queried, the corresponding host will send back its layer 2 address. Devices can find and keep track of other neighbor devices on the network in pretty much the same way. When I talked about RA and RS messages in Chapter 17 and told you that they use multicast traffic to request and send address information, that too is actually a function of ICMPv6—specifically, neighbor discovery.

In IPv4, the protocol IGMP was used to allow a host device to tell its local router that it was joining a multicast group and would like to receive the traffic for that group. This IGMP function has been replaced by ICMPv6 and the process has been renamed multicast listener discovery.

With IPv4, our hosts could have only one default gateway configured. If that router went down, we had to fix the router, change the default gateway, or run some type of virtual default gateway with other protocols created as a solution for this inadequacy in IPv4.

Figure 18.20 shows how IPv6 devices find their default gateways using neighbor discovery.

FIGURE 18.20 Router solicitation (RS) and router advertisement (RA)

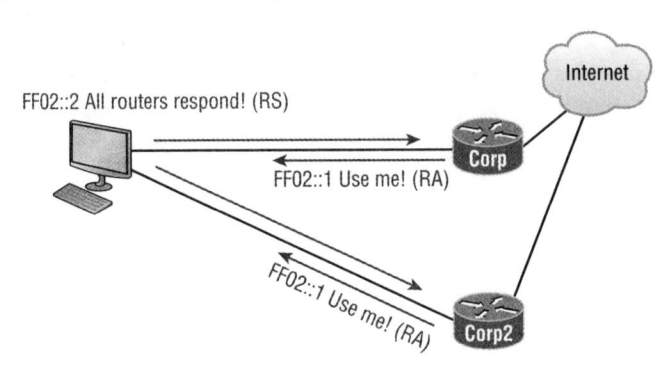

IPv6 hosts send a router solicitation (RS) onto their data link asking for all routers to respond, which they do using the multicast address FF02::2. Routers on the same link respond with a unicast to the requesting host or with a router advertisement (RA) using FF02::1.

But that's not all! Hosts can also send solicitations and advertisements between themselves using a neighbor solicitation (NS) and neighbor advertisement (NA), as shown in Figure 18.21.

FIGURE 18.21 Neighbor solicitation (NS) and neighbor advertisement (NA)

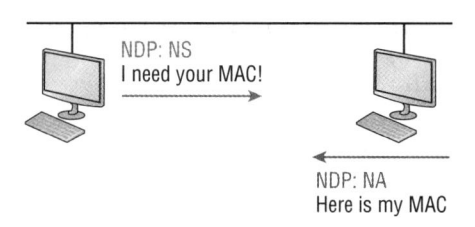

Remember that RA and RS gather or provide information about routers and NS and NA gather information about hosts. Also, remember that a "neighbor" is a host on the same data link or VLAN.

With that foundational review in mind, here are the troubleshooting steps we'll progress through during our investigation:

1. Check the cables to see if there's a faulty cable or interface. Verify interface statistics.
2. Make sure that devices are determining the correct path from the source to the destination. Correct the routing information if needed.
3. Verify that the default gateway is correct.
4. Verify that name resolution settings are correct, and especially for IPv6, make sure the DNS server is reachable via IPv4 and IPv6.
5. Verify that there are no ACLs blocking traffic.

In order to troubleshoot this problem, we'll use the same process of elimination, beginning with PC1. We've got to verify that it's configured correctly and that IP is working properly. Let's start by pinging the loopback address to verify the IPv6 stack:

```
C:\Users\Todd Lammle>ping ::1

Pinging ::1 with 32 bytes of data:
Reply from ::1: time<1ms
Reply from ::1: time<1ms
Reply from ::1: time<1ms
Reply from ::1: time<1ms
```

The IPv6 stack checks out, so let's ping the Fa0/0 of R1, which PC1 is directly connected to on the same LAN, starting with the link-local address:

```
C:\Users\Todd Lammle>ping fe80::21a:6dff:fe37:a44e

Pinging fe80:21a:6dff:fe37:a44e with 32 bytes of data:
Reply from fe80::21a:6dff:fe37:a44e: time<1ms
```

```
Reply from fe80::21a:6dff:fe37:a44e: time<1ms
Reply from fe80::21a:6dff:fe37:a44e: time<1ms
Reply from fe80::21a:6dff:fe37:a44e: time<1ms
```

Next, we'll ping the global address on Fa0/0:

```
C:\Users\Todd Lammle>ping 2001:db8:3c4d:3:21a:6dff:fe37:a44e

Pinging 2001:db8:3c4d:3:21a:6dff:fe37:a44e with 32 bytes of data:
Reply from 2001:db8:3c4d:3:21a:6dff:fe37:a44e: time<1ms
Reply from 2001:db8:3c4d:3:21a:6dff:fe37:a44e: time<1ms
Reply from 2001:db8:3c4d:3:21a:6dff:fe37:a44e: time<1ms
Reply from 2001:db8:3c4d:3:21a:6dff:fe37:a44e: time<1ms
```

Okay—looks like PC1 is configured and working on the local LAN to the R1 router. We've confirmed the Physical, Data Link, and Network layers between the PC1 and the R1 router Fa0/0 interface.

Our next move is to check the local connection on Server1 to the R2 router to verify that LAN. First we'll ping the link-local address of the router from Server1:

```
C:\Users\Server1>ping fe80::21a:6dff:fe64:9b2

Pinging fe80::21a:6dff:fe64:9b2 with 32 bytes of data:
Reply from fe80::21a:6dff:fe64:9b2: time<1ms
Reply from fe80::21a:6dff:fe64:9b2: time<1ms
Reply from fe80::21a:6dff:fe64:9b2: time<1ms
Reply from fe80::21a:6dff:fe64:9b2: time<1ms
```

And next, we'll ping the global address of Fa0/0 on R2:

```
C:\Users\Server1>ping 2001:db8:3c4d:1:21a:6dff:fe37:a443

Pinging 2001:db8:3c4d:1:21a:6dff:fe37:a443 with 32 bytes of data:
Reply from 2001:db8:3c4d:1:21a:6dff:fe37:a443: time<1ms
Reply from 2001:db8:3c4d:1:21a:6dff:fe37:a443: time<1ms
Reply from 2001:db8:3c4d:1:21a:6dff:fe37:a443: time<1ms
Reply from 2001:db8:3c4d:1:21a:6dff:fe37:a443: time<1ms
```

Let's quickly summarize what we know at this point:

1. By using the ipconfig /all command on PC1 and Server1, I was able to document their global and link-local IPv6 addresses.
2. We know the IPv6 link-local addresses of each router interface.
3. We know the IPv6 global address of each router interface.
4. We can ping from PC1 to router R1's Fa0/0 interface.

5. We can ping from Server1 to router R2's Fa0/0 interface.
6. We can eliminate a local problem on both LANs.

From here, we'll go to PC1 and see if we can route to Server1:

`C:\Users\Todd Lammle>`**`tracert 2001:db8:3c4d:1:a14c:8c33:2d1:be3d`**

```
Tracing route to 2001:db8:3c4d:1:a14c:8c33:2d1:be3d over a maximum of 30 hops

  1    Destination host unreachable.
```

Wow—that's not good. Looks like we might have a routing problem. And on this little network, we're doing static IPv6 routing, so getting to the bottom of things will definitely take a little effort! But before we start looking into our potential routing issue, let's check the link between R1 and R2. We'll ping R2 from R1 to test the directly connected link.

The first thing you need to do before attempting to ping between routers is verify your addresses—yes, verify them again! Let's check out R1 and R2, then try pinging from R1 to R2:

`R1#`**`sh ipv6 int brief`**
```
FastEthernet0/0            [up/up]
    FE80::21A:6DFF:FE37:A44E
    2001:DB8:3C4D:3:21A:6DFF:FE37:A44E
FastEthernet0/1            [up/up]
    FE80::21A:6DFF:FE37:A44F
    2001:DB8:3C4D:2:21A:6DFF:FE37:A44F
```

`R2#`**`sh ipv6 int brief`**
```
FastEthernet0/0            [up/up]
    FE80::21A:6DFF:FE64:9B2
    2001:DB8:3C4D:1:21A:6DFF:FE37:A443
FastEthernet0/1            [up/up]
    FE80::21A:6DFF:FE64:9B3
    2001:DB8:3C4D:2:21A:6DFF:FE64:9B3
```

`R1#`**`ping 2001:DB8:3C4D:2:21A:6DFF:FE64:9B3`**
```
Type escape sequence to abort.
Sending 5, 100-byte ICMP Echos to ping 2001:DB8:3C4D:2:21A:6DFF:FE64:9B3, timeout
is 2 seconds:
!!!!!
Success rate is 100 percent (5/5), round-trip min/avg/max = 0/2/8 ms
```

We can see that I now have the IPv6 addresses for both the R1's and R2's directly connected interfaces. The output also shows that I used the Ping program to verify layer 3 connectivity. Just as with IPv4, we need to resolve the logical (IPv6) address to a MAC address in order to communicate on the local LAN. But unlike IPv4, IPv6 doesn't use ARP—it uses ICMPv6 neighbor solicitations instead. After the successful ping, we can now see the neighbor resolution table on R1:

```
R1#sh ipv6 neighbors
IPv6 Address                            Age Link-layer Addr  State Interface
FE80::21A:6DFF:FE64:9B3                 0   001a.6c46.9b09   DELAY Fa0/1
2001:DB8:3C4D:2:21A:6DFF:FE64:9B3       0   001a.6c46.9b09   REACH Fa0/1
```

Let's take a minute to talk about what each resolved address state indicates has happened:

INCMP (incomplete) Address resolution is being performed on the entry. A neighbor solicitation message has been sent, but the neighbor message hasn't yet been received.

REACH (reachable) Positive confirmation has been received confirming that the path to the neighbor is functioning correctly. REACH is good!

STALE The state is STALE when the interface hasn't communicated within the neighbor reachable time frame. The next time the neighbor communicates, the state will change back to REACH.

DELAY Occurs after the STALE state, when no reachability confirmation has been received within the DELAY_FIRST_PROBE_TIME. This means that the path was functioning but it hasn't had communication within the neighbor reachable time frame.

PROBE When in PROBE state, the configured interface is resending a neighbor solicitation and waiting for a reachability confirmation from a neighbor.

We can verify our default gateway with IPv6 with the `ipconfig` command like this:

```
C:\Users\Todd Lammle>ipconfig
   Connection-specific DNS Suffix  . : localdomain
   IPv6 Address. . . . . . . . . . . : 2001:db8:3c4d:3:ac3b:2ef:1823:8938
   Temporary IPv6 Address. . . . . . : 2001:db8:3c4d:3:2f33:44dd:211:1c3d
   Link-local IPv6 Address . . . . . : fe80::ac3b:2ef:1823:8938%11
   IPv4 Address. . . . . . . . . . . : 10.1.1.10
   Subnet Mask . . . . . . . . . . . : 255.255.255.0
   Default Gateway . . . . . . . . . : Fe80::21a:6dff:fe37:a44e%11
                                       10.1.1.1
```

Remember that the default gateway will be the link-local address of the router, and in this case, we can see that the address the host learned is truly the link-local address of the Fa0/0 interface of R1. The %11 is just used to identify an interface and isn't used as part of the IPv6 address.

> **Temporary IPv6 Addresses**
>
> The temporary IPv6 address, listed under the unicast IPv6 address as, "**2001:db8:3c4d:3: 2f33:44dd:211:1c3d,**" was created by Windows to provide privacy from the EUI-64 format. This creates a global address from your host without using your MAC address by generating a random number for the interface and hashing it, which is then appended to the /64 prefix from the router.
>
> You can disable this feature with the following commands:
>
> netsh interface ipv6 set global randomizeidentifiers=disabled
> netsh interface ipv6 set privacy state-disabled

In addition to the ipconfig command, we can use the command netsh interface ipv6 show neighbor to verify our default gateway address:

```
C:\Users\Todd Lammle>netsh interface ipv6 show neighbor
[output cut]

Interface 11: Local Area Connection

Internet Address                          Physical Address    Type
---------------------------------------   -----------------   ----------
2001:db8:3c4d:3:21a:6dff:fe37:a44e        00-1a-6d-37-a4-4e   (Router)
Fe80::21a:6dff:fe37:a44e                  00-1a-6d-37-a4-4e   (Router)
ff02::1                                   33-33-00-00-00-01   Permanent
ff02::2                                   33-33-00-00-00-02   Permanent
ff02::c                                   33-33-00-00-00-0c   Permanent
ff02::16                                  33-33-00-00-00-16   Permanent
ff02::fb                                  33-33-00-00-00-fb   Permanent
ff02::1:2                                 33-33-00-01-00-02   Permanent
ff02::1:3                                 33-33-00-01-00-03   Permanent
ff02::1:ff1f:ebcb                         33-33-ff-1f-eb-cb   Permanent
```

> **NOTE** I've checked the default gateway addresses on Server1 and they are correct. They should be, because this is provided directly from the router with an ICMPv6 RA (router advertisement) message. The output for that verification is not displayed.

Let's establish the information we have right now:

1. Our PC1 and Server1 configurations are working and have been verified.
2. The LANs are working and verified, so there is no Physical layer issue.
3. The default gateways are correct.
4. The link between the R1 and R2 routers is working and verified.

So all this tells us is that it's now time to check our routing tables! We'll start with the R1 router:

```
R1#sh ipv6 route
C   2001:DB8:3C4D:2::/64 [0/0]
     via FastEthernet0/1, directly connected
L   2001:DB8:3C4D:2:21A:6DFF:FE37:A44F/128 [0/0]
     via FastEthernet0/1, receive
C   2001:DB8:3C4D:3::/64 [0/0]
     via FastEthernet0/0, directly connected
L   2001:DB8:3C4D:3:21A:6DFF:FE37:A44E/128 [0/0]
     via FastEthernet0/0, receive
L   FF00::/8 [0/0]
     via Null0, receive
```

All we can see in the output is the two directly connected interfaces configured on the router, and that won't help us send IPv6 packets to the 2001:db8:3c4d:1::/64 subnet off of Fa0/0 on R2. So let's find out what R2 can tell us:

```
R2#sh ipv6 route
C   2001:DB8:3C4D:1::/64 [0/0]
     via FastEthernet0/0, directly connected
L   2001:DB8:3C4D:1:21A:6DFF:FE37:A443/128 [0/0]
     via FastEthernet0/0, receive
C   2001:DB8:3C4D:2::/64 [0/0]
     via FastEthernet0/1, directly connected
L   2001:DB8:3C4D:2:21A:6DFF:FE64:9B3/128 [0/0]
     via FastEthernet0/1, receive
S   2001:DB8:3C4D:3::/64 [1/0]
     via 2001:DB8:3C4D:2:21B:D4FF:FE0A:539
L   FF00::/8 [0/0]
     via Null0, receive
```

Now we're talking—that tells us a lot more than R1's table did! We have both of our directly connected configured LANs, Fa0/0 and Fa0/1, right there in the routing table, as well as a static route to 2001:DB8:3C4D:3::/64, which is the remote LAN Fa0/0 off of R1.

This is good! Now let's fix the route problem on R1 by adding a route that gives us access to the Server1 network and then move on to VLANs and trunking:

```
R1(config)#ipv6 route ::/0 fastethernet 0/1 FE80::21A:6DFF:FE64:9B3
```

I want to point out that I didn't need to make the default route as difficult as I did. I entered both the exit interface and next-hop link-local address when just the exit interface or next-hop global addresses would be mandatory, but not the link-local.

Next, we'll verify that we can now ping from PC1 to Server1:

```
C:\Users\Todd Lammle>ping 2001:db8:3c4d:1:a14c:8c33:2d1:be3d

Pinging 2001:db8:3c4d:1:a14c:8c33:2d1:be3d with 32 bytes of data:
Reply from 2001:db8:3c4d:1:a14c:8c33:2d1:be3d: time<1ms
Reply from 2001:db8:3c4d:1:a14c:8c33:2d1:be3d: time<1ms
Reply from 2001:db8:3c4d:1:a14c:8c33:2d1:be3d: time<1ms
Reply from 2001:db8:3c4d:1:a14c:8c33:2d1:be3d: time<1ms
```

Sweet—we're golden with this particular scenario! But know it's still possible to experience name resolution issues. If that were the case, you would just need to check your DNS server or local host table.

We'll move on in the same way we did in the IPv4 troubleshooting section by checking into our ACLs. This would be especially important if we were still plagued with a problem after troubleshooting all your local LANs and all other potential routing issues. To do that, just use the show ipv6 access-lists command to verify all configured ACLs on a router and use the show ipv6 interface command to verify if an ACL is attached to an interface. Once you've confirmed that your ACLs all make sense, you're good to go!

Troubleshooting VLAN Connectivity

You know by now that VLANs are used to break up broadcast domains in a layer 2 switched network. You've also learned that we assign ports on a switch into a VLAN broadcast domain by using the switchport access vlan command.

The access port carries traffic for a single VLAN that the port is a member of. If members of one VLAN want to communicate to members in the same VLAN that are located on a different switch, then a port between the two switches needs to either be configured as a member of this single VLAN or configured as a trunk link, which passes information on all VLANs by default.

We're going to use Figure 18.22 to reference as we go through the procedures for troubleshooting VLAN and trunking.

FIGURE 18.22 VLAN connectivity

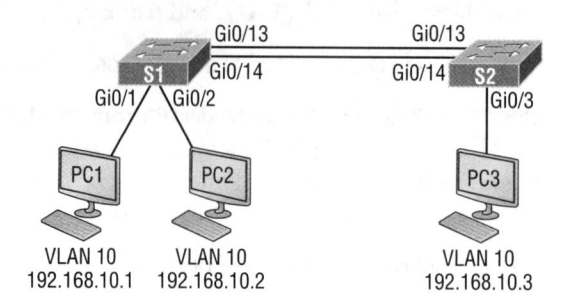

I'm going to begin with VLAN troubleshooting and then we'll get into trunk troubleshooting.

VLAN Troubleshooting

A couple of key times to troubleshoot VLANs are when and if you lose connectivity between hosts and when you're configuring new hosts into a VLAN but they're not working.

Here are the steps we'll follow to troubleshoot VLANs:

1. Verify the VLAN database on all your switches.
2. Verify your content addressable memory (CAM) table.
3. Verify that your port VLAN assignments are configured correctly.

And here's a list of the commands we'll be using in the section coming up:

```
Show vlan
Show mac address-table
Show interfaces interface switchport
switchport access vlan vlan
```

VLAN Troubleshooting Scenario

A manager calls and says they can't communicate to the new sales team member that just connected to the network. How would you proceed to solve this issue? Well, because the sales hosts are in VLAN 10, we'll begin with step 1 and verify that our databases on both switches are correct.

First, I'll use the `show vlan` or `show vlan brief` command to check if the expected VLAN is actually in the database. Here's a look at the VLAN database on S1:

```
S1#sh vlan

VLAN Name                             Status    Ports
---- -------------------------------- --------- -------------------------------
1    default                          active    Gi0/3, Gi0/4, Gi0/5, Gi0/6
                                                Gi0/7, Gi0/8, Gi0/9, Gi0/10
```

```
                                        Gi0/11, Gi0/12, Gi0/13, Gi0/14
                                        Gi0/15, Gi0/16, Gi0/17, Gi0/18
                                        Gi0/19, Gi0/20, Gi0/21, Gi0/22
                                        Gi0/23, Gi0/24, Gi0/25, Gi0/26
                                        Gi0/27, Gi0/28
10    Sales                    active   Gi0/1, Gi0/2
20    Accounting               active
26    Automation10             active
27    VLAN0027                 active
30    Engineering              active
170   VLAN0170                 active
501   Private501               active
502   Private500               active
[output cut]
```

This output shows that VLAN 10 is in the local database and that Gi0/1 and Gi0/2 are associated to VLAN 10.

So next, we'll go to step 2 and verify the CAM with the `show mac address-table` command:

```
S1#sh mac address-table
         Mac Address Table
-------------------------------------------

Vlan    Mac Address       Type        Ports
----    -----------       --------    -----
 All    0100.0ccc.cccc    STATIC      CPU
[output cut]
   1    000d.2830.2f00    DYNAMIC     Gi0/24
   1    0021.1c91.0d8d    DYNAMIC     Gi0/13
   1    0021.1c91.0d8e    DYNAMIC     Gi0/14
   1    b414.89d9.1882    DYNAMIC     Gi0/17
   1    b414.89d9.1883    DYNAMIC     Gi0/18
   1    ecc8.8202.8282    DYNAMIC     Gi0/15
   1    ecc8.8202.8283    DYNAMIC     Gi0/16
  10    001a.2f55.c9e8    DYNAMIC     Gi0/1
  10    001b.d40a.0538    DYNAMIC     Gi0/2
Total Mac Addresses for this criterion: 29
```

Okay—know that your switch will show quite a few MAC addresses assigned to the CPU at the top of the output. Those MAC addresses are used by the switch to manage the ports. The very first MAC address listed is the base MAC address of the switch and is used by STP in the bridge ID. In the preceding output, we can see that there are two MAC addresses associated with VLAN 10 and that they were dynamically learned. We can also establish that this MAC address is associated to Gi0/1. S1 looks really good!

Let's take a look at S2 now. First, let's confirm that port PC3 is connected and check its configuration. I'll use the command show interfaces interface switchport command to do that:

```
S2#sh interfaces gi0/3 switchport
Name: Gi0/3
Switchport: Enabled
Administrative Mode: dynamic desirable
Operational Mode: static access
Administrative Trunking Encapsulation: negotiate
Operational Trunking Encapsulation: native
Negotiation of Trunking: On
Access Mode VLAN: 10 (Inactive)
Trunking Native Mode VLAN: 1 (default)
[output cut]
```

Here we can see that the port is enabled and that it's set to dynamic desirable, meaning if it connects to another Cisco switch, it will desire to trunk on that link. The problem is, we're using it as an access port, which is confirmed by the operational mode of static access. At the end of the output, the text shows Access Mode VLAN: 10 (Inactive). This isn't good! Let's examine S2's CAM to see what we find out:

```
S2#sh mac address-table
          Mac Address Table
-------------------------------------------

Vlan    Mac Address       Type        Ports
----    -----------       --------    -----
 All    0100.0ccc.cccc    STATIC      CPU
[output cut]
   1    001b.d40a.0538    DYNAMIC     Gi0/13
   1    0021.1bee.a70d    DYNAMIC     Gi0/13
   1    b414.89d9.1884    DYNAMIC     Gi0/17
   1    b414.89d9.1885    DYNAMIC     Gi0/18
   1    ecc8.8202.8285    DYNAMIC     Gi0/16
Total Mac Addresses for this criterion: 26
```

Referring back to Figure 18.5, we can see that the host is connected to Gi0/3. The problem here is that we don't see a MAC address dynamically associated to Gi0/3 in the MAC address table. So what do we know so far that can help us? Well first, we can see that Gi0/3 is configured into VLAN 10, but that VLAN is inactive. Second, the host off of Gi0/3 doesn't appear in the CAM table. So now would be a good time to take a look at the VLAN database like this:

```
S2#sh vlan brief

VLAN Name                             Status     Ports
---- -------------------------------- ---------  -------------------------------
1    default                          active     Gi0/1, Gi0/2, Gi0/4, Gi0/5
                                                 Gi0/6, Gi0/7, Gi0/8, Gi0/9
                                                 Gi0/10, Gi0/11, Gi0/12, Gi0/13
                                                 Gi0/14, Gi0/15, Gi0/16, Gi0/17
                                                 Gi0/18, Gi0/19, Gi0/20, Gi0/21
                                                 Gi0/22, Gi0/23, Gi0/24, Gi0/25
                                                 Gi0/26, Gi0/27, Gi0/28
26   Automation10                     active
27   VLAN0027                         active
30   Engineering                      active
170  VLAN0170                         active
[output cut]
```

Look at that—there's no VLAN 10 in the database! Clearly this is our problem, but it's also an easy one to fix by simply creating the VLAN in the database:

```
S2#config t
S2(config)#vlan 10
S2(config-vlan)#name Sales
```

That's all there is to it. Now let's check the CAM again:

```
S2#sh mac address-table
          Mac Address Table
-------------------------------------------

Vlan    Mac Address       Type        Ports
----    -----------       --------    -----
 All    0100.0ccc.cccc    STATIC      CPU
[output cut]
  1     0021.1bee.a70d    DYNAMIC     Gi0/13
 10     001a.6c46.9b09    DYNAMIC     Gi0/3
Total Mac Addresses for this criterion: 22
```

We're good to go—the MAC address off of Gi0/3 shows in the MAC address table configured into VLAN 10.

That was pretty straightforward, but if the port had been assigned to the wrong VLAN, I would have used the `switch access vlan` command to correct the VLAN membership. Here's an example of how to do that:

```
S2#config t
S2(config)#int gi0/3
S2(config-if)#switchport access vlan 10
S2(config-if)#do sh vlan

VLAN Name                             Status    Ports
---- -------------------------------- --------- -------------------------------
1    default                          active    Gi0/1, Gi0/2, Gi0/4, Gi0/5
                                                Gi0/6, Gi0/7, Gi0/8, Gi0/9
                                                Gi0/10, Gi0/11, Gi0/12, Gi0/13
                                                Gi0/14, Gi0/15, Gi0/16, Gi0/17
                                                Gi0/18, Gi0/19, Gi0/20, Gi0/21
                                                Gi0/22, Gi0/23, Gi0/24, Gi0/25
                                                Gi0/26, Gi0/27, Gi0/28
10   Sales                            active    Gi0/3
```

Nice—we can see that our port Gi0/3 is in the VLAN 10 membership. Now let's try to ping from PC1 to PC3:

```
PC1#ping 192.168.10.3
Type escape sequence to abort.
Sending 5, 100-byte ICMP Echos to 192.168.10.3, timeout is 2 seconds:
.....
Success rate is 0 percent (0/5)
```

No luck with that, so let's see if PC1 can ping PC2:

```
PC1#ping 192.168.10.2
Type escape sequence to abort.
Sending 5, 100-byte ICMP Echos to 192.168.10.2, timeout is 2 seconds:
!!!!!
Success rate is 100 percent (5/5), round-trip min/avg/max = 1/2/4 ms
PC1#
```

That worked! I can ping a host that's a member of the same VLAN connected to the same switch, but I can't ping to a host on another switch that's a member of the same

VLAN, which is VLAN 10. To get to the bottom of this, let's quickly summarize what we've learned so far:

1. We know that the VLAN database is now correct on each switch.
2. The MAC address table shows the ARP entries for each host as well as a connection to each switch.
3. We've verified that our VLAN memberships are now correct on all the ports we're using.

But since we still can't ping to a host on another switch, we need to start checking out the connections between our switches.

Trunk Troubleshooting

You'll need to troubleshoot trunk links when you lose connectivity between hosts that are in the same VLAN but located on different switches. Cisco refers to this as "VLAN leaking." Seems to me we are leaking VLAN 10 between switches somehow.

These are the steps we'll take to troubleshoot VLANs:

1. Verify that the interface configuration is set to the correct trunk parameters.
2. Verify that the ports are configured correctly.
3. Verify the native VLAN on each switch.

And here are the commands we'll use to perform trunk troubleshooting:

```
Show interfaces trunk
Show vlan
Show interfaces interface trunk
Show interfaces interface switchport
Show dtp interface interface
switchport mode
switchport mode dynamic
switchport trunk native vlan vlan
```

Okay, let's get started by checking ports Gi0/13 and Gi0/14 on each switch because these are what the figure is showing as forming the connection between our switches. We'll start with the show interfaces trunk command:

S1>**sh interfaces trunk**

S2>**sh interfaces trunk**

Not a scrap of output—that's definitely a bad sign! Let's take another look at the show vlan output on S1 and see what we can find out:

S1>**sh vlan brief**

```
VLAN Name                             Status    Ports
---- -------------------------------- --------- -------------------------------
1    default                          active    Gi0/3, Gi0/4, Gi0/5, Gi0/6
                                                Gi0/7, Gi0/8, Gi0/9, Gi0/10
                                                Gi0/11, Gi0/12, Gi0/13, Gi0/14
                                                Gi0/15, Gi0/16, Gi0/17, Gi0/18
                                                Gi0/19, Gi0/20, Gi0/21, Gi0/22
                                                Gi0/23, Gi0/24, Gi0/25, Gi0/26
                                                Gi0/27, Gi0/28
10   Sales                            active    Gi0/1, Gi0/2
20   Accounting                       active
[output cut]
```

Nothing new from when we checked it a few minutes ago, but look there under VLAN 1—we can see interfaces Gi/013 and Gi0/14. This means that our ports between switches are members of VLAN 1 and will pass only VLAN 1 frames!

Typically I'll tell my students that if you type the show vlan command, you're really typing the nonexistent "show access ports" command since this output shows interfaces in access mode but doesn't show the trunk interfaces. This means that our ports between switches are access ports instead of trunk ports, so they'll pass information about VLAN 1 only.

Let's go back over to the S2 switch to verify and see which port interfaces Gi0/13 and Gi0/14 are members of:

S2>**sh vlan brief**

```
VLAN Name                             Status    Ports
---- -------------------------------- --------- -------------------------------
1    default                          active    Gi0/1, Gi0/2, Gi0/4, Gi0/5
                                                Gi0/6, Gi0/7, Gi0/8, Gi0/9
                                                Gi0/10, Gi0/11, Gi0/12, Gi0/13
                                                Gi0/14, Gi0/15, Gi0/16, Gi0/17
                                                Gi0/18, Gi0/19, Gi0/20, Gi0/21
                                                Gi0/22, Gi0/23, Gi0/24, Gi0/25
                                                Gi0/26, Gi0/27, Gi0/28
10   Sales                            active    Gi0/3
```

Again, as with S1, the links between switches are showing in the output of the show vlan command, which means that they are not trunk ports. We can use the show interfaces *interface* switchport command to verify this as well:

```
S1#sho interfaces gi0/13 switchport
Name: Gi0/13
Switchport: Enabled
Administrative Mode: dynamic auto
Operational Mode: static access
Administrative Trunking Encapsulation: negotiate
Operational Trunking Encapsulation: native
Negotiation of Trunking: On
Access Mode VLAN: 1 (default)
Trunking Native Mode VLAN: 1 (default)
```

This output tells us that interface Gi0/13 is in dynamic auto mode. But its operational mode is static access, meaning it's not a trunk port. We can look closer at its trunking capabilities with the show interfaces *interface* trunk command:

```
S1#sh interfaces gi0/1 trunk

Port        Mode      Encapsulation   Status          Native vlan
Gi0/1       auto      negotiate       not-trunking    1
[output cut]
```

Sure enough—the port is not trunking, but we already knew that. Now it's confirmed. Notice that we can see that native VLAN is set to VLAN 1, which is the default native VLAN. This means that VLAN 1 is the default VLAN for untagged traffic.

Now, before we check the native VLAN on S2 to verify that there isn't a mismatch, I want to point out a key fact about trunking and how we would get these ports between switches to do that.

Many Cisco switches support the Cisco proprietary Dynamic Trunking Protocol (DTP), which is used to manage automatic trunk negotiation between switches. Cisco recommends that you don't go with this and to configure your switch ports manually instead. I agree with them!

Okay, with that in mind, let's check out our switch port Gi0/13 on S1 and view its DTP status. I'll use the show dtp interface *interface* command to view the DTP statistics:

```
S1#sh dtp interface gi0/13
DTP information for GigabitEthernet0/13:
  TOS/TAS/TNS:                      ACCESS/AUTO/ACCESS
  TOT/TAT/TNT:                      NATIVE/NEGOTIATE/NATIVE
```

```
    Neighbor address 1:                      00211C910D8D
    Neighbor address 2:                      000000000000
    Hello timer expiration (sec/state):      12/RUNNING
    Access timer expiration (sec/state):     never/STOPPED
```

Did you notice that our port GI0/13 from S1 to S2 is an access port configured to auto-negotiate using DTP? That's interesting, and I want to dig a little deeper into the different port configurations and how they affect trunking capabilities to clarify why.

Access   Trunking is not allowed on a port set to access mode.

Auto   Will trunk to neighbor switch only if the remote port is set to on or to desirable mode. This creates the trunk based on the DTP request from the neighboring switch.

Desirable   This will trunk with all port modes except access. Ports set to dynamic desirable will communicate via DTP that the interface is attempting to become a trunk if the neighboring switch interface is able to become a trunk.

Nonegotiate   No DTP frames are generated from the interface. Can only be used if the neighbor interface is manually set as trunk or access.

Trunk (on)   Trunks with all switch port modes except access. Automatically enables trunking regardless of the state of the neighboring switch and regardless of any DTP requests.

Let's check out the different options available on the S1 switch with the `switchport mode dynamic` command:

```
S1(config-if)#switchport mode ?
  access         Set trunking mode to ACCESS unconditionally
  dot1q-tunnel   set trunking mode to TUNNEL unconditionally
  dynamic        Set trunking mode to dynamically negotiate access or trunk mode
  private-vlan   Set private-vlan mode
  trunk          Set trunking mode to TRUNK unconditionally

S1(config-if)#switchport mode dynamic ?
  auto       Set trunking mode dynamic negotiation parameter to AUTO
  desirable  Set trunking mode dynamic negotiation parameter to DESIRABLE
```

From interface mode, use the `switch mode trunk` command to turn trunking on. You can also use the `switch mode dynamic` command to set the port to auto or desirable trunking modes. To turn off DTP and any type of negotiation, use the `switchport nonegotiate` command.

Let's take a look at S2 and see if we can figure out why our two switches didn't create a trunk:

```
S2#sh int gi0/13 switchport
Name: Gi0/13
Switchport: Enabled
```

```
Administrative Mode: dynamic auto
Operational Mode: static access
Administrative Trunking Encapsulation: negotiate
Operational Trunking Encapsulation: native
Negotiation of Trunking: On
```

We can see that the port is in dynamic auto and that it's operating as an access port. Let's look into this further:

```
S2#sh dtp interface gi0/13
DTP information for GigabitEthernet0/3:
  DTP information for GigabitEthernet0/13:
  TOS/TAS/TNS:                              ACCESS/AUTO/ACCESS
  TOT/TAT/TNT:                              NATIVE/NEGOTIATE/NATIVE
  Neighbor address 1:                       000000000000
  Neighbor address 2:                       000000000000
  Hello timer expiration (sec/state):       17/RUNNING
  Access timer expiration (sec/state):      never/STOPPED
```

Do you see the problem? Don't be fooled—it's not that they're running in access mode; it's because two ports in dynamic auto will not form a trunk! This is a really common problem to look for since most Cisco switches ship in dynamic auto. The other issue you need to be aware of, as well as check for, is the frame-tagging method. Some switches run 802.1q, some run both 802.1q and Inter-Switch Link (ISL) routing, so be sure the tagging method is compatible between all of your switches!

It's time to fix our problem on the trunk ports between S1 and S2. We only need to fix one side of each link since dynamic auto will trunk with a port set to desirable or on:

```
S2(config)#int gi0/13
S2(config-if)#switchport mode dynamic desirable
23:11:37:%LINEPROTO-5-UPDOWN:Line protocol on Interface GigabitEthernet0/13, changed state to down
23:11:37:%LINEPROTO-5-UPDOWN:Line protocol on Interface Vlan1, changed state to down
23:11:40:%LINEPROTO-5-UPDOWN:Line protocol on Interface GigabitEthernet0/13, changed state to up
23:12:10:%LINEPROTO-5-UPDOWN:Line protocol on Interface Vlan1, changed state to up
S2(config-if)#do show int trunk

Port      Mode        Encapsulation  Status     Native vlan
Gi0/13    desirable   n-isl          trunking   1
[output cut]
```

Nice—it worked! With one side in Auto and the other now in Desirable, DTPs will be exchanged and they will trunk. Notice in the preceding output that the mode of S2's Gi0/13 link is desirable and that the switches actually negotiated ISL as a trunk encapsulation—go figure! But don't forget to notice the native VLAN. We'll work on the frame-tagging method and native VLAN in a minute, but first, let's configure our other link:

```
S2(config-if)#int gi0/14
S2(config-if)#switchport mode dynamic desirable
23:12:%LINEPROTO-5-UPDOWN:Line protocol on Interface GigabitEthernet0/14, changed state to down
23:12:%LINEPROTO-5-UPDOWN:Line protocol on Interface GigabitEthernet0/14, changed state to up
S2(config-if)#do show int trunk

Port      Mode          Encapsulation  Status      Native vlan
Gi0/13    desirable     n-isl          trunking    1
Gi0/14    desirable     n-isl          trunking    1

Port      Vlans allowed on trunk
Gi0/13    1-4094
Gi0/14    1-4094
[output cut]
```

Great, we now have two trunked links between switches. But I've got to say, I really don't like the ISL method of frame tagging since it can't send untagged frames across the link. So let's change our native VLAN from the default of 1 to 392. The number 392 just randomly sounded good at the moment. Here's what I entered on S1:

```
S1(config-if)#switchport trunk native vlan 392
S1(config-if)#
23:17:40: Port is not 802.1Q trunk, no action
```

See what I mean? I tried to change the native VLAN and ISL basically responded with, "What's a native VLAN?" Very annoying, so I'm going to take care of that now!

```
S1(config-if)#int range gi0/13 - 14
S1(config-if-range)#switchport trunk encapsulation ?
  dot1q     Interface uses only 802.1q trunking encapsulation when trunking
  isl       Interface uses only ISL trunking encapsulation when trunking
  negotiate Device will negotiate trunking encapsulation with peer on
            interface

S1(config-if-range)#switchport trunk encapsulation dot1q
23:23:%LINEPROTO-5-UPDOWN:Line protocol on Interface GigabitEthernet0/13, changed state to down
23:23:%LINEPROTO-5-UPDOWN: Line protocol on Interface GigabitEthernet0/14, changed state to down
23:23:%CDP-4-NATIVE_VLAN_MISMATCH: Native VLAN mismatch discovered on GigabitEthernet0/13 (392),
with S2 GigabitEthernet0/13 (1).
23:23:%LINEPROTO-5-UPDOWN: Line protocol on Interface GigabitEthernet0/14, changed state to up
23:23:%LINEPROTO-5-UPDOWN: Line protocol on Interface GigabitEthernet0/13, changed state to up
23:23:%CDP-4-NATIVE_VLAN_MISMATCH: Native VLAN mismatch discovered on GigabitEthernet0/13 (392),
with S2 GigabitEthernet0/13 (1).
```

Now that's more like it! As soon as I changed the encapsulation type on S1, DTP frames changed the frame-tagging method between S2 to 802.1q. Since I had already changed the native VLAN on port Gi0/13 on S1, the switch lets us know, via CDP, that we now have a native VLAN mismatch. Let's proceed to deal with this by verifying our interfaces with the show interface trunk command:

```
S1#sh int trunk
Port      Mode       Encapsulation  Status     Native vlan
Gi0/13    auto       802.1q         trunking   392
Gi0/14    auto       802.1q         trunking   1

S2#sh int trunk
Port      Mode       Encapsulation  Status     Native vlan
Gi0/13    desirable  n-802.1q       trunking   1
Gi0/14    desirable  n-802.1q       trunking   1
```

Notice that both links are running 802.1q, that S1 is in auto mode and S2 is in desirable mode. And we can see a native VLAN mismatch on port Gi0/13. We can also see the mismatched native VLAN with the show interfaces *interface* switchport command by looking at both sides of the link like this:

```
S2#sh interfaces gi0/13 switchport
Name: Gi0/13
Switchport: Enabled
Administrative Mode: dynamic desirable
Operational Mode: trunk
Administrative Trunking Encapsulation: negotiate
Operational Trunking Encapsulation: dot1q
Negotiation of Trunking: On
Access Mode VLAN: 1 (default)
Trunking Native Mode VLAN: 1 (default)

S1#sh int gi0/13 switchport
Name: Gi0/13
Switchport: Enabled
Administrative Mode: dynamic auto
Operational Mode: trunk
Administrative Trunking Encapsulation: dot1q
Operational Trunking Encapsulation: dot1q
Negotiation of Trunking: On
Access Mode VLAN: 1 (default)
Trunking Native Mode VLAN: 392 (Inactive)
```

So this has got to be bad, right? I mean really—are we sending any frames down that link or not? Let's see if we solved our little problem of not being able to ping to hosts from S1 to S2 and find out:

```
PC1#ping 192.168.10.3
Type escape sequence to abort.
Sending 5, 100-byte ICMP Echos to 192.168.10.3, timeout is 2 seconds:
!!!!!
Success rate is 100 percent (5/5), round-trip min/avg/max = 1/1/4 ms
```

Yes, it works! Not so bad after all. We've solved our problem, or at least most of it. Having a native VLAN mismatch only means you can't send untagged frames down the link, which are essentially management frames like CDP, for example. So although it's not the end of the world, it will prevent us from being able to remotely manage the switch. It will also prevent us from even sending any other types of traffic down just that one VLAN.

So am I saying you can just leave this issue the way it is? Well, you could, but you won't. No, you'll fix it because if you don't, CDP will send you a message every minute telling you that there's a mismatch and drive you mad! This is how we'll save our sanity:

```
S2(config)#int gi0/13
S2(config-if)#switchport trunk native vlan 392
S2(config-if)#^Z
S2#sh int trunk
```

Port	Mode	Encapsulation	Status	Native vlan
Gi0/13	desirable	n-802.1q	trunking	392
Gi0/14	desirable	n-802.1q	trunking	1

[output cut]

All better! Both sides of the same link between switches are now using native VLAN 392 on Gigabit Ethernet 0/13.

I want you to know that you can have different native VLANs for each link and the link will still work, however, it is best to have them the same for management purposes.

Each network is different and you have to make choices between options that will end up meeting your particular business requirements in the most optimal way.

Summary

This chapter covered troubleshooting techniques from basic to advanced. Although most chapters in this book cover troubleshooting, this one focused purely on IPv4, IPv6 and VLAN/trunk troubleshooting.

You learned how to troubleshoot step-by-step from a host to a remote device. Starting with IPv4, you learned the steps to test the host and the local connectivity and then how to troubleshoot remote connectivity.

After that we moved on to IPv6 and proceeded to troubleshoot using the same techniques that you learned with IPv4. It's important that you can use the verification commands that I used in each step of this chapter.

Lastly, I covered VLAN and trunk troubleshooting and how to go step-by-step through a switched network using verification commands and narrowing down the problem.

Exam Essentials

Understand how to Verify IP parameters for Client OS (Windows, Mac OS, Linux) To configure and verify the various OS's, use tools such as ipconfig, ipconfig /all, and ifconfig

Remember the Cisco steps in troubleshooting an IPv4 and IPv6 network.

1. Check the cables to find out if there's a faulty cable or interface in the mix and verify the interface's statistics.
2. Make sure that devices are determining the correct path from the source to the destination. Manipulate the routing information if needed.
3. Verify that the default gateway is correct.
4. Verify that name resolution settings are correct.
5. Verify that there are no ACLs blocking traffic.

Remember the commands to verify and troubleshoot IPv4 and IPv6. You need to remember and practice the commands used in this chapter, especially ping and traceroute (tracert on Windows). We also used the Windows commands ipconfig. route print and netsh, as well as Cisco's commands show ip int brief, show interface, and show route.

Remember how to verify an ARP cache with IPv6. The command show ipv6 neighbors shows the IP-to-MAC-address resolution table on a Cisco router.

Remember to look at the statistics on a router and switch interface to determine problems. You've got to be able to analyze interface statistics to spot problems if they exist, including speed and duplex settings, input queue drops, output queue drops, and input and output errors.

Understand what a native VLAN is and how to change it. A native VLAN works with only 802.1q trunks and allows untagged traffic to traverse the trunk link. This is VLAN 1 by default on all Cisco switches, but it can be changed for security reasons with the switchport native vlan vlan command.

Review Questions

The answers to these questions are found in the Appendix.

1. You need to verify the IPv6 ARP cache on a router and see that the state of an entry is REACH. What does REACH mean?
   A. The router is reaching out to get the address.
   B. The entry is incomplete.
   C. The entry has reached the end of life and will be discarded from the table.
   D. A positive confirmation has been received by the neighbor and the path to it is functioning correctly.

2. What's the most common cause of interface errors?
   A. Speed mismatch
   B. Duplex mismatch
   C. Buffer overflows
   D. Collisions between a dedicated switch port and an NIC

3. Which command will verify the DTP status on a switch interface?
   A. `sh dtp status`
   B. `sh dtp status interface` *interface*
   C. `sh interface` *interface* `dtp`
   D. `sh dtp interface` *interface*

4. What mode will not allow DTP frames generated from a switch port?
   A. Nonegotiate
   B. Trunk
   C. Access
   D. Auto

5. The following output was generated by which command?

   ```
   IPv6 Address                         Age Link-layer Addr State Interface
   FE80::21A:6DFF:FE64:9B3                0 001a.6c46.9b09  DELAY Fa0/1
   2001:DB8:3C4D:2:21A:6DFF:FE64:9B3      0 001a.6c46.9b09  REACH Fa0/1
   ```

   A. `show ip arp`
   B. `show ipv6 arp`
   C. `show ip neighbors`
   D. `show ipv6 neighbors`

6. Which of the following states tells you that an interface has not communicated within the neighbor-reachable time frame?
   A. REACH
   B. STALE
   C. TIMEOUT
   D. CLEARED

7. You receive a call from a user who says that they can't log in to a remote server, which only runs IPv6. Based on the output, what could the problem be?

   ```
   C:\Users\Todd Lammle>ipconfig
       Connection-specific DNS Suffix  . : localdomain
       IPv6 Address. . . . . . . . . . . : 2001:db8:3c4d:3:ac3b:2ef:1823:8938
       Temporary IPv6 Address. . . . . . : 2001:db8:3c4d:3:2f33:44dd:211:1c3d
       Link-local IPv6 Address . . . . . : fe80::ac3b:2ef:1823:8938%11
       IPv4 Address. . . . . . . . . . . : 10.1.1.10
       Subnet Mask . . . . . . . . . . . : 255.255.255.0
       Default Gateway . . . . . . . . . : 10.1.1.1
   ```

   A. The global address is in the wrong subnet.
   B. The IPv6 default gateway hasn't been configured or received from the router.
   C. The link-local address hasn't been resolved, so the host cannot communicate to the router.
   D. There are two IPv6 global addresses configured. One must be removed from the configuration.

8. Your host cannot reach remote networks. Based on the output, what's the problem?

   ```
   C:\Users\Server1>ipconfig

   Windows IP Configuration

   Ethernet adapter Local Area Connection:

       Connection-specific DNS Suffix  . : localdomain
       Link-local IPv6 Address . . . . . : fe80::7723:76a2:e73c:2acb%11
       IPv4 Address. . . . . . . . . . . : 172.16.20.254
       Subnet Mask . . . . . . . . . . . : 255.255.255.0
       Default Gateway . . . . . . . . . : 172.16.2.1
   ```

   A. The link-local IPv6 address is wrong.
   B. The IPv6 global address is missing.
   C. There is no DNS server configuration.
   D. The IPv4 default gateway address is misconfigured.

9. Which two commands will show you if you have a native VLAN mismatch?
   A. `show interface native vlan`
   B. `show interface trunk`
   C. `show interface` *interface* `switchport`
   D. `show switchport interface`

10. You connect two new Cisco 3560 switches together and expect them to use DTP and create a trunk. But, when you check statistics, you find that they are access ports and didn't negotiate. Why didn't DTP work on these Cisco switches?
    A. The ports on each side of the link are set to auto trunking.
    B. The ports on each side of the link are set to on.
    C. The ports on each side of the link are set to dynamic.
    D. The ports on each side of the link are set to desirable.

11. What command can used to verify the IP address on a Mac?
    A. ipconfig
    B. ifconfig
    C. iptables
    D. Get-NetIPAddress
    E. show ip int brief

Chapter 19

Wireless Technologies

THE FOLLOWING CCNA EXAM TOPICS ARE COVERED IN THIS CHAPTER:

✓ **1.11 Describe wireless principles**

- 1.11.a Nonoverlapping Wi-Fi channels
- 1.11.b SSID
- 1.11.c RF
- 1.11.d Encryption

2.0 Network Access

✓ **2.6 Compare Cisco Wireless Architectures and AP modes**

✓ **2.7 Describe physical infrastructure connections of WLAN components (AP, WLC, access/trunk ports, and LAG)**

✓ **2.8 Describe AP and WLC management access connections (Telnet, SSH, HTTP, HTTPS, console, and TACACS±/RADIUS)**

5.0 Security Fundamentals

✓ **5.9 Describe wireless security protocols (WPA, WPA2, and WPA3)**

Wireless connectivity is so everywhere these days, to really get away, I recently vacationed to a beautiful spot with no cell or Internet service on purpose! I know, crazy right? While it's true that I definitely chilled out, most of the time, I wouldn't even think of checking in anywhere that doesn't offer these things!

So clearly, those of us already in or wishing to enter the IT field better have our chops down on wireless network components and installation factors, which brings us to a great starting point: if you want to understand the basic wireless LANs (WLANs) used today, just think Ethernet connectivity with hubs—except the wireless devices we connect to are called access points (APs). This means that our WLANs run half-duplex communication—everyone is sharing the same bandwidth with only one device communicating at a time per channel. This isn't necessarily bad; it's just not good enough. Not only do we want it fast, we want it secure too!

Since I know you've crushed all of the previous chapters, you're ready to dive into this one! If that's not exactly you, just know that the two chapters on switching provide a really nice review on switching and VLANs.

Why do you need a strong background in switching and VLANs? Because if you think about it for a minute, you come to the important realization that APs have to connect to something. If not, how else would all those hosts hanging around in a wireless network area be able to connect to your wired resources, or to the Internet?

You also might be surprised to hear that wireless security is basically nonexistent on access points and clients by default. That's because the original 802.11 committee just didn't foresee that wireless hosts would one day outnumber bounded media hosts. Same thing with the IPv4 routed protocol—unfortunately engineers and scientists just didn't include wireless security standards robust enough to work in a corporate environment. These factors leave us to face this problem with proprietary solution add-ons to create a secure wireless network. The good news is that some of the standards actually do provide some solid wireless security. And they're also pretty easy to implement with a little practice.

So let's start this chapter by defining a basic wireless network as well as basic wireless principles. We'll talk about different types of wireless networks and the minimum devices required to create a simple wireless network and look at some basic wireless topologies as well. After that, I'll get into basic security by covering WPA, WPA2 and WPA3.

> **NOTE** To find your included bonus material, as well as Todd Lammle videos, practice questions & hands-on labs, please see www.lammle.com/ccna

Wireless Networks

Wireless networks come in many forms, cover various distances, and provide a wide range of bandwidth capacities depending on the type that's been installed. The typical wireless network today is an extension of an Ethernet LAN, with wireless hosts utilizing Media Access Control (MAC) addresses, IP addresses, and so forth, just like they would on a wired LAN.

Figure 19.1 shows a simple, typical WLAN.

FIGURE 19.1 Wireless LANs are an extension of our existing LANs

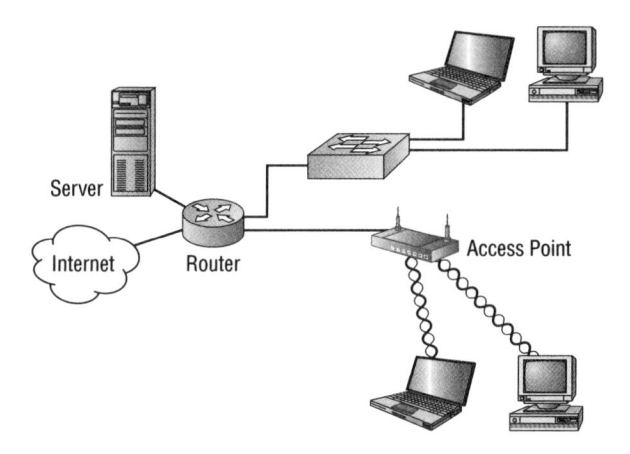

Wireless networks are more than just run-of-the-mill LANs because they're wireless of course. They cover a range of distances from short-range personal area networks to wide area networks (WANs) that really go the distance.

Figure 19.2 illustrates how different types of wireless networks look and the related distances they'll provide coverage for in today's world.

FIGURE 19.2 Today's wireless networks

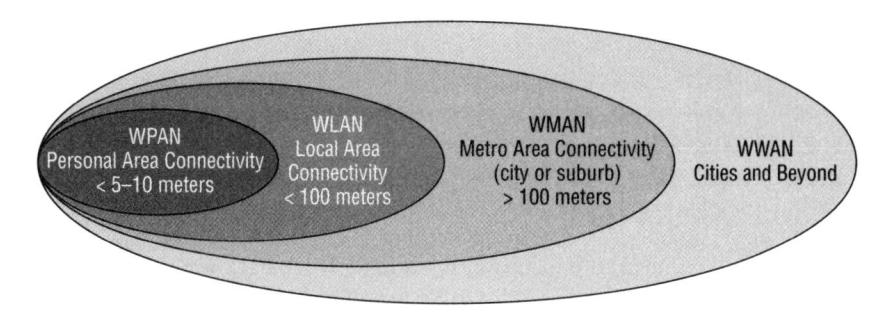

Now that you've got a mental picture, let's explore each of these networks in more detail.

Wireless Personal Area Network (WPAN)

A wireless personal area network (PAN) works in a very small area and connects devices like mice, keyboards, PDAs, headsets, and cell phones to our computers. This conveniently eliminates the cabling clutter of the past. If you're thinking Bluetooth, you've got it, because it's by far the most popular type of PAN around.

PANs are low power, they cover short distances, and they're small. You can stretch one of these to cover about 30 feet max, but most devices on a PAN have a short reach, making them popular for small and/or home offices. Bigger isn't always better—you don't want your PAN's devices interfering with your other wireless networks, or someone else's. Plus, you've got the usual security concerns to manage. So remember that PANs are the perfect solution for small devices you want to connect to your PC.

The standard use for PANs is unlicensed. This means that beyond initially purchasing PAN-typical devices, the users involved don't have to pay to use the type of devices in this network. This factor definitely encourages the development of devices that can use PAN frequencies.

Wireless LAN (WLAN)

Wireless LANs (WLANs) were created to cover longer distances and offer higher bandwidth than PANs. They're the most popular type of wireless networks in use today.

The first WLAN had a data rate up to 2Mbps, could stretch about 200–300 feet, depending on the area, and was called 802.11. The typical rates in use today are higher—11Mbps for IEEE 802.11b and 54Mbps for 802.11g/a.

The ideal for a WLAN is to have many users connect to the network simultaneously, but this can cause interference and collisions because the network's users are all competing for the same bandwidth.

Like PANs, WLANs use an unlicensed frequency band, which means you don't have to pay for the frequency band in order to transmit. And again, this attribute has resulted in an explosion of new development in the WLAN arena.

Wireless Metro Area Network (WMAN)

Wireless metro area networks (WMANs) cover a fairly large geographic area like a city or small suburb. They're becoming increasingly common as more and more products are introduced into the WLAN sector, causing the price tag to drop.

You can think of WMANs as low-budget, bridging networks. They'll save you some real cash compared to shelling out for much more costly leased lines, but there's a catch: to get your discount long-distance wireless network to work, you've got to have a line of sight between each hub or building.

Fiber connections are ideal to build an ultra-solid network backbone with, so go with them if they're available in your area. If your ISP doesn't offer the fiber option, or you just don't have the cash for it, a WMAN is a perfectly fine, economical alternative for covering something like a campus or another large area so long as you've got that vital line of sight factor in check!

Wireless Wide Area Network (WWAN)

So far, it's very rare to come across a wireless wide area network (WWAN) that can provide you with WLAN speeds, but there sure is a lot of chatter about them. A good example of a WWAN would be the latest cellular networks that can transmit data at a pretty good clip. But even though WWANs can certainly cover plenty of area, they're still not speedy enough to replace our ubiquitous WLANs.

Some people—especially those shilling stuff on TV—claim to adore their infallible, turbo-charged cellular networks. These terminally happy people are usually watching high-speed video while uploading images and gaming on their smart phones, but I don't know anyone who lives outside the TV who actually gets that kind of speed. And as for that "coverage anywhere" schtick? Off the set, dead zones and frozen phones are just reality for now.

It's possible we'll see more efficiency and growth for WWANs soon, but since WWANs are used to provide connectivity over a really large geographic area, it follows that implementing one will separate your cell service provider from a large quantity of cash. So it's going to come to motivation—as more people demand this type of service and are willing to pay for it, cellular companies will gain the resources to expand and improve upon these exciting networks.

Another set of positives in favor of WWAN growth and development: They meet a lot of business requirements, and technology is growing in a direction that the need for this type of long-distance wireless network is getting stronger. So it's a fairly good bet connectivity between a WLAN and a WWAN will be critical to many things in our future. For instance, when we have more IPv6 networks, the "pass-off" between these two types of networks may be seamless.

Basic Wireless Devices

Though it might not seem this way to you right now, *simple* wireless networks (WLANs) are less complex than their wired cousins because they require fewer components. To make a basic wireless network work properly, all you need are two main devices: a wireless AP and a wireless network interface card (NIC). This also makes it a lot easier to install a wireless network, because basically, you just need an understanding of these two components in order to make it happen.

Wireless Access Points

You'll find a central component like a hub or switch in the vast majority of wired networks, which is there to connect hosts and allow them to communicate. Wireless also have a component that connects all wireless devices together, only that device is known as a wireless *access point* (AP). Wireless APs have at least one antenna. Usually there's two for better reception (referred to as diversity) and a port to connect them to a wired network.

Figure 19.3 gives you an example of a Cisco wireless AP, which just happens to be one of my personal favorites.

FIGURE 19.3 A wireless access point

APs have the following characteristics:

- APs function as a central junction point for the wireless stations much like a switch or hub does within a wired network. Due to the half-duplex nature of wireless networking, the hub comparison is more accurate, even though hubs are rarely found in the wired world anymore.
- APs have at least one antenna—most likely two.
- APs function as a bridge to the wired network, giving the wireless station access to the wired network and/or the Internet.
- SoHo APs come in two flavors—the stand-alone AP and the wireless router. They can and usually do include functions like network address translation (NAT) and Dynamic Host Configuration Protocol (DHCP).

Even though it's not a perfect analogy, you can compare an AP to a hub because it doesn't create collision domains for each port like a switch does. But APs are definitely smarter than hubs. An AP is a portal device that can either direct network traffic to the wired backbone or back out into the wireless realm. If you look at Figure 19.1 again, you can see that the connection back to the wired network is called the distribution system (DS), and it also maintains MAC address information within the 802.11 frames. What's more, these frames are capable of holding as many as four MAC addresses, but only when a wireless DS is in use.

An AP also maintains an association table that you can view from the web-based software used to manage the AP. So what's an association table? It's basically a list of all workstations currently connected to or associated with the AP, which are listed by their MAC addresses. Another nice AP feature is that wireless routers can function as NAT routers, and they can carry out DHCP addressing for workstations as well.

In the Cisco world, there are two types of APs: autonomous and lightweight. An autonomous AP is one that's configured, managed, and maintained in isolation with regard to all the other APs that exist in the network. A lightweight AP gets its configuration from a central device called a wireless controller. In this scenario, the APs are functioning as antennas and all information is sent back to the wireless LAN controller (WLC). There are a bunch of advantages to this, like the capacity for centralized management and more seamless roaming. You'll learn all about using WLC and lightweight APs throughout this book.

You can think of an AP as a bridge between the wireless clients and the wired network. And, depending on the settings, you can even use an AP as a wireless bridge for bridging two, wired network segments together.

In addition to the stand-alone AP, there's another type of AP that includes a built-in router, which you can use to connect both wired and wireless clients to the Internet. These devices are usually employed as NAT routers and they're the type shown in Figure 19.3.

Wireless Network Interface Card (NIC)

Every host you want to connect to a wireless network needs a wireless *network interface card* (NIC) to do so. Basically, a wireless NIC does the same job as a traditional NIC, only instead of having a socket/port to plug a cable into, the wireless NIC has a radio antenna.

Figure 19.4 gives you a picture of a wireless NIC.

FIGURE 19.4 Wireless NIC

The wireless card shown in Figure 19.4 is used in a laptop or desktop computer, and pretty much all laptops have wireless cards plugged into or built into the motherboard.

> These days, it's pretty rare to use an external wireless client card because all laptops come with them built in, and desktops can be ordered with them too. But it's good to know that you can still buy the client card shown in Figure 19.4. Typically, you would use cards like the ones shown in the figure for areas of poor reception, or for use with a network analyzer because they can have better range—depending on the antenna you use.

Wireless Antennas

Wireless antennas work with both transmitters and receivers. There are two broad classes of antennas on the market today: *omni-directional* (or point-to-multipoint) and *directional* (or point-to-point). An example of omni antennas is shown back in Figure 19.3 attached to the Cisco 800 AP.

Yagi antennas usually provide greater range than omni antennas of equivalent gain. Why? Because yagis focus all their power in a single direction. Omnis must disperse the same amount of power in all directions at the same time, like a large donut.

A downside to using a directional antenna is that you've got to be much more precise when aligning communication points. It's also why most APs use omnis, because often, clients and other APs can be located in any direction at any given moment.

To get a picture of this, think of the antenna on your car. Yes, it's a non-networking example, but it's still a good one because it clarifies the fact that your car's particular orientation doesn't affect the signal reception of whatever radio station you happen to be listening to. Well, most of the time, anyway. If you're in the boonies, you're out of range you're out of luck—something that also applies to the networking version of Omnis.

Wireless Principles

Next up, we're going to cover different types of networks you'll run into and/or design and implement as your wireless networks grow:

- IBSS
- BSS
- ESS
- Workgroup bridges
- Repeater APs
- Bridging (point-to-point and point-to-multipoint)
- Mesh

Let's check out these networks in detail now.

Independent Basic Service Set (Ad Hoc)

This is the easiest way to install wireless 802.11 devices. In this mode, the wireless NICs (or other devices) can communicate directly without the need for an AP. A good example of this is two laptops with wireless NICs installed. If both cards were set up to operate in ad hoc mode, they could connect and transfer files as long as the other network settings, like protocols, were set up to enable this as well. We'll also call this an *independent basic service set* (IBSS), which is born as soon as two wireless devices communicate.

To create an ad hoc network, all you need is two or more wireless-capable devices. Once you've placed them within a range of 20–40 meters of each other, they'll "see" each other and be able to connect—assuming they share some basic configuration parameters. One computer may be able to share the Internet connection with the rest of them in your group.

Figure 19.5 shows an example of an ad hoc wireless network. Notice that there's no access point!

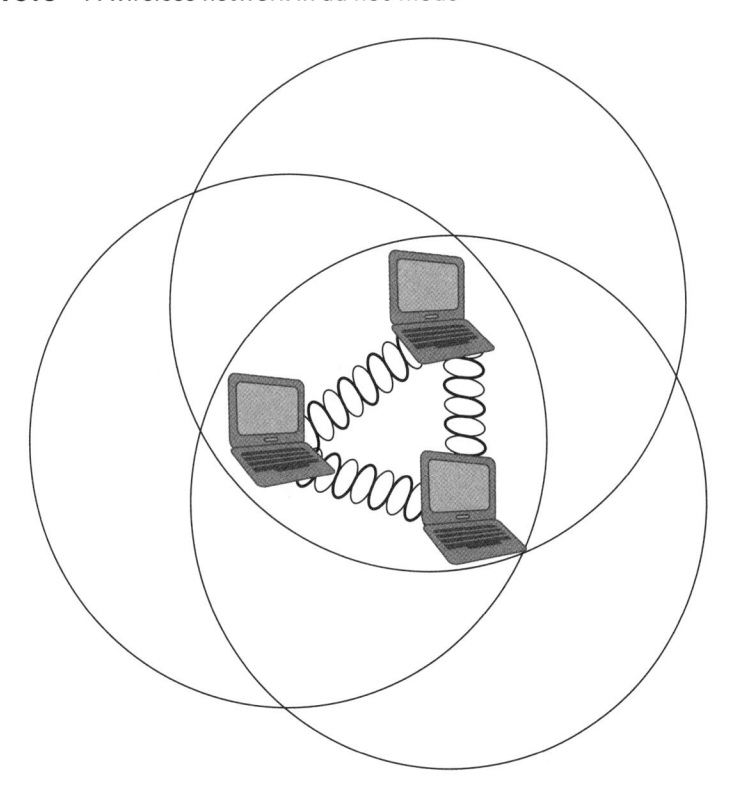

FIGURE 19.5 A wireless network in ad hoc mode

An ad hoc network, also known as peer to peer, doesn't scale well, and I wouldn't recommend it due to collision and organization issues in today's corporate networks. With the low cost of APs, you don't need this kind of network anymore anyway, except for maybe in your home—probably not even there.

Another con is that ad hoc networks are pretty insecure, so you really want to have the AdHoc setting turned off before connecting to your wired network.

Basic Service Set (BSS)

A basic service set (BSS) is the area, or cell, defined by the wireless signal served by the AP. It can also be called a basic service area (BSA), and the two terms, BSS and BSA, can be interchangeable. Even so, BSS is the most common term that's used to define the cell area. Figure 19.6 shows an AP providing a BSS for hosts in the area and the basic service area (cell) that's covered by the AP.

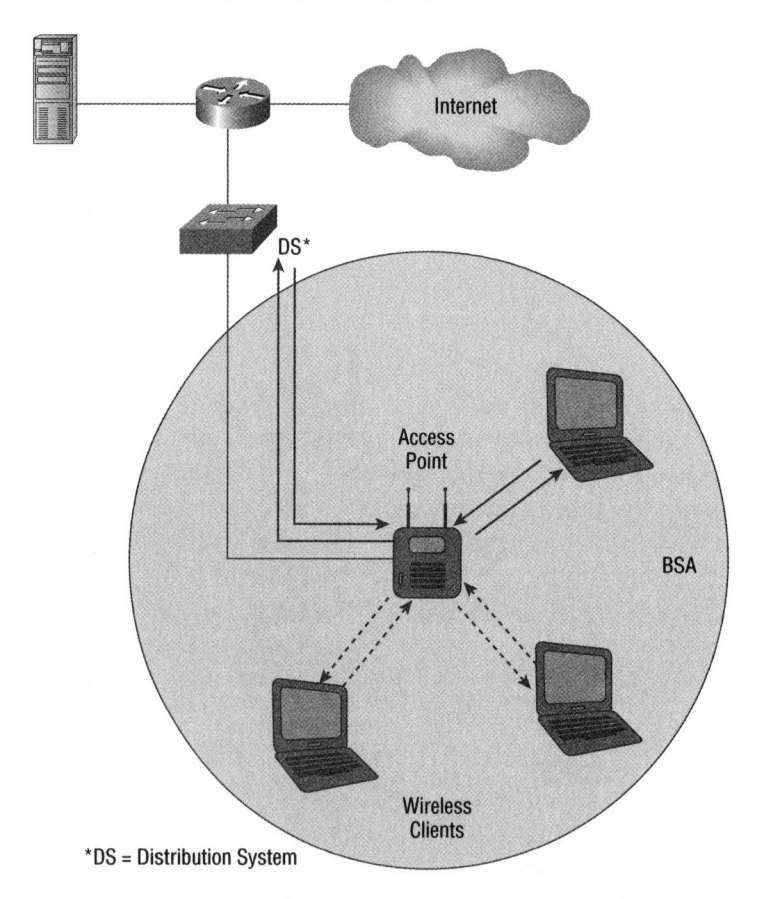

FIGURE 19.6 Basic service set/basic service area

So the AP isn't connected to a wired network in this example, but it provides for the management of wireless frames so the hosts can communicate. Unlike the ad hoc network, this network will scale better and more hosts can communicate in this network because the AP manages all network connections.

Infrastructure Basic Service Set

In infrastructure mode, wireless NICs only communicate with an access point instead of directly with each other like they do when they're in ad hoc mode. All communication between hosts, as well as any wired portion of the network, must go through the access point. Remember this important fact: in infrastructure mode, wireless clients appear to the rest of the network as though they were standard, wired hosts.

Figure 19.6 shows a typical infrastructure mode wireless network. Pay special attention to the access point and the fact that it's also connected to the wired network. This connection from the access point to the wired network is called the *distribution system (DS)* and is how the APs communicate to each other about hosts in the BSA. Basic standalone APs don't communicate with each other via the wireless network, only through the DS.

Before you configure a client to operate in wireless infrastructure mode, you need to understand SSIDs. The *service set identifier (SSID)* is the unique 32-character identifier that represents a particular wireless network and defines the BSS. And just so you know, lots of people use the terms SSID and BSS interchangeably, so don't let that confuse you! All devices involved in a particular wireless network can be configured with the same SSID. Sometimes access points even have multiple SSIDs.

Let's talk about that a little more now...

Service Set ID

So technically, an SSID is a basic name that defines the Basic Service Area (BSA) transmitted from the AP. A good example of this is "Linksys" or "Netgear." You've probably seen that name pop up on our host when looking for a wireless network. This is the name the AP transmits out to identify which WLAN the client station can associate with.

The SSID can be up to 32 characters long. It normally consists of human-readable ASCII characters, but the standard doesn't require this. The SSID is defined as a sequence of 1–32 octets, each of which may take any value.

The SSID is configured on the AP and can be either broadcasted to the outside world or hidden. If the SSID is broadcasted, when wireless stations use their client software to scan for wireless networks. The network will appear in a list identified by its SSID. But if it's hidden, it either won't appear in the list at all or will show up as "unknown network" depending on the client's operating system.

Either way, a hidden SSID requires the client station be configured with a wireless profile, including the SSID, in order to connect. And this requirement is above and beyond any other normal authentication steps or security essentials.

The AP associates a MAC address to this SSID. It can be the MAC address for the radio interface itself—called the basic service set identifier (BSSID)—or it can be derived from the MAC address of the radio interface if multiple SSIDs are used. The latter is sometimes called a virtual MAC address and you would call it a multiple basic service set identifier (MBSSID), as shown in Figure 19.7.

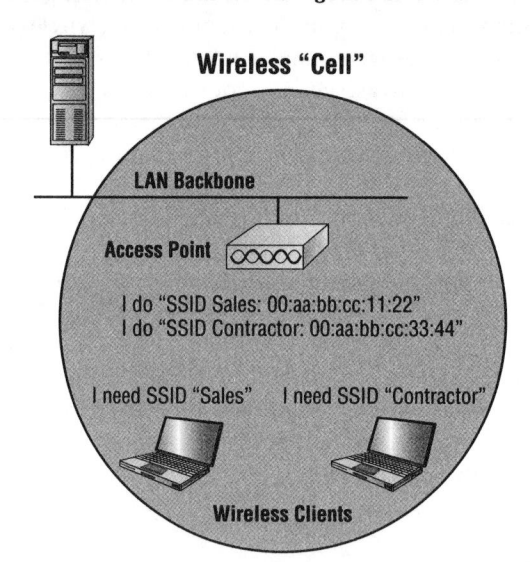

FIGURE 19.7 A network with MBSSIDs configured on an AP

There are two things you really want to make note of in this figure: first, there's a "Contractor BSSID" and a "Sales BSSID"; second, each of these SSID names is associated with a separate virtual MAC address, which was assigned by the AP.

These SSIDs are virtual and implementing things this way won't improve your wireless network's or AP's performance. You're not breaking up collision domains or broadcast domains by creating more SSIDs on your AP, you just have more hosts sharing the same half-duplex radio. The reason for creating multiple SSIDs on your AP is so that you can set different levels of security for each client that's connecting to your AP(s).

Extended Service Set

A good to thing to know is that if you set all your access points to the same SSID, mobile wireless clients can roam around freely within the same network. This is the most common wireless network design you'll find in today's corporate settings.

Doing this creates something called an *extended service set (ESS)*, which provides more coverage than a single access point and allows users to roam from one AP to another without having their host disconnected from the network. This design gives us the ability to move fairly seamlessly from one AP to another.

Figure 19.8 shows two APs configured with the same SSIDs in an office, thereby creating the ESS network.

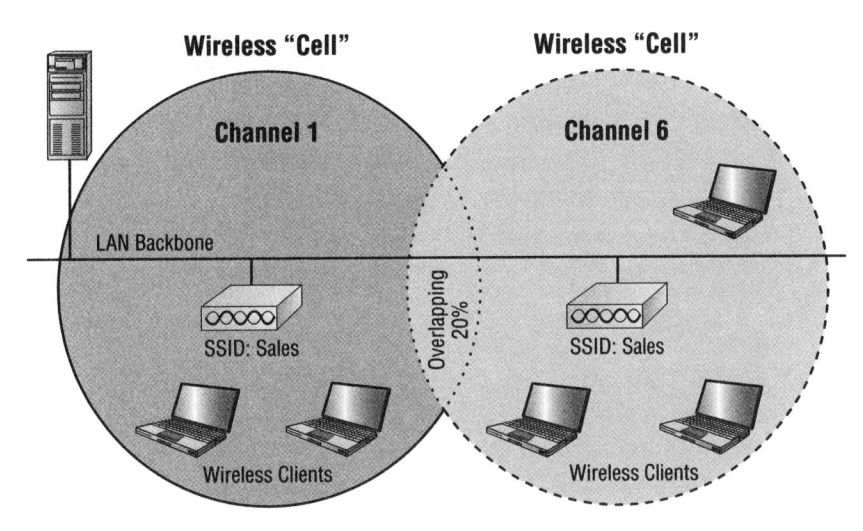

FIGURE 19.8 Extended service set (ESS)

Figure showing two overlapping wireless cells on Channel 1 and Channel 6, both with SSID: Sales, connected to a LAN Backbone, with 20% overlap between them and wireless clients in each cell.

For users to be able to roam throughout the wireless network—from AP to AP without losing their connection to the network—all APs must overlap by 20 percent of their signal or more to their neighbor's cells. To make this happen, be sure the channels (frequency) on each AP are set differently.

Repeaters

If you need to extend the coverage of an AP, you can either increase the gain of a directional antenna or add another AP into the area. If neither of those options solves your problem, try adding a repeater AP into the network and extending the range without having to pull an Ethernet cable for a new AP.

Figure 19.9 offers a picture of what this network design looks like.

A wireless repeater AP isn't connected to the wired backbone. It uses its antenna to receive the signal from an AP that's directly connected to the network and repeats the signal for clients located too far away from it.

To make this work, you need appropriate overlap between APs, as shown in Figure 19.9. Another way to get this to happen is to place a repeater AP with two radios in use, with one receiving and the other one transmitting. This works somewhat like a dual half-duplex repeater.

Seems cool, but there's an ugly downside to this design—for every repeater installed you lose about half of your throughput! Since no one likes less bandwidth, a repeater network should only be used for low-bandwidth devices, like a barcode reader in a warehouse.

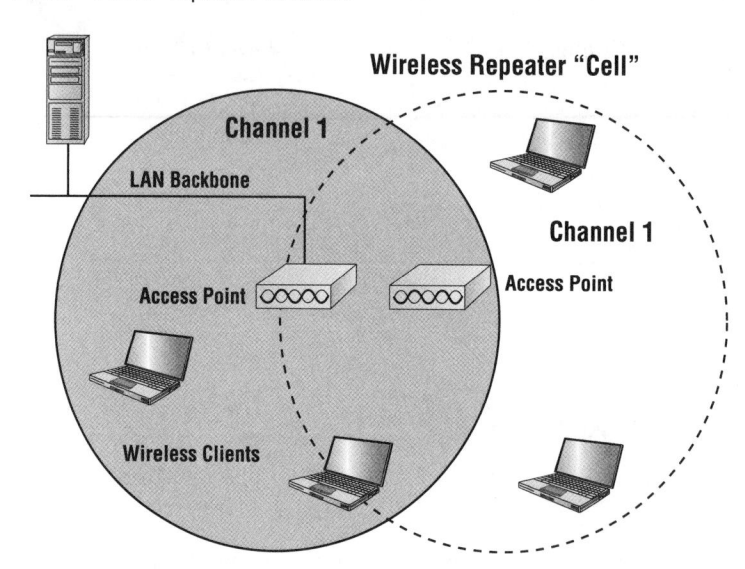

FIGURE 19.9 An AP repeater network

Bridging

Bridges are used to connect two or more wired LANs, usually located within separate buildings, to create one big LAN. Bridges operate at the MAC address layer (Data Link layer), which means they have no routing capabilities. So you've got to put a router in place if you want to be able to do any IP subnetting within your network. Basically, you would use bridges to enlarge the broadcast domains on your network. Armed with a firm understanding of how bridging works, you can definitely improve your network's capacity.

To build wireless networks correctly, it's important to have a working knowledge of root and nonroot bridges, sometimes referred to as parent and child bridges. Some bridges allow clients to connect directly to them, but others don't, so make sure you understand exactly your business requirements before just randomly buying a wireless bridge.

Figure 19.10 shows the typical bridge scenarios used in today's networks.

A point-to-point wireless network is a popular design that's often used outdoors to connect two buildings or LANs together.

A point-to-multipoint design works well in a campus environment where you have a main building with a bunch of ancillary buildings that you want to be able to connect to each other and back to the main one. Wireless bridges are commonly used to make these connections, and they just happen to be pricier than a traditional AP. The thing you want to remember about point-to-multipoint wireless networks is that each remote building won't be able to communicate directly with each other. To do that, they must first connect to the central, main point (main building) and then to one of the other ones (multipoint buildings).

FIGURE 19.10 Typical bridge scenarios

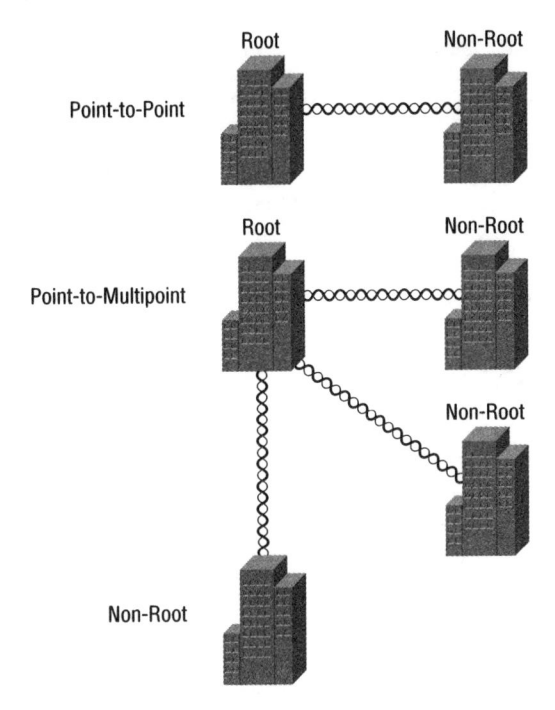

Okay—now let's get back to that root/nonroot issue I brought up a minute ago. This becomes really important to understand, especially when you're designing outdoor networks!

So look back to Figure 19.10 and find the terms root and nonroot. This figure shows a traditional point-to-point and point-to-multipoint network when one bridge, the root, accepts communications only from nonroot devices.

Root devices are connected to the wired network, which allows nonroot devices, like clients, to access the wired resources through the root device. Here are some important guidelines to help you design your wireless networks:

- Nonroot devices can only communicate to root devices. Nonroot devices include nonroot bridges, workgroup bridges, repeater access points, and wireless clients.
- Root devices cannot communicate to other root devices. Examples of devices that can be roots are APs and bridges.
- Nonroot devices cannot communicate to other nonroot devices.

But wait, there's one exception to that last bullet point. If you have a nonroot bridge set up as a repeater AP with two radios, the device must be configured as a nonroot device!

It will then repeat and extend the distance of your outdoor, bridged network, as shown in Figure 19.11.

FIGURE 19.11 A repeater AP bridge configured as a nonroot bridge

Non-Root Bridge   Non-Root Bridge   Root Bridge

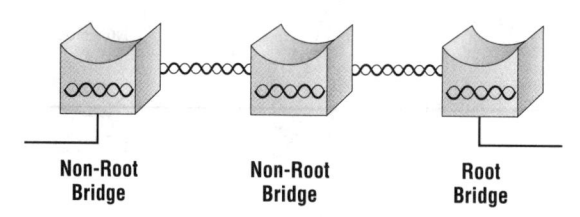

Figure 19.11 demonstrates that a nonroot bridge will communicate to another nonroot bridge only if one of the nonroot bridges has a root bridge in its uplink.

Mesh Networks

As more vendors migrate to a mesh hierarchical design, and as larger networks are built using lightweight access points that are managed by a controller, you can see that we need a standardized protocol that governs how lightweight access points communicate with WLAN systems. This is exactly the role filled by one of the Internet Engineering Task Force's (IETF's) latest draft specifications, Lightweight Access Point Protocol (LWAPP).

Mesh networking infrastructure is decentralized and comparably inexpensive for all the nice amenities it provides because each host only needs to transmit as far as the next host. Hosts act as repeaters to transmit data from nearby hosts to peers that are too far away for a manageable cabled connection. The result is a network that can span a large area, especially over rough or difficult terrain.

Remember that mesh is a network topology in which devices are connected with many redundant connections between host nodes, and we can use this topology to our advantage in large wireless installations.

Figure 19.12 shows a large meshed environment using Cisco outdoor managed APs to "umbrella" an outdoor area with wireless connectivity.

Oh, and did I mention that mesh networks also happen to be extremely reliable? Because each host can potentially be connected to several other hosts, if one of them drops out of the network because of hardware failure or something, its neighbors simply find another route. So you get extra capacity and fault tolerance automatically just by adding more hosts!

Wireless mesh connections between AP hosts are formed with a radio, providing many possible paths from a single host to other hosts. Paths through the mesh network can change in response to traffic loads, radio conditions, or traffic prioritization.

At this time, mesh networks just aren't a good solution for home use or small companies on a budget. As the saying goes, "If you have to ask..." As with most things in life, the more bells and whistles, the more it costs, and mesh networks are certainly no exception.

FIGURE 19.12 Typical large mesh outdoor environment

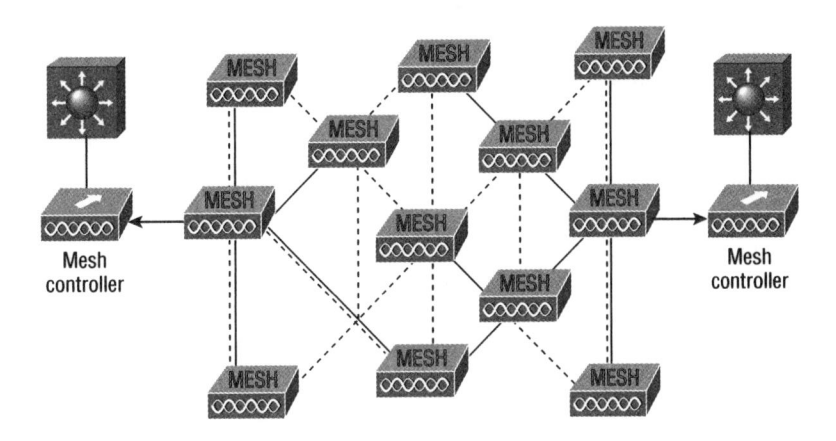

Nonoverlapping Wi-Fi channels

In both the 2.4GHz and the 5GHz frequency band, channels are defined by the standards. 802.11, 802.11b, and 802.11g use the 2.4GHz band also known as the industrial, scientific, and medical (ISM) band. 802.11a uses the 5GHz band. When two access points are operating in same area on the same channel or even an adjacent channel, they will interfere with each other. Interference lowers the throughput. Therefore, channel management to avoid interference is critical to ensure reliable operation. In this section, we will examine issues that impact channel management.

2.4GHz Band

Within the 2.4GHz (ISM) band are 11 channels approved for use in the United States, 13 in Europe, and 14 in Japan. Each channel is defined by its center frequency, but remember, that signal is spread across 22MHz. There's 11MHz on one side of the center frequency and 11MHz on the other side, so each channel encroaches on the channel next to it—even others further from it to a lesser extent.

Take a look at Figure 19.13.

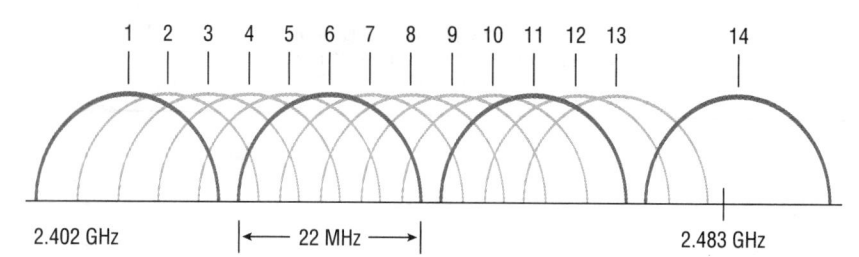

FIGURE 19.13 2.4GHz band 22MHz wide channels

This means that consequently, within the United States, only channels 1, 6, and 11 are considered nonoverlapping. So when you have two APs in the same area that are operating on overlapping channels, the effect depends on whether they're on the same channel or on adjacent channels. Let's examine each scenario.

When APs are on the same channel, they will hear each other and defer to one another when transmitting. This is due to information sent in the header of each wireless packet that instructs all stations in the area (including any APs) to refrain from transmitting until the current transmission is received. The APs perform this duty based partially on the duration field. Anyway, the end result is that both networks will be slower because they'll be dividing their transmission into windows of opportunity to transmit between them.

When the APs are only one or two channels apart, things get a little tricky, because in this case, they may not be able to hear each clearly enough to read the duration field. The ugly result of this is that they'll transmit at the same time, causing collisions that cause retransmissions and can seriously slow down your throughput—ugh! Therefore, although the two behaviors are different within these two scenarios, the end result is the same: greatly lowered throughput.

5GHz Band

802.11a uses the 5GHz frequency that's divided into three unlicensed bands called the Unlicensed National Information Infrastructure (UNII) bands. Two are adjacent to each other, but there is a frequency gap between the second and third. These bands are known as UNII-1, UNII-2, and UNII-3—the lower, middle, and upper UNII bands. Each of these bands hosts discrete channels, as in the ISM.

The 802.11a amendment specifies the location of the center point of each frequency, as well as the distance that must exist between the center point frequencies, but it failed to specify the exact width of each frequency. The good news is that the channels only overlap with the next adjacent channel so it's easier to find nonoverlapping channels in 802.11a.

In the lower UNII band the center points are 10MHz apart, and in the other two the center frequencies are 20MHz apart. Figure 19.14 illustrates the overlap of the UNII bands (top and bottom), compared to the 2.4GHz band (middle).

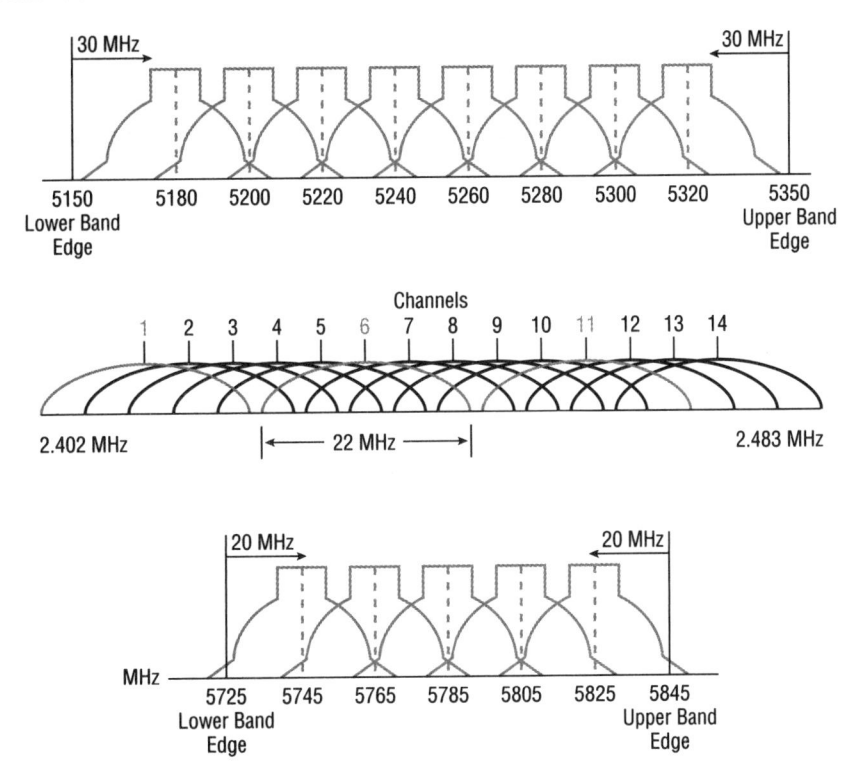

FIGURE 19.14 5GHz band 20MHz wide channels

The channel numbers in the lower UNII are 36, 40, 44, and 48. In the middle UNII, the channels are 52, 56, 60, and 64. The channels in UNII-3 are 149, 153, 157, and 161.

Channel Overlap Techniques

Sometimes it becomes necessary to deploy multiple APs, and here are two scenarios that certainly scream for doing this:

- You have a large number of users in a relatively small area. Considering the nature of the contention method used by WLANs the more users associated with a particular access point, the slower the performance. By placing multiple access points in the same area on different channels, the station-to-AP ratio improves, and performance improves accordingly.

- The area to be covered exceeds the range of a single AP and you would like to enable seamless roaming between the APs when users move around in the area.

Considering the channel overlap characteristics of both the 2.4GHz and the 5GHz bands, you must implement proper channel reuse when necessary to deploy multiple APs in the same area. It's also important if you want to deploy multiple APs within a large area to provide maximum coverage.

Multiple APs, Same Area

When deploying multiple APs in the same area, you need to choose channels that don't overlap. With the 2.4GHz band, the channels must have at least four channels' space between them, and remember—only 1, 6, and 11 are nonoverlapping.

When deploying APs in the 5GHz band (802.11a), the space between the channels can be two channels, given that there's no overlap.

Also vital to remember is that when choosing channels in a wide area, they can be reused if there's enough space between each channel's usage area or cell.

For example, in Figure 19.15 Channel 6 is used eight times, but no two areas using Channel 6 overlap.

FIGURE 19.15 Channel overlap in the 2.4GHz range

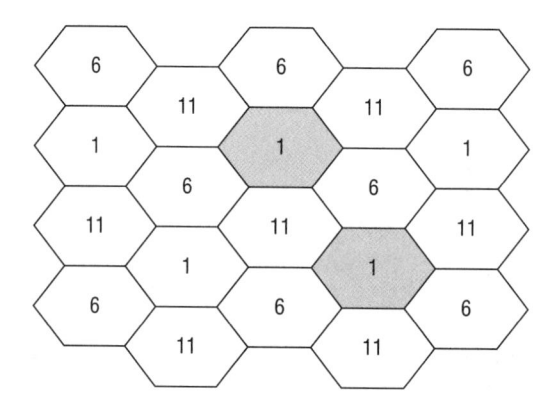

In the 5GHz band, there are two cells between cells that use the same channel, as shown in Figure 19.16.

FIGURE 19.16 Channel overlap in the 5GHz band

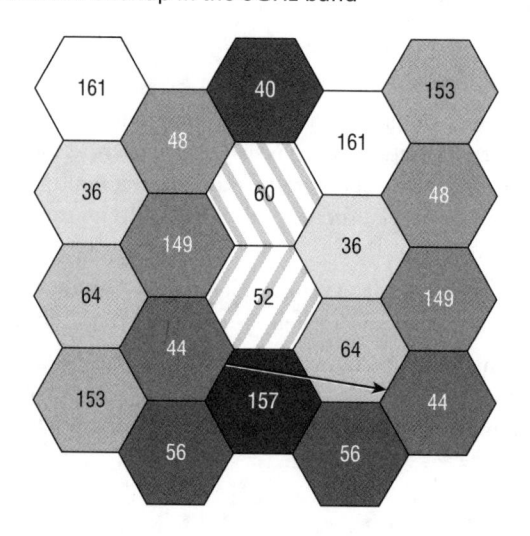

2.4GHz/5GHz (802.11n)

802.11n builds on previous 802.11 standards by adding *Multiple-Input Multiple-Output (MIMO)*, which uses multiple transmitters and receiver antennas to increase data throughput and range. 802.11n can allow up to eight antennas, but most of today's APs use only four to six. This setup permits considerably higher data rates than 802.11a/b/g does.

The following three vital items are combined in 802.11n to enhance performance:

- At the Physical layer, the way a signal is sent is changed, enabling reflections and interferences to become an advantage instead of a source of degradation.
- Two 20Mhz-wide channels are combined to increase throughput.
- At the MAC layer, a different way of managing packet transmission is used.

It's important to know is that 802.11n isn't truly compatible with 802.11b, 802.11g, or even 802.11a, but it is designed to be backward compatible with them. How 802.11n achieves backward compatibility is by changing the way frames are sent so they can be understood by 802.11a/b/g.

Here's a list of some of the primary components of 802.11n that together sum up why people claim 802.11n is more reliable and predictable:

40Mhz channels   802.11g and 802.11a use 20Mhz channels and employs tones on the sides of each channel that are not used in order to protect the main carrier. This means that 11Mbps go unused and are basically wasted. 802.11n aggregates two carriers to double the speed from 54Mbps to more than 108. Add in those wasted 11Mbps rescued from the side tones and you get a grand total of 119Mbps!

MAC efficiency   802.11 protocols require acknowledgment of each and every frame. 802.11n can pass many packets before an acknowledgment is required, which saves you a huge amount of overhead. This is called *block acknowledgment*.

Multiple-Input Multiple-Output (MIMO)   Several frames are sent by several antennae over several paths and are then recombined by another set of antennae to optimize throughput and multipath resistance. This is called *spatial multiplexing*.

Okay—now that you've nailed down our a/b/g/n networks, it's time to move on and get into some detail about RF.

Radio Frequency (RF)

It all starts when an electrical signal like one that represents data from a LAN needs to be transmitted via radio waves. First, the signal is sent to an antenna where it is then radiated in a pattern that's determined by the particular type of antenna. The pattern radiated from an antenna is an electrical signal called an alternating current, and the direction of the signal's current changes cyclically. This cycle creates a pattern known as a waveform. The waveform has peaks and valleys that repeat in a pattern, and the distance between one peak or valley and the next is known as the wavelength. The wavelength determines certain properties of the signal—for example, the impact of obstacles in the environment.

Some AM radio stations use wavelengths that stretch well over a thousand feet, or 400–500 meters, but our wireless networks use a wavelength that's smaller than your outstretched hand. Believe it or not, satellites use tiny waves that only measure about one millimeter!

Because cable, fiber, and other physical media impose various limitations upon data transmission, the ultimate goal is for us to use radio waves to send information instead. A radio wave can be defined as an electromagnetic field that radiates from a sender, which hopefully gets to the intended receiver of the energy that's been sent. A good example of this concept is the electromagnetic energy we call light that our eyes can interpret and send to our brains, which then transform it into impressions of colors.

Figure 19.17 shows the RF spectrum that we use today to send our wireless data.

FIGURE 19.17 RF spectrum

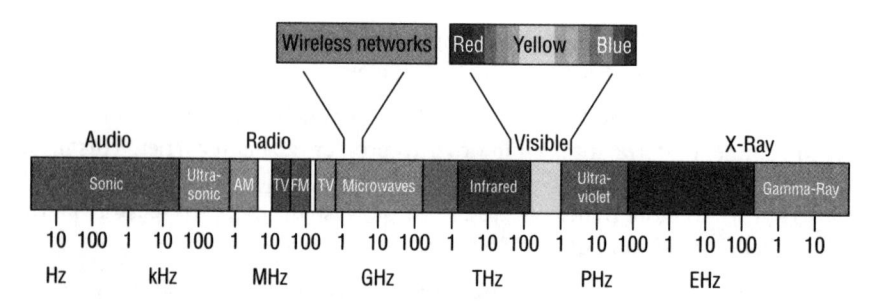

It is good that our eyes can't see these kinds of waves, because if we could, we would be so bombarded with them that we wouldn't be able to see much else!

When traveling through the air, certain wave groups are more efficient than others depending on the type of information being sent because they have different properties. So, it follows that different terms are used to define different signals generated in the transmitter when they're sent to the antenna to create the movements of the electrons generated within an electric field. This process creates an electromagnetic wave, and we use the terms frequency and wavelength to define them.

The frequency determines how often a signal is "seen," with one frequency cycle called 1 hertz (Hz). The size or distance of the cycle pattern is called the wavelength. The shorter the wavelength, the more often the signal repeats itself, and the more often it repeats, the higher its frequency is considered to be when compared with a wavelength that repeats itself less often in the same amount of time.

To get a picture of this, check out Figure 19.18.

FIGURE 19.18 Frequency

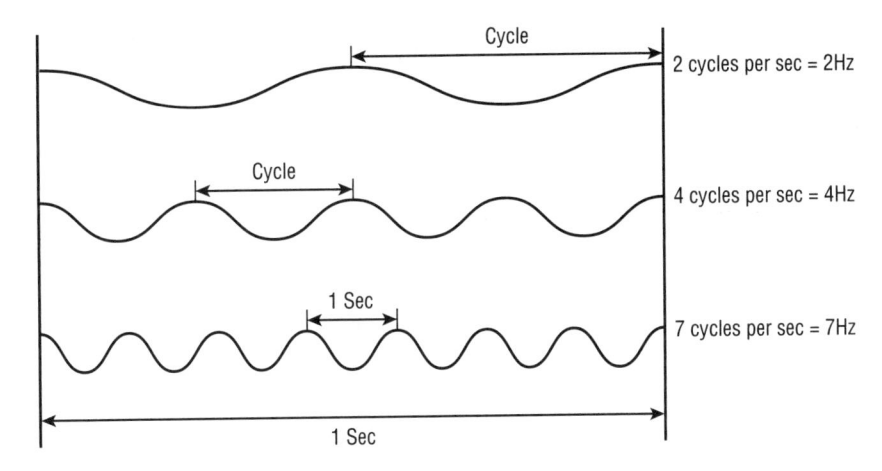

Here are some important RF terms to remember:

- 1Hz = The RF signal cycle occurs once a second
- 1MHz = The signal cycle occurs one million times a second
- 1GHz = The signal cycle occurs one billion times a second

Also good to know is that lower frequencies can travel farther, but provide less bandwidth. Higher frequencies have a wavelength with fast repeat times, which means that although they can't travel long distances, they can carry higher bandwidth. Another important term to get cozy with before we move on and talk about how RF is affected by many factors, is amplitude. Amplitude refers to the strength of the signal and is commonly represented by the Greek symbol α.

It has a profound effect on signal strength because it represents the level of energy injected into one cycle. The more energy injected in a cycle, the higher the amplitude. The term *gain* is used to describe an increase in the RF signal.

In Figure 19.19, the top signal has the least amplitude or signal strength and the bottom example has the greatest amplitude or signal strength. By the way, that's the only difference among each of these signals—all three have the same frequency because the distance between the peaks and valleys in them are the same.

Okay, let's say you're playing an electric guitar that you've plugged into your amp. If you turn up the amp's volume knob, the increased or amplified signal would look like the one on the bottom. Of note, attenuation also happens naturally the further the signal moves from the transmitter—another reason for the use of amplifiers. We can even use certain antennas to give us more gain, which in combination with the transmitter power can determine our signal's ability to go the distance.

FIGURE 19.19 Amplitude

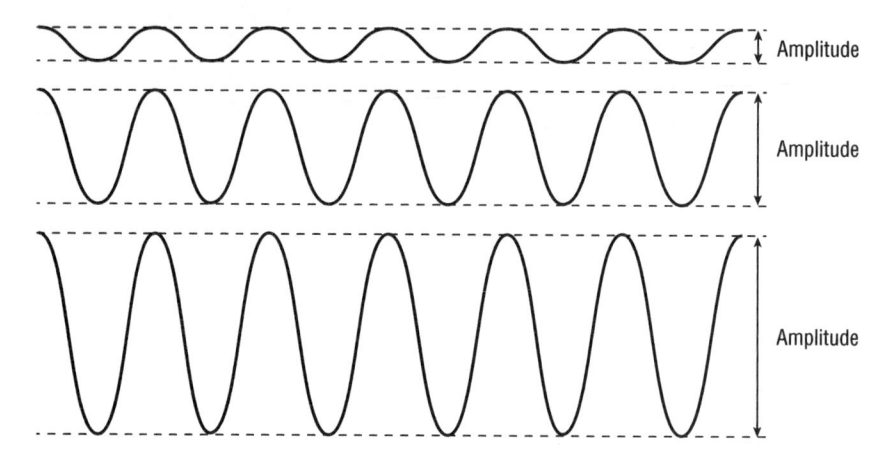

A downside to amps is that they can distort the signal and/or overload and damage the receiver if too much power is pushed into it. So finding the right balance takes experience, and yes, sometimes parting with some good ol' cash, to score better equipment.

Radio Frequency Behaviors

When you're armed with a solid understanding of RF signals, the challenges inherent to wireless networking and the things you can do to mitigate factors that negatively affect transmissions become oh-so-much-easier to deal with! So coming up next, I'm going to cover vital RF characteristics.

Free Space Path Loss

Attenuation is defined as the effect of a signal over the time, or length of a cable or other medium. The signal is weakened the further it travels from the transmitting device. Free space path loss is similar because it's a limiting factor with regard to the distance that RF signals can successfully travel and be received properly. We call it "Free Space Path Loss" because it isn't caused by environmental obstacles. Instead, it's simply a result of the normal attenuation that happens as the signal gradually weakens over the distance it travels.

Figure 19.20 shows an example of free space path loss.

FIGURE 19.20 Free space path loss

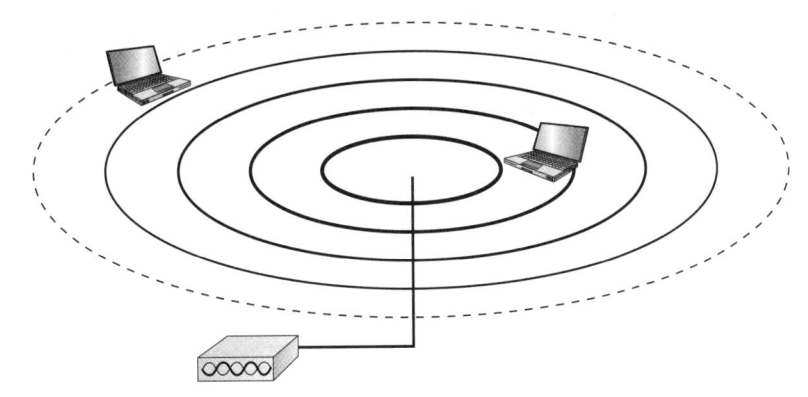

As the wave spreads away from the emitter, it gets weaker.

There are two major factors on both ends of a transmission that determine the effects of free space path loss: the strength of the signal delivered to the antenna and the type of antenna it's delivered to. The AP can amplify the signal to a certain extent because with most APs and many client devices, signal strength can be controlled. This type of signal gain is called *active* gain.

A directional antenna focuses the same amount of energy in one direction that an omnidirectional antenna sends horizontally in all directions. This results in a signal of the same strength being able to travel farther. In this scenario, the antenna provides what we call *passive* gain, which means that it comes from the particular shape of the antenna pattern itself.

On the receiving end, the same factors come into play. First, the receiver has a certain listening strength, called received sensitivity, and second, the shape of the receiving antenna has the same kind of effect on a signal that the shape of a sending antenna does. This means that two highly directional antennas that happen to be aimed perfectly at each other can carry a signal of the same strength much farther than two omnidirectional antennas.

Absorption

Since our world isn't flat and has lots of objects on it, as a signal radiates away from the antenna, it will invariably encounter obstacles like walls, ceilings, trees, people, buildings, cars—you get the idea. Even though the signal can pass through most of these obstacles, a price is paid when it does so in the form of decreased amplitude. Earlier, you learned that amplitude is the height and depth of each wave in the pattern that represents the signal strength.

So when the signal manages to pass through the object—which, surprisingly, in most cases it will—however, it always emerges on the other side weaker. This is what's referred to as *absorption*, because the people and things the signal passes through actually absorb some of its energy as heat.

To get a picture of the absorption phenomenon, check out Figure 19.21.

FIGURE 19.21   Absorption

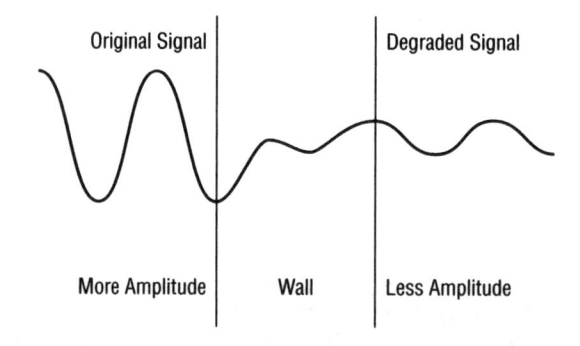

Original Signal | Degraded Signal

More Amplitude | Wall | Less Amplitude

Important to note is that the amount of signal degradation depends on the nature of what it has passed through. Clearly, drywall is not going to cause the same amount of signal degradation that concrete will, and yes, there are some materials that will block the signal completely. This is why we perform site surveys—to define where the problem areas are and figure out how to get around them by strategically placing AP(s) where they will be able to function with the least amount of obstruction.

Reflection

Now you know that absorption occurs when a signal travels through an obstacle and loses some of its energy, right? Well, *reflection* occurs when a signal strikes an object at an angle instead of directly. When this happens, some of the energy will be absorbed, but some will reflect off at an angle equal to the angle at which it struck the object.

Figure 19.22 illustrates reflection.

FIGURE 19.22   Reflection

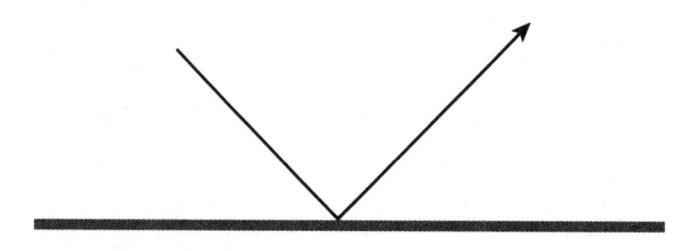

Reflection occurs when RF waves bounce off an object and are reflected into a new direction.

The exact ratio of the amount absorbed to the amount reflected depends on how porous the material is that the signal ran into and the angle at which it hit the material. The more porous the material, the more of the signal's energy will be absorbed by it.

Another thing that influences how much of the signal is reflected and how much is absorbed is the signal's frequency. Signals in the 2.4GHz range can behave differently than those in the 5GHz range. So just remember that these three factors influence absorption/reflection ratio:

- Angle of the signal
- Frequency of the signal
- Nature of the surface

One of the main problems' reflection causes is a phenomenon called multipath.

Multipath

Multipath occurs when reflection is occurring. Remember, there's lots of stuff around that reflected signals can bounce off before they finally arrive at the receiver, and since these bounced signals took a longer path to get to the receiver than the ones that took a direct path, it makes sense that they typically arrive later.

This is illustrated in Figure 19.23.

FIGURE 19.23 Multipath

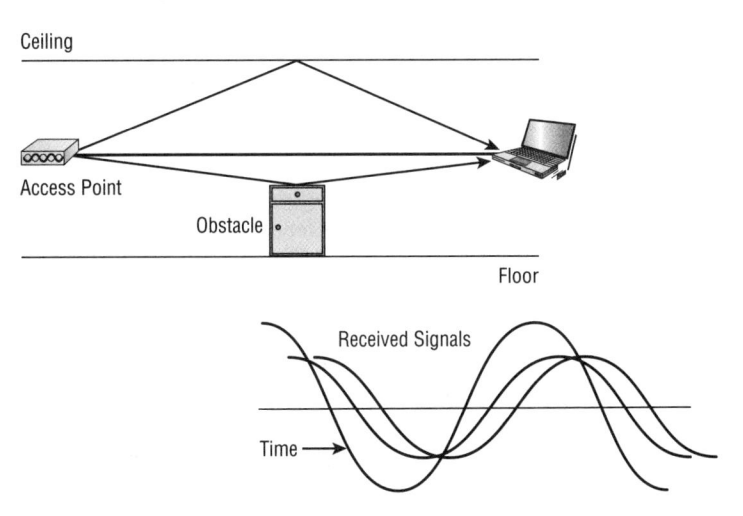

This is definitely not a good thing—because they arrive later, they'll be out of phase with the main signal, as shown in Figure 19.21. Remember how the signal wavelength has a recurring pattern? Well, if the pattern of the main signal doesn't line up with that of the reflected signal, they're out of phase—and how much they're out of phase varies in degrees.

This is ugly because out-of-phase signals are degraded signals, and if those signals are 120–170 degrees out, multipath can weaken them. This concept is known as *downfade*.

It gets worse too—if they arrive 180 degrees out, they cancel each other entirely, a nasty effect suitably called *nulling the signal*. If it's your lucky day and they go full circle, the rogue signals arrive 360 degrees out and blam—they're right back in phase and arrive at the same time. This boosts the amplitude or signal and is known as *upfade*.

Clearly, being able to deal with multipath events well is an important skill, but for now just one last thought: although I just said how bad multipath can be (and it can be!), IEEE 802.11n can take advantage of this to get higher speeds.

Refraction

Refraction refers to a change in the direction of a signal as a result of it passing through different mediums. Since this mostly happens when a signal passes from dry air to wet, or vice versa, it's more of a concern with long-range outdoor wireless links.

Figure 19.24 shows how refraction might look.

FIGURE 19.24 Refraction

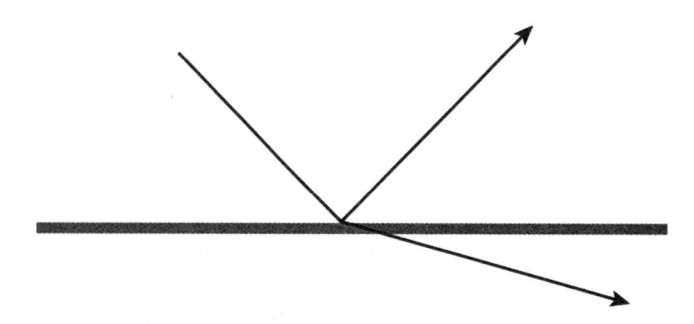

As the figure shows, refraction occurs when waves pass through a heterogeneous medium, and some of the waves are reflected and others are bent. Drier air tends to bend the signal away from the earth, whereas humid air tends to bend the signal toward earth.

Diffraction

Diffraction happens when a signal bends around an object. Think about what happens when you throw a rock into a quiet pool of water. As soon as your rock plunks in, it sends perfect rings of waves radiating outward from where it sank in all directions. If these waves slam into an object in the pool, you can see the wave bend around the object and change direction. RF signals do this too, and when they do, we experience this in the form of dead spots in places behind, say, a building.

Figure 19.25 shows a simple example of what diffraction may look like with an RF signal.

FIGURE 19.25 Diffraction

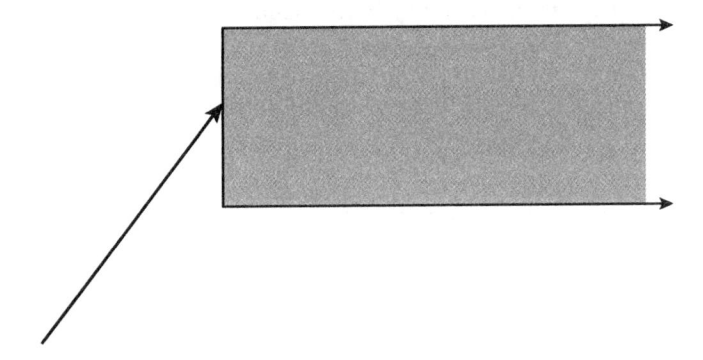

Diffraction is commonly confused with refraction, but the two are vastly dissimilar because diffraction bends the RF, whereas in refraction the RF bounces.

Scattering

Scattering is a lot like refraction, but the difference is that when signals strike an object, or objects, their scattered reflections bound off in many unpredictable directions instead of just bouncing back off at an angle pretty much equal to the angle at which it hit the object. This phenomenon is caused by the attributes of the object or objects. Here are some objects and conditions that can cause scattering:

- Dust, humidity, and micro-droplets of water in the atmosphere and rain
- Density fluctuations within a given object and its surface irregularities
- Uneven surfaces like moving water and tree leaves

Figure 19.26 shows what scatter might look like to an RF signal.

FIGURE 19.26 Scattering

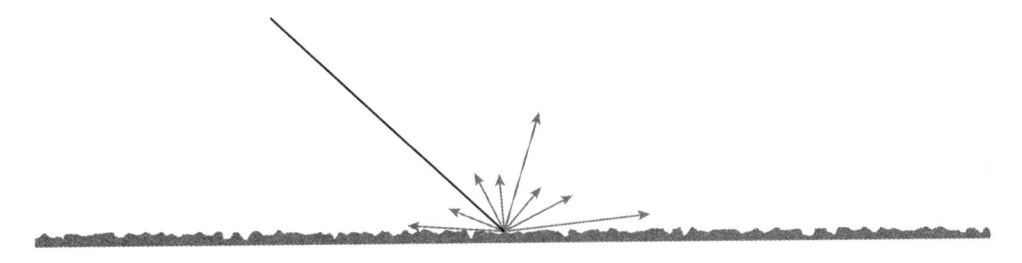

The worst thing about scattering is—you guessed it—its unpredictable nature, which makes mitigation efforts more than just a little difficult!

All this brings me back to that all-important site survey. I'm repeating this because nothing is more important than performing a thorough one before and after you design a WLAN! There's just nothing else that can help you to accurately identify, predict, and mitigate RF behaviors; determine proper AP placement; select the right type of antenna(s); or even make adjustments to the physical environment itself if possible (like trimming some trees).

RF Operational Requirements

Even in WLAN environments that exist mostly in fantasy where most or none of the aforementioned potential problems are present, there are still certain operational requirements if you want your WLAN to work well—or even at all.

Those absolute necessities that affect the performance of WLANs, and in some cases, directly affect whether or not they'll function at all, are what I'm going to cover next.

Line of Sight

Okay—so while it's true that in an indoor scenario where there are usually not as many things signals can bounce off of, they still exist there too. So again, do that site survey! Whether your WLAN will only cover a small outside or inside area, signals can usually travel through and even bounce off a few objects and still reach the receiver in fine shape. But when you're dealing with a larger coverage area using omnidirectional and semidirectional antennas, like in an outdoor area—especially when creating a point-to-point wireless bridge between, say, two buildings—something known as *line of sight* becomes critical for success. And if you're faced with creating a long-distance wireless connection using highly directional and/or dish antennas, line of sight becomes even more critical.

I want you to understand that line of sight is not as simple as having the center of the two antennas properly lined up. That's visual line of sight, and RF line of sight and visual line of sight are two different things. Regarding WLANs, RF line of sight is what you need, and to help you understand that, first let's review how spread spectrum technology works.

In narrowband RF, the signal is set to a single frequency and stays there. In spread spectrum, although people talk about channels and the like, the signal is actually being spread across a range of frequencies.

What I mean by this is that when we say that a device is using "Channel 6," that channel is actually 22MHz wide and the signal is spread across the entire 22MHz range. Furthermore, if a signal is spread out like this, it means that all of it, or at least a certain percentage of it, must be received in order for it to be interpreted well.

The following obstructions might obscure a line-of-sight link:

- Topographic features, such as mountains
- Curvature of the earth
- Buildings and other man-made objects
- Trees

Even if the visual line of sight is perfect, the RF line of sight can still be lacking if the distance is so far that the curvature of the earth gets in the way. Check out Figure 19.27.

FIGURE 19.27 Line of sight

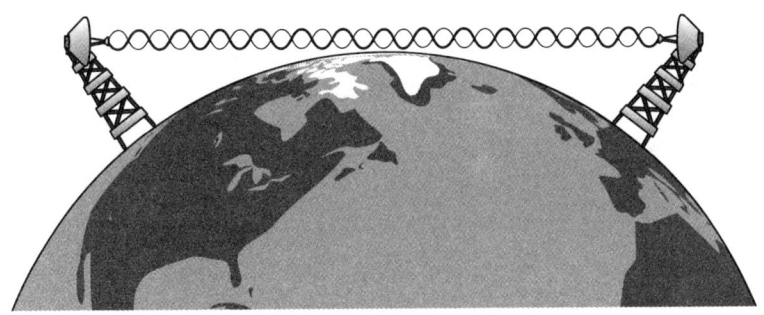

Line of sight disappears at 6 miles (9.7 km) because of the curvature of the earth.

Now, look ahead to Figure 19.28...see those trees?

FIGURE 19.28 Fresnel zone

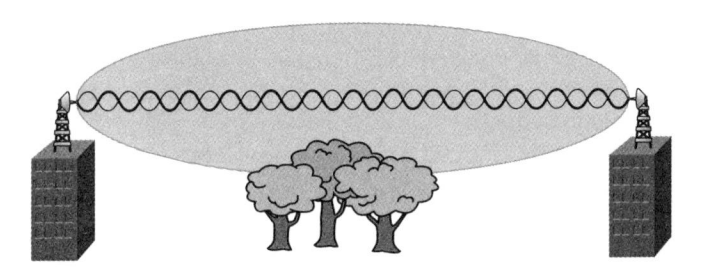

Okay, I know they're not actual size, but what it signifies is that objects can block even a small part of what we call the *Fresnel zone*, which is closely related to RF line of sight, and what you're going to learn about next.

Fresnel Zone

The Fresnel zone is an elliptical-shaped area between the transmitter and receiver that must be at least 60 percent clear for the signal to be received properly.

In Figure 19.28, even though visual line of sight looks just great, there's major blockage of the football-shaped area around the center line of the signal. This is very bad. You've personally experienced RF line-of-sight blocking if you've ever had a tree branch grow a lot over the summer and interfere with your satellite dish.

Interestingly, these zones are in alternating bands, with the inner band being in phase, the next being out of phase, and then the next one in phase again. So if one of us could figure out how to block only the out-of-phase band while leaving the in-phase bands alone, it just might be a technological breakthrough. (Hasn't happened yet!)

RSSI and SNR

We've logged a lot of ink discussing signals and signal strength, but so far, I haven't told you how these are measured. There are two terms used to discuss signal strength: received signal strength indicator (RSSI) and signal-to-noise ratio (SNR). RSSI is designed to describe the strength of the signal received, and SNR refers to the ratio of the signal to the surrounding RF noise that is always present in the environment.

First, let's talk about RSSI, which is a measure of the amount of signal strength that actually arrives at the receiving device. It's a grade value ranging from 0 to 255. For each grade value, an equivalent dBm (decibels relative to a milliwatt) value is displayed. For example, 0 in the scale may equal –95dBm and 100 might be –15dBm. So 0 would equal a much greater loss of signal than 100 would.

I'll get into dBm in more detail soon, but for now understand that dBm is not an absolute measure; it's a relative one. What I mean by *relative* is that it's a value referenced against another value—in this case, milliwatts. Decibels are used to measure an increase or decrease in power as opposed to an absolute value, meaning that decibel values come through as positive (gain) and negative (loss). RSSI values are negative and represent the level of signal loss that can be experienced en route with the card still able to receive the signal correctly. Most manufacturers will have a table listing the RSSI that's required at each frequency.

RSSI values can't be compared from one card vendor to another because each company typically uses a different scale. For example, Company A might be using a scale of 0 to 100, while Company B is using a scale from 0 to 60. Since the scales are different, the resulting RSSI values can't be compared, right?

Figure 19.29 depicts the relationship between these values.

FIGURE 19.29 SNR

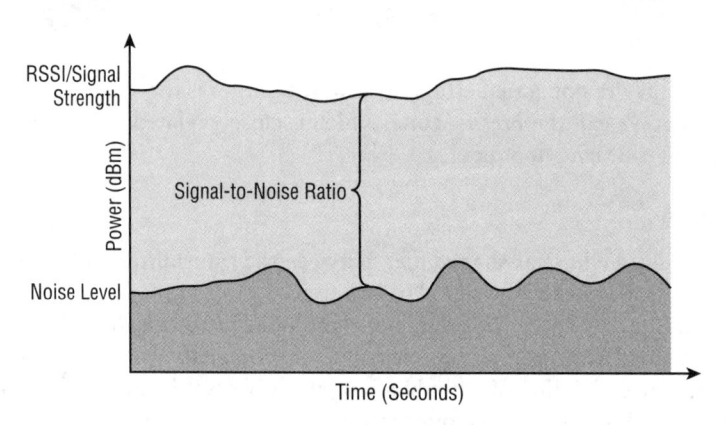

SNR is a critical comparison of the amount of signal as compared to the surrounding noise. If the level of noise is too close to the level of signal, the signal can't be picked out from the noise and understood. Think of this as someone whispering in a really loud room. A higher value is good for SNR.

Wireless Security

Now that we've covered the very basics of wireless devices used in today's networks, let's move on to wireless security.

At the foundational level, authentication uniquely identifies the user and/or machine. The encryption process protects the data or the authentication process by scrambling the information enough that it becomes unreadable by anyone trying to capture the raw frames.

Authentication and Encryption

Two types of authentication were specified by the IEEE 802.11 committee: open and shared-key authentication. Open authentication involves little more than supplying the right SSID, but it's the most common method in use today.

With shared-key authentication, the access point sends the client device a challenge-text packet that the client must then encrypt with the correct Wired Equivalent Privacy (WEP) key and return to the access point. Without the correct key, authentication will fail and the client won't be allowed to associate with the access point.

Figure 19.30 shows shared-key authentication.

FIGURE 19.30 Open access process

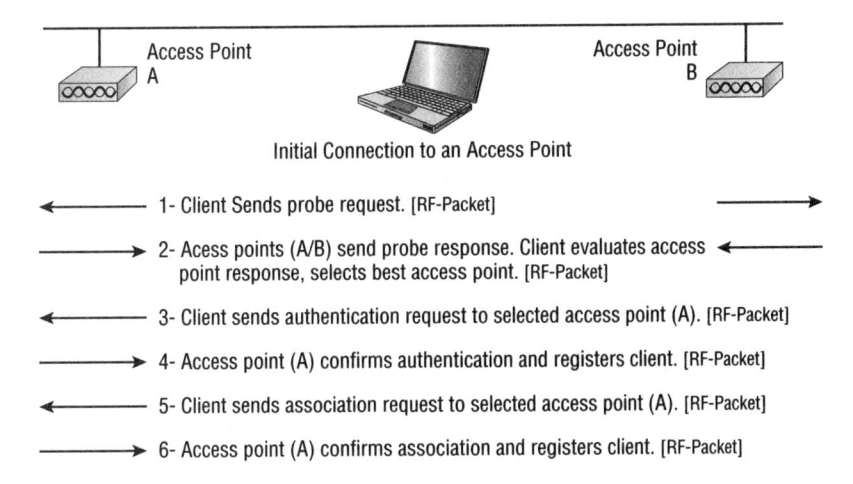

```
            Access Point                      Access Point
            A                                 B
                     Initial Connection to an Access Point

    ←———— 1- Client Sends probe request. [RF-Packet]              ————→
          ————→ 2- Acess points (A/B) send probe response. Client evaluates access ←————
                point response, selects best access point. [RF-Packet]
    ←———— 3- Client sends authentication request to selected access point (A). [RF-Packet]
          ————→ 4- Access point (A) confirms authentication and registers client. [RF-Packet]
    ←———— 5- Client sends association request to selected access point (A). [RF-Packet]
          ————→ 6- Access point (A) confirms association and registers client. [RF-Packet]
```

Shared-key authentication is still not considered secure because all a bad guy has to do to get around it is to detect both the clear-text challenge, the same challenge encrypted with a WEP key, and then decipher the WEP key. So it's no surprise that shared key isn't used in today's WLANs.

All Wi-Fi certified wireless LAN products are shipped in "open access" mode, with their security features turned off. Although open access or no security sounds scary, it's totally acceptable for places like public hot spots. But it's definitely not an option for an enterprise organization, and it's probably not a good idea for your private home network either!

Check out Figure 19.31 to see the open access wireless process.

FIGURE 19.31 Open access process

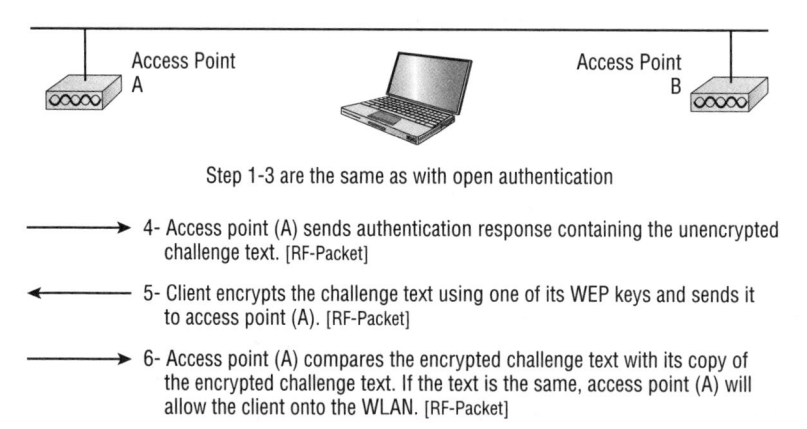

Step 1-3 are the same as with open authentication

→ 4- Access point (A) sends authentication response containing the unencrypted challenge text. [RF-Packet]

← 5- Client encrypts the challenge text using one of its WEP keys and sends it to access point (A). [RF-Packet]

→ 6- Access point (A) compares the encrypted challenge text with its copy of the encrypted challenge text. If the text is the same, access point (A) will allow the client onto the WLAN. [RF-Packet]

Here, you can see that an authentication request has been sent and "validated" by the AP. But when open authentication is used or set to "none" in the wireless controller, the request is pretty much guaranteed not to be denied. For now, understand that this authentication is done at the MAC layer (Layer 2), so don't confuse this with the higher-layer authentication we'll cover later, which occurs after the client is associated to the access point.

With what I've told you so far, I'm sure you agree that security seriously needs to be enabled on wireless devices during their installation in enterprise environments. But believe it or not, a surprising number of companies don't enable any WLAN security features, dangerously exposing their valuable data networks and resources to tremendous risk!

The reason that these products are shipped in open access mode is so that anyone, even someone without any IT knowledge, can buy an access point, plug it into their cable or DSL modem, and voilà—they're up and running. It's marketing, plain and simple, and simplicity sells. But that doesn't mean you should leave the default settings there—unless you want to allow that network to be open to the public!

WEP

With open authentication, even if a client can complete authentication and associate with an access point, the use of WEP prevents the client from sending and receiving data from an access point unless the client has the correct WEP key.

A WEP key is composed of either 40 or 128 bits, and in its basic form, it's usually statically defined by the network administrator on the access point, and on all clients that communicate with that access point. When static WEP keys are used, a network administrator must perform the tedious task of entering the same keys on every device in the WLAN.

Clearly, we now have fixes for this because tackling this manually would be administratively impossible in today's huge corporate wireless networks!

WPA and WPA2: An Overview

Wi-Fi Protected Access (WPA) and WPA2 were created in response to the shortcomings of WEP. WPA was a stopgap measure taken by the Wi-Fi Alliance to provide better security until the IEEE finalized the 802.11i standard. When 802.11i was ratified, WPA2 incorporated its improvements, so there are some significant differences between WPA and WPA2.

These are each essentially another form of basic security that are really just an add-on to the specifications. Even though you can totally lock the vault, WPA/WPA2 pre-shared key (PSK) is a better form of wireless security than any other basic wireless security method I've talked about so far. Still, keep in mind that I did say basic!

WPA is a standard developed by the Wi-Fi Alliance and provides a standard for authentication and encryption of WLANs that's intended to solve known security problems. The standard takes into account the well-publicized AirSnort and man-in-the-middle WLAN attacks. So, of course we use WPA2 to help us with today's security issues because we can use AES encryption, which provides for better key caching than WPA does. WPA is only a software update whereas WPA2 required a hardware update, but you'd be hard-pressed to find a laptop or any pc today that doesn't have WPA2 support built-in.

Pre-Shared Key (PSK) verifies users via a password or identifying code, often called a passphrase, on both the client machine and the access point. A client gains access to the network only if its password matches the access point's password. The PSK also provides keying material that TKIP or AES uses to generate an encryption key for each packet of transmitted data.

Although more secure than static WEP, the PSK method still has a lot in common with static WEP in that the PSK is stored on the client station and can be compromised if the client station is lost or stolen—even though finding this key isn't all that easy to do. This is exactly why I definitely recommend using a seriously strong PSK passphrase that includes a mixture of letters, numbers, cases, and nonalphanumeric characters. With WPA, it's still possible to specify the use of dynamic encryption keys that change each time a client establishes a connection.

> The benefit of WPA keys over static WEP keys is that the WPA keys can change dynamically while the system is used.

WPA is a step toward the IEEE 802.11i standard and uses many of the same components, with the exception of encryption. 802.11i (WPA2) uses AES-CCMP encryption. The IEEE 802.11i standard replaced WEP with a specific mode of AES known as Counter Mode with Cipher Block Chaining Message Authentication Code Protocol (CCMP). This allows AES-CCMP to provide both data confidentiality (encryption) and data integrity—now we're getting somewhere!

Wi-Fi Protected Access (WPA)

WPA was designed to offer two methods of authentication in implementation. The first, called WPA Personal or WPA (PSK), was designed to work using a passphrase for authentication, but it improves the level of protection for authentication and data encryption too.

WPA PSK uses the exact same encryption as WPA Enterprise—the PSK just replaces the check to a RADIUS server for the authentication portion. PSK offers us these benefits:

- The Initialization vector (IV) is 48 bits and not 24 bits. This increases the number of vector values from over 16 million possibilities to 280 trillion values. Also, they must be used in order and not randomly, which oddly enough increases the security because it eliminates the reuse of IVs—a condition referred to as collisions, not to be confused with collision domains.

- The key for each frame is changed for each packet, hence the term *temporal*, or temporary. A serial number is applied to each frame and the serial number, along with the temporal key, and the IV is used to create a key unique to each frame. Furthermore, each frame undergoes per-packet key hashing as well.

- Centralized key management by the AP including broadcast and unicast keys. The broadcast keys are rotated to ensure that they don't remain the same, even though at any particular point in time, they will be the same for all stations in the Basic Service Set (BSS). When a PSK is used for authentication, it's used to derive the Pairwise Master Key (PMK) as well as the resulting Pairwise Transient Keys (PTKs). No worries—I'll tell you more about those concepts later!

- Finally, we get a new form of frame check sequence (FCS). The FCS refers to the part of any packet that's used to ensure that the integrity of the packet is maintained. It's also used to determine if anything changed in the packet. Here's a scenario: Through an attack called *bit flipping*, a hacker could generate a TCP re-send message. The AP will forward this TCP re-send to the wireless space, thereby generating a new initialization vector. A bit-flipping attack allows the attacker to artificially increase the number of IVs, thus speeding up a WEP attack by increasing the chance of duplicates or collisions occurring. TKIP uses a message integrity code (MIC), instead of a regular FCS. MIC can detect almost all changes to a bit in the frame, so it can bust bit flipping much more readily than FCS. If it detects a MIC failure, it will report this event to the AP. If the AP receives two of these failures in 60 seconds, it will respond by disassociating all stations and stopping all traffic for 60 seconds. This makes it impossible for the hacker to recover the key—nice!

The only known weakness of WPA PSK lies in the complexity of the password or key used on the AP and the stations. If it happens to be one that's easily guessed, it could be susceptible to something known as a dictionary attack. This type of attack uses a dictionary file that tries out a huge number of passwords until the correct match is found. Consequently, this is very time consuming for the hacker. WPA3's big difference is how it can prevent a dictionary attack.

Because of this, WPA PSK should mainly be used in a small office, home office (SOHO) environment and in an enterprise environment only when device restrictions, such as voice over IP (VoIP) phones, don't support RADIUS authentication.

WPA2 Enterprise

Regardless of whether WPA or WPA2 is used during the initial connection between the station and the AP, the two agree on common security requirements. Following that agreement, a series of important key-related activities occur in this specific order:

1. The authentication server derives a key called the Pairwise Master Key (PMK). This key will remain the same for the entire session. The same key is derived on the station. The server moves the PMK to the AP where it's needed.

2. The next step is called the four-way handshake. Its purpose is to derive another key called the Pairwise-Transient-Key (PTK). This step occurs between the AP and the station, and of course requires four steps to complete:

    a. The AP sends a random number known as a nonce to the station.

    b. Using this value along with the PMK, the station creates a key used to encrypt a nonce that's called the snonce, which is then sent to the AP. It includes a reaffirmation of the security parameters that were negotiated earlier. It also protects the integrity of this frame with a MIC. This bidirectional exchange of nonces is a critical part of the key-generation process.

    c. Now that the AP has the client nonce, it will generate a key for unicast transmission with the station. It sends the nonce back to the station along with a group key commonly called a group transient key, as well as a confirmation of security parameters.

    d. The fourth message simply confirms to the AP that the temporal keys (TKs) are in place.

One final function performed by this four-way handshake is to confirm that the two peers are still "alive."

802.11i

Although WPA2 was built with the 802.11i standard in mind, some features were added when the standard was ratified:

- A list of EAP methods that can be used with the standard.
- AES-CCMP for encryption instead of RC4.
- Better key management; the master key can be cached, permitting a faster reconnect time for the station.

But wait, there's more! There is a new sheriff in town and its name is WPA3.

WPA3

In 2018 the Wi-Fi Alliance announced the new WPA3, a Wi-Fi security standard to replace WPA2. The WPA2 standard has served us well, but it's been around since 2004! WPA3 will improve on the WPA2 protocol with more security features just like WPA2 was designed to fix WPA.

What's fun about WPA3 is the naming used to define the handshake as well as the exploits—yes, exploits are already out there! First, remember that WPA2 uses a PSK, but WPA3 has been upgraded to 128-bit encryption and uses a system called Simultaneous Authentication of Equals (SAE). This is referred to as the Dragonfly handshake. It forces network interaction on a login so that hackers can't deploy a dictionary attack by downloading its cryptographic hash and then running cracking software to break it.

Even more fun, the known exploits of WPA3 are called Dragonblood. The reason these Dragonblood exploits are already out is because the protections in WPA2 haven't really changed that much in WPA3—at least not yet. Worse, WPA3 is backward compatible, meaning that if someone wants to attack you, they can just use WPA2 in an attack to effectively downgrade your WPA3 compatible system back to WPA2!

Like WPA2, the Wi-Fi Protected Access security includes solutions for personal and enterprise networks. But WPA3 offers up some very cool new goodies, which pave the way for more powerful authentication and enhanced cryptographic clout. It also helps to protect vital networks by preserving resiliency and offers a cleaner approach to security.

Here's a list of characteristics shared by all WPA3 networks:

- Use the latest security methods
- Don't allow outdated legacy protocols
- Require the use of Protected Management Frames (PMF)

Like us, our Wi-Fi networks have different levels of risk tolerance according to type and function. For the non-public, home or enterprise variety, WPA3 gives us some cool tools to shut down password guessing attacks. WPA3 also works with superior security protocols for networks that require or want a higher degree of protection.

As mentioned, WPA3 is backwards compatible and provides interoperability with WPA2 devices, but this is really only an option for companies developing certified devices. I'm sure that it will become a required piece over time as market adoption grows.

WPA3-Personal

So how does being able to seriously protect your individual users sound? WPA3-Personal gives us that ability by offering up powerful password-based authentication via Simultaneous Authentication of Equals (SAE). This is a big upgrade from WPA2's Pre-shared Key (PSK) and works really well even when users choose simple, easy to crack passwords!

And like I said, WPA3 frustrates hacker's attempts to crack passwords via dictionary attacks too. Some additional perks include:

- Natural password selection: Allows users to choose passwords that are easier to remember

- Ease of use: Delivers enhanced protections with no change to the way users connect to a network
- Forward secrecy: Protects data traffic even if a password is compromised after the data was transmitted

WPA3-Enterprise

Basically, wireless networks of all kinds gain a lot of security with WPA3, but those with sensitive data on them like networks belonging to financial institutions, governments and even enterprises really get a boost! WPA3-Enterprise improves everything WPA2 offers, plus it really streamlines how security protocols are applied throughout our networks.

WPA3-Enterprise even gives us the option to use 192 bit-minimum strength security protocols, plus some very cool cryptographic tools to lock things down tight!

Here's a list of the ways WPA3 beefs up security:

- *Sweet feature alert:* WPA3 uses a system called Wi-Fi Device Provisioning Protocol (DPP), which thankfully allows users to utilize NFC tags or QR codes to allow devices on the network. Like I said, sweet!
- *Authenticated encryption:* 256-bit Galois/Counter Mode Protocol (GCMP-256)
- *Key derivation and confirmation:* 384-bit Hashed Message Authentication Mode (HMAC) with Secure Hash Algorithm (HMAC-SHA384)
- *Key establishment and authentication:* Elliptic Curve Diffie-Hellman (ECDH) exchange and Elliptic Curve Digital Signature Algorithm (ECDSA) using a 384-bit elliptic curve
- *Robust management frame protection:* 256-bit Broadcast/Multicast Integrity Protocol Galois Message Authentication Code (BIP-GMAC-256)
- The 192-bit security mode offered by WPA3-Enterprise ensures that the right combination of cryptographic tools are used and sets a consistent baseline of security within a WPA3 network.

WPA3 has also improved upon 802.11's open authentication support by giving us something called Opportunistic Wireless Encryption (OWE). The idea behind the OWE enhancement option is to offer encryption communication for networks without passwords and it works by giving every device on the network its own, unique key.

This implements something called Individualized Data Protection (IDP), which happens to come in handy for password-protected networks too because even if an attacker gets a hold of the network password, they still can't access any other encrypted data!

All good—we've got WPA, WPA2, and now WPA3 covered. But how do they compare? Table 19.1 breaks them down.

TABLE 19.1 WPA, WPA2, and WPA3 Compared

Security TYPE	WPA	WPA2	WPA3
Enterprise Mode: Business, education, government	Authentication: IEEE 802.1X/EAP Encryption: TKIP/MIC	Authentication: IEEE 802.1X/EAP Encryption: AES-CCMP	Authentication: IEEE 802.1X/EAP Encryption: GCMP-256
Personal Mode: SOHO, home, and personal	Authentication: PSK Encryption: TKIP/MIC	Authentication: PSK Encryption: AES-CCMP	Authentication: SAE Encryption: AES-CCMP
	128-bit RC4 w/TKIP encryption	128-bit AES encryption	128-bit AES encryption
	Ad hoc not supported	Ad hoc not supported	Ad hoc not supported

Summary

This chapter really packed a punch! Like rock 'n' roll, wireless technologies are here to stay, and for those of us who have come to depend on wireless technologies, it's actually pretty hard to imagine a world without wireless networks—what did we do before cell phones?

So we began this chapter by exploring the essentials and fundamentals of how wireless networks function.

Springing off that foundation, I then introduced you to the basics of wireless RF and the IEEE standards. We discussed 802.11 from its inception through its evolution to current and near future standards and talked about the subcommittees who create them.

All of this lead to a discussion of wireless security—or rather, non-security for the most part, which logically directed us towards the WPA, WPA2 and WPA3 standards.

Exam Essentials

Understand the IEEE 802.11a specification.   802.11a runs in the 5GHz spectrum, and if you use the 802.11h extensions, you have 23 non-overlapping channels. 802.11a can run up to 54Mbps, but only if you are less than 50 feet from an access point.

Understand the IEEE 802.11b specification.   IEEE 802.11b runs in the 2.4GHz range and has three non-overlapping channels. It can handle long distances, but with a maximum data rate of up to 11Mpbs.

Understand the IEEE 802.11g specification. IEEE 802.11g is 802.11b's big brother and runs in the same 2.4GHz range, but it has a higher data rate of 54Mbps if you are less than 100 feet from an access point.

Understand the IEEE 802.11n components. 802.11n uses 40Mhz wide channels to provide more bandwidth, provides MAC efficiency with block acknowledgements, and uses MIMO to allow better throughput and distance at high speeds.

Understand the difference between WPA, WPA2 and WPA3 802.11n uses 40.

Review Question

You can find the answers to these questions in the Appendix.

1. Which encryption type does enterprise WPA3 use?
   A. AES-CCMP
   B. GCMP-256
   C. PSK
   D. TKIP/MIC

2. What is the frequency range of the IEEE 802.11b standard?
   A. 2.4Gbps
   B. 5Gbps
   C. 2.4GHz
   D. 5GHz

3. What is the frequency range of the IEEE 802.11a standard?
   A. 2.4Gbps
   B. 5Gbps
   C. 2.4GHz
   D. 5GHz

4. What is the frequency range of the IEEE 802.11g standard?
   A. 2.4Gbps
   B. 5Gbps
   C. 2.4GHz
   D. 5GHz

5. You've finished physically installing an access point on the ceiling of your office. At a minimum, which parameter must be configured on the access point in order to allow a wireless client to operate on it?
   A. AES
   B. PSK
   C. SSID
   D. TKIP
   E. WEP
   F. 802.11i

6. Which encryption type does WPA2 use?
   A. AES-CCMP
   B. PPK via IV
   C. PSK
   D. TKIP/MIC

7. How many non-overlapping channels are available with 802.11b?
   A. 3
   B. 12
   C. 23
   D. 40

8. Which of the following is has built-in resistance to dictionary attacks?
   A. WPA
   B. WPA2
   C. WPA3
   D. AES
   E. TKIP

9. What's the maximum data rate for the 802.11a standard?
   A. 6Mbps
   B. 11Mbps
   C. 22Mbps
   D. 54Mbps

10. What's the maximum data rate for the 802.11g standard?
    A. 6Mbps
    B. 11Mbps
    C. 22Mbps
    D. 54Mbps

11. What's the maximum data rate for the 802.11b standard?
    A. 6Mbps
    B. 11Mbps
    C. 22Mbps
    D. 54Mbps

12. WPA3 replaced the default open authentication with which of the following enhancements?
    A. AES
    B. OWL
    C. OWE
    D. TKIP

13. A wireless client can't connect to an 802.11b/g BSS with a b/g wireless card. And the client section of the access point doesn't list any active WLAN clients. What's a possible reason for this?
    A. The incorrect channel is configured on the client.
    B. The client's IP address is on the wrong subnet.
    C. The client has an incorrect pre-shared key.
    D. The SSID is configured incorrectly on the client.

14. Which two features did WPA add to address the inherent weaknesses found in WEP? (Choose two.)
    A. A stronger encryption algorithm
    B. Key mixing using temporal keys
    C. Shared key authentication
    D. A shorter initialization vector
    E. Per frame sequence counter

15. Which two wireless encryption methods are based on the RC4 encryption algorithm? (Choose two.)
    A. WEP
    B. CCKM
    C. AES
    D. TKIP
    E. CCMP

16. Two workers have established wireless communication directly between their wireless laptops. What type of wireless topology has been created by these two employees?
    A. BSS
    B. SSID
    C. IBSS
    D. ESS

17. Which two of the following describe the wireless security standard that WPA defines? (Choose two.)
    A. It specifies the use of dynamic encryption keys that change throughout the users connection time.
    B. It requires that all devices must use the same encryption key.
    C. It can use PSK authentication.
    D. Static keys must be used.

18. Which wireless LAN design ensures that a mobile wireless client will not lose connectivity when moving from one access point to another?
    A. Using adapters and access points manufactured by the same company
    B. Overlapping the wireless cell coverage by at least 15%
    C. Configuring all access points to use the same channel
    D. Utilizing MAC address filtering to allow the client MAC address to authenticate with the surrounding APs

19. You're connecting your access point and it's set to root. What does extended service set ID mean?
    A. That you have more than one access point and they are in the same SSID connected by a distribution system
    B. That you have more than one access point and they are in separate SSIDs connected by a distribution system
    C. That you have multiple access points, but they are placed physically in different buildings
    D. That you have multiple access points, but one is a repeater access point

20. What are three basic parameters to configure on a wireless access point? (Choose three.)
    A. Authentication method
    B. RF Channel
    C. RTS/CTS
    D. SSID
    E. Microwave interference resistance

Chapter 20

Configuring Wireless Technologies

THE CCNA EXAM TOPICS COVERED IN THIS CHAPTER ARE:

1.0 Network Fundamentals

✓ 1.1.e Controllers (Cisco DNA Center and WLC)

2.0 Network Access

✓ 2.9 Configure the components of a wireless LAN access for client connectivity using GUI only such as WLAN creation, security settings, QoS profiles, and advanced WLAN settings

5.0 Security Fundamentals

✓ 5.10 Configure WLAN using WPA2 PSK using the GUI

Now that you know how wireless works, I'm going to guide through configuring a wireless network from beginning to end. There's a lot of steps taken and a whole bunch of infrastructure between hooking our laptops up to a wireless connection to getting online successfully!

To start our journey, I'll tell you all about how to get a Cisco Wireless LAN Controller up and running before showing you how to join access-points to our new WLC. After that, we'll dig deep into how to configure the WLC to support wireless networks. By the end of this chapter, you'll triumph by having an actual endpoint join our wireless LAN!

> To find your included bonus material, as well as Todd Lammle videos, practice questions & hands-on labs, please see www.lammle.com/ccna

WLAN Deployment Models

Cisco's Unified Wireless Networks (CUWN) was brought into this world to save our sanity by making it a lot less painful to tackle WLAN management issues like these:

- Integrating diverse devices types into our WLANs while ensuring they play nicely and work together well
- Maintaining a consistent security configuration with a constant onslaught of APs being added into the enterprise.
- Monitoring the environment for new sources of interference and redeploying existing devices as necessary
- Properly managing channel allocation to minimize co-channel and adjacent channel interference, while ensuring that enough APs are deployed in areas requiring high capacity

And just to complicate things further, keep in mind that all these issues must be managed within a three-dimensional environment that's changing constantly. An important key to this whole puzzle is that most of the challenges I listed above exist because of an outmoded deployment model we used back in the day called the stand-alone model, sometimes called the autonomous model or design. I'll tell you more about this model soon, but for now just know that in it, APs operate as separate entities with no centralized management capabilities! What could go wrong? Not exactly much of a stretch to imagine the inherent weakness of this design, is it?

A typical stand-alone design begins with a static site survey that's basically a snapshot of the radio frequency (RF) environment at a particular moment in time. Based on this snapshot, you would then deploy devices to mitigate any existing interference to provide coverage where you need it. Because we all know that change is the constant within the RF space, the big snag lies in that word *static*. A really common RF environment change is when a new company moves into the unoccupied office next door. Clearly, that would change pretty much everything, but even tiny little things like someone bringing a new metal object into the area can also bring you some serious grief!

Introducing the new lightweight model—*lightweight* is also used to describe the type of APs used within it. It not only puts the power of centralized administration in our hands, it also brings some sweet new capabilities for addressing the snags I listed earlier to the table! Even more wonderful, this model can create an infrastructure that's able to react to changes in real time. Yes! In. Real. Time! Let's just compare these two models now.

Stand-Alone Model

Not just any kind of AP can operate in the stand-alone model—only the autonomous variety of APs can do this. I'll give you a list of all the different types soon. Figure 20.1 pictures a Cisco AP.

FIGURE 20.1 Cisco stand-alone AP

Autonomous APs use the same internetworking operating system (IOS) that your Cisco routers do, except they also have more wireless features built into the code. You configure them individually, and there's no centralized administration point.

And let me tell you—managing several Autonomous Access Points can get out of control fast because not only do you have to keep the configuration consistent between the AAPs. You also have to manually handle the security policies on each one and also potentially tune the wireless channels and features to improve performance and reliability—no small thing! Cisco came up with a couple of solutions that focused on helping with configuration and management issues, but those fixes are nothing compared with the lightweight solution. I'll only talk about them briefly here.

Basically, you can configure a feature called Wireless Domain Services (WDS) on an AP or Cisco switch that will allow for at least some crumbs to centralize services for autonomous APs.

There's also an older solution called the Wireless Solution Engine (WLSE) that can give you limited centralized control and monitoring.

Lightweight Model

Practically every the issue with the standalone model can be solved with central management—no joke! With centralized management, a controller can push configurations to APs and also intelligently tune the wireless performance for you since it can see the bigger picture of the wireless network.

The CUWN lightweight model definitely requires centralized control, which we gained via Cisco WLAN controllers (WLCs)... more on these in a bit. For now, know that APs are controlled and monitored by the WLC. All clients and APs transmit information back to the WLC, including stats about coverage, interference and even client data.

Figure 20.2 illustrates the lightweight model.

FIGURE 20.2 Cisco Lightweight AP

All transmitted data is sent between the APs and the WLCs via a mouthful of an encapsulation protocol called **Control And Provisioning of Wireless Access Point** (CAPWAP). CAPWAP carries and encapsulates control information between the APs and the WLC over an encrypted tunnel over UDP 5246 for control traffic and UDP 5247 for the data. Client data is encapsulated with an CAPWAP header that contains vital information about the client's received signal strength indicator (RSSI) and signal-to-noise ratio (SNR). Once the data has arrived at the WLC, it can be forwarded as needed, which is how the real-time processes I talked about earlier become available. A couple of great benefits gained through this kind of centralized control are improved security and traffic conditioning. For example, traffic is redirected directly to the WLC so you only need a central firewall to secure all wireless traffic instead of needing to secure each and every site!

Physical and logical security becomes a lot tighter in the CUWN because to ensure only authorized APs connect to the WLC, both devices exchange a certificate and mutually authenticate. Any APs found not to be CAPWAP capable are classified as rogues. So basically, the network forces CAPWAP-capable APs to be authenticated before they'll be permitted to download any configuration from a WLC, which helps mitigate rogue APs. For physical security reasons, the configuration of the AP resides only in RAM while in operation and connected to the WLC. That way, the configuration can't be nicked from the AP once that device has been removed from the network.

The CUWN consists of five elements that work together to provide a unified enterprise solution:

- Client devices
- APs
- Network unification
- Network management
- Mobility services

There's a variety of devices around that support these elements. Among them are Cisco Aironet client devices, the Cisco Secure Services Client (CSSC), and other Cisco-compatible devices. For APs, we can choose between the type configured and managed by a WLC and those that operate in stand-alone mode.

While it's good to know that a single Cisco WLC can manage many APs, know that you'll get to savor a major increase in capacity with a few additional Cisco WLCs in the mix. You can incorporate other devices into your basic CUWN to add more features and management capabilities too like the Cisco Wireless Control System (WCS), which facilitates the centralized management of multiple WLCs. You also need WCS in order to add a Cisco Wireless Location Appliance. These are very cool tools that provide features like real-time location tracking of clients and RFID tags.

And that's not all...Cisco also offers Mobility Express controllers—a scaled-down wireless controller that can run on a Cisco switch like the 3850 or on certain Cisco Access Points to provide virtual management. The newest type of Wireless Controller is the Cisco 9800, which is entirely built into IOS-XE instead of running AireOS like WLC uses.

Split MAC

Even more good news about lightweight architecture is that it allows for the splitting of 802.11 Data Link layer functions between the lightweight AP and the WLC.

The lightweight AP handles real-time portions of the communication, and the Cisco WLC handles the items that aren't time sensitive. This technology is typically referred to as split MAC.

Here's a list of the real-time portions of the protocol that are handled by the AP:

- Frame exchange handshake between the client and AP performed during each frame transfer
- Beacon frame transmission
- Handling of frames for clients operating in power save mode (including both buffering and transmission)

- Responses to probe request frames from clients and the relaying of received probe requests to the controller
- Transmission to the controller of real-time signal quality information for every received frame
- RF channel monitoring for noise, interference, other WLANs and rogue APs
- Encryption and decryption (Layer 2 wireless only), with the exception of VPN and IPSec clients

The remaining tasks that aren't time-sensitive are handled by the WLC. Some of the MAC-layer functions provided by WLC include:

- 802.11 authentication
- 802.11 association and reassociation (mobility)
- 802.11 to 802.3 frame translation and bridging
- The termination of all 802.11 frames at the controller

> **NOTE** Although the controller handles the authentication, wireless encryption keys for WPA2 or EAP will remain in both the AP and the client.

Cloud Model

A slick new way to manage your wireless infrastructure is by using Cisco's APs - Donald. Meraki is entirely managed by the cloud, so all you have to do is ensure the access points are able to reach the internet. From there you can now manage your entire Meraki network from a publicly accessible web interface.

This means you can make changes to your network from anywhere. Check out Figure 20.3:

A control plane is formed to the cloud to allow for management, which provides monitoring information to help with troubleshooting as well as aid to other features. The cloud provides automatic firmware upgrades, analytics, security features and updates, plus a central point for automation.

The data plane remains on the premises, so end-user traffic isn't affected by cloud management at all.

The downside to the cloud model is that APs just don't offer much local management on the devices—they don't support command line interfaces (CLI). So if the Internet connection goes down at the office, you won't be able to make many changes to your network until the Meraki device can get back online!

Another caveat with Meraki is because its focus is ease of use, it doesn't offer as many features as other Cisco controllers offer.

So basically, Meraki can be a great tool for companies that don't have a highly skilled IT team to deploy more complex solutions. It would also work for branches that just don't have IT staff to help with configurations or troubleshooting.

WLAN Deployment Models

FIGURE 20.3 The cloud model

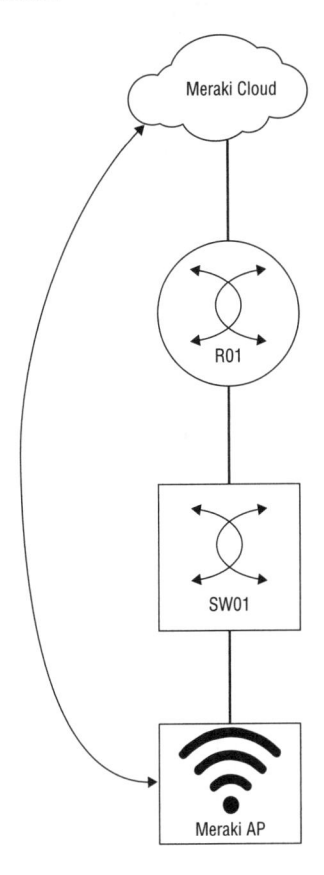

Figure 20.4 gives you a sample of the Meraki dashboard for configuring a SSID.

FIGURE 20.4 Meraki Wireless

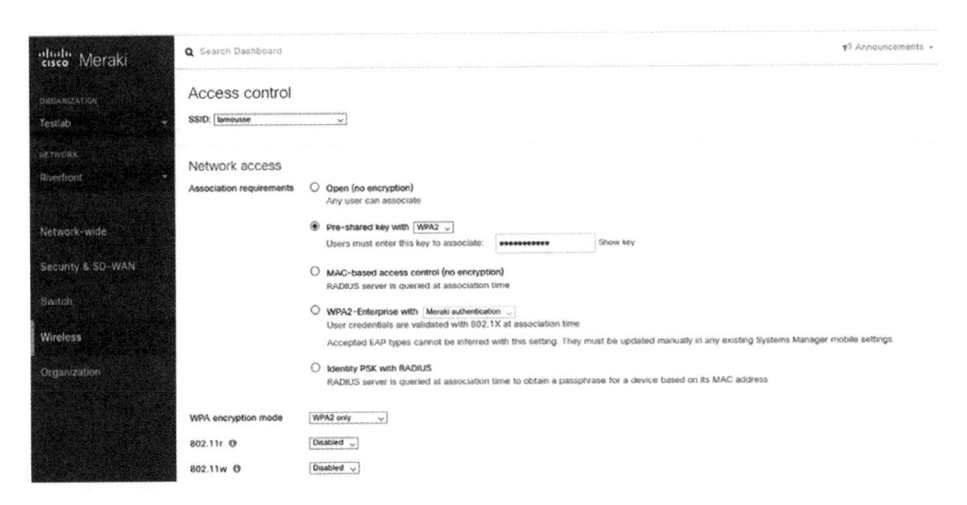

Setting Up a Wireless LAN Controller (WLC)

This is a great place to cover how to actually bring a WLC online so we can start configuring our wireless networks in our lab!

Configuring the Switch

To connect the WLC to a switch, I'm going to create some VLANs and then some trunk ports to connect to the WLC. The environment will use three interfaces because we'll be playing with port channels coming up soon as shown in Figure 20.5.

FIGURE 20.5 Example wireless network

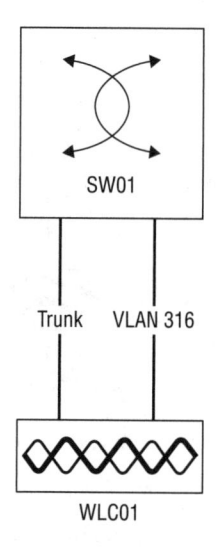

We'll also need an access port to use the service port that we'll talk about later in this chapter.

So now I'll create a VLAN for the WLC to use for its management interface and also one for out of band management used by the service port like this:

```
C3750X-SW01(config)#vlan 311
C3750X-SW01(config-vlan)#name Wireless-Controller
C3750X-SW01(config-vlan)#vlan 316
C3750X-SW01(config-vlan)#name Wireless-ServicePort
```

And while I'm here, I'll go ahead and create some other VLANs that the WLC will use as we move through this chapter like this:

```
C3750X-SW01(config-vlan)#vlan 101
C3750X-SW01(config-vlan)#name WLAN101
C3750X-SW01(config-vlan)#vlan 102
C3750X-SW01(config-vlan)#name WLAN102
C3750X-SW01(config-vlan)#vlan 103
C3750X-SW01(config-vlan)#name WLAN103
```

Of course, the switch will also need SVIs to provide connectivity to the WLC. I'll take care of that now:

```
C3750X-SW01(config)#interface vlan 311
C3750X-SW01(config-if)#description Wireless Controller
C3750X-SW01(config-if)#ip add 10.30.11.1 255.255.255.0
C3750X-SW01(config-if)#no shut

C3750X-SW01(config-if)#interface vlan 316
C3750X-SW01(config-if)#description Wireless-SP Port
C3750X-SW01(config-if)#ip add 10.10.16.1 255.255.255.0
C3750X-SW01(config-if)#no shut
C3750X-SW01(config-if)#exit

C3750X-SW01(config-if)#interface vlan 101
C3750X-SW01(config-if)#description WLAN101
C3750X-SW01(config-if)#ip add 10.30.101.1 255.255.255.0
C3750X-SW01(config-if)#no shut

C3750X-SW01(config-if)#interface vlan 102
C3750X-SW01(config-if)#description WLAN102
C3750X-SW01(config-if)#ip add 10.30.102.1 255.255.255.0
C3750X-SW01(config-if)#no shut

C3750X-SW01(config-if)#interface vlan 103
C3750X-SW01(config-if)#description WLAN103
C3750X-SW01(config-if)#ip add 10.30.103.1 255.255.255.0
C3750X-SW01(config-if)#no shut
```

The last thing I'm going to do on the switch is configure the switchports to be a trunk. My WLC is connected to ports G1/0/37 – 39, and the service port is connected to G1/0/40.

First, I'm going to add a description to each interface so I can remember how my lab is configured in a few weeks!

```
C3750X-SW01(config)#int g1/0/37
C3750X-SW01(config-if)#description Connection to WLC Port 1
C3750X-SW01(config-if)#int g1/0/38
C3750X-SW01(config-if)#description Connection to WLC Port 2
C3750X-SW01(config-if)#int g1/0/39
C3750X-SW01(config-if)#description Connection to WLC Port 3
```

To save some typing, I'll use the **range** command for the trunk configuration. Because the WLC doesn't run STP, it's safe to turn on portfast on the interface:

```
C3750X-SW01(config-if)#int ra g1/0/37-39
C3750X-SW01(config-if-range)#switchport trunk encapsulation dot1q
C3750X-SW01(config-if-range)#switchport mode trunk
C3750X-SW01(config-if-range)#spanning-tree portfast trunk
%Warning: portfast should only be enabled on ports connected to a single
host. Connecting hubs, concentrators, switches, bridges, etc... to this
interface  when portfast is enabled, can cause temporary bridging loops.
Use with CAUTION
```

The service port has to be an access port, so let's put the interface into VLAN 316:

```
C3750X-SW01(config-if-range)#int g1/0/40
C3750X-SW01(config-if)#description Connection to WLC Service Port
C3750X-SW01(config-if)#switchport mode access
C3750X-SW01(config-if)#switchport access vlan 316
C3750X-SW01(config-if)#spanning-tree portfast
%Warning: portfast should only be enabled on ports connected to a single
host. Connecting hubs, concentrators, switches, bridges, etc... to this
interface  when portfast is enabled, can cause temporary bridging loops.
Use with CAUTION
%Portfast has been configured on GigabitEthernet1/0/40 but will only
have effect when the interface is in a non-trunking mode.
```

WLC Initial Setup

Okay—so now that the switch is ready, I can console into my WLC and power it up! After a few minutes, it will boot to the setup wizard:

```
(Cisco Controller)
Welcome to the Cisco Wizard Configuration Tool
```

```
Use the '-' character to backup

AUTO-INSTALL: starting now...
Would you like to terminate autoinstall? [yes]: yes
```

The wizard to ask me to set a hostname and a username/password for the system:

```
System Name [Cisco_5e:ba:e4] (31 characters max): WLC01
Enter Administrative User Name (24 characters max): admin
Enter Administrative Password (3 to 24 characters):**********
Re-enter Administrative Password               : **********
```

Next, it'll ask for the service port IP address. We'll talk about what the port does soon I promise, but for now it needs to be on a separate subnet than the management port, so I'm going to give it **10.10.16.220/24** in my lab:

```
Service Interface IP Address Configuration [static][DHCP]: static
Service Interface IP Address: 10.10.16.220
Service Interface Netmask: 255.255.255.0
```

Don't worry—I'll get to link aggregation later in the chapter. I'll leave it disabled for now. But you can enable it right away if you want like this:

```
Enable Link Aggregation (LAG) [yes][NO]: no
```

The most important config aside from the user/pass is the management interface. Let's give it an IP address of **10.30.11.40/24**, and it will use the VLAN 311 SVI IP for the default router, also known as the default gateway. Because this is a trunk link, I've also got to set the VLAN on the port to 311 unless I want to change the native VLAN. And it's vital to tell the WLC the port we want to use for our management interface—I'm going with Port 1.

The interface will also want to know where to forward DHCP requests. I'm just going point it to the SVI for now:

```
Management Interface IP Address: 10.30.11.40
Management Interface Netmask: 255.255.255.0
Management Interface Default Router: 10.30.11.1
Management Interface VLAN Identifier (0 = untagged): 311
Management Interface Port Num [1 to 8]: 1
Management Interface DHCP Server IP Address: 10.30.11.1
```

You also need to provide a virtual gateway IP, but more on that later! For now, I'll leave high availability turned off since that's out of the scope that we need to cover:

```
Enable HA [yes][NO]: no
Virtual Gateway IP Address: 192.0.2.1
```

The Mobility/RF Group Name is feature that helps several WLCs work together. I'm not going to go into it here, but it is a mandatory field, so type in any value you want.

```
Mobility/RF Group Name: Testlab
```

Sadly, the wizard makes us configure a SSID now, but we have a lot of ground to cover before we get to that configuration step. So I'm just going to deal with that by configuring **Temp-SSID** with the default options and then delete it when the WLC is up and running like this:

```
Network Name (SSID): Temp-SSID
Configure DHCP Bridging Mode [yes][NO]:
Allow Static IP Addresses [YES][no]:
```

And yes, once again, the WLC wants to get ahead of us and wants you to configure a RADIUS server! Just say no for now. We'll be doing this manually.

```
Configure a RADIUS Server now? [YES][no]: no
```

Wireless networks need to know which country they're operating in because different countries handle things a bit differently. I'm in Canada, so I'll use CA for the code.

```
Enter Country Code list (enter 'help' for a list of countries) [US]: CA
```

Get your enter key ready because we can accept the defaults for the enable questions, which enables different types of wireless networks:

```
Enable 802.11b Network [YES][no]:
Enable 802.11a Network [YES][no]:
Enable 802.11g Network [YES][no]:
Enable Auto-RF [YES][no]:
```

WLCs use certificates to allow APs to register themselves, so it's a good idea to ensure our system time is correct. I'll use **10.30.11.10** for my lab NTP server:

```
Configure a NTP server now? [YES][no]:
Enter the NTP server's IP address: 10.30.11.10
Enter a polling interval between 3600 and 604800 secs: 3600
```

As much as we all love IPv6, I'm not going to enable it in the wizard. Doing this will just make it ask me for IPv6 configuration.

```
Would you like to configure IPv6 parameters[YES][no]: no
```

When we get to the end of the wizard, it'll ask if everything is correct—say 'yes' or you'll have to start all over again! The WLC will then restart and be ready to go after a few minutes:

```
Configuration correct? If yes, system will save it and reset. [yes][NO]: yes
Cleaning up DHCP Server

Configuration saved!
Resetting system with new configuration...
```

Joining Access Points (APs)

Joining APs isn't a CCNA topic, but our WLC just won't do us any good until we add some access points into the mix. So now that I've guided you through getting WLC interfaces up and running, its time to join a few access points to the controller.

There's more than one way to make a new AP register to a controller so I'm going to use the DNS method, the DHCP method, and also how to manually register an AP from its command line.

Manual Method

The manual method is quick and easy but can get annoying really fast if you have to log into several APs and them point them to the controller.

You can log into a Cisco AP through the serial port or SSH if the AP has an IP address, with **Cisco/Cisco** as the username and password—the enable password is **Cisco**:

```
AP7c69.f6ef.6d5f>enable
Password:
AP7c69.f6ef.6d5f#
```

Once logged into the AP, it'll have a default name "AP", followed by the mac address of the device. Assuming the AP has received a DHCP address, I just need to use this command to point to my WLC at 10.30.11.40 like this:

```
AP7c69.f6ef.6d5f#capwap ap controller ip address 10.30.11.40
```

Now if DHCP isn't running, I can set a static IP by entering these commands:

```
AP7c69.f6ef.6d5f#capwap ap ip address 10.30.20.101 255.255.255.0
AP7c69.f6ef.6d5f#capwap ap ip default-gateway 10.30.20.1
```

DNS Method

A more scalable way to configure APs is to create a DNS entry so the AP can locate the WLC and register to it.

To use the DNS method, all I have to do is create a DNS A on a DNS server for **CISCO-CAPWAP-CONTROLLER** that points to my WLC AP-Manager IP as demonstrated in Figure 20.6.

FIGURE 20.6 Configure AP with DNS

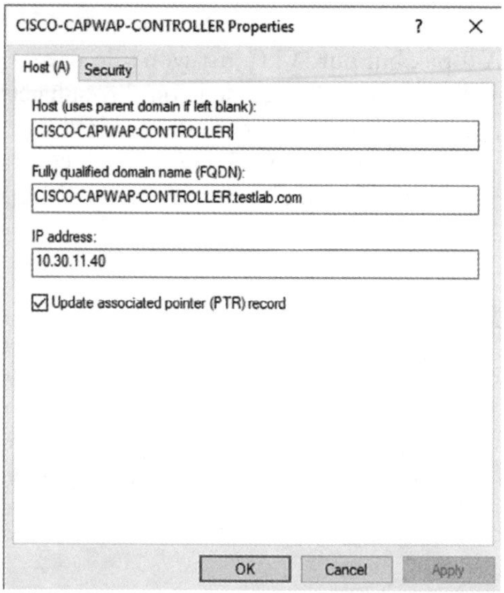

I've also got to ensure our DHCP is assigning the proper domain name to the APs so they find the correct DNS record when they perform their lookup.

DHCP Method

The DHCP method is a bit harder because we'll need to work with hex to configure the feature—yes, we do use hex addressing outside of IPv6! To get this done, I'll build the hex string, which starts with **F1** followed by **04** (4 x 1) if I have only one WLC in the list. It would be **08** (4 x 2) if I had two WLCs.

For the rest of the hex address I'll convert the WLC IP. My WLC IP is 10.30.11.40 so the conversion is:

10 = 0A

30 = 1E

11 = 0B

40 = 28

And putting it all together makes my hex address: **F1040A1E0B28**

Now if I was using two WLCs in this example and the second WLC was 10.30.12.40, that IP would then be:

10 = 0A

30 = 1E

12 = 0C

40 = 28

And the full hex would be: **F1080A1E0B280A1E0C28**

This isn't so bad when once you do it a few times, so practice if you need to! Anyway, now that I have my hex address, I'll configure DHCP and use option 43.

For this example I'm going to configure a DHCP server on my Cisco switch like this:

```
C3750X-SW01(config)# ip dhcp pool Wireless-AP
C3750X-SW01(dhcp-config)# network 10.30.20.0 255.255.255.0
C3750X-SW01(dhcp-config)# default-router 10.30.20.1
C3750X-SW01(dhcp-config)# domain-name testlab.com
C3750X-SW01(dhcp-config)# dns-server 10.30.11.10 10.20.2.10
C3750X-SW01(dhcp-config)# option 43 hex f104.0a1e.0b28
C3750X-SW01(dhcp-config)# exit
C3750X-SW01(config)# ip dhcp excluded-address 10.30.20.1 10.30.20.100
```

Configuring the VLAN

When you're adding APs to the network, it's a very good idea to create a new VLAN to keep their traffic separate and make it stand out when checking your network configuration. So for this setup, I'll create VLAN 320 and name it Wireless-AP so I know what it's for. While I'm at it, I'll also create the SVI for the VLAN like this.

```
C3750X-SW01(config)#vlan 320
C3750X-SW01(config-vlan)#name Wireless-AP
C3750X-SW01(config-vlan)#exit

C3750X-SW01(config)#interface vlan 320
C3750X-SW01(config-if)#description Wireless-AP
C3750X-SW01(config-if)#ip add 10.30.20.11 255.255.255.0
C3750X-SW01(config-if)#no shut
```

Configuring the Switchport

There's really not much to do in order to configure a switchport that's connecting an AP. If the AP is in local mode or you are using one of the diagnostic or troubleshooting interfaces, then the port simply needs to be an access port. Since the wireless traffic is tunneled to the controller through CAPWAP, it doesn't need to know about the VLANs being used by the SSIDs.

I also put Portfast on the ports so STP doesn't get in the way when the APs are trying to get an IP and register:

```
C3750X-SW01(config)#interface g1/0/7
C3750X-SW01(config-if)#description LAB-AP01
C3750X-SW01(config-if)#switchport mode access
C3750X-SW01(config-if)#switchport access vlan 320
C3750X-SW01(config-if)#spanning-tree portfast
```

The only complicating factor here comes up if you're running the AP in FlexConnect mode. Since traffic is locally switched in that setup, the AP needs to be a trunk port. A good trick for this situation is to change the native VLAN to be the Wireless-AP VLAN. Doing this allows you get the AP online without having to set up VLAN tagging on the AP port. And keep in mind that portfast will need the trunk keyword to work on a trunk link:

```
C3750X-SW01(config)#int g1/0/1
C3750X-SW01(config-if)#description LAB-AP03
C3750X-SW01(config-if)#switchport trunk encap dot1q
C3750X-SW01(config-if)#switchport trunk native vlan 320
C3750X-SW01(config-if)#switchport mode trunk
C3750X-SW01(config-if)#spanning portfast trunk
```

Wireless LAN Controllers (WLC)

In the vital world of wireless, there are two types of APs: autonomous and lightweight.

An autonomous AP is one that's configured, managed, and maintained in isolation relative to all the other APs that exist in the network.

A lightweight AP gets its configuration from a central device called a wireless controller. In this scenario, the APs essentially function as antennas with all information being sent back to the wireless LAN controller (WLC). There are a bunch of real advantages to this with a couple good examples being the capacity for centralized management and more seamless roaming.

When you're implementing the lightweight model, the centralized control system is the WLC. All device configurations are done at the WLC and then simply downloaded to the appropriate device. WLCs come with different features and price tags and many form factors that allow either stand-alone alliances or modules that integrate into routers and multi-layer switches. Did you know that WLCs can support from 6 up to 300 Aps?

Figure 20.7 pictures the Cisco Wireless LAN Controller.

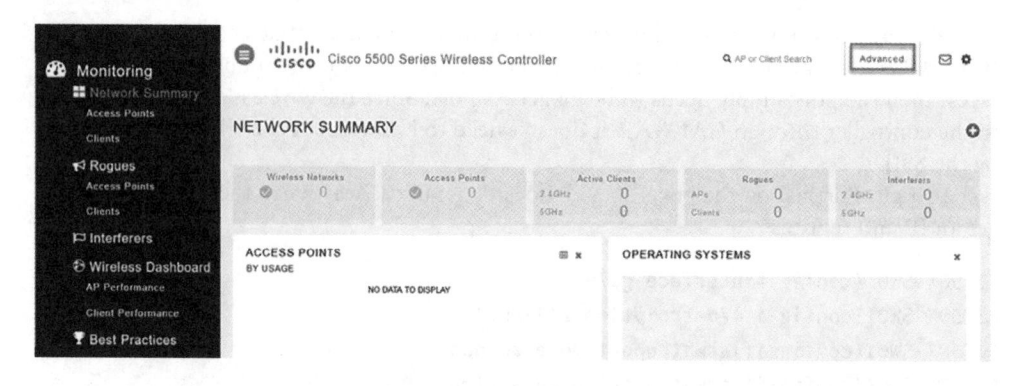

FIGURE 20.7 Cisco WLC

It's just so impressive that we can configure and control up to 16 WLANs for each AP on a single WLC! A WLAN is defined in the WLC a lot like a profile, and it has a separate

WLAN ID (1–16) and a separate WLAN SSID (WLAN name). The WLAN SSID defines where we configure unique security and quality of service (QoS) settings.

If you have clients that are connected to one AP, they'll share the same RF space and channel, but if they're connected to different SSIDs, they're in a different logical network.

And of course this means that clients in different SSIDs can be isolated from one another in the RF space and can have different VLAN and QoS tags. But they'll still be in the same collision domain, just as in autonomous AP configurations with VLANs. The SSIDs will be mapped to the VLANs in the WLC configuration.

> Even though it's not exactly required by the CCNA, I'm going to include examples of the WLC command line interface along with the web interface configurations throughout this chapter. The reason I'm doing this is that the WLC AireOS is really different from what you're used to with Cisco IOS, so it definitely won't hurt to get familiar here!

WLC Port Types

The WLC has a variety of different port types that you use to connect the WLC to the network or deploy configurations. Here's a list of them:

- Console port
- Service port
- Redundancy port
- Distribution system port
- Management interface
- Redundancy management
- Virtual interface
- Service port interface
- Dynamic interface

Console Port I'm guessing that you're already familiar with the console port. But just in case, this port works the same way as when you're dealing with a router or a switch by allowing you to configure the WLC through the CLI using out of baud access.

You can connect via a console cable and the following settings by default:

- 9600 baud
- 8 data bits
- 1 stop bit
- No Flow Control
- No Parity

You need to use the console port for initially setting up the WLC or if the WLC loses its network access for some reason. If you want to change the serial port settings, do so by clicking Serial Port in the Management menu, as shown in Figure 20.8.

FIGURE 20.8 Cisco WLC Serial Port Configuration

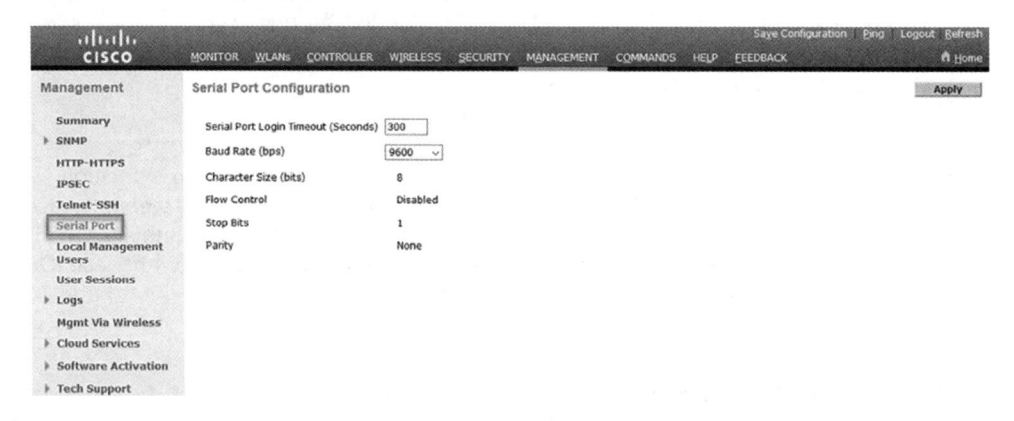

You can also adjust the baudrate with the following command:

```
(WLC01) >config serial baudrate
[1200/2400/4800/9600/19200/38400/57600/115200] Enter serial speed.
(WLC01) >config serial baudrate 115200
```

Service Port   This port is used for out of baud management of the WLC. I've got to say that this port can be a bit annoying to use though because it uses a separate routing table and can't use a default gateway. This means you've got to add static routes to use the port so it knows how to reach your management network. Figure 20.9 show the Add Route screen.

FIGURE 20.9 WLC Add Route

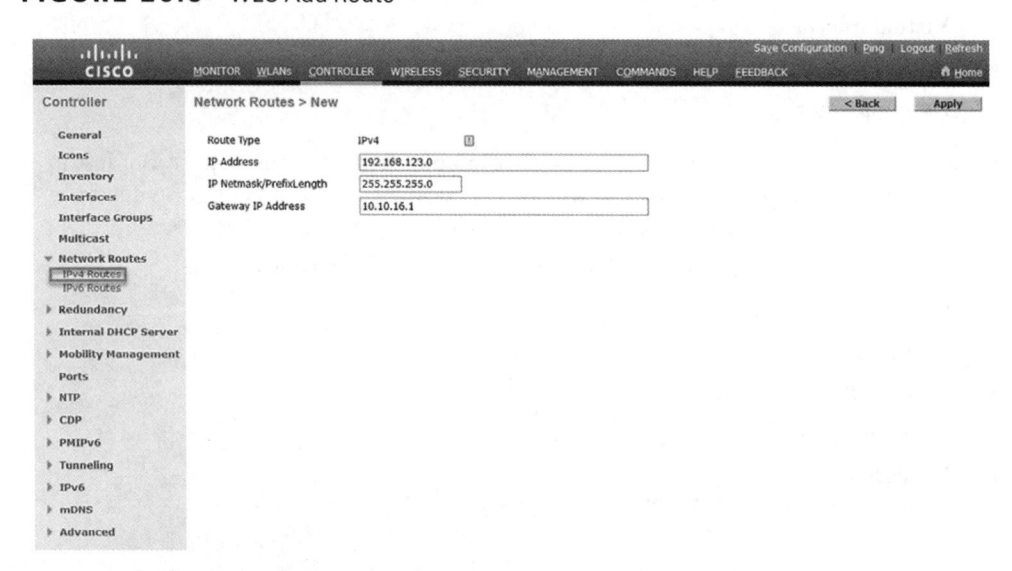

You can add routes through the CLI by using the following commands:

```
(WLC01) >config route add 192.168.124.0 255.255.255.0 10.10.16.1
(WLC01) >show route summary
Number of Routes.................................. 5
Destination Network          Netmask                Gateway
-------------------          -------------------    -------------------
192.168.121.0                255.255.255.0          10.10.16.1
192.168.122.0                255.255.255.0          10.10.16.1
192.168.123.0                255.255.255.0          10.10.16.1
192.168.124.0                255.255.255.0          10.10.16.1
```

Redundancy Port   This port can connect to a second WLC to get you high availability, ensuring your WLC is always available to serve your wireless networking needs. I'll cover this one more deeply in the interface type section.

Distribution System Port   This is just a fancy name for regular interfaces on the WLC, which can be either ethernet or SFP connections depending on the type of WLC controller you've got. You can view the Distribution System Ports, or just ports for short, via the controller page where you just click on Ports as shown in Figure 20.10.

FIGURE 20.10   Distribution system port

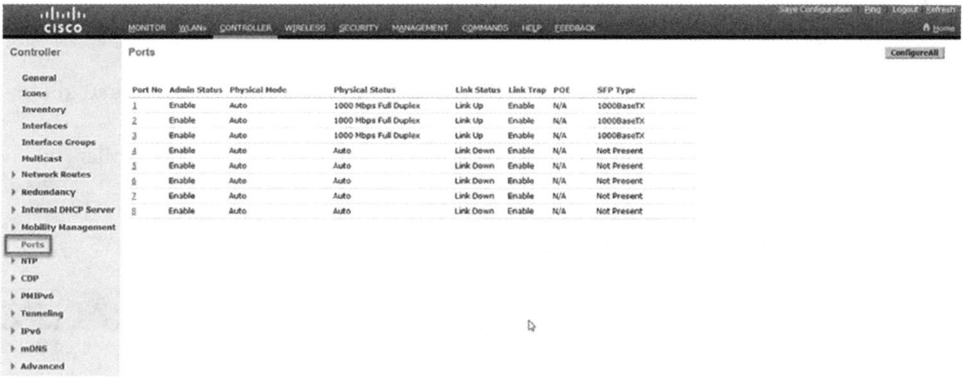

And you can also use the following CLI command to see the ports on the system:

```
(WLC01) >show port summary
     STP    Admin Physical  Physical  Link    Link
Pr   Type   Stat  Mode      Mode      Status  Status  Trap    POE   SFPType
--   ------ ----  -------   --------- -------  ------ ------- ----- ---------
1    Normal Forw  Enable    Auto      1000 Full Up    Enable  N/A   1000BaseTX
2    Normal Forw  Enable    Auto      1000 Full Up    Enable  N/A   1000BaseTX
3    Normal Forw  Enable    Auto      1000 Full Up    Enable  N/A   1000BaseTX
4    Normal Disa  Enable    Auto      Auto      Down  Enable  N/A   Not Present
```

5	Normal	Disa	Enable	Auto	Auto	Down	Enable	N/A	Not Present
6	Normal	Disa	Enable	Auto	Auto	Down	Enable	N/A	Not Present
7	Normal	Disa	Enable	Auto	Auto	Down	Enable	N/A	Not Present
8	Normal	Disa	Enable	Auto	Auto	Down	Enable	N/A	Not Present
RP	Normal	Disa	Enable	Auto	Auto	Down	Enable	N/A	1000BaseTX
SP	Normal	Forw	Enable	Auto	Auto	Up	Enable	N/A	1000BaseTX

Management interface   Used for normal management traffic including RADIUS user authentication, WLC-to-WLC communication, web-based and SSH sessions, SNMP, Network Time Protocol (NTP), syslog and so on. The management interface is also used to terminate CAPWAP tunnels between the controller and its APs.

Redundancy management   This is the management IP address of a redundant WLC that's part of a high availability pair of controllers. The active WLC uses the management interface address, while the standby WLC uses the redundancy management address.

Virtual interface   This is the IP address facing wireless clients when the controller is relaying client DHCP requests, performing client web authentication, and supporting client mobility.

Service port interface   Bound to the service port and used for out-of-band management.

Dynamic interface   Used to connect a VLAN to a WLAN.

WLC Interface Types

The WLC also has different interface types that connect to the ports we just talked about as well as provide services to the wireless networks we'll be configuring soon.

You can view the interfaces on the WLC by selecting Interfaces under Controllers as shown in Figure 20.11.

FIGURE 20.11   WLC interfaces

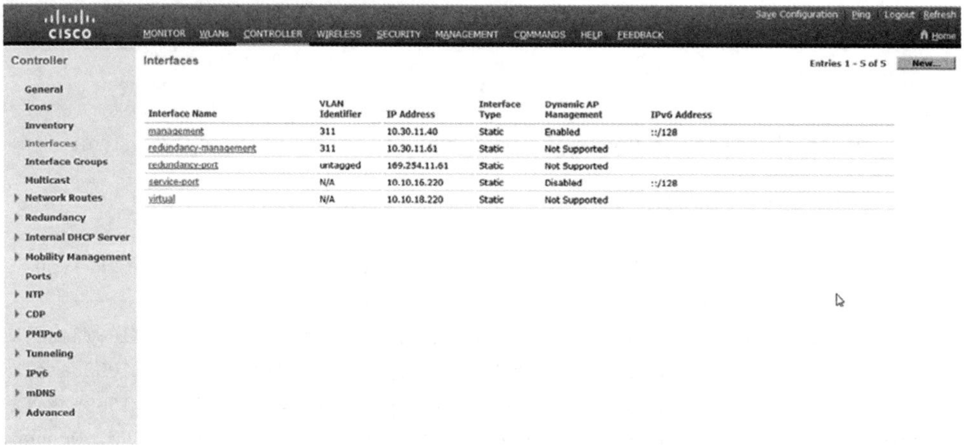

WLC Interface Types

You can also check the interfaces with the following command:

```
(WLC01) >show interface summary

Number of Interfaces.......................... 8
Interface Name                  Port  Vlan Id   IP Address       Type     Ap Mgr  Guest
------------------------------  ----  --------  ---------------  -------  ------  -----
management                      LAG   311       10.30.11.40      Static   Yes     No
redundancy-management           LAG   311       10.30.11.61      Static   No      No
redundancy-port                 -     untagged  169.254.11.61    Static   No      No
service-port                    N/A   N/A       10.10.16.220     Static   No      No
virtual                         N/A   N/A       192.0.2.1        Static   No      No
```

Management Interface

Most of the time, you'll connect to your WLC through the web interface or CLI by accessing the management interface. It needs to be given either an IPv4 or IPv6 address, and since we'll probably be trunking from the switch, we'll have to set a VLAN tag for the interface too. Because wireless traffic is brought to the controller via a CAPWAP by default, we would also set up a DHCP helper on the interface so the wireless client can get its IP address.

Aside from allowing you to configure things on the WLC, the management interface also has the Dynamic AP Manager role enabled by default. This allows APs to register to the WLC and terminates CAPWAP tunnels to the controller.

If you want to move the role to another interface, you can disable the role by unchecking the **Enable Dynamic AP Management** box, but it isn't usually worth the effort due to complexities that are out of scope here. Figure 20.12 pictures the WLC management interface.

We can also configure this through CLI with these commands.

```
(WLC01) >config interface address management 10.30.11.40

<netmask>       Enter the interface's netmask.

(WLC01) >config interface address management 10.30.11.40 255.255.255.0

<gateway>       Enter the interface's gateway address.

(WLC01) >config interface address management 10.30.11.40 255.255.255.0 10.30.11.1
```

FIGURE 20.12 WLC management interface

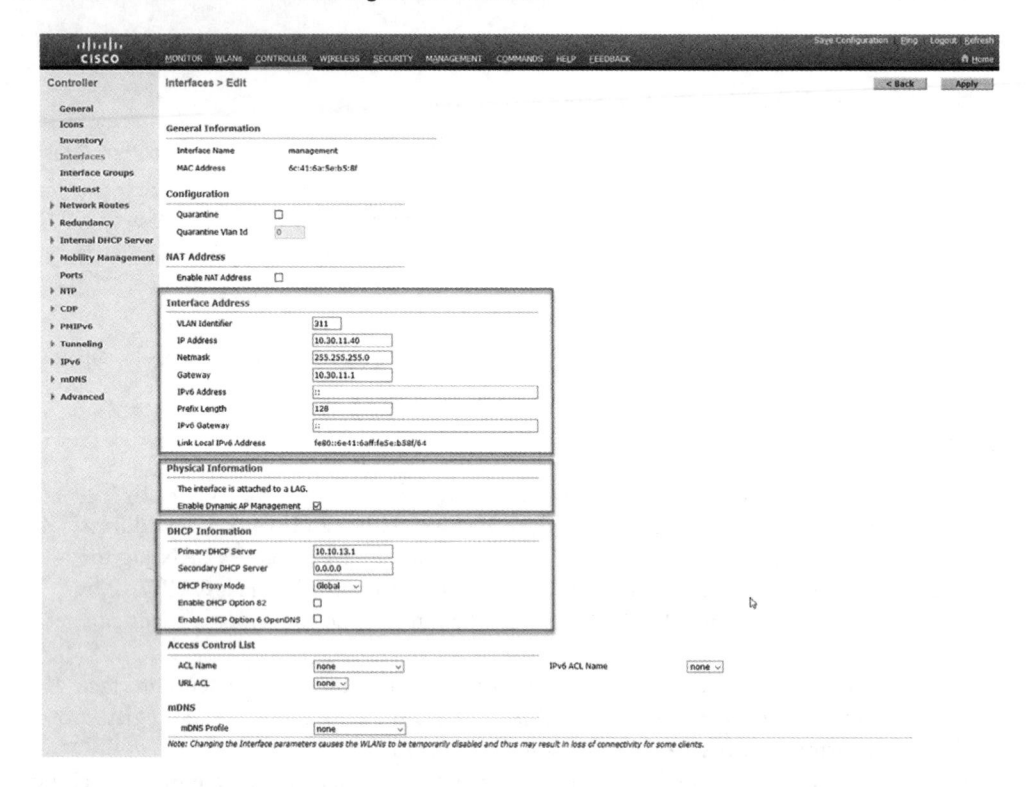

Service Port Interface

This interface is how we configure the service port I talked about in the last section. There are a lot less options available with this interface compared to the management interface, as you can see in Figure 20.13. You can set either an IPv4 or IPv6 address, or you can just use DHCP on the port to get an address.

FIGURE 20.13 WLC service port interface

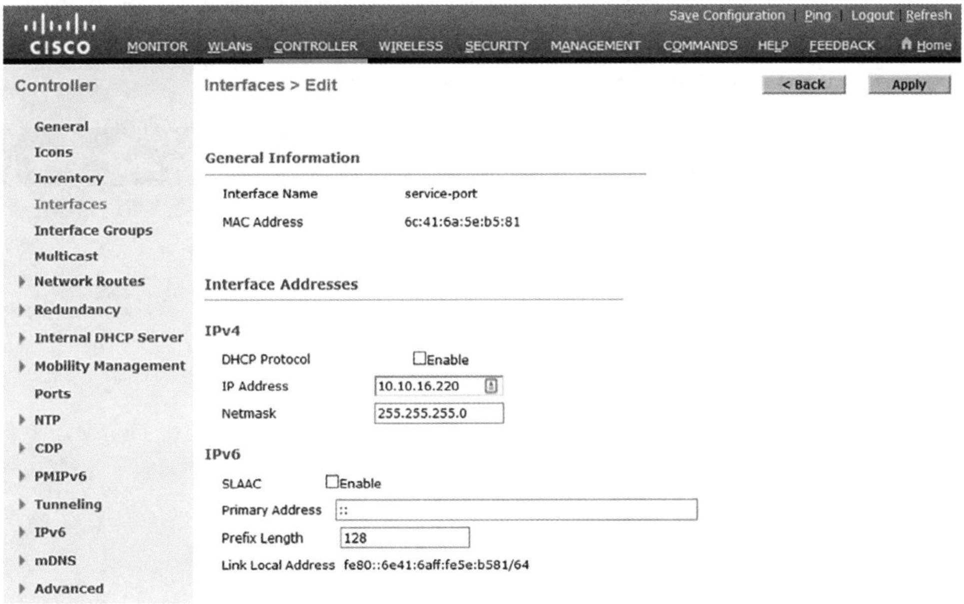

The SP interface doesn't support VLAN tagging, so you've got to configure the switch to use untagged VLANs as well.

We can also configure the service port through CLI:

```
(WLC01) >config interface address service-port

<IP address>    Enter the interface's IP Address.

(WLC01) >config interface address service-port 10.10.16.220

<netmask>       Enter the interface's netmask.

(WLC01) >config interface address service-port 10.10.16.220 255.255.255.0
```

Redundancy Management

The redundancy-management interface is used to configure the redundancy-port we talked about. It's actually the same as the service port where it's referenced in both places.

Anyway, this port is the one we use to setup high availability between two wireless controllers. Keep in mind that you need to configure an IP address in the same subnet as the management interface.

The rest of the steps are out of scope for this book, but you can probably guess the options by checking out the controller page. Figure 20.14 pictures the WLC redundancy management interface.

FIGURE 20.14 WLC redundancy management interface

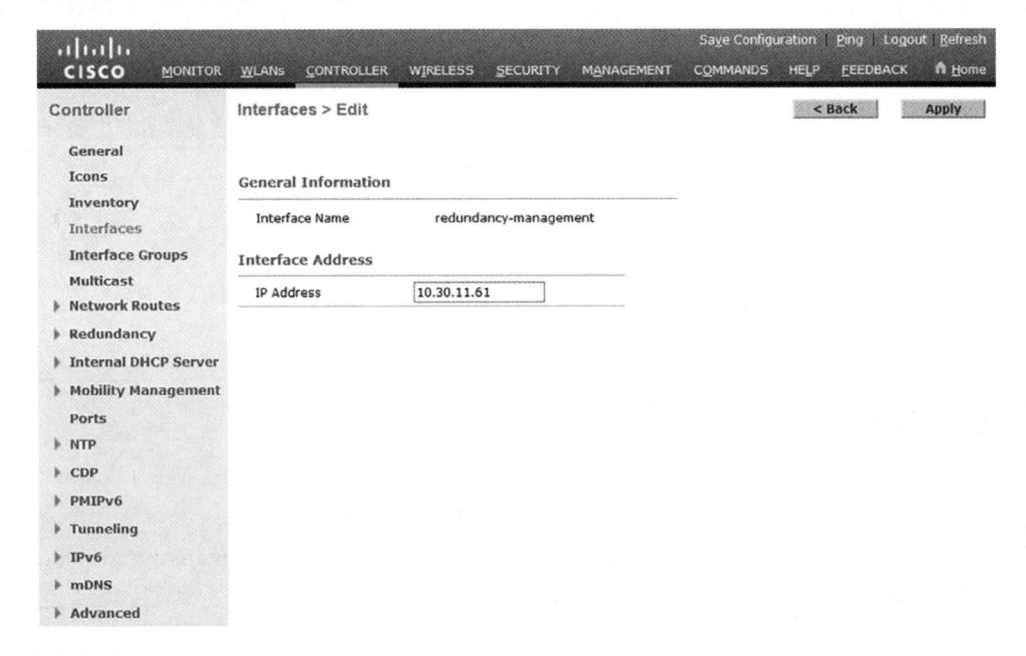

I won't show the CLI for this interface because it dives into the actual high availability configuration. Just know that follows a similar pattern as the interfaces we just covered.

Virtual Interface

The virtual interface jumps into action when the WLC needs to redirect wireless client traffic back to the controller. Remember all those times you connected to Wi-Fi at a hotel or somewhere and a website pops up asking you to agree to the rules or demanding that you fork over some money to get online? That's courtesy of the virtual interface!

Back in the day, we all used **1.1.1.1** as our redirection IP address since it was unlikely to be used by anything important…and then Cloudflare decided to launch a DNS service that uses that IP!

So, after the IT community finished ranting about that online, it was finally decided that we'll use **192.0.2.1** as the new and preferred virtual IP used for redirection.

The CLI for configuring this interface is:

(WLC01) >`config interface address virtual 192.0.2.1`

You can configure this from the GUI as shown in Figure 20.15.

FIGURE 20.15 WLC virtual interface

Dynamic Interface

When the WLC terminates the wireless traffic to the controller through CAPWAP, it will land on the management interface by default. This means that all wireless SSIDs will use the management interface's VLAN for IP addressing.

We can get more flexibility by choosing to create dynamic interfaces, which are like SVIs on a switch—a logical interface that allows you to terminate traffic to different VLANs instead of just using the management.

Whenever you create a dynamic interface by clicking the new button on the interfaces page, it's smart to give it a name that makes sense to you, plus a VLAN ID. In this case, I named the interface WLAN101 and used VLAN 101.

And depending on the controller model, the WLC can support between 16 and 4096 dynamic interfaces! Creating a Dynamic Interface can be seen on Figure 20.16.

FIGURE 20.16 WLC dynamic interface

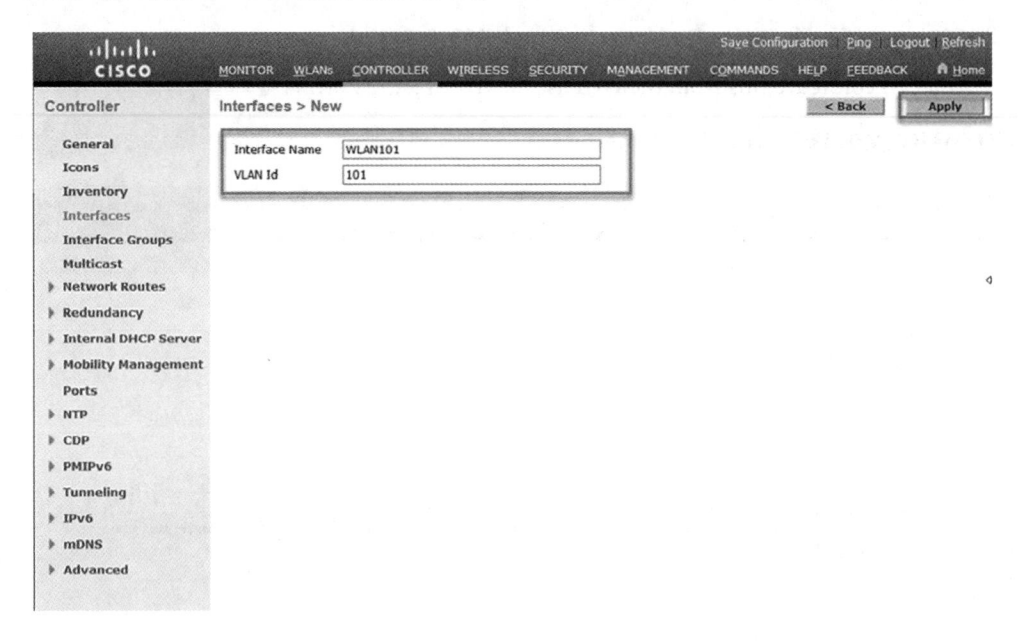

To do this in CLI I'm going to type the following:

(WLC01) >**config interface create**

<interface-name> Enter interface name.

(WLC01) >**config interface create WLAN101**

<vlan-id>   Enter VLAN Identifier.

(WLC01) >**config interface create WLAN101 101**

Once the interface is created, the configuration is really similar to the management interface, only the **Dynamic AP Management** is disabled by default.

Because the WLC does not support dynamic routing and static routes are only for the service port, it's good to put the gateway IP on the switch network instead of directly on the WLC. After all, we can't easily advertise it to the network. Figure 20.17 show the dynamic interface configuration.

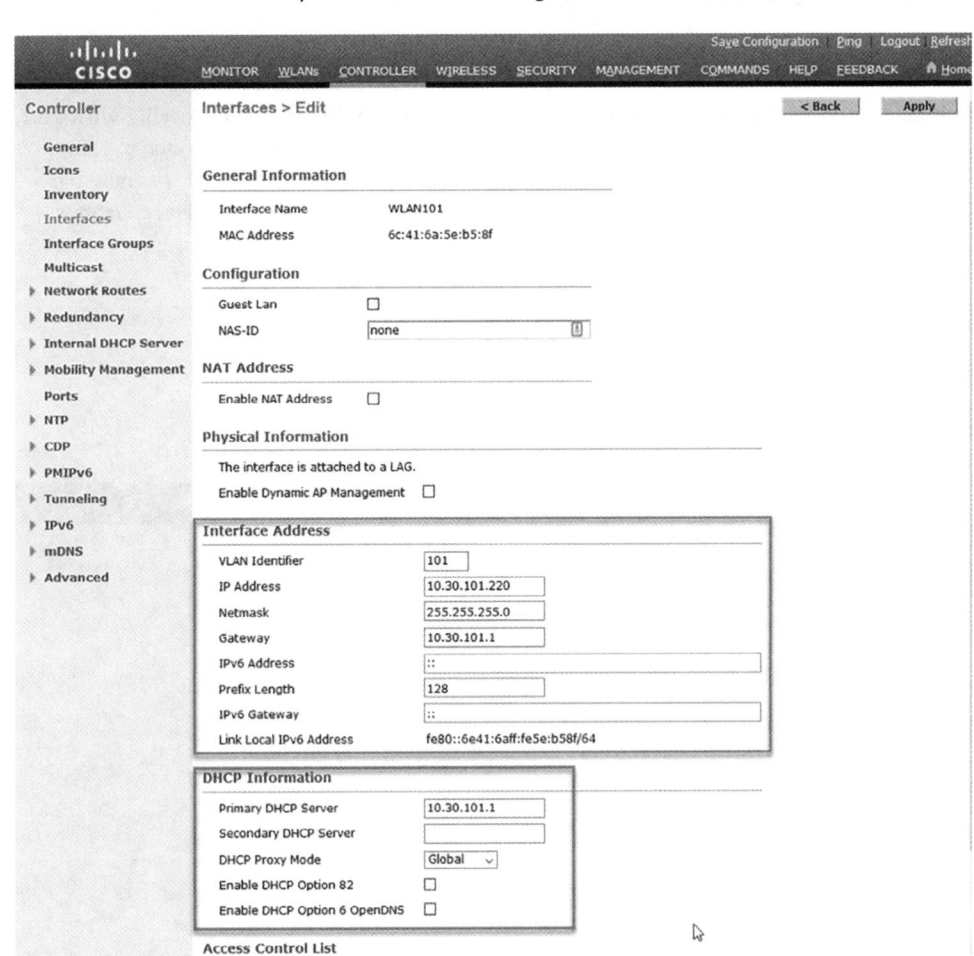

FIGURE 20.17 WLC dynamic interface configuration

The CLI for configuring an IP on the dynamic interface looks like this:

```
(WLC01) >config interface address dynamic-interface wlan101 10.30.101.220
```

<netmask>   Enter the interface's netmask.
```
(WLC01) >config interface address dynamic-interface wlan101 10.30.101.220 255.255.255.0
```

<gateway>   Enter the interface's gateway address.

```
(WLC01) >config interface address dynamic-interface wlan101 10.30.101.220 255.255.255.0 10.30.101.1
```

Interface Groups

Interface Groups is exactly what it sounds like—a way of grouping interfaces. This can come in really handy if your SSID is running out of IP addresses and you want to add more without having to change the subnet mask on the interface. Instead of bothering with that, just add more dynamic interfaces! You can even add the management interface to the pool so clients can get online, which is cool because it lets me to keep subnet sizes somewhat smaller compared to issuing one big subnet. Figure 20.18 pictures the Interface Groups configuration.

As usual, the command for getting this done is:

```
<Interface Group name> Enter interface group name.
(WLC01) >config interface group create int-group
```

FIGURE 20.18 WLC Interface Groups

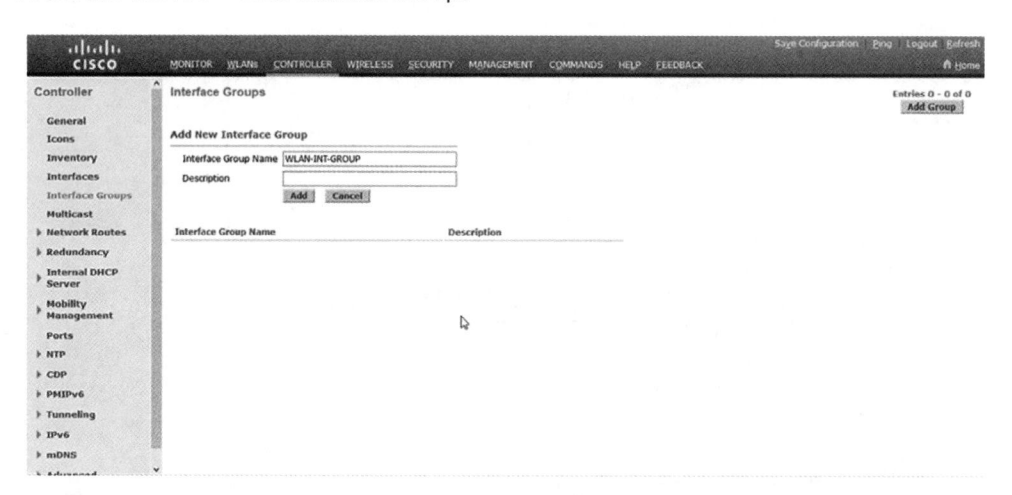

Next, you just need to pick the interfaces that will become part of the group. I'll go ahead and create some more dynamic interfaces so you can see how this works when we get to actually creating a SSID.

Now I just need to select each interface and press the **Add Interface** button as in Figure 20.19.

The CLI for adding interface groups is:

```
WLC01) >config interface group interface add wlan-int-group wlan101
WLC01) >config interface group interface add wlan-int-group wlan102
WLC01) >config interface group interface add wlan-int-group wlan103
WLC01) >show interface group summary

Interface Group Name              Total Interfaces   Total Wlans   Total AP Groups   Quarantine
--------------------------------  ----------------   -----------   ---------------   ----------
wlan-int-group                           3                2                2             No
```

FIGURE 20.19 WLC interface group configuration

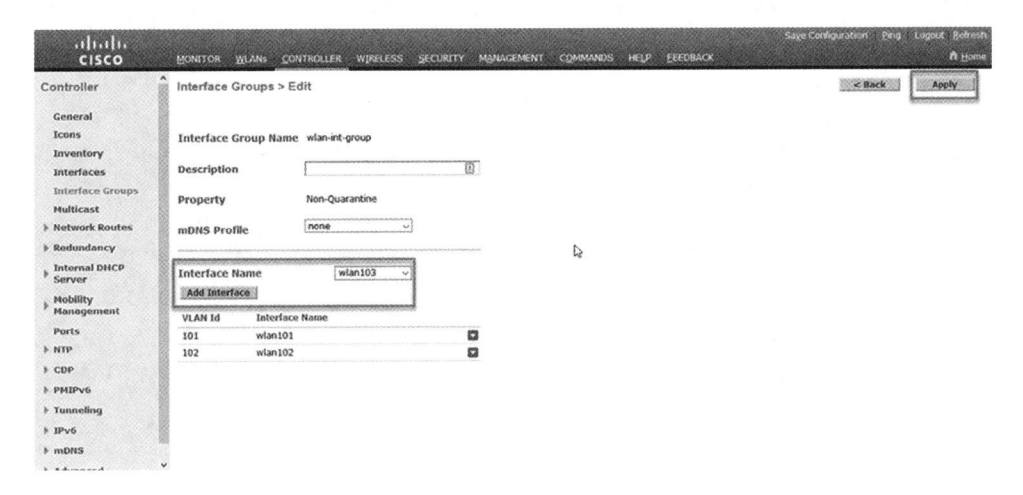

Link Aggregation Group (LAG)

Since everybody wants a high-performance, reliable network, I'm going to show you how to increase fault tolerance and optimize our WLC's network connectivity by creating a port channel. It's too bad this isn't as flexible as it is on a Cisco switch, at least not yet, but it's still worth doing.

On a WLC all Distributed System Ports are added to the Link Aggregation Group (LAG). Because the WLC doesn't support LACP or PAGP we'll have to go with **channel-group # mode on** on the switch side. Pro tip—you've got to reboot the WLC for the LAG to activate, so just don't this on a production system during the day!

624 Chapter 20 ▪ Configuring Wireless Technologies

We'll enable LAG from the Controller page, which thoughtfully reminds us to save our config and reboot the system. Be warned that if you're using any untagged interfaces for wireless traffic, they'll be deleted after rebooting! Figure 20.20 pictures the LAG configuration.

FIGURE 20.20 WLC LAN Aggregation Group

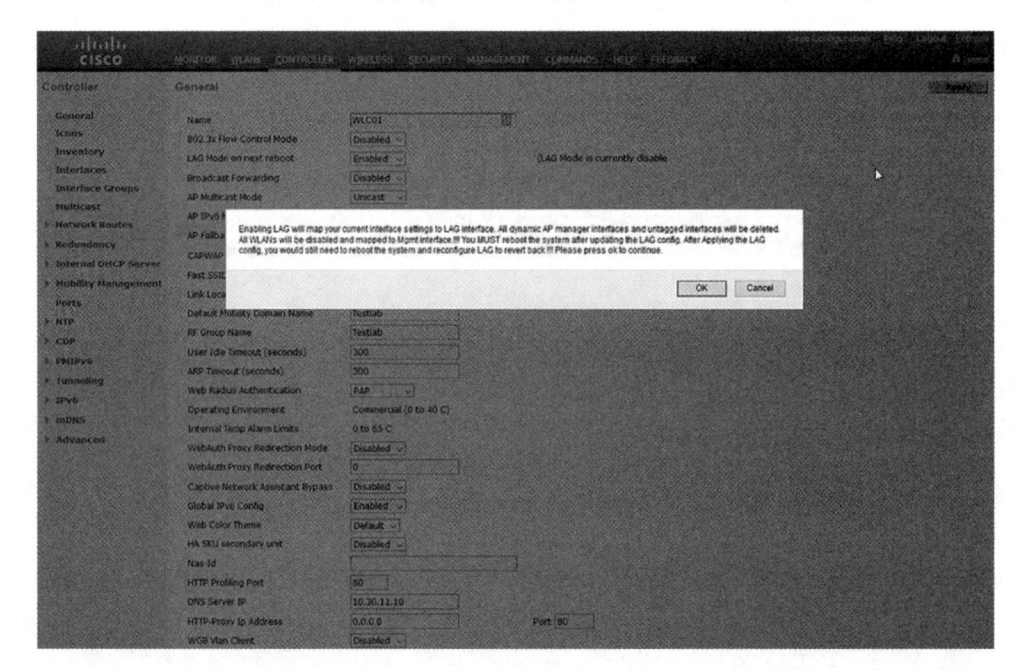

Just choose **Save Configuration** in the top right of the page, then go to **Commands** and click the **Reboot** page where you'll hit the **Reboot** button as in Figure 20.21.

FIGURE 20.21 WLC reboot

We get the same reminders if we configure this through CLI:

```
(WLC01) >config lag enable
Enabling LAG will map your current interfaces setting to LAG interface,
All dynamic AP Manager interfaces and Untagged interfaces will be deleted
All WLANs will be disabled and mapped to Mgmt interface
!!! You MUST reboot the system after updating the LAG config. !!!
!!! After Applying the LAG config, you would still need to    !!!
!!! reboot the system and reconfigure LAG to revert back      !!!
Are you sure you want to continue? (y/n) y
You MUST now save config and reset the system.
(WLC01) >save config
Are you sure you want to save? (y/n) y
Configuration Saved!
(WLC01) >reset system
Are you sure you would like to reset the system? (y/N) y
System will now restart!
```

Now on my switch, I'm going to go ahead and configure a port channel on interfaces Gig1/0/37 through Gig1/0/39 that are connected to the WLC:

```
C3750X-SW01(config)#interface range g1/0/37-39
C3750X-SW01(config-if-range)#switchport trunk encapsulation dot1q
C3750X-SW01(config-if-range)#switchport mode trunk
C3750X-SW01(config-if-range)#spanning portfast trunk
%Warning: portfast should only be enabled on ports connected to a single
host. Connecting hubs, concentrators, switches, bridges, etc... to this
 interface  when portfast is enabled, can cause temporary bridging loops.
Use with CAUTION
C3750X-SW01(config-if-range)#channel-group 11 mode on
*Jan  2 14:26:43.320: %LINK-3-UPDOWN: Interface Port-channel11, changed state to
up
*Jan  2 14:26:44.326: %LINEPROTO-5-UPDOWN: Line protocol on Interface Port-
channel11, changed state to up
```

Our port channel will be ready to rock as soon as the WLC comes back up. And since all of the interfaces have been added to the LAG, we can add more links by connecting another cable and configuring the switchport to join the channel group—nice!

Configuring the AP

So right now I've got two APs showing up on my WLC. I'm going to configure them by going to Wireless, then All APs, and then by selecting the name of the AP I want to edit. Check out Figure 20.22.

626 Chapter 20 ■ Configuring Wireless Technologies

FIGURE 20.22 WLC AP configuration screen

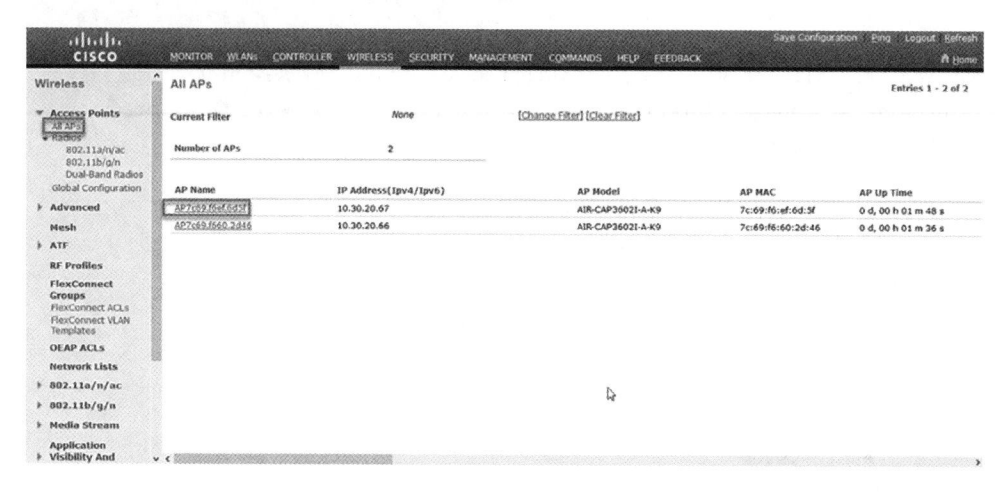

On the General page, I'm going to pick an AP name that makes sense to me. I'm also going to change the IP to static so I can keep track of the AP when I'm connecting to things in my lab better.

We won't be able to adjust the DNS address until hitting apply to commit the changes as shown in Figure 20.23.

FIGURE 20.23 WLC AP IP addressing

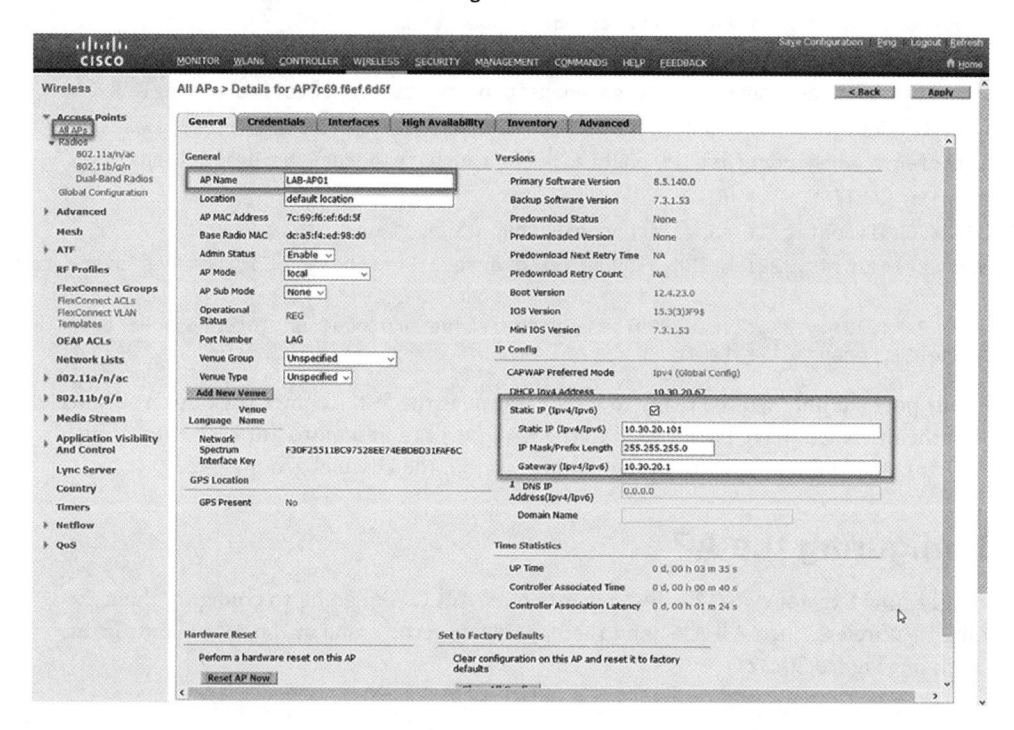

Now we can go ahead and enter the DNS server and tell the AP the domain name it should use as shown Figure 20.24.

FIGURE 20.24 WLC AP DNS configuration

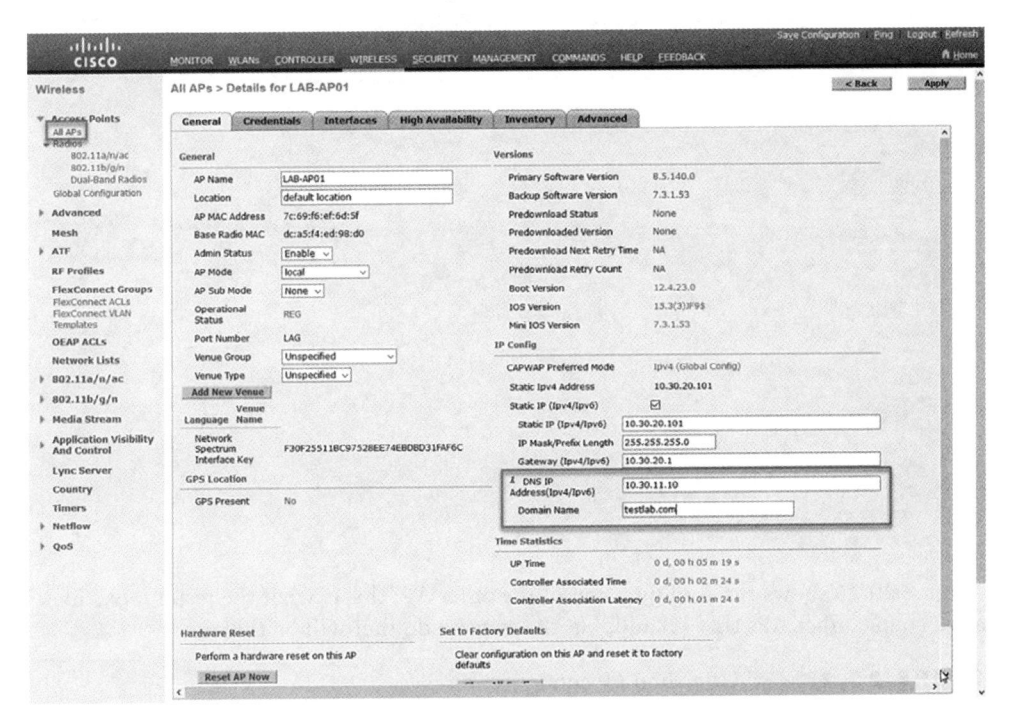

Wow! There sure are a lot of options in here, but we're going to focus in on the High Availability tab shown in Figure 20.25. This is where we can define up to three WLCs that the AP should try to connect to, which it really important because if an AP loses connection to the Primary controller, it will try the next one on the list and so on. Check out Figure 20.25.

FIGURE 20.25 WLC high availability

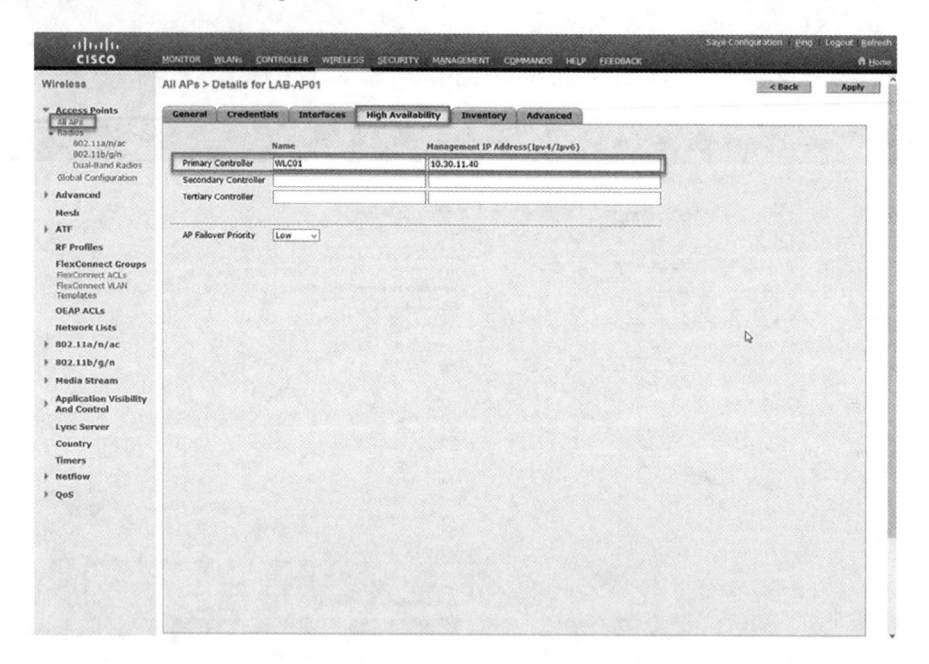

Figure 20.26 shows the configuration of the other AP; this is what the result looks like. I have a couple other APs that I'll add, but the steps to do that will be the same.

FIGURE 20.26 WLC finished AP configuration

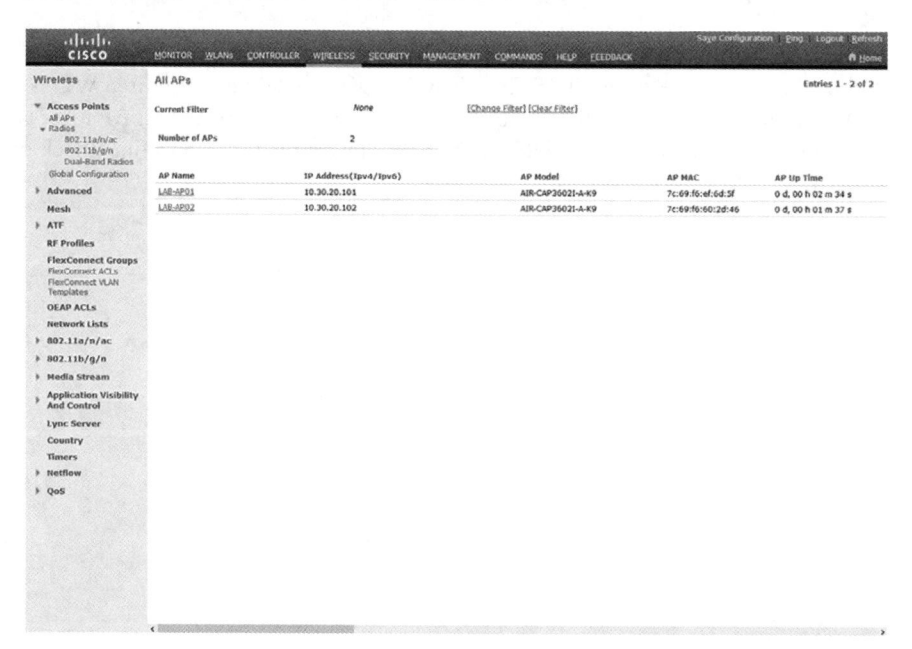

AP Modes

Access points can do more than just connect you to wireless; they also support different functions and different ways of connecting. The various options available are called modes.

The WLC supports nine AP modes depending on your specific AP model. I'm going to tell you about all the available options but just know that local is the most important for the CCNA exam and beyond.

Local This is the default mode an AP will run in. In this mode, all traffic will be carried back to the wireless controller through a CAPWAP tunnel. This is handy if you want to have a central firewall at your main office to handle all wireless traffic for all your sites. Also, when the AP isn't busy transmitting traffic, it'll actually keep itself busy by scanning the other channels for interference, measuring the noise level, checking for rogue devices, and looking for intrusion detection events. This mode can also run a Wireless Intrusion Prevention System submode, which enhances wireless security by comparing wireless traffic to IPS events and preventing bad traffic.

Monitor This mode doesn't send any wireless traffic at all; instead the AP basically acts as a dedicated sensor on your network. Just like with local mode, it will check the noise, check for interference, check for rogue devices and intrusion detection events. It will also try to provide location-based services by figuring out the location of endpoints on the network. You really only want to enable this mode if you have APs to spare or if you're troubleshooting a performance issue and need more information.

FlexConnect The problem with local mode is that sending all wireless traffic to the wireless controller may not be ideal for a site that has its own internet connection and firewall. FlexConnect allows APs to locally switch traffic rather than send it to the controller, allowing the network the AP is connected to route the traffic as it sees fit. This mode is more complex than local, but it offers more flexibility. It can also run a Wireless Intrusion Prevention System submode, which enhances wireless security by comparing wireless traffic to IPS events and preventing bad traffic.

Sniffer This mode is great when you're troubleshooting an issue with the wireless network and need to do a packet capture. It doesn't serve traffic, but it does start a packet capture that can be sent to Wireshark so you can understand what's actually going on in the network. Once the AP is in sniffer mode, just select what channel you want it to capture and give it a destination to send the captured traffic to. Figure 20.27 shows the sniffer screen.

FIGURE 20.27 WLC radio sniffer

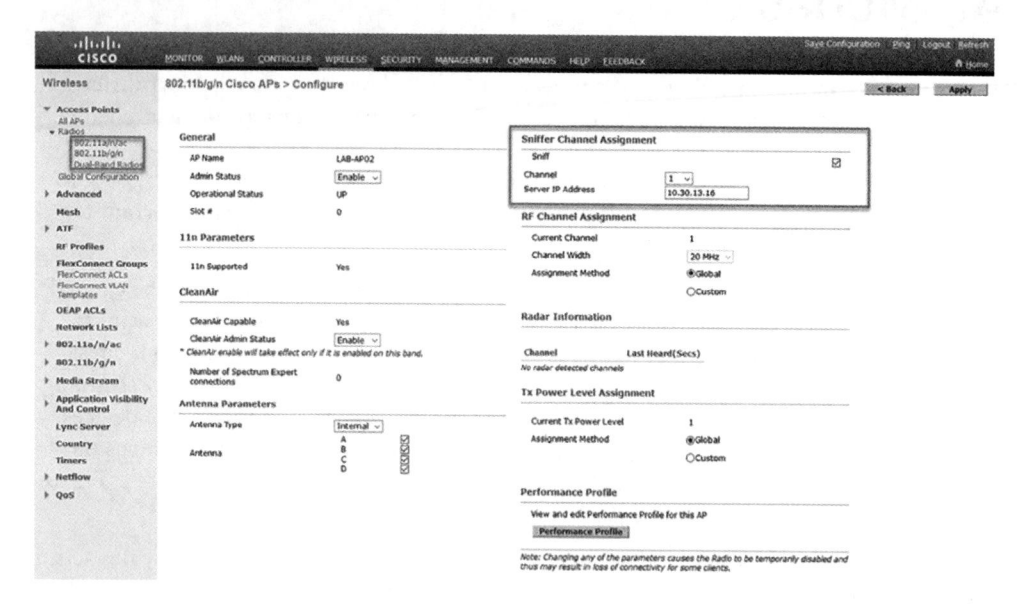

Rogue Detector This is another mode that doesn't send wireless traffic but dedicates itself to tracking access points that aren't joined to the WLC but are still possibly in your network. An example of this would be an employee bringing in a cheap wireless router from home and connecting it to his office ethernet port because he or she doesn't like all that security that IT uses. Trust me—it happens! Once the WLC detects a rogue AP, it can either notify you or try to contain the AP so it can't be used.

> Interfering with wireless connections can be against the law in some areas, so be sure to check with your company's legal team before implementing security features.

SE-Connect This mode lets you connect the AP to a spectrum analyzer to view the actual wireless spectrum. It's cool because it lets you figure out if there's any noise or interference affecting the channel and helps you find better channels for the wireless network to use instead. Cisco has a tool called Spectrum Expert that you can use to connect to APs in this mode, but it's pretty dated since the last update was in 2012! So it's best to go with other solutions like Metageek's Chanalyzer. And once again, this mode doesn't serve wireless traffic.

Figure 20.28 give you an example of Cisco Spectrum Expert that's connected to one of the APs in SE-Connect mode.

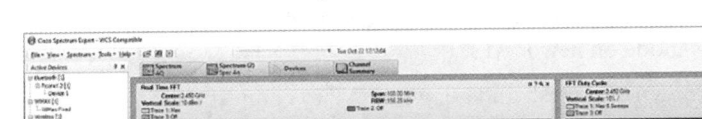

FIGURE 20.28 Cisco Spectrum Expert

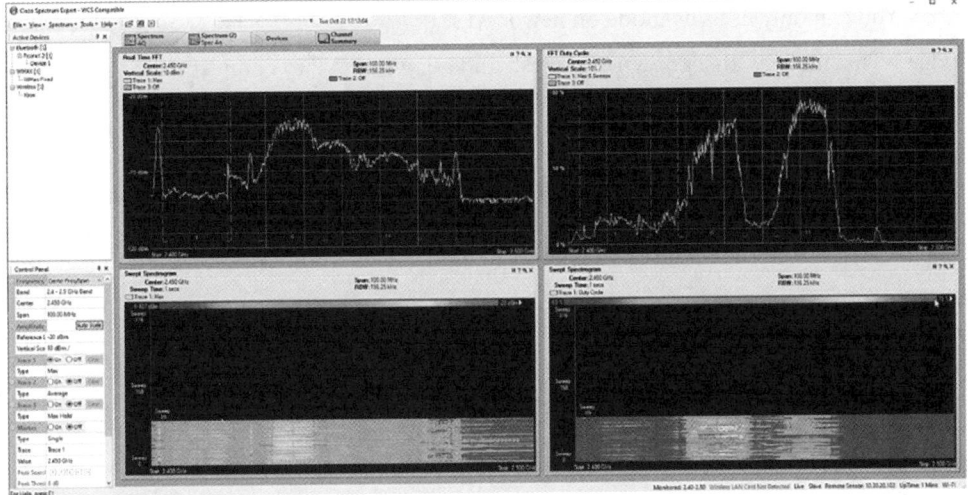

To compare, Figure 20.29 pictures an example of Metageek's Chanalyzer tool that's also connected to one of the APs in the same mode.

FIGURE 20.29 Metageek's Chanalyzer

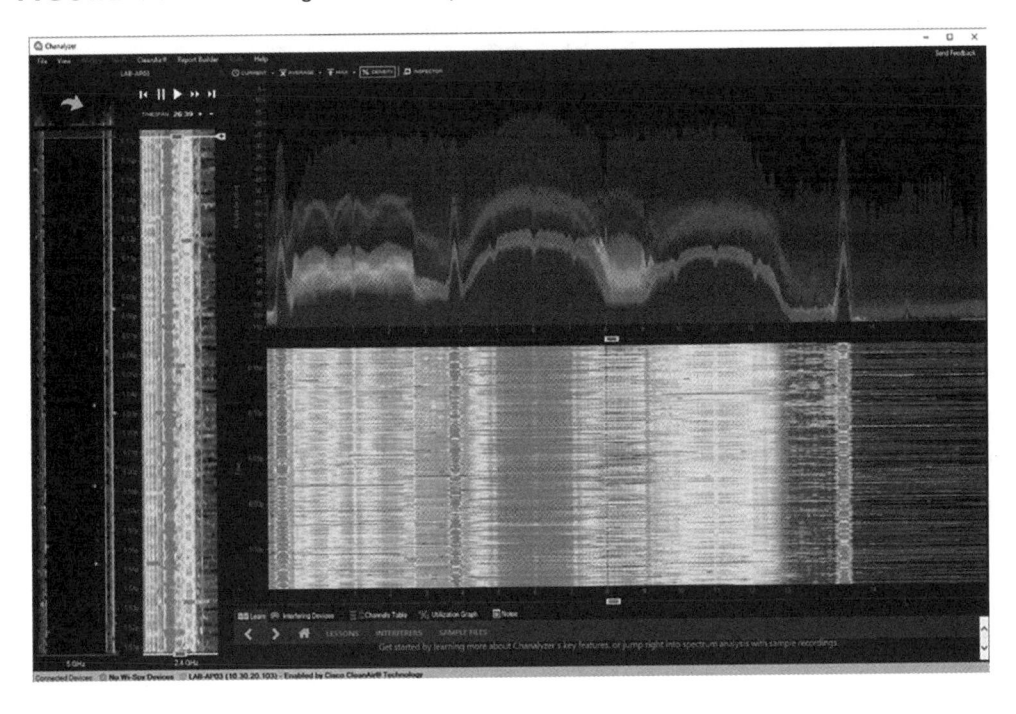

Sensor This is a newer mode that allows the AP to help out DNA Center's Assurance feature and increase the accuracy of its decisions. It's also a dedicated mode that doesn't serve traffic. You can only use this mode on newer APs.

Bridge This mode is also known as a mesh and allows an AP to connect to another AP to form a point-to-point or point-to-multipoint connection. This helps when connecting areas together wirelessly if you can't run a cable between the sites because of distance or terrain. The wireless mesh usually connects the site through ethernet to the switch but you can also allow wireless SSIDs through the mesh. The access point at the top of the mesh network is called the Root Access Point (RAP). When traffic reaches the RAP, it's sent to the controller through a CAPWAP tunnel just like with local mode. Figure 20.30 pictures a bridge layout.

FIGURE 20.30 Bridge mode

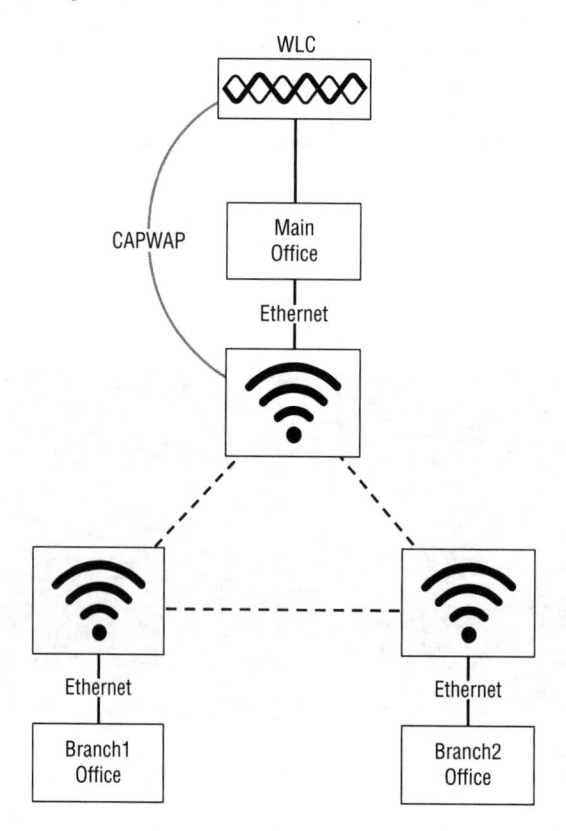

Flex+Bridge This mode adds FlexConnect to the mesh network In it, traffic is locally switched from the RAP when it reenters the network. It can also support ethernet and wireless connections. Figure 20.31 shows the kind of layout wherein Flex+Bridge would come in handy.

FIGURE 20.31 FlexConnect layout

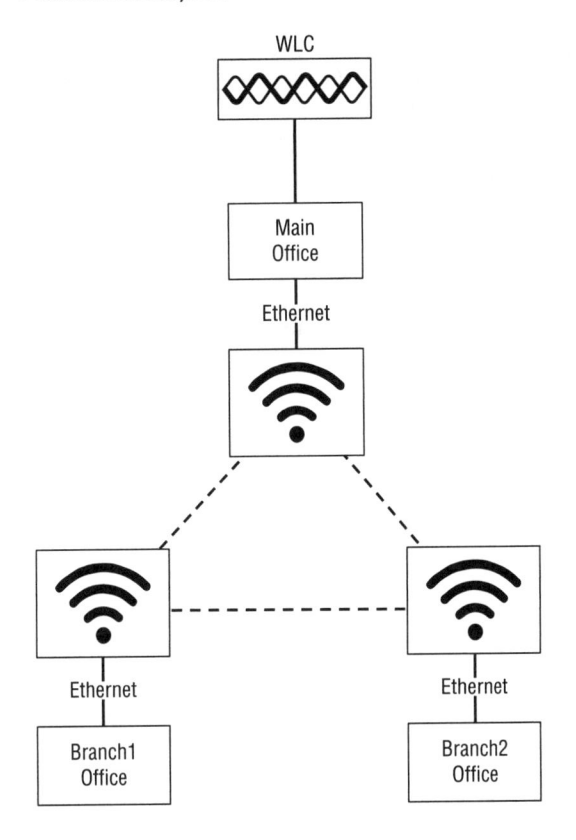

AP and WLC Management Access Connections

Okay—right now, we've got the WLC setup and some access points registered to it, so it's a great time to dive into the different kinds of management access connections available on the WLC and APs. Here's a list of the ones I'm going to cover with you:

- CDP
- Telnet
- SSH
- HTTP
- HTTPS
- Console
- RADIUS

CDP

Even though CDP doesn't technically provide management access, it's really useful if you're working on Cisco networks and need to figure out how the WLC and APs are connected to the Cisco switches.

Both the WLC and APs have CDP enabled by default, so you don't need to make any changes to make it work. But you can configure it by going to controller and then CDP to tweak the settings as seen in Figure 20.32.

FIGURE 20.32 WLC CDP configuration

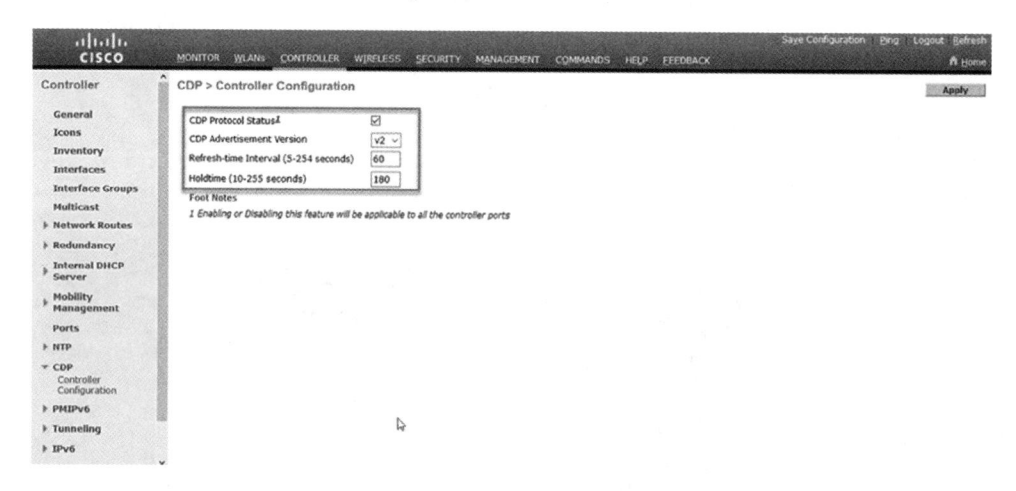

And as usual, you can use CLI to enable CDP if its disabled for some reason:

```
(WLC01) >config cdp enable
```

From the WLC you can check into CDP information from the Monitor page, then CDP Interface Neighbors, as shown in Figure 20.33.

FIGURE 20.33 WLC CDP verification

The command for this is the same one you use on a Cisco switch or router:

```
(WLC01) >show cdp neighbors
Capability Codes: R - Router, T - Trans Bridge, B - Source Route Bridge
        S - Switch, H - Host, I - IGMP, r - Repeater,
        M - Remotely Managed Device
Device ID              Local    Intrfce     Holdtme    Capability    Platform    Port ID
C3750X-SW01.testlab.com Gig 0/0/1           176        R S I         WS-C3750X   Gig 1/0/37
C3750X-SW01.testlab.com Gig 0/0/2           152        R S I         WS-C3750X   Gig 1/0/38
C3750X-SW01.testlab.com Gig 0/0/3           130        R S I         WS-C3750X   Gig 1/0/39
```

And again, just like on a switch or router, you can get more detail by clicking the neighbor on the page or by entering **show cdp neighbor detail**.

FIGURE 20.34 Show CDP neighbors

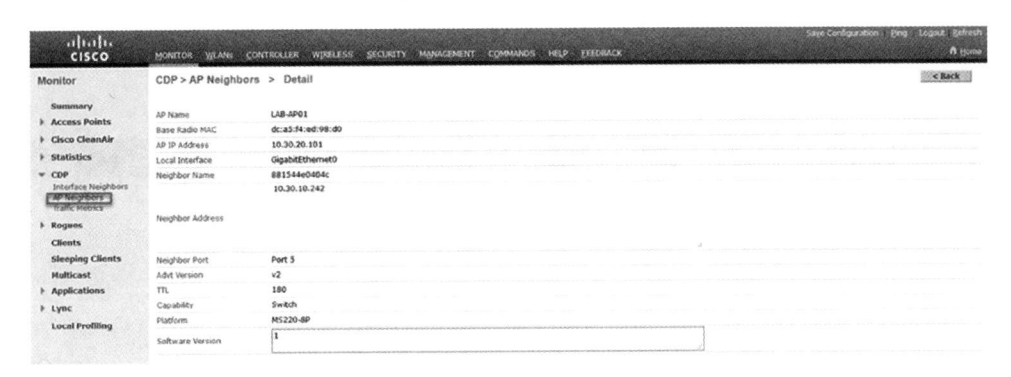

The command is also the same on Cisco APs:

```
LAB-AP03#show cdp neighbors
Capability Codes: R - Router, T - Trans Bridge, B - Source Route Bridge
        S - Switch, H - Host, I - IGMP, r - Repeater, P - Phone,
        D - Remote, C - CVTA, M - Two-port Mac Relay
Device ID              Local Intrfce    Holdtme    Capability   Platform    Port ID
C3750X-SW01.testlab.com Gig 0           148        R S I        WS-C3750X   Gig 1/0/1
```

To give you the whole picture, check out the output below. Notice that I can also see both the WLC and APs if I look at the CDP output on my switch. This makes it really easy to track down APs on your switches when you need to edit their switchports:

```
C3750X-SW01#show cdp nei
Capability Codes: R - Router, T - Trans Bridge, B - Source Route Bridge
        S - Switch, H - Host, I - IGMP, r - Repeater, P - Phone,
        D - Remote, C - CVTA, M - Two-port Mac Relay

Device ID           Local Intrfce      Holdtme     Capability   Platform    Port ID
```

```
WLC01                    Gig 1/0/37         128         H       AIR-CT550 Gig 0/0/1
WLC01                    Gig 1/0/38         128         H       AIR-CT550 Gig 0/0/2
WLC01                    Gig 1/0/39         128         H       AIR-CT550 Gig 0/0/3
LAB-AP03.testlab.com Gig 1/0/1              149         T B I   AIR-CAP37 Gig 0
LAB-AP02.testlab.com Gig 1/0/6              141         T B I   AIR-CAP36 Gig 0
LAB-AP01.testlab.com Gig 1/0/7              134         T B I   AIR-CAP36 Gig 0

Total cdp entries displayed : 11
```

Telnet

Using telnet for management is a bad idea these days since it's plaintext and the WLC turns it off by default! So most of the time, you want this setting off, disabling telnet.

But if you want to turn it on for your lab, you do that by going to the Management page, clicking Telnet-SSH on the menu and setting **Allow New Telnet Sessions** to **yes**.

Figure 20.35 shows you the WLC telnet configuration.

FIGURE 20.35 WLC telnet configuration

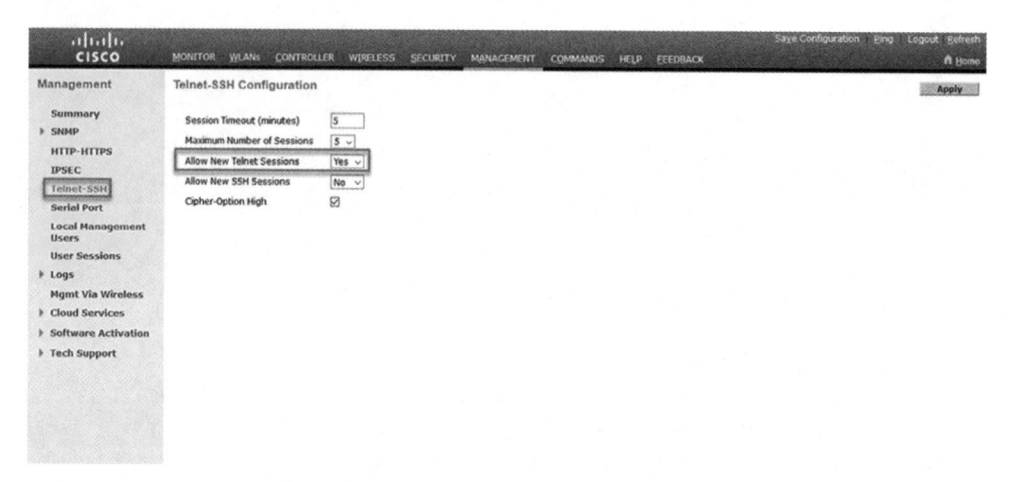

This can be configured through CLI with the following:

```
(WLC01) >config network telnet
enable          Enables this setting.
disable         Disables this setting.
(WLC01) >config network telnet enable
```

SSH

SSH is already turned on by default, so you shouldn't need to change anything to make it work. If you do want to make any changes to it, go to the same page as telnet, click the Telnet-SSH, and make sure **Allow New SSH Sessions** is set to yes as shown in Figure 20.36.

FIGURE 20.36 WLC SSH Configuration

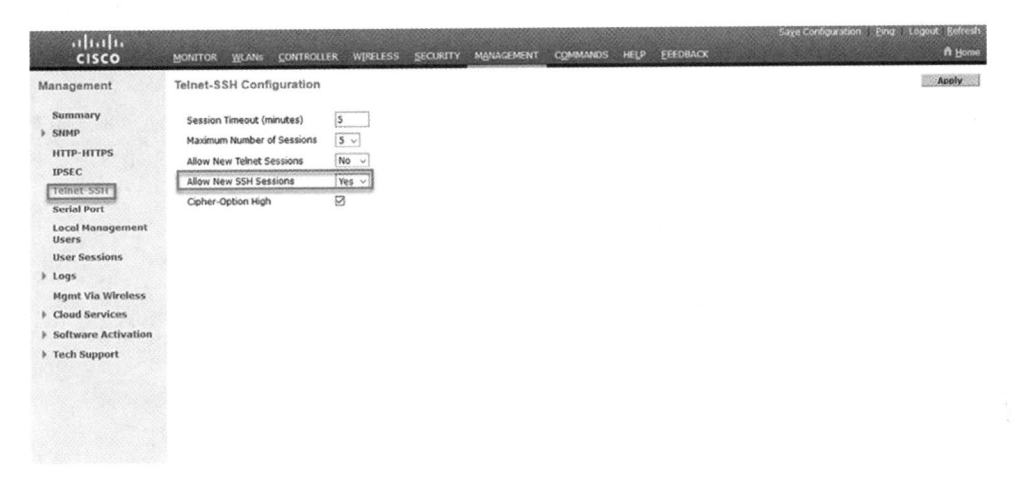

And of course you can configure SSH with CLI, but since you're probably connecting to the WLC CLI through SSH, think before you disable SSH:

```
(WLC01) >config network ssh
cipher-option   Configure cipher requirements for SSH.
delete          delete ssh public keys .
disable         Disallow new ssh sessions.
enable          Allow new ssh sessions.
host-key        Configure SSH access host key
(WLC01) >config network ssh enable
```

HTTP

HTTP is also disabled by default because it's plaintext and should really only be used in a lab setting. There's just not a great reason for using it at all. But just so you know, HTTP can be enabled or disabled by clicking HTTP-HTTPs on the Management page and confirming that **HTTP Access** is either enabled or disabled as pictured in Figure 20.37.

FIGURE 20.37 WLC HTTP configuration

Back on CLI, the command for this is a little less obvious than usual, because http access is called webmode here:

```
(WLC01) >config network webmode
enable          Enables this setting.
disable         Disables this setting.
```

HTTPS

HTTPS is your shining star—it's the main way to configure the WLC. You can also choose to enable HTTPS redirection so that if you accidentally use HTTP to access the WLC, it will automatically switch you over to HTTPS—nice! You can configure HTTPS on the same page as HTTP above, pictured in Figure 20.38.

FIGURE 20.38 WLC HTTPS configuration

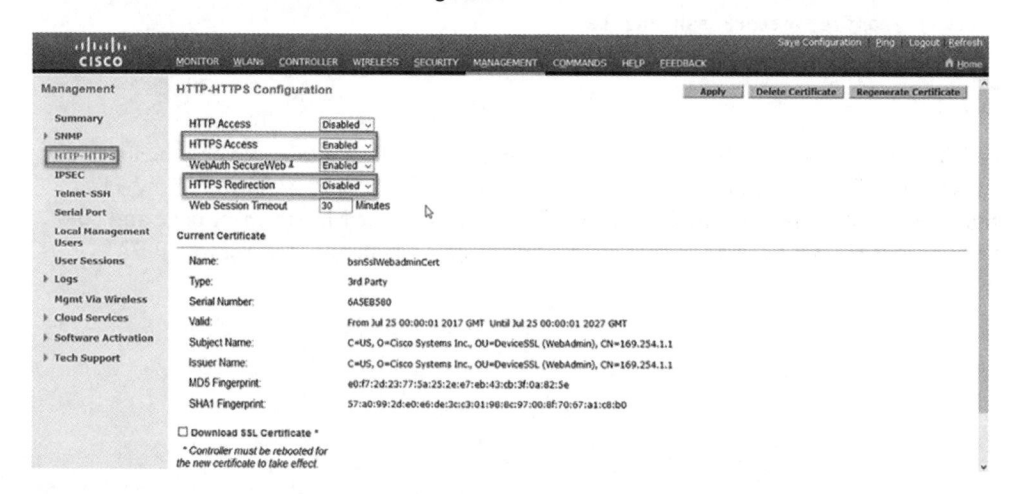

And here again, the command line uses a different keyword than you'd think; for HTTPS it is secureweb:

```
(WLC01) >config network secureweb
cipher-option   Configure cipher requirements for web admin and web auth.
csrfcheck       Enable or disable Cross-Site Request Forgery for web mode.
disable         Disable the Secure Web (HTTPS) management interface.
enable          Enable the Secure Web (HTTPS) management interface.
ocsp            Configure OCSP requirements for web admin in format http://<ip>/path
sslv3           Configure SSLv3 for web admin and web auth
(WLC01) >config network secureweb enable
```

Console

When the WLC is fresh out of the box, we use the console port to configure it. After that, it's mainly used for troubleshooting as we discussed earlier in this chapter.

RADIUS

Wireless commonly uses RADIUS servers to help secure wireless connections when using 802.1X for the SSID's security. The WLC supports up to 32 RADIUS servers, and each SSID lets us specify six RADIUS servers. This is cool because it gives us some good flexibility since we can opt for using some RADIUS servers on one SSID and different ones with another.

AAA has three components: Authentication, Authorization, and Accounting. So there's a little work for us to do configuring the Authentication section as well as the Accounting section before will work for us at all! It's nice that Cisco at least gives us a break and doesn't make us configure an Authorization section too because it just mirrors the Authentication configuration.

So let's get started—to configure RADIUS, click the Security page and then under AAA, find RADIUS and then Authentication. Once there, click **new** to start adding a new server to the WLC.

We're going to configure two RADIUS authentication servers for this chapter, and the main fields you need to really know about are:

Server Index   This is the priority of the RADIUS server. It controls the order of where the server appears in the selection list. The Server Index must be unique, so after I pick 1 for the value, the next server will need to be 2.

Server Address   This is just the IP address of the RADUS server and can be either IPv4 or IPv6. WLC does support DNS names, but it's a bit over the top for the CCNA.

Shared Secret Format   This controls which format the Shared Secret will be in—either ASCII text or hex.

Shared Secret   The password that's used between the RADIUS server and the client.

Port Number This is actually a default field, but it is good to know that RADIUS will use 1812 for all modern connections. Some legacy RADIUS configurations might use port UDP 1645 because it's the legacy RADIUS authentication number.

Support for CoA CoA stands for Change of Authorization—optional for the CCNA. It allows an 802.1X server like a Cisco Identity Service Engine (ISE) to change a RADIUS session's authorization result.

The rest of the fields can be left as default at the CCNA level.

So now I'm going add two RADIUS servers. The first one will be priority 1 and will use a server IP of 10.20.11.32, as shown in Figure 20.39.

FIGURE 20.39 WLC RADIUS configuration

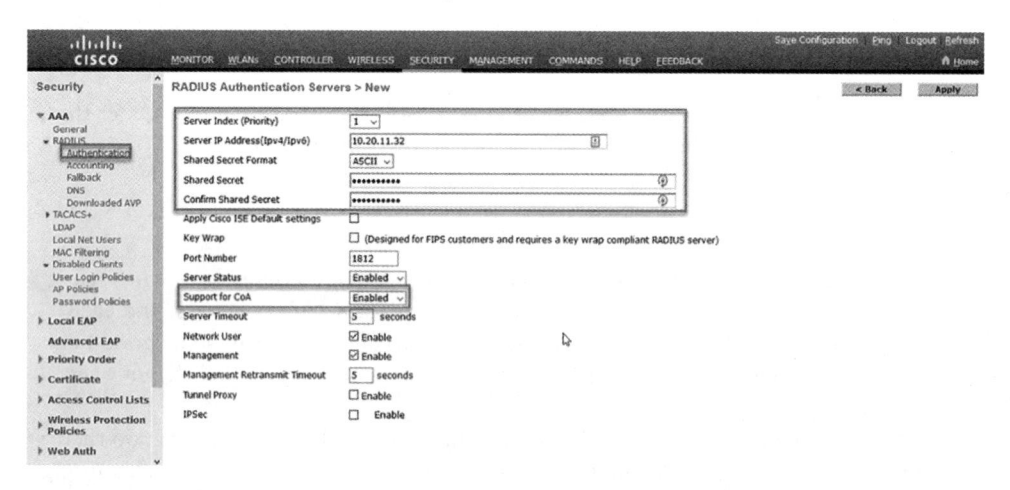

The next server is going to use a priority of 2 and have a server IP of 10.20.12.32 as I configured in Figure 20.40.

FIGURE 20.40 WLC second RADIUS configuration

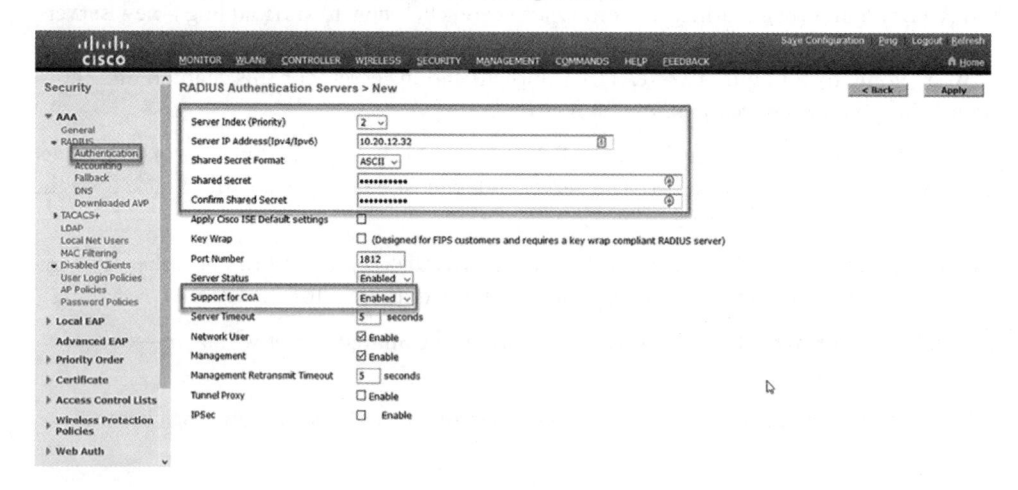

And now that I've added the servers, we can see a summary of what was configured on the Authentication page, pictured in Figure 20.41.

FIGURE 20.41 Radius configuration summary

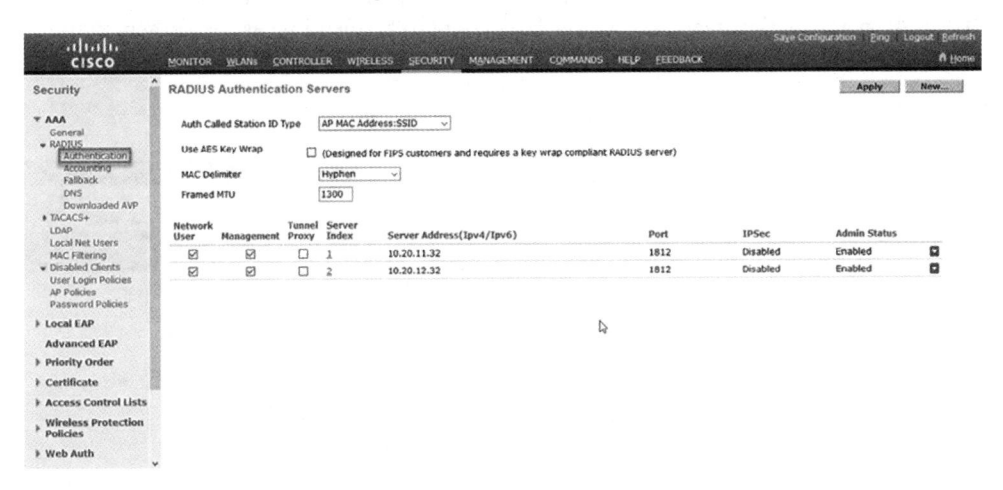

The CLI to configure the RADIUS authentication servers looks like this:

```
(WLC01) >config radius auth add 1
<IP addr>      Enter RADIUS Server IP (ipv4 or ipv6) Address.
(WLC01) >config radius auth add 1 10.20.11.32
<port>         Configures a RADIUS Server's UDP port.
(WLC01) >config radius auth add 1 10.20.11.32 1812
[ascii/hex]    The type of RADIUS Server's secret is ascii or hex.
(WLC01) >config radius auth add 1 10.20.11.32 1812 meowcatAAA
<secret>       Enter the RADIUS Server's secret.
(WLC01) >config radius auth add 1 10.20.11.32 1812 ascii
<secret>       Enter the RADIUS Server's secret.
(WLC01) >config radius auth add 1 10.20.11.32 1812 ascii meowcatAAA
(WLC01) >config radius auth add 2 10.20.12.32 1812 ascii meowcatAAA
```

Okay great—the RADIUS authentication is set up, so now we've got to go to the RADIUS accounting side of things and configure that. This is really vital because it allows the RADIUS server to track session details so that it knows who did what and when they did it!

So to configure this, click Accounting under the RADIUS section, then click **New** to get the configuration page as shown in Figure 20.42.

As we did did, I'm going to configure two RADIUS accounting servers. The only real difference is that accounting uses UDP 1813 by default, but in legacy configs, you could see UDP 1646 being used instead. The server IP is going to be the same as the authentication servers. Check out Figure 20.42.

FIGURE 20.42 WLC RADIUS accounting configuration

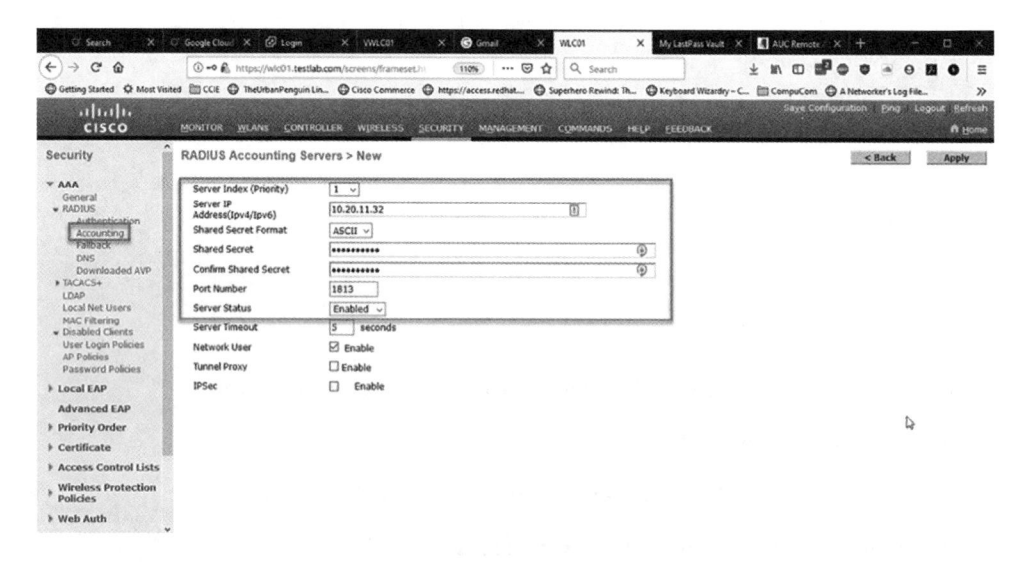

So here again, we can see the summary by looking at the Accounting page shown in Figure 20.43.

FIGURE 20.43 WLC RADIUS accounting summary

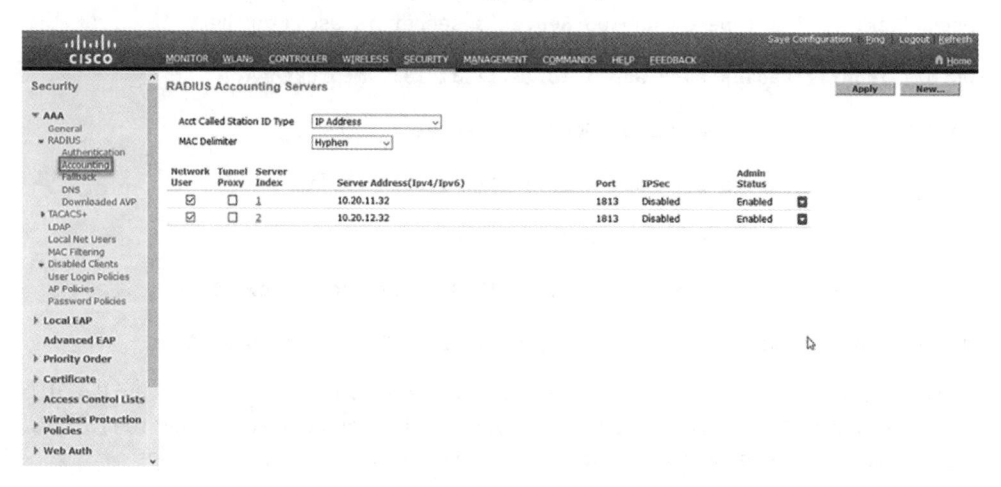

The CLI is a lot like the authentication config except it uses the **acct** keyboard:

```
(WLC01) >config radius acct add 1 10.20.11.32 1813 ascii meowcatAAA
(WLC01) >config radius acct add 2 10.20.12.32 1813 ascii meowcatAAA
```

TACACS+

Know that TACACS+ is actually better suited for device administration rather than authenticating wireless users. Because of this, the WLC supports TACACS+ for management users but not for use in WLANs. The WLC supports up to three servers, and we've got to configure authentication and authorization separately.

To create a TACACS+ authentication server, click authentication under TACACS in the AAA section, and then click **New as** demonstrated in Figure 20.44.

FIGURE 20.44 WLC TACACS+ configuration

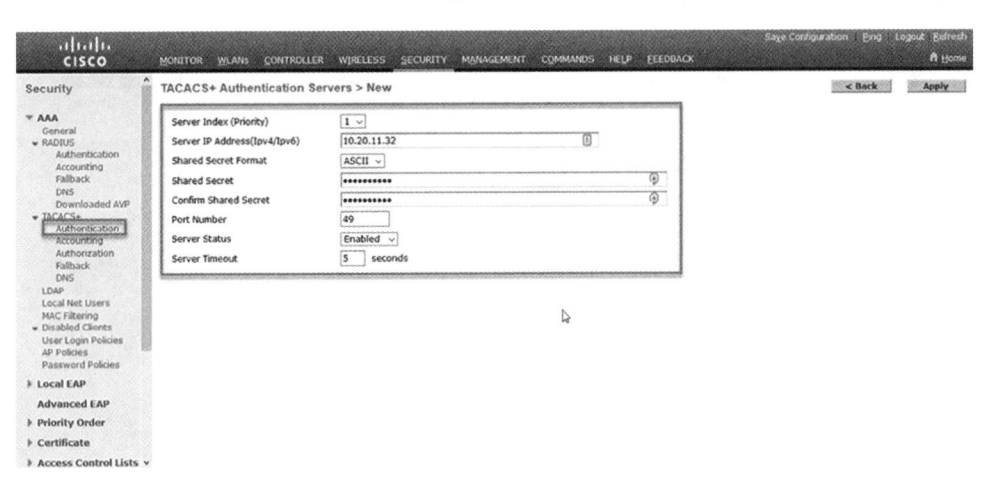

I mentioned all the fields you can configure on the new server page, but know that there are fewer options available compared to RADIUS. It's important to remember that TACACS+ uses TCP 49 for its port number.

Since I'm using Cisco ISE and it supports both RADIUS and TACACS+, let's configure TACACS+ now using the same IPs we used for the RADIUS configuration: 10.20.11.32 and 10.20.12.32.

The CLI is the same as RADIUS config, except it uses the **tacacs** keyword:

```
(WLC01) >config tacacs auth add

<1-3>        Enter the TACACS+ Server index.

(WLC01) >config tacacs auth add 1

<IP addr>    Enter TACACS+ Server IP (v4 or v6) Address.
```

```
(WLC01) >config tacacs auth add 1 10.20.11.32

<port>         Configures a TACACS+ Server's TCP port.

(WLC01) >config tacacs auth add 1 10.20.11.32 49

[ascii/hex]    The type of TACACS+ Server's secret is ascii or hex.

(WLC01) >config tacacs auth add 1 10.20.11.32 49 ascii

<secret>       Enter the TACACS+ Server's secret.

(WLC01) >config tacacs auth add 1 10.20.11.32 49 ascii meowcatAAA
```

And just like with RADIUS we can view a summary by looking at the TACACS+ authentication page shown in Figure 20.45.

FIGURE 20.45 WLC TACACS+ summary

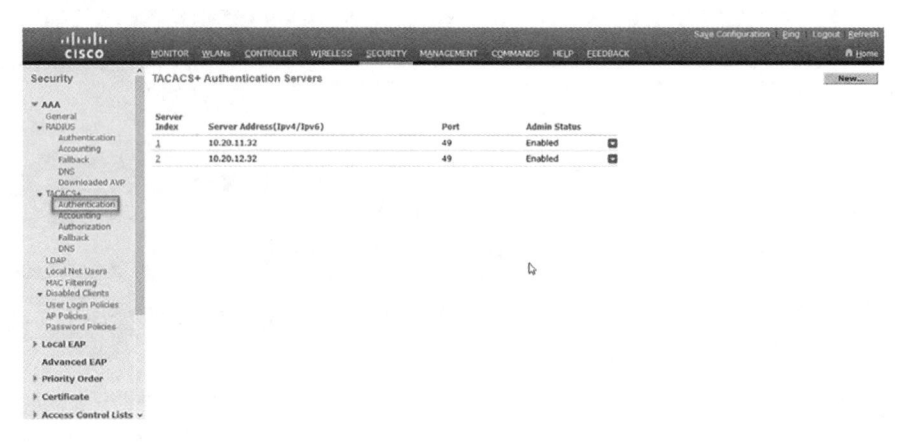

Last up, we need to configure the accounting servers and I'll use the same IPs as above. One thing to note is that TACACS+ uses TCP 49 for all operations as shown in Figure 20.46.

FIGURE 20.46 WLC TACACS+ accounting configuration

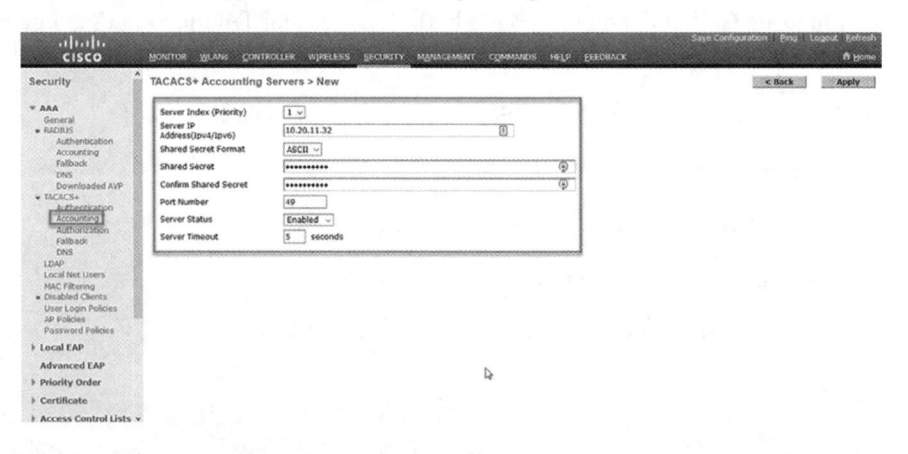

The CLI is the same except it uses the **acct** keyword:

(WLC01) >**config tacacs acct add**

<1-3>   Enter the TACACS+ Server index.

(WLC01) >**config tacacs acct add 1**

<IP addr>   Enter TACACS+ Server IP (v4 or v6) Address.

(WLC01) >**config tacacs acct add 1 10.20.11.32**

<port>   Configures a TACACS+ Server's TCP port.

(WLC01) >**config tacacs acct add 1 10.20.11.32 49**

[ascii/hex]   The type of TACACS+ Server's secret is ascii or hex.

(WLC01) >**config tacacs acct add 1 10.20.11.32 49 ascii**

<secret>   Enter the TACACS+ Server's secret.

(WLC01) >**config tacacs acct add 1 10.20.11.32 49 ascii meowcatAAA**

And of course we can verify our changes by looking at the Accounting page as demonstrated in Figure 20.47.

FIGURE 20.47 WLC TACACS+ accounting summary

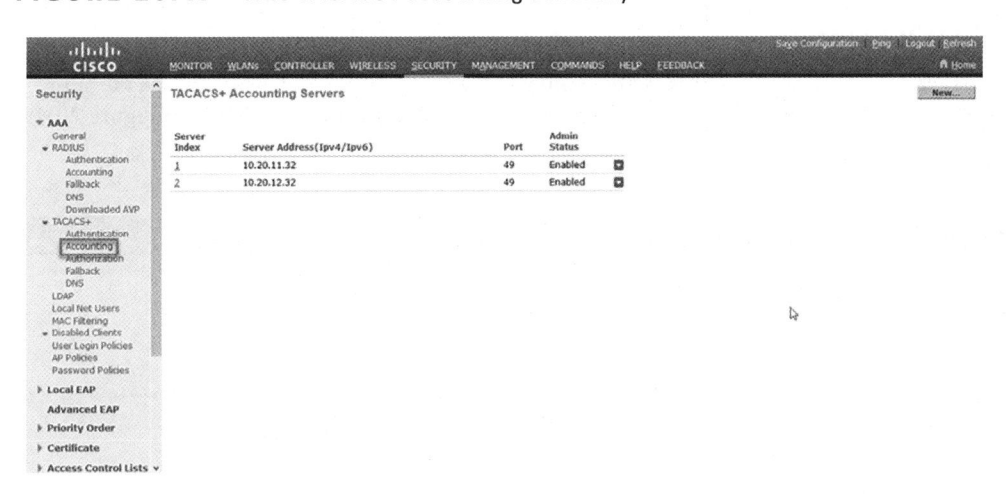

To use TACACS+ for WLC management user authentications, on the Security page, click Management User under Priority Order. Then move TACACS+ from **Not Used** to **Order Used for Authentication, and** then adjust the order.

Note: If you move LOCAL from the top of the order so that RADIUS or TACACS+ is first, LOCAL will only be used if all the remote servers are deemed unavailable. So if you have a configuration issue on the server that prevents you from logging in, you'll definitely need to resolve it before you can log in to the WLC!

Figure 20.48 pictures the authentication order that I configured.

FIGURE 20.48 WLC authentication order

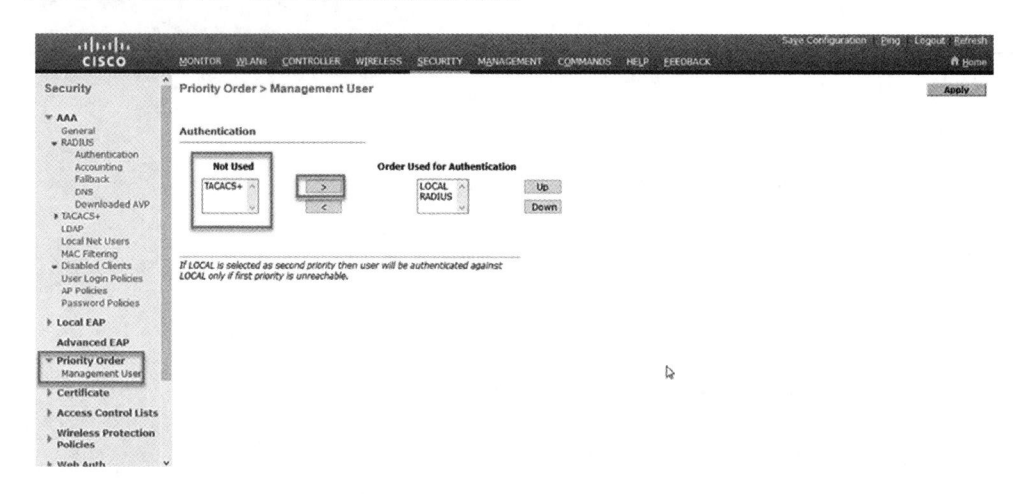

Configuring WLANs

Phew! Okay—it's finally time to create a Wireless LAN (WLAN) that we can actually connect a host to!

WLAN creation

To create a WLAN, we're predictably going to head over to the WLAN page. Make sure **Create New** is on the top right of the screen and then click on **Go** as shown in Figure 20.49.

FIGURE 20.49 WLC WLAN creation

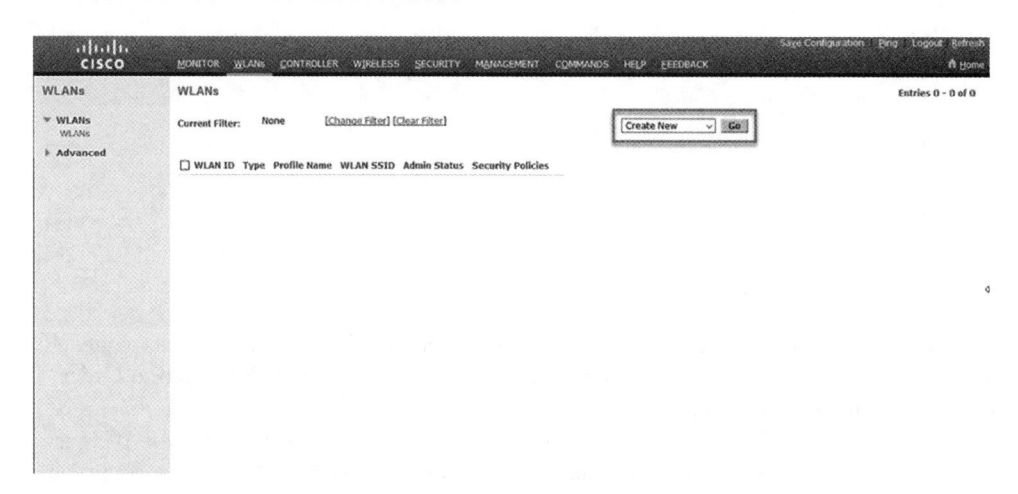

Here on the New WLAN page, we're going to give the WLAN some information. Here are the options:

Type   This controls the type of the wireless network we're creating—it will always be WLAN at the CCNA level.

Profile Name   This is just a friendly name for our WLAN, and it can be whatever you want.

SSID   This is the name of the actual SSID used by the WLAN and most of the time, people just set to this to be the same as the profile name. Again, you can pick any SSID name you want.

ID   Every WLAN needs a unique ID that's between 1 and 512. Typically, you would leave this at the default unless you need it to a certain value.

Figure 20.50 shows the WLAN configuration.

FIGURE 20.50   WLC WLAN configuration

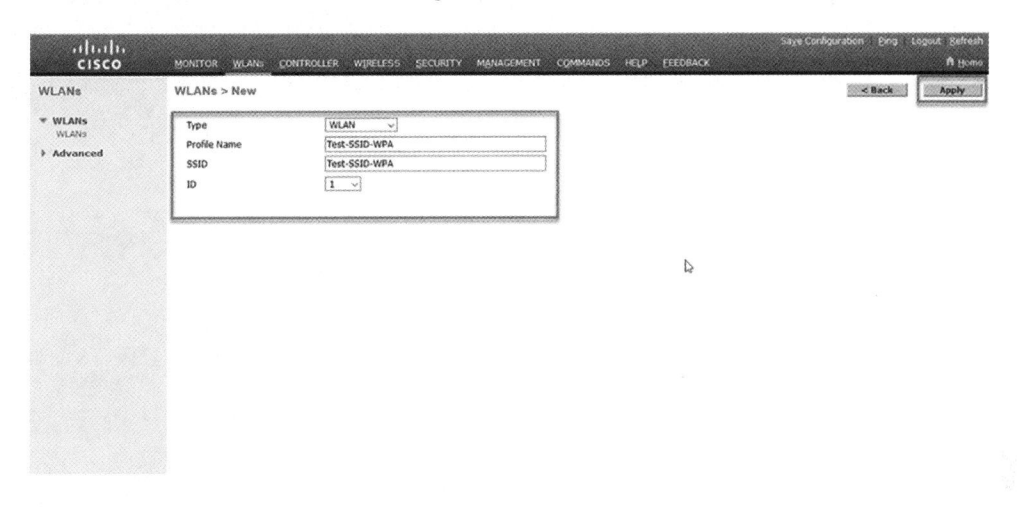

```
(WLC01) >config wlan create

<WLAN id>        Enter WLAN Identifier between 1 and 512.

(WLC01) >config wlan create 1

<name>           Enter Profile Name up to 32 alphanumeric characters.

(WLC01) >config wlan create 1 test-wlan-wpa

<ssid>           Enter SSID (Network Name) up to 32 alphanumeric characters.

(WLC01) >config wlan create 1 test-wlan-wpa test-wlan-wpa

General settings
```

So the general settings tab is where the more administrative features of the WLAN are configured. In addition to letting us change the profile and SSID name, we've got some other options open to us here too:

Status   This is like the **shutdown** command on a Cisco router—you can turn the WLAN on or off if you need to.

Interface/InterfaceGroup   This option binds the WLAN to a WLC interface or interface group. It allows you to control which VLANs the client IP will be in when they connect.

Broadcast SSID   This option controls whether the SSID is visible to everyone's wireless devices or not. It's more common to broadcast most SSIDs, but not to broadcast 802.1X wireless connections since they're usually pushed to the work laptop through Group Policy.

Figure 20.51 shows the General Tab on the WLC WLAN page.

FIGURE 20.51   WLC WLAN General tab

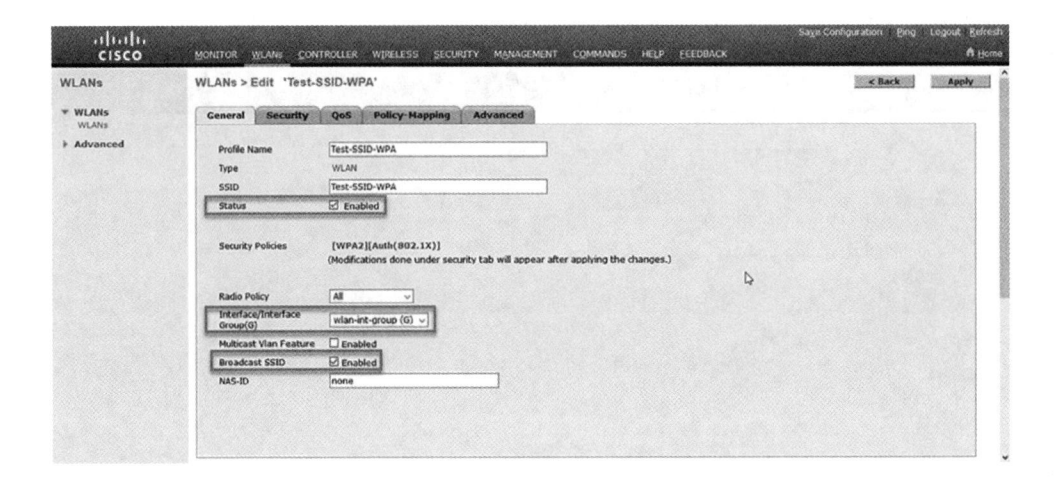

This time, CLI is a bit different from what you've been seeing. We'll use the keyword for the feature we want to configure and then reference the WLAN ID number to apply it to the right WLAN:

(WLC01) >`config wlan broadcast-ssid enable 1`

(WLC01) >`config wlan interface 1 wlan-int-group`

(WLC01) >`config wlan enable 1`

Security Settings – Layer 2

The Security tab is just what it sounds like—it controls the WLAN's security settings and yes, there are a lot of them! Fortunately for you, the CCNA is only interested in a few of the options. The WLAN will default to supporting WPA2 connections, so you don't need to make any changes to the Layer 2 Security type. The main options you've got to adjust are under the Authentication Key Management section:

802.1X This allows you to use something like a Cisco ISE server to control the WLAN connections, but you won't be using this in the CCNA. But you do need to make sure it's turned off for PSK to work!

PSK This option tells the WLAN to use a Pre-Shared Key to authenticate wireless clients.

PSK Format You can enter a pre-shared key in either ASCII format or in hex. The PSK has to be at least eight characters in length, as you can see in Figure 20.52.

FIGURE 20.52 WLC WLAN Security tab

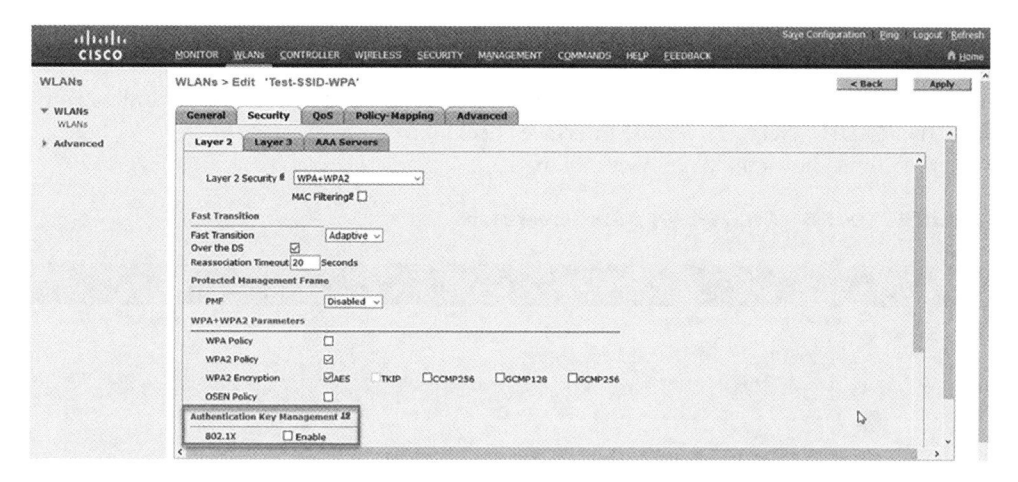

Figure 20.53 shows the PSK configuration.

FIGURE 20.53 WLC WLAN PSK configuration

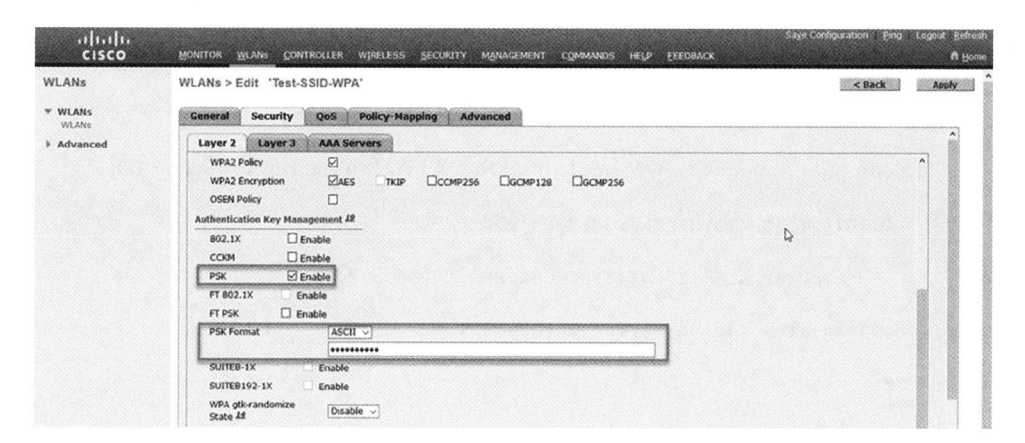

And you handle PSK configuration with the following commands:

(WLC01) >`config wlan security wpa akm psk enable 1`

(WLC01) >`config wlan security wpa akm psk set-key ascii meowcatPSK 1`

Security Settings – AAA Servers

Now if you want to use WPA2-Enterprise, the WLAN has to talk to some RADIUS servers and you can use the AAA Server subtab under Security to set that up. Since our WLAN is using a Pre-Share Key, it doesn't need AAA configuration for it to work, so I'll create a sample new WLAN to show you how to do that.

On this page, choose the RADIUS authentication and accounting servers we just created and put them in the proper order. Server 1 is used before Server 2 and so on. Remember, the WLAN can support up to 6 servers.

The WLC will use the management interface to contact the RADIUS server unless you check the **RADIUS Server Override Interface** checkbox.

Figure 20.54 shows the AAA Servers tab.

FIGURE 20.54 WLC WLAN AAA Servers tab

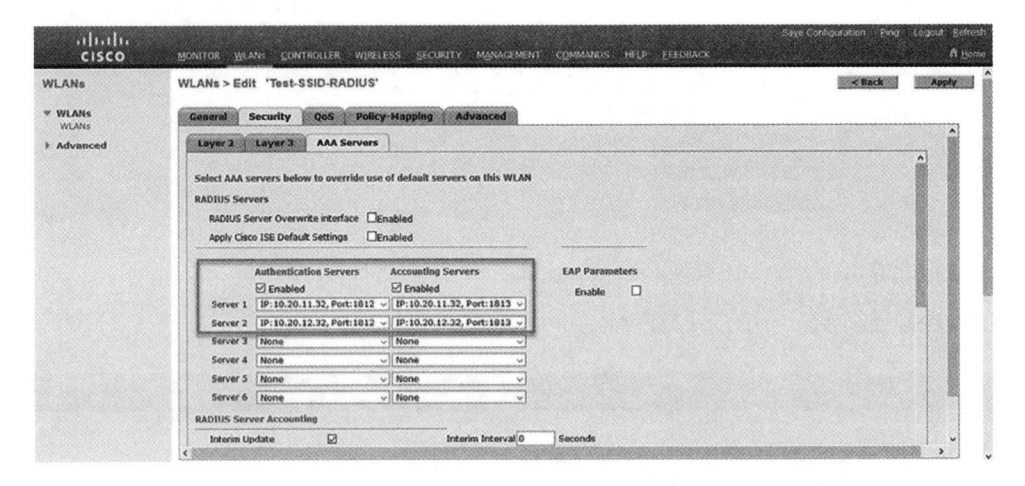

And to configure this in CLI we simply bind the WLAN to the Radius Server ID:

(WLC01) >`config wlan radius_server auth add`

<WLAN id>   Enter WLAN Identifier between 1 and 512.

(WLC01) >`config wlan radius_server auth add 1`

<Server id>   Enter the RADIUS Server Index.

(WLC01) >`config wlan radius_server auth add 1 1`

```
(WLC01) >config wlan radius_server auth add 1 2

(WLC01) >config wlan radius_server acct add 1 1

(WLC01) >config wlan radius_server acct add 1 2
```

QoS Profiles

Wireless supports Quality of Service to help prioritize important wireless traffic like wireless phones. By default, it'll use the Best Effort queue. This basically means there's no QoS policy, but you can create one either manually or via DNA Center if it's doing EasyQoS. I'll talk about this more in a later chapter.

There are four queues available for the WLC:

Bronze   This provides the lowest level of bandwidth for things like guest services or unimportant traffic. It's also known as the background queue.

Silver   This provides the normal level of bandwidth for clients and is the best-effort queue.

Gold   This provides support for high-bandwidth video applications and is also known as the video queue.

Platinum   This is the highest quality of service meant for voice over wireless connections, also known as the voice queue.

The QoS tab also supports manually adjusting the bandwidth, WMM, Call Admission Control and Lync support, which is Microsoft's Unified Communications solution commonly known as Skype for Business.

Figure 20.55 pictures the QoS tab.

FIGURE 20.55   WLC WLAN QoS tab

Policy Mapping Settings

We're going to skip over the Policy Mapping tab since it doesn't apply to at the CCNA and there isn't much to look at right now. Basically, it allows you to treat different endpoints types differently so an iPad can act differently from an Android phone.

Advanced WLAN settings

Like the name implies, the advanced tab is a collection of various advanced settings that can apply to the WLAN.

Figure 20.56 pictures the Advanced tab.

FIGURE 20.56 WLC WLAN Advanced tab

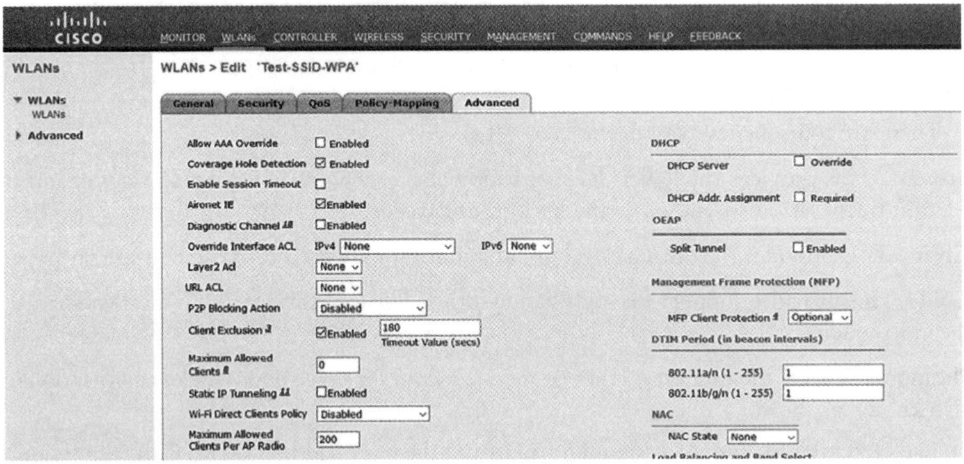

Almost all of these are beyond what you need to know for the CCNA exam, but they're interesting and important in real life. They're shown in Figure 20.56:

Allow AAA Override   This is used in connections that talk to RADIUS servers. It allows the server to tell WLC the right VLAN tagging to use for connection. It can also set the QoS settings and apply ACLs to the session.

Enable Session Timeout   This refers to the amount of time a session can be active without having to reauthenticate. When using a Pre-share key connection, it's disabled by default since the client already gave the key for the connection to work in the first place. But if using other layer 2 security options, the default is 1800 seconds or 30 min before the user needs to authenticate again.

DHCP Addr. Assignment   This option prevents clients from using static IPs. When turned on, the client must receive a DHCP offer through the wireless connection to get online. This little arrangement really helps improve security if you happen to have end users who are trying to outsmart your security policies!

DHCP/HTTP Profiling   The WLC can try to figure what endpoints are connected to the WLAN and it does this by examining the DHCP process and watching HTTP packets to identify the connection.

Connecting the Client

Okay, now that our WLAN has been created, I can finally connect to the wireless network with my laptop! Since it is a WPA2-PSK connection, I just need to enter the pre-share key to log onto the network.

Figure 20.57 shows a client connected to the WLAN.

FIGURE 20.57 Connect a client to the WLAN

Because the WLAN is using an interface group for its IP assignment, I'm getting an IP address from the WLAN102 dynamic interface. If I connect my iPhone, I might get an IP from the WLAN103 dynamic interface since the WLC will try to load balance the client traffic across all the interfaces in the interface group.

Figure 20.58 shows a client configuration.

FIGURE 20.58 WLAN client configuration

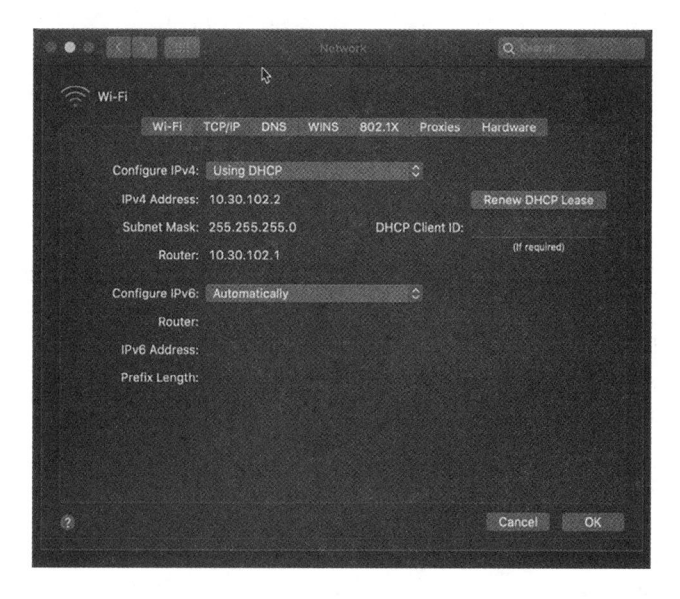

Chapter 20 ▪ Configuring Wireless Technologies

On the WLC, we can see a lot of client session details, including a network diagram that shows the CAPWAP tunnel being used by the connection and the connectivity state.

Figure 20.59 illustrates the verification of a connected client.

FIGURE 20.59 WLAN client verification

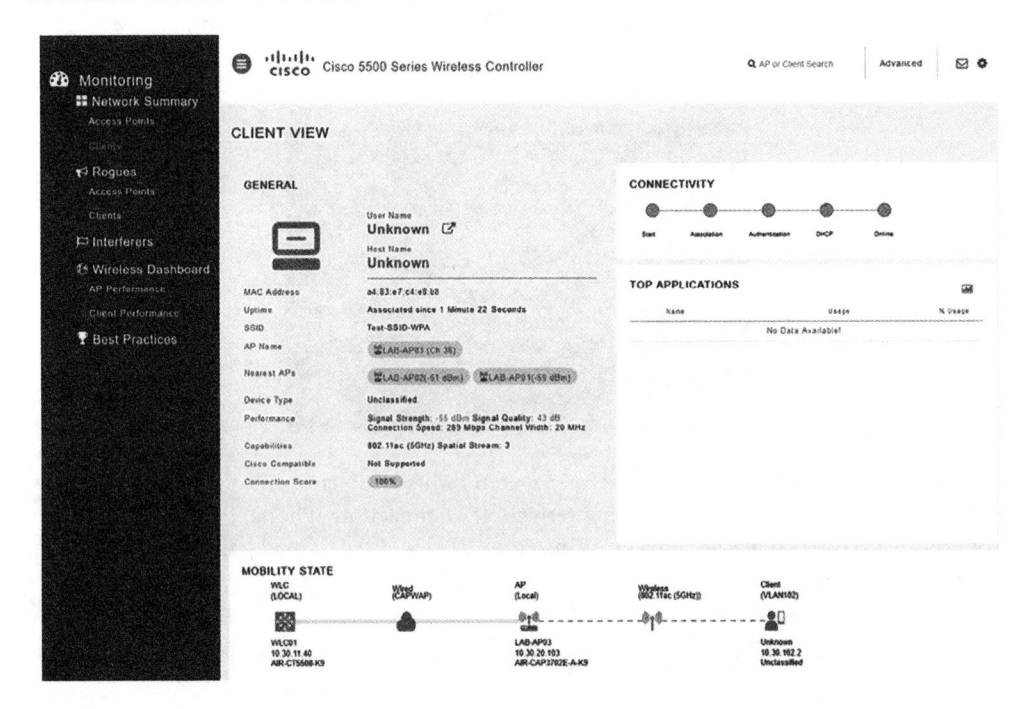

The CLI can also give us a ton of information about the client:

```
(WLC01) >show client detail a4:83:e7:c4:e8:b8
Client MAC Address............................... a4:83:e7:c4:e8:b8
Client Username ................................. N/A
Hostname: .......................................
Device Type: .................................... Unclassified
AP MAC Address................................... 7c:95:f3:31:68:00
AP Name.......................................... LAB-AP02
AP radio slot Id................................. 1
Client State..................................... Associated
Client User Group................................
Client NAC OOB State............................. Access
Wireless LAN Id.................................. 1
Wireless LAN Network Name (SSID)................. Test-SSID-WPA
Wireless LAN Profile Name........................ Test-SSID-WPA
Hotspot (802.11u)................................ Not Supported
```

```
BSSID............................................. 7c:95:f3:31:68:0f
Connected For ................................ 476 secs
Channel........................................... 52
IP Address....................................... 10.30.102.2
Gateway Address............................. 10.30.102.1
Netmask.......................................... 255.255.255.0
IPv6 Address................................... fe80::1073:3a59:a857:4647
Association Id................................. 1
Authentication Algorithm.................. Open System
Reason Code.................................... 1
Status Code..................................... 0
Session Timeout............................... 0
Client CCX version............................ No CCX support
```
Output Omitted for brevity

Summary

Wow we covered a lot of things in this chapter! I started with the various endpoints that you'd commonly see on the network and also went into how to verify and change your IP address on desktop operating systems. Then I talked about the various types of Wireless controllers that Cisco offers and then described some of the deployment models that wireless can use.

From there I took a minute to describe what a CAPWAP tunnel is and how it's used before detailing all the interfaces and ports that can be found on the WLC.

Since wireless controllers aren't very useful without any access points, I then described a few methods for joining APs to the WLC. Once that was done, we moved into talking about the different management access connections that can be used on the WLC before finally showing you how to configure a working WLAN!

Exam Essentials

Endpoints   Endpoints are just the things we connect into the network, including desktops, laptops, IP phones, access points, and IoT devices.

Server   Servers provide services to the users and devices on your network. There are several forms of these available:

Flat servers, which are typically 1 RU sized rack mounted servers and tower servers that are basically just desktops with more resources inside. And then there are blade servers that connect to a big chassis. There are also many types of server roles available including DHCP, Web, Database, and Active Directory.

Verify IP address on Windows, Mac, and Linux   You can spend the better part of your day-to-day activities either setting IP addresses on interfaces or verifying settings are correct on a device. Because of that, and also because of exam topics, I walked you through how to check the IP on Windows, Macs, and Linux desktops.

WLAN Deployment Models   Cisco uses three types of WLAN deployment models. Standalone, where the access point acts independently and must be manually configured and lightweight, where the access point registers to a controller via an encrypted CAPWAP tunnel that allows for central management and easier performance tuning. The last model we discussed is the cloud method, where the controller lives in the cloud and APs simply need to get online to be managed. Meraki is Cisco's cloud-based networking solution.

WLC Port Types   The WLC has several port types such as console ports for initial configuration: service ports for out of band management, a redundancy port to allow for high availability and distributed system ports, which is just a fancy name for regular interfaces.

WLC Interface Types   The WLC also has several interface types that provide services to the WLANs and other features. The service port interface provides access to the service port and the redundancy management port provides access to the redundancy port. The management port is used provide access to WLC. It runs the AP-Manager by default, which allows APs to register to the interface and terminates CAPWAP tunnels. Lastly, dynamic interfaces can be used to terminate WLANs to specific VLANs.

WLC and AP Management Access Connections   Cisco Wireless controllers and access points support several methods for providing management access including telnet: SSH, HTTP, HTTPS, a console port, RADIUS, and TACACS+. CDP is also very useful for managing these systems.

Joining APs   Wireless controllers require APs in order to provide network access. There are three methods for joining APs that we covered in the chapter: The manual method, where you log into the AP and type some commands, and the DNS method where you make a DNS A record to allow the AP to find the wireless controller on its own. Finally, there's also the DHCP method where we use our hex skills to provide the WLC address through option 43.

Configuring WLANs   A large part of the WLC configuration is creating the WLANs that clients can connect to. There are several parts to this including the SSID, security method, and myriad other options we can choose to enable when creating a wireless network.

Review Questions

You can find the answers in the Appendix.

1. What command is used to check the IP address on Windows 10 using CMD?
   - **A.** ifconfig
   - **B.** ipconfig
   - **C.** iwconfig
   - **D.** Get-NetIpAddress
   - **E.** iptables

2. What's required to use the Service Port on a WLC? (Choose three.)
   - **A.** The service port interface must be connected to a switch.
   - **B.** The switchport must be configured to be a trunk
   - **C.** You must add static routes to the WLC.
   - **D.** The switchport must be configured to an access port.
   - **E.** The service port interface must be configured with a subnet IP in the same subnet as the management port.

3. What DNS record do you need to create for APs to automatically discover the WLC?
   - **A.** CISCO-WLC-CONTROLLER
   - **B.** WLC-CONTROLLER
   - **C.** CISCO-AP-CONTROLLER
   - **D.** CISCO-DISCOVER-CONTROLLER
   - **E.** CISCO-CAPWAP-CONTROLLER

4. What's the default QoS queue for a WLAN?
   - **A.** Gold
   - **B.** Platinum
   - **C.** Bronze
   - **D.** Silver
   - **E.** Diamond

5. What's the QoS queue intended for video?
   - **A.** Gold
   - **B.** Platinum
   - **C.** Bronze
   - **D.** Silver
   - **E.** Diamond

6. You've been informed people are intermittently not able to connect to your office's WLAN. After some troubleshooting, you find that the VLAN is running out of IP addresses. What's the recommended solution?

    A. Create a new WLAN and have half the employees connect to it instead.

    B. Adjust the subnet mask to be larger value.

    C. Create an additional dynamic interface and use an interface group with the WLAN.

    D. Configure session timeout so idle connections will be dropped.

    E. Add more access points to the area.

7. What are three requirements of enabling a LAG on the WLC? (Choose three.)

    A. LACP must be configured on the directly connected switch.

    B. The WLC must be rebooted.

    C. All distributed system interfaces must be added to the LAG.

    D. No more than two interfaces can be in the LAG.

    E. The switch must use `channel-group # mode on`.

8. What are three drawbacks to using autonomous APs? (Choose three.)

    A. They require central management.

    B. They are independently configured.

    C. AAPs don't see the full picture of the wireless network.

    D. Security policies are harder to maintain.

    E. CAPWAP is supported.

9. Where can TACACS+ be used on a WLC?

    A. WLAN configuration

    B. Management users

    C. Interface configuration

    D. Port configuration

10. Which port does TACACS+ use for accounting?

    A. UDP 49

    B. UDP 1645

    C. UDP 1812

    D. UDP 1813

    E. TCP 49

11. Which port does RADIUS use for authentication on modern servers?

    A. UDP 1645

    B. TCP 1645

    C. UDP 1812

- D. TCP 1812
- E. UDP 1700

12. Which port does RADIUS use for authentication on legacy servers?
    - A. UDP 1645
    - B. TCP 1645
    - C. UDP 1812
    - D. TCP 1812
    - E. UDP 1700

13. What is the purpose of the virtual interface?
    - A. Management
    - B. Redirecting clients to the WLC.
    - C. Registering APs
    - D. Terminating CAPWAP
    - E. Routing

14. Which IP address is recommended for the virtual interface?
    - A. 1.1.1.1
    - B. 2.2.2.2
    - C. 192.168.0.1
    - D. 192.0.2.1
    - E. 10.10.10.10

15. What's the command used to verify the IP address on a Mac?
    - A. ipconfig
    - B. ifconfig
    - C. iptables
    - D. Get-NetIPAddress
    - E. show ip int brief

16. Telnet is enabled by default on the WLC?
    - A. True
    - B. False
    - C. Depends on version

17. A dynamic interface is similar to what kind of interface found on a Cisco switch?
    - A. Ethernet
    - B. Loopback
    - C. Switched virtual interface
    - D. Tunnel
    - E. Port-channel

18. What is the DHCP Option 43 hex value for a single WLC with the IP address 192.168.123.100?
    A. F104C0A87B64
    B. F102C0A87B64
    C. F102C0A99B70
    D. F104C0A99B70
    E. F10211BBCC88

19. What's the default AP mode?
    A. Local
    B. Monitor
    C. FlexConnect
    D. Sniffer
    E. SE-Connect

20. Which AP modes serve wireless traffic? (Choose two.)
    A. Local
    B. Monitor
    C. FlexConnect
    D. Sniffer
    E. SE-Connect

Chapter 21

Virtualization, Automation, and Programmability

THE FOLLOWING CCNA EXAM TOPICS ARE COVERED IN THIS CHAPTER:

- ✓ **1.12 Explain Virtualization Fundamentals**
- ✓ **6.1 Explain how automation impacts network management**
- ✓ **6.5 Describe characteristics of REST-based APIs (CRUD, HTTP verbs, and data encoding)**
- ✓ **6.7 Interpret JSON encoded data**

Every area of the IT sector is growing faster than ever before. Unprecedented and all encompassing, this surge is reaching into our lives in countless ways. Applications are becoming evermore complex and often require multiple servers working together to provide a useable solution to users. And of course, businesses now want their applications up and running in a matter of hours instead of weeks. Because of all this, virtualization has become an urgent need, vital to most companies due to its ability to simplify adding new servers into their networks. Making the runaway growth more manageable is key! Automation is also rapidly gaining popularity because all the changes in today's IT environment make doing everything manually too time consuming and risky.

In this chapter we'll begin to address these modern challenges by introducing you to virtualization basics. I'll walk you through its common components and features to closing the topic by comparing some of the virtualization products on the market as of this writing. After that, we'll explore important automation concepts and components to provide you with sure footing to jump into the SDN and Configuration Management chapters following this one.

> To find your included bonus material, as well as Todd Lammle videos, practice questions & hands-on labs, please see www.lammle.com/ccna

Virtual Machine Fundamentals

In the distant past of what seems like maybe a month ago, IT infrastructure was nice and straightforward, albeit a bit monotonous. If you wanted a new DHCP server on your network, you would:

- Order a new server from HP or Dell. Cisco isn't in the server market yet.
- You and a colleague would rack that server since they tend to be really heavy.
- You would ensure the server had power and network connections supplied—cabled, of course.
- You would then typically power it on for a day to see if it runs properly, known as, "burning in the server."
- You often update the server firmware so that the components are up to date.
- Install Windows Server on it.

Once all the physical stuff is done you would then work on getting the DHCP role installed by:

- Figuring out the VLAN and IP information for the server.
- Patch the server to reduce security issues before you start using it.
- Join it to the Active Directory in most cases.
- Install and configure the DHCP role of the server.

Sure is a lot of steps and time spent just to get a simple DHCP server up and running! Of course, we can make things a bit easier by using tools like Microsoft's System Center Configuration Manager (SCCM) to deploy the OS and get it patched and joined to the domain. And from there, we can use SCCM or another tool like Ansible to configure the role. But most of the time and effort is in the stuff that can't be automated like waiting for your new server to arrive, racking it, and burning it in.

Back to our stroll down memory lane... Now that we have a working DHCP server, we find we must deploy a standard 3-tier application. This is a team effort comprised of a database server, a web server, and an application server, working together to support the application.

So how would we have gone about making this happen? We could consider installing everything on our DHCP server, only the 3-tier application architecture really should be separate servers to prevent single points of failure. Plus it's just a bad idea to be adding things to infrastructure servers, leaving no option but to order up three more servers and suffer through similar steps to those I outlined. Once another week has passed and were done, we would have a network looking like the diagram in Figure 21.1.

FIGURE 21.1 Five servers and counting

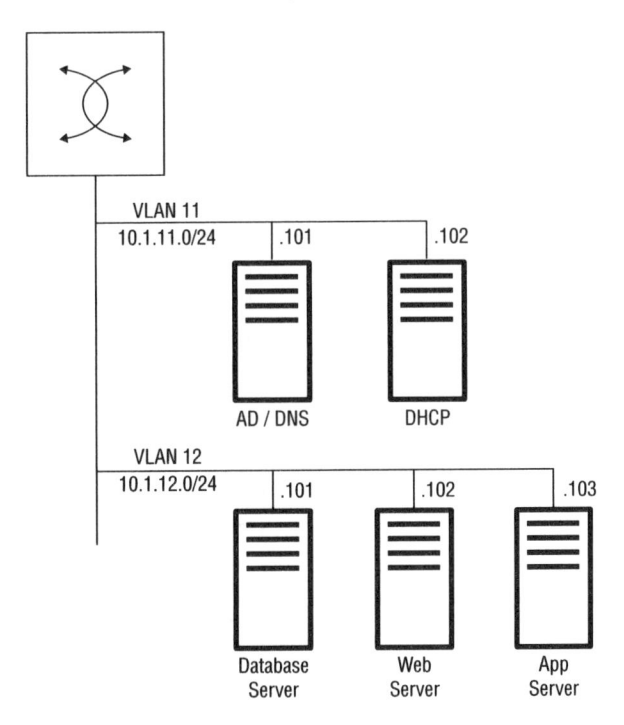

Here, we would have at least 5 physical servers connected to our network, which would grow as we added and connected new servers to our switch, eventually requiring us to add new switches to ensure we have ports for all the servers to use.

Fortunately, virtualization came along to rescue us from this plodding, expensive-in-every-way, annoying former reality! It allows us to run all of our servers on a virtualization host as virtual machines. This means that instead of the five servers and counting solution diagramed above, we're free to run everything on a single server that's running a virtualization solution. Now, if we need to add more servers into the network, we simply create the virtual machine instead of obtaining/racking/burning in a new server every time we need one. And if we need more redundancy or performance, we just add more virtualization hosts to share the load—yes!

Figure 21.2 pictures our streamlined new reality. In it, we can see our trunk link to the virtual switch (more about that later) of the virtualization host. Now, if we wanted more redundancy, we simply add more ethernet connections and possibly run something like LACP with the host.

FIGURE 21.2 Streamlined Servers

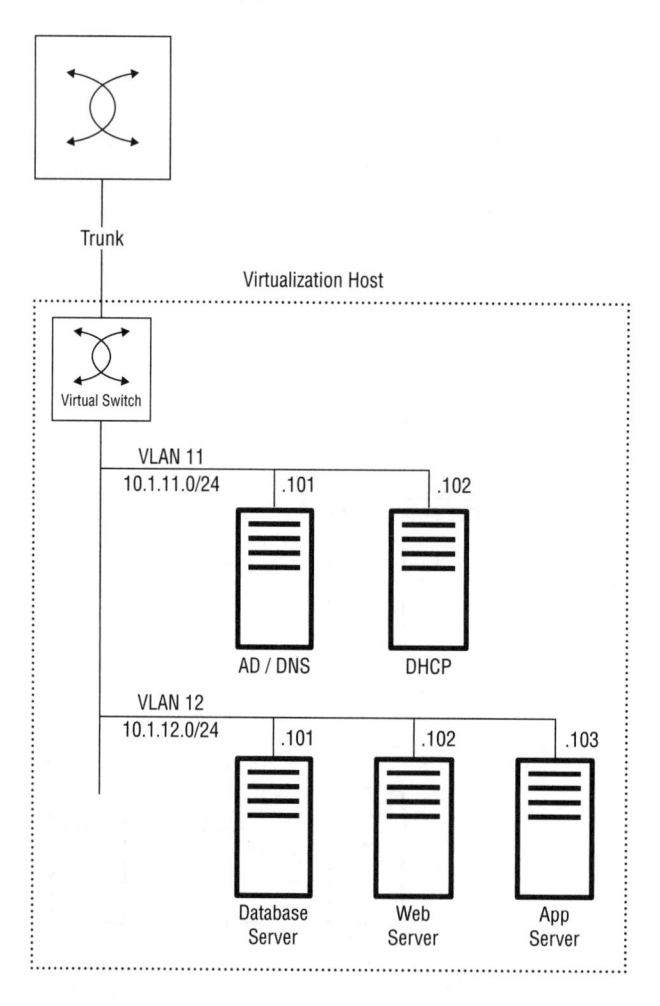

Virtualization Components

The components that virtualization solutions rely upon are:
- Hypervisor
- Virtualization guest
- Virtual appliance
- Virtual switch
- Shared storage
- Virtual storage

Let me explain each one of these now:

Hypervisor A hypervisor or virtualization host is simply the server that runs a virtualization solution. Most of the time, it's just called "the host." Typically, the host has lots of computational resources like processors, cores, and memory in order to run multiple virtual machines.

Virtualization Guest A virtualization guest, or often just "guest," is another term for a virtual machine that runs on a host. Depending on the exact virtualization solution, a guest can run practically any modern operating system.

Virtual Appliance A virtual appliance is a virtual solution provided by a vendor. Nearly all vendors provide a virtual option when you buy their product.

As for Cisco, they have an arsenal of virtual appliances. The most useful ones to remember objective-wise are:
- Cloud Service Router 1000v (CSR1000v): A virtual router that runs IOS-XE software.
- ASAv: A virtual version of Cisco's ASA firewall.
- Firepower Threat Defense Virtual: Virtual version of Cisco's Firepower firewall solution.

Virtual Switch All virtualization solutions have a virtual switch (vSwitch) that each host uses. The virtual switch acts just like a regular switch except it doesn't run STP.

vSwitches basically allow hosts to assign VLANs to virtual machines. They can also perform more advanced tricks like trunking and can even support switch features like CDP, LLDP, and SPAN, and security features like Private VLANs.

vSwitches tend to come in two forms:
- **Standard**: This is the free version switch that offers basic features. With this variety, every host will have its own independent virtual switch, meaning if you configure VLAN11 and VLAN12 on a host's vSwitch, you'll need to configure the same VLANs on any new host you add into the network that'll be sharing the workload. You do this just like you would when adding a new switch into the network if you aren't using VTP.

- **Distributed:** This option creates a single, logical, virtual switch that runs on all hosts. It supports advanced features and shares configuration between all hosts. A distributed vSwitch is just like a switch stack where all switches share the single configuration.

Shared Storage   While you can create virtual machines using a host's internal storage, this approach is very limiting when growing your virtualization environment because other virtual hosts can't easily reach the internal hard drive.

The most common solution is to use shared storage technologies like accessing a SAN or NAS through iSCSI or Fibre Channel. Doing this permits all hosts in your network to access the same common storage enabling more features, which we'll talk about a little bit further on.

VMware uses a special filesystem on its storage wherein mounted paths are called datastores. Since Hyper-V just uses the regular Windows file structure, it doesn't need this concept.

> I'm not going to venture too far into the whole storage technology arena because there are whole volumes devoted to the topic. If you're interested in going into this further, consider looking into the Cisco Data Center track.

Virtual Storage   Maybe you're thinking, "okay, you can virtualize servers and networks, but I bet you can't virtualize storage!" Actually, you can! Just know that storage area networks, or SANs will definitely shrink your bank account and they're complex too. To get around these caveats, the industry has begun embracing Hyper Converged solutions—a solution that combines computing, networking, and storage into a single server. Basically, with virtual storage, each host utilizes its local storage to create a logical SAN across the network, which all the virtual hosts can use as virtual machines.

Common solutions for this include:

- **Cisco HyperFlex:** This is Cisco's main Hyper Converged solution that runs VMware or Hyper-V with virtual storage on its Cisco Unified Computing System (UCS) servers.
- **VMware Virtual SAN:** This is a built in VMware solution that provides a virtual SAN for your VMware hosts.
- **Microsoft Storage Spaces:** Clearly a Microsoft solution that provides virtual storage, which can be generally used.

Virtualization Features

Here's a list of three components that virtualization solutions use:
- Hardware abstraction
- Snapshots
- Migrations

Hardware Abstraction

You'll appreciate this one if you've built a computer or two because computer hardware can be pretty annoying. Because hardware requires drivers that only *might be* provided by Windows Update, trying to standardize computers across your company is a bit challenging. There will always be slight differences as computers get upgraded or the manufacture adjusts the hardware components!

With virtual machines all the hardware is virtualized, so everything is always predictable even if you move the VM across several hosts.

Snapshots

Snapshots is basically an "undo" button for your virtual machine. It captures the state of a VM before you take on a task and allows you to revert to it if you need to. For instance, it's a good idea to take a snapshot of a VM before you attempt an upgrade because if the upgrade blows up the application, you can simply revert to the snapshot rather than tangle with manually undoing the upgrade.

Backup solutions such as Veeam also use snapshots to create a backup copy of the virtual machine. And of course, different vendors call features by their own names, for example, Microsoft calls their snapshot feature "checkpoints."

Note: Be aware that snapshots aren't always a magic solution! In the example above, if the failed upgrade also made changes to a database on another VM, that VM would need to have a snapshot as well to fully revert the changes.

Clones

Clones allow you to quickly create a copy of a virtual machine. They're a handy feature for creating several virtual machines based on a "golden" image that you've already patched and configured exactly the way you want it.

Migrations

Virtual machines can be migrated between hosts to balance the workload or ensure VMs are still running if the host needs to shut down for maintenance. This is cool because if shared storage is being used, the virtual machine can be migrated while it's running to avoid downtime! Otherwise, the VM most likely will need to be powered down during the move. Migrations can be manual or automatic based on performance or host availability.

Migrations come in two types:

- **Virtual Machine Migration:** Refers to when moving a virtual machine from one host to another.
- **Storage Migration:** Refers to when moving a virtual machine from one storage location to another. For example, moving a VM from internal storage to an iSCSI datastore.

Virtualization Types

There are two types of hypervisors available.

Type 1

Type 1 is also known as a bare-metal hypervisor—when the entire server and OS is dedicated to virtualization, the hypervisor can directly access all hardware on the system.

This is the most common enterprise solution since it provides the most features and the best performance.

Here are three Type 1 solutions:

- VMware ESXi
- Hyper-V
- Xen

Type 2

Type 2 is also called desktop virtualization. It refers to when the virtualization solution runs on top of your desktop OS as an application and is mostly meant for IT/developer testing since it offers a lot less features and performance. You get what you pay for—Type 2 is really simple to use and it's cheap!

These are Type 2 solutions:

- VMware Workstation/Fusion
- VirtualBox
- KVM

Hardware Virtualized Machine

Hardware Virtualized Machine (HVM) refers to when the virtual machine isn't aware it's a virtual machine. The hypervisor presents hardware to the VM that it can interact with—a hypervisor will commonly present an Intel e1000 network adapter for network connectivity, which is a widely supported NIC that should be run "out of the box" on most systems.

Paravirtualization

This virtualization type takes advantage of virtualization-aware operating systems. In this kind of system, the guest is "enlightened" to the fact that it's a VM and directly contacts the hypervisor instead of using emulated hardware. Paravirtualization can give us better performance, but the downside is that the VM needs to support the feature, so it often requires drivers to be installed on the guest operating system for it to actually function.

Virtualization Solutions

Let's look at the solutionms you can use to virualize your servers and hosts.

VMware ESXi

Pretty much everyone has heard of VMware because it's the virtualization market leader. ESXi, their Type 1, fully featured hypervisor, is based on a custom Linux OS. Management duties are carried out via either ESXi's web interface or through the VMware management solution VCenter.

While ESXi isn't free, VMware graciously provides a free license for standalone hosts for us to have some fun with.

Hyper-V

All of us have definitely heard of Microsoft, but maybe not Hyper-V, which is Microsoft's virtualization solution. It's also a Type-1 hypervisor that we run either as its own OS for a dedicated deployment, or we can install it on a Windows Server or Desktop as a role. This makes it sound sort of like it should be both Type-1 and Type-2, but Hyper-V gets full hardware access, so it's still considered a Type-1.

Management is handled either through the Hyper-V Management Tool that you install on a Windows box or via Microsoft's management solution, "System Center Virtual Machine Manager."

You can even take Hyper-V for a test drive by installing it on a Windows Server box or on Windows 10. There's a catch, though—if you install it, you won't be able to use Type-2 solutions like VMware Workstation on the computer because Hyper-V claims the hardware access. There's just never really a free lunch!

Xen/KVM

Xen and KVM are two open source Type-1 hypervisors, and arguably, they're the hardest solutions to use unless you're really strong in Linux! Other than that little hitch, they're completely free so they come in handy for labs, etc. Since this isn't a Linux course, they're out of scope for a CCNA discussion—I just wanted to mention they're out there.

VMware Workstation/Fusion

VMware Workstation is a paid Tier-2 solution for Windows and Linux that even offers a Mac version called VMware Fusion. It provides solid virtualization support with some pretty decent features too! VMware also has a free desktop solution called Player that lets you run a single virtual machine.

VirtualBox

VirtualBox is a free open source Type-2 solution from Oracle. It doesn't provide as many features as VMware Workstation does, but the price is right for a simple lab.

Automation Components

It's a Monday morning, so of course your boss asks you to add a new loopback interface with an IP in the 192.168.255.0/24 subnet on all your routers. No big deal if you have two or three routers since you can easily SSH into the devices and add the interfaces using the skills you learned from this book. But that's not the company you work at and with your 200+ routers, it would take forever to configure all the devices individually. Plus, keeping track of which IP address to use on each router is not a day at the beach, and it just gets worse if you happen to make mistakes along the way!

There are a whole bunch of surveys that put human error in the number-one spot as the cause of network outages. Sometimes it's because you accidentally shut down the wrong interface, and sometimes it's an old configuration lurking around that reacts rather poorly to your changes. And sometimes you just really needed more coffee before logging into that router!

Besides the ever-present risk when making sweeping network changes, there's the issue of your time. Getting tasked with adding 200 interfaces might be kind of cool if it's your first time, but it grows old fast, and odds are there's something a lot more interesting to spend your week on. This is a great example of when automation seriously saves the day— or week!

Network automation comes in many forms, but generally, you can boil it down to being able to apply tasks in a predictable way with increased odds of a positive outcome. And what that means for us is that instead of tediously connecting to 200 devices, we can write a script that will apply the configuration to all of the devices for us.

> **Disclaimer...** Knowing how to automate something isn't as important as understanding what it is you're automating! This is because automation will do exactly what it's told, so if you push out a broken OSPF configuration to all your production networks, you'll have a painful night ahead of you.

So now that you've got an idea why automation can be very cool, let's have a look at some of the common CCNA level components. There are almost endless options available, but we'll focus on the three main ones the exam will be picking your brain for.

Python

While Python isn't a focus of the CCNA exam, failing to mention it when talking about automation is like making a PB&J sandwich without bread. That's because Python is probably the most popular scripting language in the world for denizens of the network. It has readable syntax, is easy to use, and is very extensible. It comes in two main versions: 2x, which is on its way out, and 3x, the version you should be using now.

So let's meet the challenge I just brought up by working on actual Cisco routers and then walking through the code.

First, we're going to configure a Cisco router using netmiko, a popular python module that allows us to SSH into the device. Python modules consist of a collection of python code which happily exist to make our lives easier. We'll install it now using the pip command on a Linux system. And just to be clear, pip is a Python package manager giving us increased functionality by allowing us to install additional modules. For pip functionality in Windows, we'd go with Anaconda or just use Windows 10's Linux shells:

```
the-packet-thrower@home01:~$ sudo pip3 install netmiko
Collecting netmiko
Downloading
https://files.pythonhosted.org/packages/26/05/
dbe9c97c39f126e7b8dc70cf897dcad557dbd579703f2e3acfd3606d0cee/
netmiko-2.4.2-py2.py3-none-any.whl (144kB)
100%    153kB 1.9MB/s
Collecting scp>=0.13.2 (from netmiko)
Downloading
https://files.pythonhosted.org/packages/4d/7a/3d76dc5ad8deea79642f50a572e1c057
cb27e8b427f83781a2c05ce4e5b6/scp-0.13.2-py2.py3-none-any.whl

Successfully installed bcrypt-3.1.7 cffi-1.12.3 cryptography-2.7 future-0.17.1
netmiko-2.4.2 paramiko-2.6.0 pycparser-2.19 pynacl-1.3.0 scp-0.13.2
textfsm-1.1.0
```

Okay, so now that we have that installed, we can start working on our script file, which I'll call configure-loopback.py. Our goal is to configure a loopback interface in the 192.168.255.0/24 subnet on my 3 routers.

For the script, I'll go ahead and pick interface loopback 999 as the interface we'll create. The last IP of the loopback will be the router number. Since you don't need to learn Python for the exam, I'll just point out the script logic as we go without paying much attention to the syntax.

The first line of your script should generally be the Shebang line so that the OS knows what interpreter to use. And remember, we're using python3:

```
#!/usr/bin/env python3
```

Next, we'll import the modules we're going to work with using netmiko to connect to the routers. I'm also using getpass so we don't need to put passwords in the script, which is never a good idea! We'll start with the **from** command to tell Python which modules to use, and follow that up with the **import** command to grab a specific part of the module. Remember, I installed netmiko earlier; getpass is built into Python:

```
from getpass import getpass
from netmiko import ConnectHandler
```

It's good to put all the code inside of a main function so it can be more easily utilized. Doing this also ensures that the code will be more readable in the end:

```
def main():
```

Now, we'll stick our first real chunk of code inside the function to define the dictionaries that will store the router login information. These dictionaries are ways for Python to lookup information using key-value pairs. The key-value pairs we will need to make netmiko work are:

Device_type: cisco_ios in our case. This tells netmiko which vendor we're connecting to so it knows what kind of output to expect. Clearly, if we were connecting to another kind of system, we'd need to indicate that here instead.

IP: The device IP we're connecting to, which is also the IP we would SSH to then connect to the router.

Username: The username used to log in to the router.

Secret: This is normally the password, but it's blank since we're using getpass. We still must have the field there even if it's empty.

Port: The port we'll SSH with, by default, 22.

Know that we must define three dictionaries, one per router, and each one needs the five keys we just talked about. We create dictionaries via the command **name = {}**. You can name the dictionary whatever you want and the keys and values go between the {} with all values separated by commas.

Here's an example of how all of this looks:

```
'''
Define the routers we will connect to in dictionaries
'''
csr01 = {
    'device_type': 'cisco_ios',
    'ip': '10.30.10.81',
    'username': 'admin',
    'secret': '',
    'port': 22,
}

csr02 = {
    'device_type': 'cisco_ios',
    'ip': '10.30.10.82',
```

```
    'username': 'admin',
    'secret': '',
    'port': 22,
}

csr03 = {
    'device_type': 'cisco_ios',
    'ip': '10.30.10.83',
    'username': 'admin',
    'secret': '',
    'port': 22,
}
```

Next, we'll tell Python to create a password variable and then call getpass. Since we imported getpass already, we'll just call it by typing **getpass()** under a variable and the module will take care of everything else—nice!

```
'''
Grab the password for the routers
'''
password = getpass()
```

To get ready for the next section, we'll create a variable called IP and set it to a value of 1:

```
'''
Define IP variable as 1
'''
ip = 1
```

Okay great! Now we're ready to work on our loops—a way of cycling through data so we can do something with it like pushing router commands to our three dictionaries.

Our first loop is going to be a "for loop," which will loop through the items you provide it. Its job is change the password value in the dictionaries to our password variable set in **getpass()**.

To create a for loop, type **for** followed by the name of the looped item we want. In this case, it's **a_dict** for the name, followed by **in.** Then we'll specify the dictionaries separated by commas in between (). And don't forget—you have to end the line with a colon. Next, simply tell python that the password key in **a_dict** equals password. We're also going to tell netmiko not to be chatty:

```
# Get connection parameters setup correctly
for a_dict in (csr01, csr02, csr03):
    a_dict['password'] = password
    a_dict['verbose'] = False
```

Our next loop is actually going to push our configuration out to the routers. We'll go with the same logic as before except this time, I'm calling the loop item **a_device** because that describes what we're doing here better. Now I'll just use the **send_config_set** netmiko feature to push a variable called **config_commands**, which holds our configuration commands.

The **config_commands** variable has all the commands necessary to create our loopback999 interface and give it an ip address. The IP variable we defined adds the .1 in our 192.168.255.1 255.255.255.255 address and the end of the loop adds another 1, so the next IP will be 192.168.255.2 and then 192.168.255.3:

```
# Push Configuration
for a_device in (csr01, csr02, csr03):
    config_commands = ['interface loopback 999', 'ip address 192.168.255.' + str(ip) + ' 255.255.255.255']
    net_connect = ConnectHandler(**a_device)
    net_connect.send_config_set(config_commands)
    ip += 1
```

To finish up, I'll use a special if statement to call our main function so our script can run. We do it this way so we can make sure the script works properly before commiting to import it as a module:

```
if __name__ == "__main__":
    main()
```

Just for reference, check out the full script below. And just in case you're trying this at home, pay very close attention to the indentations because whitespace is *very* important to Python, as well as some other languages we'll talk about like YAML. Here's that script:

```
#!/usr/bin/env python

from getpass import getpass
from netmiko import ConnectHandler

def main():
    '''
    Define the routers we will connect to in dictionaries
    '''
    csr01 = {
        'device_type': 'cisco_ios',
        'ip': '10.30.10.81',
        'username': 'admin',
        'secret': '',
```

```python
        'port': 22,
    }

    csr02 = {
        'device_type': 'cisco_ios',
        'ip': '10.30.10.82',
        'username': 'admin',
        'secret': '',
        'port': 22,
    }

    csr03 = {
        'device_type': 'cisco_ios',
        'ip': '10.30.10.83',
        'username': 'admin',
        'secret': '',
        'port': 22,
    }

    '''
    Grab the password for the routers
    '''
    password = getpass()

    '''
    Define IP variable as 1
    '''
    ip = 1

    # Get connection parameters setup correctly
    for a_dict in (csr01, csr02, csr03):
        a_dict['password'] = password
        a_dict['verbose'] = False

    # Push Configuration
    for a_device in (csr01, csr02, csr03):
        print ('Creating Loopback on ' + str(a_device['ip']))
        config_commands = ['interface loopback 999', 'ip address 192.168.255.' + str(ip) + ' 255.255.255.255']
        net_connect = ConnectHandler(**a_device)
        net_connect.send_config_set(config_commands)
```

```
        ip += 1

if __name__ == "__main__":
    main()
```

Let's try it out!

To run the script, we just need to call it with python3.

```
the-packet-thrower@home01:~$ python3 configure-loopback.py
Password:
Creating Loopback on 10.30.10.81
Creating Loopback on 10.30.10.82
Creating Loopback on 10.30.10.83
```

To keep things on the simple side, I didn't add any show commands into the mix here. But we can verify things the old-fashioned way:

```
CSR01#show ip int br | in 999
Loopback999            192.168.255.1    YES manual up                    up

CSR02#show ip int br | in 999
Loopback999            192.168.255.2    YES manual up                    up

CSR03#show ip int br | in 999
Loopback999            192.168.255.3    YES manual up                    up
```

Nice—python created our interfaces for us!

This is good place to pause, and I've got something important to point out: I just wrote 60 lines of code to save from entering 3–4 lines of code (enable, conf t, interface loopback 999, and IP address) per device. So this begs the question, "how many devices does it take before our script is worth doing all that?" Like pretty much everything in this field, it depends. That's because once you get used to scripting you can do it quickly—maybe even by just editing a working script. On the other hand, if its going to take all day to get your script up and running, it might be faster to just do it manually. Especially if you don't have hundred(s) of routers to mess with!

> **NOTE** If you want to know more about Python—not a bad idea in this field—check into the Cisco Certified DevNet Associate cert.

JSON

JavaScript Object Notation (JSON) is a data exchange format that most systems have agreed to use for communicating data. Its job is to express data in a structured human-readable way.

You'll see many RESTful APIs and software defined solutions use JSON as the primary format it will send and receive data in; other formats you will see in some solutions are XML and YAML.

JSON structures data into key/value pairs separated with a colon inside of curly braces; it also requires the keys and values:

- Use double quotes, not single quotes.
- Boolean values must be lowercase; this is different from Python, which wants capitalization.
- Trailing commas must not be used; languages like Python don't care if you have a trailing comma in a dictionary but JSON does.

As an example, here is how I could express my name, age, and website in JSON.

```
{
  "name" : "Todd Lammle",
  "age" : "40",
  "website" : "www.lammle.com"
}
```

If we wanted to store more items, we can organize values between square brackets.

```
{
    "Creators": [

      {
        "name" : "Donald Robb",
        "age" : "34",
        "website" : "www.the-packet-thrower.com"
      },

      {
        "name" : "Todd Lammle",
        "age" : "40",
        "website" : "www.lammle.com"
      }
   ]
}
```

The advantage of this format is that it is very easy to read since it is a straightforward name/value pairing.

Since this is a Cisco book, let's look at the JSON output from a Cisco device. Fortunately, Cisco Nexus devices can natively convert show command output to JSON by using a handy pipe command so we can get our hands on some output pretty easily.

```
DC1-SPINE01# show ip interface brief | json-pretty native
{
        "TABLE_intf":   {
            "ROW_intf":     [{
                            "vrf-name-out": "default",
```

```
                        "intf-name":      "Lo0",
                        "proto-state":    "up",
                        "link-state":     "up",
                        "admin-state":    "up",
                        "iod": 5,
                        "prefix":         "192.168.255.11",
                        "ip-disabled":    "FALSE"
                }, {
                        "vrf-name-out": "default",
                        "intf-name":      "Eth1/1",
                        "proto-state":    "up",
                        "link-state":     "up",
                        "admin-state":    "up",
                        "iod": 6,
                        "prefix":         "10.1.11.254",
                        "ip-disabled":    "FALSE"
                }, {
                        "vrf-name-out": "default",
                        "intf-name":      "Eth1/2",
                        "proto-state":    "up",
                        "link-state":     "up",
                        "admin-state":    "up",
                        "iod": 7,
                        "prefix":         "10.1.12.254",
                        "ip-disabled":    "FALSE"
                }]
        }
}
```

This is an example of nested output; in order to access the Loopback0 IP we will need to work to extract the data. We can do this by starting at the outmost data structure and "extracting" the element till we get to the data we are interested in.

It takes some getting used to, for us to get to Loopback0's IP, we need to first

- Extract the TABLE_intf dictionary
- Extract the ROW_intf dictionary
- Select element in the index we want, 0 in this case
- Select the key we want the value of.

```
In [10]: pprint(json_data["TABLE_intf"]["ROW_intf"][0]["prefix"])
'192.168.255.11'
```

JSON on its own is very simple; we'll see more examples of it as we work through the other topics in this domain.

YAML

YAML Ain't Markup Language (YAML) is a grammatically incorrect data serialization language that is designed to be easy to for a human to read and interpret data. It is used by growing number of tools such as Ansible.

YAML is made up three main components:

- Mappings: These are simple key-value pairs such as Name: Todd.
- Lists: This works the same as any plain text bullet list, each item is on its own line and starts with a –
- Scalars: This is just a programming term...every string, Boolean, or number is a scalar. This means that the key and the value in the pair are each a scalar; also every item in a list is a scalar.

Let's look at a complete example:

```
---                     # All YAML files start with three dashs
name: Todd Lammle       # This is a mapping
books:                  # This is a list
CCNA
Sourcefire
Network+
videos:                 # This is a list
CCNA
Firepower
ISE
```

Whitespace is very important in YAML since it signifies a collection of lines; in the above example, the items under books are a different from the items under videos because of the indentation.

You must use spaces for indentation because YAML does not support tabs in the file. Also, there must be a space between the colon in a mapping and the value.

REST API

Application Programming Interfaces (APIs) allow you to quickly access an application resource without you having to manually map out the application and reverse engineer your own functionality.

For example, if you wanted to create an application that suggests restaurants near a user, you would need to have access to map information to know what restaurants are near the user.

To get map information on your own, you would have to either get your own map data, or you would have to develop your own way of accessing Google Maps through your own interface. Neither one of these is a practical option; fortunately Google offers many APIs that let you consume their map information in your application.

One of the most common ways of accessing APIs is through Representational State Transfer (REST). REST is a resource-based API, which means that URIs should be:

- Things not Actions
- Nouns not Verbs

If we break the words in Representational State Transfer apart, we have:
Representational – A resource state is transferred between a client and server.
State Transfer – Each request has all the information it needs to complete the operation.
Lastly REST has six constraints it needs to follow to be considered a Restful API.

- Client-Server – Connections are always initiated by a client requesting something from a server.
- Stateless – The server doesn't store any information from previous requests.
- Cacheable – The server response includes a version number so the client can decide if it can use the cached information or if it needs a new request.
- Uniform Interface – This defines the interface between the client and the server. This is divided into four subsections.
    - Identifying the Resource – Each resource must have its own unique URI.
    - Resource representation – This is how the resource will return data to the client; this is usually JSON or XML
    - Self-Descriptive Messages – Each message sent must have enough information in it to determine how to process the message.
    - Hypermedia as the Engine of Application State (HATEOAS) – This is a bit of a mouthful but basically means you should be able to easily discover other functionalities of the API. For example, if you are looking at a Cisco router API for viewing an interface, you should be able figure out how to view other items without needing too much documentation.
- Layered System – You can add additional layers between the API and the server data such as a firewall or a load balancer without impacting operations.
- Code on Demand – This is an optional constraint that allows REST to send executable code responses back to the client.

With all that out of the way, the REST API is a framework built on HTTP; all messages are simple text exchanged over an HTTP/HTTPS connection.

Let's look at a URI for DNA Center to see how REST API is put together.

- Protocol – This is either http for unencrypted or https for encrypted. Most restful API calls will be using HTTPS.
- URL – This is the Fully Qualified Domain Name for the server you are accessing. Depending on the solution, it may use a different port than 443.

- Resource – This is the specific path to the resource you are trying to access through the API.
- Parameter – This part of the URI allows you to filter the results using fields that the resource supports. This example is filtering to the hostname: cat_9k_2.dcloud.cisco.com

FIGURE 21.3 How a REST API is put together

```
https://sandboxdnac.cisco.com/dna/intent/api/v1/network-device?hostnamecat_9k_2.dcloud.cisco.com
|_____||_____||_____||_____|
Protocol   Server / Host URL            Resource                              Parameters
```

Now that we know what the URI looks like, it's time to discuss what actions we can do with it.

Restful architecture uses HTTP verbs to map to something called CRUD to define its common actions. CRUD is Create, Read/Retrieve, Update, Delete and it describes database actions, and the actions are shown in Table 21.1.

TABLE 21.1

HTTP Verb	Typical Action (CRUD)
POST	Create
GET	Read
PUT	Update/Replace
PATCH	Update/Modify
DELETE	Delete

REST API also gives us several common HTTP status codes that we can look for in our code if we are having problems, and the status and meaning are described in Table 21.2. You may recognize some of them from browsing the web.

TABLE 21.2

Status Code	Status Message	Meaning
200	OK	A'OK
201	Created	New resource created
400	Bad Request	Request was invalid
401	Unauthorized	Authentication issue

TABLE 21.2 *(continued)*

Status Code	Status Message	Meaning
403	Forbidden	Request was understood but you don't have permission
404	Not Found	Resource not found
500	Internal Server Error	Server issue
503	Service Unavailable	Server is unable to complete request

The last part of the request is the Content-Type; for most Cisco solutions, this will be application/json.

To try this out, I will use a commonly used program called Postman. This tool makes it easy to do RESTful API calls. For our lab we will play with Cisco's always online DNA Center.

Before we can do anything with a RESTful API, we need to authenticate. In the case of DNA Center we will do a POST to `https://sandboxdnac.cisco.com/dna/system/api/v1/auth/token`.

In the Authorization tab, we need to tell Postman the username and password for the server.

Username: **devnetuser**

Password: **Cisco123!**

Press send and you should get a token in the body window. There are several ways to be more efficient but for our example we'll just manually copy the token value without the quotes. Figure 21.4 shows the token body window.

FIGURE 21.4 Token Body Window

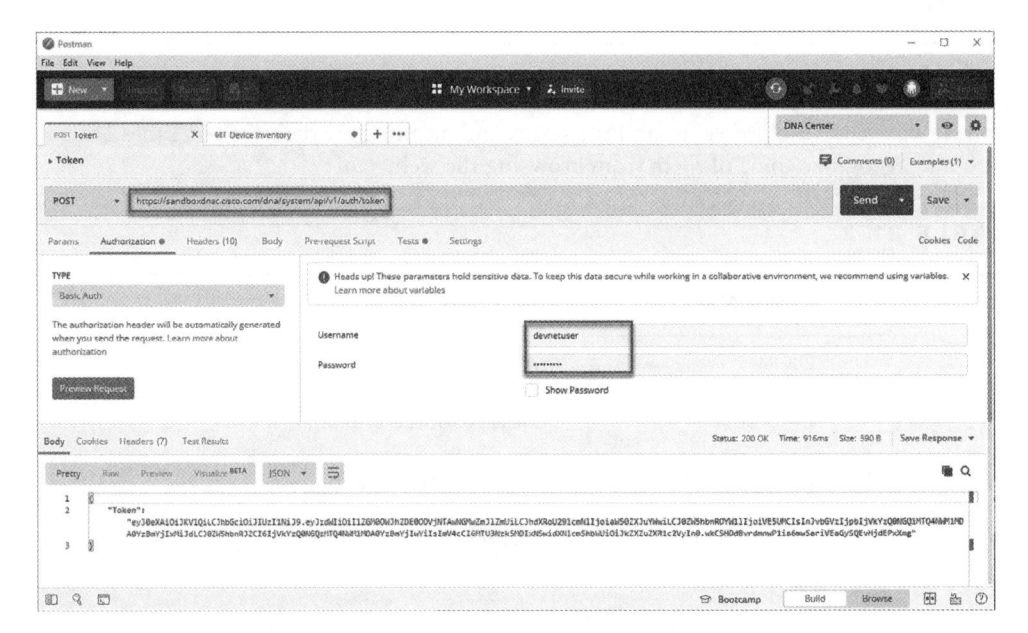

Note: The token is your only security in REST API; it provides full access to the server that issued it for the duration of its lifetime! Because of this make sure you don't share your API token with anyone who isn't trusted.

Once we have the token copied, we can create a new request to:

https://sandboxdnac.cisco.com/dna/intent/api/v1/network-device?hostname=cat_9k_2.dcloud.cisco.com

This will query the network-device resource and filter it to the cat_9k_2.dcloud.com hostname.

The content-type will be application/json.

Then we need to add X-Auth-Token, and then paste in the token value.

Finally when we press send we should get information back about that switch, as shown in Figure 21.5.

FIGURE 21.5 Device Inventory

Summary

In this chapter we had a look at virtualization fundamentals including its components, features, and the types of virtualization, and then we finished up by looking at some of the virtualization solutions on the market.

Then we looked into why automation is growing popular; then we had a look at some of the common automation components we will need to know including Python, JSON, YAML, and REST API.

Exam Essentials

Virtualization   Virtualization is a technology that allows a server to host multiple other computers as virtual machines. It does this by abstracting the host resources and sharing them with the guest machines. Virtualization provides several useful features such as the ability to clone a virtual machine in order to rapidly create new VMs.

RESTful API   A RESTful API uses common HTTP requests to GET, PUT, POST, and DELETE data from a server or device. Since HTTP is supported everywhere, it is easy to use restful APIs in practically all automation solutions.

JSON   JavaScript Object Notation (JSON) is a data exchange format that presents data in a human-readable format and is widely supported by most systems. Data is represented in key/value pairs; information can also be nested as required.

Review Questions

You can find the answers in the Appendix.

> **NOTE** The following questions are designed to test your understanding of this chapter's material. For more information on how to get additional questions, please see this book's introduction.

1. Which HTTP status code would you expect to get if the resource wasn't found?
   A. 200
   B. 201
   C. 401
   D. 403
   E. 404

2. VMware Workstation is what type of hypervisor?
   A. Type-1
   B. Type-2
   C. Type-3
   D. Type-4
   E. Type-5

3. Which of the following are JSON syntax rules? (Choose three.)
   A. Use double quotes, not single quotes.
   B. Use single quotes, not double quotes.
   C. Boolean values must be lowercase.
   D. Boolean values must be uppercase.
   E. Trailing commas must not be used.

4. Which of the following virtualization products is made by Microsoft?
   A. ESXi
   B. Workstation
   C. Xen
   D. KVM
   E. Hyper-V

5. What does REST stand for?
- **A.** Really easy stateful ticket
- **B.** Representational stateful transfer
- **C.** Representational state transfer
- **D.** Representational stateless transfer

6. Which of the following best describes a Resource in Restful API?
- **A.** The specific path to the resource you're trying to access through the API
- **B.** The security token for the request
- **C.** Filtering options for the request
- **D.** The full URL

7. A Cisco CSR1000v virtual router is which type of virtual resource?
- **A.** Virtual machine
- **B.** Virtual appliance
- **C.** Virtual network
- **D.** Virtual storage
- **E.** Type-1

8. Does YAML support tab characters?
- **A.** Yes
- **B.** No.

9. What does a mapping refer to in YAML?
- **A.** Simple value-key pairs
- **B.** Simple key-value pairs
- **C.** Complex value-key pairs
- **D.** Complex key-value pairs

10. Which of these virtualization features is useful for reverting a bad change in a VM?
- **A.** Snapshot
- **B.** Clones
- **C.** Migrations
- **D.** Hardware abstraction

11. Which HTTP operation in Restful API is most like a show command in Cisco IOS?
- **A.** POST
- **B.** DELETE
- **C.** GET
- **D.** PATCH

12. Which HTTP operation in Restful API most closely resembles a configuration command in Cisco IOS?
    A. POST
    B. DELETE
    C. GET
    D. PATCH

13. Which of the following choices best defines a token in Restful API?
    A. How you filter the response from the Restful API service
    B. How you save the output from the Restful API service
    C. How you authorize access to the Restful API service
    D. How you authenticate to the Restful API service

Chapter 22

SDN Controllers

THE CCNA EXAM TOPICS COVERED IN THIS CHAPTER ARE:

✓ **1.1.e Controllers (Cisco DNA Center and WLC)**

✓ **6.2 Compare traditional networks with controller-based networking**

✓ **6.3 Describe controller-based and software defined architectures (overlay, underlay, and fabric)**

- 6.3.a Separation of control plane and data plane
- 6.3.b North-bound and south-bound APIs

✓ **6.4 Compare traditional campus device management with Cisco DNA Center enabled device management**

Networking itself really hasn't changed all that much since the days when networks were first being rolled out. Of course it's true that a modern-day Cisco router has an endless menu of new capabilities, features, and protocols compared to older routers, but we pretty much still configure one by logging into it and making changes manually.

That said, automation has gotten popular enough to be included on the CCNA exam—it even has its own Devnet certification track! Even so, most companies still aren't keen on fully managing their network with a bunch of python scripts on a shared drive. So a better solution is to go with something called a Software Defined Networking controller to centrally manage and monitor the network instead of doing everything manually.

I'm going to introduce you to network monitoring solutions and configuration management before moving into Software Defined Networking (SDN) concepts and controller-based architecture. We'll also cover some very cool advantages a DNA Center managed network offers us over a traditionally managed network. This is going to be a great chapter!

> **NOTE** To find your included bonus material, as well as Todd Lammle videos, practice questions & hands-on labs, please see www.lammle.com/ccna

Traditional Network Monitoring Systems (NMS)

People working on a network team find out about problems affecting the network two main ways: being bombarded by angry users or via a Network Monitoring System (NMS) that alerts them when the network isn't looking so well. And even though users will probably still swarm when Facebook isn't working, I'll take the latter!

I mean, at least we get warned that the mob is coming with an NMS... A Network Monitoring System's job is to continuously poll your network devices using SNMP so it can pinpoint any misbehaving devices. Performance statistics like ICMP response times are also tracked to help us make network design decisions and troubleshoot. The NMS also keeps track of how much traffic is moving through the network, and depending on the exact solution being used, everything from applications to VoIP call quality can be tracked—nice!

By default, NMS polls the network devices every couple of minutes. Plus, when an interface goes down on a Cisco router, the router can send an SNMP trap to the NMS, alerting the system to the issue. And while we're talking about those alerts—most NMS solutions can send an email, an SMS text message if someone's on call for network support, or just display the alert so the Network Operations Center can investigate the issue.

In the upcoming examples, I'll be showing you a popular NMS solution, Solarwind's Network Performance Monitor, which is actually used by a fair amount of small to midsized companies. Know that Cisco does have a full solution called Prime Infrastructure, but we'll be talking about DNA Center that's its successor later in this chapter in detail instead. I think the contrast is really interesting!

Configuring SNMP

Configuring basic SNMP is the way we'll start configuring a Cisco device here. Doing this will be just like we did earlier only with some extra commands to set up SNMP traps.

We're going to a read-only community for basic monitoring and a read-write community in case we want more in-depth information or if the NMS needs to make any changes on the device like this:

```
C3750X-SW01(config)#snmp-server community testlabRO RO
C3750X-SW01(config)#snmp-server community testlabRW RW
To configure SNMP traps, I'll use the following command to tell the switch where
to send the traps. Here's how that looks on my SolarWinds server at 10.20.2.115:
C3750X-SW01(config)#snmp-server host 10.20.2.115 traps testlabTRAPS
```

So depending on the network environment, you might have to change the source interface that SNMP will use to send traps with the **source-interface** command:

```
C3750X-SW01(config)#snmp-server source-interface traps vlan 310
```

Each Cisco device has lots of traps you can enable that vary by platform and sometimes between IOS versions. You can see all available traps by typing a question mark after the **snmp-server enable traps** command. After that, just choose the traps you want enabled by selecting them one at time:

```
C3750X-SW01(config)#snmp-server enable traps ?
auth-framework    Enable SNMP CISCO-AUTH-FRAMEWORK-MIB traps
bridge            Enable SNMP STP Bridge MIB traps
bulkstat          Enable Data-Collection-MIB Collection notifications
call-home         Enable SNMP CISCO-CALLHOME-MIB traps
cluster           Enable Cluster traps
<trimmed for brevity>
```

If you're just not that picky, an easier way is to enter the **snmp-server enable traps** command without any options because this enables all the traps supported on the system. If you want to disable a trap later, just use the no command on it:

```
C3750X-SW01(config)#snmp-server enable traps
C3750X-SW01(config)#do sh run | in enable trap
```

```
snmp-server enable traps snmp authentication linkdown linkup coldstart warmstart
snmp-server enable traps flowmon
snmp-server enable traps transceiver all
snmp-server enable traps call-home message-send-fail server-fail
snmp-server enable traps tty
snmp-server enable traps license
snmp-server enable traps auth-framework sec-violation
snmp-server enable traps cluster

<trimmed for brevity>
```

Network Health

Okay so once the NMS has learned about the network devices in my lab—some Cisco routers, a 3750X switch, and some Meraki devices—the dashboard will display an overview of my network's health.

NMS's usually show the status of your network with three colors:

- **Green** - Healthy nodes with no reported problems.
- **Yellow** - Nodes that are up but have reported issues like interfaces that are down, or a hardware issue like a fan that isn't working.
- **Red** - Nodes that aren't reachable and are probably down.

Figure 22.1 gives you an overview of my network.

FIGURE 22.1 NMS network overview

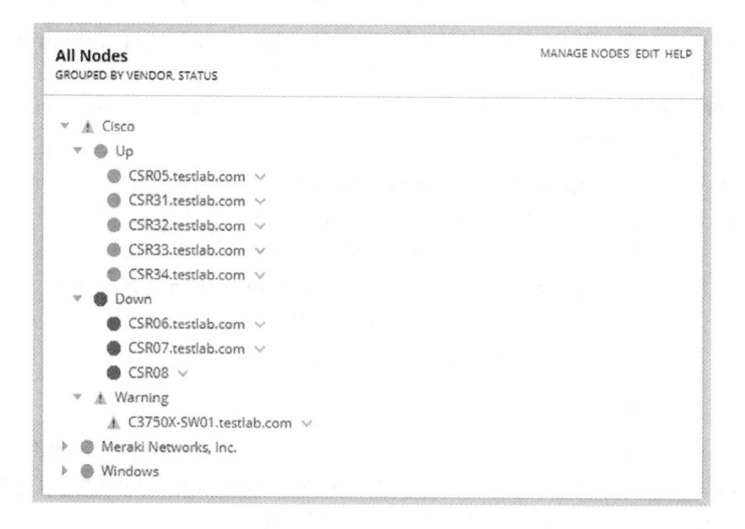

```
All Nodes                                    MANAGE NODES  EDIT  HELP
GROUPED BY VENDOR, STATUS

▼  ⚠ Cisco
    ▼  ● Up
            ● CSR05.testlab.com  ⌄
            ● CSR31.testlab.com  ⌄
            ● CSR32.testlab.com  ⌄
            ● CSR33.testlab.com  ⌄
            ● CSR34.testlab.com  ⌄
    ▼  ● Down
            ● CSR06.testlab.com
            ● CSR07.testlab.com
            ● CSR08  ⌄
    ▼  ⚠ Warning
            ⚠ C3750X-SW01.testlab.com  ⌄
▶  ● Meraki Networks, Inc.
▶  ● Windows
```

You can view more detailed information on the Alerts page, as shown in Figure 22.2.

FIGURE 22.2 NMS alert configuration

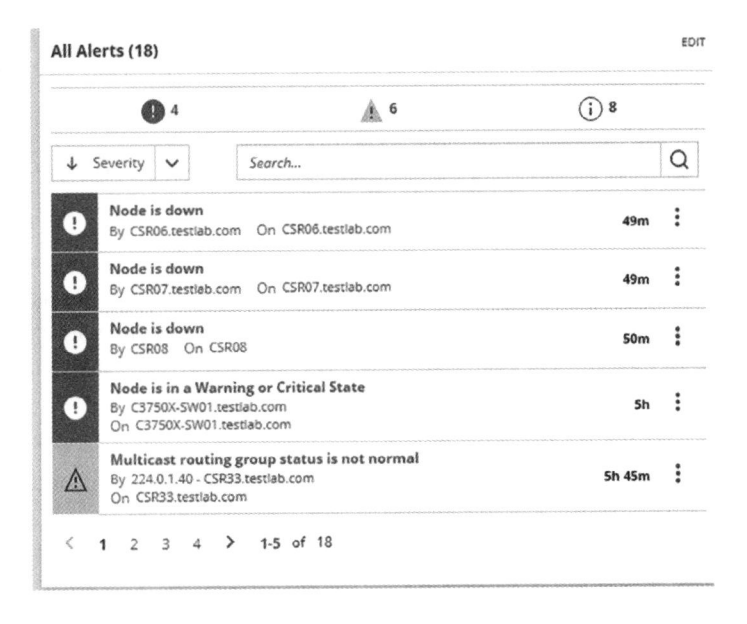

So how does an NMS make its decisions about how to handle an interface going down or what to do when a router reboots anyway? NMS is configured with lots of default rules defining how a system should treat various events discovered by the SNMP polling. And what's cool is that every NMS solution lets you customize alerts to suit your environment. Sometimes it's easy like with SolarWinds or Prime Infrastructure, but if you've gone with an open source solution, you just might find yourself writing java code at 3 a.m.!

Figure 22.3 shows the alert customization page.

FIGURE 22.3 NMS alert configuration

Central Syslog

NMS solutions can also serve as a convenient central syslog when troubleshooting. On the Syslog page, you can run searches to make it easier to filter exactly what you're looking for, which is a really good thing because there can be hundreds of syslog messages at any given time.

Syslog messages from a network device can also be used to notify the NMS there's a network issue. You can even configure rules that will determine how the syslog will react to whatever syslog messages you want. This allows you to make things happen like having the server run a script if the NMS receives an OSPF-related message.

All we have to do to configure a Cisco router to send syslog messages to the NMS is tell the router what logging level the router should send traps at. I'm going with level 7 to make sure syslog messages are sent so I can show you what the NMS side looks like. After that, I'll just tell the router how to reach my SolarWinds server like this:

```
CSR31(config)#logging trap debugging
CSR31(config)#logging host 10.20.2.115
```

Figure 22.4 gives you a look at the central syslog page.

FIGURE 22.4 NMS central syslog

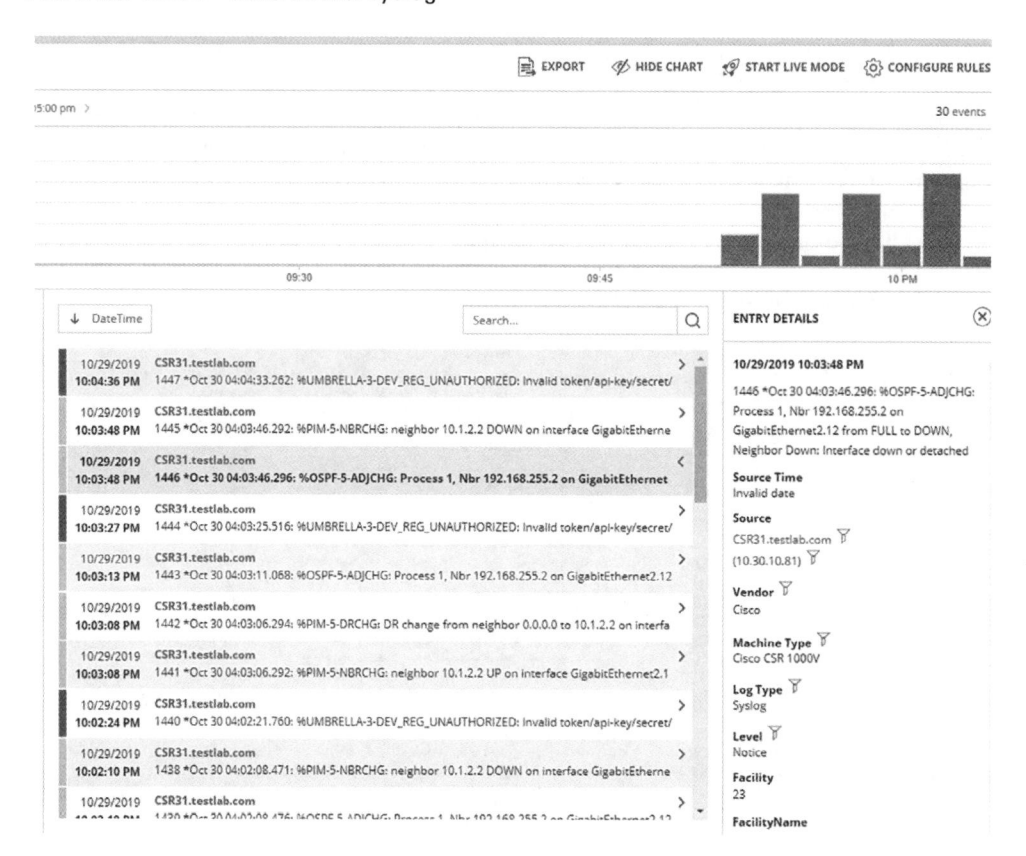

The main information shown here is that several syslog messages have been reached from my router CSR31.testlab.com, and that highlighted message tells us OSPF has gone down.

Central SNMP Traps

Now we've already covered configuring the SNMP traps that show up on the server a lot like syslog messages do. The main difference is that traps usually offer up a lot more detail than log messages.

Just like before, we can search for a keyword or filter by device to make it easier to find what we're looking for. And we can also configure rules if we want SolarWinds to do something in particular when it receives a trap.

Figure 22.5 displays the central SNMP trap page.

FIGURE 22.5 NMS central SNMP trap

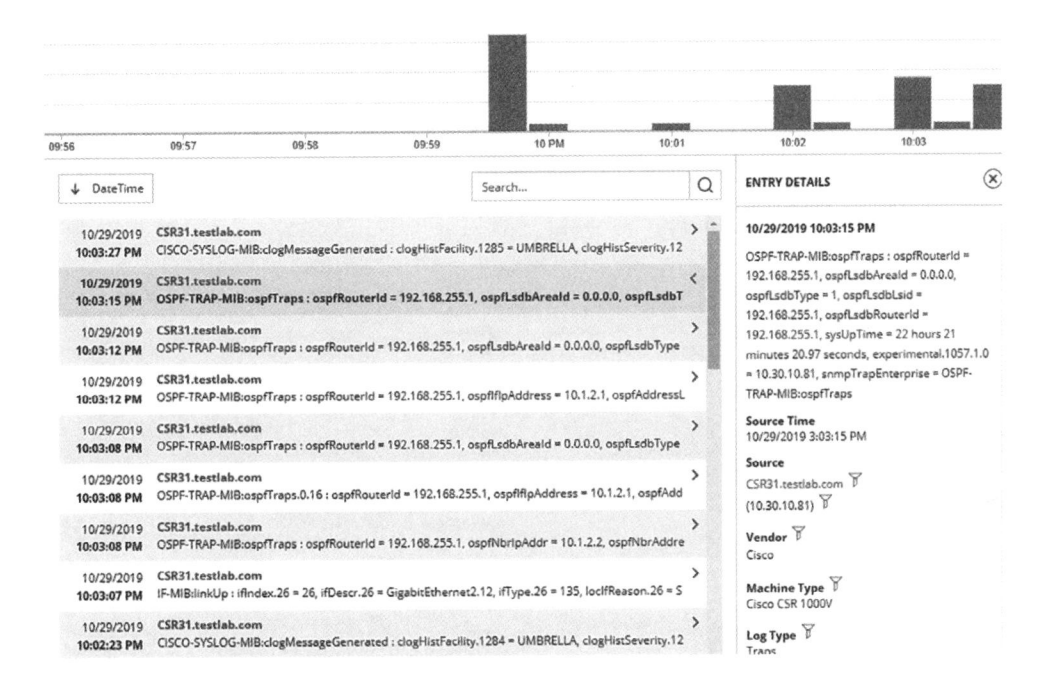

Interface Information

Another cool thing about NMS monitoring your network is that you can easily view a graphical representation of various interface information. Yes, you can actually see how busy your interfaces are by checking out the interface utilization graph; a glance at buffer misses graph tells you if your buffers are getting overloaded, and a quick look at an interface error graph shows you how many errors are on interfaces!

696 Chapter 22 ▪ SDN Controllers

So let's check out the information in the Interface Utilization graph on my switch shown in Figure 22.6.

FIGURE 22.6 NMS interface utilization

STATUS	INTERFACE	PORT MODE	ASSIGNED VLANS	TRANSMIT	RECEIVE
Up	Vlan1 - Vl1			0 %	0 %
Up	Vlan101 - WLAN101			0 %	0 %
Up	Vlan102 - WLAN102			0 %	0 %
Up	Vlan103 - WLAN103			0 %	0 %
Up	Vlan310 - Servers			0 %	0 %
Up	Vlan311 - Wireless Controller			0 %	0 %
Up	GigabitEthernet1/0/1 - Gi1/0/1	Access	Wireless-AP	0 %	0 %
Up	GigabitEthernet1/0/2 - Gi1/0/2	Access	Wireless-AP	0 %	0 %
Up	GigabitEthernet1/0/3 - Gi1/0/3	Access	Wireless-AP	0 %	0 %
Up	GigabitEthernet1/0/4 - Gi1/0/4	Access	Wireless-AP	0 %	0 %
Up	GigabitEthernet1/0/5 - Gi1/0/5	Access	Wireless-AP	0 %	0 %
Down	GigabitEthernet1/0/37 - Gi1/0/37	Trunk	default VLAN0100 WLAN101 WLAN102 WLAN103 See more...	0 %	0 %
Down	GigabitEthernet1/0/38 - Gi1/0/38	Trunk	default VLAN0100 WLAN101 WLAN102 WLAN103 See more...	0 %	0 %
Up	GigabitEthernet1/0/48 - Gi1/0/48	Trunk	default VLAN0100 WLAN101 WLAN102 WLAN103 See more...	0 %	0 %

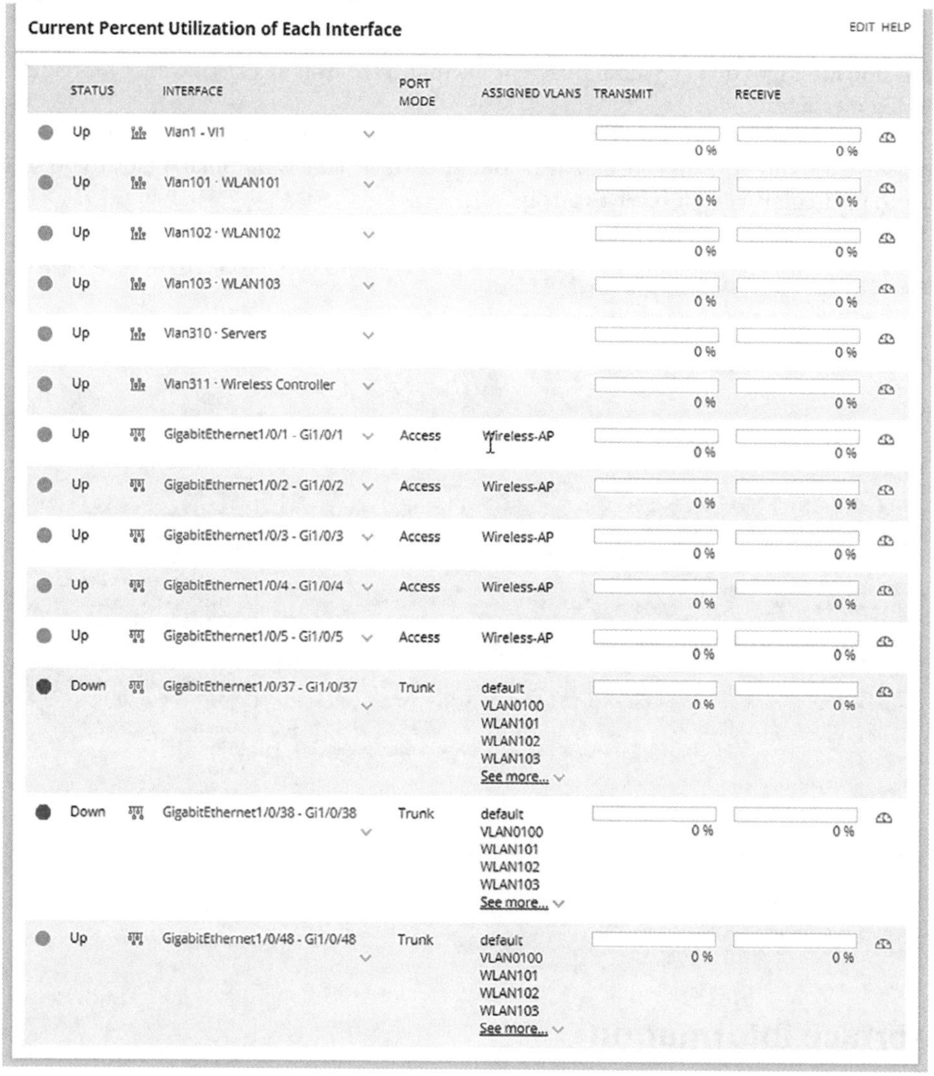

Okay, so since this is a lab, we're not seeing traffic here, but if I we're downloading something, you'd see just how busy each interface gets. There's also some good operational information like the assigned VLAN names the interface is using. SolarWinds also give us a good interface description, which really helps identify important information.

Hardware Health

When you're troubleshooting manually, hardware health is notoriously hard to keep track of. Unless you're right there on the box to troubleshoot an issue and/or happen to notice a log message about failing hardware, you probably won't realize there's a problem until the router blows up at 2 a.m.!

Again, the NMS makes life a whole lot easier by presenting us with an easy-to-read graph on our hardware health. Figure 22.7 shows what mine looks like.

FIGURE 22.7 NMS hardware health

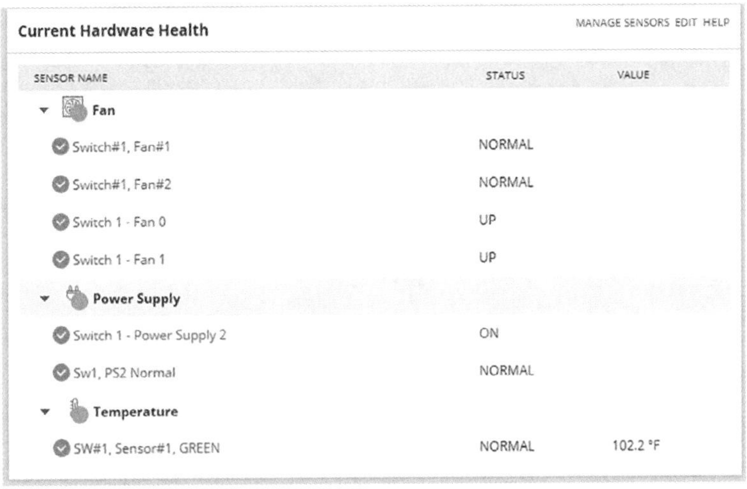

Sensor Name	Status	Value
Fan		
Switch#1, Fan#1	NORMAL	
Switch#1, Fan#2	NORMAL	
Switch 1 - Fan 0	UP	
Switch 1 - Fan 1	UP	
Power Supply		
Switch 1 - Power Supply 2	ON	
Sw1, PS2 Normal	NORMAL	
Temperature		
SW#1, Sensor#1, GREEN	NORMAL	102.2 °F

Network Information

Surprise! A network monitoring system does indeed offer a ton of information about what's generally up with the network. Two graphs I'd like to highlight are Response Time & Packet Loss, which is great for troubleshooting those "slow Internet" phone calls, and CPU Load and Memory Utilization is a snapshot of exactly how well a router is running and if it should be reconfigured or upgraded. Check out Figure 22.8 to get a picture of these.

FIGURE 22.8 NMS network graphs

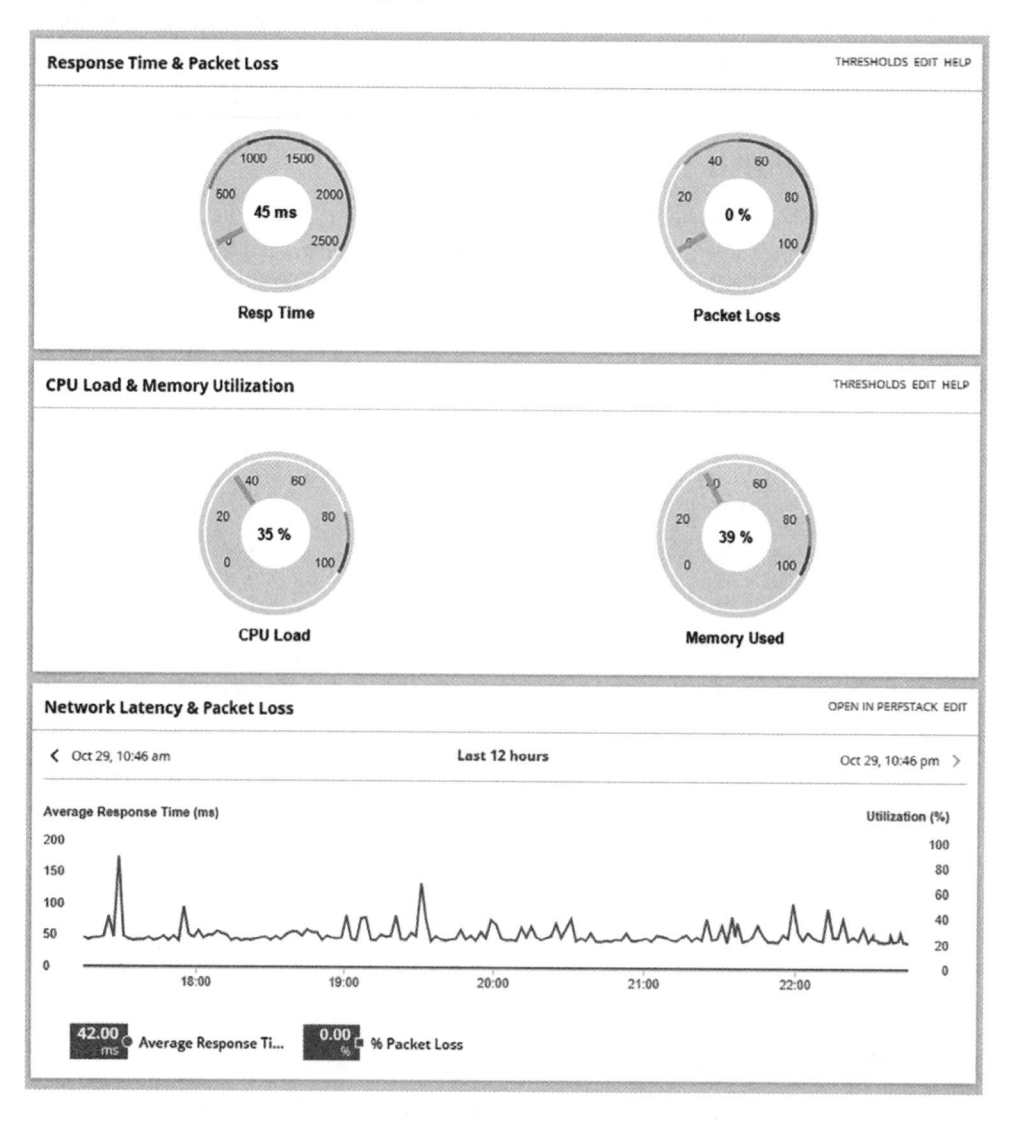

NMS also pulls in intel like CDP information to show you vitals like which devices are directly attached to the switch and which VLANs are on the switch so it can populate other graphs. It analyzes routes within the routing table so it can determine if flapping is happening in your network, where a route appears and then disappears over and over. It culls even more advanced information like if the switch is in a stack or not, revealed in the VLAN table. Figure 22.9 pictures the Network Topology and VLAN tables.

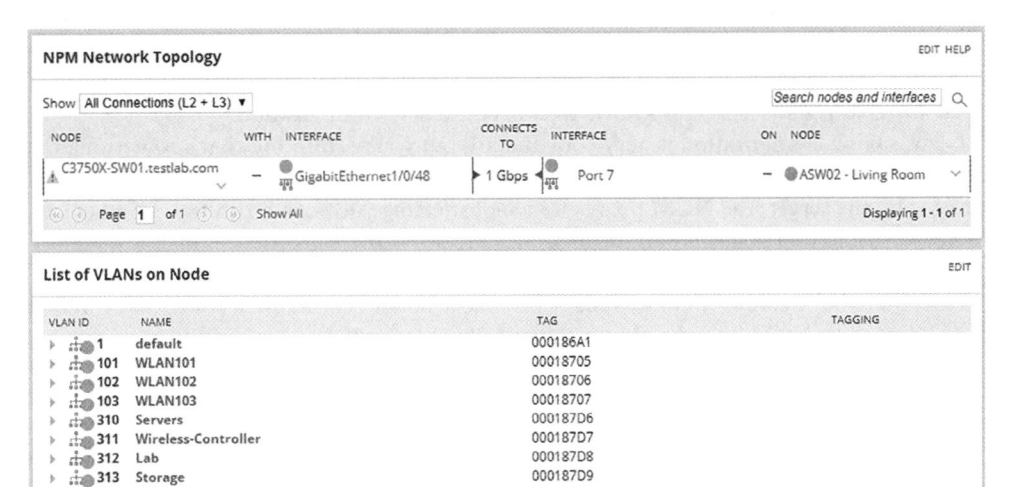

FIGURE 22.9 NMS network topology

NPM Network Topology					EDIT HELP
Show All Connections (L2 + L3) ▼				Search nodes and interfaces	
NODE	WITH INTERFACE	CONNECTS TO	INTERFACE	ON NODE	
C3750X-SW01.testlab.com	GigabitEthernet1/0/48	1 Gbps	Port 7	— ASW02 - Living Room	
Page 1 of 1 Show All				Displaying 1 - 1 of 1	

List of VLANs on Node			EDIT
VLAN ID	NAME	TAG	TAGGING
1	default	000186A1	
101	WLAN101	00018705	
102	WLAN102	00018706	
103	WLAN103	00018707	
310	Servers	000187D6	
311	Wireless-Controller	000187D7	
312	Lab	000187D8	
313	Storage	000187D9	
314	Desktops	000187DA	
316	Wireless-ServicePort	000187DC	
320	Wireless-AP	000187E0	

From this very brief look at network monitoring systems, you get the idea that we've only scratched the surface here. You can just imagine has the actual depth of the NMS, so it's no surprise that there are tons of books and certifications based upon it. The CCNA introduces DNA Center, which we will talk about later in this chapter, and the CCNP and CCIE seriously expand on the topic. Just so you know, if you feel like test-driving SolarWinds for yourself, they offer a 30-day trial you can download at www.SolarWinds.com.

Traditional Network Configuration Managers (NCMs)

Now that we've covered ways to monitor your network, we'll move on to how to handle your configuration backups. Let me start by asking you what would you do if you had to replace your main Internet router due to an outage? Would you copy and paste a hopefully up-to-date config that was saved in Notepad? Maybe... But copying and pasting tons of configuration through a console port can result in missed lines that you'd have to troubleshoot. Worse, will you actually have to configure the entire router from scratch? Rebuilding a CCNA-level device from the starting gate may not sound so bad as long as you have the proper IPs on hand. But a busy real-world router can easily have hundreds or even thousands of lines of configuration! So how would you avoid that nightmare?

Coming to the rescue of sys admins everywhere, the Network Configuration Manager does just what it sounds like it does—it manages your network configuration—yes!

Depending on the specific solution, the NCM can be the same server as your NMS, or it can even be an entirely separate server with no integration. This is so good... NCM routinely backups your configuration by connecting to each network device and copying the configuration over to the server. Network devices can also be set up to notify the NCM about any changes so the server knows to collect the new configuration.

Okay, saving configuration is very cool and all, but you're thinking that's something that can easily be done with a Python script written over a lunch break, right? Well, once the config is on the server, the NCM proves it value by letting you search through saved configs for keywords, letting you compare configuration to see if there are any changes between saved versions. And you can push out configurations too!

Now that you're sold, the commands below show how to configure a router to be added to an NCM. The NCM must be able to telnet or SSH into the box, so we'll have to create a username and password for the NCM to use like this:

```
CSR31(config)#aaa new-model
CSR31(config)#aaa authentication login default local
CSR31(config)#username ncm secret ncmPass
CSR31(config)#enable sec ncmEnable
```

NCMs can also use the SNMP Read-Write community to make changes on the box, meaning the SNMP seen in the NMS configuration may also be needed as well.

Here's a network device's configuration overview page in SolarWinds shown in Figure 22.10.

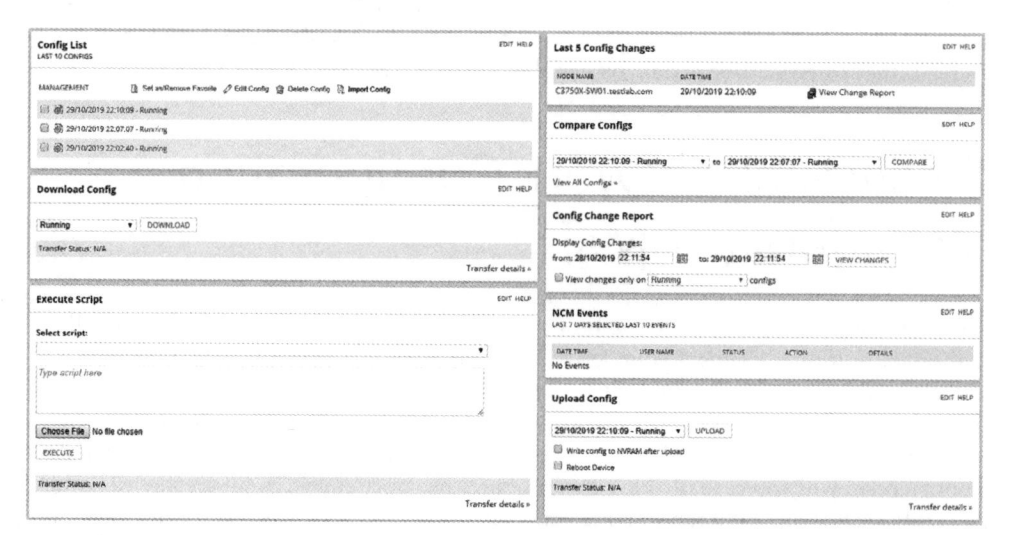

FIGURE 22.10 NCM config overview

And here's an example of the compare configs feature—key when trying to troubleshoot lost configs after a crash or even when you're just trying to determine the changes that occurred on a device before disaster struck. Check out Figure 22.11.

FIGURE 22.11   NCM compare config

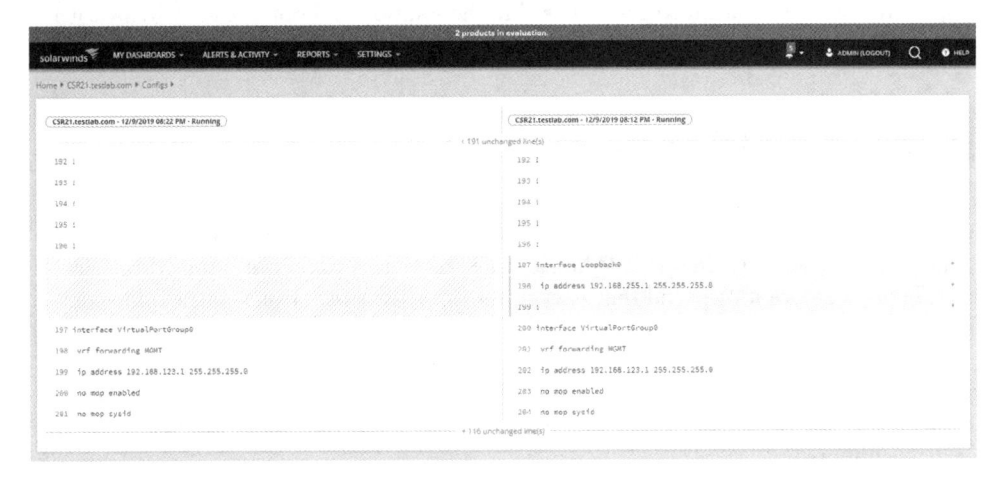

The NCM can also push out simple configurations. What's more, you can even use the NCM scripting language to make configuration templates to effect mass configuration changes across the network. Every type NCM uses a different scripting engine for the template feature. For example, DNA Center uses Apache Velocity for creating templates, Solarwind's scripting language can be seen in Figure 22.12.

FIGURE 22.12   NCM push config

Config Change Template:

```
script ChangeInterfaceDescriptionCiscoIOS (
                            NCM.Nodes @ContextNode,
                            NCM.Interfaces[] @PhysicalInterfaces,
                            string @NewInterfaceDescription    )
{
  // Enter config terminal mode
  CLI
  {
    configure terminal
  }

  foreach (@itf in @PhysicalInterfaces)
  {
    CLI
    {
      interface @itf.InterfaceDescription
      no description
      description @NewInterfaceDescription
      exit
    }
  }
  //Exit Config mode
  CLI {exit}
}
```

And again, in the real world, NCMs are actually pretty complex things. What we've covered this far is just meant to get you used to the solution and prepare for when we get into how DNA Center handles the feature later.

Traditional Networking

To really get what Software Defined Networking (SDN) is you've got to understand how a regular router sends traffic first. When a router receives a packet, it jumps through several hoops before it can send that packet out towards destination. Let's explore that process now.

Before the router can send out traffic, it has to know all the available destination routes. These routes are learned via a static route, a default route, or through a routing protocol. Because the CCNA exclusively focuses on OSPF, we've got to configure it and get the neighbors up.

Once that's done, we should have a nicely populated routing table for the router. It'll look up the proper destination route with the help of Cisco Express Forwarding, which is what Cisco uses to build the forwarding table these days. Exactly how CEF and the forwarding table works are out of scope topics for the CCNA, so I won't go into them further here.

Now that we have our route, the router will need an ARP entry for the next hop IP address before it can send the traffic. The TTL on the packet will also be decreased by one as it passes through the router, and the IP header and Ethernet frame checksum will also be recalculated before the traffic is sent over the wire.

Routers divide these different tasks into three different planes:

- The management plane
- The control plane
- The data plane

Let's explore them now.

Management Plane

The management plane controls everything about loging into a network device including telnet and SSH access—not that we would ever use telnet, right?

SNMP is also included in the management plane, which allows Network Monitoring Systems to poll the device for information.

And HTTP and HTTPs are also part of the plane. Maybe you're thinking, "Cisco has got to have a web interface on routers!" In the IOS's early days, the web interface was, um... Well, it wasn't pretty. It was really just a way to run some IOS commands through a web page and you would only turn it on if you were running an application on your router that required it like Cisco Unified Call Manager Express. But now, with modern IOS-XE, the web interface is just lovely as you can see in Figure 22.13.

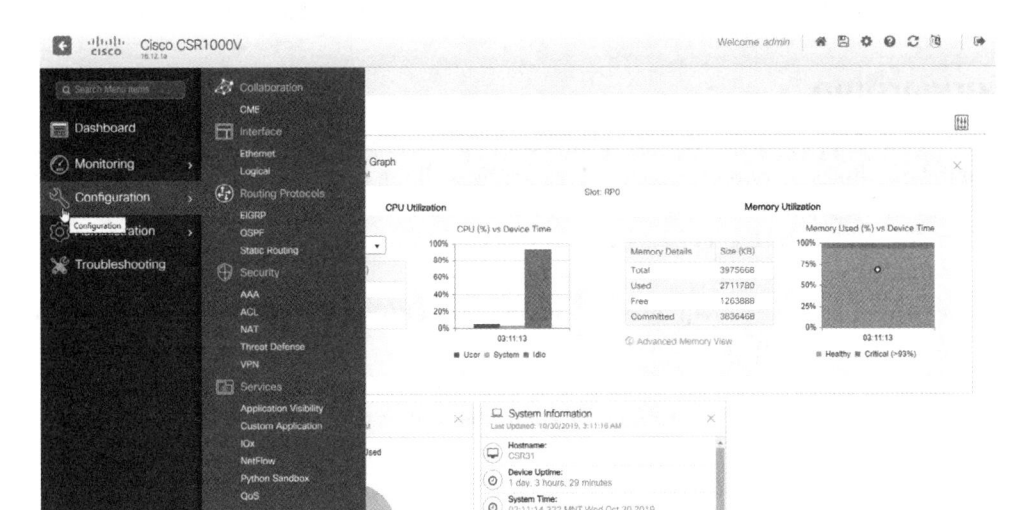

FIGURE 22.13 IOS-XE web interface

APIs are also considered management access including restful API discussed back in the Automation chapter. Ports like the console port, the AUX port, and the management port are also found here.

Control Plane

The control plane is really the brain of the router—it's where all the protocols are run and where all the decisions are made. The goal of this plane is to generate all necessary forwarding information needed to send the packet on towards its destination.

So, lots of important things happen in the control plane. Security functions like defining ACLs and NAT, if the packet needs to change its source, or if the destination changed. Of course, everything to do with routing protocols like OSFP, including forming adjacencies and learning the routes, all occur on this plane.

ARP is also a big part of the control plane, since knowing how to reach the layer 2 address of the next hop is essential for the actual routing to occur. Other control plane protocols include things like STP, VTP, and MAC address tables on switches, as well as QoS and CDP/LLDP.

Data Plane

So if the control plane is the router's brain, the data plane is its workhorse. The data plane's job is to take all the information presented from the control plane and use it to send the packet on its merry way.

Everything that happens at the data plane directly affects traffic. These are activities like encapsulating and de-encapsulating traffic as it arrives at and leaves the router, adding and removing packet headers as needed, plus actually dropping traffic that hits a deny statement on a ACL are all data plane tasks. Even the actual forwarding, where the packet moves from the inbound interface to the outbound interface, happen here as well.

Forwarding

Okay—now that you know what the planes are and what happens at each of them, let's turn to how things work on the router. I'll start by walking through the steps R02 will take when it receives a packet from R01 that needs to be sent to R03.

First, have a look at Figure 22.14 that pictures how the forwarding table is built from the routing table:

1. OSPF running on R02 will form an adjacency with R01 and R03. The control plane on R02 will then receive the routes via LSA information.
2. The Link State Advertisements go into the Link State Database on the three routers. The LSDB contains type 1 LSAs for each to the routers and type 2 for the designated routers unless the OSPF network type has been changed.
3. The Neighbor information is also kept track of in the Neighbor Table.
4. The Neighbor Table and LSDB are pushed to the routing table where the best route is chosen. From here, the normal rules you're already familiar with apply, like lowest metric, lowest administrative distance and longest match.

FIGURE 22.14 Fowarding traffic flow

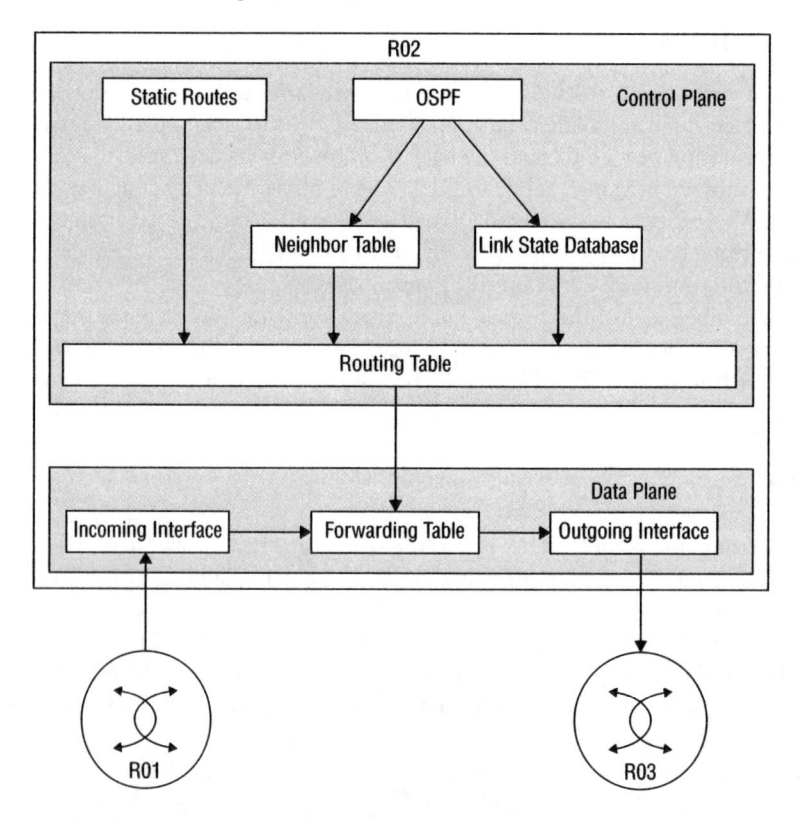

Now that the routing table has chosen routes, we can expand our diagram a bit to include more tables as shown in Figure 22.15:

1. Cisco Express Forwarding (CEF) will take the routing table's best routes and install them in the Forwarding Information Base (FIB) table.
2. The ARP Table is used to build the Adjacency Table. The forwarding table requires ARP to be resolved for a next hop before the route's considered valid. Protocols like PPP are also included in the forwarding table.
3. The information is pushed to hardware for forwarding.

FIGURE 22.15 Forwarding table

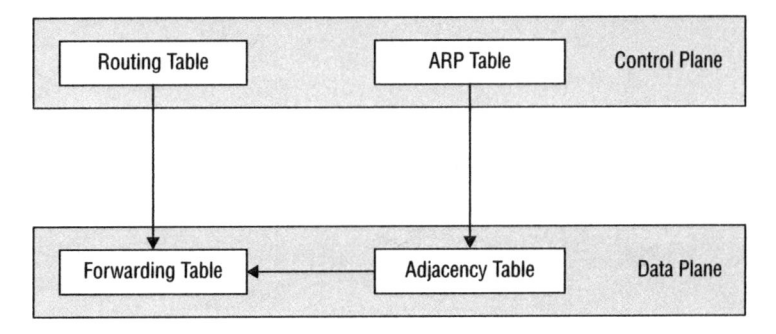

The whole story about how this works is well above the CCNA level, but packing the information I've given you will really help when we start talking about SDN because we're going to be relocating the control plane off the device and on to an SDN Controller.

Oh, and also before we get into SDN, I want to understand just how much work it would actually be to add a new virtual machine that uses a new subnet and requires Internet access into a traditional 3-tier architecture. Check out Figure 22.16.

In general, we'd have to:

1. Select a new VLAN and subnet to use—hopefully we've got an IP Address Management solution!
2. Make sure the new VLAN is on all switches. VTP can be used for this.
3. We'd probably have to configure STP to ensure the new VLAN has the proper root switch.
4. We'd need to add the new VLAN to trunk allow lists.
5. The new VLAN will also need an SVI on each distributed switch and an FHRP should be used as well.
6. The new subnet will need to be added into the routing protocol.
7. Firewall rules will have to be updated to allow the new subnet through and NAT will need to be configured too.
8. Depending on specific requirements, external routing may also need to be adjusted.

FIGURE 22.16 Full topology

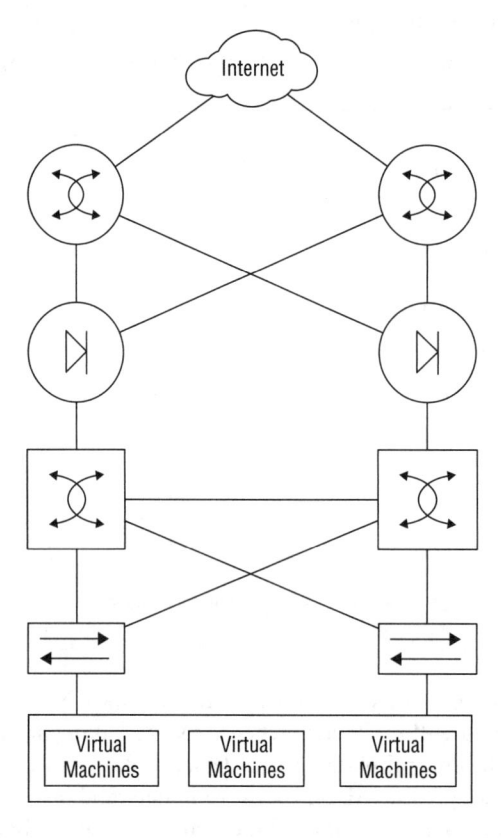

Not so bad? Well, now imagine that this just happens to be a really frequent request since most businesses constantly create new VMs! This is a very a big deal for the network team... It'll take a whole bunch of time to plan the changes, go through change control, and then actually implement them. Plus, the whole melee introduces a lot of risk with all those changes and increases the odds the network won't be cleaned up after a VM is no longer needed by the business. You get it now—adding a VM *is* no small thing!

Introduction to SDN

I'm going to begin our journey into the world of SDN by introducing you to two of its important components: the Northbound Interface and the Southbound interface. We gain access to the SDN solution via the Northbound Interface (NBI), which is actually similar to the management plane we just went over.

The SDN Controller communicates with network-level devices through the Southbound Interface (SBI). Figure 22.17 gives you a picture of the architecture.

FIGURE 22.17 SDN architecture

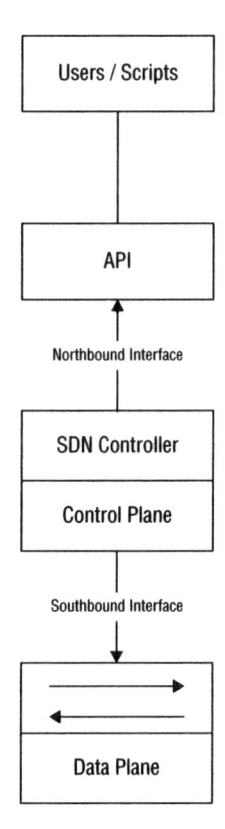

Northbound Interfaces

The reason we access the SDN Controller through the NBI is so we can deploy the SDN to get something done for us, and most of the time, we do that via a GUI in Meraki or through a restful API call inside a script. We're free to use whatever language we want for the script because all it's going to do is call the restful API.

Some of the vital things we can do through the NBI are creating VLANs, getting a list network of devices and generally polling the health of our networks. We can even automate the network in a way that would completely solve the scenario laid out at the beginning of this chapter!

Southbound Interfaces

Now as I said, the South Bound Interface (SBI) is how the SDN Controller actually talks with the network device, and there are lots of different ways it can do that depending on your specific solution. For instance, OpenDaylight, a popular open source SDN Controller, uses a protocol called OpenFlow to talk to switches. On the other hand, Meraki uses a proprietary solution right now since they manage everything themselves.

Here's a rundown of some common southbound interface protocols:

OpenFlow   Describes an industry-standard API defined by the ONF (opennetworking.org). It configures non-proprietary, white label switches and determines the flow path through the network. All configuration is done via NETCONF. OpenFlow first sends detailed and complex instructions to the control plane of the network elements in order to implement a new application policy. This is referred to as an imperative SDN model.

NETCONF   Even though all devices don't yet support NETCONF, it provides a network management protocol standardized by the IETF. With the help of RPC, you can install, manipulate, and delete the configuration of network devices using XML.

onePK   This is a Cisco proprietary SBI that allows you to inspect or modify the network element configuration without hardware upgrades. It makes life easier for developers by providing software development kits for Java, C, and Python. One PK is now legacy, but it's still possible to find it in the real world.

OpFlex   This is a southbound API that is used by Cisco ACI, OpFlex uses a declarative SDN model because the controller, which Cisco calls the Application Policy Infrastructure Controller (APIC), sends a more abstract, "summary policy" to the network elements. The summary policy makes the controller believe that the network elements will implement the required changes using their own control planes, since the devices will use a partially centralized control plane.

SDN Solutions

There are myriad SDN Controller solutions on the market today. Here's a list of the ones you might come across.

Cisco APIC-EM   This was Cisco's first real attempt at an enterprise SDN controller, and its main focus was configuring Cisco's IWAN solution. Considered legacy these days, APIC-EM was succeeded by DNA Center.

Cisco DNA-Center   This is Cisco's main enterprise SDN controller that we'll explore soon!

Cisco ACI   This is Cisco's Data Center focused SDN solution. You can learn all about ACI in the Data Center certification track.

Cisco SD-WAN   This solution brings the benefits of SDN to the WAN. You'll learn more about SD-WAN when you tackle the CCNP.

OpenDaylight   ODL is a popular open source OpenFlow controller. Cisco offers a wee bit of OpenFlow support, but Cisco definitely prefers their own SDN solutions due to OpenFlow limitations. Here's an example of OpenDaylight in Figure 22.18.

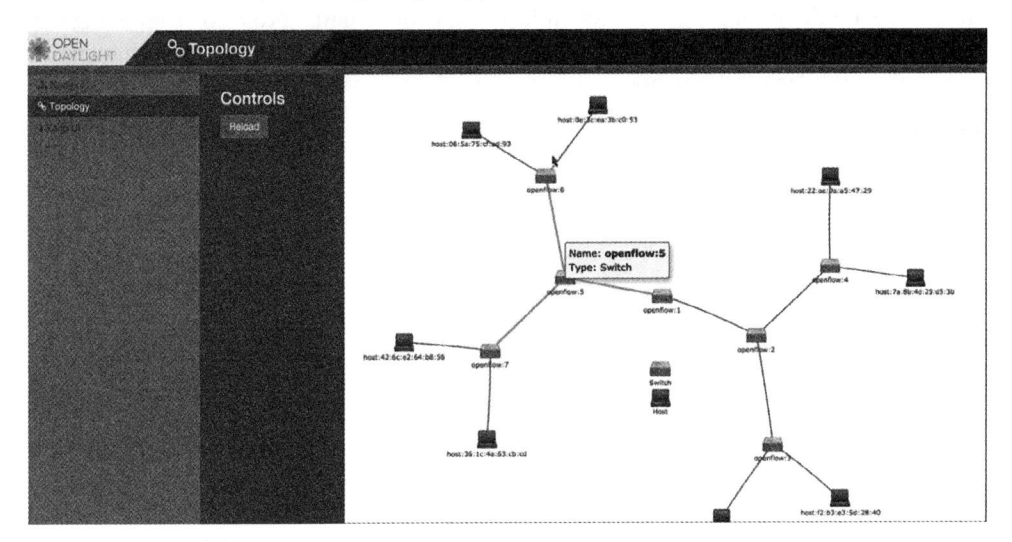

FIGURE 22.18 OpenDaylight topology

Separating the Control Plane

Software Defined Networking can actually mean lots of things, but it generally refers to separating the control plane from the data plane on a network device. Of course, this is a big help in device management because devices can be centrally managed by a controller, instead of manually.

So let's take a look at how things work on a plain, vanilla switch. Know that the control plane exists on each device independently and traffic is sent through interfaces in the data plane; see Figure 22.19.

FIGURE 22.19 SDN control plane

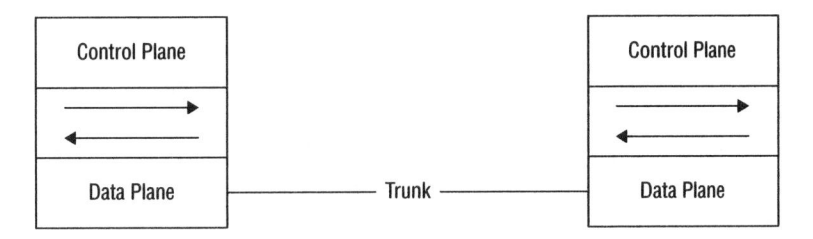

This is a great example of separating the control plane that doesn't plunge too deeply down the Cisco Meraki rabbit hole. Everything in Meraki's lineup is totally managed by the cloud, which means actual devices really only provide the data plane.

The advantage here is that you can centrally manage your equipment from anywhere—there's even an app for that, but it's pretty limited right now. The downside to the Meraki model is predictable: Because devices have to be able to reach the Meraki cloud before you can manage anything, things get awkward fast when you're flailing to resolve an outage or trying to get some pesky site online! But Meraki does equip us with basic, local management abilities that help troubleshoot connection issues as demonstrated in Figure 22.20.

FIGURE 22.20   SDN Controller

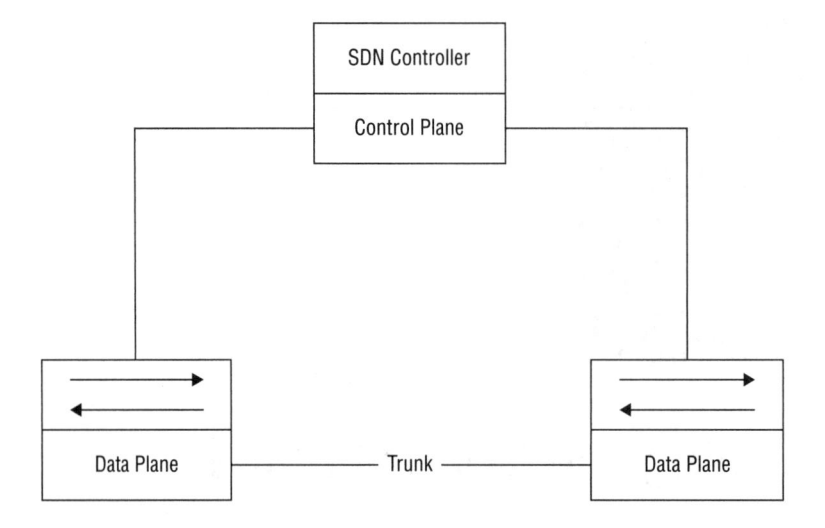

Controller-Based Architectures

Another good central management example is brought to you by the Cisco Wireless LAN Controller. The access points that join the WLC aren't to bright on their own, so they rely on the controller to push the configuration to them and tell them what to do.

Cisco SDN solutions like Digital Network Architecture (DNA) Center, which we'll talk about soon, allows you to centrally manage your network device's configuration through several applications that live on the SDN Controller.

This is better than traditional configuration because if you need to make changes to your network, you just adjust the settings in DNA Center to be replicated to your network's relevant devices.

This is a beautiful thing because it ensures configuration is consistent everywhere at once, greatly reducing the risk of death by typo when making a change on 50 switches manually—nice!

Of course, there's a downside to central management. For instance, say I were to accidentally type in "switchport trunk allowed VLAN 10" instead of "switchport trunk allowed VLAN add 10" on a switch. I'd probably cause an outage I'd have to scramble to fix, but it wouldn't be the end of the world. On the other hand, if I made that same mistake on a template that I'm pushing to all my switches? Apocalyptic—time to make sure the old resume is up to date for sure!

So fortunately, we can usually build out our configurations in the controller before applying them, maybe even getting someone to peer review things before sending away.

Anyway, controllers also give us a convenient central point for monitoring and automation since they're usually aware of a large part of the network, if not all of it.

Campus Architecture

Just so you know, the only type of architecture we've covered so far is the campus architecture that's most commonly used in traditional, enterprise networks. And just in case you need a quick review, in this kind of architecture, switches are connected to each other in a hierarchical fashion. The upside to this approach is that troubleshooting is easy since the stuff that belongs in each layer of the model is well defined, just like how the OSI model makes it easier to understand what's happening on the network and where.

All the endpoints in the network connect to the access layer where VLANs are assigned. Port-level features like port security or 802.1X are applied at this layer. Since access layer switches don't have a lot of responsibilities and generally, no layer 3 configuration aside from what's needed for managing the switch, you can usually get away with cheaper layer 2 switches and save some coin.

The Distribution layer hosts all the SVIs and provides any IP-based services the network needs like DHCP relay. The distribution switch uses layer 2 interfaces with the access layer switches to terminate the VLANs, plus layer 3 interfaces to connect to the core switches. It will also a run a routing protocol to share routes with them.

The core layer's only job is providing high speed routing between the distribution switches. It doesn't offer any other services—it just makes sure packets get from one switch to another. Here's an example campus topology in Figure 22.21.

FIGURE 22.21 Campus fabric

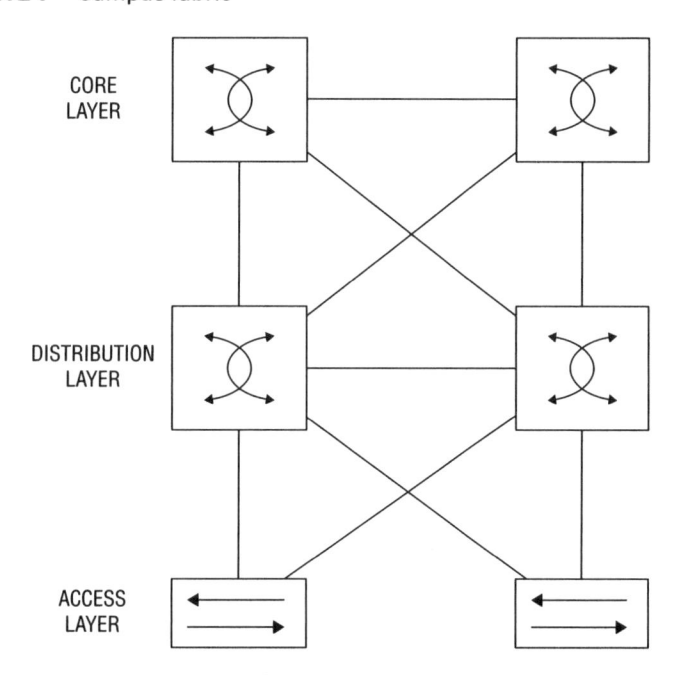

Spine/Leaf Architecture

The new and preferred architecture for controller-based networks and data centers is called CLOS, which stands for nothing other than the guy's name who thought it up. CLOS is a spine/leaf design wherein you have two types of switches: a spine and a leaf.

The Leaf switch maps to the access and distribution layers in the Cisco 3 tier model and is what you connect your devices into. Each leaf switch has a high-bandwidth uplink to each spine switch.

The spine switch is a lot like the core because its sole job is to provide super fast transport across the leaf switches. Because leaf switches only connect to the spine switches not other leaf switches, traffic is really predictable since all destinations in the fabric follow the same path: Leaf -> Spine -> Leaf. Because everything is 3 hops away, traffic is easily load balanced in the routing table via equal-cost load balancing (ECMP).

What's more, it's also very easy to expand the network. If you need more ports, just add a leaf switch. Need more bandwidth? Just add another spine switch. Figure 22.22 pictures CLOS topology.

FIGURE 22.22 CLOS topology

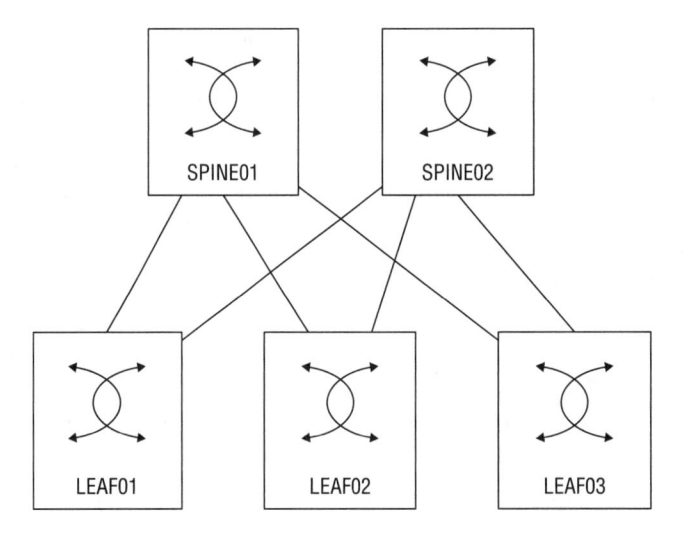

SDN Network Components

One of the benefits of Software Defined Networking is that a SDN controller can abstract away the "boring stuff" so you can focus on the fun more complex configurations.

One of the ways SDN achieves this is by dividing the network into two different parts. An underlay, this is the physical network that is focused on providing a lot of layer 3 connectivity throughout the network. The underlay typically uses the spine/leaf architecture we just discussed but can also use the campus architecture depending on the solution being used. For example, DNA Center's Software Defined Access solution is based on a typical campus topology because it is aimed at enterprise networks. SD-Access does use slightly different names though, the access layer is called the edge, and the intermediate node is the equivalent of the distribution layer but we don't need to worry too much about that architecture.

There is also the overlay component, which is where the services the SDN controller provides is tunneled over the underlay.

We'll have a closer look at the underlay and overlay in more detail.

Underlay

Underlay has its own components, and we'll cover each of them in this section:

- MTU
- Interface Config
- OSPF or IS-IS Config
- Verification

So the underlay is basically the physical network that provides connectivity so that the overlay network can be built upon, or *over* it. There's usually basic configuration on it and its focus is on advertising the device's loopback IP into OSPF or IS-IS is another link state routing protocol that is beyond what we need to learn for the CCNA.

Devices in the underlay tend to be cabled so they're highly redundant, removing single points of failure and optimizing performance. One way to implement this is via a full mesh topology, where every device is connected to every other device. Even though a full mesh network provides maximum redundancy, it can get out of hand fast because of the number of links involved as your network grows.

Figure 22.23 pictures an example of a standard underlay topology.

FIGURE 22.23 Underlay topology

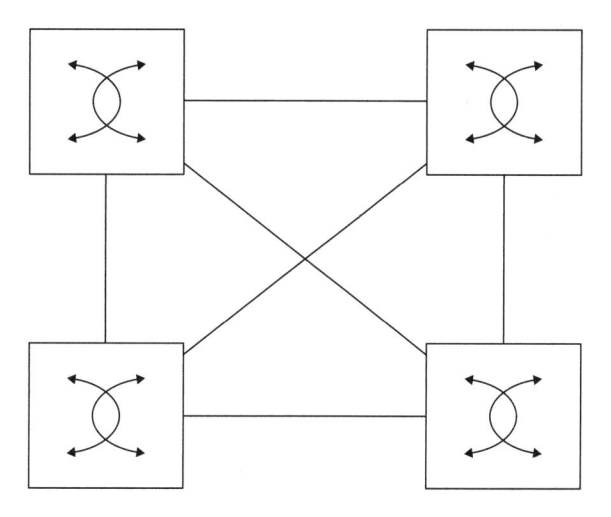

MTU

The Underlay's job it to carry a lot of traffic with larger packet payloads than you'd normally see in a standard network. Because of this, it's a good idea to raise the MTU on the underlay switches so the larger packets don't give you any grief.

You change the MTU on most Cisco IOS or IOS-XE based switches via the **system mtu** command. The switch must be rebooted for the change to take effect:

```
SW01(config)#system mtu ?
  <1500-9198>  MTU size in bytes
```

```
SW01(config)#system mtu 9000
Global Ethernet MTU is set to 9000 bytes.
Note: this is the Ethernet payload size, not the total
Ethernet frame size, which includes the Ethernet
header/trailer and possibly other tags, such as ISL or
802.1q tags.
SW01(config)#do reload
```

> **NOTE** OSPF requires the MTU to match on both ends of the neighbor adjacency to work properly, so when the MTU is changed, it has to be changed on neighboring devices too. To get around this, you can apply the **ip ospf mtu-ignore** command on neighboring interfaces to fix OSPF without changing the MTU.

Since the underlay will be running a routing protocol, **ip routing** needs to be enabled to make the act as a layer 3 switch:

```
SW01(config)#ip routing
```

Interface Config

It's a bad idea to go with Spanning Tree Protocol in an underlay topology because its job is to block redundant links—a problem, because it results in the underlay switch's superfast uplink interfaces that clock in between 10gbs, 40gbs, even 100gbs, not always being used. What a waste! You can sort of mitigate this by spending (wasting) a bunch of time adjusting the STP configuration by spreading the VLAN root across several switches, but it really won't solve the problem because each VLAN will still have blocked links.

The better way to handle this is to use only layer 3 interfaces. Doing this means STP won't run at all, meaning all the switch interfaces in the underlay will also run without being blocked. Plus, there won't be any loops to worry about since its just OSPF or IS-IS doing the routing. And as a further bonus, because the switches should all have the same number of connections, the routing table can load balance traffic using Equal Cost Load Balancing (ECMP)!

So with all that in mind, I'm going to configure the interfaces connecting the switches together as layer 3 interfaces and give them an IP address. To be more efficient, I'll also configure OSPF on the interfaces to use the point-to-point network type in order to remove the need for a designated router, like this:

```
SW01(config)#int g3/0
SW01(config-if)#no switchport
SW01(config-if)#ip address 10.1.21.1 255.255.255.0
SW01(config-if)#ip ospf network point-to-point
SW01(config-if)#int g3/1
SW01(config-if)#no switchport
SW01(config-if)#ip address 10.1.22.1 255.255.255.0
SW01(config-if)#ip ospf network point-to-point
SW01(config-if)#int g3/2
SW01(config-if)#no switchport
SW01(config-if)#ip address 10.1.31.1 255.255.255.0
SW01(config-if)#ip ospf network point-to-point
SW01(config-if)#int g3/3
SW01(config-if)#no switchport
SW01(config-if)#ip address 10.1.32.1 255.255.255.0
SW01(config-if)#ip ospf network point-to-point
SW01(config-if)#int g2/2
SW01(config-if)#no switchport
SW01(config-if)#ip address 10.1.41.1 255.255.255.0
SW01(config-if)#ip ospf network point-to-point
SW01(config-if)#int g2/3
SW01(config-if)#no switchport
SW01(config-if)#ip address 10.1.42.1 255.255.255.0
SW01(config-if)#ip ospf network point-to-point
```

Each switch in the underlay should have a loopback interface for later, when we talk about the overlay:

```
SW01(config-if)#interface loopback 0
SW01(config-if)#ip add 192.168.255.1 255.255.255.255
```

OSPF Config

Next, OSPF needs to be configured. There's really nothing wrong using another routing protocol like EIGRP here, but since the CCNA only focuses on OSPF, I' going with that. I want all IPs on the switch to run OSPF, so I'll use the **network 0.0.0.0 0.0.0.0 area 0** shortcut to enable all interfaces:

```
SW01(config-if)#router ospf 1
SW01(config-router)#network 0.0.0.0 0.0.0.0 area 0
SW01(config-router)#exit
```

Other Underlay Config

The underlay's focus is to ensure routing is working so there isn't much else to add to the configuration aside from a standard switch setup like configuring AAA or NTP. Some solutions require features like multicast routing, but that's above the CCNA level.

Verification

To save some typing time, I went ahead and configured the other switches in the topology just like I showed you with SW01. At this point, we can see that all the switch interfaces have formed an OSPF adjacency:

```
SW01#show ip ospf nei

Neighbor ID     Pri   State         Dead Time   Address     Interface
192.168.255.3   0     FULL/   -     00:00:38    10.1.32.3   GigabitEthernet3/3
192.168.255.3   0     FULL/   -     00:00:37    10.1.31.3   GigabitEthernet3/2
192.168.255.2   0     FULL/   -     00:00:37    10.1.22.2   GigabitEthernet3/1
192.168.255.2   0     FULL/   -     00:00:37    10.1.21.2   GigabitEthernet3/0
192.168.255.4   0     FULL/   -     00:00:34    10.1.42.4   GigabitEthernet2/3
192.168.255.4   0     FULL/   -     00:00:34    10.1.41.4   GigabitEthernet2/2
```

When I look at the routing table, I see that SW01 has learned each switch's loopback address and is load balancing the route across two interfaces because of ECMP:

```
SW01#show ip route ospf | b 192.168.255

         192.168.255.0/32 is subnetted, 4 subnets
O        192.168.255.2 [110/2] via 10.1.22.2, 00:11:52, GigabitEthernet3/1
                       [110/2] via 10.1.21.2, 00:12:02, GigabitEthernet3/0
O        192.168.255.3 [110/2] via 10.1.32.3, 00:04:32, GigabitEthernet3/3
                       [110/2] via 10.1.31.3, 00:04:42, GigabitEthernet3/2
O        192.168.255.4 [110/2] via 10.1.42.4, 00:01:40, GigabitEthernet2/3
                       [110/2] via 10.1.41.4, 00:01:40, GigabitEthernet2/2
```

Okay—we're done! The underlay is now all set and ready for the overlay configuration.

Overlay

Basically, an overlay is a "virtual network" that's tunneled over your underlay devices. This allows the SDN Controller to have strict control over the traffic running through the network. The type of tunnel being used varies depending on the exact SDN solution, but generally it is Virtual Extensible LAN (VXLAN) being used. VXLAN is a way of tunneling Layer 2 traffic over Layer 3, this allows you to connect VLANs across routed networks, but the details are above the CCNA level.

The overlay is where the advanced configurations like security or QoS gets introduced into the network. The underlay has no visibility into the tunneled networks so it can't effectively do things like filtering traffic.

Routing for the overlay is usually handled by BGP or EIGRP. Going with link-state protocols is a bad idea because they require all devices in an area to have the same LSAs. Plus, you can't easily improve the routing table with summaries, etc.

Dynamic Multipoint Virtual Private Network (DMVPN) is a very popular type of overlay that runs over the WAN. In this topology, each branch connects to the hub router through DMVPN using the 10.100.123.0/24 network, allowing us to run an IGP across the Internet to provide that all-important, consistent routing factor. DMVPN actually offers lots of advantages, but for now, check out Figure 22.24 for a simple example of an overlay.

FIGURE 22.24 DMVPN topology

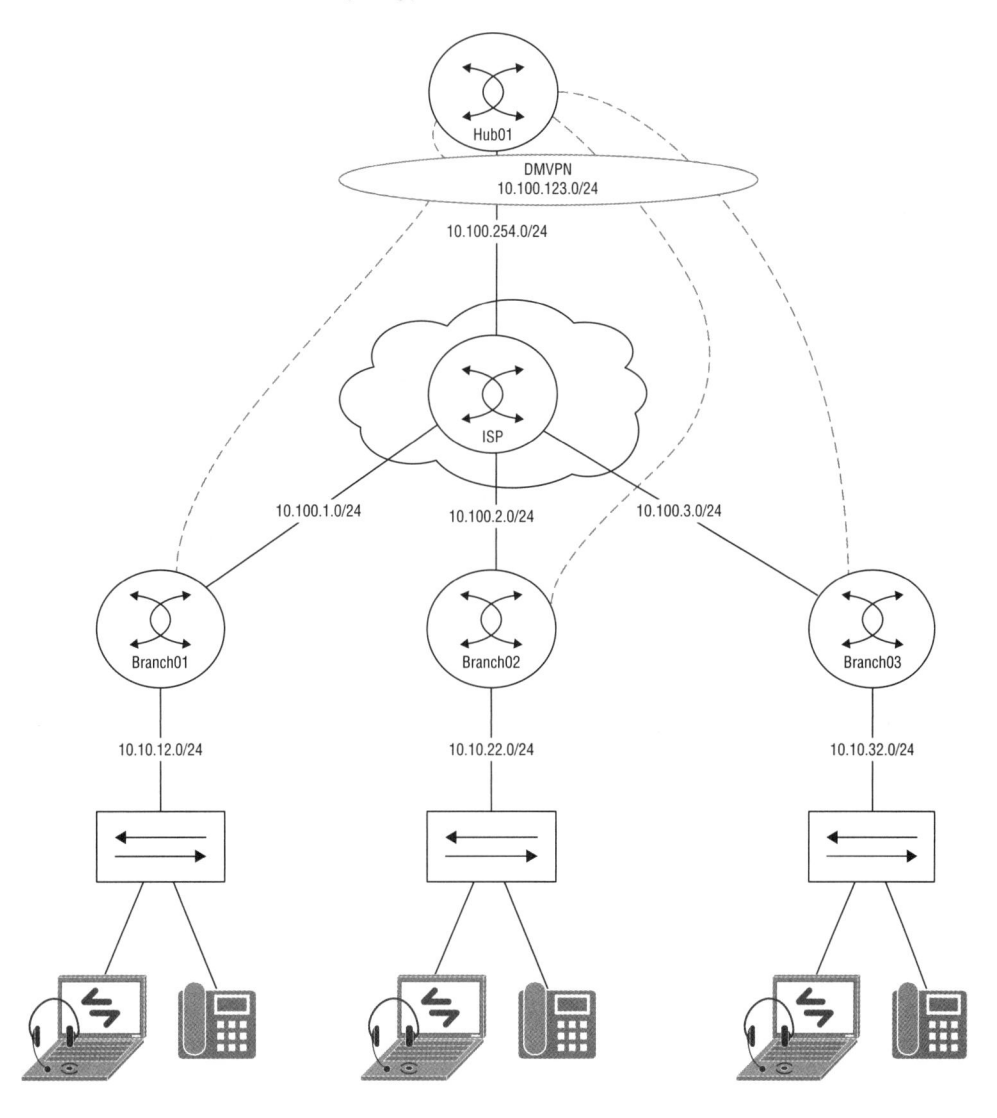

Fabric

The network fabric is actually the simplest thing in this chapter to understand. It's really just a shorthand term for all the layer 3 network devices—the routers, switches, firewalls, wireless controllers access points involved in a solution. We can refer to the network as a fabric when we're talking about SDN because the network details are abstracted by the SDN Controller.

Put another way, a fabric is a simple, high-speed, layer 3 network. The motivation behind this trend is that IP networks scale better than layer 2 networks because we don't need to work a bunch of complex engineering magic to get around STP limitations. Also, layer 3 fabric isn't usually so risky when it comes to misconfigurations because the SDN Controller dynamically builds and maintains the underlay and overlay networks for you!

DNA Center Overview

The rest of our time in this chapter is going is going to be spent on DNA Center. When we wrap it up, you'll be well up to speed on all the various services it serves up. Basically, the whole point of DNA Center is to be your one-stop shop for managing all networking and troubleshooting needs.

In that vein, DNA Center provides full network monitoring just like we talked about in the NMS section, only more. In addition to the SNMP monitoring and storage for statistics, DNA Center captures a complete snapshot of your network for up to a week—pure gold when troubleshooting network snags of any stripe! DNA Center even offers troubleshooting advice to help you resolve complex issues by taking advantage of AI/Big Data analytics to help you make decisions.

The server has a robust NCM component that can not only do configuration apply templates, it takes things much further by allowing you to automatically configure switches just by taking them out of the box, connecting the network interfaces, and powering it up!

As if that wasn't enough, DNA Center is also an actual SDN Controller, fully capable of building out underlay and overlay networks in order to support Cisco's Software Defined Access feature. And Cisco is continuously adding new features and application integration to the solution. For example, DNA Center can replace APIC-EM by managing IWAN, a legacy SD-WAN solution through an SDN application. The server can also centrally manage the WLCs in your network and will be able to eventually manage other Cisco solutions like SD-WAN or ACI down the road.

Figure 22.25 shows an example of the DNA Center dashboard, plus a sweet summary of everything going on the network.

FIGURE 22.25 DNA Overview

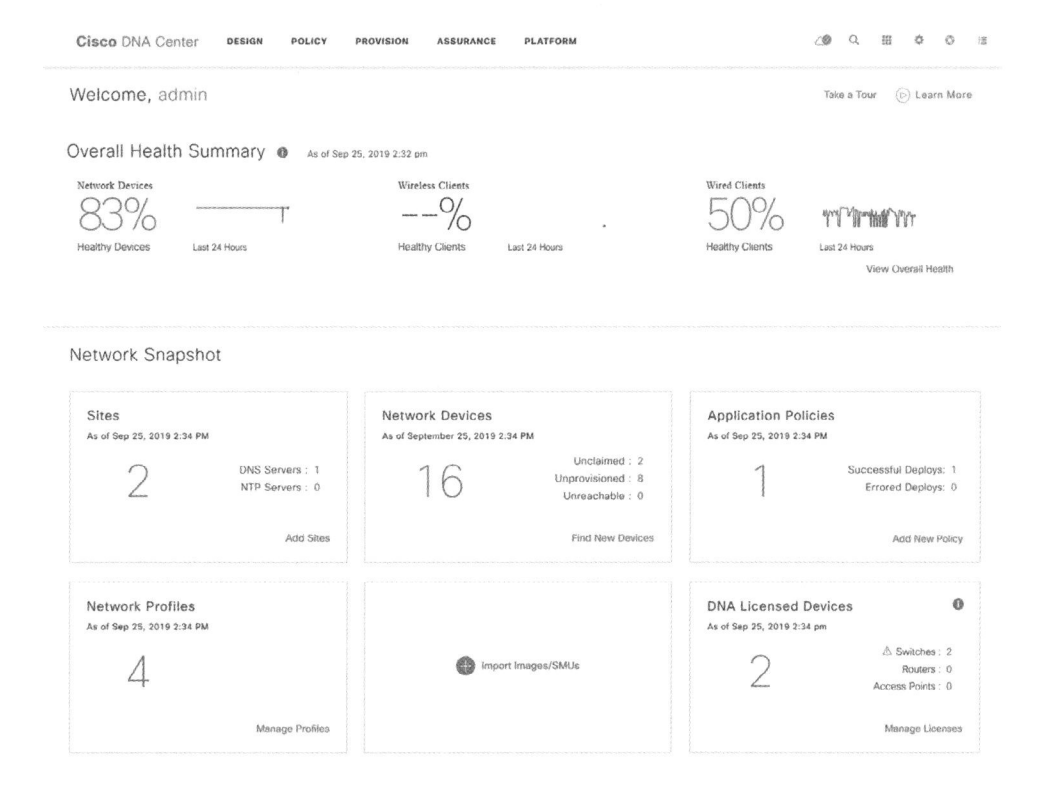

Nice, huh? Now let's walk through some of the powerful features that DNA Center brings to the table and contrast them with how we'd trudge through these same tasks in traditional network management.

Discovery

To make our lives easier, DNA Center can dynamically search the network for the devices to add so we don't have to add them all manually. The Discovery feature works by querying IP ranges you specify or by logging into a device and following its CDP/LLDP information throughout your network.

Once DNA Center has detected devices, it'll try to access them with SNMPv2, SNMPv3, Telnet, SSH, HTTP(S), and Netconf to gain control of the device and add it to the inventory.

Discovery jobs can be scheduled to run as often as you want to ensure all your Cisco devices are managed by DNA Center. You can also create multiple jobs in case you need to use different connection options in other parts of your network.

Figure 22.26 shows what the discovery page looks like.

FIGURE 22.26 DNA discovery

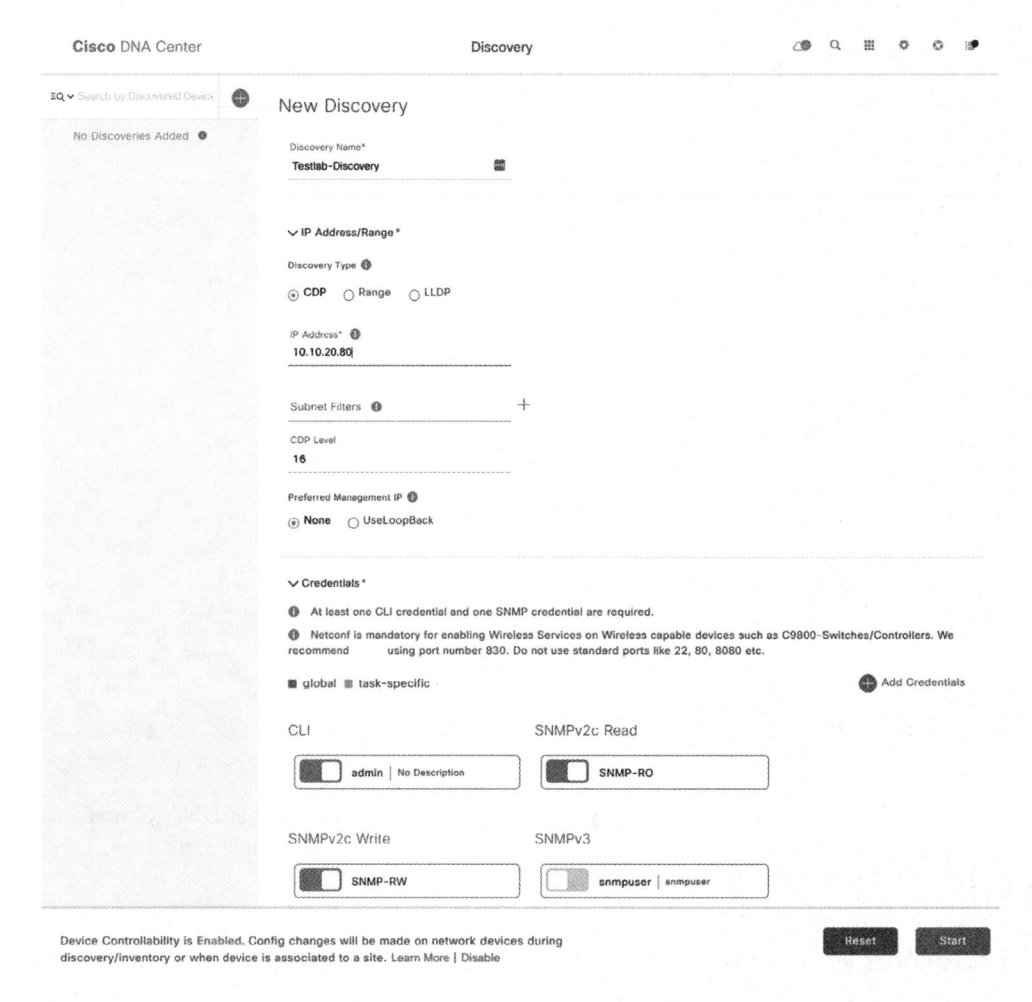

So while it's true that other NMS solutions can usually discover nodes in the network, DNA Center again takes things a step further by serving up a lot of robust options for protocol support.

Another cool factor comes down to licensing… When you buy a solution like SolarWinds or Prime Infrastructure, you've also got to pony up for licensing to be able to add nodes. And SolarWinds charges you for every little element you add, even a measly network interface. Just imagine you have four switches in a stack and each one of them has 48 interfaces. That comes to a whopping 192 licenses required to add all those interfaces into SolarWinds for monitoring! Because of this, most SolarWinds deployments focus only on adding vital interfaces like uplink ports.

But with DNA Center, life is so much better because each device has the proper license installed locally, which is something you can take care when you order the device from your Cisco partner.

Contrast all of the above if you aren't using an NMS. You'd have to manually keep track of your network devices with either an open source solution or maybe just an Excel spreadsheet that you edit when you make changes to your network!

Network Hierarchy

A wonderful benefit DNA Center brings is allowing us to organize our networks into sites and locations using the Network Hierarchy feature as pictured in Figure 22.26.

FIGURE 22.27 DNA Network Hierarchy

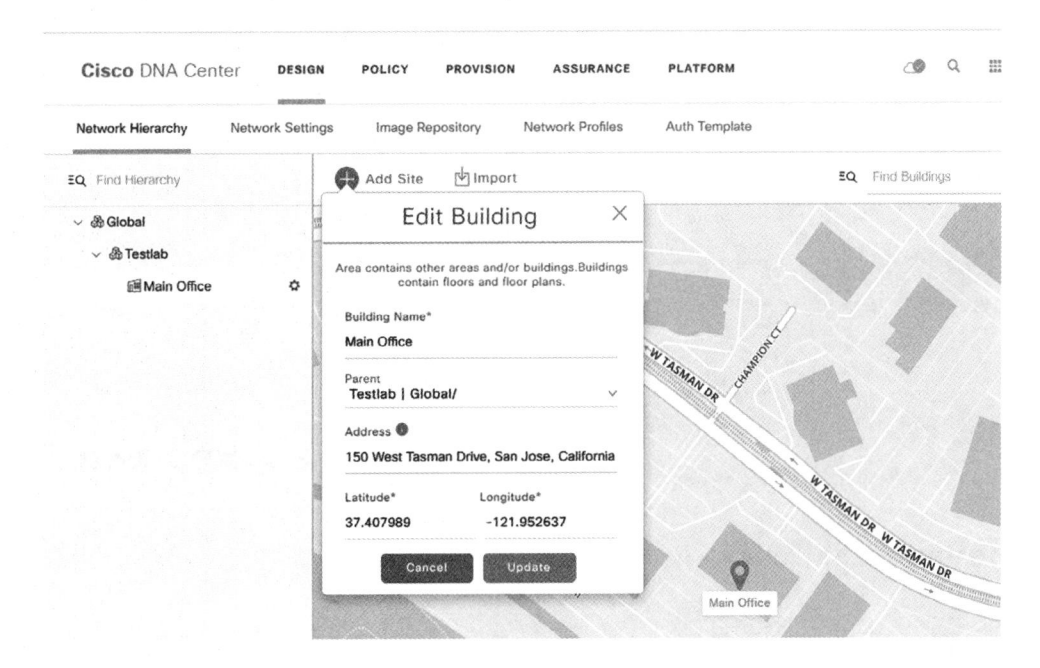

This gives us another troubleshooting advantage, provides site survey information to Wireless Controllers, and also provides configuration consistency across various locations. Common settings like Authentication, Syslog servers, NTP Servers, or the Message of the Day can be automatically pushed to network devices when they're added to the inventory. This feature ensures that there's no stale configuration on random routers after the NTP server has an IP change because we can just update the value for the DNA. Check out Figure 22.28.

DNA Center can also fully manage your wireless environment so any WLC configurations, like when you add a new SSID, can be done in the Network Hierarchy tool. This makes it easy to create wireless configurations to apply to multiple WLCs. Take a look at the Wireless settings in Figure 22.29.

FIGURE 22.28 DNA Network Settings

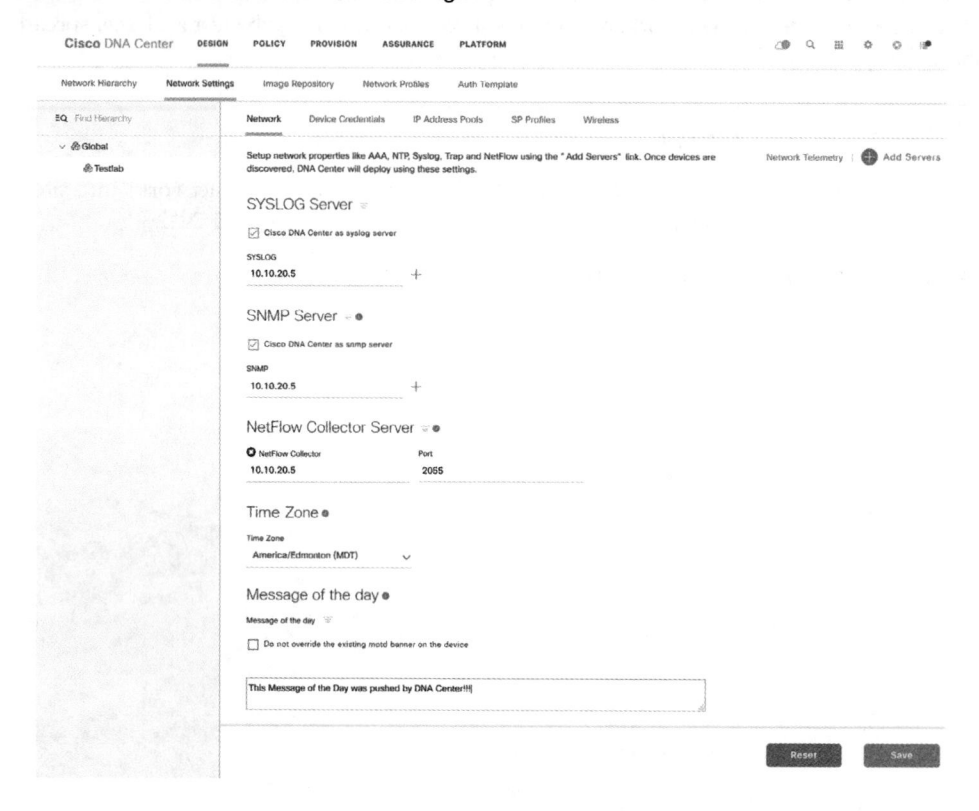

FIGURE 22.29 DNA Wireless Settings

A traditional NCM like SolarWinds has a similar feature to Network Hierarchy called Compliance. It allows you to define which configuration should appear on a network device, with the NCM alerting you if the device doesn't have that configuration. The difference here is that the compliance feature won't usually push the configuration to ensure consistency. NCMs rarely allow you to group network devices in a hierarchy. Instead, they typically make you manage each device independently.

NCMs generally can't centrally control your wireless controllers either since that requires deep vendor knowledge to make happen. Whereas, DNA Center uses that in-depth knowledge to offer plenty integrations into Cisco devices beyond just wireless!

One caveat is that DNA Center doesn't yet support device configuration backups. Because of this we still need to use SolarWinds or Prime Infrastructure to handle device backups. But there's some rapid development going on with DNA Center so maybe a nice backup feature will be available by the time you read this sentence.

It kind of goes without saying, but if you're doing all this manually, you'd have to be logging into all your network devices almost constantly to verify that the configuration is still current and meeting your needs. Configuration changes over time as you troubleshoot issues or execute changes on devices.

Templates

When you need more specific configuration pushed to network devices, you can apply Template features to a Network Hierarchy location.

The Template feature allows you to type out the IOS configuration you want applied and to make things easier it also supports the Apache Velocity scripting language. Apache lets you make your templates more powerful by adding more functionality into your configuration with some cool little tools like:

Variables Variable can be defined anywhere in the configuration by adding a dollar sign in front of a word. In the screenshot example, I created a variable called **loopback_ip** so I can have a different loopback interface IP on each network device.

Enable Mode By default, DNA Center will assume everything in the template is a configuration command. If you need to push an enable command like **clock set** you can put the command between #MODE_ENABLE before the command and #MODE_END_ENABLE after it like this:

```
#MODE_ENABLE
clock set Sept 17 2019 00:00:00
#MODE_END_ENABLE
```

Interactive commands Most commands in IOS don't prompt the user for additional input but some, like the **banner motd** or the **crypto key generate rsa general-keys** commands, do.

If you need to push such a command, you can put #INTERACTIVE at the top and #ENDS_INTERACTIVE at the bottom.

This can get a little confusing, so I'm going to give you an example to bring it all home to you. For the interactive portion, I put a <IQ> after the command, and followed by the expected prompt values, you'd enter your response after the a <R>.

To further clarify things, check out this output using the crypto key to generate rsa general-keys command:

```
CSR11(config)#crypto key generate rsa general-keys
% You already have RSA keys defined named CSR11.testlab.com.
% Do you really want to replace them? [yes/no]:
```

Okay—now you can see here that the CLI is asking us if we want to replace the keys with a yes or no prompt. To add this to a template we do the following:

```
#INTERACTIVE
crypto key generate rsa general-keys <IQ>yes/no<R> yes
#ENDS_INTERACTIVE
```

The yes/no answers are captured by the <IQ> tag (IQ standing for Interactive Question), and the response is captured by the <R> tag.

You don't need to know how to make templates for the exam, but it's good to see the functionality is there. Have a look at a template in Figure 22.30.

FIGURE 22.30 DNA Switch Template

Templates work pretty much the same with DNA Center and other NCM solutions, with the only real difference being found in the scripting engine capabilities. We usually do this manually in a sort of log by keeping text files with configurations that the network team can copy and paste into the router as they need them.

Topology

DNA Center likes to build a layer 3 diagram using the network devices it knows about. This is great because we get to reference a dynamic network diagram when troubleshooting instead of only relying on some Visio diagram that's probably way out of date! It creates its diagrams with the information provided by CDP and LLDP, and it also follows the MAC and ARP tables to figure out what's connected. If the map isn't entirely accurate, you can tweak it manually. DNA Center also needs to know the topology so it can inform other features like SD-Access.

Figure 22.31 offers a snapshot of what the topology map looks like.

FIGURE 22.31 DNA topology

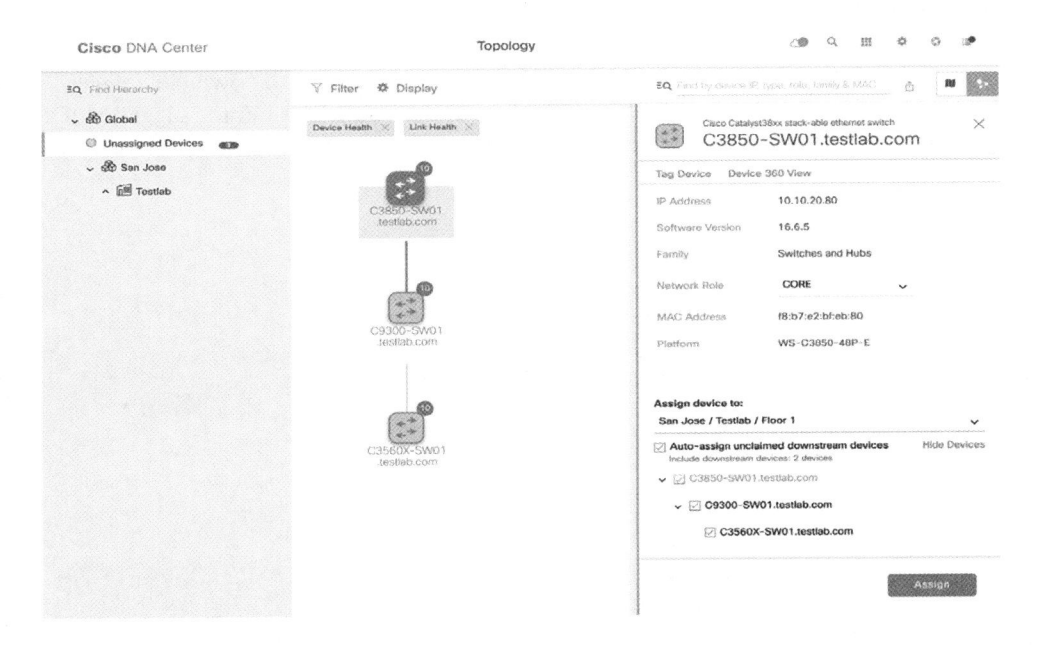

Good to know is that while NMS solutions can create network maps, they're often created manually by the network team. For instance, SolarWinds has a network map creator used to arrange the network devices into the network topology you want to see in the dashboard.

The thing is, doing this manually means maintaining a network topology made in Visio, and as implied, these almost always get out of date fast. As far as I know, no one has ever met anyone chomping at the bit to obsessively make sure the documentation is current!

To everyone's relief, DNA Center tries to improve life by dynamically creating the network topology for us. It discovers network devices and adds them to the map in an intelligent way. True—you'll definitely still need to customize the map to make sure its accurate, but it does the heavy lifting for you.

Upgrades

Another thing that will scatter everyone on your team is when you need to upgrade a device's firmware. This is painfully boring: You must find and download the proper IOS image for your device, copy the image onto the device, set the boot statement, reboot, and then... WAIT.

Now while upgrading a router or two doesn't sound so bad, things can get really get out of control if some security vulnerability is discovered within the IOS you're using. Yep—just like that, now you've got a hundred routers you need to upgrade—*fast*! Upgrading is usually a big part of onboarding a new router too since the IOS that ships on a router is probably not the same version you actually want to be using on everything.

Breathe easy because DNA Center can allow help you standardize the IOS versions you're using on all your network devices by making sure new network devices are automatically upgraded to the version you want. This feature allows us to download images directly from Cisco.com or manually upload them and it also points out the suggested IOS release for the platform. Here's an example of the repository used by the upgrade feature in Figure 22.32.

FIGURE 22.32 DNA upgrade repository

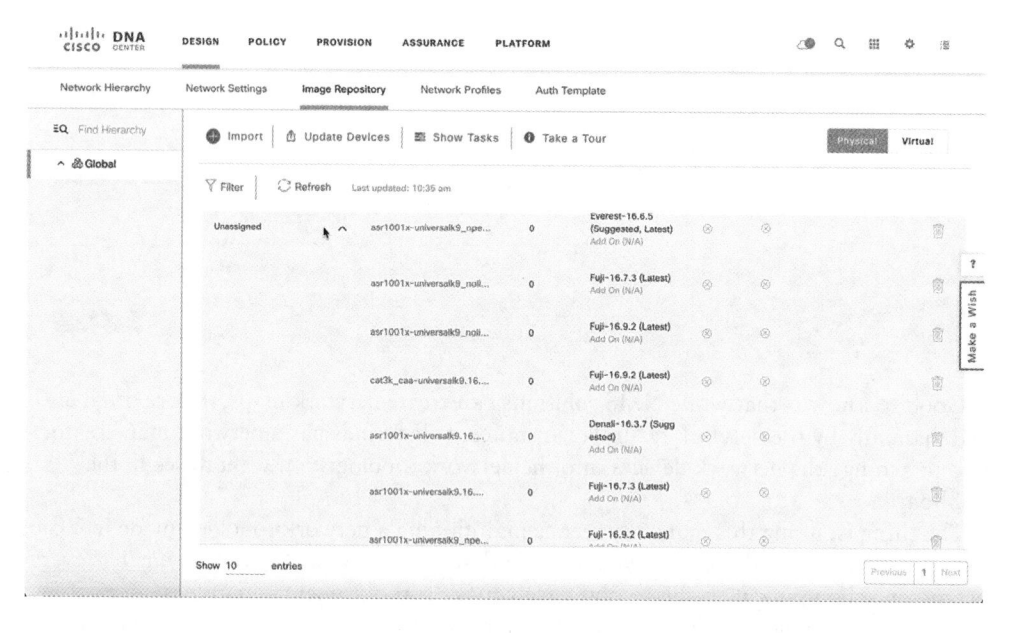

DNA Center will move the image onto the device using SCP or HTTPS, which is a heck of a lot more efficient than trying to use TFTP across the network. The example in Figure 22.33 shows DNA Center pushing an image to my Cisco switch.

FIGURE 22.33 DNA upgrading devices

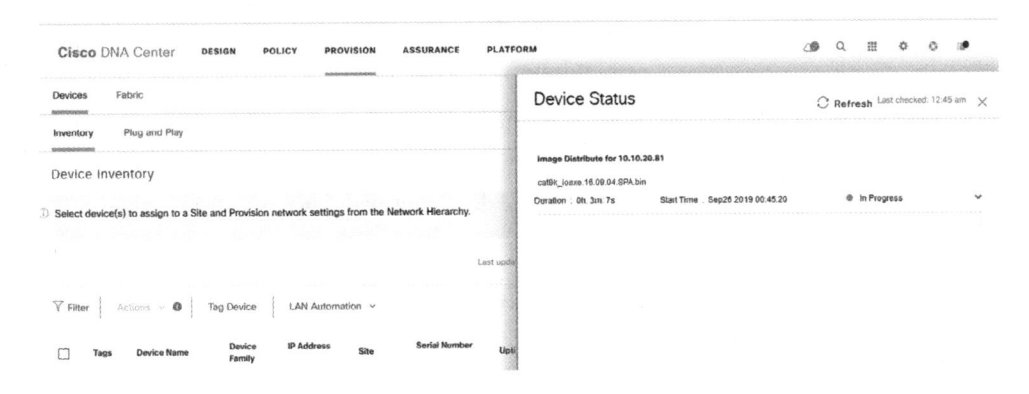

What's more, when you schedule an upgrade, DNA Center will go through a bunch of checks to make sure the device is going to support it. Here's a list of the Device Upgrade Readiness Pre-checks:

Precheck	Description
Device management status	Checks if the device is successfully managed in Cisco DNA Center.
File transfer check	Checks if the device is reachable through SCP and HTTPS.
NTP clock check	Compares device time and Cisco DNA Center time to ensure certificates from DNA Center can be installed on the device.
Flash check	Verifies if there's enough room on the device for the update. Some devices support the ability to automatically cleanup flash to try to fit the update file in by deleting unused files.
Config register check	Verifies the config registry value, ensuring the switch will boot properly if you forgot to fix the config register after a password recovery.
Crypto RSA check	Checks whether an RSA certificate is installed. This is required for SSH and HTTPs to work.
Crypto TLS check	Checks whether the device supports TLS 1.2.

Precheck	Description
IP Domain name check	Checks whether the domain name is configured, which is required for SSH and HTTPs to work.
Startup config check	Checks whether the startup configuration exists for the device.
Service Entitlement check	Checks if the device has valid license.
Interface check	Checks the status of the device's management interface.
CDP neighbors check	Displays information about the connected routers and switches in the network discovered using CDP.
Running Config check	Checks the configuration that's currently running on the device.
Spanning Tree Summary check	Checks the information about the Spanning Tree Protocol (STP).
AP Summary check	Displays the AP Summary associated with the Cisco Wireless Controllers devices.

Time for our comparison: NCMs can push IOS images to Cisco devices too, but they generally don't have as many sanity checks and safety precautions that DNA Center does. For instance, SolarWinds basically just pushes a **copy tftp** command to the device to download the firmware, and depending on your script, it'll also change the boot statement and reboot for you. And of course, SolarWinds doesn't have direct access to cisco.com to download the firmware for you, so you'll need to download the file manually and store the file on the server.

Doing this manually is fairly labor intensive because not only do you have to download the file, you'll probably need to set up a TFTP/FTP/SCP server to transfer it. Then you'll have to manually log into the device to start the upgrade.

Command Runner

One of the beautiful benefits of central management is that you can take advantage of the fact that DNA Center can access many devices at once to do get something done. The command runner tool lets you to run a bunch of commands against devices in your inventory and store the results. This comes in handy when you need to quickly verify information across your network devices, like when you want to be sure all your routers can see a new OSPF route! Another pro is that the output can also be exported as a text file in case you want to store it or use it in a document.

Configuration commands are not supported though, so you'll need to use the template feature if you want to push changes to the device. Have a look at Command Runner here in Figure 22.34.

FIGURE 22.34 DNA Command Runner

Both DNA Center and NCMs have similar functionality for this feature. Both can push commands to several devices and present the output to you all tied up in a bow.

If you aren't using a solution, though, there you would be, connecting to each device, one at a time and saving the output on a Notepad or a email to send later—ugh!

Assurance

Sadly, blaming the network when it usually isn't at fault is rampant in this field. A huge amount of your time is going to be spent troubleshooting network issues based on vague, outdated, and incorrect information.

Let's say a manager comes up to you at lunch saying he couldn't connect to the corporate wireless a few days ago on his laptop but it works fine now. How would you troubleshoot that one? Well, you could check ticketing to find out if there was an outage at the time that could explain the snag. If you don't have any tickets to rummage through, maybe your team members will remember something, right?

Of course, you could also log into the wireless controller or Cisco ISE if you're using it for wireless security and check there for any logs, but it's pretty hard to find relevant logs from a few days ago and even harder to correlate them!

What about trying to replicate the issue on your laptop? That'd be a tough one unless the issue consistently pops up. You'd be stuck trying to connect at random times in the day in different locations to try to hit the issue.

But all that was before you were armed with DNA Center's Assurance feature... This amazing tool actually gives you access to a time machine! It stores loads of network information for a week—everything from logs, network health issues seen on the network, and connection results—all stored and ready for you. Check out an overview of network health in Figure 22.35.

FIGURE 22.35 DNA Network Health

The Assurance feature also correlates issues and provides suggestions on what the cause probably was, even offering troubleshooting tips about the steps you can try. This is so good because it makes it possible to troubleshoot glitches that slipped by your radar since users can just get used to it taking three tries to connect to wireless before it works so they never even mention it!

Figure 22.36 gives you a picture of the wireless troubleshooting page.

DNA Center's Assurance feature is unique, and it's no small thing. NMS solutions can give you a lot of great information, but only DNA Center can carry out full analytics to give us a solid network time capsule snapshot right now.

And doing this manually turns you into a gumshoe relentlessly grilling users for information and stuck doing a bunch tests to possibly hit on issues. You may even be reduced to mindlessly fishing through configurations hoping something jumps out at you!

FIGURE 22.36 DNA wireless clients

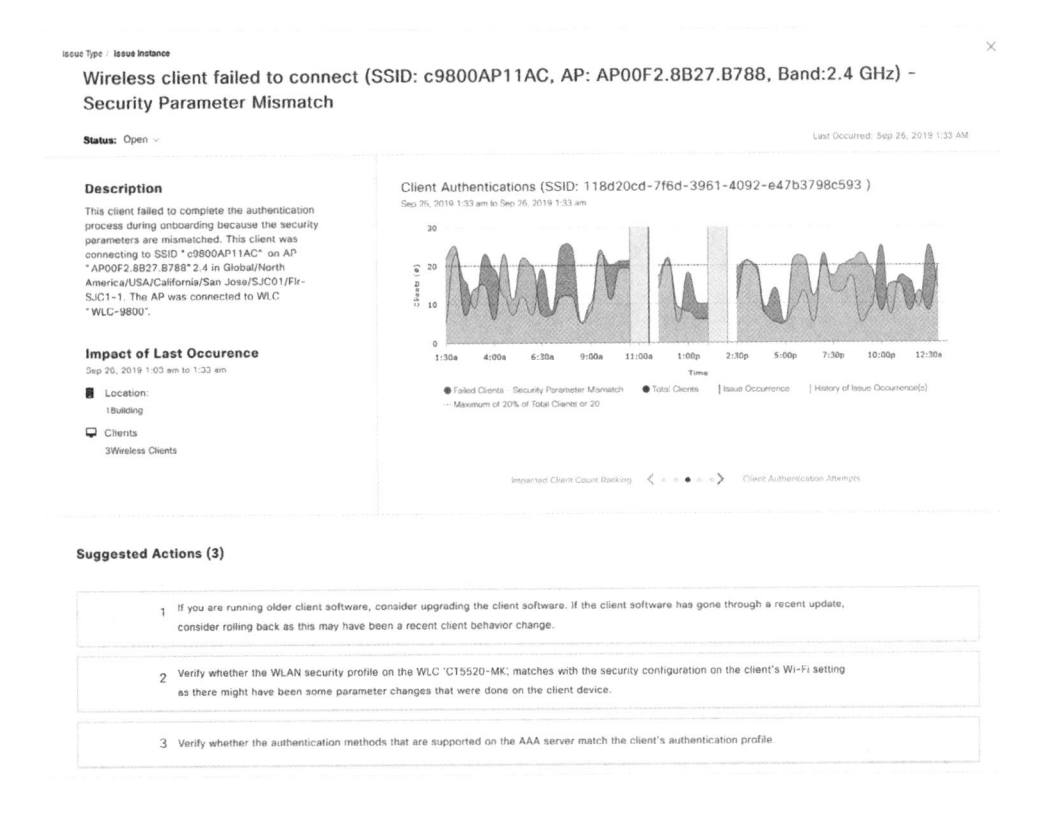

Path Trace

The path a given user's network traffic takes through the network isn't always so straightforward today. Back in the day, traceroute was a go-to way to determine the path a user is taking to get to their destination. But it won't show you that that wireless traffic is going through a CAPWAP tunnel or that a site is connected through a VPN or a DMVPN. Traceroute also won't reveal the layer 2 switches that the packet must travel through.

Path Trace is an evolution of the APIC-EM Path Trace feature that was on the previous CCNA. It takes advantage of the fact that DNA Center knows everything about all the network devices in your network and gives you a visual representation of the path taken from source to destination.

The tool reveals the true path tunnels take and shows you if any ACLs on network devices will block your traffic. You can even specify which ports you want to test. Check out Path Trace in action in Figure 22.37.

FIGURE 22.37 DNA Path Trace

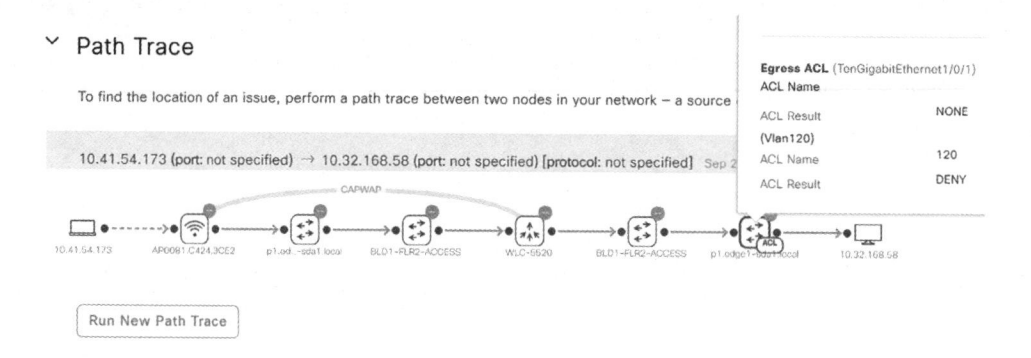

This is another feature that's unique to DNA Center and APIC-EM if you happen to have that in your network. Solarwinds has something similar called NetPath, but it works by using agents you deploy throughout your network. DNA Center uses the firsthand information it collects from the network and as said can detect ACL issues. SolarWinds can't do that.

An important point here is that the things Path Trace does can't really be done manually either. Sure, you can run some utilities like tcptraceroute or hping3 on Linux, but these methods have limitations regarding UDP traffic and they won't serve up a graphical display of the path traffic takes!

EasyQoS

Quality of Service can be tough to implement and maintain. DNA Center includes the successor to APIC-EM's EasyQoS feature, which lets you to simplify your QoS policies by grouping applications into three categories instead:

- Business Relevant: applications important to your business like Email or Active Directory.
- Business Irrelevant: applications with no business value like BitTorrent, YouTube and FaceBook.
- Default: applications that aren't in the other two categories, like DNS or Database traffic.

You can move applications into whichever category works for your network. After all, if you work for YouTube, then YouTube may very well be business relevant! The QoS Policy is shown in Figure 22.38.

FIGURE 22.38 DNA QoS Policy

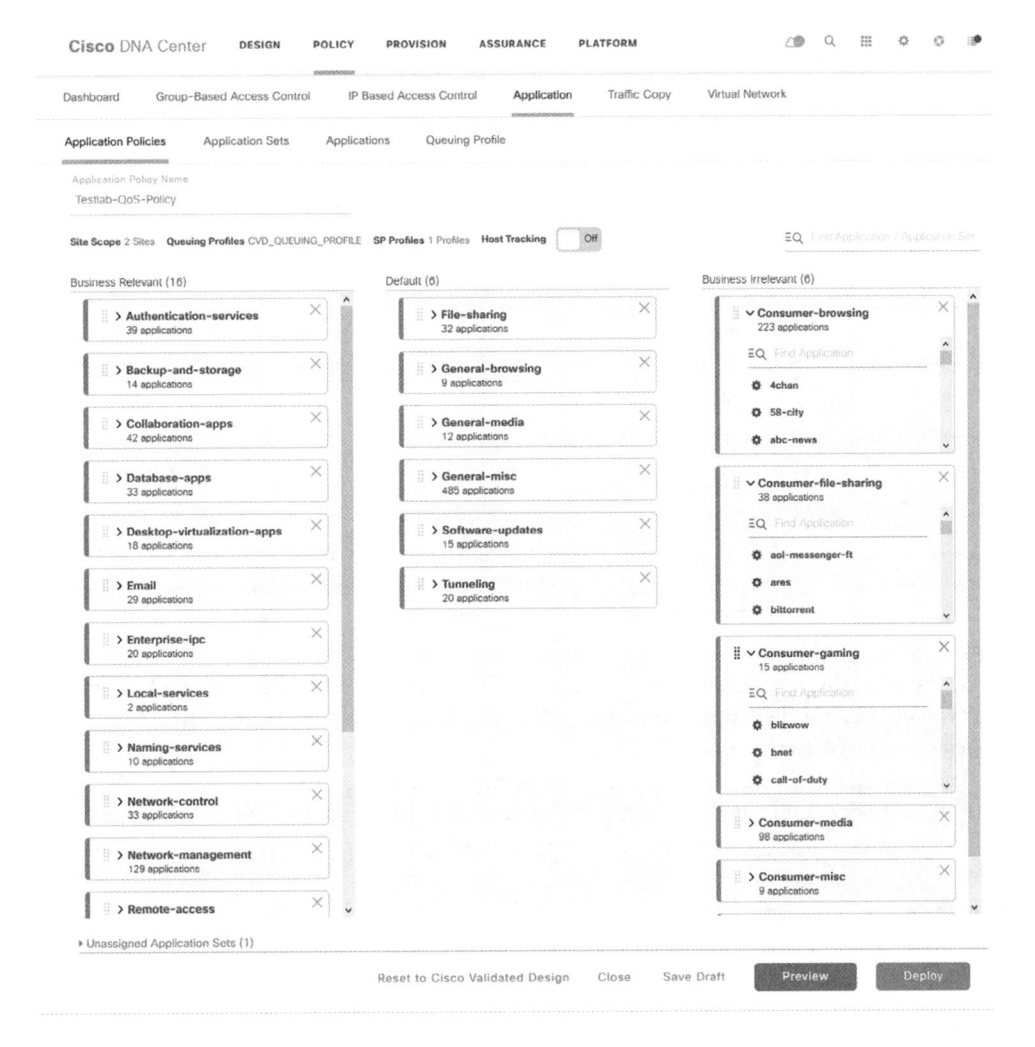

DNA Center will take your Application Policy and convert it into a QoS one that handles all the components for you. All you need is to adjust the DSCP and bandwidth allocations for your connections and you have a consistent QoS policy applied across your network. The Service Provider profiles are pictured in Figure 22.39.

FIGURE 22.39 DNA Service Provider Profiles

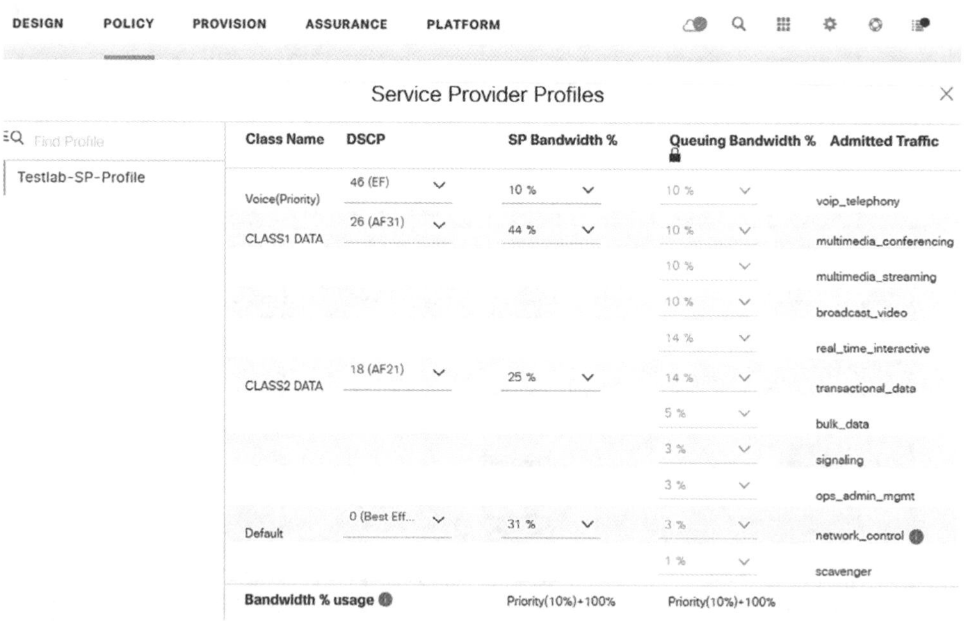

By the way, this is another feature unique to DNA Center. NCMs can push QoS policies that you create, but they aren't designed to let you to easily manage your end-to-end QoS policies like DNA Center does.

And here again, doing this manually can be majorly complex task that needs to be planned out very carefully. Every network device, including routers, switches, wireless controllers, and even firewalls can all be part of the QoS policy and therefore must be adjusted.

LAN Automation

Up until now if we wanted to add a new network device to DNA Center, we would've had to make sure the device could reach the server. We also needed to have authentication, SSH, and SNMP set up so the server could connect to the new device.

LAN Automation eases the pain by allowing new devices to be set up automatically via Cisco Plug and Play (PNP). This feature works by creating a DHCP server on the upstream network device, which then passes an IP address and the PNP server information on to the new Cisco device when it boots. From there, DNA Center automatically sets up basic routing and other things that should go on an underlay device like multicast.

Once it's done, the new device will appear in DNA Center in the proper site. LAN Automation is shown in Figure 22.40.

FIGURE 22.40 DNA LAN automation

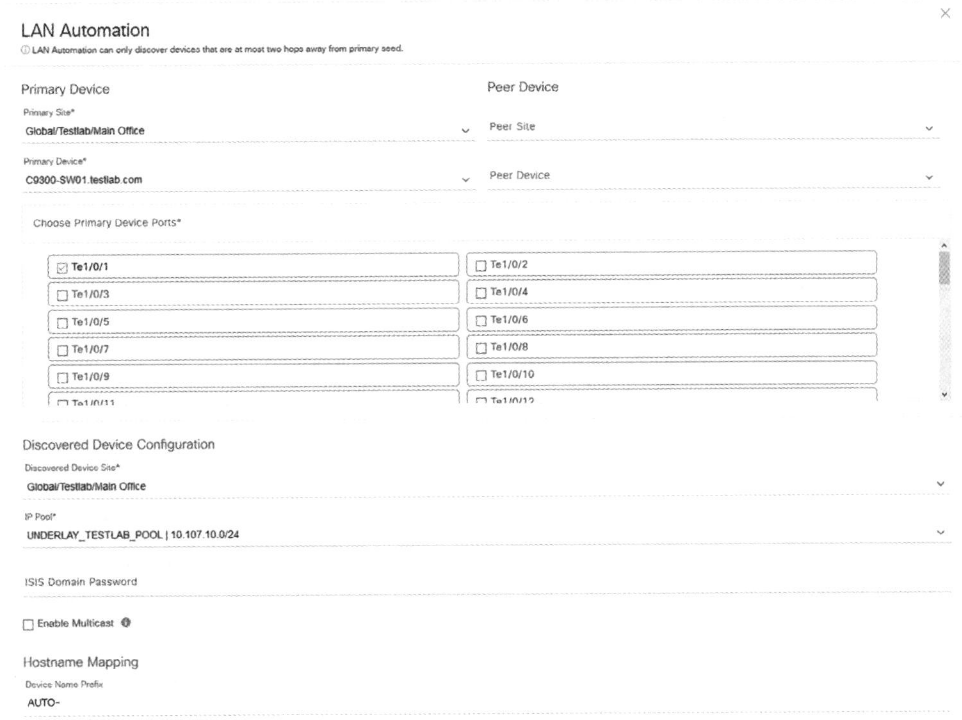

Here we have yet another feature that's unique to DNA Center. Because of the deep integration required to make PNP work, other NCMs just can't compete in this area!

To go about this manually, you'd have to manually put the configuration on the router before you ship it to its destination—the risk here being that if there are any configuration errors, a-troubleshooting you'll go before the device can get online.

SD-Access

Software Defined Access is really the flagship feature of DNA Center. Essentially, it lets you to make use of intent networking to state that the Marketing team doesn't get to access the IT team's resources—let DNA Center "figure it out."

The actual solution under the hood is extremely complex and uses a plethora of features that are well out of the scope for the CCNA. Even so, DNA Center makes it easy for even a junior to manage a network that would normally require a much more senior team to keep it up and running!

Since SD-Access is Cisco proprietary, there's no way for a NMS or NCM to do something similar. You can manually configure the network features that comprise SD-Access, but you won't be able to easily manage it with a web interface!

Restful API

We already covered restful API in the previous chapter. Everything in DNA Center can be managed by REST. This makes it really easy to have your scripts contact DNA Center instead of having to individually connect to devices to get information.

A neat feature is Code Preview. DNA Center lets you test drive Restful API through the web interface so you can get a feel for the kind of information it will give you. The web interface can even generate Restful API code snippets for you in several languages including Python!

Check out the Code Preview feature in Figure 22.41.

FIGURE 22.41 DNA Restful API

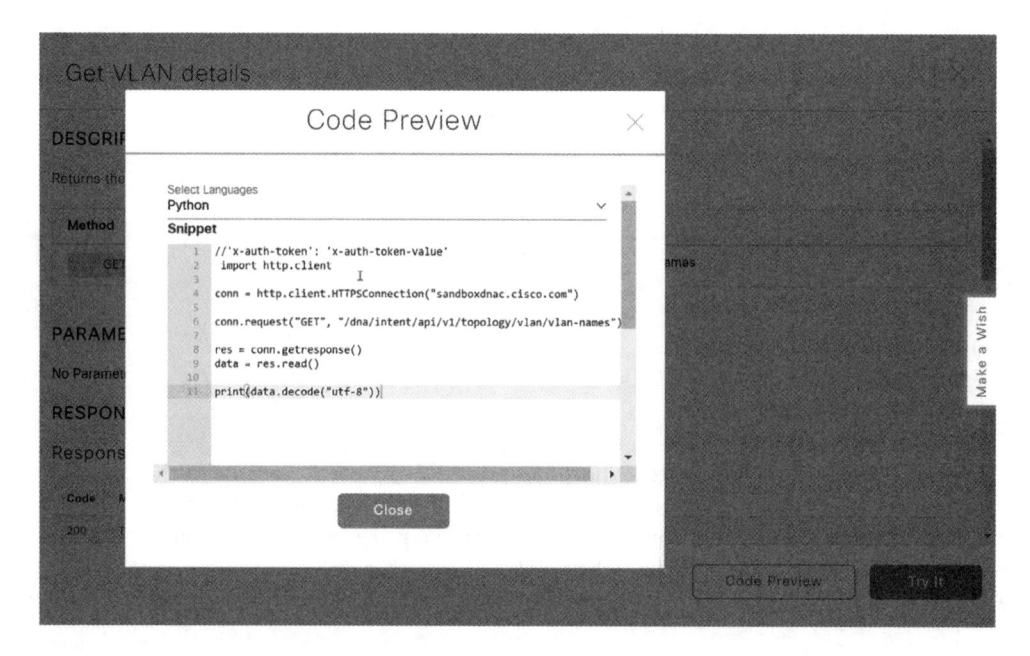

Summary

In this chapter, we covered how to traditionally manage a network using a Network Monitoring System (NMS) and a Network Configuration Manager (NCM). We also talked in a bit of detail about how a router actually sends packets because one of the goals of SDN is to separate the control plane and the data plane so that the intelligence of the network lives in the SDN Controller.

You learned about several network architectures that we can see in controller-based networks before I explained what a network fabric is what components it uses.

We closed up the chapter by going through some common DNA Center services and how they work, while comparing them with NMS/NCM solutions as well as if you were to tackle the job manually.

Exam Essentials

SDN Architecture   Software Defined Networking (SDN) solutions tunnel traffic across the underlay devices using an overlay. The underlay provides connectivity for the tunnels to be able to be formed. The overlay provides the actual services to the fabric. The fabric is simply a term for all network devices that use the SDN solution.

Controller-based Architecture   Rather than managing your network devices individually, you can use a controller-based solution that allows you to centrally manage everything instead. This improves efficiency since you can configure a large number of devices at once and also reduces the risk of configuration errors because your changes aren't applied immediately and can be reviewed. It also ensures configuration for all your network devices is consistent. Controllers also provide a great single point to monitor or script against since it knows about most or all of your network fabric. SDN Controllers communicate with the network using a southbound interface towards the devices and a northbound interface to permit access to the SDN Controller.

DNA Center   DNA Center is the successor to APIC-EM and provides SDN and controller-based features to your network. DNA Center can ensure your configuration is consistent and make sure QoS is working properly and is set up on all devices in the network. The assurance feature provides a unique time machine to view issues that happened up to a week ago.

Review Questions

You can find the answers in the Appendix.

1. What's the Northbound interface used for? (Choose one.)
   A. Communicates with the network device layer
   B. Allows users to interact with the SDN controller
   C. Tracks Access Point performance
   D. How traffic routes out the network

2. What's the network underlay?
   A. A term for everything in the SDN network
   B. A layer where tunnels are built to provide services
   C. A layer that provides connectivity throughout the fabric

3. What's an advantage of controller-based network vs. traditional networks? (Choose three.)
   A. Central management.
   B. Allows for mass configuration.
   C. Can monitor the entire network connected to the controller.
   D. Difficult to manage.
   E. Each device is independent of each other.

4. What's the name of an architecture that uses an access layer?
   A. Spine/Leaf
   B. CLOS
   C. Underlay
   D. Campus
   E. DNA Center

5. What are some protocols found in the management plane? (Choose three.)
   A. SSH
   B. CDP
   C. SNMP
   D. Telnet
   E. LLDP

6. What are some protocols found in the control plane? (Choose three.)
   A. OSPF
   B. CDP
   C. Console Port
   D. LLDP
   E. Management Port

7. What are some protocols found in the data plane?
   A. OSPF
   B. CDP
   C. NAT
   D. LLDP
   E. The Data Plane does not run protocols.

8. Which Southbound protocol is used by OpenDaylight?
   A. onePk
   B. OpenFlow
   C. Netconf
   D. Restful API
   E. Python

9. Which Southbound protocol is used by ACI?
   A. onePk
   B. OpenFlow
   C. Netconf
   D. OpFlex
   E. Python

10. Which of these are protocols commonly used with the northbound interface? (Choose two.)
    A. OnePk
    B. OpenFlow
    C. Restful
    D. OpFlex
    E. Python

11. What's the purpose of DNA Center's EasyQoS feature? (Choose three.)
    A. Automatically configure QoS
    B. Ensure best practices are being used for QoS
    C. Make it easy to adjust QoS policies.
    D. Generates a script you can apply to network devices manually
    E. Reviews your QoS Policies and recommends ways to make them simpler.

12. How long does DNA Center's Assurance feature store network data in its snapshot?
    A. One day
    B. Three days
    C. Five days
    D. One week
    E. One month

13. Which feature does LAN Automation use to configure new switches?
    A. SNMP
    B. Telnet
    C. SSH
    D. Plug and Play
    E. Restful API.

14. Which protocol does Network Monitoring Systems primarily use to monitor network devices?
    A. SNMP
    B. Telnet
    C. SSH
    D. Plug and Play
    E. Restful API

15. Which protocol does Network Configuration Manager primarily use to configure network devices? (Choose three.)
    A. SNMP
    B. Telnet
    C. SSH
    D. Plug and Play
    E. Restful API

16. What kinds of switches are found in a CLOS architecture? (Choose two.)
    A. Access Switches
    B. Leaf Switches
    C. Distribution Switches
    D. Spine Switches
    E. Core Switches

17. What kinds of switches are found in a Campus architecture? (Choose three.)
    A. Access Switches
    B. Leaf Switches
    C. Distribution Switches
    D. Spine Switches
    E. Core Switches

18. What type of switching is done in a network fabric?
    A. Layer 2
    B. Layer 3
    C. Layer 4
    D. Layer 7

19. What can the Command Runner be used for?
- **A.** Pushing OSPF configuration
- **B.** Pushing Show commands and viewing the results.
- **C.** Pushing ACL configuration
- **D.** Pushing Interface configurations
- **E.** Pushing a banner configuration

20. What can the Code Preview feature be used for? (Choose three.)
- **A.** Enrolling in beta updates for DNA Center
- **B.** Viewing what a code will do when ran against DNA Center
- **C.** Generating a simple code snippet to call the Restful API resource in the scripting language of your choice
- **D.** Viewing the source code for a DNA Center application

Chapter 23

Configuration Management

THE CCNA EXAM TOPICS COVERED IN THIS CHAPTER ARE:

6.0   Automation and Programmability

✓   6.6   Recognize the capabilities of configuration management mechanisms Puppet, Chef, and Ansible

After getting through Chapter 22, you're probably really excited about DNA Center because, well, how could you not be? It just makes our lives so much easier by centrally automating network tasks. And wow… Those templates that streamline configuration, making it predictable and consistent throughout our networks! Yep, you'd be crazy not to love it—even only with what you know about it so far.

We're going to take things to a whole new DNA Center level now, diving deeper into Configuration Management tools like Ansible, Chef and Puppet too. These great features make it possible to automate almost everything in your infrastructure!

Most Configuration Management tools like Ansible definitely help us get our networks under control, but that's not all. It can actually handle the rest of the stack! In addition to creating VLANs, it can even configure our virtual machines for us. Ansible can actually install and configure the application it'll use and can even add the new box in for monitoring and backup solutions.

What's more is that once you understand these sweet solutions, they're really easy to use. The only caveat is that it does take a good bit of effort to make the switch to a more DevOps-focused infrastructure team.

So, let's jump in and explore Ansible, Puppet, and Chef now!

> To find your included bonus material, as well as Todd Lammle videos, practice questions & hands-on labs, please see www.lammle.com/ccna

Team Silos

Before we dig into configuration management tools, let's take a minute to understand how we got here.

To be real, it's just a fantasy to think you'll only be dealing with IT-related things. That's really only possible when you're working in a small company with a simple IT infrastructure. The IT department in this type of company usually brings on only one or two IT generalists to do all the computer stuff.

So yes—you'll definitely be working on IT-related things, but it's highly likely you'll also be the only contact when things aren't working so well too. Figure 23.1 pictures the IT Generalist's career reality.

FIGURE 23.1 IT generalist

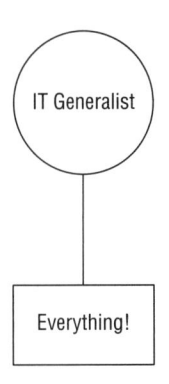

```
     ┌─────────────┐
     │ IT Generalist │
     └──────┬──────┘
            │
     ┌──────┴──────┐
     │ Everything! │
     └─────────────┘
```

Larger companies tend to be more organized by clearly defining IT team responsibilities and compartmentalizing all the work into silos. Silos exist to contain things, so calling a given department a silo is just a snappy way to say it's only responsible for certain devices, tasks, and projects. How this actually lives for IT folk translates down to a perfectly packaged reason to blame the network and its relevant staff (us) for a world of issues, fairly or not!

So yes, all things IT fall squarely on the network team, which includes everything we've covered in this book, from routers to switches, and wireless—down to faulty power strips! Anyway, you can get a picture of a typical network silo in Figure 23.2.

FIGURE 23.2 Silo network team

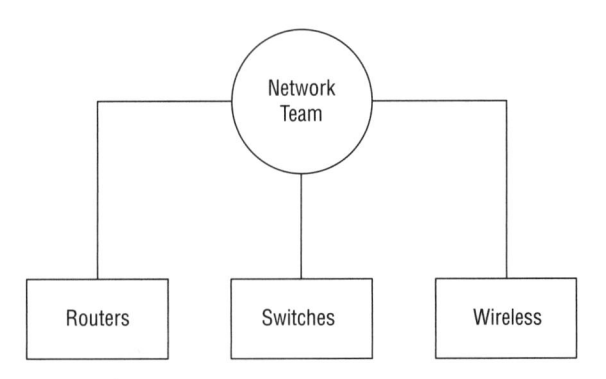

```
              ┌──────────┐
              │ Network  │
              │   Team   │
              └────┬─────┘
       ┌───────────┼───────────┐
   ┌───┴───┐   ┌───┴────┐   ┌──┴─────┐
   │Routers│   │Switches│   │Wireless│
   └───────┘   └────────┘   └────────┘
```

It's the SysAdmins in the company who tend to be responsible for the actual Windows and Linux servers in the infrastructure. In really huge companies, there could even be whole, separate teams looking after the Windows and Linux environments. Figure 23.3 shows an example of the silo systems team.

FIGURE 23.3 Silo systems team

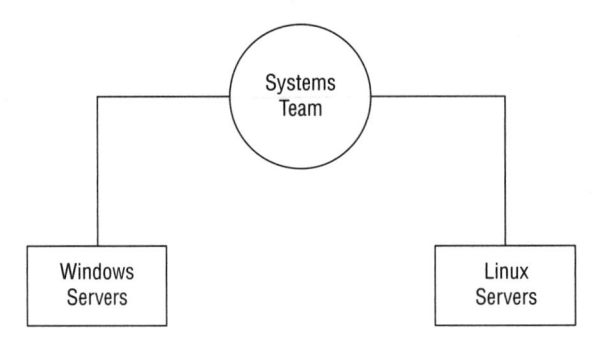

The security team usually focuses on the company's firewalls, but they can also be in charge of creating virtual private networks (VPNs) between companies for connectivity. Remote access solutions like a client VPN and things like Citrix, which allow access to the environment, can often be in their domain too. The security group is also tasked with monitoring for security events and making sure vulnerabilities are addresses as they're discovered. Figure 23.4 pictures the security silo team.

FIGURE 23.4 Silo security team

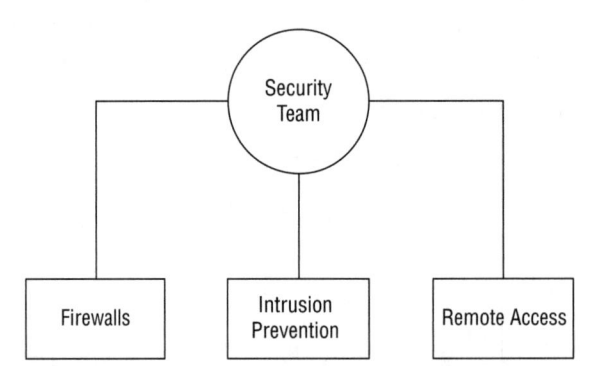

As usual, those neat little organizational silo boundaries end up to be more suggestion over time because they're just too limiting. Individual companies need customized solutions to meet their individual needs so predictably, and we're seeing a lot of cross-over between the various silos now. For instance, a network team just might be tasked with setting up VPNs because of the more advanced networking knowledge needed to pull that off well.

The waters get even muddier when we consider all the roles and services that run on servers and network devices. One company will say things like DHCP, DNS, and load balancer are the network team's responsibility, while another will let their sysadmins take charge instead. Services can even be a shared responsibility between teams, with the sysadmin team getting custody of DHCP servers while the network team is responsible for DHCP traffic leaving network devices like wireless controllers.

Figure 23.5 gives you an example of roles belonging to one silo or another being seen on network services.

FIGURE 23.5 Network services

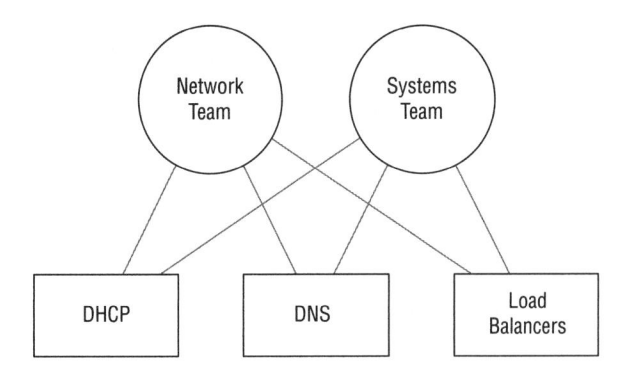

The development silo is all about the developer's complete focus on supporting their software releases. The other IT teams support them by building the infrastructure they need for their applications. For example, if a developer needs a new web server, the network team would make sure the server can get online. The systems team would install the server's operating system and the actual web server application. The security team would check the server after it's built to see it complies with their best practices, ensuring anti-malware has been installed and the host firewall has been enabled. Figure 23.6 demonstrates an example of this workflow.

FIGURE 23.6 Silo development team

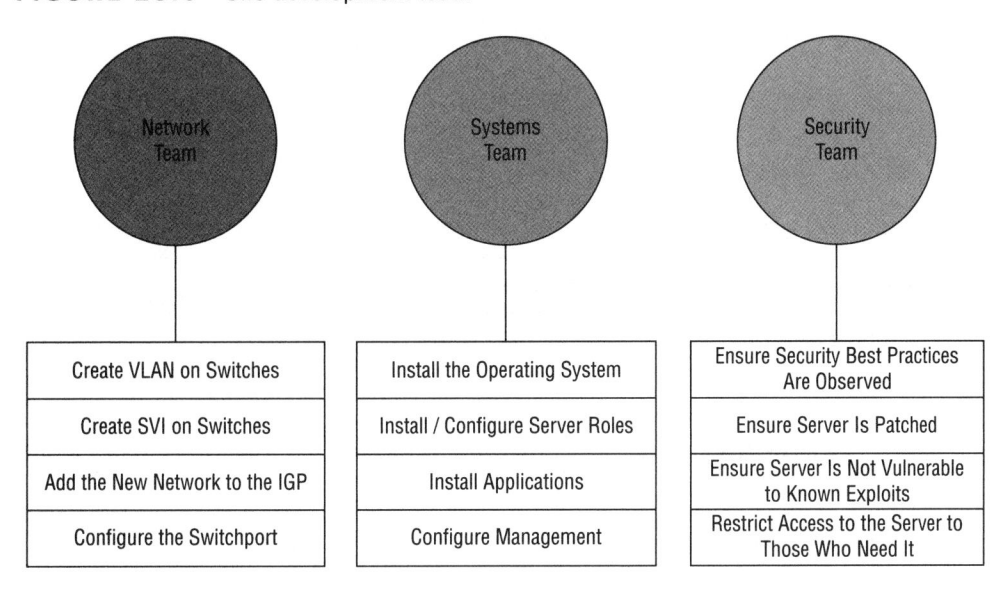

DevOps

DevOps is one of the most popular buzzwords around in IT today, but it's really one of those IT terms that means different things to different people. DevOps is actually more about a shift in corporate culture than it is about adding automation to everything, which is one reason why it's easier for a startup company to embrace it than for a larger company that's more set in its ways. Even so, most companies are working towards the goal so they can manage today's more complex IT infrastructure and cloud implementations.

So let's define DevOps for our purposes: It's basically a way to merge teams to solve some of the issues we just talked about regarding silos. A company would have DevOps engineers busy automating the infrastructure so that it can be spun up as needed for applications.

The most obvious benefit to be had here is that IT resources needed by the company can now be provisioned very quickly instead of maybe waiting weeks for all the different IT teams to complete their various tasks required to get a vital resource online. Change control is also simplified because DevOps methodology lets us test the code in different environments. It also allows us the freedom to easily back out of changes when necessary.

An example of the DevOps responsibilities is shown in Figure 23.7.

FIGURE 23.7 DevOps team

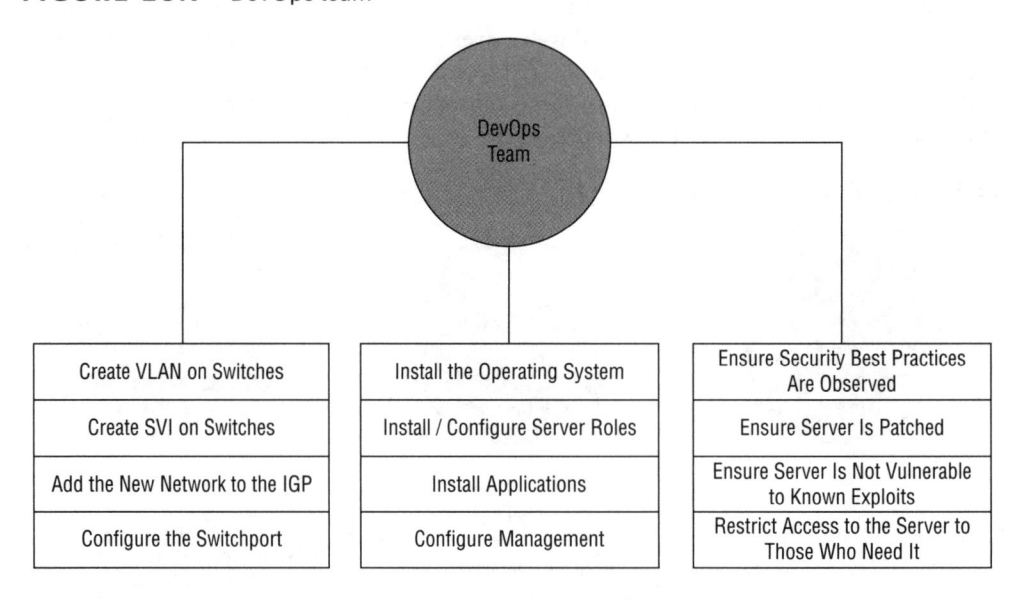

```
                    ┌──────────┐
                    │  DevOps  │
                    │   Team   │
                    └──────────┘
```

Create VLAN on Switches	Install the Operating System	Ensure Security Best Practices Are Observed
Create SVI on Switches	Install / Configure Server Roles	Ensure Server Is Patched
Add the New Network to the IGP	Install Applications	Ensure Server Is Not Vulnerable to Known Exploits
Configure the Switchport	Configure Management	Restrict Access to the Server to Those Who Need It

Infrastructure as Code (IaC)

You can think of Infrastructure as Code (IaC) as the practical output that we'd get out of a DevOps practice. IaC is the fun "automate everything" part of DevOps, with the goal being to create and maintain our IT infrastructure using the configuration managers we'll cover soon.

Aside from helping improve the speed of deployments, IaC can also help combat configuration drift—something that begins anytime you make an unintended change on a network device or a server.

But sadly, drift is a reality for companies over time. It happens when a server is removed from the network but the VLAN isn't removed from the switches. Maybe a firewall rule is added to do some troubleshooting, but it's forgotten afterwards, becoming one of hundreds—a cobweb in the rule base. Things just find their way onto servers that shouldn't be there, and one dark and stormy night, all these random cobwebs in the environment will rise up and collectively gum things up good! Now you've got a code blue as assorted IT teams clamber together to figure out why some mission-critical application suddenly crashed, desperate to fix it ASAP!

IT life isn't nearly as perilous when an application is deployed using Infrastructure as Code. Armed with this little beauty, we can skip all that troubleshooting chaos by just deleting the deviant server, then redeploying it instead. Yes, it can be fun to sleuth out exactly why Apache broke, but you can still have plenty of good times during the nice break you'll get while the virtual machine rebuilds, right?

So if you're thinking that periodically deleting the created infrastructure and remaking it can drastically reduce the amount of drifting from the intended configuration, you're right, because the new resources will be created exactly as described by the IaC solutions—genius! As a bonus, the new VMs can be automatically patched and up to date as they're being spun up by the solution. And if an agent-based configuration manager like Puppet or Chef is being used, then drift can be automatically corrected since the server will periodically check in to ensure it isn't going rogue on you.

An important principle of Infrastructure as Code is idempotence—a super fancy way of saying that the configuration will be only be applied to a target environment if it will result in a change. This means that if you make an Ansible playbook that enables NTP on a server, then start the service, Ansible will only do the install task if NTP isn't already installed on that server. Plus, it'll only do the start service task if NTP isn't currently running—nice.

Clearly this kind of behavior makes the IaC configuration much easier than trying to do the same thing with a bash script. Here's how easy it is to install NTP in an Ansible playbook—you just add these two lines to a playbook:

```
- name: Install NTP on RHEL
  yum: name=ntp state=present
```

The actual syntax doesn't matter right now, but the gist is that we're naming the task **Install NTP on RHEL**, calling the **yum** module to install NTP on the Linux box and then start the service. Because of idempotence magic, Ansible will check to see if the package is installed and will skip the step if it is already. This saves us time when we run the playbook and makes the playbook's footprint as small as possible. If you wanted to do this with bash, you would write something like this:

```
if ! rpm -qa | grep -qw ntp; then
yum install -y ntp
fi
```

The basic logic of the 'if' statement is to check the installed packages on server the for NTP. If it's not in the list, then the package will be installed. So why we wouldn't just push the install command again and let it run? Well, in this case it wouldn't cause any grief, but the command could get us a different result than we'd expect: instead of installing NTP, yum would give us a message saying NTP is already installed:

```
Package ntp-4.2.6p5-29.el7.centos.x86_64 already installed and latest version
Nothing to do
```

This is bad because it doesn't follow the idempotence principle since the command isn't doing exactly what's expected by the script, which can lead to ugly, unpredictable behavior later, when doing more advanced automation!

Hopefully that helps you get that using an IaC idempotence simplifies your deployments since you don't need to start accounting for different command results in your script logic.

Okay—so now that you're familiar with Infrastructure as Code, let's dive into the configuration management tools you'll need to know for the CCNA exam and as a modern network professional.

Ansible

Ansible is currently one of the most popular configuration management solutions for networking professionals. The tool is a Python-based solution that applies configuration found in playbook files via an SSH connection.

The solution is easy to get up and running because target systems don't require agents installed and registered to a central server before the solution can work. Instead, Ansible doesn't even require a central server—you can actually run playbooks directly off your office laptop. Even so, I recommend running Ansible from a central location because Ansible must be able to SSH to the target nodes to apply the configuration, and your network probably has some security restricting direct access.

Because Ansible primarily uses SSH to connect to nodes and doesn't require agents, it supports almost all major vendor systems in the networking community. All the vendor needs to do is provide modules for Ansible to use. A module is basically a set of instructions written in Python to be performed by Ansible. Back in the Infrastructure of Code section I briefly mentioned the yum module to show how to install NTP on a Red Hat Linux system.

Playbooks are just a set of instructions saying what should be applied to a target device. The file is written in the YAML format we talked about in the automation chapter.

Here's how Ansible and Ansible Tower/AWX compares to the other solutions:

Pros:

- Easy install and setup.
- Powerful orchestration.
- Supported by most enterprise-grade vendors on the market.
- Supports both push and pull modules.
- Agentless model is faster and less complicated than the agent model.
- Sequential execution order makes deployments predictable.

Cons:

- Requires root SSH access to Linux nodes.
- As a newer platform, it's not as mature as Puppet or Chef.
- Since Ansible has several scripting components, the syntax can vary.
- It's focused on orchestration over configuration management so Ansible doesn't protect against configuration drift.
- Troubleshooting can be tricky when compared to Puppet or Chef.
- No native config rollback on failure.

Installation

Ansible is a very lightweight solution. The tool is installed with the **pip install ansible** command. You can also use your Linux box's package manager to install Ansible, but yum and apt tend to lag behind the current release. Pip generally has the latest version:

```
[ansible@rhel01 ~]$ pip install ansible --user
Collecting ansible
Downloading
Installing collected packages: ansible
Running setup.py install for ansible ... done
Successfully installed ansible-2.9.0
```

Once Ansible is installed, it only has two setting files you must have on your computer before you try to run a playbook—a settings file called **ansible.cfg** and an inventory file typically called **hosts**. Once those two files are in place, we can run Ansible in ad-hoc mode or write a playbook. Let's have a closer look at those files now. In Figure 23.8, you can see a visualization of the Ansible components.

FIGURE 23.8 Ansible components

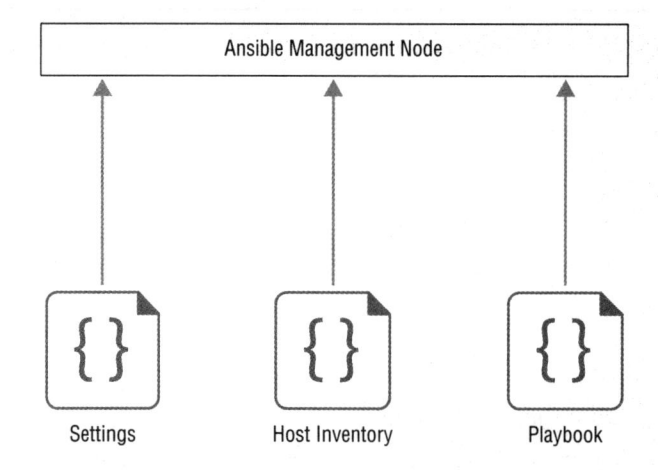

Settings

The ansible.cfg file is entirely optional because if Ansible can't find the settings file, it'll just go with default values when doing tasks.

When you install something through **pip**, it doesn't usually create folders or files for you. By default Ansible will look for the settings file by checking the **ANSIBLE_CONFIG** variable to see if a path is set. If not, it'll check for the ansible.cfg in the current directory that you're running the playbook from. If Ansible still doesn't find a path, it'll try your home directory and then finally **/etc/ansible/**. To keep things nice and easy to maintain, use the /etc/ansible folder if you can.

So even though there are loads of settings Ansible can use, we're just going to create a file that sets **host_key_checking** to false under [defaults]. Doing this makes your lab easier because Ansible won't try to verify the target node's SSH keys. If you don't turn this off, the system must have all the SSH host keys saved before the playbook will work correctly. Check it out:

```
[ansible@rhel01 ~]$ sudo mkdir /etc/ansible/
[ansible@rhel01 ~]$ cat /etc/ansible/ansible.cfg
[defaults]
host_key_checking = False
```

Inventory

The inventory file tells Ansible which target nodes to connect to and gives it information on how it should make that connection. The file also allows you to group nodes for easier administration. By default, Ansible will check the for the **hosts** file under **/etc/ansible/** when trying to access a node. You can also specify another location when you run Ansible by using a command-line switch.

Inside the hosts file we'll create two groups and a subgroup: switch, router, and a third group comprised of the router and switch groups we created for easy referencing. We'll define the variables we want the connection to use by appending "**:vars**" to the group name that's going to use them.

There are three built-in variables we'll use to tell Ansible the username and password for connecting to the Cisco devices:

ansible_connection   This defines how Ansible connects to the nodes. Local means it will SSH from the Ansible computer.

ansible_user   This is the default username variable.

ansible_password   This is the default password variable.

Here is an example of looking at an Ansible hosts file:

```
[root@rhel01 ~]# cat /etc/ansible/hosts
[switch]
sw0[1:2].testlab.com

[router]
r0[1:2].testlab.com

[cisco:children]
switch
router

[cisco:vars]
ansible_connection=local
ansible_user=ansible
ansible_password=ansible
```

Lab Setup

So we can play with Ansible, I'll configure a playbook that configures the network topology seen in Figure 23.9.

FIGURE 23.9 Ansible topology

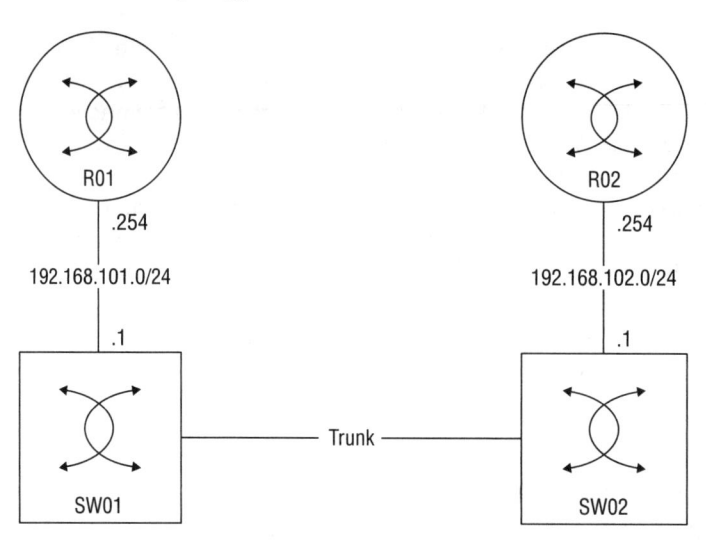

I'll use Ansible to configure routing between R01 and R02, and each router will connect to VLAN 101 and 102, respectively. The routers will have a default route that points to the SVI. By the time I'm done, our playbook should be able to ping from one router to the other.

I have to enable SSH and create a user for Ansible to use on all our Cisco devices. I'll also set the user to use privilege 15 to simplify our lab environment like this:

```
SW01(config)#aaa new-model
SW01(config)#aaa authentication login default local
SW01(config)#aaa authorization exec default local
SW01(config)#username ansible priv 15 secret ansible
SW01(config)#ip domain-name testlab.com
SW01(config)#crypto key generate rsa modulus 2048
The name for the keys will be: SW01.testlab.com

% The key modulus size is 2048 bits
% Generating 2048 bit RSA keys, keys will be non-exportable...
[OK] (elapsed time was 2 seconds)

SW01(config)#
*Sep 23 05:29:53.728: %SSH-5-ENABLED: SSH 1.99 has been enabled
SW01(config)#line vty 0 15
SW01(config-line)#transport input ssh
SW01(config-line)#do wr
Building configuration..
```

Great—now that our network is up and running, I'm also going to create some host records for my Cisco devices so we can use DNS names with Ansible. You can also just use IP addresses if you prefer:

```
[root@rhel01 ~]# cat /etc/hosts
127.0.0.1       localhost localhost.localdomain localhost4 localhost4.localdomain4
::1             localhost localhost.localdomain localhost6 localhost6.localdomain6
10.10.21.51     sw01.testlab.com
10.10.21.52     sw02.testlab.com
10.10.21.53     r01.testlab.com
10.10.21.54     r02.testlab.com
```

Modules

Ansible version 2.9.0 is the version I'm using currently, and it comes with 3387 modules. We can check them out with the **ansible-doc -l** command. Because this is a CCNA book, I'll filter the output to be just IOS-specific modules and trim it for brevity.

The modules that tell Ansible how to do a task usually come from the vendor, but you can make your own custom ones in Python. For instance, you can use the **ios_command** module to push an exec-level command to a Cisco device so you can capture show output. The **ios_config** is used to push configuration commands to the device.

The thing that makes Ansible unique compared to a regular Python script that pushes commands is the more specific modules available, which let you to complete specific tasks like adding a banner or enabling BGP just by calling the module. You'll get to see this in action when we get to our playbook example.

Here is an example:

```
[root@rhel01 ~]# ansible-doc -l | grep ^ios_
ios_banner              Manage multiline banners on Cisco IOS devices
ios_bgp                 Configure global BGP protocol settings on Cisco IOS
ios_command             Run commands on remote devices running Cisco IOS
ios_config              Manage Cisco IOS configuration sections
ios_facts               Collect facts from remote devices running Cisco IOS
ios_interface           Manage Interface on Cisco IOS network devices
ios_interfaces          Manages interface attributes of Cisco IOS network devices
ios_l2_interface        Manage Layer-2 interface on Cisco IOS devices
ios_l2_interfaces       Manage Layer-2 interface on Cisco IOS devices
ios_l3_interface        Manage Layer-3 interfaces on Cisco IOS network devices
ios_l3_interfaces       Manage Layer-3 interface on Cisco IOS devices
ios_lacp                Manage Global Link Aggregation Control Protocol (LACP)
ios_lacp_interfaces     Manage Link Aggregation Control Protocol (LACP)
ios_lag_interfaces      Manage Link Aggregation on Cisco IOS devices
```

If you want to get detailed help on a module, just add the module name to the **ansible-doc** command. For example, here's part of the output from the **ansible-doc ios_vlan** command, edited a bit for brevity:

```
EXAMPLES:
- name: Create vlan
  ios_vlan:
    vlan_id: 100
    name: test-vlan
    state: present

- name: Add interfaces to VLAN
  ios_vlan:
    vlan_id: 100
    interfaces:
      - GigabitEthernet0/0
      - GigabitEthernet0/1
```

Ad-Hoc Example

Now that you've seen how Ansible works and been acquainted with a couple modules, let's test things out without making a playbook by running ad-hoc commands. These come in handy when you're troubleshooting and you just want find out quickly if things are running well.

A really common ad-hoc module is ping, which simply tries to connect to the specified group and lets you know if it worked. Here's an example using the default localhost group that's running Ansible:

```
[ansible@rhel01 ~]$ ansible localhost -m ping
localhost | SUCCESS => {
    "changed": false,
    "ping": "pong"
}
```

Playbook Example

With our pieces in place, let's take a look at the playbook I put together. The final script is 144 lines, and I could have made things more efficient, but I wanted to keep things straightforward so you can follow along without a hitch.

Because playbooks are YAML, every file starts with --- at the top. For each section, I'll provide a descriptive name so that we all know what the playbook is doing when it's running.

The **hosts** keyword tells Ansible which group or host in the inventory file the tasks are going to run on.

Know that because we're working with Cisco devices, **gather_facts** will always be no. Ansible will try to gather facts about the host by default; otherwise, Cisco does provide an **ios_facts** module if you want similar performance for IOS devices.

Okay—so what I'm doing in the All Switches play is using a loop to create three VLANs—one for each router and one between the switches. I'm also creating the trunk between the switches and ensuring **ip routing** is enabled on the switches so they can do OSPF. Check it out:

```
---
######## All Switches ########
- name: Configure Switches
  hosts: switch
  gather_facts: no
  tasks:
  - name: Create VLANs
    ios_vlan:
      vlan_id: "{{ item }}"
      name: "ANSIBLE-VLAN{{ item }}"
    loop:
      - 101
      - 102
      - 123
  - name: Configure Trunk Port between SW01 and SW02
    ios_l2_interface:
      name: GigabitEthernet3/0
      mode: trunk
  - name: Enable IP Routing on Switches
    ios_config:
      lines: ip routing
```

In the All Devices play, I'm enabling OSPF on all devices in the cisco group in the host file, which combines the router and switch groups.

Note: Whitespace is very important in YAML, so if you're trying this out on your own, make sure to honor the spacing in the lines. Also, the TAB key is a huge no-no with playbooks…always use the spacebar!

```
######## All Devices########
- name: Configure All Devices
  hosts: cisco
  gather_facts: no
```

```
  tasks:
  - name: Enable OSPF on All Devices
    ios_config:
      lines:
        - network 0.0.0.0 0.0.0.0 area 0
      parents: router ospf 1
```

In the rest of the plays, I'm working with individual nodes since we have unique configuration on each of them. On SW01, I'll have to assign the VLANs to interfaces, create the SVIs with IPs, and enable them.

A good thing to keep in mind is that aside from the routing commands that I used the **ios_config** module for, most tasks have their own specialized module you can run to make configuration a bit cleaner. Here's a look at SW01's configuration:

```
######## SW01 ############
- name: Configure SW01
  hosts: sw01.testlab.com
  gather_facts: no
  tasks:

  - name: Assign SW01 VLANs
    ios_vlan:
      vlan_id: 101
      interfaces:
        - GigabitEthernet0/1

  - name: Create Vlan101 SVI
    ios_l3_interface:
      name: Vlan101
      ipv4: 192.168.101.1/24

  - name: Create Vlan123 SVI
    ios_l3_interface:
      name: Vlan123
      ipv4: 192.168.123.1/24

  - name: Enable SVIs
    ios_interface:
      name: "{{ item }}"
      enabled: True
```

```yaml
        loop:
          - Vlan101
          - Vlan123
```

SW02 is pretty much identical to SW01's configuration:

```yaml
######## SW02 ############
- name: Configure SW02
  hosts: sw02.testlab.com
  gather_facts: no
  tasks:

    - name: Assign SW02 VLANs
      ios_vlan:
        vlan_id: 102
        interfaces:
          - GigabitEthernet0/1

    - name: Create Vlan102 SVI
      ios_l3_interface:
        name: Vlan102
        ipv4: 192.168.102.1/24

    - name: Create Vlan123 SVI
      ios_l3_interface:
        name: Vlan123
        ipv4: 192.168.123.2/24

    - name: Enable SVIs
      ios_interface:
        name: "{{ item }}"
        enabled: True
      loop:
        - Vlan102
        - Vlan123
```

Now I'm going to add the IP to the interface and enable it on R01. I'll also add a default route to the mix like this:

```yaml
######## R01 ############
- name: Configure R01
  hosts: r01.testlab.com
  gather_facts: no
```

```yaml
  tasks:

  - name: Create R01 G0/1
    ios_l3_interface:
      name: Gig0/1
      ipv4: 192.168.101.254/24

  - name: Enable G0/1
    ios_interface:
      name: Gig0/1
      enabled: True

  - name: Add Default Route
    ios_static_route:
      prefix: 0.0.0.0
      mask: 0.0.0.0
      next_hop: 192.168.101.1
```

R02 is more of the same:

```yaml
######## R02 ############
- name: Configure R02
  hosts: r02.testlab.com
  gather_facts: no
  tasks:

  - name: Create R02 G0/1
    ios_l3_interface:
      name: Gig0/1
      ipv4: 192.168.102.254/24

  - name: Enable G0/1
    ios_interface:
      name: Gig0/1
      enabled: True

  - name: Add Default Route
    ios_static_route:
      prefix: 0.0.0.0
      mask: 0.0.0.0
      next_hop: 192.168.102.1
```

So, now that I'm done with my playbook, I'll go ahead and run it with the **ansible-playbook** command. Ansible will actually verify the file and then run it. The playbook is run one task at a time from top/down and will show feedback about each play and task that runs:

```
[root@rhel01 ~]# ansible-playbook cisco.yml

PLAY [Configure Switches]
****************************************************************************
***************************************************************

TASK [Create VLANs]
*****************************************************************************
***************************************************************
ok: [sw01.testlab.com] => (item=101)
ok: [sw02.testlab.com] => (item=101)
ok: [sw01.testlab.com] => (item=102)
ok: [sw02.testlab.com] => (item=102)
ok: [sw02.testlab.com] => (item=123)
ok: [sw01.testlab.com] => (item=123)

TASK [Configure Trunk Port between SW01 and SW02]
****************************************************************************
************************************
ok: [sw02.testlab.com]
ok: [sw01.testlab.com]
<Omitted for brevity>
PLAY RECAP
****************************************************************************
**************************************************************
r01.testlab.com            : ok=4    changed=3    unreachable=0    failed=0
skipped=0    rescued=0    ignored=0
r02.testlab.com            : ok=4    changed=3    unreachable=0    failed=0
skipped=0    rescued=0    ignored=0
sw01.testlab.com           : ok=8    changed=4    unreachable=0    failed=0
skipped=0    rescued=0    ignored=0
sw02.testlab.com           : ok=8    changed=4    unreachable=0    failed=0
skipped=0    rescued=0    ignore
```

Because I've named my plays and tasks based on what they are doing, I can tell exactly if and where something has gone off the rails during execution. This is important because when Ansible detects an error, it'll only give you its best guess about where the error happened and why. Sometimes it's helpful, other times, not so much.

For instance, if I remove the indentation on the **vlan_id** line under Create VLANs and run it, Ansible gets the approximate location right, but the interpreter thinks it's an issue with missing quotes—oops! Check it out:

```
[root@rhel01 ~]# cat broke-cisco.yml
---
######## All Switches ########
- name: Configure Switches
  hosts: switch
  gather_facts: no
  tasks:

  - name: Create VLANs
    ios_vlan:
    vlan_id: "{{ item }}"
      name: "ANSIBLE-VLAN{{ item }}"
    loop:
      - 101
      - 102
      - 123
[root@rhel01 ~]# ansible-playbook broke-cisco.yml
ERROR! Syntax Error while loading YAML.
  did not find expected key

The error appears to be in '/root/broke-cisco.yml': line 11, column 7, but may
be elsewhere in the file depending on the exact syntax problem.

The offending line appears to be:

    vlan_id: "{{ item }}"
      name: "ANSIBLE-VLAN{{ item }}"
      ^ here
We could be wrong, but this one looks like it might be an issue with
missing quotes. Always quote template expression brackets when they
start a value. For instance:

    with_items:
      - {{ foo }}

Should be written as:

    with_items:
      - "{{ foo }}"
```

While it's true no one expects to be an expert on how Ansible works for the CCNA, it's really good for you to see it in action anyway because the Infrastructure as Code concept is actually a new way of thinking for a lot people in this industry!

With that, here's a run-down of some of the terms that Ansible uses:

Inventory   Defines the nodes that Ansible knows about and groups them so they can be referenced. The inventory also includes connection information and variables.

Playbook   A file that contains a set of instructions to be executed.

Play   Multiple plays can exist in a playbook, which allows the playbook to apply configuration to different nodes in different sections.

Variables   You can use custom variables in your playbooks.

Templates   You can use Python's Jinja2 templates with your playbooks, which is really helpful for network administration.

Tasks   An action the playbook applies, like installing Apache on a Linux box.

Handlers   These are a lot like tasks, except they're only called to an event like a service starting.

Roles   Allows you to spread out playbooks across several folders to make the configurations more modular, scalable, and flexible.

Modules   Built into Ansible, modules are files that describe how Ansible will achieve a given task. You can also write your own. Cisco has 69 modules in the current version of Ansible that cover everything from IOS to their UCS server platform.

Facts   These are global variables that contain a ton of information about the system, including vital stats like the system's IP address.

Ansible Tower/AWX

Ansible has two more enterprise-focused solutions to go with if you want more central management and security controls.

- **Ansible Tower:** A paid version via Red Hat that adds central management to Ansible that improves security because you can control who can run playbooks through Role-Based Access Control (RBAC). Ansible Tower also provides a single point for integration with other tools. Red Hat offers a free version that supports 10 hosts if you want to try it.
- **AWX:** The upstream development version of Ansible Tower, that's kind of like Fedora vs. Red Hat Enterprise Linux. You can use it for free, but there's less reliability since there can be frequent changes with little testing. Be aware that there's only limited support available.

Puppet

Puppet is more popular than Ansible is with sysadmins because it's agent based and provides stronger configuration management. But Puppet used to require an agent so it could only run on devices that support that like Cisco Nexus. This fact is important for the CCNA exam—Cisco will test to see if you know Puppet generally requires agents, even though the tool now supports agentless configuration in the newer versions.

Puppet is a Ruby-based tool and uses its own declarative language (a domain-specific language) for its manifest files. These files are like Ansible playbooks.

Here's how Puppet compares to our other two solutions:

Pros:

- Prevents configuration drift through compliance automation and reporting tools because the agent continuously checks in with the Puppet master to make sure it's compliant with the manifests
- Strong web UI
- More mature solution than Ansible
- Easy setup

Cons:

- You've got to learn Ruby to get good with Puppet, and Ruby isn't as widely used by the network community. It's more of a niche skill.
- Lacks a push system, so changes occur only when nodes check in.
- The master-agent architecture complicates redundancy and scalability.

Installation

Puppet is way more complex than Ansible, with a key difference being you have to use a central server to register Puppet's agents to.

With that, I'm going to start by downloadig the install information from Puppet like this:

```
[root@rhel01 ~]# dnf install https://yum.puppetlabs.com/puppet-release-el-8.noarch.rpm
Updating Subscription Management repositories.
```

And now I'll install the server with the package management:

```
[root@rhel01 ~]# dnf install puppetserver
Updating Subscription Management repositories
```

Next up is doing a little basic server configuration by editing the **/etc/puppetlabs/puppet/puppet.conf** file.

I'm going to add a [main] section plus a few fields:

Certname: The certificate name the server will use.

Server: The Puppet server name, which doesn't need to match the actual server FQDN.

Environment: Puppet supports different development environments; we're going with "Production."

Runinterval: Dictates how often a Puppet agent checks in.

```
cat /etc/puppetlabs/puppet/puppet.conf
[master]
vardir = /opt/puppetlabs/server/data/puppetserver
logdir = /var/log/puppetlabs/puppetserver
rundir = /var/run/puppetlabs/puppetserver
pidfile = /var/run/puppetlabs/puppetserver/puppetserver.pid
codedir = /etc/puppetlabs/code

[main]
certname = rhel01.testlab.com
server = rhel01.testlab.com
environment = production
runinterval = 1h
```

Now we're going to tell the Puppet certificate authority to automatically approve node requests that come from my testlab.com domain:

```
[root@rhel01 ~]# cat /etc/puppetlabs/puppet/autosign.conf
*.testlab.com
```

And finally, I'll enable and start the service on the server:

```
[root@rhel01 ~]# systemctl enable puppetserver
[root@rhel01 ~]# systemctl start puppetserver
```

Lab Setup

For this lab we're going to use Puppet to configure a Cisco Data Center network with Nexus 9000 switches. Puppet requires an agent for configuration, so we'll need a platform that explicitly supports it. We're not going to bother configuring SSH before we start because Puppet doesn't need to SSH into the switches.

But we are going to configure VLAN 10 on the DC switches, create the interfaces trunk links and some SVIs, give them IP addresses, and then set up OSPF. Figure 23.10 pictures our Puppet Lab's network topology.

> **NOTE**
> In reality, the configuration for Puppet is a whole lot more complex than the Ansible example is, and it requires more advanced Linux configuration. I just wanted to include this lab so you can see how Puppet operates.

FIGURE 23.10 Puppet lab

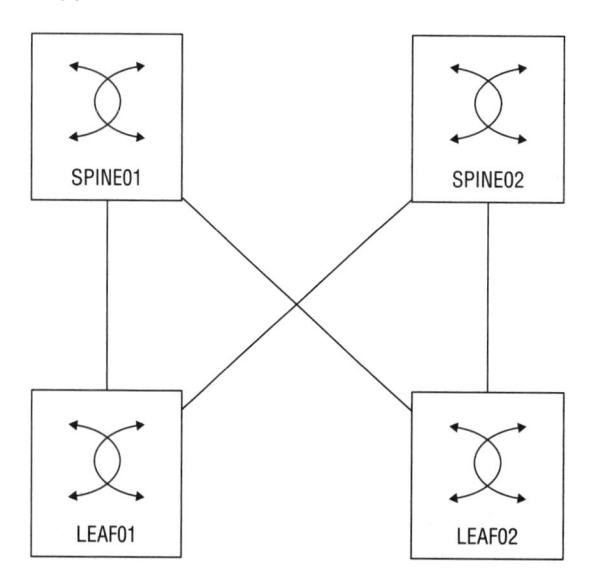

```
    SPINE01         SPINE02



    LEAF01          LEAF02
```

Site Manifest File

So, now that we've got a running server, we're going to move on to the **site.pp** manifest. This is the top-level/root configuration file where we'll decide which nodes we'll be configuring. You can pretty much think of the site manifest like the inventory in Ansible except that it also acts as the playbook!

The site manifest is generally used to define variables, and after that, it calls other manifest files to apply the actual configuration. This helps keep the file easy to understand.

These are the fields we'll be working with:

Node: The node that we'll be applying configuration to.

$last_octet: A custom variable we'll use to build IP addresses.

$int1_intf: Also a custom variable that defines an interface to be configured.

$int2_intf: Another custom variable that defines an interface to be configured.

$vlan: A custom variable that defines a VLAN number.

Include: This allows you to keep manifests clean by letting you put configuration in other manifests to import when needed. In this case, we're importing the **dc_role.pp** manifest which is where the main configuration lives:

```
node 'spine01.testlab.com' {
    $last_octet="1"
    $int1_intf="Ethernet1/1"
    $int2_intf="Ethernet1/2"
    $vlan=10
    include dc_role::dc_config
}

node 'spine02.testlab.com' {

    $last_octet="2"
    $int1_intf="Ethernet1/1"
    $int2_intf="Ethernet1/2"
    $vlan=10
    include dc_role::dc_config
}
node 'leaf01.testlab.com' {

    $last_octet="3"
    $int1_intf="Ethernet1/1"
    $int2_intf="Ethernet1/2"
    $vlan=10
    include dc_role::dc_config
}

node 'leaf02.testlab.com' {

    $last_octet="4"
    $int1_intf="Ethernet1/1"
    $int2_intf="Ethernet1/2"
    $vlan=10
    include dc_role::dc_config
}
```

DC Manifest File

The **dc_role.pp** manifest file is where we define the Nexus configuration; the basic logic of the file is:

cisco_interface   This resource is using the provided variables to configure Ethernet1/1 and Ethernet1/2 as trunk ports with a description. The resource is also used to create the SVI with an IP address and a loopback interface.

cisco_vlan   This resource is used to create VLAN 10 on all the switches.

cisco_ospf   This resource enables OSPF on the Nexus switches; in the Nexus platform you need enable features you want to use before you can configure them; it also creates **router ospf 1** in the configuration.

cisco_interface_ospf   This resource adds the SVIs and loopbacks into OSPF under area 0.

```
class dc_role::dc_config {
  cisco_interface { $int1_intf:
      shutdown         => false,
      switchport_mode  => trunk,
      description      => 'Configured by Puppet!',
  }
  cisco_interface { $int2_intf:
      shutdown         => false,
      switchport_mode  => trunk,
      description      => 'Configured by Puppet!',
  }
  cisco_vlan { "${vlan}":
      ensure           => present,
  }
  cisco_interface { "Vlan10":
      shutdown              => false,
      ipv4_address          => "192.168.10.${last_octet}",
      ipv4_netmask_length   => 24,
      description           => 'Created by Puppet!',
  }
  cisco_interface { "Loopback0":
    ipv4_address          => "192.168.254.${last_octet}",
    ipv4_netmask_length   => 32,
  }
```

```
  cisco_ospf { "1":
      ensure => present,
  }
  cisco_interface_ospf { "Vlan10 1":
     area => 0,
  }
   cisco_interface_ospf { "Loopback0 1":
      area => 0,
  }}
```

Installing the Puppet Agent

To install the Puppet agent, we're going use a feature called Guestshell, a built-in Centos 7 Linux container that's available on most modern Cisco platforms. We'll have to adjust the size of the container before we can use it with Puppet, and we'll get that done via **guestshell resize** and **guestshell enable**.

We can enter the Linux environment with the **guestshell** command on its own:

```
SPINE02(config)# guestshell resize rootfs 1500
Note: Root filesystem will be resized on Guest shell enable
SPINE02(config)# guestshell resize memory 500
Note: System memory will be resized on Guest shell enable
SPINE02(config)# guestshell enable
SPINE02(config)# guestshell
```

Okay—now that we're inside Centos, we've got to get it online. The CCNA doesn't cover virtual routing and forwarding, but it really just comes down to having multiple, separate routing tables on a device. In this case, I'm going to tell guestshell to use the management routing table with **chvrf management**.

Oh and we'll also need to configure DNS so we can download our packages. Once we're online, we can use **yum** to download the Puppet agent and install it:

```
[admin@guestshell ~]$ sudo chvrf management
[root@guestshell admin]# echo "nameserver 10.20.2.10" >> /etc/resolv.conf
[root@guestshell admin]# yum install http://yum.puppetlabs.com/puppetlabs-release-pc1-el-7.noarch.rpm
Loaded plugins: fastestmirror
puppetlabs-release-pc1-el-7.noarch.rpm
[root@guestshell admin]# yum install puppet-agent
Loaded plugins: fastestmirror
```

The Puppet agent doesn't update the path variable, so we'll have to add the Puppet directories to the path.

We also need to install **cisco_node_utils** on each switch with **gem**, a Ruby package manager. Check it out:

```
[root@guestshell ~]# echo "export
PATH=/sbin:/bin:/usr/sbin:/usr/bin:/opt/puppetlabs/puppet/bin:/opt/puppetlabs/puppet/lib:\
/opt/puppetlabs/puppet/bin:/opt/puppetlabs/puppet >> ~/.bashrc
[root@guestshell ~]# source ~/.bashrc
gem install cisco_node_utils
1 gem installed
```

Next up is configuring the Puppet agent so it knows where the Pupper Master is and which name to use on its certificate. Since Guestshell doesn't usually set a hostname, we'll use the **certname** field to identify the node to the Puppet Master. If we didn't do this, the FQDN will be used when we boot the agent:

```
[root@guestshell ~]# cat /etc/puppetlabs/puppet/puppet.conf
[main]
server = rhel01.testlab.com
certname = spine02.testlab.com
```

We can start the agent with the **puppet agent -t** command, and if all goes well, we should see the certificate being created. It will also pull the manifests and start applying them:

```
[root@guestshell ~]# puppet agent -t
Info: Creating a new SSL key for spine02.testlab.com
Info: csr_attributes file loading from /etc/puppetlabs/puppet/csr_attributes.yaml
Info: Creating a new SSL certificate request for spine02.testlab.com
Info: Certificate Request fingerprint (SHA256):
87:A0:6C:26:1B:E2:58:9E:8A:78:2A:25:75:C1:31:4E:EE:0A:93:EC:2C:76:CD:2E:77:A0:E7:C2:57:5A:8C:81
Info: Caching certificate for spine02.testlab.com
Info: Caching certificate_revocation_list for ca
Info: Caching certificate for spine02.testlab.com
Info: Using configured environment 'production'
Info: Retrieving pluginfacts
Notice: /File[/opt/puppetlabs/puppet/cache/facts.d]/mode: mode changed '0775' to '0755'
```

Verifying the Results

Once we've completed the setup on each switch in our topology, we'll verify the configuration that's been applied. The output below shows us that the SVI and Loopbacks have been created with the right IP:

```
SPINE01(config)# show ip int br
IP Interface Status for VRF "default"(1)
```

```
Interface              IP Address       Interface Status
Vlan10                 192.168.10.1     protocol-up/link-up/admin-up
Lo0                    192.168.254.1    protocol-up/link-up/admin-up
```

And OSPF is also up and running—we can see the loopbacks from all the other switches:

```
SPINE01(config)# show ip route ospf
IP Route Table for VRF "default"
'*' denotes best ucast next-hop
'**' denotes best mcast next-hop
'[x/y]' denotes [preference/metric]
'%<string>' in via output denotes VRF <string>

192.168.254.2/32, ubest/mbest: 1/0
    *via 192.168.10.2, Vlan10, [110/41], 00:06:40, ospf-1, intra
192.168.254.3/32, ubest/mbest: 1/0
    *via 192.168.10.3, Vlan10, [110/41], 00:06:38, ospf-1, intra
192.168.254.4/32, ubest/mbest: 1/0
    *via 192.168.10.4, Vlan10, [110/41], 00:09:47, ospf-1, intra
```

Here's a list of some important Puppet terms you want be familiar with:

- **Puppet Master:** The Master server that controls the configuration on managed nodes.
- **Puppet Agent Node:** A node controlled by a Puppet Master.
- **Manifest:** A file containing instructions to be executed.
- **Resource:** Declares a task that needs to be executed and how. For example, if we install apache on a Linux box, we can declare Apache and make sure its state is set to "installed."
- **Module:** A group of manifests and related files organized nicely to make life easier.
- **Class:** You can use classes to organize the manifest file just as you can use programming languages like Python.
- **Facts:** Global variables that contain a ton of information about the system, like the system's IP address.
- **Services:** Used to control services on a node.

Puppet Enterprise

Puppet comes in an open source version that's free to use on any Linux box and an upgraded version called Puppet Enterprise. You've got to pony up some cash for Puppet

Enterprise, but it adds in a web interface and more enterprise features. Puppet does provide a free version that supports 10 hosts if you want to try it.

Chef

Chef is by far the most complex configuration management tool in the box, but like Puppet, it's based in the Ruby programming language and uses agents for communication. Chef is different because it has a much more distributed architecture plus a lot more features that make it a real favorite with developers!

Chef has a central server just like Puppet does, but it also includes the concept of a Workstation node. Basically, it's a standard workstation with Chef tools installed. The idea is to build your Chef cookbooks then upload them to the "bookshelf" on the Chef Server so they can be used by all the Chef Nodes—hungry yet? I am.

The workstation creates a folder called the chef-repo (short for repository) to store cookbooks and recipes. A recipe is like an Ansible playbook, and a cookbook is the folder that holds the recipes. The idea behind all this is that a cookbook teaches you how to make several dishes. The Chef Cookbook contains directions on what to apply to server nodes.

The Chef Workstation provides tool that interacts with the Chef server called—you guessed it—a knife.

The Chef Node is the computer that Chef will control through the agent. It has two components installed: The Chef-Client is the agent that registers the node and does all the work, and another one called Ohai that monitors the server for changes in configuration that must be reported.

I know that's a lot to swallow, so here's a quick summary of Chef components:

- **Cookbook**: A file containing a set of instructions to be executed.
- **Recipe**: An action that the cookbook applies, like installing Apache on a Linux box.
- **Chef Nodes**: Computers that Chef manages.
- **Knife**: Command-line tool for managing Chef through the server API.
- **Chef Server**: The master server that manages all the nodes and cookbooks.
- **Chef Manage**: The web interface for Chef Server—the API is used for communication.
- **Workstation**: A computer you perform configuration related tasks from like when creating a cookbook.
- **Bookshelf**: A place to store cookbook content.

Figure 23.11 gives you a picture of the full Chef architecture.

FIGURE 23.11 Chef architecture

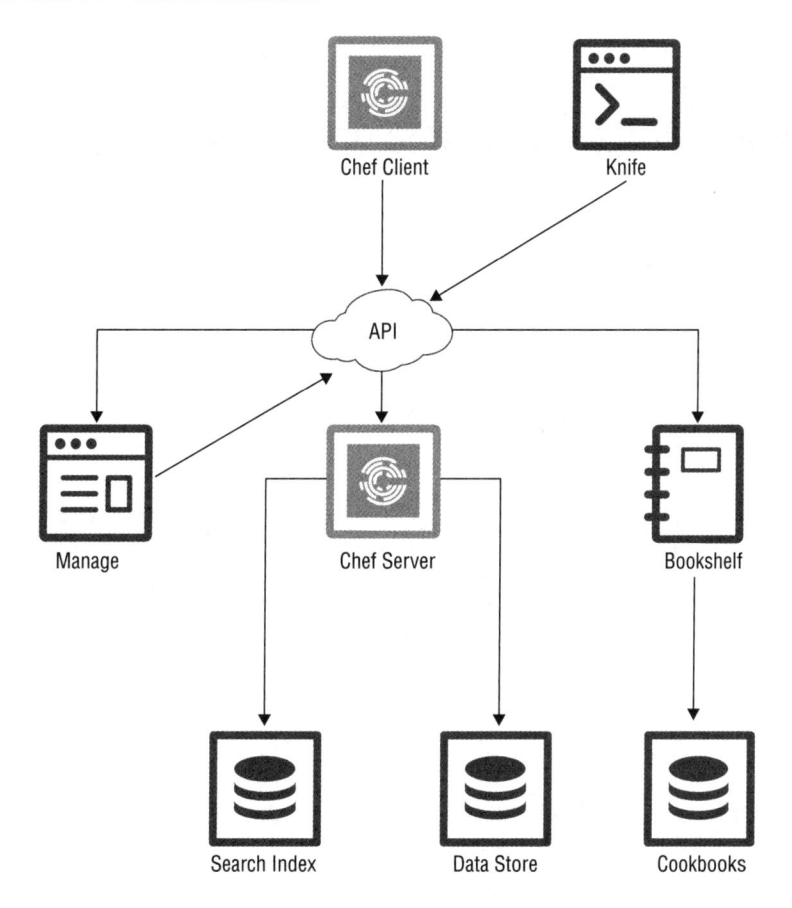

Chef Server has only a single version; the open source tool we're all free to use on any Linux box. Chef Workstation can run on both Windows and Linux. Here's a list of Chef's pros and cons:

Pros:

- Very flexible for OS and middleware management.
- Developer focused.
- The architecture suits large-scale deployments.
- Sequential execution order.
- Great reporting.
- Supports hosted cloud offerings.

Cons:
- Steep learning curve.
- Complicated install and setup.
- Lacks a push system so changes only occur when nodes check in.

Installation – Server

Now it's finally time to set up the Chef Server. And just as the Puppet example did, this gets into the weeds far deeper than what you'll need for the CCNA.

To get started, we'll download the install file from Chef:

```
[root@rhel02 ~]# wget https://packages.chef.io/files/current/chef-server/13.0.40/el/8/chef-server-core-13.0.40-1.el7.x86_64.rpm
```

And then install it with the **dnf localinstall** command:

```
[root@rhel02 ~]# dnf localinstall chef-server-core-13.0.40-1.el7.x86_64.rpm
Updating Subscription Management repositories.
```

Next, we'll set up Chef by using the **chef-server-ctl reconfigure** command. It'll ask us to accept the license:

```
[root@rhel01 ~]# chef-server-ctl reconfigure
+---------------------------------------------+
            Chef License Acceptance

Before you can continue, 3 product licenses
must be accepted. View the license at
https://www.chef.io/end-user-license-agreement/

Licenses that need accepting:
  * Chef Infra Server
  * Chef Infra Client
  * Chef InSpec

Do you accept the 3 product licenses (yes/no)?
> yes
Persisting 3 product licenses...
✓ 3 product licenses persisted.
```

We'll definitely want to allow HTTP and HTTPS traffic through the host firewall like this:

```
[root@rhel01 ~]# firewall-cmd --permanent --add-service={http,https}
[root@rhel01 ~]# firewall-cmd --reload
success
```

Now we'll create an admin user for Chef called chefadmin. The easiest way to do this is to enter in the user info and the certificate path as variables, then reference them in the **chef-server-ctl user-create** command to keep things cleaner.

We'll put the certificate in my root directory since we'll need it later:

[root@rhel01 ~]# **USERNAME="chefadmin"**
[root@rhel01 ~]# **FIRST_NAME="Todd"**
[root@rhel01 ~]# **LAST_NAME="Lammle"**
[root@rhel01 ~]# **EMAIL="todd@lammle.com"**
[root@rhel01 ~]# **KEY_PATH="/root/chefadmin.pem"**
[root@rhel01 ~]# **sudo chef-server-ctl user-create ${USERNAME} ${FIRST_NAME} ${LAST_NAME} ${EMAIL} -f ${KEY_PATH} --prompt-for-password**

Next we'll create an Organization using a short name and a long name. I'll go with testlab as the short name and Testlab as the long name. We also have to tell Chef where to export the organization validator certificate—I'll put that in /root too:

[root@rhel01 ~]# **chef-server-ctl org-create testlab 'Testlab' **
> **--association_user chefadmin **
> **--filename /root/testlab-validator.pem**

Installation – Workstation

Okay—now that the server is up, we'll configure the Chef Workstation. As usual, we'll download the RPM:

[root@rhel01 ~]# **wget https://packages.chef.io/files/current/chef-workstation/0.9.31/el/8/chef-workstation-0.9.31-1.el7.x86_64.rpm**

And then install it with the **yum localinstall** command like this:

[root@rhel01 ~]# **yum localinstall -y chef-workstation-0.9.31-1.el7.x86_64.rpm**
Updating Subscription Management repositories.

Next we need to set up the chef-repo that will store our cookbooks with the **chef generate repo chef-repo**. This will create a folder structure for us, and once its created, we'll **cd** into it:

[root@rhel01 ~]# **chef generate repo chef-repo**
Generating Chef Infra repo chef-repo
- Ensuring correct Chef Infra repo file content

Your new Chef Infra repo is ready! Type `cd chef-repo` to enter it.
[root@rhel01 ~]# **cd chef-repo/**

Next we must create a **.chef** directory to store the server and organization certificates. We can use **scp** to copy them over to the directory:

```
[root@rhel01 chef-repo]# mkdir .chef
[root@rhel01 chef-repo]# cd .chef/
 [root@rhel01 .chef]# scp rhel02:chefadmin.pem .
root@rhel02's password:
chefadmin.pem
100% 1674    674.0KB/s    00:00
[root@rhel01 .chef]# scp rhel02:testlab-org.pem .
root@rhel02's password:
testlab-org.pem
```

And of course, we've got to create a **knife.rb** file that references the certificates and points the repository to the Chef Server. The file also references where the cookbooks are stored:

```
[root@rhel01 .chef]#cat knife.rb
current_dir = File.dirname(__FILE__)
log_level :info
log_location STDOUT
node_name "chefadmin"
client_key "#{current_dir}/chefadmin.pem"
validation_client_name 'testlab-validator'
validation_key "#{current_dir}/testlab-org.pem"
chef_server_url "https://rhel02.testlab.com/organizations/testlab"
cookbook_path ["#{current_dir}/../cookbooks"]
```

With all that in place we can use the **knife ssl fetch** command to pull the Chef Server certs. After that, we can finally check communications are working with the **knife ssl check**:

```
[root@rhel01 .chef]# knife ssl fetch
WARNING: Certificates from rhel02.testlab.com will be fetched and placed in your trusted_cert
         directory (/root/chef-repo/.chef/trusted_certs).
         Knife has no means to verify these are the correct certificates. You should
         verify the authenticity of these certificates after downloading.
Adding certificate for rhel02_testlab_com in /root/chef-repo/.chef/trusted_certs/rhel02_testlab_com.crt
[root@rhel01 .chef]# knife ssl check
Connecting to host rhel02.testlab.com:443
Successfully verified certificates from `rhel02.testlab.com'
```

Lab Setup

Phew! With all that out of the way, let's talk about our lab setup for Chef. We're going to use Chef to configure an Ubuntu and Fedora server. Just so you know, Chef used to support Cisco Nexus like Puppet does, but the current version of Chef doesn't do Cisco at this time.

Chef also has a more complex infrastructure than what you've seen so far, so we'll install the Chef Workstation on my RHEL01 host and the Chef Server on RHEL02.

Our goal this time is to install Apache and generate a website that tells us which host we're connecting to. You can check out the topology in Figure 23.12.

FIGURE 23.12 Chef lab

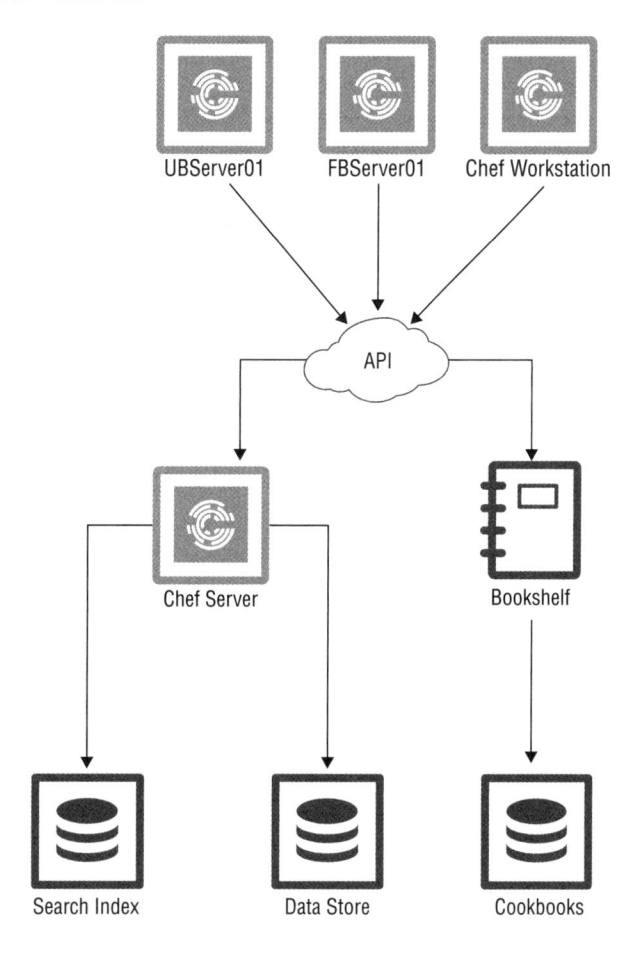

So let's create a cookbook by using the **chef generate cookbook** command, I'll name it **create-webpage**:

[root@rhel01 .chef]# **cd /root/chef-repo/**
[root@rhel01 chef-repo]# **chef generate cookbook cookbooks/create-webpage**

To generate the webpage content, we'll create an Embedded Ruby Template (ERB) with the **chef generate template create-webpage**.

Then, we'll edit the **index.html.erb** file and put in our website code. We'll add in the node name dynamically with the **<%= node['fqdn'] %>** code:

```
[root@rhel01 cookbooks]# chef generate template create-webpage index.html
Recipe: code_generator::template
  * directory[./create-webpage/templates] action create
    - create new directory ./create-webpage/templates
    - restore selinux security context
  * template[./create-webpage/templates/index.html.erb] action create
    - create new file ./create-webpage/templates/index.html.erb
    - update content in file ./create-webpage/templates/index.html.erb from none to e3b0c4
    (diff output suppressed by config)
    - restore selinux security context

[root@rhel01 cookbooks]# cat create-webpage/templates/index.html.erb
<html>
  <head><title>CCNA Fun!!!</title></head>
  <body>
      <h1>More Cisco!!!</ />
      <h2>This node is: <%= node['fqdn'] %></h2>
  </body>
</html>
```

Now it's time to create the recipe that'll install Apache based upon the Linux OS the node happens to be running:

```
root@rhel01 cookbooks]# cat create-webpage/recipes/default.rb
#
# Cookbook:: create-webpage
# Recipe:: default
#
# Copyright:: 2019, The Authors, All Rights Reserved.

#Install Web Server

package 'Install Web Server on Node' do
```

```
    case node[:platform]
    when 'redhat', 'fedora'
      package_name 'httpd'

    when 'ubuntu'
      package_name 'apache2'
    end
end

#Enable and Start the Web Service
service 'Enable and Start Web Service' do
  case node[:platform]
  when 'redhat', 'fedora'
    service_name 'httpd'
  when 'ubuntu'
    service_name 'apache2'
  end
  action [:enable, :start]
end

# Create Main Webpage
template '/var/www/html/index.html' do
  source 'index.html.erb'
  mode '0644'
  case node[:platform]
  when 'redhat','fedora'
    owner 'apache'
    group 'apache'
  when 'ubuntu'
    owner 'www-data'
    group 'www-data'
  end
end
```

We have the option to edit **metadata.db** to give us more info about the cookbook:

```
[root@rhel01 cookbooks]# cat create-webpage/metadata.rb
name 'create-webpage'
maintainer 'The Authors'
maintainer_email 'you@example.com'
license 'All Rights Reserved'
```

```
description 'Installs/Configures create-webpage'
long_description 'Installs/Configures create-webpage'
version '0.1.0'
chef_version '>= 14.0'


# The `issues_url` points to the location where issues for this cookbook are
# tracked.  A `View Issues` link will be displayed on this cookbook's page when
# uploaded to a Supermarket.
#
# issues_url 'https://github.com/<insert_org_here>/create-webpage/issues'

# The `source_url` points to the development repository for this cookbook.  A
# `View Source` link will be displayed on this cookbook's page when uploaded to
# a Supermarket.
#
# source_url 'https://github.com/<insert_org_here>/create-webpage'
```

Next we've got to upload the cookbook to the server bookshelf so we can deploy it to our servers:

```
[root@rhel01 cookbooks]# knife cookbook upload create-webpage
Uploading create-webpage [0.1.0]
Uploaded 1 cookbook.
```

To deploy the cookbook to the nodes, we'll use the **knife bootstrap** command to SSH into the host, install the agent, and trigger the deployment. Let's do the Ubuntu host first:

```
[root@rhel01 ~]# knife bootstrap 10.30.10.150 --ssh-user the-packet-thrower --ssh-password cisco1234 --sudo --use-sudo-password cisco1234 \
> --node-name UBServer01.testlab.com -r 'recipe[create-webpage]'
Connecting to 10.30.10.150
The authenticity of host '10.30.10.150 ()' can't be established.
fingerprint is SHA256:VpH/gzMW9kFZ7NMiWMRgL/B4hukaLsFYdgZhobGlT60.

Are you sure you want to continue connecting
? (Y/N) y
```

And now the Fedora server:

```
[root@rhel01 ~]# knife bootstrap 10.30.10.160 --ssh-user the-packet-thrower --ssh-password cisco1234 --sudo --use-sudo-password cisco1234 \
> --node-name UBServer01.testlab.com -r 'recipe[create-webpage]'
```

```
Connecting to 10.30.10.160
The authenticity of host '10.30.10.160 ()' can't be established.
fingerprint is SHA256:VpH/gzMW9kFZ7NMiWMRgL/B4hukaLsFYdgZhobGlT60.

Are you sure you want to continue connecting
? (Y/N) y
```

Verifying the Results

To test the whole meal, I'll plug up the pages in my browser so we can see the node name plus our "More Cisco!!!" message. Check out the results in Figure 23.13: Chef Verification.

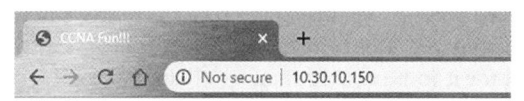

FIGURE 23.13   Chef verification

Summary

DevOps and Infrastructure as Code are becoming seriously popular ways to keep network and server configuration under control. This chapter covered the basics of DevOps and IaC and demonstrated how Ansible, Puppet, and Chef work, including the strengths and weaknesses of each.

Next, you got to have a whole bunch of fun running through the lab solutions, becoming familiar with what they look like in real-world use.

Exam Essentials

Ansible   Ansible is a Python-based configuration management tool that uses YAML playbooks to push configuration to nodes. It's an agentless solution offering wide support for network devices because it uses SSH to reach nodes. Because there's no agent, Ansible can only push configuration to nodes.

Puppet   Puppet is a Ruby-based configuration management tool that uses custom manifest files to configure devices. It requires an agent to be installed on the node, so it has less network support. Puppet also doesn't support pushing configuration to nodes. Instead, the configuration is applied when the agent checks in. Puppet does support Cisco network devices that can install the Puppet agent.

Chef   Chef is a Ruby-based configuration tool that uses cookbooks to apply configuration. Chef is the most advanced solution in this chapter and is better suited for programmers because it's more structured and has a strong developer focus. It also requires that nodes have an agent deployed for it to be able to manage them. Chef can't push configurations.

Review Questions

You can find the answers in the Appendix.

1. Which configuration management solutions require agents? (Choose two.)
   A. Puppet
   B. Ansible
   C. Chef
   D. Cisco IOS

2. What does Ansible call the file that holds the configuration that should be applied to nodes?
   A. Cookbook
   B. Manifest
   C. Playbook
   D. Inventory

3. What configuration management solution is best suited for managing Cisco devices?
   A. Puppet
   B. Ansible
   C. Chef
   D. Cisco IOS

4. What languages does Ansible use in playbooks?
   A. JavaScript
   B. Python
   C. Ruby
   D. YAML

5. Which configuration management solution uses manifest files?
   A. Puppet
   B. Ansible
   C. Chef
   D. Cisco IOS

6. Which configuration management solution is best suited for developers?
   A. Ansible
   B. Chef
   C. Puppet
   D. Cisco IOS

7. Which solution uses an inventory file?
   A. Puppet
   B. Ansible
   C. Chef
   D. Cisco IOS

8. Puppet is based on which language?
   A. JavaScript
   B. Python
   C. Ruby
   D. TCL

9. Which connection methods does Ansible use? (Choose two.)
   A. Telnet
   B. SSH
   C. Powershell
   D. Ping

10. What does Knife do in a Chef deployment?
    A. It stores the recipe files.
    B. It is the name of the main server.
    C. It is Chef's inventory file.
    D. It is the CLI utility for managing Chef.

11. What are some components used in a Chef deployment? (Choose three.)
    A. Chef server
    B. Chef workstation
    C. Bookshelf
    D. Cooktop

12. What configuration management solution is best suited for sysadmins?
    A. Ansible
    B. Puppet
    C. Chef
    D. Python

13. A YAML file can't contain which type of character?
    A. Space
    B. Tab
    C. Question mark
    D. Forward slash

14. Which command do you use to run an Ansible playbook?
    A. Ansible-doc
    B. Ansible-execute
    C. Ansible-Playbook
    D. Run-Playbook
15. Which command do you use to look up a module in Ansible?
    A. Ansible-doc
    B. Ansible-execute
    C. Ansible-Playbook
    D. Run-Playbook

Appendix

Answer to Review Questions

Chapter 1: Network Fundamentals

1. A. The core layer should be as fast as possible. Never do anything to slow down traffic. This includes making sure you don't use access lists, perform routing between virtual local area networks, or implement packet filtering.

2. C. SOHO stands for small office, home office and is a single or small group of users connecting to a switch, with a router providing a connection to the Internet for the small network.

3. A, C. The access layer provides users, phones, and other devices with access to the internetwork. PoE and switch port security are implemented here.

4. C. 1000Base-ZX (Cisco standard) is a Cisco-specified standard for Gigabit Ethernet communication. 1000Base-ZX operates on ordinary single-mode fiber-optic links with spans up to 43.5 miles (70 km).

5. D. A T3, referred to as an S3, comprises 28 DS1s bundled together, or 672 DS0s, for a bandwidth of 44.736 Mbps.

6. B. Since there is no such thing as layer 2 packets, we wouldn't be able to do packet inspection with any device on this nonexistent packet type.

7. C. The IEEE has created a standard for PoE called 802.3af. For PoE+, it's referred to as 802.3at.

8. B. In a two-tier, the design is meant to maximize performance and user availability to the network, while still allowing for design scalability over time.

9. C. 10GBase-T is a standard proposed by the IEEE 802.3an committee to provide 10 Gbps connections over conventional UTP cables (category 5e, 6, or 7 cables).

10. A. In a spine-leaf design, people refer to this as a Top-of-Rack (ToR) design because the switches physically reside at the top of a rack.

Chapter 2: TCP/IP

1. C. If a DHCP conflict is detected, either by the server sending a ping and getting a response or by a host using a gratuitous ARP (arp'ing for its own IP address and seeing if a host responds), then the server will hold that address and not use it again until it is fixed by an administrator.

2. B. The Secure Shell (SSH) protocol sets up a secure session that's similar to Telnet over a standard TCP/IP connection and is employed for doing things like logging into systems, running programs on remote systems, and moving files from one system to another.

3. C. A host uses something called a gratuitous ARP to help avoid a possible duplicate address. The DHCP client sends an ARP broadcast out on the local LAN or VLAN with its newly assigned address to find out if another host replies, and this helps solve conflicts before they occur.

4. A, B. The client that sends out a DHCP Discover message in order to receive an IP address sends out a broadcast at both layer 2 and layer 3. The layer 2 broadcast is all Fs in hex, or ff:ff:ff:ff:ff:ff. The layer 3 broadcast is 255.255.255.255, which means any networks and all hosts. DHCP is connectionless, which means it uses User Datagram Protocol (UDP) at the Transport layer, also called the Host-to-Host layer.

5. B, D, E. SMTP, FTP, and HTTP use TCP.

6. C. The range of multicast addresses starts with 224.0.0.0 and goes through 239.255.255.255.

7. C, E. The Class A private address range is 10.0.0.0 through 10.255.255.255. The Class B private address range is 172.16.0.0 through 172.31.255.255, and the Class C private address range is 192.168.0.0 through 192.168.255.255.

8. B. The four layers of the TCP/IP stack (also called the DoD model) are Application/Process, Host-to-Host (also called Transport on the objectives), Internet, and Network Access/Link. The Host-to-Host layer is equivalent to the Transport layer of the OSI model.

9. B, C. ICMP is used for diagnostics and destination unreachable messages. ICMP is encapsulated within IP datagrams, and because it is used for diagnostics, it will provide hosts with information about network problems.

10. C. The range of a Class B network address is 128–191. This makes our binary range 10xxxxxx.

Chapter 3: Easy Subnetting

1. D. A /27 (255.255.255.224) is 3 bits on and 5 bits off. This provides 8 subnets, each with 30 hosts. Does it matter if this mask is used with a Class A, B, or C network address? Not at all. The number of subnet bits would never change.

2. D. A 240 mask is 4 subnet bits and provides 16 subnets, each with 14 hosts. We need more subnets, so let's add subnet bits. One more subnet bit would be a 248 mask. This provides 5 subnet bits (32 subnets) with 3 host bits (6 hosts per subnet). This is the best answer.

3. C. This is a pretty simple question. A /28 is 255.255.255.240, which means that our block size is 16 in the fourth octet. 0, 16, 32, 48, 64, 80, etc. The host is in the 64 subnet.

4. F. A CIDR address of /19 is 255.255.224.0. This is a Class B address, so that is only 3 subnet bits, but it provides 13 host bits, or 8 subnets, each with 8,190 hosts.

5. B, D. The mask 255.255.254.0 (/23) used with a Class A address means that there are 15 subnet bits and 9 host bits. The block size in the third octet is 2 (256 − 254). So this makes the subnets in the interesting octet 0, 2, 4, 6, etc., all the way to 254. The host 10.16.3.65 is in the 2.0 subnet. The next subnet is 4.0, so the broadcast address for the 2.0 subnet is 3.255. The valid host addresses are 2.1 through 3.254.

6. D. A /30, regardless of the class of address, has a 252 in the fourth octet. This means we have a block size of 4 and our subnets are 0, 4, 8, 12, 16, etc. Address 14 is obviously in the 12 subnet.

7. D. A point-to-point link uses only two hosts. A /30, or 255.255.255.252, mask provides two hosts per subnet.

8. C. A /21 is 255.255.248.0, which means we have a block size of 8 in the third octet, so we just count by 8 until we reach 66. The subnet in this question is 64.0. The next subnet is 72.0, so the broadcast address of the 64 subnet is 71.255.

9. A. A /29 (255.255.255.248), regardless of the class of address, has only 3 host bits. Six is the maximum number of hosts on this LAN, including the router interface.

10. C. A /29 is 255.255.255.248, which is a block size of 8 in the fourth octet. The subnets are 0, 8, 16, 24, 32, 40, etc. 192.168.19.24 is the 24 subnet, and since 32 is the next subnet, the broadcast address for the 24 subnet is 31. 192.168.19.26 is the only correct answer.

Chapter 4: Troubleshooting IP Addressing

1. D. A point-to-point link uses only two hosts. A /30, or 255.255.255.252, mask provides two hosts per subnet.

2. B. With an incorrect gateway, Host A will not be able to communicate with the router or beyond the router but will be able to communicate within the subnet.

3. A. All steps will work at this point, except pinging the remote computer would fail if any of the other steps fail.

4. C. When a ping to the local host IP address fails, you can assume the NIC is not functional.

5. C, D. If a ping to the local host succeeds, you can rule out IP stack or NIC failure.

6. A. The most likely problem if you can ping a computer by IP address but not by name is a failure of DNS.

7. D. When you issue the `ping` command, you are using the ICMP protocol.

8. B. The `traceroute` command displays the networks traversed on a path to a network destination.

9. C. The `ping` command tests connectivity to another station. The full command output is shown in the question.

10. C. The `/all` switch must be added to the `ipconfig` command on a PC to verify DNS configuration.

Chapter 5: IP Routing

1. C. The ip route command is used to display the routing table of a router.

2. B. In the new 15 IOS code, Cisco defines a different route called a local route. Each has a /32 prefix defining a route just for the one address, which is the router's interface.

3. A, B. Although option D almost seems right, it is not; the mask option is the mask used on the remote network, not the source network. Since there is no number at the end of the static route, it is using the default administrative distance of 1.

4. B. This mapping was learned dynamically, which means it was learned through ARP.

5. B. Hybrid protocols use aspects of both distance vector and link state—for example, EIGRP. Be advised, however, that Cisco typically just calls EIGRP an advanced distance-vector routing protocol.

6. A. Since the destination MAC address is different at each hop, it must keep changing. The IP address, which is used for the routing process, does not. Do not be misled by the way the question is worded. Yes, I know that MAC addresses are not in a packet. You must read the question to understand of what it is really asking.

7. C. This is how most people see routers, and certainly they could do this type of plain ol' packet switching in 1990 when Cisco released its very first router and traffic was seriously slow, but not in today's networks! This process involves looking up every destination in the routing table and finding the exit interface for every packet.

8. A, C. The S* shows that this is a candidate for default route and that it was configured manually.

9. B. RIP has an administrative distance (AD) of 120, while OSPF has an administrative distance of 110, so the router will discard any route with a higher AD than 110 to that same network.

10. D. Recovery from a lost route requires manual intervention by a human to replace the lost route.

Chapter 6: Open Shortest Path First (OSPF)

1. A, C. The process ID for OSPF on a router is only locally significant, and you can use the same number on each router, or each router can have a different number—it just doesn't matter. The numbers you can use are from 1 to 65,535. Don't get this confused with area numbers, which can be from 0 to 4.2 billion.

2. B. The router ID (RID) is an IP address used to identify the router. It need not and should not match.

3. A. The administrator typed in the wrong wildcard mask configuration. The wildcard should have been 0.0.0.255 or even 0.255.255.255.

4. A. A dash (-) in the State column indicates no DR election because they are not required on a point-to-point link such as a serial connection.

5. D. By default, the administrative distance of OSPF is 110.

6. A. Hello packets are addressed to multicast address 224.0.0.5.

7. A. 224.0.0.6 is used on broadcast networks to reach the DR and BDR.

8. D. The Hello and Dead timers must be set the same on two routers on the same link or they will not form an adjacency (relationship). The default timers for OSPF are 10 seconds for the Hello timer and 40 seconds for the Dead timer.

9. A. The default OSPF interface priority is 1, and the highest interface priority determines the designated router (DR) for a subnet. The output indicates that the router with a router ID of 192.168.45.2 is currently the backup designated router (BDR) for the segment, which indicates that another router became the DR. It can be then be assumed that the DR router has an interface priority higher than 2. (The router serving the DR function is not present in the truncated sample output.)

10. A. LSA packets are used to update and maintain the topological database.

Chapter 7: Layer 2 Switching

1. A. Layer 2 switches and bridges are faster than routers because they don't take up time looking at the Network Layer header information. They do make use of the Data Link layer information.

2. A, D. In the output shown, you can see that the port is in Secure-shutdown mode and the light for the port would be amber. To enable the port again, you'd need to do the following:

    S3(config-if)#**shutdown**

    S3(config-if)#**no shutdown**

3. B. The `switchport port-security` command enables port security, which is a prerequisite for the other commands to function.

4. B. Gateway redundancy is not an issue addressed by STP.

5. A, C.
   - Protect—This mode permits traffic from known MAC addresses to continue to be forwarded while dropping traffic from unknown MAC addresses when over the allowed MAC address limit. When configured with this mode, no notification action is taken when traffic is dropped.
   - Restrict—This mode permits traffic from known MAC addresses to continue to be forwarded while dropping traffic from unknown MAC addresses when over the allowed MAC address limit. When configured with this mode, a syslog message is logged, a Simple Network Management Protocol (SNMP) trap is sent, and a violation counter is incremented when traffic is dropped.
   - Shutdown—This mode is the default violation mode; when in this mode, the switch will automatically force the switchport into an error disabled (err-disable) state when a violation occurs. While in this state, the switchport forwards no traffic. A Simple Network Management Protocol (SNMP) trap is sent.

6. C. The IP address is configured under a logical interface, called a management domain or VLAN 1.

7. B. The `show port-security interface` command displays the current port security and status of a switch port.

8. B, D. To limit connections to a specific host, you should configure the MAC address of the host as a static entry associated with the port, although be aware that this host can still connect to any other port but no other port can connect to F0/3 in this example. Another solution would be to configure port security to accept traffic only from the MAC address of the host. By default, an unlimited number of MAC addresses can be learned on a single switch port, whether it is configured as an access port or a trunk port. Switch ports can be secured by defining one or more specific MAC addresses that should be allowed to connect and by defining violation policies (such as disabling the port) to be enacted if additional hosts try to gain a connection.

9. D. The command statically defines the MAC address of 00c0.35F0.8301 as an allowed host on the switch port. By default, an unlimited number of MAC addresses can be learned on a single switch port, whether it is configured as an access port or a trunk port. Switch ports can be secured by defining one or more specific MAC addresses that should be allowed to connect and violation policies (such as disabling the port) if additional hosts try to gain a connection.

10. D. You would not make the port a trunk. In this example, this switchport is a member of one VLAN. However, you can configure port security on a trunk port, but again, that's not valid for this question.

Chapter 8: VLANs and Inter-VLAN Routing

1. D. Here's a list of ways VLANs simplify network management:
   - Network adds, moves, and changes are achieved with ease by just configuring a port into the appropriate VLAN.
   - A group of users that need an unusually high level of security can be put into its own VLAN so that users outside of the VLAN can't communicate with them.
   - As a logical grouping of users by function, VLANs can be considered independent from their physical or geographic locations.
   - VLANs greatly enhance network security if implemented correctly.
   - VLANs increase the number of broadcast domains while decreasing their size.

2. B. While in all other cases access ports can be a member of only one VLAN, most switches will allow you to add a second VLAN to an access port on a switch port for your voice traffic; it's called the voice VLAN. The voice VLAN used to be called the auxiliary VLAN, which allowed it to be overlaid on top of the data VLAN, enabling both types of traffic through the same port.

3. A. Yes, you need to do a no shutdown on the VLAN interface.

4. C. Unlike ISL, which encapsulates the frame with control information, 802.1q inserts an 802.1q field along with tag control information.

5. A. With a multilayer switch, by enabling IP routing and creating one logical interface for each VLAN by using the `interface vlan number` command, you're now doing inter-VLAN routing on the backplane of the switch!

6. A. Ports Fa0/15–18 are not present in any VLANs. They are trunk ports.

7. C. Untagged frames are members of the native VLAN, which by default is VLAN 1.

8. C. A VLAN is a broadcast domain on a layer 2 switch. You need a separate address space (subnet) for each VLAN. There are four VLANs, so that means four broadcast domains/subnets.

9. C. Frame tagging is used when VLAN traffic travels over a trunk link. Trunk links carry frames for multiple VLANs. Therefore, frame tags are used for identification of frames from different VLANs.

10. B. 802.1q uses the native VLAN.

Chapter 9: Enhanced Switched Technologies

1. B, D. The switch is not the root bridge for VLAN 1 or the output would tell us exactly that. The root bridge for VLAN 1 is off of interface G1/2 with a cost of 4, meaning it is directly connected. Use the command show cdp nei to find your root bridge at this point. Also, the switch is running RSTP (802.1w), not STP.

2. D. Option A seems like the best answer, and had switches not been configured with the primary and secondary command, then the switch configured with priority 4096 would have been root. However, since the primary and secondary both had a priority of 16384, then the tertiary switch would be a switch with a higher priority in this case.

3. A, D. It's important that you can find your root bridge and the show spanning-tree command will help you do this. To quickly find out which VLANs your switch is the root bridge for, use the show spanning-tree summary command.

4. A. 802.1w is the also called Rapid Spanning Tree Protocol. It's not enabled by default on Cisco switches, but it is a better STP to run because it has all the fixes that the Cisco extensions provide with 802.1d. Remember, Cisco runs RSTP PVST+, not just RSTP.

5. B. The Spanning Tree Protocol is used to stop switching loops in a layer 2 switched network with redundant paths.

6. C. Convergence occurs when all ports on bridges and switches have transitioned to either the forwarding or blocking states. No data is forwarded until convergence is complete. Before data can be forwarded again, all devices must be updated.

7. C, E. There are two types of EtherChannel: Cisco's PAgP and the IEEE's LACP. They are basically the same, and there's little difference to configuring them. For PAgP, use auto or desirable mode, and with LACP use passive or active. These modes decide which method you're using, and they must be configured the same on both sides of the EtherChannel bundle.

8. A, B, F. RSTP helps with convergence issues that plague traditional STP. Rapid PVST+ is based on the 802.1w standard in the same way that PVST+ is based on 802.1d. The operation of Rapid PVST+ is simply a separate instance of 802.1w for each VLAN.

9. D. BPDU Guard is used when a port is configured for PortFast, or it should be used, because if that port receives a BPDU from another switch, BPDU Guard will shut that port down to stop a loop from occurring.

10. C. To allow for the PVST+ to operate, there's a field inserted into the BPDU to accommodate the extended system ID so that PVST+ can have a root bridge configured on a per-STP instance. The extended system ID (VLAN ID) is a 12-bit field, and we can even see what this field is carrying via the show spanning-tree command output.

Chapter 10: Access Lists

1. D. It's compared with lines of the access list only until a match is made. Once the packet matches the condition on a line of the access list, the packet is acted upon and no further comparisons take place.

2. C. The range of 192.168.160.0 to 192.168.191.0 is a block size of 32. The network address is 192.168.160.0, and the mask would be 255.255.224.0, which for an access list must be a wildcard format of 0.0.31.255. The 31 is used for a block size of 32. The wildcard is always one less than the block size.

3. C. Using a named access list just replaces the number used when applying the list to the router's interface. `ip access-group Blocksales in` is correct.

4. B. The list must specify TCP as the Transport layer protocol and use a correct wildcard mask (in this case 0.0.0.255), and it must specify the destination port (80). It also should specify any as the set of computers allowed to have this access.

5. A. The first thing to check in a question like this is the access-list number. Right away, you can see that the second option is wrong because it is using a standard IP access-list number. The second thing to check is the protocol. If you are filtering by upper-layer protocol, then you must be using either UDP or TCP; this eliminates the fourth option. The third and last options have the wrong syntax.

6. C. Of the available choices, only the `show ip interface` command will tell you which interfaces have access lists applied. `show access-lists` will not show you which interfaces have an access list applied.

7. C. The extended access list ranges are 100–199 and 2000–2699, so the access-list number of 100 is valid. Telnet uses TCP, so the protocol TCP is valid. Now you just need to look for the source and destination addresses. Only the third option has the correct sequence of parameters. Option B may work, but the question specifically states *only* to network 192.168.10.0, and the wildcard in option B is too broad.

8. E. Extended IP access lists use numbers 100–199 and 2000–2699 and filter based on source and destination IP address, protocol number, and port number. The last option is correct because of the second line that specifies `permit ip any any`. (I used `0.0.0.0 255.255.255.255`, which is the same as the any option.) The other options does not have this, so they would deny access but not allow everything else.

9. D. First, you must know that a /20 is 255.255.240.0, which is a block size of 16 in the third octet. Counting by 16s, this makes our subnet 48 in the third octet, and the wildcard for the third octet would be 15 since the wildcard is always one less than the block size.

10. B. To find the wildcard (inverse) version of this mask, the zero and one bits are simply reversed as follows: 11111111.11111111.11111111.11100000 (27 one bits, or /27) 00000000.00000000.00000000.00011111 (wildcard/inverse mask). However, the answer is always one less (-1), and a /27 is a block of 32, so the answer is easily 31 in the fourth octet (no math!).

Chapter 11: Network Address Translation (NAT)

1. **A, C, E.** NAT is not perfect and can cause some issues in some networks. In most networks, it works just fine. NAT can cause delays and troubleshooting problems, and some applications just won't work with it.

2. **B, D, F.** NAT is not perfect, but there are some advantages. It conserves global addresses, allowing us to add millions of hosts to the Internet without "real" IP addresses. This provides flexibility in our corporate networks. NAT can also allow you to use the same subnet more than once in the same network without overlapping networks.

3. **C.** The command debug ip nat will show you in real time the translations occurring on your router.

4. **A.** The command show ip nat translations will show you the translation table containing all the active NAT entries.

5. **D.** The command clear ip nat translations * will clear all the active NAT entries in your translation table.

6. **B.** The show ip nat statistics command displays a summary of the NAT configuration as well as counts of active translation types, hits to an existing mapping, misses (an attempt to create a mapping), and expired translations. *

7. **B.** The command ip nat pool *name* creates the address pool that hosts can use to get onto the global Internet. What makes option B correct is that the range 171.16.10.65 through 171.16.10.94 includes 30 hosts, but the mask has to match 30 hosts as well, and that mask is 255.255.255.224. Option C is wrong because there is a lowercase t in the pool name. Pool names are case sensitive.

8. **A, C, E.** You can configure NAT three ways on a Cisco router: static, dynamic, and NAT Overload (PAT).

9. **B.** Instead of the netmask command, you can use the prefix-length *length* statement.

10. **C.** In order for NAT to provide translation services, you must have ip nat inside and ip nat outside configured on your router's interfaces.

Chapter 12: IP Services

1. **B.** You can enter the ACL directly in the SNMP configuration to provide security, using either a number or a name.

2. **A, D.** With a read-only community string, no changes can be made to the router. However, SNMPv2c can use GETBULK to create and return multiple requests at once.

3. C, D. SNMPv2c introduced the GETBULK and INFORM SNMP messages but didn't offer any more security than SNMPv1. SNMPv3 uses TCP and provides encryption and authentication.

4. C. This command can be run on both routers and switches, and it displays detailed information about each device connected to the device you're running the command on, including the IP address.

5. C. The Port ID column describes the interfaces on the remote device end of the connection.

6. B. Syslog levels range from 0–7, and level 7 (known as Debugging or local7) is the default if you were to use the `logging ip_address` command from global config.

7. D. By default, Cisco IOS devices use facility local7. Moreover, most Cisco devices provide options to change the facility level from their default value.

8. C, D, F. There are significantly more syslog messages available within IOS as compared to SNMP Trap messages. System logging is a method of collecting messages from devices to a server running a syslog daemon. Logging to a central syslog server helps in aggregation of logs and alerts.

9. D. To enable a device to be an NTP client, use the `ntp server IP_address version number` command at global configuration mode. That's all there is to it! Assuming your NTP server is working, of course.

10. B, D, F. If you specify a level with the `logging trap level` command, that level and all the higher levels will be logged. For example, when you use the logging trap 3 command, emergencies, alerts, critical, and error messages will be logged. Only three of these were listed as possible options.

11. C, D. To configure SSH on your router, you need to set the `username command`, the `IP domain name`, `login local`, `transport input ssh` under the VTY lines and the `crypto key` command. SSH version 2 is suggested but not required.

Chapter 13: Security

1. D. To enable the AAA commands on a router or switch, use the global configuration command aaa `new-model`.

2. A, C. To mitigate access layer threats, use port security, DHCP snooping, dynamic ARP inspection, and identity-based networking.

3. C, D. The key words in the question are not true. DHCP snooping validates DHCP messages, builds and maintains the DHCP snooping binding database, and rate-limits DHCP traffic for trusted and untrusted source.

4. A, D. TACACS+ uses TCP, is Cisco proprietary, and offers multiprotocol support as well as separated AAA services.

5. B. Unlike TACACS+, which separates AAA services, this is not an option when configuring RADIUS.
6. D. The correct answer is option D. Take your newly created RADIUS group and use it for authentication and be sure to use the keyword local at the end.
7. B. DAI, used with DHCP snooping, tracks IP-to-MAC bindings from DHCP transactions to protect against ARP poisoning. DHCP snooping is required in order to build the MAC-to-IP bindings for DAI validation.
8. A, D, E. There are three roles: Client, also referred to as a supplicant, is software that runs on a client that is 802.1x compliant. The authenticator is typically a switch that controls physical access to the network and is a proxy between the client and the authentication server. The authentication server (RADIUS) authenticates each client before many available any services.
9. B. MFA, biometrics, and certificates are all password alternatives.
10. A. A security program that is backed by a security policy is one of the best ways to maintain a secure posture at all times. This program should cover many elements, but three are key: user awareness, training, and physical security.
11. C, E, F. There are many problems with the IP stack, especially in Microsoft products. Session replaying is a weakness that is found in TCP. Both SNMP and SMTP are listed by Cisco as inherently insecure protocols in the TCP/IP stack.
12. B. The TCP intercept feature implements software to protect TCP servers from TCP SYN-flooding attacks, which are a type of denial-of-service attack.
13. B, E, G. By using the Cisco Lock and Key along with CHAP and TACACS, you can create a more secure network and help stop unauthorized access.
14. C. Network snooping and packet sniffing are common terms for eavesdropping.
15. C. IP spoofing is fairly easy to stop once you understand the way spoofing takes place. An IP spoofing attack occurs when an attacker outside your network pretends to be a trusted computer by using an IP address that is within the range of IP addresses for your network. The attacker wants to steal an IP address from a trusted source so it can use this to gain access to network resources.

Chapter 14: First Hop Redundancy Protocol (HSRP)

1. C. By setting a higher number than the default on a router, that router would become the active router. Setting preempt would assure that if the active router went down, it would become the active router again when it come back up.
2. C. The idea of a first hop redundancy protocol is to provide redundancy for a default gateway.

3. A, B. A router interface can be in many states with HSRP, and Established and Idle are not HSRP states.

4. A. Only option D has the correct sequence to enable HSRP on an interface.

5. D. This is a question that I used in a lot of job interviews on prospects. Show standby is your friend when dealing with HSRP.

6. D. There's nothing wrong with leaving the priorities at the defaults of 100. The first router up with be the active router.

7. C. In version 1, HSRP messages are sent to the multicast IP address 224.0.0.2 and UDP port 1985. HSRP version 2 uses the multicast IP address 224.0.0.102 and UDP port 1985.

8. B, C. If HSRP1 is configured to preempt, then it will become active because of the higher priority. If not, HSRP2 will remain the active router.

9. C. In version 1, HSRP messages are sent to the multicast IP address 224.0.0.2 and UDP port 1985. HSRP version 2 uses the multicast IP address 224.0.0.102 and UDP port 1985.

Chapter 15: Virtual Private Networks (VPNs)

1. A, D. GRE tunnels have the following characteristics: GRE uses a protocol-type field in the GRE header so any layer 3 protocol can be used through the tunnel, GRE is stateless and has no flow control, GRE offers no security, and GRE creates additional overhead for tunneled packets—at least 24 bytes.

2. C. If you receive this flapping message when you configure your GRE tunnel, it means you used your tunnel interface address instead of the tunnel destination address.

3. D. The show running-config interface tunnel 0 command will show you the configuration of the interface, not the status of the tunnel.

4. C. The show interfaces tunnel 0 command shows the configuration settings and the interface status as well as the IP address and tunnel source and destination address.

5. B. All web browsers support Secure Sockets Layer (SSL), and SSL VPNs are known as Web VPNs. Remote users can use their browser to create an encrypted connection and they don't need to install any software. GRE doesn't encrypt the data.

6. A, C, E. VPNs can provide good security by using advanced encryption and authentication protocols, which help protect your network from unauthorized access. By connecting the corporate remote offices to their closest Internet provider and then creating a VPN tunnel with encryption and authentication, you'll gain a huge savings over opting for traditional leased point-to-point lines. VPNs scale very well to quickly bring up new offices or have mobile users connect securely while traveling or when connecting from home. VPNs are very compatible with broadband technologies.

7. **A, D.** Internet providers who have an existing Layer 2 network may choose to use layer 2 VPNs instead of the other common layer 3 MPLS VPN. Virtual Private Lan Switch (VPLS) and Virtual Private Wire Service (VPWS) are two technologies that provide layer 2 MPLS VPNs.

8. **D.** IPsec is an industry-wide standard suite of protocols and algorithms that allows for secure data transmission over an IP-based network that functions at the layer 3 Network layer of the OSI model.

9. **C.** A VPN allows or describes the creation of private networks across the Internet, enabling privacy and tunneling of TCP/IP protocols. A VPN can be set up across any type of link.

10. **B, C.** Layer 2 MPLS VPNs and the more popular Layer 3 MPLS VPN are services provided to customers and managed by the provider.

Chapter 16: Quality of Service (QoS)

1. **B.** Dropping packets as they arrive is called tail drop. Selective dropping of packets during the time queues are filling up is called congestion avoidance (CA). Cisco uses weighted random early detection (WRED) as a CA scheme to monitor the buffer depth and performs early discards (drops) on random packets when the minimum defined queue threshold is exceeded.

2. **B, D, E.** Voice traffic is real-time traffic requiring consistent, predictable bandwidth and packet arrival times. One-way requirements include latency < 150 ms, jitter <30 ms, and loss < 1%. Bandwidth needs to be 30 to 128 Kbps.

3. **C.** A trust boundary is where packets are classified and marked. IP phones and the boundary between the ISP and enterprise network are common examples of trust boundaries.

4. **A.** NBAR is a layer 4 to layer 7, deep-packet inspection classifier. NBAR is more CPU intensive than marking and uses the existing markings, addresses, or ACLs.

5. **C.** DSCP is a set of 6-bit values that are used to describe the meaning of the layer 3 IPv4 ToS field. While IP precedence is the old way to mark ToS, DSCP is the new way and is backward compatible with IP precedence.

6. **D.** Class of service (CoS) is a term used to describe designated fields in a frame or packet header. How devices treat packets in your network depends on the field values. CoS is usually used with Ethernet frames and contains 3 bits.

7. **C.** When traffic exceeds the allocated rate, the policer can take one of two actions: It can either drop traffic or re-mark it to another class of service. The new class usually has a higher drop probability.

Chapter 17: Internet Protocol Version 6 (IPv6)

1. D. The modified EUI-64 format interface identifier is derived from the 48-bit link-layer (MAC) address by inserting the hexadecimal number FFFE between the upper 3 bytes (OUI field) and the lower 3 bytes (serial number) of the link-layer address.

2. D. An IPv6 address is represented as eight groups of four hexadecimal digits, each group representing 16 bits (two octets). The groups are separated by colons (:). Option A has two double colons, B doesn't have 8 fields, and option C has invalid hex characters.

3. A, B, C. This question is easier to answer if you just take out the wrong options. First, the loopback is only ::1, so that makes option D wrong. Link local is FE80::/10, not /8, and there are no broadcasts.

4. A, C, D. Several methods are used in terms of migration, including tunneling, translators, and dual-stack. Tunnels are used to carry one protocol inside another, while translators simply translate IPv6 packets into IPv4 packets. Dual-stack uses a combination of both native IPv4 and IPv6. With dual-stack, devices are able to run IPv4 and IPv6 together, and if IPv6 communication is possible, that is the preferred protocol. Hosts can simultaneously reach IPv4 and IPv6 content.

5. A, B. ICMPv6 router advertisements use type 134 and must be at least 64 bits in length.

6. B, E, F. Anycast addresses identify multiple interfaces, which is somewhat similar to multicast addresses; however, the big difference is that the anycast packet is only delivered to one address, the first one it finds defined in terms of routing distance. This address can also be called one-to-one-of-many, or one-to-nearest.

7. C. The loopback address with IPv4 is 127.0.0.1. With IPv6, that address is ::1.

8. B, C, E. An important feature of IPv6 is that it allows the plug-and-play option to the network devices by allowing them to configure themselves independently. It is possible to plug a node into an IPv6 network without requiring any human intervention. IPv6 does not implement traditional IP broadcasts.

9. A, D. The loopback address is ::1, link-local starts with FE80::/10, site-local addresses start with FEC0::/10, global addresses start with 2000::/3, and multicast addresses start with FF00::/8.

10. C. A router solicitation is sent out using the all-routers multicast address of FF02::2. The router can send a router advertisement to all hosts using the FF02::1 multicast address.

Chapter 18: Troubleshooting IP, IPv6, and VLANs

1. D. Positive confirmation has been received confirming that the path to the neighbor is functioning correctly. REACH is good!

2. B. The most common cause of interface errors is a mismatched duplex mode between two ends of an Ethernet link. If they have mismatched duplex settings, you'll receive a legion of errors, which cause ugly slow performance issues, intermittent connectivity, and massive collisions—even total loss of communication!

3. D. You can verify the DTP status of an interface with the `sh dtp interface` *interface* command.

4. A. No DTP frames are generated from the interface. Nonegotiate can be used only if the neighbor interface is manually set as trunk or access.

5. D. The command `show ipv6 neighbors` provides the ARP cache on a router.

6. B. The state is STALE when the interface has not communicated within the neighbor-reachable time frame. The next time the neighbor communicates, the state will change back to REACH.

7. B. There is no IPv6 default gateway, which will be the link-local address of the router interface, sent to the host as a router advertisement. Until this host receives the router address, the host will communicate with IPv6 only on the local subnet.

8. D. This host is using IPv4 to communicate on the network, and without an IPv6 global address, the host will be able to communicate to only remote networks with IPv4. The IPv4 address and default gateway are not configured into the same subnet.

9. B, C. The commands `show interface trunk` and `show interface` *interface* `switchport` will show you statistics of ports, which includes native VLAN information.

10. A. Most Cisco switches ship with a default port mode of auto, meaning that they will automatically trunk if they connect to a port that is on or desirable. Remember that not all switches are shipped as mode auto, but many are, and you need to set one side to either on or desirable in order to trunk between switches.

Chapter 19: Wireless Technologies

1. B. WPA3 Enterprise uses GCMP-256 for encryption, WPA2 uses AES-CCMP for encryption, and WPA uses TKIP.

2. C. The IEEE 802.11b and IEEE 802.11g standards both run in the 2.4 GHz RF range.

3. D. The IEEE 802.11a standard runs in the 5 GHz RF range.

4. C. The IEEE 802.11b and IEEE 802.11g standards both run in the 2.4 GHz RF range.

5. C. The minimum parameter configured on an AP for a simple WLAN installation is the SSID, although you should set the channel and authentication method as well.

6. A. WPA3 Enterprise uses GCMP-256 for encryption, WPA2 uses AES-CCMP for encryption, and WPA uses TKIP.

7. A. The IEEE 802.11b standard provides three non-overlapping channels.

8. C. WPA3 is resistant to offline dictionary attacks where an attacker attempts to determine a network password by trying possible passwords without further network interaction

9. D. The IEEE 802.11a standard provides a maximum data rate of up to 54 Mbps.

10. D. The IEEE 802.11g standard provides a maximum data rate of up to 54 Mbps.

11. B. The IEEE 802.11b standard provides a maximum data rate of up to 11 Mbps.

12. C. The 802.11 "open" authentication support has been replaced with Opportunistic Wireless Encryption (OWE) enhancement, which is an enhancement, not a mandatory certified setting.

13. D. Although this question is cryptic at best, the only possible answer is option D. If the SSID is not being broadcast (which we must assume in this question), the client must be configured with the correct SSID in order to associate to the AP.

14. B, E. WPA uses Temporal Key Integrity Protocol (TKIP), which includes both broadcast key rotation (dynamic keys that change) and sequencing of frames.

15. A, D. Both WEP and TKIP (WPA) use the RC4 algorithm. It is advised to use WPA2, which uses the AES encryption, or WPA3 when it is available to you.

16. C. Two wireless hosts directly connected wirelessly is no different than two hosts connecting with a crossover cable. They are both ad hoc networks, but in wireless, we call this an Independent Basic Service Set (IBSS).

17. A, C. WPA, although using the same RC4 encryption that WEP uses, provides enhancements to the WEP protocol by using dynamic keys that change constantly as well as providing a Pre-Shared Key method of authentication.

18. B. To create an Extended Service Set (ESS), you need to overlap the wireless BSA from each AP by at least 15 percent in order to not have a gap in coverage so users do not lose their connection when roaming between APs.

19. A. Extended service set ID means that you have more than one access point and they all are set to the same SSID and all are connected together in the same VLAN or distribution system so users can roam.

20. A, B, D. The three basic parameters to configure when setting up an access point are the SSID, the RF channel, and the authentication method.

Chapter 20: Configuring Wireless Technologies

1. B. Windows 10 CMD uses ipconfig to display IP information. Get-NetIPAddress is a PowerShell command and won't work in the cmd prompt.

2. A, C, D. The three things the SP needs are as follows: (1) the switch port must be a access port because VLAN tagging is not supported, (2) you need to add static routes to the network from which you are managing the WLC, and (3) the SP interface must be connected to a switch.

3. E. For the DNS method, you need to create an A record for CISCO-CAPWAP-CONTROLLER that points to the WLC management IP.

4. D. WLANs default to silver queue, which effectively means no QoS is being utilized.

5. A. WLC's gold queue is also known as the video queue.

6. C. The best solution is to use the interface group to extend the amount of IP addresses available to the WLAN. Creating a new WLAN would be a burden to the employees and would only confuse them. Adding more APs won't help the issue since we need more IP addresses, and the session timeout won't free up IP addresses.

7. B, C, E. LAGs on a WLC are fairly restrictive. All interfaces must be part of the bundle, `channel-group # mode on` must be used because LACP or PAGP isn't supported, and the WLC must be rebooted for the LAG to be enabled.

8. B, C, D. Autonomous access points (AAPs) are less desirable than lightweight because they are managed independently, which means that security policies must be manually adjusted. Since there is no central controller, AAPs can't see the bigger picture when making decisions, and CAPWAP isn't supported on AAPs since there's no controller to tunnel to.

9. B. TACACS+ is better suited for device administration, so it's used to control management user access to the WLC.

10. E. TACACS+ uses port TCP 49 for all operations.

11. C. RADIUS uses UDP 1812 for authentication.

12. A. RADIUS uses UDP 1645 for authentication on legacy servers.

13. B. The virtual interface is used to redirect client traffic to the WLC.

14. D. The recommended IP used to be 1.1.1.1 but is now 192.0.2.1.

15. B. Macs are based on Unix and use the `ifconfig` command to display IP address info.

16. B. Telnet is disabled by default on the WLC and is not recommended.

17. C. A dynamic interface is similar to a SVI on a switch because it's a virtual interface that terminates a VLAN.

18. B. The hex value is F102 because it's single controller, and 192.168.123.100 converts to A87B64.

19. A. APs use Local mode by default. This uses a CAPWAP to tunnel traffic to the controller.

20. A, C. The two AP modes listed that can serve wireless traffic are Local and FlexConnect.

Chapter 21: Virtualization, Automation, and Programmability

1. E. 404 is the status code when what you requested isn't found.

2. B. VMware Workstation is a Type-2 solution.

3. A, C, E. JSON files must use double quotes and Boolean values must be lower case. Trailing commas are not allowed.

4. E. Microsoft makes the Hyper-V.

5. C. REST stands for Representational State Transfer

6. A. The resource section of the URI points to the specific

7. B. A virtual network device from a vendor is a virtual appliance.

8. B. YAML doesn't support using the tab in the file. You must always use the spacebar, otherwise it will throw an error when you try to run it.

9. B. In YAML a mapping is a simple key-value pair such as Name: Todd

10. A. Snapshots let you restore virtual machines back to a state in time. Cloning can also be used to make a backup, but it isn't as practical as a snapshot is.

11. C. You use the GET operation to "get" information from Restful API, so it's most like a show command on a router.

12. A. You use the POST operation to "post" information to Restful API, is most like a configuration command on a router.

13. D. The token is used to authenticate you to the restful API service. Restful API does not support authorization.

Chapter 22: SDN Controllers

1. B. The north bound interface (NBI) allows users to interface with the SDN controller through a web interface or through scripts that call RESTful API.

2. C. The job of the underlay is to provide connectivity to the overlay so tunnels can be formed.

Chapter 22: SDN Controllers   807

3. **A, B, C.** A controller offers many benefits, including central management, system-wide network monitoring, and the ability to push out configuration to multiple devices.

4. **D.** The campus architecture uses an access, distribution, and core layer.

5. **A, C, D.** The management plane provides management access to the device; it contains protocols such as Telnet, SSH, and SNMP.

6. **A, B, D.** The control plane provides all protocols that live on the router, including protocols such as CDP, LLDP, and OSPF.

7. **E.** The data plane does not run protocols; rather it is concerned with forwarding traffic.

8. **B.** OpenDaylight uses OpenFlow to communicate with switches.

9. **D.** Cisco ACI uses OpFlex to communicate with switches.

10. **C, E.** You usually interact with the northbound interface of a SDN controller through Restful API, either directly or through a Python script.

11. **A, B, C.** EasyQoS is a DNA Center application that automatically configures QoS throughout your network based on best practices. It also makes it easy to adjust QoS policies by just letting you tell DNA Center what applications are important to your company.

12. **D.** DNA Center stores the network snapshot for one week, though it is possible this number will increase as DNA Center continues to improve over time.

13. **D.** LAN Automation uses the Plug and Play feature to configure new switches. It can't use any other protocol because the switch won't have any SNMP or login information out of the box.

14. **A.** NMS solutions use SNMP to poll network devices for information and to detect problems.

15. **A, B, C.** NCM solutions use Telnet or SSH to log in into network devices to do configurations. The server can also use the SNMP Read-Write community to do configurations.

16. **B, D.** CLOS architecture is also known as spine/leaf architecture, so it makes sense that it uses spine and leaf switches.

17. **A, C, E.** Campus architecture consists of access, distribution, and core switches.

18. **B.** A fabric entirely consists of layer 3 only.

19. **B.** The Command Runner is a useful tool for pushing show commands to devices and viewing the results.

20. **C.** The Code Preview feature can generate a simple code snippet for several programming languages so you can quickly add it into your script.

Chapter 23: Configuration Management

1. **A, C.** Puppet and Chef require you to install an agent on the node before the configuration server can manage it.
2. **C.** Ansible deploys playbooks to nodes.
3. **B.** Ansible is the best solution for managing Cisco solutions because it has the widest support since it doesn't require an agent.
4. **D.** While Ansible is based on python, the playbooks are written in YAML.
5. **A.** Puppet uses manifest files to apply configuration to nodes.
6. **B.** Chef is better suited for developers because while its more complex, it's more programmer-friendly than the other solutions.
7. **B.** Because Ansible pushes configuration to nodes, it needs an inventory file to keep track of the nodes since it doesn't use agents like Puppet and Chef.
8. **C.** Puppet is based on the ruby language.
9. **B, C.** Ansible uses SSH to connect to Linux and network systems and Powershell to manage Windows systems.
10. **D.** Knife is the name of the CLI utility used to manage Chef.
11. **A, B, C.** The Chef deployment uses a Chef Server, a Workstation for managing the recipes and a bookshelf for storing the recipes for use on the nodes.
12. **B.** Puppet is the solution most sysadmins prefer because it uses agents to ensure configuration doesn't drift from the desired state. Plus, it isn't as complicated as Chef.
13. **B.** YAML uses white space to properly read the configuration contents, tabs aren't allowed because it confuses the spacing.
14. **C.** Ansible uses the **ansible-playbook** command to run a playbook against a group of nodes.
15. **C.** Ansible uses the **ansible-doc** command to lookup a module and how to use it.

Index

Note to the Reader: Throughout this index **boldfaced** page numbers indicate primary discussions of a topic. *Italicized* page numbers indicate illustrations.

A

AAA. *See* Authentication, Authorization, and Accounting (AAA)
aaa authentication login command, **385–386**
aaa authentication login default local command, **700**, **754**
aaa authorization exec default local command, **754**
aaa group server radius command, **385**
aaa group server tacacs+ command, **386**
aaa new-model command
    Ansible, **754**
    NCM, **700**
    RADIUS, **384**
    TACACS+, **386**
AAPs (Autonomous Access Points), **554**, **597–598**
ABRs (Area Border Routers), **166**, *166*
absorption in RF, **573–574**, *574*
abstraction, hardware, **667**
access attacks, **365–366**
access-class command, 302
access control, physical, **376–377**, *376*
access control lists (ACLs). *See* access lists
access layer in three-layer hierarchical model, **12–13**
access links in VLANs, 225
access-list command, **295–296**, 303
access-list deny command, **296–301**, 304
access-list deny host command, 296
access-list deny tcp command, 304
access-list deny tcp any command, 304
access-list deny tcp any host command, 305–306
access-list permit command, 302
access-list permit any command, 299
access-list permit ip command, 307
access-list permit ip any command, 306
access-list remark command, 313
access lists, **290**
    exam essentials, **316**
    extended
        configuring, **519–521**, *520*
        examples, **307–310**, *307*, *309*
    overview, **303–307**
    verifying, **521–522**
    introduction, **291–294**
    masquerade attacks, 371
    monitoring, **313–315**
    named, **310–312**
    remarks, **312–313**
    review questions, **317–318**
    security issues mitigated by, **294–295**
    standard, **295–301**, *299–301*
    summary, **316**
    Telnet, **302–303**
    wildcards with, **296–298**
access points (APs)
    autonomous, **597–598**
    endpoints, **497**
    wireless channels, **568–569**, *568*
    WLCs
        configuring, **625–628**, *626–628*
        joining, **607–610**, *608*
        modes, **629–632**, *630–633*
        types, **610–611**, *610*
access ports in VLANs, **225–226**, *225*
Access switch in DTP, 540
accidental attacks, 369
ACI tool, 708
Acknowledgment number field in TCP segment, 44
ACLs. *See* access lists
Active Directory server role, 498
active gain in RF, 573
active mode in NBAR, 456
active routers in HSRP, **416–418**, *417–418*, 421
Active state in HSRP, 426
active timers in HSRP, 420
ActiveX controls, 374
AD (administrative distances)
    dynamic routing, **150–151**
    static routing, 143
ad hoc networks, **556–557**, *557*
Address Resolution Protocol (ARP)
    IP routing process, **122–126**, 130
    operation, **58–60**, *59*

addresses
   IP. *See* IP addresses
   MAC. *See* MAC (Media Access Control) addresses
addressing technique in QoS, 456
adjacencies in OSPF, **167**
Adjacency Table in forwarding traffic flow, 705, *705*
administrative distances (ADs)
   dynamic routing, **150–151**
   static routing, 143
Advanced Research Projects Agency (ARPA), 31
advertising default routes, **157–158**
AES-CCMP encryption, 583
agents in SNMP, 37, 349
Aggregation in collapsed core, 13
AHs (Authentication Headers) in IPsec, **439–440**, *439*
alerts in network health, 692–693, *693*
Allow AAA Override setting, 652
alternative ports in STP, 255
amplitude in RF, 571, *572*
anonymous FTP, 35
anonymous user accounts, **387–388**
Ansible, **750–751**
   ad-hoc example, **756**
   installation, **751–752**, *752*
   inventory, **753**
   lab setup, **753–755**, *754*
   modules, **755–756**
   playbook example, **756–763**
   settings, **752**
ansible-playbook cisco.yml command, 761
Ansible Tower, 763
antennas
   free space path loss, 573
   RF, 569
   wireless, **556**
anti-replay service in ESP, 440
any command, 299
anycasts in IPv6, 468–469, **472**
APIC-EM, 708
APIPA (Automatic Private IP Addressing), **42**
APIs (Application Programming Interfaces), **679–683**, *681–683*
appliances in virtualization, 665
Application-layer attacks, 373
application signatures in QoS, 456

application-specific integrated circuits (ASICs), 5
APs. *See* access points (APs)
Area Border Routers (ABRs), 166, *166*
areas in OSPF, 168, **172–175**, *174*
arp command, 108
ARPA (Advanced Research Projects Agency), 31
ARPAnet, 31
ASAv tool, 665
ASBRs (Autonomous System Boundary Routers), 166
ASICs (application-specific integrated circuits), 5
ASs (autonomous systems) in IGRP, 150
assurance in DNA Center, 729–730, *730–731*
asymmetric encryption in IPsec transforms, 440–441
audit trails, 370
audits in security, **392–393**
authentication
   ESP, 440
   external, **383–386**, *383*
   Kerberos, **399–400**, *400*
   local, 395
   methods, **381–382**, *382*
   multifactor, 397
   PKI, **398–399**, *398–399*
   security server, **382–383**
   Windows, 382
   wireless networks, **581–582**, *581–582*
Authentication, Authorization, and Accounting (AAA)
   components, 380
   process, 383, *383*
   RADIUS, 639
   WLAN servers, **650–651**, *650*
Authentication Headers (AHs) in IPsec, **439–440**, *439*
authentication server role in identity based networking, 380
authenticator role in identity based networking, 380
Authenticode technology, 374
Auto switch in DTP, 540
autoconfiguration in IPv6
   stateful, **476–477**, *476*
   stateless, **474–476**, *474*
automatic account lockouts, **393–394**
Automatic Private IP Addressing (APIPA), **42**

automation
 components, **670**
 exam essentials, **684**
 JSON, **676–679**
 Python, **670–676**
 REST API, **679–683**, *681–683*
 review questions, **685–687**
 summary, **684**
 YAML, **679**
Autonomous Access Points (AAPs), 554, **597–598**
Autonomous System Boundary Routers (ASBRs), 166
autonomous systems (ASs) in IGRP, 150
auxiliary passwords, **405**
AWX, 763

B

backup designated routers (BDRs) in OSPF, 167
backup ports in STP, 255
badge readers, **376–377**
bandwidth
 multimedia applications, 223
 OSPF, 170
 RF, 571
 WANs, **17**
baselines in SNMP, 37
basic service areas (BSAs), **557–558**, *558*
basic service set identifiers (BSSIDs), 559
basic service sets (BSSs), **557–558**, *558*
BDRs (backup designated routers) in OSPF, 167
Berkeley Software Distribution (BSD), 31
BGP (Border Gateway Protocol), 150
binary numbering system for IP addresses, 61
biometrics, **397–398**
BIOS passwords, **391**
BIP-GMAC-256 (Broadcast/Multicast Integrity Protocol Galois Message Authentication Code), 587
bit flipping in PSK, 584
bits in IP addresses, 60
blade servers, 497
block acknowledgments for wireless channels, 569
block sizes with wildcards, **297–298**
blocked ports in STP, 255

bookshelves in Chef, 772
Bootstrap Protocol (BootP), **40–42**, *41*
Border Gateway Protocol (BGP), 150
BPDU (Bridge Protocol Data Unit) in STP, 254, 256
BPDU Guard, **276–277**
bridge IDs in STP, 254, **267–273**, *268*
bridge mode for WLC access points, 632, *632*
bridge port roles in STP, **254–255**
Bridge Protocol Data Unit (BPDU) in STP, 254, 256
bridges
 STP, **253–254**
 transparent, 6
 wireless networks, **562–564**, *563–564*
broadcast addresses
 description, 60, 67
 Layer 2, **68**, *68*
 Layer 3, **68–69**, *69*
broadcast domains
 description, **4–5**
 flat networks, 221, *221*
Broadcast/Multicast Integrity Protocol Galois Message Authentication Code (BIP-GMAC-256), 587
broadcast SSIDs, 648
broadcast storms, loop avoidance for, 202, *203*
broadcasts
 flat networks, 221
 IPv6, 468
 multimedia applications, 223
 OSPF networks, 168
 VLANs, **223**
bronze queues, 651
brute-force attacks, 372
BSAs (basic service areas), **557–558**, *558*
BSD (Berkeley Software Distribution), 31
BSSIDs (basic service set identifiers), 559
BSSs (basic service sets), **557–558**, *558*
Buffer full/source quench message, 56
buffering
 congestion management, **458**, *458*
 IP routing process, 124
bytes in IP addresses, 60

C

cabling
    Catalyst switches, 206
    Ethernet, **19–24**, *19–24*
    overview, **17–19**
CAM (content addressable memory) table, 213
campus architecture in SDN, **711**, *711*
CAPWAP (Control And Provisioning of Wireless Access Point), 598–599
capwap ap controller ip address command, 607
CAs (certificate authorities), 396, 398
Catalyst switch configuration
    overview, **204–206**, *205*
    port security, **210–212**
    S1, 206–207
    S2, 207–208
    S3, 208–210
    verifying, **212–214**
CBAC (Context-Based Access Control), 369
CBWFQ (Class Based Weighted Fair Queuing), 459–460
CCMP (Counter Mode with Cipher Block Chaining Message Authentication Code Protocol), 583
CDP. *See* Cisco Discovery Protocol (CDP)
cdp enable command, 339
cdp holdtime command, 339
cdp run command, 339
cdp timer command, 339
CEF (Cisco Express Forwarding)
    forwarding traffic flow, 705
    router internal process, **127**
central office (CO), 17
central syslog, **694–695**, *694*
certificate authorities (CAs), 396, 398
certificates, **396–397**
Challenge Handshake Authentication Protocol (CHAP), 370
Chanalyzer tool, 631, *631*
channel-group 1 mode command, 280–281
Channel Service Unit/Data Service Unit (CSU/DSU) devices, 16
channels in wireless networks, 565
    2.4GHz band, **565–566**, *566*
    2.4GHz/5GHz, 569
    5GHz band, **566–567**, *567*
    multiple APs, **568–569**, *568*
    overlap techniques, 567

CHAP (Challenge Handshake Authentication Protocol), 370
character-mode access, 401
Chargen attacks, 369
Checksum field
    TCP segment, 44
    UDP segment, 46
chef generate cookbook command, 778
chef generate repo chef-repo command, 775
chef-server-ctl org-create command, 775
chef-server-ctl reconfigure command, 774
chef-server-ctl user-create command, 775
Chef tool, **772–774**, *773*
    lab setup, **777–781**, *777*
    server installation, 774–775
    verifying results, **781**, *781*
    workstation installation, 775–776
child bridges in wireless networks, 562
CIDR (Classless Inter-Domain Routing), **80–81**
Cisco Discovery Protocol (CDP), **338**
    neighbor information, 340–343
    timers and holdtime, **338–339**, *339*
    topology documentation, **344–346**, *344*, *346*
    WLC, **634–636**, *634–635*
Cisco Dynamic Multipoint Virtual Private Network (DMVPN), **443**
Cisco Express Forwarding (CEF)
    forwarding traffic flow, 705
    router internal process, **127**
Cisco Firepower NGFW, **8–9**, *8*
Cisco HyperFlex, 666
Cisco Secure Services Client (CSSC), 599
Cisco Unified Wireless Networks (CUWN), **596–601**, *597–598*, *601*
cladding in fiber-optic cabling, **22–23**, *22–23*
Class A addresses, **64–65**
Class B addresses
    description, 65
    subnetting, **93–101**
Class Based Weighted Fair Queuing (CBWFQ), 459–460
Class C addresses
    description, **65–66**
    subnetting, **82–93**, *85–86*, *88*
Class D and E addresses, 63
Class of Service (CoS) in QoS, 455
class selectors in QoS, 456
classes
    protocols, **152**
    Puppet, 771
    QoS, **455–456**

classful routing in RIP, 153–154
Classless Inter-Domain Routing (CIDR), **80–81**
classless routing in RIP, 153
clear ip nat translation command, 329
clients
    identity based networking, 380
    redundancy, **412–414**, *413–414*
    WLANs, **653–655**, *653–654*
clock rate command, 138
clock synchronization in NTP, **347–348**, *348*
clones in virtualization, **667**
CLOS architecture, 712, *712*
cloud deployment model, **600–601**, *601*
Cloud Service Router 1000v (CSR1000v), 665
CO (central office), 17
Code bits field in TCP segment, 44
collapsed core topologies, **13**, *13*
collision domains
    flat networks, 221
    switches for, **3–5**, *3*
colons (:)
    JSON, 677
    Python, 673
Command Runner in DNA Center, **728–729**, *729*
commas (,)
    JSON, 677
    Python, 672–673
comments for access lists, **312–313**
Common Spanning Tree (CST), **260–261**, *260*
compare configs feature, **700–701**, *701*
compatibility in VPNs, 436
complexity of passwords, **390**
confidentiality in ESP, 440
config cdp enable command, 634
config interface address dynamic-interface command, 621
config interface address management command, 615
config interface address service-port command, 617
config interface address virtual command, 619
config interface create command, 620
config interface group create int-group command, 622
config interface group interface add wlan-int-group command, 623
config lag enable command, 625
config network secureweb command, 639
config network ssh command, 637
config network telnet command, 636
config network webmode command, 638
config radius acct add command, 643
config radius auth add command, 641
config route add command, 613
config serial baudrate command, 612
config tacacs auth add command, **643–645**
config wlan broadcast-ssid command, 648
config wlan create command, 647
config wlan enable command, 648
config wlan interface command, 648
config wlan radius_server auth add command, **650–651**
config wlan security command, 650
configuration
    Catalyst switches
        overview, **204–206**, *205*
        port security, **210–212**
        S1, **206–207**
        S2, **207–208**
        S3, **208–210**
        verifying, **212–214**
    CDP, **634–636**, *634–635*
    extended access lists, **519–521**, *520*
    GRE tunnels, **443–445**
    HSRP, **423–425**, *423*
    HTTP, **637–638**, *638*
    HTTPS, **638–639**, *638*
    IP routing, **132–133**, *132*
        Corp router, **133–135**
        LA router, **139–141**
        SF router, **135–138**
    IPv6 protocol, **484**, *484*
        autoconfiguration, **474–477**, *474*, *476*
        Corp, **485**, **487–488**
        DHCPv6 servers, **476–477**
        ICMPv6 servers, **479–483**, *479*, *481–482*
        LA, **486–488**
        SF, **486**
    NAT
        dynamic, **325–326**
        overloading, **326–327**
        static, **325**
        verifying, 327
    OSPF, **175**, *175*
        areas, **172–175**, *174*
        Corp router, **175–176**
        enabling, **171**
        LA router, **177–179**, *177*

loopback interfaces, 180–182
SF router, 176–177
verifying, 182–188
port channels, 280–282
Python commands, 673–676
RADIUS, 384–385, 639–643, *640–642*
RIP
Corp router, 153–154
LA router, 155–156
SF router, 154–155
SNMP, 351–352, 691–692
SSH, 637, *637*
syslog, 354–356, *355*
TACACS+, 385–386, 643–646, *643–646*
telnet, 636, *636*
tools. *See* Configuration Management
trunk ports, 236–240
VLANs
inter-VLAN routing, 240–246, *241–242, 244, 246*
overview, 231–234
switch port assignments, 234–236
WLCs
access points, 625–628, *626–628*
switches, 602–604, *602*
Configuration Management, 744
Ansible. *See* Ansible
Chef, 772–781, *777, 781*
DevOps, 748, *748*
exam essentials, 782
IaC, 748–750
Puppet, 764–772, *766*
review questions, 783–785
summary, 781
team silos, 744–747, *745–747*
configured VLANs, 225
conflicts in DHCP, 42
congestion
avoidance tools, 460–461, *461*
management tools, 457–460, *458–460*
connectionless protocols, 45
connections
user account limits, 388
WLAN clients, 653–655, *653–654*
connectivity for IP network. *See* IP network connectivity
console passwords, 402–403
console ports
Catalyst switches, 205
WLCs, 611–612, *612*
content addressable memory (CAM) table, 213
Context-Based Access Control (CBAC), 369
contract employees, 387
Control And Provisioning of Wireless Access Point (CAPWAP), 598–599
control plane
description, 703
separating, 709–710, *709–710*
controller-based architectures, 710–712, *711–712*
convergence
OSPF, 164
RSTP, 263
STP, 256
cookbooks in Chef, 772, 778
core in fiber-optic cabling, 22–23, *22–23*
core layer in three-layer hierarchical model, 11–12
Corp router configuration
DHCP, 140–141
IP routing, 133–135
IPv6, 485, 487–488
OSPF, 175–176
RIP, 153–154
routing tables, 129
static routing, 144–146
CoS (Class of Service) in QoS, 455
costs
OSPF, 170–171
STP, 254, 256–257
VPNs, 435
Counter Mode with Cipher Block Chaining Message Authentication Code Protocol (CCMP), 583
CPE (customer premises equipment), 16
CQ (Custom Queueing), 459
CRC (cyclic redundancy check)
IP header, 53
IP routing process, 123–126
ISLs, 228
crossover cable, 20–21, *20–21*
CRUD verbs in REST API, 681
crypto key generate rsa command, 357
crypto key generate rsa general-keys command, 724
crypto key generate rsa modulus command, 754

CSR1000v (Cloud Service Router 1000v), 665
CSSC (Cisco Secure Services Client), 599
CST (Common Spanning Tree), **260–261**, *260*
CSU/DSU (Channel Service Unit/Data Service Unit) devices, 16
curl command, 109
curly braces ({}) in JSON, 677
Custom Queueing (CQ), 459
customer premises equipment (CPE), 16
CUWN (Cisco Unified Wireless Networks), **596–601**, *597–598*, *601*
cyclic redundancy check (CRC)
  IP header, 53
  IP routing process, 123–126
  ISLs, 228

D

DAD (duplicate address detection), 482, *482*, 524
DAI (Dynamic ARP Inspection), 379
DAP (Directory Access Protocol), 396
DARPA, 31
Data field
  IP header, 53
  TCP segment, 44
  UDP segment, 46
data integrity in ESP, 440
data plane, **703–704**
data traffic in QoS, 453–454, *453*
database server role, 498
DC manifest file in Puppet, **768–769**
debug ip nat command, 327, 329
debug standby command, 427
default-information originate command, 158
default-router command, 609
defaults
  administrative distances, 151
  gateways, 124–125, 510–512
  RIP routes, **157–158**
  routing, **147–148**
DELAY state in neighbor discovery, 528
delays in QoS, 452
DELETE verb in REST API, 681
demarcation points, 16
denial of service (DoS) attacks, 366, **368–370**
deny tcp host command, 520

description command
  joining APs, 609–610
  WLC switches, 603–604
Description field in syslog messages, 353
designated ports in STP, 254
designated routers (DRs) in OSPF, 167
Desirable switch in DTP, 540
desktops
  access layer, 12
  endpoints, **496**
Destination Address field in IPv6 headers, 478
destination addresses in IP routing process, 121–131
destination hosts, 124–125
Destination IP address field in IP header, 53
destination network parameter, 142
Destination port field
  TCP segment, 44
  UDP segment, 46
destination ports in TCP, **49–50**
Destination unreachable message in ICMP, 55
Device Provisioning Protocol (DPP), 587
DevOps, **748**, *748*
DHCP. *See* Dynamic Host Configuration Protocol (DHCP)
DHCP Addr. Assignment setting in WLANs, 652
DHCP/HTTP Profiling setting in WLANs, 652
DHCPv6 server configuration, **476–477**
diagnostic addresses, 107
Differentiated Services Code Point (DSCP), 455–456
diffraction in RF, **576–577**, *577*
digital certificates, **396–397**
Digital Network Architecture (DNA) Center
  assurance, **729–730**, *730–731*
  Command Runner, **728–729**, *729*
  discovery, **719–721**, *720*
  EasyQoS, **732–734**, *733–734*
  exam essentials, **737**
  LAN Automation, **734–735**, *735*
  network hierarchy, **721–723**, *721–722*
  overview, **718–719**, *719*
  Path Trace, **731–732**, *732*
  REST API, **736**, *736*
  review questions, **738–741**
  SDN, 708
  Software Defined Access, **735**
  summary, **736–737**

templates, **723–724**, *724*
topology, **724–725**, *725*
upgrades, **725–728**, *726–727*
Digital Signal 0 (DS0) connections, 17
Dijkstra algorithm, 164
directional antennas, 556, 573
Directory Access Protocol (DAP), 396
Disabled state in STP ports, 255
disabling
   telnet, 636
   user accounts, 387
discovery
   CDP. *See* Cisco Discovery Protocol (CDP)
   DNA Center, **719–721**, *720*
   neighbors, **480–483**, *481–482*, **523–531**, *524–525*
distance-vector protocols, **152**
distinguished names (DNs) in X.500 standard, 396
distributed vSwitches, 666
distribution layer in three-layer hierarchical model, **12**
distribution systems (DSs)
   access points, 554
   infrastructure basic service sets, 559
   WLC ports, **613–614**, *613*
DIX group, 17
DMVPNs (Dynamic Multipoint Virtual Private Networks), **443**, 717
DNA Center. *See* Digital Network Architecture (DNA) Center
DNA scanners, 397
dnf install https command, 764
dnf localinstall command, 774
DNs (distinguished names) in X.500 standard, 396
DNS (Domain Name Service)
   joining APs, **607–608**, *608*
   overview, **39–40**, *39*
   server role, 498
dns-server command, 609
documentation for topologies, **344–346**, *344*
DoD model, **31–33**, *32–33*
domain-name command, 609
Domain Name Service (DNS)
   joining APs, **607–608**, *608*
   overview, **39–40**, *39*
   server role, 498

domains
   broadcast, 4–5, 221, *221*
   collision, 3–5, *3*, 221
   QoS, 455
door locks, **377**
DORA process in DHCP, 41
DoS (denial of service) attacks, 366, **368–370**
dotted-decimal notation, 61
downfade in RF, 575
DPP (Device Provisioning Protocol), 5 87
Dragonblood exploit, 586
Dragonfly handshake, 586
dropped packets in QoS, 452
DRs (designated routers) in OSPF, 167
DSCP (Differentiated Services Code Point), **455–456**
DSs (distribution systems)
   access points, 554
   infrastructure basic service sets, 559
   WLC ports, **613–614**, *613*
DTP (Dynamic Trunk Protocol), 233, 238, **539–540**
duplex settings, 513
duplicate address detection (DAD), 482, *482*, 524
Dynamic ARP Inspection (DAI), 379
dynamic command, 237–238
Dynamic Host Configuration Protocol (DHCP)
   access points
      joining, **608–609**
      wireless, 554
   Corp router configuration, **140–141**
   overview, **40–42**, *41*
   server role, 498
   snooping, 378–379, *379*
   virtual machine servers, 663
dynamic interface in WLCs, 614, **619–621**, *620–621*
dynamic IP routing, **150–152**
Dynamic Multipoint Virtual Private Networks (DMVPNs), **443**, 717
dynamic NAT, 322, **325–326**
dynamic routing, 119
Dynamic Trunk Protocol (DTP), 233, 238, **539–540**

E

E1 connections, 17
EasyQoS in DNA Center, **732–734**, *733–734*
eavesdropping, **366–368**
ECDH (Elliptic Curve Diffie-Hellman) exchange, 587
ECDSA (Elliptic Curve Digital Signature Algorithm), 587
ECMP (Equal Cost Load Balancing), 714
EGP (exterior gateway protocol), 150
EIA/TIA (Electronic Industries Alliance/Telecommunications Industry Association), 18
EIGRP (Enhanced IGRP), 151
EIGRPv6 protocol, 483
Elliptic Curve Diffie-Hellman (ECDH) exchange, 587
Elliptic Curve Digital Signature Algorithm (ECDSA), 587
email
    e-mail bombs, 369
    server role, 498
enable command, 401
enable mode in DNA Center templates, 723
enable password command, 401
enable sec ncmEnable command, 700
enable secret password command, 401
Enable Session Timeout setting, 652
enabling
    OSPF, **171**
    passwords, **401–402**
Encapsulating Security Payload (ESP), **440**
encapsulation command, 240
encapsulation for VLANs, 240–242
encryption
    ESP, 440
    IPsec transforms, **440–441**, *441*
    passwords, **405–406**
    PKI, **399**, *399*
    wireless networks, **581–582**, *581–582*
    WPA3-Enterprise, 587
endpoints, **496–497**
Enhanced IGRP (EIGRP), 151
enterprise-managed VPNs, **436–438**, *436*
entrances, 377
Equal Cost Load Balancing (ECMP), 714
erase start command, 135
erase startup-config command, 133

errors in QoS, 452
ESP (Encapsulating Security Payload), **440**
ESSs (extended service sets), **560–561**, *561*
ESXi, **669**
EtherChannel, **278–279**, *279*, **283**
Ethernet cabling, **19**, *19*
    crossover cable, **20–21**, *20–21*
    fiber-optic, **22–23**, *22–23*
    Power over Ethernet, **23–24**, *24*
    straight-through cable, **20**, *20–21*
    UTP gigabit wiring, **21–22**, *22*
EUI-64 addresses, **474–476**, *474*, *476*
exec-timeout command, 403
exit interface parameter, 143
expiration of passwords, **390**, **394–395**
extended access lists
    configuring, **519–521**, *520*
    description, 292
    examples, **307–310**, *307*, *309*
    overview, **303–307**
    verifying, **521–522**
extended service sets (ESSs), **560–561**, *561*
exterior gateway protocol (EGP), 150
external authentication, **383–386**, *383*
external EIGRP, 151
external threats, 365
extranet VPNs, 436

F

fabric in SDN, 718
Facility field in syslog messages, 353
facts
    Ansible, 763
    Puppet, 771
fast switching in router internal process, **127**
FastEthernet interface, 230
FCS (Frame Check Sequence)
    IP routing process, 123–125
    PSK, 584
    UDP segment, 46
FHRP (First Hop Redundancy Protocol), **414–416**, *415*
FIB (Forwarding Information Base) table, 705
fiber-optic cabling, **22–23**, *22–23*
FIFO (First In First Out) queues in congestion management, 459

File Transfer Protocol (FTP), **35–36**, *35*
files
    server role, 498
    transferring, **35–36**, *35–36*
filters
    frame, 197
    switches, 195–196, *196*
Firepower Threat Defense (FTD) devices, 10, 294, 364
Firepower Threat Defense Virtual, 665
firewalls, **6–10**, *7*, **290–291**, *291*
First Hop Redundancy Protocol (FHRP), **414–416**, *415*
First In First Out (FIFO) queues in congestion management, 459
5GHz band, **566–567**, *567*
Flags field
    IP header, 53
    TCP segment, 44
flat networks, structure of, 221, *221*
Flex+Bridge mode in WLC access points, **632**, *633*
FlexConnect mode in WLC access points, **629**
flexibility in VLANs, **224**
floating static routes, 144
Flow Label field in IPv6 headers, 478
for loops in Python, 673–674
40Mhz channels, 569
forward/filter decisions, **197–199**
forward/filter tables, 195–197, *197*
Forwarding Information Base (FIB) table, 705
forwarding ports in STP, 254–255
forwarding traffic flow, **704–706**, *704–706*
FQDNs (fully qualified domain names), 40
fraggle attacks, 372
Fragment offset field in IP header, 53
Frame Check Sequence (FCS)
    IP routing process, 123–125
    PSK, 584
    UDP segment, 46
frame filtering, **197–199**, *197–198*
frame protection in WPA3-Enterprise, 587
frame tagging in VLANs, **227–228**
free space path loss in RF, **572–573**, *573*
frequencies, RF. *See* radio frequency (RF)
Fresnel zones, **579**
FTD (Firepower Threat Defense) devices, 10, 294, 364
FTP (File Transfer Protocol), **35–36**, *35*
fully qualified domain names (FQDNs), 40

G

gain in RF, 571, 573
Galois/Counter Mode Protocol (GCMP-256), 587
Gateway Load Balancing Protocol (GLBP), 416
gateways
    IP network connectivity, 510–512
    IP routing, 124–125
    of last resort, 147
GCMP-256 (Galois/Counter Mode Protocol), 587
Generic Routing Encapsulation (GRE), 438
GET messages in SNMP, 349–350
Get-NetIPAddress cmdlet, 503
GET verb in REST API, 681
GETBULK feature in SNMP, 37
getpass command in Python, 671–674
GLBP (Gateway Load Balancing Protocol), 416
global NAT names, 322–323, *323–324*
global unicast addresses, **471**, *471*, 473
gold queues, 651
gratuitous ARP in DHCP, 42
GRE (Generic Routing Encapsulation), 438
GRE tunnels
    configuration, **443–445**
    GRE over IPsec, **442–443**
    overview, **441–442**, *442*
    verifying, **445–447**
group roles in HSRP, **421–422**, *422*
guards, 377
guests in virtualization, 665
guestshell command, **769**

H

hand scanners, 397
hardware abstraction, **667**
hardware addresses in IP routing process, 122–126
hardware health, **697**, *697*
Hardware Virtualized Machines (HVMs), **668**
Hashed Message Authentication Mode (HMAC), 587
Header checksum field in IP header, 53
Header length field
    IP header, 53
    TCP segment, 44

headers in IPv6 protocol, **477–479**, *477*
health
    hardware, **697**, *697*
    networks, **692–693**, *693*
Hello protocol in OSPF, 167–169, *169*
hello timers in HSRP, **419**
hexadecimal numbering system for IP addresses, 61
hierarchical addressing, **61–64**
histories, password, **394–395**
HMAC (Hashed Message Authentication Mode), 587
hold timers in HSRP, **419**
holdtime in CDP, 338–339, *339*
Hop Limit field in IPv6 headers, 478
hops in distance-vector protocols, 151
Hops/time exceeded message in ICMP, 56
host IP addresses, 61
Host-to-Host layer, **42**
    description, 32
    key concepts, **46–47**, *47*
    port numbers, **48–51**
    TCP, **43–45**, *43*
    UDP, **45–46**, *46*
hostname command, 357
hostnames
    resolving, **39**, *39*
    WLCs, 605
Hot Standby Router Protocol (HSRP), **416–418**
    configuration, **423–425**, *423*
    group roles, **421–422**, *422*
    interface tracking, **422**, *422*
    load balancing, **427**, *428*
    preemption, **425**
    states, **426**
    timers, **419–421**, *420*
    troubleshooting, **428–429**
    verifying, **425–427**
    virtual MAC addresses, **418–419**
HTML (Hypertext Markup Language) attacks, 374
HTTP (Hypertext Transfer Protocol)
    overview, 37–38, *38*
    WLCs, 637–638, *638*
HTTPS (Hypertext Transfer Protocol Secure)
    overview, 38
    WLCs, 638–639, *638*
hubs, 2–3, *3*
HVMs (Hardware Virtualized Machines), **668**

Hyper-V, **669**
Hypertext Markup Language (HTML) attacks, **374**
Hypertext Transfer Protocol (HTTP)
    overview, **37–38**, *38*
    WLCs, **637–638**, *638*
Hypertext Transfer Protocol Secure (HTTPS)
    overview, **38**
    WLCs, **638–639**, *638*
hypervisors
    server role, 498
    virtualization, 665, **668–669**

I

IaC (Infrastructure as Code), **748–750**
ICMP (Internet Control Message Protocol), 122–126, 129
    attacks, 369
    in IP routing process, 122–126, 129
    smurf attacks, 372
ICMPv6 protocol
    IP network connectivity, **523–531**, *524–525*
    server configuration, **479–483**, *479*, *481–482*
Identification field in IP header, 53
identifying VLANs, **224–229**, *225–226*, *228*
identity based networking, 379–380, *380*
IDs for WLANs, 647
IEEE Ethernet standards, **17–19**
    IEEE 802.1, **228–229**, *228*
    IEEE 802.1d, 259
    IEEE 802.1s, 260, **267**
    IEEE 802.1w, 260
    IEEE 802.11i, **585**
ifconfig command, *506*, *506*
IGP (interior gateway protocol), 150
implicit denies, 292, 306
import command in Python, 672
inbound access lists, **293**
INCMP (incomplete) state in neighbor discovery, 528
independent basic service sets (IBSSs), **556–557**, *557*
Individualized Data Protection (IDP), 587
INFORM operation in SNMP, 350
Infrastructure as Code (IaC), **748–750**

infrastructure basic service sets, **558–559**
Initial state in HSRP, **426**
Initialization vectors (IVs) in PSK, **584**
input errors in IP network connectivity, **514**
input queue drops, **513**
inside global (IG) addresses in NAT, **330**
inside NAT network names, **322–323**, *323–324*
Inter-Switch Link (ISL) routing, **228**
inter-VLAN routing (IVR)
    configuring, **240–246**, *241–242*, *244*, *246*
    description, **231**, *231*
    exam essentials, **247**
    overview, **229–231**, *230–231*
    review questions, **248–250**
    summary, **247**
interactive commands for DNA Center templates, **723**
interface configuration in SDN underlay, **714**
Interface Groups
    WLANs, **648**
    WLCs, **622–623**, *622–623*
interface information for networks, **695–697**, *696*
interface loopback command, **180**, **715**
interface port-channel command, **279**, **281**
interface range command, **234–236**
interface tracking in HSRP, **422**, *422*
interface tunnel number command, **444**
interface vlan command, **603**
interior gateway protocol (IGP), **150**
internal routers, **290–291**, *291*
internal threats, **365**
Internet Control Message Protocol (ICMP), **122–126**, **129**
Internet layer, **51–52**
    ARP, **58–60**, *59*
    description, **32**
    ICMP, **55–58**, *56*, *58*
    IP, **52–55**, *53–54*
Internet of Things (IoT), **497**
Internet Protocol (IP), **52–55**, *53–54*
Intrusion Prevention Systems (IPSs), **6–10**, *8*
inventory in Ansible, **763**
IoT (Internet of Things), **497**
IP (Internet Protocol), **52–55**, *53–54*
ip access-group command, **521**
ip access-group in command, **307**

ip access-group out command, **299–300**, **307**, **312**
ip access-list command, **311**
ip access-list extended command, **315**, **520–521**
ip access-list standard command, **311**
ip add command
    joining APs, **609**
    SDN, **715**
    WLC switches, **603**
ip address command, **715**
IP addresses, **60**
    access lists. *See* access lists; extended access lists
    APIPA, **42**
    DHCP, **40–42**, *41*
    FHRP, **415**, *415*
    hierarchical scheme, **61–64**
        Class A, **64–65**
        Class B, **65**
        Class C, **65–66**
        network addresses, **61–64**, *62*
        special purpose, **63–64**
    IP routing process, **121–131**
    IPv4, **67–70**, *68–69*
    IPv6. *See* IPv6 protocol
    Layer-3 EtherChannel, **283**
    NAT. *See* Network Address Translation (NAT)
    private, **66–67**
    spoofing, **371**
    subnets. *See* subnets and subnetting
    switches, **206**
    terminology, **60**
    troubleshooting, *110–113*
        exam essentials, **114**
        Linux, **506–507**, *506–507*
        Mac OS, **504–506**, *504–506*
        OS parameters, **108–109**
        overview, **106–108**, *106*
        problem determination, **109–113**, *110–113*
        review questions, **115–116**
        summary, **114**
        Windows 10, **498–504**, *499–503*
    WLCs, **605–606**
ip default-gateway command, **210**
ip dhcp excluded-address command, **609**
ip dhcp pool command, **609**

ip domain-name command, 40, *357, 754*
IP headers, **52–54**, *53–54*
ip nat inside source command, **325–326**, 330–333
ip nat outside command, *326, 332*
ip nat pool command, **325–326**, 330–332
ip nat translation max-entries command, 329
ip nat translation timeout command, *330*
IP network connectivity
    exam essentials, **545**
    extended access lists, **519–522**, *520*
    IPv6 networks, **522–531**, *523–525*
    overview, **507–518**, *508*
    review questions, **546–548**
    SPAN, **518–519**, *518*
    summary, **544–545**
    VLANs, **531–544**, *532*
ip ospf cost command, *171*
ip ospf mtu-ignore command, *714*
ip ospf network point-to-point command, *715*
IP phone endpoints, **497**
ip route command, *142–143, 515*
IP routing
    administrative distances, **150–151**
    basics, **118–121**, *120*
    classes, **152**
    configuration, **132–133**, *132*
        Corp router, **133–135**
        LA router, **139–141**
        RIP, **153–154**
        SF router, **135–138**
    default routing, **147–148**
    DHCP, **140–141**
    distance-vector, **152**
    dynamic, **150–152**
    exam essentials, **159–160**
    examples, **127–132**, *128, 130–131*
    process, **121–127**, *121, 123*
    review questions, **161–162**
    router internal process, **126–127**
    SDN, *714*
    static, **142–143**
        Corp router, **144–146**, *144*
        LA router, **146–147**
        SF router, **145–146**
        verifying, **148–150**
    summary, **159**
ip routing command, *714*

IP services
    CDP, **338–346**, *339, 344, 346.*
    exam essentials, **358–359**
    LLDP, **346–347**
    NTP, **347–348**, *348*
    review questions, **360–362**
    SNMP, **348–352**, *349–350*
    SSH, **357–358**
    summary, **358**
    syslog, **352–356**, *355*
ip ssh version command, *357*
ip subnet-zero command, **81–82**
ipconfig command
    description, **109**
    IP network connectivity, *509, 512*
    neighbor discovery, *528*
    Windows 10, **502–504**, *502–503*
IPsec
    GRE over IPsec, **442–443**
    introduction, **438–439**
    transforms, **439–441**, *439, 441*
IPSs (Intrusion Prevention Systems), **6–10**, *8*
IPv4 addresses, **67–68**
    broadcasts, **68–69**, *69*
    multicast, **70**, *70*
    subnets. *See* subnets and subnetting
    unicast, **69**, *69*
ipv6 address command, **473–474**
ipv6 enable command, **474**
IPv6 protocol, **466**
    addresses
        manual assignment, **472–473**
        special, **472–473**
        structure, **469**, *469*
        types, **470–472**, *471*
    benefits and uses, **467–469**
    configuration, **484**, *484*
        autoconfiguration, **474–477**, *474, 476*
        Corp router, **485**, *487–488*
        DHCPv6 servers, **476–477**
        ICMPv6 servers, **479–483**, *479, 481–482*
        LA router, **486**, *486–488*
    exam essentials, **490–491**
    headers, **477–479**, *477*
    IP network connectivity, **522–531**, *523–525*
    need for, **467**
    review questions, **492–493**
    routing protocols, **483**

shortened expressions, **469–470**
static routing, **483–484**, *484*
summary, **490**
temporary addresses, *529*
ipv6 route command, **487–488**, *531*
ipv6 route static command, *488*
ipv6 unicast-routing command, *473*, **485–486**
IVR. *See* inter-VLAN routing (IVR)

J

Java blocking, *369*
JavaScript Object Notation (JSON), **676–679**
jitter in QoS, *452*
joining access points, **607–610**
JSON (JavaScript Object Notation), **676–679**

K

Kerberos protocol, **399–400**, *400*
key command, **385–386**
keys
    IPsec transforms, *441*
    PSK, *584*
knives in Chef, *772*, *776*
KVM hypervisor, **669**

L

L2F (Layer 2 Forwarding), *438*
L2TP (Layer 2 Tunneling Protocol), *438*
LA router configuration
    IP routing, **139–141**
    IPv6, **486–488**
    OSPF, **177–179**, *177*
    RIP, **155–156**
    static routing, **146–147**
LACP (Link Aggregation Control Protocol), *279*
LAG (Link Aggregation Group), **623–625**, *624*
LAN Automation, **734–735**, *735*
Land.c attacks, *369*
LANs (local area networks)
    overview, *2*, *3*
    VLANs. *See* VLANs (virtual LANs)

vs. WANs, **15–16**
wireless. *See* wireless networks
laptop endpoints, **496**
last-resort parameter for passwords, *401*
Layer 2 broadcasts, *67*, *68*
Layer 2 Forwarding (L2F), *438*
Layer 2 MPLS VPNs, *437*
Layer 2 security, **378–380**, *378–380*
Layer 2 switching
    address learning by, **195–197**, *196*
    Catalyst switches. *See* Catalyst switch configuration
    exam essentials, **215**
    forward/filter decisions, **197–199**, *197–198*
    loop avoidance, **202–204**, *203*
    port security, **199–202**, *199*
    review questions, **216–218**
    summary, **215**
    switching services, **194–195**
Layer 2 Tunneling Protocol (L2TP), *438*
Layer 3 broadcasts, **68–69**, *69*
Layer 3 EtherChannel, *283*
Layer 3 MPLS VPNs, *438*
layered approaches in topologies, *13*
LDAP (Lightweight Directory Access Protocol), **395–396**
leaf-and-spine topology, **14–15**, *14–15*
leaf switches in SDN, **712**
Learn state in HSRP, *426*
Learning state in STP ports, *255*
Length field in UDP segment, *46*
length of passwords, **391–392**
licensing in DNA Center, *720*
Lightweight Access Point Protocol (LWAPP), *564*
lightweight access points, *554*
Lightweight Directory Access Protocol (LDAP), **395–396**
lightweight WLAN deployment model, **598–599**, *598*
limits on connections, *388*
line command, **401–402**
line aux command, *405*
line console command, **402–403**
line of sight in RF, **578–579**, *579*
line vty command, *357*, *404*
Link Aggregation Control Protocol (LACP), *279*
Link Aggregation Group (LAG), **623–625**, *624*

link costs in STP, **256–257**
Link layer, 32
Link Layer Discovery Protocol (LLDP),
    346–347
link-local addresses, **471**, *471*, 474
Link State Advertisements (LSAs)
    forwarding traffic flow, 704
    OSPF, 167–168
Link State Database (LSDB), 704, *704*
link-state protocols, **152**
Link State Updates (LSUs) in OSPF, 169–170
links in OSPF, 167
Linux, IP address troubleshooting in, **506–507**, *506–507*
Listen state in HSRP, 426
Listening state in STP ports, 255
LLDP (Link Layer Discovery Protocol), **346–347**
LLDP-MED (Media Endpoint Discovery), 346
lldp receive command, 346–347
lldp run command, 346
lldp transmit command, 346–347
LLQ (Low Latency Queuing), 459, *460*
load balancing in HSRP, **427**, *428*
local area networks (LANs)
    overview, 2, *3*
    VLANs. *See* VLANs (virtual LANs)
    vs. WANs, **15–16**
    wireless. *See* wireless networks
local authentication, **395**
local loops, 17
local mode for WLC access points, **629**
local NAT names, 322–323, *323–324*
Lock and Key, 370
lockouts for user accounts, **393–394**
locks, door, 377
log command, 306
logging command, 354–355
logging buffered command, 354
logging console command, 354
logging host command, 356, 695
logging informational command, 355
logging trap command, 356
logging trap debugging command, 695
logging trap informational command, 356
logical addresses, 52
login command, 402
login local command, 357
logs for real-time alerts, 370

loopback addresses
    description, 67
    IP network connectivity, 510
    IP troubleshooting, 107
loopback interfaces in OSPF, **179–182**, *179*
loops
    avoiding, 195, **202–204**, *203*
    Python language, 673–674
Low Latency Queuing (LLQ), 459, *460*
LSA flooding, **169–170**
LSAs (Link State Advertisements)
    forwarding traffic flow, 704
    OSPF, 167–168
LSDB (Link State Database), 704, *704*
LSUs (Link State Updates) in OSPF, 169–170
LWAPP (Lightweight Access Point Protocol), 564

M

mac address-table command, 214
MAC forward/filter tables, **195–199**, *196*
MAC (Media Access Control) addresses
    Catalyst switches, **213–214**
    FHRP, 415
    HSRP, **418–419**
    IP routing process, 130–131, *130*
    IPv6 autoconfiguration, **474–475**
    learning by layer 2 switching, **195–197**, *196*
    neighbor discovery, 480, 524
    port security, 210–211
    Proxy ARP, 412–413
    RSTP, 264, 266
    SPAN, 518
    STP, 257, 259
    STP failure consequences, 273–274
    wireless channels, 569
MAC OS, IP address troubleshooting in, **504–506**, *504–506*
maintenance accounts, renaming, **388–389**
malware, **375**
man-in-the-middle attacks, **373**
Management Information Base (MIB) in SNMP, 350, *350*
management interface in WLCs, **614–615**, *616*
management plane, **702–703**, *703*
manifests in Puppet, **769–771**

mantraps, **376**, *376*
manual assignment of IPv6 addresses, 472–473
many-to-many NAT, 322
marking in QoS, **455–456**
mask parameter for static routing, 142
masks
    access lists, **296–298**
    OSPF, 172
    subnets, **78–79**
masquerade attacks, **371**
Maximum Transmission Units (MTUs)
    ICMPv6 servers, **479–480**
    SDN underlay, **714**
MBSSIDs (multiple basic service set identifiers), **559**, *560*
Media Access Control addresses. *See* MAC (Media Access Control) addresses
Media Endpoint Discovery, 346
Meraki networks, **600–601**, *601*
mesh networks, **564**, *565*
message integrity code (MIC)
    PSK, **584**
    WPA2 Enterprise, **585**
messages, syslog, **352–355**, *355*
MIB (Management Information Base) in SNMP, **350**, *350*
MIC (message integrity code)
    PSK, **584**
    WPA2 Enterprise, **585**
migrations in virtualization, **667–668**
Mills, David, 38
MILNET, 31
MIMO (Multiple-Input Multiple-Output), **569**
minimum length of passwords, **391–392**
MNEMONIC field in syslog messages, 353
mobile phone endpoints, **497**
Mobility Express controllers, **599**
Mobility/RF Group Name feature in WLCs, **606**
modules
    Ansible, **755–756**, 763
    Puppet, **771**
monitor mode for WLC access points, **629**
monitor session dest interface command, 519
monitor session source interface command, 519
MSTP (Multiple Spanning Tree Protocol), **267**

MTUs (Maximum Transmission Units)
    ICMPv6 servers, **479–480**
    SDN underlay, **714**
multi-access networks, 168
multicasts
    addresses, **70**, *70*
    IPv6, **468**, **472**
    multimedia applications, 223
    neighbor discovery, **482**
multifactor authentication, **397**
multimedia applications, 223
multimode fiber-optic cabling, **23**, *23*
multipath in RF, **575–576**, *575*
multiple APs in wireless channels, **568–569**, *568*
multiple basic service set identifiers (MBSSIDs), **559**, *560*
Multiple-Input Multiple-Output (MIMO), **569**
Multiple Spanning Tree Protocol (MSTP), **267**

N

NA (neighbor advertisement), 481, *482*, **524–525**, *525*
name command, **602–603**
named access lists, 292, **310–312**
names
    maintenance accounts, **388–389**
    NAT, **322–323**
NAT. *See* Network Address Translation (NAT)
native VLANs
    frame tagging, **227–229**
    modifying, **239–240**
NBI (Northbound Interface), **707**
NBMA (non-broadcast multi-access) network, 168
neighbor advertisement (NA), 481, *482*, **524–525**, *525*
Neighbor Discovery Protocol (NDP), **480–483**, *481–482*, **523–531**, *524–525*
neighbor solicitation (NS), 481, *482*, 524–525, *525*
neighbors
    CDP, **340–343**
    forwarding traffic flow, **704**, *704*
    IPv6 protocol, **480–483**, *481–482*, **523–531**, *524–525*
    OSPF, 167

neighborship database, 168
NETCONF protocol, 708
netmask command, 331
netmiko module, 671
netsh interface ipv6 show neighbor
    command, 529
Network Access layer, 32
Network Address Translation (NAT), 320
    access points, 554
    configuration
        dynamic, 325–326
        overloading, 326–327
        static, 325
        verifying, 327
    exam essentials, 333
    names, 322–323
    operation, 323–324, *323–324*
    private IP addresses, 66
    pros and cons, 321
    review questions, 334–335
    summary, 333
    testing and troubleshooting, 328–333,
        330–332
    types, 322
    uses, 320–321, *321*
network addresses in IP addresses, 60,
    61–64, *62*
Network Based Application recognition
    (NBAR), 456
network command
    OSPF, 172
    SDN, 715
Network Configuration Managers (NCMs),
    699–702, *700–701*
Network Control Protocol (NCP), 30–31
network fundamentals
    components, **2–6,** *3–4, 6*
    Ethernet cabling, **19–24,** *19–24*
    exam essentials, 24–25
    firewalls and IPS, **6–10,** *7–9*
    physical interfaces and cables, **17–19**
    review questions, 26–27
    summary, 24
    topologies, **10**
        collapsed core, **13,** *13*
        spine-leaf, **14–15,** *14–15*
        three-layer hierarchical model,
            10–13, *11*
        WANs, **15–17**
network interface cards (NICs), **555,** *555*

network management stations (NMSs) in
    SNMP, 349
Network Monitoring Systems (NMSs),
    690–691
    central syslog, **694–695,** *694*
    hardware health, **697,** *697*
    interface information, **695–697,** *696*
    network health, **692–693,** *692–693*
    network information, **697–699,** *698–699*
    SNMP
        configuration, **691–692**
        traps, **695,** *695*
Network Time Protocol (NTP), 38, *39*,
    347–348, *348*
networks
    attacks
        Application-layer, 373
        DoS, 368–370
        eavesdropping, 366–368
        HTML, 374
        man-in-the-middle, 373
        masquerade, 371
        passwords, 372–373
        primary, 365–366
        repudiation, 371–372
        rerouting, 371
        session hijacking, 371
        smurfing, 372
        Trojan horse, 373–374
        unauthorized access, 370
        viruses, 373–374
        WareZ, 370
        worms, 373–374
    DNA Center hierarchy, **721–723,**
        721–722
    fundamentals. *See* network fundamentals
    health, **692–693**
    information, **697–699,** *698–699*
    security threats, 365
    virtual. *See* VLANs (virtual LANs)
    wireless. *See* wireless networks
    WLCs. *See* wireless LAN controllers
        (WLCs)
Next Generations Firewalls (NGFWs),
    6–10, *7*
Next Header field in IPv6 headers, 478
next hop address parameter, 142
no cdp enable command, 339
no cdp run command, 339
no ip route command, 515

no lldp run command, 346
no logging buffered command, 355
no logging console command, 355
no login command, 404
no service password-encryption command, 406
no service timestamps command, 356
no shutdown command, 212, 245
no switchport command, 715
node addresses in IP addresses, 61
nodes in Chef, 772
non-broadcast multi-access (NBMA) networks, 168
non-designated ports in STP, 254
non-repudiation, 372
non-root bridges in STP, 254
nonegotiate command, 238
Nonegotiate switch in DTP, 540
nonroot bridges, 562–564, *564*
Northbound Interface (NBI), 707
NS (neighbor solicitation), 481, *482*, 524–525, *525*
ntp master command, 348
ntp server command, 347
nulling signals in RF, 576

O

OC-3 connections, 17
OC-12 connections, 17
OC-48 connections, 17
octets in IP addresses, 60
OIDs (Organizational IDs) in SNMP, 350, *350*
omni-directional antennas
    description, 556
    free space path loss, 573
one-time passwords (OTPs), 381
one-to-many NAT, 322
one-to-one NAT, 322
onePK protocol, 708
100Base-FX Ethernet, 18
100Base-TX Ethernet, 18
1000Base-CX Ethernet, 18
1000Base-LX Ethernet, 19
1000Base-SX Ethernet, 19
1000Base-T Ethernet, 18, **21–22**, *22*
1000Base-ZX Ethernet, 19
Open Shortest Path First protocol. *See* OSPF (Open Shortest Path First) protocol

OpenDaylight protocol, 708, *709*
OpenFlow protocol, 708
operating systems (OSs), IP parameters for, **108–109**
OpFlex protocol, 708
Opportunistic Wireless Encryption (OWE), 587
optical fiber converters, 17
Options field
    IP header, 53
    TCP segment, 44
Organizational IDs (OIDs) in SNMP, 350, *350*
OSPF (Open Shortest Path First) protocol
    basics, **164–165**
    configuration, 175, *175*
        areas, **172–175**, *174*
        Corp router, **175–176**
        LA router, **177–179**, *177*
        SDN, 715
        SF router, **176–177**
        verifying, **182–188**
    default ADs, 151
    enabling, **171**
    exam essentials, **188**
    features, **164**
    loopback interfaces, **179–182**, *179*
    LSA flooding, **169–170**
    overview, *166*
    review questions, **189–191**
    vs. RIP, **165**
    SPF tree calculation, **170–171**
    summary, **188**
    terminology, **166–169**
    wildcards, **173–175**
OSs (operating systems), IP parameters for, **108–109**
OTPs (one-time passwords), 381
out-of-order delivery in QoS, 453
outbound access lists, **293**
output errors in IP network connectivity, 514
output queue drops, 513
outside NAT names, 322–323, 325
overlap channel techniques, 567
overlay in SDN, **716–717**, *717*
overload command, 326
overloading NAT, 322, 324, *324*, **326–327**
OWE (Opportunistic Wireless Encryption), 587

P

Packet description Language Models (PDLMs), 456
packet fragmentation and reassembly, 369
packet sniffers, 366–367
PAgP (Port Aggregation Protocol), 279
Pairwise Master Key (PMK), 585
Pairwise Transient Keys (PTKs)
    PSK, 584
    WPA2 Enterprise, 585
parameters for operating systems, **108–109**
paravirtualization, **668**
parent bridges, 562
passive gain in RF, 573
passive-interface command, 157
passive mode in NBAR, 456
password aux command, 405
password console command, 402
password telnet command, 404
passwords
    attacks, 372–373
    authentication, 381
    auxiliary, 405
    BIOS and UEFI, 391
    complexity, 390
    console, 402–403
    enabling, 401–402
    encrypting, 405–406
    expiration, 390, 394–395
    histories, 394–395
    length, 391–392
    management features, 393–395
    requiring, 391
    screensavers, 390
    setting, 400–401
    single sign-on, 395
    special characters, 393
    strong, 389–390
    Telnet, 403–404
    WLCs, 605
PAT (Port Address Translation)
    configuration, 326–327
    description, 322
    overloading, **324–325**, *324–325*
PATCH verb in REST API, 681
path costs in STP, 254
Path Trace in DNA Center, **731–732**, *732*
Payload Length field in IPv6 headers, 478
PCP (Priority Code Point), 455

PDLMs (Packet description Language Models), 456
Per-VLAN Spanning Tree+, **260–261**, *261–262*
perimeters, **290–291**, *291*, 377
permanent parameter, 143
PEs (Provider Edge routers), 437
pharming, **375**
phishing, **375**
physical access control, **376–377**, *376*
physical interfaces, **17–19**
ping command
    ICMP, 56–57
    IP addresses, 107–108
    IP network connectivity, **510–516**
    neighbor discovery, 525–526, 531
    static routing, 148–150
    VLANs, 536, 544
Ping of Death attacks, 369
pip command, 671
PKI (Public Key Infrastructure), **398–399**, *398–399*
platinum queues, 651
playbooks in Ansible, 763
plays in Ansible, 763
Plug and Play (PNP) in LAN Automation, 734–735
PMFs (Protected Management Frames), 586
PMK (Pairwise Master Key), 585
PNP (Plug and Play) in LAN Automation, 734–735
PoE (Power over Ethernet)
    light, 205
    overview, **23–24**, *24*
point-to-multipoint connections in OSPF, 168–169
point-to-point connections in OSPF, 168
Point-to-Point Tunneling Protocol (PPTP), 438
points of presence (POPs), 17
policers in QoS, 457, *457*
policing in QoS, **456–457**, *457*
policy mapping settings, 651
POPs (points of presence), 17
Port Address Translation (PAT)
    configuration, **326–327**
    description, 322
    overloading, **324–325**, *324–325*
Port Aggregation Protocol (PAgP), 279

port channels
  EtherChannel, 279
  verifying, 280–282, 280
Port Number field in RADIUS, 640
port-security command, 200–201
port VLAN IDs (PVIDs), 227
PortFast standard, 275–276, 275
ports and port numbers
  Catalyst switches, 205–206, 210–212
  EtherChannel, 278–279, 279
  Host-to-Host layer, 48–51
  Layer 2 security, 378
  root bridges, 253–255
  security for, 199–202, 199, 201, 210–212
  STP
    bridges, 254–255
    costs, 254
    states, 255–256
  VLANs, 225–226, 225, 234–236
  WLCs, 605, 611–614, 612–613
POST verb in REST API, 681
Postman program, 682
Power over Ethernet (PoE)
  light, 205
  overview, 23–24, 24
powers of two, 79
PPTP (Point-to-Point Tunneling Protocol), 438
PQ (Priority Queuing), 459
pre-shared key (PSK)
  WLANs, 649, 649
  WPA and WPA2, 583–584
  WPA3, 586
preemption in HSRP, 425
prefix-length command, 331
prefix routing, 153
Priority Code Point (PCP), 455
Priority Queuing (PQ), 459
private IP addresses, 66–67
private keys in IPsec transforms, 441
PROBE state in neighbor discovery, 528
Process/Application layer, 33
  APIPA, 42
  BOOTP, 40–42, 41
  description, 32
  DHCP, 40–42, 41
  DNS, 39–40, 39
  FTP, 35–36, 35
  HTTP, 37–38, 38
  HTTPS, 38

NTP, 38, 39
SNMP, 37, 37
SSH, 34–35, 35
Telnet, 34, 34
TFTP, 36, 36
process switching in router internal process, 127
profile names in WLANs, 647
propagations in RIP, 156–157
protect violation mode for port security, 200
Protected Management Frames (PMFs), 586
Protocol field in IP header, 53–55, 54
Provider Edge routers (PEs), 437
provider-managed VPNs, 436–438
Proxy Address Resolution Protocol (Proxy ARP), 412–414, 413–414
PSK (pre-shared key)
  WLANs, 649, 649
  WPA and WPA2, 583–584
  WPA3, 586
PTKs (Pairwise Transient Keys)
  PSK, 584
  WPA2 Enterprise, 585
Public Key Infrastructure (PKI), 398–399, 398–399
public keys in IPsec transforms, 441
Puppet, 764
  agent installation, 769–770
  DC manifest file, 768–769
  installation, 764–765
  lab setup, 765–766, 766
  Puppet Enterprise, 771–772
  site manifest file, 766–767
  verifying results, 770–771
PUT verb in REST API, 681
PVIDs (port VLAN IDs), 227
PVST+ standard, 260
Python language, 670–676

Q

Quality of Service (QoS)
  classification and marking, 455–456
  congestion avoidance tools, 460–461, 461
  congestion management tools, 457–460, 458–460
  DNA Center, 732–734, 733–734
  exam essentials, 461
  overview, 452–453

policing, shaping, and re-marking, 456–457, *457*
review questions, 462–463
summary, **461**
traffic characteristics, **453–454**, *453*
trust boundaries, **454–455**, *454*
WLANs, **651**, *651*
queues
    congestion management, **458–460**, *458–459*
    IP network connectivity, 513
    WLANs, **651**

R

R1 router configuration, 514–515
R2 router configuration, 515–516
RA (router advertisement) requests
    DHCPv6 servers, 477
    ICMPv6 servers, **480–481**, *481*
    IPv6 autoconfiguration, 475
    neighbor discovery, **524–525**, *524*
rack-mounted servers, 497
Radio Frequency Identification (RFID), **376–377**
radio frequency (RF)
    absorption, *574*
    diffraction, **576–577**, *577*
    free space path loss, **572–573**, *573*
    multipath, **575–576**, *575*
    operational requirements, **578**
        Fresnel zones, **579**
        line of sight, **578–579**, *579*
        RSSI and SNR, **580**, *580*
    reflection, **574–575**, *574*
    refraction, **576**, *576*
    scattering, **577–578**, *577*
    wireless networks, **569–572**, *570–572*
RADIUS. *See* Remote Authentication Dial-In User Service (RADIUS)
radius server command, 385
range command, 234–236
RAP (Root Access Point) in WLC access points, *632*
Rapid PVST+ standard, 260
Rapid Spanning Tree Protocol (RSTP), **262–267**, *264–267*
RDNs (relative distinguished names) in X.500 standard, 396

re-marking in QoS, **456–457**, *457*
REACH (reachable) state in neighbor discovery, 528
read operations in SNMP, 352
real-time alerts logs, 370
received signal strength indicator (RSSI), **580**, *580*
receiver sensitivity, 573
recipes in Chef, 772
reconnaissance attacks, 365
Redhat Linux, IP address troubleshooting in, **506–507**, *506–507*
redistribution, 157
redundancy
    clients, **412–414**, *413–414*
    exam essentials, **429**
    FHRP, **414–416**, *415*
    HSRP. *See* Hot Standby Router Protocol (HSRP)
    review questions, 430–431
    summary, **429**
    WLCs, 613–614, **617–618**, *618*
reflection in RF, **574–575**, *574*
refraction in RF, **576**, *576*
registered jack (RJ) connectors, 18
relative distinguished names (RDNs) in X.500 standard, 396
remark command, 313
remarks in access lists, **312–313**
remote access VPNs, 436
Remote Authentication Dial-In User Service (RADIUS)
    configuration, **384–385**
    process, **384**
    server role, 498
    WLANs, **650–651**, *650*
    WLCs, **639–643**, *640–642*
renaming maintenance accounts, **388–389**
repeaters, **561**, *562*
replay attacks, 371
Representational State Transfer (REST) API
    DNA Center, **736**, *736*
    overview, **679–683**, *681–683*
repudiation attacks, **371–372**
request timed out message, 125
rerouting attacks, 371
reserved IP addresses, **63–64**, **472–473**
resolving hostnames, **39**, *39*
resources in Puppet, 771

REST (Representational State Transfer) API
    DNA Center, **736**, *736*
    overview, **679–683**, *681–683*
restrict violation mode for port security, 200
retinal scanners, 397
RF. *See* radio frequency (RF)
RFID (Radio Frequency Identification), 376–377
RIDs (router IDs) in OSPF, 167, 179–182, *179*
RIP (Routing Information Protocol), **152–153**
    configuration
        Corp router, **153–154**
        LA router, **155–156**
        SF router, **154–155**
    default ADs, 151
    default routes, **157–158**
    vs. OSPF, **165**
    propagations, **156–157**
RIPng protocol, 483
RJ (registered jack) connectors, 18
ROAS (router on a stick)
    HSRP, 427
    VLANs, 230, *230*
rogue detector mode for WLC access points, 630
roles in Ansible, 763
Root Access Point (RAP) in WLC access points, *632*
root bridges
    STP, **253**, **257–262**, *258–262*
    wireless networks, 562–564, *564*
root ports in STP, 254
round-robin scheduling, 458
route print command, 509
route tables, 509
router advertisement (RA) requests
    DHCPv6 servers, 477
    ICMPv6 servers, 480–481, *481*
    IPv6 autoconfiguration, 475
    neighbor discovery, 524–525, *524*
router IDs (RIDs) in OSPF, 167, 179–182, *179*
router on a stick (ROAS)
    HSRP, 427
    VLANs, 230, *230*
router ospf command, 171–173, 715
router rip command, 153–154
router solicitation (RS) requests
    DHCPv6 servers, 477
    ICMPv6 servers, 480–481, *481*

IPv6 autoconfiguration, 475
neighbor discovery, 524–525, *524*
routers
    internal, **290–291**, *291*
    internal process, **126–127**
    overview, **3–6**, *4*
routing. *See* inter-VLAN routing (IVR); IP routing
Routing Information Protocol. *See* RIP (Routing Information Protocol)
RS (router solicitation) requests
    DHCPv6 servers, 477
    ICMPv6 servers, 480–481, *481*
    IPv6 autoconfiguration, 475
    neighbor discovery, 524–525, *524*
RSA token cards, 382, *382*
RSSI (received signal strength indicator), 580, *580*
RSTP (Rapid Spanning Tree Protocol), **262–267**, *264–267*
running-config file, 314

S

S1 Catalyst switch configuration, **206–207**
S2 Catalyst switch configuration, **207–208**
S3 Catalyst switch configuration, **208–210**
SAE (Simultaneous Authentication of Equals), 586
SBI (Southbound Interface), **708**
scalability
    VLANs, **224**
    VPNs, 436
scattering in RF, 577–578, *577*
SCCM (System Center Configuration Manager), 663
schedules for congestion management, 458
screensaver passwords, 390
scripts in Python, 670–676
SD-Access, 735
SD-WAN, 708
SDN controllers. *See* Software Defined Networking (SDN) controllers
SE-Connect mode for WLC access points, 630, *631*
secret parameter for passwords, 401
Secure Hypertext Transfer Protocol (SHTPP), 38

Secure Shell (SSH) protocol
   overview, **34–35**, *35*, *357–358*
   WLCs, **637**, *637*
Secure-shutdown command, 211–212
Secure Sockets Layer (SSL), 435
security, **364**
   access lists. *See* access lists
   audits, **392–393**
   authentication, **381–386**, *382–383*, **398–400**, *398–400*
   biometrics, **397–398**
   Catalyst switch configuration, **210–212**
   certificates, **396–397**
   exam essentials, **407**
   Layer 2, **378–380**, *378–380*
   LDAP, **395–396**
   malware, 375
   multifactor authentication, **397**
   network attacks. *See* networks
   passwords. *See* passwords
   physical access control, **376–377**, *376*
   port, **199–202**, *199*, *201*
   REST API, 683
   review questions, **408–410**
   summary, **407**
   training, 375
   user accounts, **386–389**
   user awareness, **374–375**
   VLANs, **223–224**
   VPNs. *See* virtual private networks (VPNs)
   wireless networks
      authentication and encryption, **581–582**, *581–582*
      comparisons, **588**
      settings, **648–651**, *649–650*
      WEP, **582–583**
      WPA and WPA2, **583–585**
Security Accounts Manager (SAM), 395
security protocols in IPsec transforms, **439–440**, *439*
security server authentication, **382–383**
segment format
   TCP, **43–45**, *43*
   UDP, **46**, *46*
sensitivity of receivers, 573
sensor mode for WLC access points, 632
seq no field in syslog messages, 353

Sequence Number field
   ESP, 440
   TCP segment, 44
Server Address field in RADIUS, 639
Server Index field in RADIUS, 639
server name command, 385
servers
   Chef, 772, **774–775**
   forms, **497**
   roles, **498**
   virtual machines, **663–664**, *663–664*
service password-encryption command, 406
service ports in WLCs, 605, **612–617**, *612*, *617*
service sequence-numbers command, 356
service set identifiers (SSIDs)
   overview, **559–560**, *560*
   WLANs, **647–648**
   WLCs, 606, 611
service timestamps log datetime msec command, 347
services in Puppet, 771
session hijacking, **371**
SET messages in SNMP, **349–350**
Severity field in syslog messages, 353
severity levels in syslog, **353**
SF router configuration
   IP routing, **135–138**
   IPv6, **486**
   OSPF, **176–177**
   RIP, **154–155**
   static routing, **145–146**
shapers in QoS, **457**, *457*
shaping in QoS, **456–457**, *457*
Shared Secret field in RADIUS, 639
Shared Secret Format field in RADIUS, 639
shortened expressions in IPv6, **469–470**
Shortest Path First (SPF) algorithm, 152, **170–171**
show access-list command, **314–315**, **520–522**
show access-lists command, 516
show cdp command, 339
show cdp neighbors command, 269, **340–341**, 345, 635
show cdp neighbors detail command, 341, 346, 635
show client detail command, **654–655**

show controllers command, 138
show dtp interface command, 537, 539–541
show etherchannel port-channel command, 281
show etherchannel summary command, 282
show interface command, 212
show interface summary command, 615
show interface trunk command, 237–238
show interface tunnel command, 446
show interfaces command
    GRE tunnels, 446
    IP network connectivity, 512
show interfaces switchport command, 234, 532, 534, 537, 539–540, 543
show interfaces trunk command, 537, 539, 541, 543
show ip access-list command, 314
show ip arp command, 108, 124
show ip dhcp binding command, 149
show ip dhcp pool command, 149
show ip interface command, 314–315, 522
show ip interface brief command
    Catalyst switches, 212
    GRE tunnels, 445–446
    IP network connectivity, 514
    Puppet results, 770
show ip nat statistics command, 329
show ip nat translations command, 327–328
show ip ospf command, 180–181, **183–184**
show ip ospf database command, **184–185**
show ip ospf interface command, **185–186**
show ip ospf neighbor command, **186–187**, 716
show ip protocols command, **187–188**
show ip route command
    Corp router, 129
    IP network connectivity, 514–515
    IP routing, 120–121
    OSPF, 182–183
    routing tables, 134–135, 137–138
    static routes, 145–147
show ip route ospf command, 716
show ipv6 interface brief command, 488–489, 527
show ipv6 neighbors command, 528
show ipv6 route command, 485–487, 530
show logging command, 355
show mac address-table command, 198, **213–214**, 532–535
show monitor command, 519
show ntp command, 348

show ntp associations command, 348
show ntp status command, 348
show port-security command, 211
show port summary command, 613
show running-config command
    Catalyst switches, 212
    CDP, 344–345, *346*
    IP access lists, 314
    passwords, 405
    VLANs, 239
show spanning-tree command, 268–271
show spanning-tree summary command, 271–272
show spanning-tree vlan command, 268, 270–271
show standby command, 425
show standby brief command, 425–426
show vlan command, 233, 235, 532–534, 537
show vlan brief command, 532, 535, 538
SHTPP (Secure Hypertext Transfer Protocol), **38**
shutdown command, 212
shutdown mode in port security, 200
signal-to-noise ratio (SNR) in RF, **580**, *580*
signatures in QoS, 456
silos, **744–747**, *745–747*
silver queues, 651
Simple Network Management Protocol (SNMP), **348–349**, *349*
    configuration, 351–352, 691–692
    MIB, **350**, *350*
    overview, **37**, *37*
    traps, **695**, *695*
Simultaneous Authentication of Equals (SAE), 586
single-mode fiber-optic cabling, 23, *23*
single sign-on (SSO), **395**
site manifest file in Puppet, 766–767
site-to-site VPNs, 436
slash notation (/) for subnets, 80–81
Small Office Home Office Network (SOHO), 2–3, *3*
smart cards, **377**
smurf attacks, **372**
snapshots in virtualization, 667
sniffer mode for WLC access points, **629**, *630*
SNMP. *See* Simple Network Management Protocol (SNMP)
snmp-server community command, 351, 691

snmp-server contact command, 351
snmp-server enable traps command, 691–692
snmp-server host command, 691
snmp-server location command, 351
snmp-server source-interface traps vlan command, 691
snooping in DHCP, 378–379, *379*
SNR (signal-to-noise ratio) in RF, 580, *580*
soft tokens in authentication, 381
software addresses, 52
Software Defined Access, **735**
Software Defined Networking (SDN)
    controllers, **690**
    components, **712–713**
        fabric, **718**
        overlay, **716–717**, *717*
        underlay, **713–716**, *713*
    control plane, **709–710**, *709–710*
    controller-based architectures, **710–712**, *711–712*
    DNA Center. *See* Digital Network Architecture (DNA) Center
    exam essentials, **737**
    introduction, **706–707**, *707*
    NBI, **707**
    NCMs, **699–702**, *700–701*
    NMS monitoring, **690–699**, *692–699*
    review questions, **738–741**
    SBI, **708**
    solutions, **708**, *709*
    summary, **736–737**
    traditional networking, **702–706**, *703–706*
SOHO (Small Office Home Office Network), 2–3, *3*
solicited-node address in neighbor discovery, 481–482
Source Address field in IPv6 headers, 478
Source IP address field in IP header, 53
Source port field
    TCP segment, 44
    UDP segment, 46
Southbound Interface (SBI), **708**
SPAN feature, **518–519**, *518*
spanning portfast trunk command
    joining APs, 610
    WLCs, 625
spanning-tree bpduguard enable command, 277

spanning-tree mode rapid-pvst command, 272
spanning-tree portfast command, 276, 609
spanning-tree portfast bpduguard default command, 277
spanning-tree portfast trunk command, 604
Spanning Tree Protocol (STP), **252–253**, *253*
    BPDU Guard, **276–277**
    bridge IDs, **267–273**, *268*
    bridge port roles, **254–255**
    convergence, **256**
    exam essentials, **284**
    failure consequences, **273–275**, *273–274*
    link costs, **256–257**
    operations, **257–259**, *257–259*
    port states, **255–256**
    PortFast, **275–276**, *275*
    review questions, **285–287**
    root bridges, **257–259**, *258–259*
    summary, **284**
    terms, **253–254**
    types, **259–260**
        CST, **260–261**, *260*
        MSTP, **267**
        PVST+, **260–261**, *261–262*
        RSTP, **262–267**, *264–267*
spanning-tree vlan command, 270–271
spatial multiplexing, 569
Speak state in HSRP, 426
spear phishing, 375
special characters in passwords, **393**
special purpose IP addresses, **63–64**, 472–473
Spectrum Expert tool, 630, *631*
speed settings in IP network connectivity, 513
SPF (Shortest Path First) algorithm, 152, 170–171
spine/leaf architecture
    overview, **14–15**, *14–15*
    SDN, **712**, *712*
split MAC WLAN deployment model, 599–600
spoofing IP addresses, 371
Sputnik launch, 31
spyware, 375
square brackets ([]) in JSON, 677
SSH (Secure Shell) protocol
    overview, **34–35**, *35*, 357–358
    WLCs, 637, *637*

SSIDs (service set identifiers)
    overview, **559–560**, *560*
    WLANs, 647–648
    WLCs, 606, 611
SSL (Secure Sockets Layer), 435
SSO (single sign-on), 395
STALE state in neighbor discovery, 528
stand-alone WLAN deployment model,
    597–598, *597*
standard access lists, 292, **295–301**, *299–301*
standard vSwitches, 665
standby group ip virtual_ip command, 423
standby ip command, 425
standby name command, 424–425
standby prempt command, 425
standby priority command, 424–425
standby routers in HSRP, 416–418,
    417–418, 421
Standby state in HSRP, 426
standby timers in HSRP, 420
standby timers msec command, 421
stateful autoconfiguration in IPv6, **476–477**
stateless autoconfiguration in IPv6,
    474–476, *474*, *476*
states
    HSRP, **426**
    STP ports, **255–256**
static IP addressing, 42
static MAC address, 214
static NAT, 322, **325**
static routing, 119
    Corp router, **144–146**, *144*
    default ADs, 151
    IP routing, 148–150
    IPv6 protocol, 483–484, *484*
    LA router, 146–147
    overview, 142–143
    SF router, 145–146
stations in SNMP, 349
status messages in REST API, 681–682
Status option in WLANs, 648
sticky command, 201, 214
storage and Storage Spaces in virtualization,
    666
STP. *See* Spanning Tree Protocol (STP)
straight-through cable, **20**, *20–21*
strict priority scheduling, 458
strong passwords, **389–390**
structured threats, 365
stub routers, 147

subinterfaces in VLANs, 240
subnets and subnetting, 76
    basics, **76–77**, *77*
    CIDR, **80–81**
    Class B addresses, **93–101**
    Class C addresses, **82–93**, *85–86*, *88*
    creating, 77–78
    exam essentials, **102**
    ip subnet-zero, **81–82**
    masks, 78–79
    powers of two, 79
    review questions, **103–104**
    summary, **102**
    VLANs, 241
Support for CoA field in RADIUS, 640
SVI (switched virtual interface), 231
sweet feature alerts, 587
switch ports
    LED, 206
    VLANs, **234–236**
switched virtual interface (SVI), 231
switches
    IP addresses, 206
    overview, **3–6**, *3*, *6*
    virtualization, **665–666**
    WLCs, **602–604**, *602*
switchport command, 234–236
switchport access command, 237–238
switchport access vlan command,
    532, 536
    joining APs, 609
    WLC switches, 604
switchport mode command, 237–238, 537,
    540
switchport mode access command
    joining APs, 609
    port security, 200
    WLC switches, 604
switchport mode dynamic command, 537,
    540–542
switchport mode trunk command
    joining APs, 610
    port channels, 280–281
    WLC switches, 604
    WLCs, 625
switchport nonegotiate command, 238
switchport port-security command,
    200–201, 211
switchport port-security mac-address
    command, 210

switchport trunk allowed command, 238–239
switchport trunk allowed vlan command, 281
switchport trunk encapsulation command, 239
switchport trunk encapsulation dot1q command
   joining APs, 610
   port channels, 280–281
   VLANs, 542
   WLC switches, 604
   WLCs, 625
switchport trunk native command, 239
switchport trunk native vlan command
   joining APs, 610
   VLANs, 537, 542, 544
switchports in joining APs, 609–610
symmetric encryption in IPsec transforms, 440
SYN floods, 369
syn packet acknowledgments, 50
synchronization with NTP, 347–348, *348*
syslog, 352–354
   central, **694–695**, *694*
   configuration and verification, 354–356, *355*
System Center Configuration Manager (SCCM), 663
system LED, 205, *205*
system mtu command, 714

T

T1 connections, 17
T3 connections, 17
tablet endpoints, **497**
tacacs-server command, 386
tasks in Ansible, 763
TCP. *See* Transmission Control Protocol (TCP)
TCP/IP. *See* Transmission Control Protocol/Internet Protocol (TCP/IP)
team silos, **744–747**, *745–747*
telnet command
   extended access lists, 520–521
   IP network connectivity, 516–518
Telnet protocol
   IP access lists, **302–303**
   overview, **34**, *34*
   passwords, 403–404
   WLCs, **636**, *636*

templates
   Ansible, 763
   DNA Center, **723–724**, *724*
temporary employees, 387
temporary IPv6 addresses, 529
10Base-T Ethernet, 18
10GBase-T Ethernet, 19
Terminal Access Controller Access Control System (TACACS+), 370
   configuration, 385–386
   process, **385**
   server role, 498
   WLCs, **643–646**, *643–646*
terminal monitor command, 352
testing NAT, 328–333, *330–332*
TFTP (Trivial File Transfer Protocol), **36**, *36*
thin protocols, 45
thrashing of MAC tables, 203
three-layer hierarchical model, **10**, *11*
   access layer, **12–13**
   core layer, **11–12**
   distribution layer, **12**
tickets in Kerberos, 400
TIDs (traffic identifiers) in QoS, 456
time to live (TTL) in IP header, 53
timers
   CDP, **338–339**, *339*
   HSRP, **419–421**, *420*
Timestamp field in syslog messages, 353
token cards in authentication, 381–382, *382*
toll networks, 17
top-of-rack (ToR) design, 14–15, *14*
topologies, **10**
   collapsed core, **13**, *13*
   database, 168
   DNA Center, **724–725**, *725*
   documentation, **344–346**, *344, 346*
   spine-leaf, **14–15**, *14–15*
   three-layer hierarchical model, **10–13**, *11*
   WANs, **15–17**
ToR (top-of-rack) design, 14–15, *14*
Total length field in IP header, 53
tower end servers, 497
traceroute command
   ICMP, 56, 108
   IP network connectivity, 511
   neighbor discovery, 527
traffic characteristics in QoS, **453–454**, *453*
Traffic Class field in IPv6 headers, 478
traffic flow in ESP, 440

traffic identifiers (TIDs) in QoS, 456
training for security, **375**
transferring files, **35–36**, *35–36*
transforms in IPsec, **439–441**, *439*, *441*
translation timeout in NAT, 330
Transmission Control Protocol (TCP), **43**
    attacks, 369
    IP, **52–55**, *53–54*
    key concepts, **46–47**, *47*
    port numbers, **48–51**
    segment format, **43–45**, *43*
Transmission Control Protocol/Internet Protocol (TCP/IP)
    ARP, **58–60**, *59*
    destination ports, **49–50**
    and DoD model, **31–33**, *32–33*
    exam essentials, **71–72**
    history, **30–31**
    Host-to-Host layer. *See* Host-to-Host layer
    ICMP, **55–58**, *56*
    IP addresses. *See* IP addresses
    Process/Application layer. *See* Process/Application layer
    review questions, **73–74**
    summary, **71**
    syn packet acknowledgments, 50
    UDP, **45–46**
transparent bridging, 6
transport input command, 357–358
transport input ssh command, 404
Transport layer, 32
TRAP operation in SNMP, 350
traps
    SNMP, 37, 349, **695**, *695*
    syslog, **355–356**
Trivial File Transfer Protocol (TFTP), **36**, *36*
Trojan horse attacks, **373–375**
troubleshooting
    HSRP, **428–429**
    IP addresses, *110–113*
        exam essentials, **114**
        Linux, **506–507**, *506–507*
        Mac OS, **504–506**, *504–506*
        OS parameters, **108–109**
        overview, **106–108**, *106*
        problem determination, **109–113**, *110–113*
        review questions, **115–116**
        summary, **114**
        Windows 10, **498–504**, *499–503*

IP network connectivity
    exam essentials, **545**
    extended access lists, **519–522**, *520*
    IPv6 networks, **522–531**, *523–525*
    overview, **507–518**, *508*
    review questions, **546–548**
    SPAN, **518–519**, *518*
    summary, **544–545**
    VLANs, **531–544**, *532*
    NAT, **328–333**, *330–332*
    trunks, **537–544**
trunk command, 237–238
trunk links, **226–227**, *226*
trunk ports, **236–240**
trunk switches, 540
trunks, troubleshooting, **537–544**
trust boundaries in QoS, **454–455**, *454*
trusted domains in QoS, 455
trusted networks, **291**, *291*
TTL (time to live) in IP header, 53
tunnel destination, 445
tunnel mode command, 444
tunnel source command, 445
tunnels, GRE, **441–447**, *442*
2-tier topologies, **13**, *13*
2.4GHz band, **565–566**, *566*
2.4GHz/5GHz, **569**
Type I hypervisors, **668–669**
Type II hypervisors, **668–669**
Type of Service field
    IP header, 53
    QoS, 455

U

Ubuntu Linux, IP address troubleshooting in, **506–507**, *506–507*
UDP. *See* User Datagram Protocol (UDP)
UEFI passwords, **391**
unauthorized access, 370
underlay in SDN, **713**, *713*
    interface configuration, **714–715**
    MTU, **714**
    OSPF configuration, **715**
    verifying, **716**
unicasts
    addresses, **69**, *69*
    IPv6, 468, **470–471**, *471*

UNII (Unlicensed National Information Infrastructure) bands, 566–567, *567*
unique local addresses, **471**
UNIX Berkeley Software Distribution, 31
unshielded twisted-pair (UTP) cabling, 18
unstructured threats, 365
untrusted domains in QoS, 455
untrusted networks, 291, *291*
upfade in RF, 576
upgrades in DNA Center, *726–727*
upstream routing, 240
Urgent field in TCP segment, 44
use-tacacs parameter for passwords, 401
user accounts, 386–387
   anonymous, 387–388
   connection limits, 388
   disabling, 387
   lockouts, 393–394
   maintenance, 388–389
user awareness for security, 374–375
User Datagram Protocol (UDP), 45
   DHCP, 41
   key concepts, 46–47, *47*
   port numbers, 48–51
   segment format, 46, *46*
username command, 357
username ansible priv command, 754
username ncm secret ncmPass command, 700
usernames
   authentication, 381
   WLCs, 605
UTP gigabit wiring, **21–22**, *22*
UTP (unshielded twisted-pair) cabling, 18

V

variables
   Ansible, 753, 763
   DNA Center templates, 723
verifying
   bridge IDs, 267–273, *268*
   Catalyst switches, 212–214
   Chef results, 781, *781*
   extended access lists, 521–522
   GRE tunnels, 445–447
   HSRP, 425–427
   IP routing, 148–150
   NAT, 327

OSPF, 182–188
port channels, 280–282, *280*
Puppet results, 770–771
SDN, 716
syslog, 354–356, *355*
Version field
   IP header, 53
   IPv6 headers, 478
video traffic in QoS, 453–454, *453*
violation command, 211
virtual circuits
   port numbers, 50
   TCP, 43
Virtual Extensible LANs (VXLANs), 716
virtual interface in WLCs, 614, **618–619**, *619*
virtual LANs. *See* VLANs (virtual LANs)
virtual MAC addresses in HSRP, **418–419**
virtual machines
   fundamentals, **662–664**, *663–664*
   migrations, 667
virtual private dial-up networks (VPDNs), 438
virtual private LAN switching service (VPLS), 437
virtual private networks (VPNs)
   benefits, 435–436
   enterprise-managed and provider-managed, **436–438**, *436–437*
   exam essentials, 447
   GRE tunnels, **441–447**, *442*
   IPsec transforms, **439–441**, *439*, *441*
   overview, **434–435**, *435*
   review questions, 448–450
   summary, 447
virtual private wire service (VPWS), 437
Virtual Router Redundancy Protocol (VRRP), 416
virtual routers in HSRP, 416–417, 421
Virtual Tunnel Interface (VTI) mode, **443**
VirtualBox, 670
virtualization
   components, 665–666
   exam essentials, 684
   features, 666–667
   review questions, 685–687
   solutions, 669–670
   summary, 684
   types, 668
   virtual machines
      fundamentals, **662–664**, *663–664*
      migrations, 667

viruses, 373–375
vlan command, 232–233, 602–603, 609
VLAN Trunk Protocol (VTP), 232
VLANs (virtual LANs), 220
    broadcast control, 223
    configuration, 231–234
        inter-VLAN routing, 240–246, 241–242, 244, 246
        switch port assignments, 234–236
        trunk ports, 236–240
    exam essentials, 247
    flexibility and scalability, 224
    frame tagging, 227–228
    identifying, 224–229, 225–226, 228
    ISL for, 228
    joining APs, 609
    operation, 220–223, 221–222
    review questions, 248–250
    routing between, 229–231, 230–231
    security, 223–224
    summary, 247
    troubleshooting, 531–532, 532
        scenario, 532–537
        trunks, 537–544
    trunk links, 226–227, 226
VMware ESXi, 669
VMware virtual SANs, 666
VMware Workstation/Fusion, 669
voice access ports, 226
voice traffic in QoS, 453–454, 453
VPDNs (virtual private dial-up networks), 438
VPLS (virtual private LAN switching service), 437
VPNs. *See* virtual private networks (VPNs)
vSwitches, 665–666
VTP (VLAN Trunk Protocol), 232
VTY, access lists for, 302–303
VXLANs (Virtual Extensible LANs), 716

W

WALK operation in SNMP, 350
WANs (wide area networks), 4, 15–16
    bandwidth, 17
    terms, 16–17, 16
WAPs. *See* access points (APs)
WareZ attacks, 370
WCS (Wireless Control System), 599
WDS (Wireless Domain Services), 598
web server role, 498
Weighted Fair Queuing (WFQ), 459
weighted fair scheduling, 458
weighted random early detection (WRED), 461
WEP (Wired Equivalent Privacy), 582–583
WFQ (Weighted Fair Queuing), 459
Wi-Fi Protected Access (WPA), 583–585
wide area networks (WANs), 4, 15–16
    bandwidth, 17
    terms, 16–17, 16
wildcards
    access lists, 296–298
    OSPF, 173–175, 174
Window field in TCP segment, 44
Windows 10, IP address troubleshooting in, 498–504
Windows authentication, 382
Wired Equivalent Privacy (WEP), 582–583
wireless access points (WAPs). *See* access points (APs)
wireless antennas, 556
Wireless Control System (WCS), 599
Wireless Domain Services (WDS), 598
wireless LAN controllers (WLCs), 554–555
    access points, 610–611, 610
        configuring, 625–628, 626–628
        modes, 629–632, 630–633
    exam essentials, 655–656
    initial setup, 604–606
    interface types, 614–615, 614
        dynamic, 619–621, 620–621
        Interface Groups, 622–623, 622–623
        LAG, 623–625, 624
        management, 615, 616
        redundancy-management, 617–618, 618
        service port, 616–617, 617
        virtual, 618–619, 619
    joining APs, 607–610, 608
    management access connections, 633
        CDP, 634–636, 634–635
        HTTP, 637–638, 638
        HTTPS, 638–639, 638
        RADIUS, 639–643, 640–642
        SSH, 637, 637
        TACACS+, 643–646, 643–646
        telnet, 636, 636
    port types, 611–614, 612–613

review questions, 657–660
summary, 655
switch configuration, 602–604, *602*
WLANs
    advanced settings, **652**, *652*
    client connections, **653–655**, *653–654*
    creation, **646–648**, *647–648*
    policy mapping settings, 651
    QoS profiles, **651**, *651*
    security, **648–651**, *649–650*
wireless metro area networks (WMANs), 552
wireless network interface cards, **555**, *555*
wireless networks, 550
    channels, 565
        2.4GHz band, **565–566**, *566*
        2.4GHz/5GHz, 569
        5GHz band, **566–567**, *567*
        multiple APs, **568–569**, *568*
        overlap techniques, 567
    deployment models, **596–597**
        cloud, **600–601**, *601*
        lightweight, **598–599**, *598*
        split MAC, **599–600**
        stand-alone, **597–598**, *597*
    devices, **553–556**, *554–555*
    exam essentials, 588–589
    forms, **551–553**, *551*
    principles, 556
        basic service sets, **557–558**, *558*
        bridges, **562–564**, *563–564*
        extended service sets, **560–561**, *561*
        independent basic service sets, **556–557**, *557*
        infrastructure basic service sets, **558–559**
        mesh networks, **564**, *565*
        repeaters, **561**, *562*
        service set identifiers, **559–560**, *560*
    radio frequency. *See* radio frequency (RF)
    review questions, 590–593
    security
        802.11i standard, **585**
        authentication and encryption, **581–582**, *581–582*
        comparisons, 588
        WEP, **582–583**
        WPA and WPA2, **583–585**
        WPA2 Enterprise, 585
        WPA3, **586–588**
    summary, 588
wireless personal area networks (WPANs), 551
Wireless Solution Engine (WLSE), 598
wireless wide area networks (WWANs), 553
WLCs. *See* wireless LAN controllers (WLCs)
WLSE (Wireless Solution Engine), 598
WMANs (wireless metro area networks), **552**
Workstation nodes in Chef, 772
workstations in Chef, **772**, **775–776**
worms, 373–375
WPA (Wi-Fi Protected Access), **583–585**
WPA2
    wireless networks, 583–585
    WPA2 Enterprise, 585
WPA3, 586
    WPA3-Enterprise, 587
    WPA3-Personal, **586–587**
WPANs (wireless personal area networks), 551
WRED (weighted random early detection), 461
write operations in SNMP, 352
WWANs (wireless wide area networks), **553**

X

X.500 standard, 396
X.509 certificates, **396–397**
Xen hypervisor, 669

Y

yagi antennas, *556*
YAML Ain't Markup Language (YAML), 679
yum localinstall command, 775

Online Test Bank

Register to gain one year of FREE access to the online interactive test bank to help you study for your CCNA certification exam—included with your purchase of this book! All of the chapter review questions and the practice tests in this book are included in the online test bank so you can practice in a timed and graded setting.

Register and Access the Online Test Bank

To register your book and get access to the online test bank, follow these steps:

1. Go to bit.ly/SybexTest (this address is case sensitive)!
2. Select your book from the list.
3. Complete the required registration information, including answering the security verification to prove book ownership. You will be emailed a pin code.
4. Follow the directions in the email or go to www.wiley.com/go/sybextestprep.
5. Find your book on that page and click the "Register or Login" link with it. Then enter the pin code you received and click the "Activate PIN" button.
6. On the Create an Account or Login page, enter your username and password, and click Login or, if you don't have an account already, create a new account.
7. At this point, you should be in the test bank site with your new test bank listed at the top of the page. If you do not see it there, please refresh the page or log out and log back in.

SYBEX
A Wiley Brand